LET'S GO:
Spain & Portugal

"Lighthearted and sophisticated, informative and fun to read. *[Let's Go]* helps the novice traveler navigate like a knowledgeable old hand."

—*Atlanta Journal-Constitution*

"The guides are aimed not only at young budget travelers but at the independent traveler, a sort of streetwise cookbook for traveling alone."

—*The New York Times*

Let's Go writers travel on your budget.

"Retains the spirit of the student-written publication it is: candid, opinionated, resourceful, amusing info for the traveler of limited means but broad curiosity." —*Mademoiselle*

"The writers seem to have experienced every rooster-packed bus and lunar-surfaced mattress about which they write." —*The New York Times*

"All the dirt, dirt cheap." —*People*

Great for independent travelers.

"A world-wise traveling companion—always ready with friendly advice and helpful hints, all sprinkled with a bit of wit." —*The Philadelphia Inquirer*

"Lots of valuable information for any independent traveler."

—*The Chicago Tribune*

Let's Go is completely revised each year.

"Unbeatable: good sight-seeing advice; up-to-date info on restaurants, hotels, and inns; a commitment to money-saving travel; and a wry style that brightens nearly every page." —*The Washington Post*

"Its yearly revision by a new crop of Harvard students makes it as valuable as ever." —*The New York Times*

All the important information you need.

"Enough information to satisfy even the most demanding of budget travelers...*Let's Go* follows the creed that you don't have to toss your life's savings to the wind to travel—unless you want to."

—*The Salt Lake Tribune*

"Value-packed, unbeatable, accurate, and comprehensive."

—*The Los Angeles Times*

Let's Go Publications

Let's Go: Alaska & the Pacific Northwest 1998

Let's Go: Australia 1998 **New title!**

Let's Go: Austria & Switzerland 1998

Let's Go: Britain & Ireland 1998

Let's Go: California 1998

Let's Go: Central America 1998

Let's Go: Eastern Europe 1998

Let's Go: Ecuador & the Galápagos Islands 1998

Let's Go: Europe 1998

Let's Go: France 1998

Let's Go: Germany 1998

Let's Go: Greece & Turkey 1998

Let's Go: India & Nepal 1998

Let's Go: Ireland 1998

Let's Go: Israel & Egypt 1998

Let's Go: Italy 1998

Let's Go: London 1998

Let's Go: Mexico 1998

Let's Go: New York City 1998

Let's Go: New Zealand 1998 **New title!**

Let's Go: Paris 1998

Let's Go: Rome 1998

Let's Go: Southeast Asia 1998

Let's Go: Spain & Portugal 1998

Let's Go: USA 1998

Let's Go: Washington, D.C. 1998

Let's Go Map Guides

Berlin	New Orleans
Boston	New York City
Chicago	Paris
London	Rome
Los Angeles	San Francisco
Madrid	Washington, D.C.

Coming Soon: Amsterdam, Florence

**Let's Go
Publications**

LET'S GO
Spain
& Portugal
1998

Derek M. Glanz
Editor

Amir D. Perlson
Associate Editor

James J. Castanino
Assistant Editor

St. Martin's Press ❧ New York

HELPING LET'S GO

If you want to share your discoveries, suggestions, or corrections, please drop us a line. We read every piece of correspondence, whether a postcard, a 10-page email, or a coconut. Please note that mail received after May 1998 may be too late for the 1999 book, but will be kept for future editions. **Address mail to:**

> **Let's Go: Spain & Portugal**
> **67 Mount Auburn Street**
> **Cambridge, MA 02138**
> **USA**

Visit Let's Go at **http://www.letsgo.com,** or send email to:

> **fanmail@letsgo.com**
> **Subject: "Let's Go: Spain & Portugal"**

In addition to the invaluable travel advice our readers share with us, many are kind enough to offer their services as researchers or editors. Unfortunately, our charter enables us to employ only currently enrolled Harvard-Radcliffe students.

Maps by David Lindroth copyright © 1998, 1997, 1996, 1995, 1994, 1993, 1992, 1991, 1990, 1989, 1988 by St. Martin's Press, Inc.

Map revisions pp. xiv, xv, xvi, xvii, 52, 53, 68, 69, 127, 137, 147, 173, 175, 197, 203, 219, 221, 229, 245, 269, 300, 301, 335, 363, 387, 389, 413, 414, 415, 433, 447, 495, 515, 526, 527, 529, 577, 585, 620, 621, 633, 655 by Let's Go, Inc.

Distributed outside the USA and Canada by Macmillan.

ISBN: 0-312-15749-5

First edition
10 9 8 7 6 5 4 3 2 1

Let's Go: Spain & Portugal is written by Let's Go Publications, 67 Mount Auburn Street, Cambridge, MA 02138, USA.

Let's Go® and the thumb logo are trademarks of Let's Go, Inc.
Printed in the USA on recycled paper with biodegradable soy ink.

About Let's Go

THIRTY-EIGHT YEARS OF WISDOM

Back in 1960, a few students at Harvard University banded together to produce a 20-page pamphlet offering a collection of tips on budget travel in Europe. This modest, mimeographed packet, offered as an extra to passengers on student charter flights to Europe, met with instant popularity. The following year, students traveling to Europe researched the first, full-fledged edition of *Let's Go: Europe*, a pocket-sized book featuring honest, irreverent writing and a decidedly youthful outlook on the world. Throughout the 60s, our guides reflected the times; the 1969 guide to America led off by inviting travelers to "dig the scene" at San Francisco's Haight-Ashbury. During the 70s and 80s, we gradually added regional guides and expanded coverage into the Middle East and Central America. With the addition of our in-depth city guides, handy map guides, and extensive coverage of Asia and Australia, the 90s are also proving to be a time of explosive growth for Let's Go, and there's certainly no end in sight. The first editions of *Let's Go: Australia* and *Let's Go: New Zealand* hit the shelves this year, expanding our coverage to six continents, and research for next year's series has already begun.

We've seen a lot in 38 years. *Let's Go: Europe* is now the world's bestselling international guide, translated into seven languages. And our new guides bring Let's Go's total number of titles, with their spirit of adventure and their reputation for honesty, accuracy, and editorial integrity, to 40. But some things never change: our guides are still researched, written, and produced entirely by students who know first-hand how to see the world on the cheap.

HOW WE DO IT

Each guide is completely revised and thoroughly updated every year by a well-traveled set of over 200 students. Every winter, we recruit over 140 researchers and 60 editors to write the books anew. After several months of training, Researcher-Writers hit the road for seven weeks of exploration, from Anchorage to Adelaide, Estonia to El Salvador, Iceland to Indonesia. Hired for their rare combination of budget travel sense, writing ability, stamina, and courage, these adventurous travelers know that train strikes, stolen luggage, food poisoning, and marriage proposals are all part of a day's work. Back at our offices, editors work from spring to fall, massaging copy written on Himalayan bus rides into witty yet informative prose. A student staff of typesetters, cartographers, publicists, and managers keeps our lively team together. In September, the collected efforts of the summer are delivered to our printer, who turns them into books in record time, so that you have the most up-to-date information available for your vacation. And even as you read this, work on next year's editions is well underway.

WHY WE DO IT

We don't think of budget travel as the last recourse of the destitute; we believe that it's the only way to travel. Living cheaply and simply brings you closer to the people and places you've been saving up to visit. Our books will ease your anxieties and answer your questions about the basics—so you can get off the beaten track and explore. Once you learn the ropes, we encourage you to put *Let's Go* down now and then to strike out on your own. As any seasoned traveler will tell you, the best discoveries are often those you make yourself. When you find something worth sharing, drop us a line. We're Let's Go Publications, 67 Mount Auburn Street, Cambridge, MA 02138, USA (email fanmail@letsgo.com).

HAPPY TRAVELS!

Contents

Maps

Color Maps

Researcher-Writers

driana Abdenur   *Porutgal*

ith a few giggles and a trademark twinkle in her eye, AA had her way with Portu-
al and its men. And what an army of suitors she had—whether she needed a lift
om a motorcycling stud after her sandal was gnawed off by ravaging dogs (pup-
es?), or thirsted beer with swarthy sailors, or thirsted for more than sardines and
erry from a dashing matador, Adriana never missed a beat as she unearthed the
garve and cracked us up with the most clever stick figures since Gumby.

dam Branch   *Morocco and Algeciras*

gh-quality copy, stone-hard facts and no half-baked research made Adam a smart
y. ("Peace of cake, dude.") Adam did the work of 30 Berbers, and could write an
tire book on how to shake a guide—"just carry him on your forearm, man, or
eak into a dead sprint. Moroccans can't run." Always ahead of schedule, Branchy
en found the time to put Wittgenstein in his place—"whatever."

blo Colapinto   *Madrid, Extremadura, Castilla La Mancha, and Islas Canarias*

blito muscled up for his journey with a hearty snack of sheep's brain and sculpted
physique in Extremadura, where he nursed from the same teet as Cortés and
arro. He laid seige on Madrid, but had to flee from his (almost) harem of sultry
itresses, who hid their desires beneath tight (hair) buns. In lonelier times, he
uck up converstion with the nearest rock. With knowledge and strength, our *gran
quistador* sailed off to sea and returned with the great Canaries.

tibaliz Iturralde   *Andalucía*

told us what sucked, who sucked, and why, but left no traces of the forces that
re. Not afraid to "tailor" her act to keep herself well-nourished, *la vasca* barely
aped Malagan pirates, Alsina Graells (a rather large German woman), and research-
uced nightmares. Esti heard more *piropos* than Penélope Cruz, and her brilliant
erage earned her immortalization—she will forever be known as the Patron Saint
PAM.

zabeth Kivowitz   *Castilla y León, Navarra, Aragón, La Rioja, Costa Brava*

tía más guay del norte, Liz championed laundromats, *pintxos*, and the Spice Girls
he guided us throught the Pyrenees, only stopping for a sauna and massage along
way, and emerging as the undisputed *Campeona de las Cosas Free-bees*. She "got
nbed" in San Sebastián, left the poor city with a food shortage, and still discovered
oya del sexo. Like Brett she stole the show at the *San Fermines,* and like Ernest
didn't run.

se Lichtenstein   *Castilla y León, Galicia, Asturias and Cantabria*

piddles and diddles, spins to baseline and, Oh my God! Jesse Lichtenstein has just
ked over the five-foot-three one-armed Galician. I don't believe it!" Jesse found
y sorts of entertainment in rainy Spain, and got a hefty dose of Babel from hostel
ers in Santiago who mistook him for a *libro de reclamaciones.* Knowing what's
ortant, he never missed an opportunity to take a jab at a time chart.

an McKittrick   *Catalunya, Islas Baleares, Valencia and Murcia*

ing through Catalunya, Ryan would have qualified for a moped license if only he
t his eyes on the roads and not on the addresses of laundromats. Lover of A/C,
-sized clips (99020-BC-20), and our expert on L'Eixample, Ryan combined a little
y and a lot of chutzpah to squeeze the last bit of unspoiled coast from the Mediter-
an. After imbibing a dose of catalanismo-infused xampany, he was merciless
Mallorca and unsparing in Sitges, but found his paradise in Menorca.

haella Maloney   *Pays Basque, France*

Acknowledgments

Let's Go: Spain & Portugal is dedicated to the curious and the adventurous
who seek fun and enrichment in the Iberian Peninsula and North Africa.
                                                                —SPAM

racias sean dadas a nuestros investigadores: ¡qué jorneo! To Melissa (MR), *el
egamento.* To Menriq for mad hot Madrid nightlife. *A:* Jake, *commandante;* Cathe-
ne, Leah, and Sam, *los salvavidas; los punks de maps; el eqiupo de producción—
eniall; y* Anne, *claro.* In a pinch: Lisa filled a void; Bull brought wisdom with a great
ead and heart; Dan V.; Jace; Rachel E.; Ms. Hornby; Emily; Hillary; Drés; Stein; Weiss
. Weiss. Thanks to the founders of *Let's Go* and to the legacy of SPAM clans who
ade our job easy. **—Team SPAM.**

Congrats, Amir. James, CF, right-hand man, thanks for being a team player—this
n't JV! A whim is all it takes. *Y sobre todo, eres una máquina; fue privilegio mío.*
I Trensnochedor, veintitres abrazos y diecisiete besos: Modell, Pervil, Pintocolas,
rbs, Mai, Steinclub, Jenny, and Taya. To IES and Madrid: educación v(í)vida
Hala!).* The fam: Jay, Mom, Dad, and Lyle. **—DMG**

Well, Derek, what began as a whim turned into quite a project. A rewarding
oject and a great summer, all culminating in an actual book—amazing. To my won-
rful family: Thank you for all your support—you guys are the best. Thanks to John
 for being a fabulous teacher and a great friend. **—JJC**

Thanks to Derek and James for their dedication and hard work. Melissa, thanks for
ur smile. Dan and Dinko: maybe someone cleaned the bathroom, maybe not.
val, for telling me what time it is. YiLing, ahuvati, hayalda hachi hachi yaffa
oward. To the other baby, Ms. Cookie: now its official. Thanks Aba, Risa, Eyal, and
 backyard (dis is great! I don't hate it!), most of all for your love. **—ADP**

'itor	Derek M. Glanz
sociate Editor	Amir D. Perlson
sistant Editor	James J. Castanino
anaging Editor	Melissa M. Reyen
blishing Director	John R. Brooks
oduction Manager	Melanie Quintana Kansil
sociate Production Manager	David Collins
rtography Manager	Sara K. Smith
itorial Manager	Melissa M. Reyen
itorial Manager	Emily J. Stebbins
ancial Manager	Krzysztof Owerkowicz
rsonnel Manager	Andrew E. Nieland
olicity Manager	Nicholas Corman
olicity Manager	Kate Galbraith
w Media Manager	Daniel O. Williams
sociate Cartographer	Joseph E. Reagan
ociate Cartographer	Luke Z. Fenchel
ice Coordinators	Emily Bowen, Charles Kapelke
	Laurie Santos
ector of Advertising Sales	Todd L. Glaskin
ior Sales Executives	Matthew R. Hillery, Joseph W. Lind
	Peter J. Zakowich, Jr.
sident	Amit Tiwari
eral Manager	Richard Olken
istant General Manager	Anne E. Chisholm

Let's Go Picks

We've liked, we've disliked, and here's a dose of what we loved. Admittedly, subjective is as subjective does: how about a Reader's Picks '99? Send us a postcard of your favorite travel haunts. Key: Andorra (A), Morocco (M), Portugal (P), and Spain (S). Sorry Gibraltar, you still haven't made the cut.

Best beaches: La Concha (S), picturesque without the picture takers (p. 234). **Caminha, Tavira, Aveiro (P),** take your pick (p. 590, 617, 572). **Cala Macarella (S),** crystal blue without the party (p. 379). **Ses Salines (S),** a strip in June, in August a *fiestita* (p. 384). **O Castro de Baroña (S),** clothing optional (p. 187). **Las Canteras (S),** perpetual summer in Gran Canaria (p. 512). **Playa de Cortadura (S),** blue-banner-best (p. 484). **El Jadida (M),** especially if you beat the high seasoners (p. 661).

Best nightlife: Ibiza (S), where fashion is a contest (p. 379). **Marbella (S),** Beautiful People are always in style (p. 468). **Madrid (S),** party from 9 'til 11...that's pm 'til am (p. 67). **San Sebastián (S),** the night only begins with *pintxos* (p. 227). **Marrakech (M),** trained monkeys ans snake charmers—it's why you come to Morocco (p. 667). **Valencia (S),** *hoy fiesta, mañana resaca; pero hoy fiesta* (today party, tomorrow hangover; p. 486). **Sevilla and Granada (S),** *fiestas de proprciones andaluces* (p. 411, p. 444).

Best places with no significant sights whatsoever: Amarante (P), breath, sip, bite, kiss; repeat (p. 582). **Marbella (S),** plenty of looking, though (p. 468). **Formentera (S),** dunes, mopeds, beach (p. 383). **Camariñas (S),** cover this place in lace (p. 189). **San Sebastián (S),** the cathedral's prominent; you'll pass it on your way for pintxos and the beach (p. 227). **Chueca (S),** plenty of scenery, though (p. 103).

Best monuments/castles/architecture: Mérida (S), more to see than in El Corte Inglés (p. 499). **Fès (M),** a wack-o medina (p. 643). **Granada (S),** behold the Alhambra and Albaicín (p. 444). **Guimarães (P),** its grandeur has passed, but the town wasn't noticed (p. 583). **Barcelona (S),** *la ciudad de diseño* (p. 298). **Santiago de Compostela (S),** you might not leave till the rains pass (p. 172). **Sant Joan des Abadesses (S),** Romanesque-ness up the wazoo (p. 355).

Backpacker's best: Picos de Europa (S). La Alpujarra (S), refuge to the Moors, the Bloomsbury group, and new-age Buddhists (p. 456). **Dadès Gorge (M),** ripped earth (p. 678). **Toubkal (M),** a far out trek (p. 667). **Alto Minho (P),** the lushest greenery in Portugal (p. 590). **Cercedilla (S),** skiing, hiking, and more, just 90min. from Madrid (p. 117). **Parque Nacional de Ordesa (S),** an Alps-Rockies combo up along the French border (p. 286).

Researcher Picks: Menorca (S), the silent island (p. 372). **Trujillo (S),** west coast! (p. 507). **Sevilla (S),** boisterous, feminine, aromatic, and romantic (p. 411). **Sintra (P),** Arabia meets Bavaria (p. 546). **Formentera (S),** time is *slowly,* but surely, running out (p. 383). **San Sebastián (S),** we think you should go here (p. 227). **Morocco's Atlantic Coast during the off-season,** laid back towns and whitewashed medinas (p. 653).

Best place to have a bad hair day: Tarifa (S), surfer's heaven, model's hell (p. 481).
Best Place to "get bombed": San Sebastián (S), tastless!
Post-Pyrenees meltdown: Caldea Spa (A), steam bath? massage? (p. 295).
Largest mass of pork: Museo del Jamón, Madrid (S). Babe, we hardly knew ya (p. 86).
Best drugs: Las Palmas (S; p. 505).
Where Clinton again proved he can cry on cue: The Albaicín (S; p. 450).

TO
RABAT

Chapter Divisions

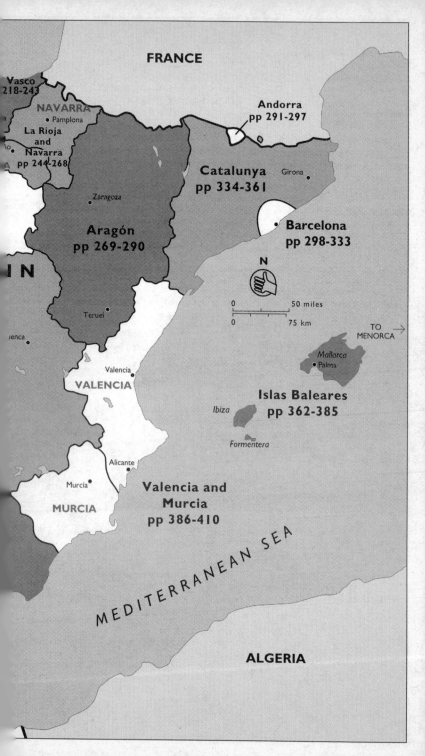

FRANCE

NAVARRA

• Pamplona

Andorra

Catalunya   Girona •

Zaragoza •

Aragón   • Barcelona

SPAIN

N

Teruel •

0 _____ 50 miles
0 _____ 75 km

TO
MENORCA →

Mallorca
• Palma

uenca •

Valencia •

VALENCIA   Islas Baleares

Ibiza

Formentera

Alicante •

Murcia •   Valencia and
       Murcia
MURCIA

MEDITERRANEAN SEA

ALGERIA

XVII

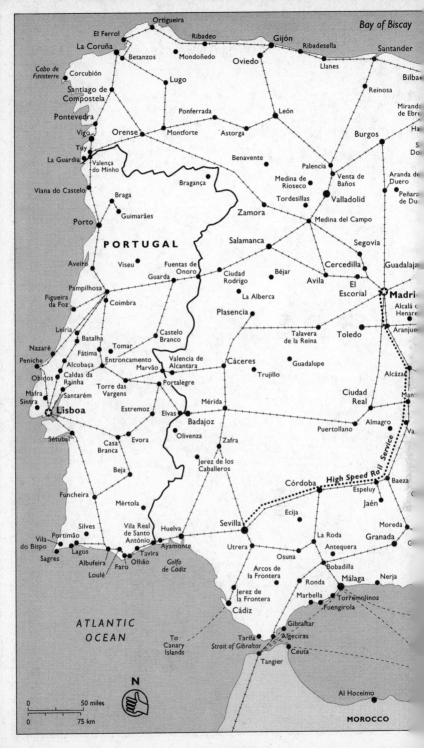

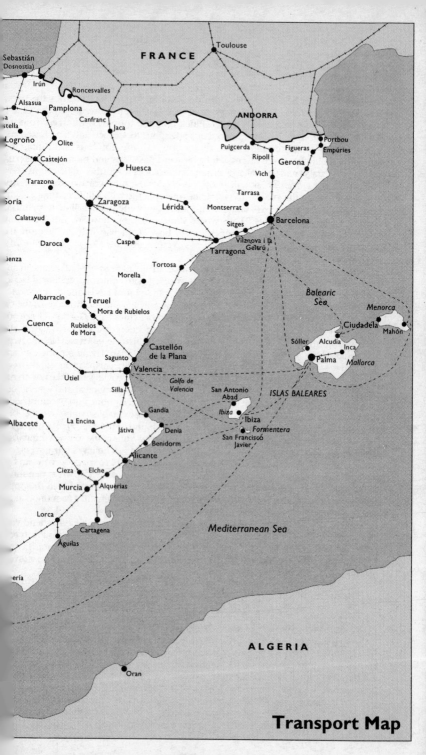

Transport Map

How to Use This Book

Or, how to digest **SPAM** (**S**pain **P**ortugal **A**ndorra **M**orocco). First, buy the book. It's physically smaller—but with more pages and juice—and more wieldly this year. It also sports a less conspicuous jacket. Pluck only the toppings you need from the **Essentials** section, which offers info that's analagous to spinach and lima beans and carrot juice—dense and difficult to digest but with the nutrients and ruffage for smoother sailing later. We discuss embassies and passports and money and alternative types of travel and special concerns and references for further information.

Next, a tasty *entremés* (side dish, Sp.), precedes the nitty gritty to each country specific section of the guide; this will whet your appetite with a little cultural enlightenment. The **Life and Times** sampler dips into history and politics, literature, music, food, language, and festivals. That's where you can find out how Spanish soccer has fared recently in international competition, or how Manueline Style architecture has altered Portugal's "look," or what type of government leads Morocco into the 21st century.

As you prepare to indulge in the main course, an all-out feast of Mediterranean and East Atlantic culture, you should familiarize yourself with some organizational tactics we use. We introduce regions and cities with a little bit of landscape description, a dash of history, and an impression of the pace of daily life and the attitudes of the citizens who populate the area. Island coverage and big cities have **Getting There** and **Getting Around** sections detailing transport connections; the earlier you dive into these the more efficient and economical thy travels will be. In cities and larger towns an **Orientation** section provides a rudimentary verbal map, laying out the city and the relative locations of key points; it is optimally read with a map at your side—it can help make a dreadful map useful. **Practical Information** provides hard data on things like tourist offices, financial services, transportation info, medical and emergency contacts, postal info (including the post office(s)), and telephone info. **Accommodations** and **Food** listings feature **ranked entries;** those establishments we feel provide the highest quality for the best price can be found at the top. **Sights** highlight the places we recommend you visit. **Entertainment** is your guide to everything from high culture and festivals to pubs and clubs, and SPAM '98 believes our coverage vastly improved after two years of focus. Many cities also have **maps** so you can better strategize how to get down from the top bunk so you can get down at that funky disco. Very small towns are not subdivided, and the text flows roughly in the opposite direction—Introduction followed by Sights and Entertainment, Accommodations and Food, Practical Information, and Transport.

Finally, a note on **how *not* to use this book.** Though you could easily spend your time visiting only the places we've covered, don't lose sight of why you're traveling—for excitement, for new and challenging experiences, for enjoyment. Don't allow *Let's Go* to substitute for your personal travel exploits; rather, let it be a diving board for your own adventures.

A NOTE TO OUR READERS

The information for this book is gathered by *Let's Go*'s researchers from late May through August. Each listing is derived from the assigned researcher's opinions based upon his or her visit at a particular time. The opinions are expressed in a candid and forthright manner. Other travelers might disagree. Those traveling at a different time may have different experiences since prices, dates, hours, and conditions are always subject to change. You are urged to check beforehand to avoid inconvenience and surprises. Travel always involves a certain degree of risk, especially in low-cost areas. When traveling, especially on a budget, always take particular care to ensure your safety.

ESSENTIALS

PLANNING YOUR TRIP

■ When to Go

In most coastal and interior regions, Spain, Portugal, and Morocco have their **high season** *(temporada alta)* in summer (roughly June-Sept.). Still, winter is high season in many high places (ski resorts). In many parts of Spain and Portugal, high season extends back to **Semana Santa** (Holy Week, the seven days leading to Easter Sunday), and includes festival days (see **Festivals and Holidays,** p. 680 Morocco's momentous religious event—Ramadan—is characteristically devoid of activity outside the sacred realm. In each country, August features slews of Europeans (including natives) on holiday, resulting somewhat surprisingly in a number of closed offices, restaurants, and lodgings.

Off-season (or "low season," *temporada baja)* trekking has many advantages, including lighter crowds, lower prices to stay and travel, and greater availability of rooms. During this period, university towns burst with students and vitality, but likewise many smaller (e.g. seaside) towns virtually shut down in winter. Tourist offices and sights cut their hours, restaurants close, and heat ceases. Furthermore, less than ideal weather in certain regions may temper your traveling (see **Climate,** p. 683

■ Useful Information

TOURIST OFFICES

Take advantage of the wealth of info tourist offices can provide, be it maps, brochures, or advice. Generally, they are less rigid and busy, more travel-oriented, and more attuned to your concerns than consulates.

Tourist Offices of Spain

U.S.: 666 5th Ave., 35th fl., **New York,** NY 10022 (tel. (212) 265-8822; fax 265-8864; email oet.ny@here-i.com; http://www.OKSPAIN.org). 845 North Michigan Ave., **Chicago,** IL 60611 (tel. (312) 642-1992; fax 642-9817). San Vincente Plaza Building, 8383 Wilshire Blvd., Suite 960, **Beverly Hills,** CA 90211 (tel. (213) 658-7188; fax 658-1061). 1221 Brickell Ave., Suite 1850, **Miami,** FL 33131 (tel. (305) 358-1992; fax 358-8223).

Canada: 2 Bloor St. W., 34th fl., **Toronto,** ON M4W 3E2 (tel. (416) 961-3131; fax 961-1992).

U.K.: 57-58 Saint James's St., **London** SW1A 1LD (tel. (171) 499 09 01; fax 629 42 57). 24hr. brochure request line (tel. 8910 66 99 20).

Ireland: Refer to Spanish Tourist Office in the U.K.

Portuguese National Tourist Offices

U.S.: 590 Fifth Ave., 4th fl., **New York,** NY 10036-4704 (tel. (212) 354-4403, 354-4404, or (800) PORTUGAL/76788425; fax 764-6137; http://www.portugal.org). Portuguese Trade & Tourism Office, 1900 L St. NW, Suite 310, **Washington, D.C.** 20036 (tel. (202) 331-8222; fax 331-8236; http://www.portugal.org).

Canada: Portuguese Trade & Tourism Commission, 60 Bloor St. W. #1005, **Toronto,** ON M4W 3B8 (tel. (416) 921-7376; fax 921-1353). 500 Sherbrooke St. W. #940, **Montreal,** QUE H3A 3C6 (tel. (514) 282-1264; fax 499-1450).

U.K.: Portuguese Trade & Tourism Office, 2nd fl., 22-25A Sackville St., **London** W1X 1DE (tel. (171) 494 14 41; fax 494 18 68).

Ireland: Portuguese Trade & Tourism Board, 54 Dawson St., **Dublin** 2 (tel. (1) 670 91 33 or 670 91 34; fax 670 91 41).

South Africa: Portuguese Trade and Tourism Office, Embassy of Portugal, 4th fl., Sunnyside Ridge, Sunnyside Drive Parktown, 2193 **Johannesburg** (tel. (27-11) 484 34 87; fax 484 54 16). Send mail to: P.O. Box 2473, Houghton 2041 Johannesburg.

Moroccan National Tourist Offices

U.S.: 20 E. 46th St., **New York,** NY 10007 (tel. (212) 557-2521; fax 949-8148). P.O. Box 22663, **Lake Buena Vista,** FL 32830 (tel. (407) 827-5337).

Canada: Place Montreal Trust, 1800 Avenue McGill Collège, #2450, **Montreal,** PQ H3A 3J6 (tel. (514) 842-8111; fax 842-5316).

U.K.: 205 Regent St., **London** W1R 7DE (tel. (171) 437 00 73; fax 734 81 72).

Australia: West St., North, **Sydney,** NSW 2060, DX 10641 Australia (tel. (2) 995 767 17; fax 992 310 53).

TRAVEL ORGANIZATIONS

American Automobile Association (AAA) Travel Related Services, 1000 AAA Dr. (Mail Stop 100), Heathrow, FL 32746-5063 (tel. (407) 444-7000; fax 444-7380). Offers emergency road services (for members), travel services, and auto insurance. The International Driving Permit (IDP), valid in most countries, is available for purchase from local AAA officers. Affiliated with Portuguese (ACP) and Spanish (RACE) driving organizations, AAA is a presence worldwide. To become a member, call (800) 926-4222.

Council on International Educational Exchange (Council), 205 East 42nd St., New York, NY 10017-5706 (tel. (888) COUNCIL (268-6245); fax (212) 822-2699; http://www.ciee.org). A private, non-profit organization, Council administers work, volunteer, and academic programs around the world. They also offer identity cards, including ISIC and GO25, and a range of publications, including the magazine *Student Travels* (free). Call or write for more info.

Federation of International Youth Travel Organizations (FIYTO), Bredgade 25H, DK-1260 Copenhagen K, Denmark (tel. (45) 33 33 96 00; fax 33 93 96 76; email mailbox@fiyto.org; http://www.fiyto.org), is an international organization promoting educational, cultural and social travel for young people. Member organizations include language schools, educational travel companies, national tourist boards, accommodation centers and other suppliers of travel services to youth and students. FIYTO sponsors the GO25 Card (http://www.go25.org).

International Student Travel Confederation, Herengracht 479, 1017 BS Amsterdam, The Netherlands (tel. (31) 20 421 2800; fax 20 421 2810; http://www.istc.org; email istcinfo@istc.org). The ISTC is a non-profit confederation of student travel organizations whose focus is to develop, promote, and facilitate travel among young people and students. Member organizations include International Student Surface Travel Association (ISSA), Student Air Travel Association (SATA), IASIS Travel Insurance, and the International Association for Educational and Work Exchange Programs (IAEWEP).

TRAVEL PUBLICATIONS

These companies hawk travel gear and accessories, travel books, guides, maps, schedules, videos, gadgets—everything except your ticket out of here.

Bon Voyage!, 2069 W. Bullard Ave., Fresno, CA 93711-1200 (tel. (800) 995-9716; outside the U.S. tel. (209) 447-8441; email 70754.3511@compuserve.com). Mail order catalogue offers products for the deluxe traveler to diehard trekker. Books, travel accessories, luggage, electrical converters, maps, videos, etc. They will match and ship the goods free if you can spot lower advertised prices elsewhere.

The College Connection, Inc., 1295 Prospect St., Suite B, La Jolla, CA 92037 (tel. (619) 551-9770; fax 551-9987; email eurailnow@aol.com; http://www.eurailpass.com). Publishes *The Passport,* listing hints for traveling and studying abroad, free for *Let's Go* readers (request by email or fax only). Its close affiliate, The College Rail Connection, sells railpasses and flights at student discounts.

Forsyth Travel Library, Inc., 1750 East 131st Street, P.O. Box 480800, Kansas City, MO 64148 (tel. (800) 367-7984; fax (816) 942-6969; email forsyth@avi.net; http://www.forsyth.com). This mail-order service stocks city, area, and country maps; guides for rail and ferry travel; rail tickets and passes. Reservation service, too. The *Thomas Cook European Timetable,* listing train schedules is available for US$28, $39 with full map, $4.50 shipping. Free catalog.

■ Internet Resources

Along with everything else in the 90s, budget travel is moving rapidly into the information age, with the **Internet** as a leading travel resource. Today, people can make their own airline, hotel, hostel, or car rental reservations on the internet, and connect personally with others abroad, allowing people to become their own budget travel planners. *NetTravel: How Travelers Use the Internet,* by Michael Shapiro, is a very thorough and informative guide which describes the different uses of the internet and how they are most useful for travelers (US$25).

There are a number of ways to access the **Internet.** Most popular are commercial internet services, such as **America Online** (tel. (800) 827-6364) and **CompuServe** (tel. (800) 433-0389). Many employers and schools also offer gateways to the Internet, often at no cost (unlike the corporate gateways above). The forms of the Internet most useful to budget travelers are the World Wide Web and Usenet newsgroups.

THE WORLD WIDE WEB

Increasingly the Internet forum of choice, the **World Wide Web** provides its users with text, graphics and sound. The Web's lack of hierarchy makes it difficult to distinguish between good information, bad information, and marketing. **Search engines** (services that search for web pages under specific subjects) can significantly aid the search process. **Lycos** (http://a2z.lycos.com), **Infoseek** (http://guide.infoseek.com), and **HOTBOT** (http://www.hotbot.com) are among the most popular. **Yahoo!** is a slightly more organized search engine; check out its travel links at http://www.yahoo.com/Recreation/Travel. Another good way to explore is to find a good site and go from there, through links from one web page to another. Check out **Let's Go's web site** (http://www.letsgo.com) and find our newsletter, information about our books, an always-current list of links, and more. Or, you can try some of our favorites sites directly:

Rent-A-Wreck's Travel Links (http://www.rent-a-wreck.com/raw/travlist.htm).
Big World Magazine (http://www.paonline.com/bigworld), a budget travel 'zine, has a web page with a great collection of links to travel pages.
The CIA World Factbook (http://www.odci.gov/cia/publications/nsolo/wfb-all.htm) has tons of vital statistics on the country you want to visit (the hyphen in the address is necessary).
The Student and Budget Travel Guide (http://asa.ugl.lib.umich.edu/chdocs/travel/travel-guide.html) gives info on accommodations, transportation, and more.
TravelHUB (http://www.travelhub.com) is a great site for cheap travel deals.

Let's Go lists relevant web sites throughout different sections of the **Essentials** chapter. Finally, web sites come and go very rapidly; a good web site one week might disappear the next, and a new one might quickly take its place.

■ Documents and Formalities

EMBASSIES AND CONSULATES

Direct questions concerning visas and passports go to consulates, not embassies (which handle more weighty matters). For info on your home country's embassies and consulates in Spain, Portugal, and Morocco see p. 36.

Spain

U.S.: Embassy, 2375 Pennsylvania Ave. NW, Washington, D.C. 20037 (tel. (202) 452-0100). **Consulates,** 150 E. 58th St., 30th fl., **New York,** NY 10155 (tel. (212) 355-4080, -81, -82; fax 644-3751). **Others** in Boston, Chicago, Houston, Los Angeles, Miami, New Orleans, Puerto Rico, San Francisco, and Washington, D.C.

Canada: Embassy, 74 Stanley Av., Ottawa, ON, K1M 1P4 (tel. (613) 747-2252 or 747-7293; fax 744-1224). **Consulates,** 1 Westmount Sq., Suite 1456, **Montreal,** PQ H3Z 2P9 (tel. (514) 935-5235, -36; fax 935-4655). 1200 Bay St., Suite 400, **Toronto,** ON M5R 2A5 (tel. (416) 967-4949 or 967 4960; fax 925-4949).

U.K.: Embassy, 39 Chesham Pl., **London** SW1X 8SB (tel. (171) 235 55 55; fax 259 53 92). **Consulates,** 20 Draycott Pl., **London** SW3 2RZ (tel. (171) 589 89 89; fax 581 78 88). Suite 1A, Brook House, 70, Spring Gardens, **Manchester** M2 2BQ (tel. (161) 236 12 33; fax 228 74 67). 63 N. Castle St., **Edinburgh** EH2 3LJ (tel. (131) 220 18 43, 220 14 39, or 220 14 42; fax 226 45 68).

Ireland: Consulate, 17A Merlyn Park, Balls Bridge, Dublin 4 (tel. (035) 269 1640; fax 269 1854).

Australia: Embassy, 15 Arkana St., **Yarralumla,** ACT. 2600 (tel. (02) 6273 3555). Mailing address: P.O. Box 9076, Deakin, ACT 2600. **Consulates:** Level 24, St. Martins Tower, 31 Market St., **Sydney,** NSW 2000 (tel. (02) 9261 2433 or 9261 2443; fax 9283 1695). 3rd. floor, 766 Elizabeth St., **Melbourne,** VIC 3000 (tel. (03) 9347 1966 or 9347 1997; fax 9347 7330).

New Zealand: Embassy, check Spanish Embassy in Australia. **Consulates,** Pararekau Island, P.O. Box 71, Papakura, **Aukland** (tel. (9) 298 51 76; fax 299 80 57).

South Africa: Embassy, 37 Shortmarket St., **Cape Town** 8001 (tel. (012) 222 326; fax 222 328). 169 Pine St., Arcadia, **Pretoria** 0083 (tel. 344 3875/76; fax 343 4891).

Portugal

U.S.: Embassy, 2125 Kalorama Rd. NW, Washington, D.C. 20008 (tel. (202) 328-8610; fax 462-3726). **Consulates,** 630 5th Ave., 3rd fl., #310, **New York,** NY 10111 (tel. (212) 246-4580 or 246-4582; fax 459-0190). Others in Boston, Chicago, Coral Gables (FL), the Dominican Republic, Houston, Honolulu, Los Angeles, Newark, New Bedford (MA), New Orleans, Philadelphia, Providence, San Francisco, San Juan (PR), Waterbury (CT), and Washington, D.C.

Canada: Embassy, 645 Island Park Dr., Ottawa, ON K1Y OB8 (tel. (613) 729-0883; fax 729-4236). **Consulates,** 2020 University St. #1725, **Montréal,** QU H3A 2A5 (tel. (514) 499-0621 or 499-0359; fax 499-0366). 121 Richmond St. W., 7th fl., **Toronto,** ON M5H 2K1 (tel. (416) 360-8260 or 360-8261; fax 360-0350). 700 West Pender St., #904, **Vancouver,** BC V6C 1G8 (tel. (604) 688-6514). 167 Lombard Ave. #908, **Winnipeg,** MB R3B OV3 (tel. (204) 943-8941).

U.K.: Embassy, 11 Belgrave Sq., **London** SW1X 8PP (tel. (171) 235 53 31; fax 245 1 87). **Consulate,** Silver City House, 62 Brompton Road, **London** SW3 1BJ (tel. (171) 581 87 22).

Australia: Embassy, 23 Culgoa Circuit, O'Malley A.C.T. 2606 Deakin, [or] P.O. Box 92, A.C.T. 2600 **Canberra** (tel. (02) 6290 1733; fax 6290 1957). **Consulate,** 13 Ocean St., **Edgecliff,** NSW 2027 (tel. (02) 9326 1844; fax 9282 3705 or 9327 1607). Mailing address: G.P.O. Box 4219, **Sydney,** NSW 2001.

New Zealand: Embassy, 117 Arney Road, Remuera, **Auckland** 5 (tel. (9) 22 34 50). **Consulate,** Delloitte Hosking and Sells, Southpac House, Victoria St., 1 **Wellington** 1 (tel. (4) 72 16 77).

South Africa: Embassy, 599 Leyds Street, Mucklenuk, **Pretoria** (tel. (012) 341 2 40; fax 341 39 75). **Consulates,** 701 Van Erkom Building, 217 Pretorius St., **Pretoria** (tel. (012) 262 141 or 323 55 54). 3rd fl., Diamond Corner Building, 63 Strand St., **Cape Town** (tel. (021) 24 24 54 or 24 24 56). 16th fl., 320 W. St., **Durban** (tel. (031) 305 75 11).

Morocco

U.S.: Embassy, 1601 21st St. NW, **Washington, D.C.** 20009 (tel. (202) 462-7979; fax 452-0161). **Consulates,** 10 East 40th. St., 24th fl., **New York,** NY 10016 (tel. (212

213-9644; fax 779-7441). 1821 Jefferson Place NW, **Washington, D.C.** 20036 (tel. (202) 462-7979; 452-0106).
Canada: Embassy, 38 Range Rd., **Ottawa,** ON. K1N 8J4 (tel. (613) 236-7391/92). **Consulate,** 1010 Sherbrooke West Street 1510, **Montreal,** QU H3A 2R7 (tel. (514) 288-8750).
U.K.: Embassy, 40 Queens Gate Gardens, **London** SW7 5NE (tel. (171) 581 50 01; fax 225 38 62).

PASSPORTS

Travelers need legal passports or visas to enter and leave Spain, Portugal, and Morocco. A passport allows **U.S., Canadian, British,** and **New Zealand citizens** to remain in all three for 90 days. **Australian citizens** may remain in Portugal and Morocco for 90 days with a passport, but need a visa to enter Spanish territory. **South African** citizens need a visa to get into all three countries (see **Visa,** p. 7). In all three, your passport must be valid for a minimum of six months after your planned end of stay. Carry your passport and/or visa at all times; police have the right to examine it on demand. Furthermore, admission as a visitor does not include the right to work, which may be authorized only with a work permit. Lastly, be mindful that entering certain countries to study requires a special visa.

Australia Citizens must apply for a passport in person at a post office, a passport office, or an Australian diplomatic mission overseas. An appointment may be necessary. Passport offices are located in Adelaide, Brisbane, Canberra City, Darwin, Hobart, Melbourne, Newcastle, Perth, and Sydney. A parent may file an application for a child who is under 18 and unmarried. Adult passports cost AUS$120 (for a 32pg. passport) or AUS$180 (64pg.), and a child's is AUS$60 (32pg.) or AUS$90 (64 page). For more info, call toll-free (in Australia) 13 12 32.

Canada Application forms in English and French are available at all passport offices, Canadian missions, many travel agencies, and Northern Stores in northern communities. Citizens may apply in person at any 1 of 28 regional Passport Offices across Canada. Travel agents can direct applicants to the nearest location. Canadian citizens residing abroad should contact the nearest Canadian embassy or consulate. Children under 16 may be included on a parent's passport. Passports cost CDN$60, are valid for 5 years, and are not renewable. Processing takes approximately 5 business days for applications in-person; 10 days if by mail. For additional info, contact the Canadian Passport Office, Department of Foreign Affairs and International Trade, Ottawa, ON, K1A 0G3 (tel. (613) 994-3500; http://www.dfait-maeci.gc.ca/passport). Travelers may also call (800) 567-6868 (24hr.); in Toronto (416) 973-3251; in Vancouver (604) 775-6250; in Montréal (514) 283-2152. Refer to the booklet *Bon Voyage, But...,* free at any passport office or by calling **Info-Centre** at (800) 267-8376, for further help and a list of Canadian embassies and consulates abroad. You may also find entry and background information for various countries by contacting the **Consular Affairs Bureau** in Ottawa (tel. (800) 267-6788 (24hr.) or (613) 944-6788).

Ireland Citizens can apply for a passport by mail to either the Department of Foreign Affairs, Passport Office, Setanta Centre, Molesworth St., Dublin 2 (tel. (01) 671 1633), or the Passport Office, Irish Life Building, 1A South Mall, Cork (tel. (021) 272 525). Obtain an application at a local Garda station or request one from a passport office. The new **Passport Express Service,** available through post offices, allows citizens to get a passport in 2 weeks for an extra IR£3. Passports cost IR£45 and are valid for 10yr. Citizens under 18 or over 65 can request a 3yr. passport that costs IR£10.

New Zealand Application forms for passports are available in New Zealand from travel agents and Department of Internal Affairs Link Centres in the main cities and towns. Overseas, forms and passport services are provided by New Zealand embassies, high commissions, and consulates. Applications may also be forwarded to the

Passport Office, P.O. Box 10526, Wellington, New Zealand. Standard processing time in New Zealand is 10 working days for correct applications. The fees are adult NZ$80 and child NZ$40. An urgent passport service is also available for an extra NZ$80. Different fees apply at overseas post: nine posts including London, Sydney, and Los Angeles offer both standard and urgent services (adult NZ$130, child NZ$65, plus NZ$130 if urgent). The fee at other posts is adult NZ$260, child NZ$195, and a passport will be issued within three days. Children's names can no longer be endorsed on a parent's passport—they must apply for their own, which are valid for up to 5 years. An adult's passport is valid for up to 10 years.

South Africa Citizens can apply for a passport at any **Home Affairs Office** or **South African Mission.** Tourist passports, valid for 10 years, cost SAR80. Children under 16 must be issued their own passports, valid for 5 years, which cost SAR60. If a passport is needed in a hurry, an **emergency passport** may be issued for SAR50. An application for a permanent passport must accompany the emergency passport application. Time for the completion of an application is normally 3 months or more from the time of submission. Current passports less than 10 years old (counting from date of issuance) may be **renewed** until December 31, 1999; every citizen whose passport's validity does not extend far beyond this date is urged to renew it as soon as possible, to avoid the expected glut of applications as 2000 approaches. Renewal is free, and turnaround time is usually 2 weeks. For further information, contact the nearest Department of Home Affairs Office.

United Kingdom British citizens, British Dependent Territories citizens, British Nationals (overseas), and British Overseas citizens may apply for a **full passport** valid for 10 years (5 years if under 16). Application forms are available at passport offices, main post offices, many travel agents, and branches of Lloyds Bank and Artac World Choice. Apply in person or by mail to one of the passport offices located in London, Liverpool, Newport, Peterborough, Glasgow, or Belfast. The fee is UK£18. Children under 16 may be included on a parent's passport. Processing by mail usually takes 4-6 weeks. The London office offers same-day, walk-in rush service; arrive early. The formerly available **British Visitor's Passport** (valid in some western European countries and Bermuda only) has been abolished; every traveler over 16 now needs a 10-yr., standard passport. The U.K. Passport Agency can be reached by phone at tel. (0990) 21 04 10, and information is available on the Internet at http://www.open.gov.uk/ukpass.

United States Citizens may apply for a passport at any federal or state **courthouse** or **post office** authorized to accept passport applications, or at a **U.S. Passport Agency,** located in Boston, Chicago, Honolulu, Houston, Los Angeles, Miami, New Orleans, New York, Philadelphia, San Francisco, Seattle, Stamford, or Washington, D.C. Refer to the "U.S. Government, State Department" section of the telephone directory or the local post office for addresses. Parents must apply in person for children under age 13. You must apply in person if this is your first passport, you're under age 18, or if your current passport is more than 12 years old or was issued before your 18th birthday. Passports are valid for 10 years (5 years if under 18) and cost US$65 (under 18 US$40). Passports may be **renewed** by mail or in person for US$55. Processing takes 3-4 weeks. **Rush service** is available for a surcharge of US$30 with proof of departure within 10 working days (e.g., an airplane ticket or itinerary), or for travelers leaving in 2-3 weeks who require visas. Given proof of citizenship, a U.S. embassy or consulate abroad can usually issue a new passport. Report a passport lost or stolen in the U.S. in writing to Passport Services, 1425 K St., N.W., U.S. Department of State, Washington D.C., 20524 or to the nearest passport agency. For more info, contact the U.S. Passport Information's **24-hour recorded message** (tel. (202) 647-0518). U.S. citizens may receive consular information sheets, travel warnings, and public announcements at any passport agency, U.S. embassy, or consulate, or by sending a self-addressed stamped envelope to: Overseas Citizens Services, Room 4811, Department of State, Washington, D.C. 20520-4818 (tel. (202) 647-5225; fax 647-3000). Additional information (including publications) about documents, formalities and travel abroad is available

through the Bureau of Consular Affairs homepage at http://travel.state.gov, or through the State Department site at http://www.state.gov.

VISAS

If you wish to stay longer than your passport allows, apply for a visa at a Spanish, Portuguese, or Moroccan embassy or consulate in your own country well before departing (see p. 3). A visa is an endorsement stamped into your passport by a foreign government allowing you to stay in their country for a specified time, period, and purpose. Unless you're a student, extending your stay abroad may be difficult. Contact the country's immigration officials or local police before your passport expires.

For more information, send for *Foreign Entry Requirements* (US$0.50) from the **Consumer Information Center,** Department 363D, Pueblo, CO 81009 (tel. (719) 948-4000; http://www.pueblo.gsa.gov), or contact the **Center for International Business and Travel (CIBT),** 25 West 43rd St. #1420, New York, NY 10036 (tel. (800) 925-2428 or (212) 575-2811 from NYC), which secures visas for travel to and from all countries for a variable service charge.

CUSTOMS: INTO SPAIN, PORTUGAL, & MOROCCO

Anything beyond each country's allowance must be **declared** and is charged a **duty.** In **Spain,** for instance, personal belongings, radios, recorders, and sporting goods for personal use are admitted duty-free, are up to 200 cigarettes, 100 cigars, 2L of wine, 1L of liquor, and two cameras. Those coming to **Morocco** can freely import clothes, sporting equipment, small camping objects, "personal effects" (one camera, pair of binoculars, musical instrument, radio, and typewriter), 200 cigarettes, and 50 cigars or 400 grams of pipe tobacco. Presenting receipts from purchases made abroad will help establish values when you return. It is wise to make a list, including serial numbers, of any valuables that you have on you from home. If you register this list with customs before your departure and have an official stamp it, you will avoid import duty charges and ensure an easy passage upon your return. Be especially careful to document items manufactured abroad.

CUSTOMS: RETURNING HOME

Upon returning home, you must declare all articles you acquired abroad and pay a **duty** on the value of those articles that exceed the allowance established by your country's customs service. Goods and gifts purchased at **duty-free** shops abroad are not exempt from duty or sales tax at your point of return; you must declare these items as well. "Duty-free" merely means that you need not pay a tax in the country of purchase.

It is illegal to export **Moroccan dirhams,** Morocco's currency. On leaving Morocco, you may convert 50% of the *dirhams* in your possession by presenting exchange slips (to prove they were purchased at the official rate) to an authorized bank at your point of departure. Save your receipts as proof each time you change money, and try not to end up with too many extra *dirhams*.

Australia Citizens may import AUS$400 (under 18 AUS$200) of goods duty-free, in addition to 1.125L alcohol and 250 cigarettes or 250g tobacco. You must be over 18 to import alcohol or tobacco. There is no limit to the amount of Australian and/ or foreign cash that may be brought into or taken out of the country, but amounts of AUS$10,000 or more, or the equivalent in foreign currency, must be reported. All foodstuffs and animal products must be declared on arrival. For information, contact the Regional Director, Australian Customs Service, GPO Box 8, Sydney NSW 2001 (tel. (02) 9213 2000; fax 9213 4000).

Canada Citizens who remain abroad for at least 1 week may bring back up to CDN$500 worth of goods duty-free any time. Citizens or residents who travel for a period between 48 hours and 6 days can bring back up to CDN$200. Both of these exemptions may include tobacco and alcohol. You are permitted to ship goods except tobacco and alcohol home under the CDN$500 exemption as long as you declare them when you arrive. Goods under the CDN$200 exemption, as well as all alcohol and tobacco, must be in your hand or checked luggage. Citizens of legal age (which varies by province) may import in-person up to 200 cigarettes, 50 cigars or cigarillos, 400g loose tobacco, 400 tobacco sticks, 1.14L wine or alcohol, and 24 355mL cans/bottles of beer; the value of these products is included in the CDN$200 or CDN$500. For more information, write to Canadian Customs, 2265 St. Laurent Blvd., Ottawa, ON K1G 4K3 (tel. (613) 993-0534), phone the 24hr Automated Customs Information Service at (800) 461-9999, or visit Revenue Canada at http://www.revcan.ca.

Ireland Citizens must declare everything in excess of IR£142 (IR£73 per traveler under 15 years of age) obtained outside the EU or duty- and tax-free in the EU above the following allowances: 200 cigarettes, 100 cigarillos, 50 cigars, or 250g tobacco; 1L liquor or 2L wine; 2L still wine; 50g perfume; and 250mL toilet water. Goods obtained duty and tax paid in another EU country up to a value of IR£460 (IR£115 per traveler under 15) will not be subject to additional customs duties. Travelers under 17 may not import tobacco or alcohol. For more information, contact The Revenue Commissioners, Dublin Castle (tel. (01) 679 27 77; fax 671 20 21; email taxes@iol.ie; http://www.revenue.ie) or The Collector of Customs and Excise, The Custom House, Dublin 1.

New Zealand Citizens may import up to NZ$700 worth of goods duty-free if intended for personal use or are unsolicited gifts. The concession is 200 cigarettes (1 carton) or 250g tobacco or 50 cigars or a combination of all 3 not to exceed 250g. You may also bring in 4.5L of beer or wine and 1.125L of liquor. Only travelers over 17 may import tobacco or alcohol. For more info, contact New Zealand Customs, 50 Anzac Ave., Box 29, Auckland (tel. (09) 377 35 20; fax 309 29 78).

South Africa Citizens may import duty-free: 400 cigarettes, 50 cigars, 250g tobacco, 2L wine, 1L of spirits, 250mL toilet water, 50mL perfume, and other consumable items up to a value of SAR500. Goods up to a value of SAR10,000 over and above this duty-free allowance are taxable at 20%; such goods are also exempted from payment of VAT. Items acquired abroad and sent to the Republic as unaccompanied baggage do not qualify for any allowances. You may not export or import South African bank notes in excess of SAR2000. For more information, consult the free pamphlet *South African Customs Information,* available in airports or from the Commissioner for Customs and Excise, Private Bag X47, Pretoria 0001 (tel. (12) 314 99 11; fax 328 64 78).

United Kingdom Citizens or visitors arriving in the U.K. from outside the EU must declare goods in excess of the following allowances: 200 cigarettes, 100 cigarillos, 50 cigars, or 250g tobacco; still table wine (2L); strong liqueurs over 22% volume (1L), or fortified or sparkling wine, other liqueurs (2L); perfume (60 cc/mL); toilet water (250 cc/mL); and UK£136 worth of all other goods including gifts and souvenirs. You must be over 17 to import liquor or tobacco. These allowances also apply to duty-free purchases within the EU, except for the last category, other goods, which then has an allowance of UK£71. Goods obtained duty and tax paid for personal use (regulated according to set guide levels) within the EU do not require any further customs duty. For more information, contact Her Majesty's Customs and Excise, Custom House, Nettleton Road, Heathrow Airport, Hounslow, Middlesex TW6 2LA (tel. (0181) 910-3744; fax 910-3765).

United States Citizens may import US$400 worth of accompanying goods duty-free and must pay a 10% tax on the next US$1000. You must declare all purchases, so have sales slips ready. The US$400 personal exemption covers goods purchased

for personal or household use (this includes gifts) and cannot include more than 100 cigars, 200 cigarettes (1 carton), and 1L of wine or liquor. You must be over 21 to bring liquor into the U.S. If you mail home personal goods of U.S. origin, you can avoid duty charges by marking the package "American goods returned." For more information, consult the brochure *Know Before You Go,* available from the U.S. Customs Service, Box 7407, Washington D.C. 20044 (tel. (202) 927-6724), or visit the Web (http://www.customs.ustreas.gov).

YOUTH, STUDENT, & TEACHER IDENTIFICATION

Student identification cards entitle youthful travelers in **Spain, Portugal,** and occasionally **Morocco** to many discounts and some freebies. The most widely accepted is the **International Student Identity Card (ISIC),** put out by the **International Student Travel Confederation (ISTC).** For US$19 or CDN$15, cardholders readily receive student discounts off of tickets for sights, theaters, and museums; accommodations; train, ferry, and airplane travel; and other goodies across Europe. The ISIC also provides a toll-free Traveler's Assistance Hotline, whose multilingual staff can help in medical, legal, and financial emergencies overseas. It also provides insurance benefits, including US$100 per day of in-hospital sickness for a maximum of 60 days, and medical/accident insurance up to US$3000 (see **Insurance,** p. 19). Many student travel agencies around the world issue ISICs, including STA Travel in Australia and New Zealand; Travel CUTS in Canada; USIT in Ireland and Northern Ireland; SASTS in South Africa; Campus Travel and STA Travel in the U.K.; Council Travel, Let's Go Travel, and STA Travel in the U.S.; and any of the other organizations under the auspices of the International Student Travel Confederation (ISTC). Prospective members must prove they are enrolled in school—many airlines and some other services require other proof of student identity, such as a signed letter from the registrar attesting to your student status and stamped with the school seal or your school ID card. The card is valid from September through December of the following year. For more information on these cards, consult the organization's web site (http://www.istc.org; email isicinfo@istc.org). Another option for the under-26 crowd is the 1-year **GO25 Card,** put out by FIYTO. The GO25 card provides discounts similar to those available with the ISIC and is available through many travel agencies (Europeans may contact FIYTO directly), yet its members need not be enrolled students. The fee is US$19, CDN$15, or UK£5. Refer to **Budget Travel Agencies** on p. 30 (particularly student travel services) for a corps of companies which vend ISIC, ITIC (International Teacher Identity Card), and GO25 cards.

DRIVING PERMITS AND CAR INSURANCE

In **Spain** and **Portugal**, travelers often drive with a valid American or Canadian license or officially with an **International Driving Permit (IDP)** for a limited number of months; most car rental agencies don't require the permit, nor does either government—most valid home-spun licenses will work. In **Morocco,** an IDP is officially required but chances are it won't matter. At the same time, though, it's a good idea to get one anyway; it also serves as a credible ID.

Your IDP, valid for one year, must be issued in your own country before you depart. A valid driver's license from your home country must always accompany the IDP. An application for an IDP usually needs to be accompanied by one or two photos, a current local license, an additional form of identification, and a fee. Australians can obtain an IDP by contacting their local **Royal Automobile Club (RAC),** or the **National Royal Motorist Association (NRMA)** if in NSW or the ACT, where a permit can be obtained for AUS$12. Canadian license holders can obtain an IDP (CDN$10) through any **Canadian Automobile Association (CAA)** branch office in Canada, or by writing to CAA Central Ontario, 60 Commerce Valley Drive East, Thornhill, ON L3T 7P9 (tel. (416) 221-4300). Citizens of Ireland should drop into their nearest **Automobile Association (AA)** office where an IDP can be picked up for IR£4, or phone (1) 283 3555 for a postal application form. In New Zealand, con-

tact your local **Automobile Association (AA),** or their main office at 99 Albert Street, PO Box 5, Auckland (tel. (09) 377 4660; fax 309 4564). IDPs cost NZ$8 ĞNZ$2 for return postage. In South Africa visit your local **Automobile Association of South Africa** office, where IDPs can be picked up for SAR25, or for more information phone (011) 466 6641, or write to P.O. Box 596, 2000 Johannesburg. In the U.K. IDPs are UK£4 and you can either visit your local **AA Shop** or call (01256) 49 39 32 and order a postal application form (allow 2-3 weeks). U.S. license holders can obtain an IDP (US$10) at any **American Automobile Association (AAA)** office or by writing to AAA Florida, Travel Agency Services Department, 1000 AAA Drive (mail stop 28), Heathrow, FL 32746-5080 (tel. (407) 444-4245; fax 444-4247).

Most credit cards cover standard **insurance.** If you rent, lease, or borrow a car, you will need a **green card,** or **International Insurance Certificate,** to prove that you have liability insurance. Obtain it through the car rental agency; most include coverage in their prices. If you lease a car, you can obtain a green card from the dealer. Some travel agents offer the card; it may also be available at border crossings. Verify whether your auto insurance applies abroad; even if it does, you will still need a green card to certify this to foreign officials. If you have a collision abroad, the accident will show on your domestic records if you report it to your insurance company.

HOSTELING PREP

For tight budgets and those lonesome traveling blues, hostels can't be beat. Hostels are generally dorm-style accommodations, often in single-sex large rooms with bunk beds, although some hostels do offer private rooms for families and couples. There can be drawbacks: some hostels close during certain daytime "lock-out" hours, have a curfew, impose a maximum stay, or, less frequently, require that you do chores. Fees range from US$5 to $25 per night, and hostels associated with one of the large hostel associations often have lower rates for members. If you have Internet access, check out the **Internet Guide to Hostelling** (http://hostels.com), which includes hostels from around the world in addition to lots of information about hostelling and backpacking worldwide. **Eurotrip** (http://www.eurotrip.com/accommodation/accommodation.html also has information on budget hostels and several international hostel associations. Reservations for over 300 **Hostelling International (HI)** hostels (see listing below) may be made via the International Booking Network (IBN) a computerized system which allows you make hostels reservations months in advance for a nominal fee (tel. (202) 783-6161). If you plan to stay in hostels, consider joining one of these associations:

An Óige (Irish Youth Hostel Association), 61 Mountjoy St., Dublin 7 (tel. (01) 830 4555; fax 830-5808; anoigeşiol.ie. One-year membership is IR£7.50, under 18 IR£4 family IR£7.50 for each adult with children under 16 free. Prices from IR£4.50-9.50 a night. 37 locations.

Australian Youth Hostels Association (AYHA), Level 3, 10 Mallett St., Campendown NSW 2050 (tel. (02) 565 1699; fax 565 1325; email YHA@zeta.org.au). Memberships AUS$42, renewal AUS$26.

Hostelling International-American Youth Hostels (HI-AYH), 733 15th St. NW Suite 840, Washington, D.C. 20005 (202-783-6161; fax 783-6171; email hiayh serv@hiayh.org; http://www.hiayh.org). Maintains 35 offices and over 150 hostels in the U.S. Memberships can be purchased at many travel agencies (see **Budget Travel Agencies,** p. 30) or the national office in Washington, D.C. One year membership US$25, under 18 US$10, over 54 US$15, family cards US$35; includes *Hostelling North America: The Official Guide to Hostels in Canada and the United States.* Reserve by letter, phone, fax, or through the International Booking Network (IBN), a computerized reservation system which lets you book from other hostels worldwide up to 6 months in advance. Basic rules (with much local variation): check-in 5-8pm, check-out 9:30am (although most urban hostels have 24-hour access), max. stay 3 days, no pets or alcohol allowed on the premises. Fees US$ 22 per night.

Hostelling International-Canada (HI-C), 400-205 Catherine St., Ottawa, Ontario K2P 1C3, Canada (tel. 613-237-7884; fax 237-7868). Maintains 73 hostels throughout Canada. IBN booking centers in Edmonton, Montreal, Ottawa, and Vancouver; expect CDN$9-23/night. Membership packages: 1-yr, under 18 CDN$12; 1yr., over 18 CDN$25; 2yr., over 18 CDN$35; lifetime CDN$175.

Scottish Youth Hostels Association (SYHA), 7 Glebe Crescent, Stirling FK8 2JA (tel. (01786) 891400; fax 891333; email syha@syha.org.uk; http://www.syha.org.uk). Membership UK£6, under 18 UK£2.50.

Youth Hostels Association of England and Wales (YHA), Trevelyan House, 8 St. Stephen's Hill, St. Albans, Hertfordshire AL1 2DY, England (tel. (01727) 855215; fax 844126). Enrollment fees are: UK£9.50; under 18 UK£3.50; UK£19 for both parents with children under 18 enrolled free; UK£9.50 for one parent with children under 18 enrolled free; UK£130 for lifetime membership. Overnight prices for under 18 UK£4.25-17.20, for adults UK£6.25-20.50.

Youth Hostels Association of Northern Ireland (YHANI), 22 Donegall Rd., Belfast BT12 5JN, Northern Ireland (tel. (01232) 324733 or 315435; fax 439699). Prices range from UK£8-12. Annual memberships UK£7, under 18 UK£3, family UK£14 for up to 6 children.

Youth Hostels Association of New Zealand (YHANZ), P.O. Box 436, 173 Gloucester St., Christchurch 1 (tel. (643) 379 9970; fax 365 4476; email info@yha.org.nz; http://www.yha.org.nz). Annual membership fee NZ$24.

Hostel Association of South Africa, P.O. Box 4402, Cape Town 8000 (tel. (021) 24 2511; fax 24 4119; email hisa@gem.co.za; http://www.gen.com/hisa). Membership SAR45, group SAR120, family SAR90, lifetime SAR250.

CURRENCY AND EXCHANGE

> NOTE: This book was researched in the summer of 1997. Since then, prices may have risen by as much as 5-15%. The **exchange rates** (listed in each country's Essentials section) were compiled in early September. Since rates fluctuate considerably, check before you go. In Spain the unit of currency is the *peseta* (pta); in Portugal, the *escudo* ($); in Morocco, the *dirham* (dh).

If you stay in hostels and eat out at low-price establishments, expect to spend around US$40 a day in **Spain,** slightly less in **Portugal,** and less than US$20 in **Morocco.** No matter your budget, carry surplus cash and be prepared to get more. And look out for crooks and hustlers (especially in Morocco)—tourists are often targets. Be aware that personal checks may not be accepted, even at some banks.

When to exchange?—that is the question. Doing so abroad may be cheaper, but doing it before prevents headaches. Bring enough foreign currency to last at least through the first 24-72 hours of a trip, depending on which day you arrive. Also, observe commission rates closely and check newspapers to get the standard exchange rate. Banks generally have the best rates, but shop around. Morocco eases the process somewhat: rates are uniform, and banks do not charge commission. Since you lose money with every transaction, convert in large sums (unless the currency is depreciating rapidly). But control yourself!—it may be difficult to change pesetas, dirhams, or escudos back to your home currency. Also, the more money you have, the more that can be stolen. Especially in Morocco, do not try the black market for currency exchange—chances are good that you will be swindled.

If you are using traveler's checks or bills, carry some in small denominations (US$50 or less). These are especially useful when exchange rates are bad.

Avoid using Western money when you can. Throwing dollars around to gain preferential treatment is offensive, and it can attract thieves (one Morocco research-writer learned this the hard way). Also, many locals may raise prices for foreigners. Bargaining is common, especially at bazaars and street fairs. As the Moroccan embassy in Washington, D.C. writes, "You ought not forget to bargain over the prices"—in Morocco or Iberia.

Banking hours in **Spain** from June through September a re Monday through Friday 9am-2pm; from October 1 to May 31, banks are also open Saturday 9am-1pm. Some banks are open in the afternoon as well. Banks charge a minimum commission for currency exchange. Banco Central Hispano is the place to exchange American Express traveler's checks, not American Express offices. Hispano branches, marked by blue signs with a yellow seashell symbol, do not charge commission and offer the best rates. In **Portugal,** official hours are Monday through Friday 8:30am-3pm, but play it safe by giving yourself some extra time. In **Morocco,** banking hours are Monday through Friday 8:30-11:30am and 2:30-4:30pm, during Ramadan from 9:30am-2pm. In the summer, certain banks close at 1pm and do not re-open in the afternoon. Exchange offices often lie near harbors and airports; at Casablanca-Mohammed V Airport, the exchange office is open 24 hours. Hotels, often with longer hours, are another alternative; some exchange money at the same rate as banks, but watch for high commissions, particularly when cashing traveler's checks.

In larger cities in Spain and Portugal, you may stumble across handy, high-tech **automatic exchange machines.** Like ATMs, these machines provide 24-hour service. Insert American bills, add water (no, don't), and *pesetas* or *escudos* pop out. Unless you use the AmEx service (see below), avoid cashing checks in foreign currencies; they usually take weeks and US$30 to clear.

TRAVELER'S CHECKS

Traveler's checks are a smart way to manage your money. TIVE, Tagus, most other travel agencies, and many banks sell them, usually at face value plus a 1% commission. American Express and Visa are the most widely recognized, though other major checks are sold, exchanged, cashed, and refunded with almost equal ease. Each agency refunds lost or stolen checks, and many do more snazzy things. You will almost always need a police report to verify loss or theft of checks, credit cards, or insurance-prone mishaps. Ask about toll-free refund hotlines, emergency message relay services, and stolen credit card assistance when purchasing checks.

Expect red tape and delays in the event of lost or stolen traveler's checks. To expedite the refund process, keep check receipts separate and store them in a safe place or with a traveling companion; record check numbers when cashing them; leave a list of check numbers with someone at home; and ask for a list of refund centers. American Express and Bank of America have over 40,000 centers worldwide. Plan for emergencies by carrying extra checks and cash. Never countersign your checks until you are prepared to cash them. Lastly, bring your passport when using them.

American Express: Call (1800) 25 19 02 in Australia; in New Zealand (0800) 44 10 68; in the U.K. (0800) 52 13 13; in the U.S. and Canada (800) 221-7282). Elsewhere, call U.S. collect (801) 964-6665. American Express traveler's checks are now available in 10 currencies: Australian, British, Canadian, Dutch, French, German, Japanese, Saudi Arabian, Swiss, U.S., and soon South African. They are the most widely recognized worldwide and the easiest to replace if lost or stolen. Checks can be purchased for a small fee (1-4%) at American Express Travel Service Offices, banks, and American Automobile Association offices (AAA members can buy the checks commission-free). Cardmembers can also purchase checks at American Express Dispensers at Travel Service Offices at airports and by ordering them via phone (tel. (800) ORDER-TC (673-3782)). AmEx offices cash their checks commission-free (except where prohibited by national governments), although they often offer slightly worse rates than banks. You can also buy *Cheques for Two* which can be signed by either of two people traveling together. Request the AmEx booklet *"Traveler's Companion,"* which lists travel office addresses and stolen check hotlines for each European country. Visit their online travel offices (http://www.aexp.com).

Citicorp: Call (800) 645-6556 in the U.S. and Canada; in Europe, the Middle East, or Africa call (44) 171 508 7007; from elsewhere call U.S. collect (813) 623-1709.

Thomas Cook MasterCard: For 24hr. cashing or refund assistance, call (800) 223-9920 in the U.S. and Canada; elsewhere call U.S. collect (609) 987-7300; from the

U.K. call (0800) 622 101 free or (1733) 502 995 collect or (1733) 318 950 collect. Offers checks in U.S., Canadian, and Australian dollars, British and Cypriot pounds, French and Swiss francs, German marks, Japanese yen, Dutch guilders, Spanish pesetas, South African rand, and ECUs. Commission 1-2% for purchases. Thomas Cook offices may sell checks for lower commissions and will cash checks commission-free.

Visa: Call (800) 227-6811 in the U.S.; in the U.K. call (0800) 895 492; from anywhere else in the world call (01733 318 949) and reverse the charges. Any of the above numbers can tell you the location of their nearest office. Any type of Visa traveler's checks can be reported lost at the Visa number.

You can exchange traveler's checks for currency at American Express offices and most banks. *Let's Go* lists exchange locales. Bring your passport for check-related transactions. If you bring checks, cash from home is not a necessity (except for emergencies, in which case it should be stored separately from traveler's checks). Most all major check brands (such as American Express and Visa) may be brandished across Spain and Portugal. In Morocco, many smaller establishments may only accept American Express, if anything at all. Oddly, some banks do not take American Express traveler's checks but will accept other brands.

CREDIT CARDS

Depending on the country you are dealing with, credit cards are either accepted in all but the smallest businesses or, in some places, only recognized in fancy hotels and restaurants. However, some benefits of credit cards can be reaped just about everywhere. Major credit cards, especially **MasterCard** and **Visa,** can be used to extract cash advances from associated banks and teller machines throughout Canada, the U.S., and Western Europe (France, Germany, Italy, Portugal, Spain, the U.K., and elsewhere, though it varies by country) in local currency. Credit card companies get the wholesale exchange rate, which is generally 5% better than the retail rate used by banks and even better than that used by other currency exchange establishments. However, you will be charged ruinous interest rates if you do not pay the bill quickly, so be careful when using this service. **American Express** cards also work in some ATMs, as well as at AmEx offices and major airports. You must ask your credit card company to assign you a PIN before you leave; without it, you will be unable to withdraw cash with your credit card outside the U.S. Keep in mind that MasterCard and Visa have different names elsewhere ("EuroCard" or "Access" for MasterCard and "Carte Bleue" or Barclaycard" for Visa).

Credit cards are also invaluable in an emergency—an unexpected hospital bill or ticket home or the loss of traveler's checks—which may leave you temporarily without other resources. Furthermore, credit cards offer an array of other services, from insurance to emergency assistance, which depend completely on the issuer.

American Express (tel. (800) 843-2273) has a hefty annual fee (US$55) but offers a number of services. AmEx cardholders can cash personal checks at AmEx offices outside the U.S., and U.S. Assist, a 24-hr. hotline offering medical and legal assistance in emergencies, is also available (tel. (800) 554-2639 in U.S. and Canada; from abroad call U.S. collect (301) 214-8228). Cardholders can take advantage of the American Express Travel Service; benefits include assistance in changing airline, hotel, and car rental reservations, baggage loss and flight insurance, sending mailgrams and international cables, and holding your mail at one of the more than 1700 AmEx offices around the world.

MasterCard (tel. (800) 999-0454) and **Visa** (tel. (800) 336-8472) are issued in cooperation with individual banks and some other organizations; ask the issuer about services which go along with the cards.

CASH CARDS

Automatic Teller Machines (ATMs) are abundant in Spain, Portugal, and (although there are less) Morocco. Depending on the system that your bank at home uses, you

will probably be able to access your own personal bank account whenever you are in need of funds. (Be careful, however, and keep all receipts–even if an ATM won't give you your cash, it may register a withdrawal on your next statement). Happily, ATMs get the same wholesale exchange rate as credit cards. There is often a limit on the amount of money you can withdraw per day (usually about US$500, depending on the type of card and account), and computer network failures are not uncommon. Be sure to memorize your PIN code in numeral form since machines outside the U.S. and Canada often don't have letters on the keys. Also, if your PIN is longer than four digits, ask your bank whether the first four digits will work, or whether you need a new number. The two major international money networks are **Cirrus** (U.S. tel. (800) 4-CIRRUS (424-7787)) and **PLUS** (U.S. tel. (800) 843-7587).

MONEY FROM HOME

Money can also be wired abroad through international money transfer services operated by Western Union (tel. (800) 325-6000; Visa, MC, Discover). In Spain or Portugal, consult the local operator or phone directory. Credit card transfers do not work overseas; you must send cash. Rates for sending cash are generally $10 cheaper than with a credit card. The money is usually available in Spain within minutes, though most likely considerably longer in Portugal or Morocco.

In emergencies, U.S. citizens can have money sent via the State Department's **Overseas Citizens Service,** American Citizens Services, Consular Affairs, Room 4811, U.S. Department of State, Washington, D.C. 20520 (tel. (202) 647-5225; nights, Sundays, and holidays (202) 647-4000; fax (on demand only) (202) 647-3000; http://travel.state.gov). For US$15, the State Department will forward money within hours to the nearest consular office, which will then disburse it instead of instructions. The office serves only Americans in the direst of straits abroad; non-American travelers should contact their embassies or information on wiring cash. The quickest way to have the money sent is to cable the State Department through Western Union.

VALUE-ADDED TAX (VAT)

The Value-Added Tax (VAT; in Spain IVA) is a sales tax tagged on all goods and services in the European Union (EU). The standard rate is 7% (4% on the Canary Islands, Ceuta, and Melilla), although a reduced rate applies to goods such as food, water, books, newspapers, (prescription) drugs, and hotel stays. Foreigners (non-EU) who have stayed in the EU less than 180 days can claim back the VAT paid on purchases which exceed 15ptas at the airport. Ask the shop where you have made the purchase to supply you with a tax return form. Stores, restaurants, and lodgings include VAT in their prices, unless otherwise noted. The tax on accommodations and other services is not refundable. In **Portugal,** the rate wavers between 2-16%. In **Spain,** the *factura* is the "official bill," the price of your purchase excluding the VAT.

■ Safety and Security

Emergency phone numbers are **091** and **092** for **Spain, 112** in **Portugal,** and **19** and **15** in **Morocco.** Memorize these on the road, plane, and everywhere in between.

PERSONAL SAFETY

Tourists are particularly vulnerable to crime for two reasons: they carry comparatively large amounts of cash (crooks think so at least) and are not as street savvy as locals. To avoid unwanted attention blend in, dress conservatively, and use common sense: Check maps in safe places; avoid nervous, over-the-shoulder glances; and remember those guys waiting for you around the corner may not be good friends after all. New surroundings may require added vigilance. When you get to a place where you will be spending some time, find out about unsafe areas from the tourist office, the (hostel, hostal, etc.) manager, a local whom you trust, or *Let's Go.* Especially when traveling alone, be sure someone at home knows your itinerary. And

never say that you are traveling alone. Whistles may be a good idea, be it to scare off attackers or otherwise attract attention. Also, be sure to jot down and/or memorize local police numbers.

When walking at night, turn day-time precautions into mandates. Stick to busy well-lit streets and avoid dark alleyways. Do not cross through parks, parking lots or any other large, deserted areas. Whenever possible, *Let's Go* warns of unsafe neighborhoods and areas, but only your eyes can tell you for sure if you have wandered into one—buildings in disrepair, vacant lots, and general desertedness are all bad omens. A place can change character drastically in a single block. On the flip side, look for children playing, women walking freely, and an otherwise active community. If you feel uncomfortable, then get out. Nevertheless, a fearful traveler is a dull and unhappy one. Especially in Iberia, explore like there is no tomorrow.

If you are driving a **car,** be sure to learn local driving signals. Motor vehicle accidents are the top cause of tourist fatalities, so be alert. Park in a garage or well-traveled area. Learn your route before cruising; some roads have poor (or nonexistent) shoulders, others have few gas stations. For country-specific precautions, look at each country's **By Car** section. All told, buckle up, do not sleep in the car, drive safely, and call your mother.

Sleeping out in the open can be very dangerous—camping is recommended only in official, supervised campsites. Overnight trains merit added safeguards as well.

Exercise extreme caution when using pools or beaches without lifeguards. Hidden rocks, dangerous undertows, and otherwise unknown terrain may cause serious injury or even death. If renting scuba diving equipment, make sure it is up to par before taking the plunge. Also, cliffs can be high—jumping off them can be painful.

There is no sure-fire set of precautions that protect you from everything. A good self-defense course will give you more concrete ways to react to different types of aggression, but costs tend to be high. **Impact, Prepare, and Model Mugging** can refer you to local self-defense courses in the United States (tel. (800) 345-KICK). Course prices vary from $50-400, and women's and men's courses are offered. Community colleges frequently offer inexpensive self-defense courses.

For official **United States Department of State** travel advisories, call their 24-hour hotline at (202) 647-5225 or check their website (http://travel.state.gov), which provides travel information and publications. Alternatively, order publications, including a free pamphlet entitled *A Safe Trip Abroad*, by writing to Superintendent of Documents, U.S. Government Printing Office, Washington, DC 20402, or by calling them at (202) 512-1800. Official warnings from the **United Kingdom Foreign and Commonwealth Office** are on-line at http://www.fco.gov.uk; you can also call the office at (0171) 238 4503. The **Canadian Department of Foreign Affairs and International Trade** (DFAIT) offers advisories and travel warnings at its web address (http://www.dfait-maeci.gc.ca) and at its phone number ((613) 944-6788 in Ottawa, (800) 267-6788 elsewhere in Canada). Their free publication, *Bon Voyage, But....*, offers travel tips to Canadian citizens; you can receive a copy by calling them at (613) 944-6788 from Ottawa or abroad, or at (800) 267-6788 from Canada.

FINANCIAL SECURITY

Among the more colorful aspects of large cities are **con artists.** Hustlers often work in groups, and children, unfortunately, are among the most effective at the game. Be aware of certain classic tricks: the good and bad guy team, sob stories, seemingly innocent "deals," distractions, and out-and-out thieves. Morocco is the worst of the three countries when it comes to such shenanigans. As our research writer mentioned, there is a 50% chance the guides following you will rip you off, and a 50% chance they will buy you dinner.

First off, try not to keep your wallet in your back pocket. Moreover, counting your money in public and carrying large quantities is a bad idea wherever you go. Try to get a purse that is sturdy, has a secure clasp, and should be carried crosswise on the side away from the street with the clasp on *your* side. As far as securing your backpack is concerned, buy small combination padlocks which slip through the zippers.

A money belt is *the* way to carry cash. You can get one at Forsyth Travel Library (see p. 2), or at most camp supply stores. Avoid keeping anything especially precious in a fanny-pack; your valuables will be highly visible. City crowds and public transportation can be spawning grounds for pickpockets, so be careful. Plus, a joyous phone call can be ruined by rough-housers; if you must say your calling card number, do so quietly; watch over your shoulder when punching it in. Lastly, as said previously, photocopy any important documents—bring one with you, leave another at home.

On buses, carry your backpack in front of you. Avoiding checking baggage on trains, especially if you are switching lines. Trains are notorious hot spots for practicing criminals. Professionals may wait for tourists to fall asleep and then steal your stuff. When traveling in pairs, sleep in alternating shifts. When alone, use good judgment in selecting a train compartment—do not stay in an empty one. Keep all valuables on your person, and try to sleep on top bunks with your luggage stored above (if not in bed with you).

Let's Go lists locker storage locations, generally in hostels or train and bus stations, but bring your own padlock anyway. Never leave bags unattended, or with your new friend—you may regret it. If you feel particularly unsafe, look for places with a curfew or night attendant. Leave the gold watches and diamonds at home.

Travel Assistance International by Worldwide Assistance Services, Inc. provides its members with a 24-hour hotline for assistance. Their year-long frequent traveler package ($235-295) includes medical and travel insurance, financial assistance, and help in replacing lost documents. Call (800) 821-2828 or (202) 828-5894, fax (202) 828-5896, or write them at 1133 15th St. NW, Suite 400, Washington, D.C. 20005-2710. The **American Society of Travel Agents** provides extensive informational resources, both at their web-site (http://www.astanet.com) and in their free brochure, *Travel Safety*. You can obtain a copy by sending a request and self-addressed, stamped envelope to them at 1101 King St., Alexandria, VA 22313.

DRUGS AND ALCOHOL

Laws vary from country to country, but, needless to say, **illegal drugs** are best avoided altogether. Don't forget, you are subject to the laws of the country you are traveling in, not those of your home country, and it is your responsibility to familiarize yourself with these laws before leaving. In Spain, Portugal, and Morocco all recreational drugs—including marijuana—are illegal. In Morocco, foreigners with drugs have regularly been arrested and then forced to shell out ridiculous amounts of money as bribe/bail equivalent. Avoid **public drunkenness**; it is against the law in many countries. In Spain and Portugal, for instance, consuming alcohol may be a national pastime, but flat-out drunkenness is definitely frowned upon. To quote Sir Budweiser know when to say when.

If you carry **prescription drugs** while you travel, it is vital to have a copy of the prescriptions readily accessible at country borders and everywhere else you go.

■ Health Concerns

Common sense is the simplest prescription for good health when you travel: eat, sleep, and drink enough; but everyone has their limits, so do most everything in moderation. At the same time, a number of organizations and reminders can help make your trip happy and healthy. On the whole, Spain and Portugal conform to most Western standards of health, while Morocco—although better than much of Africa—presents more potential problems health wise.

First off, a handy **first-aid kit** may prove invaluable for minor problems (paper cuts, etc.). Moreover, in your passport, write the names of any people you wish to be contacted in a medical emergency, and also list any allergies or medical conditions you would want doctors away from home to be aware of. If you wear glasses or contact lenses, carry an extra prescription and pair of glasses Be sure to have up-to-date, legible prescriptions or a statement from your doctor, especially if you use insulin or

syringe. While traveling, keep all medication with you in carry-on luggage so it will not be knocked around or lost.

Peruse your **immunization** records before you go; make sure you are up to date on normal "childhood" shots and tetanus. Before you go, check that Morocco does not require any health particulars, like a yellow fever vaccination certificate, as do most African countries. Still, traveling in Africa puts you at a statistically higher risk for typhoid fever, hepatitis A (getting a dose of Harvix or IG is a good idea—consult a doctor), parasites, or Hepatitis B. Generally, "tourist" itineraries—meaning visits to modern, densely populated cities and minimal mixing with rural populations—put you at less risk. Also, take precautions to prevent insect bites.

Particularly in Iberia, **tap water** should be fine, although be more careful in rural areas and Morocco. The village pump may not be as friendly as the villagers, especially in Morocco. *Sidi Ali* and *Sidi Harazem* are heavily chlorinated mineral waters, available for about 5dh per 1.5L bottle. To make sure you're not getting tap water, insist on breaking the plastic seal on the bottled water yourself before paying. Remember: if you can't drink the water, you can't suck the ice. Hikers in all countries should beware the dreaded diarrhea-inducing parasite **giardia,** contracted through untreated lake or stream water, which has an icky staying power of years.

Food- and water-borne diseases are the number one cause of illness in North Africa, so watch out. **Food poisoning,** particularly, can spoil your trip. Street vendors, especially in more run-down locales or Morocco, may sell aged or otherwise bad food; avoid unpeeled fruits and vegetables, in particular hard-to-wash greens.

Coincidentally, any food you are not accustomed to—such as rarer meat in Portugal or the oil- and grease-fest that defines many Spanish dishes—can cause stomach troubles. **Traveler's diarrhea,** an offshoot ailment, can last from three to seven days, and symptoms include diarrhea, nausea, bloating, and malaise. If the nasties hit you, have quick-energy, non-sugary foods with protein and carbohydrates to keep your strength up. Over-the-counter remedies (such as Pepto-Bismol or Immodium) may counteract the problems, but they can also complicate serious infections. Avoid antidiarrheals if you suspect you have been exposed to contaminated food or water, which puts you at risk for other diseases. The most dangerous side effect of diarrhea is dehydration, making water-gorging the best recipe for health. If you develop a fever or your symptoms don't go away after four or five days, consult a doctor. Also consult qualified medical personnel if children develop traveler's diarrhea, since treatment is different than for adults.

Several organizations provide health-related help. The **United States Center for Disease Control and Prevention,** an excellent source of info for travelers around the world, maintains an international travelers' hotline (tel. (404) 332-4559; fax 332-4565; http://www.cdc.gov). The CDC publishes the booklet *Health Information for International Travelers* (US$20), an annual global rundown of disease, immunization, and general health advice, including risks in particular countries. This book may be purchased by phone (tel. (202) 512-1800) with a credit card (Visa Mastercard, Discover), or get their address. The **U.S. State Department** compiles Consular Information sheets on health, entry requirements, and other issues for all countries of the world. For quick information on travel warnings, call the **Overseas Citizens' Services** (tel. (202) 647-5225). To receive the same Consular Information sheets by fax, dial (202) 647-3000 directly from a fax machine and follow the instructions. The State Department's regional passport agencies in the U.S., field offices of the U.S. Chamber of Commerce, and U.S. embassies and consulates abroad provide the same data; otherwise, send a self-addressed, stamped envelope to the Overseas Citizens' Services, Bureau of Consular Affairs, Room 4811, U.S. Department of State, Washington, D.C. 20520. If you are HIV positive, call (202) 647-1488 for country-specific entry requirements or write to the Bureau of Consular Affairs, CA/P/PA, Department of State, Washington, D.C. 20520. For more general health info, contact the **American Red Cross.** The ARC publishes a First Aid and Safety Handbook (US $5) available by calling or writing to the American Red Cross, 285 Columbus Ave., Boston, MA 02116-3114 (tel. (800) 564-1234).

Those with medical conditions (e.g. diabetes, allergies to antibiotics, epilepsy, heart conditions) may want to obtain a stainless steel **Medic Alert** identification tag (US$35 the first year, and $15 annually thereafter), which identifies the disease and gives a 24-hour collect-call information number. Contact Medic Alert at (800) 825-3785, or write to Medic Alert Foundation, 2323 Colorado Ave., Turlock, CA 95382. Diabetics can contact the **American Diabetes Association,** 1660 Duke St., Alexandria, VA 22314 (tel. (800) 232-3472) to receive copies of the article "Travel and Diabetes" and a diabetic ID card, which carries messages in 18 languages explaining the carrier's diabetic status.

If you are concerned about being able to access medical support while traveling, contact one of these two services: **Global Emergency Medical Services (GEMS)** has products called *MedPass* that provide 24-hour international medical assistance and support coordinated through registered nurses who have on-line access to your medical information, your primary physician, and a worldwide network of screened, credentialed English-speaking doctors and hospitals. Subscribers also receive a personal medical record that contains vital information in case of emergencies. For more information call (800) 860-1111, fax (770) 475-0058, or write: 2001 Westside Drive, #120, Alpharetta, GA 30201. The **International Association for Medical Assistance to Travelers (IAMAT)** offers a membership ID card, a directory of English-speaking doctors around the world who treat members for a set fee schedule, and detailed charts on immunization requirements, various tropical diseases, climate, and sanitation. Membership is free, though donations are appreciated and used for further research. Contact chapters in the **U.S.,** 417 Center St., Lewiston, NY 14092 (tel. (716) 754-4883; fax (519) 836-3412; email iamat@sentex.net; http://www.sentex.net/~iamat), **Canada,** 40 Regal Road, Guelph, Ontario, N1K 1B5 (tel. (519) 836-0102) or 1287 St. Clair Avenue West Toronto, M6E 1B8 (tel. (416) 652-0137; fax (519) 836-3412), or **New Zealand,** P.O. Box 5049, Christchurch 5.

WOMEN'S HEALTH

Women traveling in unsanitary conditions are vulnerable to urinary tract and bladder infections, common and severely uncomfortable bacterial diseases which cause a burning sensation and painful and sometimes frequent urination. Drink tons of vitamin-C-rich juice, plenty of clean water, and urinate frequently, especially right after intercourse. Untreated, these infections can lead to kidney infections, sterility, and even death. If symptoms persist, see a doctor. If you often develop vaginal yeast infections, take along enough over-the-counter medicine, as treatments may not be readily available in Central America. Women may also be more susceptible to vaginal thrush and cystitis, two treatable but uncomfortable illnesses that are likely to flare up in hot and humid climates. Wearing loosely fitting trousers or a skirt and cotton underwear may help. Tampons and pads are sometimes hard to find when traveling; certainly your preferred brands may not be available, so it may be advisable to take supplies along. Refer to the *Handbook for Women Travellers* by Maggie and Gemma Moss (published by Piatkus Books) or to the women's health guide *Our Bodies, Our Selves* (published by the Boston Women's Health Collective) for more extensive information specific to women's health on the road.

HOT AND COLD

Take steps to prevent **heat exhaustion,** particularly dangerous during Iberian and Moroccan summers. Relax in hot weather, drink lots of non-alcoholic fluids, and lie down indoors if you feel awful. Continuous heat stress can lead to **heatstroke,** characterized by rising body temperature, severe headaches, and cessation of sweating. Wear a hat, sunglasses, and light longsleeve shirt to avoid heatstroke. Cool sufferers with wet towels and take them to a doctor.

Always drink enough liquids to keep your urine clear. Alcoholic beverages are dehydrating, as are coffee, strong tea, and bubbly caffeinated sodas. If you plan on sweating, be sure to eat enough salty food to prevent electrolyte depletion, which

causes severe headaches. Less debilitating, but still dangerous, is **sunburn.** Bring sunscreen with you (it's often more expensive and hard to find when traveling), and apply it liberally to avoid burns and risk of skin cancer. If you get sunburned, load up with more fluids than usual.

Less relevant, but nonetheless important at high altitudes and certain northern areas of Spain and Portugal, is **hypothermia.** Warning signs are easy to detect: body temperature drops rapidly, resulting in the failure to produce body heat. You may shiver, have poor coordination, feel exhausted, or have slurred speech, feel sleepy, hallucinate, or suffer amnesia. *Do not let hypothermia victims fall asleep.* Dress in layers, and watch for **frostbite,** evidenced by numbness and/or pain. Take serious cases, especially children, to a doctor as soon as possible.

■ Insurance

Beware of buying unnecessary travel coverage—your regular policy may well apply even as you jaunt through foreign lands. Most **medical insurance** (especially university policies) cover costs incurred abroad, but nonetheless check with your provider. **ISIC** and **ITIC**, **STA** and **Council** offer a range of different plans. Most **American Express** cardholders have automatic car rental (collision and theft, but not liability) and travel accident insurance on flight purchases made with the card. Insurance companies usually require a copy of the police report for thefts, or evidence of having paid medical expenses before they will honor a claim and may have time limits on filing for reimbursement. Always carry policy numbers and proof of insurance.

The Berkely Group/Carefree Travel Insurance, 100 Garden City Plaza, P.O. Box 9366, Garden City, NY 11530-9366 (tel. (800) 323-3149 or (516) 294-0220; fax 294-1096). Two comprehensive packages. 24hr. emergency hotline.

Globalcare Travel Insurance, 220 Broadway, Lynnfield, MA 01940 (tel. (800) 821-2488; fax (617) 592-7720; email global@nebc.mv.com; http://www.nebc.mv.com/globalcare). Complete medical, legal, emergency, and travel-related services. Special student programs.

Travel Assistance International, by Worldwide Assistance Services, Inc., 1133 15th St. NW, #400, Washington, D.C. 20005-2710 (tel. (800) 821-2828 or (202) 828-5894; fax (202) 828-5896; email wassist@aol.com). 24hr. free hotline. Their Per-Trip (starting at US$65) and Frequent Traveler (starting at US$235) plans include medical, travel, and communication assistance services.

■ Alternatives to Tourism

TUDYING

or a college experience with spice, look into studying abroad. Foreign study programs vary tremendously in expense, academic quality, living conditions, degree of ontact with local students, and exposure to local culture and languages. To immerse ourself in **Spain** this way, try U.S. university programs and youth organizations hich set students up at Spanish universities and language centers for foreign students. If you are fluent, enroll directly in a Spanish colleges (non-Spanish students ave practically taken over Salamanca). Most universities in **Portugal** open their gates foreign students, and foreigners can enter language and cultural studies programs most of them.

American Field Service (AFS), 198 Madison Ave., 8th Fl., New York, NY 10016 (tel. Students (800) AFS-INFO (237-4636), Administration (800) 876-2376; fax (503) 241-1653; email afsinfo@afs.org; http://www.afs.org/usa). AFS offers summer, semester, and year-long homestay international exchange programs, for high school students and recent high school graduates. Financial aid available.

Council, sponsors over 40 study abroad programs throughout the world. Contact them for more info (see **Travel Organizations,** p. 2).

Peterson's Guides, P.O. Box 2123, Princeton, NJ 08543-2123 (tel. (800) 338-3282; fax (609) 243-9150; http://www.petersons.com). *Study Abroad* (US$30) annual guide lists programs all over the world and essential information on the study abroad experience in general. *Learning Adventures Around the World* (US$25), an annual guide to "learning vacations," lists volunteer, museum-hopping, study and travel programs.

Education Office of Spain, 150 5th Ave. #918, New York, NY 10011 (tel. (212) 741-5144 or 741-5145); and in the Spanish Embassy, 2375 Pennsylvania Avenue NW, Washington, D.C. 20037 (tel. (202) 728-2335). British may contact the education Office in the Spanish Embassy in London (see p. 3; tel. (171) 727 24 62; 229 49 65).

WORKING

There is no better way to immerse yourself in a foreign culture than to become part of its economy. It's easy to find a **temporary job,** but it will rarely be glamorous and may not even pay for your plane fare, let alone your accommodation. Officially, you can hold a job in Iberia and Morocco only with a **work permit.** Your employer must obtain this document, usually by demonstrating that you have skills that locals lack—not the easiest of tasks. There are, however, ways to make it easier. Friends in your destination country can help expedite work permits or arrange work-for-accommodations swaps. Many permit-less agricultural workers go untroubled by local authorities. European Union citizens can work in any EU country, and if your parents were born in an EU country, you may be able to claim dual citizenship or at least the right to a work permit. Students can check with their universities' foreign language departments, which may have connections to job openings. Call the Consulate or Embassy of the country in which you wish to work to get more information about permits.

If you are a **U.S. citizen** and a full-time student at a U.S. university, the simplest way to get a job abroad is through work permit programs run by **Council on International Educational Exchange (Council)** and its member organizations. For a US$225 application fee, Council can procure three- to six-month work permits (and a handbook to help you find work and housing) for Australia, Costa Rica, France, Germany, New Zealand, Spain, and the U.K. Vacation Work Publications publishes *Work Your Way Around the World* (UK£11, UK£ 2.50 postage, UK£1.50 within U.K) to help you along the way (see below).

InterExchange, 161 Sixth Ave., New York, NY 10013 (tel. (212) 924-0446; fax 924-0575; email interex@earthlink.net; http://www.interexchange.org) offers *au pair* and teaching opportunities. Places *au pairs* for 2-18 month placements in Spain.

International Schools Services, Educational Staffing Program, 15 Roszel Road, P.O. Box 5910, Princeton, NJ 08543 (tel. (609) 452-0990; fax 452-2690; e-mail: edustaff-ing%ISS@mcimail.com). Recruits teachers and administrators for schools in Europe. All instruction in English. Applicants must have a bachelor's degree and two years of relevant experience. Nonrefundable $75 application fee.

Tagus-Youth Student Travel, (p. 30). Has *muito* info on paid and volunteer work in Portugal.

Useful Publications

Transitions Abroad Publishing, Inc., 18 Hulst Rd., P.O. Box 1300, Amherst, MA 01004-1300 (tel. (800) 293-0373; fax (413) 256-0373; email trabroad@aol.com; http://www.transabroad.com). Publishes *Transitions Abroad*, a bi-monthly magazine listing all kinds of opportunities and printed resources for those seeking to study, work, or travel abroad. They also publish *The Alternative Travel Directory*, a truly exhaustive listing of information for the "active international traveler." For subscriptions contact them at Transitions Abroad, Dept. TRA, Box 3000, Denville, NJ 07834 (tel. (800) 293-0373).

Vacation Work Publications, 9 Park End St., Oxford OX1 1HJ, U.K. (tel. (01865) 24 19 78; fax 79 08 85). Publishes a wide variety of guides and directories with job listings and info for the working traveler, including *Teaching English Abroad*

(UK£10, UK£2.50 postage, UK£1.50 within U.K.) and *The Au Pair and Nanny's Guide to Working Abroad* (UK£9, UK£2.50 and 1.50 postage).

VOLUNTEERING

Volunteer jobs are readily available almost everywhere. You may receive room and board in exchange for your labor; the work can be fascinating (or stultifying). You can sometimes avoid the high application fees charged by the organizations that arrange placement by contacting the individual workcamps directly; check with the organizations. Listings in Vacation Work Publications's *International Directory of Voluntary Work* can be helpful (see above).

Council has a Voluntary Services Dept., 205 E. 42nd St., New York, NY 10017 (tel. (888) COUNCIL (268-6245); fax (212) 822-2699; email info@ciee.org; http://www.ciee.org), which offers 2- to 4-week environmental or community services projects in over 30 countries. Participants must be at least 18 years old. Minimum US$295 placement fee; additional fees may also apply for various countries.

Eurocentres, 101 N. Union St. #300, Alexandria, VA 22314 (tel. (800) 648-4809 (recorded info.), (888) 387-6236, or (703) 684-1494; fax (703) 684-1495); http://www.clark.net/pub/eurocent/home.htm) or Eurocentres, Head Office, Seestrasse 247, CH-8038 Zurich, Switzerland (tel. (01) 485 50 40 (country code: 41); fax 481 61 24). Language programs and homestays (US$500-5000) of two weeks to a year, all over the world. Some financial aid available.

Peace Corps, 1990 K St. NW, Room 8508, Washington, D.C. 20526 (tel. (800) 424-8580; fax (202) 606-4469; email msaucier@peacecorps.gov; http://www.peacecorps.gov). Opportunities available in developing nations in agriculture, business, education, the environment, and health. Volunteers must be U.S. citizens, age 18 and over, and willing to make a 2-year commitment. A bachelor's degree is usually required.

Volunteers for Peace, 43 Tiffany Rd., Belmont, VT 05730 (tel. (802) 259-2759; fax 259-2922; email vfp@vfp.org; http://www.vfp.org). A nonprofit organization that arranges speedy placement in 2-3 week workcamps comprising 10-15 people. VFP offers over 1,000 programs in 70 countries. Most complete and up-to-date listings provided in the annual *International Workcamp Directory* (US$15). Registration fee US$200. Some work camps are open to 16 and 17 year olds for US$225. Free newsletter.

■ Specific Concerns

WOMEN TRAVELERS

Women going it alone are often forced to cope with several unique, almost always difficult circumstances. Tourists—particularly those who look or sound "foreign"—are more frequently subject to especially unwarranted harassment. Trust your instincts; if you don't feel safe, leave. Consider staying in places offering single rooms which lock from the inside, and avoid potentially pesky communal showers. Always carry extra money for emergencies. Hitching is a definite *"NO!"* even for a pair of females. Stick to centrally situated accommodations and avoid late-night treks and metro/train rides, if possible. Lastly, choose your train compartment wisely; look for one occupied by other women or ask the conductor to organize one.

And, of course, look the part. This means appearing as un-touristy as possible, looking as if you know where you are going, and dressing conservatively (especially in rural areas). Still, much is beyond your control. A wedding band may thwart many an advance. When confronted, the best response may be none at all—walk away. Blank stares—thus, eschewing eye contact—are a ready way to discourage bad guys. Sunglasses are thus a big plus. If need be, turn to an older woman for support—her rebukes will subdue most. Carry a whistle or airhorn—and don't hesitate to blow or yell. Also, wearing tighter or more revealing **clothes** means more hassle. Annoying

Semester In Spain

A Program of Trinity Christian College

*Spend a fall or spring semester,
or a short-term program in Seville, Spain!*

Semester dates:
January 28—May 23, 1998
August 31—December 18, 1998

Short term dates:
January 5—23, 1998
June 1—June 25 and
June 28—July 18, 1998
(all dates are subject to change)

General Information
- Beginning, intermediate and
  advanced Spanish classes
- Home stay/small classes
- Experienced staff—native Spaniards
- Credit transfers by transcript
- Some financial aid available

Semester Information
- Cost is approximately $7,600
- 16 semester hours credit

Short term Information
- Cost is approximately $2,000
- 4 semester hours credit

Call: (800) 748-0087
Write: Trinity Christian College
SIS—Dept LGO
6601 West College Drive
Palos Heights, IL 60463
email: spain@trnty.edu
on the web: www.trnty.edu/spain

garb and anything that makes you stick out is better off avoided. Also, take heed of the wise words in **Safety and Security** (p. 14), and **Clothing and Footwear** (p. 29).

For general information, contact the **National Organization for Women (NOW)**, which boasts branches across the country that can refer women travelers to rape crisis centers and counseling services, and provide lists of feminist events. Main offices include 22 W. 21st St., 7th Fl., **New York,** NY 10010 (tel. (212) 260-4422); 1000 16th St. NW, 7th Fl., **Washington, D.C.** 20004 (tel. (202) 331-0066); and 3543 18th St., **San Francisco,** CA 94110 (tel. (415) 861-8960; fax 861-8969; email sfnow@sirius.com; http://www.sirius.com/~sfnow/now.html). *Directory of Women's Media* is available from the National Council for Research on Women, 530 Broadway, 10th fl., New York, NY 10012 (tel. (212) 274-0730; fax 274-0821. This publication lists women's publishers, bookstores, theaters, and news organizations (mail orders, $30). Thalia Zepatos's *A Journey of One's Own,* (US$17 from Eighth Mountain Press, 624 Southeast 29th Ave., Portland, OR 97214 (tel. (503) 233-3936; fax 233-0774); email eightmt@aol.com), gives advice plus a helpful bibliography of books and resources. *Women Going Places* (US$15 from Inland Book Company, 1436 W. Randolph St., Chicago, IL 60607 (tel. (800) 243-0138; fax (800) 334-3892) or from local bookstores) is a women's travel and resource guide. Geared primarily to lesbians, it nonetheless offers good advice applicable to all women.

In **Portugal,** women are generally treated with respect (blondes, an anomaly among these dark-headed people, may be the occasional exception). Men in **Spain** are freer with unwanted comments and gestures than you may be accustomed to; be alert, smart, and avoid awkward situations as much as possible.

Morocco is a special case. Islamic culture requires women to be veiled and secluded even in their own homes. Generally, people may conform by skirting short skirts, sleeveless tops, shorts, and the like; moreover, females should always wear a bra. Women—particularly non-Moroccans—may be gawked at, commented upon, approached by hustlers, and have their butts and breasts squeezed while in a crowd. Moroccan women may hiss at "indecently" clad female travelers. Exercise extreme caution: don't walk in deserted areas or alone. Again, the best response may be silence. Yelling *"shuma"*—meaning shame—will frequently embarrass harassers, especially in the presence of onlookers. If maltreatment persists, protest loudly and often. Strolling arm in arm with another woman, common in Europe and North Africa, can lessen the risk of harassment or violence; so can wearing a head scarf. In larger, inland cities other subtler forms of discrimination may arise, such as being refused a room in a vacant hotel; proprietors would rather not be responsible for your well-being. Many bars do not admit women.

OLDER TRAVELERS

Senior citizens are eligible for a wide range of discounts on transportation, museums, movies, theaters, concerts, restaurants, and accommodations. If you don't see a senior citizen price listed, ask, and you may be delightfully surprised. Agencies for senior group travel (like **Eldertreks,** 597 Markham St., Toronto, Ontario, Canada M6G 2L7, tel. (416) 588-5000, fax 588-9839, email passages@inforamp.net, and **Walking the World,** P.O. Box 1186, Fort Collins, CO 80522, tel. (970) 225-0500, fax 225-9100, email walktworld@aol.com; travel to North America, Europe, New Zealand, and Central America) are growing in enrollment and popularity.

Elderhostel, 75 Federal St., 3rd Fl., Boston, MA 02110-1941 (tel. (617) 426-7788, fax 426-8351; email Cadyg@elderhostel.orghttp://www.elderhostel.org).For those 55 or over (spouse of any age). Programs at colleges, universities, and other learning centers in over 70 countries on varied subjects lasting 1-4 weeks.

Gateway Books, 2023 Clemens Rd., Oakland, CA 94602 (tel. (510) 530-0299, credit card orders (800) 669-0773; fax (510) 530-0497; email donmerwin@aol.com; http://www.discoverypress.com/gateway.html. Publishes *Europe the European Way: A Traveler's Guide to Living Affordably in the World's Great Cities* (US $14).

Pilot Books, 127 Sterling Ave., P.O. Box 2102, Greenport, NY 11944 (tel. (516) 477-1094 or 1(800) 79PILOT (7974568); fax (516) 477-0978; email feedback@pilot-books.com; http://www.pilotbooks.com). Publishes a large number of helpful guides including *Doctor's Guide to Protecting Your Health Before, During, and After International Travel* (US$10, postage US$2)

Unbelievably Good Deals and Great Adventures That You Absolutely Can't Get Unless You're Over 50, by Joan Rattner Heilman, Contemporary Books, US$10.

BISEXUAL, GAY, AND LESBIAN TRAVELERS

Some consider the gay scene in **Spain** the most open in Europe; in the major cities (Madrid, Barcelona), people are characteristically tolerant. Sitges and Ibiza have particularly vibrant gay communities. Scour bookstores, bars, and kiosks for the bimonthly magazine *Entiendes...?,* with articles in Spanish about gay issues and a comprehensive list of gay services, groups, activities, and—yes, even personal ads.

Portugal is more conservative. Gays and lesbians are generally accepted in Lisbon and, increasingly, in Porto, but are invisible elsewhere in the country. No law promotes anti-gay discrimination, but social traditionalism—particularly strident Catholicism—may foster prejudice. Nonetheless, Lisbon staged its first gay rights parade in 1995, manifesting a burgeoning collective gay identity. In **Morocco,** don't be deceived by men holding hands; civil and Islamic law prohibit homosexuality.

Are You Two...Together? A Gay and Lesbian Travel Guide to Europe, gives anecdotes and tips for homosexuals traveling in Europe. Includes overviews of regional laws, lists of organizations, and establishments catering or friendly to gays and lesbians. Available in bookstores or from Random House, US$18.

Giovanni's Room, 345 S. 12th St., Philadelphia, PA 19107 (tel. (215) 923-2960; fax 923-0813; email gilphilp@netaxs.com). An international feminist, lesbian, and gay bookstore with mail-order service that carries many publications listed here.

International Gay Travel Association, P.O. Box 4974, Key West, FL 33041 (tel. (800) 448-8550; fax (305) 296-6633; email IGTA@aol.com; http://www.rainbow-mall.com/igta). An organization of over 1300 companies serving gay and lesbian travelers worldwide. Call for lists of travel agents, accommodations, and events.

Spartacus International Gay Guides (US$33), published by Bruno Gmunder, Postfach 61 01 04, D-10921 Berlin, Germany (tel. (30) 615 00 3-42; fax (30) 615 91 34). Lists bars, restaurants, hotels, and bookstores around the world catering to gays. Available in bookstores and in the U.S. by mail from Lambda Rising, 1625 Connecticut Ave. NW, Washington D.C., 20009-1013 (tel. (202) 462-6969).

DISABLED TRAVELERS

Accessibility varies widely in Iberia and Morocco. Guidebooks and brochures may not give accurate accounts on ramps, door widths, and elevator dimensions. Directly asking restaurants, hotels, railways, and airlines about their facilities works best. Handicapped access is common in **Madrid's** museums and in modern museums elsewhere. As for getting around, rail is usually most convenient besides a van rental. Contact **Rail Europe** (see **By Train,** p. 38) for info on discounted rail travel.

Those bringing **guide dogs** must abide by the general procedure for pets. All three countries require veterinarian-issued health and rabies inoculation certificates for pets; well before your departure, send or take these to the nearest consulate to be stamped. (Fee: US$5.60 for Spain; Portugal US$5.80; Morocco US$3.)

The following organizations provide additional info for disabled travelers:

American Foundation for the Blind, 11 Penn Plaza, New York, NY 10011 (tel. (212) 502-7600). Info and services for the visually impaired. Contact Lighthouse, 36-20 Northern Boulevard, Long Island City, NY 10011 (tel. (800) 829-0500) for a catalog. Open Mon.-Fri. 8:30am-4:30pm.

Facts on File, 11 Penn Plaza, 15th Fl., New York, NY 10001 (tel. (212) 967-8800). Publishers of *Disability Resource,* a reference guide for travelers with disabilities (US$45 plus shipping). Available at bookstores or by mail order.

ESSENTIALS

Graphic Language Press, P.O. Box 270, Cardiff by the Sea, CA 92007 (tel. (760) 944-9594; email niteowl@cts.com; http://www.geocities.com/Paris/1502). Comprehensive advice for wheelchair travelers including accessible accommodations, transportation, and sight-seeing for various European cities. Their web site Global Access features worldwide trip reports from disabled travelers, tips, resources, and networking.

Mobility International, USA (MIUSA), P.O. Box 10767, Eugene, OR 97440 (tel. (514) 343-1284 voice and TDD; fax 343-6812; email info@miusa.org; http://miusa.org). International Headquarters in Brussels, rue de Manchester 25 Brussels, Belgium, B-1070 (tel. (322) 410-6297; fax 410 6874). Contacts in 30 countries. Information on travel programs, international work camps, accommodations, access guides, and organized tours for those with physical disabilities. Membership US$30 per year. Sells *A World of Options: A Guide to International Educational Exchange, Community Service, and Travel for Persons with Disabilities* (US$30, nonmembers US$35; organizations US$40).

Moss Rehab Hospital Travel Information Service (tel. (215) 456-9600, TDD 456-9602). A telephone info resource line on international travel accessibility and other travel-related concerns for people with disabilities.

Society for the Advancement of Travel for the Handicapped (SATH), 347 Fifth Ave. #610, New York, NY 10016 (tel. (212) 447-1928; fax 725-8253; email sath-travel@aol.com; http://www.sath.org). Publishes quarterly travel newsletter *OPEN WORLD* (free for members, US$13 for nonmembers) and info booklets with advice on trip planning for people with disabilities. Annual membership US$45, students and seniors US$30.

Twin Peaks Press, PO Box 129, Vancouver, WA 98666-0129 (tel. (360) 694-2462, orders with MC and Visa (800) 637-2256; email 73743.2634@compuserve.com; http://netm.com/mall/infoprod/twinpeak/helen.htm). Publishes *Travel for the Disabled* ($20), *Directory for Travel Agencies of the Disabled* ($20), *Wheelchair Vagabond* ($15), *Directory of Accessible Van Rentals* ($10). Postage US$3.50 for first book, US$1.50 for each additional book.

Tour Companies

Directions Unlimited, 720 N. Bedford Rd., Bedford Hills, NY 10507 (tel. (800) 533-5343; in NY (914) 241-1700; fax 241-0243). Specializes in arranging individual and group vacations, tours, and cruises for the physically disabled. Group tours for blind travelers.

The Guided Tour Inc., Elkins Park House, 114B, 7900 Old York Rd., Elkins Park, PA 19027-2339 (tel. (800) 783-5841 or (215) 782-1370; fax 635-2637). Organizes travel programs for persons with developmental and physical challenges and those requiring renal dialysis. Call, fax, or write for a free brochure.

TRAVELING WITH CHILDREN

They can't drive or drink, but they can have an ID. Given their relative fragility and penchants to get lost, kids especially need identification of their own. Check for children's discounts on everything from international commercial flights to museums to restaurants. Kids under two generally fly for 10% of the adult fare (no seat guaranteed). Children 2-11 often get 25% off the adult fare; it's up to the airline.

The following publications offer tips for adults traveling with children and distractions for the kids. Their publishers are also a source for more generic information.

Backpacking with Babies and Small Children (US$10). Published by Wilderness Press, 2440 Bancroft Way, Berkeley, CA 94704 (tel. (800) 443-7227 or (510) 843-8080; fax 548-1355; email wpress@ix.netcom.com).

The **Kidding Around** series (US$10-13, postage under US$5). Educational (and distracting) illustrated books, including one for Spain. From John Muir Publications, P.O. Box 613, Santa Fe, NM 87504 (tel. (800) 285-4078; fax (505) 988-1680).

Take Your Kids to Europe by Cynthia W. Harriman (US$17). A budget travel guide geared towards families. Published by Globe-Pequot Press, 6 Business Park Rd., Old Saybrook, CT 06475 (tel. (800) 285-4078; fax (860) 395-1418; email charriman@masongrant.com).

MINORITY TRAVELERS

Spanish people suffer from little interaction with other races. It shows in some expressions, like "Don't be a Moor," meaning mind your manners. Infrequent incidents are never violent or threatening, just a little awkward. They occur out of naivete or ignorance. You'll find that younger generations are open-minded. Don't be struck by a Spaniard's unabashed eagerness when meeting a foreigner who is not caucasian. This is not ethnic insensitivity, but rather curiosity, as odd as it may seem. **Portugal** is comfortably anti-racist. Its ethnic composition reflects its rich colonial history (in Africa and the Americas), complementing a healthy indigenous mix (see **Portugal: History and Politics,** p. 517) People of various ethnicities should have little to fear, since post-Salazar Portugal is eager to liberalize. In **Morocco,** generally, nationality more than ethnicity may invite harassment. Asian and blond travelers, and those who flaunt their wealth or national identity are targets.

VEGETARIAN AND KOSHER TRAVELERS

If it's **kosher,** chances are it's not in Spain, Portugal, or Morocco. Nevertheless, for tips and establishments, buy *The Jewish Travel Guide* (US$15, US$2.50 shipping), which lists kosher restaurants, synagogues, and other Jewish institutions in over 80 countries. Available from Ballantine-Mitchell Publishers, Newbury House 890-900, Eastern Ave., Newbury Park, Ilford, Essex, U.K. IG2 7HH (tel. (0181) 599 88 66; fax 599 09 84). It is available in the U.S. from Sepher-Hermon Press, 1265 46th St., Brooklyn, NY 11219 (tel. (718) 972-9010).

Vegetarians, too, may find cooking their new pastime after trekking through Spain, Portugal, and Morocco. Inexpensive produce and cow/pig-friendly delectables are available at the many local markets, locations and hours of which are listed in *Let's Go* with each town entry. Nonetheless, at restaurants often the closest you'll get to a vegetarian plate is the plate itself. Asking for two first courses *(primer platos)* may work; the main dish *(segundo plato)* will invariably contain meat. *Let's Go* lists some exceptions, especially with vegetarian inclined restaurants in larger cities and tourist resorts. For more information, call (800) 435-9610 to order *The European Vegetarian Guide to Restaurants and Hotels* (US$14, plus US$1.75 shipping).

For a description of typical cuisine in Spain, Portugal, and Morocco, refer to the **Food** section preceding each country segment. Health-related concerns, such as diabetes, are dealt with in Health, p. 16.

■ Packing

Some credos to pack by: "If you want to get away from it, don't take it with you;" or, "Lay out what you need—take half the clothes, twice the money." Consider how much you will want to carry day in and out and weigh the trials and tariffs of storage. Finally, be sure to leave room for souvenirs and gifts.

LUGGAGE

Backpack: If you plan to cover most of your itinerary by foot, a sturdy backpack is unbeatable. Many packs are designed specifically for travelers, while others are for hikers. In any case, get a pack with a strong, padded hip belt to transfer weight from your shoulders to your hips. Good packs cost from US$150 to US$420.

Suitcase or trunk: Fine if you plan to live in one or two cities and explore from there, but a bad idea if you are going to be moving around a lot. Make sure it has wheels and consider how much it weighs even when empty.

Duffel bag: If you are not backpacking, an empty, lightweight duffel bag packed inside your luggage will be useful: once abroad you can fill your luggage with purchases and keep your dirty clothes in the duffel.

Daypack, rucksack, or courier bag: Bringing a smaller bag in addition to your pack or suitcase allows you to leave your big bag behind while you go sight-seeing. It can be used as an airplane carry-on to keep essentials with you.

Moneybelt or neck pouch: Guard your money, passport, railpass, and other important articles in either one of these, available at any good camping store, and keep it with you *at all times.* The moneybelt should tuck inside the waist of your pants or skirt; you want to hide your valuables, not announce them with a colorful fanny- or butt-pack.

CLOTHING AND FOOTWEAR

Clothing: When choosing your travel wardrobe, aim for versatility and comfort, and avoid fabrics that wrinkle easily. Always bring a jacket or wool sweater.

Walking shoes: Well-cushioned **sneakers** are good for walking, though you may want to consider a good water-proofed pair of **hiking boots.** A double pair of socks—light silk or polypropylene inside and thick wool outside—will cushion feet, keep them dry, and help prevent blisters. Bring a pair of flip-flops for protection in the shower. Talcum powder in your shoes and on your feet can prevent sores, and moleskin is great for blisters. Break in your shoes before you leave.

Rain gear: A waterproof jacket and a backpack cover will take care of you and your stuff. Gore-Tex is a miracle fabric that's both waterproof and breathable; it's mandatory if you plan on hiking. Avoid cotton as outerwear if you will be outdoors a lot.

In Spain, Portugal, and Morocco, contrary to American custom, **shorts** are uncommon. Beyond this fact, standard Western wear works in Iberia, although extremes of any kind may draw unwanted attention, especially away from big cities. Morocco has different, slightly stricter standards, and it may prove harder to blend in there. On the whole, dressing conservatively is the best bet for safety and sanity.

MISCELLANEOUS

Sleepsacks: If you plan to stay in **hostels,** don't pay the linen charge; make the requisite sleepsack yourself. Fold a full size sheet in half, then sew it closed along the open long side and one of the short sides. Or, buy it at HI outlet stores.

Contact lenses: Machines which heat-disinfect contact lenses will require a small converter (about US$20) if you are visiting an area with a different current. Consider switching temporarily to a chemical disinfection system—check with your lens dispenser to see if it is safe to switch. Contact lens supplies are sometimes rare or expensive. Bring enough saline and cleaner for your entire vacation, or wear glasses. In any case, bring a backup pair of glasses.

Washing clothes: *Let's Go* attempts to provide information on laundromats in the Practical Information listings for each city, but sometimes it may be easier to use a sink. Bring a small bar or tube of detergent soap, a rubber squash ball to stop up the sink, and a travel clothes line.

Electric current: In most European countries, electricity is 220 volts AC, enough to fry any 110V North American appliance. 220V Electrical appliances don't like 110V current, either. Visit a hardware store for an adapter (which changes the shape of the plug) and a converter (which changes the voltage). Don't make the mistake of using only an adapter (unless appliance instructions explicitly state otherwise), or you'll melt your radio.

Film is expensive just about everywhere. Bring film from home and, if you will be seriously upset if the pictures are ruined, develop it at home. If you are not a serious photographer, you may want to consider bringing a **disposable camera** or two rather than an expensive permanent one. Despite disclaimers, airport security X-rays *can* fog film, so either buy a lead-lined pouch, sold at camera stores, or ask the security to hand inspect it. Always pack it in your carry-on luggage, since higher-intensity X-rays are used on checked luggage.

Other useful items: first-aid kit; umbrella; sealable plastic bags (for damp clothes, soap, food, shampoo, and other spillables); alarm clock; waterproof matches; sun hat; moleskin (for blisters); needle and thread; safety pins; sunglasses; a personal stereo (Walkman) with headphones; pocketknife; plastic water bottle; compass; string (makeshift clothesline and lashing material); towel; padlock; whistle; rubber bands; toilet paper; flashlight; cold-water soap; earplugs; insect repellant; electrical tape (for patching tears); clothespins; maps and phrasebooks; tweezers; garbage

bags; sunscreen; vitamins. Some items not always readily available or affordable on the road: deodorant; razors; condoms; tampons.

Stores across Europe and Morocco stock most **toiletries.** In **Morocco,** toilet paper is scarce at hostels, and sold at grocery stores, many newsstands, and tobacco shops.

Check our Orientation and Practical Information listings of each town to find out whether and where English language books are sold.

GETTING THERE

■ Budget Travel Agencies

Campus Travel, 52 Grosvenor Gardens, London SW1W 0AG (http://www.campus-travel.co.uk). Forty-six branches in the U.K. Student and youth fares on plane, train, boat, and bus travel. Skytrekker, flexible airline tickets. Discount and ID cards for students and youths, travel insurance for students and those under 35, and maps and guides. Puts out travel suggestion booklets. Telephone booking service: in Europe call (0171) 730 34 02; in North America call (0171) 730 21 01; worldwide call (0171) 730 81 11; in Manchester call (0161) 273 17 21; in Scotland call (0131) 668 33 03.

Council Charter, 205 E. 42nd St., New York, NY 10017 (tel. (212) 661-0311; fax 972-0194). Inexpensive charter and scheduled airfares between the U.S. and Europe. Also, one-way fares and open jaws (fly into one city and out of another).

Council Travel, the travel division of Council, is a full-service travel agency specializing in youth and budget travel. They offer discount airfares on scheduled airlines, railpasses, hostelling cards, low-cost accommodations, guidebooks, budget tours, travel gear, and international student (ISIC), youth (GO 25), and teacher (ITIC) identity cards. U.S. offices include Emory Village, 1561 N. Decatur Rd., **Atlanta,** GA 30307 (tel. 404-377-9997); 729 Boylston St., **Boston,** MA 02116 (tel. 617-266-

1926); 1153 N. Dearborn, **Chicago,** IL 60610 (tel. 312-951-0585); 10904 Lindbrook Dr., **Los Angeles,** CA 90024 (tel. 310-208-3551); 205 E. 42nd St., **New York,** NY 10017 (tel. 212-822-2700); 3606A Chestnut St., **San Diego,** CA 92109 (tel. 619-270-6401); 530 Bush St., **San Francisco,** CA 94108 (tel. 415-421-3473); 1314 N.E. 43rd St., **Seattle,** WA 98105 (tel. 206-632-2448); 3300 M St. NW, **Washington, DC** 20007 (tel. 202-337-65464). For U.S. cities not listed, call 800-2-COUNCIL/226-8624. Overseas offices include: 28A Poland St. (Oxford Circus), **London,** W1V 3DB (tel. (0171) 437 77 67); 22 Rue des Pyramides 75001 **Paris** (tel. 1 44 55 55 65); **Munich** (tel. (089) 39 50 22); **Tokyo** (tel. 3 35 81 55 17); **Singapore** (tel. 65 738 70 66). Visit their website at http://www.ciee.org/cts/ctshome.htm.

Educational Travel Centre (ETC), 438 North Frances St., Madison, WI 53703 (tel. (800) 747-5551; fax (608) 256-2042; email edtrav@execpc.com; http://www.edtrav.com). Flight info, HI-AYH cards, Eurail, and regional rail passes, plus the free pamphlet *Taking Off.*

Let's Go Travel, Harvard Student Agencies, 17 Holyoke St., Cambridge, MA 02138 (tel. (617) 495-9649; fax 495-7956; email travel@hsa.net; http://hsa.net/travel). Railpasses, HI-AYH memberships, ISICs, ITICs, FIYTO cards, guidebooks (including every *Let's Go* at a substantial discount), maps, bargain flights, and a complete line of budget travel gear. All items available by mail; see the catalog tucked into this publication.

Rail Europe Inc., 226 Westchester Ave., White Plains, NY 10604 (tel. (800) 438-7245; fax 432-1329; http://www.raileurope.com). Sells all Eurail products and passes, national railpasses, and point-to-point tickets. Gives you up-to-date info on all rail travel in Europe, including Eurostar, the English Channel train.

STA Travel, 6560 Scottsdale Rd. #F100, Scottsdale, AZ 85253 (tel. (800) 777-0112 nationwide; fax (602) 922-0793; http://sta-travel.com). A student and youth travel organization with over 150 offices worldwide offering discount airfares for young travelers, railpasses, accommodations, tours, insurance, and ISICs. 16 offices in the U.S. including: 297 Newbury Street, **Boston,** MA 02115 (tel. (617) 266-6014); 429 S. Dearborn St., **Chicago,** IL 60605 (tel. (312) 786-9050); 7202 Melrose Ave., **Los Angeles,** CA 90046 (tel. (213) 934-8722); 10 Downing St., Ste. G, **New York,** NY 10003 (tel. (212) 627-3111); 4341 University Way NE, **Seattle,** WA 98105 (tel. (206) 633-5000); 2401 Pennsylvania Ave., **Washington, D.C.** 20037 (tel. (202) 887-0912); 51 Grant Ave., **San Francisco,** CA 94108 (tel. (415) 391-8407); **Miami,** FL 33133 (tel. (305) 461-3444). In the U.K., 6 Wrights Ln., **London** W8 6TA (tel. (0171) 938 47 11 for North American travel). In New Zealand, 10 High St., **Auckland** (tel. (09) 309 97 23). In Australia, 222 Faraday St., **Melbourne** VIC 3050 (tel. (03) 349 69 11).

Students Flights Inc., 5010 East Shea Blvd., #A104, **Scottsdale, AZ** 85254 (tel. (800) 255-8000 or (602) 951-1177; fax 951-1216; email jost@isecard.com; http://isecard.com). Also sells Eurail and Europasses and international student exchange identity cards.

Tagus-Youth Travel, R. Camilo Castelo Branco, 20 1150 **Lisbon** (tel. (1) 352 59 86). R. Padre António Vieira, 3000 **Coimbra** (tel. (39) 349 99, fax (39) 349 16). Portugal's youth travel agency. Geared mainly toward Portuguese youth, but great for booking student airline tickets. Info on workcamps and *au pair* positions, discount transportation, HI and student ID cards, student residences, camping, and study visits in Portugal. English, Italian, Spanish, and French spoken.

Travel CUTS (Canadian Universities Travel Services Limited), 187 College St., Toronto, Ont. M5T 1P7 (tel. (416) 979-2406; fax 979-8167; email mail@travelcuts). Canada's national student travel bureau and equivalent of Council, with 40 offices across Canada. Also in the U.K., 295-A Regent St., **London** W1R 7YA (tel. (0171) 637 31 61). Discounted domestic and international airfares open to all; special student fares to all destinations with valid ISIC. Issues ISIC, FIYTO, GO25, and HI hostel cards, as well as railpasses. Offers free *Student Traveller* magazine, as well as information on the Student Work Abroad Program (SWAP).

Unitravel, 117 North Warson Rd., St. Louis, MO 63132 (tel. (800) 325 2222; fax (314) 569 2503). Budget fares on major airlines from U.S. to Europe and Africa.

Viajes TIVE, one office at C. José Ortega y Gasset, 71, **Madrid** 28006 (tel. (1) 347 77 78; fax 401 81 60). Spain's national chain of student travel agencies, with offices

most everywhere. They peddle discount travel tickets, ISIC cards, and HI memberships, and dispense transportation info.

Wasteels, 7041 Grand National Drive #207, Orlando, FL 32819 (tel. (407) 351-2537; in **London** (0171) 834 70 66). A huge chain in Europe, with over 200 locations. Info in English can be requested from the London office (tel. (0171) 834 70 66; fax 630 76 28). Sells Wasteels BIJ tickets, discounted (30-45% off regular fare) 2nd class international point-to-point train tickets with unlimited stopovers (must be under 26 on the first day of travel). Stuff sold *only* in Europe.

■ By Plane

Airlines will gleefully squeeze every dollar from customers; the path to cheap fares thus leads through a deliberately confusing jungle. Call toll-free numbers and always ask about discounts. Have several knowledgeable **travel agents** guide you; those specializing in travel to locales in and around Iberia and Morocco are better. Students and "youth" (people under 26) need never pay full price. Seniors can also get great deals; many airlines offer senior traveler clubs, airline passes, and discounts for their companions. Moreover, Sunday newspapers often have travel sections that list bargain fares from the local airport.

Outsmart airline reps with the phone-book-sized *Official Airline Guide* (check your local library; at US$359/yr, the tome costs as much as some flights), a monthly guide listing nearly every scheduled flight in the world (with fares, US$479) and toll-free phone numbers for all the airlines which allow you to call in reservations directly. More accessible is Michael McColl's *The Worldwide Guide to Cheap Airfare* (US$15), an incredibly useful guide for finding cheap airfare.

There is also a steadily increasing amount of travel information to be found on the Internet. The *Official Airline Guide* now also has a website (http://www.oag.com) which allows access to flight schedules. (One-time hook-up fee US$25 and a user's fee (17¢-47¢/min)). The site also provides information on hotels, cruises, and rail and ferry schedules. **TravelHUB** (http://www.travelhub.com) will help you search for travel agencies on the web.

Most airfares peak between mid-June and early September. Midweek (Monday through Thursday mornings) round-trip flights run about US$40-50 cheaper than on weekend flights. Hub-hopping is another budget strategy; rather than flying to Madrid or Lisbon (pin-sized cities by airline standards), consider a less direct but likely cheaper flight across the Atlantic to London, Amsterdam, Brussels, or Luxembourg. Flying to London is usually the cheapest way across the Atlantic. "Open return" tickets are usually pricier than purchasing ones with a fixed-return date and paying to change it. Whenever flying internationally, pick up your ticket well in advance, have the flight confirmed within 72 hours of departure, and arrive at the airport at least two hours before your flight.

Commercial airlines' lowest regular offer is the **Advance Purchase Excursion Fare (APEX)**. Specials advertised in newspapers may be cheaper, but have more restrictions and fewer available seats. APEX fares provide you with confirmed reservations and allow "open-jaw" tickets (landing in and returning from different cities). Generally, reservations must be made seven to 21 days in advance, with a seven to 14-day minimum and up to 90-day maximum stay limits, and hefty cancellation and change penalties (fees rise in summer). Book APEX fares early during peak season; past May you may have a difficult time getting the departure date you want.

Look into flights to less traveler targeted destinations or on smaller carriers. **Icelandair** (tel. (800) 223-5500) has last-minute offers and a stand-by fare from New York to Luxembourg (April-June 1 and Sept.-Oct. US$410; June 1-Aug. US$610). Reservations must be made at least three days before take-off time.

Local connections may work as well. **Iberia** flies out of hubs Madrid and Barcelona on both international and domestic routes (in Madrid tel. (1) 902 40 0500, in Barcelona tel. (3) 902 400 500; to reserve from the U.S. call (800) 772-4642; from South Africa 9 2000 931 61). **Aviaco,** a subsidiary of Iberia, covers only domestic routes

Better Safe than Sorry

Everyone who flies should be concerned with airline safety. The type and age of the aircraft used often indicate the airline's safety level—aircraft not produced by one of the major manufacturers sometimes fall below acceptable standards, and aircraft over 20 years old require increased levels of maintenance. If you're flying a foreign airline, especially to Third World countries, consult one of the following organizations. Travel agencies can tell you the type and age of aircraft on a particular route, as can the *Official Airline Guide* (http://www.oag.com); this can be especially useful in Eastern Europe where less reliable equipment is often used for inter-city travel. The **International Airline Passengers Association** (tel. (972) 404-9980) publishes a survey of accident rates on foreign airlines and provides safety information on carriers worldwide. The **Federal Aviation Administration** (http://www.faa.gov) reviews the airline authorities for countries whose airlines enter the U.S. and divides the countries into three categories: stick with carriers in category 1. Call the **U.S. State Department** (tel. (202) 647-5225; http://travel.state.gov/travel_warnings.html) to check for posted travel advisories which sometimes involve foreign carriers.

Prices at charter companies such as Air España (Palma), Aviación y Comercio (Madrid), and Euskal Air (Vitoria) are often lower than Iberia's. Travelers ages 12-25 are eligible for discounts with Iberia and other lines offer similar deals, possibly as high as 25% (21-day minimum advance purchase for Iberia). Recent EU regulations may introduce outside competition to national routes (keyword: cheaper rates); so it's best to go through a travel agency or thumb through newspapers. **Royal Air Maroc** (in Casablanca tel. (2) 31 41 41; in U.S. tel. (800) 344-6726; in U.K. tel. (0171) 439 43 61), the national carrier of Morocco, flies to most major cities in Europe, including Madrid and Lisbon. Domestically, a network of flights radiates from posh Mohammed V Airport outside Casablanca. Flights fly daily to Marrakech, Agadir (a resort on the south coast), Tangier, Fès, and less regularly to Ouarzazate.

TICKET CONSOLIDATORS

Ticket consolidators resell unsold tickets on commercial and charter airlines at unpublished fares. The consolidator market is by and large international. Consolidator flights are the best deals if you are traveling on short notice, on a high-priced trip, to an offbeat destination, or in peak season. There is rarely a maximum age or stay limit, but unlike tickets bought through an airline, you cannot use your tickets on another flight if you miss yours—in such a case, ask the consolidator rather than the airline for a refund. Keep in mind these tickets are often for coach seats on connecting (not direct) flights on foreign airlines, and that frequent-flyer mile tabs may not carry over. Consolidators come in three varieties: wholesale only, which sell to travel agencies; specialty agencies (both wholesale and retail); and **"bucket shops"** or discount retail agencies. You, as a private consumer, can deal directly only with retail agencies, but can access a larger market through a travel agent, who can get tickets from wholesale consolidators. Look for bucket shops' ads in weekend papers (in the U.S., the Sunday *New York Times* is best). In London, the bucket shop center, the Air Travel Advisory Bureau (tel. (0171) 63 50 00), lists consolidators.

Be a smart and careful shopper. Mixed among the many reputable and trustworthy companies are some shady dealers. Contact your local Better Business Bureau to scan company's track record. Ask the consolidator to send your tickets as quickly as possible so you have time to fix any problems. Also, get the company's policy in writing: insist on a **receipt** giving full details about the tickets, refunds, and restrictions, and record whom you talked to and when. It may be worth paying with a credit card (despite the 2-5% fee) so you can stop payment if you never receive your tickets. Beware of the "bait and switch" gag: shyster firms will advertise a super-low fare and then tell callers it has been sold. Although this is a viable excuse, if they can't offer you a price near the advertised fare on *any* date, it is nothing more than a scam to

lure customers—report them to the Better Business Bureau. Ask about accommodation and car rental discounts—some consolidators have their fingers in many pies.

Several consolidators sell tickets to Spain, Portugal, and Morocco, best reached by their 800 numbers. Among these are: **AESU** (tel. (800) 638-7640 or http://www.aesu.com); **Air Travel Discounts, Inc.** (tel. (800) 888-2621); **Alpha Travel** (tel. (800) 793-8424); **Campus Travel** (tel. (800) 328-3359); **Central Holidays** (tel. (800) 935-5000); **Central Tours** (tel. (800) 783-9882); **4th Dimension Tours** (tel. (800) 343-0020); **Millrun Tours** (tel. (800) 645-5786); **Picasso Travel** (tel. (800) PICASSO (742-2776)); **Plus Ultra** (tel. (800) FOR-SPAIN (367-7724)).

Kelly Monaghan's *Consolidators: Air Travel's Bargain Basement* (US$7 plus US$2 shipping) from the Intrepid Traveler, P.O. Box 438, New York, NY 10034 (e-mail intreptrav@aol.com), is an invaluable source for info. Cyber-stuff worth browsing includes **World Wide** (http://www.tmn.com/wwwanderer/).

STAND-BY FLIGHTS

Airhitch, 2641 Broadway, 3rd Floor, New York, NY 10025 (tel. (800) 326-2009 or (212) 864-2000, fax 864-5489) and Los Angeles, CA (tel. (310) 726-5000), will add a certain thrill to the prospects of when you will leave and where exactly you will end up. Complete flexibility on both sides of the Atlantic is necessary; flights cost US$175 each way when departing from the Northeast, $269 from the West Coast or Northwest, $229 from the Midwest, and $209 from the Southeast. Travel within the USA and Europe is also possible, with rates ranging from $79-$129. The snag is that you do not buy a ticket, but the promise that you will get to a destination near where you're intending to go within a window of time (usually 5 days) from a location in a region you have specified. You call in before your date range to hear all of your flight options for the next seven days and your probability of boarding. You then decide which flights you want to try to make and present a voucher at the airport which grants you the right to board a flight on a space-available basis. This procedure must be followed again for the return trip. Be aware that you may only receive a monetary refund if all available flights which departed within your date-range from the specified region are full. However, future travel credit is always available. There are several offices in Europe, so you can wait to register for your return; the main one is in Paris (tel. (1) 47 00 16 30). **Air-Tech, Ltd.,** 588 Broadway #204, New York, NY 10012 (tel. (212) 219-7000, fax 219-0066) offers a very similar service; their Travel Window is one to four days. Rates to and from Europe (continually updated; call and verify) are: Northeast US$169; West Coast US$239; Midwest/Southeast US$199. Upon registration and payment, Air-Tech sends you a FlightPass with a contact date falling soon before your Travel Window, when you are to call them for flight instructions. You must go through the same procedure to return—and that no refunds are granted unless the company fails to get you a seat before your Travel Window expires. Air-Tech also arranges courier flights and regular confirmed-reserved flights at discount rates.

Be sure to read all the fine print in your agreements with either company—a call to The Better Business Bureau of New York City may be worthwhile. Be warned that it is difficult to receive refunds, and clients' vouchers will not be honored if an airline fails to receive payment in time.

CHARTER FLIGHTS

With **charters,** a tour operator contracts with an airline to fly extra loads of passengers to peak-season destinations. These fly less frequently and have more restrictions than major airlines and are particularly strict with their refund policies. Charters are almost always booked, and schedules and itineraries may change or be cancelled at the last moment (as late as 48 hours before the trip, and without a full refund). Always pay with a credit card, and consider travelers' insurance against trip interruption.

Try **Interworld** (tel. (305) 443-4929, fax 443-0351); **Travac** (tel. (800) 872-8800, fax (212) 714-9063; email mail@travac.com; http://www.travac.com) or **Rebel**

Valencia, CA (tel. (800) 227-3235; fax (805)-294-0981; http://rebeltours.com; e-mail travel@rebeltours.com) or Orlando, FL (tel. (800) 732-3588). Don't be afraid to call every number and hunt for the best deal.

Eleventh-hour **discount clubs** and **fare brokers** offer members savings on European travel, including charter flights and tour packages. Research your options carefully. **Last Minute Travel Club,** 100 Sylvan Rd., Woburn, MA 01801 (tel. (800) 527-8646 or (617) 267-9800), and **Discount Travel International** New York, NY (tel. (212) 362-3636; fax 362-3236; see **Ticket Consolidators** above) are among the few travel clubs that don't charge a membership fee. Others include **Moment's Notice,** New York, NY (tel. (718) 234-6295; fax 234 6450; http://www.moments-notice.com), air tickets, tours, and hotels; US$25 annual fee. **Travelers Advantage,** Stamford, CT (tel. (800) 548-1116; http://www.travelersadvantage.com; US$49 annual fee); and **Travel Avenue** (tel. (800) 333-3335; see **Ticket Consolidators** above). Study these organizations' contracts closely; you don't want to end up with an unwanted overnight layover.

COURIER COMPANIES AND FREIGHTERS

Those who travel light should consider flying internationally as a **courier.** The company hiring you will use your checked luggage space for freight; you are only allowed to bring carry-ons. You are responsible for the safe delivery of the baggage claim slips (given to you by a courier company representative) to the representative waiting for you when you arrive—don't screw up or you will be blacklisted as a courier. You will probably never see the cargo you are transporting—the company handles it all—and airport officials know that couriers are not responsible for the baggage checked for them. Restrictions to watch for: you must be over 21 (18 in some cases), have a valid passport, and procure your own visa (if necessary); most flights are round-trip only with short fixed-length stays (usually one week); only single tickets are issued (but a companion may be able to get a next-day flight); and most flights are from New York. Round-trip fares to Western Europe from the U.S. range from US$250-400 (during the off-season) to US$400-550 (during the summer). For an annual fee of $45, the **International Association of Air Travel Couriers,** 8 South J St., P.O. Box 1349, Lake Worth, Florida 33460 (tel. (561) 582-8320) informs travelers (via computer, fax, and mailings) of courier opportunities worldwide. Steve Lantos publishes a monthly update of courier options in **Travel Unlimited** as well as general information on low-budget travel (write P.O. Box 1058A, Allston, MA, 02134 for a free sample newsletter; subscription runs US$25 per year). Most flights originate from New York or London and travel to Europe, Asia, or South America, although flights to Australia and South Africa exist. **NOW Voyager,** 74 Varick St. #307, New York, NY 10013 (tel. (212) 431-1616; fax 334-5243); email info@nowvoyagertravel.com; http://www.nowvoyagertravel.com), acts as an agent for many courier flights worldwide primarily from New York and offers special last-minute deals to such cities as London, Paris, Rome, and Frankfurt for as little as US$200 round-trip plus a US$50 registration fee. (They also act as a consolidator; see **Ticket Consolidators** above.) Other agents to try are **Halbart Express,** 147-05 176th St., Jamaica, NY 11434 (tel. (718) 656-5000; fax 917-0708; offices in Chicago, Los Angeles, and London) and **Discount Travel International** (tel. (212) 362-3636) (see **Ticket Consolidators** above).

You can also go directly through courier companies in New York, or check your bookstore or library for handboks such as *Air Courier Bargains* (US$15 plus$2.50 shipping from the Intrepid Traveler, P.O. Box 438, New York, NY 10034; email intreptrav@aol.com). *The Courier Air Travel Handbook* (US$10 plus $3.50 shipping) explains how to travel as an air courier and contains names, phone numbers, and contact points of courier companies. It can be ordered directly from Bookmasters, Inc., P.O. Box 2039, Mansfield, OH 44905 (tel. (800) 507-2665).

ONCE THERE

■ Tourist Offices

Spain

Most towns have a centrally located **Oficina de Turismo** (called **Turismo**) which distributes info on sights, lodgings, and events, and sometimes a free map here and there. Bigger cities may have more than one, and there is often a regional office; the branches' services and brochures don't always overlap. *Turismos* are also handy places to check phone numbers. Although they do not explicitly book accommodations, many will list establishments or show you the way to a *casa particular*. In smaller towns the staff, maps, and/or brochures may not be available in English.

Portugal

The national tourist board is the **Direcção Geral do Turismo (DGT).** Their offices are in virtually every city; look for the **"Turismo"** sign. Services offered are similar to those in Spain. Finding an English speaker at bigger offices is usually no problem, and French and German speakers should also take heart. The principal student travel agency is **TAGUS-Youth Student Travel (see Budget Travel Agencies, p. 30).**

Morocco

Most cities have a centrally located **Office Nationale Marocaine de Tourisme (ONMT).** They may offer a free map and information on sights, markets, accommodations, and official guides. Some even store luggage and change money when banks are closed. Many cities also have a **Syndicat d'Initiative,** a city tourist office, with the same services. Both offices are not really geared for the budget traveler.

■ Embassies and Consulates

Foreign embassies are in Madrid, Lisbon, and Rabat; consulates are usually in other major cities. In Spain and Portugal, embassies and consulates usually are open Monday through Friday, with *siestas* (breaks; in Portuguese, *sestas*) each day; call for specific hours, though some are listed. In Morocco, the standard business hours of embassies and consulates are Mon.-Fri. around 8am, out to lunch around noon—some open after until 6pm, some do not. Consulates give legal advice, medical referrals, and can readily contact relatives back home. In extreme cases, they may offer emergency financial assistance. For the embassies and consulates of Spain, Portugal, and Morocco in your home country (for other useful resources, see page 5).

Spain

U.S. Embassies: C. Serrano, 75, **Madrid** 28006 (tel. (1) 587 2200; telex; fax (1) 58 23 03). **Consulates:** Po. Reina Elisenda 23, **Barcelona** 08034 (tel. (93) 280 22 27 fax 205 52 06). Open 9am-12:30pm, 3-5pm. **Consular Agencies:** Po. Delicias, **Sevilla** 41012 (tel. (95) 423 18 85). Av. Jaime III, 26, Entresuelo, **Palma de Mallorca** 07012 (tel. (971) 72 50 51). Centro Comercial "Las Rampas," Fase 2, Planta Locales 12G7 & 12G8, **Málaga** 29640 (tel. (95) 247 48 91; fax (95) 246 51 89); Mail only: Calle Paz 6, 5 local 5, **Valencia** 46003 (tel. (96) 351 69 73). Cantón Grande 16-17, **La Coruña** 15003 (tel. (981) 21 32 33).

Canadian Embassies: Edificio Goya, C. Núñez de Balboa, 35, **Madrid** 28001 (tel. (1) 431 43 00; fax 577 98 11; http://info.ic.gc.ca/Tourism). **Consulates:** Passeig de Gracia, 77-30. **Barcelona** 08008 (tel. (3) 215 0704; fax 487 9117). Edificio Horizonte, Pl. Malagueta, 3-1, **Málaga** 29016 (tel. (5) 222 3346; fax 222 4023).

British Embassy: C. Fernando el Santo, 16, **Madrid** 28010 (tel. (1) 319 02 00; fax 308 10 33). **Consulates:** Centro Colón, Marqués de la Ensenada, 16, 2nd fl., **Madrid** 28004 (tel. (1) 308 52 01; fax 308 08 82). **Consulate-General,** Edificio Torre de Barcelona, Av. Diagonal, 477, 13th fl., **Barcelona** 08036 (tel. (3) 419 90 44; fax 40

24 11; email brconbcn@alba.mssl.es). Pl. Nueva 8B, **Sevilla** 41001 (tel. (5) 422 88 75; fax 421 03 23). Alameda de Urquijo, 2, 8th fl., **Bilbao** 48008 (tel. (4) 415 76 00; fax 416 76 32). Pl. Mayor, 3D, **Palma de Mallorca** 07002 (tel. (71) 71 24 45; fax 71 75 20). Av. Isidor Macabich, 45, 1st. fl., Apartavo 307, **Ibiza** 07800, Balearic Islands (tel. (71) 30 18 18); not a full consulate, but sends passport application forms to Palma or Madrid. Pl. Calvo Sotelo, 1/2, **Alicante** 03001 (tel. (65) 21 60 22; fax 14 05 28). Po. de Pereda, 27, **Santander** 39004 (tel. (42) 22 00 00; fax 22 29 41). Duquesa de Parcent, 8, Edificio Duquesa, Apartavo 360, **Málaga** 29001 (tel. (5) 221 75 71; fax 221 11 30).

Irish Embassy: Claudio Coello, 73, **Madrid** 28001 (tel. (1) 576 3500; 435 1677).

Australian Embassy: Po. Castellana, 143, **Madrid** 28046 (tel. (1) 579 04 28; fax 570 02 04; http://www.embaustralia.es). **Consulates:** Gran Vía Carlos III, 98, **Barcelona** 08028 (tel. (3) 330 94 96; fax 411 09 04). Federico Rubio, 14, **Sevilla** 41004 (tel. (5) 422 02 40; fax 421 11 45).

New Zealand Embassy: Pl. de La Lealtad, 2, **Madrid** 28014 (tel. (1) 523 02 26; fax 523 01 71). **Consulate:** 4th fl., Traversa de Gracia, 64, **Barcelona** 08006 (tel. (93) 209 03 99; fax 202 08 90).

South African Embassy: Claudio Coello, 91, 6th fl., **Madrid** 28006 (tel. (1) 435 66 88; fax 577 7414). **Consulates:** Teodora Lamadrid, 7-11, **Barcelona** 08022 (tel. (3) 418 6445; fax 418 0538). Las Mercedes, 31, 4th fl., Las Arenas, **Bilbao** (Vizcaya) 48005. Franchy y Roca, 5, 6th fl., **Las Palmas de Gran Canaria** 35007 (tel. (28) 22 60 04; fax 22 60 15).

Portugal

U.S. Embassy: Av. das Forças Armadas, 1600 **Lisbon** (tel. (1) 727 33 00; fax 726 91 09).

Canadian Embassy: Av. Liberdade, 144, 4th fl., #4, 1250 **Lisbon** (tel. (1) 347 48 92; fax 347 64 66).

British Embassy: Rua São Bernardo, 33, 1200 **Lisbon** Codex (tel. (1) 392 4000; fax 392 41 86; Britembassy@mail.telepac.pt). **Consulates:** Av. Zarco, 2, CP 417, 9000 **Funchal, Madeira** (tel. (91) 22 12 21; fax (91) 23 37 89).

Irish Embassy: Rua da Imprensa à Estrela, 4 fl., #1, 1200 **Lisbon** (tel. (1) 396 15 69; fax (1) 397 73 63).

Australian Embassy: Refer to the Australian Embassy in Paris: 4 Rue Jean Rey, 75724 Paris Cedex 15, Paris, France (tel. (331) 405 933 00; fax 405 933 10).

New Zealand Embassy: Refer to the British Embassy in Lisbon or the New Zealand Embassy in Italy at Via Zara, 28, **Rome** 00198 (tel. (396) 440 29 28; fax 440 29 84; nzemb.romşagora.stm.it). **Consulate:** Av. Antonio Augusto de Aguilar, 122-9th floor, 1050 **Lisbon** (tel. 351-1-3509690; fax 351-1-3572004).

South African Embassy: Av. Luis Bivar, 10, 1097 **Lisbon** (tel. (1) 353 50 41; fax 353 57 13; email SAfrican.Embassy@individual.EUnet.pt). **Consulate,** Rua do Campo Alegre, 1306-Sala 405, 4150 **Porto** (tel. (02) 600 2023); Rua Pímenta Aguiar, Bloco C-30, 9000 **Funchal, Madeira** (tel. (091) 742 825).

Morocco

U.S. Embassy: 2 Av. de Marrakech, **Rabat** (tel. (7) 76 22 65; fax 76 56 61). Open Mon.-Fri. 9:30am-noon. 24-hr. emergency phone (tel. 76 96 39). **Consulate:** 8 Blvd. Moulay Youssef, **Casablanca** (tel. (2) 26 45 50; fax 20 41 27).

Canadian Embassy: 13 Bis, Jaafar Assadik, B.P. 709, Agdal, **Rabat** (tel. (7) 67 28 80; fax 67 21 87). **Consulate:** 31 Rue Hanza Agdal, **Rabat** (tel. (7) 67 23 75 or 67 23 77; fax 67 24 31).

British Embassy: 17 Blvd. de la Tour Hassan, B.P. 45, **Rabat** (tel. (7) 72 09 05, 72 09 06, 73 14 03, or 73 14 04; fax 70 45 31 or 2025 62). **Consulates:** 43 Blvd. d'Anfa, B.P. 13762, **Casablanca** (tel. (2) 22 16 53, 22 17 41, 22 31 85, or 29 58 96; fax 26 57 79). 41 Bd. Mohammed V, B.P. 2122, **Tangiers** (tel. (9) 94 15 57; fax 94 22 84). Hours for the consulates are the same as those for the embassy.

Irish Embassy: Refer to British Embassy and Consulates (above).

Australian Embassy: Refer to Canadian Embassy (above).

New Zealand Embassy: Refer to British Embassy and Consulates (above).

■ Getting Around

BY TRAIN

To this day trains remain the budget travelers' preferred mode of travel through Europe. Bring food and water with you on trips; the on-board cafes can be pricey, and train water can be undrinkable. Trains are far from theft-proof, so lock your compartment door if you can, and always keep valuables on your person.

Many train stations have different counters for domestic and international tickets, seat reservations, and information. On major lines, reservations are always advisable (US$3-10), and often required, even with a railpass. Also, while the use of many of Europe's high speed or quality trains (such as EuroCity, InterCity, or France's TGV) are included in the railpass price, a supplement is then required to ride some city-to-city trains, including Spain's AVE (usually around US$10). A sleeping berth in a couchette car is a recommended perk (about US$20; reserve several days in advance).

Railpasses Buying a railpass is both a popular and sensible option under many circumstances. Ideally, a railpass allows you to jump on any train in Europe, go wherever you want whenever you want, and change your plans at will. The handbook that comes with your railpass tells you everything you need to know and includes a timetable for major routes, a map, and details possible ferry, steamer, bus, car rental, hotel, and **Eurostar** (the high speed train linking London and Paris or Brussels) discounts. In practice, it's not so simple. You still must stand in line to pay for seat reservations, supplements, and couchette reservations, as well as to have your pass validated when you first use it. More importantly, railpasses don't always pay off. For ballpark estimates, consult Rick Steve's **Europe Through the Back Door** newsletter, or the **DERTravel** or **RailEurope** railpass brochure for prices of point-to-point tickets.

Add them up and compare with railpass prices. If you're under age 26, the BIJ tickets are probably a viable option (see **Rail tickets,** p. 39).

You may find it tough to make your railpass pay for itself in Portugal and Spain, where train fares are reasonable or distances are short. If, however, the total cost of your trips nears the price of the pass, the convenience of avoiding ticket lines may be worth the difference. Try to avoid obsessing about making the pass pay for itself; you may come home with only blurred memories of train stations.

Eurailpass remains the best option for non-EU travelers. Eurailpasses are valid in most of Western Europe (except Britain). Eurailpasses and Europasses are designed by the EU itself, and are available only by non-Europeans almost exclusively from non-European distributors. The EU sets the prices, so no one travel agent is better than any other for buying a Eurailpass.

The first class Eurailpass rarely pays off; it is offered for 15 days (US$522), 21 days (US$678), one month (US$838), two months (US$1188), or three months (US$1468). If you are traveling in a group you might prefer the **Eurail Saverpass,** which allows unlimited first-class travel for 15 days (US$444), 21 days (US$576), one month (US$712), two months (US$1010), or three months (US$1248) per person in groups of two or more. Travelers under age 26 can buy a **Eurail Youthpass,** good for 15 days (US$365), 21 days (US $475), one month (US$587), two months (US$832), or three months (US $1028) of second-class travel. The two-month pass is most economical. **Eurail Flexipasses** allow limited first-class travel within a two-month period: 10 days (US$616), 15 days (US$812). **Youth Flexipasses,** for those under 26 who wish to travel second-class, are available for US$431 (10days) or US$568 (15days), respectively.

The **Europass** combines France, Germany, Italy, Spain, and Switzerland in one plan. With a Europass you can travel in any of these five countries from five to fifteen days within a window of two months. First-class adult prices begin at US$316 and increase incrementally by US$42 for each extra day of travel. With purchase of a first-class ticket you can buy an identical ticket for your traveling partner for 40% off. Second-class youth tickets begin at US$210 and increase incrementally by $29 for each extra day of travel. Children between the ages of 4-11 travel for half the price of a first-class ticket. You can also add associate countries (Austria/Hungary, Belgium/Luxembourg/Netherlands, Greece, and Portugal) for a nominal fee. The Europass introduces planning complications; you must plan your routes so that they only make use of countries you've "purchased." They're serious about this: if you cut through a country you haven't purchased you will be fined.

You should plan your itinerary before buying a Europass. It will save you money if you limit yourself to travel between three and five adjacent Western European countries, or if you know that you want to go only to large cities. Europasses are not appropriate if you like to take lots of side trips—you'll waste rail days. If you're tempted to add lots of rail days and associate countries, consider the Eurailpass.

You'll find it easiest to buy a Eurailpass before you arrive in Europe; contact Council Travel, Travel CUTS, Let's Go Travel (see **Budget Travel Agencies,** p. 27), or any of many other travel agents. If you're stuck in Europe and unable to find someone to sell you a Eurailpass, call an American railpass agent who can send a pass by express mail. Eurailpasses are non-refundable once validated; you can get a replacement for a lost pass only if you have purchased insurance on it under the Pass Protection Plan (US$10). All Eurailpasses can be purchased from a travel agent, or from **Rail Europe, Inc.,** 226-230 Westchester Ave., White Plains, NY 10604 (tel. (800) 438-7245; fax (800) 432-1329 in the U.S.; and tel. (800) 361-7245; fax (905) 602-4198 in Canada; http://www.raileurope.com), which also sells point-to-point tickets. They offer special rates for groups of six or more travelling together. **DERTravel Services,** 9501 W. Devon Ave. #400, Rosemont IL, 60018 (tel. (800) 421-2929; fax (800) 282-7474; http://www.dertravel.com) also deals in rail passes and point to point tickets.

For EU citizens, there are **InterRail Passes,** for which six months' residence in Europe makes you eligible. The Under 26 InterRail Card (from UK£189) allows either 5 days or one month of unlimited travel within one, two, three or all of the seven

zones into which InterRail divides Europe; the cost is determined by the number of zones the pass covers. The Over 26 InterRail Card offers unlimited second-class travel in 19 countries in Europe for 15 days or one month for UK£215 and UK£275, respectively. For information and ticket sales in Europe contact **Student Travel Center,** 1st Fl. 24 Rupert St., London, W1V7FN (tel. (0171) 437 01 21, 437 63 70, or 434 13 06; fax 734 38 36; http://www.hols.com/student/). Tickets are also available from travel agents or major train stations throughout Europe.

If your travels will be limited to one country, consider a national railpass or regional passes. In addition to simple railpasses, many countries (and Europass and Eurail) offer rail-and-drive passes, which combine car rental with rail travel—a good option for travelers who wish both to visit cities accessible by rail and make side trips into the surrounding areas. Several national and regional passes offer companion fares, allowing two adults traveling together 50% off the price of one pass. Some of these passes can be bought only in Europe, some only outside of Europe, and for some it doesn't matter; check with a railpass agent or with national tourist offices.

Rail Tickets For travelers under 26, **BIJ** tickets (*Billets Internationals de Jeunesse,* sold under the names **Wasteels, Eurotrain,** and **Route 26**) are a great alternative to railpasses. Available for international trips within Europe and for travel within France as well as most ferry services, they knock 25-40% off regular second-class fares. Tickets are good for two months after purchase and allow a number of stopovers along the normal direct route of the train journey. Issued for a specific international route between two points, they must be used in the direction and order of the designated route and must be bought in Europe. They are available from European travel agents, at Wasteels or Eurotrain offices (usually in or near train stations), or directly at the ticket counter in some nations. Contact Wasteels in Victoria Station, adjacent to Platform 2, London SW1V 1JT (tel. (0171) 834 70 66; fax 630 76 28).

Useful Resources The ultimate reference for planning rail trips is the **Thomas Cook European Timetable** (US$28; with a map of Europe with all train and ferry routes US$39; postage US$4.50). This timetable, updated regularly, covers all major and most minor train routes in Europe. In the U.S. and Canada, order it from **Forsyth Travel Library** (see **Travel Publications,** p. 2). In Europe find it at any **Thomas Cook Money Exchange Center.** Also from Forsyth is **Traveling Europe's Trains** (US$15), by Jay Burnoose, which includes maps and sight-seeing suggestions. Available at most bookstores or from **Houghton Mifflin Co.,** 222 Berkeley St., Boston, MA 02116 (tel. (800) 225-3362; fax (800) 634-7568) is the annual **Eurail Guide to Train Travel in the New Europe** (US$15), giving timetables, instructions, and prices for international train trips, day trips, and excursions in Europe. The annual railpass special edition of the free Rick Steves' **Europe Through the Back Door** travel newsletter and catalogue, 120 Fourth Ave. N., P.O. Box 2009, Edmonds, WA 98020 (tel. (425) 771-8303; fax 771-0833; email ricksteves@aol.com; http://www.ricksteves.com) provides comparative analysis of European railpasses with national or regional passes and point-to-point tickets.

BY BUS

Though European trains and railpasses are extremely popular, the long-distance bus networks of Portugal and Morocco are more extensive, efficient, and often more comfortable than train services; in Spain, the bus and train systems are on par. The biggest problem with European bus travel is deregulation; it can be difficult to negotiate the route you need, but short-haul buses reach rural areas inaccessible by train. Amsterdam, Athens, Istanbul, London, Munich, and Oslo are centers for lines that offer long-distance rides across Europe; see the Bus listings in the **Practical Information** sections for these cities, as well as the openings to each country chapter.

Eurolines, 4 Cardiff Rd., Luton LU1 1PP (tel. (01582) 40 45 11; fax (01582) 40 04 94; in London, 52 Grosvenor Gardens, Victoria; (tel. (0171) 730 82 35), is Europe's largest operator of Europe-wide coach services, including Eastern Europe and Russia.

A Eurolines Pass offers unlimited 30-day (under 26 and over 60 UK£159; 26-60 UK £199) or 60-day (under 26 and over 60, UK£199, 26-60 UK£249) travel between 20 major tourist destinations. Eurolines also offers **Euro Explorers,** eight complete travel loops throughout Europe with set fares and itineraries. **Eurobus,** P.O. Box 3016, Workingham, Berkshire RG40 2YP (tel.(0118) 936 23 21; fax (0118) 936 23 22; http:/ /www.eurobus.uk.com), offers cheap bus trips in 25 major cities in 10 major European countries for those between ages 16 and 38. The buses, with English speaking guides and drivers, stop door-to-door at one hostel or budget hotel per city, and let you hop on and off. Tickets are sold by zone; for any one zone US$225, for any two zones US$400, for all three zones US$525.Travelers under 26 are eligible for discounts on all tickets. For purchase in the United States contact Council Travel or STA; in Canada contact Travel CUTS (see **Budget Travel Agencies,** p. 30).

BY CAR

Cars offer access to the countryside and an escape from the town-to-town mentality of trains. Unfortunately, they also insulate you from the camaraderie that European rail travelers enjoy. Although a single traveler won't save by renting a car, four usually will. If you can't decide between train and car travel, consider a combination of the two; Rail Europe and other railpass vendors offer economical rail-and-drive packages for both individual countries and all of Europe. Travel agents may have other rail-and-drive packages.

A good source of information on driving in each country are automobile clubs like AAA, CAA, etc.—you can get most relevant material from such organizations in your own country. **Automóvel Club de Portugal (ACP)** based at Rua Rosa Araújo, 24, Lisbon 1250 (tel. (351-1) 356 3931; fax (357 4732), provides breakdown and towing services to members or to AIT and FIA affiliated Club members at any time.

Rental offices can be found at most airports in Spain, Portugal, and Morocco, although check at home for certainty's sake. **Tax** on rentals can be as much as 16% in Spain, 17% in Portugal, and 19% in Morocco (plus the airport tax, US$11 in Spain and US$13 in Portugal). Most companies require that you be at least 21 in Spain (23 for Avis), 21 in Portugal and Morocco, and that you have had a driver's license for at least one year. Morocco has a few other restrictions. **Rent** a car from a U.S.-based firm (Alamo, Avis, Budget, or Hertz) with its own European offices, from a European-based company with local representatives (Europcar), or from a tour operator (Auto Europe, Bon Voyage By Car, Europe By Car, and Kemwel), which arranges rentals at its own rates. Not surprisingly, multinationals offer greater flexibility, but tour operators often strike better deals. Rental prices vary by company, season, and pick-up point. Expect to pay US$80-400 a week, plus tax (5-25%), for a teensy car. Reserve well before leaving for Europe and pay in advance if possible. Always check if quoted prices include tax and collision insurance; some credit card companies cover this automatically. Ask about discounts, and be flexible in your itinerary. Ask your airline about special packages; you may get up to a week of free rental. Minimum age varies by agency.

Try **Auto Europe,** 39 Commercial St., P.O. Box 7006, Portland, ME (tel. (800) 223-5555; fax (800) 235-6321; http://www.auto-europe.com); **Avis Rent a Car** (tel. (800) 331-1084; http://www.avis.com); **Bon Voyage By Car** (tel. (800) 272-3299; in Canada (800) 253-3876); **Budget Rent a Car** (tel. (800) 472-3325); **Europe by Car,** One Rockefeller Plaza, New York, NY 10020 (tel. (800) 223-1516 or (212) 581-3040; fax 246-1458; http://www.europebycar.com); **Europcar,** 145 Avenue Malekoff, 75016 Paris (tel. (800) 227-3876; (800) 227-7368 in Canada; (1) 45 00 08 06 in France); **Hertz Rent a Car** (tel. (800) 654-3001; http://www.hertz.com); **Payless Car Rental** (tel. (800) 729-5377).

For longer than 17 days, **leasing** can be cheaper than renting and it is sometimes the only option for those ages 18-21. The cheapest leases are agreements to buy the car and then sell it back to the manufacturer at a prearranged price. Leases include insurance coverage and are not taxed. The most affordable ones usually originate in France, Belgium, Germany, or Italy. Expect to pay at least US$1200 for 60 days. Con-

tact **Bon Voyage By Car, Europe by Car, France Auto-Vacance,** or **Auto Europe.** You will need to make arrangements in advance.

If you're brave and know what you're doing, **buying** a used car or van in Europe and selling it just before you leave can provide the cheapest wheels for longer trips. Check with consulates for import-export laws concerning used vehicles, registration, and safety and emission standards. Camper-vans and motor homes give the advantages of a car without the hassle and expense of finding lodgings. David Shore and Patty Campbell's *Europe by Van and Motorhome* (US$14; postage US$2, overseas US$6) guides you through the entire process of renting, leasing, buying, and selling vehicles in Britain and on the Continent, including buy-back options, registration, insurance, and dealer listings. To order, write or call Shore/Campbell Publications, 1842 Santa Margarita Dr., Fallbrook, CA 92028 (tel./fax (800) 659-5222 or (760) 723-6184). In Morocco, selling imported cars or other goods may land you in jail.

Eric Bredesen's *Moto-Europa* (US$16; shipping US$3, overseas US$7), available from Seren Publishing, 2935 Saint Anne Dr., Dubuque, IA 52001 (tel. (800) 387-6728; fax (319) 583-7853), is a thorough guide to all these options and includes itinerary suggestions, a motorists' phrasebook, and chapters on leasing and buying vehicles. More general info is available from the **American Automobile Association (AAA),** Travel Agency Services Dept., 1000 AAA Dr., Heathrow, FL 32746-5080 (tel. (800) 222-4357 or (417) 444-7380; http://www.aaa.com). For regional numbers of the **Canadian Automobile Association (CAA),** call (800) 222-4357.

Before setting off, be sure you know the laws of the countries in which you'll be driving. Be careful: road conditions in Europe are rarely as driver-friendly as they are in the States. On top of that, Portugal has the highest accident mortality rate in Europe. The **Association for Safe International Road Travel (ASIRT)** can provide more info about conditions in specific countries. They are located at 5413 West Cedar Lane, Suite 103C, Bethesda, MD 20814 (tel. (301) 983-5252; fax 983-3663; http://www.horizon-web.com/asirt). Western Europeans use unleaded gas almost exclusively.

BY PLANE

Unless you're under 26, flying across Europe on regularly scheduled flights will devour your budget. Student travel agencies sell cheap tickets, and budget fares are frequently available in the spring and summer on high-volume routes to resort areas in Spain and possibly Portugal. Consult budget travel agents and local newspapers and magazines. The **Air Travel Advisory Bureau** in London (tel. (0171) 636 50 00), can put you in touch with discount flights to worldwide destinations for free. In addition, many European airlines offer visitor ticket packages, which give intercontinental passengers discount rates on flights within Europe (as well as on accommodations and car rentals) after arrival. Check with a travel agent for details.

BY FERRY

Travel by boat is an enchanting alternative much favored by Europeans but overlooked by most foreigners. The majority of European ferries are comfortable and well-equipped. Check in at least two hours early for a prime spot. Avoid the astronomically priced cafeterias by bringing your own food. Ask for discounts; ISIC holders can often get student fares, and Eurail passholders get many reductions and free trips. You'll occasionally have to pay a small port tax (under US$10). Advance planning and reserved ticket purchases through a travel agency can spare you days of waiting in dreary ports for the next boat to embark.

Ferries in Europe divide into four major groups. **Mediterranean** ferries may be the most glamorous, but they are also the most treacherous in terms of ride safety. Reservations are recommended, especially in July and August, when ships are insufferably crowded and expensive. Bring toilet paper—there is a dearth on board. Ferries run on erratic schedules, with varying prices, so shop around for the best deal. Beware of dinky, unreliable companies which often do not take reservations.

Transmediterránea offers sea service around the edges of Spain, Portugal, and Morocco, including service between the Islas Baleares (Balearic Islands) and Islas Canarias (Canary Islands). Those interested can ring Transmediterránea in Madrid (tel. (1) 322 91 00; 322 91 10); Barcelona (tel. (3) 443 25 32; fax 443 27 81); Ceuta (tel. (56) 50 94 39, fax 50 95 30), and Tangier (tel. (9) 93 36 25). Frequent ferries shuttle back and forth between Spain and Morocco; the cheapest runs two hours between Algeciras (Spain) and Tangier. Tangier also has ferry connections to Málaga, Gibraltar, and elsewhere. (For more details, see **Tangier: Orientation and Practical Information,** p. 631.) Taking a ferry to Spain's Mediterranean and Atlantic islands is scenic, romantic, and sunny. Also investigate smaller companies such as **Flebasa** and **Pitra.**

BY BICYCLE

Today, biking is one of the key elements of the classic budget Eurovoyage. A few simple tools and a good bike manual will be invaluable. For information about touring routes, consult national tourist offices or any of the numerous books available. **The Mountaineers Books,** 1001 S.W. Klickitat Way #201, Seattle, WA 98134 (tel. (800) 553-4453 or (206) 223-6303; fax 223-6306; mbooks@mountaineers.org) offers several nation-specific tour books (especially France, Germany, Ireland, and the U.K.), as well as **Europe By Bike,** by Karen and Terry Whitehill (US$15; shipping $3), a great source of specific area tours in 11 countries. Send for a catalogue. **Cycling Europe: Budget Bike Touring in the Old World** (US$13), by N. Slavinski and available from National Book Network, 15200 NBN Way, PO Box 190, Blue Ridge Summit, PA 17214-0190 (tel. (800) 462-6420), may also be a helpful addition to your library. **Michelin road maps** are clear and detailed.

Blue Marble Travel (in U.S. tel. (800) 258-8689 or (201) 326-9533; fax 326-8939; in Paris (01) 42 36 02 34; fax 42 21 14 77; http://www.blumarbl.com) offers travel discounts and bike tours, but not necessarily group trips (it's up to you), through Spain and Portugal.

Many airlines will count your bike as your second free piece of luggage, a few charge. The additional or automatic fee runs about US$60-110 each way. Bikes must be packed in a cardboard box with the pedals and front wheel detached; airlines sell bike boxes at the airport (US$10). Most ferries let you take your bike for free or a nominal fee. You can always ship your bike on trains, though the cost varies from small to substantial.

Riding a bike with a frame pack strapped on it or your back is about as safe as pedaling blindfolded over a sheet of ice; panniers are essential. The first thing to buy, however, is a suitable **bike helmet.** At about US$25-50, they're a better deal than head injury or death. U-shaped **Citadel** or **Kryptonite locks** are expensive (starting at US$30), but the companies insure their locks against theft of your bike for one to two years. **Bike Nashbar,** 4111 Simon Rd., Youngstown, OH 44512 (tel. (800) 627-4227; fax (800) 456-1223; http://www.nashbar.com), has excellent prices and cheerfully beats advertised competitors' offers by US$.05. They ship anywhere in the U.S. or Canada.

Renting a bike generally beats bringing your own. *Let's Go* lists bike rental shops for most larger cities and towns. Some youth hostels (including many in Spain and Portugal) rent bikes for low prices. Also check train stations for deals.

In both **Spain** and **Portugal,** back roads in flatlands and coastal areas are best for cycling. A **mountain bike** adds the off-road riding option, and is sturdier than a road bike. This is especially useful in Morocco, where it is often safer to ride on the dirt shoulder than on the road. Watch out for motorists who aren't used to driving alongside cyclists, particularly in Portugal, where bicycling has only recently gained disciples. Summertime pedal-pushers should be careful the scorching Mediterranean climate; the north is much cooler and generally less crowded.

BY MOPED AND MOTORCYCLE

Motorized bikes offer an enjoyable, relatively cheap way to tour coastal areas and countryside, particularly where there are few cars. They don't use much gas, can be put on trains and ferries, and are a compromise between the high cost of car travel and the limited range of bicycles. Yet, they're uncomfortable for long distances, dangerous in the rain, and unpredictable on rough roads and gravel. Always wear a helmet, and never ride with a backpack. If you've never been on a moped before, a twisting mountain road is not the place to start. Expect to spend about US$20-35 per day; try auto repair shops, and bargain. Motorcycles normally require a license. Before renting, ask if the quoted price includes tax and insurance, or you may be hit with an unexpected additional fee. Avoid handing your passport over as a deposit; if you have an accident or mechanical failure you may not get it back until you cover all repairs. Pay ahead of time instead.

In **Spain**, mopeds are thick on the coast and not uncommon on highways. Most cities have rental agencies (US$30 per day, less in coastal areas where tourist rentals are more common). **Portugal,** too, is revving up its engines. Though two-wheeling is less popular here than in the rest of Europe, rental places have opened up in most cities and many tourist centers. Ask at the local tourist office for details.

BY THUMB

Let's Go strongly urges you to consider seriously the risks before you choose to hitch. We do not recommend hitchhiking as a safe means of transportation, and none of the info presented here is intended to do so.

No one should hitch without carefully considering the risks involved. Not everyone can fly a plane, but almost any bozo can drive a car. Hitching means entrusting your life to a random person who happens to stop beside you on the road, thus risking theft, assault, sexual harassment, and unsafe driving. There are, however, pluses to hitching. Favorable hitching experiences allow you to meet local people and get where you're going when public transportation is sketchy. The choice is yours.

Women traveling alone should not hitch. It's too dangerous. A man and woman are a safer combo. Two or more men will have a tough time getting picked up.

If you do decide to hitch, consider where you are. Hitching in Iberia is generally not the quickest, most reliable, or safest means of transportation. In Morocco hitching is inadvisable.

Where you stand is vital. Experienced hitchers pick a spot outside of built-up areas, where drivers can stop, return to the road without causing an accident, and have time to look over potential passengers as they approach. Hitching (or even standing) on super-highways is usually illegal: you may only thumb at rest stops or at the entrance ramps to highways. In the **Practical Information** section of many cities, we list the tram or bus lines that take travelers to strategic points for hitching out.

Finally, success will often depend on what you look like. Successful hitchers travel light and stack their belongings in a compact but visible cluster. Most Europeans signal with an open hand, rather than a thumb; many write their destination on a sign in large, bold letters and draw a smiley-face under it. Drivers prefer hitchers who are neat and wholesome. Almost no one will stop for anyone wearing sunglasses.

Safety issues are always imperative, even for those who are not hitching alone. Safety-minded hitchers avoid getting in the back of a two-door car, and never let go of their backpacks. Hitchhiking at night can be especially dangerous; experienced hitchers stand in well-lit places. They don't get into a car they can't get out of again in a hurry. If they ever feel threatened, they insist on being let off, regardless of where they are. Acting as if they are going to open the car door or vomit on the upholstery will usually get a driver to stop. Look for ride services, a cross between hitchhiking and the ride boards common at many university campuses, pairing drivers with riders with a fee to both agency (about US$20) and driver (per km). **Eurostop International** is one of the largest in Europe. Not all such organizations screen drivers and riders.

In **Spain,** hitchers report that Castilla and Andalucía offer little more than a long, hot wait, and that hitchhiking out of Madrid—in any direction—is virtually impossible. The Mediterranean Coast and the islands rate as more promising. Approaching people for rides at gas stations near highways and rest stops reportedly gets results.

In **Portugal,** hitchers are a rare commodity. Beach-bound locals occasionally hitch in summer but otherwise stick to the inexpensive bus system; most of the thumbers you'll see are tourists. Rides are easiest to come by between smaller towns. Again, best results are at gas stations near highways and rest stops.

Almost no one in **Morocco** hitches, although often flagging down buses and trains may feel similar. Transportation are dirt cheap by European and North American standards. If Moroccans do pick up a foreigner, they will most likely expect payment for the ride. Hitching is somewhat popular in the south and in the mountains.

OFF THE BEATEN PATH: WALKING AND HIKING

Europe's grandest scenery can often be seen only by foot. *Let's Go* describes many daytrips for those who want to hoof it, but native inhabitants (many Europeans are fervent hikers), hostel proprietors, and fellow travelers are the best source of tips. Many European countries have hiking and mountaineering organizations; alpine clubs provide inexpensive, simple accommodations in splendid settings. *Walking Europe from Top to Bottom* by S. Margolis and G. Harmon details one of Europe's most popular trails (US$11).

■ Keeping in Touch

MAILING FROM HOME

Mail can be sent internationally through **Poste Restante, Posta Restante,** or **Lista de Correos** in Spain (all equivalent to General Delivery) to any city or town. Mark the envelope "HOLD" and address it with the last name capitalized and underlined.

Spain, mail should be addressed as follows: <u>HAYWARD</u>, John; Lista de Correos; City Name; Postal Code; SPAIN; AIR MAIL.

Portugal, general delivery mail is *Posta Restante.* There is a 60$ charge per piece picked up, and mail should be addressed as follows: <u>BROYLES</u>, Tyler; Posta Restante; Post Office Street Address; City Name; Postal Code; PORTUGAL; AIR MAIL. Be warned, the system is far from efficient.

Morocco, general delivery mail is *Poste Restante.* There is a 2dh fee per item picked up, and mail should be addressed as follows: <u>BOWIE</u>, Elizabeth; Poste Restante; Post Office Address; City Name; MOROCCO; AIR MAIL. The mail will go to a special desk in the central post office, unless you specify a post office by street address or postal code. As mail is sometimes misfiled, request your mail under both first and last names (also in Morocco try "M" for "Mr." or "Ms."). Bring a passport or international student ID card for identification. If you must leave town while expecting mail, you can have that mail forwarded to another general delivery address. Packages, letters, etc. too commonly get lost or misplaced.

Another reliable option for mail collection in all three countries is **American Express,** whose various offices can act as a mail service for cardholders if you contact them in advance. Under this free **"Client Letter Service,"** they will hold mail for 30 days, forward upon request, and accept telegrams. Just like General Delivery, the last name of the person to whom the mail is addressed should be capitalized and underlined. Some offices will offer these services to non-cardholders (especially those who have purchased AmEx Travelers' Cheques), but you must call ahead to make sure. Check the Practical Information section of the countries you plan to visit; *Let's Go* lists AmEx office locations for most large cities. A complete list is available free from AmEx (tel. (800) 528-4800) in the booklet *Traveler's Companion* or online at http://www.americanexpress.com/shared/cgi-bin/tsoserve.cgi?travel/index.

Government fixed prices, specifically postage or calling rates, are as a rule adjusted—to rise, fall, or stay the same—on January 1. The listed prices, compiled in summer 1997, are estimates. Thus, expect some change.

MAILING HOME

Spain

Air mail *(por avión)* takes 4-7 business days to reach the U.S. and Canada; service is faster to the U.K. and Ireland and slower to Australia and New Zealand. Standard postage is 87ptas. **Surface mail** *(por barco)*, albeit considerably less expensive than air mail, takes one month or more, and some packages take two to three months. **Registered or express mail** *(registrado* or *certificado)*, the most reliable way to send a letter or parcel home, takes 4 to 7 business days (letter postage 237ptas). Spain's **overnight mail** is not worth the added expense nor does it work much quicker. For similar rates and better service than the post office for big packages, try private companies such as DHL, UPS, or the Spanish company SEUR. Look under *mensajerías* in the yellow pages. Drop **letters** in yellow post boxes along main streets.

Stamps are sold at post offices and tobacconists *(estancos* or *tabacos;* identified by the brown sign with yellow lettering and an icon of a tobacco leaf; they always have postal scales). *Let's Go* lists post offices, including phone and address.

Portugal

Don't expect official time estimates to jive with the actual ones. The following are our estimates as to when a package should get to North America. People in Europe should expect a shorter wait, Australia and N.Z. a longer one. **Air mail** *(via aerea)* takes 8 to 10 business days to reach the U.S. or Canada. Postage costs 140$ to U.S. and Canada for a postcard ($210 for a standard letter) and 80$ within Europe. **Surface mail** *(superficie)*, for packages only, may take two months. **Registered** or **blue mail**,

takes 6-8 business days (for roughly three times the price of air mail). **EMS** or **Express Mail** will probably get there in 3 to 4 days, for more than double the blue mail price.

Stamps are available at post offices *(correios)* and automatic (surprisingly efficient) stamp machines outside all post offices and in central locations around cities. Prices are 80$ for Europe and Portugal, 140$ for elsewhere.

Morocco

Air mail *(par avion)* can take anywhere from 7 to 31 to an infinite number of days to reach the U.S. and Canada (about 10dh for a slim letter, postcards 4-7dh). Less reliable **surface mail** *(par terre)* takes up to two months. **Express mail** *(recommande* or *exprès postaux),* slightly faster than regular air mail, is the most reliable way to send a letter or parcel. Post offices, shops, and some *tabacs* sell postcards and **stamps.** Unfortunately, you cannot count on your mail getting to your destination in a set time; faxes, e-mail, phone calls, and jaunts to Spain are more reliable options.

TELEPHONES

Let's Go lists the city **telephone code** under **Practical Information** in each city. The code includes a bracketed 9 for Spanish codes, a bracketed 0 for Portugal and Morocco codes. **You will need the parenthesized number only if you are calling from a different area code within the same country.** However, if you are calling from another country, you will not need to dial the parenthesized number. For example, we have listed the telephone code for Madrid as (9)1. To reach Madrid from elsewhere in Spain, dial 91, then the number. To reach Madrid from another country, omit the 9; simply dial 1, then the number. The same goes for the (0) in Portugal and Morocco phone codes. In Morocco, you must dial 12 plus another number (001 for AT&T, for instance) to reach an international operator. **In this Essentials section, Let's Go has included city codes but omitted such parenthesized long-distance code numbers.** For example, we have not included the 1 necessary to dial long-distance within the United States; nor have we included the 0 necessary for internal long-distance calls within the U.K., Australia, or New Zealand. Such codes are unnecessary for making international calls.

To place a direct international call, dial the international access code (wait for a possible high-pitched dial tone), then country code + city code + local number. You can call the operator beforehand to get an idea of how much your call will cost. The relevant codes and operator numbers are listed below.

Country Codes: See **Appendix,** p. 684
International Access Code: Spain: 07. **Portugal:** 00. **Morocco:** 00.
International Operator: Spain: 9198 inside Europe; 9191 for intercontinental calls. **Portugal:** 099 inside Europe; 098 for intercontinental calls. **Morocco:** 12.
Directory Assistance: Spain: 003. **Portugal:** 118. **Morocco:** 16.

Times, They Are a Changin'

Portugal's phone system is undergoing a drastic change. Not only are all numbers supposed to be upped to seven digits (an evolving, eerily incomplete process), but there is no standard scheme for these additions. *Let's Go* has tried to amend all the numbers we list but, inevitably, some may fall through the cracks and others will change from now until your travels. Be mindful, and be happy.

TELEPHONE SERVICES

Grande companies run the whole phone show in both Spain and Portugal. **Telefónica** is the central phone company in Spain, with calling services throughout the world (and Spain) and offices most everywhere. Just take a number, then a seat, and the doting staff does the legwork—this is why you pay the IVA. Every office comes equipped with a complete set of phone books for all of Spain. Some are open 24 hours; Visa is accepted. **Telecom Portugal** is Telefónica's equivalent in Portugal; it offers like services, both of which are characterized by ritzy telephone offices.

By calling the numbers below, you may access English-speaking AT&T or MCI operators, and then use a calling card to finance the call. The connection to the operator is free. Calling cards allow you to make international calls without having to lug loads of coins. For more info, call **AT&T** about **USADirect** and **World Connect** services (tel. (800) 331-1140), **Sprint** (tel. (800) 877-4646), or **MCI WorldPhone** and **World Reach** (tel. (800) 996-7535). MCI's WorldPhone also provides access to MCI's Traveler's Assist, which gives legal and medical advice, exchange rate info, and translation services. For similar services for countries outside the U.S., contact your local phone company. In Canada, Contact Bell Canada **Canada Direct** (tel. (800) 565 4708); in the U.K., British Telecom **BT Direct** (tel. (800) 34 51 44); in Ireland, Telecom Éireann **Ireland Direct** (tel. (800) 250 250); in Australia, Telstra **Australia Direct** (tel. 13 22 00); in New Zealand, **Telecom New Zealand** (tel. 123); and in South Africa, **Telkom South Africa** (tel. 09 03). These companies can prove invaluable when making emergency **collect calls,** especially overseas. In Spain, each has a toll-free 900 number; in Portugal each has a comparable 05 number; and in Morocco the company or local operator can provide more information.

Pay Phones

In **Spain,** phone booths are marked by signs that say *Teléfono público* or *Locutorio.* Most bars have pay phones. Local calls cost 20ptas. An international connection is 500ptas. **Phone cards** in 1000 and 2000pta denominations are more convenient than feeding coin after coin into a pay phone; they're sold at tobacconists and most post offices. Watch out—it's easy to leave them in phone booths. **AmEx** and **Diner's Club** cards now work as phone card substitutes in most pay phones.

In **Portugal,** phone booths are located at phone offices, on the street, and in all post offices. Coin-operated phones are essentially non-existent; you'll need phone cards. The **Credifone** system uses magnetic cards sold at drugstores, post offices, and locations posted on phone booths. By Credifone and its counterpart Portugal Telecom, the basic unit for all calls (and the price for local ones) is 18$. Telecom phones, using "patch" (not strip) cards, are most common in Lisbon and Porto, and increasingly elsewhere. Credifone cards, with magnetic strips, are most useful outside these two hubs. While Telecom is gaining ground, travelers should tote both cards—Credifone and Telecom. Private calls from bars and cafes cost whatever the proprietor decides, typically 30-40$; usually a posted sign indicates the rates.

In **Morocco,** pay phones accept either coins (2dh will cover most local calls) or Moroccan phone cards; the rates are the same, and the latter are more common. However, phone cards, available at post offices, are in generally too large a denomination to be practical. Entrepreneurial Moroccans hang around phone banks (found near all post offices) and let you use their phone cards. You pay them only for the units used—typically 2dh per unit, a rate not much worse than the coin-operated rate. To use the card, insert and dial 00. The dial tone will turn into a catchy tune: whistle along (or don't) while dialing the country code and the number.

Collect Calls

In **Spain,** collect calls *(cobro revertido)* are billed according to pricier person-to-person *(persona a persona)* rates but may still be cheaper than calling from hotels. (1) Dial 005. (2) State the number you want to call and your name. (3) Hang up the phone. (4) The phone magically rings when your call is accepted.

In **Portugal,** collect calls *(pago no destino)* are charged at person to person *(chamada pessoa à pessoa)* rates, cheaper than from hotels; dial 18 01 23 for operators.

To make a collect call in **Morocco,** ask the desk attendant at the local telephone office to place a call *en P.C.V.* ("ahn PAY-SAY-VAY"). Write down your name and the country, state, city, and telephone number you want to call (see above). Calling cards and their parent companies—such as AT&T, BT Direct, etc.—are the best means to call in emergencies. Call the companies above for details and numbers.

FAX

Most **Spanish** post offices have fax services. Some photocopy shops and some telephone offices *(Telefónica)* also offer fax service, but they charge more than the post office (whose rates are standardized by the government), and faxes can only be sent, not received. To send to North America, expect to spend around 1600ptas for the first page, 500ptas each additional page. Prices do not include 16% IVA. Fax is also becoming more common in **Portuguese** businesses, and is frequently used by hotels and other accommodations locales. But, if no better option is available, go to the large cities' post offices, which have fax machines available for public use at roughly 2500$ for the first page; 1700$ for each additional page.

OTHER MEANS OF COMMUNICATION

Domestic and international **telegrams** offer an option slower than phone but faster than post. Fill out a form at any post or telephone office; cables to North America arrive in one or two days. Telegrams can be quite expensive, so consider **faxes.**

Between May 2 and Octoberfest, **EurAide,** P.O. Box 2375, Naperville, IL 60567 (tel. (630) 420-2343; fax (630) 420-2369; http://www.cube.net/kmu/euraide.html), offers **Overseas Access,** a service useful to travelers without a set itinerary. The cost is US$15 per week or US$40 per month plus a US$15 registration fee. To reach you, people call, fax, or use the internet to leave a message; you receive it by calling Munich whenever you wish, which is cheaper than calling overseas. You may also leave messages for callers to pick up by phone.

Daily newspapers including the London *Times,* the *Wall Street Journal* (International Edition), and the *New York Times* are available at train stations and kiosks in major European and U.S. cities, but elsewhere often only in the capital city and airports. The *International Herald Tribune* is available just about everywhere. *The Economist* and international versions of *Time* and *Newsweek* are also easy to find in Europe and the U.S., a little less so elsewhere.

If you're spending a year abroad and want to keep in touch with friends or colleagues, **electronic mail (email)** is an attractive option. With a minimum of computer knowledge and a little planning, you can beam messages anywhere for no per-message charges. One option is to befriend college students as you go and ask if you can use their email accounts. If you're not the finagling type, **Traveltales.com** (http://traveltales.com) provides free, web-based email for travelers and maintains a list of cybercafes, travel links, and a travelers' chat room. **Katchup** (http://www.katchup.co.nz) offers a similar service for NZ$50 per year. Other free, web-based email providers include **Hotmail** (http://www.hotmail.com), **RocketMail** (http://www.rocketmail.com), and **USANET** (http://www.usa.net).

SPAIN

US $1 = 156.53pesetas (ptas)
CDN $1 = 112.31ptas
UK £1 = 249.15ptas
IR £1 = 226.16ptas
AUS $1 = 116.83ptas
NZ $1 = 100.20ptas
SAR = 41.74ptas
POR 1$ = 0.83ptas
ECU $1 = 166.36ptas

100ptas = US $0.64
100ptas = CDN $0.89
100ptas = UK £0.40
100ptas = IR £0.44
100ptas = AUS $0.85
100ptas = NZ $0.99
100ptas = SAR 2.40
100ptas = POR 119.87$
100ptas=ECU $0.60

ESSENTIALS

Spanish organizations are not known for their efficiency. Relish the journey, block out the superfluous concept of time, and maintain your sanity. Buses are probably the best option for short trips, trains for longer ones, although this rule is by no means steadfast throughout Spain. Like most everything else, the degree of hospitality you'll encounter depends on the region: locals in less touristy locales are more likely to go out of their way, while those in tourist havens are generally more business-like.

■ Getting Around

MAIN TRAINS

Spanish trains are clean, relatively punctual, and reasonably priced, although they bypass many small towns. **Viajes TIVE,** the student travel agency, can help clarify Spain's complex, ever-changing rail system. Spain's national railway is **RENFE (RE** **N**acional de los **F**errocarriles **E**spañoles). RENFE offers numerous **discounts,** bu unfortunately no youth discount exists for foreign travelers. The **Tarjeta Turística** (a.k.a. the Spanish Flexipass) permits unmitigated travel for 3-10 days (US$144-368 Buy tickets within 60 days of departure at RENFE travel offices, RENFE train station and authorized travel agencies. RENFE offers partial refunds (75% off on red days) fo cancellations up to 5 minutes before train departure; 85% for cancellations more tha 24 hours ahead. Watch out for big differences in prices and avoid *tranvía, semia recto,* or *correo* trains—these are turtle slow.

AVE (Alta Velocidad Española): Shiny high-speed trains that dart between Madri and Sevilla (hitting Ciudad Real and Córdoba). Service to Barcelona and Paris *still* the works. AVE soars above other trains in comfort and price, not just spee Amenities are abundant: headsets, newspapers, drinks, snacks, plus ample le room. The early bird saves: the cheapest run, *"valle,"* leaves at 7am; more expe sive trains go at 8am, 2, and 7pm. Reservations (including fee) required.

Talgo 200: *Talgo* trains on AVE tracks. These currently service only Madrid-Málaga and Madrid-Cádiz-Huelva. Changing a Talgo 200 ticket carries a 20% fine.

Talgo: Sleek trains zip passengers in A/C compartments. It's more comfortable, po sibly faster, and twice as pricey as *Cercanías-Regionales* trains.

Intercity: Talgo's neglected cousin. Few stops, cheaper, but not as nice. A/C a comfy. Five lines cover: Madrid-Valencia-Castellón, Madrid-Zaragoza-Barcelon Madrid-Zaragoza-Logroño-Pamplona, Madrid-Alicante, and Madrid-Murcia/Carte ena.

Estrella: A pretty slow night train that comes equipped with *literas* (bunks).

Cercanías: Wide commuter trains traveling from larger cities to suburbs and near *pueblos,* with frequent stops. Passes are available.

Regional: Like *cercanías*, but older; trains offering multi-stop, cheap rides to small towns and cities.

The other train company in Spain is **FEVE** (Ferrocarril de Vía Estrecha), which runs short routes between northern towns not served by RENFE (mostly around Cantabria). FEVE is like an old dog: sluggish, but dependable. Stations can be inconveniently located. For assistance, contact FEVE at C. General Rodrigo, 6, Madrid (tel. (1) 533 70 00 or 9(8) 534 24 15; open Mon.-Fri. 8am-8pm).

HOP ON THE BUS

Higher rates and fewer discounts on train tickets have led many budget travelers to prefer from buses to trains as their preferred mode of transport. Bus routes, far more exhaustive than the rail network, provide the only public transportation to many isolated areas and almost always cost less than trains. Comfort standards tend to be high, especially for longer journeys, and some buses. Particularly for those traveling within a single region, buses are likely the best way to go.

Spain has numerous private companies; lack of centralization may make trip planning an ordeal. **Viajes TIVE** or bus station info windows can help. Companies' routes rarely overlap; it's unlikely that more than one will serve your intended destination. In many cities, each has its own station. In Madrid, most buses use the **Estación Sur de Autobuses** (tel. (1) 468 45 11). *Let's Go* lists major companies (all based in Madrid except Linebús) below (for **bus stations** in Madrid see p. 70). Still, most regional companies work from other cities.

ALSA, Estacion Sur (tel. (1) 528 28 03). Service between Madrid, Galicia, Asturias, and Castilla-León; also Portugal, France, Italy, Switzerland, and Belgium.

Auto-Res/Cunisa, S.A. (tel. (1) 559 96 05). From Madrid to Castilla-León, Extremadura, Galicia, and Valencia and nearby beaches.

Auto Transporte Julia, S.A. (tel. (1) 541 91 25). Runs a fleet of buses to and from Portugal, France, Italy, Switzerland, Belgium, and other countries.

Continental-Auto, Alenza, 20 (M: Cuatro Caminos) (tel. (1) 356 23 07). Drives buses to many *pueblos* of interest near Madrid, including Toledo, Guadalajara, and Alcalá de Henares, as well as north to País Vasco.

Enatcar (tel. (1) 527 99 27 or 467 35 77). Offers routes (in new buses) from Madrid to Andalucía (Granada), Valencia (Alicante), and Catalunya (Barcelona).

Julia Via Internacional, C. Viriato (tel. 490 40 00) in Barcelona, and Est. Sur de Autobuses in Madrid. Buses run throughout Western Europe.

Linebús (tel. (3) 265 07 00 in Barcelona). Serves passengers going to (or from) France, U.K., Holland, Belgium, and Italy; also to, from, and in Morocco.

SAIA (International Autocares), Est. Sur de Autobuses (tel. (1) 530 76 00). Drives to Belgium, Germany, France, Holland, and Andorra.

Samar, S.A. (tel. (1) 468 48 39). Runs to Aragón—it also crosses borders north to Andorra and Toulouse and west to Portugal.

Sevibus, S.A. (tel. (1) 530 44 17). Go between Madrid and Sevilla (including Huelva and Ayamonte) in festive-hued buses, most with movies and headsets.

TIBUS, Po. Habana, 26 (tel. 562 78 03). Jettisons buses off to gay Paris.

N THE DRIVER'S SEAT

ain's improved highway system connects major cities by four-lane *autopistas* with nty of service stations (still uncommon on back roads). Fast is vogue, but **speeders** ware: police can "photograph" the speed and license plate of your car, issuing you cket without pulling you over. And don't cruise in the passing lane; police and fel-w motorists won't appreciate it. Purchase **gas** in super (97 octane), normal (92 tane), diesel, and—more than ever—unleaded. Prices are astronomical by North nerican standards: 115ptas per liter, or slightly over US$3.50 per gallon. **Renting** a r in Spain is considerably cheaper than in many other European countries. You may nt to check with Atesa, Spain's largest national car rental company. The Spanish A/CAA is **Real Automóbil Club de España (RACE),** C. Jose Abascal, 10, 28003, drid (tel. (1) 447 32 00; fax 447 79 48).

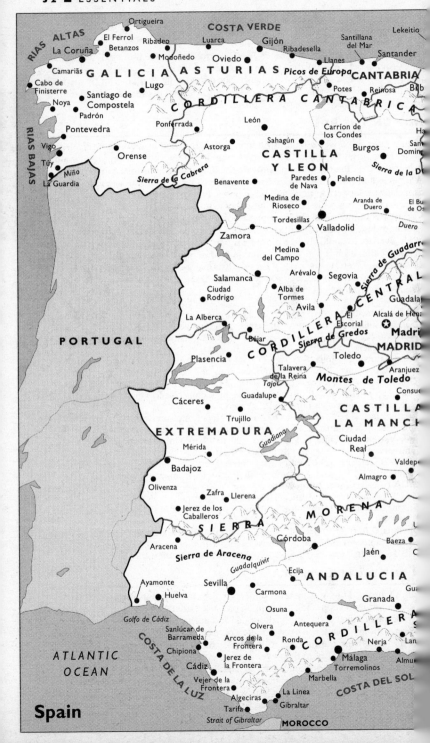

Spain

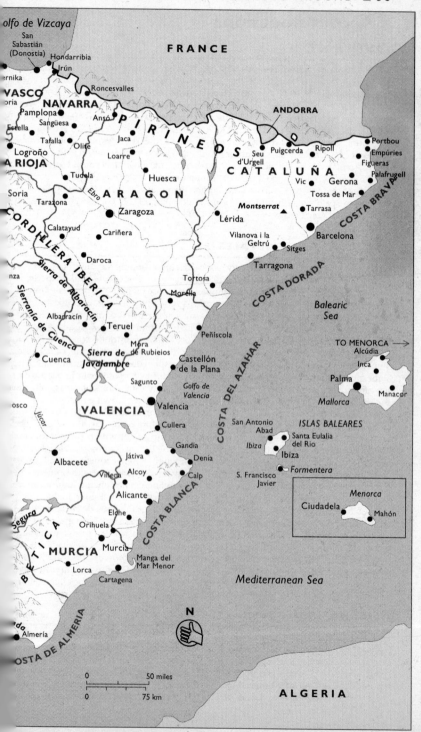

■ Accommodations

YOUTH HOSTELS

Red Española de Albergues Juveniles (REAJ), the Spanish Hostelling International (HI) affiliate, runs 165 youth hostels year-round. The price depends on location (typically some distance away from town center) and services offered. Rates tend to be higher for guests 26 or older. **Pensión completa** (full board: a bed and 2 meals), **pensión media** (half board: a bed and 1 meal), and breakfast (typically 150-200ptas) are sometimes available. Hostels usually lock out around 11:30pm in high season, and neighbors' sleep must be respected until 7am. As a rule, don't expect much privacy. To reserve (particularly important for big groups) a bed in high-season (July-Aug. and during *fiestas*), call well in advance. If you do not have a national **Youth Hostel Card** (valid for your country and HI network), an **HI card** (1800ptas) is required. You can usually get one in hostels, from your home HI association (see **Hostelling Prep,** p. 10), and in Spain's main youth and/or travel company, TIVE. For more info, contact REAJ, C. Jose Ortega y Gasset, 71, Madrid 28006 (tel. (1) 347 76 29 or 347 76 30; fax (1) 401 81 60).

PENSIONES AND HOSTALES

Spanish accommodations have many aliases, distinguished by the different grades of rooms. The cheapest and barest options are **casas de huéspedes** and **hospedajes.** Step up a notch with **pensiones** and **fondas.** These are all basically boarding houses, often with curfews, without heat, and with a fondness for long-term guests (*estables*). Higher on the ladder, **hostales** have sinks in their bedrooms, whereas **hostal-residencias** rival *hoteles* in overall quality. The government rates *hostales* on a two-star system; even one-star places in this category are typically quite comfortable. The system also fixes each *hostal*'s prices, posted in the lounge or main entrance. *Hostal* owners invariably dip below the official rates, especially when tourism sags. The highest-priced accommodations are **hoteles** which have a bathroom in each room but often overwhelm budget travelers' budgets. Many establishments are family-run and make their own rules. When in doubt, ask as to a place's own guidelines.

Frequently you'll have to hand over your passport (or, at hostels, an HI card) for the night; foot the bill the next morning to get it back. Before doing anything drastic (like choosing to stay), ask to see a room and verify the price, which proprietors are required by law to post visibly in every room and by the main entrance. Haggling for prices, especially in small inns, is common practice. Single rooms may be hard to come by, so solo travelers should be ready to pay for a double. An establishment cannot turn away a lone traveler from a double room and cannot charge him/her more than 80% the double price. Some kind souls charge half—chalk it up to luck.

If you have any troubles (with rates or service), ask for the **libro de reclamaciones** (complaint book), which by law must be produced on demand. The argument will usually end immediately, since all complaints must be forwarded to the authorities within 48 hours. Report any problems to tourist offices who may help resolve disputes for you. In the text, **full bath** or **bath** refers to a shower and toilet, while **shower** means just a shower stall. Most rooms that *Let's Go* lists have winter heating, as Spanish winters (particularly in the north and the mountains) can be chilly; on the brighter, hotter side, A/C is documented in *Let's Go* on a case-by-case basis.

ALTERNATIVE ACCOMMODATIONS

To promote tourism in rural areas, tourist authorities may suggest alternative (perhaps more traditional) accommodations. **Casas particulares** (private residences) may be the only choice in less touristed towns. Listings for major cities are posted at many foreign language schools and institutes; you can also ask restaurant proprietors and bartenders for names and directions. Unfortunately, most tourist offices, will not assist you in this endeavor. **Casas rurales** (rural cottages) and **casas rústicas** (farm-

houses), officially referred to as *agroturismo,* have overnight rates from 1000 to 3500ptas. Rent *casa rurales,* well-suited for large groups and families, piece-meal or whole. Look for these in northern Asturias and Castilla y León. **Refugios** are rustic mountain huts most frequented by hikers.

Colegios mayores (state university dorms) open their doors to summer travelers; the Consulate General of Spain (see **Embassies and Consulates,** p. 4) should have more info. Likewise, many private universities rent out rooms in their **residencias** (dorms); ask the proximate tourist office for details. **Monasteries**—Benedictine and Cistercian—and **convents** house less rowdy travelers (along with a diet of monks and nuns). Impressive architecture and unmatched tranquility often accompany this experience—though silence, prayer, and seclusion are the rule. Some lodgings are single-sex. Several monasteries refuse to charge, instead suggesting a donation (about 1700ptas). Both national and local tourist offices keep lists of holy lodgings broken down by religious order, number of rooms, and gender stipulations. Make reservations well in advance, for God's sake.

The cream of the accommodation crop remain **Paradores Nacionales**—castles, palaces, **convents,** and historic buildings since converted into luxurious hotels. Count your *pesetas* carefully before banking on this; consider 12,000ptas a bargain.

■ Camping

In **Spain,** campgrounds are generally the cheapest choice for two or more people. They either charge separate per person, per tent, and per car fees, or for a *parcela*—a small plot of land—plus possible per person fees. Prices can add up for lone travelers, and even for pairs. The law is on your side: campgrounds are categorized on a three-class system, with rating and pricing based on amenity quality. Like *hostales,* they must post fees within view of the entrance. They must also provide sinks, showers, and toilets. Ritzier ones may even have a playground, grocery store, cafe, restaurant, post office, bike or moped rentals, car wash, and/or pool. Most tourist offices provide info on official camping areas, including the hefty *Guía de campings.* It's wise to schedule reservations and arrive early, especially in high season.

LIFE AND TIMES

With a history that spans over 50 constitutions, an endless array of amorphous kingdoms controlled by Arabs, Visigoths, Germans, French, Celts, and indigenous peoples, and an empire that spread to the Americas, Spain can only be described imprecisely, as a *mestizo* culture.

■ History and Politics

Spain was colonized and came to be characterized by a succession of civilizations—**Basque** (considered indigenous), **Tartesian, Iberian, Celtic, Greek, Phoenician,** and **Carthaginian**...before the Romans dropped by with a vengeance in the 2nd century BC. In close to nine centuries, the **Romans** drastically altered Spain, particularly its language, architecture, roads, irrigation techniques, and use of grapes, olives, and wheat. A slew of Germanic tribes, including Swabians (in Galicia) and Vandals, swept over Iberia in the early 700s AD, but the **Visigoths,** born-again Christians, emerged above the rest.

Moors in Store

Following Muslim unification, a small force of Arabs, Berbers, and Syrians invaded Spain in 711. Practically welcomed by the divided Visigoths, the Moors encountered little resistance, and the peninsula soon fell under Damascus's dominion. These events precipitated the infusion of Muslim influence (although Catholics and Jews

were tolerated for the most part), which peaked in the 10th century. The Moors set up their Iberian capital in Córdoba. During Abderramán III's rule, some considered Spain the wealthiest and most cultivated country in the world.

Tension between Moors and Christians was never continuous; most of the time, in fact, both peoples lived in peace. The turning point in Muslim-Christian relations came when Sultan Almanazor died, leaving a power vacuum in Córdoba. At this point, Caliphate holdings shattered into petty states called *taifas*. With power less centralized, Christians soon got the upper hand. Christian policy officially (though not always *de facto*) tolerated Muslims and Jews, a policy which fostered a syncretic culture and even a style of art, **Mudéjar.** Later, though, countless Moorish structures were ruined in the Reconquista, at the expense of many Muslims. In this game of life-and-death and convert-or-get-out, relations were not cordial.

Estranged People in a Spain Place

For some time, **Jews** were peacefully settled throughout Iberia. A 15th-century rabbi noted that the Jews in Castile "have been the most distinguished in all the realms of the dispersion: in lineage, in wealth, in virtues, in science." Yet in 1369, **Enrique de Trastámara** defeated his half-brother **Pedro el Cruel** (a legendary Richard III type) at Montiel, inaugurating the Trastámara dynasty that was to spawn **Isabel la Católica.** Always a bit precarious, tolerance in Castile was substituted by Christian rigidity akin to the scene in 14th century France. The 1391 pogroms started soon after, as thousands of Jews were massacred and many more forcibly converted. Even those who did convert, *conversos,* were persecuted and tortured. Paradoxically, *converso*s could rise to the high ranks of political, ecclesiastical, and intellectual institutions and become connected with Christian aristocratic and merchant classes. Catholic saint and author **Teresa of Avila** (1515-1582), for example, was the daughter of a *converso,* as was **Luis de Santángel,** the secretary of Isabel and a big promoter of Columbus. The mass conversion led to a complex situation as a "tainted" upper class desperately disavowed its Semitic heritage by devising false genealogies, among other tactics. As a result, *converso* culture became neither entirely Jewish nor Christian.

The Catholic Monarchs: Dispersal and Discovery

In 1469, the marriage of **Fernando** de Aragón and **Isabel** de Castilla joined Iberia's two mightiest Christian kingdoms. By 1492, the dynamic duo had captured Granada (the last Moorish stronghold) and shuttled off Columbus, and later many others, to explore the New World. By the 16th century, the duo's strong leadership made Spain's empire the world's most powerful. The Catholic Monarchs introduced the **Inquisition** in the 1480s, executing and then burning Jews who were earlier forced to convert. The Spanish version had dual aims: to strengthen the authority of the Church and to better unify Spain. In approximately 90 years of rule, the Catholic Monarchs greatly heightened Spain's position as a world economic, political, and cultural power—made all the more enduring by conquests in the Americas. Spain proved braver than neighboring countries in financing such risky endeavors and—over the next 300 years—would reap the rewards.

Habsburgs in the House

The daughter of Fernando and Isabel, **Juana la Loca** (the Mad), married **Felipe el Hermoso** (the Fair) of the powerful Habsburg dynasty. Mr. Handsome (who died playing jai lai) and Mrs. Crazy (who refused to believe he died and dragged his corpse through the streets) spawned **Carlos I** (Charles V, 1516-1556), who reigned over an immense empire (as the last official Holy Roman Emperor) comprised of modern-day Holland, Belgium, part of Germany, Austria, Spain, and the American colonies. Fortunately, he spent more time in Spain than any other country, but the task of maintaining political stability was monumental. Carlos did his part: as a good Catholic, he embroiled Spain in a war with France; as an art patron of superb taste, he nabbed

Titian as his court painter; as a fashion plate, he introduced Spain to the Habsburg fashion of wearing all black.

But trouble was a-brewing in the Netherlands (then called the Low Countries and Flanders). After Carlos I died, his son **Felipe II** (Philip II, 1556-1598) was left holding the bag full of rebellious territories. More conservative (and faithful to Spain) than his father, he still would not stand still, sweeping Portugal after the ailing King Henrique died in 1580. One year later the Dutch declared their independence from Spain and Felipe began warring with the Protestants, spurring an embroilment with England. The war with the British ground to a halt when Sir Francis Drake and bad weather buffered the **Invincible Armada** in 1588. His enthusiasm (and much of his empire) sapped, Felipe retreated to his grim, newly built palace, El Escorial, through the last decade of his reign.

Felipe III (1598-1621), preoccupied with many of the finer aspects of life, in turn allowed his adviser, the Duque de Lerma to pull the governmental strings. Following the popular trend, Felipe III and the Duke expelled nearly 300,000 Moors. Mustached **Felipe IV** (1621-1665) painstakingly held the country together through his long, tumultuous reign. In the beginning of his rule, the **Conde Duque de Olivares** manipulated the impressionable young king, but Felipe's somber blood came to the fore as he settled in (and set Olivares out). He discerningly patronized the arts (painter Diego Velázquez and playwrights Lope de Vega and Calderón de la Barca were in his court) and architecture (the Buen Retiro in Madrid). Then the Thirty Years' War (1618-1648) broke out over Europe, and defending Catholicism sapped Spain's resources. It ended with the marriage of Felipe IV's daughter and Louis XIV. His successor **Carlos II,** the *"hechizado"* (bewitched), was epileptic and impotent, the product of generations of inbreeding. From then on, little went right: Carlos II died, Spain fell into a depression, and cultural bankruptcy ensued.

From France: Bourbons and Constitutions

The 1713 Treaty of Utrecht seated **Felipe V,** a Bourbon grandson of Louis XIV, on the Spanish throne. The king built huge, showy palaces (to ape Versailles in France) and cultivated a flamboyant, debauched court. Despite his hardly disciplined example, the Bourbons who followed Felipe ably administered the Empire, at last beginning to regain control of Spanish-American trade lost to northern Europeans. They also constructed scores of new canals and roads, organized settlements, instituted agricultural reform and industrial expansion, and patronized the sciences and arts (via centralized academies). Next up, **Carlos III** was probably Madrid's finest "mayor," radically transforming the capital. Spain's global standing recovered enough for it to team with France to aid the 13 Colonies' independence from Britain, symbolized by Captain Gálvez' heroically engineered victories in the South.

Napoleon then popped in as part of his world domination kick. The French occupation ended, ironically enough, when the Protestant Brits beat up the Corsican's troops at Waterloo. This led to the restoration of arch-reactionary **Fernando VII,** who sought to revoke the progressive Constitución de Cádiz of 1812. As a result of Fernando's ineptitude and inspired by liberal ideas in the new constitution, most of Spain's Latin American empire soon threw off its yoke. Domestically, Parliamentary Liberalism was restored in 1833 upon Fernando VII's death; it would predominate Spanish politics until Primo de Rivera's mild dictatorship in the 1920s. Rapid industrialization and prosperity marked 19th century Spain. Case in point: Catalunya's *Renaixença* (Renaissance) produced the **Modernista** movement in architecture and design, led by the innovative Antoni Gaudí. But Spain's defeat to the U.S. in the 1898 Spanish-American War cost them Cuba, the Philippines, and Puerto Rico. Meanwhile, most of Spain remained indigent and agricultural.

> The French occupation of Spain ended, ironically enough, when the Protestant Brits beat up Napoleon's troops at Waterloo.

Civil War

In April 1931, **King Alfonso XIII** ignominiously fled Spain, thus giving rise to the Second Republic. Republican Liberals and Socialists established safeguards for farmers and industrial workers, granted women's suffrage, assured religious tolerance, and chipped away at traditional military dominance. However, national euphoria faded fast. The 1933 elections split the Republican-Socialist coalition, in the process increasing the power of right wing and Catholic parties in the parliamentary *Cortes*. Military dissatisfaction led to a heightened profile of the fascist *Falange*, which further polarized national politics. By 1936, Radicals, Anarchists, Socialists, and Republicans had formed a loose, federated alliance to win the next elections. But the peace was a tease. Once **Generalísimo Francisco Franco** snatched control of the Spanish army, militarist uprisings uprose, and the nation plunged into war. The three-year **Civil War** ignited worldwide ideological passions. Germany and Italy dropped troops, supplies, and munitions into Franco's lap, while the stubbornly isolationist U.S. and liberal European states were slow to aid the Republicans. Although Franco enjoyed popular support in Andalucía, Galicia, Navarra, and parts of Castilla, the Republicans controlled population and industrial centers. The Soviet Union, somewhat indirectly, called for a so-called **Popular Front** of Communists, Socialists, and other leftist sympathizers to stave off Franco's fascism. But soon after, the West abandoned the coalition, and aid from the Soviet Union waned as Stalin, disgruntled by the Spanish left's insistence on ideological autonomy and increasingly convinced that he might actually benefit from an alliance with Hitler, lost interest. All told, bombing, executions, combat, starvation, and disease took 600,000 lives.

Transition to Democracy

Brain-drain (as leading scientists, artists, and intellectuals emigrated or were assassinated en masse), worker dissatisfaction, student unrest, regional discontent, and international isolation characterized the first decades of Franco's dictatorship. Several anarchist and nationalist groups, notably the Basque ETA, resisted the dictatorship throughout, often via terrorist acts. In his old age, Franco tried to smooth international relations by joining NATO and encouraging tourism, but the "national tragedy" (as it was later called) did not officially end until Franco's death in 1975. **King Juan Carlos I**, grandson of Alfonso XIII and officially a Franco protégé, carefully set out to undo Franco's damage. In 1978, under centrist premier Adolfo Suárez, Spain adopted a new constitution in a national referendum that led to the restoration of parliamentary government and regional autonomy. The post-Franco years have been marked by progressive social change. Divorce was finally legalized in 1981 and women now vote more and comprise over 50% of universities' ranks. Problems do still plague Spain, but violent regionalists remain in the minority. Most, in fact, seem satisfied with the degree of regional cultural autonomy. By the early 1980s, many regions controlled everything but foreign relations.

> King Juan Carlos I, grandson of Alfonso XIII and officially a Franco protégé, carefully set out to undo Franco's damage.

Charismatic **Felipe González** led the PSOE (Spanish Socialist Worker's Party) to victory in the 1982 elections. González opened the Spanish economy and championed consensus policies, overseeing Spain's integration into the EU in 1986. Despite his support for continued membership in NATO (he had originally promised to withdraw if he won) and unpopular economic stands, González was reelected in 1986 and continued a program of massive public investment. The years 1986-1990 were outstanding for Spain's economy, as the nation enjoyed an average growth rate of 3.8% a year. By the end of 1993, recession set in. In 1993, González and the PSOE only barely maintained a majority in Parliament by allying with the Catalan nationalist party, Convergencia i Unió (CiU), against the increasingly popular conservative Partido Popular (PP). Revelations of massive corruption led to a resounding socialist defeat in the 1994 European parliamentary elections at the hands of the Popular Party. Negative attention triggered losses in regional elections in the president's homeland and traditional Socialist stronghold, Andalucía. A second cascade of high

profile scandals in late 1994 further destabilized the PSOE government. Most damaging of these was the arrest of four interior ministry officials charged with organizing an illegal clandestine organization, GAL (Anti-terrorist Liberation Groups), in the 1980s to combat Basque separatists. González was pestered into admitting his complicity in GAL "death squads." José María Aznar led PP into power after González's support eroded as measures to reduce unemployment rates, which reached well above 20 percent, proved inneffective. Still, the overall outlook is bright. Most Spaniards seem pleased with the process of Parliamentary Democracy, if not always with its results and policies. Despite notable exceptions, most regional movements have been more cooperative than subversive to the central government in Madrid.

■ The Arts

PAINTING

Spanish painting flourished in the Golden Age of the Spanish empire (roughly 1492-1650). Maestro of mannerism **El Greco** (1541-1614) skillfully used color, light, and elongated figures to provide illusions of space and mysticism, as in Toledo's Santo Tomé altar. Philip II's foremost court painter **Diego Velázquez** (1599-1660) prided himself on precision and accuracy, whether in countless royal portraits or the brilliant *Las meninas* (The Maids of Honor, 1656) in Madrid's Prado. His contemporaries created religious work for all tastes: **Francisco de Zurbarán** (1598-1664) a mystical austerity, **José Ribera** (1591-1652) a crude realism, and **Bartolomé Murillo** (1617-1682) a bland sentimentalism. During the Neo-Classical era, noted genius and libertarian **Francisco de Goya** (1746-1828) used the canvas to upstage French contemporaries and publicize his political views. Funded by the court, Goya mocked his corrupt patrons in *The Family of Charles IV*. *El tres de mayo de 1808* comments on Napoleon's invasion of Spain. Madrid's Prado also houses an entire room of Goya's Black Paintings, nightmarish visions such as *Bobabilicón*.

Spanish artists (often working in France) rebounded from centuries of mediocrity in the early 20th century. **Pablo Picasso** (1881-1973) inaugurated his "Blue Period" while in Barcelona and later co-pioneered Cubism, in which he shows objects from all angles in space. His 1937 *Guernica* portrays the horrible bombing of the village in the Civil War. **Joan Miró** (1904-1983) explored playful, colorful abstract compositions. Fellow Catalan, mustached **Salvador Dalí** (1904-1991), was a Surrealist star, flamboyantly depicting, among other things, melted clocks. His wild autobiography (precursor of the Warhol Diaries) *Diary of a Genius*, remains popular.

Antoni Tàpies, Antonio Saura, and hyperrealist **Antonio Lopez** have recently emerged, as have sculptors **Chillida** and **Oteiza,** as Spain's artistic heavies. Since Franco's death in 1975, a new generation of artists—*chicos* and *chicas* in the dictator's reign—has thrived. With new museums in Madrid, Barcelona, Valencia, Sevilla, and Bilbao, Spanish painters and sculptors once again have a national forum for their work. Some upstarts include **Miquel Barceló** (whose portraits resemble swarms of black flies), abstract artist **José María Sicilia,** and sculptor **Susana Solano.**

ARCHITECTURE

Scattered **Roman ruins**—aqueducts, temples, theaters—lie principally in Tarragona, Segovia, and Mérida. Since Islam banned representations of humans and animals, sculpture and painting were out in **Moorish Spain** and spectacular buildings and ornately patterned surfaces (such as Granada's Alhambra and Córdoba's Mesquita) were in. Christians under Muslim rule did not rest, ushering in the **Mozarabic** style. After the Reconquista, they combined to develop **Mudéjar**, mixing Gothic and Islamic influences (in the Alcazars at Sevilla and Segovia). Islamic and Christian ideas further meshed in the 11th and 12th centuries in **Spanish Romanesque** style, producing heavy stone monasteries and churches such as Salamanca's *catedral*. Toledo, cen-

ter of Spain's Jewish culture, boasts some of the oldest **synagogues** in the world. **Neoclassical** examples also span the landscape.

New World riches funded the **Plateresque** ("in the manner of a silversmith") movement, a showy extreme of Gothic which transformed wealthier parts of Spain. Gold and silver ornamentation adorned much of Plateresque Salamanca. Influenced by the Italians, Jaén's Andrés de Vandelvira pioneered the decidedly plainer **Spanish Renaissance** style, best exemplified in Felipe II's El Escorial. Opulence retook center stage in 17th and 18th-century **Baroque Spain,** typified by the compressed ornaments, shells, and garlands of **Churrigueresque** works. Flamboyant examples pepper the peninsula, a prime example being Toledo's cathedral's altar.

In the late 19th and early 20th centuries, Catalan's **Modernista** brand burst on the scene at Barcelona, led by the eccentric genius of **Antoni Gaudí, Luis Domènich i Montaner,** and **José Puig y Caldafalch.** Modernista structures defy any and all previous standards, trademarked by voluptuous curves and abnormal textures. The new style was inspired partly by Mudejar relics, but far more so by organic forms and unbridled imagination. Spain's outstanding architectural tradition continues to this day with such trendsetters as **Josep María Sert, Ricardo Bofill,** and **Rafael Moneo.**

LITERATURE

Spain's literary tradition first blossomed in the late Middle Ages, from 1000-1500. The 12th-century *Cantar de Mío Cid* (Song of My Cid), a sober yet suggestive epic poem and Spain's oldest surviving work, chronicles national hero El Cid's life and military battles, from his exile from Castilla to his return to grace in the king's court. *La Celestina,* a soap opera-esque dialogue, paved the way for the picaresque novel (like *Lazarillo de Tormes, Guzmán de Alfarache*), American Dream-type stories about poor boys *(pícaros)* who overcome huge odds to attain great wealth. This literary form, among others, surfaced during Spain's **Golden Age.** Poetry particularly thrived in this era. Some consider the sonnets and romances of **Garcilaso de la Vega** the most perfect ever written in Castilian. Along with friend **Joan Boscán,** Garcilaso introduced the "Italian" style (Petrarchan love conventions, etc.) to Iberia. The reverend **Sta. Teresa de Ávila** and **San Juan de la Cruz** blessed Spain with mysticism. This period also bred outstanding dramas, including works from **Calderón de la Barca** and **Lope de Vega,** who personally knocked off over 2000 plays. Both promoted the neo-platonic view of love, claiming it always changes one's life dramatically and eternally. Francisco de Quevedo contributed to the rebirth of sonnets, treating erotic themes with a sardonic twist. **Miguel de Cervantes'** two-part *Don Quixote de la Mancha—* often considered the world's first novel—is the most famous work of Spanish literature. Cervantes relates the hilarious parable of the hapless, marble-missing Don and his sidekick, Sancho Panza, bold *caballeros* (knights) out to save the world.

The 19th century inspired contrast, from the biting journalistic prose of **Larra** to **Zorrilla's** romantic *Don Juan Tenorio* to the classic *La Regenta* by **Leopoldo Alas "Clarín."** The modern literary era began with the **Generación del '98,** a group led by essayist **Miguel de Unamuno** and cultural critic **José Ortega y Gasset.** Reacting to Spain's embarrassing defeat in the Spanish-American War (1898), these nationalistic authors argued, through essays and novels, that each individual must spiritually and ideologically attain internal peace before society can do the same. The new kids on the block claimed membership in the **Generación del 1927,** experimental lyric poets who used surrealistic and vanguard poetry to express profound humanism. This group included **Pedro Salinas, Federico García Lorca** (assassinated at the start of the Civil War), **Rafael Alberti,** and **Vicente Aleixandre.** In the 20th century, the Nobel Committee has honored playwright and essayist **Jacinto Benavente y Martínez,** poet **Vicente Aleixandre,** and novelist **Camilo José Cela** (author of *La Familia de Pascal Duarte*). Women writers, like **Mercè Rodoreda** and **Carmen Martín Gaite,** have earned critical acclaim. As Spanish artists are again flocking to Madrid, like they were in the early part of the century, a new avant-garde spirit has been reborn in the capital. **Ana Rossetti** and **Juana Castro** led a new generation of women erotic poets into

the 80s. The newest group of poets represents the first time in panorama of Spanish literature that women are at the forefront.

MUSIC

Flamenco, the combination of *cante jondo* (melodramatic song), guitar, and dancing continues to work into the 1990s. **Paco de Lucía,** an internationally renowned guitarist who experiments in jazz-*flamenco* crossover, rattles *flamenco* purists. Singer **Camerón de la Isla,** who died young in 1992, maintains a devoted following throughout the peninsula. (As to *flamenco*'s dance side, see below.) **Singer-songwriters** of the Franco years voiced underground discontent and became outwardly famous afterwards. **Joan-Manuel Serrat** is perhaps the biggest name; other singers of note are **Albert Pla, María del Mar Bonet, Lluís Llach,** and **Ana Belén.** American rock is ubiquitous in Spain, but Spanish rock sometimes holds it own. **Mecano** hypnotizes audiences beyond peninsular bounds, and Barcelona band **El Último de la Fila** and big-forum **Héroes del Silencio** are well worth a listen. Other popular groups and soloists are **Presuntos Implicados, Los Rodríguez,** and **Manolo Tena. Jose Carreras,** of "three Tenors" fame, is now among the world's finest opera singers. And we cannot forget **Julio Iglesias,** loved the world over.

Flamenco Frills and Drills

Few things are more exciting than a free-wheeling *sevillana,* part of why the feisty *flamenco* dancer is Spain's beloved cultural icon. The woman's *bata de cola*—a colorful 19th-century style dress with trains, frills, ribbons, and polka-dots—immediately catches the eye. But *flamenco* is not limited to *sevillanas;* numerous variations form the core of any master's repertoire. What follows is hardly complete; think of it as a mere sampling:

Soleares (Soléas): One of the oldest and most dignified *flamenco* forms, it reduces even stoic onlookers to tears. **Bulerías:** Near the end of a performance, the rhythm picks up and the entire company gets down in this—the *bulería.* **Alegrías:** The brisk pace and liveliness of *alegrías* (joy) make them crowd-pleasers. **Fandango:** The *fandango* dance may have originated in Huelva, but nearly every town in Andalucía has added a twist. **Farruca:** Boundless strength and refined beauty generally make strange bed-fellows, but not in the *farruca.*

FILM

One of the greatest influences on Spanish film was not a filmmaker, but a politician. Franco's regime of censorship (1939-1975) defined Spanish film both during and after his rule. The Franco regime rewarded filmmakers who reflected fascist values and punished those who spoke against them. **Luis Buñuel,** a crony of Dalí and García Lorca and Spain's first filmmaker of note, produced surrealist films, most notably *Un chien andalou.* When censorship slacked in the 1960s, **Carlos Saura** emerged, with such mesmerizing hits as *El jardín de las delicias* (1970) and *Cría cuervos* (1975). Still, the public could not view most of his work, left instead with James Bond-type spy flicks and *chonzos* (cheap Westerns).

In 1977, censorship laws were finally revoked. The pent up energy of the stifling Franco era was unleashed in a frenzy of movie-making. Post-Franco Spanish film often tackles risque themes. **Pedro Almodóvar** expressed post-Franco disillusion in kitschy, fashion-conscious Madrid with films like *Mujeres al borde de un ataque de nervios* (*Women on the Verge of a Nervous Breakdown,* 1988) and *¿Qué he hecho yo para merecer esto?* (*What Have I Done to Deserve This?,* 1984). Other directors to look for in Spain include Bigas Luna (scatological *Jamón Jamón* was a notorious hit), Fernando Trueba, Vicente Aranda, and Victor Érice. *Belle Epoque* won an Oscar in 1994, focusing some long-awaited international attention on Spain's film industry and exemplifying its rise in respect and strength globally.

LORDS OF THE RING

Bullfighting as we know it started in the 17th century, to the partial dismay of the Church which feared the risks made the activity tantamount to suicide (ergo sinful). Although anti-bullfighting arguments have persisted and evolved (in the Age of Reason they bemoaned the irrational use of land to raise bulls; now animal rights activists chain themselves to ring entrance gates), the fascination with the "spectacle" or "rite" (it's not considered a sport) prevails. The activity has been analyzed as everything from a mythical to psycho-sexual to Nationalist phenomenon. The recent bullfighting renaissance has been accompanied by books by English-speakers. We would be negligent not to plug Ernest Hemingway's accounts (and *machismo*) in *The Sun Also Rises* and *Death in the Afternoon*.

PROSE TO PERUSE

Travel Literature

English scribes have penned several top-notch Spanish travel narratives. Richard Ford's witty, 19th-century account, *Handbook for Travellers in Spain and Readers at Home,* remains a fan-favorite. Most time-honored classics are region-specific, including Washington Irving's *Tales of the Alhambra,* Bloomsbury-Circle-expatriate Gerald Brenan's *South from Granada,* Robert Graves' Mallorcan stories, and Laurie Lee's *As I Walked Out One Midsummer Morning.* For native flavor, read Nobel prize-winning Camilo José Cela's *Journey to the Alcarria,* based on rural Castilla.

Fiction, Spanish and Foreign

Start with *Poema del Mio Cid* and Cervantes' *Don Quixote.* Among the most popular modern novelists are the moving Carmen Laforet *(Nada)*, post-modern Juan José Millás *(El desorden de tu nombre)*, lyrical Esther Tusquet *(El mismo mar de todos los veranos)*, and amusing Manuel Vázquez Montalbán (Murder in the Central Committee). Spain has also inspired a number of prominent American and British authors. Ernest Hemingway immortalized bullfighting, machismo, and Spain itself in *The Sun Also Rises* and *For Whom the Bell Tolls.* Graham Greene takes a walk (via a priest, all around Spain) on the lighter side in the humorous *Monsignor Quixote.*

Art and Architecture

The best bibliographies and accounts of political, architectural, and art history are in *The Blue Guide*—especially reliable since they're written by specialists. The standard work on Spanish architecture is Bernard Bevan's *History of Spanish Architecture.* For the latest (1980s and 90s) scoop, peruse Anatxu Zabalbeascoa's *The New Spanish Architecure.* Fred Licht's collection of essays, *Goya,* is a must-read for fans of the artist, and books on Picasso, Dalí, and Gaudí can be had with minimal fuss.

History and Culture

Written in 1968, James Michener's best-seller *Iberia* continues to captivate audiences for its thoroughness, insight, and style. *Barcelona,* by Robert Hughes, delves deep into the culture of Catalunya. George Orwell's *Homage to Catalonia,* a personal account of the Civil War, rivals *Iberia* and *Barcelona* in quality and fame. A handful of other historians stand out—Richard Fletcher on Moorish Spain, J.H. Elliot's work *Imperial Spain 1469-1716,* and Raymond Carr and Stanley Payne on the modern era.

▓ Language(s)

The five official languages in Spain differ far more than cosmetically, although some spelling variations are but superficial compared to their Castilian counterparts. **Castilian** *(castellano)*, almost always spoken, is as sure a ticket as you'll get. **Catalan** *(català)*, retaining its prestige among the elite, is spoken in all of Catalunya and has given rise through permutations to **Valencian** *(valenciá)*, the regional tongue of Valencia

in the east, and **Mallorquín,** the dialect of the Balearic Islands. The once-Celtic northwest corner of Iberia gabs in **Galician** *(gallego),* closely related to Portuguese. Although more prevalent in the countryside than cities, Galician is now spreading among the young, as is **Basque** *(euskera),* formerly confined to País Vasco and northern Navarra. These languages have standardized grammars and, with the exception of Basque, ancient literary traditions. Regional television broadcasts, native film industries, strong political associations, and extensive schooling have saved these from extinction—for how long is anybody's guess.

City and provincial names in this text are listed in Castilian first, followed by the regional language in parentheses, where appropriate. Info within cities (i.e. street names or plaza names), on the other hand, is listed in the regional language. Generally when traveling throughout Spain, Castilian names will suffice and are universally understood. However, it is wise within the specific regions to exercise caution, politeness, and respect to the home language.

Let's Go provides a glossary and pronunciation guide in the back of the book for all terms used recurrently throughout the text (see p. 686).

■ Food and Drink

The Spanish prize fresh ingredients, light sauces, and pig products. Each region has its own repertoire of dishes based on indigenous produce, meats, and fish. While the best-known Spanish dishes—*paella, gazpacho,* and *tortilla española*—are from Valencia, Andalucía, and Castilla respectively, País Vasco, Navarra, Catalunya, and Galicia traditionally cook up many of Spain's most intriguing dishes.

TYPICAL FARE

The wilds of the sea are tamed deliciously and distinctively throughout the Spanish rim. **País Vasco** masters *bacalao* (cod), *chipirones en su tinta* (squid in its own ink), *sopa de pescado* (fish soup), mouthwatering *angulas a la bilbaína* (baby eels in garlic), earthier *pimientos del piquillo* (roasted red peppers), and sumptuous *rellenos* (stuffed peppers). **Galicians** savor *empanadas* (pastry) with particularly tasty *bonito* (tuna), *pulpo* (octopus), *mejillones* (mussels), and *santiaguiños* (spider crabs). **Catalunya** has blessed the world with *zarzuela,* a seafood and tomato bouillabaisse, and its own brand of *langosta* (lobster). One favorite includes *torradas,* hearty toast spread with crushed tomato and often topped with *butifarra* (sausage) or ham. **Menorca** miraculously whips up mayonnaise (named for its capital Mahón), while **Mallorca's** *ensaimada,* angel hair pastry smothered in powdered sugar, sweetens breakfasts. **Islas Baleares's** chefs also stir up various fish stews, while **Andalucíans** have famously—and lightly—mastered the art of frying fish.

Valencia glories in countless uses of rice; its *paella,* the saffron-seasoned dish made with meat, fish, poultry, vegetables, or snails, is world famous (there are over 200 varieties alone throughout the region). In the north, **Asturias** warms to *fabada* (bean stew), complemented by *queso cabrales* (blue cheese). Landlocked **Castilla** churns out a dense *cocido* (stew) of meats, sausage, and chick-peas, as well as *chorizo,* a seasoned savory sausage. For pork lovers, oh-so-tender *cochinillo asado al horno* (roast suckling pig) is a glutton's delight. Adventurers shouldn't miss **Navarra's** quirky *perdiz con chocolate* (partridge in chocolate).

> Spain's most omnipresent edible manifestation crosses all regional bounds: jamón serrano or jamón del país.

Spain's most omnipresent edible manifestation crosses all regional bounds: *jamón serrano* or *jamón del país* (the best of which comes from pigs fed only acorns) is cured and zestier than regular ham, itself known as *jamón york* or *jamón dulce.* Or, you may enjoy sinking your teeth into *queso* (cheese). The best known is *queso de Burgos,* a soft, mild cheese thought to better the invalid (and pamper the healthy), and *queso manchego,* a fairly sharp brand made from sheep's milk.

SPAIN INTRODUCTION

Consumed in bars and *tascas* (*tapas* bars), **tapas** tantalize taste buds all around Spain. *Tapas* are bite-sized servings, while **raciones** are bigger portions (sometimes equal in size to entrees). These munchables (*pinchos* in Basque) come in countless varieties, often region-specific. Served around dinner time, they are appetizers and the main course in one. *Tabernas* serve *tapas* from a counter, while *mesones* bring them to the table. *Tortilla de patata* (potato and egg omelette) and *tortilla francesa* (plain omelette) are ubiquitous. *Bocadillos* (thick baguette sandwiches) and *sandwiches* (the flimsier white bread version, often grilled) are abundant. Our **Glossary of Food and Restaurant Terms** lists helpful food terms and translations (p. 688).

MEALS AND DINING HOURS

Spaniards start their day with a continental breakfast of coffee combos or thick, liquid chocolate and *bollos* (rolls), *churros* (lightly fried fritters), or other pastries. As in most of Europe, Spaniards devour their biggest meal, dinner ("lunch" to Americans), at midday (around 2-3pm). This traditionally consists of several courses: an *entremesa* (appetizer) of soup or salad; a main course of meat, fish, or a twist like *paella;* and a dessert of fruit, *queso* (cheese), or some sweets. Supper at home is light, consumed near 8pm. Eating out time is after 9pm. Rendezvous at one or more *tascas*—featuring *tapas* and drinks—are common supper substitutes.

RESTAURANTS

While some restaurants open from 8am-1 or 2am, most serve meals from 1 or 2-4pm only and in the evening from 8pm until midnight. Some hints: eating at the bar is cheaper than at tables, and the check won't be brought to your table unless you request it. Most city tourist office's rate nearby *restaurantes* on a fork system, five forks meaning gourmet. Full *restaurante* meal prices range from about 800ptas to perhaps 1800ptas in a four-forker. *Cafeterías* are ranked by cups, one to three. Also, many *bar-restaurantes* (and some *hostales*) have cozy *comedors* (dining rooms) on the premises. Diners will repeatedly come across three options. **Platos combinados** (combination platters) include a main course and side dishes on a single plate, plus bread and sometimes a drink. The **menú del día**—two or three dishes, bread, wine/ beer/mineral water, and dessert—is Spaniards' common choice for the *comida* (midday meal), at roughly 800-1500ptas. Generally, you'll have several options, although advertised items are periodically not available. Those dining **a la carte** choose from individual entrees. A full meal ordered this way typically runs twice as much, if no more, than the *menú*.

TIPS ON TIPPING

Most restaurants add a service charge to your bill. It's customary to round off the sum of the next highest unit of currency and leave the change as a tip. You should generally tip 5-10%, more if the service is exceptional. Also tip-worthy are: train or airport porters (100-150ptas per bag); taxi drivers (10% of the meter fare, if they're nice); hotel porters 100-150ptas; parking lot attendants 15-25ptas; and cloakroom attendants 25-100ptas. Most Spaniards do not expect big tips, as in some countries.

DRINKS

Spanish **wine** is uniformly good. When in doubt, the *vino de la casa* (house wine) is an economical, often delectable choice. Also good is *vino tinto* (red wine), *vino blanco* (white wine), or *rosado* (rosé). For a taste, get a *chato* (small glass). Mild, fragrant reds are Spain's best vintages, but the corps of fine wines is vast. La Mancha's Valdepeñas are light, dry reds and whites, drunk young. Catalunya's whites and **cava** (champagnes) and Aragón's Cariñena wines pack bold punches. The fresh Ribeiro and delicate Albariño from Galicia, the muscatel of Málaga, and Castilla's Valle de Duero all pleasingly quench the palate. **Sidra** (alcoholic cider) from Asturias and País Vasco, and **sangría** (a red-wine punch with sliced peaches and oranges, seltzer, sugar

and a dash of brandy) are delicious alcoholic options. A light drink is *tinto de verano,* a cool mix of red wine and carbonated mineral water.

Jerez (sherry), Spain's most famous wine, hails from Jerez de la Frontera in Andalucía. Tipple the dry *fino* and *amontillado* as aperitifs, or finish off a rich supper with the sweet *oloroso* or *dulce.* The *manzanilla* produced in Sanlúcar (near Cádiz) has a salty aftertaste, ascribed to the region's salt-filled soil.

Wash down your *tapas* with a *caña (de cerveza),* a normal sized draft-beer. A *tubo* is a little bigger than a *caña,* and small beers go by different names—*corto* in Castilla, *zurito* in Basque. Pros refer to **mixed drinks** as *copas.* Beer and Schweppes is a **clara.** A **calimocho,** popular with young crowds, mixes Coca-Cola and red wine. Older drinkers prefer **sol y sombra** (literally sun and shade—brandy and anise).

Spain whips up numerous non-alcoholic quenchers, notably **horchata de chufa** (made by pressing almonds and ice together) and the flavored crushed-ice **granizados.** Shun the machine-made version of either drink—it doesn't do either justice. Coffee and milk *do* mix. *Café solo* means black coffee; add a touch of milk for a *nube;* a little more and it's a *café cortado;* all's fair with *café con leche*—half coffee, half milk—often imbibed at breakfast; savor steamed milk with a dash of coffee, a *leche manchada;* and top it off with a *blanco y negro,* an ice cream and coffee float.

■ Today's Spain: 1998 and Beyond

NEWSPAPERS AND MAGAZINES

ABC, palpably conservative and pro-monarchist, is the oldest national daily paper. It jostles with the more liberal *El País* for Spain's largest readership. *El Mundo* is a younger left-wing daily renowned for its investigative reporting. Barcelona's *La Vanguardia* maintains a substantial Catalan audience, while *La Voz de Galicia* dominates the northwest. *Diario 16,* the more moderate counterpart to *El Mundo,* publishes the popular newsweekly *Cambio 16,* whose main competition is *Tiempo. Hola,* the original *revista del corazón* (magazine of the heart), caters to Spaniard's love affair with aristocratic titles, Julio Iglesias, and "beautiful" people. The nosier, less tasteful tabloid *Semana* has gossip galore and readers aplenty.

TELEVISION

Channel surf to the state-run TVE1 and La2 or private stations Tele5 and Antena3. Each region has its own network, broadcast in the local vernacular. In Madrid, the local channel is TeleMadrid (TM3). Canal Plus is Spain's top-notch HBO equivalent. It appears scrambled during movies, but features free sit-coms and music videos on Sunday mornings. Tune in to news at 3 and 8:30pm on most stations. Programming includes well-dubbed American movies, sports, steamy Latin American *telenovelas* (soaps), game shows, jazzed-up documentaries, and cheesy three-hour variety extravaganzas. View fab American series like *Baywatch* and *Fresh Prince of Bel Air* and Spanish equivalents. If all else fails, *fútbol* games and bullfights are guaranteed to hold your attention. Check newspapers for listings.

SPORTS

¡Viva España! True to form, the beat—and the glory—go on for Spanish sports. Gold medalist Miguel Indurain, Spain's most decorated athlete, remains a Basque hero despite his inability to capture an unprecedented sixth straight Tour de France title. Spaniards, like Aranxta Sanchez Vicario and Conchita Martinez, star in tennis.Seve Ballesteros, the country's ace on the golf links, putts with the best of 'em. As with cuisine, regional specialties spice the sports scene, including jai alai from Basque country, wind surfing along the south coast, and skiing in the Sierra Nevadas and the Pyrenees. The men's water polo team shocked the world by winning the gold at the '96 Olympics. Still, *fútbol* pumps the blood of this country, uniting Spaniards who agree to disagree, vehemently, on local teams' fates. Their pro game ranks with the

finest in the world, featuring clubs such as F.C. Barcelona and Real Madrid whose rosters read like an all-star scroll. On top of that, the entire country revels in the travails of the national team. This squad advanced to the quarterfinals of the '94 World Cup and advanced to the semis of the '96 European Championships, much to the joy of its countrymen. F.C. Zaragoza won the European championship in '95. Should an entire city seem desolate one Saturday afternoon, don't fret—go to a bar and prepare for ensuing emotional eruptions as the game unfolds.

EL FUTURO

Recently, political scandal has scarred Spain's improving reputation coming out of the Franco dictatorship, as have the rash of ETA bombings which regularly pockmark the headlines. April of 1997 was an exceptionally violent month. Still, in the grand scheme, the nation is in good shape, spiritually and physically. Its economy, if not booming, has been bolstered by links with the European Union, and the standard of living remains quite high. Inflation figures earlier in 1997 indicate that Spain will qualify for entrance into the EMU in 1999. País Vasco and Catalunya continue to develop more quickly than the rest of the nation, as evidenced by the 1992 Summer Olympics in Barcelona and the unveiling of Richard Gehry's new Guggenheim Museum in Bilbao. Tourism continues to rise. Spain's popularity among northern Europeans attests to its multitude of beachfront resorts, and its interest to the rest of the world has has increased dramatically with new attractions like the Guggenheim and cutting edge architecture to complement the country's generally safe, care-free environment.

Madrid

The stately grandeur of Old Madrid's palaces and museums rapidly dissipates as one enters the smaller avenues and encounters the libertarian *joie-de-vivre* of its transplanted citizens. After decades of totalitarian repression under Franco, Madrid's youth burst out laughing and crying during the 1980s, an era known as *la Movida* ("Shift" or "Movement") that was exemplified by Pedro Almodóvar's cinematic portrayals of frenetic lives and passionate colors.

Madrid's cultural renaissance did not stand behind a totemic figure like Almodóvar, however; or Gaudí as in Barcelona or Hemingway as in Pamplona. Rather, a 200,000-strong student population has taken to the streets, shed the decorous reserve of their predecessors, and captured the present. These *madrileños* are the chosen generation who are too young to recall the forbidding Franco years. They seem neither cognizant of their city's historic landmarks nor preoccupied with the future, even with unemployment rates reaching thirty percent.

One might expect a chasm between the radical young generation and their elders, but these young people are clearly affected by the countryside disposition of their parents and grandparents. Because Madrid is a city of migrants—one rarely meets a *madrileño* who is more than two generations removed from the outlying regions of Spain—Madrid does not exemplify the chaos of more experienced European capitals. Like in any Spanish town, *madrileños* rush home for the afternoon meal and flood the streets for their ritualistic evening stroll; but unlike most of the world, Madrid still works to live, not the reverse.

Arrivals and Departures

BY PLANE

All flights land at **Aeropuerto Internacional de Barajas,** 30 minutes northeast of Madrid by car. In the airport, a branch of the **regional tourist office** (tel. 305 86 56; see **Tourist Offices,** p. 74), in the international arrivals area, has **maps** and other basics (open Mon.-Fri. 8am-8pm, Sat. 9am-1pm). In the airport and at the Bus-Aeropuerto stop in Pl. Colón, branches of the **Brújula** accommodations service can find visitors places to stay immediately (See **Accommodations,** p. 78).

The green **Bus-Aeropuerto** (look for EMT signs just outside the doors) leaves from the national and international terminals and runs to the city center (1 per hr. 4am-5:17pm, every 15min. 6:17-10pm, every 25min. 10pm-1:45am; 370ptas). It stops underground beneath the Jardines del Descubrimiento in **Plaza de Colón** (M: Colón). After resurfacing in Colón, walk towards the neo-Gothic statue on the opposite side of the Jardines. The statue overlooks **Paseo de Recoletos.** The Colón Metro station (brown line, L4) is across the street. Fleets of **taxis** swarm the airport. The ride to **Puerta del Sol** costs 2000-2500ptas, depending on traffic and the number of bags (50ptas per bag). The fare to downtown Madrid should cost no more than 3000ptas with the 350ptas airport surcharge.

Airlines

Iberia: C. Goya, 29 (tel. 587 81 09). M: Serrano. Open Mon.-Fri. 9:30am-2pm and 4-7pm. For reservations call 24hr. tel. (902) 400 500. **Aviaco** (tel. 554 36 00), associated with Iberia, sends planes to the Islas Baleares.

American Airlines: C. Pedro Texeira, 8 (tel. 597 20 68). M: Lima. Open Mon.-Fri. 9am-5:30pm. Telephone reservations Mon.-Fri. 9am-6:30pm, Sat. 9am-3pm.

British Airways: C. Serrano, 60 (tel. 431 75 75). M: Serrano. Open Mon.-Fri. 9am-5pm. Telephone reservations Mon.-Fri. 9am-7pm.

Continental: C. Leganitos, 47, 9th fl. (tel. 559 27 10). M: Pl. España. Open Mon.-Fri. 9am-6pm. Telephone reservations till 7pm.

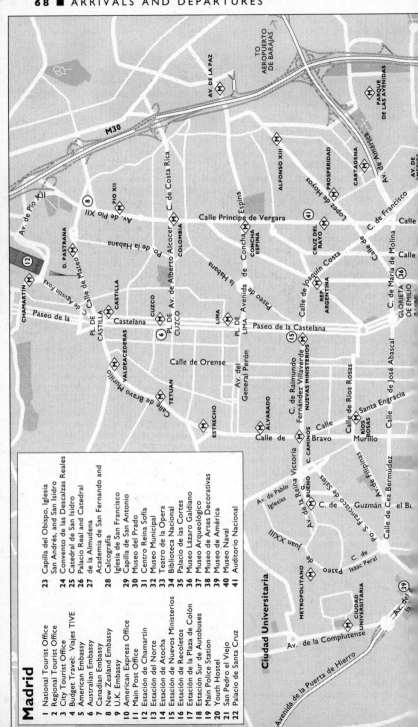

Madrid

1 National Tourist Office
2 Regional Tourist Office
3 City Tourist Office
4 Budget Travel: Viajes TIVE
5 American Embassy
6 Australian Embassy
7 Canadian Embassy
8 New Zealand Embassy
9 U.K. Embassy
10 American Express Office
11 Main Post Office
12 Estación de Chamartín
13 Estación del Norte
14 Estación de Atocha
15 Estación de Nuevos Ministerios
16 Estación de Recoletos
17 Estación de la Plaza de Colón
18 Estación Sur de Autobuses
19 Main Police Station
20 Youth Hostel
21 San Pedro el Viejo
22 Palacio de Santa Cruz
23 Capilla del Obispo, Iglesia
   San Andrés, and San Isidro
24 Convento de las Descalzas Reales
25 Catedral de San Isidro
26 Palacio Real and Catedral
   de la Almudena
27 Academia de San Fernando and
28 Calcografía
29 Iglesia de San Francisco
   Capilla de San Antonio
30 Museo del Prado
31 Centro Reina Sofía
32 Museo Municipal
33 Teatro de la Opera
34 Biblioteca Nacional
35 Palacio de las Cortes
36 Museo Lázaro Galdiano
37 Museo Arqueológico
38 Museo de Artes Decorativas
39 Museo de América
40 Museo Naval
41 Auditorio Nacional

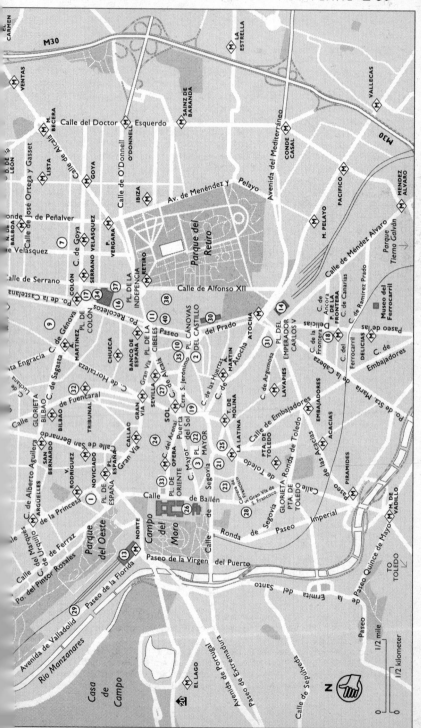

Air France: Pl. España, 18, 5th fl. (tel. 330 04 40). M: Pl. España. Open Mon.-Fri. 9am-5:30pm.

BY TRAIN

Two *Largo Recorrido* (long distance) **RENFE** stations, **Madrid-Atocha** and **Madrid-Chamartín,** connect Madrid to the rest of the world. Two intermediate stations, **Recoletos** and **Nuevos Ministerios,** connect Atocha and Chamartín. RENFE *Cercanías-Regionales* (commuter rails) tickets can also be purchased and trains boarded at the following Metro stations: Embajadores, Méndez Alvaro, Laguna, Aluche, and Principe Pío (access via M: Ópera). You can purchase *Cercanías-Regionales* tickets from automatice vendors. Prices are detemined by number of zones crossed; Madrid's stations are in the middle zone (100ptas to travel within zone C-1). These trains are generally comfortable and have A/C. Hold on to your ticket. Principe Pío also has separate lines running to Northern Spain. Call RENFE (tel. 328 90 20) for reservations and reliable info. **RENFE Main Office,** C. Alcalá, 44, at Gran Vía (M: Banco de España), is a useful place. They sell tickets for departures from Chamartín. Schedules and **AVE** (Alta Velocidad Española) and **Talgo** tickets are also available (open Mon.-Fri. 9:30am-8pm).

Estación Chamartín: Agustín de Foxá (24hr. tel. 328 90 20; Spanish only). M: Chamartín. Bus #5 runs to and from Sol (45min.); the stop is just beyond the lockers. Ticket windows open 8:30am-10:30pm. Chamartín services towns throughout Spain—mostly northeast and south. International destinations include Lisbon and Paris. Most Cercanías trains can be boarded here (see **Cercanías,** below). Chamartín has a **tourist office, currency exchange,** accommodations service, post office, **telephones,** car rental, **lockers** (300ptas), bookstores, *cafeterías,* and police.

Estación Atocha: (tel. 328 90 20). M: Atocha-Renfe. Ticket windows open 6:30am-11:30pm. No international destinations. Trains head to: Andalucía, Castilla-La Mancha, Extremadura, and Valencia, Castilla y León, and El Escorial. **AVE** service (tel. 534 05 05) to Sevilla via Córdoba. The cast-iron atrium of the original station has been turned into a simulated rainforest; the sound of sprinklers behind the station's Art Deco facade makes for a soothing if humid wait between trains. Art galleries, boutiques, restaurants, and cafes are additional diversions. **Luggage storage** is by the rain forrest.

Estación de Recoletos: Po. Recoletos, 4. M: Colón. Entrance is on the middle segment of a split boulevard. Cercanías trains every 5-10min.

Estación Nuevos Ministerios: C. Raimundo Fernández Villaverde, at Po. Castellana. M: Nuevos Ministerios. Cercanías trains every 5-10min.

BY BUS

Most intercity buses pass through the **Estación Sur de Autobuses,** C. Méndez Alvaro, s/n, (tel. 468 42 00 or 468 45 11; M: Méndez Álvaro; info open daily 7am-11pm). Numerous private companies, each with its own station and set of destinations, serve Madrid (see **By Bus,** p. 40).

Estación Auto Res, Pl. Conde de Casal, 6 (tel. 551 72 00). M: Conde de Casal. To Salamanca (1690ptas, 3¼hr; express 2210ptas, 2½hr.) and Cuenca (1300ptas; 2½hr.; express 1600ptas, 2hr.).

Estación Empresa Alacuher, Po. Moret (tel. 376 01 04). M: Moncloa. To El Pardo (6am-11pm every 13min., 20min., 135ptas).

Estación Empresa Continental Auto, C. Avenida de América, 34 (tel. 356 23 07). M: Cartagena. To Alcalá de Henares (every 15min. 6am-midnight, 40 min., 250ptas) and Guadalajara (475ptas, every hr., 1hr.); Toledo (570ptas, every ½hr, 1½hr.).

Estación Empresa Larrea, Po. Florida, 11 (tel. 530 48 00). M: Príncipe Pío (via extension from M: Ópera). To Ávila (10am, 2:30, 3:45, and 8pm, 2hr., 910ptas).

Estación Herranz, C. Princesa, in the Intercambio de Moncloa. M: Moncloa. To El Escorial (about every hr., 1hr., 380ptas) and Valle de los Caídos via El Escorial

(leaves El Escorial 3:15pm, returns 5:30pm, 20min.). Return buses to Madrid from El Escorial, every hr. until 9pm. El Escorial tel. 890 41 00.

Estación La Sepulvedana: Po. Florida, 11 (tel. 530 48 00). M: Príncipe Pío (via M: Ópera). To Ávila (3 per day, 2hr.) and Segovia (every hr. till 10:15pm, 1½hr.).

BY THUMB AND RIDESHARE

Hitchhiking is legal only on minor routes (though always a risk). The Guardia Civil de Tráfico picks up would-be highway and turnpike hitchhikers and deposits them at either nearby towns or on a bus. No official organization exists to arrange shared journeys to destinations inside and outside Spain. Try the message boards at HI hostels, the TIVE travel agency (see **Budget Travel,** p. 75), and English language bookstores for rideshare offers (see **Shopping,** p. 111).

■ Getting Around Madrid

MAPS

The *Plano de Madrid* and the *Plano y Guía de Transportes,* free at city tourist offices, are out of sight. For a more comprehensive map with street index, purchase the *Almax* map at a newsstand (375ptas). Convenient one-page maps of Madrid are free at any **El Corte Inglés** (see p. 75).

METRO

Madrid has a fabulous and fun metro that puts almost every other big-city subway system to shame. The free *Plano del Metro* (available at any ticket booth) is also clear and helpful. Trains are clean and run frequently; only on Sundays and late at night is a wait more than five minutes. Green timers hanging boastfully above most platforms show when the last train departed. Wall maps of the Metro and of surrounding neighborhoods abound in every station, as do signs with info on fares and schedules. Up-to-the-minute schedules for late-night trains list arrival times for every stop.

Ten lines connect Madrid's 126 stations. Lines are distinguished by color and number. An individual Metro ticket costs 130ptas, but savvy riders opt for the *bonometro* (ticket of 10 rides) at 660ptas. Both can be purchased at self-service machines in any metro stop and at *estancos* and news kiosks. Monthly passes, including discounted youth passes, are good for both the Metro and city buses. For more details, call Metro info at tel. 552 59 09 or ask at any ticket booth. Remember to hold on to your ticket or pass until you leave the Metro—riding without a receipt incurs an outrageous fine.

Trains run everyday from 6am-1:30am, not late enough on Madrid time to be deserted. Violent crime in the Metro stations is almost unheard of and women usually feel safe traveling alone. Do watch out for pickpocketing attempts in crowded cars. Ride in the first car where the conductor sits if you feel uncomfortable, do not ride with your wallet pocket facing a doorway, and avoid empty cars at night. Some stations, particularly those connected to two or more lines, have long tunnels and series of escalators; exercise caution here and stick with people. Stations to the north are less-frequented than most at night, and are often deserted by midnight. Metro stations Chueca, Gran Vía, Sol, Tirso de Molina, La Latina, and Plaza de España surface in areas which can be intimidating after midnight. Still, to reiterate, generally the Metro is clean, efficient, and worry-free.

BUS

Unlike the Metro, buses provide you with a a view of Madrid and a sense of direction. Like the Metro, the system is exceptional. Most stops are clearly marked. For extra guidance in finding routes and stops, turn to the handy *Plano de Los Transportes,* available for purchase at newsstands (200ptas), or the free *Madrid en Autobús,* available at bus kiosks.

The fare is 130ptas and a 10-ride *bonobus* pass, sold at newsstands and *estancos* (tobacco shops), costs 660ptas. Buses run from 6am to midnight. Between midnight and 3am, nocturnal buses travel from Pl. Cibeles to the outskirts every half-hour; after that, every hour until 6am. Nocturnal buses (N1-N20) are listed on a special section of the *Plano* (cut it out and keep it with you). Buses stop all along the marked routes, not just in Pl. Cibeles, but make sure to signal your stop. For more info, call **Empresa Municipal de Transportes (EMT)** at tel. 401 99 00 (Spanish only).

TAXI

Zillions of taxis zip around Madrid at all hours. If by some freak chance one does not appear when you need it, or if you want to summon one to your door, call tel. 445 90 08 or 447 51 80. A green *libre* sign in the window or a lit green light indicates availability. Taxis are affordable for groups of two to four people, and are particularly useful late at night when only night buses run. The base fare is 170ptas, plus 50-75ptas per kilometer. Common fare supplements include: airport (350ptas); bus and train stations (150ptas); luggage charge (50ptas per bag); Sundays and holidays (6am-11pm, 150ptas); nighttime (11pm-6am, 150ptas). The fare from the city center to the airport is about 2500ptas. To Estación Chamartín from Pl. Colón costs about 900ptas.

Taxi drivers in Madrid rarely cheat passengers. You can, however, request an estimate before entering the cab and make sure that the driver turns on the meter. Also, don't rely on a driver's hostel, restaurant, or club recommendations as they sometimes have deals going with the owners of such establishments. If you have a complaint or think you've been overcharged, demand a *recibo oficial* (official receipt) and *hoja de reclamaciones* (complaint form), which the driver is required to supply. Take down the license number, route taken, and fare charged. Drop off the forms and info at the Ayuntamiento (City Hall), Pl. Villa, 4 (tel. 447 07 15 or 447 07 14), to possibly get a refund.

To request taxi service for the disabled, call tel. 547 82 00, 547 85 00, or 547 86 00. Rates are identical to those of other taxis. If you leave possessions in a taxi, visit or call the **Negociado de Objetos Pududos,** Pl. Legazpi, 7 (tel. 588 43 44), between 9am and 2pm. Drivers are obligated to turn in any items within 48 hours.

CAR RENTAL

What on earth do you want to rent a car for? If congested traffic and nightmarish parking doesn't unnerve you, aggressive drivers and bratty moped maniacs will (pedestrians have learned to keep out of the way). Don't drive unless you're planning to zoom out of the city. To rent a car you must be over 21 and have an International Driver's Permit and major credit card (or leave a deposit equal to the estimated rental fee). Gas is not included in the price, and averages 150ptas per liter. Per kilometer surcharges apply to rentals of less than a week. Tobacco shops sell parking permits.

Autos Bravo: C. Toledo, 136 (tel. 474 80 75). M: Puerta de Toledo. Medium-sized car 11,500ptas per day, 74,900ptas per week; insurance included, unlimited mileage. Cheapest rental 9728ptas per day, 51,156ptas per week. Open Mon.-Fri. 9am-2pm and 4:30-8pm, Sat.-Sun. 9am-1pm.

Autos Viaducto: C. Segovia, 26 (tel. 548 48 48), C. Martín de los Heros, 23 (tel. 541 55 41), and Av. Mediterráneo, 4 (tel. 433 12 33 or 552 10 44). Cheapest rate 6400ptas per day, including insurance, 100km free, then 15ptas per km after that. IVA not included. Open Mon.-Fri. 9am-1pm and 4-7:30pm.

MOPED RENTAL

Popular with Madrid's residents, mopeds are swift and easy to park. A lock and helmet are needed. Try **Motocicletas Antonio Castro,** C. Conde Duque, 13 (tel. 542 06 57), at C. Santa Cruz de Marcenado. M: San Bernardo. A 49cc Vespino costs 4500ptas per day (8am-8pm) plus 16% IVA; 19,500ptas per week. Deposit is 70,000ptas. Prices

include mileage and insurance but not gas. Renters must be at least 18 and have a driver's license and photo ID (open Mon.-Fri. 8am-1:30pm and 5-8pm).

■ Orientation

The "Kilómetro 0" marker in front of the police station signals the city's epicenter at **Puerta del Sol,** an intersection of eight major streets. Sol is the city's transportation hub. Below ground, three Metro lines (blue #1, red #2, yellow #3) converge and transport people to within walking distance of any point in the city; above ground, buses and taxis swarm. Sol is packed with restaurants, *cafeterías,* shops, tourists, banks, *hostales,* and services of all kinds, including theft.

Madrid is divided into distinct neighborhoods. **Old Madrid** is the nucleus of neighborhoods clustered around Sol. Four of Madrid's five most prominent monuments surround Sol, each in a different direct compass direction and within walking distance: the **Palacio Real** is to the west via **Calle de Arenal;** the **Gran Vía** to the north by way of **Plaza del Carmen** and a pedestrian shopping extravaganza, where you'll find **El Corte Inglés** and **FNAC;** the **Museo del Prado,** reached by way of the eastward descent of **Calle de San Jerónimo;** and to the south the **Museo Reina Sofía** is right near **Madrid-Atocha** (the older train station), reached by way of **Calle de Atocha;** C. Atocha does not run from Sol, but rather the **Plaza Mayor,** the fifth of the great monuments within walking distance of Sol. Pl. Mayor is part of the larger nucleus to the west of Sol, consisting of the two **Royal Madrids:** red brick **Madrid de los Austrias** around **Plaza de la Villa** and Pl. Mayor, and granite **Madrid de los Borbones,** around **Ópera.** Both neighborhoods are relatively quiet, given over to churches and historical houses, but *hostales* huddle among the monuments.

East from Sol, the majestic **Calle de Alcalá** leads out of Old Madrid towards broader avenues, eventually passing by the **Parque del Buen Retiro.** C. Alcalá is the northern boundary of the wedge formed along with Po. Prado to the east, Sol to the west, and C. Atocha to the south. Once the literary district of Madrid and now the theatre district, the neighborhood is known as **Huertas.** It is crowded with some of the best hostel values in the city, as well as some of the best bars and cafes, centered around **Plaza Santa Ana.**

Fewer tourists venture directly south of Sol into the area around **La Latina** and **Tirso de Molina** Metro stops. This area has less wealth and prestige than the rest of Old Madrid. **El Rastro,** a gargantuan ancient flea market, is staged here every Sunday morning. Farther south lies **Lavapiés,** a working-class neighborhood.

The newer points of interest lie mainly to the east and north of the old city. To the northwest, the Gran Vía runs up to **Plaza de España;** its tall **Torre de Madrid** is the pride of 50s Spain. Moving westward from Pl. España, the Gran Vía turns into **Calle de Princesa,** a bustling middle-class shopping avenue leading directly into **Argüelles,** an energetic neighborhood of families and students spilling over from **Moncloa,** the student district, whose nerve center is the McDonald's on **Calle de Isaac Peral.** Isaac Peral continues north past **Ciudad Universitaria** (University City).

East of Argüelles (and north of the Gran Vía linked by **Calle de Fuencarral**), are the three hyper-cool club and bar-hopping districts of **Malasaña, Bilbao,** and **Chueca,** where *la marcha madrileña* is in full effect until late morning. Bilbao, Tribunal, and Alonso Martínez form a nifty triangle of action o' plenty. Malasaña, behind the Parque de Tribunal, is grungier, and **Chueca,** to the east of C. Fuencarral, is the hippest (and naughtiest), bordered by the great north-south backbone of the **Paseo de la Castellana-Paseo de Recoletos-Paseo del Prado,** which runs from Atocha in the south to **Plaza de Castilla** in the north, passing the Prado, the fountains at the *plazas* of **Cibeles, Colón, Cánovas del Castillo** (popularly referred to as **Plaza Neptuno**), and the elaborate skyscrapers beyond Colón. East of the Po. Castellana and behind the Museo del Prado, the lush Parque del Retiro functions as an exaggerated front yard for the posh shopping and residential streets of the **Barrio de Salamanca.**

Madrid is much safer than most other major European cities, but the Pta. del Sol, Pl. Dos de Mayo in Malasaña, Pl. Chueca, and Pl. España are still intimidating late at night.

As a general rule, avoid the parks and quiet residential streets after dark. Watch out for thieves and pickpockets in the Metro and on crowded city streets, and be wary of opportunists who target tourists with their clever scams. Con artists are a tradition in Madrid's *centro*.

Publications About Madrid

Because you will be a lost puppy without it, the weekly entertainment magazine **Guía del Ocio (125ptas) should be your first purchase in Madrid.** It has concert, theater, sports, cinema, and TV schedules, as well as sections listing exhibits, restaurants, bars, and clubs under various specific categories. Brief articles highlight new establishments and special events. The *Guía* comes out on Thursday or Friday for the week beginning the following Monday, so be careful which edition you buy on Friday for information on weekend entertainment tips. The *Guía* is available behind the counter of any news kiosk. For a good supplement with articles on new finds in and around the city, pick up *In Madrid*, an interesting English monthly distributed free at tourist offices and many restaurants and bars. (Reach the greater English-speaking minority in Madrid by placing a free classified ad in the back.) *En Madrid*, a monthly available at the tourist office, lists up-to-date hours and telephone numbers of monuments and some practical information, as well as a calendar of events. *The Broadsheet*, free at bookstores, is a no-frills listing of English classifieds with headings like "For Sale" and "Wanted." This self-proclaimed "lifesaver for English speakers in Madrid" is geared toward long-term residents of Madrid. The weekly *Segundamano*, on sale at kiosks, is essential for apartment or roommate seekers. The best full-length city guides to Madrid are *Time Out: Madrid* and the *Guía del Trotamundos: Madrid* (in Spanish).

For exciting info on Madrid check out the website: http://www.munimadrid.es.

■ Practical Information

Tourist Offices: English is spoken by all. Those planning trips outside the Comunidad de Madrid can visit region-specific offices within Madrid; ask the tourist offices below for their addresses. **Municipal,** Pl. Mayor, 3 (tel. 366 54 77 or 588 16 36; fax 366 54 77), on the Pl. Mayor. M: Sol. Hands out **indispensible city and transportation maps,** a complete guide to accommodations, as well as *En Madrid,* a monthly activities and information guide (open Mon.-Fri. 10am-8pm, Sat. 10am-2pm). **Oficinas de Información,** C. Princesa, 1 (541 23 25), off Pl. España. M: Pl. España. Has the same fabulous maps as the Municipal. **Regional/Provincial Office of the Comunidad de Madrid,** Mercado Pta. de Toledo, Ronda de Toledo 1, stand #3134 (tel. 364 1876). M: Pta. de Toledo. In a gallery with large banners on a *plaza* by the public library (across from the metro station). Brochures, transport info, and maps for towns in the Comunidad. Also has brochures about towns, campsites, highways, daytrips, and *paradores* throughout the Comunidad de Madrid. Open Mon.-Fri. 9am-7pm, Sat. 9:30am-1:30pm. A **second office** is at C. Duque Medinaceli, 2 (tel. 429 49 51, 429 31 71, or 429 37 05), just off Pl. Cortes. M: Sol. Open Mon.-Fri. 9am-7pm, Sat. 9am-1pm. Other offices at **Estación Chamartín** (tel. 315 99 76, open Mon.-Fri. 8am-8pm, Sat. 9am-1pm) and the **airport** (tel. 305 86 56), in the international arrivals area (same hr. as Chamartín). **El Corte Inglés** also good **free maps** and info (see below).

Tours: Read the fine print before pledging to pay an arm and a leg to take a walk around the block. The following are geared towards tourists, and are given in English. **Pullmantur,** Pl. Oriente, 8 (tel. 541 18 05, 541 18 06, or 541 18 07). M: Ópera. Several tours of Madrid, averaging around 4000ptas. Also excursions to outlying areas. **Trapsatur,** San Bernardo, 23 (tel. 542 66 66). M: Santo Domingo. **Julia Tours,** Gran Vía, 68 (tel. 792 01 77). M: Callao. Also offers tours of Andalucía, Portugal, and Morocco.

General Info Line: tel. 010. Min. deposit 20ptas. Run by the Ayuntamiento, they'll tell you anything about Madrid, from the nearest police station's address to zoo hours. **Tel Info:** tel. 003. No English spoken. Min. deposit 10ptas.

Budget Travel: Viajes TIVE, C. Fernando el Católico, 88 (tel. 543 02 08 or 543 74 12; fax 544 00 62). Exit M: Moncloa at C. Isaac Peral, walk straight down C. Arcipreste de Hita, turn left on C. Fernando el Católico, across from the double underpass. Office is on your left. **Branch office,** José Ortega y Gasset, 71 (tel. 347 77 78). M: Lista. Run by the Comunidad de Madrid, so no commissions. Discount airfares and ticket sales. BIJ train tickets. InterRail pass for 1 month of train travel (under 26 eligible after min. 6 months of residence in Madrid or if country of residence participates in the program—the U.S. does not). Price depends on length of stay and countries involved (31,920-52,920ptas). ISIC 700ptas. HI cards 1800ptas. Organized group excursions and language classes. Thriving message board with rides, cheap tickets, and roommate notices. Lodgings and student residence info. Both offices open Mon.-Fri. 9am-2pm, Sat. 9am-noon. Arrive early, or count on long lines. English spoken. **Comunidad de Madrid, Dirección General de Juventud,** C. Alcalá, 30 and 32 (tel. 580 40 00 or 580 42 42). M: Banco de España. Same type of documentation as TIVE, though no tickets sold here. **Viva,** Pl. Callao, 3 (tel. 902 32 52 75; fax 531 76 95). Arranges trips, car rentals, and documentation. **Viajes Lanzani,** Gran Vía, 88 (tel. 541 47 32). M: Gran Vía. Info on discount and student airfare; bus and train tickets. Also discounted tours, excursion packages, and accommodations info.

Currency Exchange: Banco Central Hispano charges no commission on traveler's checks and cash and offers the best rates on AmEx traveler's checks. Open in summer Mon.-Fri. 8:30am-2:30pm; in winter Mon.-Thurs. 8:30am-4:30pm, Fri.-Sat. 8:30am-1pm. Banks (1-2% commission, 500ptas min. charge), El Corte Inglés, and even 4- and 5-star hotels offer exchange services at varying rates. Monkey observation booths in Sol and Gran Vía open Sat.-Sun. and as late as 2am, such as Exact Change, Cambios-Uno, and Chequepoint, are not a good deal for cashing traveler's checks. They have no commission and small (250-300ptas) minimum charges, but poor rates. On the other hand, for small-denomination bills (e.g., US$20 or US$50) they may be the best option. **ATMs** are plentiful in Madrid. **Servi Red, Servi Caixa,** and **Telebanco** machines accept bank cards with one or more of the Cirrus, PLUS, EuroCard, and NYCE logos. Be forewarned: use only the first 4 digits of your PIN code. Also, Spanish machines operate only with numbers, not letters, so if your PIN code is your cat's name, be sure you know its numerical translation. ATM-inspired crime is on the rise, so avoid nighttime ATM sprees.

American Express: Pl. Cortes, 2 (tel. 322 55 00 or 572 03 03 for main info). M: Sevilla. On the corner of C. Marques de Cubas, 1 block uphill from Pl. Cánovas de Castillo (a.k.a. Pl. Neptuno). From M: Sevilla, go down C. Cedaceros and turn left on C. San Jerónimo; office is on the left. The office has Agencia de Viajes written in big letters on the windows. In addition to currency exchange (1% cash and 2% traveler's check commission; no commission on AmEx traveler's checks; no min. charge), they'll hold mail for 30 days and help send and receive wired money. In an emergency, AmEx cashes personal checks up to US$1000 for cardholders only. 24hr. Express Cash machine outside. To report or cancel lost traveler's checks, call 24hr. toll free tel. (900) 99 44 26. To report other problems, call 24hr. toll free tel. (900) 94 14 13. Open Mon.-Fri. 9am-5:30pm, Sat. 9am-noon.

El Corte Inglés: C. Preciados, 3 (tel. 532 18 00). M: Sol. **C. Goya, 76** (tel. 577 71 71). M: Goya. **C. Princesa, 42** (tel. 542 48 00). M: Argüelles. **C. Raimundo Fernández Villaverde, 79** (tel. 556 23 00). M: Nuevos Ministerios. Giant chain of department stores. "A place to shop. A place to dream." **Currency exchange:** Commission included in their mediocre rates. Good **map,** haircutting, cafeteria-restaurant, **supermarket, telephones,** tapes and CDs, **books in English,** electronics, and **sycophantic salespeople.** Open Mon.-Sat. 10am-9pm, Sun. 10am-2pm.

Luggage Storage: Estaciones Chamartín, self-serve, automatic lockers in the *consigna* area by the bus stop. Lockers 300-600ptas per day. Open 6:30am-12:30am. Lockers may be opened once with each payment. **Estación Atocha,** same services, prices, and hours. Exiting the *largo recorrido* area, lockers are to the left of the rainforest display. **Estación Sur de Autobuses,** bags checked (800ptas).

Message Boards: Librería Turner and **Booksellers** (see **Shopping: Books,** p. 112). **TIVE** travel agency (see **Budget Travel,** p. 75) also has a board brimming with cheap travel tickets and rideshare offers. **Albergue Juvenil Santa Cruz (HI)** has

fewer of the same types of notices (heavy on the rideshare offers). Also check the classifieds in *En Madrid*.

Laundromats: All laundromats have drying services—price varies depending on size of load or drying time (about 100ptas). **Lavandería Donoso Cortés,** C. Donoso Cortés, 17 (tel. 446 96 90). M: Quevedo. From the Metro, walk down C. Bravo Murillo to C. Donoso Cortés. Self-service. Wash 600ptas. Detergent 70ptas (open Mon.-Fri. 9am-2pm and 3:30-7:45pm, Sat. 9am-1:30pm). **Lavomatique** (tel. 448 40 02). C. León at C. Cervantes, near Pl. Santa Ana. M: Antón Martín. Walk up C. Amor de Dios, turn left on C. Las Huertas and right on C. León. Self service. Wash 600ptas. Open daily 9am-2pm and 4:30-8pm. **Lavandería Automática SIDEC,** C. Don Felipe, 4. M: Gran Vía. Wash 600ptas; detergent 25ptas; dry 100ptas (open Mon.-Fri. 10am-9pm). **Maryland,** C. Meléndez Valdés, 52 (tel. 543 30 41). M: Argüelles. Go up C. Princesa, turn right on C. Hilarión, which then intersects C. Meléndez Valdés. Self service. Wash including detergent 725ptas. Open Mon.-Fri. 10am-8pm, Sat. 10:30am-2pm.

Libraries: Bibliotecas Populares (info tel. 445 98 45). A big, airy branch is at M: Puerta de Toledo (tel. 366 54 07). English-language periodicals. If you bring your passport and two ID-size photos, they'll issue a card on the spot. Free. Open Mon.-Fri. 8:30am-8:45pm, Sat. 9am-1:45pm. Closed Sat. in summer. **Biblioteca Nacional,** C. Serrano, next to the Museo Arqueológico (tel. 580 78 23). M: Serrano. Not open for reading or browsing (but its bookstore is). Limited to scholars doing doctorate and post-doctorate research. To use the facilities, bring letters of recommendation and a project proposal. Basically, overinflate your importance. It will work. Open Mon.-Fri. 9am-9pm, Sat. 9am-2pm. **Washington Irving Center,** C. Marqués Villamagna, 8 (tel. 587 22 00). M: Serrano or Colón. From the station, walk up C. Serrano, and turn left on C. Marqués de Villamagna. Good selection of U.S. magazines and books. Anyone over 16 can check books out for 2 weeks by filling out a simple application form. Allow about a week for processing. Open Mon.-Fri. 2-6pm.

English Bookstores: See **Shopping: Books,** p. 112.

English-Language Periodicals: International edition dailies and weeklies available at kiosks on the Gran Vía, Paseos del Prado, Recoletos, and Castellana, and around Pta. del Sol. If you're dying for the *New York Times* (425ptas), try one of the **VIPS** restaurants (see **Red-Eye Establishments,** p. 85)

Language Service: Ferocio (*For*eign *Ocio*), C. Mayor, 6, 4th fl. (tel. 522 56 77), is an organization dedicated to bringing foreigners and natives together to share languages (and anything else). Sponsors weekly international parties (see **Entertainment,** p. 109) and organizes group trips to other parts of Spain.

Women's Services: Librería de Mujeres, C. San Cristóbal, 17 (tel. 521 70 43), near Pl. Mayor. M: Sol. Walk down C. Mayor, make a left on C. Esparteros, the first right on C. Postas, 1st left onto C. San Cristóbal. Gloria Steinem and Susan Faludi in translation. The shop's motto: *"Los libros no muerden, el feminismo tampoco."* (Books don't bite, neither does feminism.) Books and gifts; more of a resource for Spanish speakers. Open Mon.-Fri. 10am-2pm and 5-8pm, Sat. 10am-2pm. Check out the mural. **Women's Issues,** tel. 900 19 10 10 or 347 80 00.

Gay and Lesbian Services: The Colectivo de Gais y Lesbianas de Madrid (COGAM), C. Fuencarral, 37 (tel./fax 523 00 70), directly across from the Ministry of Justice. M: Granvía. Provides a wide range of services and activities of interest to gays, lesbians, and bisexuals (reception open Mon.-Fri. 5-9pm). English usually spoken. Free screenings of gay-interest movies, COGAM youth group (25 and under), and HIV-positive support group (tel. 522 45 17; Mon.-Fri. 6-10pm). Free counseling Mon.-Thurs. 7-9pm. Library open daily 7-9pm. COGAM publishes the semi-monthly *Entiendes...?,* a magazine in Spanish about gay issues, as well as a the *Pink and Black Pages* listing gay services, groups, activities, and personals (magazine available at many kiosks and in Berkana Librería Gai y Lesbiana and Librería El Galeón; see **Books,** p. 112). **GAI-INFORM,** a gay info line (tel. 523 00 70; daily 5-9pm), provides info in Spanish (and sometimes French and English) about gay associations, leisure activities, and health issues. The same number has info on sports, workshops in French and English, and dinners. Info on Brujulai, COGAM's weekend excursion group. Dispenses free prophylactics. Their cafe, **Urania,** is unaffiliated but is used as a social gathering center.

Religious Services: Our Lady of Mercy English-Speaking Parish, C. Alfonso XIII, 165 (morning tel. 533 20 32; afternoon tel. 554 28 60), on the corner of Pl. Habana. Mass in English daily at 11:30am. **Immanuel Baptist Church,** C. Hernández de Tejada, 4 (tel. 407 43 47). English services Sun. 11am and 7pm. Prayer services Wed 7:30pm. **Community Church of Madrid,** C. Bravo Murillo, 85 (tel. 838 55 57). M: Cuatro Caminos. At the Colegio El Porvenir. Multidenominational Protestant services in English Sun. 10am. **British Embassy Church of St. George,** C. Núñez de Balboa, 43 (tel. 576 51 09; call 8am-4pm). M: Velázquez. Services Sun. 8:30, 10, 11:15am, and noon; Fri. 10:30am. **Sinagoga Beth Yaacov,** C. Balmes, 3 (tel. 445 98 43 or 445 98 35), near Pl. Sorolla. M: Iglesia. Services Fri. 8pm, Sat. 9:15am. Also small chapel, 2 social halls, room for Sun. classes, mikvah, library, and kosher catering. Kosher restaurant can be reserved. Passport sometimes required. Spanish only. **Centro Islámico,** C. Alonso Cano, 3 (tel. 448 05 54). M: Iglesia. Services and sessions of language classes Mon.-Fri. 9am-2pm and 5-8pm.

Help Lines: 20ptas min. charge for all non-900 numbers. **AIDS Info Hotline** (tel. 445 23 28; Mon.-Fri. 9am-2pm). **Detox** (tel. 900 16 15 15) English spoken. 9am-9pm daily. **Alcohólicos Anónimos,** C. Juan Bravo, 40, 2nd fl. (tel. 309 19 47 in English; crisis line in Spanish tel. 532 30 30). M: Núñez de Balboa. **English-Language Helpline** (tel. 559 13 93) for confidential help from trained volunteers 7-11pm.

Crisis Lines: Poison Control (24hr. tel. 562 04 20). **Rape Hotline** (tel. 574 01 10) available Mon.-Fri. 10am-2pm and 4-7pm; other times machine offers emergency instructions. No English spoken.

Late-Night Pharmacy: (Info tel. 098). Check *Farmacias de Guardia* listings in local papers to find pharmacies open after 8pm. Listings of the nearest on-duty pharmacy are also posted in all pharmacy windows. Contraceptive products are sold over the counter in most Spanish pharmacies.

Hospitals: Most are in the north and east ends of the city. Prompt appointments are hard to obtain (emergency rooms are the best option for immediate attention), but public hospitals treat patients without advance payment. **Anglo-American Medical Unit,** Conde de Aranda, 1, 1st fl. (tel. 435 18 23). M: Retiro. Doctors, dentists, optometrists. Run partly by British and Americans. Regular personnel on duty 9am-8pm. *Not* an emergency clinic. Embassies and consulates also keep lists of English-speaking doctors in private practice. **Hospital Clínico San Carlos,** Pl. Cristo Rey (tel. 330 30 00; 24hr.). M: Moncloa.

Emergency Clinics: In a **medical emergency** dial 061. **Equipo Quirúrgico Municipal No. 1,** C. Montesa, 22 (tel. 588 51 00). M: Manuel Becerra. **Hospital Ramón y Cajal,** Ctra. Colmenar Viejo, km 9100 (tel. 336 80 00). Bus #135 from Pl. Castilla.

Red Cross: (tel. 522 22 22).

Police:. C. Luna, 17 (tel. 521 12 36). M: Callao. From Gran Vía walk down C. Arenal. This station has forms in English. To report crimes committed in the Metro, go to the office in the Sol station (tel. 521 09 11). Open daily 8am-11pm. **Guardia Civil** (tel. 062 or 534 02 00). **Protección Civil** (tel. 588 91 15).

Emergency: tel. 091 (national police) or 092 (local police).

Post Office: Palacio de Comunicaciones, Pl. Cibeles (tel. 396 24 43). M: Banco de España. Enormous, ornate palace on the far side of the plaza from the Metro. Info (door E) open Mon.-Fri. 8am-10pm or call the useful info line (tel. 537 64 94). Open for stamp purchase and certified mail (main door) Mon.-Fri. 8am-10pm, Sat. 8:30am-8:30pm, Sun. 9:30am-1:30pm. **Lista de Correos** (window 18) open Mon.-Fri. 8am-9:30pm, Sat. 8:30am-2pm. Sending packages (door N) open Mon.-Fri. 8am-9pm, Sat. 8:30am-1:30pm. Telex and **fax** service (door H, right of main entrance); open Mon.-Fri. 8am-midnight, Sat.-Sun. 8am-10pm. Windows may change. English and French spoken at info desk. **Postal Code:** 28070.

Telephones: Telefónica, Gran Vía, 30, at C. Valverde. M: Gran Vía. Direct-dial lines to the U.S. at exorbitant rates. Almodóvar worked here. Open daily 9:30am-11:30pm. Calls over 500ptas can be charged to a credit card. Open Mon.-Fri. 8am-midnight, Sat.-Sun. and holidays 8am-10pm. Long-distance calls may also be placed at Po. Recoletos, 43, off Pl. Colón (same hours). **Tarjetas telefónicas** (telephone cards) sold at Telefónica or any **estanco** (tobacco shop) in 1000ptas and 2000ptas denominations, save you from change-guzzling public phones, and *tarjeta*-only phones are usually unoccupied. **Telephone Code:** (9)1.

■ Accommodations and Camping

The demand for rooms is always high and it increases dramatically in summer. Never fear, Madrid is inundated with *hostales*. Prices average about 2400ptas per person for a basic *hostal* room, a bit more for a two-star *hostal*, slightly less for a bed in a *pensión*, and even less when visiting during the off season. Bargaining is a good idea, and perfectly acceptable, especially if you are sharing a room with two or more friends or are planning to stay for more than a few days.

ACCOMMODATIONS SERVICE

Viajes Brújula: Torre de Madrid, 6th fl. #14 (tel. 559 97 04 or 559 97 05; fax 548 46 24). M: Plaza España. Located in a huge building with signs for Alitalia and Kuwait Airlines on the ground floor. For 300ptas, they make reservations for any participating locale in Spain. *You must go in person.* You pay a deposit of about one-third of the room price, which is then subtracted from the price of the accommodation. They charge a commission, so room prices may be higher in addition to the 300ptas commission. Not every establishment is signed up with Brújula (no HI youth hostels). Nevertheless, it's a good deal if you are tired and need to secure a bed. English spoken. Open Mon.-Fri. 9am-2pm and 4:30-7pm. Branch offices located at: Estación Atocha at the AVE terminal (tel. 539 11 73; open daily 8am-10pm); Estación Chamartín (tel. 315 78 94; open 7:15am-11:30pm); and the airport bus terminal in Pl. Colón (tel. 575 90 57; open 8am-10pm).

YOUTH HOSTELS

Madrid has two HI hostels. While neither is centrally located, the Albergue Juvenil Richard Schirrman in the Casa de Campo is located in a particularly isolated and dangerous spot, and therefore is not recommended by *Let's Go.*

Albergue Juvenil Santa Cruz de Marcenado (HI), C. Santa Cruz de Marcenado, 28 (tel. 547 45 32; fax 548 11 96). M: Argüelles. From the Metro, walk 1 block down C. Alberto Aguilera away from C. Princesa, turn right at C. Serrano de Jóven, and left on C. Santa Cruz de Marcenado. Modern, recently renovated facilities near the student district. Seventy-two firm beds in airy rooms fill quickly, even in winter. Rooms have cubbies; lockers (outside rooms) 200ptas extra. An HI card is required and can be purchased for 1800ptas. Sheets, but not towels, provided. 3-day max. stay. Reserve a space (by person, mail, or fax only) 15 days in advance, or arrive early and pray. Message board. English spoken. Reception open daily 9am-9:30pm. Silence after midnight, very strict 1:30am curfew and 2:30am lights out. 950ptas, over 26 1300ptas. Breakfast included. Visa, MC. Closed Christmas and New Year's. If you can't get a bed at Santa Cruz, **Hostal-Residencia La Montaña,** C. Juan Álvarez Mendizábal, 44, 4th fl. (tel. 547 10 88), and the 4 other *pensiones* in the same building are a short jaunt away. From the HI, cross the busy C. Princesa, turn left, go right on C. Rey Fancisco, then left on C. J.A. Mendizábal. From M: Ventura Rodríguez: Facing the park (green shrubbery), walk up C. Princesa to your left, 3 blocks to C Rey Francisco, turn left, go 3 blocks to J. A. Mendizábal, turn left again. Rooms are immaculate, ample, sunny, and in relatively low demand. Single by the front door is a bit cramped. One of five *hostales* at this address. Singles 1800ptas, with shower 2000ptas. Doubles with shower 3400ptas, with bath 3700ptas. Triples 5800ptas.

HOSTALES AND PENSIONES

In Madrid, the difference between a one-star *hostal* and a *pension* is often minimal. A room in a one- or two-star *hostal* has at least these basics: bed, closet space, desk with chair, sink and towel, window, light fixture, fake flowers, and a lock on the door (religious icons are popular but not standard). Winter heating is standard, air-conditioning is not. Unless otherwise noted, communal bathrooms (toilet and shower) are the rule. Most places accept reservations, but they're never required. Reservations are recommended in summer and on weekends year-round, especially in the Puerta de

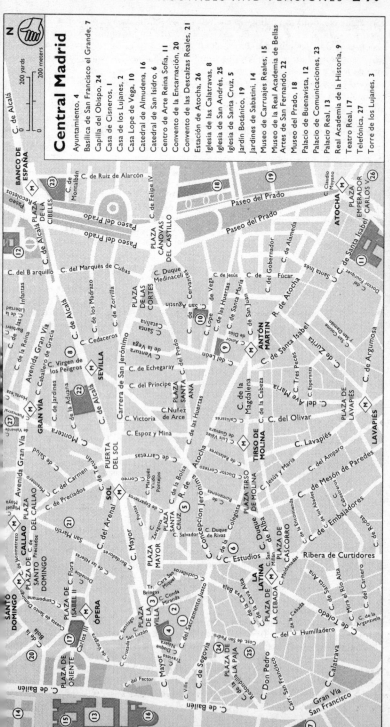

Central Madrid

Ayuntamiento, 4
Basílica de San Francisco el Grande, 7
Capilla del Obispo, 24
Casa de Cisneros, 1
Casa de los Lujanes, 2
Casa Lope de Vega, 10
Catedral de Almudena, 16
Catedral de San Isidro, 6
Centro de Arte Reina Sofía, 11
Convento de la Encarnación, 20
Convento de las Descalzas Reales, 21
Estación de Atocha, 26
Iglesia de las Calatravas, 8
Iglesia de San Andrés, 25
Iglesia de Santa Cruz, 5
Jardín Botánico, 19
Jardines de Sabatini, 14
Museo de Carruajes Reales, 15
Museo de la Real Academia de Bellas
Artes de San Fernando, 22
Museo del Prado, 18
Palacio de Buenavista, 12
Palacio de Comunicaciones, 23
Palacio Real, 13
Real Academia de la Historia, 9
Teatro Real, 17
Telefónica, 27
Torre de los Lujanes, 3

MADRID

Sol area and at our top listings in each district. As a rule in Madrid, especially in competitive central zones, *hostales* are well-kept and comfortable. Owners are usually accustomed to opening the doors, albeit groggily, at all hours, or providing keys for guests, but ask before club-hopping until the wee hours; late-night lockouts or confrontations with irate owners are no fun.

Pensiones are like boarding houses: they sometimes have curfews, and often host longer-term guests *(estables)*. Winter heating is not standard, but readers can assume there's heat unless otherwise noted. Towels and sheets are provided, but not always changed daily. The same goes for *casas de huéspedes* or simply *casas*. The best deals are found outside the most central locations, but remember that Madrid's stellar public transportation makes virtually any locale central.

SOL AND ÓPERA

Puerta del Sol is the center of the city in the center of the country. All roads converge here (it's Spain's km0) and all tourists ramble through at least once. Signs indicating *hostales* and *pensiones* stick out from flower-potted balconies and decaying facades on narrow, sloping streets. For better deals, stray several blocks from Sol. The following listings fall in the area west of Sol, between Sol and the Palacio Real. Bus #3, 25, 19, and 33 serve Ópera, #5 (from Atocha), 15, 20, 50, 51, 52, 53, and 150 serve Sol.

Hostal-Residencia Paz, C. Flora, 4, 1st and 2nd fl. (tel. 547 30 47). M: Ópera. On a quiet street parallel to C. Arenal, off C. Donados or C. Hileras. Firm beds in 10 recently-renovated, brilliant rooms—some overlooking a courtyard, others with access to terrace. Singles 2300ptas. Doubles 3500ptas, with shower 4100ptas. Triples with shower 5100ptas. Laundry 1000ptas. Reservations encouraged. Visa, MC

La Pensión Luz, C. Fuentes, 10, 3rd fl. (tel. 542 07 59). M: Sol. Twelve sunny, inviting rooms in an elegant old building off C. Arenal. The bathrooms sparkle so much you won't mind sharing. Singles 2500ptas. Doubles 3700ptas, made into triples for 5300ptas. Discounts available for long stays (15 days or more).

Hostal Cruz-Sol, Pl. Santa Cruz, 6, 3rd fl. (tel. 532 71 97). M: Sol. Pleasant, ample rooms with parquet floors and cavernous ceilings. Many overlook the picturesque plaza. No winter heating, but warm beige interior with sudden bursts of red and sweet baby blue. Singles 2000ptas. Doubles 2500ptas, with bath 4000ptas. Triples 3000ptas; 5000ptas. Showers 200ptas per person, free for singles.

Hostal-Residencia María del Mar, C. Marqués Viudo de Pontejos 7, 2nd and 3rd fl. (tel. 531 90 64). M: Sol. Off C. Correo from Pta. del Sol. Thirty recently-renovated rooms with high ceilings, shiny floors, and shapely furniture—just don't get stuck in one of the 2 windowless singles. Lounge with TV, no smoking in common areas, 2am curfew. Singles with sinks (no hot water) 1700ptas. Doubles 2900ptas, with bath 4500-5000ptas. Hot showers 200ptas.

Hostal Santa Cruz, Pl. Santa Cruz, 6, 2nd fl. (tel./fax 522 24 41). M: Sol. In the mellow Pl. Santa Cruz, next to the Pl. Mayor. Sky-high ceilings and a palatial lounge. Tiny, sinkless singles 2800ptas, with shower 3200ptas. Doubles 3800ptas, with bath or shower 4800ptas. Triples 5000ptas, with shower 6000ptas. Reservations accepted by fax.

Hostal Madrid, C. Esparteros, 6, 2nd fl. (tel. 522 00 60; fax 532 35 10). M: Sol. Off C. Mayor. Spacious rooms with shiny wood floors and large windows. All have TV and new bathrooms. Telephones, A/C. Friendly, multilingual proprietors. Cold drinks 150ptas. Singles 4000ptas. Doubles 7000ptas. One triple with balcony 8000ptas. Reservations recommended. Visa.

Hostal-Residencia Miño, C. Arenal, 16, 2nd fl. (tel. 531 50 79 or 531 97 89). M: Ópera or Sol. A melting pot of rooms ranging from large with hardwood floors and balconies to tight quarters with vinyl underfoot. Some rooms overlook busy C. Arenal, others have a quieter but darker patio. Singles 2200ptas, with shower 2900ptas. Doubles with shower 3900ptas, with bath 4500ptas. Triples 5400ptas.

Hostal-Residencia Rober, C. Arenal, 26, 5th fl. (tel. 541 91 75). M: Ópera. The variety of patterns on the rugs and bed coverings give that grandparent feel. Smoking is strictly prohibited. All 14 pristine rooms have their own tiny TVs. Fans. Single

3200ptas, with bath 4000ptas. Doubles with bath 5000ptas. Triples with bath 7000ptas. Prices don't include 7% IVA. Visa, MC, AmEx.

Hostal-Residencia Encarnita, C. Marqués Viudo de Pontejo, 7, 4th fl. (tel. 531 90 55). M: Sol. Above the María del Mar. Standard *hostal* charm: claustrophobic rooms, tired beds, dark halls, cheap nature posters. Singles 1500ptas. Doubles 2600ptas, with bath 2900ptas. Triples 3600ptas, with bath 4000ptas. Quad 4800ptas. Showers 200ptas.

HUERTAS

Although *madrileños* have never settled on a nickname for this neighborhood, it's generally referred to as Huertas and is known as Madrid's theater district. It rings all day and night with bar-crawlers nibbling on *tapas*, especially on Wednesdays, when show tickets are discounted. Sol, Pl. Mayor, *El triángulo de arte,* and Atocha train station are all within walking distance. Sol-bound buses stop near accommodations on C. Príncipe, C. Nuñez de Arce, and C. San Jerónimo; #14, 26, 37 (passing Est. Atocha and Est. Sur de Autobuses), and 45 run along Po. del Prado.

Hostal R. Rodríguez, C. Nuñez de Arce, 9, 3rd fl. (tel. 522 44 31). off Pl. Santa Ana. Alluring rooms, including two snazzy triples with classic columns and wispy curtains. 24hr. reception. Shared baths only. English spoken. Singles 2300ptas. Doubles 3300ptas. Triples 4300ptas.

Hostal Aguilar, C. San Jerónimo, 32, 2nd fl. (tel. 429 59 26). M: Sol. More than 50 modern rooms, all with telephone, A/C, coin-operated TV, and shower. Singles with shower 3200ptas, with bath 3500ptas. Doubles: 4400ptas; 5500ptas. Quads with bath 8000ptas. 1500ptas more for each extra person. Visa, MC.

Hostal Agential, C. Cervantes, 34, 3rd fl. (tel. 429 27 14). M: Antón Martín. Off C. León, which is off C. Atocha. Newly-renovated by friendly proprietors. Two windowless singles share one bath for 2200ptas, with private bath 3800ptas. Doubles 5000ptas. Triples with bath 6000ptas. Ask about discounts.

Hostal Lucense, C. Núñez de Arce, 15, 1st fl. (tel. 522 48 88). M: Sol. Go down C. San Jerónimo, turn right on C. Cruz, and left on C. Nuñez de Arce. The sign outside reads "Speaking Englisch," which turns out to be about right. Best for skinny people with lots of clothes—narrow rooms with huge closets. Singles 1300ptas. Doubles 2000ptas, with bath 2800ptas. Triples: 3000ptas; 3600ptas. If you don't have a shower in your room, you can bathe for 200ptas.

Pensión Poza, C. Núñez de Arce, 9, 1st fl. (tel. 522 48 71). M: Sol. Under the same management as Hostal Lucense (see above), but an even better deal—larger rooms, same prices. No winter heating.

Hostal-Residencia Sud-Americana, Po. Prado, 12, 6th fl. (tel. 429 25 64). M: Antón Martín or Atocha. Across from the Prado on Pl. Cánovas de Castillo. Eight rooms total—all with faux-leather armchairs and some with balconies. Face the Po. de Prado and enjoy a magnificent view, though in the summer you can't see the Prado through the trees. Singles 2400ptas. Doubles 4600ptas. One triple 5600ptas.

Hostal Abulense, C. Nuñez de Arce, 15, 3rd fl. (tel. 522 81 44). M: Sol. Upstairs from the Hostal Lucense, a friendly proprietress runs this simple and slightly cramped *hostal* at very cheap rates. The doorbell chimes "Jingle Bells" and Beethoven's Fifth. Communal bathroom. Small singles 1400ptas. Fair-sized doubles 2400ptas. Triples 3300ptas. Showers 150ptas. Cheaper for longer stays.

Hostal Villar, C. Príncipe, 18, 1st-4th fl. (tel. 531 66 00 or 531 66 09; fax 521 50 73). M: Sol. Walk down C. San Jerónimo, turn right on C. Príncipe. The 70s stormed through this old building, leaving in their wake 46 comfortable rooms with TVs, telephones, and a whole lotta brown. Singles 2300ptas, with bath 3000ptas. Doubles: 3300ptas; 4200ptas. Rooms can be made into triples for 4480ptas, with bath 5800ptas. Visa, MC.

Hostal Casanova, C. Lope de Vega, 8, 1st fl. (tel. 429 56 91). Simple rooms, all with sink and hot water, some with a stunning view of the neighbor's brick wall. Spacious communal bathrooms, and large single beds. No heating. Nice floor patterns, though. Singles 1600ptas. Doubles 2800ptas, made into triples for 3500ptas.

Hostal Carreras, C. Príncipe, 18, 3rd fl. (tel. 522 00 36). M: Antón Martín, Sol, or Sevilla. Off San Jerónimo, between Pl. Santa Ana and Pl. Canalejas. House rules are posted throughout, including no noise after midnight. Spacious rooms lit with fluorescent bulbs. Advance payment required. A more modern **annex,** C. Príncipe, 20, is equipped with full modern baths and fewer fluorescent bulbs. Three singles 2000ptas each. Doubles 3500ptas, with shower 4000ptas, with bath 4500ptas. Triples with shower 4500ptas. Quads 6000ptas.

Hostal-Residencia Regional, C. Príncipe, 18, 4th fl. (tel. 522 33 73). M: Antón Martín, Sol, or Sevilla. Same building as Carreras. If you're lucky (and pay more), you'll get a futuristic shower pod. Singles 2400ptas, with shower 3500ptas. Doubles: 3400ptas; 4400ptas. Triples: 4500ptas; 5500ptas.

Hotel Lido, C. Echegaray, 5, 2nd fl. (tel. 429 62 07). M: Sol. Off C. San Jerónimo near Pl. Canalejas. The rickety steps don't seem to keep guests away. Smallish rooms, some without windows, others with big, arboreal balconies. Long-term guests (month-stays) are preferred; they can use the kitchen. Singles: 2000ptas, 35,000ptas per month. Doubles: 3500ptas; 65,000ptas. Breakfast 350ptas.

Hostal Armesto, C. San Agustín, 6, 1st fl. (tel. 429 90 31). M: Antón Martín. In front of Pl. Cortés. A small establishment with well-coordinated furniture, wallpaper, curtains, and carnation-pink bedspreads. Several rooms look out onto a garden. All rooms with bath. Singles 4500. Doubles 5800ptas. Triples 7000ptas.

Hostal León, C. San Jerónimo, 32, 4th fl. (tel. 429 67 78). M: Sol. On the same floor as the Mondragón. Cupid carvings adorn the ceilings of this simple *hostal.* Authentic 70s decor and attractive tiling in the common bathroom. Some rooms open up into the scenic elevator shaft. Singles 1700-1800ptas. Doubles 3400ptas. Triples 4500-5200ptas. Sizeable quad 6000ptas.

Hostal-Residencia Mondragón, C. San Jerónimo, 32, 4th fl. (tel. 429 68 16). M: Sol. In the same building as the Aguilar and several other *hostales.* Spain's first motion picture was filmed in this building in 1898. Some rooms open on to a gardenia-filled terrace. Hot water runs only in communal bathrooms. Singles 1900-2000ptas. Doubles 2800ptas, with shower 3000ptas. Triples 3900ptas.

GRAN VÍA

Screaming lights, flashing cars, swishing skirts, and heavy-healed shoes swirling in cigar smoke and exhaust fumes. The Gran Vía is macro-Madrid, its Broadway or Champs-Elysées. Like those avenues, it is busy and international. It has sex shops, McDonald's, ritzy theaters, and steel chairs reflecting the neon glow. It is vertical and cosmopolitan in a city that spreads outward, neighborhood by neighborhood. *Hostal* signs scatter the horizon. Accommodations tend to be expensive. If you're shown to a streetside room, you may wish to check it for well-fortified windows. Bus #75, 149, 143, 146, 147, and 148 reach Callao; #1, 2, 44, 46, 74, 75, and 133 service both Pl. España and Callao.

Hostal Lauria, Gran Vía, 50, 5th fl. (tel./fax 547 35 49). M: Callao. Ultra-comfortable rooms have oriental rugs and random artwork. Homey *salón* with stereo and TV. Use of kitchen and refrigerator. English spoken. All rooms with shower. Singles 3700ptas. Doubles 4500ptas, with toilet 4700ptas. Triples 6000ptas. Laundry 1200ptas. Visa, MC. Reservations recommended a week in advance.

Hostal Margarita, Gran Vía, 50, 4th fl. (tel. 541 91 82; fax 541 91 88). M: Callao. Stucco walls, light wood shutters and baby blue beds create an airy, Californian ranch house feel. Rooms are tastefully sparse, with big windows, pretty little bathrooms, TVs, and telephones. The owner is eager to please—show him your *Let's Go.* Singles 3500-3800ptas. Doubles 5000ptas. Triples 6500ptas. 20% off stays longer than a week. Laundry service available.

Hostal-Residencia Josefina, Gran Vía, 44, 7th fl. (tel. 521 81 31 or 531 04 66). M: Callao. Heavy gray drapes, peeling paint, and dramatic candelabra give the hallways a mysterious feel. The rooms, however, all have happy colors; most have balconies, though some only a view of a dark gray wall. Room 15 is a dream trip, with a spacious lounge. Common bathrooms. Singles 2700ptas, with shower 3200ptas. Doubles with shower 4000ptas. Triples with shower 6000ptas.

Hostal-Residencia Alibel, C. Gran Vía, 44, 8th fl. (tel. 521 00 51). M: Callao. Well-lit rooms with great views and polished armoires; a column here, an archway there. Will do laundry and offer drinks. French spoken. Doubles 3700ptas, with shower 4200ptas, with bath 4500ptas. Triples with shower 5500ptas.

Hostal A. Nebrija, Gran Vía, 67, 8th fl., elevator A (tel. 547 73 19). M: Pl. España. Pleasant and spacious rooms, heavily furnished in medieval style and with huge windows revealing great views; a great place to read. Singles 3100ptas. Doubles 4100ptas. Triples 5900ptas. Quads 6500ptas. Visa, AmEx.

Hostal-Residencia Delfina, Gran Vía, 12, 4th fl. (tel. 522 64 23 or 522 64 22). M: Gran Vía or Sevilla. Old-fashioned charm in a stately building is spiced with parquet floors and neon paint on the walls. All rooms have bath, telephone, TVs, and A/C. Singles 3200ptas. Doubles 4700ptas. Triples 6500ptas. Slightly cheaper in winter.

Hostal-Residencia María, Miguel Moya, 4, 2nd fl (tel. 522 44 77). M: Callao. Located just off Pl. Callao, set 20m back from the noisy Gran Vía, directly across Pl. Callao. Airy, spacious rooms, all with TVs and some with fans or attractive cut-glass fixtures. Whole place has a neutral yellow-beige color. Singles 2700ptas, with bath 3100ptas. Doubles with bath 4500ptas. Triple with bath 6000ptas. Visa, MC.

Hostal-Residencia Lamalonga, Gran Vía, 56, 2nd fl. (tel. 547 26 31 or 547 68 94). M: Callao. Crowded TV lounge with a neat row of fancy chairs, stained glass windows, and ubiquitous fake flowers. Walls meet at odd angles; elevators also a perk. All rooms have telephone and private bath. Singles 4300ptas. Doubles 5700. Triples 7200ptas. Cheaper in winter. 10% discount for stays over 5 days. Visa, MC.

FUENCARRAL

The most attractive characteristic of C. Fuencarral, north of Sol between metro stops Gran Vía and Tribunal, is the wealth of *hostales* and *pensiones* residing in practically every portal. Narrow, crowded, and commercial, C. Fuencarral is the main traffic pipeline to the Gran Vía. It is noisier and more odoriferous than the Gran Vía, but it's less expensive and closer to the nightlife hubs of Malasaña and Chueca. Bus #3, 7, 40, and 149 run south along C. Fuencarral.

Hostal Palacios and Hostal Ribadavia, C. Fuencarral, 25, 1st-3rd fl. (tel. 531 10 58 or 531 48 47). M: Gran Vía. Both *hostales* are run by the same cheerful family. **Ribadavia** (3rd fl.) has pleasant, bright rooms with old furniture. **Palacios** (1st and 2nd fl.) flaunts brand new rooms, all with baths. Two singles with private bath just outside room 2400ptas, with bath inside 2800ptas. Doubles with shower 3800ptas, with bath 4400ptas. Triples with bath 6400ptas. Quad with shower 7500ptas.

Hostal Medieval, C. Fuencarral, 46, 2nd fl. (tel. 522 25 49). M: Tribunal. On the corner with C. Augusto Figueroa. Don't think Dark Ages, think pink. The lounge honors the Spanish royal couple and Real Madrid (¡Hala Madrid! ¡Hala Vikingos!). Singles with shower 3000ptas. Doubles with shower 4000ptas, with bath 5000ptas. Triples with shower 6000ptas.

Hostal-Residencia Abril, C. Fuencarral, 39, 4th fl. (tel. 531 53 38). M: Tribunal or Gran Vía. Nice and simple—light wood, low prices, and random baby posters. Redone in 1994. Singles 1900ptas, with shower 2200ptas, with bath 2500ptas. Doubles: 2900ptas; 3200ptas; 3400ptas. Triples 3100ptas, with bath 4300ptas.

Hostal-Residencia Domínguez, C. Santa Brígida, 1 (tel. 532 15 47). M: Tribunal. Go down C. Fuencarral toward Gran Vía, turn left on C. Santa Brígada, up one flight of dark steps. Modern bathrooms almost as big as the quiet, spartan rooms. Narrow hallways lead to a free luggage storage area. Singles 1700ptas, with shower 1900ptas. Doubles 2800ptas, with shower 3200ptas, with bath 3400ptas. Reservations recommended.

ELSEWHERE

Near Chamartín train station budget lodgings are rare. **Chueca,** the area behind Gran Vía and along and near C. las Infantas, is about as rich in *hostales* (not to mention restaurants, bars, and nightlife) as any of the above districts. It's hip and fun but can be dangerous, especially for solo travelers. Other lightly touristed zones include the middle-class commercial **Gaztambide,** east of Argüelles and Moncloa and C. Princesa; the

mainly residential **Chamberí,** north of M: Iglesia and C. General Martínez Campos, and south of M: Ríos Rosas; and **La Latina,** the area around the Metro stop stretching to M: Tirso de Molina and the Glorieta Puerta de Toledo. Near the **Madrid-Atocha** train station are a handful of *hostales,* the closest down Po. Santa María de la Cabeza.

Hotel Mónaco, C. Barbieri, 5 (tel. 552 46 30 or 552 46 38; fax 521 16 01). M: Chueca. A former brothel catering to Madrid's high society (Alfonso XIII, the king's grandfather, is rumored to have been a frequent visitor). The hotel's decor still encourages naughtiness. Frescoes of Eve-like temptresses prod and pry the imagination while hundreds of mirrors keep watch to ensure the realization of fantasy. Each room is a different adventure. Ostentatiously risquée first-floor bedrooms. Singles are simple. All rooms with bath. Treat yourself. This isn't Spain anymore—indeed, the owner's Portuguese—welcome to Monaco, room 34. Singles 7000ptas. Doubles 10,000ptas. Triples 11,500ptas. Accepts all major credit cards.

Hostal Greco, C. las Infantas, 3, 2nd fl. (tel. 522 46 32 or 522 46 31; fax 523 23 61). M: Gran Vía or Chueca. You get lots of bang for your buck at this art-nouveau *hostal.* Enormous rooms with large bathrooms, telephones, TVs, and personal safes (100ptas). Most rooms are carpeted. No main-door keys distributed; the owner prefers quiet clientele. Singles (only 2—call for a reservation) 3400ptas. Doubles 5600ptas. Triples 7500ptas. Visa, MC.

Hostal Lorenzo, C. las Infantas, 26, 3rd fl. (tel. 521 30 57; fax 532 79 78). M: Gran Vía or Chueca. Tastefully redecorated rooms, TVs, telephones, A/C, real plants on real balconies, and sound-proof windows. Turn the knob by the bed to hear music through ceiling speakers. Singles with bath 3800ptas. Doubles with bath 5800ptas. Triples with bath 7000ptas. Breakfast 300ptas. Credit cards accepted.

Hostal Central, C. Palma, 2, 1st fl. (tel. 447 00 47). M: Tribunal. Off Fuencarral, just after the Metro stop. In the center of one of the most vibrant areas in Madrid, one block from C. San Vicente Ferrer and 2 blocks from Pl. 2 de Mayo—caution advised in this part of town at night. Simple and worn, but clean, well-lit, and cheap. Singles 1500ptas. Doubles 2500ptas. Triples 3000ptas. Showers 200ptas.

CAMPING

Tourist offices can provide info about the 13 or so campsites within 50km of Madrid. Similar info is in their **Guía Oficial de Campings, España '98,** a big book which they gladly let you look through, but don't give away (most bookstores carry it). The **Mapa de Campings** shows the location of every official campsite in Spain. Also ask for the brochure **Hoteles, Campings, Apartamentos, España '98,** which lists and describes hotels, campsites, and apartments in and around Madrid. For further camping info contact the Consejería de Educación de Juventud, C. Fernando el Católico (tel. 522 29 41 or 521 44 27). **Camping Osuna** (tel. 741 05 10; fax 320 63 65) is located on Av Logroño (8km). Take the Metro to Canillejas, then cross the pedestrian overpass walk through the parking lot, and turn right along the freeway. Pass under two bridges (the first a freeway and the second an arch) and look for campground sign on the right (600ptas per person, per tent, and per car, plus 7% IVA). **Camping Alph** (tel. 695 80 69) hides on a shady site 12.4km down the Ctra. de Andalucía in Getafe From the Legazpi Metro station take bus #447, which stops next to the Nissan dealership (every 30min. until 10pm, 10min.). Ask the driver to let you off at the pedestria overpass near the Amper building. After crossing the bridge, take an enchantin, 1.5km walk back toward Madrid along the edge of the busy highway. Alpha has pool (590ptas per person and car, 640ptas per tent; plus IVA). Both campground could pass as autonomous cities: each has phones, hot showers, washers and dryer, safes, currency exchange, medical care, a playground, a bar, and a restaurant.

■ Food

In Madrid, it's not hard to fork it down without forking over too much, and betwee *churro*-laden breakfasts, two-hour lunches, *meriendas* (snacks), dinner, and *tapa* it's a wonder Madrid gets anything done at all—if it weren't for the *movil* (cellul:

phones), Madrid wouldn't function. You can't walk a block without tripping over at least five *cafeterías*, where a sandwich, coffee, and dessert sell for around 600ptas. Fresh produce in Madrid's center is scarce. There's **Mercado San Miguel,** listed below, as well as some fruit stands north of Sol, in Pl. Carmen, but neighborhood markets lie in residential areas like Argüelles. Vegetarians may shrink a size: this book alone lists most of the vegetarian restaurants available. For a full meal at a *restaurante* or *casa,* one step up from the hegemonic *cafetería,* expect to spend at least 1100ptas. Keep in mind the following essential buzz words for quicker, cheaper *madrileño* fare: *bocadillo* (a sandwich on hard role 350-400ptas); *sandwich* (a sandwich on sliced bread, ask for it *a la plancha* if you want it grilled, 300ptas); *croissant* (with ham and cheese 250ptas); *ración* (a large *tapa* served with bread 300-600ptas); and *empanada* (a puff pastry with tuna, hake, or other fillings 200-300ptas). See the **Glossary of Food Terms** (p. 688) for additional useful translations.

In general, *restaurantes* open from 1 to 4pm and 8pm to midnight; in the following listings, such is the case unless otherwise noted. More casual establishments such as *mesones, cafeterías, bares, cafés, terrazas,* and *tabernas* serve drinks and foodstuffs all day until midnight; some are closed on Sundays. For a nibble pop into a **Rodilla,** an all-purpose food chain. It's green (in color) and sells sticky tarts, 85ptas sandwiches, coffee, and croissants for about 100ptas. There's one in Pl. Callao (C. Preciados, 25) and another in Argüelles, on C. Princesa near El Corte Inglés. Open Mon.-Sat. 8:30am-10:30pm, Sun. 9am-10:30pm. (Delivery tel. 544 88 28. 300ptas service charge for orders less than 1500ptas. Delivery 11am-4pm and 5:30-10pm.)

Groceries: **%Dia** and **Simago** are the cheapest city-wide supermarket chains. More expensive are **Mantequerías Leonesas, Expreso,** and **Jumbo.** Every **El Corte Inglés** has a huge food market with an excellent selection, located either on the basement or top floor (open Mon.-Sat. 10am-9:30pm; see **Practical Information,** p. 75 for addresses).

Markets: **Mercado de San Miguel,** a covered market on Pl. San Miguel, off the northwest corner of Pl. Mayor, sells the finest seafood and produce in the city at high prices. There's a **%Dia** right behind it (San Miguel open Mon.-Fri. 9am-2pm and 5:30-8pm, Sat. 9am-3pm). **Mercado de la Cebada** is a less expensive covered market, at the intersection of C. Toledo and C. San Francisco. Open Mon.-Sat. 8am-2pm and 5:30-8pm. **Mercado Antón Martín** is just south of M: Antón Martín. Open Mon.-Sat. 8am-2pm and 6-8pm.

Specialty Shops: Excellent pastry shops abound in Madrid's streets. The sublime **Horno La Santiaguesa,** C. Mayor, 73, hawks everything from *roscones de reyes* (sweet bread for the Feast of the Epiphany) to *empanadas* to chocolate and candy. Open Mon.-Sat. 8am-9pm, Sun. 8am-8pm. **Horno San Onofre,** C. San Onofre, 4, off C. Fuencarral, serves sumptuous fruit tarts and *suspiros de modistilla* (seamstress's sighs), a *madrileño* specialty (open Mon.-Sat. 9am-9pm, Sun. 9am-8pm). A super mouth-watering, tooth-rotting candy store is **Carmelos Paco,** C. Toledo, 53 (tel. 365 42 58). **El Gourmet de Cuchilleros,** just through Pl. Mayor's Arco de Cuchilleros, is a gourmet store stocking Spanish jams, honey, candy, and cheese. For goofy mugs and **Velveeta,** try **Taste of America,** Po. Castellana, 28 (tel./fax 435 70 39), an American grocery store also offering barbecue and Tex-mex products, and brownie mix. Open Mon.-Sat. 10am-9pm, Sun. 10:30am-9pm.

Red Eye Establishments: *Guía del Ocio* lists late-night eateries under *Cenar a última hora.* **VIPS: Gran Vía, 43** (tel. 542 15 78; M: Callao); **Serrano, 41** (M: Serrano); the deluxe version at **C. Princesa, 5** (M: Ventura Rodríguez), or any of the other orange-sign branches around the city are late-night options. Everything from sandwiches to full dinners served, with an American twist—in other words, its a diner with cushioned booths, serving Hawaiian Burgers and Cheese Fries. The food is average and the prices are a tad high. VIPS also carries English books and magazines, records, chocolate, and canned food. Open daily 9am-3am. **7-Eleven** stores are scattered about in Ópera, Alonso Martinez (C. Mejía Lequerida), and Av. America, selling **Don Simón** *sangría* for about 169ptas. Sweet *sangría.* **Hot & Cool,** C. Gaztambide, in Mocloa-Argüelles, stays cool and hot with fresh *bocadillos de lomo y queso* (450ptas) until 3am on weekends.

SOL AND PLAZA MAYOR

Choose carefully, although you'll inevitably pay for ambience. This area is overrun by tourists, *típico* fare abounds, and prices run fairly steep. Cruise to nearby Pl. Santa Ana for better deals, but don't miss the Museo del Jamón.

Museo del Jamón, C. San Jerónimo, 6 (tel. 521 03 46). M: Sol. Five other much-loved locations throughout the city, including one on Gran Vía. If for some reason the pork perfume and the in-your-face slabs of *jamón serrano* are rattling your nerves, head upstairs to the dining room (opens at 1pm). Succulent Iberian ham is served up in any and every form your piggish little heart could possibly desire: *bocadillo* (200ptas), *chiquito* (100ptas), *croissant* (200ptas), *ración* (550ptas). *Tapas maestro* and cold, frothy mugs of Mahou beer. It's noisy by sundown. Open Mon.-Sat. 9am-12:30am, Sun. 10am-12:30am. Visa, AmEx.

El Estragón, Costanilla de S. Andrés, 10 (tel. 365 89 82), Pl. Raja . M: La Latina. Uphill off C. Segovia, facing La Capilla del Obispo. **Vegetarian** food that will make die-hard meat-eaters reconsider. Delicious platefuls of beautiful food; give a go at the zesty lentil salad (with yogurt sauce), included in the *menú* (1000-1500ptas).

Lhardy, C. San Jerónimo, 8 (tel. 521 33 85), at C. Victoria. M: Sol. 1839-style dining at 2039-style prices in one of Madrid's oldest restaurants. The 3600ptas house specialty *cocido* is guarded by uniformed men. Former Prime Minister Felipe González comes here on occasion for power lunches. Budget hounds congregate in the ground floor store for cognac, sherry, *consomé* (200ptas each), and the best hors d'oeuvres in town. Gourmet foodstuffs for sale. Open Mon.-Sat. 1-3:30pm and 9-11:30pm, Sun. 1-3:30pm. Visa, MC, AmEx.

Casa Botín, C. Cuchilleros, 17 (tel. 366 42 17). Looks, smells, and is expensive—but in a good way. Four floors of *comedores* (each with its own name) are guaranteed to make you gasp in delight and sigh romantically, and spending 4080ptas on the *menú* (which includes the house specialty—*cochinillo asado*) will stuff your pidgeon. The best restaurant in Madrid, and maybe all of Spain, and worth the ducats. Founded in 1725, it's the **oldest restaurant in the whole wide world,** according to Guiness. Hemingway loved it, and wrote about in *A clean, well-lighted place*. Reservations recommended.

Taqueria La Calaca, C. Fuentes, 3 (tel. 541 74 23), off C. Arenal. M: Sol. Save yourself a flight to Mexico. Delicious nachos (their specialty) 875ptas. Tamales 800ptas. Entrees 1150ptas. Open till 1am.

Restaurante-Cafetería Sabatini, C. Bailén, 15 (tel. 547 92 40), opposite the Sabatini Gardens which are next to the Palacio Real. M: Ópera. Come at sunset and bring a date—sidewalk tables face some of Madrid's most famous (and romantic) sights. Portly portions of *paella* (900ptas) and garlic chicken (900ptas). *Menú* 1300ptas. Open daily 9am-1am. Dinner served 8pm-midnight.

Can Punyetes, C. Señores de Luzón, 5 (542 09 21), off C. Mayor. M: Ópera. Simpl Catalan cuisine. Locals gather here for *tostadas* (grilled meat, pâtés, and cheese on toast). A/C. Average meal 1500ptas, *menú* 1350ptas. Open Mon.-Sat. 1-4pm an 8pm-midnight.

SANTA ANA

Plaza Santa Ana is a favorite spot to kill a couple hours with a beverage and a snack It's green, shady, and generally a happy place. Unlike Puerta del Sol, you might s next to a real live Spanish person. **Calles Echegaray, Ventura de la Vega,** and **Man uel Fernández González** are the budget streets. Quality is high and prices are low.

Gula Gula, C. Infantes, 5 (tel. 420 29 19) off C. Echegaray, near C. Huertas. M: Antó Martin. Food is fun! This place has lost its mind. Your waiter/waitress may be wear ing a bikini. All you can eat from the exotic salad bar 1500ptas (the banana dish particularly delectable). *Spectáculos* Sun. at 11pm might include storytellers drag queens. Open until 3am. Another Gula Gula is at on Gran Via, 1, near Accacá (tel. 522 8764). Make reservations on weekends.

Mesón La Caserola, C. Echegaray, 3 (tel. 429 39 63), off C. San Jerónimo. M: Sol. Bustling, crowded joint serves a solid *menú* (975-1500ptas) to ravenous locals. Despite its proximity to Sol, La Caserola's prices and atmosphere remain more *madrileño* than *turístico.* Also serves breakfast, *tapas,* and hefty bocadillo-and-beer combos named after relatives (you can eat your *suegra,* or mother-in-law, the form of pork loin and lettuce). A/C. Many entrees around 900ptas. Open Tues.-Sun. until 1:30am, Mon. opens at noon.

Restaurante Integral Artemisa, C. Ventura de la Vega, 4 (tel. 429 50 92), off C. San Jerónimo. M: Sol. Tasty **veggie** food unspoiled by nicotine (no smoking). Its sibling, off the Gran Vía (Tres Cruces, 4, tel. 521 8721), is even more politically correct. All proceeds from Wed. dinners go to humanitarian organizations. Salads 800-1100ptas. Entrees 995-1350ptas. *Menú* 1200ptas. Non-vegetarian entrees 1150-1350ptas. A/C. Visa.

Taberna D'a Queimada, C. Echegaray, 17 (tel. 429 32 63), 1 block down from C. San Jerónimo. M: Sol. Little nuggets and knickknacks from all over Spain. A cauldron of *paella* waits by the door. *Menú* 975ptas. Entrees 900-2700ptas. Across the street and closer to C. San Jerónimo is the nearly identical **Taberna D'a Queimada II,** under the same management. A/C.

Roma Ristorante Pizzería, C. Núñez de Arce, 14 (tel. 521 53 35), off Pl. Santa Ana. M: Sol. A pleasant, family-owned refuge from Spanish cuisine. Fun, comfortable seating. Pizzas 775-950ptas. Pasta 750-950ptas. Entrees 1100-1950ptas. Salads 575-900ptas. Visa, MC.

LAVAPIÉS-LA LATINA-ATOCHA

The neighborhoods south of Sol, bounded by C. Atocha and C. Toledo, are residential and working class. No caviar or champagne here, but plenty of *menús* for around 1000ptas. A la carte is often a better bargain. *Bocadillo* joints along **C. Santa Isabel,** by Madrid-Atocha and the Reina Sofía, slap together greasy sandwiches and garlicky *tapas* at scrumptious prices.

El Granero de Lavapiés, C. Argumosa, 10 (tel. 467 76 11). M: Lavapiés, off the plaza. Old world charm and new world food on a tranquil tree-lined street. Gazpacho 475ptas. Vegetarian *menú* 1200ptas. Open for lunch Sun.-Fri. 1-4pm.

La Farfalla, C. Santa María, 17 (tel. 369 46 91). M: Antón Martín, 1 block south following C. Huertas. La Farfalla's specialty is Argentine-style grilled meat (1100-1750ptas), but true love is one unforgettable mouthful of their thin-crust pizza: *erótica* or *exquisita* 700ptas. Pastas 625-850ptas. Open for dinner Sun.-Thurs. until 3am, Fri.-Sat. until 4am.

La Biotika, C. Amor de Diós, 3 (tel. 429 07 90), at C. Santa María. An intimate haven for the **tofu**-deprived. Wide selection from the macrobiotic *carta* served until 11:30pm. *Menú* (1100ptas) served until midnight. Open for lunch 1-4:30pm.

Cafetería-Restaurante El Encinar del Bierzo, C. Toledo, 82 (tel. 366 23 89). M: La Latina. Recent renovations now match the quality of the food. House specialties: *conejo al ajillo* (rabbit with garlic 2000ptas) and *gambas a la plancha* (fried shrimp 1100ptas). *Menú* 1300ptas, *del día* (daytime only) 1100ptas. Closed Wed.

GRAN VÍA

If you came to Spain to escape the Power of the Big Mac, run away from the Gran Vía. Luckily, **C. Fuencarral** is lined with cheap *mesones.*

Costa Del Sol, (tel. 52202 82 or 531 01 79) M: Gran Vía. Opposite C. Valverde. A well-kept secret. Its worn front hides a ship-shape restaurant with deliciously inexpensive meat and loads of it. Salads 250-450ptas. Carnes 400-875ptas. Lunchtime *menú* 1000ptas.

Mesón Altamar, C. Luna, 28 (tel. 521 03 51), off C. San Bernardo, which is off Gran Vía. M: Santo Domingo. Fried fish amid high seas decor. House specialty *calamares mexicanos* (Mexican squid). *Paella* Thurs. and Sun. *Menú* 875ptas.

MADRID

Restaurante-Cafetería El Valle, C. Fuencarral, 8. M: Gran Vía. Local shoppers and businessfolk make it a midday hideaway in the cozy back room. Many a *pulpo* (octopus) dish. *Raciones* 250-1300ptas. *Menú* 1050-1750ptas.

CHUECA

The fantastically gay district, where the only thing in the closet is a cabaret of clothes and glam, glam, glam. Lots of good places to wine and dine, especially the former.

El 26 de Libertad, C. Libertad, 26 (tel. 522 25 22), off C. las Infantas. The lunchtime *menú* (1250ptas) is spectacular. In a restaurant designed like an art gallery, where entrees average 1800ptas, one would expect the food to be pretty good. Rest assured. Dinner *menú* is double the price.

Nabucco, C. Hortaleza, 108 (tel. 410 06 11), a few blocks off Pl. Santa Bárbara. M: Alonso Martínez or Chueca. Upscale clientele, excellent food, and affordable prices, all with a burnt-orange backdrop, inspired by the dirt of Sevilla's Plaza de Toros and a chorus of seductive cupids. Pizzas 640-870ptas. Pasta 690-910ptas. Salads 370-755ptas. Visa, MC, AmEx, DC.

La Carreta, C. Barbieri, 10 (tel. 532 70 42 or 521 60 97), off C. las Infantas. M: Gran Vía or Chueca. Specializes in Argentine, Uruguayan, and Chilean meals; lots of meat on wooden platters. If your budget allows it, try the delicious Martín Fierro dessert (890ptas), named after the Argentine national novel, or skip dessert and hit the Tango. Classes and performances offered Mon.-Tues. 7pm. Performances from 8:30pm-5am on weekends. Lunch *menú* 1500ptas. Entrees around 900ptas. *Menú* 1500ptas. Visa, MC, AmEx, DC.

Taberna Carmencita, C. San Marcos, 36 (tel. 531 66 12), on the corner with C. Libertad. M: Chueca. Popular with tourists and businesspeople, this classic restaurant, founded in 1850, evokes pre-Civil War Madrid: brass fixtures, black and white photos of bullfighters, polychrome glazed tiles, lace curtains, and iron and marble tables. *Menú* 1300ptas, but doesn't include 7% IVA. Lunchtime *menú* 1070ptas includes IVA. Excellent house wines. Entrees 900-2600ptas. Visa, MC, AmEx, DC.

Restaurante Zara, C. las Infantas, 5 (tel. 532 20 74), off C. Hortaleza. M: Gran Vía. An island of colorful and delicious Cuban cuisine. Daily "tropical" specials 1400ptas. Meat entrees 700-1100ptas. Closed Sat.-Sun. Visa, MC, AmEx, DC.

Chez Pomme, C. Pelayo, 4 (tel. 532 16 46), off C. Augusto Figueroa. M: Chueca. **Vegetarian** food and a pretty good *menú* 950ptas. Salads 650-900ptas. Entrees 700-800ptas. Closed Sun.

Tienda de Vinos, C. Augusto Figueroa, 35 (tel. 521 70 12), off C. Hortaleza. M: Chueca. Look for the red doors facing Mercado de San Antón. Once a major leftist hangout, now a good place for cheap food. Entrees 400-800ptas.

MALASAÑA

Streets radiating from **Plaza 2 de Mayo** drown in a sea of *cafeterías,* bars, restaurants, and pubs. **Calle San Andrés** is the most densely populated, but **Calles San Bernardo** and **Manuela Malasaña,** on the fringes of this neighborhood, shouldn't be overlooked. Many spots here are more imaginative in their cuisine and setting than those serving "regional specialties" and more likely to offer vegetarian options. Watch the colorful characters who fill the maze of tiny streets; watch them closely after dark.

La Gata Flora, C. Dos de Mayo, 1, and across the street at C. San Vicente Ferrer, 3 (tel. 521 20 20 or 521 27 92). M: Noviciado or Tribunal. Huge servings. Pizzas and pastas 825-1000ptas. Luscious, verdant salads 550-700ptas. *Sangría* 600-900ptas. Open Sun.-Thurs. 2-4pm and 8:30-midnight, Fri.-Sat. until 1am. Visa, MC, DC.

La Granja Restaurante Vegetariano, C. San Andrés, 11 (tel. 532 87 93), off Pl. 2 de Mayo. M: Tribunal. Candles and incense for a romantic vegetarian encounter. Salads 650ptas. Entrees like *arroz con algas* (rice with seaweed) 600-750ptas. Lunch *menú* 900ptas. Closed Tues. Visa.

El Restaurante Vegetariano, C. Marqués de Santa Ana, 34, off Pl. Juan Pujol on the corner with C. Espíritu Santo. M: Tribunal. Another sanctuary for vegetarians

though smaller and a tad pricier than La Granja. Homemade bread. Soups 500-600ptas. Salad bar 550-775ptas. Main dishes 1000ptas. Closed Mon. Visa, MC.

BEYOND BILBAO

The area north of Glorieta de Bilbao (M: Bilbao) in the V formed by **Calles Fuencarral** and **Luchana,** and including **Plaza de Olavide,** is swarming with bars, clubs, cafes, and restaurants. Most bars and *mesones* purvey splendid, cheap *tapas* to feed an energized crowd that cruises the streets come evening. Lunch gets pricier farther north in more gentrified territory.

La Tarterie, C. Cardenal Cisneros, 24 (tel. 593 85 27), right off C. Luchana, which is off Glorieta de Bilbao. M: Bilbao. This restaurant/art gallery likes to consider itself an art gallery/restaurant and features temporary exhibits of experimental art. The not-so-great interior is full of skinny artists. Great quiches (675ptas), salads (650ptas), and pizzas (775-1050ptas).

Pizza Buona, C. Hartzenbusch, 19 (tel. 448 23 87), off C. Cardenal Cisneros, which is just off C. Luchana. M: Bilbao. A patriotic green, red, and white decorated Italian restaurant on a German-named street in the heart of Spain. Tasty pizzas 525-825ptas. A/C.

Bar Samara, C. Cardenal Cisneros, 13. M: Bilbao. Bills itself as Egyptian, but offers Middle Eastern staples. Hummus, baba ghanoush, and tahini salads 475-525ptas. Kabobs and other entrees from 1500ptas. Gets crowded after dark. A/C. Open Sun. and Tues.-Thurs. until midnight, Fri.-Sat. until 1am.

ARGÜELLES

Argüelles is a middle-class *barrio* near the Ciudad Universitaria. It's full of inexpensive markets, moderately priced restaurants, and unshaven neighborhood bars.

Cáscaras, C. Ventura Rodríguez, 7 (tel. 542 83 36). M: Ventura Rodríguez. Sleek interior that kind of looks like a tortilla, which, coincidentally, is also what they serve (725-955ptas). *Cáscaras* are eggshells. Vegetarian dishes 675-975ptas. *Tortillas* 745-955ptas. Salads 675-850ptas. Breakfast and non-vegetarian fare as well. Popular for *tapas, pinchos,* and ice-cold Mahou beer in the early afternoon and evening. The Fugees ate here.

La Crêperie, Po. Pintor Rosales, 28 (tel. 548 23 58). M: Ventura Rodríguez. Affordable crepes on the chic Po. Rosales (has *terraza*). Menus covered with Cupids and grease. Salty crepes 515-670ptas. Dessert crepes 360-625ptas. Coffee 135ptas. Open Sun.-Thurs. until 1am, Fri.-Sat. until 1:30am. Not open for breakfast.

Ristorante Capriccio, C. Rodriguez San Pedro, 66 (tel. 549 91 16). M: Argüelles. Exit at C. Alberto Aguilera. Italian countryside meets urban pastel decor. Fresh pasta 800-1000ptas. Gourmet pizzas 700-1000ptas. Open until midnight. Delivery. A/C. Visa, MC, AmEx.

TAPAS

Not so long ago, bartenders in Madrid used to cover *(tapar)* drinks with saucers to keep the flies out. Later, servers began putting little sandwiches on top of the saucers, and there you have it: *tapas.* Hopping from bar to bar gobbling *tapas* is an active alternative to a full sit-down meal, and a fun way to try random food you would never dream of putting near your mouth. Most *tapas* bars (a.k.a. *tascas* or *tabernas*) are open noon-4pm and 8pm-midnight or later. Some double as restaurants, like **Museo del Jamón,** and cluster around **Plaza Mayor** (tourist alert!) and **Plaza Santa Ana,** which is very hip on Sunday.

La Toscana, C. Manuel Fernández González, 10-17 (tel. 429 60 31), on the corner with C. Ventura de la Vega. M: Sol. Friendly *mesón* with a friendly bull's head and dangling crockery. Beautiful *tapas* like *morcilla* (250ptas). Jam-packed on weekends. Open Thurs.-Tues. noon-4pm and 8pm-midnight.

MADRID

La Trucha, C. Nuñez de Arce, 6 (tel. 532 08 82). M: Sol. Cramped but cheap, and popular with locals. Open Mon.-Sat. 12:30-4pm and 8pm-midnight.

El Anciano Rey de los Vinos, C. Bailén, 19 (tel. 248 50 52), 1 block from where C. Mayor hits C. Bailén. M: Sol. A bright, lofty-ceilinged bar, with cider on tap and a wide selection of house wines. Open Thurs.-Tues. 10am-3pm and 5:30-11:30pm.

La Chuleta, C. Echegaray, 20 (tel. 429 37 29). Spacious and modern with psychotic hours. Savory *tortillas, calamares* (squid), and peppers. Open Sun.-Thurs. 9am-3am, Fri.-Sat. 9am-5am. AmEx and traveler's checks accepted.

Los Caracoles, Pl. de Cascorro, 18 (tel. 365 94 39). M: La Latina. Use whatever money wasn't stolen during El Rastro to dine on *caracoles* (snails, 675ptas) in the company of old men and one particularly loud one (the owner). Open daily 10:30am-4pm and 7-11:30pm.

La Princesita, C. Princesa, 80 (tel. 545 70 71). M: Argüelles. Finding a seat is nearly impossible, but bar fare is cheaper anyway. Specialties are *queso de Cabrales* (goat cheese 100ptas) and their *empanada asturiana* (250ptas). Open daily 10am-11:30pm.

CLASSIC CAFES

Coffee at these places is expensive (200-450ptas), but the price includes atmosphere. It's customary to linger for an hour or two in these historic cafes and can actually be an economical way to soak up a little of Madrid's culture (and a lot of secondhand smoke).

Café Círculo de Bellas Artes, C. Alcalá, 42 (tel. 531 77 00). M: Banco de España. Tourists rest weary museum feet outside (no cover charge there). For 100ptas cover you can lounge on leather couches beneath high, frescoed, ceilings among nude sculptures and clothed sculptors from the Círculo. Coffee or tea 200ptas inside. The 100ptas also lets you see temporary exhibitions, and you'll feel like a real-live artist. Cover 100ptas.

Café Gijón, Po. Recoletos, 21 (tel. 521 54 25). M: Colón. On its 100th anniversary in 1988, the Ayuntamiento designated Gijón an historic site, easing the blow of the expensive coffee (300ptas). If you want to get something to eat, forget about sending your kids to college. Choose between a breezy terrace and a smoky bar-restaurant. Marble tables, white-uniformed waiters. Long a favorite of the literati. Open daily 9am-1:30am.

Café de Oriente, Pl. Oriente, 2 (tel. 547 15 64). M: Ópera. A beautiful, old-fashioned cafe catering to a ritzy older crowd. Spectacular view of the Palacio Real from the *terraza,* especially at night when the palace is spotlighted. Quite pricey (coffee on the terrace is 400ptas, entrees start at 1500ptas)—so sneak a lot of free peeks at the palace. Open daily 8:30am-1:30am.

Nuevo Café Barbieri, C. Av. María, 45 (527 36 58). M: Lavapiés. Intellectuals lurk here, fingering stiff drinks and specialty coffees on balding velvet cushions. Art films some nights in the back room—pick up a schedule. Drinks 500-600ptas.

Café Comercial, Glorieta de Bilbao, 7 (tel. 531 34 52). M: Bilbao. Traditional cafe with high ceilings and huge mirrors. Frequented by artists and Republican aviators. Anti-Franco protests started here. Plays host to frequent *tertulias* (gatherings of literati and intellectuals). A/C. Sandwiches from 200ptas. Beer 300ptas. Open 8am-2am, Fri.-Sat. until 3am.

■ Sights

You need good shoes to walk around in.

—A shoemaker

Madrid, large as it may seem, is a walker's city. It has a fantastic public transportation system but you should use it as little as possible. In fact, the word *paseo* refers to a major avenue—like *Paseo de la Castellna* or *Paseo del Prado*—but it more literally means a "stroll." We recommend that you do just that from Sol to Cibeles and from the Plaza Mayor to the Palacio Real and sights will kindly introduce themselves. The city's art and architecture and its culture and air will convince you heartily that it was once the capital of the world's greatest empire. Madrid is a lounger's city, too—i

offers some of the world's best places to stop strolling. When you're panting for a break after perusing the Triángulo de Arte or suffering from *resaca* after a rough night in Chueca, you can head for Schweppes and shade at the Parque del Retiro.

For psycho sightseers with a checklist of destinations, the municipal tourist office's *Plano de Transportes* map, marking monuments as well as bus and Metro lines, is indispensable. For the rest, it's just damn useful. In the following pages, sights are arranged by a combination of geographical location and historical consistency. The first section, Puerta del Sol, is the heart of the city. Four of the eight neighborhoods that follow—Madrid de los Austrias, Madrid de los Borbones, Huertas, and Gran Vía—bud directly off Sol. A walking tour of any of those five areas can naturally begin there. Prado-Recoletos, Retiro, and Argüelles-Moncloa are each just a step away from Sol, bridged to the magnificent plaza by one of the other four zones. El Pardo falls last, and buses destined for its palace and pastures leave from the penultimate neighborhood, Moncloa.

PUERTA DEL SOL

Kilómetro 0—the origin of six national highways fanning out to the rest of Spain—marks the figurative and definitive center of the country in the most chaotic of Madrid's infinite plazas, **Puerta del Sol.** Sol races all day and night with taxis and pickpockets, lottery vendors and newsstands. The sunset here is spectacular, as the Tío Pepe sign begins to glow. A web of pedestrian-only tributaries originating at the Gran Vía lead a rush of consumers down a gallery of shoe boutiques and department stores and funnel them into Puerta del Sol. The broad alleyways culminate at **El Oso y el Madroño,** the bronze symbol of Madrid and the city's universal meeting place. Sol saw its greatest moment when *madrileños* triumphantly preserved their nation from the throes of Napoleon in 1808. The Frenchman struck a nerve when his plan to kidnap the royal children leaked, sparking the city to revolt. Two of Goya's paintings in the Prado, *El dos de mayo* (May 2, 1808) and *Los fusilamientos del tres de mayo* (The Execution of the Rioters: May 3, 1808), commemorate the episode. On New Year's Eve, citizens congregate in Sol to gobble a dozen grapes as the clock strikes midnight, one per strike. Literally the "Sun's Gateway," the giant plaza derives its name from an old gateway to the Alcázar that faced the Orient.

MADRID DE LOS AUSTRIAS

Also known as Habsburg Madrid and Old Madrid, the center of the city is most densely packed with monuments and tourists. The Habsburgs (1516-1700) built the Plaza Mayor and the Catedral de San Isidro from scratch, but many of Old Madrid's buildings date much earlier than the 16th century, some to the age of the Moors (c. 860-1086). After Phillip II moved the seat of Castile from Toledo to Madrid in 1561 (pop. 20,000), he and his descendants commissioned the court's architects to update many of these edifices to fit the latest mode, like the Iglesia de San Francisco el Grande's upgrade to Neoclassicism. Plaza de la Villa is the last sight listed, but you may wish to design your own walking tour of Habsburg Madrid to begin there. Geographically, it fits more snugly into a tour of Madrid de los Borbones (see p. 93), but for historical consistency it belongs with Madrid de los Austrias.

La Latina: Plaza Mayor to Puerta de Toledo

With lances of exaggerated length, 17th-century nobles on horseback spent Sunday afternoon chasing bulls in the **Plaza Mayor** (M: Sol). The nobility had such a jolly time giving a go at it that eventually everyone joined in the fun; on foot, and with sticks, running hither and thither after those pesky bulls. The tradition came to be known as the *corrida,* from the verb *correr* (to run), which is why bullfights and Pamplona-like street frenzies are called *corridas de toros.* When tired, the commoners would relax and enjoy a good public execution. The plaza, like Sol, is an easy orientation point for any walking expedition through Madrid. It is elegantly arcaded and topped with Habsburg' *herrerense* (after Juan de Herrera, architect of El Escorial) black slate roofs,

spindly towers, and iron verandas. These properties would define "Madrid-style" architecture and inspire every peering *balcón* constructed in Spain and abroad. The plaza was completed in 1620 for Felipe III. His statue, installed in 1847, graces Pl. Mayor's center. Towards evening, *madrileños* resurface, tourists multiply, and cafe tables fill with lively patrons. During the annual **Fiesta de San Isidro** (May 15-22), the plaza explodes. The plaza's surrounding streets, especially those through the **Arco de los Cuchilleros** on the southwest corner of the Plaza, house old specialty shops and renowned *mesones,* where you can enjoy garlicky *tapas* and pitchers of *sangría* in a festive, albeit touristy, atmosphere.

Just east of Pl. Mayor via **Calle de Gerona, Plaza de Santa Cruz** cradles **the Palacio de Santa Cruz,** a former prison. The palace's alternation of red brick and granite corners and black-slate towers exemplify the Habsburg style.

The **Catedral de San Isidro** (M: Latina) commemorates Madrid's patron saint on C. Toledo, directly south off Pl. Mayor. Pedro Sánchez, Francisco Bautista, and Juan de Harro designed the cathedral in Jesuit Baroque style at the beginning of the 17th century. San Isidro's remains landed here in 1769. It reigned as the cathedral of Madrid from the late 19th century until the Catedral de la Almudena was consecrated in 1993. In 1936, rioting workers burned the exterior; it has since been restored (open for mass only; see p. 93 for cathedral hours). Continuing down C. Toledo, turn right on the **Carrera de San Francisco** (M: Latina) and pass the **Mercado de la Cebada** on your left. Turn right up Cost. San Andrés to see the **Iglesia de San Andrés** (open for mass only). Mussulmans originally constructed the Gothic-Mudéjar red brick and granite building as a mosque. Its 17th-century overhaul infused Baroque intricacies and posited the sarcophagus of San Isidro in the **Capilla de San Isidro.** The **Museo de San Isidro** sits next door. Francisco Giralte designed San Andrés's polychrome alabaster. Continuing up Cost. San Andrés, the mannerist **Capilla del Obispo** will greet you with its imposition. The chapel is a remnant of the **Vargas Palace.** Giralte designed its Renaissance portals and the tombs of Madrid's elite Vargas family. The palace forms the upper left corner of **Plaza de la Paja** (straw square), Madrid's main square and grain distributor during the Middle Ages, when Mudéjar Muslims inhabited the area. From Pl. Paja, turn left on C. Redondilla and take the third right after Pl. Granado Redondilla onto C. Don Pedro. Crossing C. Bailén and continuing along C. Don Pedro will take you to Pl. Gabriel Miró and the **Parque de las Vistillas** (so called for the tremendous *vistillas,* or little views of Palacio Real, Nuestra Señora de la Almudena, and the countryside).

Doubling back along C. Don Pedro, turn right on C. Bailén to reach the **Plaza de San Francisco** and its **Iglesia de San Francisco el Grande** (St. Francis of Assisi), whose most outstanding feature is its Neoclassical facade. Carlos III commissioned the fructiferous Francisco Sabitini, the third of four architects to work on the church since its origination in the 12th century, to reconstruct the facade in its present form (M: Puerta de Toledo or Latina). Inside, Goya's *Saint Bernard of Siena Preaching* hangs alongside Velázquez's *Aparition of the Virgen before Saint Anthony* (open in summer Tues.-Sat. 11am-1pm and 5-8pm). St. Francis himself allegedly built a convent next door in the 13th century, where the **Capilla de Cristo de los Dolores** stands today. Follow Gran Vía de San Francisco downhill to reach Pl. Puerta de Toledo where the **biblioteca publica** resides. Across the plaza sprawls the **Mercado de Puerta de Toledo,** inside is the **tourist office.**

Past the Pta. de Toledo, the **Río Manzanares,** Madrid's notoriously dinky river snakes its way around the city. But the broad Baroque **Puerta de Toledo** makes up for the river's inadequacies. Sandstone carvings on one side of the bridge depict San Isidro rescuing his son from a well, and his wife Santa María de la Cabeza on the other. Renaissance **Puente de Segovia,** which fords the river from C. Segovia, was conceived by Juan de Herrera, the talented designer of El Escorial. Both bridges afford gorgeous views (and fertile ground for the blossoming of young love).

Plaza de la Villa

When Felipe II made Madrid the capital of his empire in 1561, most of the town huddled between Pl. Mayor and the Palacio Real, stretching north to today's Ópera and south to Pl. Puerta de Moros. Only a handful of medieval buildings remain, but the labyrinthine layout is unmistakable. **Plaza de la Villa**—west of Pl. Mayor on C. Mayor—marks the heart of what was old Madrid. The **Torre de los Lujanes,** a 15th-century building on the eastern side of the plaza (left side if looking from C. Mayor), is the sole remnant of the once lavish residence of the Lujanes family. Note the original horseshoe-shaped Gothic door on C. Codo (there aren't many examples of Gothic-Mudéjar left in Madrid). Across the plaza, the characteristically Habsburg 17th-century **Ayuntamiento** (Casa de la Villa) on the plaza was both the mayor's home and the city jail. As Madrid (and its bureaucracy) grew, officials annexed the neighboring **Casa de Cisneros,** a 16th-century house built in the Plateresque style (Cisneros was the architect).

MADRID DE LOS BORBONES

Weakened by plagues and political losses, the Habsburg era in Spain ended with the death of Carlos II in 1700. Felipe V, the first of Spain's Bourbon Monarchs, ascended the throne in 1714 after the 12-year War of Succession. The Decree of *Nova Plata* (1715), dissolved the remaining Aragonese territories into Castile. The move essentially solidified the territory now known as Spain. Bankruptcy, industrial stagnation, military incompetence, and widespread moral disillusionment compelled Felipe V to embark on a crusade of urban renewal. His successors Fernando VI and Carlos III in the 18th century fervently pursued the same ends with wonderful results.

Ópera

At the end of C. Mayor, the impossibly luxurious **Palacio Real** (M: Ópera) lounges at the western tip of central Madrid, overlooking the **Río Manzanares.** Felipe V commissioned Giovanni Sachetti to replace the burned Alcázar with a palace that would dwarf all others. Sachetti died and Filippo Juvara took over the project, basing his new facade on Bernini's rejected designs for the Louvre. Although only a fragment is complete, it's still one of Europe's most grandiose residences. The shell took 40 years to build and the decoration of its 2000 rooms with 20 square km of tapestry dragged on for a century. The Monarchy abandoned the venture in the war-torn 1930s. To see the collection of porcelain, tapestries, furniture, armor, and art, stroll on your own or take a guided tour (in Spanish, 40min.).

The palace's most impressive rooms include the raucously Rococo **Salón de Gasparini,** with a Mengs ceiling fresco, and the **Salón del Trono** (Throne Room) with a Tiepolo ceiling fresco. Hundreds of ornate timepieces, collected mainly by Carlos IV, are strewn about the palace. The **Real Oficina de Farmacia** (Royal Pharmacy) features crystal and china receptacles used to cut royal dope. The **Biblioteca** shelves first editions of *Don Quijote* and a Bible in the gypsy language Romany. The **Real Armería** (Armory) displays El Cid's swords, the armor of Carlos I and Felipe II, and other instruments of medieval warfare and torture. (Palace open, except during royal visits, Mon.-Sat. 9am-6pm, Sun. 9am-3pm; Oct.-March Mon.-Sat. 9:30am-5pm, Sun. 9am-2pm. 950ptas, students 350ptas, Wed. free for EU citizens. Arrive early to avoid lines.)

Beautiful gardens and parks swathe the Palacio Real. The **Plaza de Oriente** spans the foreground, a semicircular space lined with statues of monarchs. The sculptures were originally intended for the palace roof, but planners feared that the objects would fall off and hit the Queen. To the northwest are the **Jardines de Sabatini,** the park of choice for romantics. King Juan Carlos I opened **Campo del Moro** (facing the canal) to the public only 13 years ago; the view of the palace rising majestically on a dark green slope is straight out of a fairy tale. The **Catedral de Almudena** rises from behind a stone pavilion. The controversy surrounding the cathedral's face-lift after a 30-year hibernation is obvious. Its new psychedelic stained-glass windows clash jarringly with a more conventional altar. (Open Mon.-Fri. 10am-1:30pm and 6-8:45pm, Sun. 10am-2pm and 6-8:45pm, closed during mass.) If relics are your style, the **Con-**

vento de la Encarnación, with 700 saintly bones, awaits just to the north of the Jardines de Sabatini on Pl. Encarnación. Pedro de Ribera's elegant *Ermita de la Virgen del puerto* lies next to the canal, west of the palace.

PRADO-RECOLETOS-CASTELLANA

The most striking feature on any map of Madrid is the one grand avenue that splits the city in two, running from the city's northernmost tip at Madrid-Chamartín to its southern extreme, Madrid-Atocha. Madrid's great thoroughfare is really three fused segments that represent three eras of urban expansion. Carlos III, the city's urban visionary, laid the Paseo del Prado from 1775-1882 to espouse community among the elite. The road connects Atocha to Plaza de Cibeles, passing the Museo del Prado, Thyssen-Bornemisza, and the Ritz along the way. The newest members of the *clase alta* (upper class) congregate at the luxuriously shaded *terrazas* along Paseo de Recoletos, extending from Cibeles to Plaza de Colón. Contemporary Madrid stretches along Paseo de la Castellana, lined with the bank buildings commissioned during the 70s and 80s and culminating with the Puerta de Europa's twin towers. If you're designing a walking tour around central Madrid over the span of a few days, the Castellana sights may be out of reach. Recoletos and Prado combine well with the Huertas section and the Retiro route to form a manageable axis of sights.

Paseo del Prado and Paseo de Recoletos

With virtually every major museum in the vicinity, this "museum mile," or Triángulo de Rate, is the cultural axis of Madrid. Beginning from **Estación de Atocha's** iron-framed atrium, you'll see the ceramic tiles and stained glass of **Ministerial de Agricultura** on Po. Infanta Isabel. Home to Picasso's *Guernica,* the **Centro de Arte Reina Sofía** (p. 100) and its glass-enclosed elevators vogue directly across from the station, on **Plaza Emperador Carlos V.**

Walking up Po. Prado, you'll pass the **Jardín Botánico** on the right. Next to it the **Prado** stands correct, and behind it lies the **Iglesia de San Jerónimo,** built by Hieronymite monks and re-endowed by the Catholic Monarchs. The church has witnessed a few joyous milestones: Fernando and Isabel were crowned here and it saw the marriage of King Alfonso XIII (open 8am-1:30pm and 5-8:30pm). To the north, in Pl. Lealtad, stands the **Obelisco a los Mártires del 2 de Mayo,** filled with the ashes of those who died in the 1808 uprising against Napoleon. Its four statues represent Constance, Virtue, Valor, and Patriotism. Behind the memorial sits the colonnaded Greco-Roman style **Bolsa de Madrid** (Stock Exchange), a work by Repullés, architect of the Vienna Stock Exchange. The Ventura Rodríguez's **Fuente de Neptuno,** in Pl. Cánovas de Castillo, one of three aquatic masterpieces along this avenue.

The tulip-encircled **Fuente de la Cibeles** (Fountain of Cybele) spews water at the intersection of Recoletos and **Calle de Alcalá.** It depicts the fertility goddess's triumphant arrival in a carriage drawn by lions. Myth has it that the fleet-footed Atalanta would only take as her lover the man who could outrun her. No man was up to the challenge until one cunning suitor instructed his cohorts to scatter golden apples in Atalanta's path to distract her from running. The goddess Cibeles, watching the prank, was overcome with wrath at men's evil ways. She punished the plotters—who protested that "she was asking for it"—by turning them into lions, and made them pull her carriage. Madrid residents successfully protected this emblem of their city during Franco's bomb raids by covering it with a pyramid of sandbags.

To the right are the **Museo Naval** (see **Museums,** p. 99) and the eye-popping **Palacio de Telecomunicaciones,** where you can mail your letters in style and waft through its stamp museum. Antonio Palacios and Julián Otamendi of Otto Wagner's Vienna School designed the neo-Baroque structure in 1920. On the northeastern corner of the intersection (behind black gates) is the former **Palacio de Linares,** a 19th century townhouse built for Madrid nobility (M: Banco de España). Long abandoned by its former residents and proven by a team of scientists to be inhabited by ghosts, it was transformed into the **Casa de América,** with a library and lecture halls for the

study of Latin American culture and politics. It sponsors art exhibitions, tours of the palace, and guest lectures, mostly on Latin American subjects.

Continuing north towards the brown **Torres de Colón** (Columbus Towers), you'll pass the **Biblioteca Nacional** (entrance at #20), whose sleek **Museo del Libro** displays treasures from the monarchy's collection, including a first-edition copy of *Don Quijote de la Mancha.* Behind it the lies huge **Museo Arqueológico** (see **Museums,** p. 102), whose collections are managed by Lauro Olmo Enciso. The museum is on **Calle de Serrano,** a thoroughfare lined with expensive boutiques beset in the posh neighborhood **Barrio de Salamanca.**

The museum and library huddle just south of the **Plaza Colón,** where jetlagged moles resurface from the airport bus drop-off to the **Jardines del Descubrimiento** (Gardens of Discovery). Huge clay boulders loom at one side (near C. Serrano), inscribed with odd trivia about the New World, like Seneca's prediction of the discovery, the names of all the mariners on board the caravels, and citations from Columbus's diary. A neo-Gothic monument to Columbus rises from a thundering fountain whose spray can be very refreshing in Madrid's dry summer heat. Concerts, lectures, ballet, and plays are performed in the **Centro Cultural de la Villa** (tel. 575 60 80; M: Colón), beneath the statue and the waterfall.

Paseo de la Castellana

Nineteenth- and early 20th-century aristocrats dislocated themselves from Old Madrid to settle along **Paseo de la Castellana.** During the Civil War, Republican forces used the mansions as soldier's barracks and most were torn down in the 60s by the banks and insurance companies who would commission new and innovative structures in the following decadence. Competition begot architectural excellence, offering the lowly pedestrian a rich man's spectacle of architecture as fashion (rose aluminum with pink glass, pink granite with green glass, and so on). Some notables include Moneo's **Bankinter** at #29, the first to integrate rather than demolish a townhouse; **Banco Urquijo,** known as "the coffeepot"; **Banca Catalana Occidente,** #50, the delicate ice cube on a cracker on Glorieta de Emilio Castelar near the American Embassy; the oh-so-pink **Edificio Bankunion,** #46; **Edificio La Caixa,** #61; and the Sevillian-tiled **Edificio ABC** at #34, the conservative monarchical newspaper's former office.

Just south of the American Embassy, between Pl. Colón and Glorieta de Emilio Castelar and under the C. Juan Bravo overpass is an **Open-air Sculpture Museum** with works by Miró, González, and Chillida (hanging from the bridge).

Much farther north of Pl. Emilio Castelar, look for the **Museo Nacional de Ciencias Naturales** (with cupola). Turning right on C. Juan Bravo you'll find the elaborate **Museo Lázaro Galdiano.** Left on Po. General Martínez Campos is the **Museo Sorolla** (see **Museums,** p. 99). Much, much farther up the street, past Torres Picasso and Europa at **Plaza de Lima,** squats the 110,000-seat **Estadio Santiago Bernabéu** (M: Nuevos Ministerios, Lima, or Cuzco), home to **Real Madrid,** champions of the *Liga Española* in 1997 (for more info, see **Fútbol,** p. 113). Fans of modern skyscraper architecture will get goosebumps at the sight of the **Puerta de Europa,** two 27-story leaning towers connected by a tunnel. American John Bergee designed it to look like a doorway to the city (M: Pl. Castilla).

RETIRO

Felipe IV originally intended the 300-acre **Parque del Buen Retiro** (1630; M: Retiro) to be a *buen retiro* (nice retreat). Before that it was hunting territory, and now it's a place to get your palm read, play a soccer or basketball match, or soak the rays reflecting off the **Estanque Grande,** a rectangular lake in the middle of the park. The lake has been the social center of the Retiro ever since aspiring caricaturists, fortune-tellers, Michael Jackson impersonators, sunflower-seed vendors, and illicit drug vendors (they're the pesky ones hissing at passers-by after sundown at the Monument to Alfonso XII) parked their goods along its marble shore. (Boat rentals open 9:30am-8:30pm, cool paddle boats 550ptas for 4 people, less cool motorboat 150ptas per person.) Ricardo Velázquez built the steel and glass **Palacio de Cristal,** south of the lake

by the boat rental center, to exhibit Philippine flowers; it now hosts a variety of art shows with subjects from Bugs Bunny to Spanish portraiture. (Open Tues.-Sat. 11am-2pm and 5-8pm, Sun. 10am-2pm. Admission varies, but often free.) A few steps away, the **Palacio de Velázquez** (named after the Ricardo; tel. 573 62 45), north of the *estanque*, exhibits works in conjunction with the Museo de Arte Reina Sofía. The northeast corner of the park swells with medieval monastic ruins and waterfalls. At nightfall during the summer (when only the north gate remains open), Retiro becomes a lively bar and cafe hangout; avoid venturing into the park alone after dark.

Bullets from the 1921 assassination of prime minister Eduardo Dato permanently scarred the eastern face of **Puerta de Alcalá** (1778), outside Retiro's Puerta de la Independencia. The imposing five-arch monument honors Carlos III. The area south of C. Alcalá and to the west of Retiro is littered with popular museums. The **Museo Naval** is on Po. Prado, next to the Palacio de Comunicaciones. Farther south, the **Casón del Buen Retiro** faces the park (see p. 100); behind its sits the **Museo del Ejército,** resting place of El Cid's sword (see p. 103). The three buildings are remnants of Felipe IV's palace, which burned down in 1764. South of Retiro, on Av. Alfonso XII, Villanueva's **Observatorio Astronómico** reaches for the stars at the summit of a grassy slope. The 18th-century structure is considered one of the most elegant examples of Spanish Neoclassicism (open Mon.-Fri. 9am-2pm).

HUERTAS

The area east of Puerta del Sol is a wedge bounded by **Calle de Alcalá** to the north, C. Atocha to the south, and Po. Prado to the east. From the wedge's western apex at Sol, a myriad of streets slope downward, outward, and eastward toward various points along Po. Prado. **Carrera de San Jerónimo** splits the wedge a bit north of center, running directly from Sol down to Pl. Cánovas de Castillo. **Plaza de Santa Ana** is nestled below C. Nuñez de Arce and off **Calle del Prado** (not to be confused with Po. Prado).

The grand C. Alcalá leads from Sol's northeast and dips down to Po. Recoletos at Pl. Cibeles before ascending again to the Puerta de Alcalá and Parque del Buen Retiro (see p. 94). Banks inhabit most of its beautiful statue-festooned baroque buildings. The **Círculo de Bellas Artes** (tel. 531 77 00), at #42, has undergone a recent resurgence and is again the gathering place of Madrid's high society of the arts. From the street you can see into its luxurious cafe through its enormous windows. Designed by Antonio Palacios, the building encloses two stages and several salons and studios for lectures and workshops run by prominent artists. Many facilities are for *socios* (members) only, but exhibition galleries for all media are open to the public. If you've a few hours to spare and some spiffy threads stashed away, the extra few hundred *pesetas* will buy you a cup of coffee and reward you with a sublime taste of decadent lifestyle. Also on C. Alcalá is Curriguera and Diego Villanueva's **Museo de la Real Academia de Bellas Artes de San Fernando** (Palacio Gayeneche; see **Museums,** p. 102).

Looping back westwards towards Sol on C. San Jerónimo (off Pl. Neptuno) will take you through the center of Madrid's foregone literary district that saw its heyday during the Siglo de Oro as home to Cervantes, Góngora, Quevedo, Calderón, and Moratín. It returned to literary prominence in the late 19th and early 20th centuries when Hemingway frequented its pubs among other establishments. At #19 is the **Palacio Miraflores,** designed by the premier 18th-century architect, Pedro de Ribera. Ribera's **Palacio del Marqés de Ugena,** C. Príncipe, 28, rises off Cra. San Jerónimo on the left. Follow C. Príncipe downhill to the enchanting **Plaza Santa Ana** and its hopping bar and cafe scene (see p. 86). C. Prado on the southeast (left) side of the plaza leads to the **Ateneo,** C. Prado, 21, a onetime hangout for intellectual Madrid at the close of the 19th century and again during the Second Republic following the Dictatorship of Primo de Rivera. The Ateneo is a private library, but its evening concert and symposia are often open to the public. Two blocks south, at C. Huertas and C. León, Juan de Villanueva's austere **Real Academia de la Historia** houses a magnificent old library of its own. The edifice's red brick and granite exterior exemplifies Madrid-style architecture. Although Golden Age playwright Lope de Vega and Miguel de Cervantes were bitter rivals, the 17th-century **Casa de Lope de Vega** (tel. 429 9

16) is ironically located at C. Cervantes, 11 (off C. León, a few blocks south of C. San Jerónimo). The prolific playwright and poet spent the last 25 years of his life here (open Tues.-Fri. 9:30am-2pm, Sat. 10am-1:30pm; 200ptas, students free). Odder still, Cervantes is purportedly buried on C. Lope de Vega.

GRAN VÍA AND CHUECA

Gran Vía

Urban planners paved the Gran Vía in 1910 to link **Calle de Princesa** with Cibeles. After Madrid won new riches as a neutral supplier during World War I, the city funneled its earnings into developing the Gran Vía into one of the world's great thoroughfares. At its highest elevation in **Plaza de Callao** (M: Callao), the Gran Vía branches southward onto C. Postigo San Martín, where you'll find the famed **Convento de las Descalzas Reales** (**Museums,** p. 99). Returning to Pl. Callao and proceeding westward (left facing the conspicuous Sex Shop), the Gran Vía makes its descent toward **Plaza de España** (M: Pl. España), where a row of olive trees surrounds a grandiose **Monumento a Cervantes.** Next to the plaza are two of Madrid's tallest skyscrapers, the **Telefónica** (1929) and the **Edificio de España** (1953). Louis S. Weeks of the Chicago School designed the former, which was the tallest concrete building in existence at the time (81m). Franco built the *edificio* and its 32 elevators in a boastful gesture toward the rest of the world (there's a **cafe** on the 26th; 100ptas cover). Tucked between the two skyscrapers on C. San Leonardo is crafty little **Iglesia de San Marcos,** a Neoclassical church composed of five intersecting ellipses; a Euclidean dream, there's not a single straight line in sight. **Museo de Cerralbo** lingers near Pl. España on C. Ventura Rodríguez (see p. 102).

Chueca

By night, Chueca bristles with Madrid's alternative scene of tourists, immigrants, homosexuals, and the hopelessly fashion conscious in search of a common end—fun. By day, the area between **Calle de Fuencarral** and **Calle de San Bernardo** beholds some of the most avant-garde architecture and current art exhibitions in the city. Bourbon King Fernando VI commissioned the **Iglesia de las Salesas Reales** (1758), Pl. Salesas (M: Colón or Alonso Martínez), at the request of his wife Doña Bárbara. The Baroque-Neoclassical domed church is clad in granite, with facade sculptures by Alfonso Vergaza and a dome painting by the brothers González Velázquez. Its ostentatious facade and interior prompted critics to pun on the queen's name: "Barbaric queen, barbaric tastes, barbaric building, barbarous expense," giving rise to the expression, *"¡qué bárbaro!"* which can exclaim absurdity or extravagance. Bárbara and Fernando are buried in the *iglesia.*

You can double back on C. Fernando VI to see the **Palacio de Longoria** (a.k.a. Sociedad General Autores, or writer's union) for a sleek preview of Barcelonan *modernisme* (M: Tribunal or Alonso Martínez). If you walk one block past C. Hortaleza and turn left, you'll fall in love with the **Museo Romántico** (see p. 103).

ARGÜELLES-MONCLOA

The 19th century witnessed the growth of several neighborhoods around the core of the city, north and northwest of the Palacio Real, and northwest of Pl. España where the Gran Vía becomes C. Princesa. Today, the area known as **Argüelles** and the zone surrounding **Calle San Bernardo** form a cluttered mixture of elegant middle-class and student housing, bohemian hangouts, and cultural activity. Heavily bombarded during the Civil War, Argüelles inspired Chilean poet Pablo Neruda, then a resident, to write *España en el corazón.* Although the area boasts lots of hip stores and innovative restaurants, the areas around Pl. 2 de Mayo are known as Madrid's drug-dealing center. It is always busy, but caution is advised, especially at night.

Parque del Oeste is a large, sloping park north of the Palacio Real cared for by transvestites and full of quiet voyeurs with dogs. All sorts of people flop on the hillsides, but more noteworthy is the **Rosaleda** (rose garden; open 10am-8pm) at the

MADRID

bottom of the park (M: Argüelles or Moncloa). A yearly competition determines which award-winning rose will be added to the permanent collection. Nearby on Po. Pintor Rosales in **Parque de la Montaña** stands the 4th-century BC **Templo de Debod** (tel. 409 61 65). Built by Pharaoh Zakheramon, it's the only Egyptian temple in Spain, with hieroglyphics on the interior walls. The Egyptian government shipped the temple stone by stone from the banks of the Nile in appreciation of Spanish archaeologists who helped rescue a series of monuments from advancing waters near the Aswan Dam. (Open Tues.-Fri. 10am-2pm and 6-8pm, Sat.-Sun. 10am-2pm; off-season 10am-2pm and 4-6pm, Sat.-Sun. 10am-2pm. 300ptas, students 150ptas, free Wed.)

On **Paseo Rosales** away from the city center and past the *terrazas* is the *teleférico* (cable car) running between Po. Rosales and **Casa de Campo,** the city's largest park. (Open daily 11am-9pm, ff-season Sat.-Sun. noon-8pm. 355ptas one way, 505ptas round-trip.) Inside, the "amusement" park **(Parque de Atracciones)** can be traced to its roller-coaster's pathetic creak (M: Batán; open Sun.-Fri. noon-11pm, Sat. noon-midnight). The **Zoo/Aquarium** is five minutes away (open daily 10am-9pm, off-season 10am-6:30pm; 1560ptas).

Ermita de San Antonio de la Florida (tel. 542 07 22; M: Príncipe Pío), containing Goya's pantheon, is close to Parque del Oeste at the end of Po. Florida. Goya's frescoed dome arches above his own buried corpse—but not his skull, which was missing when the remains arrived from France (it was apparently stolen by a phrenologist; open Tues.-Sun. 10am-2pm; free).

Ciudad Universitaria (University City) is quite a distance north of the Parque del Oeste and Pl. España. A battleground in the Civil War and resistance center during Franco's rule, Spain's largest university educates over 120,000 students per year. The Prime Minister's official residence, the **Palacio de la Moncloa,** can be seen—but not touched—from the road through these grounds (M: Moncloa).

A prime example of Fascist Neoclassicism, the arcaded **Cuartel General del Aire** (Ejército del Aire) commands the perspective on the other side of Arco de la Victoria by the Moncloa Metro station. The complex was to form part of the "Fachada del Manzanares" urban axis linking Moncloa, the Palacio de Oriente, San Isidro, and the Iglesia de San Francisco. The building looks suspiciously like El Escorial. **Museo de América** (see p. 102) is a bit farther down the avenue, by the **Faro de Moncloa,** a 92m-high metal tower which you can pay to ascend (200ptas). You can supposedly see El Escorial on a clear day.

EL PARDO

Built as a hunting lodge for Carlos I in 1547, **El Pardo** was enlarged by generations of Habsburg and Bourbon royalty into a magnificent country palace. Franco resided here from 1940-1975. Although politics have changed, the palace is still the official reception site for distinguished foreign visitors who wine, dine, and politic amid gorgeous Renaissance and Neoclassical furniture, chandeliers, and other works. Renowned for its collection of tapestries—several of which were designed by Goya—the palace also holds a little-known Velázquez depiction of a deer slain by Felipe IV and Ribera's *Techo de los hombres ilustres* (Ceiling of the Illustrious Men). During his stay, Franco fitted the palace with modern amenities such as TVs and air conditioning, which are cunningly camouflaged so as not to clash with the elegant decor. You can also see the bedroom cabinet in which he kept Santa Teresa's silver-encrusted hand. (Open Mon.-Sat. 9:30am-6pm, Sun. 9:30am-2pm. Compulsory 45min. guided tour in Spanish. 650ptas, students 250ptas, Wed. free for EU citizens. Catch bus #601 from the stop in front of the Ejército del Aire building above M: Moncloa. 15 min., 150ptas each way.) The palace's **capilla** and the nearby **Casita del Príncipe,** created by Villanueva of El Prado fame, are both free.

▓ Museums

EL TRIÁNGULO DEL ARTE

Don't miss the **Paseo del Arte** ticket that grants admission to the Museo del Prado, Colección Thyssen-Bornemisza, and Centro de Arte Reina Sofía for 1050ptas. Passes are available at the three museums.

Museo del Prado

The Prado (tel. 420 37 68), on Po. Prado at Pl. Cánovas del Castillo (M: Banco de España or Atocha), is Spain's premier museum and one of Europe's finest. Carlos III commissioned Juan de Herrera to construct the Neoclassical building as the Museum of Natural Sciences. The Prado had housed the royal painting collection since the time of Fernando VII, who cared precious little for art and rather more about making an impression at home and abroad. The Prado's collection of over 3000 paintings, many collected by Spanish monarchs between 1400 and 1700, includes Spanish and foreign masterpieces, with particular strengths in the Flemish and Venetian Schools.

Hours of jostling through herds of schoolchildren will not allow every canvas in the Prado its due. Don't feel bad about striding through rooms full of imitation Rubens. The museum is laid out in a logical fashion with rooms numbered and indexed in a free brochure. Nevertheless, once inside it's easy to lose sight of the forest for the groves of Goyas and Velázquezes. Guidebooks can be helpful and informative. They vary in size and detail, ranging from 150ptas "greatest hits" brochures to weighty 2000ptas tomes packed with serious art criticism.

The second floor houses Spanish and Italian works from the 16th and 17th centuries, most notably an unparalleled collection of works by **Diego Velázquez** (1599-1660), court painter and interior decorator for Felipe IV. Within are several of his most famous paintings, including *Las hilanderas* (The Tapestry Weavers), *Los borrachos* (The Drunkards), and *La fragua de Vulcano* (Vulcan's Forge). To achieve what some consider to be an effect of continuous movement with the viewer, Velazquez repositioned the horse in *Las lanzas* (The Spears or The Surrender of Breda) several times before its completion. The complex and oft-imitated *Las meninas* (The Maids of Honor), widely considered Velázquez's *magnum opus*, occupies an entire wall. The complicated web of stares and glances has led many critics to insist that it's not a painting, but an "encounter." Exquisite portraits of the royal family, including Velázquez's affectionate renderings of the foppish and fey Felipe IV, are legion. Velázquez is renowned for his masterful manipulations of light and perspective, and is credited with radicalizing portraiture with his unforgiving realism.

The far-reaching influence of Velázquez's technique is evident in the work of **Francisco de Goya y Lucientes** (1746-1828), especially in his two hilariously unflattering depictions of Carlos III and his satirical masterpiece *La familia de Carlos IV*. Many wonder how he got away with depicting the Royal family the way he did; some suggest that in the *La familia de Carlos IV* he manipulated light and shadow to focus the viewer's gaze on the figure of the queen, despite the more prominent position of the king, thus supporting contemporary popular opinion about who truly powered the monarchy without violating protocol. In addition to his *Dos de Mayo* and *Fusilamientas de Tres de Mayo* that depict the Revolution of 1808, Goya's paintings have got people talking. Many gossipers surmise that Goya's mysteriously expressionless *La maja vestida* (Clothed Maja) and *La maja desnuda* (Nude Maja) depict the Duchess of Alba. That speculation has been ruled out by experts—but they Veloázquez and the Duchess did have a *hot* affair. Goya's *Cartones para tapices* (Cartoons for Tapestries)—so called because they were models for tapestries destined for El Escorial, not because they merited any knee-slapping—depict light-hearted scenes of provincial people cavorting in pastoral settings. Don't miss the large room downstairs devoted to Goya's *Pinturas Negras* (Black Paintings). These works date from the end of his life, when the artist was in declining health and living in a small country house outside Madrid, since nicknamed the *Quinta del Sordo* (the deaf man's house). Goya

painted these chillingly macabre scenes on the walls of his house; years after his death they were transferred to canvases and restored.

The Prado also displays many of **El Greco's** (Domenico Theotocopulo, 1541-1614) religious paintings. *La Trinidad* (The Trinity) and *La adoración de los pastores* (The Adoration of the Shepherds) are characterized by El Greco's unusually luminous colors, elongated figures, and mystical subjects. You can also find **Murillo's** *Familia con pájaro pequeño* (Family with Small Bird), **Ribera's** *El martirio de San Bartholomeo* (Martyrdom) and *La Trinidad*, and **Zurbarán's** *La inmaculada* on the second floor.

The Prado has a formidable collection of Italian works, including **Titian's** portraits of Carlos I and Felipe II, and **Raphael's** *El cardenal desconocido* (The Unknown Cardinal). **Tintoretto's** rendition of the homicidal seductress Judith and her hapless victim Holofernes, as well as his *Washing of the Feet* and other works are here. Some minor **Botticellis** and a slough of his imitators are also on display. Among the works by **Rubens**, *Un Satiro* (A Satyr) stands out.

Because the Spanish Habsburgs long ruled the Netherlands, the Flemish holdings are also top-notch. **Van Dyck's** *Marquesa de Legunes* is here, as well as **Hieronymus Bosch's** harrowing triptych, *The Garden of Earthly Delights*, and works by **Albrecht Dürer** and **Peter Breughel the Elder.**

Among the Byzantine medieval and Renaissance Spanish works, check out **Alfonso Sánchez Coello's** amusing *Las infantas Isabel Clara Eugenia y Catalina Micaela*, painted around 1500, and the two small chapels of 11th- and 12th-century paintings from the Mozarabic Church of San Baudelio de Berlanga and the Ermita de la Cruz de Maderuelo. The Spanish government gave two New York art speculators a monastery in exchange for some of these paintings. (Open Tues.-Sat. 9am-7pm, Sun. 9am-2pm. Admission including the Casón del Buen Retiro (see below) 500ptas, students 250ptas. Free entrance Sat. 2:30-7pm and all day Sun.)

Next door to the Prado, the lush and shady **Jardín Botánico** (tel. 420 30 17) awaits with 30,000 species of plants. Imported trees, bushes, and flowers from occident to orient please everybody. (Open daily 10am-9pm; winter 10am-6pm; spring and fall 10am-7 or 8pm. 200ptas, students 100ptas.)

Casón del Buen Retiro

With your ticket stub from the Prado, walk the three minutes to C. Alfonso XXII, 28 (tel. 330 28 60). Once part of Felipe IV's Palacio del Buen Retiro, the Casón was destroyed in the war against Napoleon. The rebuilt version has a great collection of 19th-century Spanish paintings. Enter the *Sección de Arte Español del Siglo XIX* from the side (open Tues.-Sat. 9am-6:45pm, Sun. 9am-1:45pm).

Museo Nacional Centro de Arte Reina Sofía

A marvelous permanent collection of 20th-century art occupies two floors in a renovated hospital, located on C. Santa Isabel, 52 (tel. 467 50 62), opposite Estación Atocha at the south end of Po. Prado (M: Atocha). Its three floors also host rotating exhibits, a library and archives specializing in 20th-century art (open Mon. and Wed.-Fri. 10am-9pm), photography archives, music library, repertory cinema (art films in Spanish at noon and 4:30pm, 150ptas), cafe, and flashy gift shop. The museum surrounds a gorgeous courtyard and sculpture garden.

Viewed only from a distance, **Picasso's** master work *Guernica* is the centerpiece of the Reina Sofía's permanent collection. When the Germans bombed the Basque town of Guernica as a military exercise at the bequest of Franco during the Spanish Civil War, Picasso painted this huge colorless work of contorted, agonized figures to denounce the bloodshed. The screaming horse in the center represents war, and the twisted bull, an unmistakable national symbol, places the scene in Spain. When asked by Nazi officials whether he was responsible for this work, Picasso answered, "No, you are." He gave the canvas to New York's Museum of Modern Art (MOMA) on the condition that it return to Spain when democracy was restored. In 1981, five years after Franco's death, *Guernica* was brought to Madrid's Casón del Buen Retiro. The later move to the Reina Sofía sparked an international controversy—Picasso's other

stipulation had been that the painting hang only in the Prado, to affirm his equivalent status with Titian and Velázquez. The masterpiece is currently accompanied by a large, fascinating array of preliminary sketches and drawings, and the bullet-proof glass that once shielded the enormous work and created disturbing reflections has recently been removed.

Spain's contribution to the early avant-garde and the essential role of Spanish artists in the cubist and surrealist movements are illustrated by the works of **Miró, Julio González, Juan Gris, Dalí,** and **Picasso** in the Reina Sofía's permanent collection. The increasing prominence of abstract movements during the 20th century is well-chronicled. Especially impressive are the exhibits of Miró's paintings from the 70s and Dali's work as a young artist. (Open Mon. and Wed.-Sat. 10am-9pm, Sun. 10am-2:30pm. 500ptas, students 250ptas, free entrance Sat. after 2:30pm and Sun. all day.)

Museo Thyssen-Bornemisza

Without missing a step, the 775-piece Thyssen-Bornemisza collection (tel. 369 01 51) surveys over 600 years of art in the world's most extensive privately owned showcase. The museum is located on the corner of Po. Prado and C. San Jerónimo (M: Banco de España, bus #6, 14, 27, 37, and 45). The 18th-century Palacio de Villahermosa houses Baron Hans-Heinrich Thyssen-Bornemisza's collection. Rafael Moneo remodeled its interior in 1992, adding marble floors and blushing terra-cotta walls, and retaining a flat, spacious layout. Madrid won the bidding for the baron's collection largely because the magnificent space was available for use. (Open Tues.-Sun. 10am-7pm. No one admitted after 6:30pm. 600ptas, students with ISIC and seniors 350ptas, children under 12 free. You can be stamped for same-day re-entry.)

After passing by portraits of the royal couple on the bottom floor, the tour begins on the top floor with a brief look at the Middle Ages. The **Old Masters collection,** including a Van Eyck Diptych**,** and Holbein's portrait of *Henry VIII,* stands out where the Prado is relatively weak. Domenico Ghirlandalo's profile portrait of Giovanni Tornabuoni has graced the cover of a few publications (another portrait of her, by Botticelli, hangs in the Louvre). Jan de Beer's *The Birth of the Virgin* is a marvel of odd period techniques. Works by Derick Bagert stand out among the **16th-century German** paintings. The Titians and Tintorettos surpass those at the Prado, as do works from the early **Baroque** period, especially those by Caravaggio.

Winding through the centuries, one is eventually met with more vibrant splashes of color. **Impressionist** and **Post-Impressionist** collections include works by Manet, Pisarro, Gauguin, Van Gogh, Monet, Renoir, Degas, Cezanne, and drawings by Toulouse-Lautrec (famous from their days as Parisian theatre posters). A Modigliani work hangs out amongst other Fauvists, and Feiningu's *White Man* lights up the **Expressionist** section. The collections of **17th-century Dutch** (including work attributed to Frans Hals) and **19th-century North American** paintings are also excellent.

The breadth of the **20th-century collection** is a wonder to behold. A great many of the towering names of this century are represented: Picasso, Chagall, Max Ernst, Paul Klee, Miró, Léger, Juan Gris, Mondrian, Maholy-Nagy, Magritte, Giacometti, Kandinsky, Lichtenstein, David Hockney, Hopper, Rauschenberg, Stella, Dalí, Tanguy, O'Keefe, Andrew Wyeth, Rothko, Jackson Pollock…and the list goes on. Among the standouts of this brilliant group are Richard Estes's *Telephone Booths,* Mondrian's *New York City, New York,* and Domenico Gnoli's *Armchair.* Ben Shahn contributes two excellent pieces: *Four Piece Orchestra,* and *Carnival.* The array of cubist works includes several important Picassos and Braques. Hockney's coffin-shaped *In Memory of Cecchino Bracci,* and Richard Lidner's *Moon Over Alabama* are also here.

OTHERS

Calle de Claudio Coello (M: Goya), **Calle de Barquillo** (M: Chueca), and **Calle de Galileo** (M: Quevedo) pack in the most **Art Galleries.** (generally open Tues.-Fri. 11am-2pm and 5-9pm, Mon. 5-9pm; free). Again, *Guía del Ocio* is vital.

MADRID

Monasterio de las Descalzas Reales, Pl. Descalzas (tel. 559 74 04), between Pl. Callao and Sol. M: Callao or Sol. Juana of Austria, daughter of Carlos I, converted the former royal palace into a monastery in 1559. La Roldana, one of the few known 17th-century female artists, designed a chapel in the upper cloister. The Salón de Tapices contains 10 renowned tapestries woven from cartoons by Rubens (some of which now hang in the Prado), as well as Santa Ursula's jewel-encrusted bones and a depiction of *El viaje de Santa Ursula y las once mil vírgenes* (The Journey of Santa Ursula and the Eleven Thousand Virgins). Zurbarán, Titian, and Rubens are all represented in the museum. The convent is still home to 26 Franciscan nuns. Tours are conducted in Spanish (45min.; 30min. max. wait while a tour group assembles). Open Tues.-Thurs. and Sat. 10:30am-12:45pm and 4-6pm, Fri. 10:30am-12:45pm, Sun. 11am-1:45pm. 650ptas, students 250ptas, Wed. free for EU citizens. Convent's church free when mass is being given (Mon.-Sat. 8am and 7pm, Sun. 8am and noon.).

Convento de la Encarnación, in Pl. Encarnación (tel. 542 00 59), off C. Bailén just east of Palacio Real. M: Ópera. Juan de Herrera's disciple Juan de Gómez constructed the convent with representative *herrerense* austerity. The macabre *relicuario* houses about 1500 relics of saints, including a vial of San Pantaleón's blood, believed to liquify every year on July 27th. In 1995 alone, 30,000 people showed up to gawk. The *Exchange of Princesses on the Bidasoa* depicts the swap weddings of French King Louis XII's sister Isabel to Felipe IV, and Felipe IV's sister Anne to Louis XII. Open Wed. and Sat. 10:30am-12:45pm and 4-5:45pm, Sun. 11am-1:30pm. 425ptas, students 225ptas. Wed. free for EU citizens.

Museo Cerralbo, C. Ventura Rodríguez, 17 (tel. 547 36 46). M: Ventura Rodríguez. Once home to the Marquis of Cerralbo XVII (1845-1922), the palatial residence-turned-museum displays an eclectic assemblage of period furniture and ornamentation. Beautiful Venetian glass chandeliers and a so-called "mysterious" clock by Barbedienne stand out within a labyrinth of marble, mirrors, and mahogany. The ballroom is an aesthetic feast, the music room has a Louis XVI-style French piano, and the chapel houses El Greco's *The Ecstasy of Saint Francis.* Open Tues.-Sat. 9:30am-2:30pm, Sun. 10am-2pm. 400ptas, students 200ptas. Free Wed. and Sun.

Museo de América, Av. Reyes Católicos, 6 (tel. 549 26 41), near Av. Puerta de Hierro and next to the conspicuous *Faró de Moncloa,* the futuristic metal tower. M: Moncloa. This underappreciated museum recently reopened after painstaking renovations and is now a can't-miss. It documents the societies and cultures of pre-Columbian civilizations of the Americas, as well as the Spanish conquest. Newly renovated to include state-of-the-art multi-media exhibits. Open Tues.-Sat. 10am-3pm, Sun. 10am-2:30pm. 500ptas, students 200ptas, free on Sun.

Museo de la Real Academia de Bellas Artes de San Fernando, C. Alcalá, 13 (tel. 522 14 91). M: Sol or Sevilla. A beautiful museum with an excellent collection of Old Masters surpassed only by the Prado. The Royal Academy of San Fernando was founded in 1752 by Ferdinand VI, and served as a pedagogical institution under royal patronage until the 1960s, when the teaching facilities transferred to the University of Madrid. Goya was a director and famous prodigies include Dalí and Picasso. Velázquez's portraits of Felipe IV and Mariana de Austria and Goya's *La Tirana* are masterpieces; the Rafael and Titian collections are strong. Other notable works are the Italian Baroque collection and 17th-century canvases by Ribera, Murillo, Zurbarán, and Rubens. Large collection of Picasso prints. Open Tues.-Fri. 9am-7pm, Sat.-Mon. and holidays 9am-2:30pm. 300ptas, students 150ptas, Sat.-Sun. free. The **Calcografía Real** (Royal Print and Drawing Collection) in the same building houses Goya's studio and some of his equipment, and organizes temporary exhibitions. Free with museum admission.

Museo Arqueológico Nacional, C. Serrano, 13 (tel. 577 79 12), behind the *Biblioteca Nacional.* M: Serrano. The history of the entire western world is on display in this huge museum. Amid other astounding items from Spain's distant past smirks the country's most famous archaeological find, *Dama de Elche,* a 4th-century funeral urn. Beneath the garden is a replica of the Cantabrian *Cuevas de Altamira* with reproductions of cave drawings. Museum also displays ivories from Muslim Andalucía, Romanesque and Gothic sculpture, and Celtiberian silver and gold. Call

ahead for a schedule of available exhibits. Open Tues.-Sat. 9:30am-8:30pm, Sun. 9:30am-2:30pm. 500ptas, students 250ptas, Sat.-Sun. free after 2:30pm.

Museo Lázaro Galdiano, C. Serrano, 122 (tel. 561 60 84). M: Rubén Darío. Beautiful interior with frescoes, the walls and doorframes with elaborate woodwork. Among the riches are an overwhelming display of Italian Renaissance bronzes, ancient jewels, Gothic reliquaries, and Celtic and Visigoth brasses. Array of paintings includes canvases by Velázquez, Zurbarán, Ribera, El Greco, Mengo, Bosch, and Goya, plus a Da Vinci. Brits are well-represented—Gainsborough, Reynolds, Constable, Turner, and T.H. Lawrence. Top floor devoted to antique brocades, tapestries, and weaponry. Open Sept.-July Tues.-Sun. 10am-2pm. 300ptas, Sun. free.

Museo Sorolla, Po. General Martínez Campos, 37 (tel. 310 15 84). M: Rubén Darío or Iglesia. Former home and studio of Joaquín Sorolla, the acclaimed 19th-century Valencian painter. Tranquil garden and uncrowded halls are a change from crowded museums. Sensual paintings of the Valencian shores, sunbathers, and pre-WWI society portraits. Open Sept.-July Tues.-Sun. 10am-3pm, Sun. 10am-2pm. 400ptas, students 200ptas.

Museo Romántico, C. San Mateo, 13 (tel. 448 10 71). M: Alonso Martínez. Housed in a 19th-century mansion built by a disciple of Ventura Rodríguez, this museum is an exquisite time capsule of the Romantic period (early 19th century) decorative arts and painting. Open Sept.-July Tues.-Sat. 9am-3pm, Sun. 10am-2pm. 400ptas, students 200ptas. Sun. free.

Museo del Ejército, C. Méndez Núñez, 1 (tel. 522 89 77), just north of Casón del Buen Retiro. M: Retiro or Banco de España. Vast collection of military paraphernalia in a stately fragment of the Palacio del Buen Retiro. Plans are to annex this museum to the Prado and recreate its original appearance as the Buen Retiro's Hall of Thrones (with painting cycles by Zurbarán and Velázquez). Open Tues.-Sun. 10am-2pm. 100ptas, students 50ptas, under 18 and Sat. free.

Museo Naval, C. Montalbán, 2 (tel. 379 52 99), across from Palacio de Comunicaciones. M: Banco de España. Models of ships from the olden days. A globe of the sky dating from 1693 gives a taste of 17th-century cosmology, and an enormous map charts Spanish expeditions from the 15th to 18th centuries. Open Sept.-July Tues.-Sun. 10am-1:30pm. Free.

Museo Municipal, C. Fuencarral, 78 (tel. 588 86 72). M: Tribunal. Basement exhibit traces the evolution of Madrid from ancient times, with an enormous diorama of the city in 1830, a model of 17th-century Pl. Mayor, and a variety of documents. Undistinguished collection of 16th- to 18th-century Spanish works. Great gift shop. Open Tues.-Fri. 9:30am-8pm, Sat.-Sun. 10am-2pm. 300ptas, Wed. and Sun free.

■ La Marcha (Nightlife)

In Madrid, a perpetual stream of automobile and pedestrian traffic blur the distinction between 4pm and 4am. During the summer, after the sun has mellowed out, *terrazas* (a.k.a. *chiringuitos,* outdoor cafes) sprawl across sidewalks all over Madrid. Colder weather sends *madrileños* scrambling into bars and *discotecas.*

For clubs and discos, life begins around 2am. Many discos have "afternoon" sessions for teens (7-10pm; cover 250-1000ptas). But the "night" sessions (lasting until dawn) are when to really let your hair down. Don't be surprised if at 5:30am there's a line of people waiting to get into a hipster club. The *entrada* (cover; often includes a drink) can be as high as 2000ptas, and men may be charged up to 500ptas more than women, if women are charged at all. Keep an eye out for *invitaciones* and *oferta* cards—in stores, restaurants, tourist publications, tourist offices, or handed out in the streets—that offer discounts or free admission.

Spaniards get an average of one less hour of sleep than other Europeans. People in Madrid claim to need even less than that. Proud of their nocturnal offerings (they'll tell you with a straight face that they were bored in Paris or New York), *madrileños* insist that no one goes to bed until they've killed the night—and a good part of the following morning. Some clubs don't even bother opening until 4 or 5am. The only (relatively) quiet nights of the week are Sunday and Monday. For current info on the

goings on, scan Madrid's entertainment guides (see p. 74). **Forocio,** C. Mayor, 6 (tel. 522 56 77), organizes special events for foreigner visitors.

Madrid's nightlife is without peer. *La marcha,* as students call it, is concentrated in several distinct neighborhoods. Everyone has a favorite neighborhood, and while hip clubs change with season, year, and time of day (night, morning), the personality of each zone evolves slowly. Once you've found the neighborhoods that suit your tastes, you'll find there's plenty of night to be spent hopping from place to place and *barrio* to *barrio.* **Goa After Club** (Centro), **Heaven** (Centro), and **Midday** (Malasaña) are the top after-hours clubs. Don't forget the *Guía del Ocio,* which runs features on the hottest locales and lists basic information on practically every nightspot worth the ink on its recycled paper.

Plaza 2 de Mayo in Malasaña, Plaza Chueca, Plaza de España, and the Gran Vía can be intimidating; their smaller streets can be sleazy. Madrid is fairly safe for a city of its size, but one should always exercise caution. The only really fearsome places late at night are the parks

CENTRO

The area of El Centro encompasses Sol, Atocha, Ópera, Quevedo, and Tirso de Molina. The imposition of high prices and tourists are nuisances only to those who aren't in the know. So here's the scoop, don't pollute.

Kapital, C. Atocha, 125 (tel. 420 29 06). M: Atocha. A block off Po. Prado. One of the most extreme results of *La Movida,* this place tries really hard to impress. Two dance floors, a sky-light lounge, and tons of bars amount to a total of seven floors of pseudo-fun. Packed with white 20-year-olds willing to pay the 1200ptas cover. Includes 2 drinks if you have their invite from the tourist office, 1 drink without. Don't lose your ticket or they'll fine you 5000ptas when you leave. Drinks 800-1000ptas. Thurs. parties. Open Thurs. 12:30-6am, Fri.-Sun. 6-11pm and 12:30-6am.

Mogador, C. Magallanes, 1 (tel. 448 94 65). M: Quevedo. Mature crowd gets down and dirty to salsa Tues.-Thurs. and you can rub your ass against the red velvet walls. Happy happy. Hot hot. Free salsa classes Tues. 11pm-midnight. Open Mon. 9:30pm-5:30am, Tues.-Thurs. 11pm-5am, Fri.-Sat. midnight-5am, Sun. 7:30pm-3am. Cover 1000ptas includes 1 drink, 1200ptas for 2 drinks.

Las Noches de Babel, Ronda de Toledo, 1 (tel. 366 49 23). M: Puerta de Toledo. *Pijolandia*—where a sleek and sheik young (23-28-years-old) "beautiful people" wiggle around in tight clothes to light funk and house. Vegetable decor a quirky surprise. Concerts. Open daily 11pm-6am.

Refugio, C. Dr. Cortezo, 1. M: Tirso de Molina. The most outrageous gay men's scene in the…you decide. Famous for *fiestas de espuma* (suds parties) and racy Fri.-Sat. night "shows," like the *concurso de pollas* (penis competition). It's got a dark room for the shadiest of affairs. Open Tues.-Sun. midnight-morning. Cover 1000ptas includes a drink.

Joy Eslava, C. Arenal, 11 (tel. 366 37 33). M: Sol or Ópera. A 3-tiered theater turned disco; 3 bars, laser lights, video screen, live entertainment. Young crowd of all types groove to disco. Cover 2000ptas includes one drink. Open Mon.-Thurs. 11:30pm on, Fri.-Sat. 7-10:15pm and 11:30pm-5:30am.

Heaven, C. Veneras, 2 (tel. 548 20 22). M: Santo Domingo. Heavenly party when you're still floating at 8am. **After-hours.** Open Sat.-Sun. 6-10:30am. Cover 1000ptas. Drinks 600-900ptas.

Azúcar, Po. Reina Cristina, 7. M: Atocha. The only place up to date on top Latin American rhythms. Leave your Air Jordans in the hostel—no sneakers, jockstrap. Salsa classes daily 9:30-11pm. Cover 1200ptas, Sat. 1500ptas. Open Mon.-Thurs. 11pm-5:30am, Fri.-Sat. till 6:30am, Sun. 8pm-5am.

Torero, C. Santa Cruz, 26 (tel. 523 11 29). M: Sol. Late 20s early 30s crowd a little off from the cutting edge and all the more festive for being a little out of sync. Spanish pop, Latin rhythms, and *funky.* Thurs. a veritable cabaret, with drag queens and wacky theater spectacles. Open daily 11pm-6am.

The (Bowel) Movement

Imagine some potential pork—a pig to represent Madrid, plugged in the rear by its owner (Generalísimo Francisco Franco) who wants to make it bigger than all the other pigs. Forty years of Franco-imposed constipation were bound to end in an explosion—and indeed, his death proved quite the laxative; not so much as a day had passed when every newspaper printed a pornographic photo on its front page. This period of the happy pig is known commonly as "*el destapeo*" (the uncorking or uncovering). Then came the 80s and *la Movida* (the Movement) and Pedro Almodóvar's films about loony grandmothers, outgoing young women, typified animated homosexuals, and electric students. Nightlife was given a dose of the movement, but in many areas it was still a bit too much a bit too fast, resulting in today's golden age of overly ambitious clubs and gimmicky bars. The legendary nightlife, however, existed *before* Franco's rule. Royal fiestas filled Parque del Retiro's lake with silver gondolas and chaotic reenactments of naval battles, while El Capricho Park near the airport almost surely hosted of the Queen's orgies.

Black Jack, C. Príncipe, 11 (tel. 521 02 06). M: Sevilla. A mating frenzy of mainstreamers. Twenty- and thirtysomethings groving to disco-pop love to stare. Open Wed.-Thurs. 11pm-5am, Fri.-Sat. till 6am.

Kathmandú, C. Señores de Luzón, 3 (tel. 541 52 53), off C. Mayor, facing the Ayuntamiento. M: Sol. A hole-in-the-wall offering high-energy techno and acid jazz. 1000ptas includes 1 drink. Open Thurs. till 5am, Fri. and Sat. until 6am.

Max, C. Aduana, 21 (tel. 522 98 25). M: Sevilla. Known as an **after hours** club. Open Fri.-Sat. 4am-10am. Live rock 'n' roll.

Palacio Gaviria, Arenal, 9 (tel. 526 60 69/70/71). Former palace turned ballroom haven for Chachachá. Fun Thurs. when **Forocio** (see p. 109) throws its international festivals; nearly all groups and nationalities represented. Pick up an invitation at the tourist office on C. Mayor, 6.

GRAN VÍA

This street just won't go away. "Hello, it's me again," it says, and you think to go run and hide. These night spots provide great shelter. Although none is located directly on the Gran Vía, all are just a skip away. Don't wander around dark side streets looking for a bar; admit that you are lost and head back to Papa Vía.

Tierra, Cabarello de Gracia, 20 (tel. 532 72 71). M: Gran Vía. Off C. Montera, but best to go over 1 block to C. Peligios. Cow patterned upholstery. Black interior with psychedelic glow-in-the-dark design plays host to wicked good house. Open Thurs.-Sat. midnight-4:30am. Beer 500ptas.

Flamingo Club, Mesoneros Romanos, 13 (tel. 532 15 24). M: Gran Vía or Callao. Rather like a chameleon, the Flamingo is home to a variety of late-night fun. It's at its best as **Soul Kitchen** on Wed. and Sat. (midnight-5:30am), where *"la musica es funky."* The only real hip-hop club in town. A bit sketch. Same crowd heads to Goa After Club afterward. Before midnight on Soul Kitchen days, it's the Dark Hole Gothic Club, and the crowd is Goth (like Robert Smith). Club Shangay Tea Dance is saved for Sun. from 9pm-2am and draws a gay crowd. Cover always 1000-2000ptas includes 1 drink.

Goa After Club, C. Mesonero Romanos, 13 (tel. 531 48 27). M: Callao or Gran Vía. "Psychodelic trance atmosphere." **After-hours** party for the artificially energized. Open Sat.-Sun. 6-10am. Cover 1000ptas. **Copas** 700-1000ptas.

Calentito, C. Jacometrezo connects the Gran Vía to Pl. Sto. Domingo. Latin rhythms so hot, "Calentito" has to be written backwards (to fool the uncool). For Brazilian beats try **Oba-Oba,** across the street. No cover for either.

MADRID

SANTA ANA

Plaza Santa Ana's many bars and small *terrazas* are the preferred jumping-off point for an evening of bar- and club-hopping. Tourists and *madrileños* mingle, chat, smoke, and drink here, the heart of Huertas, Madrid's erstwhile literary district and now the cafe spot for the theater crowd. It's also a place for first-session dance clubs. **Calle de Huertas** is the main street, just off the plaza.

Discotecas

No Se Lo Digas a Nadie, C. Ventura de la Vega, 7, next to Pl. Santa Ana. M: Antón Martín. Not the best kept secret in Madrid; this place, with its bright blue sign and bright blue garage doors, is conspicuous. Billiards upstairs. Live mellow music starts around 12:15am. Drinks 500-800ptas.

Angels of Xenon, C. Atocha, 38 (tel. 369 38 81). M: Antón Martín. Threatening black walls enclose a mostly gay crowd, dancing hard under two big-ass disco balls. Too cool for the likes of you. 1500ptas cover with 1 drink, 1000ptas without.

Bar-Musicales

Kasbah, C. Santa Maria, 17. M: Antón Martín. Dazed aliens and other funked out decorations look on as house DJs spin some of the best jungle and techno in Madrid. On Sun., amateurs are invited to give it a whirl. No cover. Beer 300ptas.

Café Jazz Populart, C. Huertas, 22 (tel. 429 84 07). Jazz aficionados (to some extent) in a smoky bar decorated with brass instruments. Live music daily (except Thurs.): jazz, blues, swing, reggae, *flamenco*, and Latin jazz. No cover. Pitcher of beer 300ptas, but prices sometimes double during performances (Sun.-Thurs. 11pm, Fri.-Sat. 11pm and 12:30am). Open 6pm-12:30am, until 3am Fri.-Sat.

Café Central, Pl. Angel, 10 (tel. 369 41 43), off Pl. Santa Ana. M: Antón Martín or Sol. Jazz club of such high class that the middle-aged audience has no rhythm whatsoever. Still, it's packed during performances (10pm-2am). Cover charge 800-1000ptas. Cheaper Mon. Beer 300-500ptas.

El Mosquito, Torrecilla de Leal, 13. M: Antón Martín. Rap, soul, and funk draw a lesbian and gay crowd. Drinks 300-700ptas. Open Sun.-Thurs. 6pm-12:30am, Fri.-Sat. 6pm-3am.

Bars

Naturbier, Pl. Santa Ana, 9 (tel. 429 39 18). M: Antón Martín. Locally brewed *bier,* inspired by the credo: "beer is important to human nutrition." Superior lager 225-500ptas. Open Sun.-Thurs. 11:30am-1am, Fri.-Sat. 11am-3am.

Viva Madrid, C. Manuel Fernández González, 7 (tel. 429 36 40), next to Pl. Santa Ana. M: Antón Martín. Tiled and classy U.S. expat hangout. You'll still hear Spanish, though, because they're louder. Packed. Beer 300-400ptas, mixed drinks 700-800ptas. Open 1pm-7am.

Cervecería Alemana, Pl. Santa Ana, 6 (tel. 429 70 33). M: Antón Martín. Naturbier's neighbor. A former Hemingway hangout with a slightly upscale crowd. Open Sun.-Fri. noon-12:30am, Sat. noon-2am.

El Oso y el Madroño, C. Bolsa, 4 (tel. 522 77 96). A hand organ and old photos of Madrid. Try the potent Licor de Madroño, an arbutus-flavored Spanish liqueur (150ptas). Open 10am-midnight.

El Café de Sheherezade, C. Santa María, 18, a block south of C. Huertas. M: Antón Martín. Recline on opulent pillows as you sip exotic infusions (tea 350ptas). Moorish arches and Persian rugs in a dark, mellow atmosphere. Thurs. features Middle Eastern music. For similar drinks with Arabic dance on Sat., head to **Damasco,** C. Infante, 4 (tel. 554 88 26). Both also offer *pira* (pipe 600-1000ptas.)

LA CASTELLANA

The fashionable *terrazas* lining Madrid's most modern drag come alive every night around 11:30pm in July and August. Drinks can be quite pricey, reaching 600ptas for beer, 1000ptas for mixed drinks. There's no cover, plus, if you want anybody to talk to you, you'll have to spend a few extra *pesetas* on clothes, preferably a brilliant Lacoste-tee.

Bolero, Po. Castellana, 33 (tel. 554 91 51). M: Colón. An ultra-fashionable *terraza*. Claw your way to the bar with your exquisitely manicured hands. Drinks 1000ptas. Open 7:30pm-3am.

Boulevard, Po. Castellana, 37 (tel. 302 52 08). M: Colón. More *gente guapa* (beautiful people); loud music. Drinks 1000ptas. Open noon-3am.

BagëLus, C. María de Molina, 25 (tel. 561 61 00). M: Av. América. Three sumptuous floors of *pijolandia* (rich kid land)—restaurant, cafe, art gallery, club (techno on one floor, Latin on another), *terraza,* and even a travel agency. Be forewarned that *bagëlus* means "virility." Beer 600ptas, mixed drinks 800ptas.

CHUECA

Several years ago the site of a trendy, ritzy series of pubs and clubs (their remains are still open on C. Costanilla Capuchinos), Chueca is now home to an outrageous mostly male gay scene. Pl. Chueca's *terrazas* are becoming more and more popular among all youths, who've realized that the rest of Madrid isn't bizzare. Clubs may come and go, but **Calle de Pelayo** is clearly the main drag. Beers cost about 400ptas.

Entiendes...?, published by COGAM (see p. 76), Madrid's gay and lesbian coalition, lists clubs and bars in this area. *El Mundo's* Friday supplement, Metropoli, the *Guía del Ocio* and *In Madrid* also note gay and lesbian clubs. Look at **Berkana Librería Gai y Lesbiana** for more guides or listings (see **Shopping,** p. 111.). The safest walking route at night is up C. Fuencarral from Gran Vía and right on C. Augusto Figueroa, though you should still take proper precautions.

Rick's, C. Clavel, 8. M: Chueca. Chueca's hottest bar in '97 sure to be fired up for '98. Mostly gay men but women mingle comfortably in a bar of multifaceted tastes, where you can dance, schmooze, smooch, or knock around a foosball. Look good, be happy. Open 11:30am-morning. Beer 600-900ptas.

Black & White, C. Libertad, 34 (tel. 531 11 41). M: Chueca. Top and bottom floors are stark contrasts. Upstairs a more mature crowd mingles and downstairs the young ones whoop it up on the dance floor. Gays and lesbians, but not exclusively. Open daily 8pm-5am. Beer 500ptas. Mixed drinks 800ptas.

Heaven, C. Veneras, 2. Versatile like the drag queens pack it in Thurs.-Fri.—gay, lesbian, and straight crowd commingling to house and underground spun by the city's best DJs. Club functions both as a first-session spot and afterparty. Open Mon.-Wed. 1-5am, Thurs. and Sun. till 8am, Fri.-Sat. till 10am. Cover 1000ptas includes 1 drink.

Kingston's, C. Barquillo, 91 (tel. 521 15 68). M: Chueca. Reggae and Hip Hop. Word to the wise: it draws a shady crowd. Open 10pm-morning. Min. consumption 500ptas.

Finnegan's Irish Pub, Pl. Salesas, 9 (tel. 310 05 21). M: Chueca. Welcoming atmosphere popular with Americans. Open Thurs.-Mon. 11pm-5am. Beer 400ptas.

Café Figueroa, C. Augusto Figueroa, 17 (tel. 521 16 73), on the corner with C. Hortaleza. M: Chueca. Smoke-filled, dimly lit cafe is otherwordly. Low lounge-couches and lacy curtains emanate a dream-like elegance. Pop in after lunch at Nabucco's. Gay clientele. Beer 300-425ptas. Coffee 250-450ptas. Open Sun.-Thurs. 3pm-1am, Fri.-Sat. 3pm-2:30am.

Acuarela, C. Gravina, 8, off C. Hortaleza. M: Chueca. Very chill cafe an alternative to the cruising scene. Crowded. Beer 400ptas. Open 4pm-4am.

Ambient, C. San Mateo, 21 (tel. 448 80 62), off C. Hortaleza. M: Chueca or Alonso Martínez. A lesbian *bar-pizzería* that takes pool very seriously. Look out for the Pool Championships in March.

El Truco, C. Gravina, 10 (tel. 532 89 21). M: Chueca. Classy bar featuring local artists' works. Lesbian-friendly. Open 8pm-2am, till 4am Fri.-Sat. Same owners run **Escape,** a club down the street. Both are strong enough for a man, but designed particularly for a woman. Open Fri. and Sat. 1am-7am.

Big Bamboo, C. Barquillo, 42 (tel. 562 88 38) M: Chueca. Three blocks east of C. Pelayo down C. Gravina, and left on C. Barquillo. It's not who you dance with, it's what you dance to: reggae all the way. DJ accepts requests. African immigrants and tons of tourists. Usually no cover unless there's a live band.

MADRID

ALONSO MARTÍNEZ-BILBAO

Plenty of discos and bars shake around **Glorieta de Bilbao,** especially along and between **Calles Fuencarral**and **Luchana.** *Terrazas* on **Pl. Olavide** have a mellower drink-sipping scene (drinks outside 150-250ptas). Being frugal is no trouble in these high school and college-student-filled streets. Bars and clubs are boisterous and packed year-round. In **Alonso Martínez,** the university crowd sweats out strong drinks in tight spaces.

Barnon, C. Santa Engracia, 17 (tel. 447 38 37). M: Bilbao. Real Madrid's stud forward Raúl owns this hip-hop bar of VIPs that attracts *vikingos,* his teammates and American hoops players. High fashion crowd jets to Soul Kitchen once they get their buzz on. Open 10pm-3am, Fri.-Sat. till 4. No cover. Hip hop Wed. and Sat.

Vaivén, Travesía de San Mateo, 1. M: Alonso Martínez. The most exclusive salsa club in the city. If you've got the goods, it's a great place to meet someone of the opposite sex. Mid-week concerts. Open 9pm-4am. Beer 600ptas. Drinks 900ptas.

Bocaccio, C. Marqués de la Ensenada, 16 (tel. 308 49 81). M: Colón. Insider glamour scene of beautiful people. Alcohol is not the drug of choice for the folk who come here. Open Fri.-Sat. 7-11pm and midnight-6am, Mon.-Thurs. 7-11pm, Sun. 10pm-3am. Afternoon session 600ptas includes 1 drink. Night session 1000ptas. Sun. 500ptas.

Clamores Jazz Club, C. Albuquerque, 14 (tel. 445 79 38), off C. Cardenal Cisneros. M: Bilbao. Swanky (pink neon) setting and some of Madrid's more interesting jazz. The cover (600-1200ptas) gets slipped into the bill. *Codas* 500-800ptas. Live jazz daily except for Mon. Open 7pm-3am. Fri. and Sat. till 4am. July -Aug. closed Sun.

Archy, C. Marqués de Riscal, 11 (tel. 308 31 62), off C. Almagro from Pl. Alonso Martínez. M: Alonso Martínez. Dress to kill or the fashion police at the door might point and laugh. Beautiful people only. Also a fancy restaurant. No cover, but drinks cost 700-900ptas. Open noon-morning.

Cambalache, C. San Lorenzo, 5 (tel. 310 07 01). M: Alonso Martínez or Tribunal. Tango classes 7-9pm, live tangos 11pm-midnight. Argentine food served 6-11pm. You might want to reserve ahead. Open 8:30pm-5am.

Cervecería Ratskeller's, C. Luchana, 15 (tel. 447 13 40), at C. Palafox (by the cinema Palafox). M: Bilbao. Barfing, pinching, white hats, jams, flannels, and Bud t-shirts. You're in…Cancún (Madrid).Open 5pm-3am.

MALASAÑA

Malasaña is darker, more bohemian, and more sedate(d) than Pl. Santa Ana. Entertainment guides don't list the heaps of small, crowded pubs in this area, most of which play great music (jazz and blues). Hippies, intellectuals, and junkies and hippy-intellectual-junkies, check each other out in **Pl. 2 de Mayo. C. San Vincente Ferrer,** with its tattoo parlors, secondhand clothing and leather stores, motorcycle repair shops, and countless pubs, is prime Malasaña. On **C. Barceló,** kids run an open-air narcotics market. Most people in Masalaña are drunk, high, or both, or both. Pretend you're particularly bad-ass (or at least a little confident), and be wary here at night.

Café de la Palma, C. La Palma, 62 (tel. 522 50 31). M: San Bernardo or Noviciado. Rugs and throw pillows in an Moroccan-style atmosphere, or air, or aura, or cloud. Open 6pm-morning.

Midday, C. Amaniel, 13 (tel. 547 25 25). M: Noviciado. *The* **after-hours** club for Madrid's *gente guapa.* Techno and house and very exclusive. Open Sun. 6am-3pm.

Vía Láctea, C. Velarde, 18 (tel. 466 75 81). M: Tribunal. This deservedly famous club is almost always jam-packed. The "Milky Way's" loudspeakers and slightly expensive drinks will make you think you're a comet. Open Tues.-Sun. 7pm-3:30am.

La Tetera de la Abuela, C. Espíritu Santo, 19. "Granny's Teapot" attracts twentysomething angst and a pseudo-intellectual crowd. Open Sun.-Thurs. 7:30pm-1am, Fri.-Sat. 7:30pm-2am.

Manuela, C. San Vicente Ferrer, 29 (tel. 531 70 37). Old-looking cafe-bar with dirty mirrors is elegant in a "this-must-have-been-elegant-quite-some-time-ago" sort of

If you're stuck for cash on your travels, don't panic. Western Union can transfer money in minutes. We've 37,000 outlets in over 140 countries. And our record of safety and reliability is second to none. Call Western Union: wherever you are, you're never far from home.

WESTERN UNION | MONEY TRANSFER®

The fastest way to send money worldwide.

Austria 0660 8066 Canada 1 800 235 0000* Czech 2422 9524 France (01) 43 54 46 12 or (01) 45 35 60 60 Germany 0130 7890 or (0180) 522 5822 Greece (01) 927 1010 Ireland 1 800 395 395* Italy 167 22 00 55* or 167 464 464* Netherlands 0800 0566* Poland (022) 636 5688 Russia 095 119 82 50 Spain 900 633 633* or (91) 559 0253 Sweden 020 741 742 Switzerland 0512 22 33 58 UK 0800 833 833* USA 1 800 325 6000*.

*Toll free telephone No.

Get the MCI Card.
The Smart and Easy Card.

The MCI Card with WorldPhone Service is designed specifically to keep you in touch with people that matter the most to you. We make international calling as easy as possible.

The MCI Card with WorldPhone Service....

- Provides access to the US from over 125 countries and places worldwide.
- Country to country calling from over 70 countries
- Gives you customer service 24 hours a day
- Connects you to operators who speak your language
- Provides you with MCI's low rates with no sign-up or monthly fees
- Even if you don't have an MCI Card, you can still reach a WorldPhone Operator and place collect calls to the U.S. Simply dial the access code of the country you are calling from and hold for a WorldPhone operator.

For more information or to apply for a Card call:
1-800-444-1616

Outside the U.S., call MCI collect (reverse charge) at:
1-916-567-5151

Pick Up The Phone.
Pick Up The Miles.

You earn frequent flyer miles when you travel internationally, why not when you call internationally? Callers can earn frequent flyer miles with one of MCI's airline partners:

- American Airlines
- Continental Airlines
- Delta Airlines
- Hawaiian Airlines
- Midwest Express Airlines
- Northwest Airlines
- Southwest Airlines

Please cut out and save this reference guide for convenient U.S. and worldwide calling with the MCI Card with WorldPhone Service.

Your MCI Worldphone Access Numbers

COUNTRY	WORLDPHONE TOLL-FREE ACCESS #
# South Africa (CC)	0800-99-0011
# Spain (CC)	900-99-0014
# Sri Lanka (Outside of Colombo, dial 01 first)	440100
# St. Lucia ⌦	1-800-888-8000
# St. Vincent (CC)	020-795-922
# Sweden (CC) ◆	0800-89-0222
# Switzerland (CC) ◆	0800
# Syria	0080-13-4567
# Taiwan (CC) ◆	001-999-1-2001
# Thailand ★	1-800-888-8000
# Trinidad & Tobago ⌦	00-8001-1177
# Turkey (CC) ◆	1-800-888-8000
# Turks and Caicos ⌦	☎ 10-013
# Ukraine (CC) ⌦	800-111
# United Arab Emirates ◆	0800-89-0222
# United Kingdom (CC) To call using BT ■	0500-89-0222
To call using MERCURY ■	1-800-888-8000
# United States (CC)	000-412
# Uruguay	1-800-888-8000
# U.S. Virgin Islands (CC)	172-1022
# Vatican City (CC)	800-1114-0
# Venezuela (CC) ⌦ ◆	1201-1022
Vietnam ●	008-00-102
Yemen	

Automation available from most locations.
(CC) Country-to-country calling available to/from most international locations.
⌦ Limited availability.
▶ Wait for second dial tone.
◀ When calling from public phones, use phones marked LADATEL.
■ International communications carrier.
★ Not available from public pay phones.
◆ Public phones may require deposit of coin or phone card for dial tone.
● Local service fee in U.S. currency required to complete call.
▲ Regulation does not permit intra-Japan calls.
⌦ Available from most major cities

And, it's simple to call home.

1. Dial the WorldPhone toll-free access number of the country you're calling from (listed inside).

2. Follow the voice instructions in your language of choice or hold for a WorldPhone operator.
   - Enter or give the operator your MCI Card number or call collect.

3. Enter or give the WorldPhone operator your home number.

4. Share your adventures with your family!

The MCI Card with WorldPhone Service... The easy way to call when traveling worldwide.

MCI — Calling Card
415 555 1234 2244
J.D. SMITH
WorldPhone

For more information or to apply for a Card call:
1-800-444-1616

Outside the U.S., call MCI collect (reverse charge) at:
1-916-567-5151

Please cut out and save this reference guide for convenient U.S. and worldwide calling with the MCI Card with WorldPhone Service.

COUNTRY	WORLDPHONE TOLL-FREE ACCESS #
#American Samoa	633-2MCI (633-2-624)
#Antigua (Available from public card phones only)	#2
#Argentina ◆	0800-5-1002
#Aruba ÷ ◆	800-888-8
#Australia (CC) ◆ To call using OPTUS ■	1-800-551-111
To call using TELSTRA ■	1-800-881-100
#Austria (CC) ◆	022-903-012
#Bahamas	1-800-888-8000
#Bahrain	800-002
#Barbados	1-800-888-8000
#Belarus (CC) From Brest, Vitebsk, Grodno, Minsk	8-800-103
From Gomel and Mogilev regions	8-10-800-103
#Belgium (CC) ◆	0800-10012
#Belize From Hotels	815
From Payphones	817
#Bermuda ÷	1-800-888-8000
#Bolivia ◆	0-800-2222
#Brazil (CC)	000-8012
#British Virgin Islands ÷	1-800-888-8000
#Brunei	800-011
#Bulgaria	00800-0001
#Canada (CC)	1-800-888-8000
#Cayman Islands	1-800-888-8000
#Chile (CC) To call using CTC ■	800-207-300
To call using ENTEL ■	800-360-180
#China ✦	108-17
#Colombia (CC) ◆ (Available from most major cities)	980-16-0001
To call using a Mandarin-speaking Operator	108-12
Colombia IIIC Access in Spanish	980-16-1000
#Costa Rica ◆	0800-012-2222
#Cote D'Ivoire	1001
#Croatia (CC) ★	0800-22-0112
#Cyprus ◆	080-90000
#Czech Republic (CC) ◆	0-42-000112
#Denmark (CC) ◆	8001-0022
#Dominica	1-800-888-8000
#Dominican Republic (CC) ÷	1-800-888-8000
Dominican Republic IIIC Access in Spanish	1121
#Ecuador (CC) ÷	999-170
#Egypt ◆ (Outside of Cairo, dial 02 first)	355-5770
El Salvador ◆	800-1767
#Federated States of Micronesia	624

— FOLD —

COUNTRY	WORLDPHONE TOLL-FREE ACCESS #
#Fiji	004-890-1002
#Finland (CC) ◆	08001-102-80
#France (CC) ◆	0800-99-0019
#French Antilles (CC) ◆ (includes Martinique, Guadeloupe)	0800-99-0019
#French Guiana (CC)	0-800-99-0019
#Gabon	00-005
#Gambia ◆	00-199
#Germany (CC)	0130-0012
#Greece (CC) ◆	00-800-1211
#Grenada ÷	1-800-888-8000
#Guam (CC)	950-1022
#Guatemala (CC) ◆	99-99-189
#Guyana	177
#Haiti ÷	193
Haiti IIIC Access in French/Creole	190
#Honduras ÷	122
#Hong Kong (CC)	800-96-1121
#Hungary (CC) ◆	00▼800-01411
#Iceland (CC) ◆	800-9002
#India (CC) ✦ (Available from most major cities)	000-127
#Indonesia (CC)	001-801-11
#Iran ÷ (SPECIAL PHONES ONLY)	(SPECIAL PHONES ONLY)
#Ireland (CC)	1-800-55-1001
#Israel (CC)	177-150-2727
#Italy (CC) ◆	172-1022
#Jamaica ÷ (From Special Hotels only)	873
Jamaica IIIC Access	#2-from public phones
#Japan (CC) ◆ To call using KDD ■	0039-12▼
To call using IDC ■	0066-55-121
To call using ITJ ■	0044-11-121
#Jordan	18-800-001
#Kazakhstan (CC)	8-800-131-4321
#Kenya ◆ (Available from most major cities)	08011
#Korea (CC) To call using KT ■	00309-14
To call using DACOM ■	00309-12
Phone Booths÷ Press red button, 03, then ★	Press red button, 03, then ★
Military Bases	550-2255
#Kuwait	800-MCI (800-624)
#Lebanon ÷	600-MCI (600-624)
#Liechtenstein (CC) ◆	0800-89-0222
#Luxembourg	0800-0112

— FOLD —

COUNTRY	WORLDPHONE TOLL-FREE ACCESS #
#Macao	0800-131
#Macedonia (CC)	99800-4266
#Malaysia (CC) ◆	800-0012
#Malta	0800-89-0120
#Marshall Islands	1-800-888-8000
#Mexico ▲ Avantel (CC)	91-800-021-8000
Telmex ▲ Mexico IIIC Access	95-800-674-7000
	91-800-021-1000
#Micronesia	624
#Monaco (CC) ◆	800-99-019
#Montserrat	1-800-888-8000
#Morocco	00-211-0012
#Netherlands (CC) ◆	0800-022-912
#Netherlands Antilles (CC) ÷	001-800-888-8000
#New Zealand (CC)	000-912
#Nicaragua (CC) (Outside of Managua, dial 02 first)	166
Nicaragua IIIC Access in Spanish	*2 from any public payphone
#Norway (CC) ◆	800-19912
#Pakistan	00-800-12-001
#Panama	108
Military Bases	2810-108
#Papua New Guinea (CC)	05-07-19140
#Paraguay ÷	008-11-800
#Peru	0-800-500-10
#Philippines (CC) ◆ To call using PHILCOM ■	105-15
To call using PLDT ■	105-14
Philippines IIIC via PLDT in Tagalog	1026-12
Philippines IIIC via PhilCom in Tagalog	1026-11
#Poland (CC) ÷	00-800-111-21-22
#Portugal (CC) ÷	05-017-1234
#Puerto Rico (CC)	1-800-888-8000
#Qatar ★	0800-012-77
#Romania (CC) ÷	01-800-1800
To call using ROSTELCOM ■	747-3322
#Russia (CC) ÷ To call using ROSTELCOM ■ (for Russian speaking operator)	747-3320
To call using SOVINTEL ■	960-2222
#Saipan (CC) ÷	950-1022
#San Marino (CC) ◆	172-1022
#Saudi Arabia (CC)	1-800-11
#Singapore	8000-112-112
#Slovak Republic (CC)	00421-00112
#Slovenia	080-8808

MCI

way. Live music (usually folksy) begins at 10pm. Cover for performances 300-400ptas. Open 6pm-3am.

ARGÜELLES-MONCLOA

"Los jóvenes, los jóvenes" (the kids, the kids). The young aspiring students inundate the streets wearing banana-peel-tight jeans, halter tops, denim jackets, and pony tails. This place will make you feel sorry for Spanish mothers. The area clears out weekdays in June (when exams hit) and everyday in August (when they leave town for vacation). In July, the weekend is a call to arms.

Chapandaz, C. Fernando Católico, a block from Arcipreste de Hita, down the stairs to the right. M: Moncloa. Strip mall by day, student hub by night (Fri.-Sat.) Lined with several bars and clubs, but only Chapandaz has stalactites and the mysterious *leche de pantera* (panther's milk). Large mixed drinks 500ptas. Open until 2am.

Galileo Galilei, C. Galileo, 100 (tel. 534 75 57 or 58) M: Guzmán el Bueno, or bus #2 from Gran Vía. At the top of the street, off C. Alberto Aguilera. Soft 80's decor plays host to some of Madrid's most fervent pop bands. Cover free-1500ptas.

El Pez Gordo, C. Pez, 6 (tel. 522 32 08) M: Santo Domingo. North of Gran Vía, off C. San Bernardo. (Don't try short cuts at night. Stick to the main streets.) This fat fish has blue and yellow innards and plenty of floor space to stare at. With surround-sound jazz, coffee for 125ptas, and a variety of wine (100-300ptas per cup) and cheese (200-300ptas). Open daily 1-3pm and 6pm-2am.

Palio, Isaac Peral, 38 (tel. 543 13 49). M: Moncloa, up C. Peral on the right. Glowing fluorescence of the zodiac is only just the entryway. No cover. Beer 500ptas.

Chema's Bar, Colegio Mayor San Agustín, Av. Séneca. M: Moncloa. Just a mole in the wall bar at the Complutense. Disproportionate ratio of male Spanish students to American exchange students. Frequented by illuminati Susan Parada, Esteban Rodriguez Marcos Roca Sierra, and Lauro Olmo Enciso. Beer 100ptas. Open Mon.-Fri. 10am-9pm.

■ Entertainment

MUSIC

In summer the city sponsors free concerts, ranging from classical to jazz to bolero and salsa, at **Plazas Mayor, Lavapiés,** and **Villa de París.** See **Entertainment,** p. 109 for informative publications, and check out the preceding clubs and bars for live rock and jazz performances.

The **Auditorio Nacional,** C. Príncipe de Vergara, 136 (tel. 337 01 00; M: Cruz del Rayo), hosts the finest classical performances (800-4200ptas). Home to the Orquesta Nacional, it has a magnificent hall for symphonic music and a smaller one for chamber recitals. The **Fundación Juan March,** C. Castelló, 77 (tel. 435 42 40; M: Núñez de Balboa), sponsors free weekly concerts (Fri.-Sun.) and hosts a university lecture series (Tues.-Wed 7:30pm). The **Conservatorio Superior de Música** (M: Atocha) recently moved into the 18th-century medical building next door to the Centro Reina Sofía, hosts free student performances, professional traveling orchestras, and celebrated soloists. **Teatro Monumental,** C. Atocha, 65 (tel. 429 81 19; M: Antón Martín), is home to Madrid's Orquesta Sinfónica. Reinforced concrete—a Spanish invention—was first used in its construction in the 20s; prepare for unusual acoustics. Most of the above organizations shut down activity in July and August.

For opera and *zarzuela* (Spanish light opera), head for the ornate **Teatro de la Zarzuela,** C. Jovellanos, 4, M: Banco de España (tel. 429 82 25), modeled on La Scala. The grand 19th-century granite **Teatro de la Ópera,** on Pl. Ópera (tel. 559 35 51), is the city's principal venue for classical ballet.

Flamenco in Madrid is tourist-oriented and expensive. It's like looking for pasta at McDonald's. **Café de Chinitas,** C. Torija, 7 (tel. 547 15 01 or 547 15 02; M: Santo Domingo), is as overstated as they come. Shows start at 10:30pm and midnight; the memories last forever (they'd better—the 4300ptas cover includes one drink). At

Corral de la Morería, C. Morería, 17 (tel. 365 84 46 or 365 11 37; M: La Latina), by the Viaducto on C. Bailén, shows start at 10:45 and last till 2am. The 4000ptas cover includes one drink. **Casa Patas,** C. Ceñizares, 10 (tel. 369 04 96; M: Antón Martín), is a more down-to-earth flamenco club. The shows start at midnight on Thurs-Sat. nights. The cover charge varies (open Mon.-Sat. 8pm-2:30am). **Teatro Albéniz,** C. Paz, 11 (tel. 531 83 11; M: Sol), hosts a yearly *Certamen de Coreografía de Danza Española y Flamenco* which features original dance and music, including a good portion of extraordinary flamenco (tickets 700-2000ptas).

The **Johnnie Walker Music Festival** in June and July brings big-name musicians from around the world—Herbie Hancock and Ray Charles last year (1000-1500ptas). Madrid's big rock 'n' roll stadium, **Palacio de los Deportes,** Av. Felipe II (tel. 401 91 00; M: Goya), generally rings in American groups. More alternative groups play at **Aqualung Universal,** Po. Ermita del Santo, 45 (tel. 470 23 62). Rock to the likes of the Lemonheads, Nick Cave, and Arrested Development. For information and tickets, try **FNAC** (tel. 595 62 00), **Madrid Rock** (tel. 523 26 52), **Virgin Megastore** (tel. 431 74 44), **Libreria Crisol** (tel. 322 47 00), or **TelEntrada** (tel. 902 38 33 33).

FILM

In summer, the city sponsors free movies and plays, all listed in the *Guía del Ocio* and entertainment supplements in all Friday papers. Look out for the **Fescinal,** a film festival at the Parque de la Florida in July. The **Parque del Retiro** sometimes shows free movies at 11pm. The **Centro Reina Sofía** has a repertory cinema of its own. The university's **colegios mayores** sponsor film series and jazz concerts.

Most cinemas show three films per day at around 4:30, 7:30, and 10:30pm. Tickets cost 600-700ptas. Some cinemas, like the Princesa, offer weekday-only matinee student discounts for 500ptas. Wednesday is *día del espectador:* tickets cost around 500ptas—show up early. Check the *versión original* **(V.O. subtitulada)** listings in entertainment guides for subtitled movies. Most Spanish theaters will not allow entrance to a movie past showtime. You can't go wrong if you hop off at M: Ventura Rodríguez, between Pl. España and Argüelles, site of three excellent theaters: **Princesa,** C. Princesa, 3 (tel. 559 98 72), shows mainstream Spanish films and subtitled foreign films. **Alphaville,** C. Martín de los Heros, 14 (tel. 559 38 36), behind Princesa passing underneath the large patio, has a bar and shows films suited to alternative tastes (*Mallrats* played for over a year) and current Spanish titles. (**Lumière,** in the underpass, shows V.O. films but the crowd is less hip.) **Renoir** (tel. 559 57 60) is a few doors down by the *palomitas* (popcorn) vendor, but the erudite theater won't let you eat inside. Renoir shows highly acclaimed recent films; many are foreign and subtitled. The state-subsidized *filmoteca española* in the Art Deco **Ciné Doré,** C. Santa Isabel, 3 (tel. 369 11 25; M: Antón Martín), is Madrid's finest repertory cinema (tickets 200-400ptas). It also has a comfortable bar, restaurant, and bookstore. Subtitled films are shown in many private theaters, including Alphaville, **Multicines Ideal,** C. Dr. Cortezo, 6 (tel. 369 25 18; M: Sol), is an anglophile favorite with 9 screens. To experience Spain's flawless dubbing industry, renowned world-wide, change over to **Gran Vía's** plush cinemas.

THEATER

In July and August, **Plaza Mayor, Plaza de Lavapiés, Plaza Villa de París** frequently host plays; some *teatros* close for vacation. During the rest of the year, theater-goers can consult the well-illustrated magazines published by state-sponsored theaters—which also sell posters of their productions for next to nothing—such as **Teatro Español, Teatro de la Comedia,** and the superb **Teatro María Guerrero.** Buy tickets at theater box offices or at agencies (**FNAC** tel. 595 62 00; **Libreria Crisol** tel. 322 47 00; **TelEntrada** tel. 902 38 33 33). **Huertas,** east of Sol, is the theater district (see p. 96). For a complete listing of theaters and shows, consult the *Guía del Ocio.*

Main Stages

Centro Cultural de la Villa, Pl. Colón (tel. 575 60 80). M: Colón or Serrano. City-run performance center showing ballet and plays. Tickets 2000ptas. Summer venue.

Sala Olimpia, C. Valencia (tel. 527 46 22). M: Lavapiés. National troupe produces avant-garde theatrical works. Tickets 2200-2600ptas. 30% student discounts. Summer venue.

Teatro Bellas Artes, C. Marqués de Casa Riera, 2 (tel. 532 44 37). M: Banco de España. Private theater devoted to staging new works.

Teatro de Cámara, C. San Cosme y San Damián, 3 (tel. 527 09 54). M: Atocha or Antón Martín. Classic repertory theater company produces canonical dramas and comedies by the likes of Gogol, Cervantes, Chekov…and Raymond Carver. Poetry recitals. Tickets 1000-1500ptas. Summer venue.

Teatro de la Comedia, C. Príncipe, 14 (tel. 521 49 31). M: Sevilla. The traveling *Compañía Nacional Teatro Clásico* often performs classical Spanish theater here. Tickets 1300-2600ptas, reduced prices Thurs. Ticket office open 11:30am-1:30pm and 5-9pm.

Teatro Español, C. Príncipe, 25 (tel. 429 62 97). M: Sol. Site of 16th-century Teatro de Príncipe, the Teatro Español dates from the 18th century. Established company run by city hall regularly showcases winners of the prestigious Lope de Vega award. Tickets 200-2000ptas. 50% discount on Wed. Excellent, traditional **Café del Príncipe** inside. Summer venue.

Teatro María Guerrero, C. Tamayo y Baus, 4 (tel. 319 47 69). M: Colón or Banco de España. Excellent state-supported repertory company. Tickets 1400-2400ptas. Ticket office open 11:30am-1:30pm and 5-6pm. Summer venue.

Teatro La Latina, Pl. Cebada, 2 (tel. 365 28 35). M: Latina. A varied repertoire of works by new and established playwrights. Tickets 1800-3000ptas. Office open 11am-1pm and 6-8pm. Summer venue.

Teatro Nacional Clásico, C. Príncipe, 14 (tel. 521 49 31). Works by great Spanish dramatists of the past. Tickets 1300-1600ptas. Visa, AmEx.

Alternative Theater

Teatro El Canto de la Cabra, C. San Gregorio, 8 (tel. 310 42 22). M: Chueca. Avant-garde troupe, offering interesting open-air performances in July and August. Tickets 1500ptas; students 1000ptas. Summer venue.

Teatro Cuarta Pared, C. Ercilla, 17 (tel. 517 23 17). M: Embajadores. Storytelling performances and experimental theater. Tickets 1200ptas.

Teatro Maravillas, C. Manuela Malasaña, 6 (tel. 446 71 94). M: Bilbao. Popular commercial theater; mostly musicals and comedies. Tickets 1500-2500ptas; under 20 1000ptas.

Teatro Estudio de Madrid, C. Cabeza, 14 (tel. 539 64 47). M: Tirso de Molina. Amateur studio theater; avant-garde works and performance art. Tickets 1200ptas; students 800ptas. Summer venue.

Teatro Triángulo, C. Zurita, 20 (tel. 530 68 91). M: Lavapiés. Experimental takes on some classics, but mostly theater of the absurd. Tickets 1200ptas; students 800ptas. Summer venue.

SHOPPING

Most shops open in the morning, then roll up their awnings and drop their metal grates for *siesta* from two to five in the afternoon and re-open till eight o'clock. Major department stores, such as **El Corte Inglés** and **FNAC** (see p. 75) open from around 10am to 9pm. Some enterprising shops have begun to stay open on Saturday afternoons and a few during lunch. Many close in August, when practically everyone flees to the coast. By law, *grandes almecenes* (department stores) may only open the first Sunday of every month, a law that reflects the State's reluctance to make the capitalistic plunge. **Inal** publishes a yearly *Guía Esencial para vivir en Madrid*, which includes descriptions of most stores

MADRID

El Rastro

Every Sunday morning for hundreds of years, **El Rastro** has been *the* place to sell stolen watches and buy battered birdcages. Old shoes and cheap jewelry abound, but the intrepid shopper will find good deals on second-hand leather jackets, leather bags, and canaries (on their own special sidestreet). Students and their propaganda of discontent congregate around *Tirso de Molina*. Antiquarians contribute their peculiar mustiness to Calle (not Salón or Paseo) del Prado and adjacent streets—some Spaniards pride themselves on equipping an entire apartment with antique sideboards and cauldrons from the Rastro. From Pl. Mayor, walk down C. Toledo to Pl. Cascorro (M: La Latina), where the market begins, and follow the rest of the world to the end, at the bottom of C. Ribera de Curtidores. Unless you enjoy being crushed in a river of solid flesh, arrive no later than 10am and drift off to an air-conditioned bar when you get sticky (**Los Caracoles** is convenient; see **Tapas**, p. 89). The flea market is a den of **pickpockets,** so wear your backpack backwards (that is, frontwards), and be very discreet when taking out your wallet or money. El Rastro is open Sun. and holidays 9am-2pm.)

Boutiques

From Sol to the Gran Vía and along C. Princesa, the main department stores float in a sea of smaller discount stores. Budgeters with weary spirits and scraped soles shop at **Los Guerrilleros** (a huge store with quite low prices), Puerta del Sol, 5, diagonally across from El Corte Inglés.

Lines of outlets with garments at wholesale prices mingle with young designer boutiques on **C. Conde de Romanones** (M: Tirso de Molina). Shopping here means fishing through a sea of funky to undesirably tacky clothes to find what meets your fancy. For die-hard club gear head to **Glam** on C. Fuencarral, 35 (tel. 522 80 54), or the naughtier **Come** on C. Hortaleza, 38—nothing but platforms and vinyl here. On Almirante, 22 is crazy, modern, unisex **Plan 2** (tel. 522 33 11).

For a designer look and semi-affordable prices, there's **Zara,** a retail store found throughout Madrid (C. Fuencarral, 126-128; Gran Vía 32; and C. Princesa, 45). Zara's factory reject branch, **Lefties,** is cheap-cheap-cheap, and located on C. Carretas, 10, a block and a half off Sol. **Kameleón,** Arenal, 8 (tel. 523 21 63), and Preciados, 32 (tel. 522 35 93), sells second-hand clothes.

The embassy quarter north of C. Génova is decidedly more haughty. Madrid's poshest shopping areas are Jerónimos and Salamanca. In the latter, couture and near-couture boutiques vogue on **Calles Serrano, Príncipe de Vergara, Velázquez, Goya, Ortega y Gasset, Coello, and Alfonso XII** (M: Serrano or Velázquez).

Malls

La Vaguada (M: Barrio del Pilar; bus #132 from Moncloa), in the northern neighborhood **Madrid-2,** is Madrid's first experiment with Americana. It offers everything a homesick Michigonian could want: 350 shops, including the Body Shop, Springfield, Burberry's, and confectionery bazaars; a food court with Colonel Sanders and Ronald McDonald; multicinemas; and a bowling alley/arcade. Open daily 10am-10pm.

By far the poshest shopping mall belongs to the **Galería del Prado,** Pl. Cortes (M: Banco de España), located beneath the crusty Hotel Palace and across the Castellana from the Ritz, no less. It's on the way to AmEx and the Triángulo de Arte, and let's face it, it's fun to handle furs and suedes while poopy attendants look on scornfully. Open Mon.-Sat. 10am-9pm. Of course, don't forget El Corte Inglés (see **Practical Information,** p. 75)

Books

FNAC, C. Preciados, 28 (tel. 595 62 00). M: Callao. The 1995 opening of this French megastore was a media event. The best music and book selection in town. Also sells books in English and CDs. Open Mon.-Sat. 10am-10pm.

Librería Turner, C. Genova, 3 (tel. 319 09 26). M: Alonso Martínez. Brand-new editions (more expensive) of classics and new releases in English, French, German, and Spanish. Also books on tape and a sci-fi collection. Strong reference section

with phrasebooks and dictionaries. Open Mon.-Fri. 10am-8pm, Sat. 10am-2pm. The companion store next door carries music and English-language videos for rent.

Casa del Libro, Gran Vía, 29 (tel. 521 21 13). M: Gran Vía or Callao. A tradition. Six stories of books, including a selection in English. Open Mon.-Sat. 10am-8:30pm.

Librería Crisol, C. Juan Bravo, 38 (tel. 322 48 00). A high-powered place with futuristic interior design; service and prices to match. Great hours: open Mon.-Sat. 10am-10pm, Sun. 11am-3pm and 5-9pm. Many other locations around Madrid.

La Casa del Libro, Gran Vía, 29 (tel. 521 20 37). M: Callao or Pl. España. One of the best selections in town. They'll order it if you've got the time.

Booksellers, C. José Abascal, 48 (tel. 442 79 59 or 442 81 04). M: Iglesia. From the Metro station, walk down C. Santa Engracia five blocks and take a right on C. José Abascal. A vast array of new books in English, plus American and English magazines. Open Mon.-Fri. 9:30am-2pm and 5-8pm, Sat. 10am-2pm

Librería de Mujeres (Women's Bookstore), C. San Cristóbal, 17 (tel. 521 70 43), near Pl. Mayor. International bookstore. English spoken. (See p. 76).

Berkana Librería Gai y Lesbiana, C. Gravina, 11 (tel./fax 532 13 93). M: Chueca. Gay and lesbian bookstore. Open Mon.-Fri. 10:30am–2pm and 5-8:30pm, Sat. noon-2pm and 5-8:30pm.

Cuesta de Moyano, along the southern border of the Jardín Botánico (M: Atocha), 30 open-air wood stalls hawk new and used paperbacks and rare books. Best buying day is Sunday.

Librería Felipa, C. Libreros, off Gran Vía. M: Callao or Pl. España. The entire street is books, but only Felipa gives a 20% discount off list price. Generations of students have bought their textbooks here.

English Editions, Pl. San Amaro, 5 (tel. 571 03 21). M: Estrecho. In the tiny Pl. San Amaro, off C. General Perón. Used novels bought and sold—excellent selection. Also a mini-mart featuring English and American specialties such as Skippy peanut butter. Open Mon.-Fri. 11am-2pm and 5-8pm, Sat. 11am-2pm.

Altair, C. Gaztambide, 31. M: Arguelles. Street heads north from intersection of C. Princesa and C. Aguilera. New travel-book bookstore. Carries guides to almost everywhere. Open Mon.-Sat. 10am-2pm and 4:30-8pm.

VIPS mega-convenience-stores also stock novels and guidebooks in English. See **Red-Eye Establishments,** p. 85

El Corte Inglés, granted (see **Practical Information,** p. 75), sells books and CDs.

Capes and Pets

The classic Spanish **cape store** Seseña is at C. Argensola, 2 (tel. 319 59 40; M: Alonso Martínez). A quick gander at **ZooPark,** C. Fernando Catolica, 77, M: Moncloa, or **NaturaPark,** C. Fuencarral, 42, is harmless, unless you get too close to the large reptiles or small monkeys).

ATHLETICS

Fútbol

Spaniards obsess over **fútbol** (soccer). If either **Real Madrid** or **Atlético de Madrid** wins a match, count on streets being clogged with screaming fans and honking cars (more so than is usual). Every Sunday and some Saturdays between September and June, one of these two teams plays at home. *Los vikingos,* fans of El Madrid, supported Raúl and the boys to the title of *la Liga Española* in 1998, and Kiko and Atlético won it all in '97 after almost being demoted to second division the year before. Real Madrid plays at **Estadio Santiago Bernebéu,** Po. Castellana, 104 (tel. 457 11 12; M: Lima). Atlético de Madrid plays at Estadio Vicente Calderón, C. Virgen del Puerto, 67 (tel. 366 47 07; M: Pirámides or Marqués de Vadillos). Tickets for seats cost 3000-7000ptas. If tickets are sold out, shifty scalpers lurk around the stadium during the afternoon or evening a few days before the game. These tickets cost only 25-50% more, whereas on game day prices become astronomical. For the big games— Atlético vs. Real, either team vs. F.C. Barcelona *(La Barça),* key matches in April and May, summer *Copa del Rey* and *Copa de Europa*—scalpers are really the only

option, so be wary. Betting is legal with the state-run lottery; department stores and *estancos* distribute gamecards.

Recreation

For **cycling** info and bicycle repair, spin over to **Ciclos Muñoz,** C. Pablo Ortiz (tel. 475 02 19; M: Usera). **Swimmers** splash in the outdoor pools (open 10:30am-8pm, 500ptas, ages 4-13 225ptas) at: **Casa de Campo** (tel. 463 00 50) on Av. Angel (M: Lago); the indoor **Municipal de La Latina,** Pl. Cebada, 2 (M: La Latina); **Aluche** (tel. 706 28 28) on Av. General Fenjul (bus #17, 34, or 139); and **Peñuelas,** C. Arganda (tel. 474 28 08, M: Delicias or bus #18). Gallop over to the **Hipódromo de Madrid,** Ctra. de La Coruña, km 7800 (tel. 357 16 82), for **horse-racing.** Call the **Dirección General de Deportes** (tel. 409 49 04) for more sporting info.

LA CORRIDA (THE BULLFIGHT)

Bullfighters are loved or loathed. If the crowd thinks the *matador* is a man of mettle and style, they exalt him as an emperor. If they think him a coward or a butcher, they whistle cacophonously, chant *"Vete"* (Get out!), throw their seat cushions (40ptas to rent) at him, and wait outside the ring to stone his car. A bloody killing of the bull, instead of the swift death-stab, can upset the career of even the most renowned *matador* or *matadora*—in 1996, **Cristina** entered the ring as Spain's first female bullfighter of premier rank.

Corridas (bullfights) are held during the Festival of San Isidro and every Sunday in summer, less frequently the rest of the year. The season lasts from March to October, signalled by posters in bars and cafes (especially on C. Victoria, off C. San Jerónimo). **Plaza de las Ventas,** C. Alcalá, 237 (tel. 356 22 00; M: Ventas), east of central Madrid is the biggest ring in Spain. Metro or bus rides, even 90 minutes before the fight, can be asphyxiating.n Seats run for 450-15,200ptas, depending on its location either in the *sombra* (shade) or the blistering *sol.* Tickets are usually available the Friday and Saturday before and the Sunday of the bullfight. If you're intrigued by the lore but not the gore, head to the **Museo Taurino,** C. Alcalá, 237 (tel. 725 18 57), at Pl. Monumental de Las Ventas. The museum displays a remarkable collection of *trajes de luces,* capes, and posters of famous *corridas.* (Open Mon.-Fri. 9:30am-2:30pm. On fight days it opens 1hr. before the *lidia.* Free.) The bullfighting school where teenagers graduate to become *novilleros* (novice bullfights), is tucked away by the amusement park at M: Batán. Bulls are kept there before being transported to the big time bull ring, and the school often has its own *corridas* for free (tel. 470 19 90).

From May 15-22, the **Fiestas de San Isidro** bring a bullfight every day with top *toreros* the and fiercest bulls. The festival is nationally televised, and most of those without tickets crowd into bars. **Bar-Restaurante Plata,** C. Jardines, 11 (tel. 532 48 98; M: Sol), has cheap *tapas* and a loud television. **Bar El Pavón,** C. Victoria, 8, at C. Cruz (M: Sol); **El Abuelo,** C. Núñez de Arce, 5, where aficionados brandish the restaurant's famous shrimp during arguments over bullfighters; and **Bar Torre del Oro,** Pl. Mayor, 26 (tel. 366 50 16; open 10am-1am; M: Sol or Ópera), are all local favorites. The bar of ritzy **Hotel Wellington** on C. Velázquez is also known to have its share of *matadores* and their groupies. During the *fiestas* it's unusual to enter a bar and not find the TV tuned to the bullfight.

No Bull! Bull Facts

1—Kids can start bullfighter training at age 12, but its against the law to pace a *toro vivo* (live bull) until they're 16. Before that, they practice with cows.

2—An authentic *traje de luces* (suit of lights) Matador-costume sells for around 200,000ptas; about as much as it costs to stuff a bull's heads.

FESTIVALS

The brochure *Las Fiestas de España,* available at tourist offices and the bigger hotels, contains historical background and general info on Spain's festivals. Madrid's **Carnaval** was inaugurated in the Middle Ages then prohibited during Franco's dictatorship. The city bursts with street fiestas, dancing, and processions. The Fat Tuesday celebration culminates with the mystifying "Burial of the Sardine." In late April, the city bubbles with the high quality **Festival Internacional de Teatro.** The May **Fiestas de San Isidro,** in honor of Madrid's patron saint, bring concerts, parades, and Spain's best bullfights. Throughout the summer, the city sponsors the **Veranos de la Villa,** an outstanding variety of cultural activities, including free classical music concerts, movies in open-air settings, plays, art exhibits, an international film festival, opera and *zarzuela* (Spanish operetta), ballet, and sports. In August, the neighborhoods of **San Cayetano, San Lorenzo,** and **La Paloma** have their own festivities in a flurry of *madrileñismo:* Processions, street dancing, traditional games, food, and drink are combined with home-grown hard rock and political slogans. The **Festivales de Otoño** (Autumn Festivals) from Sept.-Nov. also conjure an impressive array of music, theater, and film. On Nov. 1, **Todos los Santos** (All Saints' Day), an International Jazz Festival brings great musicians to Madrid. The **Día de la Constitución** (Day of the Constitution, or National Day) on Dec. 6 heralds the arrival of the National Company of Spanish Classical Ballet in Madrid. Tourist offices in Madrid have all the grit.

ELSEWHERE IN THE COMUNIDAD DE MADRID

The Comunidad de Madrid is an autonomous administrative region, shaped like an arrowhead and pointing right at the heart of Castilla y León. Historically, Madrid and Castilla La Mancha were known as Castilla La Nueva (New Castile), while the Castilla north of Madrid was called Castilla La Vieja (Old Castile, now part of Castilla y León).

■ Alcalá de Henares

The people of Alcalá (pop. 165,000) pride themselves on their town's distinguished progeny (Miguel de Cervantes, Catherine of Aragon, Juan Ruiz "Azorín," Rocío Rodríguez Salceda), as well as the university's famed alumni (Francisco de Quevedo) and professors (Lope de Vega). Exceptional architectural examples, especially the university's Renaissance facade (1499) and the Capilla de San Ildefonso draw tourists. Better yet, visitors return to Alcalá to satisfy their sweet tooth, munching on *almendras garrapiñadas* (honey and sugar coated almonds) and *churros y chocolate.*

Orientation and Practical Information Plaza de Cervantes is the main square. To get there from the **train station,** turn left as you exit and follow Po. Estación for a few blocks. Take a right on C. Libreros and the plaza will be on your left. The **tourist office,** Callejón de Santa María, 1 (tel. 889 26 94), at the corner of Pl. Cervantes, has a list of tourist sites and a detailed map of Alcalá (open daily 10am-2pm and 4-6:30pm, July-Sept. 10am-2pm and 5-7:30pm). The **Red Cross,** Pl. Cervantes, 12 (tel. 883 60 63 or 881 40 83), has an emergency line (tel. 888 15 02). For an **ambulance** or other medical emergencies, dial 061. The **police** answer at (tel. 881 92 63; all 091 or 092 in an **emergency**). The **post office** (tel. 889 23 34) is located on Pl. Cervantes between the intersection of C. Libreros and the tourist office (open Mon.-Sat. 8:30am-7pm, Sat. 9:30am-1pm). The **train station** is located on Po. Estación. Trains run from Madrid's Atocha and back every 15 minutes (30min., 610ptas round-trip). The Continental-Auto **bus station,** Av. Guadalajara, 36 (tel. 888 16 22), runs buses every 15 minutes between Alcalá and Madrid (20min., 250ptas). To reach the city center, turn right on Av. Guadalajara and fork left onto C. Libreros.

Accommodations and Food The town is small and the number of hostels limited, so reservations are recommended. Some of the least expensive rooms can be found at **Hostal Jacinto,** Po. Estación, 2, 2nd staircase, 1-D (tel. 889 14 32), three blocks from the train station. This quirkily decorated *hostal* is close to Pl. Cervantes. (Singles 2000ptas, with shower 2200ptas. Doubles with shower 3600ptas, with bath 4500ptas. Triples 4500ptas. Quads 6000ptas. Accepts reservations, but not credit cards.) **Restaurante Topeca '75** (tel. 888 45 25), on C. Mayor, half a block from Pl. Cervantes, is a mirrored bar with a classy dining room upstairs (*menú* 800ptas,enormous jugs of *sangría* 800ptas). **Mesón Las Cuadras de Rocinante,** C. Carmen Calzado, 1 (tel. 880 08 88), is off C. Mayor. If it's good enough for Don Quijote's horse, it's good enough for you. Huge, delicious, and cheap *raciones* are 325-1000ptas; *sangría* 650-1300ptas.

Sights **Plaza de Cervantes** is filled with rose bushes and outdoor cafes. At its south end cluster the **Ruinas de Santa María,** the remains of a 16th-century church destroyed during the Civil War. In the surviving **Capilla del Oidor,** white Gothic plaster works surround the fountain where Cervantes was christened. Just east of Pl. Cervantes in Pl. San Diego sits the **Colegio Mayor de San Ildefonso,** fulcrum of the once-illustrious university. Pioneering humanist Cardinal Cisneros founded the college in 1499, 13 years before he created the university itself. Cisneros now decays in the altar of the adjoining **Capilla de San Ildefonso** (tel. 882 13 54). Although the whole university was transferred to Madrid in 1836, several academic departments returned to Alcalá in 1977. Tours are the only way to get in. (Open Mon.-Fri., tours at 11:30am, 12:30, 1:30, 5 and 6pm; Sat.-Sun. at 11, 11:45am, 12:30, 1:15, 2, 4:30, 5:15, 6, 6:45 and 7:30pm; 300ptas.). The town's **Catedral Magistral** is one of the few in the world with this title; to be so named every priest must be a university magistrate. The cathedral was built between 1497 and 1514, its tower added in the 1600s.

Down C. Mayor from Pl. Cervantes is **Casa de Cervantes** (tel. 889 96 54), the reconstruction *in situ* of the house where the author was born. A collection of furniture, pottery, and other artifacts fills 13 rooms. Although they are all originals (including the map downstairs), none belonged to Cervantes or his father who owned the house. *Don Quijote* editions in every language are displayed upstairs (open Tues.-Fri. 10:15am-2pm and 4-6:45pm, Sat.-Sun. 10:15am-2pm and 4-6:30pm; free). The **Open Air Sculpture Museum** begins at the Puerta de Madrid and follows the town wall along C. Andrés Saborit and Vía Complutense. It pays tribute to contemporary Spanish artists (and beautifies the less attractive section of town).

Happy times are here again

Alcalá's native son Azorín, of the Generation of '98, wrote embittered novels that criticize his nation's moral decay and lagging industrialization following the devastating loss to the U.S. in the Spanish-American War:

> *¿Para qué hacer nada? Yo creo que la vida es el mal, y que todo lo que hagamos para acrecentar la vida, es fomentar esta perdurable agonía sobre un átomo en lo infinito...Lo humano, lo justo sería acabar el dolor acabando la espaecie.*

> [Why do anything? I believe that life is the misfortune, and that everything we do to advance life is to foment this everlasting agony atop an atom in infinity...The humane, the just thing would be to end the pain ending the species.]

> Juan Ruiz "Azorín," *La Voluntad*

■ Sierra de Guadarrama

The Sierra de Guadarrama is a pine-covered mountain range halfway between Madrid and Segovia. Its dark geological shapes loom large in local imagination, as well as the local economy. With La Mujer Muerta (The Dead Woman) to the west, the Sierra de la Maliciosa (Mountain of the Evil Woman) to the east, and, between the two, the Siete Picos (Seven Peaks), it's a bit scary out there. Yet none of these portents of doom deter the influx of summer and winter visitors who come to hike and ski.

CERCEDILLA

Cercedilla sucks in city slickers yearning for fresh air. A picturesque town of Alpine chalets, Cercedilla's attractions change with the seasons: during the summer, vacationers seek the cooler, more relaxed living of the Sierra; during the winter, skiers crowd nearby resorts.

Orientation and Practical Information Cercedilla is the easiest town in the Sierras to reach by **train** as a daytrip from Madrid or Segovia. To get to town from the station, go uphill, fork right at the top, and continue straight on at the train track (15-20min.). Frequent **Buses** from Madrid drop you off in the center of town. Most of the hiking action begins up the **Carretera las Dehesas,** beyond the intersection, uphill from the train station. A strenuous hike leads past the Hospital de Fuenfrías to the meadow of Navarrulaque. The **Calzada Romana,** atop of the Carretera, offers weird hiking along an ancient Roman road that once connected Madrid to Segovia.

The **Consejería de Medio Ambiente,** Ctra. las Dehesas (tel. 852 22 13), a wooden chalet 3 km up the road (30min. from the train station), functions as a tourist office and offers hiking info. The free leaflet *Senderos Autoguiados* (self-guided trails) is especially good. From July to October, free guided tours of the valley depart from the shelter across the road from the chalet at 10am (open daily 9am-6pm; winter 9am-4pm). For **medical assistance,** call the Centro Médico (tel. 852 30 31; **emergency** tel. 852 04 97). The **police** are in the Ayuntamiento, Pl. Mayor, 1 (tel. 852 02 00, 852 04 25, or (90) 871 65 22). In an **emergency,** dial 091 or 092. The **telephone code** is (9)1.

The **train station** (tel. 852 00 57) is at the base of the hill on C. Emilio Serrano. Service to: Madrid (over 30 per day, 1½hr., 465ptas); Segovia (9 per day, 45min., 290ptas); Los Cotos (9 per day, 45min., 465ptas); and Puerto de Navacerrada (9 per day, ½hr., 125ptas, round-trip 440ptas). The **bus station,** Av. José Antonio, 2 (tel. 852 02 39), is across the street and to the left of the Ayuntamiento.

Accommodations and Food On Ctra. Las Dehesas, two **HI youth hostels** have views of the Sierra, group meals, and lockout. The **Villa Castora (HI)** (tel. 852 03 34) is closest to the train station, about 1½km up Ctra. Las Dehesas on the left. The pool is open in summer. Rooms have baths and the first floor has a terrace. Reservations 15 days in advance are recommended. (Reception open 8am-10pm. Doubles 1275ptas per person, over 26 1725ptas. Quads: 950ptas; 1300ptas. Breakfast included.) The same prices and hours can be found at **Las Dehesas (HI;** tel. 852 01 35) along with spartan but sunny and clean rooms, tucked back among the trees just beyond the Agencia del Medio Ambiente on Ctra. las Dehesas; it's closer to the hiking trails and farther from the highway. (Midnight curfew. Make reservations one week ahead. HI cards, required at both, are available on the spot for 1800ptas.) **Camping** is strictly controlled throughout the Sierra de Guadarrama, and is no longer allowed within Cercedilla's town limits, which extend far beyond the town. A list of campsites is available at the Agencia del Medio Ambiente. Reaching most of these rather remote sites requires wheels (tires, not roller skates).

Supermarket **Maxcoop,** C. Docta Cañados, 2 (tel. 852 00 13), is in the town center off Av. Generalísimo (open Mon.-Sat. 9:30am-2pm and 5:30-9pm, Sun. 9:30am-2pm). Hordes of bars peddle inexpensive *bocadillos* and *raciones* in the town proper.

PUERTO DE NAVACERRADA AND LOS COTOS

A magnet for outdoorsy types year-round, **Puerto de Navacerrada** offers bland **skiing** in the winter and beautiful **hiking** in the summer—backpackers use Navacerrada as a starting point to roam the peaks. A little engine leaves for Navacerrada from the Cercedilla station. In addition, the same Cercanías line that travels from Madrid to Cercedilla passes through Navacerrada a few stops later (1¾hr., 440ptas). The ski season lasts from December to April; there are special areas for beginners and competitions for the more accomplished. For hiking, exit the station, turn left at the highway, and turn left again (off the road) at the large intersection marking the pass. The dirt path leads uphill. Many hiking routes lead through the pine forests; the **Vía de Schmidt** (or Smit) to the left leads back to Cercedilla.

Los Cotos is another popular winter resort. Nearby **Rascafría** in Los Cotos has two well regarded ski stations: **Valdesqui** (tel. 852 04 16) and **Valcotos** (both open in winter roughly 10am-5pm). For detailed info on winter sports, call the Madrid office of the Dirección General de Deportes (tel. 409 49 04). Cercanías run from Madrid to Los Cotos, through Cercedilla and Navacerrada (2hr., 435ptas).

■ San Lorenzo del Escorial

In the shadow of Felipe II's somber colossus El Escorial—half monastery and half mausoleum—the town of San Lorenzo is usually neglected by daytrippers from Madrid, although within easy striking distance. Arrive early and stay late to make the most of the Spanish "eighth wonder of the world," a fascinating, severe complex

including a monastery, two palaces, a church to die for, two pantheons, a magnificent library, and innumerable artistic treasures. Above all, *don't* come on Monday, when the whole complex and most of the town is closed.

ORIENTATION AND PRACTICAL INFORMATION

Autocares Herranz **bus** is the easiest way to travel between El Escorial and Madrid. Buses leave from the Mocloa metro Station and whisk travelers to El Escorial's **Plaza Virgen de Gracia**. The Autocares Herranz office, C. Reina Victoria, 3 (tel. 890 41 00, 890 41 22, or 890 41 25), and the **bar/casino** at C. Rey, 3, sell tickets to Madrid (Mon.-Sat. over 40 per day, Sun. 10 per day, 1 hr., 720ptas round-trip). Confirm your return ticket before boarding the bus for Madrid at the bar/casino. Exit the bus station to the left and turn right up C. Florida Blanca to get to the **tourist office** (½block), C. Floridablanca, 10 (tel. 890 15 54), where you can pick up a **map.** (On Sun. ask for a map at the hotel next door. *Turismo* open Mon.-Fri. 10am-2pm and 3-5pm, Sat. 10am-1:45pm.)

El Escorial's **train** station, Ctra. Estación (tel. 890 04; RENFE info tel. 328 90 20), is two kilometers from town. Shuttle buses run frequently between the station and Pl. Virgen de Gracia. (Most trains run to Madrid-Atocha but a few go to Madrid-Chamartín, every 20min., 9am-3pm, 1hr., 750ptas round-trip.) Those with **medical problems** should consult the **Red Cross,** Ctra. Guadarrama, km7 (tel. 890 41 41), or call an **ambulance** (tel. 896 11 11). The **police,** C. Gobernador, 2 (tel. 890 52 23), have an **emergency** line (tel. 091 or 092). Change money at **Banco Central Hispano,** C. Rey, 11. There are **ATMs** outside the **Post Office,** C. Juan de Toledo, 2 (tel. 890 26 85; open Mon.-Fri. 8:30am-2pm, Sat. 8:30am-1pm). The **Postal Code** is 28200. **Telephone Code** (9)1.

ACCOMMODATIONS AND FOOD

Rooms fill up quickly in July and August, however, the situation gets dire only during the festivals (Aug. 10-20). The center's many cafes are busy throughout the day. Purchase *pan, queso, y vino* (bread, cheese, and wine) at the **Mercado Público,** C. Rey, 7, two blocks off C. Floridablanca (open Mon.-Wed. and Fri.-Sat. 9:30am-1:30pm and 6-9pm, Thurs. 6-9pm). To reach the **Residencia Juvenil "El Escorial" (HI),** C. Residencia, 14 (tel. 890 59 24; fax 890 06 20), walk up C. Rey, past the *Mercado Publico,* turn right at C. San Pedro Regalado, and go up the steps with the stone balls. When the road forks, go right (C. Millan); when it forks again, take C. Residencia. (HI card required. Singles and doubles 1275ptas per person, over 26 1725ptas. Quads 950ptas per person, over 26 1300ptas. Breakfast included; lunch, dinner available. Reservations accepted.) From the bus stop to **Hostal Vasco,** Pl. Santiago, 11 (tel. 890 16 19), walk up C. Ray two blocks and turn right. The hostel has a terrace on the plaza. Some rooms sport small balconies and excellent views of the monastery. (Singles 3000ptas. Doubles with shower 4500ptas, with full bath 4700ptas. Triples 5700ptas. Breakfast 425ptas.) To sleep under the stars, go to **Camping Caravaning El Escorial** (tel. 890 24 12), seven kilometers away on Ctra. de Guadarrama al Escorial. (625ptas per person, per tent, per car; reservations accepted).

SIGHTS

El Escorial

The entire El Escorial complex (tel. 890 59 03, 890 59 04, or 866 02 38—it's that big) is open Tues.-Sun. 10am-7pm; Oct.-March 10am-6pm. Last admission to palaces, pantheons, and museums is 1hr. or 30min. before closing. (Monastery 850ptas, students 350ptas, guided tour 950ptas, Wed. free for EU citizens. *Casitas* 325ptas.)

The Monastery

The **Monasterio de San Lorenzo del Escorial** was a gift from Felipe II to God, the people, and himself, commemorating his victory over the French at the battle of San Quintín in 1557. It was a jubilant occasion, but Felipe squelched any frivolous exuberance in the design of what was to be first his royal monastery and then his mauso-

leum. Juan Bautista de Toledo was commissioned to design the complex in 1561; when he died in 1567, Juan de Herrera inherited his mantle. Except for the Panteón Real and minor additional work, the monastery was finished in a speedy 21 years.

According to tradition, Felipe oversaw much of the work from a chair-shaped rock 7km from the construction site. That stone is now known as **Silla de Felipe II** (Felipe's Chair), and the view is still regal.

Considering the resources Felipe II—son of Carlos I, who had ruled the most powerful empire in the world—commanded, the building is noteworthy for its austerity, symmetry, and simplicity—in Felipe's words, "majesty without ostentation." Four massive towers pin the corners and the towers of the basilica that rise from the center are surmounted by a great dome, giving the ensemble a pyramidal shape. At Felipe II's behest, steep slate roofs were introduced from Flanders—the first of their kind in Spain. Slate spires lend grace to the grim structure, further mellowed by the glowing *piedra de Colmenar,* a stone hewn from nearby quarries. Variations of this Habsburg style (or *estilo herrerense*) of unadorned granite and red brick, slate roofs, and corner towers, appear throughout Spain—particularly in Madrid and Toledo

To avoid the worst of the crowds, enter El Escorial by the traditional gateway on the west side (C. Floridablanca). After marvelling over the collection of Flemish tapestries and paintings, including El Greco's *Martirio de San Mauricio y la Legión,* then enter the **Museos de Arquitectura and Pintura.** It has an outstanding exhibition on the construction of El Escorial, comparing it to other related structures and with wooden models of 16th-century machinery and of the buildings themselves. The Museo de Pintura features masterpieces by Bosch, Dures, El Greco, Titian, Tintoretto, Velázquez, Zurbarán, Van Dyck, and others.

The **Palacio Real,** lined with XVI century *azulejos* (tiles) from Toledo, includes the **Salón del Trono** (Throne Room) and two **dwellings**—Felipe II's spartan 16th-century apartments and the more luxurious 18th-century rooms of Carlos III and Carlos IV. The Bourbon half is distinguished by the sumptuousness of its furniture and **tapestries.** Copies of works by Goya, El Greco, and Rubens done in intricate detail and brilliant wool yarn cover the walls. Pastoral images cover the **Puertas de Marguetería,** German doors made from 18 different types of trees—some from as far as America.

The long **Sala de Batallas** (Battle Room) links the two parts of the palace. A huge fresco here depicts some of Castile and Spain's greatest victories: Juan II's 1431 triumph over the Muslims at Higueruela (note the fleeing townsfolk), Felipe II's two successful expeditions to the Azores, and the battle of San Quintín. Downstairs, in the royal chambers, Felipe II's miniscule bed attests to his (relative) asceticism.

The **Biblioteca** (library) on the second floor holds numerous priceless books and manuscripts despite several fires which have reduced the collection. Alfonso X's *Cantigas de Santa María,* the Book of Hours of the Catholic monarchs, Saint Teresa's manuscripts and diary, the gold-scrolled *Aureus Codex* (by German Emperor Conrad III, 1039), and an 11th-century *Commentary on the Apocalypse* by Beato de Liébana are just a small selection of the choice readings.

Death Royale

The **Panteón Real** was another brainchild of Felipe II. Though he didn't live to see it finished, he's buried here along with Carlos I and most of their royal descendants. Servants dumped bygone nobles in the small adjoining rooms so that the bodies could dry before being stuffed into their permanent tombs; drying time varied based on climate conditions and fat content (about 15-20 years).

The stairway and the crypt are elegantly adorned with black and red marble and jasper—a colorful combination which, combined with the gold cherubs and high ceiling, resembles a deathly *discoteca.* Of the 26 gray marble sarcophagi, 23 contain the remains of Spanish monarchs, and three are still empty. All the late Spanish kings except for Felipe V and Fernando VI are buried here—only those whose sons become monarchs can join the macabre club.

The lower main cloister is a segue into the cool and magnificent **basílica**. Marble steps lead to an altar adorned by two groups of elegant sculptures by Pompeo Leoni. The figures on the left represent assorted relatives of Felipe II: parents Carlos I and Isabel, daughter María, and sisters María (Queen of Hungary) and Leonor (Queen of France). Those on the right depict Felipe II with three wives and his son Carlos. The **Coro Alto** (High Choir) has a magnificent ceiling fresco of heaven filled with choirs of angels. The **cloister** shines under Titian's fresco of the martyrdom of St. Lawrence.

Casitas

Commissioned by the Prince of Asturias, who later became Carlos IV, the **Casita del Príncipe** has a splendid collection of ornaments, including chandeliers, lamps, rugs, furniture, clocks, tapestries, china, and engraved oranges. The French roughed up the *casita* during the Napoleonic invasions, but many rooms were redecorated by Fernando VII in the then-popular Empire style. To get to the *casita,* follow the right side of the Ctra. Estación to the corner of the monastic complex, turn the corner, and fork left (15min.). Closed for repairs in '97, but should be open by '98. Three kilometers down the road to Avila is the simpler **Casita del Infante,** commissioned by Gabriel de Borbón, Carlos's brother, in the mid-16th century.

ENTERTAINMENT

San Lorenzo is not the fossilized tourist trap one might expect—throngs of young people make for a vibrant night life. **C. Floridablanca** and **C. Rey** overflow with *cervecerías* and cafes. Teens and twenty-somethings head a little farther uphill. **Pub la Jara,** C. Floridablanca, 34, a small, quiet place with a youngish clientele and a foosball table, mixes strong drinks. Open daily 6pm-3am. **Jandro's Bar,** Pl. Animas, is next door to a good *tapas* joint, **Bar-Restaurant Cueva.** A popular place for the young to build a buzz, Jandro's drinks are a tad expensive (beer 400ptas) and the music blares (open 7:30pm-4am). The *bakalao* (techno) joint of choice, **Disco-Pub Que Mas Da,** C. Santiago, 11, pours cheap beer without a cover (open Sun.-Thurs. 8pm-midnight, Fri.-Sat. 8pm-4:30am). During the **Festivals of San Lorenzo** (Aug. 10-20), parades of giant figures line the streets and fireworks fill the sky. Folk dancing contests and horse-drawn cart parades mark **Romería a la Ermita de la Virgen de Gracia,** the second Sunday in September. Ceremonies are held in the forest of Herría.

■ Near El Escorial

EL VALLE DE LOS CAÍDOS

In a previously untouched valley of the Sierra de Guadarrama, 8km north of El Escorial, Franco built the overpowering monument of **Santa Cruz del Valle de los Caídos** (Valley of the Fallen) as a memorial to those who gave their lives in the Civil War. Naturally, the massive granite cross (150m tall and 46m wide) was meant to honor only those who died "serving *Dios* and *España,*" i.e. the fascist Nationalists. This thing is big—birds build their nests between the statue's eyes. Apocalyptic tapestries line the cave-like **basilica,** which is also decorated with death-angels with swords and angry light fixtures. Behind the chapel walls lie a multitude (nine levels) of dead. The high altar is located directly underneath the mammoth cross with its mammoth statues, and is testimony to modern Spain's view of Franco; despite the fact that Franco lies buried underneath, there is no mention of his tomb in tourist literature. (Mass daily at 11am. Open daily 9:30am-7pm; in winter 10am-6pm. 650ptas; students and seniors 250ptas; free Wed. for EU citizens. Funicular ride up to the cross 350ptas.)

El Valle de los Caídos is accessible only via El Escorial. **Autocares Herranz** runs one **bus** to the monument. (Leaves El Escorial Tues.-Sun. at 3:15pm and returns at 5:30pm, 15min., round-trip plus admission 870ptas. Funicular not included.)

MADRID

■ Aranjuez

Two rivers converge at the heart of green Aranjuez, a getaway for generations of Habsburg and Bourbon royalty, now a perfect place for more common folk to stroll through wondrous gardens and dazzling palaces. Famed for its delicious strawberries and asparagus, Aranjuez and its verdant splendors inspired Rodrigo's classical guitar piece, *El Concierto de Aranjuez.*

Practical Information The **tourist office** (tel. 891 04 27), in Pl. San Antonio, supplies a map and brochures (open Mon.-Fri. 10am-2pm and 4-6pm). From the **train station** (tel. 891 02 02), it's a pleasant 10-minute walk to the town center. With your back to the station, turn right, walk to the end of the street, then turn left onto tree-lined Ctra Toledo. Municipal bus L2 stops outside the station and on C. Stuart. Trains roll to: Madrid (45 Cercanías per day to Atocha, 45min., 740ptas round-trip, plus 7 *regionales* to Chamartín); Toledo (4-8 per day, 30min.); and Cuenca (6 per day, 2hr.). AISA and SAMAR park in Aranjuez's **bus station,** C. Infantas, 8 (tel. 891 01 83 or 530 46 06). Both companies leave from C. Infantas. Madrid's Estación Sur de Autobuses (Mon.-Sat. 20-30 per day, Sun. 10 per day, 1hr., 355-390ptas).The **Red Cross** (tel. 891 02 52) is at C. Rey, 7. Contact the municipal **police** at C. Infantas, 36 (tel. 891 00 22 or 891 00 55); **emergency** numbers are 091 and 092. The **post office** (tel. 891 11 32) is at C. Peña Redonda, 3, off C. Capitán Gómez (open Mon.-Fri. 8:30am-1:30pm, Sat 9:30am-1pm). The **postal code** is 28300.

Accommodations and Food Accommodations in Aranjuez tend to be costly yet luxurious. **Hostal Rusiñol** (tel./fax 891 0155), C. San Antonio at C. Stuart, offers rooms with TVs (singles 1850ptas; doubles 2900ptas, with shower 4200ptas; Visa). **Camping Soto del Castillo** (tel. 891 13 95), across the Río Tajo and off the highway to the right (2km from palace, watch for the signs), is a first-class site amid lush fields (600ptas per person, 500ptas per car, 525-650ptas per tent, electricity 500ptas).

The town's **strawberries** and **asparagus** have been famous for centuries. Nowadays, many of Aranjuez's strawberries are actually grown in other areas of Spain to be sold (to unsuspecting tourists) as *fresón con nata* (strawberries with cream 350-450ptas) at kiosks and cafes throughout town. Imitations are huge—real Aranjuez strawberries are on the smaller side. Aranjuez's restaurants, with views of the Tajo, are plentiful and expensive. Foreign food is more affordable. At **Ristorante Italiano Il Brigantino,** C. Abastos, 64 (tel. 892 48 89), off C. Infantas, down tasty food to lively Italian pop tunes. (Pizzas 725-1000ptas, pasta 850-1100ptas, salads 375-800ptas. Open Mon.-Fri. 7:30-11:30pm, Sat.-Sun. 1:30-4pm and 7:30pm-1am.)

Sights The Tajo and its tributary, the Jarama, water the palace's beautiful gardens (and also add undesirable humidity to the summer air). River walkways run from the **Jardín de la Isla,** which sprouts banana trees and a mythological statuary, to the huge **Jardín del Príncipe,** created originally for the amusement of Carlos IV (both open daily 8am-8:30pm; Oct.-May 8am-6:30pm; free). Inside the park, the **Casa del Labrador,** a mock laborer's cottage, is a treasure trove of Neoclassical decorative arts destined for courtly galas. The queen's private quarters overflow with knick-knacks such as Roman mosaics from Mérida and views of Madrid embroidered in silk. Also in the park, the **Casa de Marinos,** once the quarters of the Tajo's sailing squad, stores royal gondolas. (*Casas* open Tues.-Sun. 10am-6:15pm. 600ptas for both, individual *casa* 425ptas, students 225ptas.) Nearby is the *embarcadero* from which the royal family set sail on the swampy river (**paddleboats** 350ptas per person per hr.).

The stately **Palacio Real** also warrants an excursion. A marvel in white brick, the palace was originally designed by Juan de Herrera—chief architect of El Escorial—under the aegis of Felipe II. In the years to come, both Felipe VI and Carlos III had their minions enlarge and embellish the palace. Now, room after opulent room displays Vatican mosaic paintings in natural marble, crystal chandeliers and mirrors from the La Granja, Buen Retiro porcelain, Flemish tapestries, and ornate French clocks.

The Oriental porcelain room with 3-D wallpaper has a dash of Rococo ceramic work while the Mozarabic smoking room is a gaudy copy of the Alhambra. (Open Wed.-Mon. 10am-6:15pm; Oct.-May Wed.-Mon. 10am-5:15pm. Compulsory tour in Spanish. 500ptas, students 250ptas, Wed. free for EU citizens.

Near Aranjuez

Tiny, tranquil **Chinchón** lies 15 minutes away from Aranjuez. While not as splendorous as its regal neighbor, Chinchón makes for an enchanting visit. Among its assets are *anis,* a savory liquor famed in the region, and a picturesque Plaza Mayor. Chinchón also boasts a castle, a frescoed monastery/hotel, and charming views. Buses run to and from Chinchón twice a day Mon.-Fri. and to Chinchón (but not from it) on Saturdays. They leave Aranjuez from C. Almíbar, next to the Plaza de Toros. Bus schedules are erratic, so call in advance (tel. 891 39 37; 170ptas each way).

Strawberries and Steam

Spain's second locomotive, which first ran from Madrid to Aranjuez on February 9, 1851, was dubbed the **strawberry train.** Built during the reign of Isabel II, it became all the rage, carting Aranjuez strawberries to Madrid during the week and *madrileños* to Aranjuez on weekends. For the past 10 years, tourists have relived those bygone days in an exact replica of that first steam train, complete with obsequious, officious costumed porters. (For info call tel. 902 22 88 22. Train runs April 13-Oct. 20 Sat.-Sun. and holidays only. Leaves from Madrid-Atocha at 10am, returns at 7:30pm. Round-trip fare including admission to all sights and plenty of strawberries 2900ptas, children 1800ptas.)

MADRID

Castilla La Mancha

Cervantes chose to set Don Quijote's adventures in La Mancha (*manxa* is Arabic for parched earth) to evoke a cultural and material backwater. No overworked fantasy of the Knight of the Sad Countenance is needed to transform the austere beauty of this battered, windswept plateau. Its tumultuous history, gloomy medieval fortresses, arid plains, and awesome crags provide grist for the imagination. The 500 castles that lend the region its name served as models for Disney World's medieval castle.

Long, long ago, this area was the battleground for conflicts between Christians and Muslims. The Christians captured Toledo in 1085 by plowing through Magerit, which would later be called Madrid. As Christian forces pranced into Muslim Spain (Toledo was captured in 1085), La Mancha became the domain of the military orders Santiago, Calatrava, Montesa, and San Juan, which were modeled after crusading institutions such as the Knights Templar, a society of powerful warrior-monks. In the 14th and 15th centuries, the region bared fearsome struggles between the kingdoms of Castilla and Aragón. All this warring left the region looking like the mess left over from a child's toy battleground: castles, fortresses, churches, walls, and ramparts scattered hither and yon, with a few windmills thrown in for good measure.

The region is Spain's largest wine-producing area (Valdepeñas and Manzanares are common table wines), and its abundant olive groves and excellent hunting provide for many local repasts. Stews, roast meats, and game are *manchego* staples. *Gazpacho manchego,* a hearty stew of rabbit, lamb, chicken, and pork, and *queso manchego,* Castile's beloved cheese, are indigenous specialties.

▨ Toledo

For Cervantes, Toledo was a "rocky gravity, glory of Spain and light of her cities." To Cossío, it was "the most brilliant and evocative summary of Spain's history." Successively a Roman settlement, capital of the Visigoth kingdom, stronghold of the Emirate of Córdoba, and imperial city under Carlos V, Toledo (pop. 60,000) may be marred by armies of tourists and caravans of kitsch, but it remains a treasure-trove of Spanish culture. Or, stated a little less optimistically, and to quote another novelist-playwright, Benito Pérez Galdos, Toledo is a "town with a great history, but only a history." Emblematic of a past *convivencia,* when Spain's three religions peacefully coexisted together, are the numerous churches, synagogues, and mosques that huddle in shared alleyways. Visitors pay monetary homage to Toledo's damascene swords and knives, colorful pottery, and almond-paste *mazapán.* Many streets clank with junky gift shops, selling everything from miniature suits of armor to cheesy ceramic pigs. Accordingly, prolonged stays and winter visits afford a more authentic sense of place.

ORIENTATION AND PRACTICAL INFORMATION

Toledo is well-connected to Madrid, as several buses and trains make the 1½hr. trip daily, but getting here from anywhere else is more difficult. To get to **Plaza de Zocodóver** in the town center, take bus #5 or 6 (110ptas) from the stop to the right exiting the **train station** or from the stop directly outside the **bus station.** Alternatively, it's not a bad walk from either station, albeit completely unshaded and mostly uphill (15min.). From the bus station, exit on the side with trees, walk right, and take the first right along the highway that surrounds the city. Pass through a gate across from the **tourist office** and continue up to the plaza. From the train station, *do not* take the big bridge across the Tajo; although this may seem like the most obvious route, it's long and unpleasant. Instead, turn right leaving the station and follow Po. Rosa to a smaller bridge, Puente de Alcántara. Cross the bridge to the Puente's stone staircase (through a set of arches); the left-hand fork after climbing the stairs leads directly to Pl. Zocodóver. You will **get lost** in Toledo, the city could not be more labyrinthine if it contained an actual Minotaur. Streets are well-labeled, and the tourist

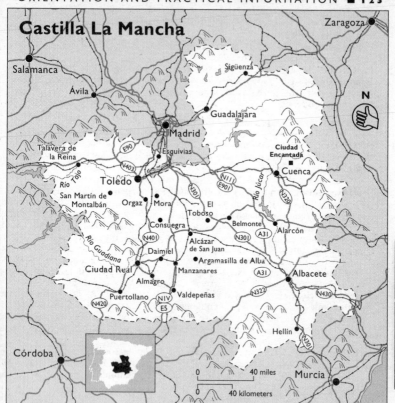

Castilla La Mancha

office distributes a fairly detailed map, but there is little you can do to avoid a wrong turn. Accept it as part of the package, it's the best way to discover the town's beauty.

Tourist Office: (tel. 22 08 43; fax 25 26 48), just outside the Puerta Nueva de Bisagra on Po. Merchán, on the north side of town. From Pl. Zocodóver, take C. Armas, the main street with many name changes leading downhill to the gates (Puetas de Bisagra); pass under and cross the intersection (10 min.). From the RENFE station, turn right and take the busy right-hand fork across the bridge (Puente de Azarquiel); follow the city walls until you reach the gateway. The office is across the road, outside the walls. Open Mon.-Fri. 9am-6pm, till 7pm in summer, Sat. 9am-7pm, Sun. 9am-3pm. For a map without the walk, queue up at the **info booth,** Pl. Zocodóver. Open Mon.-Fri. 10am-6pm, Sat. 10am-7pm, Sun. and holidays 10am-3pm.

Trains: Po. Rosa (tel. 22 30 99), in a simply exquisite neo-Mudéjar building opposite the Puente de Azarquiel. Its only line runs to Madrid's Atocha (9 per day 7am-9:50pm, 8:30am-8:30pm on weekends, 1½hr., 575ptas), passing through Aranjuez (35min., 290ptas). To get elsewhere, transfer in Madrid or Aranjuez.

Buses: (tel. 21 58 50), in the Zona Safón, 5min. from the city gate and tourist office (from Pl. Zocodóver, take C. Armas). Serviced by various companies. To Madrid (Mon.-Sat. 5:30am-10pm, Sun. 8:30am-11:30pm, every 30min., 1½hr., 575ptas) and Cuenca (Mon.-Fri. 1 per day, 3hr., 1565ptas).

Luggage Storage: At the bus station (100-200ptas).

Public Transportation: Buses 110ptas. #5 and 6 stop to the right of the train station and directly outside the bus station, and head straight to Pl. Zocodóver. The stop in Pl. Zocodóver is on C. Comercio.

Taxis: Radio Taxi (tel. 25 50 50).

Red Cross: (tel. 21 60 60).

Medical Services: Hospital Virgen de la Salud (tel. 26 92 00), toward the Ávila highway on Av. Barber.

Police: Municipal (tel. 26 97 13). **Local police,** Ayuntamiento, 1 (tel. 21 34 00 or 092). **Emergency:** tel. 091 or 092.

Post Office: C. Plata, 1 (tel. 22 36 11 or 25 10 66), off Pl. Zocodóver via C. Comercio and then C. Toledo. Open for all services, including Lista de Correos, Mon.-Fri. 8am-9pm, Sat. 9am-2pm. **Postal Code:** 45001.

Telephone Code: (9)25.

ACCOMMODATIONS AND CAMPING

Toledo is chock-full of accommodations, but finding a bed during the summer, especially on weekends, can be a hassle. The tourist office provides an invaluable list of *hoteles, hostales,* and *pensiones.*

Residencia Juvenil San Servando (HI), Castillo San Servando (tel. 22 45 54), uphill from the train station (15min.). Cross the street from the station, turn left and immediately right up Callejón del Hospital. When the steps reach a road, turn right, then right again following the signs to Hospital Provincial. The steep walk uphill just past the hospital leads to a 14th-century castle—that's not for you; you're going to the annex. If alone at night, take a cab. 96 rooms, each with 3 bunk beds, some with views. No lockers. Pool in summer, TV room, Coke machine. Curfew 11:50pm. Reception open 7am-11:50pm. 1100ptas, over 26 1350ptas. Laundry service 500ptas. No reservations accepted. Closed mid-Aug. to mid-Sept.

Pensión Nuncio Viejo, C. Nuncio Viejo, 19, 3rd fl. (tel. 22 81 78), on a street leading off the cathedral. Sweet-smelling entrance by a flower shop. Only 6 rooms—you'll feel like one of the family. Rooms are a bit cramped, but your new mom is a great cook. TV room. Singles 1300ptas. Doubles 2900ptas, with bath 3200ptas. Breakfast 190ptas. Lunch and dinner 750ptas each.

La Belviseña, Cuesta del Can, 7 (tel. 22 00 67). From the Zocodóver, walk down the Cuesta Carlos V (a.k.a. Cuesta del Alcázar), past the Alcázar and through the small plaza beyond it. Take C. Soledad, the street left of the hotel, and go left on C. San Miguel, continuing until you get to C. San Justo. Turn left and go uphill. Cuesta del Can is on the right. The cheapest *pensión* in Toledo. The Ritz it's not, but still clean. Singles 1000ptas. Doubles 2000ptas.

Pensión Lumbreras, C. Juan Labrador, 9 (tel. 22 15 71), 2 blocks from Pl. Zocodóver. Courtyard spotted with ceramic plates and plants leads to simple rooms. Some with views of the Toledo skyline. Singles 1700ptas. Doubles 3000ptas. One ample triple 4200ptas. 7% IVA not included.

Segovia, C. Recoletos, 2 (tel. 21 11 24), on a tiny street off C. Armas. Airy rooms with low doors and loud tiles, some with balcony. Singles 1900ptas. Doubles 2500ptas. Triples 3500ptas. Showers 200ptas.

Pensión Descalzos, C. Descalzos, 30 (tel. 22 28 88), down the steps off Po. San Cristóbal or down the Bajada Descalzos near the Casa del Greco. A chill abode; views of San Martín Bridge. Rooms with bath have TVs. Singles 2500ptas. Doubles 3500ptas, with bath or shower 5600ptas. Low season: 2200ptas; 3000ptas; 5000ptas. Breakfast 175-600ptas. 7% IVA not included. Closed Feb. Visa, MC.

Camping: Camping El Greco (tel. 22 00 90), 1½km from town on the road away from Madrid (C-401). Bus #7 (from Pl. Zocodóver) stops just up the hill and to the left. Wooded and shady 1st-class site between the Tajo and an olive grove. 650ptas per person (children 450ptas), 570ptas per tent, and 550ptas per car. 7% IVA not included. **Circo Romano,** Av. Carlos III, 19 (tel. 22 04 42). 2nd-class site. Close but noisier. 550ptas per person, 570ptas per tent, and 550ptas per car.

Buenas Noches

"Pasar una noche Toledana" (spend a Toledan night) refers to a sleepless night. One explication for the phrase's origin is that the expression arose out of the shrill screaming caused by the Inquisition. Another is that nights in Toledo were unbearable after Amru-Al-Lendi Yusef slit the throats of his adversaries during dinner in 800 AD. But don't worry, a final version attributes it all to those pesky mosquitoes down by the Tajo. Or maybe it's just the heat. Sleep it off.

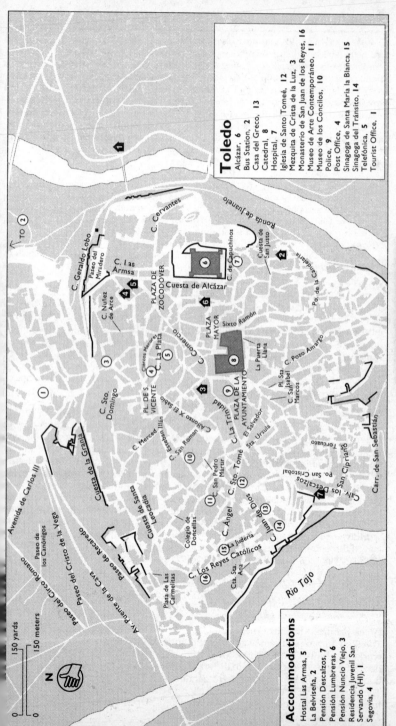

CASTILLA LA MANCHA

Toledo

Alcázar, 6
Bus Station, 2
Casa del Greco, 13
Catedral, 8
Hospital, 7
Iglesia de Santo Tomeé, 12
Mezquita de Crista de la Luz, 3
Monasterio de San Juan de los Reyes, 16
Museo de Arte Contemporáneo, 11
Museo de los Concilos, 10
Police, 9
Post Office, 4
Sinagoga de Santa Maria la Blanca, 15
Sinagoga del Tránsito, 14
Telefónica, 5
Tourist Office, 1

Accommodations

Hostal Las Armas, 5
La Belviseña, 2
Pensión Descalzos, 7
Pensión Lumbreras, 6
Pensión Nuncio Viejo, 3
Residencia Juvenil San
Servando (HI), 1
Segovia, 4

FOOD

Toledo grinds almonds into *mazapán* delights of every shape and size, from colorful fruity nuggets to half-moon cookies, and *pastelerías* (pastry shops) beckon on every corner. If your pocket allows, dining out in Toledo could be an ecstatic culinary experience (*menús* 1400-1600ptas). Regional specialties include *perdiz* (fowl), *cuchifritos* (a melange of sheep, eggs, tomato, and white wine), *venado* (venison), and *carcamusas* (mystery meat). Buy fresh fruit and basics at **Frutería-Pan,** C. Real Arrabal, inside the Puertas de Bisagra (open daily 9am-10pm). The smelly **mercado** is in the Pl. Mayor, behind the cathedral (open Mon.-Sat. 8:30am-2pm). You can find similar stores on the corner of most plazas. **Udaco** is a mini-market on Pl. San Jose, southeast of the cathedral, down C. Sixto R. Parro from Puerta Llana (open Mon.-Fri. 8:30am-2:30pm and 5-8pm, Sat. 8:30am-2:30pm).

> **Pastucci,** C. Sinagoga, 10 (tel. 21 48 66). From Pl. Zocodóver, take C. Comercio. Keep to the right of the Lacoste store and turn right through an underpass (5min.). A colorful and popular Italian eatery tucked away from touristy sites. Pizzas priced by size (900-2150ptas). Pasta 850-950ptas. Salads 600-950ptas. Open Mon.-Fri. noon-4pm and 7pm-midnight, Sat. 8pm-1am.Visa, MC.
>
> **Restaurante El Zoco,** C. Barrio Rey, 1 (tel. 22 20 51), off Pl. Zocodóver. Attractive and reasonably priced. And your countrymen know it! Expect to hear English at lunch. *Menús* 800-1500ptas. A/C. Open daily 1-4pm and 8-11pm.

SIGHTS

Toledo has an excellent collection of museums, churches, synagogues, and mosques, as well as some less historic sights, such as the Museo de Arte Erotico. Within the city's fortified walls, attributed to the 7th-century King Wamba, Toledo's major attractions form a belt around its fat middle. An east-west tour, beginning in Pl. Zocodóver, is mostly downhill. If you're not a student, a *conjunto* pass (available at all of these museums, 300ptas) is a good deal; it gets you into the Museo de Santa Cruz, Museo del Taller del Maro, Museo de la Cullera Visigótica, and Museo de Arte Contemporáneo. Be aware that most sights are closed Mondays.

La Catedral

In the city center, southwest of Pl. Zocodóver, hides the grandiose **cathedral,** with five naves, delicate stained glass, and ostentation throughout. Built between 1226 and 1498, it is the seat of the Primate of Spain. Noteworthy pieces are the 14th-century Gothic **Virgen Blanca** by the entrance and, above all, Narciso Tomés's **Transparente** (1732), a Spanish Baroque whirlpool of architecture, sculpture, and painting showing the way to heaven. In the **Capilla Mayor,** the enormous Gothic altarpiece stretches to the ceiling. Cardinal Mendoza, private confessor to the queen and big time Inquisitor, lies dead on the left. Beneath the dome is the **Capilla Mozárabe,** the only venue where the ancient Visigoth mass (in Mozarabic) is still held. The **tesoro** flaunts worldly accoutrements, including a 400-pound, 16th-century gold monstrance lugged through the streets during the annual Corpus Christi procession. The **Sacristía** holds eighteen El Grecos and two Van Dycks, along with the portraits of every archbishop of Toledo that hang in the **Sala Capitular.** (Cathedral open Mon.-Sat 10:30am-1pm and 3:30-7pm, Sun. 10am-1:30pm and 4-7pm; Sept.-June closes 1hr earlier. Sala Capitular, Capilla del Rey, *tesoro, coro,* and Sacristía 500ptas.)

El Greco

Greek painter Domenico Theotokopulus (a.k.a. El Greco) lived most of his life in Toledo, churning out eerie canvases and portraits of willowy saints. Many of his works are displayed throughout town. The majority of his masterpieces, however have long since been carted off to the Prado and elsewhere. The **Iglesia de San Tomé** houses El Greco's famous *El entierro del Conde de Orgaz* (Burial of Count Orgaz). The stark figure staring out from the back is El Greco himself, and the boy his son Jorge Manuel, who built Toledo's Ayuntamiento. (Open Tues.-Sat. 10am-2pm and

3:30-6:45pm, till 5:45pm in winter, Sun. 10am-2pm. 150ptas.) There's also the **Casa Museo de El Greco,** C. Levi, 3, downhill from the Ayuntamiento. This oddly arranged museum has 19 works of El Greco, including a copy of the *Vista y mapa de Toledo* ("Landscape of Toledo"; 1200ptas, students free).

El Alcázar

South and uphill from Pl. Zocodóver sits the **Alcázar,** Toledo's most formidable landmark. The site was a stronghold of Visigoths, Muslims, and Christians, who each rebuilt it in their own style. Little remains of Carlos V's 16th-century structure; the building was virtually reduced to rubble during the Civil War as besieged Fascist troops held out against an acute Republican bombardment. The father-son telephone drama of the Moscardós is posted in 19 different languages: when the Republicans attacked the Alcázar, they ordered Colonel Moscardó to surrender or lose his son. You can also visit the dark, windowless basement refuge where over five hundred civilians hid during the siege. The rooms above ground are now a nationalistic military museum with armor, swords, guns, knives...and dried plants. (Open Tues.-Sat. 10am-2pm and 4-6pm, Sun. 10am-1:30pm and 4-6:30pm; July-Aug. Tues.-Sun. 9:30am-2:30pm. 125ptas, free Wed. for EU citizens.)

Judería

Samuel Ha-Leví, diplomat and treasurer to Pedro el Cruel, built the **Sinagoga del Tránsito** (1366). Its simple exterior hides an extraordinarily ornate sanctuary with Mudéjar plasterwork and an *artesonado* (ornately designed wood) ceiling. The walls are crawling with Hebrew inscriptions, mostly taken from Psalms. Inside, the **Museo Sefardí** (Jews of Spanish descent) is packed with artifacts, including a *torá* (parts of which are over 400 years old) and a beautiful set of Sephardic wedding costumes. (Open Tues.-Sat. 10am-1:45pm and 4-5:45pm, Sun. 10am-1:45pm. 400ptas, students 200ptas, free Sat. after 4pm and Sun.) **Sinagoga de Santa María la Blanca** (1180), down the street to the right, was originally meant to be a mosque, but was then purchased by Jews, used as the city's principle synagogue, and in 1492 was converted into a church. Now, the Moorish arches and a tranquil garden make a welcome (secular) retreat. (Open 10am-1:45pm and 3:45-6:45pm; off season until 5:45pm. 400ptas, students 200ptas.)

Tolerance in Sepharad

Toledo fell to Alfonso VI in 1085, and Jewish culture blossomed under his tolerant reign. Jewish poets, including Yehuda Halevi, doctors, translators, and bankers rose to prominence, even intermarrying with noble Christian families and serving in royal courts. This period of *toledancia*--a pun on Toledo and tolerance—would not last, however. Mounting nationalism and anti-semitism led to the persecution, forced conversion, expulsion, and massacre of Jews during the 1492 Inquisition. Today, only two of eight synagogues remain in what was once Spain's (Sepharad in Hebrew) largest Jewish community. Jews of *toledano* descent have come back to visit in recent years, some of whom still speak *Ladino,* a variation on 15th-century Spanish. An American Jewish woman made headlines when she entered a Toledo home with the same key her ancestors had used 500 years ago.

Muslims and Visigoths

Less touristed are the remnants of the city's Islamic past, near the Puerta del Sol, off C. Real de Arrabal. Alternating as a Muslim and Christian house of worship, the striking 10th-century **Mezquita del Cristo de la Luz** is the only surviving building in Toledo built before the *Reconquista.* Its columns support arches inspired by the mosque at Córdoba. The emirate was also responsible for the **hammams** (baths) on C. Angel. The site does not open to tourists, but you can peek inside.

Toledo was the seat of Visigothic rule and culture for three centuries prior to the 711 Muslim invasion. The **Museo de los Concilios y de la Cultura Visigótica,** C. San

CASTILLA LA MANCHA

Clemente, 4 (tel. 22 78 72), is set in a 13th-century Mudéjar church. Its exhibits can't compete with the surrounding architecture and frescoes. The **Museo del Taller dei Moro,** on C. Bulas near Iglesia de Santo Tomé, features outstanding woodwork, *yesería* (plasterwork), and *azulejos* (tiles). (Both open Tues.-Sat. 10am-2pm and 4-6:30pm, Sun. 10am-2pm. 100ptas, students 50ptas, free Sat. after 4pm and Sun.)

Elsewhere

At the far western bulge of the city, with views of the surrounding hills and Río Tajo, stands the Franciscan **Iglesia de San Juan de los Reyes** (tel. 22 38 02), commissioned by Isabel and Fernando to commemorate their victory over the Portuguese in the Battle of Toro (1476). The light-filled cloister, covered with the *Reyes Católicos*'s initials, mixes Gothic and Mudéjar architecture, in contrast with the super-Gothic plateresque church interior. The Catholic monarchs had planned to use the church as their burial place, but changed their minds after their victory over Granada (open 10am-2pm and 3:30-7pm, off season until 6pm; 150ptas).

Impressive and untouristed, the **Museo de Santa Cruz,** M. Cervantes, 3 (tel. 22 14 02), off Pl. Zocodóver, is a former hospital (1504). The thick building is shaped like the Greek cross. Its 15th-century Flemish *Astrolabio* tapestry of the zodiac could entrance practicing astrologers, causing them to trip over the sarcophagus lids and fragments of carved stone that litter the well-preserved patio. The basement contains the remains from archaeological digs throughout Toledo province, including elephant tusks (open Mon.-Sat. 10am-6pm, Sun. 10am-2pm; 200ptas, students 100ptas).

Outside handsome Puerta Nueva de Bisagra on the road to Madrid is the 16th-century **Hospital Tavera.** Constructed under the auspices of the Cardenal de Tavera, buried here in a mausoleum, the building is now a private museum with five El Grecos and some Titians. The left-hand part was once the home of the Dukes of Lerma; a portrait of the last one (executed in the Civil War) eyes the gift shop (museum open 10:30am-1:30pm and 3:30-6pm; 500ptas).

ENTERTAINMENT

The best area for the city's trademark souvenirs is **Calle de San Juan de Dios,** by the Iglesia de Santo Tomé. The shop owners are aggressive, but are willing to haggle. The town is cuckoo for **Corpus Christi,** celebrated the eighth Sunday after Easter. Looking like they just stepped out of an El Greco, citizens parade through the streets alongside the cathedral's weighty gold monstrance. Most night spots cater to tourists—local nightlife tends to disappear down the following side streets:

Calle de Santa Fe, east of Pl. Zocodóver, through the arch. Filled to the brim with beer and youth and home to a few *discotecas*. Look for **Bar Black and Blue** (tel. 22 21 11), a busy blues bar, on the small Pl. Santiago Caballeros off C. Santa Fe. Performances Thurs. at 10:30pm. No cover. Beer 300ptas.

Calle de la Sillería and **Calle de los Alfileritos,** west of Pl. Zocodóver. Twenty-something crowd. Home to more upscale bars and clubs, including **Bar La Abadía,** Nuñez de Arce, 5 (tel. 25 11 40), whose cavernous basement makes for great hide-and-seek. Open Mon.-Thurs. 8am-midnight, Fri.-Sun. noon-midnight.

Zaida, in the Centro Comercial Miradero, downhill on C. Armas from Pl. Zocodóver. A perennial hot spot for dancing.

Sidi-Buo Tunisian Teahouse, Alfonso XII, 3, a glowing blue pastel. Dancer comes every other Saturday. Arabic tea 150ptas. Open till 3am.

■ Near Toledo

Plan around inconvenient bus departure times so you don't spend the night where you only wanted to stay several hours. For greater flexibility, rent a car and use Toledo as a base for excursions into this region. Cervantes freaks come to **La Mancha** to follow his footsteps and those of his most famous creations, Don Quijote and the faithful Sancho Panza. Cervantes met and married Catalina de Palacios in the main church in **Esquivias** in 1584. Supposedly he began writing his masterpiece while

imprisoned in the **Cueva del Medrano,** in the town of **Argamasilla de Alba.** It was in **El Toboso,** 100km southeast of Toledo, that Quijote fell nobly in love with Dulcinea. El Toboso hosts the **Centro Cervantino,** which displays a fine collection of Cervantes ephemera, including translations of *Don Quijote* into 30 different languages. A hop, skip, and jump south of Toledo lands you at the small but fierce **San Martín de Montalbán,** home to an amazing castle whose origins are shrouded in mystery and intrigue. The castle stands poised on an enormous pile of gray granite rocks, leaning out over an abysmal gorge of the River Torión. It was first a Visigothic, then an Arab fortress, and later an enclave of the cabalistic Knights Templar. Legend has it that somewhere inside its walls lies a cache of buried treasure.

Of all Manchegan villages, tiny **Consuegra** provides perhaps the most raw material for an evocation of Quijote's world. The **castle,** called the "Crestería Manchega" by locals, was a Roman, then Arab, then Christian fortress. El Cid's only son, Diego, died in the stable; you can visit a lavish monument in his honor near the Ayuntamiento. The castle keeps erratic hours, but the view of the surrounding plains justifies a climb anytime. Also within its diminutive circumference, Consuegra has a palace, a Franciscan convent, a Carmelite monastery, and more. Learn more about it in the **Museo de Consuegra** (tel. 47 37 31), next to the Ayuntamiento (hr. not fixed, 100ptas.) Consuegra is an easy daytrip from Toledo. **Samar buses** (tel. 22 39 15) depart from the bus station (10 per day, 585ptas). Buses return to Toledo from C. Castilla de la Mancha (7 per day). Purchase tickets from the driver when returning from Consuegra; when coming from Toledo, purchase them at the bus ticket office. Alcázar de San Juan is the primary junction for southbound trains from Madrid.

■ Almagro

Classical theater buffs and city slickers seeking solace will find sleepy Almagro (pop. 9000) appealing. A famed theater festival attracts hundreds of visitors in July. Cobblestoned streets, whitewashed houses and immaculate monuments date from the 16th century, but infrequent bus and train services pose a challenge to potential visitors.

Orientation and Practical Information The **train station** (tel. 86 02 76) awaits at the end of the tree-lined Po. Estación. To get from the station to the **Plaza Mayor,** walk down Po. Estación and turn left onto C. Rondo de Calatrava (a sign points to the **Centro Urbano**); turn right onto C. Madre de Dios (another Centro Urbano sign) which leads to the plaza (10min.). Trains run to: Madrid-Atocha (2 per day, 3hr., 1720-1975ptas); Ciudad Real (5 per day, 20 min., 240-280ptas); Alcázar de San Juan (5 per day, 1 hour, 680-785ptas); and Aranjuez (2 per day, 2hr., 1325-1520ptas). Change at Aranjuez, Ciudad Real, or Alcázar de San Juan for connections to other cities. **Buses** (tel. 86 02 50) stop at the brick building at the far end of Ejido de Calatrava across from the Hospedería Municipal. To get to Pl. Mayor, turn left on C. Madre de Dios (follow the sign) to the Centro Urbano and take the road until you reach the plaza (5 min.). **Aisa** buses leave for Madrid (3 per day, 2¼hr., 1505ptas) and Ciudad Real, for connections to Toledo (6 per day, 20min., 230ptas). All are less frequent on weekends. **Sepulvedena** goes to Jaén on weekdays (10am, 2hr., 1455ptas). Check the bus schedule ahead of time, especially on weekends when service is less frequent or non-existent. Some try **hitching** to Valdepeñas (36km), where buses to Andalucía down highway Nacional IV are more common.

The **tourist office,** C. Bernardas, 2 (tel. 86 07 17), sits inside the Palacio del Conde de Valdeparaíso. From Pl. Mayor, take a right on C. Mayor de Carnicerías, another right on C. Bernardas. They have a helpful brochure with a map and descriptions of all the sights in Almagro (Open Tues.-Fri. 10am-2pm and 5-8pm, Sat. 10am-2pm and 5-7pm; holidays 11am-2pm; during July festival Tues.-Fri. 10am-2pm and 6-9pm, Sat. 10am-2pm and 6-8pm). A **Banco Central Hispano** (tel. 86 00 04) sits alongside Pl. Mayor (open 8:30am-2:30pm). A **health clinic,** C. Mayor de Carnicerías, 11 (tel. 86 10 26 or 88 20 16), heals on the site of a 10th-century jail. The **police** (tel. 86 00 33) survey Almagro from the Ayuntamiento in Pl. Mayor. Dial 006 in an **emergency.** The

post office (tel. 86 00 52) is on C. Mayor de Carnicerías (open Mon.-Fri. 8:30am-2:30pm, Sat. 9am-1pm). The **postal code** is 13270, the **telephone code** (9)26.

Accommodations and Food Hospedería Municipal de Almagro, Ejido de Calatrava, s/n (tel. 88 20 87; fax 88 21 22), wears its five hundred years boldly. Dark hallways and antique furnishings exemplify the building's past. Firm beds, telephones, TVs, and private baths. (Singles with bath 2000ptas. Doubles with shower 3200ptas, with bathtub 3500ptas. Breakfast 250ptas. Lunch and dinner 1000ptas each. Call ahead for reservations.) Travelers wishing to attend the July theater festival should make reservations two to three months in advance.

The Plaza Mayor has several *terazzas* with *menús* featuring *platos típicos manchegos*. One such establishment is the lively **Restaurante Airén**. The *menús* start at 1200ptas, but it's hard to resist extra dishes when the bartender offers them as "something my Grandma made." **Bar-restaurants** line C. Bolaños and Ejido de Calatrava, both facing the Hospedería Municioal (see above).

Sights Every July, Spain's most prestigious theater companies and players from around the globe descend on the Almagro for the **Festival Internacional de Teatro Clásico de Almagro.** Daily performances of Spanish and international classics take place in the Corral de Comedias, the Hospital de San Juan de Dios, and the Claustro de los Domínicos. The **box office** (tel. (902) 38 33 33) is at the Teatro municipal. (Open Tues. 11am-2pm. Tickets should be purchased before the festival. Shows are at 10:45pm. Tickets 1600-2200ptas; ½-price on Tues. There are also free outdoor performances in Pl. Mayor.)

In the 13th century, tiny Almagro became the seat of the vast and powerful **Orden de Calatrava,** the oldest fraternity of militaristic monks and fuelers of the *Reconquista*. Connected to the Hospedería Municipal (see Accommodations and Food) is the **Convento de la Asunción de Calatrava.** Its cloistered courtyard was built in 1519—renovations are still underway and no set hours exist. Visit in the morning when one of the Dominican fathers, who own the convent, can admit you.

The centerpiece of Almagro is its **Plaza Mayor,** whose long balconies with green window frames are characteristic of Fugger-style architecture. The Fuggers were a 16th-century family of German bankers who lent money to the monks of Calatrava and Emperor Carlos V, who wasn't a Fugger himself, although some people thought so. The **Fugger house,** C. Arzobispo, 6, is also the Universidad Popular, and is open to the public. From Pl. Mayor, take C. Fería and make a left onto C. Arzobispo. The other hometown hero is, of course, Diego de Almagro, hailed as the conquistador of Chile, but less patriotic accounts reveal that he was executed for conspiracy against the conquistador Francisco Pizarro. In the great Pl. Mayor stands the **Corral de Comedias,** an open-air multilevel theater resembling Shakespeare's Globe. It is the only one left intact from the Golden Age (*Siglo de Oro*) of Spanish drama. Here, performers act out the works of Cervantes and Lope de Vega, who were once fierce literary rivals. Directly across the plaza from the *corral* and through some arches, the new **Museo del Teatro** displays the history of Spanish drama. Your ticket to the museum allows access to the Corral de Comedias and the **Teatro Municipal** (up C. San Agustín, from the plaza on the right), a crimson building with white trim that houses a renovated theater. Inside there's a collection of elaborate costumes. (Admission 400ptas. Students 200ptas. Seniors and under 18 free. Sat. afternoons and Sun. mornings free.)

▓ Cuenca

Cuenca (pop. 40,000) is up there, flung sky-high due to lack of space. Perched atop a hill, the vertical city overlooks the two rivers that confine it and the stunning rock formations they created. These natural boundaries have served the city well; Muslims and then Christians settled in Cuenca because it was nearly impregnable. Cuenca strains against these borders, forcing much of the city's modern commercial life to spill down the hill into New Cuenca. However, the enchanting old city safeguards

most of Cuenca's unique charm, including the famed *casas colgadas* (hanging houses) that dangle high above the Río Huécar.

ORIENTATION AND PRACTICAL INFORMATION

To get to the bus station from the train station, turn right and cut left through the Plaza—the bus station is around the corner to the right. To get to **Plaza Mayor** in the old city from either station, go left until you hit the first bus shelter and catch bus #1 or 2 —it's the last stop (#1 every 30min., 80ptas). On foot to Pl. Mayor, walk left from the bus shelter along **Calle Fermín Caballero,** which becomes C. Cervantes and then C. José Cobo, which continues through Pl. Hispanidad before turning into **Calle Carretería,** the town's main drag. From here, turn right on any street (C. Fray Luis de León is the most direct) and begin trudging upward; it's a twisty and grueling walk (20-25min.) to the plaza and the old city.

Tourist Office: González Palencia, 2 (tel. 17 88 00), in the new city near C. Carretería. No English. Supposedly open daily 8am-3pm. You'll do better at the **Municipal Tourist Office,** C. San Pedro, 6 (tel. 23 21 19), right next to the cathedral in Pl. Mayor. Brochures, maps, a video, hiking and excursion routes, and lots of info about goings on about town. Open daily 9:30am-2pm and 4-7pm.

Currency Exchange: ATMs abound on C. Parque de San Julián and at a Banco Central Hispano on C. Carretería in New Cuenca.

Trains: Po. del Ferrocarril, in the new city (tel. 22 07 20). To: Madrid, Estación Atocha (8 per day, 2½-3hr., 1325ptas); Aranjuez (8 per day, 2-2½hr., 260ptas); Valencia (5 per day, 2¾-3¾hr., 1455ptas). To get to Toledo, transfer in Aranjuez; to get anywhere else, transfer in Madrid.

Buses: C. Fermín Caballero (tel. 22 70 87 for departure times; call **Auto Res** at 22 11 84 for their prices). Down the street from the train station; look for the orange canopy. To: Madrid (8 per day, 2½hr., 1305-1600ptas); Toledo (Mon.-Fri. at 5:30am, 3hr., 1600ptas). **La Rapida** goes to Barcelona Mon., Thurs.-Fri. (4170ptas).

Taxis: Radio-Taxi Cuenca (tel. 23 33 43). 24hr. service. Fare from RENFE station to Pl. Mayor: 500-600 ptas.

Luggage Storage: train station (400ptas per day) or bus station (200ptas per day).

Red Cross: Dr. Chirino, 4 (tel. 22 22 00), in the new city.

Pharmacy: Farmacia Castellano, C. Cervantes, 20 (tel. 21 23 37). List of late-night pharmacies in the window.

Police: C. Hermanos Valdés, 4 (tel. 21 21 47), within sight of the **Municipal Police,** C. Martínez Kleiser, 4 (tel. 22 48 59). **Emergency:** tel. 091 or 092.

Post Office: Parque de San Julián, 18 (tel. 22 10 00). Open Mon.-Fri. 8:30am-8:30pm, Sat. 9:30am-2pm. Smaller branch with fewer services up the street from the RENFE station. Open Mon.-Fri. 9am-2pm. **Postal Code:** for the large post office, 16070.

Telephones: C. Colón, 70. Open Mon.-Sat. 9:30am-2pm and 5-11pm. A/C. **Telephone Code:** (9)69.

ACCOMMODATIONS

Although there are no cheap accommodations in the old part of town, lots of cheap, adequate rooms collect in the new city. Rooms on the hill with spectacular views of the old town and gorge exact a bit more money. The tourist office has a complete list of places to stay.

Hostal-Residencia Posada de San José, C. Julián Romero, 4 (tel. 21 13 00; fax 23 03 65), just up the street from the cathedral. Cash in a few extra *pesetas* for cushy beds, amazing water pressure, historic echoes (it's a 17th-century convent), and gorgeous views of the Puente de San Pablo. And why not let loose with a bottle of wine (650ptas) on the cafe's terrace? Singles 2600ptas, with shower 4300ptas. Doubles 4300ptas, with shower 7400ptas, with bath 8400ptas. Triples 5800ptas, with bath 11,000ptas. One quad with bath 13,200ptas. Prices vary by season and are higher on weekends. Reserve 2-3 weeks in advance. Visa, MC, AmEx. Cafe open Tues.-Sun. 6-10pm.

CASTILLA LA MANCHA

Pensión Cuenca, Av. República Argentina, 8 (tel. 21 25 74), in the new city. Take Hurtado de Mendoza from the train or bus station. Matching, shiny new furniture and frilly curtains make this two-star *pensión* one of the most comfortable in its price range in the new city. Images of Jesus; images of romance. Some rooms could be better ventilated. TV lounge. Singles 1600ptas, with shower 1900ptas. Doubles 2300ptas; 3500ptas.

Pensión Central, C. Alonso Chirino, 9 (tel. 21 15 11), off C. Carretería. Clean rooms with huge beds and high ceilings. Neon green patio light mystifies the moment. Singles 1400ptas. Doubles 2500ptas. Bargain doubles without running water 2100ptas. Triples 3450ptas. Lunch or dinner 900ptas.

Pensión La Mota, Pl. Constitución, 7, 1st fl. (tel. 22 55 67), at the end of C. Carretería. Attractive, sparkling, and huge new bathrooms in a *hostal* catering to doubles. Doubles 3300ptas, with bath 4500ptas. Breakfast 200ptas. Shower 200ptas. Solo travelers get little or no discount.

FOOD

Cuenca's inexpensive restaurants are mediocre; around **Pl. Mayor,** they're expensive and mediocre. Budget eateries line **C. Cervantes** and **C. República Argentina.** A few places still dish out *zorajo* (lamb tripe) and *morteruelo* (a paté dish), rare regional specialties. Be happy about *resoli,* a typical liqueur of coffee, sugar, orange peel, and eau-de-vie; and *alajú,* a sticky sweet nougat made with honey, almonds, and figs. The morning **market** is held in Pl. Carros, behind the post office. **Heladería Italianas** scoop out excellent and cheap ice cream (small scoop 100ptas); there are two within a block of each other on C. Carretería (open daily 9:30am-midnight; Fri.-Sat. until 3am). **Groceries** are to be had at **Supermercado Alconsa,** C. Fermín Caballero at C. Teruel, a two minute walk from either station (open daily 9:30am-2pm and 5-8pm). Or try discount supermarket **%Día,** Av. Castilla La Mancha at the corner of Av. República Argentina (open Mon.-Thurs. 9:30am-2pm and 5:30-8:30pm, Fri.-Sat. 9am-2:30pm and 5:30-9pm).

El Mesón (tel. 21 41 61), C. Colón, which intersects Av. República Argentina at C. Hurtado Mendoza. A communist hangout during the Civil War. Hand tools hang from the ceiling, and paintings of workers adorn the walls. Still attracts workers of all stripes with its *manchego* cuisine at decent prices. Several vegetarian starters. *Menú* 1300ptas. No dinner Sun..

Posada de San José, C. Julian Romero, 4 (tel. 21 13 00). The cafe at this former convent boasts spectacular views and delicious regional *tapas.* Great *ensalada mixta* for two, 850ptas. Wonderful *pisto* (stew made of tomatoes, peppers, and onions) 800ptas. *Raciones* about 750ptas. Open Tues.-Sun. 6-10:30pm.

Restaurante Italiano Piccolo, Av. República Argentinal, 14 (tel. 23 20 35). Waiters and waitresses are eager to tell the stories that the black and white family photos on the walls only hint at. Ask Pica for the real scoop. Great thin-crust pizzas 700-975ptas. Pasta 750-975ptas. Visa, MC, AmEx.

Mesón Casas Colgadas, C. Canónigos (tel. 22 35 09), to the left of the Museo de Arte Abstracto. The best you'll ever eat in an original, 14th-century *casa colgada* (hanging house). Bypass the expensive restaurant for the bar (opens at 1pm); it's the same fabulous view, simpler fare, and an affordable price. *Raciones* 200-1000ptas. *Bocadillos* 350-1100ptas. Coffee or tea 150-175ptas.

SIGHTS

The town's major museums are located in Cuenca's **casas colgadas.** Down C. Obispo, they dangle over the riverbanks as precariously today as they did six centuries ago. In his memoirs, Surrealist filmmaker Luis Buñuel recalled a pre-war visit to one of the *casas,* in which he spied birds flying beneath the toilet seat (see **Livin' on the Edge,** p. 135). Walking along **Hoz del Júcar,** or preferably along **Hoz del Huécar,** the two roads that surround Cuenca's old city, is a treat. The side of Hoz del Huécar opposite the *casas colgadas* affords the best views of the valley. To get there, walk carefully

---

Livin' on the Edge

Very little is known about Cuenca's unique 14th-century *casas colgadas*. Supposedly, they were originally built to house kings, giving name to **Casa del Rey. Casa de las Serenas,** the only other remaining original hanging house, got its name from the screams emitted by Menosprecío when she flung herself out of the window after her lover Enrique Trastamara had killed their son. Her voice sounded like a siren. Despite legendary conjectures and the *casas'* striking appearance, these architectural phenomena did not become famous until recently. Indeed, the *casas* were completely run down when the city of Cuenca decided to rehabilitate them early in this century, transforming them into magnificent museums—and tourist attractions. Drawing thousands of visitors each year, the *casas* have become emblems for the city.

---

across the terrifying Puente de San Pablo. Many good hiking trails etch the hill and stone cliffs opposite the old city and footbridge. The tourist office gives out trail maps. Remember to bring food and sturdy shoes.

Inside one of the *casas* at Pl. Ciudad de Ronda, the award-winning **Museo de Arte Abstracto Español** (tel. 21 29 83) displays important works by the wacky and internationally known "Abstract Generation" of Spanish painters. All pieces were chosen by artist Fernando Zóbel, a major figure in the school. Striking views of the gorge are also on display. The well designed museum exhibits works by Zóbel himself, Canogar, Tápies, and Chillida. Don't miss the "White Room" upstairs. (Open Mon.-Fri. 11am-2pm and 4-6pm, Sat. 11am-2pm and 4-8pm, Sun. 11am-1:30pm. 500ptas, students 150ptas.)

Nearby on C. Obispo Valero, the **Museo Municipal** (tel. 21 30 69) is a treasure-trove of archeological finds, including Roman mosaics, ceramics, coins, and other items from local excavations, including some excellent Visigoth jewelry (open Tues.-Sat. 9am-2pm and 4-6pm, Sun. 11am-2pm; 200ptas, students 100ptas). Perhaps the most beautiful of the museums along this short street is the **Museo Diocesano** (tel. 22 92 10). Exhibits are imaginatively displayed and include Juan de Borgoña's *retablo* from local Convento de San Pablo, many colossal Flemish tapestries, splendid rugs, and two El Grecos (*Oración del huerto* and *Cristo con la cruz*). (Open Tues.-Fri. 11am-2pm and 4-6pm, Sat. 11am-2pm and 4-8pm, Sun. 11am-2pm. 200ptas.)

The 18th-century **Ayuntamiento** is built into a Baroque arch at the Pl. Mayor's southern end; the **cathedral,** constructed under Alfonso VIII six years after he conquered Castile (1183), dominates the other side. A perfect square, 25m on each side, this is the only Anglo-Norman Gothic cathedral in Spain. A Spanish Renaissance facade and tower were added in the 16th and 17th centuries, only to be torn down when deemed inappropriate. A 1724 fire cut short the latest attempt to build a front, leaving the current exterior incomplete and thus reminiscent of a Hollywood set. Psychedelic contemporary stained glass windows complete the jumble (open daily 8:45am-2pm and 4-7pm, winter 8:45am-2pm and 4-6pm; free). Inside, the **Museo del Tesoro** houses some late medieval Psalters and a great deal of gold jewelry; more impressive is the **Sala Capitular** and its positively edible ceiling (open Tues.-Sun. 11am-2pm and 4-6pm, 200ptas).

ENTERTAINMENT

Nightlife in new Cuenca is basically a bar scene which extends into the wee hours. Several bars with loud music and young, snazzily dressed crowds line small **Calle Galíndez,** off C. Fray Luis de León—a long and dark but sweet walk down the hill from Old Cuenca; a taxi will cost about 500ptas. The Pl. Mayor boasts several pleasant, if touristy cafes. For more bars and nightclubs, take the winding street/staircase just off Pl. Mayor across from the cathedral down toward the Río Júcar, where you'll encounter an army of empty bottles.

Cuenca rings with song during the **Festival de Música Sagrada.** This famous celebration, with Spanish and international groups, occurs the week before Holy Week. The *Auditorio* hosts several music concert series throughout the year (tel. 23 27 97).

■ Sigüenza

Sleepy Sigüenza tumbles down a gentle slope halfway between Madrid and Zaragoza. Pink stone buildings cluster around a gothic cathedral, all of which are embedded in serene farmland. No modern buildings or cement companies have yet to mar the landscape; even frequent train traffic is drowned out by the tranquility of the town and its 5000 inhabitants.

Practical Information The **train station** (tel. 39 14 94) is on Av. Alfonso VI. Sigüenza is on the Madrid-Zaragoza train line; about 10 trains per day head in either direction (to Madrid 1½-2hr., 1060ptas). **Luggage storage** is available at the station for 300ptas. To get from the station to the cathedral, follow Av. Alfonso VI up hill (it changes to C. Humilladero), then take the first left onto C. Cardenal Mendoza. On your way up the hill you will pass el Parque de la Alameda and the **tourist office** (tel. 39 32 51), on the left on Po. Alameda where C. Humilladero begins. Maps and guidance are available (open Tues.-Fri. 10am-2pm and 4:30-7pm; Sat.-Sun. 9am-2:30pm and 4:30-7pm). For **currency exchange,** find banks along C. Humilladero and C. Cardenal Mendoza. Many banks have **ATMs. Taxis** are at (tel. 39 14 11). The **Red Cross** (tel. 39 13 33) is on Ctra. Madrid. The **police,** Carretera de Alcolea-Aranda de Duero, can be reached at (tel. 39 01 95). In an **emergency,** call 091 or 092. The **post office** (tel. 39 08 44) is on C. Villaviciosa off Pl. Hilario Yabén (open Mon.-Fri. 8:30am-2:30pm, Sat. 9:30am-1pm).

Accommodations and Food Although you can "do" Sigüenza in a couple of hours, it's pleasant to loiter for a while, or even spend the night. **Pensión Venancio,** C. San Roque, 3 (tel. 39 03 47), near the Alameda de la Parque from the train station, is charming. Rooms are spacious and well-lit (singles 2200ptas, doubles 3400ptas). Most restaurants are linked to *hostales* in Sigüenza. The most popular among locals is **Restaurante El Mesón,** Roman Pascual, 14 (tel. 39 06 49), serving a wide selection of Spanish wine. (soups 300-500ptas, meat entrees 800-1600ptas; Visa). To get there, walk down C. Serrano Sanz from the cathedral and take your first left.

Sights From the bottom of the hill, two imposing sights break Sigüenza's low skyline: the **cathedral,** with its magnificent gothic *rosetones* (rose windows) and the fortified **castillo,** a 12th-century castle-turned-hotel. Work on the cathedral began in the mid-12th century and continued until 1495. The building combines Romanesque, Mudéjar, and Plateresque styles. The structure's most renowned feature is the 15th-century **Tumba del Doncel,** commissioned by Isabel la Católica in memory of a favorite page who died fighting the Muslims in Granada. The young man rests contentedly dead, reading a book. Three-hundred-four stone portraits jut out of the **sacristy's** elaborate Renaissance ceiling. The staring faces include pious bishops, uppity soldiers, and local women. Nearby is an El Greco *Anunciación.* The **Capilla de las Relicas** does not in fact have any relics, but does house beautiful reliquaries, a silver *custodia* (tabernacle), and a ceiling so magnificent that the church thoughtfully provides a mirror on the floor to help you view it. Just off the **cloister,** one room is decorated with Flemish tapestries and houses an assortment of documents from the cathedral archives, including a 13th-century codex. (Open daily 11am-1:30pm and 4-7pm. Ask a cathedral employee for a tour of the best parts; 300ptas, free tours Tues. at 4, 5, and 7pm. No entry during services unless you wish to participate.) Opposite the cathedral, the small **Museo de Arte Antiguo,** a.k.a. Museo Diocesano (tel. 39 10 23), exhibits medieval and early modern religious works. The highlight is Ribera's *Jesús despojado de sus vestiduras* (Jesus Dispossessed of His Garments). (Open Tues.-Fri. noon-2pm and 4:30-6pm, Sat.-Sun. 11am-2pm and 5-7pm; Sept.-Semana Santa 11am-2pm and 4-6pm, Sun. noon-2pm. 200ptas.)

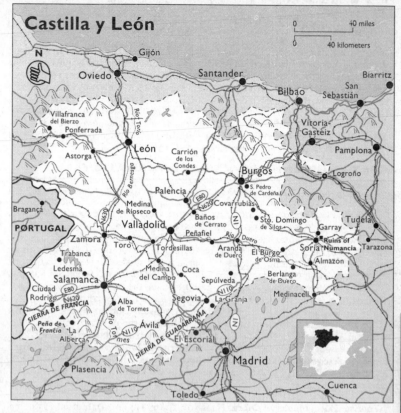

Castilla y León

Castilla y León's cities emerge like islands from a sea of burnt sienna. Reigning strong in the region, these urban personages survey their surroundings from splendid cathedrals and sumptuous palaces. The monuments—the majestic Gothic cathedrals of Burgos and León, the slender Romanesque belfries along the Camino de Santiago in León, the intricate sandstone of Salamanca, and the proud city walls of Ávila—have emblazoned themselves as national as well as regional images.

Well before Castilla's famous 1469 confederation with Aragón, when Fernando of Aragón and Isabel of Castilla were united in world-shaking matrimony, it was clear that Castilla had its act together. In the High Middle Ages, the region emerged from obscurity to lead the Christian charge against Islam. Castilian nobles, sanguine from the spoils of combat, introduced the concept of a unified Spain (under Castilian command, of course), and *castellano* ("Spanish") became the dominant language throughout the nation. Imperious León, Castilla's comrade at arms, though chagrined to be lumped with Castilla in a 1970s provincial reorganization, has much in common with its co-province. Neither has been as economically successful as their more high-tech northeastern neighbors.

Castilian gastronomy favors red meats and vegetables that can be grown in relatively cold climates, such as potatoes. *Cocido castellano* is beef, ham, potatoes, sausage, carrots, and garlic stewed together. Castilians also tend to get hyperbolically excited about their lamb dishes.

■ Segovia

Legend has it that Segovia's famed *acueducto* was built in a day—by the Devil, trying to win the heart of a Segovian water-seller named Juanilla. When the shocked Juanilla woke up to find the aqueduct almost completed, she prayed to the Virgin Mary, who made the sun rise a bit earlier in order to foil the Devil's scheme. Segovia's aqueduct may not have won Juanilla's heart, but it has intrigued visitors ever since Roman times. The town represents Castile at its best—a magnificent castle, an impressive cathedral, and twisting alleyways filled with the aroma of *sopa castellano* and *cochinillo asado* (roast suckling pig). As always, pleasure has its price: *peseta* tags on food and accommodations are much higher than in Madrid.

ORIENTATION AND PRACTICAL INFORMATION

On the far side of the Sierra de Guadarrama, 88km northwest of Madrid, Segovia is close enough to the capital to be a daytrip, but definitely warrants a longer stay.

To get to **Plaza Mayor,** the city's *centro histórico* and site of the **tourist office,** take any bus from the station (200ptas). Weekdays some go only as far as **Paseo del Salón.** If this happens to you, go left up the steps on **Puerta del Sol,** turn right, and make the first left up to the plaza. For the fastest route from the **bus station** to Pl. Mayor, make a left from the station onto C. Ezekiel González, and walk until you get to the first round intersection with a statue. Turn right, cross the Puente de Sancti Spiritus, and take the stairs up to the park. Cross the park and go up the steps of the Puerta del Sol. Turn right on C. Judería Vieja, then make a sharp left at the first corner (15min.).

The city is impossible to navigate without a map, so be sure to get one at a tourist office. It may help to think of the old city, high above the newer barrios, as a ship, with the Alcázar acting as bow, the aqueduct as stern and the cathedral tower as mainmast. Both Pl. Mayor (10min.) and the Alcázar (20min.) are uphill treks from **Plaza de Azoguejo,** next to the **aqueduct.** Running between Pl. Mayor and Pl. Azoguejo is **Calle Isabel la Católica-Calle Juan Bravo-Calle Cervantes,** a busy pedestrian thoroughfare.

Tourist Office: Municipal Office, Pl. Mayor, 10 (tel. 46 03 34), in front of the bus stop, on the corner opposite the cathedral, about 20m uphill from Iglesia San Martín. Complete info on accommodations, bus and train schedules, and sights posted in the windows. Indispensable **map.** Some English and French spoken. Open Mon.-Fri. 10am-2pm and 5-8pm, Sat. 10am-2pm and 4:30-8:30pm, Sun. 11am-2pm and 4:30-8:30pm. **Regional Tourist Office** (tel. 44 03 02), Pl. Azoguejo, at the foot of the steps leading to the top of the aqueduct. Less crowded. Piles of glossy brochures. Staff can make reservations (open Mon.-Sat. 10am-8pm, Sun. 10am-2pm).

Currency Exchange: Banks and **ATMs** surround Pl. Azoguejo and Pl. Mayor. **Banco Central Hispano,** C. Juan Braco, closes on weekends.

Trains: (tel. 42 07 74), Po. Obispo Quesada. Only one line: the Segovia-Madrid *regional.* To Madrid (15 per day, Sun. 6 per day, 2hr., 750ptas) and Villalba (halfway along the same line, transfer for El Escorial, Ávila, León, and Salamanca, 500ptas). The bus is often a better bet unless coming directly from the airport.

Buses: Estacionamiento Municipal de Autobuses, Po. Ezequiel González, 10 (tel. 42 77 25), on Av. Conde de Sepúlveda at Av. Fernández Ladreda. To: Madrid (every hr. 6am-10pm, 1¾hr., 765ptas); Ávila (2 per day, Sat.-Sun. 1 per day, 1hr., 555ptas); Salamanca (Mon.-Fri. 4 per day, Sat. 2 per day, 3hr., 1400ptas); Valladolid (2-6 per day, 2½hr., 820ptas); La Granja (6-10 per day, 20min., 105ptas).

Public Transportation: Transportes Urbanos de Segovia, Pl. Mayor, 8 (tel. 46 03 29). Buses 85-100ptas.

Taxis: Pl. Mayor (tel. 43 66 80); Pl. Oriental (tel. 42 02 58); and Av. Fernández Ladreda (tel. 43 66 81). Taxis also pull up outside the train and bus stations. **Radio Taxi:** (tel. 44 50 00).

Luggage Storage: Lockers at the train station (300ptas; open 5:45am-10pm).

Red Cross: C. Tilos (tel. 46 00 00).

Medical Services: **Hospital Policlínico,** C. San Agustín, 13 (tel. 41 92 98). **Hospital General,** Crta. de Soria (tel. 41 91 00 or 41 90 65). Either one for **emergencies.**
Police: Municipal, C. Guadarrama, (tel. 43 12 12). **Comisaría** C. Ezekiel González, (tel. 42 51 61). **Emergency:** (tel. 091 or 092).
Post Office: Pl. Dr. Laguna, 5 (tel. 46 16 16), up C. Cronista Lecea from Pl. Mayor. Open for stamps and Lista de Correos Mon.-Fri. 8:30am-8:30pm, Sat. 9:30am-2pm. **Postal Code:** 40001.
Telephone Code: (9) 21.

ACCOMMODATIONS AND CAMPING

Finding an *hostal* during the summer can be nightmarish. The regional tourist office's help with reservations and accommodations listings is valuable, but be prepared to pay 2500ptas or more for a single, unless you're hip to a windowless, sinkless space.

Residencia Juvenil "Emperador Teodosio" (HI), Av. Conde de Sepúlveda (tel. 44 11 11), look for its huge red fire escape. From train station, go right, cross the street, and walk along Po. Obispo Quesada, which soon becomes Av. Conde de Sepúlveda (10min.). Hostel's on the left. From the bus station, go right on C. Ezequiel González, which becomes Av. Conde de Sepúlveda (10min.). Hostel is on the right. Open to travelers July-Aug., when modern amenities and hotel-like doubles and triples, all with private baths, make it nearly impossible to get a room. Max. stay 3 days. Curfew 1:30am. Lodging with breakfast 1050ptas, over 26 1450ptas.
Hostal Juan Bravo, C. Juan Bravo, 12, 2nd floor (tel. 46 34 13), on the main thoroughfare in the old town, near Iglesia de San Martín. Bright, carpeted rooms with schmaltzy pictures are cool in summer. Singles with bath 4400ptas. Doubles 3500ptas, with bath 4400ptas. Triples: 5000ptas; 6300ptas. Visa, MC.
Pensión Ferri, C. Escuderos, 10 (tel. 46 09 57), off Pl. Mayor. Central and clean. Only single 1350ptas. Doubles 2300ptas. Triples 3300ptas. Showers 300ptas.
Pensión Aragón, Pl. Mayor, 4 (tel. 46 09 14). Cheap and central. Singles 1300ptas. Doubles 2300ptas. Triples 2700ptas. Quads 3500ptas. Hot shower 200ptas.
Hostal Residencia Tagore, Santa Isabel, 13 (tel. 42 42 82; email ambito.PCS@sqv.servicom.es). Follow the aqueduct as it shrinks and turn right just before it bends for the 2nd time (10min. from Pl. Azoguejo). Huge, arching sign, garden, and pool hint at paradise, but it's still a hostel. Far from Segovia center. Teeming with students year round, so call ahead. All rooms with sinks. Singles 2500ptas. Doubles 3500ptas, with toilet 5500ptas.
Camping: Camping Acueducto, Ctra. Nacional, 601, km 112 (tel. 42 50 00), 2km toward La Granja. Take the AutoBus Urbano from Pl. Azoguejo to Nueva Segovia (150ptas). 2nd-class site shaded by the Sierra de Guadarrama. Hot water. 450ptas per person and per tent, children 350ptas. Open April-Sept.

FOOD

Choosing a restaurant in Segovia is a craps shoot. In general, steer clear of Pl. Mayor, Pl. Azoguejo, and all signs simulating worn medieval parchment. *Cochinillo asado* (roast suckling pig), lamb, and *croquetas* have always been favorites. **Panaderías** around C. Juan Bravo and off Pl. Azoguejo sell goodies for reasonable prices. **Fruit and vegetable stands** crowd C. Juan Bravo and its neighboring streets. **%Día,** C. Fernández Jimenez, 32, off C. Fernández Ladreda, is a discount supermarket (open Mon.-Thurs. 9:15am-2pm and 5:15-8pm, Fri.-Sat. 9:15am-2:30pm and 5:15-8:30pm).

Bar-Mesón Cueva de San Esteban, C. La Victoria, 9 (tel. 43 78 11), to the right off the top of Pl. San Esteban, which can be reached via C. Escuderos. Local budgeters eat at this stone- and mortar-walled retreat, complete with wooden pygmy footstools for seats. Entrees start at 675ptas. *Menú* 900ptas.
Restaurante La Almuzara, C. Marqués del Arco, 3 (tel. 46 06 22), past the cathedral toward the Alcázar. Excellent vegetarian restaurant with greenery-inspired frescoes. Big salads (400-900ptas), *platos combinados* (700-1300ptas), pizzas (850-1200ptas), pasta, and some hefty entrees.

Restaurante-Mesón Alejandro, C. Carbitrería (at its end), the first left off C. Cronista Lecea, which is off Pl. Mayor to the left of the tourist office. Excellent and inexpensive. Delicious *paella* for two, and a good *menú del día* (900ptas).

Lacosta Johnny, C. Ruiz de Alda, alongside the aqueduct. Feeds the club crowd all
night Fri.-Sat. with huge bocadillos (325ptas) named after famous musicians like
Pink Floyd. The dive is takeout only (open Fri.-Sat. 9:30pm-7am).

SIGHTS

Segovia rewards the wanderer. Whether palace, church, house, or sidewalk, almost
everything deserves close consideration. Look for *esgrafía,* lacy patterns on the
facades of buildings. Also, be sure to explore the northern parts of town, away from
the Alcázar and aqueduct.

The Alcázar

The Alcázar (tel. 46 07 59), an archetypal late-medieval castle, audaciously juts into
space at the far north end of the old quarter. The surrounding countryside is enough
to make one tremble—or at least take a picture. Alfonso X, who allegedly thought
himself greater than God, beautified the original 11th-century fortress. He was later
struck by lightning. Successive monarchs added to the Alcázar's grandeur, befitting it
for the 1474 coronation of Isabel I as Queen of Castilla. To round off its castle duties,
the Alcázar served as a prison during later centuries, and in 1764 Carlos III converted
it into the most prestigious artillery academy, graduating tough and educated **Caballeros Cadetes.** A small but marvelous museum inside the Alcázar explains the role of
science in the "enlightened" military.

Trappings from an illustrious past fill the rest of the castle: tapestries, armor,
thrones, cannons, sculpture, and paintings. The walls of the **Sala de Reyes** (royal
room) are adorned with wood and gold inlay sculptures of the monarchs of Asturias,
Castilla, and León. In the **Sala de Solio** (throne room), the inscription above the
throne reads: *"tanto monta, monta tanto"* ([She] mounts, as does [he]). This popular saying signifies not what your dirty mind suggests, but rather Fernando and Isabel's equal authority as sovereigns. The **Sala de Armas** (weapons room) holds a
veritable arsenal of medieval weaponry.

If you feel strong, climb the 140 steps up a nausea-inducing spiral staircase to the
top of the **torre,** where you will be rewarded with a marvelous view of Segovia and
the surrounding amber plains. Prince Pedro, son of Enrique IV, slipped from his
nurse's arms, fell off the balcony, and crashed onto the ramparts to his bloody death;
out of desperation the nurse leapt after him and ended her own life. (Alcázar open
daily 10am-7pm, Oct.-March 10am-6pm. 375ptas, seniors 275ptas.)

The Cathedral

Commissioned by Carlos I in 1525 to replace a 12th-century cathedral damaged during the "Comunidades" war, Segovia's huge, gothic cathedral towers over Pl. Mayor.
With 23 **chapels** and a silver and gold **tesoro,** the cathedral is a mouthful. The **Sala
Capitular,** hung with well-preserved 17th-century tapestries, displays a silver and
gold chariot, an ornate *artesonado* ceiling, and various crucifixes, chalices, and candelabras. The **museum** (tel. 46 22 05) holds an excellent collection, including
Coello's 16th-century painting *La duda de Santo Tomás,* and a series of 17th-century
paintings on marble depicting the Passion of Christ. Here also lies Prince Pedro.
Upstairs, valuables include ceremonial robes, dazzling 16th-century manuscripts, and
little saintly pieces. (Open daily spring and summer 9:30am-7pm, fall and winter 9am-
6pm. 250ptas.)

The Aqueduct and Little Churches

The serpent-like **acueducto romano,** built by the Romans around 50 BC to pipe in
water from the Rio Frio, 18 km away, casts a mean shadow. Supported by 128 pillars
that span 813m, the two tiers of 163 arches are constructed of some 200,000 blocks
of granite—without any mortar to hold them together. This spectacular feat of engi-

neering, restored by the monarchy in the 15th century, was still in use ten years ago. The grand structure reaches its maximum height of 28.9m beside Pl. Azoguejo. There is no reason to limit one's viewing to that particular spot. One can sit atop the steps on the other side of the plaza, or walk along the aqueduct's entire length until the arches become too small to pass under.

Segovia's 12th- and 13th-century Romanesque churches hold erratic afternoon hours, an impedance to whirlwind touring. Most are open for visits roughly 11am-2pm and 4-7pm, but the exterior visit is worthwhile even if you've been locked out. **San Millán,** C. Fernández Ladreda, is the finest example of Romanesque architecture in the city. Its medieval frescoes were discovered under a layer of paint about 30 years ago. During the days of mass illiteracy, the murals and frescoes replaced reading the Bible (open daily during mass only, 8pm). **La Trinidad,** C. Trinidad, in the north of the city, is relatively well-preserved. Thirteenth-century **San Esteban,** to the west on Pl. Esteban, has one of the highest towers of any church in Spain. Restored in the early 20th century, the building houses a calvary from the 1800s. Tenth-century **San Martín,** Pl. San Martín, off C. Juan Bravo, is livened by *mozárabe* touches, a Baroque *retablo,* and sepulchres of 17th-century Segovians. Other outstanding churches include **San Justo, San Andrés, San Nicolas,** and **San Sebastián.** The walk around and between La Trinidad and San Esteban is fulfilling. Go behind the first church and turn left on C. S. Quirre. Take the second left and first right onto Trav. Capuchinos; this will take you past Iglesia San Esteban. A left on C. Desamparados will bring you to the **Casa-Museo de Antonio Machado** (open daily 4-7pm; free). The poet's 13-year residency (1919-1932) has been left untouched. Go even if only to look out the windows.

A 14th- and 15th-century wave of palaces followed the spree of Romanesque-churches. **Torreón de Lozoya,** Pl. San Martín, off C. Juan Bravo, is a dandy *palacio;* it hosts art exhibitions (open Mon.-Fri. 7-9:30pm, Sat. noon-2pm and 7-9:30pm). The 16th-century **Casa de los Picos,** in the southeast, has an intriguing facade studded with rows of diamond-shaped stones. The **Palacio del Conde Alpuente,** off C. Juan Bravo a bit uphill from the Casa de los Picos, epitomizes Segovian *esgrafía.*

Outside the Walls

The walk north away from the city offers an escape from the urban environment. The meandering Eresma River and lush greenery offer a welcome change of pace, and there are several sights of interest. However, such pleasure comes at a cost— be prepared for a grueling uphill trek back to the city. If you follow C. Pozo de la Nieve (on the left with your back to the Alcázar), and head down the second stone staircase, you'll be on Po. San Juan de la Cruz. A green 20-minute walk leads to **Iglesia de la Vera Cruz,** a mysterious 12-sided basilica built by the cabalistic Knights Templar in 1208. Beneath its lofty vaults are two hidden chambers where clergymen guarded their lives and their valuables from robbers and highwaymen. The Knights Templar gathered to perform initiation ceremonies in these same rooms—step into the center for an auditory adventure. (Open April-Sept. Tues.-Sun. 10:30am-1:30pm and 3:30-7pm, Oct.-March Tues.-Sun. 10:30am-1:30pm and 3:30-6pm. 170ptas.)

ENTERTAINMENT

Packed with bars and cafes, **Pl. Mayor** and its tributaries are the center of Segovian nightlife for the older crowd. **Pl. Azagejo** and **C. Carmen,** near the aqueduct, are filled with bars as well, where those under 20 (and way under 20) gather. Club headquarters are at **C. Ruiz de Alda** off Pl. Azoguejo. *Discotecarios* shuffle their feet at **Sabbat,** Po. Salón.

In July, Segovia hosts two classical music festivals. From June 24-29, Segovia celebrates its *fiestas* in honor of San Juan and San Pedro. Look for free concerts on Pl. Azoguejo and a fireworks display on the 29th.

Three kilometers northwest of Segovia, **Zamarramala** hosts the **Fiestas de Santa Agueda** (St. Agatha) in February. Women take over the town's administration for a day, dress up in beautiful, old-fashioned costumes, and parade through the streets.

They parody men to commemorate an abortive sneak attack on the Alcázar in which the women of Zamarramala tried to distract the castle guards with wine and song.

■ Near Segovia

LA GRANJA DE SAN ILDEFONSO

The royal palace and grounds of **La Granja** (tel. 47 00 19), 9km southeast of Segovia, are the Versailles of Spain. One of four royal summer retreats (with El Pardo, El Escorial, and Aranjuez), La Granja is the most extravagant. Marble fortifications, antique lace curtains, ceiling frescoes, and lavish crystal chandeliers (made in San Ildefonso's renowned crystal factory) are its royal ornaments. Felipe V, the first Bourbon King of Spain and grandson of Louis XIV, detested the Habsburgs' austere El Escorial. Nostalgic for Versailles, he commissioned La Granja in the early 18th century. The guided tour (in Spanish) is mandatory for visitors, but worth enduring—the best exhibit comes last. A mysterious fire destroyed the living quarters of the royals and their servants in 1918. The rubble was rebuilt to house one of the world's finest collections of Flemish **tapestries.** Woven in the 16th and 17th centuries, they covered the walls of Habsburg kings Carlos I and Felipe II. The peach **iglesia** flanking the palace has a red marble interior and gilded woodwork. In a side chapel, bones of various saints and martyrs make an impressive display.

Outside, the cool and expansive **jardines** are surrounded by a forest with statues of children and animals. The flamboyant **Cascadas Nuevas,** an ensemble of illuminated fountains and pools, represents the continents and four seasons. People even yell in ecstasy when the fountain turns on. (La Granja open Tues.-Sun. 10am-6pm; Oct.-March Tues.-Sat. 10am-1:30pm and 3-5pm, Sun. 10am-2pm; April-May Tues.-Fri. 10am-1:30pm and 3-5pm, Sat. and Sun. 10am-6pm. 650ptas, students 250ptas. Gardens free except Wed. and Sat.-Sun. after 3pm; 325ptas, students 200ptas. Fountains turned on Wed. and Sat.-Sun. at 5:30pm; after 3pm 350ptas.) Frequent **buses** leave Segovia's bus station for La Granja (10-13 per day, 20min., 200ptas round-trip).

Along with water, glass is another celebrated transparency in La Granja. Follow the evolution of the wine bottle and stare wide-eyed at the collection of contemporary glass art in the **Real Fabrica de Cristales** (tel. 47 17 12; open April-Sept. 11am-8pm; Oct.-March 11am-7pm; 400ptas, students and seniors 200ptas).

■ Ávila

The walled city of Ávila revives nostalgia for medieval times, when crowds gathered around *juglares* listening to epic verses, like *El Cid,* and chivalry was alive. One of Castilla's most important cities since 1090, Ávila was the home of Santa Teresa de Jesús and San Juan de la Cruz, and a mecca for 16th-century mystics, writers, and reformers. Somehow San Juan seems to get lost in the shuffle—Ávila is crazy for Santa Teresa. Museums and monuments depict in exhaustive detail her divine visitations and ecstatic visions, as described in her autobiography, *La Vida de Santa Teresa* (The Life of Santa Teresa). It is no surprise that Ávila's 48,500 inhabitants have taken the heroine as their patron saint, referring to her as La Santa and naming everything from pastries to driving schools after her.

The city sits on a rocky escarpment high above the Río Adaja Valley. Its location keeps it cool in the summer, unlike the sweltering plain below, but freezing in the winter. Swallows and storks keep a watchful eye on tourists who crane their necks to look back up at them.

ORIENTATION AND PRACTICAL INFORMATION

Just west of Segovia and northwest of Madrid, Ávila is a reasonable daytrip from either. The city has two central squares: **Plaza de la Victoria** (known to locals as the Plaza del Mercado Chico), inside the city walls, and **Plaza de Santa Teresa,** just outside. The cathedral sits between the two plazas, in the east half of the old city. To get

to the city center from the **bus station** (east of the center), cross the intersection, turn right down C. Duque de Alba (keeping the small park to the right), and follow the street past the Iglesia de San Pedro to cafe-filled Pl. Santa Teresa (10min.). To reach Pl. Santa Teresa from the train station (northeast of the center), follow Av. José Antonio until it ends in a tangle of streets at Pl. Santa Ana. There you will find C. Isaac Peral, which leads to C. Duque de Alba; turn left and continue on to Pl. Santa Teresa (15min.). Municipal bus #1 (75ptas) runs from near the train station (bus stop one block toward town) to Pl. Victoria.

Tourist Office: Pl. Catedral, 4 (tel. 21 13 87), opposite the cathedral entrance. From Pl. Santa Teresa, go through the main gate and turn right up C. Cruz Vieja, along the walls of the cathedral. Friendly, bilingual staff. Open Mon.-Fri. 10am-2pm and 4-7pm, Sat. 9:30am-2pm and 4-7pm, Sun. 9:30am-2pm and 4:30-8:30pm; in winter Mon.-Fri. 10am-2pm and 5-8pm, Sat. 9:30am-2pm.

Trains: Av. José Antonio, 40 (tel. 25 02 02), on the northeast side of town. To: Madrid (20-30 per day, fewer on weekends, 1½-2hr., 805-1800ptas); Medina del Campo, for transfer to Segovia (16 per day, 1hr., 480-1400ptas); Salamanca (2-4 per day, 2hr., 805ptas); Valladolid (7 per day, 1½hr., 775-1700ptas); El Escorial (3 per day, 1hr., 450ptas).

Buses: Av. Madrid, 2 (tel. 22 01 54), at Av. Portugal on the northeast side of town. To: Madrid (2-3 per day, 2hr., 915ptas); Segovia (4 per day, Sat -Sun. 1 per day, 1hr., 555ptas), and Salamanca (7 per day, Sat.-Sun. 2-3 per day, 1½hr., 820ptas). Other destinations include Valladolid, Cuenca, and Sevilla.

Taxis: Pl. Santa Teresa (tel. 25 08 00), also at the train station (tel. 22 01 49). Taxi Train station to Pl. Santa Teresa 350ptas plus 25ptas per piece of luggage.

Medical Services: Red Cross, Pl. San Francisco (tel. 22 48 48; **emergency** tel. 22 22 22). **Hospital Provincial:** (tel. 35 72 00). **Ambulance:** (tel. 22 14 00).

Police: (tel. 21 11 88), Po. San Roque. **Emergency:** (tel. 091).

Post Office: Pl. Catedral, 2 (tel. 21 13 54), to the left of cathedral when facing the main entrance. Lista de Correos and all services open Mon.-Fri. 8:30am-8:30pm, Sat. 9:30am-2pm. **Postal Code:** 05001.

Telephone Code: (9)20.

ACCOMMODATIONS

Accommodations are plentiful and reasonably priced, though some fill up in summer.

Pensión Continental, Pl. Catedral, 6 (tel. 21 15 02; fax 25 16 91), next to the tourist office. Beautiful ex-hotel in ex-cellent location. Bright rooms with bouncy beds and phones. Singles 2200ptas, with bath 3900ptas. Doubles: 3700ptas; 4500ptas. Triples: 5200ptas; 6300ptas. 7% IVA not included. Visa, MC, AmEx.

Hostal Casa Felipe, Pl. Victoria, 12 (tel. 21 39 24), on the side of the plaza closest to cathedral. Conveniently located above the bar. TVs and sinks standard, many rooms have balconies. Singles 2200ptas. Doubles with shower 4000ptas, with bath 5000ptas. Prices lower in June and winter.

Hostal Santa Ana, C. Alfonso Montalvo, 2, 2nd fl. (tel. 22 00 63), from the train station, down Av. José Antonio and off Pl. Santa Ana. Clean. For quieter budget travelers. Singles 2500ptas. Doubles 4200ptas. Triples 4700ptas. Discounted in winter.

Residencia Juvenil "Duperier" (HI) (tel. 22 17 16), Av. Juventud. A bit far from the town center: from Pl. Santa Teresa, take Av. Alférez Provisional; cross C. Santa Fé onto Av. Juventud. Turn right through the gate of the Ciudad Deportiva complex; the hostel is down the short street in front of you. If returning alone at night, take a taxi. Only 6-8 beds reserved for HI purposes, so call in advance. Curfew 11pm. Pool and tennis courts nearby. Meals available. Open for travelers July-Aug. Comfortable doubles, all with bath. 1050ptas per person, over 26 1450ptas.

FOOD

Budget sandwich shops cluster around **Pl. Victoria.** Cafes and bars in **Pl. Sta. Teresa** are pricier, but dining in Ávila generally saves *pesetas*. The city has won fame for its *ternera de Ávila* (veal) and *mollejas* (sweetbread). The *yemas de Santa Teresa* or

yemas de Ávila, local confections made of egg yolk and honey, and *vino de Cebre-ros,* a smooth regional wine, are delectable. Every Friday, the mercado in Pl. Victoria sells foodstuffs at low prices (9am-2pm). **El Arbol,** C. Alfonso de Montalro, 1, off Plaza Santa Ana, is a decent supermarket (open Mon.-Sat. 9:30am-2pm and 5:30-8:30pm; in winter Mon.-Sat. 9:30am-2pm and 5-8pm). Bars and local culture can be enjoyed on Conde de Vallespin (off Pl. Victoria) and its side streets.

Restaurante El Grande, Pl. Santa Teresa, 8 (tel. 22 30 83). A festive family-style restaurant with outdoor seating on the plaza. *Raciones (*350-850ptas), *menú* (1100ptas), and specialty croissant sandwiches (285-335ptas).

Ristorante Italiano, C. San Segundo, 28 (tel. 25 28 90), facing the east wall. Vines coil up the walls. Wide selection of pricey wines. Salads (600-1200ptas), pastas (700-1000ptas), and pizzas (1200ptas).

Bocatti, C. San Segundo, 28. A bright 50s-inspired sub shop with checkered tiles, Americana inspirations on the walls, and Elvis in the jukebox. Cold (365-485ptas) and hot (295-490ptas) sub sandwiches on freshly baked bread.

Gran Muralla, C. San Segundo, facing the cathedral-side wall. One great wall meets another; this flashy Chinese restaurant sits opposite Ávila's east *muralla.* Filled with Chinese kitsch decoration. Cheap, plentiful servings, lunchtime *menú* (745ptas), combination plates (400-900ptas).

Casa Patas, C. San Millán, 4 (tel. 21 31 94), off Pl. Santa Teresa. A small, colorful restaurant with few tables and the cheapest worthwhile lunchtime *menú* in town (1000ptas). Entrees 400-2000ptas.

SIGHTS

Las Murallas

Ávila's inner city is surrounded by Spain's oldest and best preserved medieval walls. Construction of the **murallas medievales** began in 1090, and most were completed in the next century. It was this concentrated burst of activity that gave the walls their unusual uniformity. Mudéjar features suggest that *morisco* citizens helped fortify Christian Ávila. Eighty-two massive towers reinforce walls whose thickness averages 3m. The most imposing of the towers, **Cimorro,** is the cathedral's bold apse. On the inside, in the corner to the right of the cathedral, are the outlines of two windows and two balconies—all that remains of what was once an Alcázar. If you wish to walk on the walls, start from the **Puenta del Alcázar.** (Open Tues.-Sun. 11am-1:30pm and 5-7:30pm; in winter Tues.-Sun. 10:30am-3:30pm. 100ptas.)

The best view of the walls and of Ávila itself is from the **Cuatro Postes,** a tiny four-pillar structure past the Río Adaja on the highway to Salamanca, 1½km northwest of the city. At this very spot, Santa Teresa was caught by her uncle while she and her brother were trying to flee to the Islamic south to be martyred.

Inside the Walls

Some believe that the profile of the huge **cathedral** looming over the watchtowers inspired Santa Teresa's metaphor of the soul as a diamond castle. Begun in the second half of the 12th century, the cathedral shows the transition from Romanesque to Gothic style, testifying to the long, turbulent years of the *Reconquista.* It is constructed of mottled stones from the region, some of which have been painted pink. The duality of color is said to represent the liberating nature of ambiguity.

View the **Altar de La Virgen de la Caridad,** where 12-year-old Santa Teresa prostrated herself after the death of her mother. Behind the main altar is the alabaster **tomb** of Cardinal Alonso de Madrigal, an Avilan bishop and prolific writer whose dark complexion won him the label "El Tostado" (the Toasted). In fact, it became popular during the Golden Age to refer to all literary windbags by this nickname. The museum displays an enormous *libros de canti* (hymnals) and Juan Arfe's silver, six-leveled **Custoda del Corpus** with bells that still swivel. (Cathedral open daily 10am-1:30pm and 3:30-6pm; Oct.-April 10am-1:30pm and 3:30-5:30pm. 250ptas.)

Santa Teresa's admirers built the 17th-century **Convento de Santa Teresa** on the site of her birthplace and childhood home. To the right of the convent, the small **Sala de Reliquias** holds some great Santa Teresa relics, including her forefinger, the sole of her sandal, and the cord with which she flagellated herself. (Convent open daily 9:30am-1:30pm and 3:30-9pm; Oct.-April daily 9:30am-1:30pm and 3:30-8:30pm; Sala de Reliquias open daily 9:30am-1:30pm and 3:30-7:30pm. Free.)

Outside the Walls

A short distance outside the city walls on Po. Encarnación is the **Monasterio de la Encarnación,** where Santa Teresa lived for 30 years—27 as a nun and three as a prioress. The mandatory guided tour (10-15min.) visits Santa Teresa's tiny cell and the small rooms called *locutorios,* where nuns peered at their guests through little barred windows. Santa Teresa, while tied to a pole, had her vision of Christ in one of these rooms. In another room, according to a cryptic sign, "while talking to San Juan de la Cruz they were lifted in ecstasy." On the main staircase, Santa Teresa had her mystical encounter with the child Jesus:

> Jesús: ¿Quién eres tú? (Who are you?)
> Santa Teresa: Yo soy Teresa de Jesús. Y tú, ¿quién eres?
> (I am Teresa of Jesus. And who are you?)
> Jesús: Yo soy Jesús de Teresa. (I am Jesus of Teresa.)

Upstairs from the cloister, a museum features a collection of furnishings, letters, and other personal effects given to the convent by wealthier nuns as bribes (dowries if you prefer) to procure entrance. Teresa's reforms eliminated this system of preference and imposed norms of collective property and simplicity (as exemplified by her own *celda*). Currently, 27 nuns live in the monastery. (Open daily 10am-1pm and 4-7pm; winter daily 10am-1pm and 3:30-6pm. Obligatory tour in Spanish 150ptas.)

The first convent Teresa founded was the **Convento de San José** (tel. 22 21 27), C. Madres, 3, off C. Duque de Alba, also known as the Convento de las Madres. The 1608 building still a functions as a convent. The small **Museo Teresiano** displays the saddle she used while roaming around and establishing convents, the drum she played at Christmas, and a letter written in her elegant hand—not to mention one of her bones and a Zurbarán. (Open daily 10am-1:30pm and 4-7pm; in winter daily 10am-1:30pm and 3-6pm. Church and museum 50ptas.)

Casa de los Deanes, a mansion in Pl. Nalvillos with a Renaissance facade, houses the remarkable **Museo de Ávila** (tel. 21 10 03). The museum exhibits beautiful artifacts from Ávila's past, including *verracos,* pre-Roman granite works representing bulls and hogs. Upstairs is a triptych attributed to Hans Memling. (Open Tues.-Sat. 10:30am-2pm and 5-7:30pm, Sun. 10:30am-2pm; 200ptas, students free, Sat.-Sun. free to all.)

Basílica de San Vicente, a large 12th-century Romanesque and Gothic building, is dedicated to Vicente, Sabina, and Cristeta, three martyred saints buried in a triple-decker sepulchre. Triangles, circles, and a few amorphous decorations cover the stone (open daily 10am-2pm and 4-7:30pm; 50ptas).

Monasterio de Santo Tomás, Pl. Granada, 1, some distance from the city walls at the end of C. Jesús del Gran Poder (or Av. de Alférez Provisional), was the summer palace of the Catholic Monarchs, Fernando and Isabel, and a seat of the Inquisition. Incorporated into the monastery in anticipation of victory, a *granada* (pomegranate) motif recalls the monarchs' triumphant 1492 capture of Granada, the last Moorish kingdom in Spain. Inside the church and in front of the *retablo* is the tomb of Prince Don Juan, Fernando and Isabel's only son, who died in 1497 at the age of 19. To the right (when facing the altar) is the **Capilla del Santo Cristo,** where Santa Teresa came to pray and confess. Also here are the Tuscan **Cloister of the Noviciate,** the Gothic **Cloister of Silence,** and the Renaissance-Transition **Cloister of the Kings.** (Church open daily 8am-1pm and 4-8pm. Museum open daily 11am-1pm and 4-7pm. Cloisters 100ptas, museum 150ptas, church free.)

CASTILLA Y LEÓN

Fairs and parades of *gigantes y cabezudos* (giant effigies) pass through when the city gets a little crazy to honor Santa Teresa (Oct. 7-15). In the second or third week of July, the **Fiestas de Verano** bring exhibits, folk-singing, dancing, pop groups, fireworks, and a bullfight.

■ Salamanca

For centuries the "hand of Salamanca," a style of brass knockers found about Salamanca, has welcomed students, scholars, rogues, royals, and saints. The city has all the features of a great medieval city—cathedral, university, and river—all in grandiose proportions. Burning sandstone walls shape the gargoyles, arches, and bell towers of everything from its 13th-century university to Churriguera's Plaza Mayor.

During medieval times, the university joined Bologna, Paris, and Oxford as the four "leading lights" of the world. Eminent Spanish intellectuals, such as Nebrija and Miguel de Unamuno, have trod its hallowed halls. These days, a balanced life-style of active and contemplative existence is the *salamantino* way. Foreign students, especially Americans, invade year-round, but wintertime snowfalls occasionally accentuate its heavy, haunting buildings.

ORIENTATION AND PRACTICAL INFORMATION

The beaming **Plaza Mayor** is the social and geographic center of town. Most sights and budget accommodations lie south of the plaza. Areas directly to the north tend to be newer and more expensive. Farther north, beyond the **Plaza de España,** are working-class districts. The **universidad** is south of Pl. Mayor, near the **Plaza de Anaya.** From the **train station** (northeast of the center), either catch bus #1 to the Gran Vía, a block from Pl. Mercado (next to Pl. Mayor), or, with your back to the station, turn left down Po. Estación to Pl. España, and walk down C. Azafranal (or C. Toro) to Pl. Mayor (30 min.). From the **bus station,** either catch bus #4 to Gran Vía, or walk down C. de Filiberto Villalobos, cross busy Av. Alemania/Po. San Vincente, and plummet down C. Ramón y Cajal. Keep the park on your left, and at the end (just after the Iglesia de la Purís) head left and go up C. Prior, which runs to Pl. Mayor (20min.). Avoid the southwest section of town after dark unless you are accompanied by a friend or bodyguard—Salamanca's drug scene is notorious.

Tourist Office: Municipal, Pl. Mayor, 13-14 (tel. 21 83 42). Big, helpful office. Open Mon.-Sat. 9am-2pm and 4:30-6:30pm, Sun. 10am-2pm and 4:30-6:30pm. **Provincial,** C. Rua Mayor, 70 (tel. 26 85 71), at the Casa de las Conchas. Open Mon.-Fri. 10am-2pm and 5-8pm, Sat.-Sun. 10am-7pm. **Info booths,** open occasionally July-Sept. Students distribute maps, info, and accommodations listings from booths in Pl. Anaya, the train station, and the bus station. **Café Alcaraván,** C. Compañía, 12, and **Restaurante El Bardo** (see **Food,** p. 149) both have crowded message boards offering rideshares, language trades, rooms to rent, etc.

Currency Exchange: Banks and **ATMs** line C. Toro. **Banco Central Hispano** i down R. Mayor on the left.

Budget Travel: TIVE, Po. Carmelitas (a.k.a. Av. Alemania), 83 (tel. 26 77 31). Lon, lines, go early (open Mon.-Fri. 9am-2pm; ticket sales until 1:30pm). **Juventu Travel,** Pl. Libertad, 4 (tel. 21 74 07; fax 21 74 08). Open Mon.-Fri. 9:30am-2pr and 4:30-8pm, Sat. 10am-1:30pm.

Trains: (tel. 12 02 02), Po. Estación Ferrocarril, northeast of town. **RENFE,** Pl. Libe tad, 10 (tel. 21 24 54; open Mon.-Fri. 9am-2pm and 5-8pm). Two regional lines. T Madrid (3 per day, 3½hr., 1590ptas); Burgos (5 per day, 3hr., 2300ptas); Palenc (2 per day, 2hr., 1600ptas); Ávila (3 per day, 2hr., 820ptas); Valladolid for transfe (10 per day, 805ptas); Barcelona (1 per day, 12hr., 6500ptas).

Buses: Av. Filiberto Villalobos, 71 (tel. 23 67 17). Info open Mon.-Fri. 9am-1:30p and 4-7pm, Sat. 9am-1:30pm. To: Ávila (2-7 per day, 1-2hr., 820ptas); Ciudad Ro rigo (9 per day, Sat. 5 per day, Sun. 3 per day, 1hr., 715ptas); Valladolid (2-6 p day, 2hr., 915ptas); Zamora (10-15 per day, 1hr., 515ptas); Segovia (Mon.-Sat. 1 per day, 2hr., 1340ptas); Madrid (regular 7-10 per day, 3hr., 2210ptas; express 1

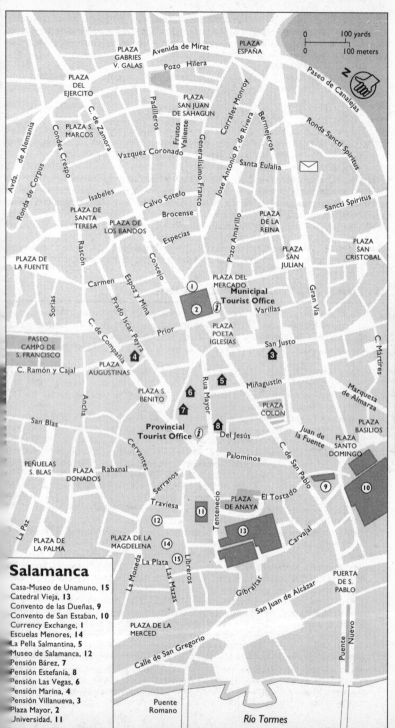

0   100 yards
0   100 meters

PLAZA
GABRIES
V. GALAS
Avenida de Mirat
PLAZA
ESPAÑA
Paseo de Canalejas
Pozo Hilera
PLAZA
DEL
EJERCITO
C. de Zamora
Padilleros
PLAZA
SAN JUAN
DE SAHAGUN
Corrales Monroy
Ronda Sancti Spiritus
PLAZA S.
MARCOS
Condes Crespo
Vazquez Coronado
Frutos
Valiente
Generalísimo Franco
Jose Antonio P. de Rivera
Bermejeros
Santa Eulalia
Avda. de Alemania
Ronda de Corpus
Isabeles
Calvo Sotelo
Sancti Spiritus
PLAZA DE
SANTA
TERESA
Brocense
Pozo Amarillo
PLAZA
DE LA
REINA
PLAZA
SAN
CRISTOBAL
PLAZA DE
LOS BANDOS
Especias
PLAZA DE
LA FUENTE
Rascón
Carmen
Concelo
PLAZA
SAN
JULIAN
Sorias
Espoz y Mina
Prado Iscar Peyra
PLAZA DEL
MERCADO
Municipal
Tourist Office ⓘ
Gran Vía
① Prior
② Varillas
PASEO
CAMPO DE
S. FRANCISCO
C. de Compañia
PLAZA
POETA
IGLESIAS
San Justo
C. Ramón y Cajal
PLAZA
AGUSTINAS
④
Miñagustin
C. Mártires
Ancha
③
Rua Mayor
⑤
Marquesa
de Almarza
San Blas
PLAZA S.
BENITO
⑥
PLAZA
COLON
PLAZA
BASILIOS
⑦
Provincial
Tourist Office ⓘ
Cervantes
⑧ Del Jesús
Juan de
la Fuente
C. de San Pablo
PLAZA
SANTO
DOMINGO
PEÑUELAS
S. BLAS
Rabanal
Palominos
PLAZA
DONADOS
Serranos
El Tostado
⑨
⑩
La Paz
Traviesa
⑫
Tentenecio
PLAZA
DE ANAYA
Carvajal
PLAZA DE
LA PALMA
⑪
⑬
PLAZA DE
LA MAGDALENA
⑭
PUERTA
DE S.
PABLO
La Moneda
La Plata
⑮ Libreros
Las Mazas
Gibraltar
San Juan de Alcázar
Puente
Nuevo
PLAZA DE LA
MERCED
Calle de San Gregorio

Salamanca

Casa-Museo de Unamuno, 15
Catedral Vieja, 13
Convento de las Dueñas, 9
Convento de San Estaban, 10
Currency Exchange, 1
Escuelas Menores, 14
La Pella Salmantina, 5
Museo de Salamanca, 12
Pensión Bárez, 7
Pensión Estefanía, 8
Pensión Las Vegas, 6
Pensión Marina, 4
Pensión Villanueva, 3
Plaza Mayor, 2
Universidad, 11

Puente
Romano
Río Tormes

15 per day, 2½hr., 1690ptas); Cáceres (8 per day, Sat.-Sun. 3 per day, 4hr., 1700ptas); León (1-3 per day, 3hr., 1675ptas); Barcelona (3 per day, 11½hr., 6220ptas). Also to: La Alberca, Bilbao, Burgos, Cuenca, Valencia, Sevilla, Mérida, Trujillo, Badajoz, Zafra, and Santander.

Taxis: tel. 25 00 00. 24hr.

Car Rental: Avis, Po. Canalejos, 49 (tel. 26 97 53). Open Mon.-Fri. 9:30am-1:30pm and 4-7pm, Sat. 9am-1:30pm. **Europcar,** (tel. 23 35 26), C. Torres Villarroel (open Mon.-Fri. 9:30am-1:15pm and 4:30-7:30pm, Sat. 9:30am-1:15pm).

Luggage Storage: At the train station (300ptas) and bus station (75ptas per item).

English Bookstores: Cervantes (tel. 21 86 02), Pl. Hermanos Jerez, near C. Azafranal. Enormous bookstore with 3 entrances, all within a block of each other (open Mon.-Fri. 9:45am-1:45pm and 4:30-8:30pm, Sat. 9:45am-1:45pm). **Portonaris,** R. Mayor, 33 (tel. 26 58 21), opposite the Casa de Conchas (open Mon.-Fri. 10am-2pm and 4:30-8pm, Sat. 10am-1:30pm).

Gay and Lesbian Services: Colectivo de Gais y Lesbianas de Salamanca (tel. 24 64 71; available Mon. 7-9pm).

Medical Services: Insalud, Av. de Mirat, 28 (tel. 29 11 00). **Red Cross:** (tel. 21 22 22), Pl. San Benito.

Police: (tel. 27 91 38), in the Ayuntamiento, Pl. Mayor, or at Ronda de Sancti-Spiritus, 8 (tel. 26 53 11). **Emergency:** (tel. 091 or 092).

Post Office: Gran Vía, 25 (tel. 26 06 07). Open for stamps and Lista de Correos (tel. 26 30 11; Mon.-Fri. 8:30am-8:30pm and Sat. 9:30am-2pm). **Postal Code:** 37080.

Telephone Code: (9)23.

ACCOMMODATIONS AND CAMPING

Thanks to floods of students, *hostales* and *pensiones* flourish in Salamanca, and prices tend to be quite reasonable. Accommodations often fill up in August, so call ahead. A tourist office brochure lists all of them. There are plenty of cheap *pensiones* on side streets off Pl. Mayor, especially on **C. Meléndez,** just south of the plaza.

Pensión Marina, C. Doctrinos, 4, 3rd fl. (tel. 21 65 69), between C. Compañía and C. Prado. A plant-filled paradise. One of the best values in town—comfortable bedrooms, bubbly owners, and 2 mammoth TV lounges. Singles 2000ptas. Doubles 2500ptas. Showers 200ptas.

Pensión Las Vegas, C. Meléndez, 13, 1st fl. (tel. 21 87 49), down C. Corrillo. Cushy beds, curtains, and tons of plants. TV lounge. Singles 1000-1500ptas. Doubles 2200ptas, with bath 3000ptas. Triples: 3600ptas; 4000ptas. Hot showers 150ptas.

Pensión Bárez, C. Meléndez, 19 (tel. 21 74 95). Romantic windows in well-ventilated, sparkling clean rooms. Generous owners provide a TV lounge. Singles 1200ptas. Doubles 2400ptas. Triples 3240ptas. Showers 150ptas.

Pensión Estefanía, C. Jesús, 3-5 (tel. 21 73 72 or 24 87 48). Floral bedspreads and tourist posters grace rooms on a quiet street off bustling R. Mayor. Single 1750ptas. Doubles with shower 3400ptas. Triples 4590. Showers 150ptas.

Pensión Villanueva, C. San Justo, 8, 1st fl. (tel. 26 88 33). Exit Pl. Mayor via Pl. Poeta Iglesias, cross the street, and take the first left. Funky beds and small showers. Singles 1200ptas, with shower 1400ptas. Doubles: 2600ptas; 2800ptas. Triples 3900ptas; 5200ptas. Prices vary with availability; less expensive on weekdays.

Hostal La Perla Salamantina, Sánchez Barbero, 7 (tel. 21 76 56). Exit Pl. Mayor via Pl. Poeta Iglesias, cross the street and take the first right. Everything sparkles. Plenty of rooms with plenty of room. Singles 1800ptas, with sink 1900ptas, with shower 2200ptas. Doubles with shower 3700ptas, with bath 4500ptas.

Camping: Regio (tel. 13 88 88), on Ctra. Salamanca, 4km toward Madrid. Alberto buses leave from the Gran Vía every 30min. A 1st-class site with all the amenities of nature, hot showers, nearby public transportation, pool, tennis courts, and currency exchange, in a luxury tourist complex with a 4-star hotel, restaurants, *terrazas,* and bars. 425ptas per person, per tent, and per car. 375ptas for a one-person tent. Visa, MC. **Don Quijote** (tel. 28 91 31), on the Ctra. Salamanca, 4km toward Aldealengua. Cabrerizos minivans leave from the Gran Vía. A small, 2nd-class camp site. 325ptas per person, 350ptas per car, 375ptas per tent. Open March-Oct.

FOOD

Every clique has its favorite cafe in **Pl. Mayor.** All serve the same decent food at slightly inflated prices. Students meet at *bar-restaurantes* lining the streets between the plaza and the university, where a full meal costs under 1000ptas. **Simago,** C. Toro, 82, has a downstairs **supermarket** with a large selection of fresh produce (open Mon.-Sat. 9:30am-8:30pm). Cheap markets abound north of Av. Mirat.

Restaurante El Bardo, C. Compañía, 8 (tel. 21 90 89), between the Casa de Conchas and the Clerecía. A traditional Spanish restaurant crowded with Americans. Lively bar downstairs. Its loud music filters through to the upstairs dining room. Meat entrees 900-1700ptas. Salads 600-850ptas. Sometimes offers a vegetarian *menú* (1000ptas). Closed Mon.

El Ave Turuta, C. Libreros, 22. Spacious, tiled, and bustling. Big-screen TV and lighter Spanish specialties. *Platos combinados* (650-700ptas), *menú* (900ptas).

Bocata World Company, C. Rua Mayor, 26. The Spanish version of "fast food." Selection of tasty, fast *bocadillos,* including some vegetarian (340-475ptas).

La Luna, C. Libreros. The bright red sign and varnished wood will make you happy. Veggie burgers, vegetarian *platos combinados* (875-975ptas). Meat meals (975-1000ptas), salads (900ptas).

SIGHTS

The Plaza Mayor

Pick a style, any style—they're all here (Roman, Romanesque, Gothic, Renaissance, and Baroque), and all in sandstone. Between the arches of the Baroque **Plaza Mayor** hang medallions with bas-reliefs of famous *españoles,* from El Cid to Franco. The plaza is the *tour de force* Alberto Churriguera, and the pinnacle of churrigueresque architecture. Andrés García de Quiñones designed the **Ayuntamiento's** facade. Churriguera's **Pabellón Real** is to its left.

The cafe-lined R. Mayor runs to the south of the plaza (the clock lies on the north side). On this road is one of Salamanca's most famous landmarks, the 15th-century **Casa de las Conchas** (House of Shells; tel. 26 93 17), adorned by scallop shells chiseled in sandstone. Pilgrims who journeyed to Santiago de Compostela wore shells as to commemorate their visit to the tomb of St. James the Apostle, and the owner of the *casa,* a knight of the Order of Santiago, wanted to create a monument to the renowned pilgrimage site. The building is now a public library and home to the Provincial Tourist Office. There are occasional art exhibits here, and the courtyard is open to visitors. (Open Mon.-Fri. 9am-9pm, Sat. 9am-2pm and 4-7pm, Sun. 10am-2pm and 4-7pm. Free.) The **Clerecía** (a.k.a. Real Colegio del Espíritu Santo; tel. 26 46 60), across the street, is a Baroque complex which was, until recently, used by a Jesuit community. It has a church, a school, and what was the community's old living quarters: 300 rooms with 520 doors and 906 windows. The narrow street prevents full appreciation of the wonderful facade. A few wealthy believers once offered a large sum of money to widen the street (open for mass only Mon.-Sat. 1:15pm and 7:30pm, Sun. 12:30pm; free).

The University

The spirit of Salamanca, this great **universidad** (tel. 29 44 00), established in 1218, has an entrance on the **Patio de las Escuelas,** off C. Libreros. The statue here represents **Fray Luis de León,** a university professor and one of the most respected literati of the Golden Age. A Hebrew scholar and a classical Spanish stylist, the Inquisition arrested Fray Luis for translating Solomon's *Song of Songs* into Castilian, and for preferring the Hebrew version of the Bible to the Latin one. After five years of imprisonment, he returned to the university and began his first lecture: *"Decíamos ayer..."* ("As we were saying yesterday...").

The university's facade is one of the best examples of Spanish Plateresque, a style named for the filigree work of *plateros* (silversmiths). The central medallion repre-

sents King Fernando and Queen Isabel, the only figures who have their mouths closed. The small frog carved into a skull is Salamanca's "gray eminence," said to represent the dankness of prison life and to bring good luck on exams. If you spot the frog without assistance you will be married within the year. The walls are marked in bold red with students' initials, painted in an ink of bull's blood, olive oil, and herbs upon graduation.

The old lecture halls inside are open to the public. (Don't miss the room of fossilized turtles, apparently the second most important of such collections in the world.) **Aula Fray Luis de León** has been left in more or less its original state. The hard benches were considered luxurious by medieval standards, when most students sat on the floor. A plaque bears Unamuno's famous love poem about the students of Salamanca. The sumptuous **Paraninfo** (auditorium) contains Baroque tapestries and a portrait of Carlos IV attributed to Goya. Fray Luis is buried in the 18th-century **chapel.** The **Antigua Biblioteca** (old library) is the most spectacular of all, located atop a magnificent Plateresque staircase whose statues and historic books can be seen through a glass cube. Reproductions of the sign in the library which threatens excommunication for those who steal or damage books has been mass marketed in souvenir shops around town. The library's original ceiling has been moved to the University Museum. (University open Mon.-Fri. 9:30am-1pm and 4-7pm, Sat. 9:30am-1:30pm and 4-6pm, Sun. 10am-1pm. 300ptas, students and seniors 150ptas.)

Also on the patio are the **Escuelas Menores,** with a smaller version of the main entryway's Plateresque facade. The **University Museum** preserves the **Cielo de Salamanca** (Sky of Salamanca), the library's famous ceiling, whose 15th-century fresco of the zodiac was painted by the celebrated Gallego brothers, Francisco and Fernando. Take a peek at the intricate strongbox with a labyrinth of locks. (Open Mon.-Fri. 9:30am-1:30pm and 4-7:30pm, Sat. 9:30am-1:30pm and 4-7pm, Sun. 10am-1:30pm.)

The **Museo de Salamanca** (tel. 21 22 35) occupies a beautiful 15th-century building once home to Álvarez Albarca, physician to the *Reyes Católicos*. Along with the *Casa de las Conchas,* this is among Spain's most important examples of 15th-century architecture. The museum has an intriguing collection of painting and sculpture, as well as some temporary exhibits in archeology and ethnology. The museum's most important canvases are Juan de Flandes' portrait of Saint Andrew and Luis de Morales's *Llanto por Cristo Muerto,* both from the 16th century, and Vaccaro's ethereal *Inmaculada.* (Open Tues.-Fri. 9:45am-1:45pm and 4-7:15pm, Sat. 10:15am-1:15pm and 4:45-7:45pm, Sun. 10:15am-1:45pm. 200ptas.)

To the right of the university's main entrance is the absorbing **Casa-Museo de Unamuno** (tel. 29 44 00, ext. 1196). Miguel de Unamuno, Rector of the University at the beginning of this century, is revered as one of the founding figures of the Spanish literary movement known as the "Generation of '98." Unamuno passionately opposed dictatorship and encouraged his students to do so as well. His stand against

---

Just Another Manic Monday

In days of old, students ages 14-25 traveled from all over Spain—by foot, mule, or wagon—to study here, one of medieval Europe's greatest universities. In order to be admitted, one had to pass a difficult set of exams and show proof of "pure blood." No trace of Moorish or Jewish ancestry was permitted. As evidenced by the University's spartan Aula de Fray Luis de León, students studied under strict ecclesiastical authority and were expected to exhibit "composure, discipline, silence, piety, confinement, chastity, humility, and obedience," and **"refrain from sport."** Well, that was the theory anyway.

Campus activities drew vigor from "fraternal brotherhoods," whose rivalries climaxed as duels at the Escuelas Menores. Rising **pheromone** levels drew **prostitutes** from nearby lands—so many that a *fiesta* celebrated them. Banished to the other side of the Río Tormes during Lent, the prostitutes were led back to the city in triumph on the second Monday following Lent. The post-festival was nicknamed *Lunes de Agua* (Water Monday), and is still celebrated.

General Primo de Rivera's 1923 *coup d'état* led to his dismissal from the rector's post, but he was triumphantly reinstated some years later. Among the more charming exhibits in the newly-restored residence are Unamuno's ruminations about his birth and his dexterous origami. (Open Tues.-Fri. 11am-1:30pm and 4:30-6:30pm, Sat.-Sun. 10am-2pm. Research room open Mon.-Fri. 8:30am-2:30pm. Mandatory guided tour in Spanish given every 30min., 300ptas. Ring the bell if the house appears closed.)

Cathedrals and Convents

Begun in 1513 to accommodate the growing number of believers, the spires of the **Catedral Nueva** were not finished until 1733. While several later architects decided to retain the original late Gothic style, they could not resist adding touches from later periods, notably its Baroque tower. The *Cristo de las Batallas,* carried by El Cid in his campaigns, is in the central chapel on the wall behind the main altar.

The smaller **Catedral Vieja** (1140) was built in the Romanesque style, with Gothic arches and vaulting. Apocalyptic angels separate the sinners from the saved inside the striking cupola. On the outside of the cupola is the scaled **Torre del Gallo** (Tower of the Rooster)—so named for the shape of its weathervane, it is best seen from the cloister courtyard. The oldest part is the **Capilla de San Martín,** with brilliantly colored frescoes dating from 1242. Off to one side is the 12th-century cloister, rebuilt after the earthquake of 1755. Here, the **Capilla de Santa Bárbara,** also called the Capilla del Título, was once the site of final exams. The **cathedral museum** (tel. 21 74 76) features a paneled ceiling by Fernando Gallegos and houses the Mudéjar Salinas organ (one of the oldest in Europe). Outside the older building is the famed **Patio Chico,** which offers a beautiful view of the two cathedrals. (Cathedrals open daily April-Sept. 10am-1:30pm and 4-7:30pm; Oct.-March 9am-1pm and 4-6pm. Old cathedral, cloister, and museum 300ptas. New cathedral free.)

Christopher Columbus might have spent time in one of Salamanca's most dramatic monasteries, the **Convento de San Esteban,** downhill from the cathedrals. During the afternoon, its monumental facade becomes a solid mass of light depicting the stoning of St. Stephen and the crucifixion of Christ. The beautiful **Claustro de los Reyes** (Kings' Cloister; tel. 21 50 00), is both Gothic and Plateresque. The huge central altarpiece in the church, crafted in 1693 by Churriguera, is a Baroque masterpiece (open daily April-Sept. 9am-1pm and 4-8pm; Oct.-March 9am-1pm and 5-6:30pm; 200ptas).

The nearby **Convento de las Dueñas** (tel. 21 54 42) was formerly the Mudéjar palace of a court official. The elegant cloister was a later addition, explaining why its five sides are of unequal length. The cloister is perhaps the most interesting, and most beautiful, in Salamanca. Medallions adorning the walls depict real *salmantinos.* Exuberantly gargoyled columns line the second floor, where every capital boasts a unique and fascinating grotesque. (Open daily 10:30am-1pm and 4:15-7pm; Oct.-March daily 10:30am-1pm and 4:15-5:30pm. 100ptas. A shop selling what appear to be antique candies is on the 1st floor.)

Elsewhere

Take a stroll down C. Rua Mayor from Pl. Mayor to the **Puente Romano,** a 2000-year-old Roman bridge spanning the scenic Río Tormes. The bridge was part of an ancient Roman road called the Camino de la Plata (Silver Way) that ran from Mérida in Extremadura to Astorga, near León. The pre-Roman **Toro Ibérico** stands on the near end of the bridge, a headless granite bull and an example of ancient *verracos.* The old bull figures in one of the most famous episodes of *Lazarillo de Tormes,* the prototype for 16th-century picaresque novel, and predecessor to *Don Quijote.* In this episode, the diminutive hero finds his head slammed into the bull's stone ear after cheating his employer.

ENTERTAINMENT

The **Plaza Mayor** is the town's social center. Locals, students, and tourists come at all hours to lounge in its cafes or *dar una vuelta* (take a stroll). At night, members of var-

ious local college or graduate school **tunas** (medieval-style student troubadour groups) often finish their rounds here. Dressed in traditional black capes, they strut around the plaza serenading women with guitars, mandolins, *bandurrias,* and tambourines. When the show is over, they make excellent drinking partners, doing their best to emulate Don Juan. People overflow from the plaza as far west as **San Vicente.** Student nightlife is also concentrated on the **Gran Vía, Calle de Bordedores,** and side streets. Bars blast music ranging from reggae to vintage rock to *nueva canción* (modern ballads). **Calle Prior** and **Calle Rua Mayor** are full of bars, and a few charming *terrazas* (and fewer Americans) gather in **Plaza de la Fuente,** off Av. Alemania. More intense partying occurs off **Calle Varillas.** Cafes and bars initiate those heading for the club scene and then reclaim them later in the evening.

Camelot, C. Bordedores. Medieval chic. This monastery-turned-club is one of the stops on the **Gatsby** and **Cum Laude** (C. Prior) club-hopping route. On weekends, places are packed by 2am. No cover.

El Corrillo Café, C. Meléndez. Live jazz for the ultra-hip in a neon setting with a Hollywood theme. 1000ptas for performances, otherwise free.

Birdland, C. Azafranal, 57, by Pl. España. Cushioned ceilings make you feel like you never left Jeannie's bottle. Drink (500ptas) to jazz greats. Open 5pm-4:30am.

De Laval Genoves, C. San Justo (crossing Gran Vía). Built in an old submarine. A gay and straight clientele grooves under black lights.

Café Novelty, on the northeast corner of Pl. Mayor, is the oldest cafe in town and a meeting place for students and professors. Miguel de Unamuno was a regular.

Pub Rojo y Negro, C. Espoz y Mina. Scrumptious coffee, liqueur, and ice cream concoctions (200-1100ptas) in an old-fashioned setting (with a dance floor) catering to couples.

Lugares, a free pamphlet distributed at the tourist office and at some bars, lists everything from movies and special events to bus schedules. Posters at the **Colegio Mayor** (Palacio de Anaya) advertise university events, free films, and student theater. During the summer, Salamanca sponsors the **Verano Cultural de Salamanca,** with silent movies, contemporary Spanish cinema, pop singers, and theater groups. On June 12, in honor of San Juan de Sahagún, there is a **corrida de toros** charity event. September 8-21, the town indulges in **festivals** and **exhibitions,** most with bull themes. Salamanca's **Semana Santa** activities are also quite famous.

■ Near Salamanca

CIUDAD RODRIGO

A medieval town 21km from Portugal, Ciudad Rodrigo's honey-colored stonework glistens from above the surrounding plains. The old city's medieval walls enclose intricate 18th-century defenses and other masonry treasures. These stone features and a quirky cathedral lure daytrippers from nearby Salamanca (1hr.).

Practical Information The **tourist office,** Pl. Amayuelas, 5 (tel. 46 05 61), is less than 1 block from the cathedral and 3 blocks from Pl. Mayor (open Mon.-Fri. 10am-2pm and 5-8pm, Sat 10am-2pm and 4-7pm). The **Red Cross,** C. Gigantes, 4 (tel. 46 12 28), is helpful. Municipal **police** patrol from Pl. Mayor, 27 (tel. 46 04 68). The **post office,** Pl. Mayor at C. Dámaso Ledesma, 12 (tel. 46 01 17), rests in a bizarre 16th-century building also known as **Casa de los Vásquez.** The interior definitely warrants a gander (open Mon.-Fri. 8:30am-2:30pm, Sat. 9am-1pm).

Ciudad Rodrigo is easily accessible by bus from Salamanca; trains are infrequent and the station is 35 minutes from the old city. The **bus station,** C. Campo de Toledo (tel. 46 10 09). To and from Salamanca (Mon.-Fri. 8 per day, Sat. 5 per day, Sun. 3 per day, 1½hr., 710ptas). Go left out of the bus station, take the second right (uphill) and pass through the stone arch ahead; the tourist office is on the left.

Accommodations and Food **Pensión Madrid,** C. Madrid, 20 (tel. 46 24 67), off Pl. Mayor, has well-ventilated rooms. (Doubles 2500ptas. One super triple with bath and kitchenette 6000ptas.) Cafes on the Plaza Mayor serve inexpensive *platos combinados;* or try hiking out to **Pizzería Gepetto,** Av. Conde Foxá, 39 (tel. 48 14 34). Go right exiting the city walls and walk a few blocks past the rotary, continuing along the road that's on the right side of the Insalud building. A variety of cheap pizzas to choose from (individual 500ptas, small 850ptas, large 1800ptas).

Sights The **cathedral** is the town's masterpiece. Originally Romanesque, the church was commissioned by Fernando II of León, who was also responsible for building the city walls. The church was substantially modified in the 16th-century Gothic style. The **coro** (chorus) was the master work of Rodrigo Alemán, from 1498-1504, and includes the sculptor's signature—a carving of his head. The two 16th-century organs star in a series of concerts every August. The **claustro** alone merits a trip to Ciudad Rodrigo. Fascinating figures festoon the columns from top to bottom—making love, playing peek-a-boo. Ears, cheeks, and breasts are all subject to nibbling. At one corner, monsters devour Muslims. The cathedral's **museum** is filled with strange and thrilling old pieces, including an ancient clavichord, the "ballot box" used to determine the cathedral's hierarchy, robes and richly embroidered slippers worn by bishops and priors, and Velázquez' *Llanto de Adam y Eva por Ariel muerto.* (Cathedral open daily 10:30am-1:30pm and 4-8pm. Free. Cloister and museum open daily 10:30am-1:30pm and 4-6pm. 200ptas, students 100ptas. Mandatory tour in Spanish.)

Few structures have appeared in Rodrigo since the days when the ornate buildings served as palaces for noble families. The **Castillo de Enrique de Trastámara,** built in the 14th and 15th centuries by Gonzalo Arias de Genizaro, crowns the battlements and commands a view of the surrounding countryside and the Agueda River. A road on the right leads to Portugal. It is now a *parador de turismo,* a government-financed luxury hotel. If you ask kindly, they might let you go up the tower.

ALBA DE TORMES

Santa Teresa left her heart in Alba de Tormes—it's in a big urn, along with her body, in the lovely **Convento de la Anunciación,** which she founded in 1571. In her autobiography, she writes that her heart was pierced by an angel of the Lord with a fiery dart. After repeated stabbings, she was left "on fire with the great love of God." The convent is in the Plazuela de Santa Teresa, two blocks from the peaceful Plaza Mayor. If you'd like a tour, ask a guide at the **Museo Teresiano** across the street. The museum holds other parts of Santa Teresa, and bits of San Juan de la Cruz (open Tues.-Sat. 10am-1:30pm and 4-7:30pm, Sun. 10am-2pm; donation requested). A few blocks down from the Pl. Mayor is the **Castillo de los Duques de Alba,** remnants of a 15th- to 16th-century structure excavated in 1991-1993. Renaissance frescoes and an archaeological exhibit of the remains are displayed. (Open in July-Aug. Sat.-Sun. Other times, the tourist office staff can let you in.) Tiny Alba de Tormes boasts seven churches, monasteries, and convents, plus a neo-Gothic basilica.

The **tourist office,** C. Lepanto, 4 (tel. 30 00 24), is helpful when it's open. (Hours not fixed, but open daily from about 10am-2pm and 4:30-8:30pm in summer; in winter 10:30am-2pm and 4-6:30pm.) Alba de Tormes makes an easy daytrip by **bus** from Salamanca (8-12 per day, 30min., 175ptas). If you can't tear yourself away from Santa Teresa's heart, stay overnight in the **Hostal América,** C. La Guía (tel. 30 00 71 or 30 03 46), across the river from town. (Singles with shower 2000ptas. Doubles 3600ptas, with shower 3800ptas. IVA not included.)

LA ALBERCA AND THE PEÑA DE FRANCIA

Three mountain ranges to the south conceal some delightful small towns between the plains of Castilla y León and Extremadura. **La Alberca,** a charming, rustic village, was the first rural town in the country to be named an official National Historic-Artis-

tic Monument (1940). Above La Alberca in the Sierra de Francia rises the province's highest peak, the **Peña de Francia** (1723m). Determined souls can scale the mountain from La Alberca. For info about La Alberca or the Peña de Francia, contact the tourist office (tel. 41 52 91, ext. 15; open June-Sept. Mon.-Sat. 10am-1pm and 5-7pm, Sat. 10am-1pm and 4-6pm, Sun. 10am-1pm). **Empresa V. Cosme** (tel. 30 02 71) runs buses from Salamanca to La Alberca (2 per day, Sat.-Sun. 1 per day, 1½hr., 600ptas).

■ Zamora

Provincial Zamora (pop. 65,000) is a lazy crossroads of human and animal life. Dogs trot leashless past the cathedral, and white storks fashion nests atop the city's eight Romanesque churches. Zamora has not seen much action since the 12th century, when Sancho II died in Zamora while attempting to subdue his errant sister Doña Urraca and consolidate his hold on the House of Castile. Although Urraca was at first excluded from her father's will in favor of her two brothers, she managed to usurp the city by threatening to sleep with every man in the kingdom. Vestiges of this illustrious and shocking past attract history voyeurs, but not too many of them.

ORIENTATION AND PRACTICAL INFORMATION

Modern **train** and **bus** stations lounge in the northeast corner of the city, a 15-minute walk from **Plaza Mayor.** To get to the center from the train station, turn left onto C. Alfonso Peña (which becomes Av. Tres Cruces) and continue to Pl. Alemania; turn left onto C. Alfonso IX and go two blocks to **Calle de Santa Clara,** a major pedestrian street which leads to Pl. Mayor. From the bus station, turn left on C. Alfonso Peña and follow the same directions.

The municipal **tourist office,** C. Santa Clara, 20 (tel. 53 18 45; fax 53 38 13), hands out multilingual brochures, maps, and a hostel guide (open Mon.-Fri. 10am-2pm and 5-8pm, Sat. 9am-2:30pm and 5-8pm). **Currency exchange** occurs at innumerable banks grace the commercial district, many advertising no commission (C. Santa Clara, C. Alfonso IX, etc.). **Luggage storage** is in the bus station (90ptas per bag, open daily 7am-12pm) and train station (300ptas per bag, open 24hr.). The **Red Cross** is on C. Hernán Cortés (tel. 52 33 00). The **municipal police** can be reached at tel. 53 04 62. In an **emergency,** call 091 or 092. The **post office,** C. Santa Clara, 15 (tel. 51 33 71 or 51 07 67; fax 53 03 35), just past C. Benquente, opens for stamps and Lista de Correos Mon.-Fri. 8:30am-8:30pm, Sat. 9am-2pm. **Faxes** can be sent and received. The **postal code** is 49080. The **telephone code** is (9)80.

Trains leave from the station (tel. 52 19 56; 24hr. tel. 52 11 10), at the end of C. Alfonso Peña, 100m down from the bus station. To: Madrid (4 per day, 4hr., 2135ptas); Valladolid (3 per day, 1½hr., 980ptas); La Coruña (3 per day, 7hr., 3600-4000ptas); Barcelona (6 per week, 12hr., 7500-8000ptas). **Buses** depart from C. Alfonso Peña, 3 (tel. 52 12 81 or 52 12 82). To: Salamanca (13-21 per day, 1hr., 515ptas); Valladolid (7 per day, 1½hr., 775ptas); León (5 per day, 2hr., 1065ptas); Madrid (6 per day, 3½hr., 1980ptas); Barcelona (3 per day, 12hr., 6685ptas); La Coruña (2-3 per day, 7hr., 3100ptas).

ACCOMMODATIONS AND FOOD

For simple rooms at reasonable prices, investigate the streets off **C. Alfonso Peña** by the train station, or off **C. Santa Clara** near Pl. Mayor. Consider calling ahead during the *fiestas* in the last week of June. All rooms are cheaper in the off season. Catch some winks at **Pensión Fernando III,** Pl. Fernando III, 2 (tel. 52 36 88). From the bus station, take the first right uphill off C. Alfonso Peña (2min.). The large, sunlit modern rooms are a bargain and close to the stations. All rooms have sinks; bathrooms are down the hall. (Singles 1000-1300ptas. Doubles 2000-2500ptas. Triples 2900ptas. Meals available.) **Pensión Gemi,** C. Juan II, 10 (tel. 51 96 88), has similar rooms, some with showers (singles 1000-1300ptas, doubles 2000-2500ptas, triples 2900ptas). Head up C. Alfonso Poña three blocks from the bus station and turn left.

Dining in Zamora tends to be expensive. Restaurants and *mesones* rub elbows off **C. Santa Clara** and around **Pl. Mayor,** particularly on **C. Herreros.** The **Mercado de Abastos,** in a domed building just to the left off C. Santa Clara after the tourist office, purveys basics (open Mon.-Sat. 7am-3pm). Roast meats, particularly *preses de ternera* (veal) and *bacalao a la tranca* (cod), are regional specialties. Steer a shopping cart at trusty **Supermarket Simago,** on C. Victor Gallego, north of Pl. Alemania off Av. Tres Cruces (open Mon.-Sat. 8:30am-9pm). **Mesón Los Abuelos** is at C. Herreros, 30. More kids than *abuelos* (grandfathers) frequent this local hangout. *Bocadillos* run 300-450ptas, *raciones* 450-900ptas (open noon-2am).

SIGHTS

Zamora's foremost monument is its **cathedral,** begun in 1135, a stocky building topped with a Serbian-Byzantine dome. Look for the child-like paintings of angels in blue and gold to the right and left of the main altar (open 10am-1pm and 5-8pm; free). Inside the cloister, the **Museo de la Catedral** features the priceless 15th-century Black Tapestries. In the gruesome Trojan War tapestry, try to find all the warriors and princesses who are in the process of losing their heads (there are at least six). (Open Tues.-Sat. 11am-2pm and 5-8pm, Sun. 11am-2pm, Mon. 5-8pm; Oct.-March Tues.-Sat. 11am-2pm and 4-6pm, Sun. 11am-2pm, Mon. 4-6pm. 300ptas.) Just uphill from the cathedral, a medieval castle (or what's left of it) reigns over a beautiful garden. The towering walls command a fine view of the mighty Río Duero. From the castle segment with the moat, look back towards the city center at the Iglesia de San Isidoro; elegant *cigueñas blancas* (white storks) often perch there.

Remarkably, eight handsome **Romanesque churches** remain within the walls of the old city: San Ildefonso, Santa María de la Horta, Santo Tomé, La Magdalena, San Cipriano, San Juan, San Vicente, and Santiago del Burgo (open Tues.-Sat. 10am-1pm and 5-8pm; Nov.-June only during mass). Each one gleams in the wake of recent restoration. If pressed for time, or if you suspect they'll all begin to look the same, at least drop by the intricately carved porch of **La Magdalena.** The luminescent marble-veined window in **San Juan** and the bright green and orange organ in **San Ildefonso** are also worth a look.

Ruins of the mostly Roman walls are scattered about like giant crumbs, the most famous being the *Puerta del Traidor* (Traitor's Gate) near the castle, where Sancho tried to do in rebellious Urraca. El Cid was supposedly knighted in **Iglesia de Santiago de Caballeros.** Urraca wasn't.

■ León

The Seventh Roman Legion founded León in 68 AD, and its name derives from *legio,* Latin for legion. Proud *leoneses* (literally "lions") roar that their cathedral is the finest in all of Spain. Its blue stained-glass windows have earned the city the nickname *La Ciudad Azul* (Blue City). León once ruled over a substantial kingdom, but it was hardly a jungle. The king of the jungle is just their unofficial mascot, but, their carnivorous eating habits may lead you to think otherwise.

ORIENTATION AND PRACTICAL INFORMATION

Most of León lies on the east side of the **Río Bernesga,** while the bus and train stations are in the west end. Across the river from the stations is the modern commercial district, directly before the old city. **Avenida de Palencia** (take a left out of the bus station and a right out of the train station) leads across the river to **Plaza Guzmán el Bueno,** where it becomes **Avenida de Ordoño II.** The road then bisects the new city and becomes **Avenida del Generalísimo Franco** in the old town, on the other side of **Plaza Santo Domingo.** Av. Generalísimo Franco splits the old town in two.

Tourist Office: Pl. Regla, 3 (tel. 23 70 82; fax 27 33 91), in front of the cathedral. Free city maps (get the black one), regional brochures, and lodgings guide. English

spoken. Open Mon.-Fri. 10am-2pm and 5-7:30pm, Sat. 10am-2pm and 4:30-8:30pm, Sun. 10am-2pm.

Budget Travel: TIVE, C. Arquitecto Torbado, 4 (tel. 20 09 51), just off Pl. Cortes. ISIC 500ptas. HI cards 1800ptas. Open Mon.-Fri. 9am-2pm.

Currency Exchange: Banco Central Hispano, Pl. Santo Domingo, Follow Av. Ordoño II into the plaza. Open Mon.-Fri. 8:30am-2:30pm. No commission.

Telephones: Telefónica, C. Burgo Nuevo, 15. From Pl. Santo Domingo, take Av. Independencia and turn right onto C. Burgo Nuevo. Open Mon.-Fri. 9am-2:30pm and 4-11pm, Sat. 10am-2pm and 4:30-9:30pm. **Faxes** sent and received here, as well as in the **post office.**

Trains: RENFE, Av. Astorga, 2 (info. tel. 27 02 02; station tel. 22 37 04), across the river from Pl. Guzmán el Bueno, at the bend in Av. Palencia. Info 24hr. **Ticket office,** C. Carmen, 4 (tel. 22 05 25). Open Mon.-Fri. 9:30am-2pm and 5-8pm, Sat. 10am-1:30pm. To: Astorga (9 per day, 45min., 385ptas); Palencia (14 per day, 1½hr., 1095-1400ptas); Valladolid (12 per day, 2½hr., 1370-1800ptas); Oviedo (7 per day, 2½hr., 890-1400ptas); La Coruña (5 per day, 7hr., 3200-4400ptas); Madrid (11 per day, 4½-5½hr., 3190-3500ptas). **FEVE,** Est. de Matallana, Av. Padre Isla, 48 (tel. 22 59 19), north of Pl. Santo Domingo, to local destinations. A complete schedule for both trains and buses is printed daily in *Diario de León* (110ptas).

Buses: Estación de Autobuses, Po. Ingeniero Saenz de Miera (tel. 21 00 00). Info Mon.-Sat. 7:30am-9pm. To: Astorga (16 per day, 45min., 405ptas); Valladolid (8 per day, 2hr., 1060ptas); Santander (1 per day, 5hr., 2800ptas); Zamora (6 per day, 2½hr., 1125ptas); Madrid (11 per day, 4½hr., 2550ptas).

Taxis: Radio Taxi (tel. 24 24 51).

Car Rental: Hertz, C. Sampirosh (tel. 23 19 99). Must be over 25 and have had license for one year. Open Mon.-Fri. 9am-2pm and 4-7pm, Sat. 9am-1pm.

Luggage Storage: At the **train station** (lockers 400ptas). Open 24hr. At the **bus station** (25ptas per bag). Open Mon.-Fri. 9am-2pm and 6-8pm, Sat. 9am-2pm.

English Bookstore: Pastor, Pl. Santo Domingo, 4 (tel. 22 58 56). Substantial selection. Open Mon.-Fri. 10am-12:30pm and 4:30-8pm, Sat. 10am-1:45pm.

Red Cross: (tel. 22 22 22).

Medical Services: Hospital Virgen Blanca (tel. 23 74 00).

Police: C. Villa Benavente, 6 (tel. 20 73 12 or 091). **Emergency:** tel. 091 or 092.

Post Office: Jardín San Francisco (tel. 23 42 90; fax 23 47 01). From Pl. Santo Domingo, down Av. Independencia and opposite Parque San Francisco on the left. Stamps, Lista de Correos, and **faxes.** Open Mon.-Fri. 8:30am-8:30pm, Sat. 9:30am-2pm. **Postal Code:** 24071.

Telephone Code: (9)87.

ACCOMMODATIONS

Budget beds are not scarce in León, but *hostales* and *pensiones* often fill during the June *fiestas.* Look on **Av. Roma, Av. Ordoño II,** and **Av. República Argentina,** which lead into the new town from Pl. Guzmán el Bueno. *Pensiones* are also scattered on the streets by the train and bus stations, but these are less centrally located and are a bit intimidating at night. Check the black tourist office map for more *hostal* locations.

Consejo de Europa (HI), Po. Parque, 2 (tel. 20 02 06), behind Pl. Toros. Recently renovated accommodations. 850ptas per person, over 26, 1000ptas. Breakfast 300ptas. Often booked, so call ahead. Open July-Aug.

Hostal Oviedo, Av. Roma, 26, 2nd fl. (tel. 22 22 36). Funky iron headboards jazz up cozy beds. Chatty proprietors offer huge rooms, many with sinks and terraces. Singles 1900ptas. Doubles 3000ptas. Triples 4500ptas.

Hostal Europa, Av. Roma, 26 (tel. 22 22 38), downstairs from the Oviedo. There must have been a sale on iron beds. Sleep under pastel sheets and wake up to dried roses on the dresser. Singles 1600ptas. Doubles 2700ptas. Triples 3500ptas.

Fonda Condado, Av. República Argentina, 28 (tel. 20 61 60). Airy rooms in shades of beige, brown, and lumberjack red. Fuzzy kitty bathmat in huge bathroom. Singles 1500-1800ptas. Doubles 2000-2500ptas. Showers 250ptas. Meals available.

FOOD

Inexpensive eateries cluster near the cathedral and on the small streets off **Av. Generalísimo Franco;** also check **Pl. San Martín,** near Pl. Mayor. Nearly all cafes come equipped with slot machines. Pork in all possible guises tops most menus, while roast suckling lamb is almost equally popular. Thirty-five hundred kilometers of trout-fishable streams invite the wild, avant-garde **International Trout Festival** in June. Fresh produce and eels of every size are sold at the **Mercado Municipal del Conde,** Pl. Conde, off C. General Mola (open Mon.-Sat. 9am-3:30pm). Vegetable relief is provided by **markets** in Pl. Mayor (open Wed. and Sat. 9am-2pm).

Cafetería-Restaurante Catedral, C. Mariano Domínguez Berrueta, 17 (tel. 21 59 18), to the right of the cathedral. Monumental portions make the 1100ptas *menú* a great bargain. Chomp down on a *bocadillo* at the mile-long bar (350-600ptas). Open Mon.-Sat. 1-4pm and 8-11pm, closed Tues. and Wed. afternoon.

Lleras, 38, C. Burgos Nuevo, less than a block from its intersection with Av. República Argentina. Jazzy restaurant offering everything from spaghetti and trout to melon and tongue. *Menú* 1050ptas. Open daily 1-5pm and 8pm until it's empty.

Capricciosa Pizzeria, C. Rúa, 24 (tel. 21 38 10), 3 blocks off C. Generalísimo Franco, or follow your nose. Pizzas 600-875ptas, pasta entrees 660-875ptas. Open daily 1-4pm and 7:30pm-midnight.

Calle Ancha, C. Generalísimo Franco, on the block between C. General Mola and C. Conde Luna. Fill your belly with fresh veggies, quiche, and fish. Gourmet vegetarian *menú* 900ptas; non-vegetarian *menú económica* 950ptas. Both *menús* come with a **bottle** of wine. Open daily 8am-1:30am.

SIGHTS

The 13th-century Gothic **cathedral,** La Pulchra Leonina, is considered by many to be the most beautiful in Spain. Its exceptional facade depicts everything from a smiling *Santa María la Blanca* to bug-eyed monsters munching on the damned. The real attractions are the vivid stained-glass interior, the glorious rose windows with spiralling saints, and the fanciful lower windows' gardens of tiny faces amid luminous petals. The sequence of windows narrates a complicated story, deciphered in the cathedral guidebook (700ptas; open daily 8:30am-1:30pm and 4-8pm). The cathedral's **museo** (tel. 23 00 60) includes gruesome wonders, like a skeleton statue of Death and a sculpture depicting the skinning of a saint. (Museum open Mon.-Fri. 9:30am-2pm and 4-7:30pm, Sat. 9:30am-2pm; in winter closes ½hr. earlier. 450ptas.)

The **Basílica San Isidoro** was dedicated in the 11th century to San Isidoro of Sevilla, whose remains were brought to León while Muslims ruled the south. The corpses of León's royal family rest in the impressive **Panteón Real,** with ceilings covered by vibrant frescoes. Look for the black sheep arch depicting the Roman agricultural calendar and the oddly detailed depiction of an angel announcing the birth of Christ. Admission to the pantheon allows entrance to the treasury and library of rare books, some of which are waist-high. Doña Urraca's famous agate chalices outshine the rest of the treasury room. A 10th-century handwritten Bible and the intriguing ceiling are the library's highlights. (Museum open Sept.-June 10am-1:30pm and 4-6:30pm; July-Aug. 9am-2pm and 3-8pm. 350ptas.) While visiting the cathedral and San Isidoro, keep an eye out for some of the city's **murallas romanas** (Roman walls).

The **Museo de León** (tel. 24 50 61), Pl. San Marcos, holds an extensive archaeological collection with pieces dating to the Paleolithic era. The cloister is a chilling graveyard for tombstones. Isabel II's exquisite chest of drawers might draw a gasp. (Open Tues.-Sat. 10am-2pm and 5-8:30pm, Sun. 10am-2pm. 200ptas, students and over 65 free, weekends free.) Next door to the *museo,* the **Monasterio San Marcos,** once a rest stop for pilgrims en route to Santiago, is León's only five-star hotel, and sports a Plateresque facade. **Los Botines,** Pl. Santo Domingo, is one of the few buildings outside of Catalunya designed by *Renaixançista* Antoni Gaudí. The relatively restrained structure displays only hints of the wild stuff to come (see **Barcelona** p. 298).

ENTERTAINMENT

For the early part of the night the *barrio húmedo* (drinker's neighborhood), around **Plaza de San Martín**, sweats with bars, discos, and techno-pop. **El Bacanal** attracts a primarily gay crowd to its Caravaggio-covered walls. Mellower music, pastel walls, and actual breathing space characterize **El Robote** (across the square). After 2am, the crowds weave to **Calle Lancia** and **Calle Conde de Guillén**, both heavily populated with discos and bars. Plenty of cool cafes line Av. Generalísimo Franco. **La Gargola** has cushy yellow-striped sofas and a starry night painted on the ceiling. **El Gran Café**, on C. Cervantes one block off Av. Generalísimo Franco, delivers live jazz twice nightly to its chic clientele. For more romantic, secluded spots, explore C. La Paloma and other narrow streets around the cathedral which harbor quieter candle-lit cafes.

Fiestas commemorating St. John and St. Peter make up a week-long celebration (June 21-30) including a *corrida de toros* (bullfight). Highlights are the feast days of San Juan on the 25th and San Pedro on the 30th. Such notable celebrities as King Juan Carlos I and his wife Sofía attend on a yearly basis and often show up at the **International Organ Festival** at the cathedral.

■ Near León

ASTORGA

Antoni Gaudí responded to a request from his friend, the bishop of Astorga, to design a new episcopal residence with converging arches, elaborate stained glass, and jutting turrets of a fanciful **Palacio Episcopal** (Bishop's Palace). As the construction dragged on for 20 years after the bishop's death, the expense proved enormous for the poor parish, whose original residence had burned in 1886. Sadly, no bishop dared occupy the fairy-tale home upon its belated completion. Today the palace houses the decidedly eclectic **Museo de los Caminos** (tel. 61 88 82), whose ostensible purpose is to illustrate the various *caminos* (paths) that have passed through 2000-year-old Astorga. On the second floor, Gaudí's candy-bright stained glass windows dazzle and awe, especially those in the effervescent chapel and dining room. (Open daily 10am-2pm and 4-8pm; in winter 11am-2pm and 3:30-6:30pm. 250ptas, 400ptas gets you into the cathedral museum as well.)

Glance at the **cathedral,** opposite Gaudí's *palacio.* Though not as spectacular as La Pulchra Leonesa, the cathedral's ornate 18th-century facade and beautiful *coro* (choir loft) are impressive (open daily 9am-noon and 5-6:30pm; Oct.-May 9am-noon and 4:30-6pm; free). The cathedral's museum has ten rooms of relics and votive objects (open 10am-2pm and 4-6pm; 250ptas, 400ptas gets you into both museums).

The **tourist office** is inside the small stone church between the cathedral and the palace (open June-Oct. Mon.-Sat. 10am-2pm and 4-8pm). **Telephones** and **ATMs** line the main street past the palace. **Luggage storage** is at the train station (400ptas). **Police** are at Pl. San Miguel (tel. 61 60 80); for **ambulances** call tel. 61 85 85. **Taxis** can be reached at tel. 61 60 00. The **post office** is on C. Alfereces.

Rooms tend to be expensive. **Pensión García,** Bajada de Postigo, 6, has the best deals in town. Take the main street that runs past the cathedral and Gaudí's palace till you reach Pl. España, the fourth plaza, then take C. Bañeza which becomes C. Bajada de Postigo just down the hill (singles 2150ptas, doubles 3400ptas). Restaurants abound around the cathedral and on Av. Murallas, near the bus station. In addition to the famous *mantecadas* (little sponge cakes), Astorga is also home to the hefty stew *cocido maragato,* which is traditionally eaten in "reverse order" (meat to broth).

The **bus station,** Av. Ponferrada (tel. 61 91 00), across from the Palacio Episcopal, is close to the town's sights. To get to the town center from the RENFE **train station,** Pl. Estación (tel. 61 64 44), walk uphill along C. Pedro de Castro to Pl. Obispo Alcolea; turn right here and continue to walk up. Twelve buses make the 45-minute journey to and from León daily (475ptas), as do 11 trains (385ptas).

▨ Valladolid

Wealth, political prominence, and architectural grandeur once came easily to Valladolid. In 1469 Fernando and Isabel were joined here in momentous matrimony. Close to a century later, shady dealings by prime minister Conde Duque de Lerma cast a shadow over Valladolid's past glory. As the beneficiary of a whopping bribe, Lerma squeezed Valladolid (already the capital of Castilla) out of the running for capital of Spain. Madrid won, Valladolid lost, and history moved on. Even today the city has some endearing quirks. Fountains are lit in day-glo pink and green, seventies architecture challenges graceful Renaissance forms, and Supermarket Simago blasts American music up and down the main pedestrian thoroughfare while the locals hum along.

ORIENTATION AND PRACTICAL INFORMATION

Valladolid occupies a central position between León (133km) and Segovia (110km), and between Burgos (122km) and Salamanca (114km). The **bus** and **train stations** sit on the south edge of town. To get from the bus station to the **tourist office,** turn right on C. San José and take the first left onto C. Ladrillo. Angle to the right onto C. Arco de Ladrillo which cuts through the wooded park **Campo Grande,** ending at **Plaza Zorrilla** and the tourist office. From here, walk down **Calle Santiago** to get to **Plaza Mayor.** The **cathedral** is a 10-minute walk east from Pl. Mayor (right as you face the Ayuntamiento), as is **Plaza Universidad. Plaza del Val** is just behind Pl. Mayor, off the northeast corner.

Tourist Office: Pl. Zorrilla, 3 (tel. 35 18 01). Maps, museum info, and a useful hotel info booklet. English spoken. Easter-Oct. open Sun.-Fri. 10am-2pm and 5-8pm, Sat. 10am-2pm; in winter daily 10am-2pm.

Budget Travel: TIVE, Edificio Administrativo de Uso Múltiple, 3rd fl. (tel. 35 45 63). From Pl. Zorilla, take C. María de Molina to C. Doctrinos, follow it across Puente Isabel la Católica, then past the parking lot. Open Mon.-Fri. 9am-2pm.

El Corte Inglés: Po. Zorilla, 130-32 (tel. 27 23 04 or 47 83 00), a 20min. walk from Pl. Zorilla. Great **map,** novels and guidebooks in English, **currency exchange.** Open Mon.-Sat. 10am-9pm.

Currency Exchange: Banco Cenral Hispano, corner of Acera de Recoletos and C. Perú. No commission. Open Mon.-Fri. 8:30am-2:30pm. Also at the bus station.

Flights: Villanubla Airport, León Highway (N-601), km 13 (tel. 41 54 00). Daily service to Barcelona, Madrid, and Paris. Service to the Islas Baleares in summer. Info open 12:30-7:30pm. **Iberia,** C. Gamazo, 17 (tel. 30 06 66 or 30 26 39). Open Mon.-Fri. 9:30am-1:30pm and 4-7pm, Sat. 9:30am-1:30pm. Taxi to airport 1800ptas.

Trains: Estación del Norte, C. Recondo (tel. 30 35 18 or 30 75 78), at the end of Campo Grande. Info (tel. 20 02 02) open 7am-11pm. To: Zamora (3 per day, 1½hr., 980ptas); Burgos (16 per day, 2hr., 890ptas); Salamanca (10 per day, 1¾hr., 820ptas); León (14 per day, 1½hr., 1195-1370ptas); Madrid (14 per day, 4hr., 1825ptas); Santander (6 per day, 4¾hr., 1855ptas).

Buses: Puente Colgante, 2 (tel. 23 63 08). Info open 8:30am-8:30pm. From the train station, turn left and follow C. Recondo which becomes C. Puente Colgante (5min. walk). To: Zamora (8 per day, 1½ hr., 785ptas); Burgos (2 per day, 2hr., 1600ptas); León (8 per day, 2hr., 1600ptas); Oviedo (4 per day, 4hr., 2115ptas); Madrid (18 per day, 2½hr., 1470ptas); Tordesillas (12 per day, 30min., 240ptas); Barcelona (3 per day, 9hr., 5925ptas); San Sebastián (2 per day, 5hr., 2775ptas).

Taxis: Radio Taxi (tel. 29 14 11), is on call 24hr.

Luggage Storage: Estación del Norte has lockers. Counters are available at the ticket window (300ptas). Baggage check at the **bus station** (50ptas per bag, open Mon.-Sat. 9am-10pm).

English Bookstore: Librería Lara, C. Fuente Dorada, 17 (tel. 30 03 66). Two shelves of Penguin-titled goodies. Open Mon.-Fri. 10am-1:30pm and 5-8pm, Sat. 10am-2pm.

Crisis Lines: AIDS hotline (toll free tel. (900) 11 10 00 or 33 93 35). **Women's Info Line** (tel. 30 08 93). **De la Esperanza** (tel. 30 70 77) and **Voces Amigas** (tel. 33 46 35 or 33 19 13) for depression. Limited English.

Red Cross: (tel. 22 22 22).
Late-Night Pharmacy: Check local papers *El Norte de Castilla* (115ptas) or *El Mundo de Valladolid* (125ptas) for listings.
Hospitals: Hospital Pío del Río Hortega, C. Santa Teresa (tel. 42 04 00 or 22 22 50; 10pm-9am). Some doctors speak English. **Emergency:** tel. 092 or 091.
Post Office: Pl. Rinconada (tel. 33 06 60; info tel. 33 06 60; fax 39 19 87), just off the far left corner of Pl. Mayor. Open for stamps, Lista de Correos, and **fax** service. Open Mon.-Fri. 8:30am-8:30pm, Sat. 8:30am-2pm. **Postal Code:** 47001.
Telephone Code: (9)83.

ACCOMMODATIONS

Cheap lodgings, all with winter heating, are abundant. The streets off the right side of **Acera de Recoletos** as you leave the train station—though a little dark and scary—and those near the cathedral and behind Pl. Mayor at **Pl. Val,** are packed with *pensiones* and *hostales*. **Albergue Juvenil Río Esgueve (HI),** Camino Cementerio (tel. 25 15 50), will re-open in 1998. In a pinch, the tourist office's guidance is invaluable.

Pensión Dani, C. Perú, 11, 1st fl. (tel. 30 02 49), downstairs from Dos Rosas. Clean, narrow rooms. Modern baths down the hall. Singles 1450ptas. Doubles 2600ptas.
Pensión Augustias, C. Augustias, 32 (tel. 25 40 25). Take C. Ferrari from Pl. Mayor to Bajada Libertad, which becomes C. Augustias. The septuagenarian owners are rightly proud of their spacious, clean quarters. Bathrooms down the hall. Singles 1500ptas. Doubles 2500ptas. Triples 3600ptas.
Pensión Mary, C. Angustias, 32 (tel. 26 17 74), 5min. from Pl. Mayor. Follow the directions for Pensión Augustias. Newly painted rooms with dark wood furniture. Singles 2000ptas. Doubles 2500ptas. Triples 3000ptas. Open July-Dec.
Pensión Dos Rosas, C. Perú, 11, 2nd fl. (tel. 20 74 39). From the train station, walk up Av. Acera Recoletos and turn right on C. Perú. A good bargain only 2 blocks from Pl. Zorrilla. Tiny singles with shiny crimson bedsheets and hieroglyphics in some rooms. Doubles are spacious and sunny. Bathrooms down the hall. Portable heaters in winter. Singles 1450ptas. Doubles 2600ptas. Triples 3800ptas.

FOOD

Stiff competition keeps prices down, making many elegant restaurants accessible to budget diners. Restaurants abound between **Pl. Mayor** and **Pl. Val.** Explore **Pl. Universidad,** near the cathedral, for *tapas*. The **Mercado del Val,** on C. Sandoval in Pl. Val, handles fresh produce (open Mon.-Sat. 6am-3pm). Groceries are at the old standby, **Supermarket Simago,** at the corner of C. Santiago and C. Montero Calvo (open Mon.-Sat. 9:30am-9pm).

Casa San Pedro Regalad, Pl. Ochavo, 1 (tel. 34 45 06), on the corner of C. Platerías. Facing the Casa Consistorial, it's two jagged blocks off the far right corner of Pl. Mayor in Pl. Dorada. Meat hangs from the rafters and is roasted over coals to the delight of over 300 patrons, many seated downstairs. *Menú del día* Mon.-Fri. 1000ptas, Sat.-Sun. 980ptas. Open daily 1:30-4pm and 8-11pm. Visa, MC, AmEx.
Restaurante Covadonga, C. Zapico, 1 (tel. 33 07 98), up the street from Pl. Val. As elegant as a restaurant can be and still have "Polly," the talking stuffed parrot hanging in the *comedor*. *Menú* 950ptas. Lots of meat and fresh vegetables. Open Aug.-June Mon.-Sat. 1-4pm and 9-11:30pm, Sun. 1-4pm.
Restaurante Chino Gran Muralla, C. Santa María, 1 (tel. 34 23 07). Look for the hanging dragons half a block off C. Santiago, north of Pl. Zorrilla. *Menú* Mon.-Thurs. 725ptas, Fri.-Sun. 950ptas.

SIGHTS

Glory slipped through Valladolid's fingers. The **cathedral** (1580), Pl. Universidad, was designed by Juan de Herrera, also responsible for El Escorial. Its interior is typically imposing and severe, with light gray stone and large, square, colorless windows. The only other color is the gold of the *retablo*. The **Museo Diocesano** (tel. 30 43 62),

inside, is worth a look for its gruesome Jesus with real matted hair, a model of the basilica's original design, and soulful statues of Jesus, Mary, and many saints. (Open Tues.-Fri. 10am-1:30pm and 4:30-7pm, Sat.-Sun. 10am-2pm. Cathedral free, museum 350ptas.) Behind the cathedral is the Romanesque **Tower of Santa María la Antigua.**

Plush **Casa de Colón** (tel. 29 13 53), on C. Colón, is now part research library and part museum. (Open Tues.-Sat. 10am-2pm and 5-7pm, Sun. 10am-2pm, shorter hours in winter. Free.) From the looks of **Casa de Cervantes,** off C. Castro, it might be concluded that the writer died of boredom. There is an amusing collection of old books and furniture, but the medieval bed-warmer is the real highlight. (Open Tues.-Sat. 10am-3:30pm, Sun. 10am-3pm. 400ptas, students 200ptas, Sun. free.)

The **Museo Nacional de Escultura** in the **Colegio de San Gregorio** may be Valladolid's most fascinating visit. The twenty-plus rooms chart the region's religious art history through transplanted segments of now-destroyed monasteries and churches. (Open Tues.-Sat. 10am-2pm and 4-6pm, Sun. 10am-2pm. 400ptas, students 200ptas, Sat. afternoon and Sun. free.)

ENTERTAINMENT

Valladolid's cafes and bars are lively, though nothing to write home about. A young, mainly university crowd fills the countless bars on **Calle del Paraiso.** Later in the night, the youth movement heads to pubs in **Plaza de San Miguel.** Cafes on **Calle de Vincente Meliner,** in Pl. Dorado, draw an older crowd. At **Roma es Azul,** people reading newspapers by the entrance are no indication of the mayhem inside.

Schedules for movies, as well as for Valladolid's first-division soccer team, **Real Valladolid,** can be found in *El Monde de Valladolid* or *El Norte de Castilla.* There are a series of basketball courts in **Parque Campo Grande** along C. Acera de Recoletos. The presence of a local professional team and satellite hook-ups to the NBA keep youths flocking to 10-foot hoops and also mini "dunk" hoops. No need to bring your own ball—there are plenty to spare, and players are eager to share.

Valladolid's **Semana Santa** (Holy Week) is, like in every other city, one of the most fascinating festivals. Sept. 16-23 marks the **Fiesta Mayor** celebrations, featuring bullfights, carnivals, and parades.

■ Palencia

Palencia (pop. 82,000) is a town where people and cows cross paths with surprising frequency. The city's laid-back residents may ask you flatly why you have come. Though low on pizazz, Palencia pleases travelers craving a healthy dose of Romanesque and Visigothic architecture.

ORIENTATION AND PRACTICAL INFORMATION

Palencia has lots o' length but is short on width. The train and bus stations, next to the park **Los Jardinillos,** are north of **Calle Mayor,** the main pedestrian artery and shopping zone. C. Mayor runs north-south beginning at **Plaza de León,** a traffic rotary adjacent to the park. **Plaza Mayor** lies five blocks east, midway on C. Mayor Principal. The **tourist office** is a 10-minute walk farther, at the south end of C. Mayor, on the left before Av. José Antonio Primo de Rivera (where the pedestrian zone ends). Thereafter, at the corner of the rose-filled Salón Garden, C. Mayor becomes **Avenida de la República Argentina** and then **Avenida de Valladolid.** To reach the **cathedral,** take the first right off C. Mayor after leaving Pl. León and walk three blocks.

The **tourist office,** C. Mayor, 105 (tel. 74 00 68; fax 70 08 22), distributes free maps and posters (open Mon.-Sat. 10am-2pm and 5-7pm). Change currency at **Banco Central Hispano,** 37 Calle Mayor (open Mon.-Fri. 8:30am-2:30pm. No commission). The train station has **luggage storage** (300ptas per day, accessible 24hr.), as does the bus station (70ptas per day; open Mon.-Fri. 9:30am-7pm, Sat. 9:30am-2pm). The **Red Cross** is at tel. 72 22 22; in emergencies call tel. 22 22 22. In other **emergencies** dial tel. 092 or 091. Mail services are divided between two **post offices:** Pl. León, 1 (tel. 74

21 80; fax 74 22 60), sends and receives **faxes;** the second office (tel. 74 21 77), next to the train station, provides Lista de Correos (both offices open Mon.-Fri. 8:30am-8:30pm, Sat. 9:30am-2pm). The **postal code** is 34001. The **telephone code** is (9)79.

Trains steam from the park Los Jardinillos (tel. 74 30 19) to: Madrid (16 per day, 4hr., 1985-2280ptas); Valladolid (22 per day, 45min., 385-445ptas); Burgos (11 per day, 1hr., 490-565ptas); León (15 per day, 1¼hr., 890-1025ptas). The **Bus Station** is also at Los Jardinillos (tel. 74 32 22; info booth open 9:30am-8pm), to the right of the train station. To get to Pl. León and C. Mayor, exit the station and turn right; then turn left onto Av. Dr. Simón Nieto, which hits Pl. León. To: Madrid (7 per day, 3½hr., 1885ptas); Valladolid (7 per day, 45min., 385ptas); Burgos (3 per day, 1½hr., 720ptas); Carrión (3 per day, 30min., 315ptas).

ACCOMMODATIONS AND FOOD

Plenty of reasonably priced *hostales* with clean, plain rooms line side streets running from C. Mayor toward the Río Carrión. The youth hostel, **Victorio Macho (HI),** C. Dr. Fleming, s/n (tel. 72 04 62), is only open during the summer (after June 20). Prospective hostelers should call ahead, but cannot make reservations. Members only. 1000ptas, over 26 1450ptas. Bus B from Los Jardinillos (every 12min., 45ptas) saves trekkers a hike. **El Salón,** Av. República Argentina, 10 (tel. 72 64 42), has sweet owners and miniature velvet chairs. Most rooms don't have running water and the beds are a little springy, but there are four spotless bathrooms (singles 1800ptas; doubles 3000ptas). Request the *pensión,* not the hotel, at **Hostal Tres de Noviembre,** C. Mancornador, 18 (tel. 74 16 47 in the morning, tel. 70 30 35 after lunch). From C. Mayor turn right on Av. José Antonio Primo de Rivera, then right again on C. Mancornador. Modern and sterile with sinks and radios, it's Palencia's version of a motel, but without running water in the rooms (singles 2000-2500ptas). **El Edén Camping** (tel. 88 01 85), hugs the river two blocks from the central Café España in the neighboring town **Carrión de los Condes.** Follow the signs (300ptas per person, 300-400ptas per tent). Three daily buses connect Palencia to Carrión (30min., 315ptas).

Palencia's **market,** off Pl. Mayor, is well-stocked (open daily 9am-2pm). **Supermarket Simago,** on C. Menéndez y Pelayo at the corner of C. Pedro Moreno, carries a huge selection of food and a small K-mart-quality supply of clothing, stationery, games, and other goods. It's across the street from Telefónica; go down C. Mayor from Pl. León and then turn right onto C. Patio de Castaño (open Mon.-Sat. 9:30am-9pm). Numerous restaurants and *tapas* bars—most of similar price and quality—line the streets just off C. Mayor. Friendly barmen serve up cheap and tasty *tapas* at **Restaurante Skarlotas,** C. Mancornador, 1 (tel. 74 16 47). Follow directions for Hostal Tres de Noviembre (above), which has the same owner. Sit-down *menú* (800-900ptas), but choices are limited. **Papareschi Restaurante-Pizzeria,** Av. Comandante Velloso, 1 (tel. 72 80 10), serves up authentic Italian pizzas (675-825ptas), standard pastas, and Budweiser. The restaurant is on Av. José Primo Antonio de Rivera, which becomes Av. Comandante Velloso (open Wed.-Mon. noon-midnight; Visa, MC).

SIGHTS

Palencia's biggest attraction is its 14th-century Gothic cathedral, **Santa Iglesia de San Antolín** (tel. 70 13 47), where 14-year-old Catherine of Lancaster married 10-year-old Enrique III in 1388. A statue of the virgin wields a gravity-defying halo greets penitents at the **Plaza de la Inmaculada Concepción.** The cathedral's **museum** has some stellar works, including El Greco's famed .*San Sebastián,* some spectacular 16th-century Flemish tapestries, a tiny caricature of Carlos V, and medieval hymnals bound in the skin of unborn calves. This orgy of medieval religiosity ends way, way down a stone staircase at the spooky **Cripta de San Antolín,** a 7th-century sepulchre. (Cathedral open Mon.-Sat. 9:30am-1:30pm and 4-6:30pm, Sun. 9:30am-1:30pm. Free. Short guided tours in Spanish 100ptas. Museum open Mon.-Sat. 9:30am-1pm and 4-6pm. 300ptas.)

More religious artifacts languish in the **Iglesia de Santa Clara** (tel. 70 00 43), the resting place for a midget Jesus (open 8:30am-8pm). A favorite of El Cid fans, **Iglesia**

de San Miguel (tel. 74 07 69), on C. General Mola, which runs parallel to the river, is where El Campeador wed Doña Jimena (open daily 9:30am-1:30pm). Watch for the blessing of the animals ceremony in mid-January, and for **Corpus Christi,** the second Sunday in June, when hundreds of seven-year-olds in sailor suits and miniature wedding dresses receive their first communion while parading through rose-petal showers down C. Mayor.

■ Near Palencia: Carrión de los Condes

Forty kilometers north of Palencia on the **Camino de Santiago** (Road to Compostela), tiny riverside beauty Carrión (pop. 1000) safeguards some incredible sights. On the south side of the **Iglesia de Santa María** (tel. 88 00 72), a 12th-century temple, is a depiction of the legendary tribute of four Carrión maidens to Moorish conquerors. Supposedly, Santa María foiled the transaction by sending four menacing bulls to gore the Moors (open daily 8am-2pm and 5-8pm; mass held daily at 8:30am, holidays 10:30am and noon).

On the far side of the Río Carrión looms the secularized **Monasterio de San Zoilo** (tel. 88 00 49 or 88 01 35). Faces of saints and popes stare down from the ornate arches of its Renaissance cloister, which is only partially open to the public. The tombs of the notorious Infantes de Carrión (who married El Cid's daughters, deflowered them, beat them, and then abandoned them in the middle of the forest in the *Cantar del Mío Cid*) are situated near the exit (open Tues.-Sun. 10:30am-2pm and 4:30-7:30pm; 200ptas).

Carrión's hidden treasure is the **Convento de Santa Clara,** also known as Las Clarisas. The *repostería* (pastry shop) bakes scrumptious cookies. The convent has recently inaugurated a **museo** (tel. 88 01 34); ring the bell and ask for Sr. Antonio to let you in (200ptas). The eclectic collection includes shepherds' nutcrackers, a statue of baby Jesus with a toothache, and numerous baby-doll clothes made especially for *el Niño* (open Tues.-Sun. 10:30am-1:30pm and 4:30-8pm).

Carrión's **tourist office** (not a government office, so hours vary) is in a wood-frame hut across the street from **Café-Bar España,** where the bus drops you off. **Hostal La Corte,** C. Santa María, 34 (tel. 88 01 38), provides luxurious, spotless, spacious rooms, and an elegant restaurant. (Singles 2000-2500ptas. Doubles 3500-5000ptas.) Or, stay with the nuns at **Convento Sta. Clara.** For nearby **camping** sites, see Palencia: Accommodations (p. 162). Three **buses** per day (tel. 74 32 22) carry day- (or half-day-) trippers from Palencia to Carrión (30min., 315ptas).

▓ Burgos

Despite its small dimensions, Burgos (pop. 180,000) has figured prominently in Spain's history, largely as a conservative citadel. For 500 medieval years it was the seat of *Castilla Vieja* (Old Castile). During its reign, the city built an enormous Gothic cathedral and celebrated the exploits of nobleman Rodrigo Díaz de Vivar, better known as El Cid Campeador, the national hero of Spain.

The hard-line politics that justified El Cid's expulsion from his native town were revived during the Civil War when General Franco stationed Nationalist headquarters here and fortified it with a military garrison. Today's Burgos exemplifies the nation's transition to democracy. The city hosts international brigades of backpacking pilgrims passing through on the Camino de Santiago.

ORIENTATION AND PRACTICAL INFORMATION

Burgos lies about 240km north of Madrid on the main route between Madrid and the French border. The Río Arlanzón splits the city into north and south sides. The **train** and **bus stations** are on the south side, while the **cathedral** and all other sights of interest are located on the north side. From the train station, follow **Avenida Conde de Guadalhorce** across the river and take the first right onto **Avenida del Generalísimo Franco,** which turns into **Paseo del Espolón** farther down. From the bus station, follow **Calle de Madrid** through **Plaza de la Vega** and across the river, then turn

right on **Paseo del Espolón.** The cathedral, unmistakable with its massive gray spires, is several hundred meters north. cafe along the *paseo* (upstream), at C. Santander, stands a large statue of El Cid. A short walk up C. Santander leads to **Plaza de España.** Look here for signs to the tourist office, which is located in **Plaza de Alonso Martínez.** The **Plaza José Antonio** (or **Plaza Mayor**) is between the cathedral and the tourist office, just east of the former.

Tourist Office: Pl. Alonso Martínez, 7 (tel. 20 18 46). From Pl. José Antonio, take Laín Calvo for 3 blocks; or, from the statue of El Cid, follow C. Santander, turn left on C. 18 de Julio and continue for 1½ blocks. It's next to the official-looking Capitanía General building (look for the office's white *Información* sign). Patient staffers distribute a variety of multilingual brochures and maps. English spoken. Open Mon.-Fri. 9am-2pm and 5-7pm, Sat.-Sun. and holidays 10am-2pm and 5-8pm.

Budget Travel: Viajes TIVE, C. General Yagüe, 20 (tel. 20 98 81), off Pl. de España. Student IDs (700ptas). English spoken. Open Mon.-Fri. 9am-2pm.

Currency Exchange: Burgos is flooded with banks and ATMs. **Banco Central Hispano** sits at C. Vitoria, 6, next to El Cid, with another location at Pl. Vega near the bus station. Open Mon.-Fri. 8:30am-2:30pm; Oct.-April also open Sat. 8:30am-1pm. For **ATMs,** hunt down the yellow on blue Telebanco signs or the black SirviRed signs; both accept Cirrus and most major credit cards.

Trains: (tel. 20 35 60), at the end of Av. Conde Guadalhorce, across the river from Pl. Castilla. A 10min. walk southwest of the city center, or a 300-500ptas taxi ride. Info open 7am-10pm. **RENFE,** C. Moneda, 21 (tel. 20 91 31). Open Mon.-Fri. 9am-1pm and 4-7pm, Sat. 9am-1pm. To: Madrid (10 per day, 3½hr., 2515-2885ptas); Barcelona (12 per day, 8hr., 4800-5170ptas); Palencia (11 per day, 1hr., 490-565ptas); Valladolid (16 per day, 1½hr., 890ptas); San Sebastián (8 per day, 4hr., 2000-2300ptas); Logroño (4 per day, 2hr., 1800-3100ptas); León (8 per day, 2hr., 2000ptas); Bilbao (5 per day, 4hr., 1700ptas); Santiago (3 per day, 8hr., 4400ptas-5500).

Buses: C. Miranda, 4 (tel. 28 88 55), just off Pl. Vega, on the south side of the river directly south of the cathedral. Each bus company has its own ticket window, its own routes, and its own schedule. To: Madrid (12-15 per day, 3hr., 1920ptas); Barcelona (4 per day, 7½hr., 4960ptas); Bilbao (8 per day, 2-3hr., 1420ptas); Valladolid (3 per day, 2hr., 1060ptas); Santander (4 per day, 2¾hr., 1305ptas); León (2 per day, 3½hr., 1700ptas); Vitoria (8 per day, 1½hr., 940ptas); San Sebastián (5 per day, 3¼hr., 1825ptas); Pamplona (5 per day, 3½hr., 1850ptas).

Taxis: Abutaxi (tel. 27 77 77) has 24hr. service. Or try **Radio Taxi,** (tel. 48 10 10).

Car Rentals: Hertz, C. General Mola, 5 (tel. 20 16 75), on the block parallel to C. Miranda near Pl. Vega. Must be 25 or over and have had a license for over a year. A small car with unlimited mileage is 11,000ptas for one day, but much cheaper for longer rentals. Accepts all major credit cards. Open Mon.-Fri. 9am-2pm and 4-7pm, Sat. 9am-1pm. **Avis,** C. Maestro, 2 (tel. 20 06 06). Must be 23 and have had a license for over a year. Slightly more expensive than Hertz for 1-day rental, but offers special weekend rate of 21,425ptas for 3 days. Open Mon.-Fri. 8:30am-1:30pm and 4-7pm, Sat. 9am-1pm.

Hitchhiking: To Madrid, hitchers walk south along C. Madrid from Pl. Vega until highway N-1; to Santander, hitchers walk north on Av. General Vigón. But remember, your mother, the tourist office, and *Let's Go* do not advocate this.

Luggage Storage: At the **train station** lockers 400ptas. Lockers are accessible 24hr., but consider safety, too. At the **bus station** (you can check your bag (100-150ptas per bag, depending on size). Open Mon.-Fri. 9am-8pm, Sat. 9am-6pm.

Crisis Hotline: SOS Droga (tel. (900) 16 15 15) for drug issues.

Red Cross: (tel. 23 22 22).

Late-Night Pharmacy: Check the listings in *El Diario de Burgos* (local paper, 120ptas) or the sign posted in every pharmacy.

Medical Services: Ambulance: (tel. 28 18 28).

Emergency: Police (tel. 091 or 092).

Post Office: Pl. Conde de Castro, 1 (tel. 26 27 50; general info 20 41 20). El Cid points the way across the river from Pl. Primo de Rivera; the post office is the big building at the first intersection. Open for stamps and Lista de Correos Mon.-Fri. 8:30am-8:30pm, Sat. 9:30am-2pm. **Postal Code:** 09070.

Telephones: Locutorio Telefónico, Pl. Alonso Martínez (tel. 26 42 28; fax 27 93 59), opposite Capitanía General, near tourist office. Look for the blue sign. **Fax** service. Open daily 9:30am-3pm, 4:30-11:30pm. **Telephone Code:** (9)47.

ACCOMMODATIONS AND CAMPING

For rousing nightlife and good *hostal* prices, scout the streets near **Pl. Alonso Martínez** on the north side of the river. The **C. San Juan** area is also dotted with reasonably priced *hostales*. Reservations are crucial for the last week of June and the first week of July (holidays of St. Paul and St. Peter) and are advisable in August. The "Fuentes Blancas" bus leaves from Pl. España (only runs July-mid-Sept. 9:30am, 12:30, 4:15, and 7:15pm, 75ptas) and voyages to **Camping Fuentes Blancas,** 3½km outside Burgos. (Open April-Sept. 500ptas per person, per tent, and per car, plus 7% IVA.)

Pensión Peña, C. Puebla, 18 (tel. 20 63 23). From Pl. España, take C. San Lesmes; C. Puebla is the 3rd right. Small, elegant rooms with big windows. Family-owned for nearly 50 years. Singles 1300ptas, with sink 1400ptas. Doubles 2500ptas, with sink 2600ptas. Luggage and bicycle storage available.

Hostal Victoria, C. San Juan, 3 (tel. 20 15 42). From El Cid's statue, walk up C. Santander past Pl. Calvobotelo and turn right onto C. San Juan. Simple, attractive rooms with sinks. Mostly tenanted by students from mid-Oct. to late June. English and French spoken. Singles 2300ptas. Doubles 3500ptas. Triples 4500ptas. Quads 6000ptas. Luggage storage available.

Hostal Hidalgo, C. Almirante Bonifaz, 14 (tel. 20 34 81), one block from Pl. Alonso Martínez. Off C. San Juan. A dim stairway leads to a warm and friendly *hostal*. High ceilings, hardwood floors. Singles 1700ptas. Doubles 2800ptas. Triples 4800ptas. Quads 6000ptas. Primarily available from the end of June-Sept.

Hostal Joma, C. San Juan, 26 (tel. 20 33 50). From El Cid's statue, walk up C. Santander past Pl. Calvo Sotelo and turn right on C. San Juan. The poorly marked *hostal* is opposite a pharmacy. Climb two dim flights of stairs to the smoky reception area. Although the rooms are small and bare, it's the cheapest place in Burgos. Singles 1700ptas. Doubles 2500ptas. Extras include shower (250ptas), breakfast (250ptas), dinner (850ptas), and laundry (60ptas per item).

FOOD

Vegetarians take heed—Burgos specializes in meat, meat, and more meat. Try *picadillo de cerdo* (minced pork), *cordero asado* (roast lamb), or, for a taste of everything, *olla podrida*, a stew in which sausage, beans, pork, cured beef, bacon, and heart disease mingle as one. Burgos natives take pride in *morcilla*, a sausage concocted from blood and rice. Locals covet *sopa burgolesa*, made with lamb and crawfish tails. *Queso de Burgos* (cheese) is delicious. Polish off your meal with *yemas de Burgos*, sugary sweet egg yolks. The area around Pl. Alonso Martínez teems with restaurants serving these staples and C. San Lorenzo is *tapas* heaven. **Spar Supermercado,** C. Concepción, midway on the block between C. Hospital Militar and C. San Cosme, prepares you for picnics (open Mon.-Fri. 9am-2pm and 5-8pm, Sat. 9am-2pm).

Mercado de Abastos (Norte), near Pl. España, and the smaller **Mercado de Abastos (Sur),** on C. Miranda next to the bus station. Here the smell of raw meat from the numerous *carnicerías* overpowers the sweeter smelling *panaderías* (bakeries), *charchuterías* (cheese shops), and produce stalls. Good, cheap fruit. Markets open Mon.-Sat. 7am-3pm. Mercado Norte reopens Friday afternoon from 5:30-8pm.

Gaia Comedor Vegetariano, C. San Francisco, 31 (tel. 23 76 45). A little bit of Berkeley on C. San Francisco. Gazpacho, fresh salads, asparagus crepes, and creamy vegetable *pasteles*, as well as desserts and wine—a light, flavorful *menú*. Fresh roses and soothing sitar music. Gaia also posts info about tai chi, yoga, environmental causes, and the rights of indigenous South Americans. Open Mon.-Fri. 1:30-4pm.

La Riojana, C. Arellanos 10 (tel. 20 61 32). A haven for the famished. The 900ptas *menú* will fill the emptiest of stomachs with heaping platefuls of paella, codfish, pork, and other local specialties. The small, wood-panelled *comedor* hums with chatter and the TV overhead. Open daily 11:30am-2am; winter noon-5pm.

CASTILLA Y LEÓN

Mesón la Amarilla, C. San Lorenzo, 26, between Pl. Mayor and Pl. Alonso Martínez. Snack at the bar or head upstairs to dine. *Patatas bravas* (French fries in spicy orange-colored sauce) is a specialty. *Raciones* 150-750ptas, *platos combinados* 1100ptas. Open 9am-4pm and 7pm-2am.

Restaurante Shang-Hai, C. Vitoria, 51 (tel. 27 03 94), a 20min. walk from the city center. Classy Chinese restaurant serves up unique Spanophile dishes, like salted lamb and "ham Chinese style" as part of its 775ptas *menú*. Open daily noon-4:30pm and 8pm-midnight. Visa, MC.

SIGHTS

Cathedral

The spires of Burgos's magnificent Gothic **cathedral** (tel. 20 47 12) rise high above the city. Although begun in the 13th century by Fernando El Santo (Fernando III) when it was funded by gentlemen sheep farmers, the cathedral has been a work in progress for centuries. The north facade is 13th-century Gothic, stark in comparison to the intricate 15th-century towers and 16th-century Puerta de la Pellejería inside the sacristy, El Cid's wooden coffin hangs several meters overhead. El Cid's actual body (or parts of it) lies with his wife Doña Jimena beneath the eight-pointed glass skylight of **Capilla Mayor,** his final resting place after centuries of not-so-peaceful transport. Before leaving the cathedral, look for the fly-catcher high up near the main door in the central aisle. As it tolls the hours, the strange creature opens its mouth in imitation of the crowds who gawk below. (Open daily 9:30am-1:30pm and 4-7pm. Admission to sacristy, museum, and Capilla Mayor 400ptas, students 200ptas.)

Near the Cathedral

The cathedral's neighbor, the **Iglesia de San Nicolás,** cowers across the Pl. Santa María. (Open July-Sept. Tues.-Sun. 9am-2pm and 4-8pm, Mon. 9am-8pm; Oct.-June Tues.-Fri. 6:30-7:30pm, Sat. 9:30am-2pm and 5-7pm, holidays 9am-2pm and 5-6pm. Free.) Continue up Pozo Seco to the **Museo del Retablo/Iglesia de San Esteban.** Eighteen 16th- to 18th-century *retablos* depict the life of Christ and various saints. (Open summer Tues.-Sat. 10:30am-2pm and 4:30-7pm, Sun. 10:30am-2pm. Rest of the year Sat. 10:30am-2pm and 4:30-7pm, Sun. 10:30am-2pm. 200ptas, students 100ptas, under 11 free.)

The ruins of a **medieval castle** preside over Burgos from a hill high above the cathedral. From C. Esteban follow the paved road uphill for 15 minutes. Better yet, from the Museo del Retablo, climb the 200 steps which rise through spruces and bright red poppies. From atop the bleached castle rocks, the cathedral spires rise up from the red roofs of Burgos which blend into the surrounding hills. The recently restored **Arco de Santa María,** over the route from the cathedral square heading towards the river, holds exhibitions of local artists' works and provides information on local cultural events (open Mon.-Sat. 10am-2pm and 5-8pm, Sun. 10am-2pm; free).

Elsewhere within City Limits

In case you hadn't noticed, Burgos is the city of legendary hero El Cid. The **Estatua del Cid** in Pl. General Primo de Rivera is Burgos's most venerated landmark after the cathedral. Rodrigo Díaz de Vivar ("Cid" comes from the Arabic for Lord) won his fame through bold exploits in battles against the Moors, and is thought by many to be the most famous Castilian of all time. The medieval epic celebrating his life, *Cantar de Mío Cid* (c. 1140), is considered the first great work in the Castilian language. Tradition compels Burgos's youngsters to climb the statue and fondle the testicles of El Cid's horse, thus ensuring their own strength, courage, and fame.

Just up C. Santander on the other side of the statue and on the right, the restored **Casa del Cordón** glows in the sunshine. Here Columbus met with Fernando and Isabel after his second trip to America. Felipe el Hermoso (the Handsome) died here after an exhausting game of *pelota* (jai-alai), provoking the madness of his wife Juana la Loca (the Mad), who later dragged his corpse through the streets.

Renovations of the **Monasterio de San Juan** (now called **Museo de Pintura Marceliano Santa María;** tel. 20 56 87) fully recovered and enclosed the cloister but left the remaining walls in ruins. To reach the monastery, follow C. Vitoria away from the statue of El Cid and take the second left. (Open Tues.-Sat. 10am-2pm and 5-8pm, Sun. 10am-2pm. Closed holidays. Admission 25ptas, students and seniors free.)

Other Excursions

The **Museo-Monasterio de las Huelgas Reales** (tel. 20 16 30) was once a summer palace for Castilian kings and later an elite convent for Cistercian nuns. Thirty-six *monjas* (nuns) still camp out here. Islamic motifs such as peacocks and eight-pointed stars decorate the Gothic cloister's badly damaged ceiling. Perhaps the quirkiest feature of the monastery is the statue of Santiago, whose movable arms were used to knight Castilian kings. Located within the monastery, the **Museo de Telas** (Textile Museum) houses the burial wardrobe of Fernando de Cerda (1225-1275) and family. Napoleon's troops snatched the jewelry from the entombed corpses and Spaniards later stripped the bodies and put their stunning gold-silk smocks and beaded hats on display. (Open Tues.-Sat. 10:30am-1:15pm and 4-5:45pm, Sun. and holidays 10:30am-2:15pm; Oct.-Mar. Tues.-Fri. 11am-1:15pm and 4-5:15pm, Sat. 11am-1:15pm and 4-5:45pm, Sun. and holidays 10:30am-2:15pm. 650ptas, students with ID and children under 14 250ptas, children under 5 free.) To get here, take the "Barrio del Pilar" bus from Pl. España (65ptas) to the Museo stop.

The **Cartuja de Miraflores** is a Carthusian monastery that houses a dozen or so monks and the intricate tombs of King Juan II of Castile, Queen Isabel of Portugal, and their son Don Alfonso. (Open Mon.-Sat. 10:15am-3pm and 4-6pm, Sun. and holidays 11:20am-12:30pm, 1-3pm, and 4-6pm, but sometimes the monks wake up late. Free. Open for mass Mon.-Sat. 9am, Sun. and holidays 7:30am and 10:15am.) To get there, take the "Fuentes Blancas" bus and either walk 300m up the road which angles to the right, along the red-dirt path which runs parallel through the woods, or walk 3km east upstream along the Po. Quinta (bus only runs July-mid-Sept. 9:30am, 12:30, 4:15, and 7:15pm, 75ptas).

ENTERTAINMENT

Partiers inundate the city of Burgos after dark. Bars on C. San Juan and C. Puebla fill up with merrymakers aiming for an early start soon after dinner (try **Marmedi** on C. Puebla). By 11pm a steady hum rises up from **Las Llamas**, where startling numbers of teenagers swarm in search of nectar. **La Pécora** offers a solid rock 'n' roll soundtrack and comfy, cushioned seats, while **Taquería Sonora** has live music. By 2am the crowd has matured; when the "early" bars close at 4 or 5am, head to the slightly more upscale **Las Bernardas** (the general area circumscribed by C. Las Calzadas, C. Belorado, and Av. General Yagüe) for "la penúltima"—the perpetual second-to-last drink.

Nightlife switches into highest gear between June 24 and July 9, when Burgos honors patron saints Peter and Paul with concerts, parades, fireworks, bullfights, and dances. The day after Corpus Christi, citizens parade through town with the *Pendón de las Navas,* a banner captured from the Moors in 1212.

■ Near Burgos

ABADÍA DE SANTO DOMINGO DE SILOS

Located amid rolling hills 60km north of Burgos, **Santo Domingo de Silos** (tel. 39 00 68) is home to the first group of chanting monks ever to hit number one on the global pop charts. The **Benedictine Monks of Abadía** chant vespers every night at 7pm and again at 8pm on summer Thursdays; high mass is at 9am, morning song at 7:30am, and *sexta* at 1:30pm. Sit, rise, and bow along with the black-cloaked monks while their voices blend with the organ and their own echoes in soothing, transcendental tones. (Abbey open Tues.-Sat. 10am-1pm and 4:30-6pm. Admission 200ptas, under 14 free.) The church itself is nothing to look at compared to its neighbor, the bizarre

Romanesque **cloister.** Look for the parade of stylized beasts which files past on the capitals of the east gallery. Rooms are a cinch to find in this friendly town of 380 people. **Hostal Cruces** (singles 3000ptas) and **Mesón Asador** (singles 3500ptas, 2500ptas per night for 2 night stay) have cozy restaurants and the best rates. The owners recommend short hikes in the hills where grazing sheep sometimes block the paths. Ask for directions to **La Yecla,** a 2.5km walk from Silos, where two cliffs form a narrow passageway protecting nesting birds and a small waterfall. A **bus** for the monastery leaves the Burgos station Mon.-Thurs. 5:30pm, Fri. 6:30pm, and Sat. 2pm and returns Mon.-Thurs. and Sat. at 8:30am(610ptas). Because of the monastery's hours, the bus-bound should consider a two-night stay.

▓ Soria

Modern development hasn't bypassed Soria (pop. 30,000), but the city retains a leisurely pace. Black-bereted pensioners tote bundles of bread past reddish Romanesque churches, and return to the streets to religiously observe the evening *paseo,* strolling through the Soria's splendid park and cobbled streets. Soria's centrally located park, Alameda de Cervantes, is a treasure. The town's more venerable citizens have been known to commandeer a pathway for a game of *tanguilla*—similar to horseshoes.

ORIENTATION AND PRACTICAL INFORMATION

The **bus station** is a 15-minute walk northwest of the city center. From the traffic circle outside the station, signs on Av. Valladolid point the way to the *centro ciudad* (downtown). Keep walking for about five blocks, then bear right at the traffic light onto **Paseo Espolón,** which borders the **Parque Alameda.** Where the park ends you'll see the central **Plaza Mariano Granados** directly in front of you. To get here from the **train station** (south of the center), either take the shuttle (see below: **Trains**) turn left onto C. Madrid and follow the signs to *centro ciudad.* Continue on C. Almazán until it forks; take Av. Mariano Vicen on the left for four blocks, and stay left on C. Alfonso VIII at the next fork for two blocks until you reach Pl. Mariano Granados (20min.). A shuttle bus runs between the *plaza* and the **bus station,** Av. Valladolid, once an hour on the half-hour. From the side of the *plaza* opposite the park, C. Marqués de Vadillo leads to the pedestrian walkway **Calle El Collado,** the main shopping street, which cuts through the old quarter past **Plaza San Esteban** to **Plaza Mayor.**

> **Tourist Office:** Pl. Ramón y Cajal (tel./fax 21 20 52). On the side of Pl. Mariano Granados opposite the park, it's the glass hut set back from the street. Ask for the *Ruta de los poetas* map and the *Guía,* with info on the province of Soria. Open daily 10am-2pm and 5-8pm; Oct.-April Mon.-Fri. 10am-2pm and 5-8pm, Sat. 10am-2pm.
>
> **Budget Travel: TIVE,** C. Campo, 5 (tel./fax 22 26 52), up the hill from Pl. Mariano Granados at the corner of C. Mesta. ISIC 700ptas. HI cards 500ptas. Open Mon.-Fri. 8am-3pm.
>
> **Currency Exchange: Banco Hispano Central,** Av. Valladolid. Walking from the bus stop, on the right-hand side before reaching Alameda de Cervantes Park. No commission. Open Mon.-Fri. 8:30am-2:30pm.
>
> **Trains: Estación El Cañuelo,** Carretera de Madrid (tel. 22 28 67). Bus shuttles between station and Pl. Mariano Granados, 20min. before each departure (30ptas). Info booth open 7am-1pm and 4-8:30pm. To Alcalá de Henares (2-3 per day, 2¾hr., 1455ptas) and Madrid (2-3 per day, 3hr., 1720ptas).
>
> **Buses:** Av. Valladolid (tel. 22 51 60), at Av. Gaya Nuño. Shuttle bus from Pl. Mariano Granados every hour on the ½hr. (30ptas), 9:30am-2:30pm. Info open 6:30am-9pm. When bus companies have no listed phone number, call the station for info. Most tickets may be purchased a 30min. before departure, except on holidays when seats may be reserved days before. **Therpasa** (tel. 22 20 60) cruises to Tarazona (5 per day, 1hr., 525ptas) and Zaragoza (5 per day, 2hr., 1085ptas). **La Serrana** (tel. 24 09 13) to Burgos (4 per day, 3hr., 1200ptas). **Linecar** (tel. 22 51 60) to

Zaragoza (3 per day, 2-2½hr., 1100ptas) and Valladolid (3 per day, 3hr., 1460ptas). Double-decker **Continental Auto** (tel. 22 44 01) to: Pamplona (5-6 per day, 2hr., 1460ptas); Madrid (6-8 per day, 2½hr., 1680ptas); Logroño (6 per day, 1½hr., 825ptas). **RENFE-Iñigo** (tel. 22 89 89) to Salamanca (2-3 per day, 5hr., 2580ptas) and Barcelona (2-3 per day, 6hr., 3885ptas).

Taxis: (tel. 21 30 34 or 22 17 18), stands at Pl. Mariano Granados, bus, and train stations. To bus station (350-375ptas) and ruins of Numancia (negotiable 1600ptas).

Car Rental: Europcar, C. Angel Terrel, 5, off C. Sagunto. One week starting at 36,500ptas. Must be 21 and have had a driver's license for one year. Open Mon.-Fri. 9am-12pm and 4:30-8pm.

Luggage Storage: Bags checked at the bus station (75ptas first day, 25ptas per day after that). Open daily 7am-10:45pm.

24-Hour Pharmacy: Check the door of any pharmacy, call the police, or consult the local newspapers: *Soria 7 Días* and *Diario Soria.*

Red Cross: (tel. 21 26 40), for **emergencies** tel. 22 22 22.

Medical Services: Hospital General, Ctra. Logroño (tel. 22 08 50).

Police: National Police, C. Nicolás Rabal, 9 (tel. 091). **Municipal Police** (tel. 21 18 62). **Guardia Civil:** (tel. 22 03 50). **Emergency:** (tel. 091 or 092).

Post Office: C. Sagunto (tel. 22 41 14), an immediate left as you enter Pl. Mariano Granados from Po. Espolón, then the first left. Open for stamps and Lista de Correos Mon.-Fri. 8:30am-8:30pm, Sat. 9:30am-2pm. **Postal Code:** 42070.

Telephones: Look for public phone booths around the city center. **Fax** service at post office on C. Sagunto. **Telephone Code:** (9)75.

ACCOMMODATIONS AND CAMPING

Affordable *pensiones* are sprinkled in the streets around **Pl. Olivo** and **Pl. Salvador,** both near Pl. Mariano Granados. Reservations, necessary during the *fiestas* in the last week of June, are also wise mid-July through mid-September.

Residencia Juvenil Antonio Machado (HI), Pl. José Antonio, 1 (tel. 22 17 89), a seasonal hostel. From Pl. Mariano Granados take C. Nicolás Rabal until you reach Pl. José Antonio. A modern college dorm open to tourists July 1-Aug. 15. Often filled with youth groups so reserve early. 11pm curfew. Members only. 950ptas, over 26 1350ptas. Breakfast 100ptas. Run jointly with **Residencia Juvenil Juan Antonio Gaya Nuño (HI),** Po. San Francisco, 1 (tel. 22 14 66). From Pl. Mariano Granados take C. Nicolás Rabal, the second left on C. Santa Luisa de Marillac, then the next right. A modern college dorm most of the year, but open to tourists for a pittance July-Sept. Mostly doubles and quads. Closed for renovation in summer 1997, but set to re-open in October.

Pension Ersogo, C. Alberca, 4 (tel. 21 35 08). From the tourist office, head up C. Caballeros and take the first right. Ring the bell on the right-hand door on the second floor (for Americans, 3rd fl.). Clean, simple rooms, some with nice big windows. Single 1800ptas, double 2800ptas, triple 4000ptas.

Casa Diocesana Pío XII, C. San Juan, 5 (tel. 21 21 76). From Pl. Marciano Granados, head up C. El Collado past Pl. San Blas, then turn right on C. San Juan; enter through iron gates under the *Residencias* sign. Be prepared to see priests wandering the halls. All rooms with bath and crucifix. Singles 2500ptas. Doubles 3475ptas. Slightly cheaper Sept. to mid-June.

Camping: Camping Fuente la Teja (tel. 22 29 67), 3km from town on Ctra. Madrid (km233). Swimming pool. 475ptas per person and per car, 500ptas per tent. Open April 1-Sept. 30.

FOOD

Specialties such as *sopa castellana* (soup with bread, garlic, egg, *chorizo,* and ham) are the stuff of Sorian gods, and the region's butter is celebrated throughout Spain. *Paciencias* (local pastries) are hard little cookies meant to be held in the mouth, not in the hand, until they soften up. **Calle M. Vincente Tutor** is spiced with bars and inexpensive restaurants. Merchants sell fresh produce, meat, and fish at the **market** on C. Estudios, left off C. Collado (open Mon.-Sat. 9am-3pm, may close early). Cruise

the **supermarket** aisles at **Autoservicio Muñoz,** C. Collado, 36 (open in summer 9am-2:45pm and 4:30-8:45pm, in winter 9:30am-2:15pm and 4:30-8:30pm, slightly longer hours on Sat.).

Bar Restaurante Regio, Pl. Ramón y Cajal, 7 (tel. 21 30 76). A fine selection of *bocadillos* (275-650ptas), *raciones* (350-1600ptas), and *menús especiales* (500-1100ptas). The mammoth *tortilla de patata* is a steal at 300ptas. Open 7am-1pm.

Casa Garrido, C. Vicente Tutor, 8 (22 20 68). Test drive Soria's culinary specialties. *Migas* (750ptas) and *menú del día* starring *sopa castellana*, pigs' feet, and stewed quail (1000ptas), are all served in a traditional-looking *mesón*. Open Mon.-Fri. 1:30-4pm and 9-11pm, Sat. 1:30-4pm.

Nueva York, C. Collado, 14 (tel. 21 27 84), one block past Pl. San Esteban. You'll want to be a part of breakfast (served until 12:30pm) with coffee, fresh orange juice, and buttery toast or croissants (275ptas). An array of cookies and chocolate beckon. Open daily 8am-10pm; winter 8am-9:30pm.

SIGHTS AND ENTERTAINMENT

The **Río Duero,** which the great 20th-century poet Antonio Machado likened to a drawn bow, forms an arc around Soria. Gustavo Asolfo Bécquer made Soria home for a time (a plaque on Pl. Ramón Benito Aceña marks the spot); many of his 19th-century *Leyendas* are set in the hills along the Duero. To find the river from Pl. Mariano Granados, walk past the huge sign for the restaurant Nueva York and straight down C. Zapatería. Halfway down the hill, C. Zapatería changes to C. Real. Follow this to Pl. San Pedro. The **Concatedral de San Pedro** is on the left (open June 15-Sept. 14: 10am-1pm and 5-8pm; Sept. 16-June 14: 4-7pm); the bridge lies just ahead. Soria abounds in churches, like **Iglesia de Santo Domingo,** notable for its Romanesque facade, and **San Juan de Rabanera** which bears Byzantine touches. The **Concatedral de San Pedro** has a nice cloister (open erratically and daily 5-7pm, 50ptas).

The **big money,** however, lies across the river. The **Ermita de San Saturio,** 1.5km downstream (turn right after crossing the bridge), is built into the side of a cliff. The result is a heavenly retreat, with light seeping into the caves through stained-glass windows. Note the window from which a young child fell in 1772, landing on his knees unharmed. It's well worth the trek (open May-Sept. 10am-2pm and 4:30-8pm; Oct.-April 10:30-6:30pm). The **Monasterio San Juan de Duero** sits transcendentally amid cottonwoods, wild irises, and green, green grass. The church itself is stunningly simple; its cloister mixes Romanesque and Islamic arches. Inside, a small museum displays medieval artifacts. (Open June-Aug. Tues.-Sat. 10am-2pm and 5-9pm; Sept.-Oct. and April-May Tues.-Sat. 10am-2pm and 4-7pm; Nov.-March Tues.-Sat. 10am-2pm and 3:30-6pm; Sun. year-round 10am-2pm. 200ptas; under 18, over 65, and students free; Sat. and Sun. free for everyone.)

The **Museo Numantino,** Po. Espolón, 8 (tel. 22 13 97), shows off the impressive Celto-iberian and Roman artifacts excavated from nearby Numancia. (Open June-Sept. Tues.-Sat. 9am-2pm and 5-9pm, Sun. 9am-2pm; Oct.-May Tues.-Sat. 9am-8:30pm, Sun. 9am-2pm. 200ptas, under 18, over 65, student with ID or youth card, and everyone on Sat. and Sun. free.). Use the same ticket for the San Juan de Duero Monastery. Wheelchair accessibility from Pl. Rey el Sabio.

When work's over, everybody in Soria heads for the old town. Early evening finds them in either Pl. Ramón Benito Aceña or Pl. San Clemente, both off C. Collado. There locals order drinks and nibbles from bar windows and loiter outside. Late-night festivities center at the disco-bars grouped around the intersection of **Rota de Calatañazer** and **Calle Cardenal Frías** near the Pl. Toros.

Many Spanish fiestas involve watching bulls and eating, but Soria ingeniously combines the two. The **Fiesta de San Juan** (the last week in June) starts each day with a running of the bulls and ends each day with an ingestion of them.

■ Near Soria

RUINS OF NUMANCIA

Die-hard archeology fans should check out the architectural ruins (all excavated arti-facts hang at the Museo Numantino in Soria) of Numancia (tel. (908) 11 42 13), a hill-top settlement 8km north of Soria dating back more than 4000 years. The Celto-iberians had settled by the 3rd century BC and tenaciously resisted the Romans. It took 10 years of the Numantian Wars and the direction of Scipio Africanus to dislodge them. Scipio erected a system of walls 9km long, 3m tall, and 2.5m thick to encircle the town and starve its residents. High off his victory, he saved 50 survivors as tro-phies, sold the rest into slavery, burned the city, and divided its lands among his allies. Numancia, however, lived on as a metaphor for patriotic heroism in Golden Age and Neoclassical tragedies.

The ruins, though battered, are still worth a visit. Check out the foundations of the Roman houses and the underground wells. (Ruins open Tue.-Sat. 10am-2pm and 5-9pm; April-May and Sept.-Oct. Tues.-Sat. 10am-2pm and 4-7pm,; Nov.-March Tues.-Sun. 10am-2pm and 3:30-6pm. 200ptas.)

Getting to Numancia can be a problem for the carless. A **bus** runs to Garray (1km from the ruins, Mon.-Fri. at 2pm, 10min., 85ptas). Unfortunately this means you arrive 1½ to 3hrs. before afternoon opening time. Getting back from Numancia is even tougher; the buses don't return till the next day. The trek along the highway back to Soria takes two hours. Happy hiking.

EL BURGO DE OSMA

El Burgo de Osma (pop. 5000) is probably only worth the trip if you have your own wheels, although medievalists who persevere past its gritty exterior and venture into the back streets around the cathedral will be richly rewarded. Two of the more attrac-tive buildings are **Hospital de San Agustín** and the **Casas Consistoriales** in the Plaza Mayor. Fulfilling a vow, the Cluniac monk Don Pedro de Osma erected the magnifi-cent 13th-century Gothic **cathedral** on the site of an earlier one. The cathedral's two **museums** have an important collection of codices, including a richly illuminated Beato de Liébana commentary on the Apocalypse and a 12th-century charter, thought to be one of the earliest written examples of Castilian vernacular. (Open daily 10:30am-1pm and 4-7pm; closed Nov.-May. Guided tour in Spanish 150ptas, solo travelers 200ptas.)

A fairly helpful **tourist office** (tel. 36 01 16) operates from early June to early Sep-tember in the Ayuntamiento/Casa Consistorial on Pl. Mayor (open Tues. 5-8pm, Wed.-Sun. 10am-2pm and 4-8pm). The Ayuntamiento shares its phone with the **municipal police** (tel. 34 01 07). The **Red Cross** is at (tel. 34 01 51), and the **Guardia Civil** at (tel. 34 00 74). The **post office** (tel. 34 00 25) shuffles papers at C. Francisco Federico. The **postal code** is 42300. The **telephone code** is (9)75.

Calle Universidad is a good place to look for some affordable beds. The **Hostal Res-idencia La Perdiz,** C. Universidad, 33 (tel. 34 03 09), on the edge of town, has frumpy rooms with baths that overlook a gas station (singles 3210ptas; doubles 5500ptas; 7% IVA not included). Open from June to September, **Camping La Pedriza** (tel. 34 08 06) is on Ctra. El Burgo-Retortillo (350ptas per person and per car, 400ptas per tent). Gonzalo Ruiz (tel. 22 20 60) sends **buses** to and from Soria (Mon.-Sat. 2 per day, 50min., 425ptas).

Galicia (Galiza)

No, my fair lady, the rain in Spain does not fall mainly on the plain—it's here in the northwest. An anomaly to international conceptions of Spain, Galicia looks and feels like no other region of the country—often veiled in a misty drizzle, its ferny eucalyptus woods, plunging valleys, and slate-roofed fishing villages nap beside long white beaches. Rivers wind through hills, gradually widening into the famous *rías* (estuaries) that empty into the Cantabrian Sea and Atlantic Ocean.

A rest stop on the Celts' journey to Ireland around 900 BC, Celtiberian influences endure. Ancient *castros* (fortress-villages), inscriptions, *dólmenes* (funerary chambers), and *gaitas* (bagpipes) testify to Galicia's Celtiberian past, as does lingering lore about witches, fountain fairies, and buried treasure.

Galicia's lonely, drizzly existence was once a blessing, but it now hinders economic growth. Daunting mountain barriers and weaving rivers and tributaries isolated the region from medieval imperialistic efforts, but the harsh landscape that defended Galicia from Moorish and Spanish invasion continues to breed few cash crops and hampers potential trade routes. Its renowned fishing industry cannot nearly support the territory, and farming continues to stagnate with net-and-plow methods. National and regional governments are trying to upgrade Galicia's inadequate roads, in part to perpetuate a recent surge in tourism that has recently inspired features in the *Atlantic Monthly* and *The New York Times*. Santiago de Compostela, the final destination on the Camino de Santiago, is now one of the most popular cities among backpackers. Those with the patience and flexible itineraries are duly rewarded. RENFE rail is reliable but limited, while clanking FEVE serves rural areas. Bus connections are seldom and hitchhiking difficult.

Galicians speak *gallego*, a language related to Portuguese and Castilian. In fact, *gallego* is a linguistic missing link of sorts between Portuguese and Castilian. Superficially, it differs from Castilian by replacing "La" and "El" with "O"; "J's" with a preponderance of "X's", and "LL" with "L." "En el pueblo" becomes "No poblo." Most Galicians are bilingual, save for townspeople in remote areas. Conversation tends to proceed in Castilian, but newspapers print articles in both languages. Although regionalism here fails to make headlines as do Basque and Catalan nationalists, expect to see a smattering of graffiti calling for "liberdade."

Regional cuisine features *caldo gallego* (a vegetable broth), *pulpo a la gallega* (marinated octopus), *vieiras* (scallops, the pilgrim's trophy), and the *empanada* (turnover/pastry stuffed with tomato and tuna, among other fillings). Or try *tetilla*, a creamy, tangy cheese, with the area's tart and slightly cloudy Ribeiro wine.

■ Santiago de Compostela

Ever since the remains of the Apostle St. James were discovered here in 813, Santiago has drawn myriads of pilgrims, many walking for years to worship at its cathedral. The esteemed relics lifted Santiago into the ranks of one of Christianity's three holy cities, alongside Rome and Jerusalem. Its cathedral marks the end of an 800-year-old, 900km pilgrimage believed to halve one's time in purgatory (see **Pilgrim's Progress,** p. 177). Today, sunburnt pilgrims, smiling nuns, musicians, and tourists fill the granite streets by the cathedral. Students at the city's renowned university enjoy the city's modern art gallery and state-of-the-art concert hall, as well as an active nightlife.

ORIENTATION AND PRACTICAL INFORMATION

Street names in Santiago can be confusing—Galician and Castilian do not always coordinate between street signs and maps. Yet the two languages are similar: *Calle* in Castilian becomes *Rúa* in Galician, *del* becomes *do*. The **cathedral** marks the center of the old city, which sits higher than the new city. Three main streets lead to the

Galicia

cathedral from the south (train station) end of town: **Rúa do Franco** (Calle del Franco), **Rúa do Vilar** (Calle del Vilar), and **Rúa Nova** (Calle Nueva).

From the **train station,** turn right at the top of the stairs and take C. Hórreo to **Praza de Galiza** (do *not* take Av. de Lugo), then go one more block to **Calle Bautizatos,** where three cathedral-bound streets originate. From the **bus station,** take bus #10 to Pr. Galiza (every 10-15min., 85ptas).

Tourist Office: (tel. 58 40 81). Take your pick. R. Vilar in the old town under the arches of a colonnade (Mon.-Fri. 10am-2pm and 4-7pm; Sat. 11am-2pm) or the little modernist structure in the center island of Pr. Galizia (open Mon.-Fri. 10am-2pm and 5-8pm, summer also Sat. 11am-2pm).

Budget Travel: TIVE (tel. 57 24 26), Plazuela del Mataderox. Turn right up R. Fonte Santo Antonio from Pr. Galiza. Train, bus, and plane tickets for international destinations. ISIC 700ptas. HI card 500ptas. Open Mon.-Fri. 9am-2pm.

Currency Exchange: Banco Central Hispano Americano, R. Vilar, 30 (tel. 58 16 12). No commission. Plus, if you act now, they will throw in a handy all-purpose kitchen utensil. Open Mon.-Fri. 8:30am-2:30pm; Oct.-April also Sat. 8:30am-1pm.

American Express: Ultratur Viajes, Av. Figueroa, 6 (tel. 58 70 00). Open Mon.-Fri. 9:30am-2pm and 4:30-7:30pm, Sat. 10am-12:30pm.

Flights: Aeropuerto Lavacolla (tel. 59 74 00), 10km away on the road to Lugo. A bus connects it to Santiago, stopping at the bus station, train station, and C. General Pardiñas, 26 (8 per day, 125ptas). Schedule printed daily in *El Correo Gallego* (daily paper, 125ptas). Info open 24hr. **Iberia,** C. General Pardiñas, 36 (tel. 57 20 24). Open Mon.-Fri. 9:30am-2pm and 4-7:15pm.

GALICIA (GALIZA)

Trains: (tel. 52 02 02), R. General Franco. Open Mon.-Sat. 7am-9pm, Sun. 7am-1pm. To: La Coruña (16 per day, 1hr., 490-565ptas); Vigo (14 per day, 2hr., 750-865ptas); Pontevedra (14 per day, 1½hr., 490-565ptas); Madrid (2 per day, 8hr., 4700-5500ptas); and León (2 per day, 6½hr., 2800-3300ptas). Schedule printed daily in *El Correo Gallego.*

Buses: Estación Central de Autobuses (tel. 58 77 00), C. San Cayetano. Nothing central about it: a 30min. walk from downtown. Bus #10 leaves every 15min. for the *real* center and leaves just as frequently from the R. Montero Río side of Pr. Galiza for the station (35ptas). On foot, exit the station onto R. Angel Castro, then turn left onto R. de Pastoriza. Continue for about 20min. as the street changes names like a chameleon. Turn right onto R. da Atalia, then left after one block onto Pr. da Pena. Follow this through Pr. de San Mariño right into the cathedral's Pr. da Immaculada. Info open daily 6am-10pm. **ALSA** (tel. 58 61 33). To: Madrid (3 per day, 8-9hr., 5010ptas); San Sebastián (2 per day, 6hr., 6910ptas); Bilbao (3 per day, 9½hr., 6170-6340ptas). **Castromil** (tel. 58 90 90) to: La Coruña (6-10 per day, 1½hr., 650-800ptas); El Ferrol (4 per day, 2hr., 950ptas); Pontevedra (15 per day, 1½hr., 600ptas); Noya (13 per day, 1hr., 380ptas); Muros (12 per day, 2hr., 750ptas); Vigo (15 per day, 2½hr., 900ptas). **Finisterre** (tel. 58 73 16) to Camariñas (3 per day, 2hr., 1015ptas) and Finisterre (3 per day, 2½hr., 1350ptas). **Empresa Freire** (tel. 58 81 11) to Lugo (9 per day, 890ptas).

Public Transportation: (tel. 58 18 15). Bus #6 goes to the train station, #9 to the campgrounds, #10 to the bus station. All buses stop in Pr. Galiza; check the signs to see which side. 85ptas. Buses run 7am-10:30pm (#6 from 10am; #9 until 8pm).

Taxis: tel. 59 84 88 or 58 24 50.

Car Rental: Autotur, C. General Pardiñas, 3 (tel. 58 64 96), 2 blocks from Pr. Galiza in the new town. Must be 21, and have had a license 1yr. Rent small car with unlimited mileage for 7600ptas per day—price depends on duration of rental and time of week. Open Mon.-Fri. 9am-2pm and 4-8pm.

Luggage Storage: At the train station (lockers 400ptas). Open 7:30am-11pm. At the bus station (75ptas per bag). Open daily 8am-10pm.

Laundromat: Lavandería Lobato, C. Santiago de Chile, 7 (tel. 59 99 54), one block from Pr. Vigo in the new city. Self-service wash and dry 650ptas per 4kg load. Full service 800ptas per load. Open Mon.-Fri. 9:30am-2pm and 4-8:30pm, Sat. 9am-2pm.

English Bookstore: Librería Galicia, Pr. Universidad, 2 blocks east of R. Nova. Excellent selection of classic English novels and a smattering of poetry. Open Mon.-Fri. 9:30am-2pm and 4-8pm.

Religious Services: Pilgrim's mass in the cathedral Mon.-Sat. 9:30am, noon (featuring the *botafumeiro,* an incense burner on steroids) and 7:30pm, Sat. also 6pm. Sun. masses at 9, 10:30am, 1, 5, and 7pm.

Drug Crisis Line: UMA Drogodependencia (tel. 58 86 56).

All Night Pharmacy: Bescansa, Pr. Toural, 10 (tel. 58 59 40), one block toward the cathedral from Pr. Galiza.

Medical Assistance: Hospital Xeral, C. Galeras (tel. 54 00 00).

Police: Guardia Civil: tel. 58 22 66 or 58 16 11. **Emergency:** tel. 091 or 092.

Post Office: Travesa de Fonseca (tel. 58 12 52; fax 56 32 88), on the corner of R. Franco. Open for stamps, Lista de Correos (around the corner, R. Franco, 6). **Faxes** Mon.-Fri. 8:30am-8:30pm, Sat. 9:30am-2pm. **Postal Code:** 15080. **Telephone Code:** (9)81.

ACCOMMODATIONS AND CAMPING

Santiago's rooms are not the cheapest, but they are plentiful. *Hospedajes* and *pensiones* conglomerate around **R. Vilar** and **C. Raíña** (between R. Vilar and R. Franco), and hand-drawn *habitaciones* signs are just about everywhere else.

Hospedaje Ramos, C. Raíña, 18, 2nd fl. (tel. 58 18 59), above O Papa Una restaurant. Spacious rooms (some with views of a cathedral tower—stick your head *way* out the window) with large windows and lots of pilgrim shell decor. Singles 1600ptas, with bath 1750ptas. Doubles: 3000ptas; 3500ptas.

Hospedaje Viño, Pr. Mazarelos, 7 (tel. 58 51 85). At Pr. Galiza, take a right onto R. Fonte San Antonio, then the 1st left up a diagonal granite street. Rooms with wood

Santiago de Compostela

Casa del Cabildo, 20
Casa del Dean, 19
Cathedral, 13
Centro Gallego de Arte
Contemporáneo, 6
Convento de Belvís, 4
Convento de Santo
Domingo de Bonaval, 5
Convento de las Madres
Mercedarias, 26
Galacian Parliament, 2
Hospedaje Ramos, 22
Hospedaje Santa Cruz 23
Hospedaje Sofía, 28
Hospedaje Viño, 31
Hotel de los Reyes
Catolicos, 14
Iglesia de Santa María
del Camino, 8
Iglesia de Santa María
Salome, 24
Monasterio de San
Martín Pinario, 11
Plaza Cervantes, 9
Plaza da Immaculada, 12
Plaza da Quintana, 17
Plaza das Prateiras, 16
Plaza de Faxeiras, 29
Plaza de Feijo, 18
Plaza de Fonseca, 21
Plaza de Galicia, 27
Plaza de San Martiño, 10
Plaza do Obradoiro, 15
Plaza Roja, 30
Porta do Camino, 7
Seminario Menor, 3
Train Station, 1
Universidad, 25

GALICIA (GALIZA)

floors and velvet chairs overlook a tranquil plaza. Bathrooms down the hall. Singles 1500ptas. Doubles 3000ptas.

Hospedaje Sofía, C. Cardenal Paya, 16 (tel. 58 51 50). Within sight of Hospadaje Viño, off Pr. Mozarelos. Enter the restaurant on the ground floor, but head directly upstairs (*hospedaje* and restaurant are not related) for spic'n'span, old-style rooms, each with a battery of knick-knacks. Practice your French with the owners. Bathrooms down the hall. Singles 2500ptas. Doubles 3600-4000ptas. Cheaper in winter.

Hospedaje Santa Cruz, R. Vilar, 42, 2nd fl. (tel. 58 28 15). Newly renovated rooms have big windows overlooking the most popular street in Santiago. Singles 2000ptas. Doubles 2500ptas. Winter: 1500ptas; 3000ptas.

Camping: Camping As Cancelas, R. 25 de Xullo, 35 (tel. 58 02 66), 2km from the cathedral on the north edge of town. Take bus #6 or 9. Souvenirs, laundry, supermarket, and pool make this the Club Med of camping. 425ptas per person, per car, and per tent. Electricity 450ptas. Open year-round.

FOOD

Let's Go disciples breathe—and eat—easy in Santiago. Bars and cafeterias line old town streets, proffering a glorious variety of finned *raciones* and remarkably inexpensive *menús*. Most restaurants here lie south of the cathedral, notably on **Rúa do Vilar, Rúa Franco,** and **Calle Raíña.** For more local flavor, try the streets radiating from Pr. Roxa in the new city. End your meal with a *tarta de Santiago,* rich almond cake emblazoned with a stylized cross.

Santiago's **market** is a sight in its own right. Produce carts, meat stalls, fresh cheese baskets, and everything from flowers to baby clothes line streets from Pr. San Felix to Convento de San Augustín (open Mon.-Sat. 7:30am-2pm). **Supermercados Lorenzo Froiz,** Pr. Toural, one block into the old city from Pr. Galiza, does not have peanut butter (open Mon.-Sat. 9am-3pm and 5-9pm). For the cheapest bread and *empanada* in town, check **Supermercado Victoria,** C. Horreo (2 blocks off Pr. Galicia).

Casa Manolo, R. Traviesa, 27 (tel. 58 29 50), near the market and Pr. San Augustín. Great deal. Come early and come often to sample the innumerable combinations on their 650ptas *menú* (wine not included, homemade flan is). Open Mon.-Fri. 1-4pm and 8pm-midnight.

Restaurante-Bar Los Caracoles, C. Raíña, 14 (tel. 56 14 98). Head for the cozy *comedor* in back, and chow down on the 700ptas *menú.* Entrees 500-2000ptas. Bocadillos from 175ptas. Open daily 10am-4pm and 7pm-midnight. Visa, MC.

Café-Bar El Metro, R. Nova, 12 (tel. 57 65 38). Snag a table under the archway outside. *Menú del día* (825ptas). *Menú del estudiante,* with a main *plato* of hake or steak rings up at 600ptas. Entrees 350-600ptas. Open 1-5pm and 8-10pm. Closed Christmas week and Semana Santa.

Casa Parades, C. Carretas, 1 (tel. 58 59 20), off the west corner of Pr. Obradoiro. *Menú del día* (1200ptas) served in a stylish *comedor* with pink tablecloths. If you are pining for your mother tongue, staff speaks a species of English. Open daily 1-4pm and 7-11pm.

Pizzeria Oasis, R. Nova de Abaixo, 3 (tel. 59 73 38). In the quiet downstairs dining room, a plaque recognizes Oasis as a Galician pizza champion (competition was, no doubt, fierce). Pizzas 700-900ptas, hearty calzones 750-850ptas. Open Wed.-Sun. 1-4:30pm and 8pm-midnight. Mon. 8pm-midnight.

Cafeteria Restaurante Donás, República del Salvador, 30 (tel. 59 06 54). Right in the middle of the new city, Dona serves up an 800ptas menú of *croquetas, pollo asado,* and assorted pig parts at its long bar and in its packed *comedor.* Open 24hr., closed Sat.

SIGHTS

The Cathedral

Standing in a mob of tourist shops and enthusiastic hawkers, Santiago's **cathedral** rises above everything, offering cool, quiet sanctuary to priest, pilgrim, worshiper

and tourist alike. Gloriously alive, every candle is lit and every pew bursts at mass. Pilgrims in t-shirts and shorts speak at the altar during services and hug the jewelled bust of St. James with special fervor. The cathedral has four facades, each a masterpiece from a different period and with entrances opening to different plazas: Platerías, Quintana, Obradoiro, and Azabaxería. From the southern **Praza de Platerías** (with the spitting sea horse), enter the cathedral through the Romanesque arched double doors set in the oldest facade, crusted over with columns and assorted icons in various stages of undress. The **Torro do Reloxio** (clock tower), Pórtico Real, and Porta Santa face the **Praza da Quintana,** to the east of the cathedral. Crowning the door is a 17th-century rendering of Santiago in *mufti.* To the north, the **Azabaxería** facade combines Romanesque and neoclassical styles in a headache-inducing blend of Doric and Ionic columns, plus a smattering of familiar religious icons.

Consecrated in 1211, the cathedral later acquired Gothic chapels in the apse and transept, a 15th-century dome, a 16th-century cloister, and the Baroque **Obradoiro** facade and its two grand towers soaring above the city. This faces **Praza da Obradoiro** (to the west), where camera-snappers, souvenir hawkers, and *tunas* (young men in medieval garb strumming lutes) coexist in a Baroque frenzy of faith, travel, and tourism. Encased in this facade, the **Pórtico de la Gloria** by Maestro Mateo is considered the crowning achievement of Spanish Romanesque sculpture. This unusual 12th-century amalgamation—angels, prophets, saints, sinners, demons, and monsters—forms a compendium of Christian theology. Unlike most rigid Romanesque statues, those in the *Pórtico* smile, whisper, lean, and gab, leaving Galician author Rosalía del Castro to proclaim, "It looks as if their lips are moving…might they be alive?" The *catedral* includes a bust of Mateo—unusual considering artists in the Middle Ages were rarely recognized in sculpture. Visitors knock their heads three times against Mateo's, hoping that some of his talent will rub off in the process.

Inside the cathedral, the **organ pipes** protruding from stone arches reputedly resemble trumpet horns echoing over the congregation's heads. St. James's revered remains lie beneath the high altar in a silver coffer, while his bejeweled bust, polished by thousands of pilgrim embraces, sits above. The **botafumeiro,** an enormous silver censer supposedly intended to overpower the pilgrims' stench, swings from the transept during high mass and major liturgical ceremonies. The **museo** and **claustros** have gorgeous and intricate 16th-century tapestries and two especially poignant statues of the pregnant Virgin Mary with her hand on her expanding belly. The museum

Pilgrims' Progress

Around St. James's tomb grew a cathedral, and around this, a **pilgrimage.** The most common route of **El Camino de Santiago, La Ruta Francesa,** leads from Roncesvalles, Navarra (near the French border) to Santiago. Since the 12th century, voluminous numbers have followed the Camino, many as true believers, others as a stipulation to inheritance, an alternative to prison, or a lucrative venture. Chaucer's wife of Bath in *The Canterbury Tales* sauntered to Santiago in bright red stockings to find a husband! Clever Benedictine monks built monasteries along the way to host pilgrims, giving rise to the first large-scale travel industry in Europe. Romanesque art, Provençal lyric, epic, legend, and music were introduced to Spain by way of El Camino de Santiago.

Pilgrims, identified by their **crook-necked staffs** and **scallop shell necklaces,** follow the superhighway (Crta. 120) and back roads leading to Santiago. Tourist offices across northern Spain advise on how and where to join El Camino on foot, bike, or horse—the only vehicles true *romeros* can use. Guides list numerous *refugios* (shelters) where pilgrims stay for free, and get stamped to certify them as legitimate. At a foot rate of about 30km per day, the entire Camino takes just under a month. Few Americans join the pilgrimage, more appealing to pockets of European students. Still, in 1994, guru Shirley MacLaine walked the walk, surprising locals and fellow *romeros* along the way with her huge backpack.

also houses manuscripts from the *Códice Calixtino* and Romanesque remains from one of many archaeological excavations here. The early 12th-century *Códice*, five volumes of manuscripts on the stories of the Apostles, includes traveling information for pilgrims. (Museum open June-Sept. Mon.-Sat. 10am-1:30pm and 4-7:30pm; Oct.-May Mon.-Sat. 11am-1pm and 4-6pm; Sun. and holidays year-round 10am-1:30pm and 4-7pm. Admission to museum and cloisters 400ptas.)

Much older than the towers that house them, the bells of Santiago were stolen as souvenirs by Moorish invaders and transported to Córdoba on the backs of Christian slaves. Centuries later, when Spaniards conquered Córdoba, they took back their bells, using some unlucky Moors as pack horses to complete their revenge.

Architecture Elsewhere

Indulge your art-historian heart in the old town, all of which has been designated a national monument. Across Pr. Obradoiro, facing the cathedral, the majestic facade of the former **Pazo de Raxoi** (Royal Palace) shines with gold-accented balconies and monumental neo-Classical columns. The bas-relief inside of the Battle of Clavijo in the same style is likewise remarkable. It now houses the Ayuntamiento and office of the president of the Xunta de Galiza. The 15th-century Renaissance **Hospital Real,** now **Hotel dos Reyes Católicos,** a ritzy *parador,* is also in Pr. Obradoiro. It upholds an ancient tradition of feeding 10 pilgrims per day (in the employee dining hall). The doorway is a carved masterpiece; linger longingly enough and you may be let in to see its four courtyards, chapel, and sculpture (open daily 10am-2pm and 4-7pm). On the other side of the cathedral off Pr. Immaculada, the **Mosteiro de San Pelayo** displays a striking statue of Mary holding Jesus and clubbing a demon (open Mon.-Sat. 10am-1pm and 4-8pm, Sun. 10am-2pm; 200ptas).

Off Pr. Platerías, residential architecture holds its own in the Baroque **Casa de Deán** and **Casa del Cabildo,** now the pilgrim info headquarters. West of the old town, a neo-Classical **universidad** weaves into an otherwise Romanesque and Baroque warp. Located one kilometer from the cathedral, the 15th-century **Colexiata de Santa María do Sar** has a disintegrating Romanesque cloister—it started crumbling in the 12th century and never stopped. Inside, pillars lean at frightening angles, forebodingly leaving visitors wary (open Mon.-Sat. 10am-1pm and 4-7pm; 50ptas).

Respite: Ethnography, Modern Art, and a Park

You will find out everything you have ever wanted to know (and more) about ship building, blacksmithing, and wooden-shoe making at the **Museo de Pobo Gallego** (tel. 58 36 20), just past the Porto de Camino inside the Gothic Convento de Santo Domingo de Bonavad. Although most exhibits stress how-to over aesthetics, several rooms devoted to contemporary Galician painting provide an artistic breather. Next door, the expansive galleries and rooftop *terraza* of the sparkling new, white stone **Centro Gallego de Arte Contemporáneo (CGAC)** house bizarre, multi-media exhibitions of international modern art. (Open Tues.-Sat. 11am-8pm, Sun. 11am-4pm. Free. Small selection of striking, dirt-cheap posters.) A walk in the **Caballeira de Santa Susana,** between the new and old cities, is a lovely way to stave off monument overdose. Its manicured gardens and eucalyptus-lined walkways open onto gorgeous views of the cathedral, the university, and rolling farmland.

ENTERTAINMENT

The local newspaper *El Correo Gallego* (125ptas) lists art exhibits and concert information. Consult three local monthlies *Santiago Dias Guía Imprescindible, Compostelán* (both available at the tourist office), and *Modus Vivendi* for updates on the live music scene. *La Voz de Galicia* (125ptas) offers a more regional focus.

At night, crowds flood cellars throughout the city. **Bars** on **Rúas Nova, Vilar,** and **Franco** are packed all night. (Clubs open roughly 11pm-4am, the real action starting well after midnight. Women generally free, men 500-800ptas.) At **Cervecería Dakar,** R. Franco, 13, rich *batidos* (milkshakes 300ptas) of nutmeg and delicious liqueur (five flavors) entice, as students spread their papers all over the tables (open Fri.-We-

8am-midnight, closed last 2 weeks of Sept.). **Cervecería Dakar,** R. Franco, 13, is a fitting example of an "early" bar (open Sun.-Fri. 8am-midnight). The house specialties, rich *batidos* (milkshake 350ptas), are made with a tasty liquor and a dash of cinnamon. **Modus Vivendi,** Pr. Feixoo, five minutes from Pr. Praterías on R. Conga, is Santiago's nightlife headquarters. This eclectic dungeon strikes a balance between Galician bagpipes, Aretha Franklin, and local art. Occasional concerts mob the outdoor dance floor. Check the entryway for listings of *música en directo* (live music) at other local spots. **Borriquita de Belén,** R. San Pelayo, 22, **Crechas,** San Pelayo, **Joam Airas,** Rúa Traviesa, and **Retablo,** Rúa Nueva, give local musicians an intimate forum. If you prefer music from a can, spin over to **Casting Araguaney,** C. Montero Rios, 25 (tel. 59 96 72), a few blocks west of Pr. Galiza in Hotel Araguaney. **Discoteca Libertí** rumbles just across the street. All ages kiss sanity good-bye at **Discoteca Black,** C. Rosalía de Castro, a popular, primarily gay club inside Hotel Peregrino. The *galerías* on R. Nova de Abaixo, in the new city, are mobbed with students on Friday nights.

In between clubs or beneath the columns of the Pazo de Raxoi in Pr. Obradoiro, **tunas** in medieval garb sing ribald songs and serenade selected beauties. Starting in the Middle Ages, *tunas* traditionally performed to earn their board while in school; today their flirtatious aims are less lofty—think of them as frat boys with lutes.

Ten minutes from the old town, the recently unveiled **Auditorio** schedules classical music interrupted by an occasional Ray Charles concert (shows Oct.-June; check the tourist office and newspaper). The **Teatro Principal,** R. Nova, 21 (tel. 58 19 28), lines up a mix of puppet shows, ballet, and Shakespeare (tickets at the box office daily 12:30-2pm and 6pm-showtime). To check out schedules before you come, visit http://www.xunta.es/consello/cultura. August brings an international folk music festival to town; Santiago's major **fiestas** are July 18-31.

RÍAS BAJAS (RÍAS BAIXAS)

According to Gallegan lore, the Rías Bajas (Low Estuaries) were formed by God's tremendous handprint. Each *ría*, or estuary, stretches like a finger through the territory. Coves and picturesque islands lure Galicians for weekend visits. Foreign tourists have recently caught on, and tourism may soon eclipse fishing as the region's top industry. Public transportation between towns is often sparse, so rent a car or plan ahead.

■ Vigo

Vigo most enticing characteristic of Vigo is that it has a well-developed service economy. The sprawling city (pop. 300,000) is noisy and polluted, but ferries, buses, and trains mercifully and efficiently shuttle visitors to the surrounding Ría de Vigo and nearby Río Miño, while a network of hotels and shops pamper tourists between excursions. Elegant cafes near the water provide soothing spots to while away an evening.

■ ORIENTATION AND PRACTICAL INFORMATION

The **Gran Vía** is Vigo's main thoroughfare, stretching south to north from **Pr. América,** through **Praza de España,** and ending at the perpendicular **Rúa Urzáiz.** A left turn (west) onto R. Urzáizone takes you all the way to **Porta do Sol** and into the **casco antiguo.**

As you exit the **train station** to R. Urzáiz, go right two blocks to reach the central Gran Vía-Urzáiz. The **bus station** is a 25-minute trek away from the city center. Exit left and follow Av. Madrid for 10 minutes to Pr. España. Go right on Gran Vía and continue until you come to the naked man sculpture, which marks Gran Vía's intersection with Rúa Urzáiz. The L7 city bus from the bus station goes to El Corte Inglés (105ptas).

Tourist Office: Av. Avenidas (tel. 43 05 77). Take R. Urzáiz to R. Colón, follow Colón to the water, turn left onto R. Montero Ríos and walk 6 blocks. The office is in the long cement building next to the ferry station. Lots of brochures and maps. English spoken. Open Mon.-Fri. 9am-2pm and 4:30-6:30pm, Sat. 10am-12:30pm.

El Corte Inglés: Gran Vía, 25-27 (tel. 41 51 11). Three blocks uphill from R. Urzáiz. Novels and guidebooks in English, haircutting, cafeteria, restaurant, **telephones,** and **maps.** Open Mon.-Sat. 10am-9:30pm.

Currency exchange: Banco Central Hispano, R. Urzáiz 20. No commission. Open Mon.-Fri. 8:30am-2:30pm.

Flights: Aeropuerto de Vigo, Av. Aeroporto (tel. 48 74 09). Daily flights to Madrid, Barcelona, Bilbao, and Valencia. A **bus** runs regularly from the Estación Marítima to the airport, stopping also at the train and bus stations (100ptas). **Iberia's** office is at Marqués de Valladares, 17 (tel. 22 70 05).

Trains: RENFE, Pr. Estación (tel. 43 11 14), downstairs from C. Lepanto. Info open 10am-11pm. To: Pontevedra (14 per day, 35min., 240-280ptas); Valladolid (2 per day, change at Medina del Campo, 4015-4665ptas); Túy (3 per day, 45min., 315ptas); Santiago de Compostela (13 per day, 2hr., 750-865ptas); La Coruña (12 per day, 3hr., 1195-1370ptas); Madrid (2 per day, 8-9hr., 4700-5500ptas); Porto, Portugal (3 per day, 2½hr., 1665ptas).

Buses: Estación de Autobuses, Av. Madrid (tel. 37 34 11), on the corner with R. Alcalde Gregorio Espino. **Castromil** (tel. 27 81 12). To: Santiago de Compostela (14 per day, 2hr., 900ptas); La Coruña (10 per day, 2½hr., 1685ptas); Pontevedra (27 per day, 45min., 300ptas). For **ATSA buses** (tel. 61 02 55), go downstairs to gates and buy tickets upon boarding. To: Túy (every 30min. 7:30am-10pm, 45min., 315ptas); La Guardia (every 30min. 7:30am-10pm, 1hr., 585ptas); Bayona (every 30min. 7am-10pm, 30min., 240ptas). **Travel Bus** (tel. 37 78 78). To Madrid (7 per day, Mon. 1 per day, 9hr., 4025ptas).

Ferries: Estación Marítima de Ría, As Avenidas (tel. 43 77 77), just past the nautica club. To: Cangas (every 30min. 6am-10:30pm, 20min., round-trip 400ptas); Moaña (every hr. 6am-10pm, 30min., round-trip 375ptas); Islas Cíes (June-Sept. only, 5 per day, round-trip 2000ptas).

Public Transportation: Red and green Vitrasa **buses** (tel. 29 16 00) run to every corner of the city (100ptas). **Taxis: Radio Taxi** (tel. 47 00 00).

Car Rental: Atesa, R. Urzáiz, 84 (tel. 41 80 76). Must be 21 and have had license one year. Open Mon.-Fri. 9am-1:30pm and 4:30-7pm, Sat. 10am-noon.

Luggage Storage: Lockers at the **train station** (400ptas). Open daily 7am-9:45pm. At the **bus station** (60ptas per bag). Open Mon.-Fri. 9:30am-1:30pm and 3-7pm, Sat. 9am-2pm. The train station is infinitely more convenient.

Red Cross: (tel. 22 22 22).

24-Hour Pharmacy: Check *Farmacias de Guardia* listings in the newspaper *Faro de Vigo* (120ptas), or the sign posted in all pharmacy windows.

Hospitals: Hospital Xeral, C. Pizarro, 22 (tel. 81 60 00). **Hospital Municipal,** C. Camelias, 109 (tel. 41 12 44). **Ambulance:** (tel. 41 64 29 or 22 60 31).

Police: Policía Municipal, Pr. Rèi (tel. 43 22 11). **Emergency:** tel. 091 or 092.

Post Office: Pr. Compostela, 3 (tel. 21 70 09 or 43 40 09; fax 37 47 26). Open for stamps and Lista de Correos Mon.-Fri. 8:30am-8:30pm, Sat. 9am-2pm; for **faxes** Mon.-Sat. 9am-9pm. **Postal Code:** 36200.

Telephone Code: (9)86.

ACCOMMODATIONS AND FOOD

Vigo's inexpensive rooms make the city a logical base for exploring surrounding areas. **C. Alfonso XIII** (to the right upon exiting the train station) is full of cheap sleeps, as are streets around the **port,** particularly **C. Carral** and **C. Urzáiz.** The **Gran Vía** and **C. Venezuela** are brimming with bright *cafeterías* and *terrazas.* Streets leading away from the port hide a seafood paradise. For **groceries, El Corte Inglés** is a sure bet (see **Orientation and Practical Information,** p.179).

Hostal Ría de Vigo, C. Cervantes, 14 (tel. 43 72 40), left off C. Alfonso XIII. Spacious and squeaky clean with balconies and private bathrooms. Singles 1500ptas. Doubles 2000ptas. July-Aug.: 2000ptas; 3000-3500ptas.

Hostal Savoy, C. Carral, 20 (tel. 43 25 41), 1 block up from R. Montero Ríos. Classy rooms with wood floors, muted colors, and free-standing showers just inches from the beds in some rooms. Singles 2000ptas. Doubles 3500ptas.

Luces de Bohemia, C. Colón, 34 (43 00 20). A classy, mirrored interior and plenty of good eats. *Platos combinados* (500-1200ptas), salads (250-650ptas), and several *menús* to choose from. Delicious desserts and specialty drinks.

Mesón Don Sancho, C. García Olloqui, 1 (tel. 22 76 46), at the end of Pr. Compostela, and one block up from R. Montero Ríos. Almost as good as being on a boat: fresh seafood (grilled shrimp 600ptas, clams steamed in wine and garlic 650ptas) and shiploads of ocean decor. Open daily 11:30am-4pm and 8:30pm-midnight.

SIGHTS AND ENTERTAINMENT

Hitting the sack early to dream of Madrid's nightlife may be your best option. Starting in the late afternoon, students pack the *casco antiguo* (left of Pr. Compostela, facing the water). Cafes, bars, and discos abound just off the steep mossy steps. You can always catch a flick at **Multicines** at the base of C. Maria Berdiales.

In honor of its notorious past as a center for witches (good and evil), in mid-June Vigo hosts *Expomagia*, a celebration of all things occult. Tantric yogis and *umbanda* (a Brazilian cult similar to voodoo), practitioners demonstrate and sell their wares down at the port. Watch for the **Fiesta de San Juan** (Xuan) in late June, when neighborhoods light huge cauldrons of *aguardiente* (the best are in the *casco antiguo*) and revel in traditional song and dance.

■ Near Vigo

Ría de Vigo's fat mouth (as if, according to a brochure, "it were about to swallow up a big piece of ocean") and lively port nourish several towns which have mushroomed in the past half century. Las Islas Cíes—Cangas, Bayona, Túy, and La Guardia—are easy daytrips from Vigo. Also, the **Río Miño** marks a quiet and porous national border. A lone bridge bearing trains, automobiles, and pedestrians spans the river between Túy in Galicia and Valença do Minho in Portugal.

ISLAS CÍES

Guarding the mouth of the Ría de Vigo, the Islas Cíes offer irresistible beaches and cliff-side hiking trails for *turismo*-weary travelers. Believe it or not, there's no tourist office on these islands and not a single postcard rack. Because of the islands' natural refuge status, only 2200 people are allowed in per day, ensuring wide stretches of uncrowded beach. **Playa de Figueiras** and **Playa de Rodas** gleam with fine sand and sheltered turquoise waters. For smaller, wavier, and more secluded spots, walk along the trail beyond Playa de Figueiras which leads to a plethora of coves and rocky lookouts. Hiking about 4km to the left of the dock on the main "road" leads to a lighthouse and breathtaking views. Watch out for territorial seagulls that dive-bomb hikers too close to their spotted chicks.

For budget food (*bocadillos* and ice cream), head to **Restaurante Playa de Rodas** or **Restaurante Camping** on the other side of the Playa de Rodas. Octopus, chicken, *calamares*, and more ice cream come cheaply considering the restaurants' prime location. A **mini-market** is next door, as are **campsites** (tel. 43 83 58). Space is limited, so call up to 15 days in advance for reservations (525ptas per person and 535ptas per tent). Seven **ferries** per day make the 50-minute trip to and from the island, sometimes more in nice weather. Though fairly expensive, the trip is worth every *peseta*, especially when you chance on schools of dolphins leaping in the waves at the *ría*'s mouth (2000ptas per adult, 1000ptas per child).

CANGAS

A 20-minute ferry ride across the Ría de Vigo, Cangas is hardly unspoiled paradise, but its attractive **beach** and small-town feel do offer respite from the urban bustle of Vigo. **Turismo** welcomes visitors upstairs from the ferry ticket office (open Mon.-Fri. 10:30am-2pm and 4-8pm). To find the **post office** from the dock, take a right on C. Baiona, a left on Av. María, and then another left onto C. Baiona (open Mon.-Fri. 8:30am-2:30pm, Sat. 9:30am-1pm). Inexpensive lodging is scarce—spend the night in Vigo. If you find yourself needing a place to sleep in Cangas, a central, relatively cheap option is **Hostal Belén** (tel. 30 00 15), on C. Antonio Nores, a tiny alley off C. Baiona before it intersects with Av. Marin. Ask for the restaurant owner (doubles 4000ptas; mid-Sept. to June 3500ptas). **Camping Cangas** (tel. 30 47 26), Playa de Limens, has beach-front sites for tent-pitching (525ptas per person and per car; open May-Sept. 9). **Mesón O Batel,** half a block behind the market, off of Pr. Constitución on R. Real, is popular with locals (*platos combinado*s 850ptas). Simple, cheap *cafeterías* scatter along Av. Ourense behind the path to the beach. **Ferries** travel from Vigo to Cangas and back again (every 30min., 20min., round-trip 400ptas). La Unión **buses** (tel. 30 01 22) run from Cangas to Pontevedra several times a day. Look for the blue Parada sign on C. Montero Ríos near the beach or in the lot by the ferry.

BAYONA (BAIONA)

Twenty-one km southwest of Vigo, snug in its own mini-estuary, Bayona was the first European town to receive word from the New World when La Pinta returned to its port in March 1493. Now a seductive beach town, Bayona (pop. 10,000) boasts one **parador nacional** and a handful of churches. A two-kilometer *paseo peatonil* (foot path) loops around the grounds of the **parador nacional** along the shore, passing barrier rocks for picnics and sunbathing. **Turismo** camps out in the stained wood shack just before the *parador* gates (open July-Aug. Mon.-Sat. 9am-2pm). During other months, get info in the Ayuntamiento (open Mon.-Sat. 9am-1pm). C. Eldouayan, the major street, abuts the waterfront, becoming C. Ramon y Cajal. The **post office,** C. Ciudad de Vigo, 3 (tel. 35 63 50), does the basics (open Mon.-Fri. 8:30am-2:30pm, Sat. 9:30am-1pm).

Bayona's budget accommodations don't live up to *parador* splendor. **Hospedaje Kin,** C. Ventura Misa, 27 (tel. 35 72 15), has TVs, sinks, and knit bedspreads. (Singles 1200-1500ptas. Doubles 2500-3000ptas, with bath 3800ptas. Prices may be flexible.) **Camping Bayona Playa** (tel. 35 00 35), is open June-Sept. (650ptas per person, 670ptas per tent and per car). For *comida,* check out **C. Ventura Misa** (parallel to C. Eldouayan, one block inland), lined with *mesones* and *cafeterías*. **Buses** run to and from Vigo (every 30min., 1hr. depending on traffic, 295ptas). Those coming for the **beach** would do better to get off at Praia América, about 4km before Bayona.

TÚY (TUI)

The small border town of Túy (pop. 16,000), while charming, offers tourists little more than the opportunity to walk into Portugal. The 1km stroll to Valença do Minho across a metal walkway over the Río Miño and through carbon monoxide clouds ends on the Portuguese side, which looks exactly like the Spanish side. Túy's small **cathedral** is a mix of Gothic and Romanesque, reflecting the town's Portuguese, Spanish, and Galician roots. Inside are relics of San Telmo, the patron saint of sailors.

An ATSA **bus** (tel. 60 00 22) from Vigo stops on C. Calvo Sotelo at Hostal Generosa, and returns to Vigo from the other side of the street (every 30min., 45min., 315ptas). Three **trains** per day (tel. 60 08 13) run from Vigo to Túy, then on to Valença and Viana do Castelo, Portugal. They stop for 15 minutes on each side for customs and passport inspections. The train stations in each town are far from the border and the center of town; taking the bus or walking across makes more sense.

LA GUARDIA (A GUARDA)

Perched between the mouth of the Río Miño and the Atlantic Ocean, La Guardia (pop. 11,000) thrives on an active fishing industry and the 500,000 tourists who annually invade its little beach and large mountain. The **bus** stops at the corner of C. Domínguez Fontela and C. Concepción Arenal. Take C. Domínguez Fontela to the central C. José Antonio and turn right to reach majestic **Monte Santa Tecla.** Bear right onto C. Rosalía de Castro to start the 6km mountain ascent. For a smooth, paved route, bear right on C. Rosalía de Castro. Alternately, hike five minutes up the road and look for the wooden archway opposite the park that marks the start of a shorter (and much steeper) 3km pathway through the woods. Near the peak is a **chapel** dedicated to Santa Tecla, the patron saint of headaches and heart disease. When you start hearing bagpipe music, you're near the tourist office (at the top). Prepare to be ambushed with sodas, postcards, and "genuine" Mt. Tecla witches. Run for cover to the old *castro* (Celtic village), with its circular stone houses covered by *pallazos* (thatched roofs). The wax body parts inside are not for sale. The hearts, heads, and feet are thank-you gifts to Sta. Tecla from cured worshipers.

La Guardia's **tourist office** (tel. 61 00 00), sits in the cultural center on C. Rosalía de Castro during the summer (mid-June to mid-Sept. open Mon.-Sat. 11am-2pm and 5-8pm), and in the Ayuntamiento in Pr. España the rest of the time (open Mon.-Sat. 8am-3pm). Change lead into gold at **Banco Central Hispano,** C. José Antonio, 11 (Mon.-Fri. 8:30am-2:30pm). In La Guardia proper, **Hostal Martírrey,** C. José Antonio, 8 (tel. 61 03 49), doubles as a beer stein mausoleum. It offers posh rooms, many with TV (singles 2000-2500ptas; doubles 4000-4600ptas; breakfast 300ptas). The one hotel on the mountain, **Hotel Pazo Santa Tecla** (tel. 61 00 02), overlooks the spectacular valley. (Singles with bath 3400ptas; doubles with bath 4650ptas. In off season: 3100ptas; 4200ptas. Breakfast 350ptas. Open Semana Santa-Oct.) The **market** is on C. Concepción Arenal, but those hungry for seafood should try **Bar Bodegón Puerto Guardés,** C. Calvo Sotelo, 1 (tel. 61 16 47), at the port (400ptas; open 10am-3pm and 7-10:30pm). La Guardia hosts a **lobster festival** the last Sunday in June, as well as the mysterious "Burial of the Swordfish" during *Carnaval.* Pilgrimages, *fútbol,* and folk festivals mark the **Feria de Monte de Santa Tecla** in the second week of August.

■ Pontevedra

Twenty-six kilometers to the north and a full decibel quieter than Vigo, Pontevedra (pop. 74,000) is a hub to its own set of villages, ports, and beaches. Tourists roost in the city center, bombarded by postcard racks, gold jewelry, and overpriced pastries.

ORIENTATION AND PRACTICAL INFORMATION

The center of town is **Praza Peregrina,** from which six streets radiate. The main ones are **Calle de la Oliva, Calle Michelena, Calle Benito Corbal,** and **Calle de la Peregrina. Praza Galiza** is a five-minute walk south of Pr. Peregrina (from Pr. Peregrina, take C. Peregrina one block and turn right onto C. Andrés Muruais, which leads to Pr. Galiza). The **train** and **bus stations,** located across from each other, are about 1km from town. To get to the city **center,** turn left exiting the bus station (go with the flow of buses). Continue on this street for 12 minutes as it changes from Av. Alféres Provisionales to Av. de Vigo to C. Perefrina, which deposits you in Pr. Peregrina.

Tourist Office: C. General Mola, 3 (tel. 85 08 14), one block from Pr. Peregrina, it's a left off C. Michelena. Tons of slick brochures and maps. English spoken. Open Mon.-Fri. 9:30am-2pm and 5-7pm, Sat. 10am-12:30pm.

Budget Travel: TIVE, C. Benito Corbal, 47, 2nd fl. (tel. 80 55 32), hidden inside a larger regional office. Open Mon.-Fri. 9am-2pm.

Currency Exchange: Banco Central Hispano (tel. 85 38 12), Pl. Peregrina. No commission. Open Mon.-Fri. 8:30am-2:30pm.

Trains: C. Alféreces Provisionales (tel. 85 13 13 or 43 11 14). A lengthy walk from town. Info open daily 7:30am-1:30pm and 3:30-9:30pm. To: Madrid (2 per day, 11hr., 5200ptas); Santiago (16 per day, 1½hr., 565ptas); La Coruña (16 per day, 3hr., 1110ptas), and Vigo (16 per day, 30min., 280ptas).

Buses: C. Alféreces Provisionales (tel. 85 24 08; fax 85 25 30). Info open Mon.-Sat. 8:30am-9pm. Service is more frequent than rail service. To: Santiago (every hr. 8am-9pm, 1hr., 600ptas); La Coruña (9 per day, 2¼hr., 1395ptas); Cambados (11 per day, 1hr., 350ptas); Sangenjo (every 30min., 30min., 230ptas); El Grove and La Toja (every 30min., 1hr., 430ptas), and Madrid (4 per day, 8hr., 3445ptas).

Taxis: (tel. 85 12 85 or 85 12 00), 350ptas from the train station downtown.

Car Rental: Avis, C. Peregrina, 47 (tel. 85 20 25). Rates vary with duration of rental and time of week. One day unlimited mileage 11,832ptas. Must be 23 and have had a license for one year. Open Mon.-Fri. 9am-1pm and 4-7pm, Sat. 9am-12:45pm.

Luggage Storage: Lockers at the train station 400ptas; at the bus station 70ptas per bag. Both open daily 8am-10pm.

English Bookstore: Librería Michelena, C. Michelena, 22 (tel. 85 87 46). Astounding selection of classics and contemporary works in Spanish, French, and English. Auster to Morrison to Pynchon. Open 9am-1:30pm and 4:30-8pm.

Red Cross: (tel. 86 54 50), C. Padre Gaile.

Hospital: Hospital Provincial, C. Doctor Loureiro Crespo, 2 (tel. 85 21 15).

Police: C. Joaquín Costa, 19 (tel. 85 38 00). **Emergency:** tel. 091 or 092. **Medical emergencies** tel. 061.

Post Office: C. Olivia, 21 (tel. 86 54 53). For stamps and Lista de Correos open Mon.-Fri. 8:30am-8:30pm, Sat. 9am-2pm. **Postal Code:** 36001.

Telephone Code: (9)86.

ACCOMMODATIONS AND FOOD

Rooms, although generally inexpensive, are not easy to find—calling ahead is a good idea. **C. Michelena, C. Peregrina,** and the area around **Pr. Galiza** are dotted with *fondas* and *pensiones*. Like many towns in Galicia, Pontevedra prides itself on seafood. In the evenings, locals crowd tiny bars on **C. Figueroa** to munch on an endless variety of fishy tapas, washed down with the local Albariño wine. For land-based goods, there's **Supermercado Froiz,** C. Benito Corbal, 28 (tel. 86 52 51), at the corner of C. de Sagasta (open Mon.-Sat. 9am-9pm).

Pensión La Cueva, C. Andrés Mellado, 7 (tel. 85 12 71), in Pr. Galiza. Aptly named, with large, dim rooms. The pensión squeezes the electric bill, but passes the savings on to you: singles 1000ptas; doubles 1500-2500ptas. Bathrooms down the hall.

Pensión Florida, C. García Camba (tel. 85 19 79), just off C. Peregrina. Clean, modern, high-altitude rooms compensate for the long flights of stairs. Singles 1500ptas; doubles 2500-3500ptas.

Mesón Pontesampaio, C. Joaquín Costa, 24 (tel. 86 40 77), from C. Peregrina turn onto C. Sagasta, then the 2nd right onto C. Joaquín Costa. Greasy regional specialties in a 700ptas *menú* (1100ptas at night). Open daily 7:30am-2am.

Bodegón Micota, C. Peregrina, 4 (tel. 85 59 17). This intriguing alternative to the cafe-bar scene, borders on "cuisine," the great temptress of the budget traveler. Carrot soup (385ptas), cheese plates (385ptas), barbecued ribs (1250ptas), mango pie (425ptas), and runty *bocadillos* (585ptas). Open daily 1:30-6pm and 7pm-2am.

SIGHTS AND ENTERTAINMENT

Pontevedra's old town is built almost entirely from granite. In the evening its arcades and stone walls emit a luminescent glow. Commissioned by the Sailors' Guild in the 16th century, the **Basílica Menor de Santa María** has a golden Plateresque door that's floodlit at night, and wax figures (men, pigs, arms) left as *ex-votos* in the chapels. The tiny 18th-century **Basílica de la Peregrina's** roundness simulates the scallop shell associated with Santiago. It houses Pontevedra's patron saint, the Virgin Mary, disguised as a pilgrim. To imagine the look of an open-air Gothic cathedral, tour the

ruins of the **Ruinas de Santo Domingo,** in a corner of Pr. España (open in summer 10am-2pm and 5:15-8:30pm; other times by organized tours).

When it's raining in El Grove, head to the **Museo Provincial** in Pr. Leña. The museum, primarily archaeological, has Roman hatchets, glasswork, modern Galician art, and traveling exhibits. The basement features a reproduction of the cabin of Mentez-Nuñez's ship. (Open Tues.-Sat. 10am-2:15pm and 5-8:45pm, Sun. 11am-1pm. 200ptas. EU members free.) The **Sala de Exposicións Teucro** on C. Javier Puig (around the corner from TIVE), holds traveling modern art shows from around the world (open Mon.-Fri. 7-9:30pm, Sat. noon-2pm and 7-9:30pm; free). The very cool free color booklet features every painting on display.

If it's sunny, head to the **beaches** of nearby **Marin.** A fleet of red APSA buses makes the 30min. journey from Pr. Galicia every 15min., 7am-10pm (110ptas). You'll endure the horrid stench of a paper mill along the way, but the beaches are clean, inviting, and popular locally. From the bus stop in Marin, facing the water, head left on C. Angusto Miranda, around the track and up the hill. To arrive at Playa Porticelo, turn right on C. Tiro Naval Janer, continue for 12 minutes bearing right where the road splits. Another seven minutes on foot brings you to the larger **Playa Mogor.** Both beaches come equipped with bar-cafes. More walking leads to more beaches.

Pontevedra's modest **nightlife** is focused on bars that dot the streets and around the Basílica de Santa María and the Parador Nacional. Should you hanker for dubbed American flicks, a movie theater sits on C. Fray Juan de Navarrete where it splits from C. Peregrina (tickets 565ptas; check local papers for other theaters and daily listings).

■ Near Pontevedra: Ría de Arousa

EL GROVE (O GROVE) AND LA TOJA (A TOXA)

Every July and August, vacationing Europeans come in Land Rovers and BMWs to seaside El Grove (pop. 11,000) and its island partner, La Toja. Charming El Grove, west of Pontevedra on a tranquil strait, is lined with mussel farms, colorful boats, and torsos of clam-diggers. La Toja, across the bridge, lures the wealthy with a casino, lavish housing developments, aggressive vendors in "typical Galician dress," and a mediocre beach. The seashell-covered church and funky-smelling black soap (Magno) produced there redeem the town's detractions (iron oxide, not dye, tints the soap).

From July to mid-October **turismo** in El Grove has its own little office in the square near the Ayuntamiento and the bus stop. The rest of the year brochures are dispensed on the second floor of the Ayuntamiento (July-Oct.15 Mon.-Sat. 10am-9pm, Sun. 10am-2pm; Oct. 16-June Mon.-Fri. 8am-3pm). **Buses** run from El Grove to Pontevedra (17 per day, 1 hr., 430ptas) and to Cambados on the way to Vilagarcía (4 per day, more July-Aug., 30min., 230ptas). Schedules are posted inside and on the door of the bus office, 50m left. All buses depart from the end of the waterfront. The **police** answer at tel. 73 33 33.

Rooms in El Grove are not cheap, and you'll need a royal flush at the casino to stay in La Toja. **Hostal Miramar** (tel. 73 01 11), Rúa Teniente Dominguez, one block from the bridge to La Toja, offers TVs and private bathrooms (singles 1800-2500ptas; doubles 3500-5000ptas). The **mercado** sits along the water's edge (open Mon.-Sat. 9am-1:30pm). A lively local restaurant, **Taberna O Pescador,** C. Pablo Iglesias, 9 (see directions to post office), serves heaping sea specialties including *chipirones* (400ptas) and *pulpo* (750ptas; open daily 11am-midnight). **Gadis Supermercado,** Rúa Castelao, 73, has the staples (open Mon.-Sat. 9am-2pm and 5-9pm).

Unless you absolutely must sample "the most delicious octopus in Galicia," skip the tourist flocks and head to the tranquil beach. Five kilometers toward Pontevedra from El Grove, **La Lanzada beach** lures topless bathers with its fine white sands and irresistible waves. Two hundred meters past the end of La Lazada revels **Restaurante La Lanzada,** accessible by beach or road, a white *cabaña* with simple, spacious rooms 50m from the surf. (Doubles with one large bed 3000ptas, with two beds 4000ptas, with large bed and bath 5000ptas.) **Camping Muiñeira** (tel. 73 84 04), roosts a short

way past Restaurante La Lanzada. Sites with soft grass and wildflowers are not particularly private, but a gorgeous beach is just a street-crossing away (500ptas per person and per tent, 400ptas per car).

CAMBADOS

For a glimpse of small-town life and a glass of good wine, head to harborside Cambados (pop. 14,000), 26km northwest of Pontevedra. Lack of a beach has left Cambados out of the tourist loop—its taxi drivers play cards all afternoon. On a quiet hill 15 minutes from the center, the **Iglesia Santa María** watches over the town's cemetery. The **Pazo de Fefiñanes,** an attractive 16th-century palace-turned-*bodega,* brims with gigantic sweet-smelling barrels of wine. The lively **Praza de Fefiñanes** is filled with bar-restaurants serving the pride of Cambados. For a lovely view of the town and the *ría,* climb the steps to the left of the ruins up to the small park.

Two **tourist offices** serve the town's visitors: one in Pr. Mercado, on Av. Galicia (open July-Sept. 10 Mon.-Sat. 10am-1:30pm and 5-8pm); the other at Rúa Novedades, 13 (open Mon.-Fri. 10am-1:30pm, Sat. 10am-1:30pm). Marble-floored, shiny rooms with baths can be found at **Hostal Pazos Feíjoo,** C. Curros Enríquez, 1 (tel. 54 28 10), one block behind the bus stop off Pr. Concello (doubles 3000-4000ptas). For food head to the **Plaza de Fefiñanes.** (Walk towards Pontevedra, turn right on Av. Vilariño, then go left on Av. Madrid, which becomes Rúa Real.) The friendly folks at **Los Amigos Hamburguesería-Pizzería,** Rúe Real, stuff patrons with pizza (600-875ptas), *platos combinados* (500-750ptas), and cheap *bocadillos.* **Supermercado Vego** vends various goodies on Rúa Nova (open Mon.-Sat. 9am-2pm and 5-9pm).

Cambados throws a *fiesta* virtually every night in mid-summer, beginning with the July celebration of **Santa Mariña,** and culminating the first weekend in August with an official tasting of the previous year's local Albariño, a light fruity wine. Plus Ultra **buses** trek to Pontevedra from the blue Parada La Unión sign on Av. Galicia near Pr. Concello (9 per day, 1 hr., 350ptas). The last bus leaves at 7pm.

■ Ría de Muros y Noya

The northernmost of the Rías Bajas are not very touristed. Frequent buses make these towns easy daytrips, though transportation must be planned precisely.

MUROS

Sitting pretty 65km west of Santiago on the north side of the *ría,* Muros combines exquisite mountain views with the warmth and friendliness of a fishing village. Stone houses, winding, hilly streets, and several chapels characterize this lively little town set in the wilds of Galicia. Historically, Muros served as a leper hospital and pilgrim pit stop before Cabo Finisterre. The town's church, the **Colexiata do Santa María,** sports Romanesque and Gothic vestiges, thanks to Lope de Mendoza's 1400 refurbishing. The **Paseo Marítimo,** along the port where the bus stops, crackles with action in summer. Watch for the **Fiesta de San Pedro** during the last few days in June, with outdoor theater and traditional Galician music in the central square, and firecrackers, merry-go-rounds, and ferris wheels at the port.

The **Ayuntamiento,** at the right end of the street as you face the water, has maps and brochures (supposedly open Mon.-Fri. 8:30am-2:30pm). The **municipal police** (tel. 82 72 76) hide out in the same building. In an **emergency,** call 091 or 092.

Hostal Ría de Muros, R. Castelao, 53 (tel. 82 60 56), located where the bus stops, proffers huge rooms, big baths, TV, and swell views (June-Sept. doubles with bath 5000ptas; Sept.-May 3000-3250ptas). Up the street, **Hospedaje A Vianda,** R. Castelao, 47 (tel. 82 63 22), has airy rooms, most with bathrooms (singles 1500-2000ptas, doubles 3000-4000ptas). Downstairs they serve a 800ptas *menú.* More restaurants line Rúa Castelao. Try the egg, tuna, and asparagus pizza at **Pizzería Pulpería** (*pulpo* 800ptas, pizzas 600-800ptas). On Friday mornings, you can buy beachwear you forgot to pack for low prices at the **outdoor market** behind R. Castelao.

Castromil **buses** run from Santiago (12 per day, 2hr., 750ptas). **Transportes Finisterre** buses (tel. 82 69 83) serve Muros and nearby towns, passing the **Playa San Francisco,** 3km away, en route to Cée (10 per day, 10min., 60ptas). Catch them in front of Banco Pastor on R. Castelao.

LOURO

Four kilometers from Muros, little **Louro's** isolated beaches hug an untamed forest. Some say these are the most virginal beaches in the Rías Bajas. **Camping A Bouga** (tel. 82 60 25) with a **supermarket** and free hot showers, packs you in right near the water (435ptas per adult, per tent, and per car; electricity 400ptas; open year-round). Take the five-minute Finisterre **bus** ride to Cée (see above).

NOYA (NOIA)

Nicknamed "the little Compostela" for its density of monuments, Noya may actually be better distinguished by its braided straw hats. Gothic arcades and 15th-century stone houses surround Noya's many small squares. The 14th-century **Igrexa de Santa María** houses a bulky collection of tomb-lids; the 16th-century **Igrexa de San Francisco** keeps the **Ayuntamiento** company while the latter undergoes construction. Well-preserved statues of curly-bearded saints compose the Galician Gothic facade of **Igrexa de San Martín.** The **tourist office** (open Mon.-Sat. 9am-2pm) and local **police** (tel. 82 27 03) are in the Ayuntamiento. For **tourist information** head to La Casa de la Cultura on Corredoira de Cadarso (open Mon.-Fri. 9:30am-1:30pm and 5-8pm). Multilingual brochures put the town's monuments in an art historical context. Call the local **police** at tel. 82 00 50. For **medical emergencies** call 82 33 10. The **Red Cross** answers at tel. 22 22 22. The bus station has **luggage storage** (75ptas; open Mon.-Fri. 9am-2:30pm and 3:30-8pm). **Hostal Valadares** (tel. 82 04 36), Rúa Edgar Moniz, is a two-minute walk from the bus station and is the best deal in town. Shiny rooms with sinks. (Singles 1500ptas. Doubles 2500ptas; cheaper when staying for more than one night.) The restaurant downstairs serves up an 1000ptas *menú*. The Castromil **bus** (tel. 58 90 90 from Santiago; tel. 82 05 19 from Noya), which runs from Santiago to Muros, stops in Noya (every hr. 8am-8pm, 1hr., 680ptas). Fourteen buses return daily. Ten Hefesl buses run daily to Riveira, stopping on the way at O Castro de Baroña.

O CASTRO DE BAROÑA

Nineteen kilometers south of Noya lies a little-known treasure of historical intrigue and mesmerizing natural beauty—the seaside remains of a 5th-century Celtic fortress known as O Castro de Baroña. The circular foundations of the houses dot the neck of an isthmus, ascending to a rocky promontory above the sea and descending to a crescent beach (clothing very optional). Catch the sunset, then pitch a tent at the free public campsite in the forest just 300m from shore. **Café-Bar O Castro** (tel. 76 74 30), the single building of the O Castro bus stop, offers spotless rooms upstairs (doubles 3000-3500ptas, winter 2500-3000ptas). There are bathrooms down the hall and bargains for longer stays (*menú* 800ptas; without dessert or coffee). Ten **buses** run daily between Noya and Riveira, stopping (but often passing—tell the driver where you are going) on the road in front of Café-Bar O Castro (250ptas from Noya). Catch the bus across the road on the way back. The nearest town, **Baroña,** 1km north, has a small supermarket, a restaurant, and a bus stop. Five kilometers north of Baroña basks more populous **Porto do Son,** with an exquisite beach of its own.

SOUTH RÍAS ALTAS

If Galicia is the forgotten corner of Spain, then the small *rías* of the Costa de la Muerte are the forgotten corner of Galicia. Beaches here are arguably the emptiest, cleanest, and loveliest in all of Spain. The local population still plows with oxen, and women tote homegrown produce to market in head-held baskets.

GALICIA (GALIZA)

Although its appellation "Coast of Death" refers to the many shipwrecks along the rocky coast, it could just as well apply to tragedy bred by gourmet tastes. Several fishers pass away each year while attempting to extract the expensive and highly sought-after delicacies, *percebes* (barnacles), from sharp rocks on the coast. The fiercest challenge for travelers, thankfully, is finding quick transportation to these remote Elysian fields. Both Cabo Finisterre and Camariñas can be reached by bus from Santiago and La Coruña, but bus service to the smaller towns and isolated beaches is infrequent. The roads, tortuous and sometimes poorly paved, have vague road signs and thick mists which often settle in the morning. Campgrounds along the coast tend to be overpriced, dirty, and amenity-free. But maybe that's part of the charm.

■ Cabo Finisterre (Cabo Fisterra)

No, you haven't died and gone to heaven—you've reached the end of the world. To the left of Cabo Finisterre spreads the Ría de Corcubión and its attractive beaches, **Sardineiro** and **Langosteira;** to the right, jagged mountains meet the unforgiving landscape of the open sea. Straight ahead and 4km from town stands the lighthouse that beckoned ships for years, offering stunning views. The wooded path off the road may look tempting, but beware of brambles, thorns, and thistles. Coastal hazards have kept the region from becoming another Club Med. Hidden turquoise beaches seduce such travelers as Spain's Nobel Prize winning novelist Camilo José Cela.

Besides glorious views from the lighthouse, there's not much in town. The **Capilla de Santa María das Areas** contains a painting of the "Christ of the Golden Beard," purportedly thrown off a British ship and found by a local fisherman. A 12th-century **church** stands beside the road to the cape. To reach the beach, proceed uphill from the statue at the port past C. Carrasqueira, then turn right at the first dirt road. After about 50m, turn left at the white house with blue trim onto the seaward path.

The **Casa do Concello** (tel. 74 00 01), C. Santa Catalina, has nice stickers but only the barest minimum of **tourist information.** As you head uphill from the statue, turn right and walk two blocks (open June-Sept. Mon.-Fri. 8:30am-2:30pm, Sat. 8am-1pm; Oct.-May Mon.-Fri. 9am-2pm and 5-7pm, Sat. 9am-2pm). An **ATM** hides out in Caixa Galicia in the main square off C. Santa Catalina (left turn coming from the statue). The Casa del Mar Clínica (tel. 74 02 52), next door to the tourist office, offers **medical assistance.** In an **emergency,** call 091 and 092. The **telephone code** is (9)81.

While Finisterre is a feasible daytrip from Santiago, **Hospedaje López,** C. Carrasqueira, 4 (tel. 74 04 49), has cheap, immaculate, light-filled rooms (some with ocean views), and Disney cheer. Head uphill away from the main statue at the port, then turn right onto C. Carrasqueira and walk for five minutes. Two of the seven dwarfs happily guard the entrance. (Singles 2000ptas. Doubles 2500-3500ptas. Triples 4500ptas. Cheaper in winter, but call first since they may close.) Many plump lobsters wave from the mirrored tanks at the entrance to **Hotel Cabo Finisterre** (tel. 74 00 00), C. Santa Catalina, 50m uphill from the statue at the port. Rooms come with bath, telephone, and TV (6000ptas). For organized camping and more temperate water, head to the opposite side of the isthmus connecting Finisterre with the mainland. **Camping Ruta Finisterre** (tel. 74 63 02), Ctra. Coruña, is east of Finisterre on the Playa del Estorde in Cée (450ptas per person, per tent, and per car; open April-Sept. 15). A small supermarket sits on C. Santa Catalina. **Supermercado Froiz,** a five-minute walk left of the statue along the shore, is the big fish (open Mon.-Sat. 9am-2pm and 5-9pm). Although most restaurants along the dock are overpriced, **Restaurante O Centalo** (tel. 74 04 52) serves a 1100ptas *menú* and many good *raciones* (300-900ptas; open daily1-4:30pm and 9pm–midnight).

Three Finisterre **buses** make the trip from Santiago daily, and two return (2½hr., 1350ptas). Buses often require a transfer in Vimianzo, but there is rarely a wait. If you plan Finisterre as a daytrip from Santiago, check return times carefully—the last bus may leave in mid-afternoon. Eight Finisterre buses travel to Cée daily, a good place for connections to towns south along the coast.

The Place for Lace

While most four-year-olds are mastering the fine art of shoelace tying, the little girls of Camariñas are perfecting their first attempts at lace-making. They sit with their mothers and grandmothers on the front steps of the whitewashed houses, lacing for hours at a time. Instead of contending with one shoelace, *palilleiras* manipulate up to 40 threads at a time, passing wooden spools dexterously between their fingers seemingly at the speed of light. Amazingly, few seem to mind the summer influx of over-the-shoulder gawkers who stand in awe, mesmerized by the flurry of pins, spools, threads, and fingers. During summer *fiestas*, contests are held to determine the fastest lacer. If it were televised, stations would need slow-motion cameras to catch the action. The lace *(encaje)* is expensive, but before complaining about the price of that table cloth, understand that it took weeks to make. Often Camariñas families' sole income is lace-making and, though some blush to admit it, many men lace, too.

■ Camariñas

Showing shades of Penelope, who wove and wove as her husband Odysseus sailed the seas, the women in Camariñas (pop. 3250, north of Cabo Finisterre on the other side of the *ría*) knit the intricate, expensive, and delicate *encaje de bolillos* lace, an activity introduced by the Celts. The difference is that these women are not waiting for their seafaring husbands; rather, they are keeping this whitewashed town afloat economically. The *palilleiras* (lace-makers) are the town's secret weapon; they are honored by a statue in the town square.

To the left of the port, the **faro** (lighthouse) looms on a wind-swept cliff 5km above frothy waves; a 1hr. walk up a windy road through fields of wildflowers and space-age windmills (hold on to your hat and lightweight loved ones). Toward Ctra. General (the main highway) are **Area da Vila** and **Lingunde,** two virtually untouched beaches, approachable only via a sandy, rocky cliffhanger of a path (off the road to the lighthouse). This area has its share of watery tragedies: the wreck of the British ship *The Serpent* is marked by a tombstone for the sailors who died when the ship approached Camariñas one cold, rainy night in 1890. Only three of over 300 men survived. Across the *ría* from Camariñas on a rocky point in **Muxía,** historic model ships hang from the ceiling of **Igrexa de Nossa Señora da Barca** (Our Lady of the Ship). The rocks in front of the church supposedly hum when innocent people walk by (although they didn't hum for us...).

Behind the statue of the *palilleira* stands the **Casa Consistorial** (tel. 73 60 00 or 73 60 25), purveyor of tourist tips (open Mon.-Fri. 8am-2pm, Sat. 9am-2pm) and **Guardia Civil,** C. Generalísimo Franco, 5 (tel. 73 62 62; or try tel. 66 86 02; open 9am-2pm and 4-7pm). For **emergencies** call 062. The **telephone code** is (9)81.

Hostal La Marina, Cantón Miguel Freijo, 4 (tel. 73 60 30), offers large rooms, many with views of the water (singles 1500-1900ptas, with bath 2100-2700ptas; doubles 2450-3350ptas, with bath 3100-4200ptas). Restaurants serving fresh seafood line the dock along C. Miguel Freijo. **Supermercados Más y Más,** on Pr. Insuela by the *palilleira* statue, sells picnic fixings (open Mon.-Fri. 9am-2pm and 4:30-8:30pm). **La Marina's** restaurant downstairs serves a filling *menú* (850ptas).

Transportes Finisterre **buses** (tel. 74 51 71) run three times daily from Santiago (2hr., 1200ptas), returning twice. They also travel twice daily from La Coruña. Camariñas can be reached from Finisterre, but if you leave Finisterre in the morning, you'll have to wait 1½ hours in the tiny town of Vimianzo for a transfer.

NEAR CAMARIÑAS

The minor coastal road passes isolated beaches such as **Praia Traba** on its way to the Ría de Laxe-Corme. At **Laxe** on the west side of the *ría*, a vast, open stretch of sand separates the geological institute at one end from the fishing fleet at the other.

GALICIA (GALIZA)

Corme, on the other side of the *ría,* is famous for its delicious *percebes* (barnacles), which are pried off rocks in treacherous waters. Try them or whatever else is swimming in the tanks at **O Biscoiteiro** (tel. 73 83 76), C. Remedios. But don't pass up the freshly baked tart bread and bountiful entrees (600-900ptas).

■ La Coruña (A Coruña)

Although the newer parts of La Coruña are gray and mundane, recent massive efforts by the city have made *la ciudad vieja* (the old city) and port areas more attractive to visitors. Sailboats line the north end of the port, and gardens and parks lie tucked within the old city. Many of La Coruña's 250,000 residents while away afternoons at pleasant waterfront cafes along the brand new Paseo Marítimo, which winds around the isthmus along marinas, rocky cliffs, and beaches. An excellent base for exploring, La Coruña's stellar night life, historic old town, and pleasant beaches more than make up for the dingier parts of town.

ORIENTATION AND PRACTICAL INFORMATION

La Coruña's new city sprawls across the mainland; an isthmus and peninsula contain the *ciudad vieja.* **Avenida de la Marina** leads past the tourist office into the lovely old city, with shaded streets and old stone buildings filling the peninsula's south tip overlooking the port. Surfboard haven **Praia del Orzán** and **Praia de Riazor** are 10-minute walks northwest from the tourist office, on the other side of the peninsula's neck. The **bus** and **train stations** are 40-minute walks from the old city, and 25-30 minutes to *hostal*-heaven on C. Riego de Agua. If your backpack weighs a ton, take bus #1 or 1A straight to the tourist office (90ptas). Otherwise, from the train station, walk in the direction of El Corte Inglés, and take a pedestrian overpass leading to the bus station. From here, walk down C. Ramón y Cajal, take a left at the commercial train station onto Av. Primo de Rivera, and follow it through five name changes up to the port. Walk (with the water on your right) until you reach the **tourist office,** on **Dársena de la Marina. Praza de María Pita** is one block from the port.

Tourist Office: (tel. 22 18 22) Dársena de la Marina, connecting the peninsula and mainland, near the waterfront. Full of tips on daytrips, brochures, and an accommodations guide. Open Mon.-Fri. 9am-2pm and 4:30-6:30pm, Sat. 10:30am-1pm.
Currency exchange: Banco Central Hispano, Canton Grano, 9-12. No commission. Open Mon.-Fri. 8:30am-2:30pm.
El Corte Inglés: C. Ramón y Cajal, 57-59 (tel. 29 00 11). A sharp right from the bus station exit. **Currency exchange:** No commission, but a poor rate. Also maps, novels and guidebooks in English, haircutting, cafeteria, **supermarket,** restaurant, **telephones,** and **bad furniture.** Open Mon.-Sat. 10am-9:30pm.
American Express Travel: Viajes Amado, C. Compostela, 1 (tel. 22 99 72). Open Mon.-Fri. 9:30am-2pm and 4:30-8pm, Sat. 9:45am-1:30pm.
Flights: Aeropuerto de Alvedro (tel. 18 72 00), 9km south of the city. Served only by Aviaco. **Iberia,** Pr. Galiza, 6 (tel. 22 56 36). Open Mon.-Fri. 9:30am-1:30pm and 4:30-8pm, Sat. 9:30am-1:30pm.
Trains: (tel. 15 02 02), Pr. San Cristóbal. Buses #1 and 1A (100ptas, 110ptas) run from here to the tourist office and the *marina.* Info open 7am-11pm. To: Santiago (13 per day, 1¼hr., 490-565ptas); Vigo (13 per day, 3hr., 1195-1370ptas); Pontevedra (13 per day, 2½hr., 1060-1215); El Ferrol (2 per day, 1¾hr., 490ptas); Madrid (3 per day, 11hr., 5000-7700ptas); Barcelona (2 per day, 16-17hr., 6600ptas). **RENFE,** C. Fonseca, 3 (tel. 22 19 48).
Buses: (tel. 23 96 44), C. Caballeros, across Av. Alcalde Molina from the train station. Buses #1 and 1A (100ptas, 110ptas) run from here to the tourist office. **ALSA-Intercar** (tel. 23 70 44). To: Madrid (4 per day, 8½hr., 4800ptas); Oviedo (4 per day, 5hr., 3600ptas); and San Sebastián (1 per day, 14hr., 6330ptas). **Castromil** to: Santiago (6-10 per day, 1½hr., 650-900ptas). **IASA** (tel. 23 90 01). To: Betanzos (on the ½hour, 45min., 240ptas); Vivero (with stops at O Barqueiro, Ortigueira, El Fer-

rol, Vicedo, Betanzos; 4 per day, 4hr., 1600ptas); and El Ferrol, with transfer to Cedeira (every hr., 1¾hr., 700ptas). Other companies have routes to Vigo, Camariñas, and other destinations.

Public Transportation: Red buses run by **Compañía de Tranvías de la Coruña** (tel. 25 01 00; about 7am-11:30pm; 100ptas). Bus stops post full itineraries.

Taxis: Radio Taxi (tel. 24 33 33 or 24 33 77). **Tele Taxi** (tel. 28 77 77).

Car Rental: Autos Brea, Av. Fernández Latorre, 110 (tel. 23 86 45). Must be at least 21 and have had license 1yr. 3-day min. rental, starting from 2060ptas per day, unlimited mileage. Open Mon.-Fri. 9am-1pm and 4-7pm, Sat. 9am-2pm.

Luggage Storage: At the train station (lockers 400ptas). Open 6:30am-1:30am. At the bus station (70ptas per checked bag). Open 8am-10pm.

Laundromat: Lavandería Glu Glu, C. Alcalde Marchesi, 4 (tel. 28 28 04), off Pr. Cuatro Caminos. Wash and dry self-serve 800ptas per 5kg load. Full service 950ptas per load. Open Mon.-Fri. 9:30am-8:30pm, Sat. 9:30am-6pm.

English Bookstore: Librería Colón, C. Real, 24 (tel. 22 22 06), a few blocks from the tourist office. Assorted novels and a large selection of international newspapers. Open Mon.-Fri. 10am-1:45pm and 5-8:30pm, Sat. 10am-2pm and 5-8pm.

Red Cross: C. Curros Enríquez (tel. 22 22 22).

Late-Night Pharmacy: Check listings in *La Voz de Galicia* (125ptas) or in any pharmacy window. **Medical Services:** Ambulatorio San José, C. Comandante Fontanes, 8 (tel. 22 63 35).

Police: Av. Alférez Provisional (tel. 22 61 00). **Guardia Civil** C. Lonzas (tel. 062). **Municipal** C. Miguel Servet (tel. 18 42 25). **Emergency:** tel. 091 or 092.

Post Office: C. Alcalde Manuel Casas (tel. 22 19 56), past Teatro Colón on Av. Marina. Open for stamps, Lista de Correos, and **faxes** Mon.-Fri. 8:30am-8:30pm, Sat. 9:30am-2pm. **Postal Code:** 15070. **Telephone Code:** (9)81.

ACCOMMODATIONS

The best and most convenient area for lodging is one block back from **Av. Marina,** near the tourist office. **C. Riego de Agua** and the surrounding area (from Pr. María Pita down to Pr. San Agustín) always have available rooms. There are many *pensiones* near the stations, though miles away from the *ciudad vieja.*

Marina Española (HI) (tel. 62 01 18), in Sada, about 20km east of La Coruña. The Empresa Calpita bus (tel. 23 90 72) runs to Sada (30min., 240ptas). 3-day max. stay. 750ptas, over 26 1100ptas. Meals available. Call first, especially in summer.

Albergue Xuvenil "Gandario" (HI) (tel. 79 10 05) in Gandario, 19km outside La Coruña. Take the bus to Gandario (30min., 215ptas). 3-day max. stay. 750ptas, over 26 1100ptas. They pack' em in six per single-sex room.

Hospedaje María Pita, C. Riego de Agua, 38, 3rd fl. (tel. 22 11 87), one block behind Av. Marina, above Hospedaje Moran. María Pita held off the attacking British; now white lace curtains, cheery rooms, and pristine bathrooms invite them (and others) in. There are 3 other *hostales* in this building. Doubles 2700ptas, in off season 2200ptas. Arrangements for singles may be made.

Hostal Castelos, C. Real, 14 (tel. 22 29 06), one block behind Av. Marina. Original 1890s mahogany wainscoting and velvet armchairs. Sashay into cavernous rooms through hand-carved door frames. Doubles 3300-3800ptas.

Pensión la Alianza, C. Riego de Agua, 8, 1st fl. (tel. 22 81 14). Dark wood and homemade oil paintings in quiet, simple rooms. Spotless gray-tiled bathroom down the hall. Singles 1500-2000ptas. Doubles 2500-3500ptas. One room has no windows.

FOOD

Sustenance for Scrooges comes easy in *mesónes* on **C. Estrella, C. de la Franja,** and nearby streets. For snazzier cafes and pizzerias, head to the area around C. Rubine off Playa de Raizor. Fresh fruit and vegetables shine in the big **market** in the oval building on Pr. San Agustín, near the old town (open Mon.-Sat. 8am-3pm). If you roll out of bed after 3pm, buy your groceries downstairs at **Supermercados Claudio** (open daily 9am-3pm and 5-9pm).

GALICIA (GALIZA)

Mesón Trotamundos, Pr. España, 9 (tel. 22 16 09). A *ración* of 6 grilled sardines costs just 400ptas. Sit at wooden tables under hunks of beef and hundreds of wine bottles, and watch the staff snip arms off octopi to make *pulpo a la gallega.* *Raciónes* 250-1100ptas. *Menú* 800ptas (except Sun.). Open daily 10am-2am.

Cafetería SouSantos, C. Fransisco Mariño, 10 (tel. 22 76 09). Near Pl. de Pontevedra and Pl. de Riazor. During *mediodía* seemingly half of La Coruña crowds this classy cafeteria for *raciónes* of clam pasta (650ptas), lasagna (650ptas), and *croquetas* (300ptas). Vegetarians will rejoice over the *gazpacho* (300ptas). Open daily 8am-3am. Closed Thurs. Sept.-June .

Pizzería Bingo, Av. de Rubine, 11 (tel. 26 18 00). No numbers or door prizes here, but you might just shout "Bingo!" when you sink into their shrimp, salmon, and caviar pizzas (700-1000ptas). Open daily 1:30-4pm and 8pm-midnight.

Cervecería-Jamonería Otros Tiempos, C. Galeria, 54 (tel. 22 62 97). Festive and light, with enough beer paraphernalia to make your ex-roommate weep for joy. Bocadillos 250-500ptas. *Raciónes* 425-750ptas. Open daily 11am-2am.

SIGHTS

La Coruña's famous tourist magnet, the **Torre de Hércules,** towers over rusted ship carcasses on the west end of the peninsula. Hercules allegedly erected the tower upon the remains of his defeated enemy Gerión. Although the original Roman section is visible only from within, this 2nd-century structure is the last Roman lighthouse still shining. Enter through the lower of two entrances to creep around the original foundation, then climb a claustrophobic 237-step tunnel to the pinnacle. (Open daily July-Sept. 10am-7pm; Oct.-June 10am-6pm. 250ptas, children and seniors free.) Take the seaside path from the beaches (2km); walk or take bus #9 or 13 (100ptas).

At the other end of the peninsula, the 16th-century **Castelo de San Antón,** home of the **Museo Arqueológico** (tel. 20 59 94), juts into the bay. There is more than a 14th-century stone pig stuck with a large cross—the Bronze Age artifacts and phallic idols may make you go wild. (Open July-Sept. Tue.-Sat. 11am-9pm; Oct.-June Tue.-Sat. 10am-7pm; Sun. and holidays 11am-2:30pm. 300ptas.)

In the old town, simple arches and windows surround the cobbled **Praza de María Pita,** named for the heroine who held off attacking Brits in 1589. The three domes of the **Pazo Municipal** rise majestically from the north side. Close by, **Prazuela Santa Bárbara** borders a 15th-century convent of the same name. A small Gothic doorway opens to **Igrexa de Santa María del Campo,** with granite columns and a rose window. The **Real Academia Gallega** (Royal Galician Academy; tel. 20 73 08) decided to make the family seat of 19th-century novelist **Condesa Emilia Pardo Bazán** its headquarters. Its library contains 25,000 volumes on Galician literature, history, and culture. Next door, at C. Tabernas, 11, the academy devotes part of a museum to Pardo Bazán's work and part to a rotating exhibition of modern and 19th-century Galician art (open July-Sept. Mon.-Fri. 10am-1pm; Oct.-June Mon.-Fri. 10am-noon; free).

The **Orzán** and **Riazor beaches,** on the northwest side of the isthmus, pack in tanners, volleyball players, and surfers. A brand new **esplanade** connects the two and is already popular for family strolls and teenage groping. An original statue of two surfers hanging ten sits on the north end of the *paseo.*

Just up the esplanade from Pl. Orzán, the brand new **Museo Domus** (Museum of Man; tel. 22 89 47) houses three floors of interactive, high-tech exhibits on the human body. Watch "blood" spurt at 30mph from a pretend heart, hear "Hello, I love you" in over 30 languages (sadly, from a computer), and spend hours playing with microscopes, computers, and other fun gizmos. The entrance fee gets you into the Science Museum/Planetarium (tel. 27 91 56) in Parque de Santa Margarita as well. (Open July-Aug. Tues.-Sat. 11am-9pm, Sept.-June 10am-7pm, Sun. and festivals 11am-2:30pm. 400ptas, with student ID 100ptas.)

Back on the other side of the peninsula, the elegant **Jardín Méndez Núñez,** sandwiched between Av. Marina and the dock, has a clock snipped to botanical perfection, with arms that really do tell the correct time. Soothing **Jardín de San Carlos,** in the old part of the city, was originally planted in 1843 on the site of old Forte San Carlos and shelters the tomb of Sir John Moore. Locals say killing this incompetent gen-

eral cost Napoleon his crown, since Wellington took over Moore's command. Take a stroll and smell the eucalyptus in the **Parque de Santa Margarita.**

ENTERTAINMENT

Summer nightlife in La Coruña reflects the cheerful nature of the peninsula. **Cafe-Bar La Barra,** C. Riego de Agua, 33, offers innocent entertainment all day long. After about 10am, students and old men gather around its wood tables to play cards, dominoes, and parcheesi (open 9am-2am). The **Teatro Principal** on Av. Marina, next door to the post office, stages local plays and international productions. Residents bar hop around **C. Franja, C. La Florida, C. San Juan,** and surrounding side streets. When bars die down at around 2am, discos along the **two beaches** start making a ruckus. Also try the discos and cafes on **C. Juan Florez** and **C. Sol. Pirámide,** Juan Florez, 50 (tel. 27 61 57), which play dance music to rouse the dead. **Picasso** and **Lautrec,** opposite each other on C. Sol, attract the artistically inclined.

Although celebrated in many parts of Europe, **La Noche de San Juan** (June 23) is greeted with particular fervor in La Coruña since it coincides with the opening of sardine season. Locals light the traditional *aguardiente* bonfires and spend the night leaping over the flames (contrary to the image that comes to mind, the rite ensures fertility) and gorging on sardine flesh. If you drop an egg white in a glass of water on this night, it will assume the form of your future spouse's occupation; many are led to believe they'll marry a dairy farmer or a cow. The last two weeks of August bring concerts, parades, folk dancing, and a mock naval battle to honor María Pita.

La Coruña's **soccer** team, Deportivo de La Coruña, the 1995 Spanish first-division champions, plays by the beach in **Estadio de Riazor** from April through June; check local papers or any bar for information.

■ Near La Coruña

Betanzos (pop. 12,000) assumes an isolated persona despite its position at a crucial transportation intersection, 23km east of La Coruña and 38km south of El Ferrol. Cafes line the central **Praza García Hermanos,** where a statue of the brothers García, the city's great benefactors, stands. One block behind the statue to the left, the **tourist office** in the *biblioteca-museo* offers a map with a walking tour of the old city (open July-Sept. Mon.-Fri. 10am-1pm and 4-8pm, Sat.-Sun. 10am-1pm). **Igrexa de San Fransisco,** located several blocks down the hill from Praza Hamanos, features a stunning number of carved pigs, bulls, and dogs. San Fransisco de Batanzos himself rests on the backs of a huge bear and boar, surrounded by his faithful puppies. The old **Jewish quarter** lies across R. Cruz Verde, at the bottom of the hill leading to the old city. Houses here all have two or three stories, since the first floor was always used as a stable. Betanzos's great **festival** involves the launching of the world's largest paper balloon (about 25m high) on the night of San Roque on August 16th. On the 18th and 25th, watch for the boat festival, *Romería*, during which Betanzos's natives adorn their tiny fishing boats with flowers and float down the river Mandeo to Canarias for feasts, wine, and gleeful insanity.

For **currency exchange,** try **Banco Central Hispano,** on the Central Plaza (open Mon.-Fri. 8:30am-2:30pm; no commission). For **ATM** access, head across the Plaza to Banco Bilbao Vizcaya. Eggs, cheese, and produce arrive in wheelbarrows at the plaza's **market** (Mon., Thurs., and Sat. 9am-1pm). For medical assistance, call the **Red Cross** at tel. 77 15 15. **Police** answer at tel. 77 06 02. The **telephone code** is (9)81.

Betanzos is a half-day trip from La Coruña. **Buses** run from La Coruña and El Ferrol (every 30min., Sun. every hr., 45min., 230ptas). IASA (tel. 23 90 01) buses also run elsewhere along the *rías*. The **train station** sits across the river. Two trains per day go between La Coruña and El Ferrol, stopping in Betanzos. The bus is easier.

Some think **Miño,** 12km north of Betanzos, has the nicest beach in the Rías Altas. On Saturday afternoons in **Pontedeume,** 22km from Betanzos, workers at the town market cook *pulpo* (octopus) in huge copper urns and mock the citizens of Betanzos for making that ridiculously huge balloon. You can reach both towns on bus lines heading to El Ferrol (every 30min., 280ptas).

NORTH RÍAS ALTAS

Not as isolated as the Costa de la Muerte, these urbane *rías* become calmer as they moving eastward. Old lighthouses, churches, and the remains of a wall or two dot the green countryside. In the misty mountains of Galicia, the weather is anything but predictable (even in summer), but views are spectacular year-round. Thanks to increasing popularity among vacationing Spaniards, the north Rías Altas have the capital resources that enabled them to create a transportation system, rendering the unspoiled coastline accessible (see **La Coruña: Buses**, p. 190).

■ Rías de Cedeira and Vivero

Where buses and trains seldom tread, hitchhiking is futile, and ferny rainforests give way to soft, empty beaches. Welcome to Cedeira and Vivero. Thick mists veil the valleys of these northernmost *rías*. Buses and FEVE trains run inland to Vivero from El Ferrol, but the sporadic coastal bus is preferable, allowing you to hop off anytime.

CEDEIRA

When cuckolding Lancelot fled England to escape the ire of King Arthur, he allegedly landed in Cedeira (pop. 8000), founding the town and sowing his seed. Set on its own *ría* 32km northeast of El Ferrol and 84km northeast of La Coruña, this small town offers pretty beaches and breathtaking scenery. There's not much to do except watch the tide, but no one seems to mind.

Near the second bus stop, the **tourist office**, C. Ezequiel Lopez, 22 (tel. 48 21 87), hands out snazzy brochures. (Open July-Aug., Mon.-Fri. 10:30am-2pm and 6-9pm, Sun. and holidays 12-2pm; May-June and Sept., Mon.-Fri. 10:30am-2pm and 4:30-8pm, Sat. 10:30am-2pm, Sun. and holidays noon-2pm.) **Bus** service is fairly sparse. To get to Vivero or Ortigueira, take an **IASA** bus from C. Ezequiel Lopez, 28, to Campo do Hospital (5 per day, 15min., 120ptas), where you change to another IASA bus (Campo do Hospital-Viviero: 1¾hr., 535ptas). Seven RIALSA buses per day run from Cedeira to El Ferrol (1hr., 490ptas). For medical care, call the **Red Cross**, C. Muelle, at tel. 48 26 22, and for other dangers call the **police** (tel. 48 07 25). The **post office** is on Av. Zumalacárrequi, 17 (tel. 48 05 52; open Mon.-Fri. 8:30am-2pm, Sat. 9am-2pm). The **postal code** is 15350. The **telephone code** is (9)81.

Hostal Chelsea, Pr. Sagrado Corazón, 9 (tel. 48 23 40), hosts guests in light-filled rooms around the corner from the first bus stop and near the beach (doubles with shower and TV 3500-3700ptas). For a small town, Cedeira has amassed a surprising number of local specialties. Open-faced *empanadas* are unique to the town, and locals love to snack on S-shaped sugar cookies *("eses")*. Commendable *bodegas* and *mesones* line both sides of the *ría*. **Taberna da Calexa,** Tras. Elrexa, 7 (tel. 48 20 09), up a tiny staircase off the road leading to the church, serves Galician wine (100ptas per glass) behind medieval stone walls, complemented with a wide variety of homemade *raciones* (mussels in vinaigrette 400ptas).

The **Santuario de San Andrés de Teixido** (a steep 12km hike from town) looks out over the sea from 620m above, the highest coastline in Europe. Closer to town lies the hermitage of **San Antonio de Corbeiro,** an easy two-km walk up a gentle slope. From the tourist office, turn left and follow signs to the turnoff (0.5km farther on the left), then it's up, up, and away. The hermitage is a white structure above the *ría*, high enough to send any acrophobe into a cold sweat. A steep tortuous 6km climb past the turnoff for San Antonio is the lighthouse **Faro de Punta Candieira.** The **Curro festival** (4th Sun. in June) entails a round-up of the wild horses that live nearby. Mid-August, meanwhile, is devoted to the **Feria de la Virgen del Mar.**

VIVERO (VIVEIRO)

The tourist brochure's assertion *"No es un sueño. Existe."* ("It's not a dream. It exists.") may seem a bit much, but seaside Vivero (pop. 14,000) does have a timeless quality. It is almost impossible for visitors to picture the town without envisioning fishing poles arching off a bridge. Peace, nearby beaches, and July *fiestas* draw a flotilla of Spanish tourists every summer. The nearest beach is in the resort town of **Covas**, 1km across the river from Vivero. If you tire of Covas, **Playa de Area** suns itself 4km from Vivero, and **Playa de Sacido** is farther away (6km). The first weekend of July is marked by the *Rapa das Bestas* but the main *fiestas* take place the last week in July. Vivero's *encierro* (running of the bulls) cures even the worst hangover.

Vivero's **tourist office** (tel. 56 08 79), Av. Ramón Canosa, hands out a decent map and posts *pensiones* on their bulletin board (open daily 11am-2pm and 5-7pm). **Banks** and **ATMs** line Av. Galicia. For the **Red Cross,** dial 56 22 00; for the **police,** call tel. 56 29 22 (091 or 092 in **emergencies**). The **post office** (tel. 56 09 27), is 20m past the market away from town (open Mon.-Fri. 8:30am-2pm, Sat. 9:30am-1pm). This is the only town in the Rías Altas with **motorcycle rentals.** They **rent cars** and **bikes** as well at Viajes Arifran, C. Rosalía de Castro, 54 (tel. 56 04 97 or 56 06 89). (Open Mon.-Fri. 9:30am-1pm and 4-7pm, Sat. 9:30am-1:30pm; July-Aug. only. Motorcycle about 9000ptas per day, bicycle 1000ptas per day.)

Fonda Bossanova, Av. Galicia, 11 (tel. 56 01 50), one block from the bus station in the direction of Covas, has small, mostly interior rooms (singles 2000ptas, doubles 3000ptas). On the first floor, the owner pleases locals with a 1000ptas *menú* and delicious desserts. On the same road heading toward Vivero is **Camping Vivero** (tel. 56 00 04). Follow the signs to the flagged reception hut. A cafe and broad beach are just steps away from this second-class campsite. (Reception open 9am-11pm. 425ptas per person, per tent, and per car. Electricity 425ptas. Open June-Sept.)

The obscenely huge Mega-Claudio **supermarket** is beside the bus station (open Mon.-Sat. 9:30am-9pm). Budget *mesones* proliferate around Pr. Maior. **Mesón Xoaquín,** R. Irmans Vilarponte, 19 (tel. 56 27 56), up from the square, serves an 850ptas *menú* in a stone *comedor* with stuffed boars and snazzy red tablecloths (open daily 1-4pm and 8-10pm). **A Cepa,** R. Fernández Victorio, 7, dishes out incredibly cheap tapas: *chipirones* 200ptas, *patatas bravas* 110ptas, and the mysterious *bikini* 150ptas (open noon-3pm and 7:30pm-midnight).

Bus companies **IASA** (tel. 56 01 03), Trav. Marina, and **ERSA,** Pr. Lugo, 2 (tel. 56 03 90), recently merged. Together, they serve: La Coruña (5 per day, 4hr., 1590ptas); El Ferrol (5 per day, 2hr., 950ptas); Lugo (5 per day, 2½hr., 1100-1250ptas); and Ribadeo (2 per day, 1½hr., 575ptas). **ALSA** buses go from Ribadeo to Oviedo. **FEVE trains** (tel. 55 07 22; down Trav. Marina past Pr. Lugo), chug twice daily to: Oviedo (2 per day, 5hr., 1805ptas); Ribadeo (3 per day, 1hr., 485ptas, connections to Ortigueira, Barqueiro, and Vicedo); and El Ferrol (3 per day, 2hr., 6750ptas).

■ Ría de Ribadeo

Even when inundated with summer residents, Ribadeo's stunning Galician scenery gives the town a ghostly, deserted air. It is the last *gallego* outpost before the Asturian border. Choose your mountain, *ría*, Cantabrian Sea view, or enjoy more than one, then pray for a clear day—the town has little else to offer.

At the water's edge, both the **Paseo Marítimo** and the **Praia Os Bloques,** just past the dock, harbor spectacular views. High above the *ría*, a three-kilometer walk from town through farm land (follow the signs), sits the **Igrexa de Santa Cruz.** If the climb doesn't take your breath away, the view of the eucalyptus countryside and crazy-blue ocean will. Three kilometers in the other direction, at the **Praia de Rocas Blancas,** a red and white *faro* (lighthouse) towers above the water.

The **tourist office** (tel. 12 86 89), in the center of Pr. España, distributes a decent map. (Open summer Tues.-Sat. 9:30am-1:30pm and 4-7pm, Mon. 4-7pm; in winter Mon.-Fri. 4-7pm; Sun. and holidays 11am-1pm.) Change money at **Banco Central His-**

pano, C. San Rogue, 17. **Rent a car** at Autos Eo, Pasarón Ilasta (tel. 11 04 89). In an **emergency,** call 091 or 092. The **post office,** Av. Asturias, 17 (tel. 12 82 48), is under-appreciated (open Mon.-Fri. 8:30am-2:30pm, Sat. 9:30am-1pm). The **postal code** is 27700. The **telephone code** is (9)82. Several hostels sit on C. San Roque, on the way from the train station. On Pr. España across from the church is **Hostal Costa Verde,** 13 (tel. 12 86 81; inquire in the bar downstairs). Its rooms and bathrooms are pristine, and some rooms have balconies. (Singles 1500ptas. Doubles 3000-4500ptas.) **Camping Ribadeo** (tel. 13 11 67), charges 425ptas per person, tent, and car. **Supermercado El Arbol** (tel. 72 58 50), on Av. Galicia, is well-stocked (open Tues.-Sat. 9am-2pm and 5-8pm, Mon. 9:30am-2pm). Low-priced *cafeterías* pepper Pr. España. **Restaurante Ros Mary,** C. San Francisco, 3, has an 900ptas *menú* of hake, steak, and *fabadas* (open daily 8am-2pm).

Getting in and out of here isn't that hard. The **FEVE train station** (tel. 13 07 39), is a 15-minute walk from Pr. España along R. Villafranco Bierzo (and through 4 name changes; info open daily 6am-9pm). Trains crawl east on the coastal route from Oviedo (2 per day, 4hr., 1290ptas) and El Ferrol (3 per day, 3½hr., 1140ptas). Trains stop at Ortigueira and Vivero, too. **IASA buses** (tel. 22 17 60) run to: Viver (2 per day, 1250ptas); La Coruña (10 per day, 3hr., 1000ptas); and El Ferrol (4 per day, 1025ptas). The **ALSA** station off Pr. España runs buses to Oviedo (4 per day, 4hr., 1550ptas). Buses leave from Av. Rosalía de Castro, in front of Viajes Terra y Mar. From Pr. España, take C. San Roque (the upper left corner), head left for two blocks, turn right, go downhill, and walk about 150m to the travel agency.

No More Bull

Instead of typical Spanish *corridas* (bullfights), Galician *pueblos* Vivero and San Lorenz host an event in the first weekend of July called *La Rapa das Bestas.* This spectacle involves capturing and breaking in wild mountain horses. A dozen or so men attempt to brand and cut hair from the manes and tales of galloping, bucking, kicking equines in a ring much smaller than a *plaza de toros.* Both horses and men frequently suffer serious injuries. A famous picture depicts a fiery one-armed man biting the horse's mane with his teeth—mmm, mmm good.

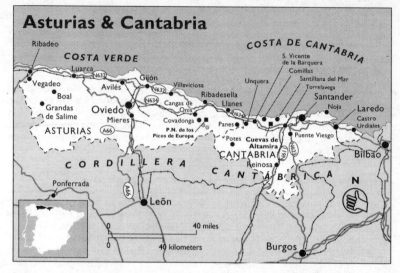

Asturias and Cantabria

Seething cliffs and hell-reaching ravines mutilate the lands of Asturias and Cantabria, wedged between País Vasco and Galicia. Their National Parks, especially the Picos de Europa, linking the two regions, are popular spots for hunting, fishing, and hiking.

Apart from industrial centers and prosperous dairy farms, Cantabria has grown rich as a summer getaway for the Spanish elite. Meanwhile, a decline of the mining, steel, and shipping industries has crippled Asturias, where traditional crafts-making techniques are charming but debilitating. Authorities have recently focused economic resources on scientific research and green tourism. They actively promote an extensive network of country inns in old mansions, cottages, and *casas de indianos*, rambling Victorian houses built by Asturians who scored big in the Americas.

The Reconquest against the Moors began in Asturias. Agricolar Moors had little use for the rough northern terrain, so the Christians made it their northern base. As the Christian kingdoms expanded southward, Asturias was gradually absorbed into the Kingdom of León, and later Castile. Its legendary blue collar resistance to the Fascists during the Civil War inspired Republican forces throughout the peninsula. Cantabria was the only region never to fall to the Moors. It was always Castile's outlet to the sea.

Because of the variegated terrain, public transportation in the Asturias and Cantabria regions can be erratic, and the weather unpredictable. But the roads are striking, winding through deciduous and alpine forests or green valleys quilted with cornfields and pastures.

Resurrecting a Tower of Bable

Galicians have Gallego, Catalans have Catalan, and Asturians have...Bable? Though it's not an official language, the dialect has returned with the sweeping post-Franco reassertion of regional tradition. You will not hear it on the street, even though it is taught to children in Bable class. Rather, Bable is a codification of a hodge-podge of more than 10 distinct traditional dialects originating in different corners of Asturias—grammar borrowing from many while belonging to none. As a result, almost no one is fluent in the tongue, and more than a handful of grandmothers express bewilderment at their grandchildren's *bable*-ing.

ASTURIAS

■ Oviedo

Smack in the middle of Asturias's plunging green valleys sits the region's capital and transportation hub—gray, urban Oviedo (pop. 200,000), where cars roar down the four-lane streets of the new city and exhaust mingles with industrial filth. Oviedo's monastic origins are mostly buried beneath cement and smokestacks, but the old city is still worth a gander. Stock up on info and supplies for your trip to the Picos de Europa, then wander through the *sidieria*-lined streets and look in on the city's celebrated cathedral.

ORIENTATION AND PRACTICAL INFORMATION

Calle de Uría bisects the city, running northwest to southeast from its origin at the **RENFE station.** On the west side of C. Uría is the leafy, luscious **Campo de San Francisco;** on the east side is the old city, with **Plaza Mayor** and **Plaza de Alfonso II,** known to locals as **Plaza de la Catedral** and to tourists as **Turismo** turf.

The **first FEVE train station** (serving Cantabria and País Vasco) is to the left as you leave RENFE, on **Avenida Santander.** To reach the **bus stations** from FEVE, take **Calle Jerónimo Ibrán,** on which Económicos (EASA) and Turytrans buses stop, to **Plaza General Primo de Rivera,** where the bus biggie, ALSA, has its unmarked station underneath the shopping arcade. To reach C. Uría from Pl. General Primo de Rivera, take a soft left onto C. Fray Ceferino, which ends at C. Uría.

The **second FEVE** train station (serving the Galicia-Asturias route) is way east of the bus stations on **Calle Victor Chávarri.** To reach C. Uría from here, take C. Victor Chávarri, which becomes Alcalde García Conde and ends at Pl. Carbayón. On the far side of the plaza, pick up C. Argüelles and you'll hit C. Uría. The ALSA bus station's info office has a good **map** on the wall.

Tourist Office: Pl. Alfonso II (tel. 521 33 85). Busy staff has maps and advice on Picos treks. English spoken. Open Mon.-Fri. 9:30am-1:30pm and 4:30-6:30pm, Sat. 9am-2pm, Sun. 11am-2pm.

Telephones: Telefónica, C. Foncalada, 6. **Faxes** sent to US (754ptas first page, 580ptas per additional page plus phone charge). Open Mon.-Fri. 9:30am-2pm and 4-10:30pm, Sat. 10am-2pm; off-season Mon.-Sat. 10am-2pm and 5-10pm. The phone company recently added a 5 as the first digit to all regional phone numbers. If you see a number without a 5 in an old publication, tack one on.

Budget Travel: TIVE, C. Calvo Sotelo, 5 (tel. 523 60 58), past the Campo San Francisco, up from C. Marqués de Santa Cruz. Info on nearby hiking and travel; excursions. ISIC 700ptas. HI card 500ptas, over 26 1000ptas. Open Mon.-Fri. 8am-3pm.

Trekking: Dirección Regional de la Juventud, C. Calvo Sotelo, 5 (tel. 523 11 12). A comprehensive pamphlet on camping, youth hostels, and hiking plus info on cultural activities. Open Mon.-Fri. 10am-1pm. **Federación Asturiana de Montaña,** C. de Julián Clavería (tel. 525 23 62), is a 30min. walk from the city center near the bull ring, or take bus #2. Call first; if you walk, get the big map from Turismo. They organize excursions, stock good trail maps, and provide mountain guides, info about weather conditions, and the best hiking routes. Open Mon.-Fri. 6-8:30pm.

Currency Exchange: Banco central Hispano, on the corner of C. Uría and C. Argüelles. Open Mon.-Fri. 8:30am-2:30pm. Oct.-May 8:30am-4:30pm.

El Corte Inglés: The feudal lord of superstores, now at two convenient locations. **C. General Alorza,** opposite the ALSA station, and **C. Uría. Currency exchange, telephones,** groceries. Open Mon.-Sat. 10am-9:30pm.

Flights: Aeropuerto de Ranón/ Aeropuerto Nacional de Asturias (tel. 555 18 33), in Avilés, northwest of Oviedo. **Aviaco** (tel. 512 76 03) flies to Madrid, Barcelona, and London. **Prabus,** C. Marqués de Pidal, 20 (tel. 525 47 51), runs frequent buses from the ALSA station to the airport. **Iberia** (tel. (985) 12 76 07).

Trains: RENFE, C. Uría (tel. 524 33 64 or 525 02 02), at the junction with Av. Santander. Pay attention to the kind of train: a slow local through the mountains can double your travel time. Info open daily 7:45am-11:15pm. To: Gijón (every 30min. until 11pm, 30min., 300-345ptas); León (8 per day, 2½hr., 850-1470ptas); Madrid (6 per day, 6½-8hr., 4200ptas); Barcelona (2 per day, 13hr., 6000ptas). **FEVE,** Av. Santander (tel. 528 40 96 or 529 76 56; from RENFE, turn left as you exit and walk downhill; 2min. To: Llanes (3 per day, 4½hr., 870ptas); Santander (2 per day, 5-7½hr., 1650ptas); Bilbao (1 per day at 8:15am, 7hr., 2570ptas). Another **FEVE,** C. Victor Chavarri, 19 (tel. 521 90 26), for trains running west as far as Ferrol. To Ferrol (2 per day, 7½hr., 2420ptas) and Ribadeo (2 per day, 4hr., 1290ptas).

Buses: ALSA, Pl. General Primo de Rivera, 1 (tel. 528 12 00), unmarked, on the lower level of a shopping arcade. To: Barcelona (2 per day, 12hr., 4850ptas); Burgos (2 per day, 4hr., 1630ptas); León (8 per day, 2hr., 1005ptas); La Coruña (3 per day, 6hr., 1360ptas); Madrid (7 per day, 6hr., 3655-5800ptas); Vigo (2 per day, 9hr., 4210ptas); Santiago (3 per day, 8hr., 3620ptas); Santander (1 per day, 3hr., 1755ptas). **Económicos (EASA),** C. Jerónimo Ibrán, 1 (tel. 529 00 39). To: Cangas de Onís (12 per day, 1½hr., 670ptas); Covadonga (5 per day, 1¾hr., 785ptas); Arenas de Cabrales (4 per day, 2¼hr., 945ptas); Llanes (11 per day, 2½hr., 1000ptas). Significantly fewer buses Sat.-Sun.

Public Transportation: TUA (tel. 522 24 22) runs **buses** (110ptas). 8am-10pm. #4 goes to bus, FEVE, and RENFE stations; #2 goes to the youth hostel/hospital; #2, 3, 5, and 7 run from RENFE to near the old part of the city.

Taxis: Radio Taxi (tel. 525 00 00 or 525 25 00).

Car Rental: Avis, C. Ventura Rodríguez, 12 (tel. 524 13 83). From 9600ptas per day. Weekend specials. Open Mon.-Fri. 9am-1pm and 4-7:30pm, Sat. 9am-1pm.

Luggage Storage: At RENFE station (lockers 300ptas). Open daily 7am-11pm. At ALSA bus station (lockers 200-300ptas). Open daily 7am-11pm.

Red Cross: (tel. 521 60 93).

Late-Night Pharmacy: Check listings in *La Voz de Asturias* (110ptas), or *La Nueva España* (110ptas).

Hospital: Hospital General de Asturias, C. J. Clavería (tel. 510 61 00).

Police: Policía Municipal, C. Quintana (tel. 521 80 29). **Lost Property:** (tel. 521 32 05). **Emergency:** tel. 091 or 092.

Post Office: C. Alonso Quintanilla, 1 (tel. 521 41 86). From C. Uría, turn left onto C. Argüelles and left again. Open for stamps and Lista de Correos Mon.-Fri. 8:30am-8:30pm, Sat. 9:30am-2pm. **Postal Code:** 33060.

Telephone Code: (9)8.

ACCOMMODATIONS

A plethora of *pensiones* pack the new city near the transport stations. Accommodations are generally much cleaner than their facades suggest. Try **C. Uría, C. Campoamor** (1 block east), and **C. Nueve de Mayo** (a continuation of C. Manuel Pedregal, 1 block farther east). Near the cathedral, try C. Jovellanos.

Residencia Juvenil Ramón Menéndez Pidal, C. Julián Clavería, 14 (tel. 523 20 54), across from the hospital. Take bus #2 from C. Uría. TV room, library, and dining room. Call first; few beds in summer. 720ptas, over 26 1000ptas.

Pensión Pomar, C. Jovellanos, 7 (tel. 522 27 91). Super-clean, airy rooms with big windows and blue sinks in a spacious old building. Singles 1500-2000ptas. Doubles 3000-3500ptas. Triples 4500ptas. Prices fluctuate with demand.

Pensión Martinez, C. Jovellanos, 5 (tel. 521 53 44). Clean rooms with sinks. Communal bathrooms. Singles 1500ptas. Doubles 3000ptas. Triples 3000ptas.

Pensión Riesgo, C. Nueve de Mayo, 16, 1st fl. (tel. 521 89 45). Long oriental rug in foyer leads to smallish, clean, unglamorous rooms with cool bedside lamps. Singles 1800ptas. Doubles 3500ptas.

Hospedaje Central, C. Dr. Casal, 8, 2nd fl. (tel. 522 30 55), 2 blocks up on the right coming from the RENFE station along C. Nueve de Mayo. On a quiet pedestrian street opposite a church. Hardwood floors, interior singles, and beds that go squishhhh. Slightly worn, but cleaner than the stairway suggests. Singles 1500ptas (often full). Doubles 2500-3000ptas. Cheaper without a shower.

FOOD

Order *sidra* by the bottle (usually 250ptas)—it goes fast, and much of it ends up on the floor. For the best *sidra* experience, head to the wooden-beamed, ham-hung **sidrerías** where waiters pour *sidra* from above their heads into your glass to release its aroma. This is no cheap New England brew—it's as tart and tangy as the local pastry, *carbayon*. Try the almond and egg yolk delight at **Camilo de Blas** (C. Jovellones). Asturias's typical dish is the meaty, bean-based *fabada*, with chunks of sausage and ham. Cheap restaurants line **C. Fray Cegerino,** running between the bus and train stations. **Gran Oleada,** C. Fr. Ceterino, 30, is a Chinese restaurant advertising a 495ptas *menú*—check for yourself, it's hard to believe. The posh indoor **market** (with an **ATM**), is on C. Fontán, off Pl. Mayor (open Mon.-Sat. 8am-8pm). For groceries, try **El Corte Inglés** (see p. 198) or C. La Lila.

Mesón Luferca, a.k.a. **La Casa Real del Jamón,** C. Covadonga, 20 (tel. 521 78 02). You may be used to those hanging hams, but nothing can prepare you for the sheer quantity and density of the pig parts in this place. Many meaty *tapas* from 400ptas. Open Mon.-Sat. 8:30am-10:30pm.

Sidrería Astoria, C. Santa Clara (tel. 21 16 09). There's ham hanging from the ceiling, ham on your plate, *sidra*-drenched sawdust on the floor. Ham, pork, or sausage, and—of course—*sidra* for 500ptas. *Menú* 900ptas. Open daily 9am-3am.

Restaurante Pinochio, C. Altamirana (tel. 522 35 21), a block up from the cathedral heading toward Pl. Mayor. A giant Pinocchio (honestly) watches the airy *comedor*. 1100ptas *menú* includes steak topped with cheese and a delicious nut tart. An array of Italian specialties. Open Tues.-Sun. 1-4pm and 8pm-midnight.

Casa Albino, C. Gascona, 15 (tel. 521 04 45), a right turn from the FEVE-Galicia station. Bullfights on TV and a few Real Madrid photos for atmosphere, but the 990ptas *menú* extends to *fabada* and braised lamb. Two dozen shrimp and *sidra* for an unbelievable 575ptas. Open daily 9:30am-5pm and 7pm-1am.

ENTERTAINMENT

The streets south of the cathedral, around **Plazas Riego, da Fontán,** and **del Paraguas,** teem with noisy *sidrerías* and clubs. **Bar Riego,** on Pl. Riego, serves rich *batidos* (milkshakes) on a breezy *terraza*. This place oozes style. Wine connoisseurs follow **la ruta de los vinos,** from *bodega* to *bodega* along C. Rosal, with *copas* 100-200ptas. On C. Cuna, between Alcalde García Conde and C. Jovellanos, **Danny's Jazz Café** soothes guests lounging on red velvet couches with a cool dose of jazz recordings and videos. The **Teatro Filarmónica,** C. Mendizábel, 3 (tel. 521 27 62), hosts dramatic productions in September, and musical concerts the rest of the year. Check the local paper for playhouse listings. Oviedo celebrates its **patronal fiesta** in honor of San Mateo on September 13-22.

SIGHTS

In Clarín's 19th-century novel *La Regenta*, Ana Osorio throws herself at the feet of her ecclesiastical lover in Oviedo's **cathedral,** Pl. Alfonso II (tel. 522 10 33). Finished for the most part in 1388, the cathedral's 80m **tower** offers great views of the city's rooftops. The exterior seems charred due to excessive pollution, but stained-glass windows illuminate the stone interior. Painted with crushed lapis lazuli stone, the brilliant blue ceiling above the altar seems to shed its own light. In the north transept, the **Capilla del Rey Castro** houses the royal pantheon, designated by Alfonso II as the resting place of Asturian monarchs. The more unusual **Capilla de San Pedro** houses an intense sculpture in metal relief depicting Simon Magnus being dropped from the sky by hideous demons (cathedral open daily 10am-1pm and 4-7pm; free). The cathedral complex also houses a museum, a *cámara santa* (holy chamber), and a cloister. The museum holds a fine collection of scepters, chalices, candelabras, processional crosses, and liturgical formal wear. (All three open Mon.-Fri. 10am-8pm, Sat. 10am-6:30pm. 400ptas, youngsters 300ptas. Thurs. free.)

Just up C. Santa Ana from Pl. Alfonso II is the **Museo de Bellas Artes,** C. Santa Ana, 1, and C. Rúa, 8 (tel. 521 30 61). The two-building, three-story complex displays ample Asturian art and a small collection of 16th- to 20th-century (mainly Spanish) art. (Open Tues.-Fri. 10:30am-1:30pm and 5-8pm, Sat.-Sun. and holidays 11am-2pm. Free.) For a change of pace, check out the temporary exhibits at the **Centro de Arte Moderno,** C. Alonso Quintanilla, 2, opposite the post office (open Mon.-Sat. 5:30-9pm). Asturian Pre-Romanesque—the first European attempt to blend architecture, sculpture (including human representations), and mural painting since the fall of the Roman Empire—was developed under Alfonso II (789-842) and perfected under his son Ramiro I, for whom the style is named *Ramirense.* Two beautiful examples of that style, **Santa María del Naranco** and **San Miguel de Lillo,** tower above Oviedo on **Monte Naranco.** (Both open Mon.-Sat. 9:30am-1pm and 3-7pm, Sun. 9:30am-1pm; Oct.-April Mon.-Sat. 9:30am-1pm and 3-5pm, Sun. 10am-1pm. 200ptas, Mon. free.)

HIKING

A good **English guidebook** to the trails and towns of the area is Robin Walker's *Picos de Europa.* If you read *castellano,* check out the many publications of **Miguel Ángel Andrados.** Helpful organizations and businesses are listed below, all based in Oviedo unless otherwise noted. Most base towns in the Picos support excursion-organizers; check specific towns for listings (see **Camping,** p. 55).

Federación Asturiana de Montaña, Dirección Regional de la Juventud, and **TIVE** travel agency (see p. 198 for addresses and phone numbers). Referral to mountain guides, organized tour groups, and instructors in everything from paragliding to kayaking and spelunking.

ICONA, C. Arquitecto Reguera, 13, 2nd fl. (tel. 524 14 12). Excursions, camping and trail info, and a 30min. video on flora, fauna, and cheese. Another office in Cangas de Onís (Av. Covadonga, 35; tel. 584 91 54).

Dirección Regional de Deportes, Pl. España (tel. (527 23 47). Info and referrals for outdoor sports and mountaineering.

Oxígeno, C. Manuel Pedregal (tel. 522 79 75), a continuation of C. Nueve de Mayo, past C. Fray Ceferino heading toward RENFE. A hardcore mountaineer shop with two walls of maps and guides; Andrados' hiking books. Staff of Picos veterans enthusiastically doles out advice. Open Mon.-Sat. 10am-1:30pm and 4:30-8:30pm.

Deportes Tuñon, C. Campoamor, 8. Sells camping gear on the block between C. Dr. Casal and C. Fray Ceferino. Extensive selection of camping and rock-climbing gear, long underwear, and a few maps. Open Mon.-Sat. 10am-1:30pm and 4:30-8:30pm.

PICOS DE EUROPA

As the crow flies, it is a scant 25km from sea level to the 2600m heights of the Picos de Europa. Other European ranges may be higher, but few match the beauty of the Sierra's abrupt, jagged profile. Intrepid mountaineers, novice trekkers, and even idle admirers flock to the Picos, which compose the most notable section of the Cordillera Cantábrica, a larger range that extends across northern Spain. Most of the Picos area has been granted maximum environmental protection as the Picos de Europa National Park. Buses from Santander and León cover the range, but the best place to start is Oviedo, base-camp of many *federaciones* (hiking organizations).

■ Orientation

Route AS-114 runs along the north edge of the Picos, intersecting Route N-621 at Panes. N-621 continues north and east toward the coast and Santander. To the south and west, N-621 leads past a turnoff for Palencia in León, on to Potes, and then deadends 25km later at **Fuente Dé.** On the west edge of AS-114 sits **Cangas de Onís,** 10 km north of **Covadonga.** Sixty kilometers east, **Arenas de Cabrales** is a prime base

ASTURIAS AND CANTABRIA

¡Expansión!

Hikers rejoice—in May 1995, the Spanish Parliament approved the creation of the 160,500-acre **Picos de Europa National Park,** quadrupling the former 40,000-acre Covadonga National Park in one giant leap of the pen. The area is now the largest national park in continental Europe, extending into Asturias, Cantabria, and Castilla y León, from just below Route AS-114 to several kilometers above N-621. The brown bear, capercaillie (a bird), and wild mountain goat are all stamped with the park's protective seal. Certain measures are enforced within the park's boundaries (4-wheel drive vehicles banned, camping only permitted in designated sites, and construction strictly regulated), but the main object of the park is to preserve endangered species, not to fence in natural beauty.

---

for hiking. Larger **Potes,** 50km south of Panes on N-621, is a less convenient, more touristy, and more expensive take-off point. Most trails in the Picos traverse the region's north-south axis between Arenas de Cabrales and Fuente Dé. Getting to the Picos is relatively easy. The bus company **ALSA,** and its subsidiary **Económicos,** are the best way to get around. The Oviedo and Cangas de Onís tourist offices stock schedules.

Albergues are ancient, non-heated buildings with bunks and access to cold water. **Casas** have hot water and wood stoves. In both cases you should bring a sleeping bag. Often only campers can find beds during July and August, and even this endeavor can be touch and go—many campgrounds and **refugios** (usually cabins with bunks but not blankets) fill up in high season. Call *hostales* or *pensiones* in June or earlier to make reservations. *Refugios* can generally only be contacted by portable phone or short-wave radio (the Guardia Civil can often help). In a jam, tourist offices can help you find a bed in a private residence.

Plan ahead! Covadonga does not have an ATM or a supermarket. Arenas has an **ATM,** but its small shops, while conveniently often open on Sunday, are pricey and limited. Stock up in Oviedo. If you set off alone (not recommended), leave a copy of your planned route so a rescue squad can be alerted if you don't return or call by a certain time. Always pack **warm clothes** and **rain gear.** If a heavy mist descends en route (as often happens), don't continue unless you know exactly where you're going. Just be patient and wait for the mist to clear (see **Camping,** p. 55).

■ Cangas de Onís

Founded after the Castilian victory over the Moors at Covadonga in 722, Cangas de Onís (pop. 3500) was the first capital of the Asturian monarchy and a launching pad for the Reconquest. Now the gateway to the **national park** spread across the Picos, this town of many postcard racks, though not as central as Arenas de Cabrales, is a great place to eat and sleep between excursions. The bus from Oviedo passes by the Romanesque **Puente Romano,** which arches gracefully over the Río Sella; it's worth backtracking the 300m from the bus stop just for a glimpse.

Practical Information The **tourist office** (tel. 584 80 05), in a glass kiosk in the park by the Ayuntamiento (on Av. Covadonga), has a map but little else (open daily 10am-2pm and 5-10:30pm; Oct.-April 10am-2pm and 4-7pm). One block toward Arenas de Cabrales from the tourist kiosk, the Covadonga National Park **Visitors Center,** in the Casa Daga, has a list of mountain *refugios* and a collection of maps (open daily 9am-9pm; fall and winter 9am-2pm and 4-6:30pm). Take a look at their large contour map in the courtyard in front, wander through the nature exhibit upstairs, and sit in on a short video description of the park. Down the street in the opposite direction from the kiosk, **Librería Imagen** stocks guides and maps. (Open daily 7am-9pm; Oct.-June Tues.-Sat. 8am-1:30pm and 3:30-7:30pm, Sun. 8am-3pm.) **Adventura,** Av. Covadonga, s/n (tel. 584 92 61 or 584 85 76), sets up various expeditions, including hik-

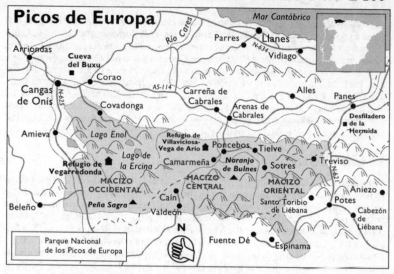

ing, canyoning, spelunking, canoeing, horseback riding, and bungee jumping (3000ptas per jump).

EASA, Av. Covadonga (tel. 584 81 33), across from the tourist office, regularly runs **buses** to: Oviedo (11 per day, 1½hr., 670ptas); Arenas de Cabrales (4 per day, 1hr., 280ptas); Llanes (3 per day, 2hr., 550ptas); and Madrid (1 per day, 10:50am, 7½hr., 3600ptas). **Municipal police,** in the Ayuntamiento, answer at tel. 584 85 58. The **Red Cross** is just above the **post office** (tel. 584 81 96), which is down Av. Covadonga. Take a right after two blocks (toward Oviedo) onto Av. Constantino González; it's on the left (open Mon.-Fri. 8:30am-2:30pm, Sat. 9:30am-1pm). The **postal code** is 33550. The **telephone code** is (9)8.

Accommodations and Food A few clean *pensiones* welcome guests on the main street, Av. Covadonga. With a sign on Av. Covadonga, but with its entrance on Av. Castilla, is the newly remodelled **Pensión Yolanda Labra,** Av. Castilla, 1, 1st fl. (tel. 90 44 33; doubles 3500ptas). Smaller operations, above restaurants and bars with signs reading *Hay Camas,* tend to be cheaper. **Restaurante El Choffer** (tel. 584 83 05) has smallish, clean rooms, firm beds, Oriental rugs, and hall baths. In the bar downstairs hangs a cigar-smokin' boar's head with hat and sunglasses (singles 1500ptas, doubles 3000ptas). Two-and-a-half kilometers down the road toward Covadonga (30min. on foot), at the turn-off for the cave, **Pensión Susierra** has clean, big doubles with baths and TVs (singles 3000ptas, doubles 5000ptas). Campers frequent the second-class **Camping Covadonga** (tel. 594 00 97), on Soto de Cangas about 5km up the road toward Covadonga (5 buses per day). Amenities include a cafeteria, bar, and showers. (525ptas per person, 400ptas per car, 450ptas per tent. Open Semana Santa and June-Sept. 20.) Some people camp illegally in a secluded meadow by the river.

After a rousing hike, few pleasures surpass a substantial meal in the land of *fabes* (beans) and *sidra.* Left of the park, **Supermercados El Arbol** sells preparations for a do-it-yourself meal (open Mon.-Fri. 9am-2pm and 5-8pm, Sat.-Mon. 9am-2pm). Most restaurants on Av. Covadonga serve *menús* slightly over 1000ptas; cheaper places with fewer tourists hide on side streets. By the church off Av. Coratorga, **Mesón El Overtense,** C. San Pelayo, 15 (tel. 584 81 62), serves up a 900ptas *menú* of *fabada,* trout, spaghetti, and fish soup.

Sights Walking into Cangas from the Roman bridge, turn left opposite the park and cross a modern bridge to **Capilla de Santa Cruz.** This Romanesque chapel sits atop the town's oldest monument, a Celtic *dolmen* (monolith). Priests hid from invading Moors in a cave underneath. Also check the **Cueva del Buxu** (BOO-shoo; 5km away), with walls adorned by 15,000-year-old paintings. Only 25 people are admitted to the cave each day, so arrive early (open Wed.-Sun. 10am-2pm and 4-6pm; 200ptas, Tues. free). To reach the cave, follow the main road to Arenas de Cabrales for 3km until the sign for the *cueva* directs you left. From here, it's a gradual two-kilometer climb past pastures and chicken coops. **Buses** to Covadonga, Llanes, and Arenas run near the Cueva del Buxu (ask to be dropped off at the Cruce de Susierra).

■ Covadonga

"This little mountain you see will be the salvation of Spain," prophesied Don Pelayo to his Christian army in 718, gesturing to the rocky promontory that soon would be the site of the first successful rebellion against the Moors. The *Reconquista* started in what is now the tiny town of Covadonga *(la donga),* about 10km east of Arenas. Nationalistic legend claims that the Virgin interceded with God on behalf of Don Pelayo's forces. Covadonga has a few impressive sights, but only the lakes will to occupy you for more than a couple of hours. With but a few permanent residents, the area is primarily a tourist magnet and training ground for young boys who enter the choir school at age 8 or 9 and are subsequently abandoned to the ravages of puberty.

Don Pelayo prayed to the Virgin perched atop a gushing waterfall in the **Santa Cueva** (Holy Cave). It now beckons pilgrims who crawl up its 50 steps, sometimes on their hands and knees. The virgin changes her lovely cloak every few days in the summer. Pilgrims and tourists now crowd the sanctuary (open daily 8am-10pm; free). The **Santuario de Covadonga,** a pale pink neo-Gothic basilica (1901), towers above the town (open daily 8am-10pm). The *Corona de la Virgen,* a crown of gold and silver studded with 1109 diamonds and 2000 sapphires, is on display in the **Museo del Tesoro,** across the square from the basilica. Underneath lies Jesus's crown, encrusted with sparklers (open daily 11am-2pm and 4-7pm; 200ptas). September 8 is the annual *Día de Covadonga,* the local festival.

Mountain climbers, go to the **info office** (tel. 584 60 35), across from the basilica, to be filled in on local accommodations and sights. This office, like the **tourist office** at the entrance to Covadonga, is open Tues.-Sun. 10am-2pm and 3-7pm. That is all. Spending the night in Cangas is cheaper than in *la donga,* but the light blue shutters of **Hospedería del Peregrino** (tel. 584 60 47), on the main highway downhill, open onto swoon-inducing views of the mountains and basilica (singles 2525-4175ptas, doubles 3120-5200ptas). The only **groceries** in town arrive twice a week (Wed. and Sat.) by truck—buy them from the driver at the Hospedería del Peregrino. Knock on the last door on the right. **EASA buses** (tel. 584 81 33), traveling from Oviedo (7 per day, 1¾hr., 785ptas) and Cangas (20min., 105ptas), grace Covadonga with two stops: one at the Hospedería and one uphill at the basilica. To reach Llanes or Arenas from Covadonga, you must backtrack to Cangas and catch a bus there.

■ Near Covadonga: Los Lagos de Enol y Ercina

Two buses per day (5 in July-Aug., 220ptas) run from Oviedo to Cangas and continue 12km higher, past Covadonga, en route to the sparkling **Lagos de Enol y Ercina** (Lakes of Enol and Ercina). Buses leave from the basilica at Covadonga, and return from a mountain traverse on a spectacular road hemmed in by cliffs and precipitous pastures. Along the way, cows and striking rock formations surround the crystal blue lakes. Don't make the trip if it's cloudy or else you will be *in* the clouds, guided and misguided by invisible mooing cows.

Two mountain *refugios* lie off the paths leading from the lakes. In summer, reserve in advance since food has to be brought in by helicopter. The **Refugio de Vega de Enol** (tel. 584 85 76) has 30 spots open year-round, with meals and guides provided.

Take highway C-6312 (Cangas de Onís-Panes, *desvío hacia* Covadonga y Lagos), go right at Lago Enol, and keep going to the *refugio* (450ptas per person, *pensión completa* 2500ptas). The **Refugio de Vegarredonda** (contact Refugios de Montaña de Asturias, tel. 584 89 16 or 908 47 18 84) is also two hours away, open year-round, and has guides, meals, hot showers, and kitchens (800ptas per night; breakfast 350ptas; from Lago Enol take highway A-6).

■ Arenas de Cabrales

If tourists valued natural beauty as much as paintings and monuments, Arenas (pop. 800) would be as packed as the Louvre in July. As it is, a fair number of outdoor enthusiasts come to this tiny town between Cangas and Potes in late summer to take advantage of the excellent hiking and climbing—Arenas makes an ideal, untouristed base for exploring the central Picos. It is also the place to try *queso de cabrales*, the local, pungent blue cheese created by mixing goat, cow, and sheep's milk, wrapping the mush in leaves, and stewing the whole mess in nearby caves for a few months.

Practical Information The **tourist office** (tel. 584 64 84), in Arenas, is small but helpful (open July-Sept. Tues.-Sun. 10am-2pm and 4-8pm). U.K. natives Jim and Peter at **Hotel Torrecerredo** (tel. 584 66 40) organize hiking/off-road excursions. They also dole out detailed trail guides for short hikes from Arenas; get one, because it's easy to get temporarily lost. Caja de Asturias has an **ATM.** For **police,** call the Guardia Civil in Carreña de Cabrales (tel. 584 50 04). The **post office** is up the street toward Cangas from the bus stop (open Mon.-Fri. 9am-1pm, Sat. 10am-noon). The **postal code** is 33554. Económicos (EASA) **buses** go west to Cangas de Onís and Oviedo four times a day. They run twice a day in the other direction to Unquera (1¼hr., 240ptas) and on to Santander (2 per day, 1½hr., 650ptas). The bus stops in Panes en route to Unquera (45min. from Arenas, 220ptas), at a restaurant over a bridge from the town center. Palomera buses (tel. 88 06 11), leave from the center of Panes to Potes (2 per day, 45min., 220ptas). The two companies' schedules are not well-coordinated; you may be in for a longish lay-over. If you are stuck in Panes for a night, the spacious rooms, private baths, and TVs at **Hostal Covadonga** (tel. 541 40 35 or 541 41 02) will ease your ire. (Singles 2000-3000ptas, doubles 3000-4000ptas, triples 6000-7500ptas.) The 1200ptas *menú* at the affiliated restaurant features delicious homemade desserts.

Accommodations and Food While many of Arenas's visitors settle down in campsites, the town also has several reasonable *hostales.* Near the tourist office is **El Castañeu.** (Tel. 584 65 73. Singles 1500ptas. Doubles 4500ptas. Triples 5000ptas. Off-season: 1200ptas; 2800ptas; 3300ptas.) **Naranjo de Bulnes** (tel. 584 65 78) has a cozy TV room, cafeteria, bar, shower facilities, and reams of info on hiking and assorted mountain sports. Spelunkers should ask about trips to **Cueva Jou de Alda,** a fascinating nearby cave. A **message board** lists excursions and local guides. Also, **mountain bikes** can be rented here (open March-Oct.; 600ptas per person, 475ptas per tent and per car).

A few grocery-*queso de Cabrales*-postcard shops make a killing selling essentials. For a *menú* (900ptas), try **Restaurante Castañeu,** under the pensión. Or head to **Restaurante Naranjo de Bulnes** (tel. 584 65 19), on the second floor of the hotel. They serve a killer 1100ptas *menú* in an elegant comedor with a gorgeous view of the Picos. For a lot of cozy after-dinner atmosphere, **Bar La Panera** has the feel and the look of an alpine lodge, perched on a small hill to the left of Banco Bilbao Vizcaya.

Hikes The area's hiking trails begin 6km away, in **Poncebos.** The walk to the trail-head is breathtaking, and after an all-day hike it's relatively easy to get a ride back to Arenas from tired fellow hikers. If you're looking to get an early start on the trail, two hostales in Poncebos, **Hostal Poncebos** (tel. 584 64 47), and **Hostal-Restaurante-**

Bar Garganta del Cares (tel. 584 64 63), keep comfortable, scenic rooms (single 2000-2500ptas, double 3500-4000ptas). Check with **Turismo** about refugio options.

Poncebos marks the start of one of the Picos's most famous trails, the 12km **Ruta del Cares.** Hewn and blasted out of mountain and sheer rock faces, at points the gorges' vertical walls drop straight down to the Río Cares 150m below. After a steep, rocky climb, the trail descends gradually behind small waterfalls and through tunnels opening onto spectacular views of lush cliffs and the river far below. In July and August, start early to avoid crowds but see (almost) tame mountain goats. Upon return to Poncebos, consider taking the path along the river, reached by descending the sometimes slippery path which starts just before the main path begins its steep ascent about 2-3km before Poncebos. Bring snacks and water, but don't bother packing a lunch—restaurants in Caixa offer 900ptas *menús* and plenty of cold drinks. The trail crosses the gorge twice, ending in **Caín,** a micro-town only recently linked to civilization by road. The walk takes about five hours, and the only way back is by foot. **Poncebos-Bulnes** is a shorter and less-traveled path which leads south along the Río Tejo to **Bulnes,** a microscopic, roadless village. The blistering hike takes one-and-a-half hours out and one hour back, and is actually more difficult than the Ruta del Cares. If Bulnes seduces you, consider tucking in at the **Albergue de Bulnes** (tel. 536 69 32). It has 20 beds in three rooms, a bar, a library, games, showers, guides, and meals (1000ptas per night; reservations suggested). The **Poncebos-Camarmeña** path shoots straight up a cliff on the way to terrific views.

A killer 17km hike, the **Poncebos-Invernales de Cabao-Naranjo de Bulnes** route (10-12hr.), crawls to Invernales de Cabao, then inches 9km more to the Picos's most famous mountain, **Naranjo de Bulnes.** From here you can see all the major *picos* in the area as well as the blue waves of the Cantabrian Sea in the distance.

Trouts of the Trade

The pristine waters and shiny white creekbeds characteristic of the Picos may yield a few clean glimpses of fish cruising along in their natural state, but don't count on seeing them on your plate. Although *trucha* (trout) is a staple of every mountain *mesón menú,* it has probably been trucked in from afar. The eco-laws of the protected Picos region preclude large commercial takes. Restaurateurs claim to have access to black market local stock for "special occasions," but they don't advertise it, and they probably don't know you well enough to let you in on the deal. However, the trout on most *menús,* usually fried unless you request *a la plancha* (grilled), is still quite good.

■ Potes

The cobbled streets of Potes (pop. 2000), while quiet and snow-bound in winter, shimmer in summer with city-fleeing climbers. This way-station between excursions to the southeast and central Picos, although surrounded by beautiful peaks, overdoes its touristy charm. Typical Asturian specialty shops crowd the town center, tempting visitors with overpriced walnut honey and do-it-yourself *fabada* kits.

PRACTICAL INFORMATION

The **tourist office,** Pl. Jesús de Monasterio (tel. 73 07 87), across the bridge and near the church, has general info about the region, though very little on Potes itself. Ask here about mountain *refugios,* but you'll have to reserve by shortwave radio at the Guardia Civil (open Semana Santa and June-Sept. Mon.-Fri. 10am-2pm and 4-8pm, Sat. 10am-2pm). **Palomera buses** (tel. 88 06 11 or 50 30 80) travel from Santander and back (3 per day, 2½hr., 815ptas), stopping along the way at San Vicente de Barquera. Buses run to and from Fuente Dé (3 per day, 45min., 245ptas), but the timing makes this almost a full-day adventure. An **Empresa Fernández** bus (tel. 21 00 00) leaves from Hotel Rubia in the end of town toward Panes for León (in summer daily at 10am). Coming into town, Palomera buses stop twice—once in front of Hotel Rubio,

and again farther into town across from Pl. Jesús de Monasterio and the tourist office. They leave from the *plaza* near the tourist office.

Wentura (tel. 73 21 61), at the end of C. Dr. Encinas toward Panes, organizes expeditions. (One-day **mountain bike rental** 2000ptas. One-day horseback trip 4600ptas. Parachuting 6500ptas. Canyon descending—combining swimming, rock-climbing, and loads of adrenaline—prices vary.) **Bustamante,** C. Dr. Encinas, 10, sells **maps** and guidebooks. **Change money** at Caja de Madrid, Pl. Jesús de Monasterio (open Mon.-Fri. 8:15am-2:30pm, Thurs. also 5-7:30pm). The **post office** is across from Pl. Jesús de Monasterio (open Mon.-Fri. 8am-2:30pm, Sat. 9am-1pm). The **telephone code** is (9)42.

ACCOMMODATIONS AND FOOD

Several *hostales* and *pensiones* line the main road. The cheapest rooms fill early in the day, so consider reserving in advance. **Hostal Lombraña,** C. el Sol, 2 (tel. 73 05 19), through a passageway off the main road, offers capacious rooms, some overlooking the river. (Singles 2600ptas, with bath 3200ptas. Doubles: 3200ptas; 3900ptas. IVA not included.) **Casa Cayo,** C. Cántabra, 6 (tel. 73 01 50), has quaint rooms in its old wing, and bright modern ones in the new part. Enjoy in-room TVs, phones, bathrooms, and a cozy lounge with an even bigger tube. Look for their sign on your right as you walk from second bus stop to town (singles 3000-3500ptas, doubles 5000-5500ptas, triples 6500-7000ptas). Closer to Panes off C. Dr. Encinas and under the tweeting canaries, **Fogon de Cus** (tel. 73 00 60) has sunny, airy rooms (singles 2500ptas, doubles 4000ptas; everything 500ptas less in off-season). There are also several *casas de labranza* (farm houses for rent) in the area. Ask at the tourist office for details.

There's no official camping in Potes proper. The closest site is first-class **Camping La Viorna** (tel. 73 20 21 or 73 21 01), about 2km up the road to Monasterio Santo Toribio. Besides its restaurant, supermarket, and swimming pool, it also organizes hiking, climbing, mountain biking, spelunking, and horseback excursions. Five kilometers down the road from Potes to Fuente Dé is **Camping San Pelayo**. Both campgrounds cost 425ptas per person, per tent, and per car and are open April-Oct.

The road through town brims with cafes and restaurants. Classy **Restaurante El Fogón de Cus** (tel. 73 00 60) is in a quiet corner below the eponymous *pensión*. Its *menú* (1150ptas) of fresh trout, *fabada,* and macaroni nourishes famished hikers. Sit out on the *terraza* or be eyed by a stuffed boar. Ravenous hikers continue to **Cafetería La Plaza,** on C. Dr. Encinas, and gorge on an 850ptas all-you-can-eat buffet of regional specialties (buffet available July noon-5pm, Aug. noon-midnight). **Supermercado Lupa** is near the second (main) bus stop. (Open Mon. 9:30am-3pm and 5pm-8:30pm, Tues-Fri. 9:30am-2pm and 5pm-8:30pm, Sat. 9am-2pm and 5-8:30pm.)

EXCURSIONS

Lucky for the touristophobe, there are many different opportunities to get out of Potes and explore some of the fascinating surrounding areas.

Fuente Dé A mind-blowing 800m *teleférico* glides up the lunar-like mountain face to a fancy *parador* and spectacular views. There are usually huge lines for the lift in the middle of summer. Open daily 9am-8pm; Sept.-June 10am-6pm. Round-trip 1200, one way 800ptas. Under 10: 500ptas; 300ptas. From the top, it's a 4km walk to **Refugio de Aliva** (tel. 73 09 99). Don't be fooled by the name—it's a *parador* (singles 5000ptas, doubles 7500ptas). To return to road-level, retrace your steps to the *teleférico* or walk (3hr.) to **Espinama.** In early July, a rowdy **festival** brings horse racing and dancing to Aliva. Three **buses** per day traverse the 23km route from Potes to Fuente Dé.

Monasterio de Santo Toribio de Liébana, 3km west of Potes, claims to hold part of the true cross.

Urdón, 15km north of Potes and on the road to Panes, is the start of a challenging hike to **Treviso,** a tiny town with far more chickens than humans. Trail details (steepness and turns) are on posters all over Potes. About 6km away; 4 hr.

Peña Sagra is about 13km east and a 2hr. walk from the towns of **Luriezo** or **Aniezo.** From the summit, you can survey all the Picos and the sea 51km away. On your way down, visit **Iglesia de Nuestra Señora de la Luz,** where the beautifully carved patron saint of Picos lives 364 days a year. The Virgin, known affectionately as *Santuca* (tiny saint), is honored on May 2.

Panes, on the routes to Santander and Cabrales, is near some spectacular scenery. The Potes-Panes drive through the **Desfiladero de Hermida** (a sharp gorge carved by the Río Deva) is stunning, but the terrifying continuation of that route to Cabrales has been reported to induce vomiting.

ASTURIAN COAST

Plunging eucalyptus forests in the west and rolling pastures in the east distinguish the calm Asturian coast, while filthy industrial centers Avilés and Gijón (above Oviedo) anchor the industrial nexus.

■ Llanes

The most popular **beaches** on the Asturian coast can be found in the secluded, monument-speckled coves of Llanes. **Playa Sablón** and **Playa Puerto Chico** host beach parties all summer long on their small, wavy shores. **Paseo de San Pedro,** an elevated grassy path along a bluff above Playa Sablón, is perfect for a quiet picnic (if you don't mind sharing with seagulls). Plateresque fans should peek at the **Iglesia de Santa María del Conceyu's** early 16th-century altar and ornate (but badly worn) portal. Violets creep across the walls of the white church in summer. Inside, stained-glass windows spill colorful light across the pews. (Open for mass Mon.-Fri. 7:30pm; Sat. 11am, 8, and 9pm; Sun. 11:30am, 1, and 7pm.)

Busy **Turismo** (tel. 540 01 64), in the *torreón* (13th century tower) on C. Afonso IX, around the corner from the yellow Ayuntamiento off the main street, hands out **maps.** From the train station, exit perpendicular to the tracks and turn right at C. Egidio Gavito. (Open summer Mon.-Sat. 10am-2pm and 5-9pm, Sun. 10am-3pm; winter Mon.-Fri. 10am-2pm and 4-6:30pm, Sat. 10am-1:30pm and 4:30-6:30pm.) Change money at **Banco Central Hispano,** C. Nemesio Sobrino, a block past the Ayuntamiento (open Mon-Fri. 8:30am-2:30pm). For medical services, call the **Red Cross** (tel. 540 18 57). The **Policía Municipal** (tel. 540 18 87) is on C. Nemesio Sobrino (near the tourist office); in an **emergency,** dial 091 or 092. The **post office** (tel. 540 11 14) is on C. Pidal; from the tourist office, head left in the direction of the bus station (open Mon.-Fri. 8:30am-2:30pm, Sat. 9:30am-1pm). The **postal code** is 33500. The **telephone code** is (9)8.

Rooms fill early in the day during the summer. **Casa del Río,** Av. San Pedro, 3 (tel. 540 11 91), in a cute red house behind light blue iron gates (facing the Ayuntamiento, hang a left to the first real street) has wonderful rooms, some with *two* balconies, is near the beach, and has communal bathrooms. (Singles 2000-2500ptas. Doubles 4000-5000ptas. Triples 5000-7000ptas. May be cheaper in the off-season). Newly renovated **Pensión La Guía,** Pl. Parres Sobrino, 1 (tel. 540 25 77), lies beneath the stone archway in the thick of the action. (Singles 2000-3500ptas. Doubles 4000-7000ptas. Triples 6000-9000ptas. All rooms with bath. Open Semana Santa-Oct.) Campers can pick and choose from nearby sites. First-class **Las Barcenas** (tel. 540 15 70), with showers and currency exchange, sits 200m past the bus station, heading out of town toward Santander. The view of the Picos in the distance helps you forget your neighbor is four feet away. (Reception open daily 8am-11pm. 450ptas per person, 400ptas per car, 550ptas per tent; Sept. and June 400ptas per person, 350ptas per car, and 500ptas per tent. Open June-Sept.) They also rent four-person *refugios* (cabins) with

bunks but no blankets. **El Brao** (tel. 540 00 14), a large site with showers, currency exchange, cafeteria, and supermarket, is a mere 15m outside town, past the bus station; go past Las Barcenas, then turn left. (Reception open daily 8:30am-midnight. 470ptas per person, per tent, and per car. Open June-Sept.)

Besides many small grocery stores spotting the main street, biggie **El Árbol** has a branch on the plaza at the intersection of C. Manuel Romano and C. Román Romano (open Mon.-Sat. 9am-9pm). Next door, independent **Café del Árbol** bakes its own bread and serves an 1100ptas *menú* on the *terraza*. Reasonably priced outdoor cafes cluster in Manuel Cué, a tiny street off C. Muelle which runs parallel to the river. **El Pescador, Colón,** and **Puerta del Sol** each serve a seafood-heavy 1000ptas *menú*.

The bus and train stations are at opposite ends of town. ALSA-Turytrans (tel. 540 23 27) runs **buses** to: Santander (11 per day, 2hr., 825ptas); Cangas de Onís (1 per day, 1¾hr., 600ptas); Oviedo (6 per day, 2hr., 1000ptas); and Madrid (1 per day, 4095ptas). To reach the town center from the bus station exit, take a left and go down C. Cueto Bajo to the post office, then turn left and keep going. The capricious FEVE **train** station (tel. 540 01 24) sits at the end of Av. Estación. Trains chug to Santander (2 per day, 2hr., 795ptas) and Oviedo (3 per day, 2½hr., 870ptas).

CANTABRIA

■ Santander

In 1941, an enormous fire gutted Santander (pop. 200,000), Cantabria's capital. Local visionaries rebuilt their peninsular city with cosmopolitan predilections. Their commercial dreams were realized with an inventory of trendy beaches, promenades, a swish casino, and an upscale shopping district. Streamline beaches alongside fax facilities make Santander a favorite seaside resort among Europeans. The active fisherman's wharf and other less-trafficked sectors of town add industrial charm to the blandness of more commercialized areas. The Universidad Internacional Menéndez Pelayo attracts artists and scholars keeping things lively in the off-season

ORIENTATION AND PRACTICAL INFORMATION

This slender, elongated city sits on the northwest side of a bay. The small **Plaza Porticada** is its heart. **Avenida de Calvo Sotelo** becomes **Paseo de Pereda** to the east, then runs along the waterfront. Buses and trains arrive at **Plaza de Estaciones,** about six blocks west of Pl. Porticada. Beach activity centers in the neighborhood **El Sardinero,** in the east part of town. Municipal buses run throughout the city (frequent service from 6-8am to midnight, Sept.-June until 10:30pm; 100ptas). The beach is bordered by lengthy **Avenida Reina Victoria** and **Avenida de Castaneda.** Midway along the Sardinero beachfront lies the swanky **casino** in **Plaza de Italia.**

Tourist Office: Jardines de Pereda (tel. 21 61 20). From the stations, follow C. Calderón de la Barca into the park; the office is off Po. Pereda. Maps and info on Santander and Cantabria. English spoken by a team of uniformed models. Open daily 9am-2pm and 4-9pm, Oct.-June 9am-1:30pm and 4:30-7:30pm. Other **offices** in the ferry station and El Sardinero across from Pl. Italia. Same services and hrs.

Budget Travel: TIVE, C. Canarias, 2 (tel. 33 22 15), a 20min. walk northwest from the center. Or take bus #5 just off Av. General Camilo Alonso Cela. Travel discounts and flights. ISIC 700ptas. HI card 1800ptas. Open Mon.-Fri. 9am-2pm.

Currency Exchange: Banco Central Hispano, C. Calvo Sotelo across from the post office (open 8:30am-2:30pm, Oct.-Apr. additionally Sat. 8:30am-1pm).

American Express: Viajes Altair, C. Calderón de la Barca, 11 (tel. 31 17 00; fax 22 57 21). Standard services and mail-holding for members. Open Mon.-Fri. 9:30am-1:30pm and 4:30-8pm, Sat. 10am-1:30pm.

Flights: Aeropuerto de Santander (tel. 25 10 07 or 25 10 04), 4km away. Daily to Madrid and Barcelona. Accessible by taxi only (1300-1500ptas). **Iberia,** Po. Pereda, 18 (tel. 22 97 00). Open Mon.-Fri. 9am-1:30pm and 4-7pm.

Trains: Pl. Estaciones, on C. Rodríguez. **RENFE station** (tel. 28 02 02). Info open 7:30am-11pm. Santander is the north terminus of one RENFE line. For service to points north, take FEVE to Bilbao and then pick up RENFE again. To: Madrid (3 per day, 7hr., 3900-4100ptas); Salamanca (5 per day, with change at Valladolid, 7hr., 3155-3900ptas); Valladolid (8 per day, 5hr., 1855-2600ptas); Palencia (8 per day, 2¼hr., 1455-2200ptas). **RENFE ticket office,** Po. Pereda, 25 (tel. 21 23 87). Open Mon.-Fri. 9am-2pm and 5-7pm, Sat. 9am-1:30pm. **FEVE station** (tel. 21 16 87). Info open 9am-2pm and 4-7pm. To Bilbao (3 per day, 2½hr., 910ptas) and Oviedo (2 per day, 5hr., 1610ptas).

Buses: Pl. Estaciones (tel. 21 19 95), across C. Rodríguez from the train station. Info open Mon.-Sat. 8am-10pm, Sun. 9am-9pm. To: Santillana del Mar (7 per day, 45min., 270ptas); Bilbao (24 per day, 3hr., 900-1475ptas); Oviedo (8 per day, 4hr., 1710ptas); La Coruña (2 per day, 12hr., 4745ptas); Madrid (6-9 per day, 6hr., 3255-4550ptas); Llanes (10 per day, 2hr., 825ptas); San Vicente (12 per day, 1½hr., 530ptas); León (1 per day, 3½hr., 2740ptas).

Ferries: Brittany Ferries, Muelle del Ferrys, near the Jardines de Pereda. To Plymouth, England (2 per week, 12,900-14,900ptas, plus 1400ptas for seat reservation). Get tickets at Modesto Piñeiro (tel. 36 06 11), at the ferry station. Info open Mon.-Fri. 9am-3:30pm and 4:30-7:30pm. In summer reserve 2 weeks ahead. **Las Reginas** (tel. 21 66 19), from Embarcadero by the Jardines de Pereda. Across the bay to Pedreña and Somo (in summer every 15min., 45min., round-trip 340ptas). Tours of the bay (in summer 3-6 per day, 1½hr., 625ptas).

Public Transportation: Buses #1, 3, 4, 5, 7, and 9 run between the city center and El Sardinero (every 15min. from around 6am-midnight, 100ptas).

Taxis: Radio Taxi (tel. 33 33 33 or 22 20 46).

Car Rental: Avis, C. Nicolás Salmerón, 3 (tel. 22 70 25). Must be at least 23, and have had license for one year. From 9000ptas per day. Open Mon.-Fri. 8am-1pm and 4-7:30pm, Sat. 9am-1pm.

Luggage Storage: At the train station, by the counter at the ticket window (lockers 400ptas). Open daily 7am-11pm. At the bus station (lockers 300ptas). Open daily 7:30am-10:30pm.

Laundromat: El Lavadero, C. Mies del Valle, 1 (tel. 23 06 07), just off C. Floranes west of the train station. Wash 350ptas, dry 200ptas per 6kg load. Soap 50ptas. Open Mon.-Fri. 9:30am-1:30pm, Sat. 5-8pm.

English Bookstores: Estudio Santander, C. Calvo Sotelo, 23. A selection of random English novels, not particularly cheap. **Hispano Argentina,** San Francisco, 13 (tel. 21 17 65). Two small shelves of Danielle Steele and friends (open Mon.-Fri. 9:45am-1:30pm and 4:30-8pm, Sat. morning only).

Red Cross: Ambulance, C. Marqués de la Hermida, 23 (tel. 27 30 58).

Medical Emergencies: Hospital Valdecilla-Cantabria (tel. 20 25 20).

Police: Pl. Verlade (tel. 33 73 00 or 22 07 44). **Emergency:** tel. 091 or 092.

Post Office: Av. Alfonso XIII (tel. 21 26 73; fax 31 02 99), near the Jardines de Pereda on the water. Open for stamps, Lista de Correos, and **fax** Mon.-Fri. 8:30am-8:30pm, Sat. 9:30am-2pm. **Postal Code:** 39080.

Telephone Code: (9)42.

ACCOMMODATIONS AND CAMPING

There are slim lodging pickings in July and August, especially late in the day. The highest hotel densities are near the market, around **C. Isabel II,** across from the train station on **C. Rodríguez,** and along elegant **Av. Castros** in **El Sardinero.** If you've come with the beach in mind, the splendor is worth the schlep.

The Monolith at Calle Rodríguez, 9

Cross the street and turn right from the train station to reach this hostelers haven. The *hóspedes* on the sixth floor offer more informal (no keys) lodging at the same price as the *pensiones* below.

Pensión Angelines, C. Rodríguez, 9, 1st fl. (tel. 31 25 84). Exuberant color scheme of tan, beige, or brown. Singles 1500-2000ptas. Doubles 2500-4000ptas. Baths down the hall.

Pensión Fernando, C. Rodríguez, 9, 3rd fl. (tel. 31 36 96). Elmer Fudd fantasy land—beware of the boar's head in the foyer and animal skin rugs in some of the newly tiled rooms. Be vewy, vewy quiet. Singles 1500-2500ptas. Doubles 3000-4500ptas. Triples 4500-6000ptas. Bathrooms down the hall

Fonda María Luisa, C. Rodríguez, 9, 5th fl. (tel. 21 08 81). Rustic carved headboards and lively wallpaper. Singles 1500-2500ptas. Doubles 3000-4500ptas.

City Center

Hostal Real, Pl. Esperanza, 1, 3rd fl. (tel. 22 57 87), in the peach building at the end of C. Isabel II. Curtained hallways lead to large doubles with wood-carved ceilings and balconies. Spartan, tiny singles upstairs. Singles 2000-3500ptas. Doubles 3000-5000ptas. Triples 5000-6750ptas.

Hostal Botín, C. Isabel II, 1, 1st fl. Satiny beds, huge rooms, and balconies overlooking the bustling market. Singles 1900ptas. Doubles 3200ptas. Triples 4320ptas. Aug.: 3100ptas; 5200ptas; 7020ptas. Quads 6720-8320ptas.

El Sardinero

Hostal-Residencia Luisito, Av. Los Castros, 11 (tel. 27 19 71), one block from the beach. Take bus #4 to Hotel Colón (Pl. Brisas). A 3min. walk on El Sardinero's rose-colored sidewalks to the beach. Huge, bright yellow rooms, many with huge balconies overlooking the owners' mini-orchard. Bathroom in the hall. Singles 2150ptas. Doubles 3855ptas. 7% IVA not included. Breakfast 205ptas. Open July-Sept.

Pensión Soledad, Av. Castro, 17 (tel. 27 09 36), next door to Luisito. Simple, plain, large rooms with sinks. Breakfast in the dining room downstairs. Singles 2150ptas. Doubles 3850ptas. Breakfast 200ptas. 7% IVA not included.

Camping: Two back-to-back sites on the scenic bluff called Cabo Mayor, 3km up the coast from Playa de la Magdalena. Both are *enorme.* Take the Cueto-Santander bus (100ptas) from in front of the Jardines de Pereda. **Camping Bellavista** (tel. 39 15 36). A 1st-class site on the beach. 600ptas per person and per car, 650ptas per tent. Reception open 8am-midnight. **Camping Cabo Mayor** (tel. 39 15 42). Pool and tennis courts. 500ptas per person and per car, 550ptas per tent. Open mid-June to Sept. Most expensive in Aug. Reception open 8am-11pm.

FOOD

Seafood restaurants crowd the **Puerto Pesquero** (fishing port), grilling up the day's catch on a small stretch at the end of **C. Marqués de la Ensenada.** From the train station, walk eight blocks down C. Castilla and turn left on C. Héroes de la Armada; cross the tracks and turn right after about 100m (20min.). Don't walk here alone at night, since parts are deserted. Closer to the city center, reasonable *mesones* and bars line **C. Hernán Cortés, C. Daóiz y Velarde,** and **Pl. Cañadío.** The **Mercado de Plaza Esperanza,** C. Isabel II, sells produce near Pl. Generalísimo behind the police station (open Mon.-Fri. 8am-2pm and 5-7:30pm, Sat. 8am-2pm). There's a lively lingerie/sandal/bikini/clothes market here every Thursday. **Supermercado BM,** C. Calderón de la Barca, 12, is one block from the train and bus stations (open Mon.-Fri. 9am-1:30pm and 5:15-7:45pm, Sat. 9am-2pm).

Bar Restaurante La Gaviota, C. Marqués de la Ensenada (tel. 22 10 06), at the corner of C. Mocejón in the *barrio pesquero* (fisherman's neighborhood). Fresh grilled sardines (12 for 600ptas) and *paella de mariscos* (1000ptas) are delicious specialties. Women traveling alone may get extras: i.e., the phone numbers of flirtatious fishermen. Watch your 1000ptas *menú* being prepared smack in the middle of the cavernous dining room. Open daily 1-4:30pm and 7:30-11:30pm.

La Cueva, C. Marqués de la Ensenada (tel. 22 20 87), next door to La Gaviota. Cozier than its neighbors, with many options on its 900ptas *menú. Chipirones encebollados* (baby squid fried in onion 650ptas). The gigantic frying pan outside brims with

steaming *paella* and lures many a hungry sailor to blissful surrender. Open daily noon-5pm and 7:30pm-midnight.

Cervecería Aspy, C. Hernán Cortés, 22 (tel. 31 45 95), off C. Lope de Vega. Elegant dining room has it all: wine rack, paintings, and a signed photo of golf star Seve Ballesteros. *Platos combinados* 650-800ptas. *Menú* 1000ptas. Open daily 8am-1am.

Restaurante Cruz Blanca, C. Hernán Cortés, 16 (tel. 36 42 95), just up from Aspy. Rice dish *arroz a la cubana* and chicken breasts pack their 1000ptas *menú*. Prussiaphiles dig the Teutonic decor, *bier,* and bratwurst (425ptas). Standing room only after 9pm. Open noon-4pm and 8pm-midnight.

Bar-Restaurante Silverio, Pl. Esperanza, 1 (tel. 21 31 25). *Raciones* at the bar are innovative and reasonable. Weird Egyptian statues. Stewed quail 400ptas. Garlic snails 500ptas. Open daily 12:30-4pm and 8pm-midnight.

SIGHTS AND BEACHES

Santander's sights scene is small on architecture, big on seaside beauty, and balanced by pleasant, though unspectacular, free museums. Jutting into the sea between El Sardinero and Playa de la Magdalena, the **Península de la Magdalena** is crowned by an early 20th-century neo-Gothic fantasy **palacio.** Originally Alfonso XIII's summer home, the cliff-top palace is a classroom building and dorm for the university. The peninsula is a **park** of beautiful lawns, hedges, and gardens overlooking the sea. A **mini-zoo** on the edge of El Sardinero holds a polar bear, sleepy lions, pot-bellied penguins, and literally tons of honking sea lions. (Peninsula de Magdalena open daily 8am-10pm. The *palacio* doesn't have scheduled visiting hours.)

Santander's **beaches** are truly spectacular. **El Sardinero's** powdery sands seem to stretch on forever. But in July and August, every inch is covered by fluorescent tourist sardines marinating in cocoa butter. Less crowded beaches—**Playas Puntal, Somo,** and **Loredo**—line the other side of the bay. In summer, Las Reginas **boats** (tel. 21 66 19) run across to the beaches of Pedreña and do 80-minute sailing tours around the bay (see **Practical Information: Ferries,** p. 210).

The **Museo Marítimo,** C. San Martín de Bajamar (tel. 27 49 62), stands beyond the *puerto chico* (little port). The top floors chart regional fishing-boat evolution, while the bottom floor, quaking under mammoth whale skeletons, highlights the sea's living creatures. *Far Side*-esque formaldehyde fishes in contorted positions peer out from glass jars, and a small aquarium shows life at sea levels. (Open Tues.-Sat. 11am-1pm and 4-7pm, Sun. 11am-2pm; mid-Sept. to mid-June Mon.-Sat. 10am-1pm and 4-6pm, Sun. and holidays 11am-2pm. Free.) Paleolithic skulls and tools rattle at the **Museo de Prehistoria y Arqueología,** C. Casimiro Sáinz, 4 (tel. 20 71 05). Artifacts from and photographs of the Cuevas de Altamira (see p. 214) are truly spectacular especially considering the sad fact that they're probably as close as you'll get to the real thing. (Open June 15-Sept. 15 10am-1pm and 4-7pm, rest of the year 9am-1pm and 4-7pm, Sun. and holidays 11am-2pm. Free.) The 1941 fire scorched the **cathedral's** facade (tel. 22 60 24), but the downstairs chapel is worth visiting for its unusually low Romanesque vaulting. (Open Mon.-Fri. 10am-1pm and 4-7:30pm, Sat.-Sun and holidays all-yr. 10am-1pm and 4:30-9pm.)

ENTERTAINMENT

As night falls, Santander goes Bacchanalian. Students forget their studies in the area around **Plaza de Cañadío, Calle de Pedrueca,** and **Calle de Daóiz y Velarde,** and up the hill from Pl. Cañadío on **Pasadillo de Zorilla.** At **Blues** on C. Gomez Areña in Pl. Cañadío, jazz and blues fans mingle under the huge plastic statues of a jazz combo.

In **El Sardinero,** tourists, students, and spirits mingle all night long. **Plaza de Italia** and nearby **Calle de Panamá** are neighborhood hotspots. The **Gran Casino** on Pl. Italia brings out the card shark in everyone. Passport, proper dress (pants and shoes) and minimum age (18 to gamble) required (open daily 7pm-4am; 600ptas). Student crowd bars **Gloria** and **Albatros** on C. Panamá. The **Cotton Pub,** set back in the hill side off C. Panamá, draws a thirtysomething crowd to its black and white *terraza.*

The August **Festival Internacional de Santander** brings myriad music and dance recitals. The events culminate in the **Concurso Internacional de Piano de Santander.** Daily classical **concerts** ring through Pl. Porticada; recent festivals have featured the London Symphony Orchestra and the Bolshoi Ballet. Ridiculously high-priced tickets are sold in booths on Po. Pereda and Pl. Porticada; a precious few are under 1500ptas. (Consult the Oficina del Festival, Palacio de Festivales de Cantabria, on C. Gamazo at tel. 21 05 08 or 31 48 53; fax 31 47 67.) Concerts rock the **Palacio,** a grand pink- and white-striped auditorium. The *barrio pesquero* celebrates its patron of fishing safety, Carmen, the third week in July with sardine fests, soccer tournaments, music, and carnival rides. For info about concerts, festivals, and movies, check the local paper *El Diario de las Montañas* (110ptas).

■ Near Santander

Since only a handful of people each day get into the Cuevas de Altamira, many spelunk in the lesser known town of **Puente Viesgo,** about 30km south of Santander. The **Cuevas del Castillo** (tel. 59 84 25) display paintings nearly as well-preserved as those in Altamira (open 10am-12:15pm and 3-7:15pm; 225ptas, free with EU ID). Continental-Auto **buses** stop in Puente Viesgo en route from Santander to Burgos (2 per day, 45min., 475ptas).

CANTABRIAN COAST

Fishing villages and beach towns await daytrippers on the soft, sandy shores of Cantabria. Quiet dairy farming towns plug away slightly inland. La Cantábrica buses follow the coast and link most of these towns with Santander.

■ Santillana del Mar

Like Voltaire's Holy Roman Empire, Santillana del Mar is none of the above. Neither *Santa* (holy), *llana* (flat), nor *del mar* (on the sea), the entire town is still a national historical monument, crowded with stone houses and cobblestone streets. Opportunistic residents have converted their entryways into souvenir shops and *comida típica*. The winding side passages, however, are blissfully quiet, save for the whistling of flirtatious parrots from geranium-covered balconies.

Practical Information The **tourist office,** Pl. Mayor, supplies a map and frank opinion of the region's sights. When the bus drops you off (and continues to Comillas), go to Hotel Santillana on the corner, then head uphill. (Open summer daily 9:30am-1:30pm and 3:30-7:30pm; in winter Mon.-Fri. 9:30am-1pm and 4:30-7pm, Sat. 9:30am-1pm.) Change money at **Banesto,** also in Pl. Mayor (open Mon.-Fri. 9am-2pm). **Telephones** snooze next to the post office; from June to September a phone stand operates by the municipal parking lot (open daily 11am-10pm). In **medical emergencies,** dial 82 06 94 or 81 82 76. Go left exiting the tourist office for the **post office** (open Mon.-Fri. 8:30am-2:30pm, Sat. 9:30am-1pm). The **postal code** is 39330. The **telephone code** is (9)42. Santillana is a short trip from Santander (26km away) by **bus.** La Cantábrica (tel. 72 08 22) sends buses from Pl. Estaciones in Santander (6 per day; Sept.-June 4 per day, 45min., 270ptas). The tourist office has a schedule.

Accommodations and Food Santillana's few budget rooms fill fast in July and August, so consider daytripping from Santander. Don't be lured by the *hostales* on the highway near the bus stop; *casas particulares* in town are sure to be cheaper. The tourist office can help find one. **Pensión Angélica** (tel. 81 82 38), on C. Hornos off Pl. Mayor (next to the post office, look for the crescent *habitaciones* sign), is as beautiful inside as out. Lacy blue rooms with animal rugs. Bathroom in the hall (singles 2900ptas, doubles 2900-3500ptas, triples 3000-4000ptas). Nearby **Posada Santa**

Juliana, C. Carrera, 19 (tel. 84 01 06), is equally endearing. Some rooms have exposed wood beams, and all have TVs, quilts, and downy pillows (doubles 5000-7500ptas; Sept.-June 4000ptas). Less than 1km away on the road to Comillas is **Camping Santillana** (tel. 81 82 50). It would be easy to mistake this deluxe first-class site for a *parador;* it boasts a panoramic view of the town, a supermarket, shiny cafeteria, pool, miniature golf, and tennis courts. (Reception open daily 8:30am-8:30pm. 525ptas per person, 500ptas per tent and per car. Mini-golf 300ptas per person per hr., tennis 600ptas per person, per hr.)

Most everyone who comes to **Casa Cossío,** Pl. Abad Francisco Navarro (tel. 81 83 55), across from the church, orders the 1050ptas *menú* for the ribs. Grilled with a tasty paprika sauce in the open fire downstairs, they're served in the shadows of stone walls and bubbly lobster tanks (bar open daily 10:30am-11:30pm; *comedor* open 1-4pm and 8-11pm). **Bodega El Porche,** Pl. Juan Infante, has sandwiches (300-500ptas) and *platos combinados* (600-800ptas; open daily 1-3:30pm and 8-10:30pm). The **SPAR** supermarket at Pl. Rey (big parking lot on C. Jesús de Tagle heading away from Pl. Mayor) sells staples (open daily 9am-11pm).

Sights Emblazoned above the door of virtually every house is a heraldic shield proclaiming the rank and honor of former noble residents. Many residents have converted their doorways into storefronts, selling ceramics and local delectable (if overpriced) sweet milk and *bizcocho* (sponge cake).

The **Colegiata de Santa Juliana,** a 12th-century Romanesque church, occupies one end of C. Santo Domingo. The charming ivy-covered **claustro** has some fragmented capitals of angels, beasts, and Jesus and his disciples. The 12th-century reform of the Cistercian Order prohibited the representation of any human form on pillars—hence the ropy vegetable patterns. (Open daily 9:30am-1pm and 4-7:30pm; in winter 10am-1pm and 4-6pm. 300ptas also gets you into the Museo Diocesano.)

In a town that's a museum itself, the **Museo Diocesano** (tel. 581 80 04) is one of only two official exhibits. Religious art and artifacts are spread throughout the harmonious Romanesque cloister and corridors of the Monasterio Regina Coeli (open daily 10am-1pm and 4-8pm, in winter 10am-1pm and 4-6pm; 100ptas). The **Museo Regional,** in the Casa del Aguila y la Parra, across from the *parador,* is Santillana's other indoor exhibition. The eclectic collection contains everything from Roman artifacts to 19th-century tools, with a few stuffed boars' heads thrown in for good measure (open 10am-1:30pm and 4-7:30pm; free).

■ Near Santillana del Mar: Cuevas de Altamira

Bison roam, horses graze, deer prance, and goats butt on the ceilings of the limestone **Cuevas de Altamira** (2km from Santillana del Mar), sometimes called the "Sistine Chapel of Primitive Art." The large-scale polychrome paintings are renowned for their scrupulous attention to naturalist detail (such as genitalia and the texture of hides) and resourceful use of the caves' natural texture. The 25 animals are so realistic and carefully wrought that they were thought to be a hoax when first discovered at the beginning of this century. To catch a glimpse, you must obtain written permission from the Centro de Investigación de Altamira, Santillana del Mar, Cantabria, Spain 39330 (tel. ((9)42) 81 80 05). **You must write one year in advance.** Send a photocopy of your passport. Since the caves have been debased by excessive tourism, only 20 people per day get to take the 15-minute tour (Tues.-Sun. 9:30am-2:30pm). If you don't get in, join fellow unfortunates in the **museum** of prehistory (open Mon.-Sat. 10am-1pm and 4-6pm, Sun. 10am-1pm; free). To walk here, follow the signs from Santillana past the abandoned **Iglesia de San Sebastián,** a hotspot for picnickers. Make a detour through the streets of Herrán, and turn right into the corn field at the wooden barrier on the other side of town.

■ Comillas

Comillas is an understated resort favored by Spain's noble families, who retain their modest palaces along with their anachronistic titles. Among the few places in historically leftist northern Spain where people can legitimately refer to themselves as count or duchess, the town has a conservative nature diluted only by thousands of young people tracking sand through the streets each summer.

ORIENTATION AND PRACTICAL INFORMATION

Tans are acquired at the broad port **Playa Comillas,** or on the longer, quieter beach of **Oyambre,** 4km away, which offers a protected lagoon and huge waves for surfers. Many petite **palaces** and an enormous Jesuit **university,** the site of summer classes, rise in Gothic splendor between the sea and the Picos de Europa. The neo-Gothic **Palacio de Sobrellano,** on the outskirts of town, dominates a pretty park. Inside, the **Capilla-Pantheon** contains furniture designed by Gaudí (open Wed.-Sun. 11am-1pm and 4-8pm; free). More Gaudí awaits at multi-colored **El Capricho,** a small stone-and-sunflower-tiled palace that has metamorphosed into a fine (read: expensive) restaurant. It's one of only three Gaudí creations outside of Cataluña. The other two are in León and Astorga.

The **tourist office,** C. de Maria del Piélago, 2 (tel. 72 07 68). From the bus stop near the Palacio, continue on the main road past the turn-off for the beach, into the plaza, then uphill (still on the main road) one block, at which point a sign directs you left. If you got off the bus at the top of the hill, walk down 25m until the sign directs you right. The office stocks bus and excursion info, as well as a list of *hostales*. The only map costs 100ptas; stare at theirs for five seconds or pick one up at your *hostal* (open May-Sept. Mon.-Sat. 10am-1pm and 5-9pm, Sun. 11am-1pm and 5-8pm). The **post office,** C. Antonio López, 6, is on the main road uphill from the tourist office turnoff (open Mon.-Fri. 8:30am-2:30pm, Sat. 9:30am-1pm). The **postal code** is 39520. The **telephone code** is (9)42.

At 18km from Santillana del Mar and 49km from Santander, Comillas is an easy daytrip. La Cantábrica **buses** (tel. 72 08 22) run between Santander and San Vicente de la Barquera, stopping at Comillas, and an equal number return (6 per day, Sept.-June 3 per day, from Santander 270ptas, from San Vicente 105ptas). The **train** goes as far as **Torrelavega,** where you can catch a bus to Comillas.

ACCOMMODATIONS AND FOOD

Comillas's budget lodgings are few and fill quickly in summer. Call ahead, especially if you're coming during the *fiestas* on July 16. At **Pensión Bolingas,** C. Gonzalo de la Torre de Trassiera El Corro (tel. 72 08 41), downhill from the tourist office, the enthusiastic owner leads you through the lobby to sagging leather furniture and relatively bare, clean rooms, some with gorgeous views of the hillside university. Enjoy a sack lunch at the tables in her garden (doubles 3300ptas open Jun. 15-Sept. 15). **Pensión la Aldea** (tel. 72 10 46), one block off C. Infantas, opposite Supermercado Greyfuss, greets with more serene browns and grays (doubles with bath 3500ptas, 2500ptas in early July and Sept). **Camping de Comillas** (tel. 72 00 74) is a first-class site on the water. It has a supermarket, cafeteria, laundromat, and beautiful views (475ptas per person, 1600ptas per *parcela;* open June-Sept.). Nearby **Camping El Helguero** (tel. 72 21 24), 3km east in **Ruiloba,** rivals the Comillas site, parading the same amenities, plus a swimming pool (450ptas per person and per car, 450ptas per tent; reception open **Semana Santa**-Oct. 9am-11pm). The La Cantábrica **bus** from Santander to San Vicente de la Barquera stops at the grounds. While upscale restaurants dot the small streets of Comillas, less expensive bars and *cafeterías* jockey for your business in Pl. Corro (1000ptas *menús*). Just outside the plaza toward the bus stop, the lively **Bar-Restaurant Filipino** serves up heaping plates of *paella* on its 1000ptas *menú*. Try **Restaurante-Pizzeria Quo Vadis,** C. Marqués de Comillos, for *molto* Italian treats (pastas 650-900ptas, pizzas 600-1000ptas). **Supermercado Grey-**

fuss, at the turnoff to the beach, replenishes beachgoers with fluids and fruits (open Mon.-Sat. 9am-2pm and 4:30-8pm). **El Árbol,** on C. Cervantes near Pl. de Joaquin de Piélago, has longer hours (open Mon.-Fri. 9am-9pm, Sat. 10am-2pm).

Come July 16, the **fiestas** go up in a blaze of fireworks and spur-greased pole-walking, goose-chasing, and dancing in the plaza.

■ San Vicente de La Barquera

The view from San Vicente's (pop. 4800) crescent beach scans a rapidly growing jigsaw of modern hotels and older houses, governed by a hillside castle framed by the Picos de Europa. This might be as close as you want to get to San Vicente in July and August, when tourists crowd the town's every street and ring every postcard rack with clicking cameras and humming camcorders.

Orientation and Practical Information The **tourist office** (tel. 71 07 97), on Av. Generalísimo (the main street running perpendicular to the waterfront), helps with accommodations (open Semana Santa and July-Sept. Wed.-Sat. 9am-2pm and 4-9pm, Sun.-Tues. 10am-2pm and 4:30-8:30pm). The **Red Cross** (tel. 79 24 50) is at the bus stop on Av. Generalísimo. For **medical** situations call the Centro de Salud (tel. 71 24 50 or 71 24 56). In an **emergency,** dial 091 or 092. The **post office,** C. Miramar, 16 (tel. 71 02 19), along the waterfront, has workers (open Mon.-Fri. 8:30am-2:30pm, Sat. 9:30am-1pm). The **postal code** is 39540. The **telephone code** is ((9)42).

Reaching this paradise/zoo is not that difficult, although traffic may be horrendous on warm weekends. ALSA-Turytrans (tel. 21 56 50) **buses** run from Santander to San Vicente in July and August (12 per day, 1½hr., 530ptas); they continue as far as Llanes (3hr., 825ptas). La Cantábrica buses (tel. 72 08 22) travel between San Vicente and Santander, stopping at Comillas (6 per day, Sept.-June 3 per day, 20min., 105ptas to Comillas; to Santander, 1½hr., 550ptas). For La Cantábrica buses, buy tickets on board. For ALSA-Turytrans buses, buy a ticket or scan a schedule at Fotos Noly, on C. Miramar next to the post office.

Accommodations Budget accommodations in San Vicente are a precious few, so in August make reservations weeks ahead. But don't despair if you forgot. Room hawkers are sure to approach backpackers with *habitación* offers. Just remember to ask for their prices before following them. In town, **Hostal La Paz,** C. Mercado, 2 (tel. 71 01 80), off the plaza at the intersection of C. Miramar and C. Generalísimo, has big airy rooms with sinks and balconies. (Singles 2000-2800ptas. Doubles 3000-4200ptas. A few doubles with showers and TV 4000-5000ptas.) Along the port, awash in its own flower gardens, sprawls the *parador* of San Vicente's lodgings, **Hostal La Barquera** (tel. 71 00 75), which sports enormous rooms, some with balconies. You might feel as if you need a lantern, but this place has electricity, perfectly functional plumbing, and overlooks San Vicente's exquisite beach—a 30-minute walk or a three-minute swim (doubles with bath 7000ptas; reception at Hotel Miramar). **Camping El Rosal** (tel. 71 01 65) is near the beach without the swim. From the bus stop, cross the bridge and keep going (20min.). Stores surround the second-class site, including a lively *cafetería* and bar, supermarket, laundry, currency exchange, and camping equipment rental. They also provide info on excursions. (Reception open 10am-10pm. 575ptas per person and per car, 475ptas per tent. Open April-Oct.)

Food Most restaurants off C. Miramar and Av. Generalísimo serve 900-1000ptas *menús* featuring *comida típica*. Tiled **Café Bar Folia,** Av. Generalísimo, 7, serves fresh *raciones* at reasonable prices (steamed razor clams 500ptas, fresh grilled sardines 470ptas, octopus 750ptas). **Supermercado Greyfuss,** C. El Arenal, 9, a block off Av. Generalísimo, stocks picnic supplies (open Mon.-Sat. 9am-2pm and 4:30-9pm).

Sights For those venturing downtown, the 12th-century church-fortress **Santa María de los Angeles** shows off a handsome Romanesque portico and the Renaissance tomb of Antonio Corro, the infamous 16th-century Grand Inquisitor. His effigy lounges jauntily, reading about a nun from Soria whom he ordered burned for heresy. The 8th-century **castillo** above town can be seen from the outside only. For silicon-enhanced fun, try **beaches Merón** and **El Rosal.** From the expansive sands of Playa Merón, a 15-minute walk over the 15th-century stone Puente de la Maza leads to fabulous views of the Picos de Europa.

ASTURIAS AND CANTABRIA

País Vasco (Euskadi, Euskal Herria, Basque Country)

"Before God was God and the rocks were rocks, the Basques were Basque." Although País Vasco is officially composed of the provinces Guipúzcoa, Alava, and Vizcaya, the Basques define themselves ethnically, not nationally, extending *Euskadi* (Basque Country) into parts of Navarra and southwestern France. The varied landscape of País Vasco resembles a nation complete unto itself, combining large, cosmopolitan cities, lush, verdant hills, industrial wastelands, and quaint fishing villages. The people are united by their deep attachment to the land, an almost spiritual appreciation of fine food and drink, and immense cultural and national pride.

País Vasco homepage: http://www.euskadi.net

Basque nationalism began in the 1890s. Their culture and language are much older—many believe that Basques are the native people of Iberia. Nationalism grew out of the combination of military defeat (the region lost three Carlist civil wars in the late 19th century) and Castile's attempts to modernize Spain rapidly; these factors were seen as threats to their traditional values, provoking a renascence of pre-modern identities. During Franco's regime, Euskadi eta Askatasuna (ETA; Euskadi and Liberty) began an anti-Madrid terrorist movement that has lasted over 30 years. Most Basque Nationalists are critical of ETA and prefer to seek independence through politics. The radical ETA-affiliated party, Herri Batasuna (the United People), has recently declined in popularity, but still draws support that is both loud and substantial in numbers. Vandalism, demonstrations, bus-burnings, and other forms of nationalist activity remain common. Until recently, violence has generally been directed at Spanish officials. However, in the past few years, ETA has bombed heavily touristed areas in order to arouse international attention.

The preservation of cultural identity is a universally shared sentiment of the Basques. Language, history, dance, sport, and music have all enjoyed a strong resur-

¡Basta ya!

On July 10, 1997, at 4pm, Miguel Àngel Blanco, 29, disappeared near his hometown from his city council seat of Ermua in the Basque province of Vizcaya. The kidnappers were members of the Basque separatist group ETA (Eskadi ta Askatasuna). ETA's plea was that the government stop incarcerating ETA members in the Canary Islands rather than in their home nation. The demand was not new, and the government was still adamant in refusing it. The dramatic circumstances of the act riveted the nation's attention and stirred its passions—all pleas, protests, and prayers were set against the cold-blooded punctuality of a clock. On July 12, at 5pm, the news came: Àngel Blanco had been shot in the head and died soon after in the hospital. The anger over the murder was palpable. Heads of government in País Vasco expressed regret, outrage, and the solidarity of the Basque people against ETA. Blue ribbons, symbols of hope before the murder, turned black, and millions took to the streets. The cry of both Spaniards and Basques was one and the same: "¡Basta ya!" (Enough already!). "¡Libertad!" (Freedom!). The majority agree that violence is not the way to affect change and gain further autonomy. Time will tell if Spain's new activism can sustain itself, or if Blanco's candles will burn out like so many before his.

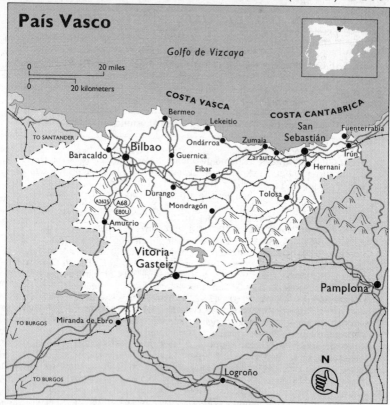

País Vasco

Golfo de Vizcaya

COSTA VASCA

COSTA CANTÁBRICA

0   20 miles

0   20 kilometers

TO SANTANDER

Bermeo
Lekeitio
San Sebastián
Fuenterrabía
Baracaldo
Bilbao
Ondárroa
Zumaia
Guernica
Zarautz
Irún
Eibar
Hernani
Durango
A2625 A68 E80U
Mondragón
Tolosa
Amurrio
Vitoria-Gasteiz
Pamplona
TO BURGOS
Miranda de Ebro
N
TO BURGOS
Logroño

gence since Franco's death. Few traditions match the breadth and sophistication of Basque cuisine. Spaniards prize *bacalao a la vizcaina* (salted cod in a tomato sauce), dishes *a la vasca* (in a delicate parsley-steeped white wine sauce), and *chipirones en su tinta* (baby squids in their own ink). *Tapas* in País Vasco, considered regional specialties, are called *pintxos* (or *pinchos*); locals wash them down with *sidra* (cider) and the local white wine, *txacoli*.

Tourist offices stock a guide for Compostelan pilgrims and art lovers called *Los Caminos de Santiago* (The Roads to Saint James) and the comprehensive *Guía de Recursos* (Guide to Tourist Resources). Rural tourism is being heavily promoted by regional authorities and tourist offices in Basque cities have brochures on *agroturismo*. In general, buses are faster and cheaper than trains in the region.

■ Bilbao (Bilbo)

Bilbao (pop. 380,000) defines bourgeois. As the industrial engine of the Basque country, it has been making men wealthy since the 16th century. Its ports served as the key shipping link between Castile and Flanders, and the city established mercantile and commercial laws that were emulated all over the world.

Bilbao doesn't rest on its economic laurels; the city has bought respectability by investing heavily in the arts. One of the finest collections of painting in all of Spain resides in its Museo de Bellas Artes, and the city supports an impressive array of theater and opera. The most radiant feather in Bilbao's cap is its new Guggenheim Museum, scheduled to open in October of 1997. Along with a new concert hall and plans for a stylish riverwalk, the Guggenheim promises to bring the cultural esteem for which Bilbao yearns.

PAÍS VASCO (EUSKADI)

ORIENTATION AND PRACTICAL INFORMATION

If it means enduring a thousand plagues, procure a map of Bilbao; this is not a compact city. Bilbao's main artery, the **Gran Vía (de Don Diego López de Haro)**, leads east from the oval **Plaza de Federico Moyúa** to the **Plaza de España (Plaza Circular)**, the axis for many important stops and stations. Past Pl. España, you will cross **Ría de Bilbao** on **Puente del Arenal**, which deposits you on the **Plaza de Arriaga**, the entrance to the **casco viejo** and home of the tourist office.

> Bilbao homepage: http://www.bm30.es/socios/instituciones/bilbao_uk.html

Tourist Office: Oficina de Turismo de Bilbao, Pl. Arriaga (tel. 416 00 22; fax 416 81 68; http://www.bm30.es/socios/instituciones/bilbao_uk.html), on the right-hand side of the ornate Teatro Arriaga. Helpful staff speaks English and issues a monthly bulletin of events. Their booklet about Bilbao is excellent. Open Mon.-Fri. 9am-2pm and 4-7:30pm, Sat. 9am-2pm, Sun. 10am-2pm. You can call the omnipotent **info service** from outside Bilbao at tel. (0)10 424 17 00.

Budget Student Travel Office: TIVE, C. Iparraguirre, 3. Expect a wait—the line can go down the block. ISIC and HI cards for sale. Open Mon.-Fri. 9am-1pm.

Currency Exchange: Banks have the best rates. Open in summer Mon.-Fri. 9am-2pm; in winter Mon.-Thurs. 9am-5:30pm, Fri.-Sat. 9am-2pm. **Banco Central Hispano,** in Pl. España. Open Mon.-Sat. 8:30am-2:30pm. **El Corte Inglés** (see below) is open for exchange Mon.-Sat. 10am-8pm.

El Corte Inglés: Gran Vía, 7-9 (tel. 424 22 11), on the east side of Pl. España. Distributes **maps. Currency exchange** (1% commission, 250ptas min. charge). They also offer novels and **guidebooks in English,** haircuts, a **supermarket,** cafeteria, restaurant, and **telephones.** Open Mon.-Sat. 10am-9pm.

American Express: Viaca, Alameda de Recalde, 68 (tel. 444 48 62), off C. Autonomía. Open Mon.-Fri. 9am-1:30pm and 4:30-7:30pm, Sat. 10am-1pm.

Flights: Airport (tel. 453 06 40), is 9km from Bilbao in Sondica (Sondika). Take the Bizkai Bus A-3247 (Transportes Colectivos, tel. 475 82 00) from C. Sendeja next to the Ayuntamiento, on the left after crossing Puente Arenal into the old town (every 40min. 6am-10:30pm, 40min., 125ptas). Buses return to the city 6:40am-11pm. Served by all major European airlines. **Iberia office,** C. Ercilla, 20 (tel. 424 10 00, airport tel. 471 12 10), at C. Colón de Larreátegui. Open Mon.-Fri. 6:30am-8:30pm.

Trains: Bilbao has 6 train stations, each with at least 2 names; the major ones huddle near Puente del Arenal. All this confusion should subside sometime in 1997 when the city inaugurates its **Estación Intermodal,** which will house all major bus and train lines under one roof in what is now **Estación de Abando.**

RENFE: Estación de Abando/del Norte, Pl. España, 2 (reservations tel. 423 86 36; info tel. 423 86 23). Ticket booth open 7am-11pm. To: Madrid (2 per day, 6-9hr., 4000ptas); Barcelona (2 per day, 11-11½hr., 4800-4900ptas); Sevilla (1 per day, 14hr., 13,200ptas); Salamanca (2 per day, 6¼hr., 3300ptas).

FEVE: Estación de Santander, C. Bailén, 2 (tel. 423 22 66). From Pl. España walk down C. Navarra toward the river and take a right just before the bridge. A huge gilded building on the water. FEVE is less efficient than RENFE. Info open Mon.-Fri. 7am-9pm. To Santander (3-4 per day, 910ptas).

Ferrocarriles Vascongados (FV)/Eusko Trenbideak (ET): 3 stations. Obscenely slow—take the bus instead. To: Guernica (27-29 per day, 1hr., 285ptas) from **Atxuri Station,** Cl. Atxuri, 6-8 (tel. 433 95 00); Plentzia beaches and regional towns from **San Nicolas Station,** Pl. San Nicolas, 3 (tel. 416 13 12). For info, call tel. 433 95 00 or ask at tourist office.

Buses: Bilbao's bus system is even harder to figure out than the trains but has improved with the construction of the **Terminbus terminal,** C. Gurtubay, 1, (tel. 439 50 77), in the west side of town near the fairgrounds. The system will hopefully improve even more with the **Intermodal** (see **Trains,** above). The tourist office can help. Of the 20 lines with departure points in the city, 6 stand out: **ANSA (GETSA, VIACAR),** C. Autonomía, 17 (tel. 444 31 00). From Pl. España, go down C. Hurtado de Amézaga to Pl. Zabálburu, bearing right on C. Autonomía for

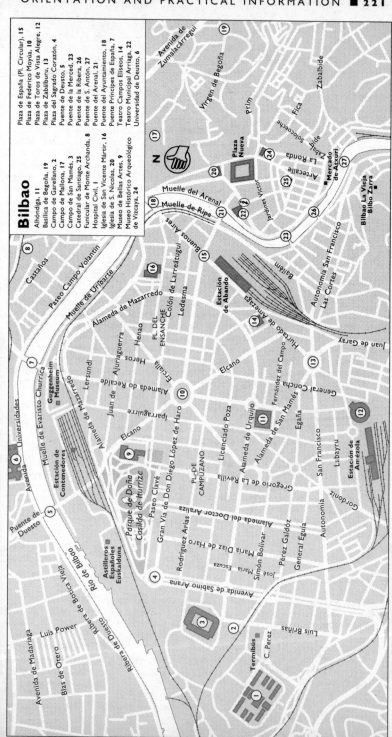

Bilbao

Alhóndiga, 11
Basílica de Begoña, 19
Campo de Garellano, 2
Campo de Mallona, 17
Campo de San Mamés, 3
Catedral de Santiago, 25
Funicular de Monte Archanda, 8
Hospital Civil, 1
Iglesia de San Vicente Mártir, 16
Iglesia de S. Nicolás, 20
Museo de Bellas Artes, 9
Museo Histórico Arqueológico
de Vizcaya, 24

Plaza de España (Pl. Circular), 15
Plaza de Federico Moyúa, 10
Plaza de Toros de Vista Alegre, 12
Plaza de Zabálburu, 13
Plaza del Sagrado Corazón, 4
Puente de Deusto, 5
Puente de la Merced, 23
Puente de la Ribera, 26
Puente de S. Antón, 27
Puente del Arenal, 21
Puente del Ayuntamiento, 18
Puente Príncipes de España, 7
Teatro Campos Elíseos, 14
Teatro Municipal Arriaga, 22
Universidad de Deusto, 6

2 blocks; enter through Bar Ansa. To: Burgos (3-4 per day, 2hr., 1400ptas); Madrid (9 per day, 5hr., 3215ptas); Barcelona (4 per day, 7hr., 4750ptas); León (Mon.-Sat. 1 per day, 6½hr., 2890ptas).

Compañía Automóviles Vascongados (CAV), C. Hurtado de Amézaga, Túnel de RENFE (tel. 423 78 60). In Estación de Abando (see **Trains,** above). To Guernica (Mon.-Sat. 28-37 per day, Sun. 3 per day, 45min., 290ptas).

ENATCAR, C. Autonomía, 4 (tel. 439 51 11), off Pl. Zabálburu (from which buses depart). Ticket booth open Mon.-Sat. 9am-1pm and 4-8pm, Sun. 9am-noon.

PESA, C. Hurtado de Amézaga, Edificio RENFE (tel. 424 88 99, info tel. (902) 10 12 10), in Estación de Abando (see **Trains**). Go straight past the station entrance; PESA is a ½block farther up. To San Sebastián (16-25 per day, 1¼hr., 1060ptas).

La Unión, C. Henao, 29 (tel. 424 08 36). From Pl. España walk down Gran Vía to Pl. Federico de Moyúa, turn right on Alameda de Recalde and go 2 blocks to C. Henao. To: Vitoria-Gasteiz (8-10 per day, 1hr., 655ptas). Leaving from Termibús (tel. 439 50 77) to: Logroño (3-4 per day, 1½hr., 1430ptas); Pamplona (3-5 per day, 2hr., 1530ptas); Zaragoza (2 per day, 3½hr., 2300ptas).

ALSA Grupo, C. Gurtabay, 1 (tel. 439 50 77). To: Santander (18 per day, 2¼hr., 900ptas); Irún (8 per day, 2hr., 1125ptas); La Coruña (2 per day, 10hr., 5585ptas); Zaragoza (6 per day, 4hr., 2300ptas).

Public Transportation: Bilbao opened an attractive and user-friendly **metro** (tel. 425 40 25) in Nov. 1995. The system has 1 line with terminal points in the suburbs. Trains leave every 5-30min. from the *casco viejo* and run through the new city. Hang on to your ticket after entering—you'll need it again to exit. Travel within one zone, 130ptas; 2 zones 155ptas; 3 zones 185ptas. 10-trip ticket: 770ptas; 925ptas; 1105ptas. Trains run Mon.-Sat. 6am-2am, Sun. 7am-11pm. **Bilbobús** (tel. 475 82 00) runs 23 lines across the city (6am-11:30pm; 110ptas, 10-ride coupon 645ptas). The tourist office has a detailed map. **Bizkai Bus** connects Bilbao to suburbs and the airport in Sondica (125ptas).

Taxis: Teletaxi (tel. 410 21 21). **Radio Taxi Bilbao** (tel. 444 88 88). Some cluster directly behind the Teatro Arriaga. To airport 1500-1700ptas.

Car Rental: Europcar, C. Rodríguez Arias, 49 (fax 442 28 49), 3 blocks past the AmEx office at C. Máximo Aguirre. Must be 21. Peugot 205 4300ptas per day, 43ptas per km. Open Mon.-Fri. 9am-1pm and 4-7:30pm, Sat. 9am-1pm.

Luggage Storage: In **Estación de Abando** lockers are 400ptas. Get tokens at the *cercanías* booth. Open daily 7am-11pm. In **Termibús,** officials will guard your luggage for 50ptas (20kg or less) for the 1st day, then 35ptas, 70ptas, and 105ptas per day. *Consigna* booth open 8:30am-8pm daily.

Lost Property: (tel. 445 03 00).

English Bookstores: Casa del Libro, C. Colón de Larreátegui, 44 (tel. 424 07 04), off Alameda de Recalde. Terrific selection of guidebooks, literature, and trashy novels. Open Mon.-Fri. 9:30am-1:30pm and 4-8pm, Sat. 9:30am-1:30pm.

Bisexual-Gay-Lesbian Organizations: EHGAM, Escalinatas de Solokoetxe, 4 (tel. 415 07 19). Open Mon.-Fri. 8-10pm, or write them at Apdo. 1667, 48080 Bilbao. Fri.-Sat. it's a gay and lesbian disco. **Gays por la Salud, Asociación T4,** C. Autonomía, 56, 3rd fl. (tel. ((9)08) 67 58 80). Open daily 10am-10pm. Support groups and health info.

Red Cross: C. Ondarrolo (tel. 422 22 22).

24Hr. Pharmacy: Check any pharmacy's door, or call the municipal police.

Medical Services: Hospital Civil de Basurto, Av. Montevideo, 18 (tel. 441 88 00 or 442 40 51). **Ambulance:** (tel. 473 16 34).

Police: Municipal, C. Luis Briñas (tel. 441 10 04). **National** (tel. 431 00 00).

Emergency: tel. 091 or 092.

Post Office: Main office, Alameda Urquijo, 19 (tel. 422 05 48; fax 443 00 24). Walk one block down Gran Vía from Pl. España and turn left after El Corte Inglés; it's on the corner with C. Bertendona. Open for info, **fax,** and Lista de Correos Mon.-Fri. 8:30am-8:30pm; for stamps only Sat. 9:30am-2pm; for **fax** Mon.-Fri. 8:30am-8:30pm. **Postal Code:** 48005.

Telephone Code: (9)4.

ACCOMMODATIONS

At any time other than during the August festival season (when rates can be higher than those listed below), most areas have never heard the words *temporada alta*. With the new Guggie, though, you may want to call ahead. The tourist office has a list of recommended budget *pensiones*, almost all of which are in the *casco viejo*. Starting points are **Plaza Arriaga,** at the base of the bridge and down the stairs to the right, and **Calle Arenal,** which runs up to the left.

Pensión de la Fuente, C. Sombrería, 2 (tel. 416 99 89). From C. Arenal, turn left on C. Correo, follow it 1 block, then turn left again. Pleasant and spacious, with a TV room and a friendly owner. Singles 1500-2000ptas. Doubles 2500-3000ptas, with bath 4000ptas. Heating extra.

Hostal Mardones, C. Jardines, 4, 3rd fl. (tel. 415 31 05). From the bridge, turn right onto C. Bidebarrieta and right again. Gorgeous rooms, some with balconies, all with polished wood floors and marble sinks. Delightful owners. Singles 2000-2700ptas. Doubles 3000ptas, with bath 3500ptas. Triples 4500-5500ptas.

Pensión Ladero, C. Lotería, 1, 4th fl. (tel. 415 09 32). From Pl. Arriaga, take C. Bidebarrieta and turn left onto C. Lotería. A bit dark, but that's no hindrance to a good night's sleep. Very clean, occasionally huge rooms, all with TV. Singles 1800ptas. Doubles 3000ptas.

Pensión Mendez, C. Santa María, 13, 4th fl. (tel. 416 03 64). From the bridge, turn right on C. Ribera; C. Santa María is on the left. Five floors insulate the *pensión* from raging nightlife below. Clean, comfy, and one of the cheapest in town. Most rooms have balconies. Singles 2000ptas. Doubles 3000ptas. Triples 4500ptas.

Hostal Arana, C. Bidebarrieta, 2 (tel. 415 64 11), at Pl. Arriaga. Pink arched halls and nautical-style reception area. Many airy, white-walled rooms, some overlooking the river (for what it's worth). All rooms have TV and phone. Showers are certainly not scalding. Singles 3000ptas, with bath 4000ptas. Doubles: 4000ptas; 5500ptas. Prices don't include 7% IVA. Closed Dec. 20-Jan. 8.

Hostal-Residencia Jofra, C. Elcano, 34, 1st fl. (tel. 421 29 49), in the new city. From Pl. España, walk 5 blocks down C. Hurtado de Amézaga past Estación de Abando and turn right. Pleasant rooms off a quiet street. Singles 2000ptas. Doubles 3200ptas. Open Sept.-July.

FOOD

Restaurants and bars near the sights on the "seven streets" offer hearty local dishes in spaces as cramped as the medieval *casco viejo* itself. Dining in the modern quarter offers more variety and amenities but perhaps less in the way of down 'n' dirty ambience. **Mercado de la Ribera,** on the bank of the river heading left from the tourist office, is the biggest indoor market in Europe. It's worth a trip even if you're not eating. Upstairs, on tables at the far end of the building, local farmers sell just-picked produce at lower, bargainable prices (open Mon.-Thurs. and Sat. 8am-2pm, Fri. 7:45am-2pm and 4:30-7:30pm). Round up **groceries** at **El Corte Inglés** (see p. 220).

In the Casco Viejo

Aitxiar, C. María Muñoz, 8 (tel. 415 09 17). Ambrosial food in a lively setting. Try the *merluza a la vasca* (hake in a wine, garlic, and parsley sauce with clams) and you'll know why this dish is so popular in País Vasco. The *tostadas* dessert is the French toast of your dreams, with anise-scented cream. Three-fork lunch *menú* 1000ptas. Open Tues.-Sun. 1-4pm and 8-11:30pm. Visa.

Restaurante Kaltzo, C. Barrencalle Barrena, 5 (tel. 416 66 42). A super pick on a street lined with many inexpensive options. Sedate dining room removed from the hysteria below. 950ptas *menú del día* includes a delicious *arroz a la marinera*, laden with shellfish. Open Tues.-Sat. 1-4pm and 8:30-11pm, Mon. 1-4pm. Visa, MC.

Restaurante Juanak, C. Somera, 10. Hand-painted menu on the wall and lively twentysomething crowd. Fifty-four *bocadillos* include vegetarian options (325-500ptas). Open Sun.-Wed. 1pm-12:30am, Thurs. 1pm-1am, Fri.-Sat. 1pm-3am.

In the New City

Restaurante Zuretzat, C. Iparraguirre, 7 (tel. 424 85 05), down the street from the Guggenheim. The 1000ptas *menú* (served 1-4pm) is a jewel that includes *marmitako*, a tomato- and potato-based Basque soup with chunks of fresh tuna, as well as a delicious chicken with walnut sauce, all served in a high-stepping atmosphere. Bar open daily 1-4pm and 8:30-11pm. Dinner served Fri. and Sat. nights only. Visa.

Restaurante-Bar Al Jordan, C. Elcano, 26 (tel. 410 42 55), on a side street near the train station. Middle Eastern food with vegetarian options. Falafel sandwiches (400ptas) and kebabs (200ptas each). Veg and non-veg *menú* 975ptas. Breakfast with mint tea, Arabic pastries, and fresh juice 300ptas. Belly dancing on Fri. and Sat. nights—call for reservations. Open daily 9am-noon or 1pm. Visa, MC, AmEx.

Café La Granja, Pl. España, 3 (tel. 423 08 13), opposite Estación de Abando. One of Bilbao's classic cafes. Breakfast of *café* and *tostadas* 235ptas. *Menú* 1300ptas (available 1:30-4pm). Open Mon.-Thurs. 7am-11:30pm, Fri.-Sun 7am-2:30 or 3pm.

SIGHTS

An undulating structure of multiple levels and unexpected curves, the new **Guggenheim Museum** will attract contemporary architecture pilgrims to see its glistening titanium skin and art aficionados to its rotating collection of modern and contemporary art. The metal edifice reflects both Bilbao's industrial repute and the city's new identity as a 21st-century metropolis. Designed by American Frank O. Gehry, the building's interior features a light-filled atrium and the world's first gallery with adjustable dimensions. Gehry designed one salon specifically to house Picasso's *Guernica*, now housed in Madrid's Reina Sofía (see **Madrid,** p. 100). Officials in Madrid have declined to relocate Picasso's enormous commemoration of the tragic World War II bombing of Guernica, claiming that its condition is too fragile to endure the journey (see **Guernica,** p. 225). Basque officials have criticized Madrid's deliberation, and with good reason—*Guernica* has already traveled to 15 different national and international locations. Drawing from the vast collections of New York's two Guggenheims, the fourth Guggenheim (the third is in Venice) will feature American abstract art and works by European and Basque artists of international acclaim. The museum will open its doors on October 3, 1997. Admission is expected to be around 600ptas.

Bilbao's **Museo de Bellas Artes,** Pl. Museo, 2 (tel. 441 95 36), hoards aesthetic riches behind an unassuming facade. Among its 12th- to 19th- century Spanish and Flemish holdings are works by El Greco and Zurbarán, Goya's *María Luisa* (wife of Carlos IV), a Gauguin, and numerous canvases by Basque painters. A substantial contemporary abstract art collection and a detail of one of Velázquez's red-nosed portraits of *Felipe IV* are some of its highlights. The ivy-covered building sits on the edge of Parque de Doña Casilda de Iturriza, on the west end of the city. From Pl. Federico Moyúa (with Pl. España behind you), angle right on C. Elcano and follow it to Pl. Museo, or take bus #10 from Puente del Arenal (open Tues.-Sat. 10am-1:30pm and 4-7:30pm, Sun. 10am-2pm; free).

Dip into Basque culture and history at the **Museo Arqueológico, Etnográfico, e Histórico de Vizcaya,** C. Cruz, 4 (tel. 415 54 23), housed in a beautiful old stone cloister. The exhibits cover hand-weaving, blacksmiths, pastoral life, and—naturally—the sea. Check out the display case on Basques in America. The museum is in the old city; walk past Pensión de la Fuente away from C. Correo to Pl. Miguel de Unamuno, from whence C. Cruz springs (open Tues.-Sat. 10am-1:30pm and 4-7pm, Sun. 10:30am-1:30pm; free). The best view of Bilbao (which isn't saying a lot) is from the *mirador* on **Monte Archanda,** north of the old town. For the *funicular* to the top, turn left from Pl. Arenal with your back to the new town and follow the riverside road past the Ayuntamiento. On Po. Campo de Volantin, turn right on C. Espalza and zig-zag left at its end (*funicular* every 15min., Mon.-Sat. 7:15am-10pm, Sun. 8:15am-10pm; June-Sept. till 11pm; one-way 95ptas).

A short train ride leads to beaches north of the city at **Plencia** (Plentzia) or at **Sopelana** along the way. Plencia's beach is a bit rough. **Getxo** lies just a little nearer to the surf; its illuminated **Puente Colgante** (suspension bridge) fords the river, leading to a

spate of all-night bars. You can also take a **bus** here from Pl. Ensanche in Bilbao (150ptas), near the market. Revelers who miss the midnight train will find themselves obliged to taxi home (2000-2500ptas). Also nearby in the region of Vizcaya is the rock-climbing fishing village of **Elantxobe,** the surfing capital of **Mundaka.**

ENTERTAINMENT

A city with so many comfortable bars can be expected to have a thriving after-dark scene, especially (but not exclusively) on the weekends. In the **casco viejo** revelers spill out into the streets to tipple *chiquitos,* small glasses of beer or wine characteristic of the region (the sport of tippling is called *chiquiteo*). Teenagers and twentysomethings jam at **Calle de Licenciado Poza** and **Calle de Barrencalle.** With 200 bars, **Calle de Ledesma** exerts a similar pull. Upscale Bilbao retires to the **Jardines de Albia** to get its *copas,* or frequents one of the city's elegant 19th-century cafes like **Café Boulevard,** C. Arenal, 6 (tel. 415 31 28), home to Miguel de Unamuno's *tertulia* (workshop). The coolest, most radical bar in town is **Herriko Taberna** (The People's Tavern), C. Ronda, 20. Unmarked, save for an outer wall splattered with militant graffiti, its interior is papered with political posters and photos of Basque detainees.

The city is sports-crazy. Watch **Atlétic de Bilbao** electrify *fútbol*-frenzied crowds at Campo de San Mamés, C. Luis Briñas (ticket info tel. 441 14 45), or witness native Miguel Indurain on TV wow locals (and the world) in July cycling at the Tour de France. The massive blowout *fiesta* in honor of Nuestra Señora de Begoña takes place during **Semana Grande** (actually two *semanas,* beginning the weekend after Aug. 15). Music, theater, and bullfights climax with fireworks. Documentary filmmakers the world over gather from October to November for the **Festival Internacional de Cine Documental de Bilbao.** Until then, you can watch original version (not dubbed) movies regularly at **Cines Abra,** C. Nicolas Alcorta, 5 (tel. 443 65 21), or the **Fas Film Club,** C. San Vicente, 2 (tel. 423 59 49), which screens art films every Monday at 7:30pm and hosts a discussion group afterward. During the summer, there are free **concerts** every Sunday evening at the bandstand in the Parque Arenal.

■ Guernica (Gernika)

On April 26, 1937, the Nazi "Condor Legion" released an estimated 29,000kg of explosives on Guernica, obliterating in three hours all but thirty percent of a city long considered the spiritual and historical center of the Basque country. The legacy of Europe's first mass civilian aerial bombardment smoulders beneath the surface in the eerily modern streets of this reincarnated town. The tragedy moved Pablo Picasso to paint his stark epic *Guernica,* now in Madrid's Reina Sofía. Fascists pointed to the painting and asked Picasso whether he had done it. "No, you did," he replied. Today, Guernica emphasizes not its victimization but its historical glory and peaceful parks, directing its visitors to focus on less dramatic times.

Practical Information To reach the **tourist office,** C. Artecalle, 8 (tel. 625 58 92; fax 625 75 42), from the train station, walk straight two blocks up C. Adolfo Urioste and turn right onto C. Artecalle; the office is on column-lined C. Andra María Walk. They relay transportation info and shuffle accommodations and restaurant listings and a multilingual map. (Open in summer Mon.-Sat. 9:30am-1pm and 4-7:30pm, Sun. 10am-2:30pm; in winter Mon.-Sat. 10am-1pm and 4-7:30pm, Sun. 10:30am-1:30pm). **Medical services,** C. San Juan, 1 (tel. 625 42 46), are available at the *ambulatorio.* **Municipal police** are at C. Artecalle, 8 (tel. 625 05 54). In an **emergency,** call tel. 091 or 092. The **post office** C. Iparragirre, 26 (tel. 625 03 87), is an institution. Make an immediate left as you exit the train station. The office is three blocks down on the right (open Mon.-Fri. 8:30am-2:30pm, Sat. 9:30am-1pm). The **postal code** is 4830. The **telephone code** is (9)4. **Trains** (tel. 625 11 82) journey to Bilbao (5 per day, 50min., 285ptas). Compañía de Automóviles Vascongados (tel. 454 05 44) sends **buses** from a spot one block left of the train station. To Bilbao (28-37 per day, 45min., 290ptas). Hail a **Taxi** by calling tel. 625 10 02.

PAÍS VASCO (EUSKADI)

Accommodations and Food Guernica is best as a daytrip, but if you dally, try **Hostal Iratxe,** C. Industria, 4 (tel. 625 64 63). If nobody's home, knock at Bar Frontón (tel. 625 31 34), down the street; the ownership is the same (singles 2000ptas, doubles 3500-4000ptas, triples 4500ptas). From the train station, go up C. Urioste and turn left on C. Pablo Picasso, which becomes C. Industria.

Market mavens go to the huge round building on the pedestrian street next to the tourist office (open Mon.-Fri. 9am-1:30pm and 4:30-8:30pm, Sat. 9am-1:30pm). **Supermercado Tutoricagüena,** C. Ciudad de Berga, 2 (across from the bus stop), is a surprisingly large supermarket but has a piddling pile o' produce. Family-run **Restaurante Zallo Barri,** C. Juan Calzada, 79 (tel. 625 18 00), left off C. Urioste as you exit the train station, dishes out a tasty 800ptas *menú* (open Tues.-Sat. 1-4pm and 8:30-11pm, Sun. 1-4pm).

Sights The emotional focus of the town is **El Arbol.** The remains of this 2000-year-old oak tree stand beneath an eight-pillared dome next to the **Casa de Juntas,** where the Vizkaya General Assembly meets. Medieval Basques gathered to debate community issues under the oak. Later, Guernica became the political center of Vizcaya. When the area passed into Castilian hands, the monarchs were expected to make a ritual voyage to Guernica and its oak to swear their respect for the autonomy of the *juntas* (local governments) and local *fueros* (laws). The oak's offspring, an august tree of 300 years, grows next to the building behind the fence. A grandchild oak was planted in 1979 to celebrate the region's restored autonomy (open June-Sept. 10am-2pm and 4-7pm; Oct.-May 10am-2pm and 4-6pm; free). Paintings and artifacts on display inside the **Museo de Euskal Herria** help fill visitors in on Basque history (open Tues.-Sat. 10am-2pm and 4-7pm, Sun. 10am-1:30pm; free).

Eduardo Chillida's arresting sculpture **La casa de nuestro padre** (*Gure aitaren etxea,* Our Father's House) was commissioned for the 50th anniversary of the city's bombing. It stands side by side with Henry Moore's perplexing **Large Figure in a Shelter.** Both pose in the bucolic **Parque de los Pueblos de Europa** (open daily in summer 10am-9pm; in winter 10am-7pm). From the FV (EuskoTren) station, follow C. Adolfo Urioste as far as it goes (4-5 blocks). At the top, enter the park and cross the little wooden bridge to the right. The only other memorial to the bombardment, the **Exposición del Bombardeo de Gernika** appears temporarily for a month annually in July or August in the Gernika Museum.

To watch the fastest Basque sport (a local invention and passion known alternatively as Jai Alai, Pelota Vasca, or Cesta), head for the **Frontón de Jai-Alai,** C. Carlos Gongoti (tel. 625 62 50; Sat.-Mon. nights 1500ptas).

■ Near Guernica

People settled in the area at least 17,000 years ago, and the **Cueva de Santimamiñe,** 5km north of Guernica, preserves a set of prehistoric paintings on its cave walls. Thirteen-thousand-year-old bison, horses, bears, and deer frolic in spite of their advanced age. Some (mainly nationalists) argue that the Basque language originated here when the population abandoned the caves in the Neolithic period, spreading their tongue throughout País Vasco. (Guided tour in Spanish only. Mon.-Fri. 10, 11:15am, 12:30, 4:30, and 6pm. 20 people max. per tour. Free.) No public transportation comes near the cave, although the bus to Lekeitio might let you off half-way there; the carless must hike or take a cab.

A 3km hike from the caves, the colorful **Bosque Pintado de Oma** has been called a metaphor for the Basque Country. Completed in 1987, the arboreal artwork is the creation of Basque artist Agustín Ibarrola, who spent years painting the several hundred pine trees. Different groupings of trees make up independent compositions; the intended observation spots are clearly marked. To get to the forest from the caves, follow the well-delineated trail from the parking lot (about 30min.).

What the Devil are they Txpeaking?

Linguists still cannot pinpoint the origin of *euskera*, an agglutinate non-Indo-European language. Its commonalties with Caucasian and African tongues regarding root structures suggest that prehistoric Basques may have migrated from the Caucasus through Africa. Historically referred to by other Spaniards as *la lengua del diablo* (the devil's tongue), *euskera* has come to symbolize cultural self-determination. Only half a million natives speak the language, chiefly in País Vasco regions Guipúzcoa and Vizcaya, and northern Navarra. Franco banned *euskera* and forbid parents to give their children Basque names. Nowadays usage spreads through *ikastolas* (all-Basque schools), TV, and Basque publications. As a result, mostly the young and elderly speak the language. The younger generations listen to rock music in *euskera*, conduct normal conversations in the language, and give their kids traditional names such as Iñaki, Idoya, and Estibaliz.

■ San Sebastián (Donostia)

Rita Hayworth, who visited San Sebastián, embodied the cool elegance and extravagant beauty of this seaside town. Glittering on the shores of the Cantabrian Sea, San Sebastián (pop. 180,000) is a city of broad boulevards, garden avenues, ornate buildings, and radiant beaches. But despite its wealth of ritzy boutiques and sheik restaurants, the city is no snob. Every day before lunch and every evening after *paseo*, locals and vacationers down *pintxos* and *txacoli* in old quarter bars that are neither touristy nor cliquish. San Sebastián is a place to fall in love with a people and their land, if only because they pay little mind to their foreign company.

Beneath its tranquil facade, San Sebastián is passionately, and sometimes violently, involved with Basque Nationalism. There is a good chance you will be awakened by a peaceful demonstration marching past your hostel window, but violent expressions are infrequent.

ORIENTATION AND PRACTICAL INFORMATION

Street and plaza signs are often in both **castellano** and **euskera.** The street guide on the tourist office map gives both versions in its index, so don't despair if you see "kalea" and "tx" everywhere. The **Río Urumea** splits San Sebastián in two. The city center, most monuments, and the two most popular beaches are on the peninsula on the west side of the river. The tip of the peninsula is **Monte Urgulla.** Inland is the **parte vieja** (old city) where night life rages and budget accommodations and restaurants cluster. South of the *parte vieja*, at the base of the peninsula, is the commercial district. In the heart of the district sits the **Catedral de Buen Pastar,** bordered by **Calle San Martin** to the north, **Calle Urbieta** to the west, **Calle Urdaneta** to the south, and **Calle Fuenterrabla** to the east. East of the river lies the **RENFE station,** the **Barrio de Gros,** and **Playa de la Zurriola.** The west and east sides of the river are connected by three bridges: Puente Zurriola, Puente Santa Catalina, and Puente María Cristina (listed from north to south). To get to the *parte vieja* from the train station, head straight to Puente María Cristina, cross the bridge, then turn right at the fountain and walk four blocks north to Av. Libertad. Turn left and follow it to the port; the *parte vieja* fans out to the right, La Concha to the left.

The **bus station** is in the south of the city in Pl. Pío XII. **Avenida de Sancho el Sabio** runs to the right (north) straight toward the cathedral, ocean, and old town (or hop on bus #28 straight to Alameda del Boulevard). To get to the tourist office, go down Av. Sancho el Sabio about four blocks; at Pl. Centenario, bear right onto C. Prim and follow it to Puente María Cristina which is on the right when you hit Pl. Bilbao. Then follow the directions above.

Tourist Office: Municipal: Centro de Atracción y Turismo, C. Reina Regente (tel. 48 11 66; fax 48 11 72), in the vast Teatro Victoria Eugenia. From the train station, turn right immediately after crossing Puente María Cristina and continue past Puente Santa Catalina; C. Reina Regente will be on the left where Puente Zurriola crosses the river. English-speaking staff, indexed map, transit and accommodations info, and a message bulletin board. Open June-Sept. Mon.-Sat. 8am-8pm, Sun. 10am-1pm; Oct.-May Mon.-Fri. 9am-2pm and 3:30-7pm, Sat. 8am-8pm. **Regional: Oficina de Turismo del Gobierno Vasco,** Po. Fueros (tel. 42 62 82), is farther down the river from the above office, heading toward the train station. Info on Guipuzcoa, including *sidrerías* (see **Entertainment,** p. 234). Open Mon.-Fri. 9am-1:30pm and 3:30-6:30pm, Sat.-Sun. 9am-1pm. Closed Sun. in winter.

Budget Travel: TIVE, C. Tomás Gros, 3 (tel. 27 69 34; fax 32 04 94), below street level a block off Pl. Euskadi down C. Miracruz and then right. ISIC 700ptas. HI card 1800ptas. They process train, bus, and plane tickets to international destinations only. Message board with travel info. Open Mon.-Fri. 9am-2pm.

Currency Exchange: Banco Central Hispano sits on Av. Sancho el Sabio just as you exit the bus station to the right. Open Mon.-Fri. 9am-2pm.

Flights: Airport (tel. 66 85 00), in Fuenterrabía (Hondarribia), 22km east of the city. **Interurbanos** buses to Fuenterrabía pass by the airport (every 12min., 7:48am-10pm, 45min., 215ptas). Info open 8am-1pm and 4-8pm. To Madrid (1-2 per day) and Barcelona (1 per day Mon.-Fri.). **Iberia** office at the airport (tel. 64 34 64).

Trains: RENFE, Estación del Norte, Po. Francia (tel. 28 30 89), on the east side of Puente María Cristina. Info desk (tel. 28 35 99) open daily 7:30am-11pm. To: Vitoria-Gasteiz (12-13 per day, 1¾hr., 1105-1500ptas); Pamplona (4 per day, 2hr., 1400ptas; take the bus to Pamplona—it costs half as much and takes half the time); Burgos (4-8 per day, 3-4hr., 2400-2500ptas); Zaragoza (3-4 per day, 4hr., 2600ptas); Madrid (6 per day, 6-9hr., 4700ptas); Barcelona (1-2 per day, 9½-11hr., 4700ptas); Paris (7 per day, 11,000ptas; change at Hendaye). **Estación de Amara (Euskotren),** Pl. Easo (tel. 47 08 15). Frequent commuter trains to Irún (25min., 120ptas) and Hendaye (40min., 120ptas). **RENFE office,** C. Camino, 1, at C. Oquendo, a block north of Puente Santa Catalina and 1 block west of the river. Open Mon.-Fri. 9am-1pm and 4-7pm, Sat. 9am-1pm.

Buses: Several private companies run from different points in the city. Most companies pass through the central station, on Pl. Pío XII, about 13 blocks south of Av. Libertad on Av. Sancho el Sabio. Buy tickets at the offices of each company.

PESA, Av. Sancho el Sabio, 33 (tel. 902 10 12 10). To Bilbao (9-29 per day, every 30min., 1¼hr., 1060ptas) and Vitoria-Gasteiz (12 per day, 1¾hr., 1010ptas).

Continental Auto, Av. Sancho el Sabio, 31 (tel. 46 90 74). To: Madrid (6 per day, 6hr., 3685ptas); Burgos (4-6 per day, 3¼hr., 1825ptas); Vitoria-Gasteiz (4-6 per day, 1¾hr., 1010ptas).

La Roncalesa, on Po. Vizcaya (tel. 46 10 64). To Pamplona (4-8 per day, 1½hr., 750ptas).

Irbarsa, Po. Vizcaya, 16 (tel. 45 75 00). To Barcelona (3 per day, 7hr., 2450ptas).

Turytrans (tel. 46 23 60). To Paris (6 per week, 10hr., 7300ptas).

Interurbanos, Pl. Guipozcoa (tel. 64 13 02). Pay on board. To: Fuenterrabía (45min., 190ptas) and Irún (35min., 180ptas). Bus leaves every 15min. 7:45am-10:45pm daily.

Public Transportation: Nineteen bus routes (100ptas, 10-ride pass available at *tabaco* stores 570ptas). List of routes available at the tourist office or call tel. 28 71 00. Bus #28 goes to center from bus station, #16 goes from Alameda del Boulevard to campground and beaches.

Taxis: Santa Clara (tel. 31 01 11), or **A.D.** (tel. 42 66 42). Try Alameda del Boulevard or Av. Libertad. About 3200ptas to the airport.

Car Rental: Europcar, C. San Martín, 60 (tel. 32 23 04; fax 29 07 00). Must be 21 or older. Open Mon.-Fri. 8am-1pm and 4-7:30pm, Sat. 9am-1pm.

Mountain Bike Rental: Comet, Av. Libertad, 6 (tel. 42 66 37). Half-day 2500ptas, 1 day 3000ptas, additional day(s) 2000ptas. Open in summer Mon.-Sat. 9:30am-1pm and 4-8pm; in winter Mon.-Sat. 9:30am-1pm and 3:30-7:30pm. Closed Mon. mornings.

Luggage Storage: Lockers at RENFE station, 400ptas per day. Open 7am-11pm.

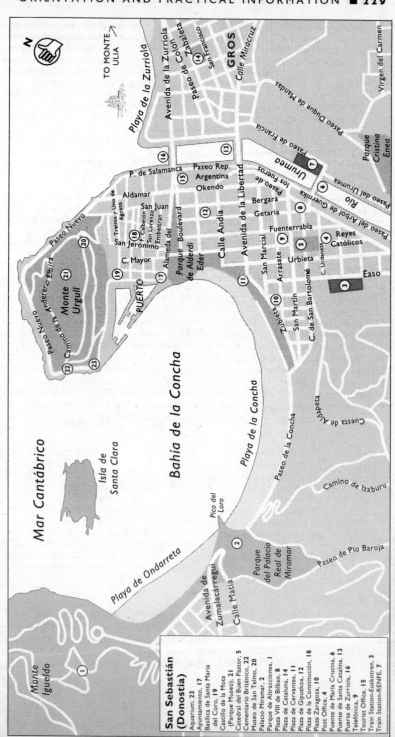

Mar Cantábrico

Isla de Santa Clara

Bahía de la Concha

GROS

TO MONTE ULIA

Virgen del Carmen

Parque Cristina Enea

Playa de la Zurriola

Avenida de la Zurriola

Paseo de Colón

San Francisco

Calle Miracruz

Paseo Duque de Mandas

Paseo de Francia

Río Urumea

Paseo del Urumea

Paseo del Árbol de Guernika

Paseo de los Fueros

P. de Salamanca

Paseo Rep. Argentina

Okendo

Aldamar

San Juan

F. Calbetón

San Lorenzo

Embeltran

San Jerónimo

C. Mayor

Treinta y Uno de Agosto

Paseo Nuevo

Monte Urgull

Camino de la Andereño Elbira

Paseo Nuevo

Castillo de la Mota

PUERTO

Alameda del Parque Boulevard de Aldebi Eder

Calle Andía

Avenida de la Libertad

Bergara

Getaria

Fuenterrabía

San Marcial

Arrasate

Reyes Católicos

C. Urdaneta

Easo

Urbieta

San Martín

Zubieta

C. de San Bartolomé

Playa de la Concha

Paseo de la Concha

Cuesta de Aldapeta

Camino de Izaburu

Pico del Loro

Parque del Palacio Real de Miramar

Avenida de Zumalacárregui

Calle Matía

Playa de Ondarreta

Monte Igueldo

Paseo de Pío Baroja

San Sebastián (Donostia)

Aquarium, 23
Ayuntamiento, 17
Basílica de Santa María del Coro, 19
Castillo de la Mota (Parque Museo), 21
Catedral del Buen Pastor, 5
Cementerio Británico, 22
Museo de San Telmo, 20
Palacio Miramar, 2
Parque de Altracciones, 1
Plaza VIII de Bilbao, 8
Plaza de Cataluña, 14
Plaza de Cervantes, 11
Plaza de Gipuzkoa, 12
Plaza de la Constitución, 18
Plaza Zaragoza, 10
Post Office, 4
Puente de María Cristina, 6
Puente de Santa Catalina, 13
Puente de Zurriola, 16
Telefónica, 9
Tourist Office, 15
Train Station-Euskotren, 3
Train Station-RENFE, 7

PAÍS VASCO (EUSKADI)

Laundromat: Lavomatique, C. Iñigo, 13, off C. S. Juan. Self-serve. Soap and ironing available. Open Mon.-Fri. 10am-1pm and 4-7pm, Sat.-Sun. and holidays 10am-1pm.

English Bookstore: Donosti, Pl. Bilbo, 2 (tel. 42 21 38), 1 block west of Puente María Cristina near the cathedral. Modern fiction. Open Mon.-Fri. 9am-1pm and 4-8pm, Sat. 9am-1pm. **Azoka,** C. Fuenterrabía, 19 (tel. 42 17 45), off Av. San Martín. Penguin Classics and bestsellers. Open Mon.-Sat. 10am-1:30pm and 4-8pm.

Hiking Info: Club Vasco de Camping, San Marcial, 19 (tel. 42 84 79), one block south of Av. Libertad. Below street level. Organizes excursions. Open Mon.-Fri. 7am-8:30pm. **Izadi,** Po. Ramón, 20 (tel. 29 35 20). Bookstore with travel guides, hiking guides, and maps. Many publications in English. Organizes tours and rents skis, wetsuits, and hiking equipment. Open Mon.-Sat. 10am-1pm and 4-8pm.

Red Cross: C. Matías, 7 (tel. 21 46 00). **Ambulance:** (tel. 28 40 00).

24-Hour Pharmacy: Ask the **municipal police** or check p. 2 of *Diario Vasco.*

Medical Services: Casa de Socorro, C. Pedro Egaño, 8 (tel. 46 63 19).

Police: Municipal, C. Larramendi, 10 (tel. 45 00 00).

Emergency: tel. 091 or 092.

Post Office: C. Urdaneta (tel. 46 49 14; fax 45 07 94), the street just south of the cathedral. Heading toward the beach on Av. Libertad, take a left on C. Fuenterrabía and walk 5 blocks. Open Mon.-Fri. 8:30am-8:30pm, Sat. 9:30am-2pm. Lista de Correos at window #3; stamps #9-12. **Postal Code:** 20007.

Telephone Code: (9)43.

ACCOMMODATIONS AND CAMPING

Desperate backpackers must scrounge for rooms in July and August—particularly during *San Fermines* (July 6-14) and *Semana Grande* (starts Sunday during the week of Aug. 15). September, the film festival season, can also be difficult. If you get away with 3000ptas per night, consider yourself lucky. Budget options center in the **parte vieja** and around the **cathedral;** there are often a few per entryway—look for signs in doorways. Many places don't take reservations in the summer. The tourist office has lists of budget accommodations, and most *pensión* owners know of **casas particulares**—don't be afraid to ask for help. Owners of *casas particulares* often solicit guests at the RENFE. Be wary that such solicitations are officially illegal and filthy floors can go for stratospheric prices. Some people choose to sleep on the beach, but the police will kick beach-sleepers out, and the area is reputedly full of shifty characters.

Albergue Juvenil la Sirena (HI), Po. Igueldo, 25 (tel. 31 02 68; fax 21 40 90), near the beach at the far west end of the city. Bus #24 runs from the train and bus stations to Av. Zumalacárregui (the stop in front of the San Sebastián Hotel). Bus #5 drops you off 1 street away on C. Matia (the stop right after tunnel). From Av. Zumalacárregui, take the street that angles toward the mountain (Av. Brunet) and turn left at its end. The hostel is the big pink building. Modern dorm-style rooms. HI members and ISIC-carriers only. Arrive before 11am. Reception closed and access to rooms restricted 11am-3pm. Curfew in summer 2am; in winter Sun.-Thurs. midnight, Fri.-Sat. 2am. In summer 1850ptas, over 26 2100ptas. In winter: 1525ptas; 1850ptas. Breakfast included. Lunch 750ptas, dinner 850ptas. Sheets 375ptas. Luggage storage, laundry facilities, and kitchen available. Visa. All rooms and facilities wheelchair accessible.

In the Parte Vieja

A lengthy walk from both stations, the *parte vieja* is brimming with reasonably priced *pensiones.* Its proximity to Playa de la Concha and the port makes this area a prime nightspot; scores of *pensiones* offer a night's sleep above loud *pintxos* bars. The smart money calls in advance. **Alameda del Boulevard,** just west of Puente Zurriola, marks the south border and is a major artery.

Pensión Loinaz, C. San Lorenzo, 17 (tel. 42 67 14). From Alameda del Boulevard, go up Calle Narrica and make a right on C. San Lorenzo. Attentive, English-speaking owners have bright rooms that will make you want to stay—forever. July-Aug. dou-

bles 4200-4700ptas. Triples 6200ptas. Semana Santa-June: 3200ptas; 4500ptas. Sept.-Semana Santa: 2700ptas; 3800ptas. Singles sometimes available. 3-bedroom apartment available upstairs for groups. *Let's Go* discount. Laundry 800ptas.

Pensión Amaiur, C. 31 de Agosto, 44, 2nd fl. (tel. 42 96 54). From Alameda del Boulevard, go up C. San Jerónimo to the end and turn left. You'll know it when you see the flower-obscured facade. The floral motif continues in the rooms decorated in High Laura Ashley, many with balconies facing the street or the mountain. Delightful owner is also a water conservationist—showers last 10min. Semana Santa and June 22-Sept. 21: doubles 4800ptas, triples 6300ptas. After Semana Santa-June 21: 3300ptas; 4500ptas. Sept. 22 until Semana Santa: 2800ptas; 3600ptas. Oct. 15-March 15 stay 3 nights and get the 4th free. *Let's Go descuento* 300ptas.

Pensión San Lorenzo, C. San Lorenzo, 2 (tel. 42 55 16), a right off C. Narrica from Alameda del Boulevard at C. San Juan. Cozy rooms and a guests-only kitchen that's also a chatty community center. 1000-1250ptas per person, depending on time of year and number of people sharing a room. Owner hires one student at a time to live in and care for the *pensión.*

Pensión Larrea, C. Narrica, 21, 1st fl. (tel. 42 26 94). Simple, appealing rooms. Bathrooms hit 10 on the Clean-O-Meter, so you won't mind sharing them. Singles 2500ptas. Doubles 4500ptas. Sept.-June: 2000ptas; 3000ptas. *Let's Go descuento.*

Pensión Puerto, C. Puerto, 19, 2nd fl. (tel. 43 21 40). Go up C. Mayor from Alameda del Boulevard and you'll run into C. Puerto. Motherly owner boasts clean rooms with big closets. Some rooms have balconies. 1500-2000ptas per person.

Pensión Arsuaga, C. Narrica, 3, 3rd fl. (tel. 42 06 81), off Alameda del Boulevard. Charming, homey rooms. Singles 2500ptas. Doubles 5000ptas. Sept.-June: 2000ptas; 4000ptas. Breakfast 300ptas. Lunch or dinner 1000ptas. Sometimes fills with students Oct.-May.

Pensión Boulevard, Alameda del Boulevard, 24 (tel. 42 94 05). Beautiful, modern rooms overlooking the leafy boulevard. Radios in all rooms, balconies in some, and a fireplace in one. Doubles 6000ptas (one person pays 4500ptas), with bath 8000ptas. In winter: 3000-3500ptas; 4500-5000ptas.

Hostal-Residencia Alameda, Alameda del Boulevard, 23, 2nd fl. (tel. 42 16 87), across from the old quarter. Faded elegance, with emphasis on the faded. Thirty-odd rooms (and they are somewhat odd). Singles 3700ptas. Doubles 5600ptas, with bath 7400ptas. Sept.-June (when open): 2800ptas; 4300ptas; 5500ptas. Everything else: 2500ptas per person, with bath 3500ptas. Consecutive days often cost less. Closed Oct. 16-March 14.

Near the Cathedral

These *bostales* lie in the heart of the commercial zone. They tend to be quieter than those elsewhere in the city, yet still fairly close to buses, trains, port, beach, and within easy walking distance of all the action in the *parte vieja.*

Pensión Urkia, C. Urbieta, 12, 3rd fl. (tel. 42 44 36). C. Urbieta borders the cathedral on the west side; the *pensión* is one block north at C. Arrasate. Polished knick-knacks and gilt mirrors in the foyer, and rooms with lovely blue and white linens, full bathrooms, and TV. July-Sept: singles 3500ptas, doubles 5000ptas, triples and quads 2000ptas per person. Oct.-June: singles 3000ptas, doubles 3200-3500ptas.

Pensión La Perla, C. Loyola, 10, 2nd fl. (tel. 42 81 23), on the street directly ahead of the cathedral. Grand stairway leads to attractive rooms with polished floors. All rooms have bath and TV; #7 is a gem. Friendly, English-speaking owner. Singles 3000ptas. Doubles 5000ptas. Oct.-June: 3000ptas; 3500ptas. 7% IVA not included.

Hostal Residencia Easo, C. San Bartolomé, 24 (tel. 45 39 12). From C. San Martín, heading toward the beach, turn left on C. Easo and right on C. San Bartolomé. Dingy neighborhood, but near the beach. Prim beds in wooden-floored rooms with huge windows. Garage 1500ptas per day. Singles 3500ptas. Doubles 5500ptas, with bath 6500ptas. Oct.-June: 2000ptas; 3500ptas; 4000ptas. Triples 5000ptas.

Pensión Añorga, C. Easo, 12, 1st fl. (tel. 46 79 45), at C. San Martín. Shares entryway with 2 other *pensiones.* Basic, but clean and breezy. Arrive early for a room with a window. Some rooms have TVs. Singles 3000ptas. Doubles 4000ptas, with bath 5000ptas. Sept.-June: 2000ptas; 3000ptas; 4000ptas.

Camping: Camping Igeldo (tel. 21 45 02), 5km west of town. 268 *parcelas* fill in the blink of an eye. Bus #16 "Barrio de Igueldo-Camping" runs between the site and Alameda del Boulevard (every 30min. 6:50am-10:30pm, 95ptas). Keep in mind San Sebastián's quirky weather. Bar-restaurant and supermarket. Reception open 8am-midnight. *Parcela* (including tent and up to 2 people) 2700ptas. Semana Santa 3100ptas. Oct.-June 1300ptas. 395ptas per extra person. 7% IVA not included.

FOOD

Pintxos (*pinchos* in *castellano*), chased down with the fizzy regional white wine *txacoli*, are a religion here; bars in the lively old city spread an array of enticing tidbits on toothpicks or bread. *Pintxos* start simple, like the popular "Gilda" (pronounced HEEL-da, named after the Rita Hayworth movie)—which consists of a pickled pepper, an anchovy, and an olive—and build to unparalleled heights of culinary extravagance. In the harbor, many small places serve tangy sardines with strong, slightly bitter **sidra** (cider), another regional specialty. Custom insists on pouring it with one's arm extended upward so the force of the stream hitting the glass will release the *sidra's* bouquet. Street vendors sell portions of *gambas* (shrimp) in egg cups and *caracolillos* (periwinkles) in paper cones (100-200ptas).

Close to 40 restaurants and bars clamor for attention on **Calle Fermín Calbetón,** in the old quarter. In fact, the entire *parte vieja* seems to exist for no other purpose than to feed. The least expensive hunting ground for a full meal at a *jatetxea* (restaurant in *euskera*) is the **Gros** neighborhood on the east side of the river. The majority of restaurants offer their best deals on lunchtime *menús del día*.

Mercado de la Bretxa inhabits imposing buildings on Alameda del Boulevard at C. San Juan. Farmers sell their own produce on the tables outside. **Mercado de San Martín** is on C. San Marcial, one block left of Av. Libertad toward the beach, between C. Loyola and C. Urbieta (both markets open Mon.-Fri. 7:30am-2pm and 5-7:30pm, Sat. 7:30am-2pm). **Groceries** near the *albergue* await at **Todo Todo 3,** C. Serrano Anguta, between C. Zumalacárregui and C. Matia (open Mon.-Fri. 9am-1pm and 4-8pm, Sat. 9am-1pm). Those staying in the old city will find **Iñigo Saski,** C. Iñigo, 7, more convenient (open Mon.-Fri. 9am-1:30pm and 4:45-7:30pm, Sat. 9am-1:30pm).

For Pintxos in the Parte Vieja

Bar La Cepa, C. 31 de Agosto, 7-9 (tel. 42 63 94). For history's greatest *pintxos* tour, start here with the to-die-for peppers and a host of other delicacies (*pintxos* 150-250ptas, *bocadillos* 350-700ptas, *menú del día* 1500ptas).

Bar Intza, C. Esterlines, 12 (tel. 42 48 33). In addition to its tasty *pintxos*, this place is notable for its outdoor seating under a (real?) grape arbor. Try the mussels stuffed with spinach and cheese (150ptas each). Open daily 10am-4pm and 6:30-11:30pm, later on weekends. In April closes at 10pm. Closed Oct.

A Man's Place Is in...the Kitchen?

In a society like the Basques', where sexually segregated roles permit men to skirt the domestic sphere without doing so much as washing a salad plate, what would you expect the men to do in their free time? Certainly not...cook?

All-male *sociedades gastronómicas,* or *txokos,* are a staple of Basque culture and are nowhere more predominant than in San Sebastián, where they play a key role in the city's social and ceremonial life. Every society has a kitchen and communal dining area where members play cards, chat, and cook for one another. These exclusive clubs reputedly produce the finest cuisine in the city. Not surprisingly, as no *txoko* member would ever whip up dinner at home, neither would he allow a woman into his society's kitchen. Until recently, the *sociedades* prohibited women from ever entering the club; members share apocryphal stories about a society excluding even Queen Victoria Eugenia. Nowadays, in trying to lure younger members with more "tolerant" ideas about women, most clubs will allow ladies in to eat but not to cook.

Bar Juantxo, C. Embeltrán, 6, at C. Esterlines in the *parte vieja*. Crammed with locals. *The* place for *bocadillos* (270-465ptas)—they sell an estimated 1000 a day! And with good reason. *Pintxos* 130ptas. Open daily 9am-3pm and 7pm-11:30pm.

Ganbara, C. San Jerónimo, 21 (tel. 42 25 75). Extremely popular place where Juan the chef looks—and cooks—like a chef should. Sitting down may be out of the question (financially), but the affordable *pintxos* are exquisite. Don't miss the *gambas rebozadas* (200ptas). Open Tues.-Sun. noon-4pm and 7-11:30pm.

Restaurants in the Parte Vieja

Jatetxea Morgan, C. Narrica, 7 (tel. 42 46 61). Way more than you can afford, except for the scene-stealing *menú del día*, 1355ptas plus IVA. Classy, *muy* classy. Visa, MC. Open daily 1:30-4pm and 8:30-11:30pm. In winter closed Sun.

Pizzeria Trattoria Capricciosa, C. Fermín Calbetón, 50 (tel. 43 20 48). Italian basics done well. Pastas 600-900ptas, pizzas 750-1000ptas. Open Mon.-Sat. 1-4pm and 8:30pm-midnight; Sun. 1:30-4pm and 8:30pm-midnight. Visa, MC.

Gaztelu, C. 31 de Agosto, 22 (tel. 42 14 11). Exquisite seafood concoctions (*pintxos* 150ptas, lunch *menú* 950ptas).

Near the Cathedral

Zakusan and **Cachón,** at C. San Marcial, 52 and 40 (tel. 42 61 46 or 42 75 07), are perfect stops on a creative, marine-inspired *pintxos* tour. Yum's the word. *Pintxos* and *canapés* 140-180ptas. Open daily 8:30am-11pm. Visa, MC.

Casa Valles, C. Reyes Católicos, 10 (tel. 45 22 10). Heavenly *pinchos*, 100-200ptas. Well-trodden by locals. Open Thurs.-Tues. 11:30am-4pm and 7pm-midnight.

La Barranquesa, C. Larramendi, 27 (tel. 45 47 47), 2 blocks down Reyes Católicos from the cathedral. One of the cheapest restaurants in town. *Lomo de cerdo* 450ptas, *bacalao a la vizcaina* 750ptas, *menú del día* 900ptas. Open Mon.-Sat. 1:15-3:30pm and 8:15-11:30pm.

Caravanseri Café, Pl. Buen Pastor. To the east of the cathedral. Salads, baked potatoes, burgers, and fabulous vegetarian options including tofu burgers and veggie sausages (600ptas). Open daily for lunch at 12:15pm.

Near the Beach

Pizzería La Pasta Gansa, Po. Concha. Fresh pasta (695-775ptas) and wood-oven pizzas (775-795ptas) served in a cool, bright locale right next to La Concha. Open Wed.-Mon. 1:30-3:30pm and 8:30pm-midnight.

SIGHTS

San Sebastián's most attractive sight is its scenery—its green walks and parks, grandiose buildings, and exuberant geography, encircling a placid, fan-shaped bay. Although the sightlines from nearby Monte Urgull are nothing to sneeze at, the best view may be from the top of **Monte Igueldo** at the east side of the bay. From here you can see the countryside meet the ocean in a line of white and azure. The view of the bay is spectacular after dark, when Isla Santa Clara, lit by floodlights, seems to float on a ring of light. For those making the *paseo* on foot, the walk ends just before the base of Monte Igueldo with Eduard Chillida's sculpture *El peine de los vientos* (Wind's Comb). But should clouds obstruct your view, perhaps these other attractions will help you whittle away a beachless day—we recommend you spend the day eating.

At the other end of the bay, the gravel paths through the shady woods of **Monte Urgull** are peppered with monuments, blissful couples, and stunning vistas. The overgrown **Castillo de Santa Cruz de la Mota** crowns the summit with cannons and a chapel and is itself crowned by the statue of the Sagrado Corazón de Jesús, which blesses the city. The carless can expect a real workout (castle open daily in summer 8am-8pm; in winter 8am-6pm). Halfway up, the huge **Cementerio Británico** commemorates British soldiers who died defending the Spanish monarchy from the French during the Peninsular War in 1833. A more jarring "monument" is the unmarked white-plaster **smear on a rock** near the *paseo* as it rises above the aquarium, where a member of ETA accidentally blew himself up trying to plant a bomb.

On **Paseo Nuevo**, the **Museo de San Telmo** (tel. 42 49 70) resides in an erstwhile Dominican monastery. The serene, overgrown cloister is strewn with Basque funerary relics. The main museum beyond the cloister comprises a fascinating array of Basque artifacts dating to prehistory, a couple of dinosaur skeletons, some El Grecos, and contemporary art (open Tues.-Sat. 10:30am-1:30pm and 4-8pm, Sun. 10am-2pm; 350ptas, students 200ptas).

Once Isabel II started vacationing here in 1846, fancy buildings sprung up like wildfire. Even the railings on the boardwalk hark back to a time when the city belonged to the elite. **El Palacio de Miramar,** built on the land that splits Playa de la Concha and Playa de Ondarreta, passed through the hands of the Spanish court, Napoleon III, and Bismarck. Visitors can stroll through the grounds (open daily in summer 9am-9pm; in winter 10am-5pm). A 30-minute walk from the cathedral up Cuesta de Aldapeta (or a 90ptas bus ride on #19) leads to the **Palacio de Ayete.** The residence is closed to the public, but the trails are not (grounds open in summer 10am-8:30pm; in winter 10am-5pm).

Thirty minutes from the town center between a lush hill and a dark, gray-green bay, the one-cobbled-street town of **Pasajes de San Juan.** The charming fishing village's wood-balconied houses and small bay crowded with colorful *chalupas* (little boats) make for an enchanting time warp. To get there, take the Areizaga **bus** (tel. 45 27 08) from C. Regina Regente in front of the tourist office to **Pasajes de San Pedro** (every 10min. daily 5:30am-11pm, 95ptas). From here, follow the road toward the sea until you can see Pasajes de San Juan across the bay. Steps lead down to the swift blue boat that will whisk you across for a small fee.

ENTERTAINMENT

The **parte vieja** pulls out all the stops after dark. **Calle Fermín Calbetón,** three blocks in from Alameda del Boulevard, sweats in a pool of bars. **Bar Uraitz** and **Bar Eibartarra,** C. Fermín Calbetón, 26, are human zoos and virtually impassable after dark. Shed your voice and (some of) your clothing before heading to **Bars Sariketa** and **Txalupa,** C. Fermín Calbetó, 23 and 3; you won't need either in the deafening swelter. If you prefer to whisper intimately, listen for the background jazz of **Bar Kai,** C. Juan de Bilbao, 2 (open 6pm-12:30am; later on weekends). Locals and techno fans head to **Akerbeltz** and **Etxe Kalte,** both on C. Mari near the port. These bars are sleek, black, and cave-like. Akerbeltz is a *bodega.*

At around 2am, San Sebastián's small but mighty disco scene starts thumping. Many discos crowd along the beach. **Bataplán,** Po. Concha, opens at midnight (cover and one drink 2000ptas). **Kabutzia,** Muelle, s/n (tel. 42 97 85), and **Ku,** atop Monte Igueldo, both open at 8pm. Covers can be exorbitant; the smart club-goer keeps an eye out for free "invitations" at bars, record shops, etc. Tune in to live jazz at **altxeri galeria,** (which means "jazz gallery") C. Reina Regente, 2 (tel. 42 29 31; open daily 5pm-2:30am, Fri.-Sat. until 3:30am).

From January through April, the fastidious gourmets of San Sebastián turn their attention to **sidrerías,** where the slightly bitter *sidra* is brewed. The *sidrerías* are open to the public and all provide the same, standard meal (*bacalao*, beef chop, *queso con membrillo*) to complement their own delicious *sidra.* Favorite local *sidrerías* are in nearby **Astigarraga.** The regional tourist office has transportation info and an extensive list of near, far, and isolated *sidrerías.*

Playa de la Concha curves from the port to the **Pico del Loro,** the beak-shaped promontory dwelling of the Palacio de Miramar. Unfortunately, the virtually flat beach disappears during high tide and each year erosion shortens the beaches a little farther. Crowds and parasols jam onto the shorter but steeper **Playa de Ondarreta,** beyond Miramar. Here **Windsurf Donostia** rents **windsurfing** equipment, surfboards, and kayaks in the summertime. Picnickers can head for the alluring **Isla de Santa Clara** in the center of the bay. Frequent **motorboats** leave for the island (July-Sept. only, 5min., 250ptas round-trip), or power yourself and rent a **rowboat.** Check at the portside kiosk for info on both options. Numerous sports-related groups offer short courses in a variety of activities all summer long. For **windsurfing** and **kayaking,** call

the Real Club Nautico, C. Igentea, 9 (tel. 42 35 75). For **parachuting,** try **Urruti Sport,** C. José Maria Soroa, 20 (tel. 27 81 96). And for **surfing,** check out the **Pukas Surf Club,** C. Mayora, 5 (tel. 42 12 05). For info on all sports, pick up a copy of the *UDA-Actividades deportivas* brochure at the tourist office. **Scuba Du,** Muelle, 23 (tel. 42 24 26), rents **scuba** equipment and offers classes and certification.

The tourist office prints a 10-page booklet (in Spanish and *euskera*) with the year's schedule of events, promoting everything from music to regattas to sculpture exhibitions. Or, pick up *El Tubo* in bookstores. The city hosts a **marathon** in mid-October; **El Día de San Sebastián** (Jan. 19-20) brings traditional parades; a **carnival** feasts in February; and a **Festival Internacional de Danza** leaps in May (contact Diputación Foral de Guipúzcoa at tel. 42 35 11).

San Sebastián's five-day **Festival de Jazz,** in mid to late July, is one of Europe's most ambitious. Such giants as Art Blakey, Wynton Marsalis, and Dizzy Gillespie have played here. For info on the 1998 festival, contact the Oficina del Festival de Jazz (beneath the tourist office) at C. Reina Regente, 20003 San Sebastián (tel. 48 11 79). The tourist office also has the scoop on concerts and schedules. For tickets call tel. 48 11 93. Movie stars and directors own the streets for a week in September during the **Festival Internacional de Cine,** deemed one of the four most important in the world (along with Venice, Cannes, and Berlin). For info about this year's film festival, which runs September 21-30, call the Victoria Eugenia Theater (tel. 48 12 12; fax 48 12 18), or write to Apartados de Correos, 397, 20080 San Sebastián; the office shares the building with the tourist office. The week of August 15, **Semana Grande** (Big Week) is ablaze with concerts, movies, and an international fireworks festival. The **Fiestas de San Juan,** on and around June 24, bring their own share of folklore performances, Basque sports competitions, and general revelry. **La Quincena Musical,** in the **Teatro Victoria Eugenia,** C. Reina Regente, sponsors more than two weeks of classical music concerts in late August, most of them free.

■ Near San Sebastián: Fuenterrabía (Hondarribia)

Less than an hour east of San Sebastián by bus, Fuenterrabía (pop. 180,000) is a European beach town designed the way European beach towns should be. Stretching along the Franco-Spanish Txingudi Bay, the town flaunts not only a silky beach but also brightly painted houses, flower-filled streets, and a gorgeous stone-and-timber *casco antiguo.* After the chic atmosphere of San Sebastián, Fuenterrabía is refreshingly simple. The beach, which lies at the far end of town past the fisherman's marina and at the end of a long seaside walk, can become ridiculously crowded with vacationing *madrileños* in the peak days of summer. The *casco antiguo,* centered around Charles V's palace (now a *parador*) in Pl. Armas, provides welcome relief from Coppertone fumes. The **Parroquia de Nuestra Señora de la Asunción** in the Pl. Armas is the oft-remodeled Gothic church where Louis XIV of France married, by proxy, Spanish Habsburg Infanta María Teresa (open for mass only).

Fuenterrabía offers several excursion possibilities. Six kilometers up Av. Monte Jaizkibel, **Monte Jaizkibel,** the highest mountain on the Costa Cantábrica, guards the **Ermita** and **Fuente de Guadalupe.** The latter is currently closed to visitors, but the environs offer mind-blasting views of the coast. On a clear day you can see as far as Bayonne, France, 45km away. **Boats** (tel. 61 64 47) shuttle to Hendaye, a French town with a bigger beach, from the pier at the end of C. Domingo Egia, off La Marina (every 15min. daily 10am-midnight; reduced service in winter; 190ptas).

The entire bay, containing both Fuenterrabía and Irún, is called **Bidasoa.** The **tourist office** for the region is **Bidasoa Turismo,** C. Javier Ugarte, 6 (tel. 64 54 58; fax 64 54 66), on Pl. San Cristobál, where the bus stops. English-speaking staff doles out maps and lodging lists. (July-Aug. open daily 10am-8pm; off season Mon.-Fri. 9am-1:30pm and 4-6:30pm, Sat. 10am-2pm.) The **Red Cross** at El Puntal can be reached at tel. 64 40 39. The **police** are at tel. 64 43 00. In an **emergency,** dial tel. 091 or 092. The **postal code** is 20280. The **telephone code** is (9)43.

The scramble for budget rooms isn't pretty; reservations are vital in the summer. State-of-the-art **Albergue Juan Sebastián Elcano (HI),** Ctra. Faro (tel. 64 15 50; fax 64 00 28), perches on a hillside overlooking the sea. From the town center, head to the beach or take the "Playa" bus; turn left where the road forks right near the beach entrance (also where the bus swivels) and follow signs to the hostel. Two hundred beds wait for travelers. Try to finagle a room with a view of the beach; others are a little cramped. Only same-day reservations are accepted, so call early. (Members only. 3-night max. stay when full. Curfew midnight, but doors open at 1 and 2am. 1100ptas per person, over 30 1625ptas. Breakfast included. Sheets 300ptas. HI cards for sale.) A step in the other direction from Pl. San Cristóbal leads to charming **Pensión Txoko Goxoa,** C. Murrua, 22 (tel. 64 46 58), in the old quarter. Head up C. Javier Ugarte from the tourist office; take the second right, C. Juan Laborda; follow C. Juan Laborda until it ends at C. Murrua. The *pensión* is on the right. Some rooms overlook the old city walls (July-Sept. doubles with bath 5700ptas, Oct.-June 5500ptas; breakfast 500ptas; Visa). **Casas rurales** provide alternative accommodations (consult the tourist office). **Camping Jaizkibel** (tel. 64 16 79; fax 64 26 53) spreads 2km from town on Ctra. Guadelupe toward Monte Jaizkibel. They also rent bungalows (24hr. reception; 495ptas per person, per tent, and per car).

Several **markets** spill onto on C. San Pedro, three blocks inland from the port. **Market Goikoetxea** (tel. 64 10 29) includes flowers and fresh bread among its luscious outdoor offerings (open Mon.-Fri. 7:30am-2pm and 4-8pm, Sat. 7am-2pm). Beach bums refuel at **Gaxen,** C. Matxin Arzu, 1, a cafe six blocks from the beach and two from the bay. Serves full breakfasts, fresh fruit shakes (325ptas), and 30 kinds of sandwiches (300-675ptas). (Open Mon.-Thurs. 9am-10pm, Fri. 9am-11pm, Sat. 9am-2pm and 5-11pm, Sun. 9am-2pm and 5-10pm.) There is a similar menu at **Kaiela,** C. Itxas Argi, 4, a bit closer to the beach than Gaxen (sandwiches 325-500ptas, salads 375-500ptas). Try C. Mayor in the **casco antiguo** for various affordable *menus del día.*

Interurbanos buses (tel. 64 13 02) run to San Sebastián from the main plaza and from C. Bernat Etxepare (every 15min. until 9:45pm, 45min., 190ptas). **AUIF** buses (tel. 64 27 91) go to Irún (every 15min. until 10pm, 10min., 100ptas).

■ Near San Sebastián: Irún

As if Irún meant what the word looks like in English, travelers who come here are usually rushing somewhere else. And with good reason: besides the transportation services that connect to Paris, Madrid, and San Sebastián, Irún has only a vast urban sprawl to recommend it.

Irún's **Ayuntamiento** (tel. 64 92 00) at Pl. San Juan Harria dispenses eye-crossing maps (open Mon.-Fri. 8:30am-2pm and 4-7:30pm, Sat. 8:30am-1:30pm). RENFE **trains** (tel. 61 67 08) fan out to all of Spain; connections to San Sebastián are frequent (25min., 150ptas). The station has **currency exchange,** a **post office,** and **luggage storage** (400ptas, ask for token at the bar; station open daily 7am-11pm). For **taxis** call 61 22 29 or 62 29 71. The **Red Cross** can be reached at 61 03 56. The **police** (tel. 62 02 39; in **emergency** tel. 091 or 092) are stationed in Pl. Ensanche. For other services, call Fuenterrabía (see above). The main **post office** (tel. 61 12 07) is down the street at Pl. Ensanche, 7 (open Mon.-Fri. 8:30am-7:30pm, Sat. 9am-2:30pm).

Several *hostales* near the train station fill quickly in summer. Some people use Irún as a base for visiting San Sebastián to avoid the pricier *hostal* climate. Bear in mind, however, that Irún is not cheap or charming, and public transport back from San Sebastián is scarce after 10pm. One street over from C. Estación lies **Hostal Residencia Lizaso,** C. Aduana, 5 (tel. 61 16 00), with a TV room and clean, unremarkable rooms (singles 2250ptas, with shower 3900ptas; doubles 3600ptas, 5100-5300ptas). **Restaurante Gwendo,** C. Estación, 13, has a 1000ptas *menú* and outdoor seating in back. The **mercado** is at C. República de Argentina, 12 (open daily 8:30am-1:30pm).

Insert Body Here.

Prodigy Internet puts you where you want to be.

Yes, I want Prodigy Internet for ne month FREE* to help plan my next vacation.

Name		
Address		
City	State	Zip
Home: ( )	Work: ( )	
Email address		

To request a CD-ROM of free software by phone, call **1-800-PRODIGY, ext. 3302.**

prodigyinternet™

System Requirements:

- Microsoft® Windows® 95 using Microsoft® Internet Explorer: 486 PC-compatible processor or higher, 16 MB RAM, 30 MB available hard drive space, 28.8 Kbps modem (14.4 Kbps minimum), CD-ROM drive.
- Microsoft® Windows® 3.1 using Netscape Navigator™: 486 PC-compatible processor or higher, 16 MB RAM, (8 MB minimum), 25 MB available hard drive space, 28.8 Kbps modem (14.4 Kbps minimum), CD-ROM drive.
- Macintosh® System 7.5 or higher using Netscape Navigator™: 68030 or higher processor, 16 MB RAM, 20 MB available hard drive space, 28.8 Kbps modem (14.4 Kbps minimum), CD-ROM drive.

*For complete details on the one month trial offer and the membership plans, see online Customer Service or Help Sites.

LETSGO/PIMAB01

Use Prodigy Internet to plan your next vacation.

Before you go on your next vacation, use Prodigy Internet to help make your trip a lot less expensive and a lot more fun. You'll be able to plan your entire vacation online, including:

• Booking air, hotel and car reservations
• Finding money-saving cruise packages
• Accessing Internet travel guides, such as **Let's Go** (www.letsgo.com)
• Receiving low-fare alerts via email

Plus, you'll have access to **Traveling Lite** (http://travelinglite.prodigy.com), a student/budget site brought to you by Prodigy Internet.

To get your Prodigy Internet software with one FREE* month, call 1-800-PRODIGY, ext. 33 Or simply return the attached card below.

http://travel.prodigy.net

NO POSTA
NECESSARY
MAILED IN
UNITED STA

BUSINESS REPLY MAIL
FIRST CLASS MAIL   PERMIT NO. 10   PLYMOUTH, MA

POSTAGE WILL BE PAID BY ADDRESSEE

 prodigyinternet™

PRODIGY SERVICES CORPORATION
PO BOX 1740
PLYMOUTH, MA 02362-9903

■ Pays Basque, France

Have a hankering for some brie? The Spain-France border dividing *Euskadi* (Basque country), considered arbitrary by the Basque, invites jaunts into France. The gorgeous beaches of Bayonne and St-Jean-De-Luz are easily accessible via the French border town of Hendaye, a quick commuter train ride from San Sebastián (see San Sebastián: Trains, p. 228). Trade in your *pesetas* and run for the border.

■ Bayonne

A grand port with small-town appeal, Bayonne enjoys a prominent position on the Gulf of Gascony, close to the Spanish border. Its spiny twin steeples biting into the skies, the 13th-century **Cathédrale Ste-Marie** intimidates from afar and impresses from within. (Cloister open daily 9:30am-12:30pm and 2-5pm. 5F. Church open Mon.-Sat. 10am-noon and 3-6pm, Sun. 3:30-6pm.) Highlights of the unbeatable **Musée Bonnat**, 5, rue Jacques Laffitte, in Petit-Bayonne, include the lecherous mythical men in the Rubens room, a ghoulish El Greco, and Goya's grim *La Dernière Communion de San José de Calasanz* (open Wed.-Mon. 10am-noon and 2:30-6:30pm, Fri. until 8:30pm; 20F, students 10F).

Bayonne is linked by **train** to Paris (5½hr., 406-456F), Bordeaux (1½-2½hr., 130-138F), and Biarritz (10min.,12F). The **tourist office** (tel. 05 59 46 01 46; fax 05 59 59 37 55), pl des Basques, provides a free map and can help find rooms. (Open July-Aug. Mon.-Sat. 9am-7pm, Sun. 10am-1pm; Sept.-June Mon.-Fri. 9am-6:30pm, Sat. 10am-6pm.) In St-Esprit, decent lodgings dot the train station area. The **Hôtel Paris-Madrid**, pl. de la Gare (tel. 05 59 55 13 98), has cheerful rooms. (Reception open July-Sept. 24hr.; Oct.-June daily 6am-12:30am. Singles and doubles 90-165F.) Huge portions of delicious regional cuisine are served in a classy atmosphere at **Le Bistrot Ste-Cluque**, 9, rue Hugues, across from the station (*menu* 55F; duck 55F; *paella* 65F; open daily noon-2pm and 7-11pm).

■ St-Jean-de-Luz

Sheltered in a natural port with the Pyrenees looming above, St-Jean prospered on lucrative New World whaling rights until France signed them away in 1713, but by pirating and profiteering they scavanged a wealthy existence. Separated from Spain by an arbitrary border separating French and Spanish Basque Country, St-Jean (pop. 13,000) cultivates its Basque heritage in the shadows of and ice cream stands. Each summer, sardines become guests of honor (and projectiles) at riotous Basque festivals, including a fish soup bash and the *Nuit de la Sardine*.

ORIENTATION AND PRACTICAL INFORMATION

From the station, turn left onto blvd. Commandant Passicot, then bear right around pl. Verdun to get to av. Verdun, which leads to the tourist office on pl. Foch. From pl. Foch, rue de la République runs two blocks to **place Louis XIV**, the center of town. The beach is a minute away.

Tourist Office: pl. Foch (tel. 05 59 26 03 16; fax 05 59 26 21 47). Maps and info on accommodations, events, and excursions. Open July-Aug. Mon.-Sat. 9am-8pm, Sun. 10:30am-1pm and 3-7pm; Sept.-June Mon.-Sat. 9am-12:30pm and 2-6:30pm.

Currency Exchange: Change Plus, 32, rue Gambetta (tel. 05 59 51 03 43). Fair rates, no commission. Open July-Aug. Mon.-Sat. 8am-8pm, Sun. 10am-1pm and 4-7pm; Sept.-June Mon.-Sat. 9am-12:30pm and 2-7pm.

Buses: Pullman Basque, 33, rue Gambetta (tel. 05 59 26 03 37), runs to Pamplona, San Sebastián, and Spanish villages (July-Sept. Fri., full day, 140F). Ticket office open July-Sept. daily 8:30am-12:30pm and 2:30-7:30pm; Oct.-June 9:30am-noon and 2:30-7pm.

Bike Rental: Ado Peugeot, 5-7, av. Labrouche (tel. 05 59 26 14 95) Bikes 60F per day. *VTTs* 80F per day. Open Mon.-Sat. 8:30am-noon and 2-7pm.

Emergency: tel. 17. **Medical emergency:** tel. 15.
Police: av. André Ithurraide (tel. 05 59 26 08 47). On the left, just past the *fronton municipal*, heading away from the tourist office.
Post Office: 44, blvd. Victor Hugo (tel. 05 59 51 66 50). **Currency exchange** (*pesetas* only). Poste restante. Open July-Aug. Mon.-Fri. 9am-6pm, Sat. 9am-noon; Sept.-June Mon.-Fri. 9am-noon and 1:30-5:30pm, Sat. 9am-noon. **Postal code:** 64500.

ACCOMMODATIONS AND CAMPING

Hotels fill up rapidly in summer, and it might be tough to reserve since budget places host long-term guests. Arrive early, especially in August. You may have better luck commuting from Bayonne or Biarritz.

Hôtel Verdun, 13, av. Verdun (tel. 05 59 26 02 55), across from the *gare*. Clean, pretty rooms and oddly appealing, Brady-era TV lounge. Reception open 7:30am-9:30pm. Singles and doubles 155-180F, with shower 170-230F; triple with bath 260F. Off-season singles 130F, with shower 180F; triples 170F. Call early to reserve. Free showers. Breakfast 20F. Restaurant serves 3-course 65F *menu*. V, MC.
Hôtel Bolivar, 18, rue Sopite (tel. 05 59 26 02 00), off blvd. Thiers, on a central but quiet street. Clean, basic rooms without carpets. Reception open 8am-9:30pm. Singles 185F, with shower 240F; doubles 195-210F, with shower 250F, with shower and toilet 290F; triples with bathroom 330F; quads with bathroom 360F. Free showers available 8am-10pm. Breakfast 32F. Open May-Sept. V, MC, AmEx.
Camping: There are 14 sites in St-Jean-de-Luz and 13 more within 13km, most of them 3-star. To walk to most of the campsites, take blvd. Victor Hugo, continue along av. André Ithurraide, then veer left onto chemin d'Erromardie (20min.). Or take an ATCRB bus headed to Biarritz or Bayonne and ask to get off near the *camping,* then walk the extra 800m.

FOOD

St-Jean-de-Luz's Basque and Spanish specialties are the best north of the border. The port's famous seafood is kept on ice outside the expensive restaurants on rue de la République and pl. Louis XIV (*menus* 75-250F). Most are heavy on ambience. Informal **Relais de St-Jacques,** 13, av. de Verdun (tel. 05 59 26 02 55), across from the train station, serves an ever-changing 65F *menu*. (Open July-Aug. daily noon-2pm and 7-8:45pm; Sept.-June closed Sat. night and Sun. V, MC.) **Margarita,** 4, rue l'Eglise, prepares such one-of-a-kind South American dishes as ostrich with green peppers (80F; open daily July-Aug. noon-2:30pm and 7:15-11pm; Sept.-June closed Sun.-Mon.; V, MC, AmEx). Get your Nutella fix at **Codec,** 87, rue Gambetta (tel. 05 59 26 46 46; open Mon.-Sat. 8:30am-12:30pm and 3-7:15pm, Sun. 8:30am-12:30pm). **Chez Dodin,** 80, rue Gambetta (tel. 05 59 26 38 04), scoops its own ice cream in its 1960s-style *salon de thé* and taunts cultural purists with its *beret basque* (chocolate mousse shaped like a beret and rolled in chocolate sprinkles, 13F; 11F per scoop; open daily 9:45am-12:30pm and 2:45-7:30pm; V, MC).

SIGHTS AND ENTERTAINMENT

Although young Louis XIV was smitten with the charms of Marie Mancini, he was convinced to iron out border disputes by marrying Maria Teresa of Spain. Lovesick Louis sojourned in St-Jean-de-Luz in 1660, reluctantly awaiting his wedding. Fortunately, the union proved successful; upon the queen's death, the Sun King sighed, *"C'est le premier chagrin qu'elle me cause"* ("This is the first time she has caused me sorrow"). The **Maison Louis XIV,** pl. Louis XIV (tel. 05 59 26 01 56), is frozen in its glory days as Louis' lair. (Open June-Sept. Mon.-Sat. 10:30am-noon and 2:30-5:30pm, Sun. 2:30-5:30pm; July-Aug. until 6:30pm. Admission 15F, students 12F.)

Before heading to the beach, take time to walk through the tiny streets overlooking the port, shining with half-timbered, whitewashed houses trimmed in red. Rumor has it that residents used ox blood to get the colors just right. Sheltered by protective

dikes off **promenade Jacques Thibaud**, St-Jean-de-Luz's beach and harbor provide prime conditions for sailing and windsurfing.

Summer rollicks with Basque festivals, concerts, and the championship of *cesta punta* (July-Aug. Tues. and Fri. at 9:15pm, tickets 50-120F at the tourist office). **Toro de Fuego,** with pyrotechnics, dancing, and a man in a bull costume, heats up summer nights in pl. Louis XIV (July-Aug. Wed. at 10:30pm and Sun. at 11:30pm). The biggest annual festival is the three-day **Fête de St-Jean,** the weekend closest to St-Jean's Day (June 21). At the **Fête du Thon** (the first Sat. in July), the town gathers around the harbor to eat tuna (60F), toss confetti, and pirouette to music. The fun doesn't stop as St-Jean fêtes its favorite little fish with the big **Nuit de la Sardine,** the second Saturday in July at the Campos-Berri, next to the *cesta punta* stadium. It features an orchestra, Basque songs, and, yes, **sardines** (40-60F). The fabulous **Fête du Ttoro** ffeatures exxciting acctivities innvolving ffish ssoup *(ttoro)*. The *Fête* takes place on the first Saturday in September; the next day, *Luziens* can sheepishly confess to the priests whom they pelted with fish guts hours earlier. To get in on the fishy fun at sea level, sign up for a four-hour **fishing trip** that leaves from the port (ask at the tourist office). For more water fun, hit **Le Spot,** 16, rue Gambetta (tel. 05 59 26 07 95; fax 05 59 26 62 36), for surfing lessons (180F for 2hr., including equipment) or rental equipment (wetsuit: ½-day 40F, full day 60F; bodyboard: ½-day 40F, full day 70F; open Jan.-Oct. daily 9:30am-9pm; Nov.-Dec. Sun. 10am-7:30pm; V, MC). Wiggle out of your wetsuit at the sandy, surfer-filled burger joint in back (heavenly hamburgers 32-45F; open until 10pm; V, MC).

■ Vitoria-Gasteiz

Vitoria-Gasteiz (pop. 210,000), like Bilbao and the rest of Basque Country, is up-and-coming. It is the capital of País Vasco, but anomalously preserves its greener quarters and slow pace of life. The city boasts airy shopping plazas, tree-canopied avenues, magnificent churches, and world-class museums, successfully retaining the charm of an old city packaged into a sleek cosmopolis.

Vitoria-Gasteiz's name game began in 1181 when King of Navarra Sancho "El Sabio" (the Wise) changed the town's name from Gasteiz to Villa de Nueva Vitoria, promoting it to city status with a single stroke of verbiage. Upon recovering regional autonomy in 1979, the Basques re-incorporated the original name.

The hyphenated name chosen for Vitoria-Gasteiz is indicative of the city's regional political and cultural sentiment. Vitoria retains a dedication to its regional heritage, while growing sentiment favors cooperation with Madrid's plans for the future. *Castellano* began to replace *euskera* as the language of discourse in conjunction with the improvement Castile's commercial routes in the 19th and 20th centuries. Today, Castilian is spoken almost exclusively.

ORIENTATION AND PRACTICAL INFORMATION

Vitoria-Gasteiz is sensibly arranged and user-friendly: signs to all major sights are readable and accurate, and street names are posted on clearly visible signs. The medieval **casco viejo** (old city) is the egg-shaped epicenter of the city. At its base, **Plaza de la Virgen Blanca** marks the center of town. Wide tree-lined pedestrian streets surround the old city.

From the **train station,** follow **Calle Eduardo Dato** to its end, turn left on C. Postas, and head straight to the plaza. The old **bus station** on C. Francia won't re-open for another year or so. Until then, buses park 'n' roll from a temporary glass building on **Calle de los Herrán,** between C. Prudencio María Verástegui and C. Arana. **All directions below will be given assuming you exit on its west side,** facing the stores across the street (there are none on the east side), with C. Verástegui on your left. To get to Pl. Virgen Blanca, follow C. Verástegui to its end and turn left on C. Francia; follow C. Francia for four blocks as it becomes C. Paz and turn right onto C. Postas, which leads straight to the plaza.

Tourist Office: Parque de la Florida (tel. 13 13 21; fax 13 02 93), from the train station follow C. Eduardo Dato (go straight exiting the station) and take the 2nd left onto C. Florida; follow it to the edge of the *parque*. From the bus station, head towards Pl. Virgen Blanca, but follow C. Francia/Paz 2 blocks past C. Postas to C. Ortiz de Zárate on the right, which leads to C. Florida. In the park, follow the tree-lined path to the left; the tourist office is in a squat stone house. Open Mon.-Fri. 9am-7pm, Sat. 10am-7pm, Sun 10am-2pm; Oct.-May Mon.-Thurs. 9am-1:30pm, Fri. 8am-3pm. Get the *Paseo por el casco viejo* map. Abundant info on all of Spain. If the office in the park is still being renovated, head to the **municipal tourist office** (tel. 16 15 98; fax 16 11 05), on Av. Gasteiz. From the edge of the park, bear right on C. Luis and continue in the same direction through Pl. Lovaina when C. Luis Heinz changes into C. Sancho el Sabio. Make a right when you hit Av. Gasteiz. The office is on the left on the corner of Av. Gasteiz and C. Chile in Palacio Europa.

Budget Travel: TIVE, C. General Alava, 10, 2nd fl. (tel. 14 22 20). ISIC (500ptas). Open Mon.-Fri. 9am-2pm.

Flights: Aeropuerto Vitoria-Foronda (tel.16 35 00), 5km out of town. Accessible only by car or taxi (1600-1800ptas). **Iberia** (tel. 22 82 50), info open 7am-11pm. Check page 2 of *El Correo Español* (local paper) for current flights.

Trains: RENFE, Pl. Estación (tel. 23 02 02), at the end of C. Eduardo Dato, south of the old city. Info open 8am-10pm. To: Pamplona (4-5 per day, 1-1½hr., 490-1000ptas); San Sebastián (7-9 per day, 1¼-2½hr., 1105-1500ptas); Burgos (12-15 per day, 1½-2hr., 1025-1500ptas); Zaragoza (2-3 per day, 3hr., 1620-2300ptas); Madrid (7 per day, including 3 night trains, 5-6hr., 3800 4000ptas); Barcelona (1 per day, 7hr., 4700ptas).

Buses: C. Herrán, on a traffic island east of the old city. General info (tel. 25 84 00), open Mon.-Fri. 9am-1pm and 3-7pm. Tons of companies. **La Burundesa** (tel. 25 55 09) to: San Sebastián (10 per day, 1½hr., 935ptas); Pamplona (6-10 per day, 1½hr., 875ptas); Zaragoza (5-8 per day, 3hr., 1900ptas). **La Unión** (tel. 26 46 26), to Bilbao (8-17 per day, 1hr., 655ptas). **Continental Auto** (tel. 28 64 66), to: Burgos (7-8 per day, 1½hr., 940ptas); San Sebastián (8-10 per day, 1½hr., 930ptas); Madrid (9-10 per day, 4½-5hr., 2800ptas).

Public Transportation: Buses cover the metropolitan area and suburbs (80ptas). The tourist office has a pamphlet with routes. Bus #2 goes from the bus station to C. Florida (home of many *pensiones*). City buses run approximately 6:30am-11pm.

Taxis: Radio-Taxis (tel. 27 35 00 or 25 30 33.)

Car Rental: Avis, 53 (tel. 24 46 12), just past C. Adriano VI. From 9727ptas per day (includes mileage, insurance, and tax). Must be at least 23 and have had license for 1 yr. Open Mon.-Fri. 9am-1:30pm and 4-7pm, Sat. 9am-1pm.

Luggage storage: At the train station (400ptas).

English Press: Linacero, C. Fueros, 17-19 (tel. 25 06 88), left off C. Postas heading toward Pl. Virgen Blanca. Classics, travel guides, and some juicy stuff. **Study,** C. Fueros, 14, across the street, vends Penguin Classics. Both open Mon.-Fri. 9:45am-1:30pm and 4:30-8pm, Sat. 10:30am-1:30pm; Sept.-May also open Sat. 5-8pm.

Youth Center: Instituto Foral de la Juventud, Pl. Provincia, 18 (tel. 18 18 18). From Pl. Virgen Blanca, turn left onto C. Diputación, which ends at Pl. Provincia. Info on trips, camping, and travel. Open Mon.-Fri. 9am-2pm; Sept.-June Mon.-Fri. 9am-2pm and 5-7pm.

Red Cross: Portal de Castilla (tel. 13 26 30); **emergency:** (tel. 22 22 22).

24-Hour Pharmacy: Call tel. 23 07 21 for a recording. Check pharmacy doors (one at C. Eduardo Dato, 24, another at C. Postas, 34) or p.2 of *El Correo Español*.

Medical Services: Hospital General de Santiago, C. Olaguíbel (tel. 25 36 00). With your back to the bus station, go left 1 block after C. Francia becomes C. Paz.

Police: Municipal (tel. 16 11 11).

Emergency: tel. 091 or 092.

Post Office: C. Postas, 9 (tel. 23 05 75; fax 23 37 80), on the pedestrian street leading to Pl. Virgen Blanca from the east. Open Mon.-Fri. 8:30am-8:30pm, Sat. 9:30am-2pm. For Lista de Correos, walk around the corner to the C. Nuestra Señora del Cabello side of the building to the unmarked door (open Mon.-Fri. 8:30am-2pm, Sat. 9:30am-2pm). **Postal Code:** 01008.

Telephone Code: (9)45.

ACCOMMODATIONS AND CAMPING

There aren't many bargains in Vitoria-Gasteiz, but rooms are of the highest quality in Spain. The tourist office has an up-to-date listing of budget *pensiones* and *casas de huéspedes*. Most are clustered near the bus and train stations. If you plan to drop in during the *fiestas* in early August, make reservations at least a month in advance.

Pensión Zurine, C. Florida, 24 (tel. 14 22 40), across the street from Pensión Araba. Baby-pink rooms contrast with the ice-blue bathrooms. Low, firm beds. Winter heating. Singles 2300ptas. Doubles 3500ptas.

Hostal-Residencia Nuvilla, C. Fueros, 29, 3rd fl. (tel. 25 91 51), from the bus station follow directions to Pl. Virgen Blanca (see **Orientation,** p. 239) but take the first left off C. Postas. Large and always well-kept rooms. Rare singles 2500ptas. Doubles 3500ptas. Triples 5000ptas. Bathrooms in hallway are very clean.

Casa 400, C. Florida, 46, 3rd fl. (tel. 23 38 87), a right turn off C. Eduardo Dato coming from the train station. A private college dormitory during the school year. Completely renovated with a youthful atmosphere. Some rooms have big, glassed-in balconies. Dining room, coffee machine, and laundry service. Rooms available only July 1-Sept. 30. Singles 2500ptas. Doubles 3200ptas. Breakfast 250ptas. *Pensión completa* (room and board) 3950ptas per person.

Pensión Araba (2), C. Florida, 25 (tel. 23 25 88), on the road to the tourist office from the bus station; from the train station, turn right onto C. Florida. Trés posh. Persian-style rugs, wood floors, dark furniture, and beautifully tiled bathrooms. Elevator and parking garage. TVs for all. Doubles 3500ptas, with bath 4500ptas. Triples 4725ptas; 6075ptas.

Hostal Savoy, C. Prudencio María de Verástegui, 4 (tel./fax 25 00 56). Turn left from the bus station then take an immediate right. Large, modern rooms with phones and baths, all in a new building. Singles 3500ptas. Doubles 5200ptas. Triples 7000ptas. Breakfast 250ptas. Other meals 1000ptas. Rooms in **Residencia Fuentes,** on the 4th fl., lack these amenities, but they are comfortable and far cheaper. Singles 2000ptas. Doubles 3300ptas. Triples 4775ptas. Breakfast 250ptas.

Camping Ibaya (tel. 14 76 20), 5km from town toward Madrid. Follow Portal de Castilla west from the tourist office intersection. Supermarket, cafe/restaurant, hot showers. Reception open daily 8am-2pm and 4-10pm. 500ptas per person, per tent, and per car. Open year-round.

FOOD

Plunge into the **casco viejo** for the most interesting options. Interesting, however, doesn't necessarily equate to better; the new city reputedly offers the better restaurants. Nonetheless, **C. Cuchillería,** uphill from the post office off C. Francisco, is crowded by students. From the train station, take C. Eduardo Dato, turn right on C. Postas, then left past the post office and uphill, where C. Cuchillería and other old-town streets radiate from C. San Francisco. Fresh produce is traded at the two-level market, **Mercado de Abastos,** on Pl. Santa Bárbara (open Mon.-Fri. 9am-2pm and 5-8pm, Sat. 8am-3pm). There's always the **grocery** option at **Simago,** C. General Alava, 10, between C. Eduardo Dato and C. San Antonio (open Mon.-Sat. 9am-9pm). **Tierra Viva,** C. Portales, 4, sells organic fruits and veggies, whole grain breads, and smoked tofu (open Mon.-Fri. 9:30am-1:30pm and 4:30-8:30pm, Sat. 10am-2pm).

Casco Viejo

Restaurant Hirurak, C. Cuchillería, 26 (tel. 25 65 55), off C. San Francisco on the right. Funky, young clientele bops to reggae and blues. Entrees 950-1400ptas. Open Tues.-Fri. 1-3:30pm and 9-11pm, Sat.-Sun. 2-3:30pm and 9-11:30pm.

Amboto Oleagarena, C. Cuchillería, 29 (tel. 25 00 93). Small dining room in a stone tavern with benches that jut out from the wall. Modern music and traditional food. *Menú* 1000ptas (1200ptas on Sat.). Open Mon.-Fri. 1-3:30pm, Sat. 2:30-3:30pm, Sun. 1:45-3:30pm.

Bar Kirol, C. Cuchillería, 31. Nothing fancy, but you can't beat the prices. *Chatos* of beer or wine 65ptas. *Bocadillos* 275ptas and up. *Tapas* 375-600ptas.

PAÍS VASCO (EUSKADI)

Elsewhere

Museo del Organo, C. Manuel Iradier, 80. Take C. Florida east from the park to the Pl. Toros, then turn right. Healthy hipsters come here for vegetarian delights. 4-course *menú* which changes daily, but usually includes a salad bar with fresh vegetables. Come early, or be prepared to wait. Lunch only, open Mon.-Sat. 1-4pm.

Restaurante Bilbaína, C. Prudencio María Verástegui, 2 (tel. 25 44 00). Recommended by bus drivers and frequented by businessmen, so you know it's good. Exceptional *menú* includes a savory *merluza a la rancha* (ranch-style hake) and baked cinnamon apples for dessert (1075ptas plus 7% IVA). Open Mon.-Sat. 1-4pm and 9-11pm, Sun. 1:30-4pm.

Bar Restaurante Poliki, C. Fueros 29 (tel. 25 05 19). Tasty dishes populate the *menú del dia* (1100ptas) while the *tapas,* especially *boquerones en vinagres* (anchovies in vinegar 300ptas) and *patatas picantes* (spicy french fries, 300ptas) are delish. Open 1:30-4:30pm and 8-11:30pm. AmEx, Visa, MC.

SIGHTS

Vitoria-Gasteiz is to be digested slowly—by foot, stopping periodically for a few *copas.* Vast and airy **Plaza de la Vírgen Blanca** is the focal point of the *casco viejo* and site of Vitoria-Gasteiz's *fiestas.* Beside Pl. Virgen Blanca is the broad, arcaded **Plaza de España.** It divides the old town's concentric streets and balconied houses on the hill from the new town's broad, gridded avenues. Many of the old quarter's Renaissance *palacios* are open to the public.

When Gasteiz became Vitoria-Gasteiz, the hill was connected more gracefully with the rest of the town below. Architects Sefurola and Olaguíbel accomplished the union by constructing **Los Arquillos,** a set of arches that merges the old and new cities through stairs and streets arrayed like terraces, just above C. Mateo de Moraza. The *casco viejo* begins uphill through the arches. Down C. Cuchillería, the 15th-century **Casa del Cordón,** so-called because of the stone *cordón* (rope) that embellishes its central arch, is open to all (Mon.-Sat. 7-9pm). On parallel C. Herrería, the **Casa-Torre de Doña Ochanda** invites visitors up to its 15th-century tower, now home of a **Museum of Natural Science** (open Tues.-Fri. 10am-2pm and 4-6:30pm, Sat. 10am-2pm, Sun. 11am-2pm). Construction of the Gothic **Catedral de Santa María** (also known as the Catedral Vieja, or Old Cathedral), at the top of the *casco viejo,* began in the 13th century, and today flaunts two especially expressive *portales*—it's a good thing, since the rest of the cathedral is closed for restoration. The Old Cathedral faces off with the neo-Gothic **New Cathedral,** in the new part of town on C. Monseñor Cadena y Eleta.

The gorgeous, stained-glass Casa de Araba on Po. Fray Francisco de Vitoria houses the **Museo de Bellas Artes,** with sculptures in the front garden, and a display of Romanesque and polychromatic works by Ribera, Miró, El Greco, and Picasso inside. A collection of playing cards dates back six centuries and an impressive exhibit traces the history of coinage in Spain from the Celtiberians to the 19th century (open Tues.-Fri. 10am-2pm and 4-6:30pm, Sat. 10am-2pm, Sun. 11am-2pm; free).

Other sites of interest in the province of Alava include the **natural parks** of Urquiote, Urbea, and Valdrejo, and the town of La Guardia, which, though in Alava, produces Rioja wine with *denominación de orígen calificada.*

ENTERTAINMENT

Come any evening of the year to see all of Vitoria-Gasteiz head like lemmings to the watering holes in the *casco viejo.* On weekdays the action settles down by midnight but the thrashing weekend scene rumbles till dawn. Early in the evening, the ba scene centers on **Calle Cuchillería.** For more space but no less attitude, head fo **Calle Herrería,** where many bars have courtyard seating. The scene migrates to **Calle Zapatería,** also in the *casco viejo,* and **Calle San Antonio,** where *la marcha* contin ues through the morrow. Pirates and other rebel types frequent the **Taberna de Tuerto,** C. Zapatería, 151, featuring purple lighting and pounding music after mid

night. The more refined, if no less exotic, **El Jardín de Atras,** C. Correrea, is a Moroccan tea room that pipes in Arabic music and puts out delicious pastries.

The monthly *Guía del Ocio* (125ptas) is an excellent guide to bars, entertainment, and special events in the city. World class jazz grooves into Vitoria-Gasteiz in mid-July for the week-long **Festival de Jazz de Vitoria-Gasteiz.** Tickets for big name performers cost 500-2000ptas, but there are plenty of free performances on the street. July also brings an **International Folklore Festival** to Bilbao, with more free performances. For info call (tel. 14 19 19) or write to C. San Antonio, 16, 01005 Vitoria-Gasteiz. The **Fiesta de la Virgen Blanca** (Aug. 4-9), includes dancing and *a capella* singing. Rockets launch the revelry in Pl. Virgen Blanca.

■ Near Vitoria

Tucked inside a quiet wood overlooking fields of grain, the **Santuario de la Virgen de Estíbaliz** (tel. 29 30 88) has long attracted caravans of singing ruins and casual Sunday picknickers. Eight kilometers on the road to San Sebastian, the site hosts a monastery an impeccably restored 12th-century Roman basilica whose primitive statue of the Virgin remains emblematic of Basque autonomy (inspiring the name of many a little Basque girl in the process). Alfonso XI of Castrilla (1312-1350) crossed his heart and swore to Estíbaliz to respect Basque laws of self-governance or fueros. The refuge today occasional performances of traditional music and dance. Drivers should follow signs to Estella and Argandoña. Pinedo buses (tel. 25 89 01) at the Vitoria-Gasteiz station runs 4 per day as far as the Argandoña crossroad (115ptas) a 2km walk to the sanctuary. Tell the driver you are heading to Estibaliz. A sign points the way from the Argandoña stop. (Basilica open daily 8am-8pm. Free. Push on front door even if it looks closed).

La Rioja and Navarra

The Navarrese countryside slopes down from delicate Pyrenean villages on the French border, through Pamplona's elegance, to the dusty villages in the south featured in the film *Jamón, Jamón*. Bordered by Basque Country to the west and Aragón to the east, the infrequently visited region greets tourists with gentle landscapes and welcoming villages.

Navarra has an unfortunate legacy of siding with losers. In 1512 Fernando el Católico annexed it to a newly unified Spain. He granted the Navarrese partial autonomy, permitting the sustainment of *fueros* (traditional medieval laws), but more generally treated them with hostility for their opposition to centralist efforts in the Peninsular War. Navarrese misfortune continued into the Modern Age when the region supported the losing conservative cause in the 19th-century Carlist wars. They finally sided with "winners" in the 20th century by allying themselves with General Francisco Franco's Nationalist forces, victors of the Spanish Civil War.

The Navarrese have continued to support controversial political causes since the re-establishment of the Bourbon Monarchy in 1975. Many of the region's northern inhabitants are ethnically Basque and align themselves with Basque independence movements. Basque Nationalists in Navarra are thus dually concerned with their regional exclusion from País Vasco and the Basque movement for independence.

In areas where Navarra sees few tourists, locals receive guests with exceptional warmth. An extensive network of government subsidized *casas rurales* host backpackers in private homes, and their proprietors often invite guests to home-cooked meals. The region's epicurean specialty is *trucha a la Navarra* (trout stuffed with ham) but anything that finds its way onto your plate here is likely to be good. The *Guía de alojamientos de turismo rural* is available at any tourist office.

Tucked under Navarra, La Rioja is famous for great wine. "Rioja" is an internationally acclaimed wine classification with an 800 year tradition. The western farmlands owe their fertility to their close proximity to the rainy hills of País Vasco, while extensive irrigation ensures that even the acrid plains near Navarra produce bumper crops. The name "La Rioja" derives from the Ebro tributary Río Oja, whose muddy waters trickle through the vineyards. 1994 was an excellent year; try also 1987 and 1991. At home and abroad, look for the label of authenticity *denominación de origen calificada*.

Logroño, capital of La Rioja, lies in the region's center. The best *bodegas* (wine cellars) siphon off the lands in western Rioja Alta, around Haro. Trying to find a picturesque town with a *bodega* here is like trying to find a tipsy tourist in Pamplona during *los San Fermines*. El Camino de Santiago (St. James' Way) passes through much of La Rioja, and tourist offices provide useful information on understanding its history and participating in its continuing tradition. The mountainous Sierra region with tranquil fields at the feet of lunar-like peaks, lines La Rioja's southern border where dinosaur tracks have been discovered. Ask at any tourist office about the *Ruta del dinosaurio*, as well as the *zonas de acampada,* three scenic zones where the government has provided basic camping facilities on the unspoiled land.

LA RIOJA

▪ Logroño

Logroño's tourist office brochure proclaims that Logroño (pop. 110,000) feeds both the body and the soul. But unless your soul thrives on commerce and industry, you may not find spiritual nourishment; your body, however, will have plenty to be happy about. As the best entry point into the vineyard towns of La Rioja, even

La Rioja & Navarra

Logroño's hole-in-the-wall bars serve the region's fine wine, complemented with savory, inexpensive *tapas*. Taking strides to dismantle its over-industrialized image, Logroño has begun restoring its *casco antiguo* (old quarter), and in the serene after-glow of a hearty meal Logroño's few monuments take on a certain charm.

ORIENTATION AND PRACTICAL INFORMATION

Both the old and new towns radiate from the **Parque del Espolón,** a tree-lined set of gravel paths with a large fountain at the center. The **casco antiguo** stretches between the park and the **Río Ebro,** on the far north side of the city.

To reach the park from the **train station,** cross the major traffic artery of **Avenida de Lobete** and angle left on **Avenida de España.** Continue past the **bus station** which is at the next major intersection, connecting Av. España and **Calle del General Vara de Rey** (hereafter C. General Vara), which runs north-south. A right onto C. General Vara leads north to the park (8min. walk) and the *casco antiguo.*

Tourist Office: C. Miguel Villanueva, 10 (tel. 29 12 60; fax 25 60 45), left off C. General Vara coming from the bus and train stations; it borders the south end of Parque Espolón. Helpful staff doles out excellent **maps** and brochures. Open Mon.-Sat. 10am-2pm and 4:30-7:30pm, Sun. 10am-2pm; Nov.-May Mon.-Fri. 9am-2pm.
Currency Exchange: Many banks crowd the broad avenues surrounding the park. Open Mon.-Fri. 8:30am-2:30pm; in winter open Sat. also. All have **ATMs.** One **Banco Central Hispano** is on C. Bretón de los Herreros, just past C. Sagasta.
Trains: RENFE, Pl. Europa (tel. 24 02 02), off Av. España on the south side of town. Info open 7am-11pm. To: Haro (4-5 per day, 40min., 385-1100ptas); Burgos (4 per

day, 2¼hr., 2800ptas); Zaragoza (6 per day, 2-2½hr., 1200-1800ptas); Bilbao (2-3 per day, 3hr., 2000ptas); Madrid (1 per day, 5¼hr., 4000ptas); Barcelona (4 per day, 7hr., 3900-4200ptas).

Buses: Av. España (tel. 23 59 83), on the corner of C. General Vara and Av. Pío XII. Several companies. Check info board for the appropriate counter. Info open daily 6-11pm. To: Haro (5 per day, 45min., 345ptas); Santo Domingo de la Calzada (7 per day, 1hr., 360ptas); Vitoria-Gasteiz (4-5 per day, 2hr., 970ptas); Soria (4-5 per day, 2hr., 820ptas); Pamplona (5 per day, 2hr., 890ptas); Zaragoza (6 per day, 2hr., 1400ptas); Bilbao (5 per day, 2¼hr., 1430ptas); Burgos (7 per day, 3-5hr., 810ptas); Madrid (4-5 per day, 5hr., 2415ptas); Barcelona (2-4 per day, 6hr., 10,900ptas).

Car Rental: Avis, Gran Vía del Rey Don Juan Carlos I, 67 (tel. 20 23 54), left off C. General Vara. Open Mon.-Fri. 9am-1pm and 4-6pm, Sat. 10am-1pm. **Hertz,** Av. España, 1 (tel. 25 80 26), in the bus station. Open Mon.-Fri. 9am-2pm and 4-7pm.

Public Transportation: All buses run to the Parque Espolón, and lines #1 and 2 pass the bus station (75ptas).

Taxis: (tel. 22 42 99), stands at the northwest corner of the park and the bus station.

Luggage Storage: At the bus station (200ptas; open Mon.-Sat. 6am-11pm) and train station (400ptas; open 24hr.; tokens available daily 7am-11pm).

Public Toilets: In Parque del Espolón. Open 9am-8pm; 25ptas.

Red Cross: C. Saturnino Ulargui, 5 (tel. 22 22 22).

Medical Services: Hospital de la Rioja, Av. Viana, 1 (tel. 29 11 94), on the edge of town in the direction of Pamplona. **Emergency:** (tel. 091 or 092).

Post Office: Pl. San Agustín (tel. 22 00 66 or 22 89 06), next to the *museo*. Open for stamps and Lista de Correos Mon.-Fri. 8:30am-8:30pm, Sat. 9:30am-2pm. **Postal Code:** 26070.

Telephone Code: (9)41.

ACCOMMODATIONS AND CAMPING

The *casco antiguo* brims with budget *pensiones* and *hostales.* Try **C. San Juan,** the second left past Parque de Espolón from the stations, and **C. San Agustín** and **C. Laurel,** a little deeper into the old quarter past the far corner of the park. Although some lodgings look a bit shabby from the street, most are family-run and very clean. Reservations are crucial for the *fiesta* week ending Sept. 21. There's an *albergue* for Santiago pilgrims only, on C. Ruavieja, 3 (reception open 5-9pm).

Residencia Universitaria (HI), C. Caballero de la Rosa, 38 (tel. 29 11 45 or 26 14 22). Open as *albergue* June-Sept. 1000ptas per person, *pensión completa* 2400ptas. Breakfast 200ptas.

Fonda Bilbaína, C. Capitán Eduardo Gallarza, 10, 2nd fl. (tel. 25 42 26), take C. Sagasta into the *casco antiguo,* turn left on C. Portales and then left again on C. Capitán Eduardo. High ceilings, shiny wooden floors, and bright rooms, some with glass-enclosed balconies, make up for halls that smell like cigarettes. Singles 1700ptas. Doubles 3000ptas, with bath 3500ptas.

Hostal Sebastián, C. San Juan, 21 (tel. 24 28 00). Large doubles with sinks and industrial strength beds. Sparkling bathrooms. Front rooms have balconies looking out over the *tapas* scene. Winter heating. Singles 2000ptas. Doubles 3500ptas.

Pensión "El Revellín", C. Norte, 50 (tel. 22 02 31). Friendly couple runs *pensión* with dark-but-clean doubles and triples without baths. Doubles 3500ptas. Triples 4500ptas. Solo travelers pay 1700-2300ptas for a double room.

Camping La Playa, Av. Playa, 6 (tel. 25 22 53), off the main highway across the river from the *casco antiguo.* Riverbank site with sandy beach. Laundromat, too. Municipal swimming pools next door (free). 480ptas (plus 7% IVA) per person, per tent, per car. Prices are higher from Aug. 1 to mid-Sept. Open year-round.

FOOD

Logroñeses take their grapes seriously. Wine is the quaff of choice for everyone from patrons of the most elegant restaurants to the juiceheads pounding *chatos* in the street. Restaurants in the *casco antiguo* stock La Rioja's veggie-heavy delights, including *patatas en salsa picante* (potatoes with melted cheese in a spicy sauce) and

pimientos a la riojana (sweet peppers with minced meat). **C.'s Laurel** and **San Juan** brim with bars and cafes—many have little windows serving giddy passers-by. The local **market** is in the large concrete building on C. Capitán Eduardo Gallarza, left off C. Sagasta en route to the river (open Mon.-Sat. 7:30am-1:30pm and 4-7:30pm). For half a block's worth of groceries, head to supermarket **Simago**, Av. La Rioja, a left off C. Miguel Villanueva past the tourist office (open Mon.-Sat. 9am-9pm).

Bar Soriano, Travesía de Laurel, 2 (tel. 22 88 07), where C. Laurel makes its 90° turn. Specialty *pincho* is *champiñones con gambas* (sauteed mushrooms and shrimp on bread; with *chato* of wine or beer 130ptas). It borders on the transcendental. Bartenders shovel shrimp and 'shrooms out the window to eager crowds in the street. A proper place to whet your appetite. Open 11am-1am.

Restaurante Ruiz, C. San Juan, 11 (tel. 23 18 64). Filling meals in a monochromatic brown dining room. Delicious *menú* (1100ptas) includes a tasty *patatas a la Riojana* (starch with chorizo in a paprika-flavored broth). Open daily 1-3pm. Visa, MC.

Mesón Ríos, C. Oviedo, 15 (tel. 23 89 72), a left off Av. España as you exit the bus station. All-you-can-eat buffet 1000ptas, Sat. 1200ptas. Open Mon.-Sat. 1-4pm.

Bocatas Riojas, C. Portales, 39 (tel. 25 40 55). Across from the cathedral. Stuffs just about anything between two slices of hot bread—try the *logroñesa* with tomato, bacon, and cheese (350ptas), or the *cordobesa* with tomato and a skewer of spicy grilled beef (400ptas). Long hours satisfy wandering youth with the munchies. Open Sun.-Thurs. 10am-midnight, Fri.-Sat. 10am-3am.

SIGHTS AND ENTERTAINMENT

Catedral de Santa María de la Redonda towers over Pl. Mercado, its 18th-century facade the *casco antiguo's* highlight. From C. General Vara turn left on C. Portales; the cathedral is two blocks away on the right (open daily 8am-1pm and 6-8:30pm; free). Another three blocks along C. Portales sits the **Museo de La Rioja,** Pl. Agustín, 23 (tel. 29 12 59), which continues to subsist on the fruitful 1835 looting of regional monasteries and convents, a move sanctioned by the Disentailment Law (open Tues.-Sat. 10am-2pm and 4-9pm, Sun. 11:30am-2pm; free).

The grassy knolls along the **Río Ebro** are good strolling ground. A pedestrian path and the bridges **Puente de Hierro** and **Puente de Piedra** cross the river.

At night, the **partying** begins in the *casco antiguo,* especially in the bars lining **Calle Mayor** (which get progressively hipper the farther east you go) moving later to **Calle Argentina** (across Gran Vía del Rey Don Juan Carlos I). Dusk-till-dawn revelry characterizes the **Fiestas de San Bernabé** (June 11), which is capped by an awesome fireworks display. The **Ferias de la Vendimia,** complete with bull-running, are held a few days before and on Sept. 21.

■ Near Logroño: Santo Domingo de la Calzada

A symbolically important stop along the Camino de Santiago, Santo Domingo de la Calzada owes its existence to the pilgrimage. Eleventh-century Santo Domingo retired to the woods southwest of Logroño in search of ascetic solitude, but he didn't stay lonely for long. Seeing first-hand the trials and travails of pilgrims crossing the river, and being a good-hearted sort of chap, he built a bridge for them, drove a road (the *calzada,* or causeway) through the woods, and converted his hermitage into a hospice. Soon, business was booming in Santo Domingo (pop. 5000—now, not then). The town honors its founder for five days in May with a series of rituals that re-enact episodes of his life.

King Alfonso VI noticed the work of this monastic reject and donated resources for the construction of the grand **Catedral de Santo Domingo** on the site of the original temple. The king set the first stone himself in 1098. With some Romanesque features, the current form dates from the 12th and 13th centuries. The *retablo mayor* was removed for restoration and can be seen, in pieces, in the museum's *claustro* (open daily 9am-8pm; 250ptas, over 65 150ptas, under 18 100ptas). Engraved Romanesque pillars have been discovered behind where the *retablo* stood. Because of this discov-

A Little Something to 'Cock About

In the cathedral museum and throughout town, the casual visitor happens upon depictions of a hen and a rooster. The reference alludes to the miracle of Santo Domingo, known as "the cock that crows after it has been roasted." As the legend goes, an innkeeper's daughter fell madly in (unrequited) love with a pilgrim named Hugonell. The rejected, heartbroken girl slipped a silver cup into Hugonell's bag and reported the "robbery" to the mayor. Hugonell was found guilty and hanged. When his distraught parents visited the gallows, they heard their son's voice insisting that he was alive, and that Santo Domingo had saved him. They rushed to the mayor's house and related the bizarre series of events. The skeptical mayor, his meal of fowl and greens interrupted, scoffed and insisted that Hugonell was as dead as the roasted chicken on his plate. The mayor ate his words when the cooked cock suddenly sprouted feathers and crowed Hugonell's innocence.

Tourists who wish to engage in their own culinary commemoration of the miracle can pick up bags of the local pastry, called *ahorcamientos,* or hangings.

ery, the provincial government has decided not to put the *retablo* back up, and is discussing moving it altogether, a decision which disturbs local Santo Domingans. To reach the cathedral from the **bus stop** at Pl. Beato Hermosilla, cross Av. Juan Carlos I and follow C. Alcalde Rodolfo Varona. Take the next left (unmarked C. Pinar) for one block, then turn right on C. Hilario Perez, which ends at the cathedral square. The entrance to the cathedral is from C. Cristo (open during mass and *claustro* hours).

The town's **tourist office** sits in Casa de Trastámara, C. Mayor, 70 (tel. 34 33 34), under the long stone arch to the left of the cathedral as you face its main portal. Their map is not worth its 100ptas price tag, but the staff is worth its salt (open Mon.-Sat. 6-9pm, Sun. 12-2pm and 6-10pm). The **Red Cross** answers at tel. 34 03 34. **Police** push files at tel. 34 00 05. In an **emergency**, call 091 or 092. The **post office** (tel. 34 14 93), is on Av. Burgos (open Mon.-Fri. 8:30am-2:30pm, Sat. 9am-1pm). The **postal code** is 26250, the **telephone code** (9)41.

Unless you're planning to withdraw in contemplation, Santo Domingo is best as a daytrip. If you do hang around, **Hostal Miguel,** C. Juan Carlos I, 23 (tel. 34 32 52), is clean and comfy. From the bus stop, walk straight down C. Juan Carlos. It's on the left (singles 2000ptas, doubles 3500ptas). The **Casa del Santo** (a.k.a. Casa de Ofradías), C. Mayor, 42 (tel. 34 33 90), off the cathedral square, has info for pilgrims in the Federación de Asociaciones Jacobeas office (open Mon.-Fri. 10am-2pm and 4-7pm, Sat 10am-2pm) and runs an *hospedería,* where 40 beds and kitchen use are free, but only for those heading to Santiago. (Reception open daily 9am-10pm, though the schedule varies. Strict 10pm curfew.) The nearest camp site is 5km away toward Logroño at **Camping Bañares** (tel. 34 28 04; 575ptas per person, per tent, and per car; 7% IVA).

Several restaurants hover near the cathedral on C. Mayor and adjoining plazas, luring hungry pilgrims with generous *menús.* Try **La Taberna,** C. Mayor, 56, for owner Emilio's 1000ptas *menú* or **El Meson del Abuelo,** Pl. Alameda, for a 975ptas meal (1150ptas on Sunday). The town market is held near Pl. Beato Hermosilia.

Buses run from Pl. Beato Hermosilla to Logroño (Mon.-Sat. 9 per day, Sun. 2 per day, 1hr., 350ptas) and Haro (Mon.-Sat. 3-5 per day, Sun. 1 per day, 25min., 160ptas).

■ Near Logroño: Calahorra

When Hannibal besieged the city of Calahorra in 72 AD, he found only one inhabitant. While the rest had died from starvation, this old man survived by eating human flesh. But "Calahorran hunger" is a thing of the past. The city is known for its *huertas,* or market gardens which have been held in the **Plaza del Raso** since the Middle Ages. Spring sprouts and asparagus are combined with artichokes, cauliflower,

peas, carrots, green beans, and lamb to make *la menestra de verduras,* a typical Calahorran dish. Food in Calahorra is complemented by an array of wines, made from five varieties of grapes harvested by the San Isidro Cooperative. The annual harvesting commences the wine-making process.

Calahorra is not just a great place to chow. Historical landmarks including a Roman villa and sewers date from its 200-year history as a Roman metropolis. Its two museums, the **Convento del Carmen** and, of course, a **catedral** make this city as sweet as the fruit of its vines.

Attendants in the **Ayuntamiento** will give you a map of the city. From the train station walk along Av. Estación and continue as it turns into Po. Mercadal. The building is at the end of the *paseo,* in Pl. Tierno Galván. (Open Mon.-Fri. 8am-3pm, Sat. 8am-2pm.) The **Red Cross,** C. Dr. Fleming, 10 (tel. 13 53 13), heals. The **municipal police** are in the Ayuntamiento, through an entrance on the right side of the building (tel. 13 01 87). **Luggage storage** at the bus station costs 100ptas. In an **emergency** call 091 or 092. The **post office,** C. General Gallarza, 6, behind the Ayuntamiento, does stamps and Lista de Correos (open Mon.-Fri. 8:30am-2:30pm, Sat. 9:30am-1pm) The **postal code** is 26500, the **telephone code** is (9)41.

Budget accommodations are not superabundant. Calahorra is best visited for the day from Logroño. **Hostal Teresa,** Santa Domingo de la Calzada, 2 (tel. 13 03 32), has clean, acceptable rooms and is a brief walk from the Ayuntamiento (singles 2000ptas; doubles 3000ptas, with bath 4200ptas). Various **restaurants** along Po. Mercadal and in Pl. Raso offer tasty regional delights in reasonably priced *menús.* **Garcés,** on Av. Ebro (tel. 14 72 74) and **Viana,** C. Bebricio, 3 (tel. 13 00 08), tempt tummies with meals concocted from the spring harvest.

The Gothic **Catedral de Santa María** is deep within the *casco antiguo.* From the Ayuntamiento, walk up C. Martines and C. Grande through Pl. Raso. Continue straight, taking C. Mayor to Cuesta de la Catedral. The cathedral is built on the site where the city's two patron saints, Emeterio and Celedonio, were reportedly killed. Their decapitated heads continued to preach Christianity so they were thrown into the Río Ebro. The **Iglesia de Santiago,** Pl. Raso, is a neoclassical church with an impressive porch. Just to the left of the church on C. Angel Oliván is the **Museo Municipal,** which houses a permanent archaeological collection and temporary modern art exhibitions (open Tues.-Sat. noon-2pm and 6-9pm, Sun. noon-2pm). "**La Clínica,**" the Roman site, lies on the northern boundary of the *casco antiguo.* From the Ayuntamiento, walk towards the train station and veer right off Av. Estación onto C. Carretil. **Roman sewers** are on C. San Andrés and other Roman remains are in Parque de la Era Alta and on Po. Mercadal, including a statue of *La Matrona.* **El Convento de Carmen** lies outside the city walls, a short taxi ride away (1000ptas).

RENFE trains (tel.13 19 46) run to: Logroño (2-3 per day, 40min., 385ptas). The **bus station** is on C. Miguel de Cervantes. To get to the Ayuntamiento, hang a right out of the station and an immediate left onto C. Bebricio. The Ayuntamiento lies just ahead. The last bus to Logroño leaves at 8:30pm (6-7 per day, 1hr., 430ptas).

■ Haro

Ninety-six wine-makers overwhelm Haro (pop. 10,000), drawing international acclaim and merchants from abroad. Most **bodegas** offer tours of their facilities, in the large warehouses on the outskirts of town (several are grouped around the RENFE station, across the river from the town center). Tours are usually held between 9am-2pm. Calling a day or two in advance is a good idea; the tourist office can help. **Bodegas Bilbaínas** (tel. 31 01 47) and **Carlos Serves** (tel. 31 02 94) have English-speaking guides. With a bit more *confianza* in your Spanish, try **Bodegas Martínez Lacuesta** (tel. 31 00 50), a century-old winery whose founder brought Haro its original fame.

Between 7 and 10pm, while the rest of Spain goes on their evening *paseo,* Haro's citizenry opts for the sedentary custom of *chiquiteo*—drinking wine in the **bars** on the streets between Pl. Paz and Pl. Iglesia. The tourist office distributes an official

classification of vintages (the *Vinícola Riojana Comercial* booklet). On June 24-29 the wine flows profusely in honor of patron saint San Felices, culminating in the skin-staining **Batalla del Vino** on June 29, and it cascades during the **Fiesta Mayor** (on and around Sept. 8), which honors the Virgen de la Vega.

A bi-lingual staff at the **tourist office,** Pl. Monseñor Florentino Rodríguez (tel. 30 33 66), dispenses information on La Rioja and a rudimentary map. With your back to the Ayuntamiento, take C. Vega from the far left corner of Pl. Paz. The office is in the plaza to the left around the bend. (Open June-Oct. Mon.-Sat. 10am-2pm and 4:30-7:30pm, Sun. 10am-2pm. If closed, get info from the Ayuntamiento.) The **Red Cross,** C. Siervas de Jesús, 2 (tel. 31 18 38), fights antigens. The **municipal police,** is at C. Sanchez del Río, 11 (tel. 31 01 25). **Luggage storage** in lockers at the bus station costs 100ptas per day. In an **emergency,** call 091 or 092, bleeds blue. The **post office** (tel. 20 50 88), at the corner of Av. Rioja and C. Alemania, a left from C. Ventilla, is open for stamps and Lista de Correos Mon.-Fri. 8:30am-2:30pm, Sat. 9:30am-1pm. The **postal code** is 26200. The **telephone code** is (9)41.

There are fewer accommodations than *bodegas* in Haro; you might try daytripping from Logroño. **Hostal Aragón,** C. Vega, 9 (tel. 31 00 04), between the tourist office and Pl. Paz, repainted and redecorated, has spacious old rooms with high ceilings, wood floors, and winter heating. Don't be scared by the stairway (singles 1700ptas; doubles 3000ptas). **Camping de Haro,** Av. Miranda (tel. 31 27 37), is on the train station side of the river, left of the bridge from town (465ptas plus 7% IVA per person, per car, and per tent). **Restaurants** in the side streets off **Pl. Paz** offer satisfying meals at good prices and—surprise!—great wine. For an excellent lunch and an even better bargain, join Haro's upper crust at **Mesón Atamauri,** Pl. Juan Garcia, Gato 1 (tel. 30 32 20). The *menú del día* (1300ptas) changes daily but often features a slightly spicy *lomo a la riojana* (pork loin in red pepper sauce) and a rich *tarta de queso* (cheese tart). Bars in the **Herradura** quarter around the Iglesia Parroquial de Santo Tomás serve more modest meals and excellent *tapas.* Also on C. Santo Tomás, many **wine shops** sell the region's fruit of the vine. The best vintages start at around 3500ptas per bottle, but others cost as little as 200-500ptas.

Haro is so thoroughly steeped in wine-making that some streets emit a winey bouquet. Still, it's possible to enjoy yourself without so much as sniffing a cork. Light filtered through a beautiful stained-glass window radiates through the *retablo* of the **Basílica de Nuestra Señora de La Vega.** The church gardens command a view of the surrounding valley and vine-tangled hills. To find the church from the tourist office, turn left and follow C. Vega for about three blocks (church open daily 8am-1:30pm and 5-8:30pm). Past the basilica, in the Estación Etnológica, is the **Museo del Vino.** Guess the theme! (Open Mon.-Sat. 10am-2pm and 4-8pm, Sun. 10am-2pm. 300ptas, Wed. free.) The **Iglesia Parroquial de Santo Tomás** has an appealing Plateresque exterior; it's on Pl. Iglesia, a left from Pl. Paz as you face the Ayuntamiento.

RENFE trains (tel. 31 15 97) run to: Logroño (4-5 per day, 1hr., 385-1000ptas); Bilbao (2-3 per day, 2¼hr., 1300ptas); Zaragoza (4-5 per day, 3½hr., 1590-2200ptas); Tudela (4-5 per day, 2-2½hr., 1060-1700ptas). To reach Pl. Paz from the train station, take the road downhill, turn right and then left across the river, and let C. Navarra lead you uphill to the plaza. Haro's spankin' new **bus station** gleams at C. Ventilla. The last bus to Logroño leaves Haro around 9pm (5-6 per day, 1hr., 345ptas). To get to Pl. Paz from the bus stop, follow the signs to *centro ciudad* along C. Ventilla and bear left from Pl. Cruz along C. Arrabal.

NAVARRA

■ Pamplona

The dancing kept up, the drinking kept up, the noise went on. ...
Everything became quite unreal finally and it seemed as though nothing
could have any consequences. It seemed out of place to think of
consequences during the fiesta. All during the fiesta you had the feeling,
even when it was quiet, that you had to shout any remark to make it
heard.

Ernest Hemingway, *The Sun Also Rises*

And thus Ernest Hemingway made the *San Fermines* (July 6-14) legend—the festival that sends savage beasts through the narrow streets of a pretty normal town and invites its guests to get in the way. At the bullring, where the daily *encierro* ends, a huggable statue of Papa Hemingway welcomes aficionados—but mostly just rowdy blowhards—to Europe's premier festival: eight days of gaiety, drinking, screaming, dodging, slipping, falling, and passing out.

Like Hemingway, Pamplona doesn't nurse its hangover for more than a night's rest. The other 357 days of the year, Pamplona is still worth a visit, when university students crowd bars, get tight, and even pass out in one of the town's lush parks. Pamplona is the capital of the province of Navarra, but its roots are Basque. Although the city was named after Pompeii by its Roman "founders," the area had actually been settled centuries earlier by the Basques. The city is visibly involved with the several Basque Nationalist and Separatist movements.

ORIENTATION AND PRACTICAL INFORMATION

Almost everything of interest to visitors is in the **casco antiguo,** the northeast quarter of this provincial capital. **Plaza del Castillo,** marked by a bandstand, is its center. From the **bus station,** turn left onto Av. Conde Oliveto. At the traffic island on Pl. Príncipe de Viana, take the second left onto Av. San Ignacio, follow it to the end of pedestrian thoroughfare **Paseo Sarasate,** and bear right. From the **train station,** take bus #9 (90ptas); disembark at the last stop, traverse Po. Sarasate, then walk diagonally left to Pl. Castillo. North of Pl. Castillo, the Baroque **Casa Consistorial** (a.k.a. Ayuntamiento) makes a handsome marker amid the swirl of medieval streets.

Although Pamplona is usually a very safe city, crime skyrockets during the *San Fermines,* when assaults and muggings do occur. Some come to the *fiesta* only to take advantage of awe-struck tourists. Do not roam alone at night, and take extreme care in the parks and shady streets of the *casco antiguo.* Enthused revelers who pass out can often say good-bye to their wallet, money belt, and, thanks to savvy thieves, luggage they left in *consigna.* Some stores close during the *San Fermines,* and many restaurants and bars close after the *fiestas* for a well-deserved rest.

Tourist Office: C. Duque de Ahumada, 3 (tel. 22 07 41; fax 21 14 62). From Pl. Castillo, take Av. Carlos III 1 block, turn left on C. Duque de Ahumada, and cross C. Espoz y Mina. Adequate **map** and minute-by-minute guides to the festivities. During *San Fermines,* the line forms by 9am. English spoken. **Currency exchange,** public baths, and buses to campsite are posted on a bulletin board outside. Open Mon.-Fri. 10am-2pm and 4-9pm, Sat. 10am-2pm; during *San Fermines* daily 10am-5pm. **City Info Office,** in the rear of the Ayuntamiento (tel. 42 01 00), off the plaza by the market, offers a map and basic city info. Open Mon.-Fri. 8am-3pm.

Budget Travel: TIVE, C. Paulino Caballero, 4, 5th fl. (tel. 21 24 04; fax. 22 12 65). Take Av. San Ignacio toward Pl. Castillo, turn right on C. Roncesvalles and go 1

block, then turn right on C. Paulino Caballero. Discount travel tickets, ISIC (700ptas), and HI cards (1800ptas). Open Mon.-Fri. 9am-1:30pm. During *San Fermines* open Mon.-Fri. 10am-noon.

Currency Exchange: Reception desk at **Hotel Tres Reyes,** Jardines de la Taconera (tel. 22 66 00), changes money 24hr. From the bus station turn right, then right again on Av. Taconera for 5 blocks, and bend left; the hotel is to the left where the road forks. **Banco Central Hispano** branches sit on Pl. Castillo, 21, and in Pl. Vinculo, on the corner of C. Estella and C. Alhondiga by the post office. Open Oct.-April Mon.-Fri. 8:30am-2:30pm, Sat. 8:30am-1pm. May-Sept. closed Sat.

Flights: Aeropuerto de Noaín (tel. 16 87 00), 6km away, accessible only by taxi (about 1200ptas). To Madrid (1-2 per day) and Barcelona (Mon.-Fri. 1 per day, 30min.). Rates subject to change.

Trains: Estación RENFE, off Av. San Jorge, 20min. from the *casco antiguo* by bus #9 from Po. Sarasate (90ptas). Info (tel. 13 02 02) open Mon.-Fri. 8:30am-1:30pm and 4-7pm. Another **ticket/info office,** C. Estella, 8 (tel. 22 72 82), is 2 streets behind the bus station. Exit the bus station and go around the right corner; the office is 2 blocks down, on the left side of C. Estella. Open Mon.-Fri. 9am-1:30pm and 4:30-7:30pm, Sat. 9:30am-1pm. Pamplona is miserably connected by rail. Reservations are often mandatory on longer trains during *San Fermines;* it's much faster and easier to take the bus. To: Olite (2-3 per day, 45min., 450ptas); Tudela (6-8 per day, 2hr., 1300ptas); Vitoria-Gasteiz (4-5 per day, 1hr., 500ptas); Zaragoza (4-7 per day, 2-3hr., 1800ptas); San Sebastián (3 per day, 1¾hr., 1500ptas); Madrid (3 per day, 5-6hr., 4100ptas); Barcelona (2-3 per day, 7-9hr., 4100ptas).

Buses: Estación de Autobuses, C. Conde Oliveto at the corner with C. Yanguas y Miranda. Nearly 20 companies. Consult the bulletin board's list of destinations. Ticket booths for less frequent buses usually open 30min. before departure. To: Olite (2-7 per day, 50min., 220ptas); Jaca (2-3 per day, 2hr., 855ptas); Tudela (5-7 per day, 1½hr., 800-880ptas); Roncal (Mon.-Sat. 1 per day, 2hr., 880ptas); Vitoria-Gasteiz (7-11 per day, 1¼hr., 875ptas); San Sebastián (9 per day, 1½hr., 750ptas); Zaragoza (5-7 per day, 3½hr., 1450-1605ptas); Bilbao (5-7 per day, 2¼hr., 1530ptas); Barcelona (2 per day, 6hr., 2135ptas); Madrid (4-5 per day, 3140ptas). Also service to Burguete, Orbaiceta, Ochagavía, and Logroño.

Public Transportation: Fourteen bus lines cover all corners of the city. Route guide is available at the tourist office. Bus #9 from Po. Sarasate to train station (every 10-15min., 6:30am-10:30pm, 20min., 90ptas). During *San Fermines* some routes run night shifts (night fare 125ptas).

Taxis: (tel. 23 21 00 or 23 23 00). Stand at Pl. Castillo.

Car Rental: Europcar, Hotel Blanca Navarra, Av. Pío XII, 43 (tel. 17 60 02). Buses #1, 2, and 4 go here; get off after the traffic circle on the way out of town. Must be 21. Seat Ibiza 7000ptas per day. **Hertz** is in Hotel Tres Reyes (tel. 16 87 00). Must be at least 25. **Avis** (tel. 17 00 68) rents from the airport. Ask for discounts.

Hitchhiking: Word has it that hitching to Logroño and France is easier from here than from elsewhere.

Luggage Storage: At the bus station (tel. 22 20 08). 115ptas per bag per day, large packs 170ptas. Open Mon.-Sat. 6:15am-9:30pm, Sun. 7am-9:30pm. During *San Fermines,* open 24hr. (200ptas). Also during *San Fermines,* **RENFE** (tel. 13 02 02) stores bags (300ptas per day). Lockers (400ptas). Open daily 5:30am-1:30am.

Lost Property: Check Monasterio de Irache, 2, at the police station (tel. 42 06 12).

Laundromat: Lavomatique, C. Descalzos, 28 (tel. 22 19 22). From Pl. San Francisco follow C. Hilarión Eslava to the end, then turn right. Harried staff during *San Fermines* can even get the blood out: wash, dry, and soap for 800ptas.

Public Toilets and Baths: Squat **toilet booths** are set up for *San Fermines*. Use them! (25,000ptas fine for using the street.) Permanent bathrooms in the Jardines de Taconera let you sit. **Casa de Baño** (tel. 22 17 38), C. Hilarión Eslava, 2, at the corner with Jarauta; up from Pl. San Francisco, on the left past C. Mayor. Showers 110ptas, with towel and soap 190ptas. Open daily 8am-8pm.

Swimming Pool: Piscinas de Aranzadi (tel. 22 30 02), 15min. from Pl. Castillo on Vuelta de Aranzadi. Open daily 10:30am-8:30pm. Mon.-Sat. 300ptas, under 14 100ptas. Sun.: 500ptas; 100ptas. *San Fermines:* 800ptas; 250ptas.

Gay and Lesbian Organization: EGHAM, Apdo. 1667, Pamplona 31080.
Red Cross: C. Yanguas y Miranda, 3 (tel. 22 64 04 or 22 92 91). Also sets up stands at the bus station and the *corrida* during *San Fermines.*
24Hr. Pharmacy: Check the *Diario de Navarra* listings or call tel. 22 21 11.
Medical Services: Hospital de Navarra, C. Irunlarrea (tel. 42 22 00).
Police: National Police, C. General Chinchilla, to the right on Av. Tacoñera with your back to the statue on Po. Sarasate. **Municipal Police,** C. Monasterio de Irache, 2 (tel. 25 51 50). English spoken. **Emergency:** tel. 091 or 092.
Post Office: Central office is closed for renovations. Try the one on C. Estella (down C. Vincalo cross the plaza, turn right on C. Estella; it's next to the RENFE office). Open Mon.-Fri. 8:30am-8:30pm, Sat. 9:30am-2pm; during *San Fermines* 8:30am-2pm. **Postal Code:** 31001.
Telephone Code: (9)48.

ACCOMMODATIONS AND CAMPING

If you have Jedi powers of mind control, truckloads of cash, or a large gun, you *may* find a room during the first few days of *San Fermines.* For solo travelers, even these assets will probably not be enough. Diehard *sanferministas* book their rooms for next year before going home. In most cases, you must reserve at least a month ahead and pay rates (up front) up to four times higher than those listed (anywhere from 4000-8000ptas per person in most budget *pensiones*). Arriving several days before the *fiestas* may help. Check the newspaper *Diario de Navarra* for **casas particulares.** Early in the week, people accost visitors at the train and bus stations, offering couches and floor space. Be wary—accommodations and prices vary tremendously, and you might find yourself blowing your money for a blink of sleep on a dirty floor in a bad part of town. Because of past scams, the tourist office will neither recommend nor aid in this effort. Many who can't find rooms sleep outside on the lawns of the Ciudadela, Pl. Fueros (from the bus station turn left, then left again at the traffic circle), and on the banks of the river. Veteran park-sleepers recommend extreme caution. If you can't leave your belongings at the *consigna* at the bus station (it fills fast), sleep on top of them (still not foolproof). Always sleep in groups. It's safer to nap during the day when it's warmer and brighter and stay up through the night. During those months when Pamplona manages to keep its street free of pesky bulls, finding a room is no problem. Accommodations that define the word budget—in price *and* style—line **C. San Nicolás** and **C. San Gregorio** off Pl. Castillo. Beware that most hostel owners follow separate price schedules for *temparada alta (San Fermines), temparada media* (summer), and *temparada baja* (rest of the year). For last-minute accommodations during *San Fermines,* contact **Fermín** at tel. (9)89 33 30 31. The dude with the cell phone will eat up your phone card, but at least you'll have a roof over your head.

Casa Santa Cecilia, C. Navarrería, 17 (tel. 22 22 30). Follow C. Estafeta to its end in Mercaderes, turn right, then left at a 30° angle. Comfort lies behind the impressive (and spooky) portal. The most affordable prices around during "the party," plus sobering advice from the owners on running and viewing. Singles 2000-4000ptas. Doubles 3000ptas-8000ptas. Most credit cards accepted.

Hostal Otano, C. San Nicolás, 5 (tel. 22 50 95). Staying at this former prison may still feel like a punishment (many tiny, windowless rooms and weak showers), but it's slightly higher in quality than similarly priced neighbors, and at least you won't have to rob a bank to pay the going rate. Singles 1700-2000ptas, with bath 2700ptas. Doubles: 3500ptas; 4500ptas. Visa, MC, AmEx.

Hostal Bearán, C. San Nicolás, 25 (tel. 22 34 28). Squeaky-clean salmon-colored rooms with phone, TV, bath, and safebox. Singles 5500ptas. Doubles 6500ptas. Oct.-June: 4500ptas; 5500ptas. During *San Fermines:* 13,000ptas; 15,000ptas. Breakfast 450ptas. Visa, MC, AmEx.

Fonda La Aragonesa, San Nicolás 22 (tel. 22 34 28). Basic, clean rooms the way Ikea might design them. Walk across the street to Hostal Bearán for reception desk. Sin-

gles 3000ptas. Doubles 3500ptas. Oct.-June: 2500ptas; 3000ptas. *San Fermines:* 8000ptas; 9000ptas. Visa, MC, AmEx.

Fonda La Union, C. San Nicolás, 13 (tel. 22 13 19), next to Restaurante San Nicolás. Warm proprietors have recently renovated their rooms and it shows, especially in the new bathrooms. 2000ptas per person; 5000ptas per person during *San Fermines.* Visa, MC, AmEx.

Fonda La Montañesa, C. San Gregorio, 2 (tel. 22 43 80). You can't beat the price. And with several floors of beds, there may be hope for earlybirds without reservations. No heat. 1400ptas per person; 3000ptas per person during *San Fermines.*

Camping: Camping Ezcaba (tel. 33 16 65), in Eusa, 7km outside Pamplona on the road to Irún. From Pl. Toros, La Montañesa bus runs to Eusa (4 per day, get off at the gasoline station, the last stop). Capacity for 714 campers. Fills as fast as other accommodations during big bull week. 450ptas per person, per tent, and per car. Open June-Oct. No reservations accepted.

To suppress Basque nationalist activity, Pamplona recently passed a law requiring all bars (nightclubs excluded) to close at the unheard of hour of 2:30am on weekdays, 3:30am on weekends. Pause for a moment to imagine the outrage of locals forced to stop drinking before the first light. It's not pretty. Of course, all laws are temporarily ignored during *San Fermines.*

FOOD

While *San Fermines* draws street vendors selling everything from roast chicken to *churros,* the tiny neighborhoods of Pamplona advertise hearty *menús* throughout the entire year. Try side streets in the neighborhood of Casa de Huéspedes Santa Cecilia, the cathedral area above Pl. San Francisco, and C. Jarauta and C. Descalzos near **Po. Ronda. C. Navarrería,** near the cathedral, overflows with small bars and restaurants. More restaurants crank away on **C.'s Estafeta, Mayor,** and **San Nicolás;** the last is longer on crowds and alcohol than solid food. C. Navarrería, C. San Lorenzo, and Po. Sarasate house *bocadillo* bars. During *fiestas,* cheap drinks and cheaper ideology can be found at *barracas políticas* (bars organized by political interest groups that don't expect any interest in their platforms) set up next to the amusement park on the west end of the *ciudadela.* A fine Navarrese finish is the dessert liqueur *Patxaran (Pacharán).* The official soft drink of all Spanish northern *fiestas* is **calimocho,** a mixture of wine (to keep you happy) and Coca-Cola (to keep you up). Crazy Italians have been known to mix **Red Bull,** a taurine soft drink with more riboflavins, compound-complex carbohydrates, and caffeine molecules than a Centrum Silver Lab, and mix it with vodka or anything else with an 80-plus proof. Many cafes and restaurants close for one to two weeks after *San Fermines.*

The **market,** C. Mercado, is to the right of Casa Consistorial's facade and down the stairs. (Open Mon.-Thurs. and Sat. 8am-2pm, Fri. and during *San Fermines* 8am-2pm and 4:30-7:30pm.) **Supermarket** fiends should check **Autoservicio Montserrat,** at the corner of C. Hilarión Eslava and C. Mayor. (Open Mon.-Fri. 9am-2pm and 5-7:30pm, Sat. 9am-2pm; *San Fermines* Mon.-Sat. 9am-2pm. Visa, MC.)

Bar-Restaurante Lanzale, C. San Lorenzo, 31 (tel. 22 10 71), between C. Mayor and C. Jarauta, above Pl. San Francisco. No run-of-the-mill *menú:* zucchini soup, pork ribs, or *marimatako* (Basque tomato-and-tuna stew 1100ptas). Open Mon.-Sat. 1:30-3:30pm and 9-11pm.

Restaurante Sarasate, C. San Nicolás, 19-21 (tel. 22 57 27), above the seafood store. Healthful, all-vegetarian cuisine. Simply scrumptious. 1200ptas *menú.* Open Mon.-Thurs. 1:15-4pm, Fri.-Sat. 1:15-4pm and 9-11pm.

Restaurante San Vermin, C. San Nicolás, 44-46 (tel. 22 21 91). The place to celebrate your near brush with horned death or your consummate sanity in avoiding the whole thing altogether. Locals rate it as one of the best. *Menú* 2000ptas.

Hong-Kong, C. San Gregorio, 38 (tel. 22 66 35). Ignore the Chinese pop music; the 4-course, 750ptas *menú* will win you over. More authentic (oxymoron) than Pamplona's other Chinese restaurants. Open daily 12-4pm and 8pm-midnight.

Self-Service Estafeta, C. Estafeta, 57 (tel. 22 10 65). Service so quick you can stop, chow, and the bull *still* won't catch you. *Paella* (550ptas), roast half-chicken (500ptas), *menú* (1110ptas). Don't come here for atmosphere. Open Mon.-Sat. 1-4pm and 8:30-11pm, Sun. 1-4pm; in winter Fri.-Sat. 8:30-11pm. Visa, MC, AmEx.

SIGHTS

There's ample reason to visit Pamplona, even beyond that mythical week. The clatter of cranky bovines tends to obscure Pamplona's rich architectural legacy. In the late 14th century, Carlos the Noble (Carlos III) endowed the city with a proper **Gothic cathedral;** he and Queen Leonor are interred in the ornately sculpted mausoleum. The cathedral, which houses the second largest bell in Spain, perches at the end of C. Navarrería. Neighboring streets are packed with palaces, baroque mansions, and artisan houses from different periods. Aside from the cathedral, shrines to *Dios* satisfy dedicated church-goers: check out the Gothic 13th-century **Iglesias de San Cernín,** near the Ayuntamiento, **San Nicolás,** in Pl. S. Nicolás, and the 16th-century **Iglesia Santo Domingo,** with its sumptuous *retablo* and brick cloister.

The pentagonal **Ciudadela,** built by Felipe II and sprawled next to botanical highlight **Jardines de la Taconera,** hosts free exhibits and concerts in the summer. From the old quarter, the most scenic route to the Ciudadela is the *Vuelta del castillo;* it follows the city's third set of **walls,** built between the 16th and 18th centuries. When Charlemagne dismantled the walls in the 9th century, the Navarrese and Basques joined at the pass of Roncesvalles to massacre his rear guard and his nephew Roland. This violence is immortalized in the French medieval epic *La chanson de Roland* (Song of Roland). At the far end of the cathedral plaza, pick up C. Redín, which runs to the walls. A left turn follows the walls past the gardens of **Parque de la Taconera,** and along the Río Arga until they meet the Ciudadela, where there's a pond, some deer, and gravel paths (open daily 7am-10pm; closed during *San Fermines;* free).

For another view of the fortress, exit the old city by one of two gateways, **Portal de Francia** or **Portal de Guipúzcoa,** and stroll along the **Río Arga,** following the walls' curves. These awesome structures even scared off Napoleon, who refused to stage a frontal attack and staged a trick snowball fight instead. When Spanish sentries joined in, the French entered the city through its gates. The **Museo de Navarra** (tel. 22 78 31), up C. Santo Domingo from Casa Consistorial, shelters Roman funerary steles and mosaics, architectural fragments from the cathedral, mural paintings from all over the region, and a collection of 14th- to 18th-century paintings, including Goya's portrait of the Marqués de San Adrián. (Open Tues.-Sat. 10am-2pm and 5-7pm, Sun. 11am-2pm; shorter hours during *San Fermines.* 200ptas, students free.)

Throughout the year, **Plaza de Castillo** is the city's social heart, with people of all ages congregating in and around its bars and cafes. Hemingway's favorite was **Café-Bar Iruña,** the backdrop for much of *The Sun Also Rises.* It maintains a *Belle Epoque* feel, but its prices are well into the 21st century *(café con leche* 225ptas; good *bocatas* 475ptas). The cafe stays open only till 5pm. From then until 3am, it morphs into an overdressed bingo palace; the bar, a couple of doors down, stays itself.

The young and restless booze up at bars in the *casco antiguo.* **Calle de Jarauta** is a nighttime favorite. **Bodega La Ribera,** on C. Carmen, is a good place for cheap beers (175ptas) and foosball, where you can begin your evening with bacchanalian petulance. **Toki Leza** and **Imanol,** on C. Caldereria, draw an older but still hip crowd, as does **Mesón de la Navarreria,** el Navarreria, 15. Tranquil **Mesón del Caballo Blanco** serves its drinks from an outdoor patio overlooking the old city walls and surrounding countryside. Claustrophobes escape the cramped streets of San Gregorio and San Nicolás to bars in **Barrio San Juan,** beyond Hotel Tres Reyes on Av. Bayona; many draw a gay clientele. **Café Niza,** C. Duque de Ahemada, is also a gay hangout. To take the wine with you, a practical consideration during *San Fermines,* check out wineskin store **Botas las Tres ZZZ,** C. Comedias, 7, just off Pl. Castillo (open Mon.-Fri.

9:30am-1:30pm and 4-7pm). **Calle de Chapitela** and **Calle de Calcete** are filled with raging locals on weekends. For an atmosphere that's a bit more subdued and ventilated, try **Plaza de los Fueros** and the bars and restaurants on **Avenida Zaragoza.**

LOS SAN FERMINES (JULY 6-14)

> *¡Uno de enero, dos de febrero, tres de marzo, cuatro de abril,*
> *Cinco de mayo, seis de junio, siete de julio es San Fermín!*
> *¡A Pamplona hemos de ir! Con una bota, con una bota,*
> *¡A Pamplona hemos de ir! Con una bota y un calcetín.*

Visitors from the world over crowd Pamplona for the *Fiestas de San Fermín*—known to many visitors as the Running of the Bulls—in search of Europe's greatest party. Pamplona orgiastically delivers, with an eight-day frenzy of parades, wine, bullfights, parties, dancing, fireworks, wine, rock concerts, and wine to topple even the most Dionysian ne'er-do-wells. "My gosh! I'm sleepy now," says Robert Cohn in *The Sun Also Rises*. "Doesn't this thing ever stop?" "Not for a week," comes the seasoned response. Pamplonese, uniformly clad in blinding white garb with red sashes and bandanas, throw themselves into the merry-making with inspired abandon, displaying obscene levels of physical stamina and alcohol(ic) tolerance. Keep up with them at your own risk.

The mayor kicks off the festivitics at noon on July 6, firing the first rocket, or *chupinzao,* from the Ayuntamiento's balcony, and the crowd sings:

> *Pobre de mí*
> *pobre de mí*
> *ya han empezao*
> *las fiestas de San Fermín*
>
> *Voy a acabar*
> *voy a acabar*
> *con el cuerpo desecho*
> *y sin un reaaaaal.*

A barbaric howl explodes from the rolling sea of expectant *sanferministas* in the plaza below, and within minutes the streets of the *casco antiguo* flood with improvised singing and dancing troupes. The *peñas,* taurine societies more concerned with beer than bullfighting, lead the brouhaha. At 5pm on the 6th and at 9am or 9:30am every other day, they are joined by the *Comparsa de Gigantes y Cabezudos,* a troupe of *gigantes* (giant wooden monarchs) and *zaldikos* (courtiers on horseback). *Kilikis* (swollen-headed buffoons) run around chasing little kids and hitting them with play clubs. These harlequinesque misfits, together with church and Ayuntamiento officials, escort San Fermín on his triumphant procession through the *casco antiguo.* The saint's 15th-century statue is brought from the Iglesia de San Lorenzo at 10am on the 7th, the actual day of *San Fermín.*

The History of the Encierro

The **encierro,** or running of the bulls, is the focal point of the *San Fermines*. The ritual dates back to the 14th century, when it served the practical function of getting the bulls from their corrals to the bullring. These days, the first *encierro* of the festival takes place at 8am on the 7th, and is repeated at that time every day for the following seven days. Hundreds of bleary-eyed, hung-over, hyper-adrenalized runners flee from very large bulls, as bystanders cheer, provoke, and make mischief from barricades, windows, balconies, and doorways.

Rockets mark the bulls' progress on their 825m dash. Six steers accompany the six bulls—watch it, they have horns, too. Both the bulls and the mob are dangerous. Terrified runners, each convinced the bull is breathing on their tush, flee for dear life and react without concern for their peers who might get trampled in the process. Experi-

Before You Decide to Run...

Running with bulls is dangerous exercise. Every year, 10-12 people are severely gored, and many more are inadvertently crushed by fellow runners. On July 13, 1995, a 22-year-old American was killed. In the most idiotic of follies, two Australians leaped to their death trying to crowd surf. Inexperienced runners endanger not only themselves but also fellow sprinters. Although the Pamplonese are happy to share their party, they do not relish dying a bloody death because of a *guiri*'s stupidity. The tourist office dispenses a pamphlet that outlines the exact route of the three-minute run, and offers tips for inexperienced runners. Runners must be at least 18. Those who run should follow some basic rules:

- Watch an *encierro* before you run—once on TV to get an overview of what you're in for, and once in person to feel the crush and hysteria.
- Do not stay up all night drinking and carousing. Experienced runners get some sleep the night before and arrive at the course no later than 7am. Many locals recommend arriving at 6am. Access to the course closes at 7:30am.
- Stretch out.
- Give up on getting near the bulls and concentrate on getting to the bullring in one piece. Although it is acceptable to whack the bull with a rolled newspaper, runners should never touch the animals themselves; anyone who does is likely to get the bejeezus kicked out of him by locals.
- Try not to cower in a doorway; people have been trapped and killed this way.
- Be particularly wary of isolated bulls—they seek company in the crowds.
- If you fall, curl into a fetal position, lock your hands behind your head, and **do not get up** until the clatter of hooves is well past you. STAY DOWN!

enced runners, many of whom view the event as both art and sport, try to get as dangerously near the bull as possible.

After cascading through a perilously narrow opening (where a large proportion of the injuries occur), the run pours into the bullring, where scores of appreciative (and decidedly saner) spectators sit cheering the runners. Hemingway, *machismo* himself, didn't run, which may be a comforting thought if you feel like a chicken for sitting it out. Big E watched the *encierro* from the bullring and immersed himself profoundly in the customs of drinking and bullfighting. Spectators are in for at least a half-hour of amusement. One to three animals are released from their pens as runners scurry from the horny bulls. The bullring is where anyone who holds onto the horns or otherwise touches the bull for too long will get the crap beaten out of him by those runners who are carrying out the tradition in a respectable way. **Tip:** If you want to participate in the bullring excitement but are not confident in your running ability, you can line up by the Pl. de Toros before 7:30am and run in before the bulls are even in sight. Then you can "play" with the bulls in a mass of 350 people or so. Bullring spectators should arrive around 6:45am to experience the crowd heating up for the *encierro*. Music, waves, chanting, and dancing pump up the spectators until the headline entertainment arrives with the hordes.

It's a good idea to pay 450ptas for a seat in the **Grada** section of the bullring. Tickets are no problem if you arrive before 7am. You can watch for free too, but the free section is overcrowded and it can be hard to see (or breathe). To watch the running from a balcony, contact **Fermín** at tel. (9) 89 33 30 31. To watch a bullfight, you must wait in the line that forms at the bullring around 8pm every evening (tickets start at 2000ptas). As one bullfight ends, tickets go on sale for the next day. Try to avoid tickets in the *sol*, as these seats fill with *peña* members who spend more time dousing each other with wine than watching—or allowing anyone else to watch—the fight.

Day and Nightlife

After the taurine track meet, the insanity spills into the streets, gathering steam until nightfall explodes with singing in the bars, dancing in the alleyways, spontaneous parades, and a no-holds-barred party in Pl. Castillo, southern Europe's biggest open-

air dance floor. Be prepared with sturdy shoes (there's glass everywhere), a white t-shirt that will soon be soaked with wine, and a red *pañuelo* (bandana). Many English speakers dance and congregate where C. Estafeta hits Pl. Toros, an outdoor consortium of local *dicotecas*. Avoid the corner of C. Navarrería and C. Carmen, in front of Casa Santa Cecilia, where **chorizo-brained** Americans, Australians, and Kiwis jump from a 15-foot-high fountain into the crowds. Two or three die attempting this stunt each year. Don't do it, and don't encourage it.

The truly inspired **carousing** takes place the first few days of *San Fermines*. After that, the crowds thin, and the atmosphere goes from dangerously crazed to mildly insane. In between, the city eases the transition with concerts, outdoor dances, and a host of other performances. The end of the festivities culminates at midnight of the 14th with the singing of *Pobre de mí* (Poor Me): *"Pobre de mí, pobre de mí, que se han acabao las Fiestas de San Fermín."*

Nearby towns sponsor *encierros* as well: Tudela holds its festival during the week surrounding July 24; Estella for a week from the Friday before the first Sunday in August; Tafalla during the week of August 15; and Sangüesa for a week beginning September 11. Many Pamplonese opt for these, preferring to watch their own on TV.

■ Olite

Olite was a city fit for kings in the early 15th century. Its location along the Río Cidacos, its proximity to Pamplona, and its Gothic, baroque, and medieval architecture may make it fit for you, too. Intrigue and sabotage have lurked about the **Palacio Real,** the former palace of the Navarrese kings. In the early 15th century, Carlos III made this sumptuous palace and its flowery courtyards the focus of Navarrese court life. Ramparts, spiral staircases, guard towers, lookout perches, moats, alligators, distressed damsels, dragons, armored attackers, poison-dipped arrows, and court jesters make this the medieval castle of your dreams. Almost too perfect, in fact—the 1937 restoration was far from subtle. The blatantly modern palace now resembles Disneyland, complete with ice cream vendors, busloads of schoolchildren, and a highstepping *paradores* built alongside. (Palace open April-Sept. daily 10am-2pm and 4-8pm; Oct.-March 10am-6pm. 300ptas, students 200ptas, seniors and children 175ptas.) The palace chapel, **Iglesia de Santa María,** is noted for its 14th-century Gothic facade and belfry. **Iglesia de San Pedro** is fitted with an octagonal tower; for San Pedro, turn right on R. Villavieja and follow it to its end (both open during mass, 10am and 8pm).

Olite's **bodegas** specialize in *rosado* (rosé). Although the majority give tours only to groups with reservations, **Bodega Cooperativa Cosecheros Reunidos,** Av. Beire, 1 (tel. 74 00 67), on the outskirts of town, promises to show unannounced visitors around and even pour them wine to taste. Fittingly, Olite hosts **medieval tournaments** in July. Every August, the palace transforms into the outdoor backdrop for the **Festivales de Navarra,** a month-long shindig featuring concerts, theater, and dance. September 13-20 ushers in the **Fiesta de la Cruz,** a week of open air dances and various forms of taurine torment. Olite's a good base for exploring Tafalla, Artajona, Ujué, and the **Monasterio de la Oliva** (see p.259).

Orientation and Practical Information There are two **bus stops** in town. From Bar Orly (the first stop) on the edge of town, walk through the archway and follow R. San Francisco past **Plaza Teobaldos** and through another arch to **Plaza Carlos III.** To reach the plaza from the Carretera (the other bus stop), follow C. El Portillo for a block. To get from the **RENFE station** to Pl. Carlos III, take C. Estación to Bar Orly and follow the directions above. The staircase leading underground from the middle of the plaza goes to the **tourist office** (tel./fax 71 23 43; open April-Sept. Mon.-Fri. 10am-2pm and 4-7pm, Sat.-Sun. 10am-2pm). A series of *galerías* (old escape tunnels) houses art exhibitions and hold the same hours as the tourist office. **Taxis** can be hailed at tel. 74 01 43. For medical attention, call the **pharmacy** in the plaza at tel. 74 00 36. The **Centro de Salud** (medical center; tel. 71 23 64) is on the outskirts of the old city on Ctra. Zaragoza. The three **municipal police** have no permanent

office, so call the **Guardia Civil** at tel. 70 00 11. For any **emergency,** call tel. 091 or 092. The **post office** is on the far end of the plaza from the palace (tel. 74 05 82; open Mon.-Sat. 9-11:30am). The **postal code** is 31390. The **telephone code** is (9)48.

Trains (tel. 70 06 28) run to Pamplona (2-3 per day, 35min., 450ptas) Tudela, and other points on the Vitoria-Gasteiz-Zaragoza line. Do yourself a favor and take the **bus.** It's far more convenient and far less expensive. **Conda** (tel. 82 03 42) and **La Tafallesa** (tel. 70 09 79) run buses to Pamplona (6-12 per day, 50min., 220ptas) and Tudela (4-5 per day, 45min.). The return buses stop a little farther down the road.

Accommodations and Food The luxurious and refined air of the court lingers in many of Olite's restaurants and accommodations. One exception is the budget-minded **Fonda Gambarte,** R. Seco, 13, 2nd fl. (tel. 74 01 39), off Pl. Carlos III, which has basic doubles (3500ptas). The second option is **Pensión Cesareo Vidaurre,** Pl. Carlos III, 22, 1st fl. (tel. 74 05 97), to the right of the tourist office staircase with your back to the battlements. The nondescript entrance and teeny *camas* sign belie bright rooms upstairs (doubles 3000ptas, lower in the off season and for longer stays). Both are small and can fill up, especially during *San Fermines,* so call ahead. **Camping Ciudad Olite** (tel. 71 24 43), 8km northwest from Olite, has a restaurant, swimming pool, and other modern conveniences, but nary any shade. Follow the signs from the Pamplona-Zaragoza highway (450ptas per person, per car, and per tent). There are several **supermarkets** on C. Mayor, off Pl. Carlos III. Downstairs from the *fonda,* **Restaurante Gambarte** (tel. 74 01 39) serves a royal three-course *menú* for 1100ptas (open daily 1-3:30pm and 8-11pm).

■ Near Olite: Ujué

No isolated hill ever had it so good. Tiny **Ujué** drapes itself over a steep incline 20km from Olite. If you ignore an occasional TV antenna, its stone streets and houses invoke the most extreme Chaucerian nostalgia. Perched atop the village, the 11th-century **Iglesia Fortaleza de Santa María de Ujué** provides hypnotizing views. Inside, the Romanesque church has Carlos II's heart—literally (open 8:30am-dusk; call tel. 73 81 28 for more info). In late April, a solemn procession of barefoot, hooded penitents, some bearing crosses, descends on Ujué from surrounding towns. The **Romeria de Ujué** fulfills a promise made by Tafalla residents in 1043 to make an annual pilgrimage if God would help them drive out the Moors. They did, they do.

If you find yourself transfixed by the premodern light and are not afraid of having nothing to do, rustle up lodging in one of Ujué's two painfully quaint **casas rurales: Casa Isolina Jurio,** Pl. Mayor, 6 (tel. 73 90 37; singles 1900ptas; doubles 3800ptas; breakfast 400ptas); and **Casa El chofer I** (tel. 73 90 11; singles 2300ptas, doubles 3900ptas, breakfast 400 ptas). **Meson de las Torres,** C. Sta. María, s/n (tel. 73 90 52), dishes out pricey but excellent meals in one of two dining rooms (*menú* 3000ptas). Ujué's specialties are *almendras garapiñadas* (sugared almonds) and *nueces acarameladas* (carmelized walnuts).

The hard-luck **Monasterio de la Oliva,** 34km from Olite, has survived years of sackings and other forms of wear and tear since 1143. The result is an architectural palimpsest of Romanesque, Gothic, and baroque styles. Despite centuries of turbulence, Cistercian monks continue to do their thing here. (Open 9am-12:30pm and 3:30-6:30pm. Chanted prayers open to the public Mon.-Fri. at 7am, 12:45, and 6:30pm; Sat.-Sun. at 7:30am, noon, 1:45, and 6:30pm. Guided tours June-Sept. from 11am-1pm and 5-7:30pm, 1hr., 250ptas per person.) **Tafallesa buses** from Pamplona to Olite (see **Olite,** p.258) pause in Tafalla, where a bus connects to Ujué (Mon., Wed., and Fri. 7pm, 1715ptas; return to Tafalla Mon., Wed., and Fri. 8:45am).

■ Tudela

A brisk and breezy backwater, Tudela (pop. 30,000) showcases enticing versions of standard regional attractions. Its ghostly medieval churches emerge from a labyrin-

thine *casco antiguo* (ancient quarter), which throughout the Middle Ages hosted Muslim and Jewish populations. The *morería* and *judería* (Moorish and Jewish neighborhoods) were cultural hubs in Navarra, home to such figures as poet-philosopher Jehuda Haleví, scholar Abraham Ibn Ezra, and celebrated globe-trotter Benjamín de Tudela, who beat Marco Polo to China. King Alfonso I of Aragón ended the peaceful reign of Tudela's cohabiting populations when his forces outmuscled the Moors in 1114. Today, Tudela is peaceful year-round—a calm alternative to Pamplona during *San Fermines* (July 6-14).

Orientation and Practical Information Old town and new meet in **Plaza de los Fueros,** erstwhile sight of bullfights. To get to Pl. Fueros from the **bus and train station,** cross the plaza up Cuesta de la Estación, make the second right onto Av. Zaragoza, go straight for five blocks, then turn left onto C. Gaztambide-Carrera, which leads to the plaza. The **Casa del Reloj,** with its distinctive clock, presides over the city's west end. North of the plaza is the *casco antiguo,* overlooked by the **Castillo de Sancho el Fuerte** and the **Monumento al Corazón de Jesús,** which crown a hill at the edge of town. To the south stretches the modern town, capped by the lookout post of the **Torre Monreal.** These two high points face off over the plaza, offering panoramas of Tudela and surrounding areas.

The **tourist office** (tel. 82 15 39), on Pl. Vieja alongside the Cathedral, has a fax, a great map, and info on budget accommodations (open Mon.-Fri. 10am-2pm and 4-7pm, Sat.-Sun. 10am-2pm). Solid transportation connections make Tudela a good hub for exploring Navarra and nearby destinations in Aragón. Two **RENFE** train lines (tel. 82 06 46), run through Tudela: one connects La Rioja to Zaragoza, via Castejón de Ebro; the other connects Zaragoza to Vitoria-Gasteiz, via Pamplona. Four to six trains per day run to Pamplona (1¼hr., 680ptas). Conda **buses** (tel. 82 03 42), run to: Pamplona (6-9 per day, 1hr., 880ptas); Olite (4-5 per day, 45min., 455ptas); Tarazona (Mon.-Sat. 5 per day, 45min., 215ptas); and to Madrid, Soria, Zaragoza, and San Sebastián. **Luggage storage** is in lockers at the station (400ptas per day). For **currency exchange,** Banco Central Hispano is across the street from Hostal Remigio on C. Gaztambide (open Mon.-Sat. 8:30am-2:30pm). The **Red Cross** is on Po. Pamplona (tel. 82 74 50 or 82 74 11). The **municipal police,** C. Carcel Vieja (tel. 092), don't count their chickens. In an **emergency,** dial 091 or 092. To find the **post office,** C. Juan Antonio Fernandez, 4 (tel. 82 04 47), take a left at the end of C. Eza D. Miguel, off Pl. Fueros. The **postal code** is 31500. The **telephone code** is (9)48.

Accommodations and Food The tourist office has comprehensive info on accommodations, but Tudela is short on budget options. **Hostal Remigio,** C. Gaztambide, 4 (tel. 82 08 50), on the way from train and bus station to Pl. Fueros, has sleek modern rooms with phones and pristine bathrooms. (Singles 1800ptas, with bath 2600ptas. Doubles: 3600ptas; 4900ptas. Visa, MC, AmEx.) The all-purpose **Bar/Restaurant/Casa de Huéspedes Estrella,** C. Carnicerias, 14 (tel. 41 04 42), off C. Yanguas y Miranda from the northwest corner of Pl. Fueros, offers rooms overlooking a pleasant plaza (doubles 2400ptas) and homestyle meals (*menú* 1100ptas). Ask in the bar about rooms. Restaurant is closed Mondays. Chow down at the Chinese restaurant **Gran Mundo,** Av. Zaragoza, 51 (tel. 82 05 19), one block past Cuesta de Estación. The lunchtime *menú* is 850ptas. Picnickers can shop at **Supermercado Agid,** Av. Pamplona, 10 (open Mon.-Sat. 9am-1:30pm and 5-8pm, Sun. 10am-2pm), or pick up fresh local produce at the **mercado** on C. Concarera just off the plaza (open Mon.-Fri. 8am-1:30pm and 5-8pm, Sat. 8am-2pm).

Sights and Entertainment Tudela's airy Gothic **cathedral,** built on the site of the town's old mosque, rises from Pl. Vieja in the *casco antiguo.* To get there from Pl. Fueros, go north on C. Concarera to Pl. San Jaime, then turn right. An amalgam of styles from different periods, the cathedral features a rose-filled Romanesque cloister, several 15th-century Gothic *retablos* (altarpieces), a 12th-century White Virgin, and two ornate, cupola-crowned *capillas.* The more elaborate of these is the multi-col-

ored 18th-century Capilla de Santa Ana. (Open Tues.-Sat. 9am-1pm and 4-7pm, Sun. 9am-1pm. Admission to the cloister 100ptas.)

While the cathedral is a highlight, just strolling through the *casco antiguo* can be enchanting. Conspicuous purple signs mark key monuments. Try the 12th-century **Iglesia de la Magdalena** to the northeast; the 16th-century **Palacio del Marqués de San Adrián,** which houses the *Universidad a distancia;* the 18th-century **Palacio del Marqués de Huarte,** home to the town's library, archives, and a Rococo carriage that once belonged to the Marqués de San Andrián; and the **Iglesia de San Nicolás,** whose Romanesque *pórtico* (colonnade) alone is worth your while.

Tudela's **nightlife** is lively and nomadic. Early in the evening, friends gather in bars and cafes between Pl. Fueros and the cathedral to chat over a *caña* (a shorty). Then it's on to **Calle San Marcial,** east of the plaza, and **Calle Aranaz y Vides,** north from the bus station toward the old town, where pits of revelry carry on into the wee hours. For calmer enjoyment, check out the cafes on **Calle Herrerías,** off Pl. Fueros at the end of C. Yanguas y Miranda, or go for a stroll along the tree-lined Po. Pamplona, east of Av. Zaragoza along the Ebro River.

■ Near Tudela: Bardenas Reales

The awesome desert **Bardenas Reales,** with textured hills and cliffs wrought by erosion, covers over 400 square kilometers near the beginning of the Tudela-Pamplona road. The vistas are best contemplated from a mountain bike or car. To rent a bike, take the bus from Tudela to Pamplona and ask to be let off in the unremarkable, sunblasted town of **Arguedas** (15min., 120ptas). There, **Ciclos Marton,** C. San Ignacio, 2 (tel. 83 15 77 or 83 00 85), has mountain bikes for full-day rental (2000ptas for first day, 1000ptas each additional day). Cyclists should remain on the official roads to prevent damage to themselves. Don't forget that Bardenas is a desert; call ahead about weather conditions as the heat can sometimes be prohibitive. The tourist office in Tudela will provide tips and directions. We can recommend that you bring *agua.*

■ Estella

Suspended between the robust cities of Logroño and Pamplona, intimate Estella (pop. 13,000) works overtime to earn respect on the Camino block. What it lacks in size and glamour, it makes up for in hospitality toward pilgrims of all kinds—in the 17th century, the Ayuntamiento properly attired every citizen for a visit by Felipe III (and went broke doing so). A number of monuments to Estella's medieval dynamism remind visitors of its status as the second largest European market town (c. 13th century). The town bears traces of its heyday as a multi-ethnic metropolis, with teeny Jewish, Frankish, and Navarrese quarters.

Practical Information Estella snuggles into a bend in the Río Ega. Two streets form a cross through the heart of town. **Calle San Andrés/Calle Baja Navarra** runs north-south from the bus station on Pl. Coronación to **Plaza de los Fueros,** the Autobahn of the evening *paseo.* **Paseo de la Inmaculada Concepción** runs east-west from C. Dr. Huarte to the **Puente del Azucarero** (go right from the bus station), which spans the river and leads to the old town, past most sights and the tourist office.

The **tourist office,** C. San Nicolás, 1 (tel./fax 55 40 11), is a straight shot from the bridge through Pl. San Martín, around the corner to the right. The staff has a map and info on the Camino and surrounding areas (open Mon.-Fri. 10am-2pm and 4-7pm, Sat.-Sun. 10am-2pm). For the **Red Cross,** call tel. 55 10 11. The **police** (tel. 55 08 13) are at Po. Inmaculada, 1. Dial 091 or 092 in all **emergencies.** The **post office** is at Po. Inmaculada, 5 (tel. 55 17 92; open for stamps and Lista de Correos Mon.-Fri. 8:30am-2:30pm, Sat. 9:30am-1pm). The **postal code** is 31200. The **telephone code** is (9)48. All **buses** running from the station on Pl. Coronación belong to **La Estellesa** (tel. 55 01 27). Buses go to: Pamplona (5-12 per day, 1hr., 400ptas); Logroño (5-7 per day, 1hr., 500ptas); and Zaragoza (Mon.-Fri. 1 per day, 3hr., 1605ptas).

Accommodations and Food Near Pamplona, Estella is a good place to catch some shut-eye during *San Fermines*. Reservations are advisable during the August *fiesta*. **Pensión San Andrés,** Pl. Santiago, 50 (tel. 55 04 48 or 55 41 58), overlooks a pretty square and adorns its tidy rooms with little refrigerators, TVs, and woven bedspreads. (July-Aug. and Semana Santa: doubles 3200ptas, with bath 5000ptas. Sept.-June: doubles 3000ptas, with bath 4000ptas. Breakfast 350ptas.) The first left off C. Baja Navarra after crossing Po. Inmaculada takes you down C. Mayor to Pl. Santiago. **Fonda Izarra,** C. Calderería, 20 (tel. 55 06 78 or 55 00 24), off Pl. Fueros, offers simple, clean rooms with sinking beds (doubles 3000ptas; Visa). Its restaurant serves a 1000ptas *menú* and a 350ptas breakfast. **Camping Lizarra** (tel. 55 17 33; fax 55 47 55) is on C. Ordoiz, left from the tourist office and 1km down-river. The grounds have a supermarket, a huge pool, and mountain bike rentals. (475ptas per person, 1350ptas plus 7% I.V.A. per *parcela,* including tent, car, and electricity.)

Estella is known throughout the region for its *gorrín asado* (roast piglet, also called *gorrín de Estella*). If the thought of chowing on Winnie the Pooh's best buddy makes you uncomfortable, go for one of their vegetarian classics: *menestra de verduras* (mixed, cooked vegetables) or *alubias blancas* (white beans), although *chorizo* is known to find its way into these dishes too. Picnickers can stock up at **Autoservicio Moreno,** C. Zapatería, at the corner of C. Navarrería. To get there, take the first right off C. Baja Navarra and cross Po. Inmaculada, then go straight three blocks (open Mon.-Fri. 8am-1:30pm and 4-7:30pm, Sat. 8am-2pm). **Restaurante Casanova,** C. Fray Wenceslao de Oñate, 7 (tel. 55 28 09), on the left as you enter Pl. Fueros, has overwhelming portions that are sure to slow any pilgrim's progress. Lunch and dinner *menú* 1100ptas, entrees 500-1700ptas (open daily 1-3:30pm and 9-11pm, closed Mon. evenings in winter).

Sights In the "modern" quarter, the 12th century **Iglesia de San Miguel** commands a view of the town from the hilltop Pl. San Miguel. The portal depicts gripping scenes of St. Mike fighting dragons, weighing souls, etc. Up the stairs and opposite the tourist office, the **Iglesia de San Pedro de la Rúa** towers above **Calle de la Rúa,** the main street of the original mercantile center. This elderly Gothic church flaunts a Romanesque baptismal font. Behind the building, a 30m cliff rises above the cloister. Left from the tourist office at the end of C. Rúa lurks the street's crowning glory, the restoration-hungry **Iglesia del Santo Sepulcro,** whose 14th-century facade features a monstrous Satan swallowing the damned by the mouthful. Outside of mass hours, the first two churches can only be visited by taking tours in Spanish. (30min. tour of San Pedro, 200ptas. 1½hr. tour of San Pedro, San Miguel, and the outside of Santo Sepulcro 400ptas.)

Across from San Pedro and next to the tourist office, the oldest stone Roland in the world jousts with Farragut the Moor on the capitals of the 12th-century **Palacio de los Reyes de Navarra** (tel. 54 60 37; open Tues.-Sat. 11am-1pm and 5-7pm, Sun. 11am-1pm; free). Inside are whimsical Jurassic Park-esque sculptures of Gustavo de Maesta. Estella hangs by its fingernails to its mercantile history with an outdoor **market,** now only once a week, in Pl. Furos. Several **craftsmen** on C. Rúa recreate medieval Navarrese carved-wood furniture and ditties, including *templetas,* wooden knockers used to clack the hours of mass during Lent, and *argisaiolas,* human-shaped sculptures used by Navarrese witches and the Catholic clergy. Towering above, **Monte Amaya** provides a spectacular panorama of the valley.

The week-long **Fiestas de la Virgen del Puy y San Andrés** kick off the Friday before the first Sunday in August. Estella has an *encierro* with baby bulls, smaller and less ferocious than Pamplona's. Kiddie entertainment, a fair, and Navarrese dancing and *gaitas* (bagpipes without the bags) round out the *fiestas*.

NAVARRESE PYRENEES

Navarra encompasses the most topographically diverse range of the Pyrenees. While truly forbidding peaks dominate the eastern Valle de Roncal, the mountain slopes to the west are diminished in ferocity and height, allowing easier access to the streams, waterfalls, and green meadows dotting the area. Mist and fog obscure visibility even on summer mornings; bring a raincoat and sweater if you plan to rise before noon. Navarrese villages remain largely isolated, and most inhabitants settle into jobs with the cattle and logging industries.

Tourism is also a booming business. **El Camino de Santiago** is the celebrated cross-kingdom super-trek of intrepid pilgrims clambering over from France (see **Pilgrim's Progress,** p.177). The most popular pilgrim route crosses the border at Roncesvalles and continues to Santiago de Compostela in Galicia. Many free and cheap **refugios** cater to certified modern-day pilgrims along the way. To join the fun, get the best available guide (in Castilian), the *Guía práctica del peregrino,* published by Ediciones Everest (2500ptas). For info on the extensive network of Navarrese *casas rurales,* farm houses lodging travelers in either rooms or fully equipped apartments, ask for the useful *Guía de alojamientos de turismo rural,* free in any of Navarra's tourist offices. For reservations, call the multilingual office at tel. (9)48 22 93 28. *Acampada libre* (off-site camping) is legal almost anywhere in the Navarrese Pyrenees, unless there is a sign forbidding it; get guidelines from the local Ayuntamiento.

From **Pamplona,** you can head east toward Valle de Roncal (via Sangüesa), or north toward Roncesvalles. **Buses** are one-a-day affairs (if that) through most of the area; Pamplona is the only sensible base. When driving, watch for huge cows just hanging out on highways, and their dung.

■ Sangüesa

If you enter Sangüesa from the west, after Olite and Ujué, you might find yourself a little disappointed. Set in the arid foothills 44km east of Pamplona, Sangüesa (pop. 4500) isn't much to look or sniff at. Although the town flaunts its beautiful churches, its streets are drab, and on bad days they fill with the odors of a nearby paper factory. Sangüesa does make a good entry point, however, into some spectacular nearby sights—both natural and man-made—and is often a necessary stop-over for pilgrims.

The **tourist office,** C. Alfonso el Batallador, 20 (tel./fax 87 03 29), is on the right as you enter the Palacio de Vallesantoro. (Open Mon.-Fri. 10am-2pm and 4-7pm, Sat.-Sun. 10am-2pm; in winter daily 10am-2pm.) For **taxis,** ring tel. 87 02 22. The **Red Cross** (tel. 87 05 27) is on C. Mercado, past the tourist office. For **medical services,** there's a Centro de Salud (tel. 87 03 38) on the road to Cantolagua. The **municipal police** can be reached at tel. 87 03 10. In **emergencies,** dial 061, 091, or 092. The **post office,** Fermín de Lubián, 17 (tel. 87 04 27), sorts it out past the tourist office on Pl. Fueros. The **postal code** is 31400. The **telephone code** is (9)48.

Considering Sangüesa's proximity to popular tourist sites, the paucity of affordable lodging is surprising and potentially frustrating. The only real option is **Pensión Las Navas,** C. Alfonso el Batallador, 7 (tel. 87 00 77), where flamboyant pink curtains and bedspreads parade in clean, comfortable rooms, all with baths (singles 3500ptas, doubles 4000ptas; closed Sept. 18-Oct. 8). The **Albergue de Pereginos,** for Santiago pilgrims only, rests on C. Enrique Labrit. Ask at the tourist office for a guide to *casas particulares.* For campers, the only game outside of town is **Camping Cantolagua** (tel. 43 03 52), located near the Ciudad Deportivo (375ptas per person and per car, 395ptas per tent. 7% I.V.A. not included. Open year-round). The town's **market,** Pl. Toros, bustles at the end of C. Alfonso el Ballatador and away from C. Mayor (Fri. 9am-2pm). **Restaurant Acuario,** C. Santiago, 9 (tel. 87 01 02), serves a satisfying *menú*

(1100ptas) of potatoes with kale and lamb with peppers amid dulcet strains of Spanish muzak (open daily 1-4pm and 8-11pm).

The town earns its place on the Camino due to the **Iglesia de Santa María**, on C. Mayor by the bus stop. Its portal is a veritable triumph in Romanesque sculpture. The central relief depicts the Day of Judgment, with fanged devils casting the damned into the cavernous mouth of Lucifer. The woman nursing a toad on one breast and a snake on the other is a conventional iconographic rendering of Lust. Inside is a hairy Baroque Madonna whose human locks change every 10-15 years. Gothic stone St. James straddles a large conch before the **Iglesia de Santiago**. The **Convento de San Francisco** sits in Pl. Furos at the far end of C. Mayor. Behind him, two giggling cloaked pilgrims hold staffs and cockle shells in homage. St. Francis supposedly sojourned in Sangüesa on his pilgrimage to Compostela. The tourist office arranges tours of these sights and more (tel. 87 03 29; 250 ptas). Meanwhile, a traditional **metalsmith**, C. Alfonso el Batallador, 9, lets visitors into his forge. In July and August, the town hosts a series of medieval dinners—hucking half-eaten bones is totally kosher.

Veloz Sangüesina **buses** (tel. 87 02 09) go to and from Pamplona (Mon.-Sat. 3 per day, Sun. 4 per day, 45min., 420ptas) and deposit passengers on C. Mayor.

■ Near Sangüesa

Two fantastic gorges lie within 12km of Sangüesa. The **Foz de Lumbier** (Lumbier Gorge) is 2km outside of the little town of **Liédana**, on the bus route from Sangüesa to Pamplona. Fifty-meter walls tower on one side of this yawning gorge on the Río Irati. About 2km from the opposite edge sits the town of **Lumbier**. A 12km ride from Lumbier brings you to **Iso** and the mouth of an even more impressive gorge, the **Foz de Arbayún**. If the Río Salazar is low enough in the late summer, you can swim or hike your way through this 4km chasm; at other times, the ice-cold water forces hikers to raft or canoe. There is no blazed trail here, so watch your step and make sure you don't look emaciated—the gorge is home to a large colony of **griffin vultures**. Ask locals in Iso about conditions before setting up the TNT, sharpening the machete, or attempting any kind of expedition. No buses go directly to the gorges. Ask the tourist office in Sangüesa how to reach the nearby towns. If you have a car, look for the signs off N-240 in the direction of Pamplona.

■ Near Sangüesa: Castillo de Javier

Near the small village of **Yesa**, 8km from Sangüesa by the even smaller village of **Javier**, is the restored **Castillo de Javier**. On the border between Navarra and Aragón, the castle has changed hands many times over the last millennium. Today it's safe in the Jesuits' possession. Priests and apprentices lead tours of the picture-perfect castle in Spanish. The Chapel of the Holy Christ houses a 14th-century effigy that suffered a spontaneous blood-sweating fit at the moment of St. Francisco Javier's death. Marginally less gory is the **Patio de Armas's** collection of weaponry and armor (open daily 9am-1pm and 4-7pm; tours every 30min.; free, but donations requested).

La Tafallesa (tel. 22 28 86) runs a bus from Pamplona to Javier (Mon.-Fri. at 5pm, Sat. at 1pm, 1hr., 475ptas), and on to nearby Yesa, Roncal, and Isaba. From Sangüesa, taxis are the only option (5000ptas) for the carless.

■ Monasterio de Leyre

Windswept, austere, and miles from any other settlement (50km from Pamplona), the **Monasterio de Leyre** silently surveys the foothills of the Pyrenees and the fabricated lake, Lago de Yesa. **Hang-gliders** launch themselves off the hills where great wealth and power once presided. In the 12th century, medieval Navarrese kings took up residence in the **monasterio medieval**. Because monks still live at Leyre, you cannot enter this part, nor the 20th-century **monasterio nuevo**. However, the dank, subterranean **cripta** eagerly welcomes the public (tel. 88 40 11; open daily for guided

tours 10:30am-2pm and 4-7pm; 225ptas, children 50ptas). The architectural highlight of the monastic complex is the ghoulish **Portal de la Iglesia,** a landmark that is tremendously understated by tour guides. Outside the monastery is a path to the **Fuente de San Virila.** The fountain occupies the site where, according to legend, the abbot of San Virila slipped into a 300-year trance induced by the singing of a nightingale.

Connected to the monastery, the **Hospedería de Leyre** (tel. 88 41 37) offers comfortable rooms that, with cozy beds and private bathrooms, make the monks' cells look like, well, monks' cells. (Singles 4000ptas. Doubles 7000ptas. July-Aug. and Semana Santa: 4400ptas; 8500ptas.) Adopt asceticism or be ready to fork over serious bucks for sustenance; the *menú* in the Hospedería restaurant is 1500ptas, 1350ptas for lunch. The **Red Cross** (tel. 88 41 52) is back a bit towards Huesca. The **telephone code** is (9)48. The monastery lies about one hour away from Pamplona, off the highway to Huesca. If you don't have wheels, it's a 5km uphill slog from Yesa.

■ Roncesvalles and Burguette

The first stop on the Camino de Santiago, **Roncesvalles'** somber, mist-enshrouded monastery rests amid miles of thickly wooded mountains. Welcome to Avalon. The Valley of the Thorns is 48km from Pamplona, 20km from France, and eons from reality. Its stone walls are a monument to the continuing primacy of myth over history. For more than 1000 years, pilgrims, poets, and romantics have been drawn by the legend and spiritual shrine planted in the slopes of **Puerto Ibañeta** (1057m), less than 2km up the main road from the monastery.

Roncesvalles is filled with remembrances of the mythical warrior Roland. Legend has it that the stone in Ibañeta's road was split in two by Roland as he tried in vain to destroy his beloved sword Durandal lest it fall into his enemy's grasp. Another popular source claims that the Moor Marsillo killed Roland, but that Marsillo could not wrench the sword from Roland's fists even after his head had rolled down to the foothills. It is said that Roland's body was doing his soul's work. He actually fell in 778 at the hands of the ambushing Basque-Navarrese, who were perturbed that Charlemagne had razed the walls of Pamplona. No one seems to care that the battle didn't actually take place here. The heavily restored **Capilla de Sancti Spiritus** stands over the remains of a bone-heap (courtesy of dead soldiers and pilgrims), marking the spot of Roland's unanswered plea for help. The gates are always closed, as is the entrance to the tiny 12th-century **Capilla de Santiago,** next door to the left.

Inside the **Colegiata** (tel. 76 00 00), up the driveway from the *capilla,* tombs of King Sancho El Fuerte (the Strong) and his bride rest in solitary splendor, lit by huge stained-glass windows. In the decisive battle of the Navas de Tolosa, Sancho reputedly broke the chains protecting the Arab leader with his own hands. The heavy iron chains, hanging from the walls of the chamber, are represented in Navarra's flag. The monastery's Gothic **church,** endowed by the dead king and consecrated in 1219, is its main attraction; the elegant vaulting and stained-glass comic book battle scenes were ahead of their time (open daily 8am-8pm). Every church needs a cheese shop; this one's lies past the souvenir shop, specializing in *queso de Roncal.*

A **tourist office** (tel. 76 01 93), in the mill behind Casa Sabina Hostería, has maps and guides to the Camino de Santiago (open Mon.-Sat. 10am-2pm and 3-6pm, Sun. 10am-2pm). Burguete's **Guardia Civil** (tel. 76 00 06) serves the valley. The **telephone code** is (9)48.

Roncesvalles is a favorite starting point for pilgrims on their way to Santiago. The **monastery** has free lodging for official Camino followers—enter the door to the right as you face the monastery. Youth groups and hikers crowd **Albergue Juvenil Roncesvalles (HI)** (tel. 76 00 15), in an 18th-century hospital tucked to the right behind the monastery. (Lockout 10am-1pm and 5-7pm. 840ptas; *pensión completa* 2100ptas. Over 25: 1050ptas; 2625ptas. Breakfast 315ptas. Members only. Call in winter—it's sometimes closed due to weather.) Next to the tourist office, **Casa Sabina Hostería** (tel. 76 00 12 or 79 04 38), on the main road, offers doubles with baths (4500ptas) and a 1000ptas *menú.* Call first. For a **Banco Central Hispano** and other amenities

not found locally, head to nearby Burguete (2km south), where accommodations are numerous. Those following the **Camino de Hemingway** will want to check out the **Hostal Burguete,** C. Unica, 59 (tel. 76 00 56). The big boy slept here on his way back to Paris from *San Fermines.* By the looks of it, the place hasn't changed much—high, plump beds in cozy, old-fashioned rooms. (Singles 2600ptas. Doubles 4100ptas, with bath 5300ptas. Breakfast 400ptas, *menú del día* 1500ptas. Open March 15-Dec. 15.) Downhill on C. Unica, **Hostal Juandeaburre** (tel. 76 00 78) has singles for 2100ptas and doubles for 3700ptas. **Camping Urrobi** (tel. 76 02 00), 2½ kilometers downhill from Burguete in Espinal, has tennis courts, mountain bikes, horseback riding, and a grocery store (425ptas per person, per tent, and per car; open April-Oct.).

La Montañesa **buses** (tel. 22 15 84) run from Pamplona to Burguete (Fri. 4pm, Sat. 6pm; can continue to Roncesvalles; 1¼hr., 480ptas). There is no mass transportation to Roncesvalles. A **bus** goes to Burguete, then a **taxi** (tel. 76 00 07) brings you to Roncesvalles (350ptas). The return bus leaves Burguete Saturday and Monday at 7:15am.

■ Zugarramundi

According to Navarrese lore, a diabolical she-goat presided over the meetings of *brujos* (evil sorcerers and witches) in the majestic caves of Zugarramundi. The *akelarres* (meetings) in these impressive caves were so feared that in 1610 the Inquisition brought 300 alleged *brujos* to trial. Six were eventually burned alive before a crowd of 30,000 onlookers in Logroño's main plaza. Inaccessible to those without a car, the caves are about 80km from Pamplona, on highway N-121 to France, through Dancharinea. The sign to Zugarramundi is on the left just before the international bridge at the border. The caves are also approachable from San Sebastián.

■ Valle de Aézcoa

An 8km crow flight east of Roncesvalles, the Valle de Aézcoa welcomes hikers, fishermen, and nature lovers to mist-topped forests, wandering brooks, and well-tamed mountains. Quaint (let's face it) is the only word to describe the little villages built of plaster, stone, and brightly painted wood that are sprinkled throughout the valley. By car, the coffee-table-book town of **Arive,** a small collection of white houses with steep red roofs 25km from Burguete, is the entrypoint into the valley. From there, a narrow road winds north through the woods, following the Río Irati past the villages of **Orbara** and **Orbaiceta,** and on to the hamlet of **Barrio Larraún,** whose *refugio* makes a good base for hikers. About 10km from Arive, **Refugio Mendilatz** (tel. 76 60 30), offers winter heating, hot showers, and *literas* (900ptas per person). Turn right at the sign reading "Aterpea-Albergue 0.8k" and you'll see a sign for the *refugio* on the left. The restaurant downstairs has a 1100ptas *menú,* 300ptas breakfast, and 500ptas bag lunch; access to the kitchen is 300ptas. The staff is an excellent source for hiking advice. Otherwise, **casa rurales** provide most accommodations; in peaceful Orbaitzeta, try flower-filled **Casa Alzat** (tel. 76 60 55; doubles 3300ptas). Another choice is **Posada Sarobe,** C. San Martín, 1 (tel. 76 90 60), in the village of **Abaurrea Baja,** with beautiful rooms by Ralph Lauren on speed. (Doubles with TV and bath 6800ptas in Aug. and Semana Santa; 6000-6400ptas the rest of the year.) There's a lovely dining room downstairs. Breakfast is included. (4-course *menú* is worth the 2000ptas; restaurant open 1-3pm and 8:30pm-midnight; closed weekdays Sept.-May. *Posada* closed Feb.) Because of its relative proximity and connecting trails to Aézcoa, Roncesvalles can also make a good base.

The area's most traditional hike connects **Barrio Larraún** to Roncesvalles, passing through beautiful forests and meadows (5-6hr. each way). An easier, better defined trail (great by **mountain bike;** rent one at the campground in Ochagavía) leads east from Barrio Larraún to the striking **Embalse de Irabia** (Dam of Irabia), and from there to the **Ermita de Virgen de las Nieves** by following the Río Irati (8hr. round-trip from the *refugio*). The trail leans into the **Selva del Irati,** the second-largest forest in Europe. A more strenuous hike begins on the trail that leads to Roncesvalles, but con-

tinues straight north to **Monte Urkulu** (1423m). On the French border and crowned by a mysterious round tower, it provides glorious panoramas on both sides of the frontier (6hr. round-trip from the *refugio*). Shorter but more scenic excursions can be done by car. Ask at the *refugio* about road conditions.

■ Valle de Salazar: Ochagavía

On the banks of the Río Andena, **Ochagavía** (pop. 600) is the crisp mountain village you dream about on sweltering August afternoons in Manhattan. Warm clothing is a must in the evening. Forty kilometers from Pamplona, the Valle de Salazar's biggest town spans both sides of a cheerful river. Ochagavía's cobbled streets and white-washed houses lead to forested mountains. It's a wonderful base for hiking, trout fishing, and cross-country skiing. The 16th-century **hermita de Musquilda** is a 30-minute hike away; follow the stone path behind the church, or the road to the left just outside of town if you've got wheels.

The **tourist office** (tel./fax. 89 00 04), on the main road, is in the same building as the nature museum. (Tourist office open June-Aug. Mon.-Fri. 10am-2pm and 4:30-7:30pm, Sat.-Sun. 10am-2pm; Sept.-May Sat.-Sun. 10:30am-2pm. Museum open Tues.-Sun. 10:30am-2pm and 4:30-8pm, Mon. 4:30-8pm. 200ptas.) The **museum** offers multi-media displays of the area's geology, fauna, and vegetation (tel. 89 05 71). An **ATM** is located on the main road; the **pharmacy,** C. Urrutia 31 (tel. 89 05 06), waits on the other side (open Mon.-Fri. 10am-2pm and 5-8pm; Sat. 10am-2pm). For the pharmacy in an emergency, call 22 77 18. In **emergencies** call 061, 091, or 092. The **telephone code** is (9)48.

Hostal Orialde, across the river from the main road, is an especially good deal for doubles. Singles and doubles 3000ptas, with bath 4000-4500ptas. Breakfast 300ptas. I.V.A. not included. **Camping Osate** (tel. 89 01 84), at the entrance to town, provides a modern campsite on the river (475ptas per person and per car, 425 per tent). They rent **mountain bikes** (500ptas per hr., 1500ptas per ½day, 2500ptas per day). **Hikers** will find the climb up the Picode Orhy (2021m) fairly easy. The trail leaves from the parking lot at Puerto de Larrau, 9km north of Ochagavía on the highway to France. The ascent from *el puerto* takes about one hour. A good hike is along the Río Irati, through the **Selva de Irati** to Orbaiceta. Leave your car at the Ermita de las Nieves, 24km from Ochagavía, and make the 20km hike to Orbaiceta (8hr. round-trip but one needn't make the whole hike). **Cross country skiers** can enjoy two circuit trails starting a little farther down the same highway. **Río Irati** (tel. 22 14 70) runs **buses** to and from Pamplona (Mon.-Sat. 1 per day, 760ptas). Buses to Pamplona leave at 7am.

■ Valle de Roncal

Roncal (pop. 300) is home to world-renowned tenor Julián Gayarre and to *queso Roncal,* a sharp, dry cheese made from sheep's milk. Hardcore Gayarre-heads thrill at the **Casa Museo Julián Gayarre** (tel. 47 51 80), C. Arana, a museum in the singer's birth-house. Signs lead from the main (only) street. (Open April-Sept. Tues.-Sun. 11:30am-1:30pm and 5-7pm; Oct.-March Sat.-Sun. 11:30am-1:30pm and 4-6pm. 200ptas.) Hardcore cheeseheads stock up at the souvenir stores.

The extremely helpful **tourist office** (tel. 47 51 36) is on Roncal's main road. Ask about nearby hiking and *casas rurales.* (Open July-Sept. Mon.-Sat. 10am-2pm and 4:30-7:30pm, Sun. 10am-2pm; May-June and Oct.-Dec. Tues.-Sun. 10am-2pm.) **Banco Central Hispano,** on the road towards Isaba, doles out *pesetas* (open June-Sept. Mon.-Fri. 8:30am-2:30pm). The **Guardia Civil** is at tel. 47 50 05. In an **emergency,** call 091 or 092. Across the river from the *pelota* court, **Hostal Zaltúa,** C. Castillo, 23 (tel. 47 50 08), has quality rooms (singles 2000ptas; doubles 4000-5000ptas).

The more populous village of **Isaba** (pop. 500) straddles the highway 7km north of Roncal. The Ayuntamiento can answer any questions (tel. 89 30 55). **Phones** and **ATMs** huddle at the southern end of town. **Albergue Oxanea,** C. Bormapea, 47 (tel. 89 31 53), left up the stone staircase, past the Centro de Salud, and across from the

red benches, is run by young locals. Wooden *literas* (bunks) fit eight and 14 to a room and there's a TV/VCR room. (1000ptas per night, 900ptas with own sleeping bag. Hot showers and sheets included. Breakfast 300ptas. Other meals 1200ptas. I.V.A. not included.) **Camping Asolaze** (tel. 89 30 34), 6km toward the French border, houses a restaurant and a store, and offers *literas* (1000ptas per person, sheets 200ptas) in addition to regular plots of earth (open June-Sept.; 475ptas per person, 450ptas per tent, and 500ptas per car; doubles with baths 3900ptas). Eight kilometers north of Isaba, the earth opens up into the **Valle de Belagua. Refugio Angel Oloron** (tel./fax. 39 40 02) is open year-round and offers *literas* (750ptas), showers (200ptas), breakfast (300ptas), and other meals (1100ptas). The refuge is located at km 19 on the highway to France from Isaba. Check also in the guide to *Casas Rurales,* at any Navarrese tourist office, for local houses offering lodging.

The Valle de Roncal is prime **hiking** and **cross-country** land. A standard yet stunning hike goes from Isaba to Zuriza (6hr.). Shorter, but steeper, are the ascents from Collado Argibiela to **Punta Abizondo** (1676m) and **Peña Ezkaurre** (2050km). Drive to Collado Argibiela by way of the highway which connects Isaba with Ansó through Suriza. The ascent to Punta Abizondo takes about one-and-a-half hours, and the ascent to Peña Ezkaurre is a separate hike about two hours from Collado Argibiela. Ask the tourist office for other routes of differing durations and difficulty. Ski trails run north of Isaba, at the **Estación de Ski Larra-Belagna** (tel. (908) 16 51 67). The **Escuela de Esjui Valle del Roncal,** with offices in Hotel Isaba (tel. 89 32 36), offers lessons and skis in Isaba at 4000ptas per hour lesson for one or two people; **Ski-Fondo** at the entrance to Roncal (tel./fax. 47 51 94) does the same (opens 8am). Village festivals begin August 15 in Roncal, July 25-28 in Isaba. **La Tafallesa** (tel. 22 28 86) **buses** run from Pamplona and Javier and continue to Roncal (2hr., 880ptas from Pamplona) and to Isaba (1 per day Mon.-Sat., 2¼hr., 900ptas).

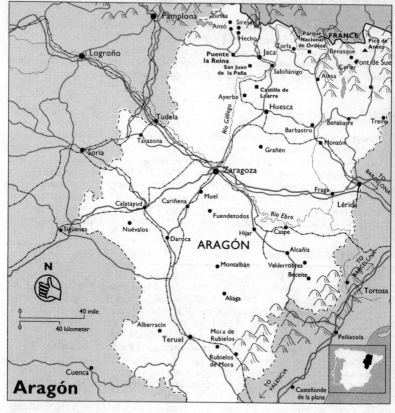

Aragón

Aragón

Traveling south to north through Aragón is like discovering that your salt-of-the-earth grandmother was quite a party girl in her younger days—it's hard to fit the pieces together. In the south, prosperous and industrious Zaragoza dominates a sun-baked assemblage of hardworking towns and flaxen plains, while in the north the exuberant peaks of the Pyrenees pop up from green, sheepherding foothills. Throughout all of Aragón's provinces, severe sandstone and slate towns are interspersed with the ornate Mudéjar architecture (a Moorish-Christian mix).

The harsh terrain and climate coupled with the region's strategic location engender a martial culture known among Spaniards for its obstinacy. Established as a kingdom in 1035 and united with enterprising Catalunya in 1137, Aragón forged a far-flung Mediterranean empire that brought Roussillon, Valencia, Murcia, the Balearic Islands, Naples, Sicily, and even the Duchy of Athens under its sway. Aragón retained the privileges of internal government even after its union with Castilla in 1469 and held them until Felipe II marched into Zaragoza in 1591 and brought the region to its knees. Economic decline followed political humiliation. As all eyes turned to the New World, many people moved in search of prosperity to the Atlantic coast.

Aragonese cuisine is as hearty as the people who make it. *Migas de pastor* (bread crumbs fried with ham) and lamb chops are predictably ubiquitous; more unexpected treats include *chi lindran* (lamb and chicken stewed with red peppers) and *melocotones al vino* (sweet native peaches steeped in wine). *Frutas de Aragón,*

another specialty, are dried fruits dipped in semi-sweet chocolate. Rough Cariña wines, produced in the south of Aragón, complement the local cuisine.

The *Guía de servicios turísticos de Aragón,* available at any tourist office in the kingdom, makes roaming easy, with information on accommodations (including *casas rurales, refugios,* and campgrounds), tourist offices, and important phone numbers.

■ Zaragoza

Whoever said God and Mammon can't peacefully co-exist never visited Zaragoza (pop. 650,000). Augustus founded the city in 19 BC—naming it Cesaragustus after himself—as a retirement colony for Roman veterans. Zaragoza gained everlasting fame some years later when the Virgin Mary dropped in for a visit; since then the city has been a pilgrimage site. Centuries later, industrial, not spiritual, vibes drove General Motors to set up shop here, cementing an already strong manufacturing sector. The city hums with prosperity, making Zaragoza a fine sample of urban Spain with the blessing of their beloved patron saint, *Nuestra Séñora,* and the convenience of lower price tags.

ORIENTATION AND PRACTICAL INFORMATION

Bordered to the north by the Río Ebro, Zaragoza is laid out like a slightly damaged bicycle wheel. Six spokes radiate from the hub at **Plaza Basilio Paraíso.** Facing the center of the Plaza with the IberCaja bank building at your back, the spokes going clockwise are: **Paseo de Sagasta; Gran Vía,** which turns into Po. Fernando el Católico; **Paseo de Pamplona,** which leads to Po. Marí Agustín and the train station; **Paseo de Independencia,** which ends at **Plaza de España** (the entrance to the *casco antiguo,* or old quarter); **Paseo de la Constitución;** and **Paseo de las Damas.** To get to Pl. Paraíso from the **train station,** start upstairs, bear right down the ramp, and walk across Av. Anselmo Clavé. Head one block down C. General Mayandía and turn right onto Po. María Agustín; continue seven blocks as the street becomes Po. Pamplona ending at Pl. Paraíso.

The *casco antiguo* lies to the north of Pl. Paraíso at the end of Po. Independencia, stretching between Pl. España and **Plaza del Pilar.** Several key museums and sights frame the plaza, the most central being the grandiose **Basílica de Nuestra Señora del Pilar.** Its blue- and yellow-tiled domes make good landmarks.

To reach Pl. Pilar from Pl. Paraíso, walk down Po. Independencia to Pl. España and take C. Don Jaime I (a bit to the right), which runs to the plaza. The user-friendly public bus system as well as city map blow-ups at major intersections make touring easy. The narrow streets to either side of **C. Conde de Aranda** may be unsafe at night, and should be avoided by women and solo travelers.

Tourist Office: City Branch: Pl. Pilar (tel. 20 12 00; fax 20 06 35), in the black glass cube in front of the basilica. Multilingual staff to help the Spanish-impaired. Request the *plano callejero* (indexed street map), as well as the tourist map, and the comprehensive *Sitios de Zaragoza* booklet set featuring info on restaurants, sights, shopping, and nightlife (available in English, 225ptas). Open Mon.-Sat. 9:30am-1:30pm and 4:30-7:30pm, Sun. 10am-2pm. **Regional Branch:** Torreón de la Zuda, Glorieta de Pío XII (tel. 39 35 37), in a squat tower at the crumbling Roman walls. From the city tourist office, proceed left along the length of the plaza. Covers all of Aragón but no city-specific info. Open Mon.-Fri. 8:15am-2:45pm and 4:30-8pm, Sat. 10am-2pm and 5-8pm, Sun. 10am-2pm; Oct.-June Mon.-Fri. 9am-2:45pm and 4-8pm, Sat. 9am-1:30pm, Sun. 9am-2pm.

Budget Travel: TIVE, Residencial Paraíso, Bldg. 4, local 40 (tel. 21 83 15 or 22 98 46). From behind El Corte Inglés (see Currency Exchange, below), through the courtyard and left. ISIC 700ptas. HI card 1800ptas. Open Mon.-Fri. 9am-2pm.

El Corte Inglés: 2 locations: Po. Sagasta, 3 (tel. 21 11 21) and Po. Independencia, 11 (tel. 23 86 44). **Currency Exchange** (no commission but lower rates), **supermar-**

ket, telephones, and a free **map.** Open Mon.-Sat. 10am-9:30pm. **Concerts and Events:** (tel. (902) 11 12 12). Ticket booth in Pl. España in front of McDonald's.

Currency Exchange: Banks open 8:30am-2pm; some open afternoons in winter. Many luxury hotels will change currency in emergencies. Banks line Po. Independencia, and ATMs are everywhere. **Banco Central Hispano,** Po. Maña Agustin, 1 (tel. 22 52 71), will exchange traveler's checks. Other locations dot the city.

American Express: Viajes Turopa, Po. Sagasta, 47 (tel. 38 39 11; fax 25 42 44), 6 blocks from Pl. Paraíso; around corner on C. de las Torres. Bus #33 from Pl. España stops nearby. Full services. Cardholder mail held. Slightly better exchange rates than most banks. Open Mon.-Fri. 9am-1:30pm and 4-8pm, Sat. 9:30am-1pm.

Flights: The Ebrobus, Pl. Aragón, 10 (tel. 32 40 09), off Pl. Paraíso at the beginning of Po. Independencia, shuttles between the airport and its terminal (3-7 per day, 7am-9:30pm, 30min., 150ptas). A taxi to the airport costs about 1000ptas. Call airport for info (tel. 71 23 00). Flights to major Spanish and European cities. **Iberia,** C. Bilbao, 11 (tel. 21 82 56; domestic and international reservations tel. (901) 40 05 00; open Mon.-Fri. 9:30am-2pm and 4-7pm, Sat. 9:30am-1:30pm).

Trains: Estación Portillo, Av. Anselmo Clavé (24hr. info tel. 28 02 02). Taxi to Pl. Pilar (550ptas) or bus #21 from Po. María Agustín. Info booth open 6am-10pm. A **RENFE** office, C. San Clemente, 13 (tel. 23 38 02), is helpful. From Pl. Paraíso, follow Po. Independencia 4 blocks, then turn right. Open Mon.-Fri. 9am-2pm and 5-7pm, Sat. 9am-2pm. To: Tudela (3-4 per day, 45min., 1000ptas); Jaca (3 per day, 3½hr., 1325ptas); Logroño (4 per day, 2hr., 1095ptas); Pamplona (5 per day, 2-2½hr., 1095ptas); Teruel (3 per day, 2½hr., 1325ptas); Madrid (8 per day, 3-4hr., 3000ptas); Barcelona (8 per day, 3½-5hr., 3000ptas); San Sebastián (2 per day, 4hr., 2700ptas); Valencia (2 per day, 5-6hr., 2385ptas). .

Buses: Various bus companies dot the city, each with private terminals.

Agreda Automóvil, Po. María Agustín, 7 (tel. 22 93 43). Bus #21 stops directly in front, across the street if coming from Pl. Pilar. To: Madrid (15 per day, 3hr., 1710ptas); Barcelona (9 per day, 3½hr., 1640ptas). From **second terminal** at Av. Valencia, 20 (tel. 55 45 88), entrance on C. Lérida (bus #38) to: Muel (5 per day, 2 per day Sun., 30min., 260ptas); Cariñena (Mon.-Sat. 5 per day, Sun. 2 per day, 1hr., 400ptas); Daroca (2-3 per day, Sun. 2 per day, 2hr., 715ptas).

Therpasa, C. General Sueiro, 22 (tel. 34 31 58), from Pl. Paraíso walk ½ block down Po. Constitución, then right for 2 blocks. Open Mon.-Fri. 7am-1pm and 3:30-9:30pm, Sat. 9am-1pm. To Tarazona (5-6 per day, 1½hr., 665ptas) and Soria (4-7 per day, 2½hr., 1075ptas).

La Oscense, Po. María Agustín, 7 (tel. 22 93 43). Shares terminal with Agreda Automóvil. To Jaca (2-3 per day, 2½hr., 1435ptas).

CONDA, Av. Navarra, 79 (tel. 33 33 72); from Pl. Paraíso follow Po. Pamplona to Po. María Agustín; turn left at 2nd major intersection onto Av. Madrid. Cross the highway and railbed on the blue pedestrian bridge; hang a right on Av. Navarra, then left after a long stretch, or take bus #25 from Po. Pamplona and watch for the station on the left. To: Tudela (5 per day, 1hr., 675ptas); Pamplona (7-8 per day, 2½hr., 1345-1600ptas); San Sebastián (5 per day, 4hr., 1795-2350ptas).

Zuriaga, C. San Juan Pablo Bonet, 13 (tel. 27 61 79). From Pl. Paraíso walk 7 blocks down Po. Sagasta, then turn right. (Bus #33 from Pl. España; find road sign for C. San Juan Pablo Bonet after 2 stops on Po. Sagasta.) To Logroño (2-6 per day, 1¾hr., 1245ptas) and Teruel (5 per day, 2¾hr., 1350ptas).

Public Transportation: Red **TUZSA** buses (tel. 41 39 00) cover the city (80ptas, 10-ride ticket 470ptas from booth in any kiosk). Tourist office offers a free map of bus routes. Bus #21 is particularly useful, running from near the train station to Po. Pamplona, Pl. Paraíso, Pl. Aragón, Pl. España, Pl. Pilar, and then up C. San Vincente de Paúl. Bus #33 is more central, going through Po. Sagasta, Pl. Paraíso, Po. Independencia, and Pl.España.

Taxis: Near the train station. **Radio-Taxi Aragón** (tel. 38 38 38). **Radio-Taxi Zaragoza** (tel. 42 42 42). Train station to Pl. Pilar about 500ptas.

Car Rental: Avis, Po. Fernando El Católico, 9 (tel. 55 50 94), from Pl. Paraíso take Gran Vía, which becomes Po. Fernando El Católico (open Mon.-Fri. 8am-1pm and 4-8pm, Sat. 8am-12:45pm). Those who are under 21 can rent a small car from **Atesa,** Av. Valencia, 3 (tel. 35 28 05). Take Gran Vía to Av. Goya, turn right, then left. Open Mon.-Fri. 8:30am-1:30pm and 4:30-7:30pm, Sat. 9am-1:30pm.

Luggage Storage: At the train station, the *equipaje* office sells locker tokens (400ptas, open 24hr.). Also storage at **Agreda Automóvil** bus station, 100ptas per piece per day (open Mon.-Fri. 10am-1:30pm and 4-7:30pm, Sat. 10am-1:30pm). At **Therpasa** bus station (tel. 22 67 10, open Mon.-Fri. 9am-1pm and 4-7:30pm, Sat.9am-noon).

Laundromat: Lavandería Rossell, C. San Vicente de Paul, 27 (tel. 29 90 34), turn right on C. Coso, go 4 blocks, then go left 4½ blocks. Wash and dry 990-1800ptas per load. Open Mon.-Fri. 8:30am-1:30pm and 5-8pm, Sat. 8:30am-1:30pm.

English Bookstore: Librería General, Po. Independencia, 22 (tel. 22 44 83). Surprisingly large selection downstairs (open Mon.-Fri. 9:30am-1:30pm and 5-8:30pm, Sat. 10am-2pm). Also **El Corte Inglés** (see **Currency Exchange** above).

Women's Services: Casa de la Mujer, Don Juan de Aragón, 2 (tel. 39 11 16), offers judicial assistance and general info (open Mon.-Fri. 9am-2pm and 4-8pm; Sept.-June Mon.-Fri. 9am-9:30pm).

Youth Organization: CIPAJ (Centro de Información y Promoción de Actividades Juveniles), C. Bilbao, 1 (tel. 21 39 60). From Po. Independencia turn left on C. Casa Jiménez, go 2 blocks past Pl. Aragón, then turn left. Classes, cultural activities, jobs, and other services for youths. Great monthly bulletin of city happenings (available at tourist office). Some English spoken. Open Mon., Wed., and Fri. 11am-2pm, Tues. and Thurs. also 6-8pm.

Public Bathrooms: Southeastern corner (facing the altar) of the Basilica and downstairs at the Mercado Central.

Medical Services: Hospital Miguel Servet, Po. Isabel La Católica, 1 (tel. 35 57 00). In **emergencies,** turn to Ambulatorio Ramón y Cajal, Po. María Agustín, 12 (tel. 43 41 11). **Ambulance** (tel. 35 85 00).

Police: Domingo Miral, s/n (tel. 092). **Lost and Found:** Mon.-Fri., tel. 55 91 76. **Emergency:** tel. 091 or 092.

Post Office: Po. Independencia, 33 (tel. 22 26 50), 1 block from Pl. Aragón on the right. Info booth open Mon.-Fri. 8:30am-8:30pm. Open for stamps, **fax,** and Lista de Correos (downstairs at window 4) Mon.-Fri. 8am-9pm, Sat. 9am-7pm. Another branch next to train station at C. Clave. Open Mon.-Fri. 8:30am-8:30pm, Sat 9:30am-2pm. **Postal Code:** 50001.

Telephone Code: (9)76.

ACCOMMODATIONS AND CAMPING

Hostales and *pensiones* pepper the narrow streets of the *casco antiguo,* especially within the rectangle bounded by **Alfonso I, Don Jaime I, España,** and **Pilar,** and in the area to the right of the train station exit. Be wary the week of October 12, when Zaragoza celebrates the *Fiesta de la Virgen del Pilar.* Make reservations as early as possible and expect to pay double some of the rates listed below; or just party the night straight through. *Ferias* (trade shows) are held from February through April. The biggest is the agricultural machinery show, FIMA, in late March or early April, when you may have to scour everything within a 100km radius to find a room.

Albergue-Residencia Juvenil Baltasar Gracián (HI), C. Franco y Lopez, 4 (tel. 55 15 04 or 55 13 88). Take bus #22 from train station, or turn right out of station onto Av. Clavé, take 2nd right onto C. Burgos, follow 6 blocks then turn right onto C. Franco y Lopez. Recently renovated. Fifty-five beds clad with sheets and blankets in sparkling rooms of 2, 4, and 8; the rest of the building is a college dormitory. Must call in the morning to make reservations for that night. No lockout, curfew midnight. 1000ptas. Over 26, 1400ptas. Closed in Aug.

Casa de Huéspedes Elena, C. San Vicente de Paúl, 30 (tel. 39 65 80), behind the cathedral and across the street from Lavandería Rossell. Often full of long-staying workers, so call first. Remarkably clean, big rooms with big furniture. All rooms are doubles and cost 2000ptas. Elena treats you like a grandchild.

Pensión Rex, C. Méndez Nuñez, 31 (tel. 39 26 33), on the corner of C. Don Jaime I. Spacious rooms, many with balconies, all with snappy red and white bedspreads and floor-to-ceiling windows. Singles 1820ptas, with shower 2350ptas. Doubles: 3420ptas; 4280ptas. 370ptas to shower in a clean common bathroom.

Hostal Ambos Mundos, Pl. Pilar, 16 (tel. 29 97 04; fax 29 97 02), at the corner with C. Don Jaime I. Bathroom fixtures emit startling noises and beds sag, but these well-worn rooms are otherwise comfortable and clean. Some doubles have balconies that overlook the plaza. Singles with shower 2355ptas. Doubles with shower or bath 4065ptas. Breakfast 400ptas; other meals 1500ptas.

Hostal Venecia, C. Estebanes, 7 (tel. 39 36 61), the first left off C. Don Jaime I heading toward Pl. Pilar. Cramped, dark rooms helped only by new-looking furniture and a bright sitting area with TV. Solo travelers might not feel completely safe on this street at night. Singles 1500ptas. Doubles 3000ptas. Breakfast 100ptas. Other meals 800ptas.

Hostal Plaza, Pl. Pilar, 14 (tel. 29 48 30 or 28 48 39; fax 39 94 06). Yellow, green, and salmon-colored rooms with tiled floors, duck decorations, and bicycle storage. This place is immaculate, and the views of the Basilica and Pl. Pilar are terrific from some rooms. Singles 3500ptas, with shower 3800ptas. Doubles: 3900ptas; 5800ptas. All rooms have phones, some have TV. Breakfast 350ptas.

Camping: Casablanca, Barrio Valdefierro (tel. 33 03 22), down Ctra. Nacional 2. Bus #36 from Pl. Pilar or Pl. España to the suburb of Valdefierro. Ask the driver to let you know when you've arrived, as it's notoriously difficult to find. By car, take the road to Madrid, then the Valdefierro Exit, and from there follow the signs. Good facilities, including pool. June 20-Sept. 20 550ptas per person, per tent, and per car; otherwise 500ptas. Open Holy Week-Oct. 15.

FOOD

For the scoop on restaurants, lay your hands on the *Places to Eat* brochure, part of the *Sitios de Zaragoza* collection. *Tapas* bars, inexpensive restaurants, and *bocadillo* factories crowd the area and the sector known as **El Tubo** (Calles Mártires, Cinegio, 4 de Agosto, and Estébanes). Several *marisquerías* serve seafood *raciones* at good prices on C. Don Jaime I, near Pl. Pilar. (Other good *tapas* bars are on C. Santa Cruz.) For those who prefer their *tapas* and *copas al fresco*, the Pl. Santa Marta (to the right and behind the Catedral del Seo) has many offerings. One typical Zaragozan *tapas* is *anchoas salmueras* (anchovies in salt). The **market** thrives in the long green building on Av. César Augusto off Pl. Pilar. Fresh fruits and veggies, cow's tongue, and live squid are available (open Mon.-Sat. 9am-2pm and 5-8pm). Zaragoza's oldest **bakery,** Fantoba, C. Don Jaime, 21, vends scrumptious pastries and chocolate-dipped strawberries (open Mon.-Sat. 10am-2pm and 5-9pm). **Supermarket** shoppers can refuel at **Galerías Primero,** C. San Jorge, the street that C. Merdeo Nuñez turns into (open Mon.-Fri. 9am-2pm and 4:30-9pm, Sat. 9am-2pm and 4:30-9pm), or at **El Corte Inglés's** well-stocked but pricey basement mega-mart (see **Orientation and Practical Information,** p. 257).

Casa Pascualillo, C. Libertad, 5. In El Tubo district, off of Méndez Nuñez. Filling, homestyle meals in a lively atmosphere. *Menú del día* 850ptas. Stewed bull meat fresh from the ring *(toro de lidia)* 750ptas—a steal considering the extravagant butchering. Open Tues.-Sat. 1:30-4pm and 7-11pm, Sun. 1:30-4pm. Visa.

Restaurante Caball, C. Don Jaime I, 3 (tel. 29 85 81). For when you're sick of the noodle soup/fried pork slice *menú del día.* Delicious *menú* (900ptas) with cauliflower au gratin and chicken breasts in Roquefort sauce. *Platos combinados* 800ptas. Open Mon.-Sat. 1-3:30pm and 9-11pm, Sun. 1-3:30pm. Visa, MC.

La Zanahoria, C. Tarragona, 4 (tel. 35 87 94). From Pl. Paraíso take Gran Vía, turn right on Av. Goya, then take the 1st left after crossing Av. Teruel/Valencia. Yuppie vegetarians come for the excellent salads, quiches, and Whitney Houston rhythms. Lunch *menú* 1000ptas. *Platos combinados* 900ptas. Two-course dinner with beverage (1500ptas). Open 1:30-4pm and 9-11:30pm. For dinner arrive before 10pm or call for reservations. Visa, MC.

Olimpo, C. Cinegio, 3 (tel. 29 50 97). In the heart of El Tubo. All manner of cheap fried things for *tapas,* and a popular *menú del día* for 850ptas. Open daily 1-4pm and 8pm-midnight Visa, MC

Taruffi, C. Alfonso I, 27. Chicken, tuna, salmon, vegetable, and BLT submarines for 300-500ptas. Breakfast specials for 250ptas. Open daily 11am-8:30pm.

SIGHTS

The main location of Zaragoza's tourist sites, the **Plaza del Pilar** is a vast square surrounded by a unique combination of architectural styles. The **Basílica de Nuestra Señora del Pilar,** the patroness whom millions of Spanish women are named after, dominates the plaza. Its massive Baroque structure (begun in 1681) defines the skyline with brightly colored tiled domes decorated with frescoes by Goya, González Velázquez, and Bayeu. Evidence of the miraculous abounds inside. Two bombs hanging to the right of the **Virgin** bear witness to her divine intervention; they were dropped on the basilica during the Civil War but failed to explode. The **Museo del Pilar** (tel. 39 74 97), displays the glittering *joyero de la Virgen* (Virgin's jewels) and a collection of original sketches of the ceiling frescoes (museum open 9am-2pm and 4-7pm, 150ptas; basilica open 6am-9:30pm; free).

On the left as you exit the basilica is Zaragoza's 16th-century Gothic and Plateresque **La Lonja** (stock exchange), distinguished by a star vaulting and a forest of soaring Ionic columns that rise to a ceiling of gilt crests. It is open for occasional art exhibits Mon.-Sat. 10am-2pm and 5-9pm, Sun. 10am-2pm. To the left of La Lonja is an outdoor **monument** where statues act out scenes from Francisco de Goya's paintings. On the other side of C. Don Jaime I, the squatting glass and marble cube houses the **Foro Romano,** site of Caesar Augustus' grave.

Following the Muslim conquest of the Iberian Peninsula in the 8th century, a crisis over succession smashed the kingdom into petty tributary states called *taifas*. The **Palacio de la Aljafería,** on C. Castillo, remains the principal relic of Aragón's *taifa*. Buses #21 and 33 stop here, or head left on Coso to the pedestrian street that leads to the castle. Previous alterations and renovations have encumbered the building's original grace, but its awesome stone exterior and serene interior are still worth a visit. The ground floor has a distinctly Moorish flavor in contrast to the Gothic second floor. The fortified tower imprisoned *el trovador* in García Gutierrez's drama of the same name, the source of Verdi's opera. (Open Mon.-Sat. 10am-2pm and 4-8pm, Sun. 10am-2pm; Oct.-May Tues.-Sat. 10am-2pm and 4:30-6:30pm, Sun. 10am-2pm. Free.)

In addition to an extensive collection of medieval Aragonese paintings, the **Museo Provincial de Bellas Artes,** Pl. Los Sitios, 6 (tel. 22 21 81), hangs works by Ribera, Lucas van Leyden, and Claudio Coello, along with a Goya self-portrait and likenesses of Carlos IV and María Luisa. From Pl. Paraíso, follow Po. Independencia about five blocks, turn right and go five more blocks on C. San Clemente. Turn left upon reaching Pl. Sitios; the museum is on your left (open Tues.-Sat. 9am-2pm, Sun. 10am-2pm, special exhibits 4-8pm; free).

The **Museo Pablo Gargallo,** dedicated to one of the most innovative sculptors of the 1920s, houses a small but marvelous collection of his works in the graceful **Palacio de Arguillo,** built in 1670. Walking down C. Don Jaine from Pl. España, turn left on C. Ménendez Núñez. The museum is on the left in Pl. San Felipe, five blocks down (open Tues.-Sat. 10am-2pm and 5-9pm, Sun. 10am-2pm; free).

The **Fundación Pablo Serrano,** Po. María Agustín, 26, honors two more artists—Pablo Serrano (1908-85) and his wife, painter Juana Francés—with racy abstract works and reinterpretations of Picasso, Velázquez, and Goya. Guided tours are in Spanish. (Museum open Mon. and Wed.-Sat. 10am-2pm and 5-8pm (summer 6-9pm), Sun. 10am-2pm. Free.)

Those hungering for green should head for the shaded walks and fountains of the **Parque Primo de Rivera,** on the end opposite the old quarter from Pl Paraíso. On summer weekends exercise your mind, body, and soul with free outdoor classes in chess, aerobics, canoeing, and tai chi.

ENTERTAINMENT

Young Zaragozans rightfully brag that their city has *mucha marcha* (lots of action). The slick brochure *Night Spots* (part of *Sitios de Zaragoza*) covers both the gay and straight scenes. Herds of *casco antiguo*-goers crawl out of their shells around midnight in the market area, on **Calles Predicadores, El Olmo, El Temple, Contamina,**

and **Manifestación.** Farther east, Pl. Santa Cruz holds the cruelly chic **Café Praga** and the tropically laid-back **Embajada de Jamaica** (frozen margaritas 450ptas). Teeny-boppers and *militares* favor **Calle Dr. Cerrada,** off Po. Pamplona, while the older and more affluent patronize **Residencial Paraíso** and **Calles Dr. Casas, Bolonia,** and **La Paz.** University students storm **Paseo Sagasta** and its offshoot, C. Zumalacárregui. Gulping beer from *litros* (about 400ptas) is the primary sport around **El Rollo,** the zone bounded by C. Moncasi, C. Bonet, and C. Maestro Marquina at the southern end of Po. Sagasta. A mixed crowd hangs out at **Club Nautico,** on the Río Ebro behind Pl. Pilar. While bars rule supreme in Zaragoza, a small disco scene draws its share of late-night (and early morning) partiers. **Torreluna,** C. Miguel Servet, 193, is the only disco with dancing *al aire libre* all night long. **KWM,** Fernando el Católico, 70, and **Babieca,** C. Dr. Riras 6-8, are popular indoor versions. Gay bars and discos are situated around the west side of the *casco antiguo.* **Atuaire,** C. Contamina, 13 and **Sphing,** C. Ramón y Cajal, are long-standing favorites. **Café Universal,** C. Fernando el Católico, 32, plays live jazz and blues Thurs.-Sat. 11pm. The **Teatro Principal,** C. Coso, 57 (tel. 29 60 90), hosts performances of all kinds (ticket booth open daily Sept. 15-June 15, noon-1:30pm and 5pm-showtime).

Flea markets pop up all over town on Sunday mornings. The biggest, **El Rastro,** occurs outside the Pl. de Toros. An **antiques market** reminisces in Pl. San Bruno (behind the cathedral), paintings are displayed in Pl. Santa Cruz, and stamp collectors indulge in the Pl. San Francisco.

The city erupts for a week of unbridled hoopla around October 12 in honor of *La Virgen Santa del Pilar.* It's one of the few full-blown Autumn *fiestas* and although you may not find lodging, you won't need it. City patrons San Valero (Jan. 29) and San Jorge (April 23) are also celebrated. In May, Zaragoza hosts an international festival of dance, music, and theater. The city tourist office distributes info on *fiestas.*

■ Near Zaragoza

The regional tourist office of Aragón has info on excursions such as the *Ruta del Vino* (wine route) and the *Ruta de Goya.* **Fuendetodos** (pop. 170), Goya's birthplace, may be difficult to reach but is worth it for diehard Goya fans. **Samar Buil buses,** C. Borao, 13 (tel. 43 43 04), run there (2 per day, 1hr., 410ptas). The humble home where Goya was born (tel. 14 38 30) and the **Museo del Granado** are open Tues.-Sun. 11am-2pm and 4-7pm. Teruel (see p. 278) and Tarazona (see p. 276) are good daytrips from Zaragoza. Fans of Romanesque should inquire about visits to the **Cinco Villas** (five villages), particularly Sos del Rey Católico and Uncastillo.

MONASTERIO DE PIEDRA

An oasis of waterfalls and trees springs out of the dry Aragón plain around the **Monasterio de Piedra** (open 9am-9pm, tel. 84 90 11), about 110km southwest of Zaragoza. Founded in 1195 by an order of Cistercian monks from Tarragona and abandoned under government orders in 1835, the monks' quarters are now three-star lodgings. The 12th-century **Torre del Homenaje,** the only part of the existing building that hasn't been restored, still towers over the valley.

The main attraction is the surrounding park and the **Río Piedra,** which casts off waterfalls and lakes as it plunges down the valley. Follow the path leading through, under, and around this aquatic paradise (park open daily 9am-nightfall; 1000ptas).

Automóviles Zaragoza buses, C. Almagro, 18 (tel. 21 93 20), leave from Zaragoza for the *monasterio* once a day on Tues., Thurs., Sat., and Sun. at 9am (1050ptas).

LA RUTA DEL VINO

The scorched countryside south of Zaragoza is surprisingly fertile, its warm days and cool nights yielding prime grape harvests. To visitors, however, the mystique of these cherished vineyards is lost to advanced wine-making machinery. Locals will graciously recommend local vintages, but if you envision taking tours through dusky

commercial wineries, think again. Several *bodegas* offer wine for tasting and for purchase out of industrial warehouses.

Ágreda Automóvil **buses** cover all three towns from Zaragoza. To: Muel (260ptas); Cariñena (140ptas); and Daroca (315ptas). Zuriaga company's bus service to Teruel from Zaragoza is faster, but doesn't necessarily include all three towns (see Zaragoza: Practical Information, p. 270).

Muel, in addition to its Dionysian excesses (during festivals, wine flows through the town's fountains), is home to a renowned school of ceramics (tel. 14 00 54). In addition, the **Ermita de la Virgen de la Fuente** features Goya frescoes. **Cariñena** is the most important wine-producer in Aragón and houses an impressive church/ Mudéjar fortress build by the Order of the Knights of St. John.

Daroca Last stop on the bus line from Zaragoza, **Daroca** is an enchanting one-street town. Cut into a dramatic gorge, the town's sanguine roofs match its surrounding cliffs. The ruins of Daroca's city walls, 4km in circumference and once punctuated with 114 towers, can be reached by footpath that rewards hikers with a sentry's-eye view of the town and valley below. The town's main artery, **Calle Mayor,** runs uphill from **Puerta Baja** (lower gate) to the other **Puerta Alta** (lower gate). C. Arrabal is one approach to the wall; exit the Puerta Baja and turn right. Go up, then up (and up and up). Along C. Mayor are several Renaissance and Baroque palaces. Otherwise, the main sight in town is the icon-filled museum of the **Colegiata de Santa María,** a 16th-century Renaissance church. (Church and museum open Tues.-Sat. 11am-1pm and 5:30-7:30pm, Sun. for mass only. 300ptas. The tourist office arranges guided tours; call ahead for more info, or ask the nuns loitering inside.) To reach the church, take either of the two C. Juan de la Huerta from C. Mayor.

Little Daroca puts on a good party during its week-long **Fiesta de Corpus Christi,** held every year in late May or early June. Daroca also hosts the annual **Curso Internacional de Música Antigua** during the first two weeks of August, when musicians from the world over gather to teach, learn, and give free ancient music concerts.

The **tourist office** is at Pl. España, 4 (tel. 80 01 29), opposite Colegiata de Santa María. From Puerta Alta, pursue the sights along C. Mayor for 4-5 blocks, and hang a right on C. San Juan de la Huerta (open Tues.-Sat. 11am-2:30pm, Sun. 11:30am-2pm.) The **post office,** C. Mayor, 157 (tel. 80 02 11), lies near Puerta Baja (open Mon.-Fri. 8:30am-2:30pm, Sat. 9:30am-1pm). The **postal code** is 50360. The **telephone code** is (9)76. The **Red Cross** (tel. 80 03 36) heals outside Puerta Alta and across the highway. **Guardia Civil** (tel. 80 01 13) headquarters are on the highway next to the swimming pool.

Sleepy travelers might try the sumptuous **Pensión El Ruejo,** C. Mayor, 88 (tel. 80 09 62), complete with spotless modern rooms, heating, A/C, a disco, and an intimate flowering courtyard. Inquire at the bar downstairs, after 9am. The **restaurant** on the first floor serves a satisfying 1000pta *menú.* The town **market** hawks its wares in Pl. Santiago, off C. Mayor (Thurs. 9am-2pm).

Buses to Zaragoza, Teruel, or Collated all depart from in front of **Mesón Felix,** C. Mayor, near Puerta Baja. Buses arriving in Daroca stop at Puerta Baja.

■ Tarazona

Tarazona is a flirt. A lovely town (pop. 10,700), she entices tourists with her fine Mudéjar architecture and cool, winding streets, but then pushes her suitors away, refusing to let them stay (there is only one hotel within city limits) or even to know her better (most monuments are closed indefinitely for restoration). It's best to visit when she's in a generous mood—during the **Tarazona Foto** festival (mid-July to mid-August), many monuments are opened for a city-wide photography exhibition.

Practical Information The **tourist office,** C. Iglesias, 5 (tel. 64 00 74), corners the left side of the cathedral. From the Therpasa bus station, turn right on Av. Navarra, and at the circular Pl. San Francisco follow the Soria/Zaragoza signs; at the

tree-shaded Pl. Seo turn left and go up the steps. Ask for an indexed map of the city (open Mon.-Fri. 9am-1:30pm and 4:30-7pm, Sat.-Sun. 10am-1pm and 4-7pm). For **currency exchange** check out the Banco Central Hispano in Pl. San Francisco (open Mon.-Sat. 8:30am-2:30pm). Therpasa **buses** (tel. 64 11 00), operate from the station on Av. Navarra; to Soria (4-7 per day, 1hr., 540ptas) and Zaragoza (4-7 per day, 1hr., 675ptas). **Conda** leaves from Parque de Estación; from Pl. San Francisco, it's up C. Carrera Zaragoza. For trips to Tudela (Mon.-Sat. 5-6 per day, Sun. 1 per day, 40min., 215ptas), buy tickets on the bus. Ask nicely and they might let you leave your **luggage** for a few hours at the ticket window in the Therpasa station, although it's not an official storage area. The **Red Cross** is outside town on Ctra. Zaragoza (tel. 64 09 26). In **medical emergencies** you can also turn to **Ambulatorio San Atilano,** Av. Paz, 29 (tel. 64 12 85). The **municipal police** are next to the library on Pl. San Francisco (tel. 64 16 91, **emergency** tel. 092). They provide maps when the tourist office is closed. The **post office** is at Pl. Seo (tel. 64 13 17), right before the cathedral (open Mon.-Fri. 8:30am-2:30pm, Sat. 9:30am-1pm). The **postal code** is 50500. **Public phones** ring in Pl. San Francisco. The **telephone code** is (9)76.

Ketchup made with pain

When José Albericio describes the evolution of Tarazona's tastes by saying, "antiguamente piedras y ahora tomates" (in ancient times stones and now tomatoes), he is, fortunately, not talking about sandwich toppings. He is pointing out a change in weaponry. During the Middle Ages, the **Moors** pelted town heretics with a barrage of bricks and stones. If the heretic lived, he was freed. Tarazonans continue the tradition during the Fiestas del Cipotegato every August 27 with a more festive (and less revolting) twist to the ceremony. They shower *el Cipotegato,* their damned citizen, with **plump, luscious** tomatoes—a thousand kilograms of them, supplied by local social clubs. Townspeople costume their scapegoat in a harlequinesque mask and colorfully quilted suit. He is then guided through the multitudes, wielding just a ball of yarn attached to a stick for protection while being showered with **fruit.** Eventually the whole shebang becomes a giant **food fight,** thus ushering in the Corpus Christi holidays.

Accommodations and Food Turn back while you can: the hotel in the town proper charges more than a raging bull. For affordable rooms, call Sr. Benio Aparacio (tel. 64 09 45) whose apartment building *might* be available for travelers by the time you read this. This future *hostal* is located amidst the labyrinth on Rúa Baja de Becquer, near the center for Tarazona studies.

Supermercado Eco-Dagesa, Av. Navarra, 9, between Therpasa bus station and Pl. San Francisco, is good for groceries, and has a deli counter in back (open Mon.-Fri. 9:15am-1:30pm and 5-8pm, Sat. 9:15am-1:30pm). The **Hotel/Restaurante Ituri-Asso,** C. Virgen del Río, 3 (tel. 64 31 96), serves an inventive, tasty *menú del día* (940ptas plus 7% IVA) featuring pasta salad and rabbit with hazelnuts. (Open Mon.-Fri. 1-4pm and 9-11pm, Sat. till 11:30pm, Sun. 1-4pm. Visa, MC, AmEx.) **S'ha Feito...Taverna,** in the Plaza de Toros, 18, is a new bar made to look old, run by hip youngsters featuring traditional Aragonese *tapas.*

Sights Like so many monuments here, the splendid Gothic 13th- to 15th-century **cathedral** is undergoing painstaking restorations. It is closed even during the photo exhibitions, but the cloister may open soon. Supposedly, the glorious towers, belfry, lantern, and plasterwork tracery in the inner cloister are particularly fine examples of Mudéjar work, but we wouldn't know. The enchanting 18th-century **Plaza de Toros Vieja,** now multi-colored private residences, has a balconied upper tier. Facing the cathedral, turn right down C. de los Laureles, then make the first right at the Olympia Gym and pass through the arch.

Tarazona was a seasonal residence of medieval Aragonese kings until the 15th century. Their Alcázar has since served as the **Palacio Episcopal.** The bishop's home lies

across the bridge from the Pl. Toros, left one block, and then up the twisting stairs of the Recodos and Rúa Baja. The former palace dungeons, known as the **Bajos del Palacio,** lie downhill on Rúa Alta de Bécquer. They now house the **Centro de Estudios Turiasonenses** (Center for Tarazona Studies) and its temporary exhibitions (open Mon.-Sat. 11am-2pm and 5-9pm, Sun. 11am-2pm; free).

Opposite the Palacio Episcopal, in the heart of El Cinto (the medieval quarter), rises **Iglesia de la Magdalena,** with a Romanesque east end and a Mudéjar tower that dominates the old town. The entrance is a left up Cuesta del Palacio and the first left thereafter (open only for mass). **Murallas** (walls) surround the quarter's heart; go uphill from La Magdalena past the remarkable Renaissance facade of **Iglesia San Atilano** and continue to Pl. Puerto, then exit left. Your reward is a panoramic vista of the broad Valle del Moncayo and, on a clear day, the distant Aragonese Pyrenees.

During Tarazona's **fiestas** (Aug. 27-Sept. 1), crowds pelt each other and *el cipotegato* with tomatoes (see **Ketchup made with pain,** p. 277).

■ Near Tarazona: Monasterio de Veruela

Travelers with cars can visit the enchanting walled monastery of Veruela (tel. 64 90 25), which slumbers in the Sierra de Moncayo, 15km south of Tarazona. Its golden stone walls guard a Romanesque-Gothic church and a transcendentally peaceful cloister. Nineteenth-century poet Gustavo Adolfo Bécquer sought the mountain air here and penned his *Cartas desde mi celda (Letters from My Cell)* within these walls. The Cistercian monastery participates in the Tarazona Foto exhibitions (grounds open Tues.-Sun. 10am-2pm and 4-7pm; winter 10am-1pm and 3-6pm; 200ptas). **Buses** leave and return sporadically from Tarazona; ask at the tourist office for more info. Also, buses on their way to Alcalá de Moncayo might stop at the monastery if you ask the driver before departure from Tarazona. Buses also run to Vera de Moncaya, 4km from the monastery.

▓ Teruel

A sleepy town that still turns in en masse for the afternoon *siesta,* Teruel's traditional Spanish habits belie the city's cosmopolitan history. But during the *Vaquillas del Angel fiestas* in July, the once communist-leaning town proudly celebrates the resilience of its dear *torico* (little iron bull) with a 168-hour anarchic liquor fest. Teruel's narrow, snaking streets are transformed into one giant, twisted outdoor *discoteca* through which *jovenes* stumble, singing Spanish classics like *"Un dos tres, un pasito para delante, María."*

From the 12th to the 15th centuries, Muslims, Jews, and Christians lived here in cultural collusion, as evidenced by the resulting Mudéjar architecture, a blend of characteristically Arab patterns with a touch of Romanesque and Gothic class.

ORIENTATION

Teruel's nonsensical layout can confound even the most finely tuned sense of direction. Maps from the tourist office direct you to the major points of interest in the historic center, but street signs, where they exist at all, are in semi-legible script. Worse yet, several major streets and plazas go by two names.

The *casco histórico* perches on a hilltop, linked to modern Teruel by bridges. The center of the *casco* is **Plaza de Carlos Castell,** affectionately known as **Plaza del Torico** for its pillar crowned by a tiny iron bull. To reach Pl. Torico from the **train station,** take the *modernisme* staircase from the park and follow signs to the *centro histórico.* The new **bus station,** Ronda de Ambeles, at the edge of town, is only a few blocks from the *casco antiguo.* To get to Pl. Torico, head straight up C. Abadía.

PRACTICAL INFORMATION

The **tourist office** resides on C. Tomás Nogues, 1 (tel. 60 22 79), at C. Comandante Fortea/del Pozo. From Pl. Torico, follow C. Ramón y Cajal/San Juan and take the first

left; the office is 1 block away on the right. (Open in summer Tues.-Sat. 8am-2pm and 4-9pm, Sun. 10am-2pm, Mon. 9am-2pm and 5-7:30pm; rest of year Tues.-Sat. 9am-2pm and 5-7pm, Sun. 9:30am-2pm.) **Luggage storage** awaits in the train station (lockers 400ptas; open 6:30am-10:30pm) and the bus station (250ptas for one piece; open Mon.-Sat. 9am-3pm and 4:45-6:30pm). For a **24hr. pharmacy,** consult page two of *El Heraldo de Aragón* or call the municipal police. The **Red Cross** is at C. San Miguel, 3 (tel. 60 97 12). **Municipal police** answer at tel. 60 21 78. In an **emergency,** call 091 or 092. The **post office,** C. Yagüe de Salas, 17 (tel. 60 11 92), sorts it out in the Seminario Conciliar building. (Open for Lista de Correos Mon.-Fri. 8:30am-8:30pm, Sat 9:30am-2pm. **Fax** available 9am.) The **postal code** is 44001. The **telephone code** is (9)78.

Trains run from Camino de la Estación, 1 (tel. 61 02 02), down the stairs from Po. Ovalo. To: Zaragoza (2-3 per day, 3hr., 1300ptas); Valencia (2-3 per day, 2¾hr., 1195ptas); Mora de Rubielos (3 per day, 45min.); Rubielos de Mora (1 per day, 50min.). Several **bus** companies work out of the new station (tel. 60 10 14; see **Orientation,** above, for directions). **La Rápida** (tel. 60 20 04) rolls to Barcelona (1-2 per day, 5½-6½hr.). **Samar** (tel. 60 34 50) runs to Valencia (3-5 per day, 2-3hr.) and Madrid (2-3 per day, 5hr.). **Magallon** (tel. 41 72 52) and **Jimenez** (tel. 60 10 40) go to Zaragoza (4 per day). **Autotransport Teruel** (tel. 60 15 90) sends buses to Albarracín (Mon.-Sat. 1 per day, 45min.). **Furio** (tel. ((9)64) 60 01 00) drives to Mora de Rubielos (1hr.) and Rubielos de Mora (Mon.-Fri. 1 per day, 1½hr.).

Star-Crossed Lovers

The tombs of Diego de Marcilla and Isabel de Segura in the **Mausoleo de los Amantes,** next to Torre San Pedro, graphically explain why Teruel is called the *ciudad de los amantes* (City of Lovers). To prove his worth to Isabel's affluent family, Diego left Teruel in search of fortune and fame, only to return five years later just in time to watch Isabel marry his rival. Diego's request for one last kiss was refused, and he promptly died. At the funeral, Isabel kissed the corpse and, overcome with grief, died herself. Life-size alabaster statues of the lovers reach out over their tombs to touch hands, but, in Grecian urn fashion, never do. For a spot-lighted peek at the lover's remains, duck down near their heads. From Pl. Torico, take the alleyway to the left of the purple *modernista* house. Stairs from there lead directly to the *mausoleo*. (Open in summer daily 10am-2pm and 5-8pm; in winter Tues.-Sat. 10am-2pm and 5-7:30pm, Sun. 10:30am-2pm. 50ptas.)

ACCOMMODATIONS AND FOOD

Lodgings are scarce during August and Semana Santa and impossible during *fiesta*-time in early July. For hotel-quality rooms at *hostal* prices, try **Hostal Aragón,** C. Santa María, 4 (tel. 60 13 87). Head in the direction the Torico faces, and take the first left as you leave the plaza. Attractive, recently renovated rooms sport ultra-firm beds. (Singles 1800ptas, 2800ptas with bath. Doubles: 2900ptas; 4700ptas. Triples 6600ptas.) The nearest **campgrounds** are in Albarracín, 37km away, and in Mora de Rubielos, 42km away (see **Mora de Rubielos,** p. 280).

Restaurant standards and prices are high. The *casco viejo* is the place to look. Teruel is famous for its salty, flavorful cured ham, *jamón de Teruel,* featured in *tapas* bars in Pl. Torico. For veggie diversion, there is a **market** on Pl. Domingo Gascón. From Pl. Torico, take C. Joaquín Costa/Tozal (open Mon.-Sat. 8am-1:30pm). **Supermercado Muñoz** at Pl. Castell/Torico, 23, is open Mon.-Fri. 9:30am-2pm and 5-7:30pm, Sat. 9:30-2pm. To get to lip-smacking **Restaurante La Parrilla,** C. Esteban, 2 (tel. 60 59 17), walk (or run) right and uphill two blocks from the tourist office. Magnificent 1200ptas *menú* is grilled before you on a stone fireplace in the dining area (open daily 11am-5pm and 8pm-midnight).

SIGHTS AND LAS VAQUILLAS

Muslim artisans built the brick-and-glazed-tile **Torres Mudéjares** (Mudéjar Towers) between the 12th and 15th centuries, and then the Christian churches adapted the

structure of the Almohad minarets to their own purposes. The more intricately designed of the three towers are the richly tiled 14th-century **Torre de San Martín,** in Pl. Pérez Prado near the post office, and the **Torre de San Salvador,** on C. del Salvador, built around 1277. In the latter, 123 skinny steps climb through several chambers to the panoramic *campanario* up top. (Open daily 11am-2pm and 5-7pm; winter Sat.-Sun. only. 250ptas includes optional guided tour.)

The alpha and zeta of Teruel's Mudéjar monuments is the 13th-century **Catedral de Santa María de Mediavilla,** in Pl. Catedral. The magnificently decorated brick tower is a mere preface to the 14th-century stylized *artesonado mudéjar* (Mudéjar coffered ceiling) roofing the central nave. All roads left of Pl. Castell/Torico lead one block away to Pl. Catedral (open 11:30am-1:30pm and 5:30-8pm; free). Behind the cathedral, the ethnographic- and archeology-oriented **Museo Provincial,** Pl. Fray Anselmo Polanco (tel. 60 11 04), is housed in the 16th-century porticoed **Casa de la Comunidad** (open Tues.-Sat. 10am-2pm and 4-7pm, Sun. 10am-2pm; free).

Teruel's Iron Calf

The drunken celebration of historical events is a Spanish tradition, and the folks of Teruel do it sublimely. In the winter of 1937, one of the Spanish Civil War's most gruesome battles was fought on Teruel's Republican ground. With temperatures reaching below -20°C, General Franco levelled the city, outdueling his military academy classmate General Rojo. When the smoke cleared, Teruel's chrome statue of a pint-sized *torico* (bull) remained perched on its doric pedestal, surveying the surrounding rubble.

Seven days of non-stop debauchery honor the *torico*'s resilience during the annual **Vaquillas del Angel,** the week following the first Monday in July. Saturday afternoon, a group of teenagers belonging to one *peña* (private social club) erects a human web around the diminutive *torico.* One lucky member dons the bull with a red bandana and smooches it silly. The bandana is removed the following night, after a raucous *encierro* (running of the bulls), while the *torico* is showered by red, yellow, and purple alcoholic concoctions. The celebration is not as grandiose or renowned as Pamplona's—you won't find any "Teruel '97 Backpackers' Club" t-shirts or ESPN2 camera crews. Papa Hemingway would be proud.

■ Near Teruel

Protected by ancient walls, medieval townships are suspended in Teruel's countryside amid acres of feral land. Getting to these mystical hamlets is less an ordeal now that **Regionales** trains from Teruel, Valencia, and Zaragoza make the journey. Only one bus per day ventures from Teruel and returns the next morning. Unless you have a car (plan ahead as there are no car rentals in Teruel), you'll have to spend the night. The almighty *Guía de servicios turísticos,* available at any Aragonese tourist office, has information on accommodations in the area. Some folks hitch, though *Let's Go* does not recommend it. Traffic is heaviest between Teruel and Albarracín; hitchers post themselves with placards at the end of Camino de la Estación, the beginning of the road to Zaragoza. For Mora de Rubielos and Rubielos de Mora, hitchers favor the end of the aqueduct bridge on the road to Valencia.

Thirty-five kilometers west of Teruel, **Albarracín,** once a powerful Islamic city, now lives mainly off the fading grandeur of its stone houses, small churches, and dispersed towers. The **tourist office,** Pl. Mayor, 1 (tel. 71 02 51), will direct you to tours of the *pinturas rupestres,* post-paleolithic shelter paintings dating from 5000 BC. (Open July-Sept. Mon.-Sat. 10am-2pm and 5-7:30pm, Sun. 10am-2pm. Free guided tours in summer at 2:30 and 5:30pm. In the off season, consult the Ayuntamiento at tel. 71 02 51. Open Mon.-Fri. 9am-3pm.) **Camping Ciudad de Albarracín** stakes out here (tel. 71 01 97; 350ptas per person, per tent, and per car).

Mora de Rubielos, 42km east of Teruel, has the largest and best-preserved 15th-century castle in the neighborhood. In the summer, a **tourist office** sets up on C.

Diputación (tel. 80 00 00). **Trains** run to Mora de Rubielos from Valencia (3 per day); Zaragoza (3 per day); Teruel (3 per day). There's **camping** at **El Morrón-Barrachinas** (tel. 80 03 62; 600ptas per person, car and tent included; open July-Aug.).

Local connoisseurs insist the most *precioso* (exquisite) of the medieval towns around Teruel is **Rubielos de Mora,** 15km east of Mora de Rubielos. Its 600 souls live in an unrestored and unscathed architectural set-piece from medieval days, complete with two city gates and a 16th-century town hall (courtyard, dungeon, and all). The **tourist office** is in the Ayuntamiento building, Pl. Hispano América, 1 (tel. 80 40 96; open 10am-2pm and 5-7pm; Sept.-June Mon.-Fri. 10am-2pm). **Trains** run to Rubielos de Mora from Teruel and Valencia (1 per day from each).

ARAGONESE PYRENEES

Political geographers look at the Aragonese Pyrenees, consider the infrequency of northern invasions into Spain, and say it all makes sense. Everyone else looks at the Pyrenees and can't say a word. Their jagged cliff faces, deep, wrenching gorges, icy snow-melt rivers, and alpine meadows have paralyzed men and women for centuries.

Despite scanty train and bus transportation, the area draws both mountaineering veterans and casual walkers to its famous peaks. These peaks are more popular with tourists than the Catalan and Navarrese ranges, but they nonetheless abound with isolated stretches. **Jaca,** the entry point, is fairly bland. To truly enjoy the area, explore the cobbled streets and meandering trails of outlying villages and valleys. The region's spectacular features crescendo at the magical **Ordesa,** a grand old national park.

Hikers should beg, borrow, or steal an *Editorial Alpina* map; buying is also an option for anywhere between 550-700ptas at bookstores, tourist offices, and many hotels. Local sports centers offer info and guides for everything from sweat-free strolls to heart-stopping rappels. In summer, the Aragonese Pyrenees are a climber's fantasy. In winter, skiers find their own brand of bliss. Six major resorts—Astún, Panticosa, Formigal, Cerler, Candanchú, and Valdelinares—lie at their pole-tips. The pamphlets *Ski Aragón* and *El Turismo de Nieve en España,* free at tourist offices, give the low-down on them all. Huesca and Jaca provide very limited access through the area by bus. The most efficient and enjoyable way to explore the valleys is by car, and even those under 21 can rent autos in Jaca. If you can't get your own wheels, Ordesa is definitely worth the sluggish connection by mail bus.

■ Jaca

For centuries, pilgrims bound for Santiago would cross the Pyrenees into Spain, crash in Jaca for the night, then be off by sunrise. They had the right idea. There is little to do in Jaca (pop. 14,000), but the city is a good place to organize transport and excursions into the Pyrenees, eat some good food, meet some hospitable people, and get a good night's rest. Jaca also opens its hostel doors to *San Fermines* fallout.

ORIENTATION AND PRACTICAL INFORMATION

If you arrive by bus, you'll be dropped conveniently at the edge of the city center onto **Avenida de la Jacetania,** which loops around downhill to become **Avenida de Oroel.** Av. Oroel connects with **Avenida Regimiento de Galicia** at the bottom of the hill, which becomes **Avenida Primer Viernes de Mayo,** a broad street that runs back uphill to Av. Jacetania. Within this circle, the central artery for shops and restaurants is **Calle Mayor.** From the bus station, walk through the plaza across the street, exit through the upper right hand corner, and go straight for two blocks. The shuttle bus from the train station will drop you off at the Ayuntamiento, in the middle of C. Mayor, or at the intersection of C. Mayor and Av. Regimiento de Galicia.

Tourist Office: Av. Regimiento Galicia, 2, local 1 (tel. 36 00 98), left off C. Mayor. English-speaking staff. Useful **map** and hiking advice. Open July to early Sept. Mon.-Fri. 9am-2pm and 4:30-8pm, Sat. 10am-1:30pm and 5-8pm, Sun. 10am-1:30pm; mid-Sept. to June Mon.-Fri. 9am-1:30pm and 4:30-7pm, Sat. 10am-1pm and 5-7pm. The **Ayuntamiento,** C. Mayor, 24, proffers a city plan when the tourist office is closed.

Currency Exchange: Banks cluster on Av. Jacetania. On afternoons and summer weekends, try **Fincas Rapitan,** Av. Primer Viernes de Mayo, 14 (tel. 36 20 59). Open daily 10am-1:30pm. **Banco Central Hispano** sits on C. Primer Viernes de Mayo (open Mon.-Fri. 8:30am-2:30pm).

Trains: Shuttle buses run from downtown to the train station roughly 30min. before each train leaves. They stop at the Ayuntamiento on C. Mayor or, if C. Mayor is closed, at the taxi stop and at the bus station. If you're walking, take Av. Juan XXIII from the station, then turn left on C. Escuela Militar (at the Monument to Nature) and go straight until you arrive at the bus station. Follow the directions below from there. **RENFE,** C. Estación, s/n (tel. 36 13 32). Ticket booth open 10am-noon and 5-7pm. To: Ayerbe to connect to Loarre (3 per day, 1½hr., 490ptas); Zaragoza (3 per day, 3hr., 1325-1900ptas); Madrid (1 per day, 6½hr., 4100ptas).

Buses: La Oscense (tel. 35 50 60). To: Sabiñánigo, where mail buses connect to Torla, near Ordesa and Aínsa (1-2 per day, 15min., 170ptas); Zaragoza (3-4 per day, 2½hr., 1450ptas); Pamplona (2-3 per day, 2hr., 855ptas). **Josefa Escartín** (tel. 36 05 08), runs 1 bus daily at 4:30pm passing through: Hecho (1¼hr.); Siresa (1¾hr.); and Ansó (2hr.). Tickets are between 400-500ptas, depending on destination.

Taxis: (tel. 36 28 48). Taxis line up at the intersection of C. Mayor, Av. Regimiento Galicia, and Av. Viernes de Mayo.

Car Rental: Don Auto, C. Correos, 4 (tel. 35 30 27). 7000ptas per day includes insurance and IVA Must be 21. Open daily.

Bike and Ski Rental: Lokoski has two locations: Av. Francia, 55B (tel. 35 59 20); Galicia, 19 (tel. 36 10 81).

Laundromat: Lavomatique, Av. Escuela Militar de Montaña, 1 (tel. 36 01 12), part of Bar Santi, to the left of the bus station. Wash 400ptas per load, dry 200ptas. Open Mon.-Sat. 10am-2pm and 6-9pm. IVA not included.

Hiking, Climbing, and X-treme Sports: Alcorce, C. Salud, 5 (tel./fax 36 39 72), off C. Mayor near Av. Jacetania. Organizes hiking, rock climbing, spelunking, rafting, and bungee-jumping trips. Wear Vans, retro T's, and wrap-around sunglasses or get no respect. Guided hiking trips start at 3000ptas per day, per person; rafting at 5500ptas. Mountain bikes 500ptas per hr. Open Mon.-Sat. 10am-2pm and 4-8pm. **Transpirineos,** Av. Primer Viernes de Mayo, 7 (tel. 35 63 85), has similar services.

Sports Center: Polideportivo, Av. Perimetral (tel. 35 56 03). Just about everything, including a pool and skating rink.

Ski Conditions: Teléfono Blanco (tel. (9)76 20 11 12), or call resorts directly.

24Hr. Pharmacy: Check listings in the local paper, *Pirineo Aragonés.*

Medical Services: Centro de Salud, Po. Constitución, 6 (tel. 36 07 95).

Red Cross: (tel. 36 11 01), outside town on Llano de la Victoria.

Police: Policía Local, C. Mayor, 24 (tel. 092), in the Ayuntamiento.

Emergency: tel. 091 or 092.

Post Office: C. Correos, 13 (tel. 36 00 85), Av. Regimiento Galicia, across from the tourist office. Open Mon.-Fri. 8:30am-2:30pm, Sat. 9:30am-1pm. Lista de Correos downstairs on the left. **Postal Code:** 22700.

Telephone Code: (9)74.

ACCOMMODATIONS AND CAMPING

Jaca's *hostales* and *pensiones* cluster around C. Mayor and the cathedral. It pays to travel in company, as doubles and triples offer the best deals around. Lodgings are scarce only during the bi-annual Festival Folklórico in late July and early August—book rooms weeks ahead. For Santiago-bound pilgrims, the **Albergue de Peregrines** sits on C. Hospital.

Albergue Juvenil de Escuelas Pias (HI), Av. Perimetral, 6 (tel. 36 05 36). From C. Mayor, turn left onto C. Regimento de Galicia and another left on C. Perimetral. Go down the road to the left of the modern metal sculpture to the rows of brightly colored bungalows. Make-shift beds and barracks-style rooms, but still a decent night's sleep. Midnight curfew. 1300ptas per person, over 26 1800ptas. Nonmembers pay 100ptas more. Sheets 300ptas. Breakfast 250ptas.

Hostal Paris, Pl. San Pedro, 4 (tel. 36 10 20). A left off Av. Jacetania as you face the *ciudadela*. Big-windowed rooms, with firm beds and winter heating. Doubles, many with balconies 3300ptas; Sept.-June 3000ptas.

Hostal Sompart, C. Echegaray, 11 (tel. 36 34 10). Several centuries of innkeeping were obliterated with the sterile swipe of renovation. Satiny bedspreads and TVs are the only frivolities in these simple rooms. Singles 3000ptas. Doubles 4500ptas, with bath 5500ptas. Off season: 2500ptas; 4000ptas; 4500ptas. Breakfast 300ptas. Restaurant downstairs (*menú* 1000ptas). Visa, MC. Closed 2 weeks in Nov.

Habitaciones Martínez, C. Mayor, 53 (tel. 36 33 74). Bright new rooms in annex down the street. 2000ptas per person. Smaller-but-cheaper rooms above the bar.

Hotel Alpina Jaca, C. Mayor, 57 (tel./fax 35 53 69). Lots of ample rooms, all with private bath and TV. Singles with bath 2800ptas. Doubles with bath 5000ptas.

Camping: Peña Oroel (tel. 36 02 15), 3½km down the road to Sabiñánigo. Wooded grounds along a riverbank shelter, market, and swimming pool. 525ptas per person, 550per tent and per car. Open Semana Santa and mid-June to mid-Sept.

FOOD

Most of Jaca's restaurants spin off **C. Mayor,** although a few line Av. Primer Viernes de Mayo and Av. Juan XXIII. Regional specialties include *costilla de cordero* (lamb chop) and *longaniza* (short spicy sausage). At any bakery try *corazones* (or *lazos*) *de Jaca,* a sugary pastry. Cans are stacked at **Supermercado ALDI,** C. Correos, 9, next to the post office (open Mon.-Sat. 9:30am-1:30pm and 5-8pm).

Restaurante Vegetariano El Arco, C. San Nicolas, 4 (tel. 36 48 64), off the bus station plaza. Tasty vegetarian *menú* changes daily—hopefully they'll have their stellar vegetable couscous. Open Tues.-Sun. 12:30-3:30pm and 8-11:30pm. *Menú* 1000ptas, *platos combinados* 850ptas.

Crepería El Bretón, C. Ramiro I, 10. French owner makes authentic dinner (*galettes* 400-1000ptas) and dessert crepes (300-700ptas), all served in a Frenchified room with lace curtains. Salads 650ptas. Open Tues.-Sat. 6pm-1am.

Restaurante La Abuela, C. Población, off C. San Nicolas from Av. Jacetania. You *wish* your grandma could cook like his. Spanish staples done well. Daytime *menú* with a flavorful *menestra de verduras* and grilled chicken (1100ptas). Nighttime *menú* 1500ptas. *Bocadillos* 250-350ptas. Open daily 1-4:30pm and 8-11:30pm.

Restaurante Shanghai, C. Valle de Labati, 6 (tel. 36 01 43), a left off C. Escuela Militar which runs beside the bus station. Stuff yourself with the carrot-laden Chinese *menú*—4 courses for 850ptas. Open noon-4:30pm and 7:30-midnight.

SIGHTS AND ENTERTAINMENT

The pentagonal fortress referred to as **La Ciudadela,** or Castillo de San Pedro, puts Jaca on the tourist map. Built by King Felipe II in 1590 and set on a grassy knoll, the citadel originally served to protect Jaca from French Huguenot attacks. It overlooks the battlefield known as *Las Tiendas* (Tents), where Moors were repelled around 760. (Open July-Aug. daily 11am-12:30pm and 5-6:30pm; Sept.-June 11am-noon and 4-5pm. By tour only. 200ptas, under 15 50ptas.)

The Romanesque **cathedral** is modestly noteworthy. Begun in 1063, it influenced most designs for churches built along the Jacobean route. (Open daily 10am-2pm and 4-9pm; in winter 11am-1:30pm and 4-6:30pm. 300ptas.) The über-tourist might take in Jaca's strangely wonderful **meaningless monument circuit,** which runs through the city and includes sculpted commemorations of Ramiro the First, The Ice Skater, Romanticism, and the touching Human Fraternity.

ARAGÓN

During every odd-numbered year at the end of July and beginning of August, people from all over the world come with bells on their toes for the **Festival Folklórico de los Pirineos.** The rest of the year, look for excitement in the many bars that fill **Calle de Gil Berges,** or while away the hours in the **Moroccan tea room,** down the alleyway in front of the cathedral.

■ Near Jaca

The **Monasterio de San Juan de la Peña** is difficult to reach—and meant to be. Determined hermits hid the original monastery in a canyon 22km from Jaca and maintained such extreme privacy that invading Moors never discovered it or the Holy Grail concealed here for three centuries. It's worth a visit not only for the 10th-century underground church carved directly into the rock, but also for the "upper" church's cloister covered nearly completely by an overhanging boulder. Don't confuse the upper and lower monasteries with the boring 10th-century *monasterio nuevo* 1km uphill. (Open June-Sept. Tues.-Sun. 10am-1:30pm and 4-8pm; Oct.-March Wed.-Sun. 11am-2pm; April-May Tues.-Sun. 10am-1:30pm and 4-7pm. Free.) In Jaca, **Viages Arán,** C. Mayor, 46 (tel. 35 54 80), schedules bus trips to San Juan in July and August (1200ptas); otherwise, the only option besides driving yourself is to hitch.

In the 11th century, King Sancho Ramírez built a castle to protect himself from Moorish attacks. Sharp cliffs at its rear and 400m of thick walls to the east make **El Castillo de Loarre** (5km from the town of Loarre) nearly impenetrable. The building's outer walls follow the turns and angles of the rock so closely that an attacker at night might have only seen the silhouette of the awesome stone monolith. A crypt opens to the right of the steep entrance staircase where the remains of Demetrius were stashed after the French saint died in Loarre. A strip of checkered masonry curves directly above the several dozen capitals lining the apse, and a maze of passages and chambers honeycombs the rest of the castle. You can climb up to the battlements of both towers, but the only access designed for the larger of the two is a precarious footbridge from the smaller tower. Be careful when climbing the wobbly steel rungs to the roof or descending into the dark and doorless **sótano** (basement). Loarre comes in first hands-down in the "Best View from a Toilet" competition (same hours as San Juan de la Peña (see above); free). Reaching the castle requires a little ingenuity. One **bus** (675ptas) per day leaves Jaca for the town of Loarre, and **trains** only go to Ayerbe, 7km away. From there, you can trek the two hours to the town of Loarre and request a taxi. In any case, the carless still face a 5km hike from the town of Loarre up to the castle. You can **camp** in the lovely surrounding pine forest.

■ Valle de Hecho

The craggy Valle de Hecho and the Río Aragón Subordán split the turf just 20km west of Jaca, the closest hiking area to the city. From early July to early August, villages in the valley host the **Simposio de Escultura y Pintura Moderna.** Artists come from far and wide, turning the surrounding hills into a huge open-air museum. Villagers come to **Hecho** to feast on roast lamb and fried bread, to serenade plazas along with flute and accordion players, and to watch traditional dances at the jolly kick-off party in early of July. By the end of August, the symposium splatters nearly all the valley's towns with modern painting and sculpture. During the rest of the year, their creations beautify the village, particularly next to the brightly painted studio on the highway. A **bus** leaves Jaca Mon.-Sat. at 4:45pm, stopping at Hecho (6:15pm) and Siresa (6:30pm), and continuing to Ansó. Every morning except Sunday the bus returns from Ansó (6:30am) through Siresa (7am) and Hecho (7:15am) on its way to Jaca. **La Oscense** in Jaca has information (tel. 35 50 60).

HECHO

Hecho (pop. 670) is the valley's geographical and administrative center, a title far too official to do justice to the town's rustic charms. Its storekeepers radiate a contagious

provincial pride, eagerly sharing the sculptural remnants from the valley's modern art festival, which splash color on Hecho's misty gray stone veneer. Hecho (a.k.a. Echo) is also home to a sporadically open **Museo Etnológico** (between Pl. Fuente and Pl. Palacio), which displays old photos of locals and the meanest collection of farm implements you'll ever see. The village is also equipped with pitstop services for Pyrenees trekkers. The **Compania de Guías Valle de Echo** (tel. 37 50 50), leads hiking trips (7900ptas for a 2-day trip to the Selva de Oza) and rents cross-country skis (1000ptas per day).

The **bus** drops off at Pl. Fuente. **Public phones** and a **bank** (open in summer Mon.-Fri. 8:30am-2pm; in winter Sat. also 8:30am-1pm) chill on Pl. Palacio, the main square. The **Ayuntamiento** answers at tel. 37 50 02, the **Guardia Civil** at tel. 37 50 04; **medical help** is at tel. 37 51 18. The **post office** sits in a small square off C. Mayor (open Mon.-Fri. 8:30am-2:30pm and Sat. 9:30am-1pm). The valley's **phone code** is (9)74.

Hecho doesn't exactly abound with accommodations, but what did you expect? One good option is **Casa Blasquico**, Pl. Fuente, 1 (tel. 37 50 07), an unmarked white house with balconies facing the bus stop. Follow your nose; the proprietor's cooking skills are formidable, as is her command of English and French. The six rooms are frequently full, so call ahead (doubles 3500ptas, with bath 6000ptas; dinner 1700ptas). A more generic choice is **Hostal de la Val,** C. Selva de Oza (tel. 37 50 28 or 37 52 51), with its simple, modern rooms, all with bath. (Singles 4000ptas. Doubles 6000ptas. In winter: 3000ptas.; 5000ptas. The restaurant serves a 1650ptas *menú*. Visa, MC.) **Camping Valle de Hecho** (Sept.-June tel. 37 53 61), at the entrance to Hecho on the Crta. Fuente la Reina, has new facilities in a lovely location (500ptas per person, per car, and per tent; IVA not included). *Literas* also available in *albergue* on same site. **Supermercado Aldi,** C. Mayor, stocks provisions (open Mon.-Fri. 8:30am-2:30pm and 4:30-8:30pm; Sat. 9am-1:30pm).

TRAILS AND PATHS

Between Hecho and Siresa, a tranquil town just 2km up the road from Hecho, carved wood signs mark trails (none of which is particularly difficult) to Picoya, La Reclusa, Lenito, Fuente de la Cruz, and Ansó. While some trails are partly eroded, all offer spectacular views of the Pyrenees. From Siresa, the road weaves up the valley, passing by the river-rock formation known as **La Boca del Infierno** (The Mouth of Hell), where the river slips into a profound gorge. After about 9km, you'll reach **Valle de Oza,** a crescent of meadows with the grounds of **Camping Selva de Oza.** (Tel. 37 51 68; open mid-June to mid-Sept. Mid-July to mid-Aug. Reception open 9am-2pm and 4-10pm. 500ptas per person and per tent, 565ptas per car; otherwise: 465ptas; 530ptas.) Hot showers, a store, and a restaurant are on the premises. Fishing is allowed in the nearby river.

Trails into the mountains leave from near the campground. Prepare yourself by acquiring the red *Guía Cartográfica de los Valles de Ansó y Hecho,* published by *Editorial Alpina;* nearly every area store carries it (550-700ptas). The campsite arranges excursions. North of the site, you can hike on the peaks along the French border, from **Pic Rouge** (2177m) to **Pic Lariste** (2168m) to **Pic Laraille** (2147m). The last allows a stupefying view of the **Ibón de Acherito,** a glimmering lake framed by alpine brush. If you follow the guidebook and take a car part of the way, the actual hiking time for these should be around three hours to the summit. To climb **Castillo de Acher** (2390m), a square-topped mountain that resembles a waitress in the sky, follow the forest road toward the **Torrente de Espata,** amble along the path by this stream, cut up the mountainside on the zig-zag path to the ridge, follow the ridge past the **Refugio Forestal,** and go left at the fork. Several steep, narrow paths ascend to the summit (4hr. to the top). For a real romp, consider scaling **Bisaurin** (2669m), the highest peak on the block. From the rocky, snow-capped summit you can practice casting parental looks over Old Aragón, the sumptuous Peña Forca (2391m), the isolated Pico Orhy (2021m), and the cosmic Castillo de Acher (2390m). Check the forecast before you depart (*Previsión meteorológica* tel. (9)76 23 43 36).

▩ Valle de Ansó

Somewhere in the world it's 1998, but that matters precious little to the welcoming town of **Ansó**. Until recently, residents wore traditional costumes and spoke their own dialect, and to this day Ansó remains peacefully removed from the rest of the world. The city relives its more traditional days during the **Fiesta del Traje**, the last Sunday in August. Come soon, though—although the town's native population (500) has plummeted in this century, a small construction boomlet suggests that the tourists hordes are not far off. At the **Museo de Etnología**, inside the **Iglesia de San Pedro**, mannequins model traditional garb next to spinning wheels, looms, costume jewelry, wood carvings, and religious books. (Open July-mid-Sept. daily Mon.-Fri. 10:30am-1:30pm and 3:30-8pm; mid-Sept.-June talk to the priest *(mosen)* in the stone house in front of the church. 200ptas.)

For info, call the **Ayuntamiento** (tel. 37 00 21). **Phones** and the **bank** are in Pl. Mayor. In an emergency, call the **Guardia Civil** (at the edge of town) at tel. 37 00 04, and for **medical services** tel. 37 00 75. The **post office** is also on Pl. Mayor (open Mon.-Fri. 8:30am-2:30pm, Sat. 10am-1pm). The **telephone code** is (9)74. Few travelers actually spend the night here, but those who do are in for a treat. The friendly owners of **Posada Magoria,** C. Chapitel, 8 (tel. 37 00 49), have restored a traditional stone house to comfortable glory, with wide-planked wood floors and antique-filled rooms. They make their own yogurt, bake bread, and grow organic vegetables, then serve up their delicious crops at familial vegetarian meals. (2400ptas per person. Hearty breakfast 700ptas, dinner 1800ptas. Reservations advisable, but it's usually booked solid in Aug.) Around the corner of the cobbled street (look for the sign) is the newer and more standard family-run **Posada Veral,** C. Cocorro, 6 (tel. 37 01 19). (Singles 1800ptas. Doubles 3800ptas. *Menú* 975 ptas for guests only. Breakfast 375ptas.). If these are full, which is likely, try **Hostal Estanés,** C. Chapitel, 9 (tel. 37 01 46; doubles 4000ptas, with bath 5700ptas). The **bus** making the rounds of these valleys from Jaca stops at C. Mayor (6:50pm), and leaves for Jaca at 6:30am (380ptas).

ZURIZA

Fifteen kilometers north of Ansó, **Camping Zuriza** (tel. 37 01 96 or 37 00 77) rubs elbows with a mountain stream 2km away from the Río Veral, suitable for fishing, rafting, or kayaking and set in a gorgeous valley. The site also provides a **supermarket** and **hostel.** (Campsite 440ptas per person and per car, tents 390ptas. *Hostal:* doubles 4000-4500ptas, with bath 5500-6000ptas; bunk in *literas* 850-1000ptas. Includes hot showers. Visa, MC.) From the campground, it's a dayhike (3½hr.) to the **Mesa de los Tres Reyes,** a series of peaks close to the borders of France, Navarra, and Aragón (ergo the three kings). From Zuriza, the **Fountain of Linza** lies north and east of the Collado de Linza, a break between two smaller peaks. There is one lean-to **refugio** 50m from Linza open to anyone, and a more substantial one, **Refugio Linza,** nearby in the **Plano de la Casa,** with winter heating, hot showers, and bunkbeds. Call tel. 37 01 12 for info and reservations. Hereabouts the terrain alternates between the shallow **Agujero de Solana** (Hole of Solana), the steep summit of **Escoueste,** and other quirky peaks. From Zuriza, you can also make the arduous trek to **Sima de San Martín,** on the French border. To enjoy the area without straining yourself, walk 2km south of Ansó to the fork in the road. Just above the tunnel toward Hecho, you can see the striking, weather-sculpted rock formation called **El Monje y la Monja** (The Monk and the Nun). Sweep all lurid thoughts from your mind and enjoy the view.

▩ Parque Nacional de Ordesa

One could mistake the uphill trails of this park as the last ascent towards heaven, offering a preview of its majesty. Nonbelievers can just bask in all its present glory. Getting to Ordesa without a car can mean riding with the mail for an hour and then hiking 9km. Well-maintained trails cut across Arthurian forests, jagged rock faces,

Far Trek

On your way to Berlin? A *Gran Recorrido* (Great Hike) trail will get you there—eventually. One of the most beautiful and rugged stretches of the *Gran Recorrido* network trudges east to west just below the French-Aragonese border. Strung together by old mountain roads, animal tracks, and forest paths, the Aragonese portion of **GR-11** passes by clear mountain lakes and under, over, and through snow-covered peaks (the highest being Mt. Aneto, at 3404m). Though some parts of GR-11 are pretty gentle, the full trek across Navarra requires hiking experience, especially early in the season when snow cover is extensive. The border-to-border route takes eight to ten days.

For detailed info on this and other GR trails (including some with cultural and historical motifs), consult tourist offices in the area or the Federación Aragonesa de Montañismo at C. Albareda, 7, Zaragoza 50004 (tel. (9)76 22 79 71), or pick up a detailed and trail-specific *Topoguía* guide.

snow-covered peaks, and alpine meadows, leading past hills jumping with all kinds of critters. Located just south of the French border and roughly midway between Jaca and Aínsa, Ordesa offers trails for hikers of all levels of experience, which accounts for the crowds in July and August.

There is talk of bus service to Ordesa in the distant future, but for now its treasures remain reserved for those with cars. **Buses** go only as far as **Torla**, a small stone village 9km short of the park; a mail-delivery bus leaves **Sabiñánigo's** bus station (Mon.-Sat. 10am), stopping in Torla at 11:55am before continuing to **Aínsa**. The bus passes through Torla again at 3:30pm on its way back to Sabiñánigo (arrives 4:30pm). Sabiñánigo connects easily by bus or train to Jaca and Huesca (2-5 buses per day from Jaca, 15 min., 160ptas; all trains on the Zaragoza-Huesca-Jaca line stop in Sabiñánigo). From Torla, the park is accessible only on foot or by car (hitchhiking is common). Drivers should arrive at the park by 9am or earlier, as parking is limited. **Taxis** (tel. 48 61 53 or 48 61 56) make the trip for about 1200ptas in July and August.

The **Instituto Nacional Para la Conservación de la Naturaleza (ICONA)** is the control center for the park. They have an office in Torla on Ctra. Ordesa, just beyond C. Francia (tel. 48 63 48; open July-Sept. Mon.-Fri. 10am-2pm and 5-7pm), or they can be reached in Huesca (tel. 24 33 61). The new **visitor center** at the park entrance has informative displays. Both centers sell a trail map (400ptas). The visitor center has a collection of pamphlets on local fauna, to say nothing of flora—you may come across wild boar, vipers, griffins, eagles, and vultures (open July 15-Dec. 15, 10am-2pm and 5-7pm). The indispensable *Editorial Alpina* guide is on sale at the souvenir shop by the parking lot (675ptas) and at the supermarket down the street (600ptas). Torla also has a **tourism hut**, on the highway at the entrance to town, that dispenses info on accommodations and such (sporadically open July-Aug. 9am-9pm).

A **supermarket** sits on C. Francia, just past L'Atalaya (open daily 9am-2pm and 4-9pm, but hr. may vary). **Jorge Soler** (tel. 48 62 43) rents **mountain bikes** (2hr. 1000ptas, half-day 1400ptas, full-day 2300ptas). He can be found at the disco on C. Fatas, on the left as you enter town from the non-park side. In an **emergency**, call the **Guardia Civil** (tel. 48 61 60), at the edge of town just before the ICONA office. The town's **post office** is on C. Francia at Pl. Ayuntamiento, behind a tiny door (open Mon.-Sat. 9-11am). The **postal code** is 22376. The **telephone code** is (9)74.

One can only **camp** in the park for the night, and only at heights over 2200m, above the Soaso Steps. Many **refugios** (mountain huts, usually without facilities) allow overnight stays. The 120-bed **Refugio Góriz** (tel. 48 63 79), about 4hr. from the parking lot, has winter heating and meager hot showers (950ptas per person).

The town of Torla has a greater range of accommodations. Cobblestoned C. Francia is the only road in Torla off the highway to the park—ascend it, and on your right after one block, under some wooden beams, lies the newly-renovated **Refugio L'Atalaya**, C. Francia, 45 (tel. 48 60 22). The 21 bunks clumped together in one room give a *refugio* feel to an urban (ha, ha) setting (900ptas per person; hot showers

included). Its owners also serve a good *menú* (1300ptas) and breakfast (500ptas). The newer **Refugio Briet,** across the street (tel. 48 62 72), has similar facilities, but its bunks are kindly dispersed through a few rooms (1000ptas; *menú* 1400ptas). Decidedly more luxurious and offering a remarkably good off-season deal (Sept.16-June), the **Edelweiss Hotel,** Avda Ordesa, 1 (tel. 48 61 73; fax 48 63 72), is just past the tunnel on the highway to the park. All the lovely rooms here have bathrooms, TVs, and country-style furniture that mercifully refrains from cutesiness. Many rooms (often the cheaper ones) have balconies with swoon-inducing views of the mountains. (Singles with shower 3100ptas, with bathtub 3900ptas. Doubles: 5800ptas; 6600ptas. Sept.15-June 30: 2600ptas; 3100ptas; 4600ptas; 5600ptas. IVA not included.) Three **campgrounds** lie just outside of town. Try angling in the river at **Camping Río Ara** (tel. 48 62 48), about 1km down the paved path from its sign off Ctra. Ordesa, right before the bridge (400ptas per person, per tent, and per car; open April-Oct.). A hotel, pool, and tennis courts await at more upscale **Camping Ordesa** (tel. 48 61 46), 750m farther along Ctra. Ordesa. (550ptas per person, per tent, and per car. Children 500ptas. IVA not included. 30% off in low-season. Open April-Oct.) Right outside town, **Camping San Anton** (tel. 48 60 63), on the Crta. Ordesa, is smaller and cheaper, but still provides jaw-dropping views (350ptas per person, per tent, and per car; open mid-April to mid-Oct.).

CIRCO DE SOASO AND OTHER HIKES

If you only have a day to spend in Ordesa, the **Soaso Circle** is the most practical hike, especially for inexperienced mountaineers. Frequent signposts along the wide trail clearly mark the six-hour journey. The six-hour trail slips through more topographical zones than Biosphere II, traversing forests, waterfalls, cliffs, and plateaus. Be forewarned that the trail becomes slippery and rather dangerous when wet. Check weather forecasts before starting out, and remember that heavy snow can make the trail impassable in winter. Less intrepid types who want to cut the hike to about two hours may return to the parking lot rather than continuing on past the tiered Grados de Soasa waterfall to Refugio Góriz. Whichever route you choose, try to arrive at the park early because by noon the entire Soaso Circle resembles Picadilly Circus.

If you prefer a private mountain hike to a multilingual parade, try the **Circo Cotatuero** or the **Circo Carriata.** Both are two- to three-hour hikes that can be combined into a single five-hour hike. More experienced hikers might attempt the **Torla-Gavarnie** trail, a six-hour haul (one-way) all the way to Gavarnie, France. The **Ordesa-Gavarnie** trail is longer; plan to spend at least 10 hours. An even more rugged climb begins at the Refugio Góriz and scales Monte Perdido (3355m; mountaineering equipment recommended). Count on eight hours there and back from the *refugio.* For any of these hikes, the *Editorial Alpina* topographical map is an absolute must. If your car can handle a very bumpy four-kilometer road, take it through the delightful **Valle de Bujaruelo,** a left at the park entrance.

■ Near the Parque Nacional: Aínsa (L'Ainsa)

Actual (not mail) **buses** run by **Compañía Hudebus** travel from Torla to Aínsa (noon daily, 1hr.). Its new town, now an unfortunate poster child for the pre-fab housing industry, is psychically and physically removed from its perfectly preserved medieval old town, where flowers spill over the stone walls into the streets. The ruins of an 11th-century **castle** crown the good face of Aínsa at the far end of its trapezoidal Pl. Mayor and offer views of the city and its surroundings. In 1181, priests consecrated the **Iglesia de Santa María,** just across the **Plaza Mayor** from the castle.

The **tourist office,** Av. Pirenáica, 1 (tel. 50 07 67), is at the highway crossroads where the bus from Sabiñánigo and Torla stops. Its helpful staff advises on transport and excursions. (Open July-Aug. Mon. 4:30-8:30pm, Tues.-Sat. 9am-2pm and 4:30-8:30pm, Sun. 9am-2pm; April-June and Sept.-Oct. Mon.-Sat. 10am-1pm and 4:30-8pm; Nov.-March closed.) The **Red Cross** (tel. 50 00 26) is located on Av. Ordesa on the outskirts of town. The **Guardia Civil** is posted in Barrio Banasto (tel. 50 00 55 or 50

01 74). In an **emergency,** dial 091. The **farmacia** waits at tel. 50 00 23. The **post office,** Av. Ordesa (tel. 50 00 71), is opposite the bus stop on the way to the old town (open Mon.-Fri. 8:30am-2:30pm, Sat. 9am-1pm). The **postal code** is 22330. The **telephone code** is (9)74.

At the crossroads is **Hostal Dos Ríos,** Av. Central, 2 (tel. 50 00 43 or 50 01 06), with well-kept modern rooms. Budget-watchers should make sure they go to the *hostal,* not the hotel of the same name. (Singles with bath 3800ptas; doubles with bath 4900ptas. Oct.-May: 3200ptas; 4100ptas. IVA not included). Those hankering for a little atmosphere can stay in **Casa Rural El Hospital,** C. Sta Cruz, 3, in the Casco Viejo (tel. 50 07 50; doubles with bath 4500ptas). If no one answers the door, try the store below called *La Botiga.* **Camping Aínsa,** Ctra. Aínsa-Campo, km1.8 (tel. 50 02 60), has a store, pool, hot showers, and a shady site. Take a left 300m after the bridge as you leave town eastward, then follow the unpaved road (500ptas per person, 500ptas per tent, and 500ptas per car).

Scads of cats prowling Aínsa's old city may attest to the abundance of fine food there, but unless someone feeds you scraps too, you may find most of it out of your price range. The one exception (barely) is **Casa Albás,** at the *castillo* end of Pl. Mayor, that offers a 1500ptas *menú* loaded with succulent Aragonese dishes like rabbit in almond sauce and peaches in wine (open 1:30-4pm and 8:30-11pm). The supermarket **Alimentación M. Cheliz,** Av. Ordesa, in the new town's main intersection, stocks beautiful produce, homemade bread, and fresh cheeses (open Mon.-Fri. 8:30am-2:30pm and 4:30-8pm, Sat. and Sun. 9am-1pm).

Oodles of outdoor adventure companies operate out of Aínsa. For **whitewater rafting, canoeing,** and **kayaking,** try Aguas Blancas, Avda Sobrabe, 4 (tel. 51 00 08). For **horseback riding,** check out Centro Ecuestre El Trio, C. Sta Tecla, 2 (tel. 50 07 52). **L'Orache,** Av. Ordesa, 16 (tel. 50 03 32), provides package deals that include camping or hostel accommodations for group trekking, rafting, spelunking, and mountain climbing. Hikers can get head out right from the Pl. Mayor for short hikes around the nearby reservoir or into the surrounding hills.

Buses leave for Barbastro (7am), where one can connect to Benasque (**Compañía Cortés,** tel. 31 15 52). A bus leaves at 2:30pm for Torla and continues on to Sabiñánigo, where trains connect to Jaca and Huesca. Fares run around 700ptas.

▓ Valle de Benasque

The Valle de Benasque is a hiker's haven. Countless trails of all levels wind through the surrounding peaks, and the area teems with *refugios,* allowing for longer expeditions. Soft-core strollers are often scared away by the valley's serious mountaineering reputation—the area has the Pyrenees' highest peak—but everyone can enjoy the beautiful Río Esera gorge and the astounding variety of landscapes. Two-kilometer-high snow-capped peaks tiptoe down the valley, and cascades shoot over the sides of pine-covered hills. As always, get *Editorial Alpina*'s excellent topographical map of the valley (at least 500ptas) in any of Benasque's stores before starting your hike.

BENASQUE

The town of Benasque (pop. 1200) is nothing exceptional—a jaunty collection of old stone houses and new outfitting stores—but the shocking peaks that soar behind it are all the reason anyone needs to come here. With its many excursion companies and nearby trailheads, Benasque makes an excellent home for hill walkers. If you start early from Benasque, you can hike just over 8km down the valley road, cross the river on the camping area bridge, and climb up, up, up, and away, following the falls of the Río Cregueña. Four sweaty hours later you'll reach **Lago de Cregueña** (2657m), the largest and, you'll be convinced, highest lake in the **Maladeta** massif.

The pilgrimage to **Mount Aneto** (3404m), the highest of the Pyrenees, begins each morning at about 5am, when the experts set out from the **Refugio de la Renclusa** to conquer the mountain. To reach the *refugio,* take the main road north, take the

fourth exit to the right, and follow the paved road for 8km. From where it ends, it's a 30-minute hike. The trek up Aneto requires technical climbing skills and gear; many companies in Benasque organize trips and can secure guides. If lugging heavy equipment up a mountain isn't your idea of fun, head downhill to the road and follow signs to **Forau de Aigualluts.** This tranquil pond, 50 minutes from the *refugio* trailhead at the end of a tumbling waterfall, is the happy recipient of hundreds of gallons of *agua* per minute. Two gaping black holes (*foraus* in Catalan) keep the pond calm by pulling the water underground and releasing it in Val d'Arán. Another strenuous hike from the *refugio* leads to the peak of **Sacroux** (2675m). Although snow may prevent you from reaching the top and peering into France, the rush of the **Torrents de Gorgutes** and the sight of Lago Gorgutes make the four-hour climb worthwhile. (*Refugio* tel. 55 11 26. 900ptas per person, 625ptas for club members. Breakfast 500ptas. No showers, but there's a nice hose. Open June 22-Sept. 24.)

Practical Information To find the **tourist office** (tel. 55 12 89 or 55 14 45) and volumes of info on local hiking, face the Galerías Barrabés mountain supply store at the main highway intersection and continue down the alley on the right for one block. (Open July-Aug. daily 9am-2pm and 5-9pm; Sept.-June Tues.-Sun. 10am-1pm and 5-8:30pm.) There's a mapboard of the town near the fountains by the bus stop. **Vit's,** Pl. Mayor (tel. 55 02 88), rents **mountain bikes** (500ptas per hr., half-day 1200ptas, full-day 2000ptas; open July-Aug. daily 9:30am-9pm, Sept.-June daily 10am-2pm and 4-9pm). **Taxis** answer at tel. 55 11 57. There is a **laundromat** (tel. 55 14 05), on the outskirts of town, Crta. de Francia (Edificio Ball Benas). The **Red Cross** is at tel. 55 12 85, the **ambulance** at tel. 55 10 01. Signs point to the **Guardia Civil** (tel. 55 10 08) from the main highway intersection. The **post office** (tel. 55 20 71) is in the Ayuntamiento building (open Mon.-Fri. 9am-noon, Sat. 11am-noon, only for stamps). The **postal code** is 22440. The **telephone code** is (9)74. La Alta Aragonesa (tel. 21 07 00) runs **buses** to and from Huesca (1-2 per day, 3hr., 1275ptas). **Jeep tours** are offered by Autotaxi Benasque (tel. 55 11 57).

Accommodations and Food Sleep for cheap in the town proper. At the literal rock bottom are the cement floors of the *literas.* In **Fonda Barrabés,** C. Mayor, 5 (tel. 55 16 54), off Pl. Mayor, a left from the bus stop and straight ahead 200m, 800ptas lands you in a *litera* (bunk) with a well-used mattress, a blanket, possibly three bedfellows, and access to a hot shower. For a bit more than twice the price, you can get a real room, floor, and winter heating, although these mattresses have also seen their share of sleepers (singles 1500ptas; doubles 3000ptas). The restaurant downstairs serves *bocadillos* (325-475ptas) and *platos combinados* (700-975ptas). **Camping Aneto** (tel. 55 11 41), 3km out of town up the hill past the Cerler turnoff, has facilities for both summer and winter camping (430ptas per person, tent, or car). **Camping Ixeia** is a little farther past Aneto. (Open June-Sept. 400ptas per person, per tent, and per car. Call tel. (9)6 154 68 09 in Valencia for info during the off season.) Both sites have stores and hot water. You can also pitch your tent in the wide open spaces, but only for a night and never in Plan del Hospital/Plan d'Estany. **Supermarket Super Spar,** C. Horno, off Pl. Iglesia, is a two-minute walk to the left from Pl. Mayor facing the main road (open July-Aug. daily 9am-2pm and 4:30-9:30pm; Sept.-June closed Sun.). **Restaurante-Crêperie Les Arkades,** hiding down a street between the post office and the church, flips all kinds of crepes (ham and cheese 395ptas, honey and nuts 400ptas) and dishes out a 4-course *menú* with roast quail (1400ptas; open 1-4pm and 8pm-midnight; creperie opens at 5:30pm). **Pepe and Co.,** C. Mayor, vends pizzas (900-1800ptas), *paellas* (975-1200ptas), and serves a 1250ptas *menú* for lunch.

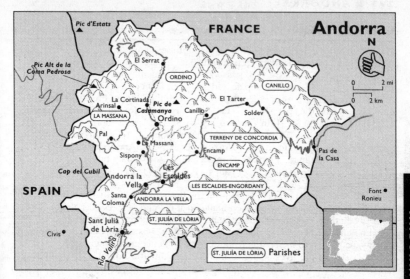

Andorra

This tiny Pyrenean country is an anomaly. The frantic atmosphere of duty-free shopping amidst neon-lit towns is cantered by the peace and serenity of breathtaking landscapes. Pragmatists might say Andorra is the best of both worlds, but a purist might beg to differ. Known officially as Principat d'Andorra (Principality of Andorra), it is ruled by two co-princes: the French president and current Bishop of Urgell, and a popularly elected *Consell General,* representing the seven parishes.

Sandwiched between France and Spain (pop. 65,000; 468sq. km), Andorra struggles to assert its identity after a long history of playing the rope in a tug of war between the Spanish Counts of Urgell, the Church of Urgell, and the French King, the latter's power invoked through a complex series of marriages. According to legend, Charlemagne founded Andorra in 784 as a reward to the valley's inhabitants for having led his army during battle against the Moors.

Andorra today is far less progressive than other industrialized western European nations. Through 1933, only third-generation Andorran men over 25 could vote. Only in the last 26 years has suffrage been extended to women, younger voters, and recent immigrants. Not until 1990 did Andorra create a commission to draft its constitution, adopted on March 14, 1993, to pave the way for political parties.

Andorra's citizenry is comfortably trilingual, but Catalan, the official language, is spoken with pride. Ask a question in Spanish, and the response will often come in Catalan. Other manifestations of cultural pride appear every summer when each of the seven parishes holds its own three-day jubilee. These spectacles start the third weekend of July and continue through mid-September. The national *festa* on December 8 honors Andorra's patron saint *Nostra Senyora de Meritxell* (Our Lady of Meritxell).

Despite Andorra's assertion of identity, the country has no currency of its own. All establishment are required to accept both *pesetas* and *francs,* although *pesetas* are far more prevalent. The absence of a sales tax draws consumers from all over Europe. With Andorran towns spaced mere minutes apart on local bus routes, a day begun wading through eight aisles of duty-free cheese may end on a hike through a pine-scented Pyrenean valley.

GETTING THERE

Planes and trains defer to automobiles and tour buses in Andorra, as the country has no airport and no train station. French and Spanish border police supposedly, if not always in practice, require a valid passport or an EU identity card to enter the country. Two highways—one from Spain and one from France—access the principality. All traffic from France must enter Andorra through the town of **Pas de la Casa;** the gateway town on the Spanish side is **La Seu d'Urgell. Andor-Inter/Samar** buses (in Madrid tel. (9)1 230 31 31; in Toulouse tel. 61 58 14 53; in Andorra tel. 82 62 89), run to Madrid (Tues., Thurs., and Sun., 9hr., 4700ptas). To go anywhere else in Spain, you must first go to La Seu d'Urgell on **La Hispano-Andorra** (tel. 82 13 72; 6-7 buses per day, 30min., 330ptas). From La Seu, **Alsina Graells buses** (tel. 82 73 79 in Andorra) continue to the rest of Spain via Puigcerdà (3 per day, 1hr., 560ptas) and Lérida (3 per day, 2½hr., 1530ptas).

Most buses leave Andorra la Vella from the **bus station,** Pl. Guillemó (known to locals as Pl. Arcades), off Av. Princep Benlloch at the end of C. Doctor Negüi. Buses from La Seu drop passengers off at the bus stop on Av. Princep Benlloch, 6, off Pl. Princep Benlloch. Madrid-bound buses leave from the bus station on C. Bonaventura Riberaygua. To get to the station from Pl. Princep Benlloch, follow Av. Meritxell to the other side of the river. Make an immediate right after crossing, an immediate left, then take the fourth right and go straight for 4-5 blocks (20min.).

GETTING AROUND

Driving in Andorra la Vella is a nightmare. The main road turns into a parking lot as red-clad traffic officers gesticulate and blow whistles in a desperate attempt to keep traffic moving. Drivers will find a map totally useless; it's best to follow signs. Trying to find **parking** is likewise a fruitless endeavor. There is, however, a totally unpublicized **parking lot** that is free for all cars for two consecutive days although it is unclear whether anyone is really counting. Use this centrally located lot, and don't make the mistake of paying a parking meter. The lot is located up the road to the right behind a big meter lot on **Av. Meritxell,** across from l'Isard Hotel.

Efficient **intercity buses** connect villages along the three major highways that converge in Andorra la Vella. The entire country is navigable in an hour or two via public transportation; most towns are only 10 minutes away. Bus rides can cost 110 to 590ptas. Bus lines are not indicated by number or color, so pay attention to the direction signs posted in the front windows. For more info, contact **Cooperative Interurbana Andorrana,** Av. Princep Benlloch, 15 (tel. 82 04 12). The tourist office's pamphlet is easy to decipher.

COMMUNICATIONS

Dual French and Spanish administration of the postal system has resulted in separate **post offices,** overseen by France and Spain, within a few blocks of one another. Correspondence forwarded to **Poste Restante** in Andorra la Vella may arrive at either post office; mail marked **Lista de Correos** arrives at the Spanish office. The tourist office recommends the French service (except for Spain-bound mail).

Phone communications in Andorra are handled exclusively by the **STA** network. To use a public pay phone, you must purchase an STA *teletarjeta* (telecard) for a minimum of 500ptas, which provides 50 units of calling time. The cards are available in any post office or kiosk. Spanish Telefónica phone cards do not work in Andorran payphones. Collect calls are not available, and AT&T does not maintain an access network with Andorra (despite what the Access Number Guide may say). For **directory assistance** within Andorra, dial 111. Andorra's **telephone code** is 376. Remember, you have to dial 07 first if calling from Spain since it's an international call.

As of 1995, all of Andorra's phone numbers, formerly 5 digits, added an 8 in front to make 6 digits. You may still occasionally see 5-digit numbers listed. Just dial 8 before any of these, or you will be subjected to a confusing Catalan recording.

■ Andorra la Vella

Andorra la Vella (Andorra the Old; pop. 20,000) is little more than a narrow, cluttered road flanked by shop after duty-free shop. Anything but *vella*, the modern city disguises—actually, suffocates—its old quarter well, upstaging it with dozens of flashing neon signs. La Vella is not completely misnamed, however, since you will probably sprout a few gray hairs just waiting to cross the street. After doing a little shopping, you're best off escaping to the countryside.

ORIENTATION AND PRACTICAL INFORMATION

Avinguda Meritxell, the city's main thoroughfare, rushes through the city beginning at Pl. Princep Benlloch in the heart of the tiny **barri antic** (old quarter) and continuing through the modern city's heart, across the **Riu Valira,** and becoming the main highway to parishes northeast of the capital. West of Pl. Princep Benlloch, to the right when facing the Església de Sant'Esteve, Av. Meritxell becomes **Avinguida Princep Belloch**. To the left (west) of the *plaça* facing the Església de Sant'Esteve, Av. Meritxell becomes **Avinguida Princep Benlloch.** C. Dr. Negüi, the first right (a sharp turn) off Av. Princep Benlloch from the *plaça*, leads to Pl. Guillemó.

Tourist Office: Av. Doctor Villanova (tel. 82 02 14; fax 82 58 23). Bucketloads of brochures—the country map and the *Hotels i Restaurants* guide are particularly useful. Open Mon.-Sat. 9am-1pm and 3-7pm; Oct.-June Mon.-Sat. 10am-1pm and 3-7pm, Sun. 10am-1pm. To get to the here from the bus stop on Av. Princep Benlloch, continue east (away from Spain) just past the *plaça* on your left, then take C. Dr. Villanova, which curves down to the right. A **second office** as eagerly awaits in Pl. Rotunda where Av. Meritxell crosses the river (same hours). There is an **info booth,** Av. Meritxell, 33 (tel. 82 71 17). Open daily 9:30am-1pm and 4-8pm. All offices, however, have been known to close suddenly for mysterious reasons.

Currency Exchange: Banc Internacional, Av. Meritxell, 32 (tel. 82 06 07). No commission. Open Mon.-Fri. 9am-1pm and 3-5pm, Sat. 9am-noon. They will exchange traveler's checks.

American Express: Viatges Pantours, Pl. Rebés, 11 (tel. 82 04 00 or 82 04 34), a bit farther down Av. Mentxell from Pl. Princep Benlloch. Open Mon.-Fri. 9:30am-1pm and 4-7:30pm, Sat. 9:30am-1pm.

Taxis: (tel. 82 69 00). Stations at Pl. Guillemó and Pl. Rebés.

Car Rental: Avis Av. Tarragona, 42 (tel. 82 00 91), at the bus station. Must be over 19 and have had a drivers license at least 1yr. Prices start at 4900ptas per day, 39ptas per km, or 19,500ptas for 3-day weekend with unlimited mileage.

Weather and Ski Conditions: In Spanish, tel. 84 88 52; in French, tel. 84 88 53.

Late-Night Pharmacy: Each pharmacy has the "duty roster" posted on its door, listing which is open on a given night. Or call the police.

Hospital: Clínica Nostra Senyora de Meritxell, Av. Fiter I Rossell (tel. 87 10 00).

Red Cross: (tel. 82 52 25).

Police: C. Prat de la Creu, 16 (tel. 82 12 22). **Emergency:** tel. 110.

Post Offices: Spanish Post Office, Carrer Joan Maragall, 10 (tel. 82 04 08). Lista de Correos. Open Mon.-Fri. 8:30am-2:30pm, Sat. 9am-1:30pm. Both at the east end of town, on the other side of the river from Pl. Princep Benlloch. **French Post Office,** *La Poste,* C. Pere d'Urg, 1 (tel. 82 02 57). Poste Restante. Open Mon.-Fri. 8:30am-2:30pm; Oct.-May Mon.-Fri. 9am-7pm, Sat. 9am-noon.

ACCOMMODATIONS, CAMPING, AND FOOD

It's as easy to find a place to drop as it is to find a place to shop—cheap pensions proliferate. Save your food budget for a different country, though, as Andorra's atyp-

ically Andorran restaurants serve mediocre food at mediocre prices. You're better off going to one of the amazing three-story supermarkets in nearby Santa Coloma (you can't miss them) or the **Grans Magatzems Pyrénées,** Av. Meritxell, 11, the country's biggest department store with one entire Kmart sized aisle dedicated to chocolate bars (open Mon.-Fri. 9:30am-8pm, Sat. 9:30am-9pm, Sun. 9am-7pm). Hunt for restaurants along the busy **Avinguda Meritxell** and in the streets around **Plaça Princep Benlloch.** Most restaurants add supplementary charges to selected items in their *menús.*

Pensió La Rosa, Antic Carrer Major, 18 (tel. 82 18 10), just south of Av. Princep Benlloch. Immaculate rooms in which blossoms of various species and colors compete for dominance over wallpaper and bed spreads. Exceptional hall bathroom. Singles 1700ptas. Doubles 3000ptas. Breakfast 350ptas.

Hotel Costa, Av. Meritxell, 44 (tel. 82 14 39), above Restaurant Mati. Big rooms, some with views of the city, are somehow both dingy and bright. Large lounges make for communal atmosphere. 1400ptas per person.

Camping: Camping Valira (tel. 82 23 84), located behind the **Estadi Comunal d'Andorra la Vella.** Shade, video games, hot showers, and an indoor pool. 500ptas per person, per tent, and per car. Reception open 8am-1pm and 3-9pm. Call ahead. 2½km down the road, **Camping Santa Coloma** (tel. 82 88 99) charges 450ptas but has no video games.

Restaurante Italiano Minim's, Antic Carrer Major, 5. Delicious pizzas (750ptas) and pastas. Homemade tortellini in tomato cream sauce (850ptas), risotto with champagne and parmesan (800ptas). Open Tues.-Sun. 1-4pm and 8-11pm.

Restaurant Marti, Av. Meritxell, 44 (tel. 82 43 84). Good, cheap victuals. *Menú* (1100ptas) topped off with *crema catalana.* Open noon-4pm and 7:30-10pm.

Mex Mex Cantina Mexicana, at the intersection of C. Antic Major and C. Fossal. Inexpensive Mexican food: enchiladas, burritos, or fajitas (400ptas); nachos and tacos (375ptas). Wash it all down with a Dos Equis or Corona.

SIGHTS AND ENTERTAINMENT

Although there is more to Andorra la Vella than shopping, there isn't *much* more. Lilliputian **Casa de la Vall** (House of the Valleys; tel. 82 91 29), home to Andorra's pocket-sized parliament, squats at the end of the stone alley winding west from Pl. Princep Benlloch and past the church. The 16th-century building, a private home until it was sold to Andorra's General Council in 1702, still has many original fixtures. Each of Andorra's seven parishes holds a key to the "seven-keyed" cupboard containing General Council documents (obligatory guided tour of the Casa every hour Mon.-Fri. 9am-1pm and 3-7pm). The tourist office sells tickets for Andorra la Vella's annual **Festival Internacional de Música i Dansa,** showcasing an international array of ballet, jazz, and classical concerts. For info, contact the **Collectiu d'Activitats Culturals,** Av. Princep Benlloch, 30 (tel. 82 02 02). The annual festival colors the capital on the first Saturday, Sunday, and Monday in August. The tourist office's monthly pamphlet *Un mes a Andorra* lists cultural activities. *7 dies a Andorra* is a free weekly with useful phone numbers and entertainment info. Its innocuous stories reflect Andorra's blissful detachment from world affairs.

■ Elsewhere in Andorra

"Elsewhere" in Andorra is where one ought to go. Escape the polluted air that drips over Andorra la Vella to ski, bike, fish, climb, ride horses, or just bask in the serenity of the rural *parròquias* (parishes).

■ The Parishes

Mountain ventures shove off from the *parròquia* of **La Massana** (pop. 5000), directly north of Andorra La Vella. It's a good 1252m above sea level but easily accessible by bus from the city (every 30min. until 9pm, 10min., 110ptas). Perambulate unhurriedly through the countryside and visit the town of La Massana's **Església Par-**

ròquial de Sant Iscle i Santa Victoria, a reconstructed Romanesque church with an impressive baroque altar. A little determined exploring in La Massana *almost* rewards with glimpses of ancestral houses and traditional tobacco farms, although the town itself feels like an overdeveloped suburb. The village *festa* is held August 15-17. The **tourist office** in La Massana (tel. 83 56 93), is in a steep-roofed cabin by the bridge, just ahead of the bus stop (open Mon.-Sat. 9am-1pm and 3-7pm, Sun. 9am-1pm and 3-6pm). For **emergency and health services,** refer to Andorra la Vella. The **Hotel Rossell,** C. Josep Rossell (tel. 83 50 92; fax 83 81 80), has big, ochre-toned rooms with baths (singles 2500ptas, doubles 4750ptas). **Restaurante Chez Gigi,** in a stone building down an alley off of Av. Sant Antoni, tosses up herby pizzas (700-950ptas). **Camping STA Catarina** is on the uphill outskirts of La Massana, on the highway to Ordino (tel. 83 50 65). The grounds are low on facilities but cost only 400ptas per person and per car (open June 26-Sept. 24). **Establiments Angrill,** on the road to Andorra la Vella across from the exit to Sispony, can fulfill your **grocery** needs (open Mon.-Sat. 8:45am-2pm and 4:30-8pm, Sun. 9am-1pm).

Sispony and the **Alberg Borda Jovell** are a 20- to 30-minute climb from La Massana, Av. Jovell (tel. 83 65 20; fax 83 57 76). To get here from La Massana's bus stop, go back towards Andorra la Vella (75m) and turn right at the main intersection. Follow the signs south for 1.3km until the *alberg,* a 700-year-old stone house, appears on the left. The renovated, all-wood interior has large bunk-bed filled rooms with tiny windows and bathrooms with stand-up toilets. The friendly owner holds court in the restaurant downstairs and is a good source of info on the area. (2200ptas per person including sheets and breakfast. Midnight curfew. Visa, MC, AmEx.)

Neither **Santa Coloma,** five minutes southwest of Andorra la Vella by bus, nor **Sant Julià de Lorià,** just north of the Spanish border, particularly merits a visit unless your urge to splurge continues unabated—both are mere annexes to the Great Mall of Andorra la Vella. To get a glimpse of what an Andorran village was like before the onslaught of Reebok and Sony, check out pretty **Ordino,** 5km northeast of La Massana. The least populated of Andorra's seven parishes, Ordino is distinguished by its status as former home to the principality's **seignorial mansions** *(pairals).* The town's nobles accrued a small fortune in the region's iron industry; the home of Don Guillem, an Andorran iron magnate, is near the church. Attached to a wall in Ordino's main square is an **iron ring** once used to chain criminals for public exposure. Ordino's **Rose Festival** takes place on the first Sunday in July.

Ordino's **tourist office,** C. Nou Desvio (tel. 83 69 63), supplies comprehensive brochures (open Mon.-Sat. 9am-1pm and 3-7pm; Sun. 9am-noon). The stone-faced **Hotel Quim** on the *plaça* (tel. 83 50 13), contains homey, comfortable rooms (doubles 4500ptas; Sept.-June 3000ptas). The incongruously postmodern **Bar Restaurante Topic** (tel. 83 76 50), serves every standard "international" food you've ever heard of: spaghetti carbonara (400ptas), fondue for two (1500ptas), and *tortilla de patatas* (500ptas; open Tues.-Sun. 9:30am-1:30pm and 3-6:30pm).

The diminutive town of **Canillo,** in the center of the country, suffers from the same architectural short-sightedness as the rest of Andorra, but is surrounded by particularly fine scenery and perhaps the principality's best skiing. The colossal **Palau de Gel D'Andorra** (Andorran ice palace; tel. 85 15 15), is an eclectic recreational facility almost as monumental as the mountains themselves. The palace's marvels, including a swimming pool, ice-skating rink, squash courts, and cinema, are accessible by individual tickets. In winter, you can swim outdoors in a heated pool while snow melts around its edges. (Palace open daily 11:30am-midnight. Each facility has its own hours. Closed Sept. 2-Oct. 6. 450ptas for pool, 900-950ptas for ice rink, 950ptas for 30min. of squash plus 250ptas for racquet rental, 525ptas for gym. Prices and hours subject to change, so call before you go.) At the edge of town on the road to Andorra La Vella, **Hotel Comerç** (tel. 85 10 20) has unmemorable rooms at memorable prices (singles 1400ptas, doubles 2750ptas).

Encamp houses the **Museu Nacional de l'Automòbil** (tel. 83 22 66) with 80 antique cars, motorbikes, and bicycles all revved up with nowhere to go. (Open Tues.-Sat. 9:30am-1:30pm and 3-6pm, Sun. 10am-2pm. 300ptas, seniors and students

ANDORRA

200ptas.) Slink toward **Escaldes-Engordany,** just outside Andorra la Vella, for the waterborn pleasures of the **Caldea Spa,** Parc de la Mola, 10 (tel. 82 86 00), if not to bathe, then to see what all the hype's about. Housed in a glass steeple, the "Centre Termolúdic" offers steam baths, hydro and human massages, tanning beds, and decadent dips in faux Roman baths. (Admission 2200ptas per 3hr., not including fees for each service. Open daily 10am-11pm.)

■ Hiking and Skiing Trails

Andorra's countryside lends itself to **mountain biking,** with a panoply of clearly marked trails. One loop trail begins and ends in Andorra la Vella, passing through La Comella for an aerial view of lazy shoppers (11km). Bikes can be rented in any parish; try **Exploramon** (tel. 86 61 82), in Andorra la Vella. For further info, contact **Federació Andorrana de Ciclisme** (tel. 82 96 92), and check out the tourist office's bike route pamphlet. **Horses** are another mane form of back-country transit. **Club Hipic L'Aldosa** (tel. 83 73 29), in La Massana, has horses and ponies available for excursions. The tourist office prints an excellent pamphlet outlining potential routes.

Hiking afficianados will find a plethora of trails. The *Grandes-Randonnées* trails #7 and 11 traverse nearly all of the country. The G-R 7 stretches from Portella Blanca on the French border to Suberri on the Spanish border, hitting an altitude of 2411m at Els Estangs, about one-third of the way through. La Massana is home to Andorra's tallest peak, **Pic Alt de la Coma Pedrosa** (2946m). The G-R 11 goes through **Arinsal,** northwest of the town on the way to Spain; a multitude of trails criss-cross the area. From the tiny **Cortals de Sispony,** 3km west of Sispony, the climb to **Cap del Cubil** (2364m), on the Spanish border, takes 1½ hours. Ordino is another base for trails of different levels of difficulty. An easy 4hr. hike tours the lakes of **Tristaina**. A very difficult 8-hour climb brings summit-oriented hikers to **Pic de Casamanya** (2740m), **Coll d' Arenas** (2539m), **Pic de l'Estanyó** (2915m), **Pic de la Cabaneta** (2863m), and **Pic de la Serrera** (2913m). Cabins and mountain refuges dot each trail. The booklet *Andorra: The Pyrenean Country,* supplied by Andorra's tourist office, lists cabin and refuge locations within the principality. Also pick up *Sports Activities,* which sketches out 52 itineraries ranging from 15-minute strolls to longer affairs. To do it all at once, try the **La Rabassa Sports and Nature Center** in the of southwest corner of Andorra (tel. 84 34 52). In addition to *refugio*-style accommodations, it offers mountain biking, guided hikes, horseback riding, archery, and all sorts of field sports.

Take a Hike

You're broke, out of shape, and there's a thickening layer of dirt, city exhaust, and last night's sangría on your forearms, enough so that you can now successfully etch your name with your fingernail in the grime. The Caldea Spa is too communal and any of Andorra's modern indoor sports centers are too modern and indoor. It's time to strap on your hiking boots, fill up the water bottle, grab some sunscreen and take a hike. The melted snow opens up a whole new country—one boasting glacial legacies, navigable peaks, fervent forests, wild meadows, and scenic vistas. Like most everything else in Andorra, few of the routes are far away, and most all can be tackled by even the least seasoned outdoorsman. An extensive system of hiking trails traverses the tiny country, ranging from short and sweet to long and rewarding. Moreover, the sights en route vary greatly as well, from heavenly lakes to lookouts onto Andorra la Vella to humble mountain shacks. Mountain bike enthusiasts can revel in their very own trails which, although less numerous than the corps of hiking routes, nevertheless provide a fresh, natural perspective of Andorra. For more info, contact one of the country's tourist offices (p. 293).

ANDORRA

And then it snows. **Skiing** opportunities heap up in the principality; the five outstanding resorts within its boundaries all rent equipment. **Pal** (tel. 83 62 36), 10km from La Massana, is a biggie. Catch the bus from La Massana at 10am; the return bus leaves Pal at 5pm (250ptas each way). On the French border, **Pas de la Casa** boasts 530 hectares of skiable land, with 42 different trails for all levels of ability. The resort (tel. 82 03 99) provides 27 mechanical lifts, downhill instruction, two medical centers, and **night skiing.** Both cross-country and downhill enthusiasts flock to the slopes of **Soldeu-El Tarter** (tel. 82 11 97), 15km from the French border, between Andorra la Vella and Pas de la Casa. **Free buses** transport skiers from their hotels in Cauillo. The resort packs an 840m vertical punch and includes 12km of cross-country trails. Other, smaller resorts are **Arinsal** (tel. 83 58 22) and **Ordino-Arcalis** (tel. 83 63 20). Andorra's tourist office publishes the rather lyrical *Mountains of Snow*, a guide to all its ski resorts. **SKI Andorra** (tel. 86 43 89) can answer questions.

ANDORRA

Barcelona

Like a Latin prize fighter swaggering into the ring, Barcelona has stepped into the international spotlight and won the world's attention. After the suffocating years of Franco's regime, Barcelona, it seemed, took only a millisecond to reclaim its role as the world's premier showcase of avant-garde architecture. Its triumphant return as host of the 1992 Summer Olympics showed the world that Barcelona was a uniquely forward-moving European city. While Europe's tourist-reliant cities stagnate behind sandblasted facades, busily preserving a past glory for Americans seeking a taste of antiquated cultures, and Spain's coastal cities play the obsequious role for northern Europeans descending upon Spain to dabble in the simpler life, Barcelona has dropped its cultural baggage to embrace contemporaneity. When President of Catalunya Jordi Pujol promoted the games to the international media as the "Catalan Games," his gesture embodied Catalan gentility. *Barcelonenses* consider themselves the privileged class of Spain, and their assertion of this seems driven by the insecurity of being Spain's figurative second capital.

The patriotic sentiment that Pujol asserted was the impetus behind Barcelona's *fin-de-siècle* rise to greatness. During the *febre d'or* (gold fever, 1875-1885), the city's financial moguls led an internal division that socially, politically, and—most visibly—geographically separated the aristocratic class from the proletariat. Josep Marià Jujol, Josep Batlló, Antoni Amatller, and their compatriots commissioned architects like Domènech Montaner, Puig i Cadafalch, and the eminent Antoni Gaudí to build private residences in L'Eixample, a spacious, gridded "upper" Barcelona, higher in elevation and status than the tangled, plebeian Barri Gòtic (Gothic Quarter). The relationship between these businessmen and their architects matured into a coalition where business leaders heavily supported the arts. Their return was *modernisme,* a movement analogous to *art nouveau* that celebrated Catalunya's past and future, incorporating tradition and innovation in a brand new style that pervaded all the arts, but with architecture clearly at the forefront.

The lasting result of this age of *Renaixença* (Renaissance) was the most extravagant display of architecture in the world. On a single block known as the *Manzana de la Discordia* (Block of Discord), works by Cadafalch, Gaudí, and Montaner battle each other for attention. Their color, flamboyance, and heterogeneity assert Barcelona's identity as a 20th-century city. While Paris, New York, and London have been described as *noir* cities, better captured in black and white, Barcelona must be seen in vibrant color.

Barcelona leaves the 20th century as a proud and prosperous middle class city, content as Spain's most powerful region outside Castile. The city's latest architectural triumph, the space-age *Maremagnum* mall, characterizes Barcelona's new age. Its experimental structure, jutting into the water, sustains the city's reputation as *"la ciudad del diseño"* (the city of design). It has a decidedly international flavor, with salsa clubs, Steven Spielberg's restaurant DIVE, and a tourist-heavy clientele. Finally, it stresses a distinct community, a place to meet and to be seen, but still detached, reaching eastward into the Mediterranean and away from Madrid.

Barcelona Tourism, http://www.bcn.es

■ Arrivals and Departures

BY PLANE

All domestic and international flights land at **El Prat de Llobregat** (tel. 478 50 00), 12km southwest of Barcelona. The most convenient way to the Pl. Catalunya (the center of town) or Estació-Sants is by **Aerobus.** (From Pl. Catalunya to the airport

Mon.-Fri. 5:30am-10pm, Sat.-Sun. 6am-10:45pm., every 15min., 40min., 465ptas. From the airport, the bus runs Mon.-Fri. 6am-11pm and Sat.-Sun. 6:30am-10:50pm.)

RENFE trains provide slightly cheaper transportation to and from the airport (every 30min., 20min., 300ptas, Sat.-Sun. 345ptas). The first train to Barcelona leaves at 6:13am and the last at 10:13pm, including stops at **Estació Barcelona-Sants** and **Plaça de Catalunya.** Buy tickets at the red automatic machines. The walkway to the trains is accessible from inside the national terminal. Trains to the airport from Pl. Catalunya and from Estació-Sants run from 6:08am to 10:13pm. Buy tickets to the airport at the "Aeroport" window in Sants (open 5am-11pm); otherwise, wait at the Recorridos Cercanías window or purchase a ticket from one of the ticket machines.

The **bus** offers the only inexpensive late-night service. From the airport to Pl. Espanya, take bus EN, which passes about every hour (daily 6:20am-2:40am), or to the airport from Pl. Espanya (daily 7am-3:15am). The stop at Pl. Espanya is on the corner between Gran Vía de les Corts Catalanes and Av. Reina María Cristina. A **taxi** ride between Barcelona and the airport costs 2000-3500ptas.

Iberia, Pg. Gràcia, 30 (tel. 412 56 67; reservations tel. (902) 400 500). M: Pg. Gràcia. To: Madrid (every hr.); Valencia (3-5 per day); Sevilla (4 per day); Lisbon (3 per day); New York (1 per day); London (3 per day); Paris (6 per day); Rome (2 per day); Geneva (1 per day); and Islas Baleares (18 per day). Students can usually get a 25% discount, except when fares are already reduced.

BY TRAIN

Call **RENFE** for general train info (tel. 490 02 02; international tel. 490 11 22; 7:30am-10:30pm). Tickets can be purchased at either of Barcelona's two stations. To: Madrid (6 per day, 7hr., 5000-7000ptas); Sevilla (4 per day, 12hr., 6400-7300ptas); Valencia (15 per day, 4hr., 3200-3900ptas); Milan (1 per day, 18hr., students 10,500ptas); Zürich (1 per day, 13hr., students 10,500ptas); Paris (3 per day, 11hr., 12,700ptas); and Geneva (2 per day, 23hr., 11,000ptas). Student discounts are usually around 25%.

Estació Barcelona-Sants, Pl. Països Catalans (tel. 490 24 00). M: Sants-Estació. For late arrivals, the N2 Nitbus shuttles to Pl. Catalunya (every 30min., 11pm-5am, 145ptas). To get to the N2, exit Sants to Pl. Joan Peiró, then walk down C. Sant Antoni to Pl. Sants. Cross C. Sants (which cuts through the plaza) to catch the bus. Sants is the main terminal for domestic and international traffic. Open daily 4:30am-12:30am.

Estació França, Av. Marqués de L'Argentera (tel. 490 02 02). M: Barceloneta. To get to Pl. Catalunya, take Metro line L4 heading towards Roquetes and switch to the red line (L1) at Urquinaona in the Feixa Llarga direction; Pl. Catalunya is the next stop. All domestic trains leaving França pass through Sants. França has international services to Milan, Zurich, and France. Open daily 7am-10pm.

Ferrocarrils de la Generalitat de Catalunya (FFCC) (tel. 205 15 15) are commuter trains with main stations at Pl. Catalunya (tel. 317 84 41) and Pl. Espanya (tel. 325 02 27), with service to Montserrat, Sant Cugat, and Tarrassa. A symbol resembling two interlocking Vs marks connections with the Metro. The commuter line charges the same as the Metro until Tibidabo (10-ride Metro pass valid).

BY BUS

Most—but not all—buses arrive at the **Estació del Nord,** C. Ali-bei, 80 (tel. 265 65 08; info open daily 7am-9pm, station open 5:30am-1am). M: Arc de Triomf (exit to Nàpols). Buses offer a cheaper and sometimes more direct mode of travel than trains. The following prices are one-way.

Enatcar, Estació del Nord (tel. 245 25 28). Open daily 6am-1am. To Madrid (5 per day, 8hr., 2690ptas) and Valencia (10 per day, 4½hr., 2690ptas). Also daily service to southern France and Italy.

Linebús, Estació del Nord (tel. 265 07 00). Open Mon.-Sat. 8am-2pm and 3-8pm. 10% discount for travelers under 26. To London (3 per week, July-Aug. 5 per week,

BARCELONA

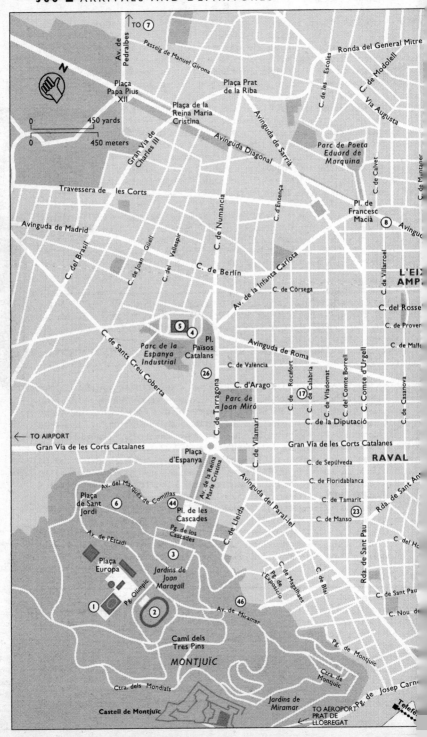

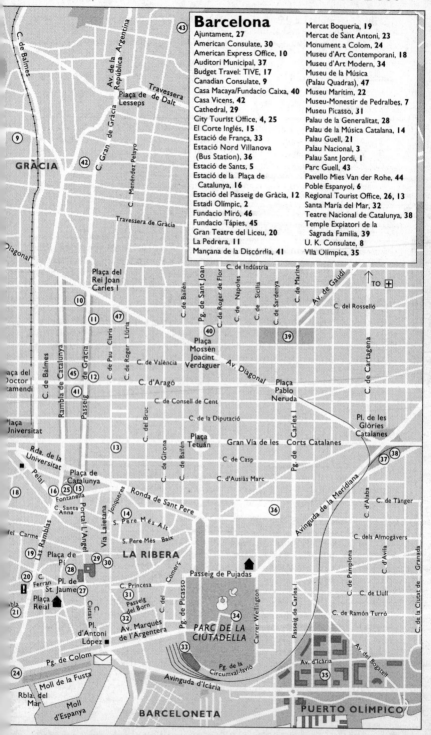

Barcelona

Ajuntament, 27
American Consulate, 30
American Express Office, 10
Auditori Municipal, 37
Budget Travel: TIVE, 17
Canadian Consulate, 9
Casa Macaya/Fundació Caixa, 40
Casa Vicens, 42
Cathedral, 29
City Tourist Office, 4, 25
El Corte Inglés, 15
Estació de França, 33
Estació Nord Villanova
  (Bus Station), 36
Estació de Sants, 5
Estació de la Plaça de
  Catalunya, 16
Estació del Passeig de Gràcia, 12
Estadi Olímpic, 2
Fundació Miró, 46
Fundació Tàpies, 45
Gran Teatre del Liceu, 20
La Pedrera, 11
Mançana de la Discórdia, 41

Mercat Boqueria, 19
Mercat de Sant Antoni, 23
Monument a Colom, 24
Museu d'Art Contemporani, 18
Museu d'Art Modern, 34
Museu de la Música
  (Palau Quadras), 47
Museu Marítim, 22
Museu-Monestir de Pedralbes, 7
Museu Picasso, 31
Palau de la Generalitat, 28
Palau de la Música Catalana, 14
Palau Guell, 21
Palau Nacional, 3
Palau Sant Jordi, 1
Parc Guell, 43
Pavello Mies Van der Rohe, 44
Poble Espanyol, 6
Regional Tourist Office, 26, 13
Santa María del Mar, 32
Teatre Nacional de Catalunya, 38
Temple Expiatori de la
  Sagrada Familia, 39
U. K. Consulate, 8
Vila Olímpica, 35

25hr., 13,450ptas) and Paris (6 per week, 14hr., 11,450ptas). Also has daily service to southern France and Morocco.

Julià Vía, C. Viriato (tel. 490 40 00). M: Estació-Sants. Open daily 8am-8pm. To: Paris (6 per week, 15hr., 11,125ptas); Frankfurt (4 per week, 19hr., 14,550ptas); and Marseille (4 per week, 10hr., 6100ptas). Student discounts.

Sarfa, Estació del Nord (tel. 265 11 58). Buses stop at many beach towns along the Costa Brava, north of Barcelona. Open daily 8am-8:30pm.

BY FERRY

Transmediterránea, Estació Marítima-Moll Barcelona (tel. 443 25 32; fax 443 27 51). M: Drassanes. Open Mon.-Fri. 9am-1:30pm and 4:30-7pm, Sat. 9am-1pm. From the Metro, head down Las Ramblas toward the Monument a Colom, which points toward the Estació Marítima. Cross Ronda Litoral and pass the Aduana building on your left. During the summer boats embark most days between Barcelona and Mallorca (8hr.), Menorca (8hr.), and Ibiza (8hr.). A *butaca,* comparable to an airline seat, is the cheapest option at 6650ptas (off season 5290ptas), but cabins are also priced reasonably. Boats fill up quickly in summer.

BY THUMB AND RIDESHARE

Those who hitch to France often take the Metro to Fabra i Puig, then Av. Meridiana to reach A-7. Those en route to Tarragona and Valencia take bus #7 from Rambla Catalunya on the side Gran Vía side. *Autopista* access lies near here. Hitchhiking on *autopistas* (toll roads, marked by the letter A) is illegal. Hitchhiking is permitted, however, on national highways (marked by N).

Barnastop, C. Sant Ramon, 29 (tel. 443 06 32), on the corner of Nou de Rambla. M: Liceu. Matches drivers with riders and can hook you up with other ride-share associations. Driver gets 3ptas per km in Spain, 4ptas per km outside Spain. 1000ptas commission paid to Barnastop for domestic travel the 1st time you use the service, 1pta per km for all subsequent travel. 2000ptas for 1st-time international travel; 1pta per km for all subsequent travel. Open Tues.-Fri. 11am-2pm and 5-7pm, Sat. noon-2pm. To: Madrid (2800ptas); Paris (7000ptas); Amsterdam (8500ptas); Rome (8000ptas); and Berlin (10,000ptas).

■ Getting Around Barcelona

MAPS

While no map does justice to the streets of the Barri Gòtic, El Corte Inglés's free map, distributed at mobile and stationary info centers, comes closest to meeting the challenge. The newsstands on Las Ramblas offer more detailed, but unwieldy, maps.

METRO AND BUS

Barcelona's extensive public transportation system (tel. 412 00 00 or 010; for disabled transportation tel. 412 44 44) will get you within walking distance of any point in the city quickly and cheaply. *Guía del Transport Públic,* available free at tourist offices, the transport info booth in Pl. Catalunya, and in metro stations, maps out all five of the city's Metro lines and bus routes. Metro and bus rides cost 135ptas. A 10-ride T2 Metro pass is 720ptas; a 10-ride T1 pass, valid for bus and Metro, is 740ptas. A T-DIA card, good for unlimited travel for a day on bus and Metro, is 550ptas. Automatic vending machines and ticket windows sell Metro passes. T1s are available at ticket windows and *estancos* (tobacco stores). Hold on to your ticket or pass until you leave the Metro—riding without a receipt carries a hefty 5000ptas fine. (Metro open Mon.-Thurs. 5am-11pm, Fri.-Sun. 6am-midnight, the day before a holiday 5am-1am, and weekday holidays 6am-11pm. Day buses usually run 5am-10pm and night buses 11pm-5am. Individual routes vary.)

The **Bus Turístic** runs four buses (marked #100) which make 15 stops at points of interest. The whole circuit (28km) takes two hours, but the full day pass (1400ptas, 2 consecutive days 1800ptas) allows you to get on and off as often as you wish. The easiest place to hop on the bus is Pl. Catalunya, in front of El Corte Inglés. Tourist offices have a free pamphlet that displays the bus route and special discounts that accompany the pass. Tickets can be purchased on the bus. Buses run from the end of March through the first week of January.

TAXIS

Taxis are everywhere. A *Libre* sign in the windshield or a lit green light on the roof means they are not occupied, while red means you're out of luck. Cabs can be summoned by phone (tel. 330 03 00, 300 11 00, 358 11 11, or 357 77 55—the last 2 are especially for disabled travelers). The first six minutes or 1.9km cost 285ptas; then 92-107ptas per kilometers, depending on when you ride.

CAR RENTAL

Docar, C. Montnegre, 18 (24hr. tel. 322 90 08; fax 439 81 19). Free delivery and pickup. From 1900ptas per day plus 19ptas per km. Insurance 1100ptas. Open Mon.-Fri. 9am-2pm and 4-8pm, Sat. 9am-2pm.

Tot Car, C. Berlín, 97 (tel. 430 01 98). Free delivery and pickup. 2300ptas per day, 21ptas per km. Insurance 1300ptas per day. Open Mon.-Fri. 8am-8pm, Sat. 9am-1pm.

BICYCLE AND MOPED RENTAL

Biciclot, Sant Joan de Malta, 1 (tel. 307 74 75). M: Clot. Leave through exit Aragó-Meridiera, turn 180 degrees at the top of the steps; take 2nd right, then 2nd left (C. Verned), then 2nd right on to S. J. de Malta. 10-speeds 350ptas per hr., 1400ptas per day. Mountain bikes 565ptas per hr., 2000ptas per day. Multi-day and group rates available. Open Mon.-Fri. 9am-2pm and 5-8pm, Sat. 10am-2pm.

Vanguard Rent a Car, C. Londres, 31 (tel. 439 38 80; fax 410 82 71). Mopeds 3000ptas per day, weekend rate (Fri.-Mon.) 5300ptas, plus 1000ptas insurance. Helmet included. 7% IVA not included.

ORIENTATION

Barcelona's layout is simple to grasp, and best pictured by imagining yourself perched atop Columbus's head at the **Monument a Colom** (on **Passeig de Colom,** which runs parallel to the shore), viewing the city with the Mediterranean at your back. From the harbor, the city slopes gently upward toward the mountains. On most *avingudas* (avenues), keeping this in mind should help you re-orient yourself. From the Columbus monument, **Las Ramblas,** the city's most lively thoroughfare, proceeds away from the harbor. It runs directly to **Plaça de Catalunya,** the city's center, and is divided into five segments: **Rambla de Santa Mónica, Rambla de Caputxins, Rambla de Sant Josep, Rambla de Estudis,** and **Rambla de Canaletas.** To the right (east) of Las Ramblas spans the **Barri Gòtic,** enclosed on the other side by **Vía Laietana. Carrer de Ferran** bisects the Barri Gòtic into north and south halves, beginning at Rambla de Caputxins and finishing at Vía Laietana, passing the **Plaça Reial** and **Plaça de Sant Jaume I,** site of the Ajuntament. Beyond Vía Laietana (farther east) lies the labyrinthine neighborhood **Ribera,** which borders **Parc de la Ciutadella** and the **Estació de França** train station. Beyond Parc de la Ciutadella (eastward still) is the **Vila Olímpica,** with its twin towers (the tallest buildings in Barcelona) and a shiny assortment of malls, discos, and hotels.

On the west side (left, with your back to the sea) of Las Ramblas is **Barri Xinès** (Barrio Chino), now officially called **El Raval.** The southern half of El Raval composes Barcelona's shrinking red-light district. In the background (farther west) rises **Montjuïc,** a picturesque hill crammed with gardens, museums (including the Fundació Miró), the '92 Olympic grounds, castles, and other tourist attractions.

L'Eixample, the gridded neighborhood created during *fin de siècle* urban expansion, fans outward from Pl. Catalunya toward the mountains. **Gran Vía de les Corts Catalanes** defines its lower edge and **Passeig de Gràcia,** the Eixample's commercial center, bisects the neighborhood. **Avinguda Diagonal** marks the oblique upper limit of the grid-planned neighborhoods, separating the Eixample from **Gràcia,** an older neighborhood in the foothills. The peak of **Tibidabo,** the northwest border of the city and the highest point in Barcelona, offers the most comprehensive view of the city.

Barcelona is fairly safe, even at night, but secure your valuables in your lap while sitting in an outdoor cafe, doing anything in the Plaça Reial, watching street shows on Las Ramblas, or wandering through the narrow streets of the Barri Gòtic. The deeper into El Raval you venture, the more unsafe it becomes. Pick-pocketers roam by day, and it can be spooky at night. Most areas with active nightlife (see p. 324) are well-patrolled, well-lit, and for the most part, safe.

■ Practical Information

Tourist Info: For general city info call 010 (110ptas charge); for destination info call tel. 412 00 00; for tourist info call tel. 412 20 01. The brand-new **Centre D'Informaciá,** Pl. Catalunya (tel. 304 31 34; fax 304 31 55), provides multilingual advice and a slew of maps, pamphlets, and guides. Hotel info and **currency exchange** also available. **Cultural events** materials are dispensed at Palau de la Virreina, Las Ramblas, 99 (tel. 301 77 75), between La Boqueria market and C. Carme (M: Liceu). Open Mon.-Sat. 10am-2pm and 4-8pm. More cultural information, including Barcelona's monthly cultural magazine in English, *Metropolitan,* is available across the street at the professional and knowledgable Centro de Informació Cultural, Las Ramblas, 118 (tel. 302 15 22 ext. 266; open Mon.-Fri. 10am-2pm and 4-8pm, Sat. 10am-2pm). **Mobile info offices** can be found at Pl. Catalunya by the Monument a Colom, and La Sagrada Familia March-June 24 10am-8pm, and are all over the place June 25-Sept. 9am-9pm. Open daily 9am-9pm. **Estació Central de Barcelona-Sants,** Pl. Països Catalans (tel. 491 44 31). M: Sants-Estació. Friendly Ajuntament staff. City-specific info only. Open in summer daily 8am-8pm; in winter Mon.-Fri. 8am-8pm, Sat.-Sun. 8am-2pm. **Aeroport El Prat de Llobregat,** International Terminal (tel. 478 47 04 or 478 0565), 25m to the left of the customs exit. Also in the departure terminal. Administered by the Generalitat de Catalunya, covers Barcelona, Catalunya, and the rest of Spain. Open Mon.-Sat. 9:30am-8:30pm, Sun. 9:30am-3pm. **Gran Vía de les Corts Catalanes,** 658 (tel. 301 74 43). M: Urquinaona or Pl. Catalunya. Two blocks from the intersection with Pg. Gràcia, in the Eixample, a few doors before the Ritz Hotel. Also run by the Generalitat. Open Mon.-Fri. 9am-7pm, Sat. 9am-2pm. **Turisme de Barcelona,** C. Tarragona 749 (tel. 423 18 00). M: Tarragona. Open Mon.-Thurs. 9am-2:30pm and 4-7pm, Fri. 9am-3pm.

Budget Travel Offices: Wasteels, Pl. Catalunya-Estació RENFE (tel. 301 18 81; fax 301 18 53). M: Catalunya. In the Metro/RENFE terminal. Enter the Metro in front of El Corte Inglés. Air and train discounts for students. Open Mon.-Fri. 8:30am-8:30pm, Sat. 10am-1pm. Visa, MC. **Unlimited Student Travel,** C. Rocafort, 116-122 (tel. 483 83 78). M: Rocafort. Two blocks from the Metro. A full-fledged travel agency overflowing with clients during the summer (expect a long wait). Open Mon.-Fri. 10am-8pm, Sat. 10am-1:30pm. **Centre d'Informació: Assesorament per a Joves,** C. Ferrán, 32 (tel. 402 78 01 or 402 78 00). More of a local student assistance office than a travel agency. No tickets for sale, but plenty of free advice and a bulletin board with youth events. Excellent library of travel guides, including *Let's Go.* Open Mon.-Fri. 10am-2pm and 4-8pm.

Consulates: See **Spain: Essentials: Embassies and Consulates,** p. 36.

Currency Exchange: The best rates can be obtained at the **banks.** General banking hours Mon.-Fri. 8:30am-2pm. **Banco Central Hispano,** Las Ramblas at C. Boqueria, is best for AmEx Traveler's Check exchange. **El Corte Inglés** and **Banco de Espanya** (tel. 453 37 18), both in Pl. Catalunya, and the **American Express** office (see below) charge no commission and have no min. on traveler's checks. On Sun. you can change money at **Estació de Sants** (tel. 490 77 70) for no commission. Open daily 8am-10pm.

El Corte Inglés: Pl. Catalunya (tel. 302 12 12) and Av. Diagonal, 617 (tel. 419 52 06). Department store behemoth with a good **map,** novels and guidebooks in English, haircutting, rooftop cafeteria, grocery store, package delivery, **travel agency, currency exchange,** and **telephones.** Open Mon.-Sat. 10am-9pm.

American Express: Pg. Gràcia, 101 (tel. 415 23 71; 24hr. tel. (91) 572 03 03; fax 415 37 00). M: Diagonal. The entrance is on C. Rosselló, around the corner from this address. Mail held 1 month free for cardholders. Open Mon.-Fri. 9:30am-6pm, Sat. 10am-noon. 24hr. **ATM** outside.

Luggage Storage: Estació Sants (M: Sants-Estació). Small lockers 400ptas, large 600ptas (open 6:30am-11pm). **Estació França** (M: Barceloneta), small lockers 300ptas, large 500ptas (open 7am-10pm). **Estació del Nord** (M: Arc de Triomf), lockers 300-600ptas (open 24hr.).

Lost Property: Objets Perduts, C. Ciutat, 9 (tel. 402 31 61), on the ground floor of the Ajuntament, Pl. Sant Jaume. M: Jaume I. Open Mon.-Fri. 9am-2:30pm.

Laundromat: Tintoreria San Pablo, C. San Pau, 105 (tel. 329 42 49). Wash, dry, and fold 1600ptas, do-it-yourself for 1200ptas. Open Mon.-Fri. 9am-1pm and 4-8pm.

Library: Institut d'Estudis Norteamericans, Vía Augusta, 123 (tel. 209 27 11). Open Sept.-July Mon.-Fri. 11am-2pm and 4-7pm. **Biblioteca Central,** C. Hospital, 57 (tel. 317 07 78), next to Hospital de Santa Creu, off Las Ramblas. Open Mon.-Fri. 9am-8pm, Sat. 9am-2pm. Closed for 3 weeks in Sept.

English Bookstore: see **Shopping,** p. 329.

Newspapers: El Periódico and **La Vanguardia** are Catalunya's leading dailies. The hip *El Periódico* leans to the left (http://www.elperiodico.es). The moderate-conservative *La Vanguardia,* founded in 1881, is more popular. Both are 125ptas.

Foreign Periodicals: Try the newsstands along Las Ramblas and Pg. Gràcia.

Women's Services: Librería de Dones Prolég, C. Dagueria, 13 (tel. 319 24 25). M: Jaume I. Women's bookstore stocks a large feminist collection with new and used books in English, French, and German. Notice board and info on workshops and seminars. Open Sept.-July Mon. 5-8pm, Tues.-Fri. 10am-2pm and 5-8pm, Sat. 11am-2pm and 5-8pm; Aug. Mon.-Fri. 5-9pm.

Gay and Lesbian Services: Coordinadora Gay Lesbiana, C. Les Carolines, 13 (tel. 237 08 69; toll-free (900) 601 601, available 6-10pm). **Cómplices,** C. Cervantes, 2 (tel. 412 72 83). M: Liceu. From C. Ferrán, take C. Avinyó, then 2nd left. A gay and lesbian bookstore with publications in English and Spanish and a map of gay and lesbian bars and discos. Open Mon.-Fri. 10:30am-8:30pm, Sat. noon-8:30pm.

Religious Services: Jewish services, Sinagoga de la Comunidad Judía, C. Avenir, 24 (tel. 200 85 13; fax 200 61 48). Services daily at 7:30am. **Muslim services,** Comunidad Musulmana, Mezquita Toarek Ben Ziad, C. Hospital, 91 (tel. 441 91 49). Open daily until 10pm.

Crisis Services: Oficina Permanente de Atención Social (24hr. toll-free tel. (900) 30 90 30). **STD treatment:** Av. Drassanes, 17-21 (hotline tel. 441 29 97). **Associación Ciutadana Anti-SIDA de Catalunya** (AIDS info), C. Tantarantana, 4 (tel. 317 05 05; open Mon.-Fri. 10am-2pm and 4-8pm). **Fundación Anti-SIDA Espaya** (national AIDS hotline toll-free tel. (900) 111 000).

Late-Night Pharmacy: Pharmacies open late on rotating basis. Check pharmacy windows for current listings.

Hospitals: Hospital Clínic, Villarroel, 170 (tel. 454 60 00 or 454 70 00). M: Hospital Clínic. Main entrance at intersection of C. Roselló and C. Casanova. **Hospital de la Santa Creu i Sant Pau** (tel. 291 90 00; emergency tel. 291 91 91), at intersection of C. Cartagena and C. Sant Antoni Moria Claret. M: Hospital de Sant Pau. **Médicos de Urgencia,** C. Pelai, 40 (tel. 412 12 12). M: Catalunya. Dial 061 for **ambulance.**

Emergency: tel. 092 or 091.

Police: Las Ramblas, 43 (tel. 301 90 60), across from Pl. Reial and next to C. Nou de La Rambla. M: Liceu. Multilingual officers.

Internet Access: El Cafe de Internet (see **Restaurants: Eixample,** p. 314)

Post Office: Pl. Antoni López (tel. 318 38 31), at the end of Vía Laietana, portside. M: Jaume I or Barceloneta. Open for stamps Mon.-Fri. 8am-10pm, Sat. 8am-2pm; Lista de Correos Mon.-Fri. 8am-9pm, Sat. 9am-2pm. Most neighborhoods have branch offices; there is a central branch at Pl. Urquinaona, 6 (tel. 301 56 27). M: Urquinaona. Open Mon.-Fri. 8:30am-2:30pm, Sat. 9:30am-1pm. **Postal Code:** 08002.

BARCELONA

Telephones: Private phone service at Estació Sants (tel./fax 490 76 50). M: Sants-Estació. **Faxes** received and sent (1st page 250ptas, each additional page 100ptas). Open 9am-10:15pm. For **directory assistance,** dial 003. **Telephone Code:** (9)3.

■ Accommodations and Camping

Although *hostales* and *pensiones* abound, visitors may end up scrambling in July and August when tourists flood every corner of the city. Room quality varies tremendously—your nighttime refuge could be a paper-thin mattress situated over a rowdy all-night restaurant or a ritzy, antique-filled room with a view.

YOUTH HOSTELS

Barcelona's *albergues* offer lodging staples (bed, shower, bath) at the lowest prices. *Let's Go* urges you to check out a room before signing your night away.

Albergue de Juventud Kabul, Pl. Reial, 17 (tel. 318 51 90). M: Liceu. As you head to the port on Las Ramblas, turn left on Pl. Reial after C. Ferrán. Kabul is on the near right corner of the *plaça*. Renowned for its social atmosphere, helpful staff, and beer vending machines, Kabul has earned a spot in Eurail lore. Satellite TV, music, and a pool table create an almost raucous environment. Those looking for sobriety might consider lodging elsewhere. A mobile police unit keeps the area relatively safe, but still use caution at night. Multilingual receptionist (24hr.). Shower heads are like elevated sink spouts. New kitchen should be ready by 1998. 1500ptas per person with a 1000ptas key deposit. Free lockers; safe deposit boxes 25-50ptas per day with 1000ptas key deposit. Sheets 200ptas. 4.5kg laundry 800ptas.

Albergue Juvenil Palau (HI), C. Palau, 6 (tel. 412 50 80). M: Jaume I. One block from Pl. Sant Jaume. Take C. Ciutat to C. Templaris, then take the 2nd left. A small, tranquil refuge in the heart of the Barri Gòtic. Offers full kitchen (open 7am-10pm) and dining salon where you can meet fellow backpackers, read a complimentary magazine, or watch the tube. 2-8 people per room. 1300ptas per bed in barracks-style rooms, breakfast included. Showers available 8-11am and 4-10pm. Winter heating. Sheets 150ptas. Flexible 5-day max. stay. Reservations with a night's deposit. Reception open 7am-3am. 3am curfew. Same-day reservations accepted.

Albergue Mare de Déu de Montserrat (HI), Pg. Mare de Déu del Coll, 41-51 (tel. 210 51 51), beyond Park Güell. Bus #28 from Pl. Catalunya stops across the street from the hostel, as does night bus N-4. Otherwise, from M: Vallcarca, walk up Av. República Argentina and across C. Viaducte de Vallcarca; signs point the way up the hill. This government-sponsored villa has its own private woods and a hilltop view of Barcelona. HI members only. 5 day max. stay. 1800ptas per person, over 25 2275ptas; breakfast included. Lunch and dinner 750ptas each. Sheets 350ptas. Reception open 8-9:30am, 5-7:30pm, and 8:30-10pm. Bedrooms closed 10am-2:pm for cleaning. No showering 10am-2pm. Move-in 5pm. Midnight curfew, but doors open every ½hr. from midnight-3am. Handicap accessible. Reservations accepted. Reception offers information on Catalunya's hostels.

Hostal De Joves Municipal (HI), Pg. Pujades, 29 (tel./fax 300 31 04). M: Arc de Triomf. From Metro, exit to C. Nápols, walk toward Parc de la Ciutadella, and turn left on Pg. Pujades. Warm, skillful staff guides you through the city. Full kitchen, dining hall, and hot showers. 5-day max. stay. 2-6 people per room at 1500ptas a head, breakfast included. Sheets 225ptas. Reception open 7am-midnight. Hostel closed 10am-3pm. Laundry (500ptas wash, 700ptas dry).

CIUTAT VELLA

The neighborhood **Barri Gòtic** spans eastward from **Las Ramblas,** and **El Raval** spans westward. The three zones, along with La Ribera to the east of the Barri Gòtic, are collectively known as the *ciutat vella* (old city). The entire zone offers a wealth of budget accommodations, although not enough to house everyone in July and August, so call ahead. Police patrol the area, but remember to watch your belongings on and

near Las Ramblas. If you are in dire straits, check Las Ramblas or C. Boqueria, but expect to pay more for less.

Lower Ciutat Vella

The following hostels are located in the southern areas of El Raval and the Barri Gòtic, below C. Portaferrissa in the Barri Gòtic, and below C. Fortuny in El Raval. They are "lower" in elevation than the Upper Ciutat Vella, and generally lower in price, but their interiors are not necessarily lower in quality. Like the hostels directly on las Ramblas, these streets can be spooky at night for solo travelers.

Hotel Call, Arco San Ramón del Call, 4 (tel. 302 11 23; fax 301 34 86). M: Liceu. On the right of Las Ramblas facing away from the water is a mini-plaza called Llano de la Boqueria. C. Boqueria enters the Barri Gòtic from the Llano. Take C. Boqueria to its end, veering left onto C. Call; the *hostal* is on the first corner on the left up C. Call. Perfect spot for the weary wayfarer craving hotel amenities. Phone and bathroom in every room. A/C. Singles 3200ptas. Doubles 4500ptas. Triples 5700ptas. Quads 6400ptas. Winter heating. Visa, MC. Call for reservations. 24hr. reception.

Pensión Fernando, C. Ferrán, 31 (tel. 301 79 93). M: Liceu. From Las Ramblas, take the 4th left off C. Ferrán. One of the best deals in the Barri Gòtic. Recent renovations have completely transformed the appearance (but not the price) of this *pensión.* Further renovations (expected to be completed end of '97) will include an elevator and a living room. Winter heating. Groups share larger rooms. Many rooms have bunk beds. 1300ptas per person, 1500ptas in room with shower.

Pensión Francia, C. Rera Palau, 4 (tel. 319 03 76). From Estació de França, cross the main avenue (Pg. Colom) and go left; C. Reva Palau is the 5th right, just one block toward the Colón Monument. A diamond in the rough, Francia is located on a pedestrian-only block near Museu Picasso and the port, but a bit off from Las Ramblas. Brand new wooden furniture, and a mini-library of English books. They'll even lend you a TV. Winter heating. Singles 1400ptas. Doubles 2500ptas, with shower 3100ptas, with bath 4600ptas. Triples with shower 3600ptas. Quads with shower 4300ptas. Breakfast 275ptas. Credit cards accepted. Keys for 24hr. entry.

Hostal Levante, Baixada de San Miguel, 2 (tel. 317 95 65). M: Liceu. Walk down C. Ferrán and turn right on C. Avinyó; Baixada de San Miguel is the first left. Ignore the shabby entrance—an oasis awaits inside. Handsome wood interior, large noise-proof windows, excellent ventilation, TV lounge, and knowledgeable owner. Safe available 7am-10pm, 24hr. reception, and winter heating. Singles 2500ptas. Doubles 4000ptas, with bath 5000ptas. Reservations encouraged July-Aug.

Hostal Residencia Rembrandt, C. Portaferrisa, 23 (tel./fax 318 10 11). M: Liceu. As you walk up Las Ramblas (away from the Mediterranean), Puertaferrisa is on your right. Clean *hostal* with large windows looking out onto the streets or one of the three charming patios. Singles 2700ptas. Doubles 4000ptas, with shower 4500ptas, with bath 5500ptas. Breakfast 350ptas.

Casa de Huéspedes Mari-Luz, C. Palau, 4 (tel. 317 34 63). M: Jaume I or Liceu. One block from Pl. Sant Jaume. Take C. Ciutat to C. Templaris, then take the 2nd left. After dark it is safer not to approach via C. Escudellers. Narrow hallways flanked by basic, barracks-style bedrooms for 2-8 inhabitants. Keys for 24hr. entry, winter heating, and kitchen use with permission. Owner posts maps and fliers for bike tours. *Guía del Ocio* is available for browsing. 1300ptas per person, 1500ptas in rooms with private showers. Laundry 800ptas per load. Reservations accepted.

Hostal Malda, C. Pí, 5 (tel. 317 30 02). M: Liceu. Take C. Portaferrisa (on the right with your back to the sea) from Las Ramblas. C. Pí is your fourth right. *Hostal* is directly above the Cine Malda. Offers simple rooms and a dining room with travel library. Singles 1300ptas. Doubles 2500ptas. Triples 3400ptas.

Hotel Rey Don Jaime I, C. Jaume I, 11 (tel. 310 62 38). M: Jaume I. Every room has a bathroom and telephone, every bed a double mattress, and every luxury a price. Winter heating and 24hr. reception with multilingual staff. Singles 3900ptas. Doubles 5700ptas. Triples 6700ptas. Visa, MC.

Pensión Bienestar, C. Quintana, 3 (tel. 318 72 83). M: Liceu. Two blocks from Las Ramblas, off C. Ferrán, with a quiet location on a pedestrian-only street. The 27 rooms may be dark, but high ceilings and freshly painted walls brighten them up.

Cheery central patio is practically a botanical garden. Bathrooms vary from elephantine to claustrophobic. Be prepared for ramshackle beds. Singles 1500ptas. Doubles 2600ptas. Triples 3900ptas.

Hostal Marítima, Las Ramblas, 4 (tel. 302 31 52). M: Drassanes. At port end of Las Ramblas; follow the signs to *Museo de Cera,* which is next door. Prime location, but a mix of street noise and intercom music clutter the airways in some spots. Bathrooms leave a bit to be desired. No heat. Singles 1500ptas. Doubles 2600ptas, with shower 3000ptas. Triples 3900ptas, with shower 4500ptas. Sketchy showers. Laundry 800ptas. 24hr. reception and security monitor.

Pensión Aviñó 42, C. Avinyó, 42 (tel. 318 79 45; fax 318 68 93). M: Drassanes. Curious reception area decor may include a framed glossy of your very own bedroom. Renovations (expected to be completed by end of '97) are giving rooms much-needed face lifts. Few singles, so arrive early. Public phones. Singles 1500ptas. Doubles 2400ptas, with shower 3000ptas. Triples 3300ptas, with bath 4200ptas. Winter heating. Prices vary according to length of stay and time of year. Visa.

Hostal Layetana, Pl. Ramón Berenguer el Gran, 2 (tel. 319 20 12). M: Jaume I. Less than a block from the Metro, on your left as you walk away from the ocean. Balconies open to contrasting scenes: the sectarian vista of the cathedral on one side and the vanity view of the fashionable plaza on the other. Luxurious living room with terrace. Singles 2300ptas. Doubles 3700ptas, with bath 5200ptas. Exterior shower 200ptas each. Reservations recommended July-Aug. Visa, MC.

Hostal Residencia Romay, C. Avinyó, 58 (tel. 317 94 14). M: Drassanes. Heading towards the seafront on Las Ramblas, turn left onto C. Josep Anselm Clavé; C. Avinyó lies on the left after the church, above Pensión Albi. A marble reception area gives way to simple rooms. Keys for 24hr. entry. Singles 1500ptas, with shower 2000ptas. Doubles 2000ptas, with bath 2500ptas. Owner promises discount with *Let's Go*.

Pensión Nogaró, C. Cervantes, 2 (tel. 318 81 48). M: Liceu. Take C. Ferrán to C. Avinyó, then the 2nd left. Small, one-man operation in the thick of the Gothic Quarter. Freshly painted hallways lead to dark rooms. One shower for nine rooms. Keys for 24hr. entry. No heat. Singles 1300ptas. Doubles 2500ptas.

Hostal Terrassa, Junta de Comerç, 11 (tel. 302 51 74; fax 301 21 88). Descending Las Ramblas, turn right on C. Hospital, then turn left after Teatre Romea. M: Liceu. Lots of rooms. Social courtyard. Winter heating. Arrive early or call ahead during summer and holidays. Singles 2000ptas, with shower 2500ptas. Doubles: 3400ptas; 4000ptas. Triples: 4400ptas; 5000ptas. Credit cards accepted.

Upper Ciutat Vella

This subdivision includes the area south of Pl. Catalunya, bounded by C. Fontanella to the north and C. Portaferrisa to the south, and enclosed by Las Ramblas to the west and Vía Laietana to the east. Portal de L'Angel is a broad pedestrian jugular running through the middle, southward from Pl. Catalunya. A bit pricier than the hostels in the Lower Ciutat Vella, accommodations here are safe, more modern, and just a skip from Las Ramblas. The nearest Metro stop is Pl. Catalunya unless otherwise specified. Reservations are almost obligatory in July and August.

Hostal Fontanella, Vía Laietana, 71 (tel./fax 317 59 43). Go 3 blocks past El Corte Inglés and hang a right. Refined owner maintains decor with soft lights, floral bouquets, lace curtains, and logo-endowed towels. Excellent beds and baths. Singles 2700ptas, with bath 3500ptas. Doubles: 4800ptas; 5900ptas. Reservations with deposit. Visa, MC, AmEx.

Residencia Australia, Ronda Universitat, 11 (tel. 317 41 77). María, the gregarious English-speaking owner, shows she cares with embroidered sheets and curtains, a spotless bathroom, ceiling fans in rooms, and winter heating. Singles 2600ptas. Doubles 3800ptas, with bath 4600ptas. Prices do not include 7% IVA.

Hostal Residencia Lausanne, Av. Portal de L'Angel, 24 (tel. 302 11 39). Restful *hostal* lives up to the building's imperial facade and entryway. Front balcony overlooks a shopping promenade and the rear terrace, a golden sanctuary. Couches and chairs in many rooms, new wallpaper, renovated baths, and a TV lounge showing

fútbol. Winter heating. Singles 2000ptas. Doubles 3000ptas, with shower 4500ptas. Triples with shower 5000ptas, with bath 6000ptas.

Hotel Toledano (Hostal Residencia Capitol), Las Ramblas, 138 (tel. 301 08 72; fax 412 31 42). As you face Las Ramblas from Pl. Catalunya, it's 50m farther on the left. This family owned, split-level hotel/*hostal* has been making tourists happy for 78 years. Rooms with cable TV, private phone, and balcony. Reception has leather couches and an English-speaking owner. Keys for 24hr. entry. 24hr. reception. Singles 2900ptas. Doubles 4600ptas, with shower 5200ptas. Triples: 5900ptas; 6500ptas. Quads: 6800ptas; 7400ptas. Quints 7000ptas; 7600ptas. Prices are for *hostal* only and don't include 7% IVA. Reservations, credit cards accepted.

Pensión Nevada, Av. Portal de L'Angel, 16 (tel. 302 31 01), just past Hostal Residencia Lausanne. Your cozy bedroom away from home, complete with matching throw pillows, firm beds, comfortable chairs, and flowers on the balcony. Knick-knacks simulate Little Bo Peep's bedroom. TV in common room. No heat. Keys for 24hr. entry. Singles 3500ptas. Doubles 5200ptas. Come early or make reservations.

Residencia Victoria, C. Comtal, 9 (tel. 317 45 97). From Pl. Catalunya, take the first left on Av. Portal de L'Angel. New owners are working to restore Victoria to a more queenly condition. Kitchen, TV, washer (100ptas), and open-air dining room. Singles 2000ptas. Doubles 4000ptas.

Pensión Santa Anna, C. Santa Ana, 23 (tel. 301 22 46). From the green line, take the Las Ramblas exit and then your 1st left onto C. Santa Anna heading toward the water. From the red line, take Pg. Gràcia exit, descend Gràcia past El Corte Inglés (on your left), cross C. Fontanella onto Portal de L'Angel, and take the 1st right on C. Santa Anna. What this place lacks in size and ambience it makes up for with clean bathrooms and the great eateries around the *pensión.* Singles 2500ptas. Doubles 4000ptas, with bath 5000ptas. Triples 5000ptas. Visa, MC.

Pensión Noya, Las Ramblas, 133 (tel. 301 48 31). Above the noisy restaurant Nuria. This 10-room retreat welcomes backpackers with open arms but no heat and cramped bathrooms (hot water 8am-midnight). Singles 1700ptas. Doubles 5200ptas. Triples 4500ptas. Reservations accepted.

Pensión L'Isard, C. Tallers, 82 (tel. 302 51 83), near MACBA, the new contemporary art museum. M: Universitat. Take Pelai exit from the metro, go left at the end of the block, then immediately left at the pharmacy. Relaxing rooms with balconies and new mattresses. Multilingual staff. Keys for 24hr. entry. Singles 2000ptas. Doubles 3700ptas, with bath 4700ptas. Triples 4800ptas. Reservations with deposit.

Pensión Arosa, Av. Puerta del Angel, 14 (tel. 317 36 87), next to Pensión Nevada. The pinkest pensión in Barcelona. Rooms are airy and clean. Singles 2200ptas. Doubles 4500 with shower. Triples 5400ptas with shower. Visa, MC.

Pensión Estal, C. Santa Anna, 27 (tel. 302 26 18), near Pensión Santa Anna. Rooms offer views of Iglesia de Santa Ana. French-speaking owner takes great pride in his establishment and happy customers attest to its merits. Singles 2200ptas. Doubles 3200ptas, with bath 4500ptas.

Pensión Aris, C. Fontanella, 14 (tel. 318 10 17), 2 blocks past Telefónica on the right. Huge, clean rooms furnished with little more than beds. Space-age windows shut out all sound. Like a big kitchen, with bright lights and quadratic floor tiling. Singles 2500ptas. Doubles 4000ptas, with bath 5000ptas. Triples: 5000ptas; 6000ptas. Open 24hr. Laundry 500-1000ptas.

Hostal Plaza, C. Fontanella, 18 (tel./fax 301 01 39), down the street from Pensión Aris. Texan couple welcomes traveling students. Eighteen rooms with American art and 3-speed fans. Public phone, fax, and TV room with music. Gets you discounts at local restaurants and discos. Singles with shower 3000ptas, with bath 3500ptas. Doubles: 4500ptas; 5000ptas. Triples: 6000ptas; 7000ptas. 5kg laundry 1000ptas. Prices may fluctuate. Room and bathroom quality vary considerably. Reservations recommended.Visa, MC, AmEx.

L'EIXAMPLE

The most beautiful *hostales* are found here along wide, safe *avingudas.* Most buildings have colorfully tiled interiors and boast large entryways with *modernista* elevators styled with wood and steel. Rooms often have high ceilings, plenty of light, and small *balcones.*

Hostal Residencia Oliva, Pg. Gràcia, 32, 4th fl. (tel. 488 01 62 or 488 17 89), on the intersection of C. Disputació. M: Pg. Gràcia. The Aerobus drops you off in the lap of luxury. Some balconies overlook the *manzana de discordia* (see p. 319). Watch Puig, Domènech, and Gaudí compete for aesthetic prominence. Posh woodwork distinguishes bureaus, bed frames, and mirrors. Funky elevator and catwalk over the central patio make leaving and returning an adventure in *modernisme*. Winter heating. Some doubles are cramped. Singles 3000ptas. Doubles 5500ptas, with bath 6500ptas.

Hostal Residencia Windsor, Rambla Catalunya, 84 (tel. 215 11 98), near the intersection of C. Mallorca. M: Pg. Gràcia. Aristocratic *hostal* lives up to its name with crimson carpets, palatial quarters, and prices to match. Expected renovations should make this Anglo-Saxon abode even more charming in '98. Winter heating. Laundry 600ptas. Singles 3300ptas, with bath 4100ptas. Doubles: 5700ptas; 6800ptas. Prices do not include 7% IVA.

Hostal Girona, Girona, 24, 1st floor (tel. 265 02 59). Located between C. Casp and C. Ausias Marc. M: Urquinaona. Carpeted hallways, large wooden doors, and affordable prices are Girona's comforts. It's directly above a branch of the University, so expect interaction with Catalan students on the street. Winter heating. Singles 2000ptas. Doubles with shower 4500ptas, with bath 5000ptas. Breakfast 200ptas.

Hostal Residencia Palacios, Gran Vía de les Corts Catalanes, 629bis (tel./fax 301 37 92), across from the tourist office. M: Catalunya or Urquinaona. Rooms are well-furnished. Winter heating. Singles 2700ptas, with shower 3500ptas, with bath 3750ptas. Doubles: 4000ptas; 4950ptas; 5250ptas. Breakfast 350ptas. Laundry 1000ptas. Reservations, credit cards accepted. Prices do not include 7% IVA.

GRÀCIA

In Gràcia, an area five to ten minutes on foot from M: Diagonal, locals outnumber travelers. Berlitz Spanish won't help in this quiet Catalan-dominated area. The accommodations listed here are small and well-kept. Quaint neighborhood bars and *pastelerías* remain "undiscovered."

Pensión San Medín, C. Gran de Gràcia, 125 (tel. 217 30 68; fax 415 44 10). M: Fontana. Delicately embroidered curtains and paintings of fox hunts adorn this family-run *pensión*. Each renovated room has new furniture and a phone. Singles 2500ptas, with bath 3500ptas. Doubles: 4500ptas; 5600ptas. Breakfast 250ptas. Winter heating. Visa, MC.

Hostal Bonavista, C. Bonavista, 21 (tel. 237 37 57). M: Diagonal. Walk toward the fountain at the end of Pg. Gràcia and make your first right; *hostal* is just off the traffic circle. Well-kept rooms with pictures of horses and their successors (old-fashioned cars). Keys for 24hr. entry. Singles 2200ptas. Doubles 3300ptas, with bath 4300ptas. Showers 300ptas.

Pensión Norma, C. Gran de Gràcia, 87 (tel. 237 44 78). M: Fontana. Rooms with life-size dressers and tables, fully approved by Mr. Clean. Arched windows and an outdoor WC provide plenty of light and air. Singles 2000ptas. Doubles 3000ptas, with bath 4000ptas.

CAMPING

Although there is no camping in Barcelona, inter-city buses (190ptas) run to all the following locations in 20-45 minutes. Campsites are classified according to size and the number of services offered. For further information, contact the **Associació de Càmpings de Barcelona,** Gran Vía Corts Catalanes, 608 (tel. 412 59 55).

El Toro Bravo (tel. 637 34 62), 11km south of Barcelona, accessible by bus L95 and L94 (summer only) from Pl. Catalunya or Pl. Espanya. Laundry and supermarket. 650ptas per person, 450ptas per child, 700ptas per tent. Reception open 8am-1:30pm and 4:30-8pm. Open year-round. 7% IVA not included. Visa, MC, AmEx.

Filipinas (tel. 658 28 95), 1km down the road from El Toro Bravo, accessible by bus L95. 650ptas per person, 450ptas per child, 700ptas per tent. 24hr. reception. Open all year. Visa, MC, AmEx.

La Ballena Alegre (tel. 658 05 04), 1km from El Toro Bravo, accessible by buses L95 and L94 (summer only). 545ptas per person, 260ptas per child, 1375ptas per tent (without car). 24hr. reception. Open March-Nov. Credit cards accepted.

Gavá, 15km south of Barcelona, has several campgrounds accessible by bus 95 from Pl. Universitat. **Albatros** (tel. 633 06 95) costs 520ptas per person, 380ptas per child, and 795ptas per tent. Reception open 8am-midnight. Camping May-Sept. Services for the disabled. **Tortuga Ligera** (tel. 633 06 42) costs 525ptas per person, 420ptas per child, and 630ptas per tent. Reception open 9am-10pm. Open year-round. Both sites are near the Tortuga Ligera bus stop. **Tres Estrellas** (tel. 633 06 37) is one stop past Ballena Alegre. 540ptas per person, 430ptas per child, and 690ptas per tent. 24hr reception. Open year-round. Services for the disabled.

■ Food

For the cheapest meals, be on the lookout for 850-950ptas *menús* posted in the restaurants in the Barri Gòtic. Small, family owned eateries serve basic but satisfying dishes. Closer to the port, bars and cafes get more crowded and harried, whereas on Rbla. Catalunya leisurely *al fresco* meals are a good excuse for people-watching. Be aware that food options shrink drastically in August, when restauranteurs and bar owners close up shop and take their vacations.

Consult the weekly *Guía del Ocio* (available at most newsstands, 125ptas) for dining options beyond those listed here. The *Guía* provides mini-reviews and listings by specialty for hundreds of restaurants, and includes sections on *servicio a domicilio* (delivery), *para llevar* (take-out), *abiertos en domingo* (restaurants open on Sun.), and *cenar de madrugada* (late-night dining). Catalan specialities include *mariluz a la romana* (white fish in tomato sauce), *butifarra con judías blancas* (sausage with white beans), and *crema catalana* (Catalan pudding).

Groceries: La Boqueria, officially Mercat de Sant Josep, off Rambla Sant Josep, 89, is Barcelona's best market, with fresh fish and produce in an all-steel modernist structure. Enough spices to have precluded Columbus's illustrious blunder (open Mon.-Sat. 7am-8pm). Supermarket **Simago,** Rambla des Estudis, 113, stocks essentials (open Mon.-Sat. 9am-9pm).

CIUTAT VELLA

El Raval

A little after 6pm, students and workers congregate in the neighborhood west of Las Ramblas, in the type of eateries where Spaniards, Catalan or otherwise, feel most at home—a simple space, simple food, full of people, noise, and unlimited bread and wine. **C. Tallers** and **Sitges,** just one block off Rbla. Canaletes, overflow with inexpensive restaurants. Good Galician food is served off **C. Lluna** and **C. Joaquín Costa.** The red-light district begins roughly south of C. Hospital.

Restaurante Pollo Rico, C. Sant Pau, 31 (tel. 441 31 84). C. Sant Pau breaks directly off Las Ramblas one street down from C. Hospital. M: Liceu. Take home your very own chicken (800ptas). Half chicken, fries, and bread 675ptas. Baked whole artichokes 150ptas. *Comer hasta que te pongas moreno.* Afternoon *menú* 900ptas. Open Thurs.-Tues. 10am-midnight.

Restaurante Riera, C. Joaquín Costa, 30 (tel. 442 50 58). M: Liceu or Universitat. Off C. Carme coming from Liceu, or off Rda. de Sant Antoni coming from Universitat. The Riera family supplies a feast fit for a poor, hungry king. Meals change daily, but a heaping plate of *paella* (500ptas) is always available. Three-course gorge-fest with dessert (690ptas) offered day and night. Open Sept.-July Sun.-Thurs. 1-4pm and 8:30-11pm, Fri 1-4pm.

La Morera, Pl. Sant Augustí, 1 (tel. 318 75 55) M: Liceu. Take C. Hospital to Pl. Sant Augustí. A friendly establishment near La Boqueria that specializes in *comida del*

mercado (fresh market food). Argentine and Catalan dishes between 600-1000ptas. Afternoon *menú* 995ptas. Open Mon.-Sat. 1-3:30pm and 8:30-11:45pm.

Restaurante Garduña, C. Morera, 17-19 (tel. 302 43 23). Inside the crowded and confusing market La Boqueria, this simple restaurant is a sight in itself—its fresh and well-priced daily produce is a tasty deal. Typical Catalan fare featured in the *menú* (975ptas) and special of the day (1375ptas). Open Mon.-Sat. 1-8pm.

Restaurante Biocenter, C. Pintor Fortuny, 25 (tel. 301 45 83). M: Catalunya (L1, L3). Across the street from the store of the same name, off Las Ramblas. This alter ego of Los Toreros sounds threateningly futuristic, but it's actually a low-key vegetarian restaurant. *Menú* with trip to the salad bar (only during the day), bowl of soup, vegetarian entree, and dessert 1125ptas. Open Mon.-Sat. 9am-5pm.

Bar Restaurante Los Toreros, C. Xuclá, 3-5 (tel. 318 23 25), on a narrow alley between C. Fortuny and C. Carme, both off Las Ramblas. M: Catalunya. The floors, faded from red to brown, would no longer anger the bull, nor would the traditional Spanish food. Who could be angry when *platos combinados* start at 500ptas? Don't be intimidated. Popular *tapas* 250-450ptas. Afternoon *menú* 800ptas. Open Tues.-Sat. 9am-midnight, Sun. 9am-5pm.

Raim D'or Can Maxim, C. Bonsuccés, 8 (tel. 302 02 34), off the right-hand side of Las Ramblas as you face the port. M: Catalunya. Smoked hams hang in hoofed glory over the bar. Multilingual staff and menu, fresh fish from 475ptas, meat dishes 600-1000ptas, and pleasing pizzas 600-875ptas. *Menú* 1000ptas. Open Oct.-Aug. Mon.-Sat. 9am-5pm and 8pm-midnight. Visa, MC, AmEx.

Barri Gòtic

The Barri Gòtic spans east of Las Ramblas and is confined by Pl. Catalunya to the north, Pg. Colom to the south, and Vía Laietana to the east. The interiors of corroding buildings are continually being disemboweled to furnish room for ever classier cafes and restaurants. *Barcelonenses* are proud of L'Eixample, but they cherish the Barri Gòtic, where one can find cheap, quality food in a familiar *barrio*.

La Fonda, C. Escudellers, 10 (tel. 301 75 15). M: Drassanes or Liceu. C. Escudellers enters Barri Gòtic between Liceu and Drassanes. Waiting in line outside is painful enough, but large windows let you watch patrons inside savoring Catalan cuisine. Try to snag a chair on the balcony and watch the tastefully presented meals (475-1200ptas) whisk by. If you're not full, try the *postre de tirentos* (pineapple, 2 truffles, strawberry ice cream, and cookies atop *creama catalana*). Visa, MC, AmEx.. Open Sept.-June 9am-1:30pm and 8:30-11:30pm.

Restaurante Bidasoa, C. Serra, 21 (tel. 318 10 63). M: Drassanes. Take 3rd left off C. Josep Anselm Clavé as you head from Las Ramblas. Locals greet the owner with hugs and kisses, and for good reason—40 years of practice have produced 43 permutations of soups, salads, and meat and fish items, all under 550ptas. A full meal runs less than 1000ptas. Go early for the famous Sun. lunch (550ptas)—it's usually devoured by locals by 3:30pm. Open Tues.-Sun. noon-midnight. Closed Aug.

Can Conesa, C. Llibreteria, 1 (tel. 310 13 94), on the corner of Pl. Sant Jaume. Classic little nook distinguishes itself with ultra-low prices and crispy grilled *bocadillos* (250-500ptas). Free map offering routes from Conesa to major sights. Cheap pizza 275-375ptas. Open Mon.-Sat. 8am-9:30pm. Closed first half of Aug.

El Gallo Kirko, C. Avinyó, 19 (tel. 412 48 38). M: Liceu. Walk down C. Ferrán, and it's the 4th right. Fill up on Pakistani rice and couscous dishes in the back room, where a 4th-century stone wall takes you back to Barcelona's Roman origins. Most dishes under 500ptas, all under 750ptas. Several vegetarian options. ISIC cardholders get a 5% discount. Open daily noon-midnight. Visa, MC, AmEx.

Les Quinze Nits, Pl. Reial, 6 (tel. 317 30 75). Streams of locals and foreigners alike wait in line every night to try this Catalan restaurant's contemporary and traditional dishes. Don't despair—the line moves quickly and it's surprisingly affordable. *Menú* 950ptas. Braised rabbit 690ptas, octopus with onions and mushrooms 756ptas. Entrees 540-1185ptas. Open 1-3:45pm and 8:30-11:45pm.

Els Quatre Gats, C. Montsió, 3 (tel. 302 41 40). M: Catalunya. Go down Av. Portal de L'Angel and take the 2nd left. This frequently touristed spot was once the hangout of Picasso, who designed the famous menu cover (on display at Museu Picasso).

Live music 9pm-1am. *Menú* 1500ptas served Mon.-Fri. 1-4pm. Entrees 1100-2600ptas. Open Mon.-Sat. 8am-2am, Sun. 5pm-2am. Visa, MC, AmEx.

Bar Restaurante Cervantes, C. Cervantes, 7 (tel. 317 33 84), 2 blocks down C. Avinyó off C. Ferran. M: Jaume I (L4). Bustling waitstaff feverishly weaves through a prattling administrative and intellectual-looking lunchtime crowd. New artist is exhibited on the walls each month. Scrumptious chicken croquettes or a gigantic plate of macaroons (275ptas). Lunch *menú* 1000ptas. Open Mon.-Fri. 7:30am-8pm.

El Gran Café, Avinyó, 9 (tel. 318 79 86). Posh turn-of-the-century interior and curtained windows shield this restaurant from dingy surroundings. Savor the romantic ambience and French-Catalan dishes. At lunchtime, *menú rapido* 1200ptas. Roast beef 1400ptas. Mon.-Sat. 1-4pm and 8-11:30pm. Visa, MC, AmEx.

Restaurant Pitarra, C. Avinyó, 56 (tel. 301 16 47). M: Drassanes. Turn left down C. Clavé at the end of Las Ramblas and take the 3rd left after a church. In the former home of great Catalan poet-dramatist Pitarra, art lives on in epic dishes concocted by Queen Sofía's former chef Señor Marc. The *escalopines ternera* (veal) is 1200ptas deliciously spent. *Paella* 1300ptas. *Vino de la casa* 750ptas. Open Sept.-June Mon.-Sat. 1-4pm and 8:30-11pm. Visa, MC, AmEx.

Restaurante Self-Naturista, C. Santa Ana, 11-15 (tel. 318 23 88). M: Catalunya. Self-service vegetarian cafeteria feels like fast food. Desserts and salads spills over the counter. Variety of breads and veggie dishes, most under 600ptas; lunch *menú* 895ptas. Open Mon.-Sat.11:30am-10pm; count on a line during *siesta*.

Around Plaza del Pí

Some of the liveliest between-meal hangouts cluster around Església Santa María del Pí. Relax at the terrazas for drinks and ice cream. From Las Ramblas, enter Llano de la Boqueria and take a left at the Banco Central Hispano onto C. Cardenal Casanyes, leading into Pl. Pí. From El Corte Inglés, follow Portal de l'Angel down to the end, veer right onto Pontaferrissa, and take the 1st left at C. Pí.

Irati, C. Cardenal Casanyes, 17 (tel. 302 30 84). A Basque *tapas* bar that attracts droves of hungry *tapas*-seekers. Bartenders pour *sidra* (cider) with the bottle pressed against their foreheads—to rid the cider of oxygen—and parade new platters of treats every 5min. Specialties include *anchoa rellena* (anchovies stuffed with ham and cheese) and *turutu* (chicken, bacon, ham, and cheese all fried into one). All *tapas* 125ptas (they count your toothpicks when you're done). Credit cards accepted. Open Tues.-Sat. noon-midnight, Sun. noon-5pm.

Osterhase, Pl. Pí, 5 (tel. 412 58 34). Gelati and drinks on the *terraza* by the church. Ice cream 200-400ptas. Yogurt shakes 325ptas.

Café de Ciutat Vella, Carrer del Pí, 5 (tel. 302 10 21). Mellow student hangout plays popular music, pleasingly low on the decibels. Hot chocolates and a variety of hot and cold coffee concoctions (100-500ptas). *Picardía* (coffee with condensed milk and whiskey) 200ptas. Pastries from 100ptas.

La Ribera

East of *la laietana* and lower in altitude than the Barri Gòtic is La Ribera, home to the Museu Picasso and Art Galleries. Families of the fishing industry once settled around Esglesia Santa Maria del Mar, the religious sponsor of fisherman. Today, some of the city's greatest art showcases and food bargains are found in the recesses of La Ribera.

Pla de la Garsa, C. Assaonadors, 13 (tel. 315 24 13). M: Jaume I. From Museu Picasso, cross C. Princesa. Assaonadors is the first street on the right. An ambrosial sampling of Catalan cheeses, meats, and salads. Lunch *menú* (990ptas) includes spinach with pine nuts, grilled meat or fish, cheese, bread, dessert (try the pears soaked in *vino*), and wine. Regular *platos* 700ptas-1000ptas. You'll be ready for a *siesta* after a meal at Garsa. Open daily 1-4pm and 8pm-2am.

Nov Celler, C. Princesa, 16 (tel. 310 47 73). M: Jaume I. From the Metro, cross Vía Laietana from Pl. Angel. C. Jaume becomes C. Princesa. Maintains a tavern atmosphere without touristy tackiness. Customers order from an eclectic list of *platos de día* and authentic Catalan specialties. *Menú* 1000ptas. Sandwiches 250-400ptas. Open Mon.-Fri. 8am-midnight, Sun. 8am-4pm. Credit cards accepted.

Luna Plena, C. Montcada, 2 (tel. 310 54 29), same street as Museu Picasso. M: Jaume I. A bit of a splurge for dinner, but afternoon *menú* 1000ptas. Looks and smells like an old brick smokehouse. Assorted Catalan *patés* and quesos 650-800ptas. Open Tues.-Sat. 1-4pm and 8-11:30pm, Sun. 1-4pm. Closed Aug.

Restaurant Milena, Vía Laietana, 6 (tel. 319 23 61), at the corner of Vía Laietana and C. Joan Hassan. M: Jaume I. Elegant restaurant with tiled bar and a varied menu. Moderately priced pastas, salads, and Catalan dishes. *Menú* 900ptas, 1200ptas on Sat. and Sun. Fresh *paella* 900-1200ptas. Open daily 8am-1am.

La Habana Vieja, C. Baños Viejos 2 (tel. 319 10 97). Baños Viejos is parallel to C. Montcada. Feast on delicious Cuban cuisine in a small but mighty wooden-beamed house. *Arroz cubano* 500-800ptas; *carnes* 1300-1600ptas; *platanos fritos* 400-600ptas. Papaya, guava, and coconut dishes are tempting tropical desserts. Open Mon.-Sat. 6pm-1am.

Peimong, C. Templarios 6-10 (tel. 318 28 73). From Pl. Sant Jaume, take C. Ciutat. C. Templaris is the 2nd right. In the mood for meat? Generous portions of hen, goat, veal, duck, and fish Peruvian-style, all under 700ptas. Vegetarians beware—you won't find anything here. Open Tues.-Sun. 1-5pm and 8pm-midnight.

L'EIXAMPLE

When dining uptown, expect restaurants to be a bit more expensive. Cheaper *bocata* fare can be found in area *patisserías*, along with croissants and desserts.

Botiga Restaurant Corts Catalanes, Gran Vía de les Corts Catalanes, 603 (tel. 301 03 76), just off Rambla Catalunya. M: Catalunya. Groceries in front, food and drink in back. Vegetarian staples include *tarta de espinacas con guarnición* (savory spinach cake) and *zumo de zanahorias* (carrot juice). Salads 525-645ptas. Pastas around 1000ptas. Restaurant open 1-4pm and 8:30-11pm. Bar and store open 9am-11:30pm. Credit cards accepted.

El Cafe de Internet, Gran Vía de les Corts Catalanes, 656 (tel. 412 19 15; www.cafeinternet.es). M: Pg. Gracia, next to the tourist office. Check your email over one of their *platos calientes* (375-1165ptas) or *tapas* (225-800ptas). Internet access 600ptas per ½hr. With student ID 800ptas for 1hr. Live concerts, poetry readings, slide shows, and art exhibits make this the city's top cyber-cultural connection. Open Mon.-Fri. 10am-midnight.

Campechano Merendero, C. Valencia, 286 (tel. 215 62 33). M: Pg. Gràcia. Through a dark tunnel enlivened by cartoons, make your way to a bamboo-topped bar and picnic tables. This lighthearted restaurant is easy on the wallet, with salad, *butifarra* (white beans), dessert, bread, and wine for 875ptas (offered Tues.-Fri. during lunchtime). Open Tues.-Sun. 1-4pm and 8-10pm. Credit cards accepted.

ba-ba-reba, Pg. Gràcia, 28 (tel. 301 43 02). M: Pg. Gràcia. Offers a wide selection of *tapas* and Catalonian *pa* (bread). Ba-ba is chi-chi, but not too expensive. Lunch *menú* 1075ptas (1-5pm). Late afternoon assorted *tapas* plate 550ptas. Outdoor dining on the *passeig* available. Open daily 7:30am-3am.

GRÀCIA

You know you are in Gràcia when you hear fellow diners speaking Catalan, instead of Spanish, English, French, or German. The food is likewise authentic.

Taverna El Glop, C. Sant Lluís, 24 (tel. 213 70 58). Near the Joanic Metro stop off C. Escorial. This 2-story rustic tavern has become super popular with the locals for its *chorizo* (Spanish sausage), cooked over an open flame. Carbo-load on gigantic *torradas* (slices of toasted Catalan bread with tomato and cheese or sausage 295-945ptas). Open Oct.-Aug. Tues.-Sun. 1-4pm and 9pm-1am. If there's a long line (as there often is after 10pm), let the staff direct you to **Taverna El Nou Glop,** C. Montmary, 49 (tel. 219 70 59), for an equally gloppy experience. Open Wed.-Sat. 8pm-1am, Sun. 1-4pm, Mon. 1-4pm and 8pm-1am.

El Tastavins, C. Ramoni Cajal (tel. 213 60 31), near Pl. Sol. M: Joanie. Admire works by local artists (and caricatures of the owners) while scarfing traditional Catalan meals. Afternoon *menú* 895ptas. Open Tues.-Sat. 8:30am-12:45am, Sun. 1-5pm.

Can Suñé, C. Mozart, 20 (tel. 218 54 86). M: Diagonal. Take C. Goya off C. Gran de Gràcia, then take the 2nd right. A petite, family-run restaurant with marble tables and ceiling fans. Neighbors gather to spin yarns and eat a different meal each day (including wine and dessert 875ptas). Fried *calamares* (700ptas). Open Tues.-Sun. 1-4pm, Fri.-Sun. also 8pm-midnight.

Restaurante Crêperie, C. Bonavista, 2 (tel. 415 44 47), off C. Gran de Gràcia. M: Diagonal (L3, L5). Crepes as a meal or just dessert start around 450-500ptas. After-noon *menú* 900ptas. Open Mon.-Fri. 8am-1am, Sat.-Sun. 6pm-1am.

■ Sights

Ruta del Modernisme passes (1200ptas, students 750ptas) allow privileged and eco-nomical access to Barcelona's architectural masterpieces. The pass allows entrance, over a 9-day period, to Casa Batlló, Casa Amatller, Casa Lleó Morera (inaccessible without pass), Palau Guell, Sagrada Familia, Casa Milá, Palau de la Música, Casa-Museu Gaudí, Fundació Antoni Tápies, and Museu d'Art Modern. Passes are sold in the Palau Güell (see below) or at Casa Lleó Morera on Pg. Grácia. During the summer, the easi-est way to take in the sights is to hop on the air-conditioned **Bus Turístic** (see p. 303). Las Ramblas and Barri Gòtic are the traditional tourist areas, but don't neglect the vibrant neighborhoods outside the Ciutat Vella.

CIUTAT VELLA

Las Ramblas

The broad pedestrian lane of Las Ramblas is a veritable urban carnival: street perform-ers dance flamenco, fortune-tellers survey palms, human statues shift poses for a small fee, and tourists hoist their packs. The tree-lined boulevard begins at Pl. Catalu-nya and comprises five distinct segments (Canaletes, Estudis, Sant Josep, Capuxtins, and Santa Monica). A portward journey begins at the Font de Canaletes (more a pump than a fountain), where visitors who wish to return someday to Barcelona tra-ditionally sample the water.

Halfway down Las Ramblas toward the port coming from Pl. Catalunya, **Joan Miró's** pavement mosaic brightens Pl. Boqueria. The **Gran Teatre del Liceu,** Las Ramblas, 61 (tel. 485 99 00), lies a few feet away to the right, on the corner of C. Sant Pau. On opening night here in 1892, an anarchist launched two bombs into the crowd of aristocrats, killing 22 and wounding many. After executing five innocents for the crime, authorities finally found the real culprit, who cried, *"Viva la anar-quía!"* before being hanged. The *teatre* was one of Europe's leading stages, having nurtured the likes of José Carreras. Ravaged by a fire on January 31, 1994, the *teatre* will hopefully reopen in October 1998 (see **Music,** p. 327). At the far end of C. Sant Pau stands Barcelona's oldest Romanesque church, the 10th-century **Església de Sant Pau** (tel. 441 00 01), in stark contrast to its setting in the red light district, **El Raval** (unofficially known as **Barri Xinès**). The church is noted for its ornate **cloister** with lobed arches, dating from the 11th and 12th centuries (visiting hours Mon.-Fri. 5-8pm).

> ### Chris-Crossed Columbus
>
> The majestic Monument to Columbus (*Colom* in *catalá*) bridges Las Ramblas with Barcelona's busy port. When *Renaxença* enthusiasts "rediscovered" the region's role in the discovery of the Americas, they convinced themselves that Colom was Catalan. Today, the knowledge that Colom was actually Genoese and that Columbus proudly points toward Libya, not the Americas, detracts from statue's historical veracity. But contemporary and past Nationalists agree that where Colom is pointing is not as important as where he is *not* pointing: Castile. (From Robert Hughes *Barcelona*, 1992)

Recently restored and free of its former tenant, the Museu de les Arts de l'Espectacle, Antoni Gaudí's **Palau Güell,** C. Nou de la Rambla, 3 (tel. 317 39 78), two streets down from Teatre Liceu, has reopened its doors. The rooftop chimneys brightly display Gaudí's first use of the *trencadís,* the covering of surfaces with irregular shards of ceramic or glass. **Plaça Reial,** on the other side of Las Ramblas, is patrolled by police cars, but still crawls with pickpockets during the day and is worse at night.

At the port end of Las Ramblas, the **Monument a Colom,** Portal de la Pau (tel. 302 52 24), towers above the city. Spotlights turn the statue into a firebrand at night. (Elevator to the top open June-Sept. daily 9am-8:30pm; Oct.-April Mon.-Fri. 10am-6:30pm, Sat.-Sun. 10am-6:30pm; May 10am-7:30pm, 10am-7pm. 250ptas, children 175ptas.) **Las Golondrinas** (tel. 442 31 06) ferries steam around Montjuïc and an isolated peninsula at the breakwater. A longer excursion includes a tour of **Port Olímpic.** Tourists sail from Portal de la Pau, in front of the Monument a Colom. (Every 30min. 11am-8:30pm; April and Oct. 11am-6pm; June 11am-7pm; Nov.-March Sat.-Sun. 11am-6pm. Round-trip 440ptas.) Ask the tourist office for information on tours by **Rampeolas** (30min., 450ptas) and **Port Olímpic** (1250ptas).

Barcelona's drive to refurbish its seafront has not only resulted in **Vila Olímpica,** but also in the amplification of **Port Vell,** the port complex and waterfront area by Pg. Colom. After moving the coastal road underground, the city opened **Moll de la Fusta,** a wide pedestrian zone that leads down to the docks past scenic, pricey restaurant-cafes and the **Museu de la Historia de Catalunya** (see **Museums,** p.322). The bridge **Rambla de Mar** links Moll de la Fusta with the **Marmagnum** mall (see **Shopping,** p.329). The cobblestone docks are ideal for an evening *passeig.*

Barri Gòtic

Carrer de la Pietat and **Carrer del Paradis** have preserved their medieval charm; meanwhile, the tourist economy has infused a liveliness—and livelihood—it would otherwise lack. The handsome **Plaça de Sant Jaume,** Barcelona's political center since Roman times, took its present form in 1823. It is dominated by two of Catalunya's most important buildings: the **Palau de la Generalitat** (seat of Catalunya's autonomous government) and the **Ajuntament** (city hall; tel. 402 72 62 to visit).

Past the Generalitat and up C. Bisbe is **Plaça de la Seu,** collision site of history and modernity cowering beneath the jagged spires of the Gothic **Església Catedral de la Santa Creu** and Picasso's *Collegi d'Arquitectes.* The cathedral's **cloister** has magnolias growing in the middle and geese waddling around the periphery (cathedral open 8am-1:30pm and 4-7:30pm; cloister open 8:45am-1:15pm and 4-6pm). Ask a guard to let you see the *coro* (choral chamber) for 125ptas, or buy a 200ptas ticket in the cloister to take an elevator to the rooftop. Palaces and museums congregate on the opposite side of the Església Catedral, on C. Comtes. The former home of the royal family, **Palau Reial** (Royal Palace), is the pearl of the *plaça.* Inside, the **Museu Frederic Marès** and the **Museu d'Historia de la Ciutat** hold court. The royal palace can be visited with admission to the history museum (see **Museums,** p.322).

Barri de la Ribera

Felipe V demolished most of La Ribera to clear space for the Ciutadela in the 18th century. The remaining neighborhood has since evolved into the Ciutat Vella's bohemian nucleus. Its ismithian streets converge at the foot of the 14th-century Gothic **Església Santa María del Mar's** octagonal towers. As its name suggests, the church once stood on the coastline of the Mediterranean, before Barceloneta's mud flats were solidified and used as foundation. **Carrer de Montcada,** beginning behind the church, exemplifies Barcelona's local reputation as *"la ciudad del diseño"* (the city of design). Museums, art galleries, art workshops, and Baroque palaces that also housed Barcelona's 16th-century bureaucrats pack its two blocks of narrow alley space. The **Museu Picasso** now stands in the stead of the Palau de Agüilar. **Galeria Maeght** (#25), one of several prestigious art galleries on the block, was once the manor of a medieval aristocrat (see **Art Galleries,** p.324).

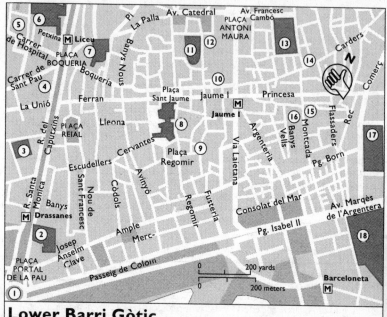

Lower Barri Gòtic

Modernist architect Lluís Domènech i Montaner designed the **Palau de la Música Catalana**, C. Sant Francesc de Paula, 2 (tel. 268 10 00), up Vía Laietana near the intersection of C. Ionqueres. The music hall is festooned with stained-glass cupolas, flowing marble reliefs, *preciosa* woodwork, and colorful ceramic mosaics. (For performance info, see **Music**, p. 327. Open Mon.-Fri. 10am-9pm. Tours normally Mon.-Fri. at 2 and 3pm; more in summer. 300ptas.)

PARC DE LA CIUTADELLA AND VILA OLÍMPICA

Barcelona's resistance to the Bourbon Monarchy convinced Felipe V to quarantine Barcelona's influential citizens in the Ciutadella, a large citadel on what is now Pg. Picasso (see **King Felipe, the John,** above). Barcelona razed the fortress in 1868 and replaced it with the peaceful promenades of **Parc de la Ciutadella**. Host of the 1888 Universal Exposition, the park now harbors several museums, well-labeled horticulture, the wacky **Cascada** fountains, a pond (rowboat rental 10am-7pm, 250ptas per person per 30min.), and a zoo. It is also a reminder the Bourbon Monarchy's harsh treatment. Buildings of note include Domènech i Montaner's modernist **Castell dels Tres Dragons** (now **Museu de Zoología**) and Josep Amergós's **Hivernacle**. Expo '88 also inspired the small **Arc de Triomf**, just across Pg. Pujades from the park. Little Snowflake *(Copito de Nieve)*, the world's only albino gorilla behind bars, vegetates in the **Parc Zoològic** (tel. 221 25 06), on the south end of the park (open daily 9:30am-7:30pm; in winter 10am-5pm; 1000ptas). On Pl. Armes is the **Museu d'Art Modern** (see **Museums,** p.322).

> ### King Felipe, the John
>
> In 1714, Barcelona fell to Bourbon King Felipe V, whose efforts to strengthen the monarchy and focus legislative power in Castile involved suppressive measures against regional administrative and aristocratic powers. Catalans today refer to the Felipe V era as the "Bourbon tyranny." The king enclosed Barcelona's residents in the walled Ciutadella (Citadel) in order to prevent urban expansion and isolate *barcelonenses* from the city's resources, thus disenabling them from organizing effectively. Out of spite toward the dastard monarch, Catalan youth used to call for a "visit to the Felipe," analogous to the British "trip to the John." (From Robert Hughes' *Barcelona* (1992), p. 186-189.)

The **Vila Olímpica,** beyond the east side of the zoo, housed 15,000 athletes for the 25th Summer Olympiad in 1992. Now a yuppie village known as **La Nova Icària,** it is home to several public parks, a shopping center, offices, strategically placed monumental buildings, in-line skate rental, and a ring road connecting the east and west ends of the city. Towards the Mediterranean, **Port Olímpic** flaunts twin towers, a golden whale-like sculpture, and waves of bars and restaurants. Beaches stretch out on both sides of the port.

L'EIXAMPLE

The *Renaixença* of Catalan culture and the growth of Barcelona during the 19th century pushed the city past its medieval walls and into ordered modernity. Ildefons Cerdà, a Catalan architect, drew up a plan with a comprehensible aerial view: a geometric grid of squares, softened by the cropped corners of streets forming octagonal intersections. Cerdà's plan attempted to relieve the stress that had festered in the old Barri Gòtic. Wide avenues and diagonal corners were intended to ease traffic flow. The original plan also called for three-sided *mançanas* (city blocks) that facilitated air circulation and imitated Catalan country-side *massas* (neighborhoods). Unfortunately, virtually every block was immediately enclosed by a fourth wall, thus sullying the genius of Cerdà's original design. But the Eixample did give rise to other, more fantastic designs. The flourishing bourgeoisie commissioned a new class of architects to build their houses, reshaping the face of the Eixample with modernist architecture that employed revolutionary shapes, materials, and spaces to reflect the signs and symbols of Catalunya. The best way to approach this macro-museum of Catalan architecture is with two handy pamphlet guides available free at the tourist office, *Discovering Modernist Art in Catalonia* and *Gaudí*. The *Route to Modernisme* pass, available at the **Palau Güell** (see **Las Ramblas,** p.315) and **Casa Lleó Morera** (see p.319), provides the most economical and privileged passage through Barcelona's modernist masterpieces.

Antoni Gaudí's serpentine rooftops, warrior-like chimneys and skeletal facades are perhaps the most famous of Barcelona's modernist gems. A staunch nationalist, Gaudí's organic architecture incorporated a vast array of Catalan symbols and myths. Gaudí designed every feature of his buildings, down to the undulating furniture, colorful mosaics, and elaborate light fixtures which fill his boisterous buildings. His methods were unconventional; he designed the vault of the Colònia Güell by hanging sand bags from a wire model of the ceiling, the inversion of which was perfectly balanced against structural stress. Although most of Gaudí's creations seem fantastical upon first glance, many, such as the attic of *La Pedrera*, which regulates heat with its vaulted ceilings, are architectural breakthroughs which have since been imitated only by advanced computer technology. Fellow modernist luminaries include **Luis Domènech i Montaner,** noted for his profusely decorated surfaces, and **Josep Puig i Cadafalch,** who developed an antiquarian style of local and foreign traditions.

Modernist buffs argue that the **Casa Milà** apartment building, popularly known as **La Pedrera** (Stone Quarry), Pg. Gràcia, 92 (tel. 484 59 80), is one of Gaudí's most refined works. The entrance to this undulating mass of granite is around the corner, on C. Provença. Note the intricate ironwork around the balconies and the irregularity

of the front gate's egg-shaped window panes. The roof sprouts chimneys resembling armored soldiers, one of which is decorated with broken champagne bottles. Rooftop tours provide a closer look at the *cascs prusians* (Prussian helmets), spiral chimneys inspired by the helmets worn in Wagner's operas. The attic (recently restored along with the rooftop if a multimillion *pesetas* project) has been transformed into the **Espai Gaudí,** a multi-media presentation of Gaudí's life and works. (Open Tues.-Sat. 10am-8pm, Sun. 10am-3pm on the hour. Same day reservations for guided tours accepted in the early morning. 500ptas, students 300 ptas.)

Only Gaudí's genius could draw thousands of tourists to a half-finished church. The architect himself estimated that the **Temple Expiadori de la Sagrada Familia** (tel. 455 02 47), on C. Marinara between C. Mallorca and C. Provença (M: Sagrada Familia), would take 200 years to complete. For 43 years, Gaudí obsessed over the Sagrada Familia, living in the complex for his last eleven until, virtually forgotten by the public, he was killed by a trolley in a possible suicide in 1926. Since then, construction has progressed erratically and with tremendous controversy. A furor has arisen over recent additions, such as the streamlined pyramid arch on C. Sardenya, which some argue doesn't flow with the structure. Of the church's three proposed facades symbolizing Jesus's nativity, passion, and glory, only the first is finished. Elevators and a maze of symmetrical staircases lead to the towers and bridges of the nativity facade. The **museum** displays a model of the completed structure and various artifacts relating to its construction. (Open Sept. and March 9am-7pm; Jan.-Feb., and Oct.-Dec. 9am-6pm; April-Aug. 9am-8pm. Admission to church and museum 800ptas.)

The odd-numbered side of Pg. Gràcia is popularly known as *la manzana de la discordia* (block of discord), referring to the aesthetic competition of the buildings on the block. Situated between C. Aragò and Consell de Cent, it offers an overview of the peak of the modernist movement. The bottom two floors of the facade of **Casa Lleó i Morera,** by Domènech i Montaner, were destroyed to house a store, but the upper floors sprout flowers and winged monsters. Puig i Cadafalch opted for a cubical pattern on the facade of **Casa Amatller** at #41. Gaudí's balconies ripple and tiles sparkle on **Casa Batlló,** #43. The rooftop is a scaly representation of Catalunya's patron Sant Jordi slaying a dragon. Although the central hallway and variegated blue-tiled stairway are open to the public, only the privileged holders of the *Route to Modernisme* pass (available two doors down at Casa Lleó Morera) can enter the *casa principal* (main apartment). **Fundació Antoni Tàpies,** designed by Domènech, is around the corner from *la manzana.* The **Museu de la Música** is nearby on Av. Diagonal, 373 (see **Museums,** p.322), and **Fundació la Caxia** in **Casa Macaya** awaits down the street on Pg. Sant Joan. Amatller and Macaya provide a rare opportunity to enter two of Puig i Cadafalch's most famous buildings.

MONTJUÏC

Throughout Barcelona's history, whoever controlled Montjuïc (hill of the Jews) ruled the city. Dozens of despotic rulers have modified the **fortress,** built atop the ancient Jewish cemetery; Franco made it one of his "interrogation" headquarters. Somewhere deep in the recesses of the structure, his *beneméritos* ("honorable ones," a.k.a. the Guardia Civil) shot Catalunya's former president, Lluís Companys, in 1941. Only in 1960 did Franco return the fortress to the city to be used for recreational purposes. This act was commemorated with a huge stone monument expressing Barcelona's thanks, a reminder of forced gratitude (it's visible from the castle battlements). Since reacquiring the mountain, Barcelona quickly made it an olympically popular attraction. To get to Parc de Montjuïc, take bus #61 from Pl. Espanya (M: Espanya), at Av. Reina María Cristina (flanked by two large brick towers). The bus runs about every 10 minutes there and back, with stops at various points on the mountain. The bus stop at Montjuïc is on . Or take the metro to Pl. Espanya, walk up Av. Reina María Cristina past the fountains, and ascend the escalators from there.

The newly reopened **Fonts Luminoses** (Illuminated Fountains), dominated by the huge central **Font Màgica** (magic fountain), are visible from Pl. Espanya up Av. Reina

María Cristina. The audio-visual show (Catalan version of the French *son et lumière*) highlights the whole mountainside and illuminates the **Palau Nacional,** home to the Museu Arqueològic (see p. 323) located directly behind the fountains. About half-way up on the right one can admire the "international style" of **Pavelló Mies van der Rohe,** designed by the German architect as his country's 1929 Expo pavilion (tel. 4423 40 16; open Nov.-March 10am-6:30pm; April-Oct. 10am-8pm; 300ptas, students 200ptas). Just across the hillside, on your right facing Palau Nacional, is **Poble Espanyol** (tel. 325 78 66), a "town" of replicas of famous buildings and sites from every region of Spain: a Pl. Mayor (with a self-service cafeteria), a C. de la Conquista, a Plazuela de la Iglesia, and so on. While this pseudo-town is great in theory, it boils down to an artificial village with a souvenir bazaar and several mediocre restaurants. (Open Sun. 9am-midnight, Mon. 9am-8pm, Tues.-Thurs. 9am-2am, Fri.-Sat. 9am-4am. Craft shops open daily 10am-8pm. 500ptas, 1900ptas per family, 1000ptas nightly.)

In 1929, Barcelona inaugurated the **Estadi Olímpic de Montjuïc** in its bid for the 1932 Olympic games. Over 50 years later, Catalan architects Federic Correa and Alfons Milá, who were also responsible for the overall design of the **Anella Olímpica** (Olympic Ring) esplanade, and Italian Vittorio Gregotti, renovated the shell (open daily 10am-8pm; free). Designed by Japanese architect Arata Isozaki, the **Palau d'Esports Sant Jordi** (tel. 426 20 89) is the most technologically sophisticated of the Olympic structures (call in advance). You can also swim in the olympic pools for a reasonable fee (see **Recreation,** p.328). To relive the 1992 Olympic experience, visit the **Galeria Olímpica** (tel. 426 06 60), at the south end of the stadium. (Open Tues.-Sat. 10am-2pm and 4-8pm, Sun. and holidays 10am-2pm; Oct.-March Tues.-Fri. 10am-1pm and 4-6pm, Sun. and holidays 10am-2pm. 390ptas, students 340 ptas.) About 100m down the road from the stadiums is the **Fundació Miró** (see **Museums,** p.322).

Parc del Migdia, on the opposite side of the Anella Olímpica from the Palau Nacional, is remote and peaceful, offering a grandiose view of the sea nibbling at the plains south of Barcelona. Bring water if you take the long, hilly walk. The **Museu Arqueològic** is on the far side of the mountain (see **Museums,** p.322). Farther along Pg. Miramar, where the park comes nearest to getting wet, is the popular **Parc d'Atraccions** (Amusement Park; tel. 441 70 24). From the Fundació Miró, walk down Av. Miramar and take the *teleferic* (cable car) halfway up (tel. 443 08 59; daily 11:30am-9:30pm; off season Sat.-Sun. 11am-2:45pm and 4-7:30pm; 400ptas, round-trip 600ptas). From Barcelona, take the funicular (tel. 412 00 00; daily 11am-10pm, off season 10:45am-8pm; 200ptas, round-trip 300ptas), from Pl. Raquel Meller (M: Parallel) to Av. Miramar, where you can hop on the *teleferic.* The park amuses with loads of rides, including bumper cars, a roller coaster, and a ferris wheel. (Open Sat.-Sun. and holidays 11:30am-10pm; in summer Tues.-Fri. 5:30pm-11:15pm, Sat.-Sun. 11:30am-11:15pm. 600ptas to get in, 1800ptas covers entrance and rides.) Uphill, at the highest *teleferic* stop, the historically rich **Castell de Montjuïc** guards over the port with a large armaments display (see **Museums,** p.322).

GRÀCIA

Located just beyond the Eixample (M: Fontana or Lesseps), Gràcia is more a down-home neighborhood than most stops on the tourist conga line. It charms even as it confuses, with narrow alleys and numerous plazas. The **Torre del Reloj** (Clocktower), on popular **Plaça Rius i Taulet,** is an emblem of the Revolution of 1868. **Plaça del Diamant,** on nearby C. Astúries, was made famous by Mercè Rodoreda's eponymous novel. At night, local youths swarm to **Plaça del Sol** and the cafes and bars that skirt its edge.

Modernisme brushed Gràcia. One of Gaudí's youthful experiments, **Casa Vicens,** C. Carolines, 24-26, may remind you of the house that Hansel and Gretel stumbled upon. The *casa* illustrates the colorful influence of Arabic architecture and a rigidness of angles that is uncharacteristic of Gaudí's later works.

PARC GÜELL

In one's first brush with Gaudí's genius, it is not so much propriety that is outraged as one's sense of probability.
        Evelyn Waugh, *Labels: A Mediterranean Journal*

Gaudí intended Parc Güell (after Eusebi Güell, its commissioner) to be a garden city, its multicolored dwarfish houses and sparkling ceramic-mosaic stairways to house the city's elite. When only two aristocrats signed on, it became a park. The park was designed entirely by Gaudí, and—in typical Gaudí fashion—not completed until after his death. The front entrance puts you face to face with a gaping, multicolored reptile. Some believe that Gaudí that the animal is a reference to the shield of the French city of Nîmes, which marks the northern limit of Old Catalunya. Two mosaic staircases flank the curious creature, leading to a *modernisme*-Roman pavilion that Gaudí originally designed as an open-air market for the park's would-be but never-were residents. From here, sweeping paths, supported by columns meant to resemble palm trees, swerve through hedges and ascend to the park's summit, which commands views of the city and Tibiado. In the midst of the Parc awaits the **Casa-Museu Gaudí** (see **Museums,** p.322).

The easiest way to reach the park is by bus #24 from Pg. Gràcia, which lets you off at the upper park entrance. You can also take the Metro to Lesseps. From the Metro, follow the signs to the stop light where you cross Av. República Argentina; follow Pl. Lesseps signs up the slight incline until it becomes Travessera de Dalt; follow Dalt past Blockbuster and go left up C. Larrard (follow the signs). The entrance is on C. d'Olot. (Like all Barcelona city parks, open 10am-9pm; April and Sept. 10am-8pm; March and Oct. 10am-7pm; Nov.-Feb. 10am-6pm. Free.)

SARRIÀ

Northwesterly Sarrià is the domain of Barcelona's old money—residents still talk about "going down to Barcelona." The last *barri* to lose its independence, Sarrià merged with Barcelona in 1921. A walk through the peaceful streets reveals elegant mansions, manicured gardens, and exclusive *modernista colegios* (private schools).

The **Monestir de Pedralbes,** Baixada del Monestir, 1 (tel. 280 14 34), at the end of Pg. Reina Elisenda, has a Catalan Gothic single-aisle church and 14th-century three-story cloister. The artistic highwater is in the **Capella Sant Miquel,** where murals by Ferrer Bassa depict Mary's seven joys as well as some of her low moments. The monastery recently received a part of the Thyssen-Bornemisza collection, purchased by Spain in 1993 (open Tues.- Sun. 10am-2pm; 300ptas, students 175ptas).

TIBIDABO

The curious name comes from the smashing view the area commands over Barcelona, the Pyrenees, the Mediterranean, and Mallorca. In St. Matthew's Gospel, the devil tempts Jesus, *"Haec omnia tibi dabo si cadens adoraberis me."* ("All this I will give to you if you fall prostrate and worship me.") Tibidabo marks the northern border of Barcelona. The souvenir shop and telescopes tucked away in the spires of the huge **Temple del Sagrat Cor's** make its religious function an afterthought. The view of Montserrat and the Pyrenees from the bust of Jesus is stunning (round-trip elevator ride 75ptas). Pay 500ptas to view the **Torre de Collserola,** 560m above sea level, a communications tower built in 1992 by British architect Norman Foster. The **Parc d'Atraccions** (tel. 211 79 42) doesn't compare to Montjuïc's (open Tues.-Sun. 11:30am-8pm; admission with unlimited use of 12 rides 2100ptas).

Designed to appeal to all ages and interests, the **Museu de Ciéncia** rests on its laurels in Tibidabo (see Museums, p. 322). The T2 Tibibus runs from Pl. Catalunya to the Torre de Collserola. (First departure from Pl. Tibidabo 30min. after the park closes; Sept. 10-June 8 bus only Sat.-Sun. and holidays.) An FFCC train or buses #17, 22, and 58 from Pl. Cataluyna run to Av. Tibidabo. To reach the mountain top, either wait 15

minutes for the **Tramvia Blau** (blue streetcar) or walk up Av. Tibidabo in almost the same time. (Tramvia runs 9:05am-9:35pm; Oct.-May Sat.-Sun. 9:05am-9:35pm. 275ptas round-trip, or use a T-1 combined train pass. At the top of the street you have to take a funicular (runs 7:15am until 30min. after the amusement park closes; one-way 300ptas).

SANTS

A quick prowl around the area surrounding the train station reveals several recently constructed concrete parks. The **Parc de l'Espanya Industrial,** a modern interpretation of Roman baths, a sunken escape from its smoggy surroundings (directly right upon exiting the train station). Down a few blocks on C. Tarragona, the **Parc de Joan Miró** (still popularly known as **Parc de l'Escorxador**) replaced a former slaughterhouse. The erect yellow, red, blue, and gray sculpture capped by a banana, Miró's *Dona i ocell* (Woman and Bird), rises triumphantly out of a small pool.

■ Museums

Barcelona's museums provides a rare opportunity to simultaneously explore the city's architectural feats and admire the works of accomplished Catalan artists. The city is traditionally forward-looking, precociously defining the rest of the world's future as its own present tense. They invest more into experimentation than preservation, a philosophy that their museums attest to. At most museums, the first Sunday of the month is free. While this section includes the more popular museums, consult the tourist office for a more comprehensive listing.

Museu Picasso, C. Montcada, 15-19 (tel. 319 63 10). M: Jaume I. A comprehensive collection of Picasso's early and late works is scattered throughout the numerous rooms of the gothic Palau Berenguer d'Aguilar. Although the museum offers little from Picasso's middle years, it boasts the world's best collection from his formative years in Galicia and Barcelona (where he began his Blue Period), and an outstanding display of lithographs and ceramics. Picasso's cubist interpretations of Velazquez's *Las Meninas* fill four rooms. Open Tues.-Sat. 10am-8pm, Sun. 10am-3pm. 500ptas, students 250ptas, under 16 free.

Museu d'Art Contemporani (MACBA), Pl. Angels, 1 (tel. 412 08 10; fax 412 46 02; email: http://www.macba.upf.es/). This bright white edifice, constructed by American architect Richard Meier, is a contrasts with the surrounding gothic neighborhood. But the museum's gentle curves and large windows are designed to make reference to, not challenge, the buildings in El Raval. Exhibitions focus on three-dimensional art, photography, video and graphic work from the past 40 yrs. Open Tues.-Fri. noon-8pm, Sat. 10am-8pm, Sun. 11am-7pm. 600ptas, students 300ptas.

Fundació Joan Miró, Parc de Montjuïc (tel. 325 80 50), Pl. Neptú on Av. Miramar. M: Espanya, then bus #61 from Pl. Espanya. Designed by Miró's friend Josep Luís Sert, the Funació, tucked into the side of Monjuïc, uses traditional elements of Mediterranean architecture to link interior and exterior spaces. Outdoor patios (offering wide-angle views of the city) and sky lights illuminate statues, paintings, and tapestries from Miró's career. The stunning *Barcelona Series* depicts Miró's personal reaction to the Spanish Civil War. Miró's preliminary sketches and thoughts for many works are also displayed. Espai 13 displays experimental work by young artists. The Fundació also sponsors music recitals and film festivals. Open Tues.-Sat. 10am-8pm, Thurs. 10am-9:30pm, Sun. 10am-2:30pm. 700ptas, students 400ptas.

Fundació Tàpies, C. Aragó, 255 (tel. 487 03 15). M: Pg. Gràcia, between Pg. Gràcia and Rbla. de Catalunya. Tàpies' wire sculpture atop Domènech's red brick building rambunctiously announces this collection of contemporary art. The top floor is dedicated to the namesake Catalan artist. The other two floors feature special exhibits of other modern artists. Open Tues.-Sun. 11am-8pm; in Aug., Sun. only 11am-3pm. 500ptas, students 300ptas.

Centre Cultural de la Fundació "la Caixa," Passeig Sant Joan, 108 (tel 207 74 75). M: Verdaguer, between C. Provença and C. Mallorca. Stroll through Puig i Cada-

falch's **Casa Macaya** as you admire the *fundació*'s permanent modern art collection and temporary exhibits of contemporary artists and photographers. Open Tues.-Sat. 11am-8pm, Sun. 11am-3pm.

Museu d'Art Modern, Plaça Armes in the Parc de la Ciutadella (tel. 319 57 28; fax 319 59 65). M: Ciutadella. A potpourri of paintings and sculptures, mostly by 19th-century Catalan artists. Noteworthy works include *Plein Air* by Casas, *Els Primers Freds* by Blay Fabregas, Josep Llimona's *Desconsol,* and Isidre Nonell's paintings of Gypsy women. Also displays furniture designed by Gaudí. Open Mon.-Sat. 10am-7pm, Sun. 10am-2:30pm. 400ptas, students 200ptas.

Museu d'Historia de la Ciutat, Pl. Rei, with entrance at C. Verguer (tel. 315 11 11; fax 315 09 57). M: Jaume I, next to Pl. Rei. In the 6th century, Visigoths buried the Roman ruins to make room for their cemetery. Their buildings, in turn, became the foundations for medieval structures. Ruins of the Roman colony are in the basement—some well-preserved floor mosaics and villa walls with interesting inscriptions are all that remain. The upper floors of the museum boast the **Capella de Santa Agueda,** built to store the king's holy relics. Get a city map at the museum and join an ancient treasure hunt: find the Roman remains in other parts of the Ciutat Vella. Open Tues.-Sat. 10am-8pm, Sun. 10am-2pm; Oct.-June Tues.-Sat. 10am-2pm and 4-8pm, Sun. 10am-2pm. 500ptas, students 250ptas.

Museu Arqueològic, Parc de Montjuïc, Pg. Santa Madruna (tel. 423 21 49). M: Espanya, then bus #61. Or take the 55 from Pl. Catalunya. East of the Palau Nacional. Collection of Carthaginian art from Ibiza. Several rooms are dedicated to relics from the excavation of the Greco-Roman city of Empúries (near Girona). Open Tues.-Sat. 9:30am-7pm, Sun. 10am-2:30pm. 200ptas, students free, all Sundays free.

Museu Nacional d'Art de Catalunya (MNAC), Palau Nacional, Parc de Montjuïc (tel. 423 71 99; fax 325 57 73). M: Espanya, then bus #61; or walk up Av. Reina M. Cristina and up the escalators. Besides housing the world's finest Romanesque art collection, the *museu* has Gothic altarpieces and paintings of Catalunya's medieval churches scavenged from museums around the world. Open Tues.-Sat. 10am-7pm, Thurs. till 9pm, Sun. 10am-2:30pm. 800ptas, students 550ptas.

Museu d'Historia de Catalunya, Pl. Pau Vila, 3 (tel. 225 47 00, fax 225 47 58). M: Barceloneta. This high-tech and hands-on museum guides you through Catalunya's Roman, Industrial, Civil War, and recent eras. Computer screens, original film clips, and music stations help narrate the region's tumultuous past. Open Tues.-Thurs. 10am-7pm, Fri.-Sat. 10am-8pm, Sun. 10am-2;30pm. 500ptas.

Casa-Museu Gaudí, Park Güell, C. Olot (tel. 219 38 11). Take bus #24 from Pl. Catalunya. Designed by Gaudí's associate Francesc Berenguer, it houses an eclectic *modernisme* collection of designs, furniture, and portraits. Open Sun.-Fri. 10am-2pm and 4-7pm. 250ptas.

Museu de la Música, Casa Vidal-Quadras, Av. Diagonal, 373 (tel. 416 11 57). M: Diagonal. An exhibit of antique instruments housed in Puig i Cadafalch's Casa Quadras. Open Tues.-Sun, 10am-2pm, Wed. 10am-2pm and 5-8pm; June 24-Sept. 24 Tues.-Sun. 10am-2pm. 300ptas, students 150ptas.

Museu de Ciéncia, C. Teodor Roviralta, 55 (tel. 212 60 50). FFCC train or buses #17, 22, and 58 from Pl. Catalunya to Av. Tibidabo. Walk 2 blocks, turn left onto C. Teodor Roviralta, then continue to the end of the street and up the stairs. Knob-twisting, button-pushing, and rod-pulling opens the doors to the mysterious world of science. If you don't understand the Catalan or Castilian instructions, let the first-graders show you the ropes. Open Tues.-Sun. 10am-8pm. 500ptas, students 350ptas. 30min. planetarium show 250ptas extra, students 200ptas extra.

Palau de la Virreina, Las Ramblas, 99 (tel. 301 77 75), on the corner of C. Carme. M: Liceu. Once a Peruvian viceroy's residence, this 18th-century palace displays temporary photographic, musical, and graphic exhibitions. It serves as the headquarters for tickets to the summer **Grec festival.** Open Tues.-Sat. 11am-9pm, Sun. 11am-3pm. 300ptas, students 150ptas.

Museu Frederic Marès, entrance at Pl. Sant Iu, 5-6 (tel. 310 58 00). M: Jaume I. Housed in the Palau Reial, on the opposite side of the cathedral. An idiosyncratic personal collection of the sculptor Marès. The first floor houses an almost over-whelming collection of crucifixions and other New Testament motifs. The 2nd and 3rd floors contain an eclectic collection of commonplace objects, such as canes,

ashtrays, and pipes–from the 15th-20th centuries. Open Tues.-Sat. 10am-5pm, Sun. 10am-2am. 300ptas, students 150ptas.

Centre de Cultura Contemporània de Barcelona (CCCB), Casa de Caritat, C. Montalegre, 5 (tel. 306 41 00). M: Catalunya or Universitat. Next to the MACBA. Temporary exhibits are only part of the brand-new CCCB. Also sponsors concerts, workshops, and lectures. Open Tues, Thurs.-Fri. 11am-2pm and 4-8pm; Wed. and Sat. 11am-8pm; Sun. 11am-7pm. 600ptas, students 400ptas, Wednesdays 400ptas.

ART GALLERIES AND CULTURAL CENTERS

As one of the world's cultural capitals, Barcelona showcases the latest artistic trends. A myriad of private galleries displays the works of budding artists and established geniuses. Galleries distribute the **Gremida de Galerías d'Art de Catalunya** which includes maps, addresses, and phone numbers.

On **Carrer de Montcada** (around the Museu de Picasso), **Galería Maeght** is Catalunya's most prestigious gallery, (#25, tel. 310 42 45; open Tues.-Sat. 10am-2pm and 4-8pm). At Moncada #14 is **Fundación La Caixa's Sala Montcada** (tel. 310 06 99; open Tues.-Sat. 11am-8pm and Sun. 11am-3pm). Both La Caixa and Maeght feature contemporary artists. Also on Montcada is the **Galería Surrealista** (#19; tel. 310 33 11), where you can purchase Dalí studies, paintings, and sculptures from 1000-50,000,000ptas (open daily 10am-2pm and 4-8pm).

A galaxy of galleries brightens the single block of **C. Consell de Cent,** between Rbla. Catalunya and C. Balmes. **Charles Taché** (#290; tel. 487 88 36; open Tues.-Sat. 10am-2pm and 4-8:30pm, closed Sat. in July) and **René Metras** (#331, tel. 487 58 74; open Tues.-Fri. 11am-1:30pm and 5-8:30pm) face each other on Cent. Around the corner is **Joan Prats,** Rambla Catalunya, 54 (tel. 216 02 90; open Sept.-July 10:30am-1:30pm and 5-8:30pm). All three exhibit the newest on the art scene.

At the **Kiku Mistu Imaginary Cultural Center,** C. de Palau, 5 (tel. 318 25 08, http://www.mister.com; M: Liceu or Jaume 1), across street from Hostel Mari-Luz, fall asleep on the *cama de sueños* (bed of dreamers). Have a drink at the shattered "Ethylic Mirages" bar, call home from the fur-line phone booth, or listen to new age music in the hanging chair. These exhibits, designed to link the world of dreams and reality, are all hands-on (email access available; open Tues.-Sat. 5-9pm; 1st entrance 200ptas).

■ Entertainment

Ocio (leisure) in Barcelona ranges from sophisticated to debaucherous. The early evening buzzes with families, the late nights are rancorous. After *siesta* the masses roll into Las Ramblas to browse magic shows and periodical stands or stroll the portside *moll*, while youngsters mill around Portal l'Angel purveying the latest fashions. To recharge, the "theatre" crowd makes conversation in cafes and *tapas* bars around Liceu, and the twenties crowd orders *copas* in the Pl. Reial. Barcelona's bar scene begins around 9pm; the discos start bumping around 2am.

For info on movies, concerts, cultural events, and bars, consult the weekly *Guía del Ocio,* available at newsstands for 125ptas. The *Cine* section denotes subtitled films with *V.O. subtitulada;* other foreign films are dubbed, usually in Catalan. The *Arte* section lists current exhibits. The *Tarde/Noche* section suggests bars and discos galore, while the *Música* section lists Barcelona's live music venues.

BARS AND DISCOS

After dinner, *bar-restaurantes* and *cervecerías* fill up. Later on, *bares-musicales* (small discos for socializing, not dancing) draw the pre-*discoteca* crowd. The masses that make it through the gauntlet hit the dance floor around 2am and jam for at least four hours (some discos don't close until 9am). The more swish bars and discos tend to discriminate on the basis of hair and dress style. Bouncers may invent a cover charge for men to meet quotas.

What's popular changes from one day to the next—do some research of your own to stay on top of things. Expect to pay around 300-400ptas for a beer and 700ptas for a mixed drink. Closing times are approximate—places don't shut down until people leave (or, more often, until the police decide they want to sleep).

Las Ramblas and Barri Gótic

Cookie-cutter *cervecerías* and *bar-restaurantes* can be found every five steps. If slabs of meat are swinging from the ceiling, you know you're in a local hang. Nightlife on and around Las Ramblas is people-packed and exciting, but not disco-oriented.

Xampanyet, C. Montcado, 15, off Pg. Borne behind La Església Santa María del Mar, and just before the Museu Picasso. George Costanza look-alike Juan Carlos is the 3rd-generation proprietor. He and his father serve *cava* and anchovies in a colorful champagne bar. *Cava* 110ptas, bottle 750ptas. Open Tues.-Sat. noon-4pm and 6:30-11:30pm, Sun. 6:30-11:30pm.

Bar Almirall, C. Joaqín Costa, 33, just up the street from Restaurante Riera (see **Food,** p. 311). A dark red cave with a decaying ceiling and weathered couches in back. They serve absinthe, the liqueur banned in France for its eerie effects on the minds of Impressionist painters. This is the oldest bar in Barcelona, and you won't find its name on neon-colored 2-for-1 fliers. Beer 250ptas.

L'Antiquari, C.Verquer, 13 (tel. 310 04 35), in Pl. Rei. M: Jaume I. A 3-floor bar housed in a former antique shop with a view of Barri Gòtic palaces. In this bar, "A" stands for anarchy (a *barcelonense* tradition). A chaotic mix of live samba, reggae, and Scottish folk. Beer 275ptas. Mixed drinks 600ptas. Open Sun.-Thurs. 10am-1am, Fri.-Sat. 10am-3:30am.

L'Ovella Negra, Sitges, 5 (tel. 317 10 87). M: Catalunya. From Pl. Catalunya, down Las Ramblas and the first right at C. Tallers; C. Sitges is the first left. Smoky tavern where locals and travelers mix freely over pool and foosball. Beer 325ptas. Open Mon.-Thurs. 9pm-3am, Fri.-Sat. 9pm-3am, Sun. 5pm-3am.

Schilling, C. Ferrán, 23 (tel. 317 67 87). M: Liceu. You'll have to push to find a seat in this chic and popular new bar. The columns, tarp-covered chandeliers, and friendly service attract a refreshingly diverse crowd. Open Mon.-Sat. 10pm-2:30am, Sun. 3pm-2:30am.

Cafe d l'Opera, Ramblas, 74 (tel. 302 41 80). M: Liceu. A drink at this cafe was once a post-opera tradition for bourgeois *barcelonenses*. Despite Liceu's recent fire, a scaled-up crowd still fills its indoor and outdoor tables. Open daily 8am-12:30pm.

Euskal Etxea, Placeta Montcada, 1-3 (tel. 310 21 85). Down the street from the Museu Picasso. This "Basque House" serves *tapas* at around 7:30pm and cheap wines (100ptas) in traditional low-ball Basque glasses. Open Mon.-Sat. 8am-5pm and 7-11:30pm, Sun. 7-11:30pm.

Cafe D'Estiu, Plaça de Sant Iu, 5-6, in the courtyard outside the Museu Marés. Tiny outdoor cafe offers a tranquil refuge from the Barri Gòtic's hustle and bustle. Sip tea (275ptas) beside a fish pond and orange trees. Open Tues.-Sun. 10am-10pm.

Jamboree, Pl. Reial, 17 (tel. 301 75 64). M: Liceu or Drassanes. Plaça Reial lies just off Las Ramblas, via C. Colom. Turn right upon entering; it's toward the end on the right. Jazz, blues, be-bop, reggae, pop-funk, and jazz-funk. Two concerts nightly, 9pm and midnight (1200ptas, drink included). Dancing after the 2nd concert. Call, visit, or call the Mas i Mas main office (tel. 318 59 66) for a schedule.

Harlem Jazz Club, C. Comtesa de Sobradiel, 8 (tel. 310 07 55). M: Liceu. Between the Pl. Reial and Via Laietana. Jazz and a variety of other live tunes. Open Mon.-Thurs. and Sun. 10:30pm-4am, Fri.-Sat. 11:30pm-4am. Sun.-Thurs. free, Sat. 500ptas with drink.

Eixample

A mod crowd: no hair products, no service. Leave your jeans and sneakers at home or face the fashion police. A slew of *bares-musicales,* disco bars, and other hybrids lie between Pg. Gràcia and C. Aribau, and C. Rossell and C. València.

Velodrom, C. Muntaner, 213. M: Diagonal. Pre-party crowd. Students meet to drink in cushioned booths and shoot pool in a weatherworn hangout with ceiling fans, monstrous windows, and a loft. *Jarras* (mugs) of beer 275ptas. Mon.-Sat. 6pm-2am.

La Fira, C. Provença, 171 (tel. 323 72 71). M: Diagonal. Between C. Aribau and C. Muntaner. Bumper cars, ferris wheel benches, and salvaged fun house mirrors meet formal dress—avoid shorts or sandals. Quieter than it should be, considering the decor. Open Tues.-Sat. 7pm-4:30am, Sun. 6pm-1am.

Dow Jones, Carrer de Bruc, 97 (tel. 207 60 45). M: Pg. Gracia, between C. Aragó and C. Valencia. Computer screens keep you posted on their beer index. Pool table. Open Mon.-Fri. 8:30am-2am, Sat.-Sun. 6pm-2am.

Montjuïc

Poble Espanyol, Av. Marqués de Comillas (tel. 322 03 26). M: Pl. Espanya. The numbers are impressive: 12 restaurants, 15 bars, 3 *bares-musicales,* and 1 large *discoteca* called **Le Fou. Hard core** scene: dancing doesn't start until 1:30am, and usually doesn't end until 9am. Open in summer nightly, in winter Thurs.-Sat. .

Firestiu, Pl. l'Univers de Fira de Barcelona. M: Espanya. An enclosed complex with a medley of bars, bungee-jumping, carnival games, and outdoor dancing. Open June-Sept. Thurs.-Sat. 10pm-4:30am. 1000ptas with drink.

Port Olímpic

Nestled among Barcelona's *platjas,* the Port Olímpic brims with glitzy restaurants that give way to dance-fiends, from the merely light-of-foot to the crackpot *discotecarios.* Fifteen *bares-musicales* occupy the strip, but many choose to dance on the port itself. If you don't like the music, take five steps to the next scene (there's no cover anywhere). Things begin at midnight and wind down at 6am. From the metro stop Ciutadella-Vila Olímpica (L4), walk down C. Marina toward the twin towers.

Panini, Moll de Mestral, 11 (tel. 221 40 40). A classy pizzeria by day, a strobe-lit beast by night. One of the hotspots. Pop/dance mixes with pumping bass and laser-lights. Disco opens Tues.-Sun at midnight.

Glub, Moll de Mestral, 13, next door, but far different from Panini. *"La mejor música española"* infuses local flavor. Don't go clubbing, go glubbing. Tues.-Sat. music starts around 11pm.

Up and Down, Moll de Mestral, 18. Heavy on the strobe, very popular. Tues.-Sat. 10pm-5am.

Maremagnum

At 1am the adults leave, the children go to bed, and the older kids party. A variety of venues for even the least mall-cultured.

Mojito Bar, Local 059 (tel. 225 80 14). The place for Caribbean music, merengue, and salsa. Free classes given on weekends. Open midnight-4:30am.

Distrito Marítimo, Moll de la Fusta, Edicles, 1 (tel. 221 55 61). Techno with gay environment and outdoor terrace. Open Fri.-Sat. midnight-5am.

Nayande!, Maremagnum (tel. 225 80 10). Indoor/outdoor dance floor hops and rocks with tunes from the 60s and 70s. Open daily 10pm-5:30am.

Insólit, Maremagnum (tel. 225 81 78). Check your email, surf the web, or boogie on down to 60s and 70s music. Open Mon.-Thurs. 11pm-3am, Fri.-Sat. 11pm-4am.

Elsewhere

Most of the larger *discotecas* are farther out of the Plaça Catalunya area.

Otto Zutz, C. Lincoln, 15 (tel. 238 07 22). M: FFCC Muntaner. Uptown near Pl. Molina where C. Balmes intersects Vía Augusta. 3 floors, 6 bars. Most lights, most dancing, most flash—yet to be matched by any other club. Live music Fri. midnight-2am. Cover 2000ptas, drink included. Open Tues.-Sat. midnight-5am.

Fibra Optica, C. Beethoven, 9 (tel. 209 52 81). M: Hospital Clinic. From the metro, walk up C. Comte Urgell, turn left at Diagonal; it's in Pl. Wagner, 1 block up on the

right. A twenty-something crowd. Cover 1700ptas. Drink included. Open Mon.-Fri. midnight-5am, Sat.-Sun. 6pm-9:30am.

Zeleste, C. Almogàvers, 122 (tel. 309 12 04), a 15min. walk from Pg. Lluís Companys; or take the NL bus (11pm-4:30am). M: Llacuna. Located in an old warehouse, this dance club sometimes has rooftop terraces and live performances for a separate charge. Cover 1000ptas. The shindig freaks around 2:30am.

La Boîte, Av. Diagonal, 477 (tel. 419 59 50). M: Hospital Clinic. More emphasis on dance than decor. Live jazz, soul, and blues Tues., Thurs., and Fri. Big names sometimes come to perform in an intimate disco setting. Open daily 11pm-5:30am.

KGB, C. Alegre de Dalt, 55 (tel. 210 59 04). M: Joanic. C. Alegre de Dalt is the first left off C. Pi i Maragall from the Metro. Caters to those who like their rock and roll loud and hard. Open Fri.-Sun. 10pm-5am.

MUSIC

The **Gran Teatre del Liceu,** Rambla de Caputxins, 61 (tel. 485 99 13; http://www.gt-liceu.es), founded in 1847, was one of the world's leading opera stages. Unfortunately, its interior was destroyed by a fire in 1994, but it will reopen in October 1998 with Puccini's *Turandant.* Many anticipated performances have been moved to the **Palau de la Música Catalana** and **Teatro Victoria** (tel. 426 20 89). Museums and parks also host concerts and recitals (Parc Güell, Parc de la Ciutadella, Fundació de Joan Miró, Fundació la Caixa, and the Centre de Cultura Contemporània). Consult the Palau de la Virreina office at Las Ramblas, 99, or check local periodicals for specific listings.

Palau de la Música Catalana, C. Francesc de Paula, 2 (tel. 268 10 00), is Lluis Domènech i Montaner's fantastic *modernisme* concert hall, illuminated by an inconceivably ornate stained-glass chandelier and tall stained glass windows, tucked away off Vía Laietana near Pl. Urquinaona. Concerts include all varieties of symphonic and choral music. Tickets run 800-1500ptas. Ask about free Tues. night winter concerts and the Oct. music festival. Box office open Mon.-Fri. 10am-9pm, Sat. 3-9pm, Sun. from 1hr. prior to the concert. Tours are offered daily around 2 and 3pm (300ptas, free with a *Ruta del Modernisme* pass).

Teatro Victoria, Avada Paral.lel, 67 (tel. 443 29 29). M: Paral.lel. Hosts many of the displaced Liceu performances.

Rock concerts are held in the main soccer stadium and in the sports palace. Get tickets in the booth on Gran Vía at C. Aribau, next to the university (open daily 10:30am-1:30pm and 4-7:30pm) or at the **Virgin Megastore** (see **Shopping,** p. 329).

THEATER

Barcelona offers multitudinous options for theater aficionados. A new, domed *auditori* (concert hall) is going up on Pl. Glòries. Next door on Pl. dels Arts will be Ricard Bofill's **Teatre Nacional de Catalunya,** a cyclopean, glass-enclosed classic-revival temple. Tickets can be reserved by phone through **TelEntrades** (tel. 310 12 12), or in any branch of the **Caixa de Catalunya** bank.

Teatre Grec turns Barcelona into a theater, musical, and dance extravaganza from June to mid-August. Some of the major venues (such as the Teatro Grec itself and the **Convent de Sant Augusti**) are open-air theaters. Be sure to ask which language the performance is in (some are in *castellano,* others in *català*). Tickets can be purchased through TelEntrades, at Palau de la Virreina (see **Practical Infomation,** p. 294), or on Portal de L'Angel, near El Corte Inglés.

Teatre de L'Eixample, C. Aragó, 140 (tel. 451 34 62). M: Urguell. This brand-new facility showcases contemporary theater, foreign and domestic. Tickets (1800-2200ptas) are available Wed.-Mon. 11:30am-noon and after 5pm.

Teatre Lliure, C. Montseny, 47 (tel. 218 92 51). M: Fontana, in Gràcia, claims notoriety and respect with years of innovative productions of contemporary theater. Tickets cost 1600-2000ptas, depending on the day. The season runs Oct.-June. Box office open Tues.-Sat. 5-8pm, Sun. and holidays 2hr. before the show.

Teatro Goya, Joajuín Costa, 68 (tel. 318 19 84). M: Universitat. Performances in *castellano* and *catalá.* Popular during the Grec festival. Tickets Tues.-Sun. after 5pm.

Mercat de les Flores, Lleida, 59 (tel. 318 85 99). M: Pl. Espanya. Hosts dance and theater performances. Tickets available at Pal. de la Virreina, Las Ramblas 99, Tues.-Sat. 11am-2pm and 4-7pm.

FILM

A myriad of cinemas screen Spanish and Catalan features, plus the latest Hollywood productions. Many theaters have a bargain ticket day. Check the schedule at the **Filmoteca,** Av. Sarrià, 33 (tel. 410 75 90), M: Hospital Clínic, run by the Generalitat, for classic, cult, exotic, and otherwise exceptional films. Films are always subtitled if they are not originally in a Spanish language (400ptas). **Alexis,** Rbla. Catalunya, 90 (tel. 215 05 06), and **Verdi,** C. Verdi, 32 (tel. 237 05 16), are both 700ptas, Fri.-Sat. 725ptas, Monday 500ptas. **Casablanca,** Pg. Gràcia, 115 (tel. 218 43 45; Sun. and Tues.-Thurs. 700ptas, Fri.-Sat. 725ptas, Mon. 500ptas). **Maldà,** C. Pí, 5 (tel. 317 85 29), has double features (Fri.-Sat. 625ptas) **Icaria-Yelmo,** C. Salvador Espira, 61 (tel. 221 75 85), in the Olympic village, has 15 screens (Tues.-Sun. 700ptas, Mon. 500ptas). **Méliés Cinemas,** Villarroel, 102 (tel. 451 00 51), M: Urgell. Screens revived classics (550ptas).

IMAX Port Vell (tel. 902 33 22 11) is the new tri-functional facility on the Moll d'Espanya (a.k.a. Maremagnum), Port Vell, featuring an IMAX screen, an Omnimax 30m in diameter, and 3-D projection. Get tickets through ServiCaixa automatic machines and by phone. Check listings for schedules (850-1500ptas).

FÚTBOL AND CORRIDAS

You may think that the lunatics running around covered head to toe in red and blue must have escaped from a nearby asylum. Chances are they are **F.C. Barcelona** fans. Grab some paint, lozenges, and some fiery locals, and head to **Camp Nou** to join fearless compatriots going berserk watching one of the finest pro *fútbol* teams on Earth. To cheer on *Los Cules* firsthand, it would be wise to go to the stadium box office at C. Aristedes Maillol well before the match or call them at tel. 330 80 52— demand for tickets is high. **R.C. Deportivo Espanyol,** a.k.a. *los periquitos* (parakeets), Barcelona's other professional soccer team, spreads its wings at Campo del Espanyol; call tel. 205 08 12 or stop by their box office on C. Ricardo Villa. You can also obtain tickets for both from Banca Catalana or by phoning TelEntrada.

Although the best *toreros* rarely venture out of Madrid, Sevilla, and Málaga, Barcelona's **Plaça de Toros Monumental** (for tickets tel. 245 58 02), on Gran Vía at Pg. Carles I (M: Marina), is an excellent facility and a joy to look at, with Arabic influence and a *modernisme* twist. Buy tickets from local travel agencies or at the box office before the start of the *corrida* (open daily 10:30am-2pm and 4-7pm; tickets 2200-12,000ptas). Bullfights normally take place from June to October on Sunday at 7pm.

POOLS AND BEACHES

Guía de l'esport, available free at the tourist offices, lists info (in Catalan) about swimming, cycling, tennis, squash, sailing, hiking, scuba diving, white-water rafting, and kayaking. Info is available over the phone (tel. 402 30 00, no English). Barcelona tends to ignore its beaches and focus more on the industrial utility of the oceanside, but there's plenty of sand. Nearby **Sitges** (see p. 332) is a popular daytrip.

Swimming Pools and Workout Facilities: Piscina Bernat Picornell, Av. Estadi, 30-40 (tel. 423 40 41). M: Espanya, then bus #61 up Montjuïc. *The* Olympic pool. Open Mon.-Fri. 7am-midnight, Sat. 7am-9pm, Sun. 7:30am-2:30pm. 1200ptas. **Club Sant Jordi,** C. París, 114 (tel. 410 92 61 or 419 66 94). M: Sants. Olympic-sized pool. Passes are available for other facilities including the sauna, universal and free weights, treadmills, and stairmaster. Bring your passport. Open Mon.-Fri. 7am-5pm, Sat. 8am-6pm, Sun. and holidays 9am-2pm (pool 500ptas per hr.).

Frontó Colon, Las Ramblas, 18 (tel. 302 32 95 or 302 40 25). M: Jaume I. Mediocre facilities but convenient location. Universal and free weights, minuscule indoor pool, and track. Open Mon.-Fri. 7:30am-10pm, Sat. 9am-8pm, Sun. 9am-2pm.

Beaches: Several lie between Vila Olímpica and the sea, all are accessible from M: Ciutadella. The closest and most populous is **Platja Barceloneta,** off Pg. Marítim. Not great surf-riding beaches, but popular with sun worshippers. **Castelldefels,** 20min. from Barcelona on the same train line as Sitges, is an enormous beach perfect for young children and hydrophobes—the water takes its time to get deep. The L93 bus leaves Barcelona's Pl. Espanya for Castelldefels (180ptas).

SHOPPING

There's a lot of style walking around Barcelona. Unfortunately, *Let's Go*ers rarely have the funds or the space. Barcelona's reputation as a fashion capital has led to outlandish prices in the elegant shops along **Pg. Gràcia** and the **Rbla. Catalunya**—but, hey, it's fun to look. Things you can probably afford—but may not want—jam the tacky tourist traps along Las Ramblas.

Carrer Portaferrissa, between Las Ramblas and Av. Portal de l'Angel. Naf-Naf, Pull & Bear, and Izod join Generation X-geared clothing stores. The area is swarming with youths from 5:30 to 8pm every weekday.

Carrer Banys Nous, in the Barri Gòtic. Prices and quality vary widely on this street of tiny antique shops. Painters gather in Pl. Pí to sell their masterpieces Sat. 11am-8pm, Sun. 11am-2pm.

El Corte Inglés, Pl. Catalunya (tel. 302 12 12). See **Practical Information,** p. 305.

Maremagnum, the new mall complex at Port Vell has restaurants (like Dunkin' Donuts and Steven Spielberg's Dive) and shops (generally open 9am-9pm).

VIPS, Rambla Catalunya, above Pl. Catalunya. A super-sized store, this late-night locale is crammed with books, records, food, alcohol, and a cafe. Open Mon.-Thurs. 8am-2am, Fri. 8am-3am, Sat.-Sun. 9am-3am.

Virgin Records Megastore, Pg. de Gràcia, 16 (tel. 412 44 77). Tons of records at regular retail prices. Better bargains are found on C. Talles off Las Ramblas. Open Sun.-Thurs. 10am-9:30pm, Fri.-Sat. 10am-10:30pm.

English Bookstores: LAIE, Av. Pau Claris, 85 (tel. 318 17 39), 1 block from the Gran Vía. M: Urquinaona or Pl. Catalunya. Extensive collection. Open Mon.-Sat. 10am-9pm. LAIE Rooftop Cafe brews aromatic teas (275ptas) in a pleasant setting. Cafe open Mon.-Sat. 9am-1am. **Librería Francesa,** Pg. Gràcia, 91 (tel. 215 14 17). M: Diagonal. Between C. Provença and C. Roselló. Good selection, including *Let's Go.* Open Mon.-Fri. 9:30am-2:30pm and 4-8:30pm, Sat. 9:30am-2pm and 5-8:30pm.

SARDANAS AND FIESTAS

The **sardana,** Catalunya's regional dance, is one of Barcelona's most popular amusements. Teenagers and grandparents join hands to dance in a circle in celebration of Catalan unity in front of the cathedral, Pl. Sagrada Familia, or at Parc de la Ciutadella, near the fountains, on Sundays at noon. Dances are also held in Pl. Sant Jaume on Sundays at 6:30pm, at Parc de l'Espanya Industrial on Fridays at 8pm, in Pl. Catedral on Saturdays at noon and 6:30pm, and in other locations throughout the city on Tuesdays, Thursdays, and Fridays. Consult papers for current info.

Fiestas are abundant in Barcelona. Before Christmas, **Feria de Santa Lucía** fills Pl. Catedral and the area around the Sagrada Familia with stalls and booths. **Carnaval** is celebrated wildly from February 7-13, but many head to the even more raucous celebrations in Sitges and Vilanova i la Geltrù. Soon thereafter the **Festa de Sant Jordi** (St. George), April 23, celebrates with a feast for Catalunya's patron saint (and Barcelona's St. Valentine's Day). Men give women roses, and women reciprocate with books. On May 11, the **Festa de Saint Ponç,** a traditional market of aromatic and medicinal herbs and honey, sets up in Carrer Hospital, close to Las Ramblas. Barcelona erupts on June 23, the night before **Día de Sant Joan.** Bonfires roar throughout the city, unsupervised children play with *petardos* (fireworks), and the fountains of

Pl. Espanya and Palau Reial light up in various colors in anticipation of fireworks on Montjuïc. August 15-21 city folk jam at Gràcia's **Festa Major.** Lights blaze in the plazas and streets, and rock bands play all night.

In September, the **Feria de Cuina i Vins de Catalunya** brings wine and *butifarra* (sausage) producers to the Rambla de Catalunya. For one week you can sample fine food and drink for a pittance. On September 24, during the **Festa de la Verge de la Mercè,** fireworks light up the city while the traditional *correfocs (*manic parades of people dressed as devils), whirl pitchfork-shaped sparklers. Buckets of water are hurled at the demons from balconies overlooking fiery streets. In October through November, a **Festival de Jazz** swings the city's streets and clubs (call tel. 232 61 67 for details).

■ Near Barcelona

MONTSERRAT

An hour northwest of Barcelona, Montserrat's unmistakable serrated profile pro-trudes from the flat Río Llobregat Valley. Sometime during the 10th century, a moun-taineer wandering the crags had a blinding vision of the Virgin Mary. When his story attracted droves of pilgrims, the opportunistic bishop-abbot Oliba founded a monas-tery to worship the Virgin, who became the spiritual patroness of Catalunya. (The present buildings date from the 19th century, although two wings of the old Gothic cloister survive.) Today 80 Benedictine monks tend the shrine and distill an indige-nous herbal liqueur, *Aromes de Montserrat.* During the Catalan *Renaixança* in the early 20th century, politicians and artists including poets Joan Maragall and Jacint Ver-daguer turned to Montserrat as a source of Catalan legend and tradition. During Franco's regime, it was the site of resistant activity. Catalan Bibles were printed here covertly and Catalan nationalist demonstrations were held on the mountain. The site still attracts devout worshippers and remains a Catalan nationalist symbol.

Practical Information For a schedule of daily religious services and help with mountain navigation, go to the **info booth** in **Plaça Creu** (tel. 835 02 51, ask for *infor-mación turística*), a providential (almost divine) and multilingual source of advice. Not all is charity, however; the *Official Guide to Montserrat* sells for 475ptas (booth open daily 9:15am-2:15pm and 3-6pm). Other conveniences in Pl. Creu include a **post office** (open Mon.-Fri. 9am-12:45pm and 2-5pm, Sat. 9am-1pm) and **currency exchange** (open Mon.-Fri. 9:15am-2pm, Oct.-May Mon.-Fri. 9:15am-2pm, Sat. 9:15am-1:30pm). La Caixa bank's automatic exchange machine (available Mon.-Fri. 9am-6pm) accepts Visa, MC, AmEx, and Eurocard. A regular ATM, Caiver Maresa, is avail-able at all hours. For an **ambulance** or **mountain rescue team,** call tel. 835 02 51 and say *ambulancia* or *socorro,* meaning emergency. The **Guardia Civil** is headquar-tered in the main square (tel. 835 01 60).

Renfe **Trains** (tel. 205 15 15) to Montserrat leave from M: Espanya in Barcelona. (Every hr., 7:10am-9:10pm, 1hr., 1720ptas round-trip; last train for Barcelona leaves at 9:42pm.) Odd-hour trains are direct on the Manresa line. Even-hour trains are des-tined for Igualada; you must transfer at the Martorell-Enllaç stop . Be sure to get off at Aeri de Montserrat, *not* Olesa de Montserrat. The trains stop at the base of the moun-tain, where a funicular (included in train fare) carries you up the slope (funiculars ascend and descend Mon.-Fri. 10am-1:45pm and 3-6:45pm; weekends and holidays 10am-1:15pm and 2:20-6:50pm). Upon exiting the upper funicular station, turn left and walk up 100m to reach Pl. Creu, Montserrat's tourist-oriented commercial area.

Accommodations and Food If you choose to spend the night, apartments for up to 10 people are available through **Administació de les Cel.les** (tel. 835 02 01; fax 835 06 59; open 9am-1pm and 2-6pm), found to your right if your back is to the corner of Pl. Creu and Pl. Santa María. The office runs three *hostales,* all with kitchen-ettes. **Abat Marcet,** the newest and nicest of the three, has rooms to accommodate

one to four people and every room has a microwave. Rooms at **Abat Oliba** accommodate two to seven people (doubles 3480ptas). **Nostra Senyora** is the oldest of the three, and has communal baths (triples and up, starting at 2965ptas). Reservations are recommended. A shower-equipped **campground** (tel. 835 02 51, ext. 582), lies five minutes up the hill beyond the St. Joan funicular (office open 8am-2pm and 4-9pm; 375ptas per person, 350ptas per tent, children 275ptas; closed in winter.)

Bar-Snack de Montserrat is cafeteria-style with an open, cool dining hall (*bocadillos* 410-445ptas; platters from 980ptas). The **pastisseria** and **autoservei,** on the right as you go up Pl. Creu, have baked goods and **groceries** (open daily 9am–5:45pm). In the bakery you'll find all sorts of indigenous treats, such as chocolates, cheeses, and wines, to appreciate on the quiet mountain paths.

Sights From Pl. Creu there are a number of options. Above Creu, the entrance to the **basilica** (open Mon.-Fri. 8-10:30am and noon-6:30pm, Sat.-Sun. 7:30-8:30pm) looks out onto Pl. Santa Noría. Right of the main chapel glimmers *La Moreneta*, Montserrat's venerated 12th-century figure of Mary and child. Legend has it that St. Peter hid the figure, which was carved by St. Luke, in Montserrat's caves. Removed from Montserrat after the Napoleonic Wars and the Spanish Civil War, the solemn black-faced figure is now showcased in an elaborate silver case. Rubbing the orb in Mary's outstretched hand brings good luck. Songs by the Escalonia (a boys' choir) ring through the basilica twice a day (Aug.-June at 1 and 7.10pm).

Also in Pl. Santa María, the **Museo de Montserrat** exhibits a wide range of art—from Mesopotamian artifacts to Torahs from Israel to paintings by El Greco, Caravaggio, and Picasso. The museum displays an excellent collection of Impressionist paintings by Catalan artists such as Joaquim Mir, Santiago Russinyol, Ramón Casas' and Isidre Nonell. Casas's famous *Madeline with cigar and absinthe* is one of many evocative portraits. For a change of pace, take a peek at the mummified Egyptian woman (open Mon.-Fri. 10am-6pm; Sat.-Sun. 9:30am-6:30pm; 500ptas, students 300ptas).

A visit to Montserrat without a meditative walk along the ridge of what Maragall called "the mountain of a hundred peaks" would be a sin. Some of the most beautiful areas of the mountain are accessible only on foot. From Pl. Creu, the Santa Cova funicular descends to paths which wind along the sides of the mountain to ancient hermitages (every 20min., 340 ptas). Take the St. Joan funicular up for more inspirational views of Montserrat (every 20min, 835ptas). The dilapidated **St. Joan monastery** and **shrine** are only a 20-minute tromp from the highest station. But the real prize is **Sant Jerónim** (the area's highest peak at 1235m), with its mystical views of Montserrat's celebrated rock formations—enormous domes and serrated outcroppings resembling human forms, including "The Bewitched Friars" and "The Mummy." The hike is about two hours from Pl. Creu (or a 1hr. trek from the terminus of the St. Joan funicular). The paths are long and winding though not necessarily difficult—after all, they were made for guys wearing long brown robes. On a clear day the spectacular views of Barcelona, the Baleares, and the eastern Pyrenees will have you singing hosannas all the way.

SANT CUGAT DEL VALLÈS

Devotees of Romanesque art and architecture can worship the church at **Sant Cugat del Vallès,** just over the Serra de Collserola and less than an hour away from Barcelona. This church boasts one of the largest Romanesque cloisters in Catalunya. Within, a double-decker forest of 13th-century columns supports the breathtaking upper gallery, completed three centuries later. The church's most striking feature, the soaring 11th-century Lombard bell tower, is visible from every corner of the town. Visigothic, biblical, and mythological motifs mingle in its intricate carvings, while a rose window breathes life into its facade. Arnau Gatell sculpted all the cloister's figures (cloister open Tues.-Sat. 10am-1pm and 3-6:30pm, Sun. 10am-1pm; 300ptas, students 200ptas, Tues. free). FFCC **trains** depart Barcelona's Pl. Catalunya (M: L1, L3) for Sant Cugat (Mon.-Fri. 5am-11:48pm, every 15min.; Sat.-Sun. 7:18am-9:18pm, every 20min. **Tourist info** is available at Pl. Barcelona, 7 (tel. 589 22 88).

BARCELONA

COSTA DE GARRAF

■ Sitges

Forty kilometers south of Barcelona, the resort town of Sitges is becoming increasingly famous for its prime tanning grounds, lively cultural festivals, international gay community, and wired nightlife. Long considered a watered-down Eivissa (Ibiza City), Sitges is gradually developing its own radical identity.

Practical Information The **tourist office** awaits on Pg. Vilafranca (tel. 894 50 04; fax 894 43 05). It has a super map with a bounty of information on accommodations, services, and festivals. From the train station, turn right on C. Salvador Mirabent Paretas and go downhill until you see the big "i." (Open daily 9am-9pm; mid Sept. to June Mon.-Fri. 9am-2pm and 4-6:30pm, Sat. 10am-1pm.) The **hospital** is on C. Hospital (tel. 894 00 33). The **municipal police,** Pl. Ajuntament, answer at (tel. 811 76 25). **Cercanías Trains** (tel. 894 98 89) link Sitges to Barcelona-Sants and M: Gràcia (every 15min., 40min., 305ptas). The **post office** (tel. 894 12 47) posts on Pl. Espanya (open Mon.-Fri. 8:30am-2:30pm, Sat. 9:30am-1pm). The **postal code** is 08870. The **telephone code** is (9)3.

Accommodations and Food Accommodations are expensive, so consider daytripping from Barcelona. As there are no lockers for luggage storage in Sitges, pack accordingly. **Hostal Parelladas,** C. Parelladas, 11 (tel. 894 08 01), one block from the beach, is dirt cheap for Sitges, with standard rooms and no surprises (singles 2300ptas, doubles with bath 4700ptas). **Hostal Mariangel,** C. Parelladas, 78 (tel. 894 13 57), just down the street, has 18 less inviting rooms of varying quality. Sea air breezes through a small lounge with wicker furniture. (Singles 2500ptas, with bath 3000ptas. Doubles: 4500ptas; 5000ptas.) Chickens roasting on an open fire at **Restaurante La Oca,** C. Parelladas, 41 (tel. 894 79 36), cause Pavlovian salivation. Succulent half-*pollo al ast* (roasted chicken) is only 690ptas (not including IVA; open daily 1pm-midnight). At the spiritual bookstore-cafe **Hatuey,** C. Sant Francesc, 44 (tel. 894 52 02), ponder the mural depicting man's evolution from primate to TV-headed yuppie while sipping *cola de caballo* (horse's tail tea 175ptas; open daily 9am-midnight).

Sights and Entertainment Plenty of soothing sand pacifies vacationing families and twenty-somethings with a *resaca* (hangover). The **beach** is a 10-minute walk from the train station via any street. In summer, the main beaches get crowded, but a quick walk brings you to quieter areas, on your right as you face the water.

Although beachgoers may consider cultural activities as frightening as rain, Sitges has some can't-miss beachside attractions—a perfect chance to let your burns cool a bit. Behind Església del Evangelista on C. Fonollar, the **Museu Cau Ferrat** (tel. 894 03 64) hangs over the water's edge. Once home to Catalan modernist Santiago Russinyol and a rendezvous point for young Catalan artists Picasso and Ramón Casas, the collection is a shrine to modernist iron and glasswork, and painting. Next door, the **Museu Maricel del Mar** (tel. 894 03 64) has a selective collection of medieval painting and sculpture. The stately **Palau Maricel** (tel. 894 03 64), built in 1910 for American millionaire Charles Deering, rivals Richie Rich's playpad. The **Museu Romàntic,** C. Sant Gaudenci, 1 (tel. 894 29 69; take C. Bonaire from the waterfront), is a 19th-century bourgeois house filled with period pieces, like music boxes and 17th- to 19th-century dolls. (All 4 museums open June 22-Sept. 10 Tues.-Sat. 9:30am-2pm and 4-9pm, Sun. 9:30am-2pm. Sept.-June Tues.-Fri. 9:30am-2pm and 4-6pm, Sat. 9:30am-2pm and 4-8pm, Sun. 9:30am-2pm. Combo entrance 700ptas, students 350ptas.)

Late-night foolhardiness clusters around **C. Primer de Maig,** which runs directly from the beach. The wild ones get radical at **Atlántida,** Sector Terramar (tel. 894 26 77), then shuffle their feet at **Pachá,** Pg. Sant Didac (in nearby Vallpineda; tel. 894 26 98). Buses run all night to the two discos from C. Primer de Maig (midnight to 4am).

1 9 9 8
TRAVEL CATALOG

EURAIL PASSES

TRAVEL

guides gear accessories ID and more

1 - 8 0 0 - 5 - L E T S G O

http://www.hsa.net/travel/letsgo.html

LET'S GO TRAVEL GEAR

P A C K S

World Journey
Equipped with Eagle Creek Comfort Zone Carry System which includes Hydrofil nylon knit on backpanel and shoulder straps, molded torso adjustments, and spinal and lumbar pads. Parallel internal frame. Easy packing panel load design with internal cinch straps. Lockable zippers. Detachable daypack. Converts into suitcase. 26x15x9" 4700 cu. in. Black, Evergreen, or Blue. $20 discount with rail pass. $205

Continental Journey
Carry-on size pack with internal frame suspension. Detachable front pack. Comfort zone padded shoulder straps and hip belt. Leather hand grip. Easy packing panel load design with internal cinch straps. Lockable zippers. Converts into suitcase. 21x15x9" 3900 cu. in. Black, Evergreen, or Blue. $10 discount with rail pass. $160

Security Items

Undercover Neckpouch
Ripstop nylon with a soft Cambrelle back. Three pockets. 5 1/4" x 6 1/2". Lifetime guarantee. Black or Tan. $10.50

Undercover Waistpouch
Ripstop nylon with a soft Cambrelle back. Two pockets. 4 3/4" x 12" with adjustable waistband. Lifetime guarantee. Black or Tan. $10.50

Travel Lock
Great for locking up your World or Continental Journey. Two-dial combination lock. $5.25

Hostelling Essentials

1997-8 Hostelling Membership
Cardholders receive priority and discounts at most domestic and international hostels
Adult (ages 18-55) $25.00
Youth (under 18) $10.00
Senior (over 55) $15.00
Family (parent(s) with children under 16)................................$35.00

Sleepsack
Required at many hostels. Washable polyester/cotton. Durable and compact. $14.95

International Youth Hostel Guide
IYHG offers essential information concerning over 2500 European hostels. $10.95

Discounted Airfares

Discounted international and domestic fares for students, teachers, and travelers under 26. Purchase your 1997 International ID card and call 1-800-5-LETSGO for price quotes and reservations.

1998 International ID Cards

Provides discounts on airfares, tourist attractions and more. Includes basic accident and medical insurance.
International Student ID Card (ISIC) $20
International Teacher ID Card (ITIC) $20
International Youth ID Card (GO25). $20

When ordering an International ID Card, please include:
1. Proof of birthdate (copy of passport, birth certificate, or driver's license).
2. One picture (1.5" x 2") signed on the reverse side.
3. (ISIC/ITIC only) Proof of student/teacher status (letter from registrar or administrator, proof of tuition, or copy of student/faculty ID card. FULL-TIME only).

Publications and More

Let's Go Travel Guides—The Bible of the Budget Traveler
- USA, Europe, India and Nepal, Southeast Asia................................$19
- Eastern Europe, France, Italy, Spain & Portugal $18
- Alaska & The Pacific Northwest, Australia, Britain & Ireland, California, Germany, Greece & Turkey, Israel & Egypt, Mexico, New Zealand $17
- Central America, Ecuador & The Galapagos Islands, Ireland, Austria & Switzerland $16
- London, New York, Paris, Rome, Washington, D.C. $14

Let's Go Map Guides
Fold out maps and up to 40 pages of text
Berlin, Boston, Chicago, London, Los Angeles, Madrid, New Orleans, New York, Paris, Rome, San Francisco, Washington D.C. $7

Michelin Maps
Know the country inside out! Great to accompany your Eurail pass—get 25% with any Eurail purchase.
Europe, Poland, Czech/Slovak Republics, Greece, Germany, Scandinavia & Finland, Great Britain and Ireland, Germany/Austria/Benelux, Italy, France, Spain and Portugal $10

1-800-5-LETSGO

http://www.hsa.net/travel/letsgo.htm

LET'S GO ORDER FORM

Last Name | First Name | Date of Birth

Street | We cannot ship to Post Office Boxes

City | State | Zip Code

Phone (very important) | Citizenship (Country)

School/College | Date of Travel

Description, Size	Color	Quantity	Unit Price	Total Price

Shipping and Handling

Eurail Passes do not factor into merchandise value.

Domestic 2-3 Weeks
Merchandise value under $30 ....$4
Merchandise value $30-$100 ....$6
Merchandise value over $100 ....$8

Domestic 2-3 Days
Merchandise value under $30 ....$14
Merchandise value $30-$100 ....$16
Merchandise value over $100 ....$18

Domestic Overnight
Merchandise value under $30 ....$24
Merchandise value $30-$100 ....$26
Merchandise value over $100 ....$28

All international shipping $30

Total Purchase Price	
Shipping and Handling	
MA Residents add 5% sales tax on gear and books	
TOTAL	

From which Let's Go Guide are you ordering? ☐ Europe ☐ USA ☐ Other_____

☐ **Mastercard** ☐ **Visa**

Cardholder name:

Card number:

Expiration date:

Make check or money order payable to:
Let's Go Travel
17 Holyoke Street
Cambridge MA, 02138
(617) 495-9649

1-800-5-LETSGO
http://www.hsa.net/travel/letsgo.html

Sitges celebrates holidays with all-out style. During the **Festa de Corpus Christi** on June 1, townspeople collaborate to create intricate fresh-flower carpets. For papier-mâché dragons, devils, and giants dancing in the streets, visit during the **Festa Major,** held August 23-25, in honor of the town's patron saint Bartolomé. Nothing compares to the **Carnaval** during the first week of Lent, when Spaniards of every ilk and province crash the town for a frenzy of dancing, outrageous costumes, and vats of alcohol. On the first Sunday of March, a pistol shot starts the **Rallye de Coches de Epoca,** an antique car race from Barcelona to Sitges. June brings the **International Theater Festival,** July and August the **International Jazz Festival,** while the **Festival Internacional de Cine Fantástico de Sitges** rolls around in October for 15 days.

■ Vilanova i la Geltrù

Catalunya's most important port after Barcelona and Tarragona, **Vilanova i la Geltrù** (90km southwest of Barcelona), is actually two cities blended into one. The industrial side does not overpower its well-groomed **beaches** (10min. from the train station). Burly Vilanovans are more likely to choose an evening of beach volleyball or soccer at the Gran Parc de Ribes over late-night madness.

An Egyptian mummy sidles up to paintings from the 17th century to the present in the **Museu Balaguer** (tel. 815 42 02), on Av. Victor Balaguer opposite the train station. The building's renovated interior is itself dazzling, seemingly straight from Barcelona. (Open Sun.-Mon. 10am-1:30pm, Tues.-Wed. and Fri.-Sat. 10am-1:30pm and 4:30-7pm, Thurs. 10am-1:30pm and 6-8:30pm; in winter Mon.-Sat. 10am-8pm, Sun. 10am-2pm. 200ptas, students 100ptas.) **Casa Papiol,** C. Major, 32 (tel. 893 03 82), is a 19th-century house that brings back the tastes of turn-of-the-century bourgeoisie (open Tues.-Sat. 9:30am-1:30pm and 4-5pm, Sun. 10am-1:30pm; 200ptas).

The **tourist office** (tel. 815 45 17), at the end of Rambla de Lluis Companys and Parc de Ribes Roges, can help find lodgings (open Mon.-Fri. 10am-1:30pm and 4:30-7:30pm, Sat. 10am-1:30pm). **Taxis** can be summoned by phone (tel. 815 50 50). **Ambulances** (tel. 904 100 904, 815 33 33, or 092) provide medical assistance. The **municipal police** can be reached at tel. 893 00 00. **Cercanías Trains** run every 15min. to and from Sitges (7min., 130ptas) and Barcelona (55min., 430ptas). Eighteen per day run from Tarragona, and 10 return (30min., 310ptas). **Ferries** run by Flebasa cruise to Alcudia (Mallorca) and Ciudadela (Menorca) via Alcudia. Flebasa also runs a **bus** service for customers between Barcelona and Vilanova (400ptas).

BARCELONA

Catalunya (Cataluña)

Catalunya's burnt-sienna, rocky Costa Brava and smooth Costa Daurada, its tranquil interior vineyards of Pendes, smooth, oval-like mountains, and cosmopolitan capital Barcelona have all kept the region physically and figuratively removed from Castilian Spain. *Catalanes* are industrious, proud, devoted to their land, and consequently privileged denizens of the richest region in the country.

Colonized by the Greeks and the Carthaginians, Catalunya was later one of Rome's favored provinces, to which scattered ruins testify. Only briefly subdued by the Moors, Catalunya's counts achieved independence in 874 and gained recognition as sovereign princes in 987. Having nabbed the throne of Aragón in 1137, Catalunya then became linked to the rest of Spain; yet Catalan *usages,* or *fueros* (legal codes), remained in effect. It took a Bourbon, King Felipe V, to suppress Catalunya as punishment for siding against him in the War of Spanish Succession (1702-1714). During the late 18th century, Catalunya developed into one of Europe's premier textile manufacturers at the same time it opened trade with the Americas. These developments led to the region's rapid revival of fortunes. Nineteenth-century industrial expansion nourished a flowering of arts and sciences, an age known as the Catalan *Renaixença* (Renaissance).

Staunch opponents of the Fascists during Spain's Civil War, Catalunya lost its autonomy in 1939 when the Republicans lost to Nationalist powers and the Falange Español took control. Franco suppressed Catalan instruction (except in universities) and clandestine publication in the language was limited to special areas. Since regaining autonomy in 1977, Catalan media and arts have flourished. The language is again official, even though the region is almost entirely bilingual. The language issue continues to fuel regional and national debates. Many Catalans, especially in Barcelona, will sooner answer inquiring visitors in English than Castilian. Some worry that the use of Catalan in institutions such as universities will discourage talented Spaniards from teaching, studying, or conducting research there, effectively isolating the principality. Others clamor for more extensive regional autonomy, arguing that Catalan regionalism has generally led to progressive ends, and that Spain should encourage rather than stifle its regional practices. The Generalitat recently mandated that all students be taught in *catalá.* The most visible display of Catalan spirit was at the 1992 Olympics, when "Freedom for Catalunya" banners were a common sight.

Lovers exchange books and roses to honor the region's patron, St. George, on the Fiesta de Sant Jordi (April 23). On September 11, *catalanes* whoop it up for *Diada,* (La Festa Nacional de Catalunya), a celebration of the region's political autonomy.

■ Girona (Gerona)

If you've come to Spain to reflect on the ages, Girona is for you. Layer upon layer of ethnic influences and epochal transitions are marked by stone alleyways twisting through the Jewish Quarter, weaving across the Riu Onyor to the modern section of Girona, on the river's west bank. Images of medieval dwellings reflecting off the Onyor's glossy waters dreamily evoke Girona's past glory as an international commercial center, when Christian, Arab, and Jewish communities settled along its shores to capitalize, as the Roman's did, on the city's favorable geography, as a gateway to Europe by land, and to the Orient by sea.

Various intellectual groups developed within those communities. The *cabalista de Gerona* originated here, practicing mystical Judaism, and later spreading the teachings of the Kaballah westward. Scholarly vivification thrives today in Girona's university, drawing intellectuals, artists, and their prodigies.

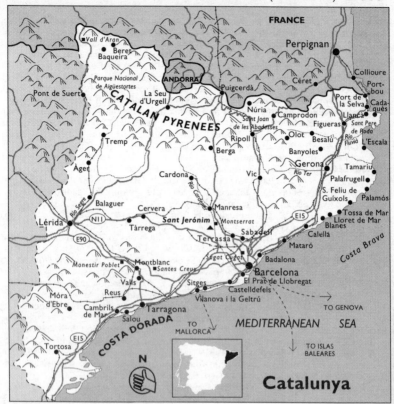

FRANCE

Perpignan

Vall d'Aran
Beret
Baqueira

Collioure

Parque Nacional
de Aigüestortes

ANDORRA
Céret

Port-
bou

Pont de Suert

La Seu
d'Urgell

Puigcerdà

Port de
la Selva

Cada-
qués

CATALAN PYRENEES

Núria
Sant Joan
de les Abadesses

Camprodon

Llançà

Sant Pere
de Roda

Figueras

Tremp

Ripoll

Olot

Besalú

L'Escala

Berga

Banyoles

Río
Fluvià

Aget

Cardona

Vic

Gerona
Río Ter

Tamariu

Balaguer

Cervera

Río Cardener

Manresa

Palafrugell

S. Feliu de
Guíxols

Palamós

Lérida

N II

Tàrrega

Sant Jerónim

Montserrat

EI5

Tossa de Mar
Lloret de Mar
Blanes

E90

Terrassa

Sabadell

Calella

Río Segre

Monestir Poblet

Montblanc

Sant Cugat

Badalona

Mataró

Costa Brava

Santes Creus

Valls

Móra
d'Ebre

Reus

Sitges

Barcelona

El Prat de Llobregat
Castelldefels

Cambrils
de Mar

Tarragona

Vilanova i la Geltrú

TO GENOVA

Salou

COSTA DORADA

TO
MALLORCA

MEDITERRANEAN   SEA

EI5

Tortosa

N

TO ISLAS
BALEARES

Catalunya

ORIENTATION AND PRACTICAL INFORMATION

Girona is the transportation hub of the Costa Brava. All trains on the Barcelona-Port-bou-Cerbère line stop here and seven different lines send buses to the Costa Brava. Transportation to Ripoll and Olot is also easy by bus, making Girona an ideal base for exploring the Catalan Pyrenees.

The cappuccino-colored **Riu Onyar** separates the new city from the old. The **Pont de Pedra** connects the two banks and leads directly into the old quarter by way of Carrers Ciutadans, Carrers Peralta, and Força, off of which branch the **cathedral** and **El Call,** the historic Jewish neighborhood. **RENFE** and **bus terminals** are situated off **Carrer de Barcelona,** in the modern neighborhood. To get to the old city from the stations, head straight out the station through the parking lot, turning left on C. Bailen, and left again on C. Barcelona. Follow C. Barcelona for two blocks until it forks at the traffic island. The right fork runs via C. Santa Eugenia to the **Gran Vía de Jaume I.** Cross this at the Banco Central Hispano to get on **Carrer Nou,** which runs directly to the Pont de Pedra.

Tourist Office: Rbla. Llibertat, 1 (tel. 22 65 75; fax 22 66 12), in a watermelon-red house directly on the left as you cross Pont de Pedra from the new town. An oasis for the directionally dehydrated. The blue and white street map is the best; the Corte Inglés's the most far-reaching. Open Mon.-Fri. 8am-8pm, Sat. 8am-2pm and 4-8pm, Sun. 9am-2pm. The **train station branch** (tel. 21 62 96) is downstairs, on the left as you face away from the RENFE ticket counter. Nifty electronic info server with zoom-able info maps. Open July-Aug. Mon.-Fri. 9am-2pm.

El Corte Inglés: (tel. 24 44 44), on C. Barcelona. Free **maps,** groceries, telephones, **currency exchange,** cafeteria, and reliability. Open Mon.-Sat. 10am-9pm.

Budget Travel: Direcció General de Juventut, C. Juli Garreta, 14 (tel. 20 15 54), 1 block from the train station, off C. Bisbe Tomás de Lorenzana. In an unmarked building on the *entresol* (mezzanine). Railpasses, buses, HI cards (500ptas), ISICs (700ptas), and the *Guide to Budget Accommodations* (500ptas). Not a TIVE office, and does not handle flight reservations. They do run Gerona's youth hostel. Open Mon.-Fri. 8am-3pm; mid-Sept. to mid-June 9am-1:30pm and 3:30-5:30pm.

Currency Exchange: If you can't find a bank in the new city, you need more help than a guidebook can give you. We recommend **Banco Central Hispano,** on the corner of C. Nou and Gran Vía de Jaume I. Another sits in the old city on Puyada Pont de Pedra, just after crossing the bridge on the right. Both open Mon.-Fri. 8:30am-2:30pm, Sat. 9:30am-1pm.

Trains: RENFE, Pl. Espanya (tel. 20 70 93), to: Figueres (26-52min., 315ptas); Portbou (1hr., 565ptas); Barcelona (1-2hr., 865ptas); Zaragoza (9 per day, 3-4hr., night train 6½hr., 4600ptas); Valencia (2 per day, 8hr., 5000ptas); Madrid (3 per day, 9hr., 6700ptas). To Jaca, change in Zaragoza.

Buses: (tel. 21 23 19), around the corner from the train station. **Sarfa** (tel. 20 17 96) to Tossa de Mar (July-Aug. 3 per day, regularly 2 per week, 1hr., 595ptas) and Palafrugell (15 per day, 1hr., 490ptas), for connections to Begur, Llafranc, Calella, and Tamariu. **Teisa** (tel. 20 02 75) to: Olot (6-12 per day, 1¼hr., 605ptas); Ripoll (4-5 per day, 2¾hr., 1050ptas); St. Feliu (15 per day, 410ptas). **Barcelona Bus** (tel. 20 24 32) express to Barcelona (995ptas) and Figueres (3-8 per day, 415ptas).

Car Rental: Most companies cluster around C. Barcelona, near the train station. Must be over 21 (some companies 24) and have had a license for at least 1-2 yr. **Hertz** (tel. 21 01 08), in the train station next to the tourist office branch. Ford Fiestas 3500-4500ptas per day (insurance not included).

Taxis: (tel. 20 33 77 or 22 10 20). Stands at Pl. Independència and Pont de Pedra.

Luggage Storage: Lockers in train station (600ptas). Open daily 6am-11pm.

English Bookstore: Gerona Books, C. Carme, 63, Rbla. Llibertat runs into C. Carme as you walk with the Riu Onyar on your right. Small but tasteful selection of new and used paperbacks. Open Mon.-Fri. 9am-1pm and 4-6:30pm.

Gay Service: Front d'Alliberament Gai de Catalunya (F.A.G.C.) (tel. 22 38 16).

Medical Services: Hospital Municipal de Santa Caterina, Pl. Hospital, 5 (tel. 20 14 50). **Hospital Doctor Josep Trueta** (tel. 20 27 00), on the highway to France. Interpreter in summer. **Red Cross:** Bonastruc de Porta, 11 (tel. 22 22 22).

Police: Policía Municipal, C. Bacià, 4 (tel. 40 90 92). From Banco Central turn right on the Gran Vía, then right on Bacià. **Emergency:** tel. 091 or 092.

Post Office: Av. Ramón Folch, 2 (tel. 20 16 87), at the beginning of Gran Vía de Jaume I. Turn right on Gran Vía coming from the old city. Open Mon.-Fri. 8:30am-8:30pm, Sat. 9:30am-2pm; July-Aug. Mon.-Fri. 8am-2pm, Sat. 9am-2pm. Letters and packages must be picked up at the **second office,** Ronda Ferrán Puig, 17 (tel. 21 07 71), but nothing may be sent (open Mon.-Sat. 8:30am-2pm). **Postal Code:** 17070.

Telephone Code: (9)72.

ACCOMMODATIONS

Rooms are most difficult to find in June and August. Most budget accommodations are sprinkled in and around the old quarter. Construction workers are jackhammering the old city, so don't be alarmed by a rude awakening at 8am.

Alberg-Residència Cerverí de Girona (HI), C. Ciutadans, 9 (tel. 21 81 21; fax 21 20 23), in the heart of the old quarter, on the street running left after Pont de Pedra. A college dorm during the year, it's ultra-modern inside. During the school year, only 8 beds are available, many more July-Aug. Sleek sitting rooms with TV/VCR; rooms of 3 and 8 beds, with lockers. Closed Aug. 1-Sep. 21. High-caliber staff, high-fashion sheets. 11pm curfew, but door opens every 30min. till 1am. 1600ptas. Over 25 2200ptas. Breakfast included. Other meals 750-800ptas. Sheets 350ptas. Laundry 500ptas. Make reservations at the Barcelona office June-Aug. (tel. (9)3 483 83 63).

Pensió Viladomat, C. Ciutadans, 5 (tel. 20 31 76). Sparkling rooms and bathrooms. Neat and well furnished with desks. Some rooms have balconies. Dining area with TV. Singles 1850ptas. Doubles 3600ptas. Triples 4200ptas. Breakfast 450ptas.

Pensió Perez, Pl. Bell-110c, 4 (tel. 22 40 08), keep straight after crossing Pont de Pedra into the old quarter onto C. Non del Teatre; Pl. Bell-110c is on the right. Elegant staircase leads to simple, clean rooms overlooking a quiet square. Singles 1500ptas. Doubles 2700ptas, with bath 3000ptas.

Pensió Reyma, Pujada Rei Marti, 15 (tel. 20 02 28), 2 blocks to the left of the cathedral (as you face it) on the corner of C. Ballaire. Bland but immaculate rooms above a plush sitting room. Singles 1600ptas. Doubles 3745ptas, with bath 5350ptas.

Hostal Residencia Bellmirall, C. Bellmirall, 3 (tel. 20 40 09), go straight from the door on the right side of the cathedral (angle left) until the blue sign appears. Stone rooms are the delightful and creative project of two Gironese artists—a florid mix of the husband's oil paintings and the wife's colorful needlework. Juice, croissants, and coffee served in an intimate breakfast room or tranquil adjoining patio. Singles 4540ptas, with bath 4800ptas. Doubles: 7200ptas; 7800ptas.

FOOD

Girona's restaurants are—almost uniformly—jewels of culinary excellence, relatively inexpensive, and outstanding places to sample innovative Catalan cuisine. Some of the best places huddle about the cathedral, especially along **C. Força.** Others—including several *al aire libre*—are found on **Pl. Independència,** at the end of C. Santa Clara in the modern section of the city. Scores of cafes line **Rbla. Llibertat,** and even more in the old quarter cater to university students. Girona's permanent **market** sits in Pl. Clave and Rubalcaba, on the new side of the city near the river (open Mon.-Sat. 8am-1pm). In summer, the **second branch** opens near the Polideportivo in Parc de la Deversa (open Tues. and Sat., 8am-1pm). One street north of C. Nou (off the Gran Vía) is supermarket **Valvi,** C. Sequia, 10. (Open Mon.-Thurs. 9am-1:30pm and 5-8:30pm, Fri. 9am-1pm and 5-9pm, Sat. 5-8:30pm.)

Café Le Bistrot, Pujada Sant Domènec, 4 (tel. 21 88 03), a right off C. Ciutadans. At lunch, hipsters and young lovers crowd marble tables and plant-filled windows to devour the inventive *platos* (*menú* 1200ptas; abridged version 950ptas). For dinner, freshly made pizzas (450-625ptas) and crepes (450ptas). Open Tues.-Thurs. 11am-2am, Fri.-Sat. and Mon. 7am-1am, Sun. 11am-4pm.

Café la Torrada, C. Ciutadans, 18 (tel. 21 71 04), a block from the youth hostel. Barely sentient lunch-time snooze-counter yields to a lively *tapas* crowd of local students and pre-yuppies. Catalan menu features almost nothing but *torradas*, those delectable toasts with toppings—order 2 or 3 (500-1300ptas) for a full meal. Open Mon.-Fri. 9am-4pm and 7pm-1am, Sat. 7pm-midnight.

L'Anfora, C. Força, 15 (tel. 20 50 10). Upstairs dining hall with wicker chairs and stone walls was once the secret site of Jewish religious ceremonies. Downstairs, large hunks of decidedly un-kosher ham hang over the bar. Mainly for tourists. Lunch *menú* 1000ptas. Open 12:30-4pm and 7-11pm. Visa, MC.

Restaurant Vegetariano La Polenta, C. Corte Reial, 6. Vegetarian fare with an international accent. Catalan rice with pine nuts 700ptas, Italian pasta 750ptas, Japanese sushi 500ptas. Plenty of no-lacto choices. *Menú* (lunch only) 1100ptas. Open Mon. and Wed.-Sat. 1-4pm and 8-11pm, Tues. 1-4pm.

Restaurante Cal'ivan, Rda. Ferrán Puig, 3 (tel. 20 14 30), in the new city. Not a tourist in sight, jammed with local businesspeople munching on one of many filling *menús* (1100-1600ptas). Open Mon.-Sat. 1-4pm and 8:30-11:30pm.

Restaurante-Cafeteria Cancarlas, C. Barcelona, 4, on the way to the train station. Lively young place serves everything from a quick sandwich (300ptas) to a variety of *platos combinados* (450-650ptas) to a stuffing *menú del dia* featuring cod with peppers and tomatoes or grilled beef with eggplant (900ptas). Shoot some pool between courses. Open daily 8am-11pm. *Menú* served 1-4pm.

Granje Mora, C. Corte Reial, 18 (tel. 20 22 38). We dare you to walk away without a smile on your face after sucking down any of their sandwiches or ice-cream drinks.

Jovial, down-to-earth owners have been a Gironan institution for 57 years. All-natural *Orxata de Xufu (horchata* 250ptas) is to die for.

SIGHTS

The old city is studded with signs for tourists. Start your self-guided historical tour at the Pont de Pedra and turn left at the tourist office down tree-lined **Rambla de la Llibertat.** At the end of the Rambla, turn right on C. Argenteria, cross C. Cort-Reial and continue on C. Carreras i Peralta. Up a flight of stairs, C. Força begins on the left.

El Call

El Call is the Jewish medieval neighborhood. ("Call" comes from *kahal,* meaning "community" in Hebrew.) It begins at C. Sant Llorenç; take a right turn off C. Força onto a narrow alleyway before the cathedral. The entrance to the **Centre Bonastruc Ça Porta** (tel. 21 67 61), also known as the **Casa de Isaac el Cec** (the Blind), is off C. Sant Llorenç about halfway up the hill. Probable site of the last synagogue in Girona, it now serves as a museum linking the baths, butcher shop, and synagogue, surrounding a serene central patio. The center honors Girona-born Rabbi Moshe ben Nahman, who in 1263 starred in a medieval version of *Crossfire,* defending his faith head-to-head with the Dominican Pau Cristià in the Disputation of Barcelona, while King Jaime I played the role of Pat Buchanan. (Open Mon.-Sat. 10am-9pm, Sun. 10am-2pm; Nov.-May Mon.-Sat. 10am-6pm, Sun. 10am-2pm. Free.)

Gerona's Jewish community became a leading center for the study of Kabbalah, an esoteric, mystical reading of the Scriptures proposing to unlock certain mysteries and foretell the future. Despite increasing conflict with the city's Christian sector, the Jewish community grew and even thrived during the Middle Ages. One century after the 1492 expulsion, however, it was eradicated by mass emigration, by forced conversion, and by the Inquisition's *autos-de-fé.* The city blocked off the *aljama*'s (neighborhood's) streets and converted the buildings for its own use. El Call's reopening began only after Franco's death in 1975. The area off C. Forçà is the best place to see what little is left of Girona's Jewish architecture.

Cathedral Complex

Farther uphill on C. Força and around the corner to the right, Girona's imposing Gothic **cathedral** rises up a record-breaking 90 steps (the largest Rococo stairway in Europe) from its *plaça.* The northern **Torre de Charlemany,** best viewed from the cloister, is the only structure left standing from the 11th century; the rest is spry, youthful, and from the 15th century. The cavernous interior has compressed the three customary naves into one, making it the world's widest Gothic vault (22m).

A door on the left leads to the trapezoidal cloister and the **Museu del Claustre** (tel. 21 44 26), which hoards some of Girona's most precious possessions, including seven 15th-century sculptures by Mercadante de Bretaña and Beato de Liébana's 10th-century *Libre de l'Apocalipsis,* an illuminated commentary on the end of the world. The museum's (and possibly Girona's) most famous piece is the intricate and animated **Tapis de la Creació,** a tapestry covering the entire wall of Room IV. Woven in the 11th or 12th century, it depicts biblical scenes and the creation cycle. The tapestry is described in Cristina Peri Rossi's novel, *La nave de los locos.* (Cathedral and museum open Tues.-Sun. 10am-2pm and 4-7pm; Sept.-June Tues.-Sat. 10am-2pm and 4-6pm, Sun. 10am-2pm. Museum 300ptas.)

Elsewhere in the Old Quarter

To reach the **Museu Arqueològic** (tel. 20 26 32) from C. Ferrán, turn left from the Banys Àrabs, descend the stairs, and pass through the gates of Pl. Jurats and over the bridge. The museum is the final resting place for medieval tombstones that once marked Jewish burial sites. A small section is dedicated to artifacts from Empúries (open Tues.-Sat. 10am-1pm and 4-7pm, Sun. 10am-2pm; 200ptas, Sun. free).

Next to the cathedral, on Pujada de la Catedral, poses the **Museu d'Art** (tel. 20 95 36), with its large collection of 12th-century Romanesque wood sculpture and the

Rebuilding Sepharad

The Jews of Girona underwent severe discrimination, ostracism, and eventual expulsion. Despite it all, they contributed inextricably to the city's culture, as poets, scientists, astronomers, rabbis, philosophers, and ministers of the court. The *aljama* (Jewish quarter), in Girona, was once populated by 300 people. It operated like a tiny independent country within the city, protected by the crown of Catalunya in exchange for financial tribute. A representative of the King ruled as mayor, answering to the crown, not the city government. This awkward balance between independence and subjugation led to continual conflicts. *Jurats* (city officials of Girona) passed oppressive measures asserting control over the Jews, in the name of protecting the Christian quarters.

Until the 11th century, Christians and Jews basically co-existed peacefully, sometimes intermarrying. Later, documented evidence cites attacks on the Jewish quarter in 8 different years, the first in 1276, the last in 1418. Attacks ranged from stone throwing to murder and looting. Eventually, the Call was enclosed and the ghetto would not be opened until August 4, 1492, after Ferdinand and Isabella expelled the Jews from Spain and the quarter had already been deserted. In recent times, eight Spanish mayors have created a network called *Caminos de Sepharad,* an organization aimed at restoring the synagogues and Jewish quarters. They hope to foster a broader understanding of the Sephardic legacy in their country.

teballa de vitraller, a 14th-century workbench for making stained-glass, and the only known vestige of the industrious medieval stained-glass industry. On the fourth floor, moody 19th-century landscape paintings of Girona hang alongside contemporary Catalan works. (Open Tues.-Sat. 10am-7pm, Sun. 10am-2pm; Oct.-March Tues.-Sat. 10am-6pm, Sun. 10am-2pm. 200ptas, Sun. free. Open Wed. nights July-Sept. till midnight.)

Near the **University of Girona** is the start of the **Passeig de la Muralla.** Railed steps lead up onto the walls of the city to a seagull's perspective of old Girona. The walk ends two blocks to the left of the Pont de Pedra. The trees and meadows of the **Vall de Sant Daniel** stretch north along the banks of the Galligants. The **Passeig Arqueològic,** partly lined with cypresses, pines, and flower beds, skirts the medieval wall on the east side of the river and overlooks the city.

ENTERTAINMENT

The **Rambla** and **Plaça de Independencia** are the places to see and be seen—to chat, gossip, politic, flirt, and dance. Most summer Fridays invite spontaneous *sardanas,* traditional Catalan dances resurrected in 19th-century Girona, involving 10-12 musicians serenading a ring of dancers. One musician plays a *tambón:* with one hand he pipes on a small flute, with the other he taps a tiny drum slung over his forearm.

After the *passeig* comes dinner, and after dinner, bar-hopping—the throngs move to the newer part of the city. Bars near Pl. Ferrán el Catòlic draw big crowds, but during the summer, **Parc de la Devesa,** across the river from the old town and several blocks to the left, has all the cachet, and often live music as well. Against a backdrop of towering old trees and broad paths, local bars stand in below their hazy splendor. Of Girona's four discos, the mightiest is **La Sala de Cel,** C. Pedret, 118 (tel. 21 26 64), off Pl. Sant Pere, in the north quarter of the city (open Sept.-July Thurs.-Sun.; 2000ptas cover includes 2 drinks). Artsy folk mill around bars and cafes in the old quarter. Two good ones to try are the **Cafe del Llibre,** C. Ferreires Vellas (parallel to C. Ciutadans), catering to chic intellectuals, and the unnamed bar at **C. Ballesteros, 21,** made popular among art-loving *amantes.*

During the second half of May, **flower exhibitions** spring up in the city, local monuments swim in blossoms, and the courtyards of Girona's fine old buildings open to the public. From July-Sept., the city hosts the **Festival de Noves Músiques,** a series of six concerts in La Mercè. The concert hall is at Pujada de la Mercé, 12 (tel. 22 33 05). In June and July, **concerts** take place in front of the cathedral, in the Jardins de la

CATALUNYA (CATALUÑA)

Devesa. From July-Sept. the Museu d'Art hosts one every other Wednesday night at 10pm. (Entrance and admission up to 1500ptas, but sometimes free or discounted for students. Check with the tourist office for an events schedule.) The **Parc de la Devesa,** on the west side of the river, is the largest urban park in Catalunya. The complete *sardana* guide, the *Guia d'Aplecs Sardanistes de les Comarques Gironines,* is available at the tourist office, along with a complete listing of observed holidays and festivals. Girona's two local holidays are July 25 for Sant Jaume, and Oct. 29 for the Fires de Sant Narcís. Like the rest of northern Spain, Girona lights up for the **Focs de Sant Joan,** an exuberant outdoor party featuring fireworks, campfires, and a long history of public merry-making.

COSTA BRAVA

The Costa Brava's jagged cliffs cut into the Mediterranean Sea from Barcelona to the French border. Though savage by name, the coast is tamed in July and August by planeloads of Europeans dumped onto its once tranquil beaches. Solitary types avoid the Costa Brava, or come in early June and late September when the water is still warm but less populated. In winter, the bitterly cold winds of the *tramontana* may intimidate even the obstinate traveler. The rocky shores have traditionally enticed artists. Chagall set up his easel here and Surrealist icon Salvador Dalí was a native of the region. Dalí's house in Cadaqués and his museum in Figueres house the largest collections of his work in Europe.

Transportation on the Costa Brava is fickle. Service is most frequent during July and August, somewhat less so the rest of the tourist season (May-Oct.), and drops to bare subsistence during winter. **RENFE trains** stop at the southern tip of the coast at Blanes, Figueres, and again at Llançà and Portbou (near the French border). **Bus** is the preferred mode of transportation here. **Sarfa** runs buses along beautiful roads. Some of the more tortuous rides might warrant anti-vomit medication. Prices, especially for lodging, vary according to season. Call ahead for precise info on accommodations and transportation. Tossa de Mar is the crown of the southern Costa Brava and a base to explore the area. To the north, Figueres is linked to Cadaqués by bus and Portbou by rail. Palafrugell is an inland connection to central Costa Brava. Local tourist offices distribute maps of off-road sights, camping areas, and coastal trails.

PORTBOU

Sitting on Catalunya's border with France, Portbou (pop. 1500) paid the price of industrial progress a hundred years ago when the Barcelona-Cerbère railroad stretched its tentacles around Portbou's delicate neck and squeezed it breathless. While Europe indecisively marches toward economic unity, Portbou faces the threat of losing its customs economy, and valuable jobs. The town is trying to flag down tourists moving between Catalunya and France, hoping to be reincarnated as a beach resort town. Still, as border towns go, Portbou is not so bad—it has preserved its pleasant pebble beach and leafy trees lining its few streets.

The **tourist office** (tel. 39 02 84), on the water, has a tidal wave of brochures (open Mon.-Sat. 9am-2pm and 3-8pm, Sun. 9am-2pm). There's **currency exchange** at the train station with fair rates, considering its location (no commission for cash, 500ptas charge for traveler's checks). The **Ajuntament,** at the end of Pg. Sardanes, at the end of the beach, houses the **police** (tel. 39 02 84), and the **health center** (tel. 12 50 58). The **Post Office** is at Pg. Enric Granades, 10 (tel. 39 01 75; open Mon.-Fri. 8:30am-2:30pm, Sat. 9:30am-1pm). The **postal code** is 17497. The **telephone code** is (9)72.

Hostal Juventus, Av. Barcelona, 3 (tel. 39 02 41), sits near the waves two blocks from the train station. The outer rooms barely manage views of the nearby bay. The same owners run a *croissanterie* downstairs (singles 1700ptas, doubles 3300ptas, triples 4800ptas). For a restorative drink, try one of many **cafes** lining Pg. Marítim. Portbou's **market** is conveniently located one block down from the train station on C.

Mercat; there's also the Can Coll **grocery store** to the immediate left upon exiting the station. Morbid, hungry types can eat cheaply from the same place philosopher Walter Benjamin ate his last meal, **Restaurant International,** C. Del Mar, 5, a left off C. Mercat as you exit the station (900-1000ptas *menú;* open daily 12:30am-4pm and 7:30-11pm). Restaurants by the waterfront offer typical tourist fare at unfortunate prices.

RENFE **trains** (tel. 39 00 99), go to Barcelona (14 per day, 2¾hr., 1200ptas) via every town with a station in western Catalunya, including Figueres (19 per day, 30min., 190ptas), as well as north to Collioure, France.

LLANÇÀ (LLANSÁ)

Nine km south of the French border, Llançà (pop. 3700) is the northernmost resort of any magnitude on the Costa Brava, with many beaches and coves and few historical sights. It's pleasant rather than scintillating, but good enough to work on your tan. The main beach, **Platja del Port,** opens onto a protected harbor. The town center lies in the opposite direction; look for the **església** and the 14th-century **Torre de Llançà** to find the central *plaça.*

From the **bus** and **train stations,** cross the highway and bridge and continue on Av. Europa until it forks: right leads into town, left to the port. For the harbor and beaches, follow the curve to the left and walk about 1km, watching for signs pointing to the port. To get to town, follow C. Rafael Estela past the **telephones** (open daily 9am-1:30pm and 4:30-10:30pm) and to **Plaça Major.** A second phone office with similar hours is at the port parking lot to the right of the beach.

The English-speaking staff in the **tourist office,** Av. Europa, 37 (tel. 38 08 55; fax 38 12 58), on the road to the port, has a detailed but superfluous map. (Open daily 9:30am-9pm, Sun. 10am-1pm only; Sept.-June Mon-Fri. 10am-1pm and 5-8pm., Sat. 10am-1pm and 5-7pm, Sun. 10am-1pm.) The **Red Cross** is at Platja Crifeu (tel. 38 08 31). The **local police** pick up at tel. 38 13 13; in an **emergency,** call tel. 091 or 092. The **post office** C. la Selva, 17 (tel. 38 12 68), is in the municipal building (open Mon.-Fri. 8:30am-2:30pm, Sat. 9:30am-1pm). The **postal code** is 17490. The **telephone code** is (9)72.

Habitaciones Ca'n Pau, C. Puig d'Esquer, 4 (tel. 38 02 70), is comfortable and quiet, with a rooftop for hanging laundry and taking in the view, and floral-bedded rooms kept clean by *Let's Go*-loving owners. Take the second left as you enter town (C. Cabrafiqa), then turn left three blocks later on C. Deciana; turn right almost immediately on C. Puig d'Esquer (singles 2035ptas, doubles 3210ptas). **Pensió Beri,** C. Creu (tel. 38 01 98), has magnificent rooms, winter heating, and huge bathrooms. Perfect your grand entrances on the wide, tile staircase. From Pl. Major, bear right and follow C. Nicolás Salmerón to the edge of town. At the crossroads take a sharp left until the sign comes into view. (Singles with bath 2800ptas. Doubles with bath 5000ptas. Sept.-June: 2000ptas; 4000ptas. Breakfast 500ptas.) **Camping L'Ombra,** Ctra. Portou, 13 (tel. 38 03 35), has 123 spaces lounging 500m from the beach (495ptas per person, 265ptas per car, and 465ptas per tent).

Llançà's waterfront *menú*-suppliers are generally overpriced, although cheap places pepper the town. Pack your picnic basket at **Valvi Supermercats,** a large supermarket on Av. Europa, on the right as you head toward the beach (open Mon.-Sat. 9am-1:30pm and 4:30-8:30pm, Sun. 9am-1:30pm). **Restaurant Grill Pati Blanc,** C. Rafael Estela, 6 (tel. 38 09 93), on the way to Pl. Major, offers just what the name says on a shaded, white patio. The meats, like grilled chicken (550ptas), are succulent, and there are plenty of veggie dishes like *escalivada* (grilled and marinated red peppers, eggplant, and onions 725ptas; open daily 1-4pm and 7:30pm-midnight).

RENFE **trains** (tel. 38 02 55) run to and from: Portbou (16 per day, 15min., 140ptas); Figueres (18 per day, 20-30min., 160ptas); Girona (18 per day, 1hr., 385ptas); and Barcelona (18 per day, 1½hr., 1105ptas). **Sarfa** (tel. 12 06 76) runs **buses** to Port de la Selva (2-6 per day, 20min., 125ptas, Sat.-Sun. 135ptas).

SANT PERE DE RODES

The glorious ruins of the **monastery** Sant Pere de Rodes, built in the 10th and 11th centuries, are 9km south of Llançà on the coast. On a clear day Portbou is easily espied to the north, and Cadaqués to the south from the Benedictine monastery.

Getting there can be something less than half the fun. The tourist office at Llançà organizes excursions every Tuesday from mid-July to August (750ptas)—anybody finding this schedule inconvenient, or lacking a car, should be prepared for some serious foot mileage. Committed hikers can trek from Llansá, a strenuous 2½-3hr. hike with splendid vistas along the way. Tenderfeet will have to take the Sarfa bus from Llançà to Port de la Selva (4 per day) and ask to be dropped off on the road to the monastery. From there, make the far less arduous 1½hr. climb. (Monastery open Tues.-Sun. 10am-7pm; Oct.-May 10am-1:30pm and 3-5:30pm. 200ptas.)

■ Figueres (Figueras)

In 1974, Surrealist Salvador Dalí chose his native Figueres (pop. 37,000) as the site to build a magnificent museum for his works. Ever since, melting clocks and poop-in-the-pants have meant fast bucks for Figueres. Thirty-six kilometers north of Girona, the city is otherwise a beachless sprawl, a convenient base for visiting the often booked-solid Costa Brava.

ORIENTATION AND PRACTICAL INFORMATION

Roughly 20km inland, Figueres marks the center of the Costa Brava's breadbasket. Trains and buses arrive at **Plaça Estació** on the edge of town. Take a left on **Carrer Sant Llàtzer**, walk seven blocks to **Carrer Nou**, and take a right. C. Nou leads directly to Figueres's arboreal **Rambla.** To reach the **tourist office,** walk up the Rambla and continue on **Carrer Lasauca.** The all-knowing big blue **"i"** beckons across the rather treacherous intersection with **Ronda Frial.**

Tourist Office: Pl. Sol (tel. 50 31 55). A good city **map** and list of accommodations and restaurants. Open July-Aug. Mon.-Sat. 9am-9pm; Easter-June and Oct. Mon.-Fri. 8:30am-3pm and 4:30-8pm, Sat. 9:30am-1:30pm and 3:30-6:30pm; rest of the year Mon.-Fri. 8:30am-3pm. In summer, **2 branch offices** open, one in front of the bus station (open July 15-Sept. 15 Mon.-Sat. 9:30am-1pm and 4-7pm), and the other a yellow mobile home by the Dalí museum (open July 15-Sept. 15 Mon.-Sat. 10am-2:30pm and 4:30-7pm).

Telephones: Pl. Sol, open Mon.-Sat. 9am-1:30pm and 4:30-9pm.

Trains: (tel. 20 70 93) chug to: Girona (24 per day, fewer Sat.-Sun. and off-season, 25min.-1hr., 370ptas); Portbou (19 per day, 30min., 300ptas); Barcelona (24 per day, 1½-2hr., 1100ptas).

Buses: All lines leave from the Estació Autobuses (tel. 67 33 54), Pl. Estació. **Sarfa** (tel. 67 42 98) to: Cadaqués (5 per day, Sept.-June 2-3 per day, 1¼hr., Mon.-Fri. 450ptas, Sat.-Sun. 510ptas) and Llançà (4 per day, 315ptas). **Barcelona Bus** (tel. 50 50 29) to Girona (4-6 per day, 1hr., 415ptas one way) and Barcelona (4-6 per day, 2¼hr., 1375ptas).

Currency Exchange: Banco Central Hispano, Rambla. Open Mon.-Fri. 8:30am-2pm.

Bike Rental: At the HI hostel (see **Accommodations and Food,** below). 400ptas per hr., 1200ptas per half-day, 1700ptas per day.

Luggage Storage: At train station, large lockers 600ptas. Open daily 6am-10pm. At the bus station 300ptas.

Red Cross: Albert Cotó, 1 (tel. 50 17 99 or 50 56 01).

Police: Ronda Firal, 4 (tel. 51 01 11), 100m from the tourist office.

Emergency: tel. 091 or 092.

Post Office: Pl. Sol (tel. 50 54 31). Open Mon.-Fri. 8:30am-2:30pm, Sat. 9:30am-1pm. **Postal Code:** 17600.

Telephone Code: (9)72.

ACCOMMODATIONS AND FOOD

Finding a place to sleep can be a surreal experience. Though the town is reorganizing to accommodate the influx of tourists, Figueres hides its affordable hotels and *pensiones* in unlikely spots. Some cluster on **C. Jonquera** and **C. Rec Arnau,** though they necessitate trekking northeast from the Dalí museum. Do not, repeat, **do not** bed down at the notoriously unsafe Municipal Park. Tourist-oriented restaurants near the Dalí museum scoop overcooked *paella* to the masses; better choices reside a few minutes away in the streets surrounding the **Rambla.** The **mercado,** is at Pl. Palmera and nearby Pl. Grano (open Tues., Thurs., and Sat. 7am-1pm). Or, mass-buy at the supermarket **MAXOR,** Pl. Sol, 6 (open Mon.-Sat. 8:30am-9pm; Visa, MC).

Alberg Tramuntana (HI), C. Anciet de Pagès, 2 (tel. 50 12 13; fax 67 38 08), one block behind the tourist office. Everything a backpacking wanderluster could want including friendly hosts, hot showers, fax service, VCR, library, board games, a restaurant that serves vegetarian meals on request, bike rentals, and laundry. Lock-in midnight (opens for 10min. at 1, 2, 3, and 4am). Lockout Mon.-Fri. 10am-4pm, Sat.-Sun. 10am-5pm. Members only, but they sell HI cards. 1600ptas, over 26 2200ptas. Oct.-April: 1375ptas; 1875ptas. Sheets 350ptas. Breakfast included. Laundry service 600ptas. Reserve 1 month in advance July-Aug. through the Barcelona office at tel. (9)3 483 83 63 or call the hostel 2-3 days prior to arrival. Visa, MC, AmEx.

Pensión Mallol, C. Pep Ventura, 9 (tel. 50 22 83), follow the Rambla toward the tourist office, turn right on Castell, and take the second left. The friendly owner keeps large rooms and holds cleanliness sacred. Long green halls contrast nicely with peppermint pink bathrooms. Singles 1800ptas. Doubles 3100ptas. Visa.

Restaurante La Torrada, La Rosa, 6 (tel. 50 95 66), left off the Rambla on C. Vilatant, then the 2nd right. The 900ptas *menú* is a meat lover's dream. Great *torradas* (toasted bread with toppings). Open Wed.-Mon. 9am-11pm. Closed July 1-14.

Pizzeria Le Setrill, C. Tortellà, 10 (tel. 50 55 40), a side street off Ronda Mosseu Cinto, which runs in front of the tourist office. Tasty Italian specialties (pizza 750-995ptas), but the real bargain is the *menú*—890ptas buys you a choice of salads, entree, and dessert. Open daily 1:30-4pm and 8pm-midnight. Closed July 1-14.

Restaurante La Pansa, C. l'Emporda, 8 (tel. 50 10 72). The back door is directly across from the youth hostel. Comfortable restaurant extremely popular with workers on their lunch break and groups of *señoras* celebrating. *Menú* (1850ptas) includes Catalan specialties like *arròs a la cassola* and a mighty fine *crema catalana* (custard). Open Mon.-Sat. 1-3:30pm and 8-11pm.

SIGHTS AND ENTERTAINMENT

Despite his reputation as a fascist and self-promoting cad and the sneers of many members of the "serious" art world that feels threatened by popular appeal, Dalí has become everybody's freshman poster choice. The **Teatre-Museu Dalí** (tel. 51 19 76; fax 50 16 66) immortalizes the man in his own style. Erotically nightmarish drawings, a sculpture garden, and a personal rock collection round out the trove of paintings which include the soul-baring *Self Portrait With a Slice of Bacon.* Dalí's cartoons are also sure to amuse. Follow C. Sant Llàtzer (from the train station) for six blocks, turn right on C. Nou, and follow it to its end at the Rambla. Go diagonally to the right and take C. Girona, which goes past Pl. Ajuntament and becomes St. Jonqueira. A flight of steps by a Dalí statue leads to the museum. (Open daily 9am-8pm; Oct.-June 11:30am-5pm. Box office closes 45min. before museum. 1000ptas, students and seniors 800ptas; Oct.-June: 800ptas; 600ptas.)

Museu de l'Empordà, Rambla, 2 (tel. 50 23 05), packs in a packrat-like assortment of archeological finds and other whatzits, including paintings from the 19th-century Catalan *Renaixença.* (Open Mon.-Sat. 11am-1pm and 4-9pm, Sun. 5-9pm; Oct.-June Mon.-Sat. 11am-1pm and 3:30-7pm, Sun. 11am-2pm. Free.)

In September, Figueres hosts classical and jazz music at the **Festival Internacional de Música de l'Empordà.** (Call Joventuts Musicals at tel. 50 01 17 for info and tickets or get a brochure at the tourist office.) In the first week of May, the **Fires i Festes de**

la **Santa Creu** sponsors cultural events and art and technology exhibitions. Merry-making at the **Festa de Sant Pere,** held June 28-29, honors the town's patron saint.

■ Near Figueres: Cadaqués

This charming cluster of whitewashed houses facing a small bay has attracted artists, writers, and musicians ever since Dalí built his summer house here in the 1930s. To preserve its facade, a largely affluent, pseudo-bohemian crowd of property owners and renters just says no to condos, huge hotels, and trains. These efforts, however, have not kept away the hordes of potential skin cancer victims from blithely burning themselves to a common crisp.

The **Museu Municipal d'Art** (or Museu de Cadaqués), C. Monturiol, a collection of local and Dalí-esque art, recently got a facelift (open daily 10:30am-1pm and 5-9pm). The **Centre d'Art Perrot-Moore,** C. Vigilant, 1 (tel. 25 82 31), near the town center, hordes Dalí memorabilia as well as some of Pablo Picasso's ephemera, including part of his sketchbook for the monumental *Guernica,* and paintings by Matisse, Duch-amp, and Dufy (open April-Oct. daily 10:30am-1:30pm and 4:30-8:30pm; 600ptas, students 400ptas). For either museum, follow the signs from the mapboard on Pl. Frederic Rahola; otherwise, head toward the bay, hang a right on the waterfront road and another on C. Vigilant. For Dalí's house, stay on the waterfront road past the bars and restaurants until C. Miranda appears on the left. Follow this road out of town and take a right onto Av. Salvador Dalí. The house is being renovated to open as a museum in Sept. 1997 (hopefully). Some of the architecture (a few oversized eggs, for example) is visible from the road that leads to the house.

The **Festival Internacional de Música** (tel. 25 83 15) sponsors 10 concerts in late July and early August, two by student groups (tickets around 2000ptas). Throughout the summer, locals dance *sardanas* outdoors (schedules listed on the **passeig** by the waterfront) and occasionally hop to live tunes. Those determined to catch some rays can try the **Platja Gran,** near the town center, or, even better, **Sa Concha,** a five-minute walk south of town.

Practical Information The bus to Cadaqués halts at a shack by a miniature two-fisted Statue of Liberty. From there, walk left and downhill along Av. Caritat Serinyana to the waterfront **Plaça Frederic Rahola.** Once there, a signboard map with indexed services and accommodations will orient you. The staff at the **tourist office,** C. Cotxe, 2 (tel. 25 83 15; fax 15 95 42), off Pl. Frederic Rahola opposite the *passeig,* is helpful, but their map falls just this side of worthless. (Open Mon.-Sat. 10am-2pm and 4-8:30pm, Sun. 10am-2pm; in winter Mon.-Sat. 10am-1pm and 4-7pm.) **Banco Central Hispano** is on C. Rieva de San Vicenç (open Mon.-Fri. 8:30am-2:30pm). **Bikes** and **in-line skates** can be rented at **Espanòbici,** C. Fort de la Vella, 2 (tel. 25 90 52), off Av. Caritat. (Open daily 9am-9pm. Mountain bikes 500ptas per hr., 2500ptas per day, 8500ptas per week. In-line skates 400ptas per hr., 2000ptas per day.) **La Sirena,** C. Riba Pitxot, along the waterfront, sells a small selection of **English books,** mostly popular, quality fiction (open June-Sept. 11am-2pm and 5-10pm; though hours may vary; Visa, MC). For **medical assistance,** call tel. 25 80 07. In an **emergency,** contact the **local police** (tel. 15 93 43), Pl. Frederic Rahola, beside the promenade, or call tel. 091 or 092. The **post office** is on Av. Rierassa, in front of Disco Paradis and far inland (open Mon.-Sat. 9am-1pm). The town's **postal code** is 17488. The **telephone code** is (9)72.

Cadaqués has no train station. Sarfa **buses** (tel. 25 87 13) run to: Figueres (5 per day, 500ptas); Girona (3 per day, summer only, 2hr., 865ptas); and Barcelona (5 per day, 1975ptas, Sat.-Sun. 2245ptas). Buses drop passengers at the junction of Ctra. Port Lligat and Pg. Caritat Serinyana, which leads to the town center.

Accommodations and Food Sleep is dear in Cadaqués—try nearby Figueres for cheaper shut-eye. Reservations are a good idea in July and August. **Hostal Marina,** C. Riera de Sant Vicenç, 3 (tel. 25 81 99), directly ahead as you face the mapboard on

Pl. Frederic Rahola, overlooks the beach. Its rooms are clean and airy, some even balconied. (Singles 2300ptas, with bath 3500ptas. Doubles: 4800ptas; 6500ptas. Breakfast 450ptas. Visa, MC.) **Hotel Ubaldo,** C. Unió, 13 (tel. 25 83 24), has brightly decorated, newly renovated digs with baths and TVs (singles and doubles 6400ptas). **Camping Cadaqués,** Ctra. Portlligat, 17 (tel. 25 81 26), is on the left on the way to Dalí's house from town; or ask the bus driver to let you off near it before you arrive in town. The grounds, only 100m from the beach, have a pool (July-Aug.), warm showers (100ptas), and a supermarket (525ptas per person, 650ptas per tent, 525ptas per car; open June-Sept. 15). Their "no frills" bungalows offer a roof over the head for the tent-deprived (doubles 3000ptas, triples 3800ptas, quads 4200ptas; two-day minimum). Cadaqués harbors the usual slew of overpriced, under-exciting tourist restaurants. For a place that tries just a bit harder, check out tiny, family-run **Can Pelayo,** C. Pruna (tel. 25 83 56), a right off of waterfront Riba Pitxot. At first glance, their *menú* (1200ptas) looks depressingly familiar, but the food goes above and beyond—try the delicious fried fish, accompanied by crisp-fried eggplant, or the fresh *paella*.

■ Palafrugell

Forty kilometers east of Girona, Palafrugell is a trampoline for takeoffs to nearby beach towns **Calella, Llafranc,** and **Tamariu,** towns that cater to wealthy Europeans whose idea of budget accommodation is any hotel that doesn't leave mints on the bed. To vacation like the Bundesbank junkies without the expense, stay in (admittedly dull) Palafrugell and daytrip to nearby beaches. Minuscule Tamariu is isolated from the other two beach towns, and thus is likely to be less crowded. Calella is the largest and liveliest of the three, and is connected to Llafranc by one of several **Caminos de Ronda,** a series of small stone footpaths allowing exploration of the coast.

ORIENTATION AND PRACTICAL INFORMATION

Turn right from the Palafrugell Sarfa **bus station,** and walk down **Carrer Torres i Jonama** to **Carrer de Pi i Maragall.** Turn right and walk past the **Guardia Civil** and the market until you hit **Plaça Nova,** pensioner and pigeon hangout.

From the Sarfa station, buses dash the paltry 3km to **Llafranc** and **Calella** (4-23 per day, 115ptas). They leapfrog Llafranc to stop in Calella first, catching Llafranc on the way back to Palafrugell. There are many stops in Calella—get off by the inflatable beach balls. Service to **Tamariu,** also by Sarfa-bus, is far less frequent (3-4 per day, 115ptas). Otherwise, spin away on moped or mountain bike, or take a pleasant—if lengthy—walk through the countryside (1hr. to each coastal town).

Tourist Office: C. Carrilet, 2 (tel. 30 02 28; fax 61 12 61). From the bus station go left on C. Torres i Jonama, left again at the traffic circle, and walk about 200m. A profoundly inconvenient location, but loaded with info. The *Guía Municipal* is indispensable, the **Catalan dictionary** is useful. (Open Mon.-Sat. 9am-9pm, Sun. 10am-1pm; Oct.-June and Sept. Mon.-Sat. 10am-1pm and 5-8pm, Sun. 10am-1pm). **Branches** with different summer hours are in **Llafranc,** C. Roger de Llúria (tel. 30 50 08); **Calella,** Les Voltes, 6 (tel. 61 44 75); and **Tamariu,** C. Riera (tel. 62 01 93). All 3 are open June-Sept. Mon.-Sat. 10am-1pm and 5-8pm, Sun. 10am-1pm.

Buses: Sarfa, C. Torres Jonama, 67-79 (tel. 30 06 23). To: Calella and Llafranc (4-23 per day, 115ptas); Tamariu (3-4 per day, 115ptas); Girona (13 per day, 1hr., 490ptas); Sant Feliu (17 per day, 45min., 245ptas); Barcelona (4-9 per day, 2hr., 1470ptas); Figueres (2-4 per day, 1½hr., 735ptas).

Taxis: Ràdio Taxi (tel. 61 00 00). 24hr. service throughout the area.

Bike Rental: Bicismarca, C. Barrisi Buixo, 55 (tel. 30 44 47). 500ptas per 2hr., 1200ptas per ½day, 1700ptas per day.

Luggage Storage: At the train ticket window in Safra station (200ptas per bag). Open 6:30am-8:30pm.

Medical services: Red Cross, C. Ample, 1. The **ambulatori,** Av. Josep Pla (tel. 30 48 16), provides general medical care.

Municipal police: Av. Josep Pla and C. Cervantes (tel. 61 31 01). Call them for 24hr. **pharmacy** info. One of 2 places on the Costa Brava with an *oficina de atención extranjera* (office for assistance to foreigners), the answer to the penniless, documentless, or clueless tourist's prayers. **Emergency:** tel. 091 or 092.

Post Office: C. Torres Jonama, 14 (tel. 30 06 07). Open for stamps and Lista de Correos Mon.-Fri. 8:30am-2:30pm, Sat. 9:30am-1pm. **Postal Code:** 17200. **Telephone Code:** (9)72.

ACCOMMODATIONS AND FOOD

Accommodation prices are reasonable. Restaurants near the beach are predictably expensive—try packing a lunch. Palafrugell has a penchant for unusual seafood variations, such as *garoines* (sea urchins) and octopus in onion sauce. Push a cart at **Super Stop,** C. Torres Jonama, 33 (open Mon.-Sat. 8am-2pm and 5-9pm, Sun.9am-2pm).

Fonda L'Estrella, C. Quatres Cases, 13-17 (tel. 30 00 05), under the pink sign at the corner of C. La Caritat, off C. Torres Jonama. Refreshing, well lit rooms off a Moorish courtyard bursting with plant life. Breakfast in the garden. If you want a romantic double, ask for room #19. 1900ptas per person. 1800ptas in low season (plus 7% IVA). Breakfast 475ptas. Parking 200ptas. Closed Oct. 15-March.

Hostal Plaja, C. Sant Sebastià, 34 (tel. 30 05 26), off Pl. Nova. Grand, frescoed foyer gives way to a broad courtyard surrounded by spiffy rooms, many with balconies, all with new beds. Singles 2600ptas. Doubles 4700ptas. Oct.-May: Singles 2400ptas Doubles 4500ptas. Breakfast 450ptas. Closed Dec. Visa, MC.

Residencia Familiar, C. Sant Sebastià, 29 (tel. 30 00 43). Halls a la Jackson Pollack, but rooms are plain, airy, and clean. Singles 2000ptas. Doubles 4000ptas (less for longer stays). Off season: 1500ptas; 3000ptas. Closed Nov.-Semana Santa.

Camping: Camping Moby Dick, C. Costa Verda, 16 (tel. 61 43 07), on bus route off Av. Costa del Sol in Calella. No Pequod in sight, but near the water (5min.) nonetheless. Plenty of shade from abundant pine trees. Good showers. 515ptas per person, 525ptas per car and per tent. Cheaper in low season. Open April-Sept.

Restaurant el Rebost del Pernil, C. Mayor, 3 (tel. 61 06 95). A new and delicious entry on the Palafrugell restaurant scene. Wide-ranging *menú del dia* (1400ptas) features truly outstanding versions of Catalan classics like *exalivada* and *fideu*. Open daily 1-4:30pm and 7:30pm-midnight.

Restaurant La Clau, C. Pi i Maragall, 31 (tel. 30 46 52), 2 blocks toward C. Torres Jonama, close to Pl. Nova. A wood and stucco eatery just a stone's throw from the plaza. *Bocadillos* 200-400ptas. Try the stuffed *calamares. Menú* 850ptas. Open Tues.-Sun. 1-4pm and 8-11pm.

Restaurant Bar L'Espasa, C. Fra Bernat Boil, 14 (tel. 61 50 32), on the seaside walk from Calella to Llafranc. Delicious food, great views. Specializes in seafood stews and *arroz negro* (black rice). *Menú* 1100ptas. Visa, MC. Closed Oct.-Semana Santa.

SIGHTS AND ENTERTAINMENT

A 40-minute walk up the road from Llafranc, the **Església de San Sebastià** crowns the mountain of the same name (50m from the lighthouse) and surveys the entire Palafrugell valley, beaches, and sea. Palafrugell proudly boasts Spain's finest cork museum (competitors: none), the **Museu del Suro,** C. Tarongeta, 31 (tel. 30 39 98), devoted to the industrial, historical, and ecological aspects of cork studies, and "cork culture." (Open Tues.-Sat. 10am-1pm and 5-9pm, Sun. 10:30am-1:30pm; Sept.-June Tues.-Sat. 5-8pm, Sun. 10:30am-1:30pm. 200ptas, students and retirees 100ptas.)

Palafrugell's Friday evening *passeig* ends up at the *plaça,* where young and old do the *sardana* at 10pm. Don't be afraid to join; all it takes is a little coordination and a truckload of chutzpah. For more familiar dancing, check out **Discoteca X qué** (pronounced *por qué*), 1km down the old road to Calella. The town's biggest party takes place July 18-20, when the dance-intensive **Festa Major** bursts into the streets. Calella's festivities take place on June 29 in honor of Sant Pere, Tamariu's on August 15, and Llafranc's on August 27-30 in honor of Santa Rosa.

In Callela

The tourist office in Palafrugell provides maps of paths and trails that criss-cross the area and join the coastal towns, including the **Rondas** (incredible climbs near the coast), as well as info on nearby **scuba diving** sites. The botanical gardens at **Castell i Jardins de Cap Roig,** a 45-minute walk from the bus stop in front of Calella's Hotel Garbí, command an excellent view of the coast. Russian Colonel Nicolas Voevodsky built the seaside castle after fleeing his homeland during the Bolshevik Revolution. He and his wife planted and pruned a splendid maze of paths and flower beds with their own hands (open dawn to dusk; 200ptas). The first sign for the castle points to the right at the fork of Av. Costa Daurada and C. Consolat del Mar. The castle also hosts the **Festival de Jazz de la Costa Brava** through July and August. On Calella's waterfront, anglers spend the first Saturday in July crooning the old sea chanties of the **Cantada d'Habaneras,** effectively scaring away most of the fish.

■ Near Palafrugell

L'ESCALA

The smell of suntan lotion permeates the remarkably tacky town of **L'Escala** (pop. 5500), 45 bus-minutes north of Palafrugell, but the nearby ruins of **Empúries** (see below) make the area an historical/beach daytrip from Figueres or Palafrugell. The HI hostel rents **mountain bikes** (250ptas per hr., 1200ptas per day), prime for whizzing down the bike/foot path to Empúries.

Orientation and Practical Information Most travelers arriving in L'Escala from Palafrugell, Figueres, Girona, and Barcelona, disembark at the Sarfa bus stop on **Avinguda Girona,** across from the **tourist office,** Plaça les Escoles, 1 (tel. 77 06 03; fax 10 33 85). The office provides a decent map, info on tourist sites, and **fax** service. (Open Mon.-Sat. 9am-8:30pm, Sun. 10am-1pm; Oct.-June Mon.-Fri. 10am-1pm and 4-7pm.) The **municipal police** (tel. 62 28 12), C. Pintor Joan Massanet, 24, are next to the to the tourist office. The **post office** is next door to the tourist office (tel. 77 16 51; open Mon.-Fri. 8:30am-2:30pm, Sat. 9:30am-1pm). The **postal code** is 17130. The **telephone code** is (9)72.

Sarfa buses (tel. 77 01 29) depart from Av. Ave María, near the tourist office, to: Figueres (4-5 per day, 45min., 460ptas); Palafrugell (4 per day, 45min., 735ptas); Girona (2-3 per day, 1½hr., 530ptas).

Accommodations and Food Although there are plenty of options, finding a room in L'Escala is taxing; many *pensiones* require summer guests to pay full board. The **HI youth hostel,** Les Coves, 41 (tel. 77 12 00), is 100m from the Empúries ruins in a grove of trees. Facing the tourist office, follow the road on the right toward the coast and the Olympic monument; from there follow signs to **Alberg De Juventut.** (Members only, though cards available at the hostel. 1600 per person, over 25 2200ptas. Oct-May: 1375ptas; 1875ptas. Breakfast included. Lunch and dinner offered. Often filled with groups mid-June to Aug. Call Barcelona's youth office (tel. ((9)3) 483 83 63) for reservations 1 month in advance.) **Pensió Torrent,** Carrer Riera, 28 (tel. 77 02 78), has pleasing whitewashed rooms at an even more pleasing price (doubles with bath 3400ptas, in winter 3200ptas). The town **market** is held daily from 7:30am-1:30pm in **Plaça Victor Català,** and a special **Sunday market** is held in summer (check tourist office for info). Or, fill your basket at supermarket **MAXOR,** Pl. Les Escoles (open Mon.-Sat. 7am-1:30pm and 4:30-9pm, Sun. 8:30am-1:30pm; MC, Visa). Nostalgic **Restaurant El Gavia,** C. Enric Serra, 16 (tel. 77 03 55), 2 blocks up from the *platja,* grooves to 40s Spanish swing. Their food is memorable, too. (*Paella* 800ptas. Open Tues.-Sun. 12:30am-3:30pm and 7:30-11:30pm. Visa, MC, AmEx.)

Sights Unless you consider neon swimwear and charbroiled Germans in dark socks and sandals an acceptable sight, head north one kilometer to Empúries.

EMPÚRIES

Just one kilometer north of L'Escala are the ruins of Empúries. In the seventh century BC, Greek traders landed on a small island on the northeast Iberian coast. As the settlement grew it moved to the mainland and became the prosperous colony of Emporion (marketplace), falling into Roman hands four centuries later. Remnants of both Greek and Roman cities, including some gorgeous mosaic floors and a Visigothic early Christian basilica, fill Empúries's 40 hectares of ruins. Excavation of the ruins continues behind profits from the 1992 Olympic Games, whose torch formally entered Spain through the ancient Greek port city. The small but rich **Museu Monogràfic d'Empúries** (tel. 77 02 08) showcases a large collection of ceramics, artifacts, and perplexing doorlocks. Plaques through the ruins indicate the ancient urban plan without marring the aura of fountains, mosaics, and columns against a backdrop of cypress trees and the breezy Mediterranean. A 300ptas audio-visual program is shown every half-hour from 10:30am to closing time. (Grounds and museum open Tues.-Sun. 10am-7:30pm; Oct.-May Tues.-Sun. 10am-7pm. 400ptas, students 200ptas.) If you cannot bear a 15-minute walk, take the *Carrilet* from **La Punta** (that's *punta*) in L'Escala (between the main beach and **Port d'en Perris**) to St. Martí d'Empúries (every hr. 9am-11pm, 200ptas, ask to get off at the ruins).

Half a kilometer north of the ruins starts the 47 sq. km **Parc Natural dels Aiguarnolls de l'Empordà,** a protected habitat with miles of marshland, lakes, and animal and plant species (the unenviably named *fartet* fish, for example). Bird-watchers should purvey the skies during the morning and early evening March-May and August-October. For more info, contact **El Cortalet info center** (tel. 25 42 22; fax 45 44 74).

SANT FELIU DE GUÍXOLS

A perilous but panoramic road twists 23km north from Tossa de Mar to Sant Feliu (pop. 17,500). While its smaller neighbors have become dependent on tourism, Sant Feliu still relies heavily on its cork and boat-building industries. The town sees its share of visitors, many towing small children along, but the calming scent of the sea still overpowers that of Coppertone.

Orientation and Practical Information Buses arrive at the Sarfa **bus station** on Ctra. Gerona. If entering Feliu by sea, you'll disembark mid-beach in front of **Passeig del Mar,** a tree-lined waterfront promenade and pedestrian path. **Rambla D'Antoni Vidal,** between the two arrival points, connects the pedestrian street to **Placeta de Sant Joan.** From the beach, take a left onto Pg. Mar, then a right onto Rbla. D'Antoni Vidal, following it to the semicircular *placeta.* Go right again at the sign for Girona to reach Ctra. Gerona and the bus station (3 blocks).

To get from the beach to the **tourist office,** Pl. Monestir, 54 (tel. 82 00 51), take a left on Pg. del Mar and a right on Av. Juli Garreta to the *plaça* (open Mon.-Fri. 10am-2pm and 4-8pm, Sat. 9:30am-1pm, Sun. 10am-2pm). **Luggage storage** is available at the Sarfa bus ticket window (200ptas per bag; open 6:30am-8:30pm). **BCH** sits on Pg. Mar. (Open Oct.-April only Mon.-Fri. 8:30am-2:30pm, Sat. 9:30am-1pm.) The **municipal police,** C. Callao (tel. 32 42 11), are on the outskirts; from Pl. Monestir, head past the theater and across the parking lot on R. Martirs. The **post office** is on Ctra. Gerona, 15 (tel. 32 11 60; open Mon.-Fri. 8:30am-2:30pm, Sat. 9:30am-1pm). The **telephone code** is (9)72. **Sarfa,** on Ctra. Gerona, 35 (tel. 32 11 87), runs **buses** to: Girona (14 per day, 1½hr., 745ptas); Palafrugell, on the Girona line (14 per day, 45min., 245ptas); Barcelona (11-14 per day, 2hr., 1240ptas); and Tossa (July-Aug. only, 3 per day, 565ptas). **Crucetours Ferry** (tel. 32 00 26), has a stand on the beach and sails south to: Tossa (5 per day, 45min., round-trip 1050ptas); Lloret (1¼hr., round-trip 1250ptas); and Blanes (4 per day, 1¾hr., round-trip 1375ptas). Round-trips on ferry are better deals than buses but one-way trips are more economical by bus.

Accommodations and Food Many hotel owners discount prices for stays of five days or more. Reservations are suggested for July and August. Two blocks from the beach and three from the Ramblas is **Pensión Geis,** C. Especiers, 27 (tel. 32 06 79). Cheerful owner keeps neat-as-a-pin rooms, all with bath and winter heating (doubles 4000ptas; Sept.-June 3600ptas; breakfast 350ptas; Visa, MC). At **Hostal Zürich,** Av. Juli Garreta, 43-45 (tel. 32 10 54), friendly, English-speaking owners rent huge, pleasant rooms with lots of light, some with balconies. One comes with an inexplicable set of stuffed dice on top of the armoire (singles 3500ptas; doubles 5500ptas, with bath 6500ptas; breakfast included). **Habitaciones El Gas Vell,** C. Sta. Magdalena, 29 (tel. 32 10 24); ring the doorbell before the Coke sign. Spartan rooms off spacious hallways reside in a working-class neighborhood 15 minutes from the beach, and near the bus station. (1500ptas per person. Or, one night stay and 3 meals 3700ptas per person. Breakfast alone 300ptas.) The **market** is in Pl. Mercat, the town's main square (Mon.-Sat. 8am-2pm). For lip-smacking *tapas,* check out **Bar El Gallo,** C. Especiers, 13 (tel. 82 23 44). Snack on grilled sardines (400ptas), grilled asparagus (750ptas), or go for the *tapeo menú* (1200ptas), which tops off 6 different *tapas* with a dessert crepe (open daily 5:30pm-midnight). **Nou Casino La Costancia,** Rambla Portalet, 2 (tel. 32 10 92), is a neo-Mudéjar cafe-bar and casino with spires and balconies. (Beers from 125ptas, coffee 80ptas. Open daily 8am-1am; Oct.-May 9am-midnight; closed one month in winter.) Many go to nearby **Platja d'Aro** for nightlife.

Sights and Entertainment Little remains to distinguish Sant Feliu from other mildly pretty Costa Brava towns, since traces of its 1000-year history have been obliterated by successive invaders. Still, the **Monestir** church and monastery at Pl. Monestir (take Av. Juli Garreta from the beach) is an architectural potpourri patched together from the remains of various buildings, including the **Torre de Fum,** which stands over Visigothic and Roman walls. (Open Mon.-Sat. 11am-2pm and 5-8pm; Oct.-May Sat. 11am-2pm and 5-8pm, Sun. 11am-2pm. 100ptas, students and retirees free.)

If you have come for Sant Feliu's three **beaches** (hardly a big "if"), stake out your grain of sand by 11am. It's a 20-minute walk to the **Platja de Sant Pol.** To the left of the central beach, a green **Viñolas** shuttle picks up beachgoers from Pg. Marítim (every 30min., 90ptas). With no commercial docking, the cove has unmediated access to the sea. Next to Sant Pol, a two-kilometer path scampers across the rocky hills, past picturesque coves and lagoons to **La Conca,** another popular beach. In summer, Sant Feliuans dance *sardanas* one block from the beach in Pl. Espanya (July-Sept. Fri. 10:15pm). Throughout July and August, classical music fills Sant Feliu's municipal theater in Pl. Monestir for the **Festival Internacional de Música de la Porta Ferrada,** the oldest in Catalunya. Every June and July local songsters get together at restaurants throughout town for the **Mostro de Cançó de Taverna,** the traditional tavern singing competition. Groups of men compete over a few accordion-assisted ditties, then enjoy a meal of bluefish. Needless to say, the wine flows freely. Contact the tourist office for exact locations and reservations.

▨ Tossa de Mar

Once upon a time, falling in love in, and with Tossa, was easy. While *The Flying Dutchman* was being filmed, Ava Gardner fell hard for Mario Cabrera, a Spanish bullfighter turned actor. Unfortunately for Ava, her husband (a.k.a. "Old Blue Eyes") found out about Tossa's spell and flew in with a group of toughies to chaperone the remainder of the filming. Nowadays, a frenetic tourist industry has transformed the "flower of the sea" from a pristine seaside village into a combination of English pubs, souvenir stores specializing in Mexican sombreros, and scads of cocoa-buttered visitors. That said, Tossa (pop. 3400) is a festive town with plenty to share: reddened cliffs and sparkling water frame its beaches, and a sun-baked cluster of 12th- to 14th-century buildings knot themselves inside the walled Vila Vella. The town lives seasonally—many *pensiones,* restaurants, and bars open only from May to October.

ORIENTATION AND PRACTICAL INFORMATION

Tossa is near the southern corner of the Costa Brava, about 40km north of Barcelona (90km of winding roads). Sarfa's **bus** service is relatively frequent from Barcelona (6-8 per day) and Girona (3 per day in summer), but is so limited during low- and mid-season that many travelers head for Lloret de Mar (about 8km farther south along the coast) and catch the bus (15min.) from there to Tossa.

Buses arrive at **Plaça de les Nacions Sense Estat,** at the corner of **Avinguda Pelegrí** and **Avinguda Ferrán Agulló;** the town slopes gently down from there to the water-front (10min.). Walk away from the station on Av. Ferrán Agulló, turn right on **Avinguda Costa Brava,** and continue until your feet get wet. **Passeig del Mar,** at the end of Av. Costa Brava, curves along the **Platja Gran** (Tossa's main beach) to the foot of the old quarter.

Tourist Office: Av. Pelegrí, 25 (tel. 34 01 08; fax 34 07 12), in the bus terminal build-ing at the corner of Av. Ferrán Agulló and Av. Pelegrí. Handy, thoroughly-indexed town map. English spoken. Open Mon.-Sat. 9am-9pm, Sun. 10am-1pm.

Buses: Av. Pelegrí at Pl. Nacions Sense Estat. **Pujol i Pujol** (tel. 36 42 36) to: Lloret del Mar (every 30min., 15min., 145ptas, Sat.-Sun. 165ptas). **Sarfa** (tel. 34 09 03) to Girona (2 per week or 3 per day depending on season, 1hr., 595ptas) and Barce-lona (every 2hr., 7:40am-7:10pm, 1½hr., weekdays 960ptas, 1735ptas round-trip; weekends 1090ptas, 1970ptas round-trip).

Ferries: Round-trip ferries are often more economical than these of the bus service. For a one-way trip, take the bus. **Crucetours** (tel. 36 23 05) runs from the main beach to St. Feliu (April-Oct., 5 per day, 45min., 850ptas, 1050ptas round-trip). Costa Brava schedules vary and Sun. service is sporadic. Poor weather may cancel all service. Check with the ticket booth near the Vila Vella end of the Platja Gran.

Mountain Bike and Moped Rentals: Road Runner, Av. de la Palma, s/n (tel. 34 05 03). Bring passport and license (for moped). 1hr. mountain bike rental 600ptas. 2hr. moped rental 1500ptas. Open April-Oct. daily 9am-9pm.

Car Rental: Europcar and Avis operate from the same storefront, Av. Costa Brava, 23 (tel. 34 28 29). One-day rentals start at 4900ptas.

Medical Services: Casa del Mar, Av. Catalunya (tel. 34 01 54). Primary health ser-vices and immediate attention. Nearest hospital is in Blanes.

Police: Municipal police, C. Església, 4 (tel. 34 01 35) in the Ajuntament. English spo-ken. They'll escort you to the **24hr. pharmacy. Emergency:** tel. 091 or 092.

Post Office: C. Maria Auxiliadora, s/n (tel. 34 04 57), one block down Av. Pelegrí from the tourist office. Open Mon.-Fri. 8:30am-2:30pm, Sat. 9:30am-1pm. **Postal Code:** 17320.

Telephone Code: (9)72.

ACCOMMODATIONS AND CAMPING

Tossa fills quickly in summer. Make reservations by phone, letter, or through the mul-titude of travel agencies, as some establishments are booked solid in July and August. The tourist office provides a list of travel agencies and helps find rooms during this period. Few rooms have winter heating. The **old quarter** hotels are the only ones worth considering.

Fonda Lluna, C. Roqueta, 20 (tel. 34 03 65). Turn right off Pg. Mar onto C. Peix-eteras, through C. Estalt until it ends, then go left and straight for the amazing bud-get find you have searched long and hard for. Delightful family keeps immaculate rooms, all with private baths. Breakfast included—eat on the rooftop terrace and take in an astonishing view of Tossa. 1600ptas per person. July-Aug. 1800ptas per person. Use of washing machine 500ptas. Hang dry. Will accept reservations only 1-2 days prior to arrival. Open March-Oct.

Pensión Moré, C. Sant Telmo, 9 (tel. 34 03 39). Downstairs, a dim and cozy sitting room. Upstairs, large rooms with wash basins and views of the old quarter. 1500ptas per person. Sept.-June 1200ptas per person. Open year-round.

Camping: Often costs as much as or more than *pensiones* for those not traveling in large groups. The tourist office has listings of nearby campgrounds. The closest is **Can Martí** (tel. 34 08 51; fax 34 24 61), at the end of Rbla. Pau Casals, off Av. Ferrán Agulló, 15min. from the bus station. June 20-Aug. 31 725ptas per person. 750ptas per tent. 500ptas per car. Rest of year: 575ptas per person 625ptas per tent, and 400ptas per car. Open May Sept.

FOOD

For the best cuisine and ambience, prowl the alleys of the old quarter, although if you're looking for that quiet, off-the-beaten track little hideaway as yet unsullied by tourist appetites, give up now. Most places specialize (though not exclusively) in local seafood. **Supermarket Valvi,** C. Enric Granados, 4, will delightedly debit your Visa or MC for your daily bread; follow beachside road to Av. Ramón Penyafort and take second left (open Mon.-Sat. 9am-9pm, Sun. 9am-2pm).

Bar Restaurante Ca Txapela, Av. Costa Brava, 3 (tel. 34 02 93). The only Basque place in town. Help yourself to delicious Basque *pintxos (tapas)* like vegetarian *pisto* or cod-filled *ajoaniro* (135ptas each), or sample a mixed plate (850ptas). Open daily 9am-2am, Sept.-June noon-11pm.

Restaurant Marina, C. Tarull, 6 (tel. 34 07 57). Faces the Església de Sant Vincenç—look for the striped awning and tables out front. Family from Fonda Lluna cooks up a *paella* as good as it gets. *Menú* 950ptas, *paella menú* 1250ptas.

SIGHTS AND ENTERTAINMENT

Inside the walled fortress of the **Vila Vella,** a spiral of medieval alleys leads to the remains of a Gothic church poised atop the cliff, the old **Església de Sant Vincenç.** Also in the Vila Vella, on tiny Plaça Pintor J. Roig y Soler, the **Museu Municipal** (tel. 34 07 09) has a nifty collection of 20s and 30s art, including—because the artist had a pad here—one of the few Chagall paintings currently in Spain (open Tues.-Sun. 10am-1pm and 3:30-6:30pm; 200ptas). Tossa's Roman mosaics, dating from the 4th to the first century BC, and other artifacts from the nearby **Vila Romana** and the excavation site off Av. Pelegrí, are displayed in the museum.

All of Tossa's **beaches** are worthwhile, as are the **calas** (small bays), accessible by foot. **Hikers** pass through on the GR-92 but several shorter trails and **mountain bike** paths also criss-cross the area; gear up with the tourist office pamphlet. Several companies send **glass-bottom boats** (tel. 34 22 99) to nearby beaches and caves (8 per day, 1hr., 850ptas one-way, up to 1250ptas round-trip to various locations). Tickets are available at booths on the Platja Gran. **Club Aire,** on the highway to Lloret (tel. 34 12 77), organizes canoeing and kayaking (2000ptas), water skiing (4250ptas for 2 lessons), scuba diving (44,000ptas 5-day certification course), sailing (1700ptas per hour), and windsurfing (1600ptas per hour) excursions.

Bar La Pirata, C. Portal, 32, has outdoor tables overlooking the sea (but no planks). **Snoopy's Bar,** C. Ignasi Meté, 6, inside the Vila Vella, is an English-style pub that packs them in like dogs for half-pints of Guinness (200ptas; open daily 6pm-3am). Fashionable discos in town are **Ely,** C. Bernats, 2 and Av. Costa Brava, 5 (tel. 34 00 09), and **Paradis,** C. Pou de la Vila, 12-14 (tel. 34 07 55), at the end of Pg. Mar in Hotel Rovira (free cover with one-drink minimum, beer 375ptas, mixed drinks 800-1000ptas). For info about outdoor concerts and cultural festivals, contact the **Casa de Cultura,** Av. Pelegrí, 8 (tel. 34 09 05), in a historic red-roof building (open 4-6pm). Local festivals take place on January 20-21, when the townsfolk make a 42km pilgrimage from Tossa to Santa Coloma in honor of St. Sebastián. The **Festa del Estiu** (Summer Fair) is held June 29-July 2 in honor of St. Peter. Tossa's residents take to the hills on Oct. 13 for a traditional picnic on **Aplec Sant Grau.** Reserve a room if you plan to come on these dates.

CATALUNYA (CATALUÑA)

CATALAN PYRENEES

Since the discovery of disposable income, tourists have flocked to Barcelona and the Costa Brava, making Catalunya holiday heaven for beach-goers. So far, though, only the discerning few have made it to the Pyrenees: hikers, Romanesque fanatics, highbrow skiers, and small town buffs. Its mountains are not as ostentatious as Aragón's, but they take their fair share of breaths away. Village life in the Catalan Pyrenees has practically stood still. Besides Catalan and Spanish, inhabitants of the ancient Catalan villages often speak (and eat) French, while people in the Val d'Aran (the westernmost area of the Catalan Pyrenees) speak Aranese, a variant of the French Gascon dialect. For each Catalan *comarca*, the Department of Commerce and Tourism distributes pamphlets with info on local winter sports or scenic areas. **Skiers** will find the English-language guide *Snow in Catalonia* (free at tourist offices) especially useful. **Cyclists** should ask for *Valles Superiores del Segre/Ariège*, which covers the Alt Urgell, Cerdanya, and the Val de Ribas. Editorial Alpina publishes a series of indispensable topographical maps bound in cranberry-red booklets.

For those coming from the east, **Ripoll** is the point of entry to the area, while those coming from the west and south enter through **Lérida** (Lleida). Lérida provides the only public transportation (bus) to the lakes and trails of the Parc Nacional d'Aigüestortes i Estany de Sant Maurici.

Isn't It Romanesque?

Romanesque castles, churches, and monasteries fill the old medieval counties of the Pyrenees region. This style emerged after the breakup of the Carolingian Empire in the latter 10th century and dominated Europe until the end of the 13th century. Romanesque architecture mixed Roman building traditions (such as the vaulted roofs) with newer techniques (such as massive masonry to uphold barrel vaults) necessary for the grandiose edifices of an expanding society. The buildings are characterized by their rounded arched doors and windows, and modest (as compared to Gothic) heights. Benedictine monks and the Knights Templar hired builders to spread Romanesque influence far and wide, making it the first truly pan-European architectural style.

VAL D'ARAN

The Catalan Pyrenees's most dazzling peaks cluster around the Val d'Aran, in the northwest corner of the province. Those peaks have proven to be sizeable barriers to outside infiltration—the Araneses have maintained not only a language distinct from both Catalan and French, but also unique festivals, music, and dances.

The Val d'Aran is especially popular in winter—the King and his family have crowned the slopes in **Baquiera-Beret** as their royal favorites. Possibly as good a place as any for snow bunnies with visions of royalty to bump into the very eligible Prince Felipe. Currently, there are about 80 alpine trails, as well as a few cross-country ones, winding down the surrounding peaks. For skiing info and reservations, contact the **Oficeria de Baquiera-Berey** (tel. 64 44 55; fax 64 44 88).

VIELHA

The biggest town in the valley (pop. 2300), Vielha suffers from the usual multi-story architectural blunders, but seems cheerfully unaware of its errors, welcoming hikers and skiers to its lively streets with every sort of service and amenity the outdoorsy might desire. Careful prowling turns up a few pretty old streets that qualify as quaint, and the town even possesses a verifiable artistic masterpiece, the 12th-century wood carving *Crist del Mig-Aran*.

Orientation and Practical Information The Ria Nere divides Vielha in two. Intersecting it and running the length of the town is Av. Castièro, which turns into Av. Pas d'Arro on the other side of the Pl. de Espanha. The **tourist office** hangs one block upriver from the *plaça* on C. Sarriulèra, 6 (tel. 64 01 10; fax 64 05 37). The multilingual staff handles spacey hikers and uptight Romanesque-seekers with equal aplomb (open daily 10am-1pm and 4:30-7:30pm). Alsina Graells runs **buses** to Vielha from Lérida (2 per day, 3hr., 1700ptas). **Taxis** answer at tel. 64 01 95. The **hospital** is on C. Espitau (tel. 64 00 06). The **pharmacy** answers at tel. 64 23 46; **Guardia Civil** picks up at tel. 64 00 05. In **emergencies,** dial 091 or 092. The **post office,** C. Sarviulèra, 2 (tel. 64 09 12), is next door to the tourist office (open Mon.-Fri. 8:30am-2:30pm, Sat. 9am-1pm). The **postal code** is 25530. The **telephone code** is (9)73.

Accommodations and Food Several inexpensive *pensiones* cluster at the end of Camin Reiau, off Pg. Libertat, which intersects Av. Casteiro at Pl. Sant Antoni. The best of the bunch is **Casa Vicenta,** Camin Reiau, 7 (tel. 64 08 19), where lovable owners let sparkling rooms (doubles with bath 5000ptas; breakfast included). **Pensión Busquets,** C. Mayor, 11 (tel. 64 02 38), hosts homey rooms in the old part of town (doubles 3800ptas). For groceries, cruise the aisles of **Supermercado Arnals,** Av. Pas d'Arros, 3 (open Mon.-Sat. 8:30am-8:30pm). **Bar-Restaurante Vidal,** C. Mayor, 6A (tel. 64 15 32), cooks a 975ptas *menú* that includes *ensalada catalana* and rotisserie chicken. If you're lucky, you might find their *olla aranesa,* a culinary hodge-podge of white beans, black sausage, cabbage, carrots, rice, noodles, and veal.

Sights and Entertainment The **Iglesia de San Miguel,** a simple 12th-century Romanesque church, is the backdrop for the intricately carved 12th-century *Crist de Mijaran* (open daily 11am-8pm). Vielha also has the **Museu de Val d'Aran,** C. Mayor (tel. 64 18 15), an ethnographic collection that sheds light on the arcane Aranese culture (open Tues.-Fri. 5-8pm, Sat. 10am-1pm and 5-8pm, Sun 10am-1pm; 200ptas).

Vielha is an excellent base for all sorts of outdoor activities, as it hosts various companies offering guides for outdoor activities. **Camins,** Av. Pas d'Arro, 5 (tel. 64 24 44; fax 64 24 97), organizes long and short treks into the Aigüestortes National Park (prices start at 1900ptas), plummets down to nearby whitewater rivers Garona and Noguera (4300ptas), and leads horseback rides (2000ptas per hour), mountain bike trips (2900-6000ptas), and mountain climbs (3500-6500ptas). **Aran Aventura,** Ed. Sapporo (tel. 64 04 44), offers similar services. Work up a sweat at the **Palai de Geu,** Eth Solan (tel. 64 28 64), on the outskirts of town. A pool, ice rink, cardiovascular equipment, and solarium are all under one massive roof. (Open Mon.-Fri. 8am-9:30pm, Sat. 11am-9pm; mid-Sept. to June Mon.-Fri. 8am-noon and 3-10pm, Sat. 10:30am-2:30pm and 4:30-9pm. One-day pass 1400ptas, includes skate rental.)

■ Parc Nacional d'Aigüestortes

Wildflowers bloom and peaks boom in Catalunya's only national park, one hundred kilometers east of Ordesa. A 2500m range divides the park into west and east halves, known respectively as the Estany de Sant Maurici and the Aigüestortes. The two halves are reached separately by motor vehicle—only a foot trail connects them. Don't rely on the freebie maps from the info offices; the red *Editorial Alpina* guides, one each for Montardo, Vall de Boí, and Sant Maurici, are essential (600ptas at any bookstore). The park brochure published by the Generalitat de Catalunya, available at tourist offices, is likewise useful. For info on the park, contact the park tourist offices (in Espot tel. 62 40 36; in Vall de Boí tel. 69 61 89; general info tel. 69 60 00). Unless otherwise noted, the **telephone code** is (9)73.

With over 10,000 hectares and 50 lakes, the park merits at least two days, and if you rely on public transport, it's hard to see much in fewer than three. There is no vehicle access to the park. Cars can only go as far as the park entrance, 1km from Espot; when the lot there fills, you must park in Espot.

The park's four *refugios* (government-maintained dormitories; about 1000ptas) and *Casas de Pagés* (like farm houses) are good **accommodation** options. For the telephone numbers of the 9 refugios in the area, contact the park tourist offices (English spoken). The mountains are deceptively placid from afar, particularly in the spring and fall. A few hikers die each year when they lose the trail during freak spring blizzards. Listen to local advice: bring warm clothing even for July and August and check with the Espot or Boi park office before heading out.

DUE EAST: ESPOT & ESTANY DE SANT MAURICI

Surrounded by buffeted terraces, the official gateway to the east half of the park is the little town of **Espot**. Espot is actually a good 4.5km from the entrance proper, an arrangement that respects the tranquility of the park but disturbs that of the traveler. The only consolation is that the hike to the entrance is quite scenic. Unfortunately, the **Alsina Graells bus** (tel. 26 85 00 or (9)33 02 65 45) from Lérida—the only mass transit in the area—only comes within 7km from the *other* side of Espot, on Highway C-147 (Mon.-Sat. 4:30pm, 3hr., 1750ptas). A **jeep service** (tel. 62 41 05) taxis into the park from Espot, and will even collect you from the bus stop if you call ahead (1500ptas to Espot per 7-8 person jeep). From Espot, jeeps run to Estany Sant Maurici (2000-3000ptas), a lake northeast in the park, and to Amitges, also in the north by the park's best and biggest *refugio* (tel. (9)3 315 23 11). Estany Sant Maurici is the launch pad for most hikes; the two-hour hike from there to Amitges is one of the park's best. The **park info office** (tel. 62 40 36), on the main road on the right as you enter town, provides good brochures and advice (open daily 9am-1pm and 3:30-7pm).

A night's rest in Espot allows hikers to start early. **Supermarkets** sell picnic supplies. Many residences in the area take in travelers (contact the tourist office for info). **Residència Felip** (tel. 62 40 93), a *Casa de Pagés*, packages rooms with breakfast (July 2000ptas per person, Aug. 2500ptas, rest of year 1500ptas). Cross the main Espot bridge, follow the road two blocks, then turn left. **Càmping la Mola** (tel. 62 40 24), 2km from Espot, has good facilities and a pool. **Càmping Sol i Neu** (tel. 62 40 01), one kilometers from La Mola en route to the village, has good facilities (both open July-Sept.; 550ptas per person, per tent, and per car).

DUE WEST: AIGÜESTORTES & VALL DE BOÍ

The western half of the park is hours away from the eastern entrance by car, but its proximity to Lérida makes it more popular with casual strollers (and cows). To savor the park's two halves, take the main trail along the Riu de Sant Nicolau from Aigüestortes to the **Portarró de Espot**, the 2400m gateway between the two sides. Heading west, the descent to Estany de Sant Maurici is steep and covered in patches of snow at higher altitudes. This six- to eight-hour hike crosses the whole park, passing the **Estany Llong**, a llong llake indeed. Near its western tip lies the park's first *refugio*, also called **Estany Llong** (tel. 69 62 84; open mid-June to Oct. 10).

Entering the park from its west side isn't much easier than the eastern approach. When it's running (July-Sept.), the bus from Lérida drops explorers off in **Boí**, a community of 150 people, seven kilometers from the park's entrance. **Taxis** (tel. 69 60 36) go from the town's *plaça* to the park (700ptas per person). The **park info office** is near the bus stop on the *plaça* (tel. 69 61 89; open 9am-1pm and 3:30-7pm).

Despite the nearby ski resort in Taüll, Boí maintains its pastoral feel. Low arches and cobblestone streets surround several family-run accommodations. The proprietor at **Casa Guasch** (tel. 69 60 42) lets you use her kitchen if the house isn't too full. Leave the plaza through the stone arch, turn right through the next arch, then bear left and turn left again where the street ends. Look for the multi-colored entryway on the left. The family knows the mountains well and can give you pointers in Spanish or Catalan (1300ptas per person).

Pont de Suert, 17km south of Boí, offers most emergency services. The **Red Cross** can be reached at tel. 69 02 85; the **Guardia Civil** at tel. 69 00 06.

SANT JOAN DE LES ABADESSES

Count Hairy was nothing if not an equal-opportunity patron. After founding Ripoll's first monastery, the Hirsute One went on to endow a convent 10km away, and appointed his daughter Emma as the first abbess. A town developed around the nuns, but not all authorities were so feminist-minded—their community was suppressed in the 11th century and it took 100 years before anyone moved in to their old digs. The Augustinians who eventually took over turned the convent, appropriately, into a monastery, and dotted the town with other Romanesque buildings. The evocative **monastery** includes a Romanesque **church,** containing the **Santíssim Misteri,** a seven-piece polychromatic modern sculpture. Admission to the church and cloister (200ptas) permits a visit to the **museu** (tel. 72 00 13; open daily 10am-2pm and 4-6pm). The monastery may be reached by following the *rambla* to the circle at the end. At the other end, make a right on the highway out of town to get to the untended ruins of **Sant Pol,** which make a beautiful unofficial picnic ground. The minuscule **tourist office** is at Rambla Comte Guifré, 5 (tel. 72 00 92; open 11am-1pm and 4-6pm; the door is left unlocked so you can get your hands on a map even during *siesta*). For **currency exchange, Banco Central Hispano** is on C. Comella, 4 (open daily 8:30am-2:30pm). **Buses** connect Sant Joan de les Abadesses to Barcelona (1 per day).

Hostal Ter, C. Vista Alegre (tel. 72 00 05), directly across the bridge at the entrance to town, has lots of aged but cute rooms viewing the river (singles 2400ptas; doubles 4100ptas, with bath 4600ptas). **Casa Rudes** is the most famous restaurant in town, but **Pizzeria La Forneria,** Carrer Major, 3 (tel. 72 06 47), is more up the budget traveler's alley. Fresh crisp pizzas (600-900ptas) and workman-like pastas (600-750ptas) are preceded by a small (free!) bowl of garlicky olives (open daily 7-11:30pm; Sept.-June Thurs.-Sun. only). Shop for your own grub at **Supermercado Super Avui,** corner of Av. Conte Guife and C. Comella (open Mon.-Sat. 9am-2pm and 5-9pm, Sun. 9am-2pm; Visa, MC, AmEx).

NÚRIA

You should be forewarned that the ascent to Núria may take your breath away but that Núria itself will not. A small valley close to the French border, these mountains are inaccessible by train or car. For centuries, only the pious and unhappily infertile (see **Our Virguin of Fertility Drugs,** p. 356) made it through the high passes to the Santuario de Sant Gil. In 1931, however, the valley installed a second-hand cable car, the *Cremallera* (the Zipper), to prepare Núria as a major ski resort in the 1940s, 50s, and 60s. Unfortunately, as bigger mountains and longer slopes grew popular, the town deteriorated, only to be revived as a Club Med-type resort with right-at-your-doorstep hiking and skiing. With a main building that resembles a poorly disguised bunker, a blatantly artificial "lake," and an air of cheerfully enforced wholesomeness, the innately suspicious might feel as though they've wandered into an alpine, Nazi version of *The Stepford Wives,* but the hundreds of happy Spaniards who flock here on weekends don't seem to mind.

In summer, picnickers come to the shores of Núria's "lake," aspiring cowboys traverse its **horseback riding** trails, and **hikers** use the valley as a base for climbing the snow-capped peaks of **Puigmal** (2913m, 4hr.) and **Eina.** Less ambitious trekkers can follow the path (2hr.) to neighboring **Queralbs,** which passes alongside waterfalls and gorges carpeted with wildflowers (the way back up to Nuna from Queralbs is significantly more challenging than the way down). In winter, ten **ski trails** offer slopes ranging from *molt facil* (very easy) to *molt difficil* (very difficult or expert) at **Estació de la Vall de Núria.** The Cremallera zips from the Ribes de Freser stop on the Ripoll-Puigcerdà line; the 45-minute ride scales 800m through virgin mountain faces to which stubborn sheep, goats, and pine trees cling (6-11 per day depending on season, 8:15am-9pm, 2150ptas round-trip). Call tel. (9)72 73 20 20 for more info.

From Núria's station, a funicular (included in price of Cremallera ticket) whisks passengers straight to **Alberg de Joventut Pic de l'Aliga** (tel. (9)72 73 00 48), the

Our Virgin of the Fertility Drugs

The Vall de Núria was just another remote mountain pass when recluse Gil of Nimes stumbled across it around the year 700 and envisioned it the perfect place for his hermitage. With nothing better to do, the soon-to-be saint carved himself a nice statue of the Virgin and child. Almost 400 years later, that statue, along with Gil's bell and cooking pot, were discovered by a local shepherd, and the hermit's isolated sanctuary became a pilgrimage destination. In a twist of events it is perhaps best not to speculate on, some daredevil pilgrim discovered her fertility increased if she put her head in the pot while ringing the bell. Ever since, barren women have been doing the same—one chime for each desired child. Visitors today can stick their own heads in the progeny-producing pot, as well as view a collection of wax body parts sent by grateful healed worshippers.

alternative route being an arduous 20-minute climb (10min. down). The modern three-story youth hostel loyally maintains Núria's training-camp atmosphere with ping-pong, volleyball, and basketball. (1600ptas per person, over 25 2200ptas. Hot showers. Breakfast included. Closed Nov.) For reservations, especially July-August and (if there's snow) January-March, call the Barcelona office at tel. (9)3 483 83 63.

The **Bar Finistrelles,** downstairs from the rudimentary souvenir store in the main complex, vends tortilla sandwiches (400ptas) and a whole roast chicken with potatoes (975ptas). The complex also offers **ski rentals, ATMS, telephones, lockers** (300ptas), and—given the rising fertility here—a **condom vending machine.**

If you find the shiny artificiality of Núria a little spooky, escape to the more honest village of **Queralbs** (pop. 124). If bare charm doesn't cut it, check out the sublime views from beside Queralbs's medieval rubble. There's one official *pensión* in town—**Hostal L'Avet,** C. Mayor, 21 (tel. 72 73 77; doubles with bath 4000ptas; dinner and breakfast 1400ptas; more per person), but **Masia Constans,** off the highway to Fontalba (tel. 72 70 13), rents full apartments with fireplaces and room for four people for 5000ptas per night. The **Cremallera** stops in Queralbs on its journey between Ribes and Núria.

■ Puigcerdà

The town with the hardest name to pronounce in all of Spain (try Pwee-chair-DAH), Puigcerdà (pop. 6300) commands the best vantage point from which to explore the teeny *comarca* of Cerdanya. Foragers and forest-types will find their niches in nearby hiking, fishing, hunting, and kayaking. The town itself is either charmingly old-world-ish or drab and decrepit, depending on your mood and your glasses' prescription, but there's no denying the beauty of the valley view. Puigcerdà sated its thirst for glory in 1993 by appearing in the Guiness Book of Records for the world's longest *butifarra* (sausage), a Freudian nightmare measuring 5200 meters.

ORIENTATION AND PRACTICAL INFORMATION

Puigcerdà's center squats squarely on a hill. **Plaça Ajuntament,** to the west, is nicknamed *el balcón de Cerdanya;* its commanding view of the valley makes it a wickedly lovely place to watch bedraggled newcomers struggle uphill from the RENFE station at the foot of the west slope. Most buses stop at the bottom of the hill.

To reach Pl. Ajuntament from the absolutely inconvenient **train station,** walk past the stairs in the station's *plaça* to the first real flight of stairs (between two buildings). Turn right at the top of these, and then look for the next set on your left, just before a sign for C. Hostal del Sol. Climb these to the top and turn left on C. Raval de les Monges, where the final set of stairs winds up to the right. With your back to the wall, **Carrer Alfons I** runs straight out of the left-hand corner of the *plaça.* It will lead you after one block to **Carrer Major,** the principal commercial street. A left on C. Major will convey you to **Plaça Santa María.** Continuing straight across C. Major on C. Alfons I brings you to **Passeig 10 d'Abril,** the other main square in town.

Tourist Office: C. Querol, 1 (tel./fax 88 05 42), a right turn off Pl. Ajuntament with your back to the view. Good map (100ptas). Lodging, entertainment, and daytrip listings. English spoken. Open Mon.-Sat. 9am-2pm and 3:30-8:30pm, Sun. 9am-2pm; Oct.-May Tues.-Fri. 10am-1pm and 4-7pm, Sat. 10am-1:30pm and 4-8pm.

Trains: RENFE (tel. 88 01 65) runs to: Ribes de Freser to connect to Núria (6 per day, round-trip train and Cremallera-Núria package 2800ptas); Ripoll (6 per day, 1¼hr., 385ptas); Barcelona (6 per day, 3hr., 1600ptas). To get to Jaca or Huesca you must first go to Zaragoza from Barcelona, a full day of travel.

Buses: Alsina Graells (tel. (9)73 35 00 20) runs buses to La Seu d'Urgell (3 per day, 1hr., 560ptas), where there is passage to Andorra and to Lérida, which connects to Aragón (1 per day, 3½hr., 1505ptas). First bus departs Puigcerdà at 7:30am; the last returns from La Seu at 7pm. **Cerdanya** (tel. 302 65 45) runs to Llívia (1-4 per day, 100ptas) and Barcelona (1-4 per day, 3hr., 1900ptas). Buses depart in front of the train station; purchase tickets on board. See schedule on the side of cigarette machine in Bar Estació, left of the station.

Currency Exchange: Central Hispano, Pl. Cabrinetty, open daily 8:30am-2:30pm.

Taxis (tel. 88 00 11), Pl. Cabrinetty.

Bike Rental: Top-Bikes, Pl. d'Avenes, 21 (tel. 88 20 42), 700ptas per hour, 1500ptas per half-day, 2500ptas per day. Visa, MC.

Red Cross: Av. Segre, 8 (tel. 88 05 47 or 89 41 53), on the outskirts of town to the right of Pl. Ajuntament with your back to the view.

24Hr. Pharmacy: C. Alfons I, 16 (tel. 88 01 60). Pharmacy doors, local paper *Reclam,* and police all list current 24hr. pharmacies.

Medical Services: Centre Hospitalari, Pl. Santa María (tel. 88 01 50 or 88 01 54). English spoken.

Municipal Police: Pl. Ajuntament, 1 (tel. 88 19 72). **Emergency:** tel. 091 or 092. **Guardia Civil:** tel. 88 01 46.

Post Office: Av. Coronel Molera, 11 (tel. 88 08 14), off Pl. Barcelona on your left after 1½ block. Open Mon.-Fri. 8:30am-2:30pm, Sat. 9:30am-1pm. **Postal Code:** 17520.

Telephone Code: (9)72.

ACCOMMODATIONS AND FOOD

Since many visitors daytrip to Puigcerdà, rooms come easily, if not cheaply. Call for reservations only in August. Most cheaper *pensiones* hole up in the old town off Pl. Santa María, and most rates drop in the off season. The neighborhood of **C. Alfons I** is a cornucopia of bakeries, markets, butcher shops, and inexpensive restaurants. The **market** is at Pg. 10 d'Abril (Sun. 9am-2pm). A **supermarket, Bonpreu,** Av. Colonel Molera, 12, packages products diagonally across from the post office (open Tues.-Sat. 9am-1pm and 4:30-8:30pm, Sun. 10am-2pm).

Mare de Déu de les Neus (HI) (tel. 89 20 12), in La Molina-Alp on Ctra. Font Canaleta, 500m from the RENFE station in La Molina. 20min. by car or 30min. by train from Puigcerdà, but only 4km from the slopes; take Alsa bus every 30min. 112 beds. Members only. 1600ptas, over 25 2200ptas. Breakfast included. Sheets 350ptas. Visa, MC, AmEx.

Hostal Núria, Pl. Cabrinetty, 18 (tel. 88 17 56), a block downhill from Pl. Ajuntament. Huge rooms, all with equally huge bathrooms. Mattresses adhere to traditional Spanish guidelines for concavity. Singles 2500ptas. Doubles 4500ptas.

Hostal Residencia La Muntanya, C. Coronel Molera, 1 (tel. 88 02 02), off Pl. Barcelona. Paintings of pearly-teared waifs weep at your pristine bedside. 3500ptas per person, including breakfast and dinner. Off season 1700ptas, without dinner.

Camping: Camping Stel (tel./fax 88 23 61). Full-service camping 1km from Puigcerdà on the road to Llívia. Supermarket and pool. 600ptas per person, per tent, and per car. Spaces fill up early in the day. Open June 21-Sept. 28 and weekends in winter.

Gourmet Cerdà, C. Alfons I, 9 (tel. 88 14 85). A well-stocked deli. Fresh bread next door at the bakery **Palau** to make a giant, self-empowered *bocadillo.* Both open Tues.-Sat. 9am-1pm and 4-8pm, Sun. 9am-2pm.

Bar-Restaurant El Meson, Pl. Cabrinetty, 11 (tel. 88 19 28). Homestyle cooking. *Menú del día* 900ptas. Open daily 1:30-4pm and 8-11:30pm.

SIGHTS AND ENTERTAINMENT

Puigcerdà calls itself the capital of snow—you can **ski** in your country of choice (Spain, France, or Andorra) at one of 19 ski areas within a 50km radius. The closest one on the Spanish side is at **La Molina.** Biking the area is also a popular option.

Between runs and two-wheeled exploration, dash over to the **campanario,** the octagonal bell tower in Pl. Santa María. This 42m-high 12th-century tower is all that remains of the **Església de Santa María,** destroyed in the 1936 Civil War (open July-Sept. daily 10am-2pm and 4-8pm; free). **Església de Sant Domènec,** the largest church in Cerdanya, hulks next door. Its most interesting holdings are several Gothic paintings, probably by Guillem Manresa, considered to be among the best of their genre. On the outskirts of town, spanning the Riu Querol, is the **Pont de Sant Martí d'Aravó,** with a Romanesque base and a Gothic superstructure.

Spend an idyllic afternoon trotting or paddling around the **Estany** (a.k.a. Lake Brilliant) up Av. Pons i Guasch from Pl. Barcelona, long a center of Puigcerdà social life—the 19th-century mansions surrounding it were summer houses for Cerdanyan elite. The **Festa de l'Estany** is held the next to last Sunday of August. On September 8, the town goes *sardanas* at the **Festivitat de la Verge de la Sagristia.** In July and August, devotees gather for the *sardana* every Wednesday at 10pm. More concentrated dancing takes place during the **Festa Major** in the first weekend of July.

COSTA DAURADA (COSTA DORADA)

▓ Tarragona

Tarragona's strategic position made the city a provincial capital in the Roman Empire, when it was known as *Tarraco.* The remains of an amphitheater, a circus, and a theater all continue to pay homage to the port's imperial days. Today, tourists climb through these jagged remnants while natives retreat to the hidden beach below. Tarragona has earned an image as younger sibling of Spain's urban elites, but vestiges of its "august" past, not its fledgling cosmopolitan character, are still Tarragona's most compelling attractions.

ORIENTATION AND PRACTICAL INFORMATION

Most sights are clustered on a hill, surrounded by the remnants of Roman walls. At the foot of the hill, **Ramblas Vella** and **Ramblas Nova** (parallel to one another) are the main thoroughfares of the new city. **Rambla Nova** runs from **Passeig de les Palmeres** (which overlooks the sea) to **Plaça Imperial Tarraco,** the monstrous rotunda and house of the bus station. To reach the old quarter's center from the **train station,** take a right and walk 200m to the killer stairs parallel to the shore.

Tourist Office: C. Major, 39 (tel. 24 52 03; fax 24 55 07), below the cathedral steps. Excellent free maps and *Routes into Catalonia's Past,* a guide to Tarragona's Roman ruins. Open June-Sept. Mon.-Fri. 9:30am-8:30pm, Sat. 9:30am-2pm and 4-8:30pm, Sun. 10am-2pm. Winter Mon.-Fri. 10am-2pm and 4:30-7pm, Sat.-Sun. 10am-2pm. **Information booths,** Pl. Imperial Terraco, at the bottom of Rbla. Vella (open May-Aug. 10am-2pm and 4-8pm). **Generalitat de Catalunya,** C. Fortuny, 4 (tel. 23 34 15). Open Mon.-Fri. 9am-2pm and 4-6pm, Sat. 9am-2pm.

Trains: Pl. Pedrera (tel. 24 02 02), on the waterfront. Info open 7am-10pm. To: Sitges (14 per day, 1hr.); Barcelona (30-40 per day, 1½hr.); Zaragoza (7-10 per day, 3½hr.); Valencia (16 per day, 4hr., 1950ptas); Madrid (5 per day, 8hr., 4300ptas).

Buses: Pl. Imperial Tarraco (tel. 22 91 26). **Transportes Bacoma** (tel. 22 20 72), serves most destinations. To: Barcelona (10 per day, 1½hr.); Valencia (9 per day, 3½hr.); Alicante (6 per day, 6½hr.).

Public Transportation: EMT Buses (tel. 54 94 80) runs 9 (in summer 11) lines all over Tarragona. Tourist offices have route info. Maps at station only. Runs 7am-10pm, some routes until 11pm. 100ptas, 10-ride "bono" ticket 695ptas.

Taxi: Radio Taxi (tel. 22 14 14 or 23 60 64).

Luggage Storage: At the train station, 24hr. lockers (600ptas).

Medical Assistance: Hospital de Sant Pau i Santa Tecla, Rbla. Vella, 14 (tel. 25 99 00). **Hospital Joan XXIII,** C. Dr. Mallafré Guasch, 4 (tel. 29 58 00). **Protecció Civil,** Pl. Imperial Tarraco (tel. 006), for any emergency. **Ambulance:** (tel. 22 22 22).

Police: Comisaría de Policía, Pl. Orleans (tel. 23 33 11). From Pl. Imperial Tarraco on the non-sea end of Rambla Nova, walk down Av. Pres. Lluis Companys, and take the 3rd left to the station. **Emergency:** tel. 091 or 092.

Post Office: Pl. Corsini (tel. 24 01 49), below Rambla Nova off C. Canyelles. Open Mon.-Fri. 8:30am-8:30pm, Sat. 9:30am-2pm. **Postal Code:** 43070.

Telephone Code: (9)77.

ACCOMMODATIONS AND CAMPING

Tarragona is not famous for its cheap beds, but search in the area behind **Pl. Pedrera,** outside the train station, in Pl. Font, or peruse the tourist office's list.

Residencia Juvenil Sant Jordi (HI), Av. Pres. Lluis Companys, 5 (tel. 24 01 95). Past Pl. Imperial Tarraco, Rbla. Nova changes into Av. Pres. Lluis Companys. Go left after leaving the train station, take the 1st right, and catch bus #2 in front of Bar Fa; it leaves you on C. Presidente Lluis Companys, 2 blocks from the bus station. Institutional dorm rooms, usually housing boisterous local college students, come with desks and large closets. Facilities include TV, table tennis, lounge, and washing machine. Reception open 7am-midnight. Doors close at midnight but open on the hour throughout the night. June-Sept. 1600ptas. Over 26 2200ptas. Oct.-May: 1375ptas; 1875ptas. Nonmembers pay a bit more. Breakfast included. Sheets 350ptas. Reserve July-Aug.

La Pilarica, C. Smith, 20 (tel. 24 09 60). From the train station, turn left and cross Pl. Pedrera to C. Barcelona, which becomes C. Sant Miguel. Turn left on C. Misericòrdia, and then take the third right. Talkative owner offers big rooms and family atmosphere near the city's nightlife. Fresh paint, funky lights, and clashing floral decor. 2000ptas per person. Winter 1500ptas per person.

Pensión Marsal, Pl. Font, 26 (tel. 22 40 69), in the heart of the historic town. Tough beds, ceiling fans. Singles 2000ptas. Doubles 4000ptas. 5th fl. rooms are cheaper. Breakfast included. Visa, MC, AmEx.

Camping: Several sites line the road toward Barcelona (Vía Augusta or CN-340) along the beaches north of town. Take bus #9 from Pl. Imperial Tarraco, opposite the market (every 20min., 80ptas). The closest is **Tarraco** (tel. 23 99 89), at Platja Rabassada. Well-maintained facilities; the beach is right out the tent door. 24hr. reception. 500ptas per person, per tent, and per car. Open April-Sept.

FOOD

Ramblas Nova, Vella, and **Pl. Font** are full of daily *menús* (800-1200ptas) and greasy *platos combinados.* Tarragona's **indoor market,** next to Pl. Corsini by the post office, hawks food and wares (open Mon.-Thurs. 8am-2pm, Fri. 8am-2pm and 5-8pm). For **groceries,** turn to **Simago,** C. Augusta at Comte de Rius (tel. 23 88 06), on a street parallel to and between Rbls. Nova and Vella (open Mon.-Sat. 9:30am-8:30pm).

La Teula, C. Merceria, 16, in the old city off Pl. Santiago Rusiñol. Salads (450-600ptas) and savory *Pan de payes* (country bread with meat or *tortilla* 675-1000ptas). Afternoon *menú* 950ptas. Open daily 11am-4:30pm and 6:30-11:30pm.

Mesón El Caserón, Trinquet Nou, 4 (tel. 23 93 28), parallel to Rbla. Vella (off Pl. Font). Ceiling fans cool stomach-stuffing, home-cooked meals. Family-run. Steak

platter 825ptas. Tantalizing seafood *paella* 1000ptas. *Menú* 1000ptas. Open Mon.-Sat. 1-3:30pm and 8:30-10:30pm, Sun. 1-3:30pm.

Universidad de Rovira i Virgil, Pl. Imperial Terraco, in the university building. Good food at student prices: 3-course *menú* with wine for 700ptas. Open summer daily 8am-5pm; termtime 8am-8pm. *Menú* served 1-3pm.

SIGHTS

Tarraco's status as provincial capital (thanks to Augustus) transformed the small military enclosure into a glorious imperial port. Countless Roman ruins stand like statues amidst 20th-century hustle and bustle. Below **Passeig de les Palmeres,** you can see the **Amfiteatre Romá** (tel. 24 25 79), where gladiators hurled each other and tossed wild animals across the arena. Above the amphitheater, across Pg. Sant Antoni, sits the **Museu de la Ronanifat** (tel. 24 19 52), which houses the **Pretori** and the **Circ Romá.** The Pretori was the governor's palace in the 1st century BC. Rumor has it that Pontius Pilate was born here. The Circ Romá, connected by vaults which both the Romans and Franco's troops used as dungeons, was once a chariot race track that extended across the old city. Most of it is buried today but some sections are still visible in the basements of restaurants and apartment buildings.

To see the remaining fourth of the 2nd-century BC walls, stroll through the **Passeig Arquelógic** (tel. 24 57 96). The walls originally stretched to the sea and fortified the entire city. The **Fórum Romá** lies near the post office, clearly demonstrating how far the walls extended. If too much Roman roamin' has left you parched, stop for a drink in the **Casa-Museu Castellarnau** (tel. 24 22 20). It housed 18th- and 19th-century *noblesa,* the Vizcondas de Castellarnau (Viscounts of Castellarnau). To get there, descend the steps in front of the cathedral and take the third right onto C. Cavellares. The six Roman sights form a consortium (open in summer Tues.-Sun. 9am-8pm; winter hours vary; 450ptas, students free).

Across Pl. Rei from the Pretori, the **Museo Arquelógic** (tel. 23 62 09) displays ancient utensils, statues, and mosaics, including a ravishing **Cap de Medusa** (Head of Medusa). (Open in summer Tues.-Sat. 10:30am-2pm and 4-7pm, Sun. 10am-2pm; winter hours vary. 300ptas; students 150ptas.) Cornered down narrow streets and lit by a huge rose window is a Romanesque-Gothic **cathedral,** on C. Major near Pl. Seu. (Open Mon.-Sat. 10am-7pm; in winter Mon.-Sat. 10am-12:30pm and 3-6pm. 300ptas.)

For a bit of the macabre, creep over to the **Necròpolis** and **Museu Paleocristià** (tel. 21 11 75), Pg. Independència, on the edge of town. The huge early Christian burial site has yielded a rich variety of urns, tombs, and sarcophagi, the best of which are in the museum. Unfortunately, the museum and burial grounds are both *de obras* (under construction) and may still be through 1998. You can still visit the major finds in a temporary exhibition hall outside the necropolis. (Both normally open Tues.-Sat. 10:30am-2pm and 4-7pm, Sun. 10am-2pm; Sept. 16-June 15 Tues.-Sat. 10am-1:30pm and 4-7pm, Sun. 10am-2pm. 150ptas, Tues. free.) The **Pont del Diable** (Devil's Bridge) is a perfectly preserved Roman aqueduct. Take municipal bus #5 from the corner of C. Christòfor Colom and Av. Prat de la Riba (every 20min., 100ptas).

The hidden access to **Platja del Miracle,** directly below town, is along Baixada del Miracle, starting off Pl. Arce Ochotorena, beyond the Roman theater. A bit farther away are the larger beaches, **Rabassada,** with dirt-like sand and the windy **Llarga.** To reach them, take bus #9 from Pl. Imperial Terraco.

ENTERTAINMENT

Nightlife in Tarragona mimics that of Barcelona, but on a smaller scale. Between 5-9pm, **Rambla Nova** and **Rambla Vella** (and the area in between) are packed with strolling families. Around 9pm, the bars liven up. **Pau de Protectorat** is the most popular street. When these bars close around 2am, everyone heads to the new Port Esporitiu, across the train tracks. Inaugurated by King Juan Carlos I last year, this strip of *bares-musicales* usually rocks until 4am.

CATALUNYA (CATALUÑA)

July and August usher in **Festivales de Tarragona** (tel. 24 47 95)—rock, jazz, dance, theater, and film—at the Auditori Camp de Mart near the cathedral. A booth on Rbla. Nova sells tickets for the 10:30pm performances (400-1800ptas). Arrive one hour before the performance. On even-numbered years, the first Sunday in October brings the **Concurs de Castells** and groups of acrobats. They appear amid dragons, beasts, and fireworks during the annual **Festa de Sant Tecla** on September 23.

Islas Baleares

Dreaming, perhaps, of the vast fortunes to be made in the 20th-century tourist industry, nearly every culture with boats and colonists to spare has tried to conquer the Baleares. English imperialist efforts notwithstanding, the isles have been Spanish since the 13th century. Today's attractions are discos and beaches, drawing nearly 2 million of the hippest European bourgeois tourists to the islands each year.

Mallorca is home to Palma, the Balearic capital, and absorbs the bulk of invaders. Its museums, architecture, and nightlife compete with Eivissa (Ibiza City) as the Baleares' cultural hub. Mallorca is not short on natural beauty, albeit in the shadows of urbanization. To the west and north, Sierra de Tramontana's jagged limestone cliffs drop abruptly into the turquoise sea. Condominiums loom over lazy bays that scoop into the coastline, while olive orchards and orange groves shade its fertile interior. Ibiza, a counter-culture haven since the 1960s, plays the entertainment capital of the islands; it may be the most radical scene on the planet. Its little neighbor, Formentera, is more peaceful, but unspoiled sands may quickly lose their charm as Italians and Germans continue flocking to Spain. Wrapped in green fields and stone walls, Menorca leads a private life with empty white beaches, hidden coves, and mysterious Bronze Age megaliths. Each island maintains its own dialect as part of its distinctive culture—*ibsenco* in Ibiza, *menorquín* in Menorca, and *mallorquín* in Mallorca, all of which derive from *catalán*.

Island cuisine is relatively simple, but mayonnaise, a Menorcan innovation, puts the Baleares in the culinary hall of fame. More substantial foods include *sopas mallorquines,* a stocky vegetable soup ladled over thinly sliced brown bread, and *escaldums,* an appetizing chicken dish. Those with a sweet tooth live and die for *ensaimadas,* doughy, candied pastries smothered in powdered sugar.

Summers tend to be hot, dry, and crowded, but fun. Spring and autumn may be gorgeous and the easiest times to find budget accommodations, but the nightlife doesn't heat up till July. There are essentially two stages of the year: uncrowded and peaceful, and mobbed and hip.

■ Getting There

Before hopping on a ferry, island-goers should always consult **Iberia/Aviaco Airlines** (tel. (902) 40 05 00) to inquire about youth discounts. Potential visitors should also seek out package deals designed for young people. **SOM** (Servicios de Ocio Marítimo; tel. (971) 31 03 99; email ibizasom@ctv.es; http//www ctv.es/USERS/ibizasom) collaborates with bus companies, ferry lines, and *discotecas* on packages to Ibiza that are specially designed for *dicotecarios* seeking transportation and an all-night party, with no particular use for lodging.

BY PLANE

Charters are the cheapest and quickest means of round-trip travel. Most deals entail a week's stay in a hotel, but some companies (called *mayoristas*) sell fares for unoccupied seats on flights booked with full-package passengers. The leftover spots, called "seat only" deals, can be found in newspaper ads or through travel agencies (check TIVE and other budget travel havens in any Spanish city). Summer and Semana Santa prices more than double standard off season (Oct.-May) fares. **Scheduled flights** are easier to book. Frequent departures soar from Barcelona, Madrid, and Valencia, as well as Düsseldorf, London, Frankfurt, Hamburg, and Paris. **Iberia** and **Aviaco** handle all flights from Spain to the Isles. Round-trip student fares (must be 22 and under or 26 and under with ISIC) are listed below. From Barcelona to: Palma (17,250ptas); Menorca (18,750ptas); Ibiza (20,050ptas). From Valencia to: Ibiza (17,550ptas); Palma (19,150ptas); Menorca (17,300ptas). From Madrid to: Ibiza

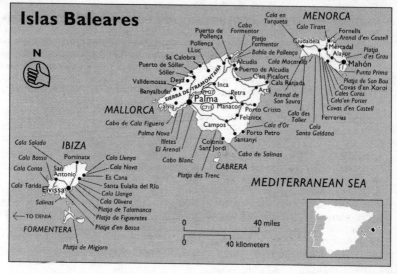

Islas Baleares

N

MALLORCA

MENORCA

IBIZA

FORMENTERA

CABRERA

MEDITERRANEAN SEA

0   40 miles

0   40 kilometers

(27,100ptas); Palma (25,500ptas); Menorca (28,750ptas). *Tarifa-mini* round-trip tickets, with 50% discounts, are sporadically available. Contact Aviaco at least six months before your departure.

BY BOAT

Ferry service is comparable in price to charter flights but longer in duration. Onboard discos and small swimming pools on some boats help ease the longer passage. Three companies compete for business: Transmediterránea is the aging champion; Flebasa the challenger; and Pitra the young upstart.

Transmediterránea ships depart from Barcelona, Est. Marítima (tel. (9)3 443 25 32), and Valencia, Est. Marítima, Pta. de Valencia, (tel. (9)6 367 65 12). Any travel agent in Spain can book seats to Palma, Mahón, and Eivissa. All connections are direct except Valencia-Mahón, a painful 18-hour trip via Palma. These are high season schedules and prices: Barcelona-Palma (8 per week, 6650ptas); Barcelona-Ibiza (5-6 per week, 6590ptas); Barcelona-Mahón (2-6 per week, 6650ptas); Valencia-Palma (6 per week, 6650ptas); Valencia-Ibiza (6 per week, 3325ptas); Valencia-Mahón (1 per week, 6650ptas). All journeys take 8-9 hours. *Fast ferries* run: Barcelona-Palma (4-5 per week, 4hr., 7875ptas); Valencia-Palma (3 per week, 4hr. 7875ptas); Valencia-Ibiza (3 per week, 3 hr., 5060ptas). You should reserve all tickets a few days in advance, but seats may be available for sale up to an hour before departure.

Flebasa (tel. (900) 177 177), leaves from Denia, in the province of Alicante. The Denia-Eivissa trip is the shortest mainland-to-island journey (1 per day, 3½hr.), and a connection in Eivissa continues to Palma. Flebasa also runs Denia-San Antonio (2 per day, 4hr.). The fare for all journeys is 5475ptas, round-trip 8760ptas. Denia lies on the FEVE rail line between Valencia to the north and Alicante to the south. In summer, ferry tickets can be supplemented with a bus connection from either of those cities or from Madrid, Albacete, or Benidorm for 350ptas extra. Flebasa also serves Vilanova i la Geltrú (p.333), just south of Barcelona, and Alcudia (p.371), a northern Mallorcan port. Offices are at the ports of Denia (tel. (9)6 578 40 11), Alicante (tel. (9)65 22 21 88), San Antonio (tel. (9)71 34 28 71), and Eivissa (tel. 31 40 05), or consult a travel agent. **Pitra** ferries (tel. (9)6 624 31 20; fax 624 28 22) also depart from Denia, running Denia-Formentera and Denia-San Antonio (3655ptas).

■ Getting Around

Flying is the most efficient way to island-hop. **Iberia** flies from Palma to Ibiza (3-4 per day, 20min., 5900ptas) and Mahón (2-3 per day, 20min., 5800ptas), and from Menorca to Ibiza, but the stop-over in Palma can last up to four hours (2-3 per day, 11,700ptas). Planes fill a few days in advance in summer, so make reservations. If flying round-trip, ask about the *tarifa-mini* fare.

Seafarers sail **Transmediterránea,** whose ships sail Palma-Ibiza (1 per week, 4½hr., 3325ptas) and Palma-Mahón (1 per week, 6½hr., 3325ptas). Transmediterránea also has summer fast ferry service running Palma-Ibiza (3 per week, 2¼hr., 5060ptas). **Flebasa** (tel. 32 29 30 in Formentera, 31 40 05 in Eivissa) ferries connect Palma-San Antonio (1 per day, 3245ptas) and Palma-Eivissa (1 per day, 3245ptas); Alcudia, Mallorca-Ciudadela, Menorca (14-35 per week, 1-3½hr., 3150ptas); and Eivissa-Formentera (16 per day, round-trip 2700-3600ptas).

All three major islands have extensive bus systems. Mallorca has two narrow-gauge train systems, but they don't accept Eurailpasses. Intra-island travel is reasonably priced—bus fares between cities range from 100-700ptas each way. You might try self-operated transport for greater mobility and access to remote areas. For groups, **car rental** may be cheapest. A day's rental of a SEAT Panda costs around 5200ptas, including insurance; Vespa or **moped rental** 2300ptas; and **bicycle rental** 900ptas.

MALLORCA

Mallorca subscribes to a simple theorem: more hotels, more tourists, more money. Charm and luxury once attracted King Juan Carlos I to vacation on Mallorca, and enchanting landscapes drew Chopin and George Sand to honeymoon there. Fortunately for some but to the chagrin of others, expanding airways and sealines have opened the island to European package tourists who suffocate Mallorca's coastline.

There are reasons for Mallorca lust. To the northwest, white sand beaches, frothy water, lemon groves, and olive trees adorn the jagged Sierra de Tramontana. To the east, expansive beaches sink into calm bays, while the southeastern coast masks its beauty underground, in a network of caves. Inland, windmills drawing water for almond and fig trees power a thriving agricultural economy. The coastline, however, has already been doomed to prospectors. Only the most persistent adventurers will find an unspoiled corner.

■ Palma

Mallorca's capital (pop. 318,875) is the showy Balearic upstart, a concrete jungle that delights in quashing every image of serene island living that could grace a travel agency's wall. Streets bustle with shoppers consuming leather accessories, designer clothes, jewelry, silverware, and car stereos. Even the city's namesake, palm trees, have gone commercial, picking up their roots and moving to hotel lobbies, replacing their cellulose with shiny, plastic roots. Palma remains one of Spain's wealthiest cities, a metropolis with large year-round population, well-preserved old quarter, fancy restaurants, and a swinging nightlife.

ORIENTATION AND PRACTICAL INFORMATION

To get to the town center from the airport, take bus #17 to **Plaça d'Espanya** (every 30min., 6:10am-1am, 15min., 285ptas). From the dock, walk out of the parking lot and turn right on Pg. Marítim, then left onto Av. Antoni Maura, which leads to **Plaça de la Reina** and **Passeig des Born.** Pg. Born leads away from the sea to **Plaça del Rei Joan Carles I. Avinguida Rei Jaume III,** the business artery, runs to the left. To the right, **Carrer de la Unió** leads (after some stairs) to the **Plaça Major,** the center of the

pedestrian shopping district. Calle Sant Miquel connects Pl. Major to Pl. Espanya, where you can catch a bus.

Tourist Office: English-speaking staff at the **municipal branch,** C. Sant Dominic, 11 (tel. 72 40 90), hands out *A Palma,* their monthly calendar/guide. Open Mon.-Fri. 9am-8pm, Sat. 9am-1:30pm. From Pl. Reina take C. Conquistador until it turns into C. Sant Dominic. The **island tourist office,** Pl. Reina, 2(tel. 71 22 16), offers info on all the islands, an fine city map, bus and train schedules, lists of all sporting and cultural events on Mallorca, and a pamphlet with hiking excursions. Open Mon.-Fri. 9am-8pm, Sat. 9am-1:30pm. **Branch office** at the airport (tel. 78 95 56) has similar info. Open Mon.-Sat. 9am-2pm and 3-8pm, Sun. 9am-2pm. The **info booth** (tel. 71 15 27) in Pl. Espanya is open Mon.-Fri. 9am-8:30pm, Sat. 9am-1:30pm.

Currency Exchange: Banco Central Hispano, Passeig de Born, 17, offers the best rates. Open Mon.-Fri. 8:30am-2:30pm.

El Corte Inglés: Av. Rei Jaume III, 15 or Av. Alexandre Rosselló, 12 (tel. 77 01 77). **Fax, phones, money exchange, supermarket,** and the **best free map** available. Both open Mon.-Sat. 10am-10pm.

Budget Travel: TIVE, C. Jerónim Antich, 5 (tel. 71 17 85), near Pl. Bisbe Berenguer de Palou and Pl. Espanya. ISIC (700ptas), HI cards (1800ptas), Interrail tickets, and mainland flights. Not for inter-island travel and charters. Open Mon.-Fri. 8am-3pm.

American Express: Viajes Iberia, Pg. Born, 14 (tel. 72 67 43). The usual services. Open Mon.-Fri. 9am-1:30pm and 4-8pm, Sat. 9:30am-1pm.

Flights: Aeroport Son San Juan (tel. 26 42 10), 8km from downtown Palma. Bus #17 goes to Pl. Espanya. **Iberia,** Joan March, 6 (tel. 75 71 51). Open Mon.-Fri. 9am-1:15pm and 4-7:15pm. Iberia's **airport office** (tel. 26 77 28). Open 6am-10:45pm. **Aviaco** (tel. 24hr. 901 333 111). See **By Plane,** p.362

Trains: Ferrocarril de Sóller, Pl. España, 2 (tel. 75 20 51), off Pl. Espanya. To Sóller (5 per day, 380ptas). Avoid the 10:40am "tourist train"—prices inflate to 735ptas for a 10min. stop in Mirador del Pujol d'en Banya. **Servicios Ferroviarios de Mallorca (SFM)** (tel. 75 22 45), in Pl. Espanya, goes to Inca (Mon.-Fri. almost every 40min., Sat.-Sun. every hr., 430ptas).

Buses: Most buses run out of the main terminal, **Estació Central D'Autobus,** Pl. Espanya (tel. 29 57 00 or 43 10 24). One company for every fannypack-wearing tourist. The tourist office has a complete schedule that orders the confusion, but the system is inefficient and restrictive. Major roads fan out from Palma like fingers, making travel to and from the capital relatively painless, but travel between most other areas is indirect and will probably route you through Palma. **Empresa Municipal de Transportes,** Pl. Espanya (tel. 75 22 45), Standard fare 170ptas, 10 tickets 780ptas. Outlying areas are slightly pricier. Buy tickets aboard or in Pl. Espanya kiosks. Buses run 6am-10pm. **Autocares Mallorca,** Pl. Espanya (tel. 54 56 96), serves Alcudia (via Inca) along with the Campsite at Cala Blava, and other ports in northern Mallorca. **Autocares Aumasa,** Pl. Espanya (tel. 55 07 30), provides links to the eastern seaboard, including Porto Cristo. **Bus Nord Belear,** C. Arxiduc Lluís Salvador, 1, at Bar La Granja (tel. 42 71 87), near Pl. Espanya, connects Valldemossa, Deyá, Soller, and Puerto de Soller. **Cladera Ferrer** (tel. 27 69 06) leaves Pl. Espanya and goes through Inca to Ca'n Picafort (10min. from Alcúdia). **Villalonga,** Pl. Espanya (tel. 53 00 57), serves Polença through Inca. **Dar Bus,** Pl. Espanya (tel. 75 06 22), serves towns in the southeast, including Sa Sapita, Es Trenc, and Colonia San Jordi. **Autocares Alorda** (tel. 50 15 03) serves Lluc and Inca from Pl. Espanya. **Playa-Sol** (tel. 29 64 17) runs tourist routes within Palma and to nearby resort areas El Arenal, Magaluf, and Palma Nova.

Ferries: Transmediterránea, Estación Marítim, 2 (tel. 40 50 14). Bus #1 runs along Pg. Marítim to Moll Pelaires. Tickets sold Mon.-Fri. 9am-1pm and 5-7pm, Sat. 9am-noon. Ferries dock at Moll Pelaires (partway around the bay south of the city); tickets sell until shortly before departure (for fares, see By Boat, p. 363).

Taxis: (tel. 75 54 40 or 40 14 14). Airport fare is about 2500ptas.

Car Rental: Mascaro Crespi, Av. Joan Miró, 9 (tel. 73 61 03). 2784ptas per day with insurance. Open Mon.-Sat. 8am-1pm and 3-8pm, Sun. 9am-1pm and 5-8pm.

ISLAS BALEARES

Moped Rental: RTR Bike Rental, Av. Joan Miró, 338 (tel. 40 25 85). From Pl. Espanya, take bus #3, 21, or 22 to Pl. Gomila. Mopeds 2150ptas per day, 5700ptas for 3 days. Open Mon.-Sat. 9am-9pm, Sun. 9am-1pm.

Luggage Storage: SFM office, Pl. Espanya. Small locker 300ptas; big 500ptas. Lockers available Mon.-Fri. 7am-8pm, Sat.-Sun. 7am-2pm.

English Bookstore: Book Inn, C. Horts, 20 (tel. 71 38 98), right off La Rambla. An impressive selection of literature. Children's books, too. Open Mon.-Fri. 10am-1:30pm and 5-8pm, Sat. 10:30am-1:30pm. Hours change in Aug.

Women's Center: Centro Informació Drets de la Mujer, C. Portella, 11, 2nd fl. (tel. 72 25 51), near Parc de la Mar. **Rape crisis** assistance available. Open Mon.-Fri. 9am-2pm. **24hr. hotline:** (tel. (900) 19 10 10).

24hr. Pharmacy: See listings in local paper, *Diario de Mallorca* (125ptas).

Medical Services: Clinic Bateau, C. Nuredduna, 4 (tel. 46 62 62 or 061). 24hr.

Police: On Av. Sant Ferran (tel. 28 16 00). **Emergency:** (tel. 091 or 092).

Post Office: C. Constitució, 6, (tel. 72 10 95), one block off Pl. Reina. Parcels upstairs. Lista de Correos downstairs at window #3. Open Mon.-Fri. 8:30am-8:30pm, Sat. 9:30am-2pm. **Postal Code:** 07001.

Telephone Code: (9)71 for all the Baleares.

ACCOMMODATIONS

As anywhere else, accommodations vary from the bed stuffed in a closet approach to the mini-villa. There aren't many of the latter—call in advance for July and August.

Albergue Residencia de Estudiantes (HI), C. Costa Brava, 13 (tel. 26 08 92), in the beach town El Arenal. Take bus #15 from Pl. Espanya (every 8 min., 170ptas) and ask to get off at Hotel Acapulco. A pristine, palatial *pensión* on the *platja*. New furniture, showers, lounge with big screen TV, library, and winter heating. HI card required. Curfew Sun.-Thurs. midnight, Fri.-Sat. 3am. Reception open 8am-3am. 1200ptas per person. Sheets included. Breakfast 300ptas. Open only July and Aug.

Hostal Bonany, C. Almirante Cervera, 5 (tel. 73 79 24), in El Terreno, 3km from the center toward the nearest beaches and 5min. from the nightlife. Take bus #3, 20, 21, or 22 from Pl. Espanya to Av. Joan Miró, walk up C. Camilo José Cela, take the 1st right, then the 1st left. Spacious rooms with bath and balcony overlook the *hostal's* pool and patio. Singles 2400ptas. Doubles 4200ptas. Hearty breakfast (bread, coffee, eggs, cheese, and juice) 400ptas. Open Feb.-Nov.

Hostal Apuntadores, C. Apuntadores, 8 (tel. 71 34 91), less than a block from the beach bus stop at Pl. Reina. Rooms are mediocre but the rooftop lounge and crowded downstairs bar raise the quality of living. Singles 2000ptas. Doubles 3500ptas, with shower 4000ptas. Discounts for longer stays. Breakfast 200ptas. Foreign currency accepted.

Hostal Cuba, C. San Magín, 1 (tel. 73 81 59), on the corner of C. Argentina. From the port, go left along Av. Gabriel Roca and turn right onto C. Argentina. Look for the blue shutters on the left. Market-conscious young owner always making improvements to stay ahead. Rooms range from dull to palatial. Smart view of cathedral and port from balconies and rooftop terrace. Great location. Singles with bath 1500ptas. Doubles 3000ptas, with full bath 3500ptas. Laundry 700ptas.

Hostal Ritzi, C. Apuntadores, 6 (tel. 71 46 10), next to Hostal Apuntadores. Lace hangings and ornate furniture give a Victorian feeling to these cozy quarters. At night, fiddle with 4 locks en route to your springy mattress. Kitchen and dining room make for a family atmosphere (available 6-8:30pm). Carpeting and lounge with English Sky TV (until 8:30pm). Ask to find out which shower works. Winter heating. Singles 2500ptas. Doubles 3500ptas, with shower 4000ptas. Continental breakfast 375ptas, English breakfast 450ptas. Credit cards.

Hostal Monleon, La Rambla, 3 (tel. 71 53 17). Tall ceilings and big windows. Some rooms somewhat dark, but big old *ventanas* (windows) make up for that. Some squeaky noise from La Rambla. Singles 2100ptas, with shower 2400ptas, with bath 2700ptas. Doubles: 3800ptas; 4100ptas; 4500ptas.

Camping: Platja Blava (tel. 53 78 63) is located at km 8 of the highway between Alcudia and C'an Picafort. Take Autocares Mallorca direct from Pl. Espanya. 550ptas per person and 1365ptas for a 6 by 6m plot. Ten buses leave daily for C'an

Picafort from Palma (595-675ptas). **Club San Pedro** (tel. 58 90 23) is a 3rd-class site 2km outside of Colònia de Sant Pere. To get here from Palma, hop on a C'an Picafort bus and take a connecting bus to Colònia de Sant Pere. 535ptas per person and 1200ptas per tent. Open April-Oct.

FOOD

Menus come in German, French, Hittite, and English, Spanish, and *mallorquín*, but the best food is rarely as international. Mom-and-Pop operations serve tourists and locals along side streets, especially around **Pg. Born.** Two **town markets** vie for customers. One is in Pl. Olivar off C. Padre Atanasio, the other is across town by Pl. Navegació in Es Jonquet (both open Mon.-Sat. 7am-3pm). For **groceries,** try **Servicio y Precios (SYP),** C. Felip Bauzà (tel. 72 78 11), around the corner from *hostal* Ritzi (open Mon.-Fri. 9am-2pm and 5:30-9pm, Sat. 9am-2pm). Bump your head on dangling sausages at **Sobrasada Colmado Santo Domingo,** C. Sto. Domingo, 1 (tel. 71 48 87), Mallorca's meat and vegetable jungle (open Mon.-Sat. 10am-8pm).

Celler Pagès, C. Felip Bauzà, 2 (tel. 72 60 36), at the end of C. Pintor Guillem Mesquida, off Pl. Reina. Disregard the exterior; a bourgeois Mallorcan crowd is all over the local cuisine. Bowl of spiced olives with every 1100ptas *menú*. Open Mon.-Fri. 1-4pm and 8:30-11pm, Sat. 1-4pm. Credit cards accepted.

C'an Joan de S'aigo, C. Sanç, 10 (tcl. 71 07 59), near Pl. Coll. Red velvet curtains, a mini-garden, and marble tables in the city's oldest house set the stage for exquisite desserts, including Mallorca's specialty *gelado de almendra* (almond ice cream 180ptas). Open Wed.-Mon. 8am-9:15pm.

Celler Sa Premsa, Pl. Bisbe Berenguer de Palou, 8 (tel. 72 35 29), between Via Roma and Pl. Espanya off Carrer OMS. Traditional *mallorquín* food on vegetable-laden platters served by superhumanly efficient waiters. *Menú del día* 995ptas. *Sopas mallorquinas* (495ptas). Open Mon.-Sat. noon-4pm and 7:30-11:30pm.

Bon Lloc, C. Sant Feliu, 7 (tel. 71 86 17), off Pg. Born. Excellent vegetarian restaurant serves up hearty morsels of protein and vitamins. Midday 4-plate *menú* 1250ptas. No smoking. Open Mon.-Sat. 1-4pm and Fri. (a la carte) 9-11pm.

Merendero Minyones, C. Minyones, 4. A teeny booth on a small street one block from C. Constitució. From Pg. Born walk up C. Constitució, then take your 1st left and 1st right. *Pa-amb-oli i tomate* (tomato and olive oil on bread 115ptas). *Sobrasada* (soft Mallorcan *chorizo* spread 155ptas). They'll wrap up sandwiches (155-210ptas) for the beach. Open Mon.-Fri. 7:30am-8:30pm, Sat. 8am-2pm.

Na Bauçano, Sta. Bárbara, 4 (tel. 72 18 86), off C. Brossa between Pl. Mercat and Pl. Cort. Homemade breads, stuffed eggplants, and vine leaves filled with falafel will make you forget about tofu. Afternoon *menú* 1050ptas. No smoking. Open Mon.-Fri. 1-4pm, Thurs.-Fri. additionally 8:30pm-midnight.

SIGHTS

Palma's architecture proudly displays Arabic, Christian, and *modernisme* influence which have passed through with the island's many conquerors. Two of the city's most important buildings share close quarters, just off Pl. Reina. **Palau Reial Almudaina** (tel. 72 71 45) was built by the Moors and later controlled by the *Reyes Católicos* (Fernando and Isabel). Guided tours, which pass through the museum, are given in numerous languages, except when King Juan Carlos I is tromping about the halls on business. (Open Mon.-Fri. 10am-6:30pm, Sat. 10am-2pm; Oct.-March Mon.-Fri. 10am-2pm. 450ptas, students 225ptas, Wed. EC members free.) Next door, one of the world's largest **cathedrals** (tel. 72 31 30) overlooks Palma and its bay. The laggard giant was begun in 1230, finished in 1601, and then modified by Gaudí in *modernisme* fashion. Now the interior and the ceiling ornamentation blend smoothly with the stately exterior. (Cathedral and **tresor** of Palma's patron saint San Sebastián open Mon.-Fri. 10am-6pm, Sat. 10am-2pm; Nov.-March Mon.-Fri. 10am-3pm, Sat. 10am-2pm. 400ptas.) The tangle of tight streets full of wide-eyed tourists around the cathedral constitutes the **Barri Gòtic** (medieval quarter). Mallorca's only well preserved

Moorish legacy is the bland **Banys Arabs** (Arab sauna baths; tel. 72 15 49), on C. Serra (open daily 9:30am-7pm, Nov.-March 9:30am-6pm; 150ptas, students free).

Palma makes up for a lack of architectural beauty by hosting a multitude of art exhibits. **Colleccio March, Art Espanyol Contemporani,** C. Sant Miquel, 11 (tel. 71 26 01), has 57 works, each by different 20th-century Spanish artists, including Picasso, Dalí, Miró, Juan Gris, and Antoni Tàpies. The curator answers the befuddled questions of those who thought art ended with Monet (open Mon.-Fri. 10am-6:30pm, Sat. 10am-1:30pm; 300ptas). The **Palau Sollerich,** C. Sant Gaietà, 10 (tel. 77 20 92), opens contemporary art exhibits to the public (open Tues.-Sat. 10:30am-1:45pm and 5-8:30pm, Sun. 10am-1:45pm; free). **Fundacio "la Caixa",** Pl. Weyler, 3 (tel. 72 01 11), hosts a permanent collection of paintings as well as other special exhibits in Domènech's *modernisme* Gran Hotel (open Tues.-Sat. 10am-9pm, Sun. 10am-2pm; free). **Centre de Cultura "Sa Nostra,"** C. Concepció, 12 (tel. 72 52 10), features rotating contemporary exhibits and sponsors cultural events such as lectures, concerts and movies. (Open Mon.-Fri. 10:30am-9pm, Sat. 10:30am-1pm. Exhibitions open Mon.-Fri. 10:30am-1:30pm and 5-9pm, Sat. 10:30am-1:30pm. Free.)

Overlooking the city and bay and set in a park, **Castell de Bellver** (tel. 73 06 57) served as summer residence for 12th-century royalty. For centuries thereafter it housed distinguished, albeit unwilling, guests. The castle contains a **Museu Municipal** of archaeological displays and several paintings. (See Fundació Miró below for transportation info. Castle, grounds, and museum open 8am-8:30pm; Oct.-March 8am-8:30pm. 150ptas, Sun. free.) Inaugurated in December 1992, **Fundació Joan i Pilar Miró,** C. Saridakis, 29 (tel. 70 14 20), is a collection of the works found in the Catalan artist's Palma studio at the time of his death. (Open Tues.-Sat. 10am-7pm, Sun. 10am-3pm, Sept. 15-May 15 Tues.-Sat. 11am-6pm, Sun. 11am-3pm. 380ptas.) Bus #3, 21, and 22 whisk you from Pl. Espanyol to C. Joan Miró. A bit outside of town is Palma's **Poble Espanyol,** C. Poble Espanyol, 39 (tel. 73 70 75), a reproduction of its parent in Barcelona, with mini samples of Spanish architecture. Bus #4 and 5 pass by along C. Andrea Doria. (Open daily 9am-7:30pm, Nov.-March 9am-6pm. Arts and Crafts 10am-7:30pm., Nov.-March 10am-5pm. 600ptas, under 12 250ptas.)

Though better **beaches** speckle the island, decent ones (sand and snacks) are a mere bus ride from Palma. The beach at **El Arenal** (Platja de Palma, bus #15), 11km to the southeast, tends to be over-touristed. The equally crowded **Palma Nova** and **Illetes** beaches (buses #21 and 3 respectively) are 15 and 9km southwest.

ENTERTAINMENT

The municipal tourist office keeps a comprehensive list of sporting activities, concerts, and exhibits. Every Friday, *El Día de Mundo* (125ptas) publishes an entertainment supplement with listings of bars and discos all over Mallorca. Look for *La Calle,* a monthly review of clubs and bars.

Enact your aristocratic fantasies in the *casa antigua*-turned-bar **ABACO,** C. Sant Joan, 1 (tel. 71 59 11), in the Barri Gòtic near the waterfront. Sip drinks amid elegant wicker and marble furniture, cooing doves, a wide array of fresh fruit, flowers, and hundreds of dripping candles, all to the accompaniment of Handel, Bach, et al. (Fruit nectars 1100ptas, potent cocktails 1700-2100ptas. Wandering the chambers is free.) The streets around **La Llotja** flow with bar-hoppers. You can't help but dance to the Cuban rhythms in **La Bodeguita del Medio,** C. Vallseca, 18 (tel. 71 78 32). Be sure to order Hemingway's favorite, *mojito* (open 8:30pm-3am). Live guitar music (Thurs., Fri., Sat. nights) gives a lift to **Barcelona** on C. Apuntadores, 5 (tel. 71 35 57; open Mon.-Sat. 10pm-3am, 450ptas minimum consumption). Slip through the hole in the wall to get to **Blues Ville** on Má Del Moro, 3, or take a dip in **El Agua,** C. Jaime Ferrer, 6. The rest of Palma's nightlife boogies near **El Terreno,** with a mother load of nightclubs centered on Pl. Gomilia and along C. Joan Miró. **Tito's Palace,** Pl. Gomilia, 1, (tel. 73 76 42), an indoor colliseum of mirrors and lights, overlooks the water (open 11am-6am, 1500ptas cover). **Plato,** across the street at Pl. Gomilia, 2, keeps a lower, more local profile. **Sa Finestra,** C. Joan Miró, 90, features live music every night after 11:30pm at. Hats off to the gay bar **Sombrero,** C. Joan Miró, 26, (tel. 73 16

00; open nightly 9pm-3am; no cover). The divine **Baccus** (tel. 45 77 89), around the corner on C. Lluis Fábregas, 2, draws lively lesbian and gay hedonists (open until 3am). Word is that **Pachá** will found its own Island by the year 2000, but for now freak out at its Av. Gabriel Roca site (open midnight-6am; cover 2000-3000ptas). **BCM** in **Magaluf** is fast becoming the hottest dig around, especially with the British—it's supposedly the biggest nightclub in Europe. (Playa-Sol bus company sends its last bus at 8pm, but you can return on bus #10 at 6:45am. Taxi from Palma 1800ptas. Open 11pm-6am. Cover 1800-2500ptas.)

Islanders use any and every occasion as an excuse to party. One of the more colorful bashes, **Día de Sant Joan** (June 24) involves a no-expense-spared fireworks display the night before, accompanied by singing, dancing, and drinking in Parc del Mar.

■ West Coast

The western end of Mallorca abruptly plunges into the water from the Sierra de Tramontana. Its hills become wavy staircase-like ridges of stone walls and olive groves with villages nestled between peaks. The best way to explore is to choose a destination along the gorgeous coast, then meander on foot. The **Playa-Sol** company (tel. 29 64 17) runs buses to the handy transport hub Andraitx, 30km from Palma.

VALLDEMOSA

Valldemosa's weathered houses huddle along the harsh Sierra de Tramontana. Little in this ancient village hints at the passion that shocked the townsfolk in the winter of 1838-39, when tubercular Frédéric Chopin and George Sand (her two children in tow) stayed in the **Cartoixa Reial** (tel. 61 21 06), loudly flouting the monastic tradition of celibacy. Chopin memorabilia includes a picture of a plaster mold of his famous hands and the piano upon which they played. Short piano recitals recapture the magic in the summer. (8 per day. Mallorcan dance Mon. and Thurs. mornings. Open Mon.-Sat. 9:30am-1:20pm and 3-6:30pm, Nov.-Feb. 9:30am-1pm and 3-5:30pm. 1100ptas, including visits to the **Museu Municipal** and the **Palau del Rei Sancho.**)

Valldemosa's low on services, but you can **exchange money** at one of the banks on Vía Blanquerra (banks open Mon.-Fri. 8:30am-2pm). Nord Balear **buses** (tel. 42 71 87) to Valldemosa leave from Palma at C. Arxiduc Salvador, 1 (5 per day, 200ptas).

If the tranquil music and floral mountain-side terraces of the Cortoixa convince you to stay, **Hostal Ca'n Mario,** C. Vetam, 8 (tel. 61 21 22; fax 61 60 29), offers the second best views in town (singles with shower 3800ptas, doubles with shower 5800ptas). Near Valldemosa, 10km north on the bus route to Sóller, is the artists' hangout, **Deyá** (5 buses per day, 110ptas). Tourists (many from the land of brie) lunch at its overpriced restaurants, all on the main road. Still, the unspoiled town and its environs afford a sensational view of miles and miles of twisted olive trees.

SÓLLER AND PUERTO DE SÓLLER

Another 30km up the coast, **Sóller** basks in a mountain valley widening to a golden port. The end of a train ride through the pine-covered mountains, the town hums with tourists all day long. Every available plot of land is lined with citrus groves, and freshly squeezed OJ is a local specialty. In August, the Ajuntament hosts an international **Festival de Dança Folclorica,** with dancers from all over Europe and Asia (1998 dates yet to be determined). The half-hour walk to **Puerto de Sóller** from the beach is free, but some prefer to rumble on the trolley (150ptas). The port, at the bottom of the valley, absorbs most of the tourists. A pebble-and-sand beach lines the small bay, where windsurfers zip back and forth.

In Sóller, the **tourist office** on Pl. Constitució, 1 (tel. 63 02 00), supplies a map and list of the few accommodations open (Mon.-Sat. 9:30am-1:30pm; info is posted at the entrance). They can suggest hikes; one manageable route steps to **Fornalutx,** an hour up the valley. The **Red Cross** is called Cruz Roja in Spanish (tel. 63 08 45). The **police** are at tel. 63 02 03; for **emergencies,** call tel. 63 11 91 or 085.

The old-school **train** (tel. 75 20 28) that runs between Palma and Sóller is a highlight in itself. Bravehearts can ride in the wind between cars through arid valleys, olive orchards, and freaky tunnels (5 per day, 1hr., 380ptas).

Numerous hotels anchor at the port base of the mountains, each flooded by package tourists. **Hotel Miramar,** C. Marina, 12-14 (tel. 63 13 50), provides modern comforts, like full baths (singles 3350ptas; doubles 4600ptas; triples 6700ptas). There are two **grocery stores** up C. Jaume Torrens, and restaurants of all sorts and sizes file along the beach. In Sóller proper, *patisseries* specialize in **Coca Mallorquina,** a cold pizza-like snack with a soft crust covered with tomato sauce and vegetables (large costs about 250ptas). **Restaurante Bar La Pirata,** C. Santa Catalina, 8 (tel. 63 14 97), near the next trolley stop, hooks customers with an 900ptas *menú* and pirate ship spoils on the walls (open Jan.-Nov. Fri.-Wed. noon-4pm and 7pm-midnight).

Exploring the rest of the coves on the coast is easiest by **boat.** Tramontana and Barcos Azules on the port near the last trolley stop (tel. 63 20 61) sail to Sa Calobra, most people's final destination (May-Oct.15 3-5 per day, round-trip 1900ptas) and Cala Deyá (June-Oct. 15, round-trip 1200ptas). Nord Balear **buses** link Puerto de Sóller to Palma via Valldemosa (5 per day, 415ptas).

SA CALOBRA

If your parents saw the road to **Sa Calobra,** a hidden cove, they'd reach for the Valium. This asphalt serpent drops 1000m to the sea over 10 hairpin kilometers, writhing back underneath itself in the process. The **boat** from Puerto de Sóller is easier on the nerves (see above). A bit of a roadway and a tunnel bored through a cliff leads to the **Torrent de Pareis,** everyone's favorite Kodak moment. Two dark, ominous cliffs sandwich a smooth pebble beach bordering the crystalline sea.

LLUC

Tucked away quietly the mountains, the **Monestir de Lluc** (tel. 51 70 25) is 20km inland in Escorca. Mallorca's Montserrat, Lluc is home of the 700-year-old *La Verge de Lluc,* whose carved wood has turned dark from age (hence its nickname, *La Moreneta,* The Dark Lady). She hibernates in the basilica. Behind the monastery, **Via Crucis** winds around a hill over the valley's olive trees and jingling goats. Gaudí designed the path's stations of the cross. Monks, pilgrims, and a few privileged guests stay at Lluc's **monastery** (tel. 51 70 25). (True pilgrims stay for a donation—others pay 2700ptas for doubles with bath; quads with bath 3500ptas.) The monks can point you to **campgrounds** nearby. The monastery's store sells **groceries,** and its **restaurant** pushes pricey food. To get here from Palma, take the **train** to Inca and catch one of the two daily connecting **buses** to Lluc, or take Autocares Alorda from Palma direct.

▓ Northern Gulfs

Longer stretches of beaches, finer sand, and a nightmarish quantity of older tourists distinguish the north edge of Mallorca. Secluded coves are tough to come by, especially with the package tours wheeling in visitors from sunless lands. Buses from Palma run through Inca to more appealing spots.

PUERTO DE POLLENÇA

Puerto de Pollença has a relatively uncrowded stretch of fine white sand. The area hosts a **festival de música** from July to September. A complete schedule of events and list of ticket vendors is available at the tourist office (tickets 1000-5000ptas).

The **tourist office** (tel. 86 54 67), behind Hotel Deia on C. Formentor, weeds through bus schedules and plans excursions in a single bound (open May-Oct. Mon.-Fri. 9am-1pm and 4-7pm, Sat. 9am-1pm, Sun. 9am-5pm). **AmEx** has an office at Viajes Iberia C. Joan XXIII, 9 (tel. 53 02 62; open Mon.-Fri. 9am-1:30pm and 4:30-7:30pm, Sat. 9:30am-1pm). **Bike** and **moped rentals** are at Rent March, C. Joan XXIII, 89.

(Open April-Oct. Mon.-Sat. 9am-1pm and 3-8pm, Sun. 9am-1pm and 6-7:30pm. Bikes 600ptas per day, 2500ptas per week. Mopeds 2500ptas per day. IVA included.)

Hostal Corro, C. Joan XXIII, 68 (tel. 53 34 00), has big rooms with sinks (doubles 4000ptas, triples with bath 5000ptas). **Supermercado Super Bosque,** C. Roger de Flor, 13, is a supermarket super forrest (open Mon.-Sat. 8:30am-1:30pm and 4:30-8:30pm, Sun 9am-1pm).

At the end of **Cabo Formentor,** 15km northeast of Puerto de Pollença, *miradores* spy on spectacular seaside cliffs. Before the final twisting kilometer, the road drops to **Platja Formentor,** where a canopy of evergreens nearly sinks into the water. Here the sand is softer, the water calmer, and the crowds smaller than in Puerto de Pollença. Autocares Villalonga sends **buses** from Palma (5 per day, 595ptas). Autocares Mall connects Alcudia and Pollença (every 15min., 25ptas). Hydrophiles can take a boat to Formentor from Puerto de Pollença (tel. 86 40 14; 5 per day, round-trip 795ptas).

PUERTO DE ALCUDIA

Hard-packed sand and tame surf stretch around the small bay. Hotels, bars, and pizzerias outnumber the boats in the marina—the best move is to steer clear. The **tourist office** (tel. 89 26 15), near the waterfront at Av. Pere Mas Reus on the corner with Ctra. Arta, has maps (open May-Oct. Mon.-Sat. 9am-7pm). Rent **bikes** from H. Herrero, C. Mariscos, 8 (tel. 54 80 86; 500ptas per day; open in summer daily 9am-9pm). **Red Cross** tel. 54 54 21. Municipal **police** answer at tel. 54 56 66 or 54 50 66.

Hostal Puerto, C. Teodoro Canet, 29 (tel. 54 54 47), on the road that leads up to Alcudia, offers hotel-quality rooms with private baths and cable TV in the lounge (singles 2140ptas, doubles 3530ptas; open May-Oct.). The only HI youth hostel outside of Palma lolls 100m from an empty beach on the Bahía de Pollença. Signs to the **Alberg Victoria (HI),** Ctra. Cap Pinar, 4 (tel. 54 53 95), lead east from the town center; 4km from Alcudia (1-hr. walk or 1000pta taxi ride). Reserve at least six months in advance for July or August (members only, 1200ptas; breakfast 300ptas).

A one-km bike ride away and well-connected by bus (every 15min.), 14th-century ramparts shelter one side of **Alcudia,** remains of the city's Roman past dating back to 2 BC. **Museu Pollentia** documents the archaeological discoveries (open April-Oct. 10am-1:30pm and 5:30-8pm, Sun. 10am-1:30pm).

Autocares Mallorca **buses** (tel. 54 56 96) for Alcudia (540ptas) and Puerto de Alcudia (560ptas) leave Pl. Espanya in Palma (Mon.-Sat. 11 per day, 1hr., Sun. 5 per day). The bus between Alcudia and Puerto de Pollença runs reliably, some continue to Cabo Formentor. Bus service to the south goes only as far as C'an Picafort.

■ Southeast

The east coast of Mallorca's southeast peninsula is a scalloped fringe of bays and caves that are the newest hotel towns. To their credit, builders have aspired to some architectural integrity. A 1- to 2-km walk puts plenty of sand between you and the thickest crowds. Rounding **Cap de Salinas,** Mallorca's southernmost point, the long leg of coastline back to Palma begins. One of Mallorca's best beaches, **Irenc,** lies between here and **Cap Blanc.** To get to Trenc, take a **Dar Bus** from Pl. Espanya in Palma to Sa Rapita, Es Trenc, or Colonia San Jordi. A 2km walk will take you away from clothes and crowds. The grandsons of Joan March, an infamous Spanish banker, own most of the southeastern interior.

Dar Buses (tel. 75 06 22) leave Pl. Espanya in Palma, for a number of worthwhile destinations in the southeast: **Santanyí,** an inland town whose Porta Murada (defensive wall) testifies to the piracy that once plagued the region; **Cala d'Or,** an inlet of pinewoods and massive boulders; **Porto Petro,** on the beach; and **Colonia Sant Jordi.** From Colonia Sant Jordi, a boat ventures to **Cabrera,** the largest island (30 sq. km) in a small archipelago of 17. Dar Buses do not arrive early enough to catch the boat. For **boat** info, call Excursiones a Cabrera (tel. 64 90 34). Uninhabited except for

a small military installation, Cabrera has a gruesome history. Besides those who perished in the many shipwrecks poking up from the ocean floor, 8000 French prisoners-of-war died here during the Peninsular War in 1809. The Spanish abandoned them on the island with no food. A monument to the dead stands by the port. Nearby looms a 14th-century **fortress** used as a pirates' den.

▨ Inland

Mallorca's heartland is a patchwork of orchards, vineyards, and wheat fields. Ancient stone walls, crumbling and rudimentary, divide inland valleys into individual farms, where windmills and haystacks dot fig, olive, and almond groves. Pastel almond blossoms flourish in February, covering the island like fragrant confetti.

INCA

Inca lies just south of the Sierra de Tramontana, panting for the moisture partitioned off by the mountains. Halfway between Palma and Puerto de Alcudia, it attracts visitors to its inexpensive leather goods and a busy Thursday morning market. Snack-food connoisseurs flock to Inca for authentic *galletes d'oli,* locally produced cookies that look like overfed goldfish crackers. The main streets parallel to the railroad tracks, **Carrer de Colom** and **Carrer de Vicent Ensenyat,** are lined with factory-outlet leather shops selling everything from books and combs to whips and chains.

Inca lies 35 minutes by **train** (tel. 50 00 59) from Palma (Mon.-Sat. 20 per day, Sun. 16 per day, 430ptas round-trip). Five **buses** per day between **Autocares Cladera Ferrer** (tel. 27 69 06) and **Autocares Mallorca** (tel. 54 56 96) journey to Alcudia (35min).

MANACOR

As part of its grand scheme to lure the masses away from the beaches, Manacor has developed a booming faux-pearl industry. Factories open for visits and purchases. The largest one, **Perlas Majorca,** Via Roma, 48 (tel. 55 09 00), is on the road to Palma on the edge of town (open Mon.-Fri. 9am-1pm and 2:30-7pm, Sat.-Sun. 10am-1pm; free). **Perlas Orquídea** (tel. 55 04 00) is located at km31 leaving Palma for Inca (open Mon.-Fri. 9am-7pm, Sat. 9am-1pm, Sun. 9:30-1pm; free). There's not much else to see except for a turreted Gothic **cathedral** and adjoining **Museu Arqueológic** (tel. 84 30 65; open Tues.-Sat. 9am-2pm).

Aumasa **buses** depart from Pl. Cos, 4 (tel. 55 07 30) for Palma (8 per day, Sun. 3 per day, 545ptas) and Porto Cristo (8 per day, Sun. 3 per day, 145ptas).

PETRA

Petra was the birthplace of Fray Junípero Serra, who established Franciscan missions all over California. His house is now a museum. The unadorned **Ermita de Bonany,** or "cathedral of the mountains," is a 1-hr. walk into the gorgeous hills. Aumasa **buses** leave from Pl. Espanya in Palma and go to Petra (3 per day, Sun. 2 per day, 530ptas).

MENORCA

In 1287 Alfonso II "the liberal" added Menorca to the Catalan kingdom. The island has since endured a succession of foreign invaders. Arab, Turkish, French, and British occupations have all left their mark on Menorca. All told, the Brits have reaped the most capital success in Menorca. After occupying the island for three separate stints during the 18th century, the Anglos have returned as tourists and restaurateurs. Menorca's raw beaches and rustic landscape spark the diverse interests of ecologists, sun worshippers, and photographers.

UNESCO's (an arts and sciences agency of the UN) 1993 declaration of Menorca as a 702-square-mile biosphere reserve has prevented British ecological and cultural sov-

ereignty. Since the declaration, public administrators have invested their efforts into preserving the island's natural harbors, pristine southerly beaches, rocky northern coastline, and latticed network of farmlands. The act has also encouraged further protection, excavation, and study of what archaeologists call the *museo al aire libre* (open air museum). The nickname refers to stone burial chambers and homestead complexes, remnants of a mysterious Talayotic stoneage culture that have been on exhibit since 1400 BC. Despite strict regulations, many of these Bronze Age relics are open to visitors. Some are even home to contemporary cave-dwellers who originally sought a communal life-style in the dwellings during the 1960s.

Menorca's two main cities, Mahón in the east and Ciudadela in the west, serve as gateways to the island's natural wonders. A small chapel dedicated to Menorca's saint caps Mont Toro, the island's highest peak. At the foot of the road leading to the shrine is Mercadal, a brilliantly white town and departure point for Fornells. Excellent topographical maps (350ptas per quadrant) are sold at **Cós 4**, Cós de Gràcia, 4, in Mahón (tel. 36 66 69; open Mon.-Fri. 10am-1pm and 5:30-8:30pm, Sat. 10am-1pm).

■ Mahón (Maó)

Perched atop a steep bluff, Mahón's (pop. 22,150) white-splashed houses overlook a well-trafficked harbor. The British occupied Menorca's verdant capital for almost a century in the 1700s, leaving Georgian doors, brass knockers, and wooden shutters in their wake. Gin distilleries, British-style pubs, and the city's early bedtime testify to a continuing influence, as do elite visitors who spend money almost as old as the island. Vacationers from the coasts of France, Italy, and Spain cruise in on mammoth yachts and leave the port in luxury sedans and private helicopters. Plan to rent a moped or a car, or take a bus to the nearby beaches—there is no sand within easy walking distance.

ORIENTATION AND PRACTICAL INFORMATION

If you arrive in Mahón by air, you must take a taxi into town (7km, 1000ptas). If you arrive by sea at the **ferry station,** walk to your left (with your back towards the water) about 150 yards, then turn right at the steps which cut through the serpentine **Costa de ses Voltes.** The steps top off between Pl. Conquesta and Pl. Espanya. From here, take Portal de Mar to Costa de sa, which becomes Hannover. Continue *todo recto* (straight ahead) to reach **Plaça de s'Esplanada.**

Mahón is a maze of narrow, one-way streets lined with whitewashed houses. Luckily for new arrivals, there are map kiosks with street indexes everywhere.

Tourist Office: Pl. s'Esplanada, 40 (tel. 36 37 90; fax 36 74 15), across the plaza from the taxi stand. Pamphlets, bus schedules, and a free **map.** English spoken. Open Mon.-Fri. 9am-2pm and 5-7pm, Sat. 9:30am-1pm. Summer office at the **airport** (tel. 15 71 15) purveys similar materials. Open May-Oct. 8am-11pm.

American Express: Viajes Iberia, C. Nou, 35 (tel. 36 28 48), 2 doors from Pl. Reial. No commission on traveler's checks. Cardholder mail held for 2 months. Open Mon.-Fri. 9am-1:30pm and 5-8pm, Sat. 9:30am-1pm.

Airport: (tel. 15 70 00), 7km out of town. Main office open 7:15am-10pm. **Aviaco/ Iberia** (reservations tel. 36 56 73, info tel. 36 90 15). To Palma (4 per day, 20min., 5800ptas), Barcelona, and Madrid. In summer advance booking is essential. Many travel agencies book charter flights.

Banks: La Caixa, C. Nou, 27 open Mon.-Fri. 8:15am-2pm, Thurs. also 4:30-7:45pm).

Buses: Transportes Menorca (TMSA), C. Josep M. Quadrado, 7 (tel. 36 03 61), off Pl. s'Esplanada. To: Alaior (7 per day, 140ptas); Son Bou (5 per day, 240ptas); Mercadal (6 per day, 220ptas); Ferrerias (6 per day, 290ptas); Ciudadela (6 per day, 450ptas); Platja Punta Prima (9 per day, 200ptas); Castell (every 30min. from 7:20am-8:45pm, 100ptas). Some depart from Pl. s'Esplanada, some from C. Quadrado; check signs at the bus stop. Buy tickets at the TMSA office, except for Punta Prima and Castell, which you buy on the bus. **Autocares Fornells** (tel. 37 66 21) depart from C. Vassallo, diagonally across from Pl. s'Esplanada. To Fornells (2 per

day, 325ptas); Arenal d'en Castell (2per day, 255ptas); San Parc (3 per day, 325ptas); Es Grau (150ptas). The tourist office and the *Menorca Diario Insular* (125ptas) have schedules with exact times. Buy all tickets on the buses.

Ferries: Transmediterránea, Nuevo Muelle Commercial (info tel. 36 60 50, reservations tel. 36 29 50), at Estació Marítima along Moll (Andén) de Ponent. To Barcelona (6 per week, Oct.-May 2 per week; 9hr.; *butaca* 6650ptas) and Palma (1 per week, 6½hr., 3325ptas), continuing to Valencia (18hr., 6650ptas). Open Mon.-Fri. 8:30am-1pm and 5-7pm, Sat. 8:30am-noon, Sun. 3-4:30pm.

Taxis: (tel. 36 12 83 or 36 28 91), or **radio taxi** from anywhere on the island (tel. 36 71 11). Flat rates for all routes. To: Airport (1025ptas); Cala Mesquida (1125ptas); Cala'n Porter (1700ptas); Es Castell (675ptas). Taxi stop at Pl. s'Esplanada.

Car Rental: English-speaking car rental at **British Car-Hire G.B. International,** Pl. s'Esplanada (tel. 36 24 32, 24-hr. tel. 26 85 24). 15,000ptas for 3 days in high season (will vary). Tourist office has list of all rental places and gas stations on Menorca. **Gas stations** open 6am-10pm; Oct.-May 7am-9pm. Rotating 24-hr. service (one of them is always in Mahón) is listed in *Menorca Diario Insular*. Some gas stations have 24hr. automatic machines which accept 1000 and 3000ptas bills.

Bike and **Moped Rental:** Scores of places, all with similar prices. For a bike, try **Just Bicicletas,** C. Infanta, 19 (tel. 36 47 51), run out of Hostal Orsi (1 day 800ptas, 3 days 2000ptas). **Autos y Motos Valls,** Pl. Espanya, 4 (tel. 36 28 39) rents scooters for 3000ptas per day. Open 9am-2:30pm and 5-8pm.

English Bookstore: English Language Library, C. Vasallo, 48 (tel. 36 27 01), a few blocks off Pl. s'Esplanada. Sells and lends. **Fax** service. Open Mon.-Sat. 9am-1pm.

Red Cross: tel. 36 11 80.

24-Hour Pharmacy: See listings in *Menorca Diario Insular,* or look in the window of Farmacia Segui Chinchilla, Ses Moreres, 30.

Medical Assistance: Residencia Sanitaria, C. Barcelona (tel. 15 77 00), near the waterfront, 1 block inland from Pg. Marítim. English spoken. **Ambulance:** 061.

Police: Municipal, Pl. Constitució (tel. 36 39 61). **Guardia Civil,** Ctra. Sant Lluís (tel. 36 32 97 or 062). **Emergency:** (tel. 091, 092 or 112).

Post Office: C. Bonaire, 11-13 (tel. 36 38 95), on the corner of C. Esglésias. From Pl. s'Esplanada, take C. Moreres until it turns into C. Hanover, then take the 1st left. Open Mon.-Fri. 8:30am-8:30pm, Sat. 9:30am-2pm. **Postal Code:** 07700. **Telephone Code:** (9)71.

ACCOMMODATIONS

Space is a problem only in August, but call a few days in advance. The tourist office keeps a complete listing of accommodations. Prices listed below are for high season only, unless otherwise specified.

Hostal-Residencia Jume, C. Concepció, 6 (tel. 36 32 66; fax 36 48 78), near Pl. Miranda. TV room downstairs, lounges on each floor, restaurant, and pool table. Rooms in tip-top shape, all with full baths. Heating in winter. Fax service. Toiletries on sale at reception. 2750ptas per person with breakfast, 3600ptas with dinner. Off season: 2100ptas; 2980ptas.

Hostal Orsi, C. Infanta, 19 (tel. 36 47 51), from Pl. s'Esplanada, take C. Moreres as it becomes C. Hannover. Turn right at Pl. Constitució, and follow C. Nou through Pl. Reial. The warm British owners are in the "they were *so* nice" Hostal Owners Hall of Fame. Complimentary breakfast and clean, sunlit rooms. Rooftop terrace with a view of colorful backyard gardens and church. Discounts on bicycle rentals. Singles 2200ptas. Doubles 4000ptas, with shower 4600ptas. Laundry 750ptas. Keys for 24hr. entry. Reservations and credit cards accepted.

Hotel la Isla, C. Santa Catalina, 4 (tel. 36 64 92), take C. Concepció from Pl. Miranda. This family-run bar-restaurant-hotel has emerged from extensive renovations. All rooms with bath and powerful water pressure. Singles 2200ptas. Doubles 4000ptas. Breakfast 300ptas. Keys for 24hr. entry. Reservations accepted.

FOOD

Bars around **Pl.'s Constitució** and **s'Esplanada** serve filling *platos combinados* (400-850ptas). Restaurants on the port have scenic views, but the prices will keep your wallet anchored in your pocket. Restaurants here hop, flop, and change hands with hyperspeed. Take a stroll by the port to see what's hot and what's cold squid.

Mahón-*esa* was invented in Mahón, and mayonnaise lends its subtle overtones to a wide variety of edibles in this city. Local favorites *sobrasada* (soft *chorizo* spread), *crespells* (biscuits), and *rubiols* (pastry turnovers filled with fish or vegetables). Be sure to order dessert, as Menorca is well-known for its pastries, including *ensaimada* and *mantecados.* Cheese lovers worship *formatge maonès.*

A fresh fruit and vegetable **market** meets in the cloister of the church in Pl. Espanya (open Mon.-Sat. 9am-2pm). Get your **groceries** at **Miny Prix**, C. J.A. Clavé and Av. Menorça (open Mon.-Sat. 8am-2pm and 5-8:30pm).

Ristorante Pizzeria Roma, Ander de Levante, 295 (tel. 35 37 77). On the port, it's the next best thing to dining on your very own yacht. Authentic Italian pizzas (650-900ptas) and *coctel de gambas* (shrimp cocktail). Fresh ingredients and speedy service that puts its overpriced neighbors to shame. Expect a wait for terrace dining at night. Open noon-midnight, closed Thurs. for lunch.

Hostal Jume (see **Accommodations**, above). For those wanting nothing more than a fresh, filling meal, Jume's waiter-cook-manager-bus boy will adroitly serve all your needs, even if the ambiance gets a -3 on a scale of 10. Spaghetti carbonara, baked chicken, salad, bread, wine, and a bowl of cherries for 950ptas.

El Turronero, C. Nou, 22-26 (tel. 36 28 98), off Pl. Reial. An old fashioned parlor with home-made *turrón* (nougat) and ice cream. If the taste of almondy play-doh still tempts your tummy, try the *turrón* ice cream. Double scoops 175ptas. *Bocadillos* 300ptas. Stock up on Menorcan munchies in connected grocery store. Open Mon.-Fri. 9am-3pm and 4-10pm, Sat. and Sun. 10am-2pm and 7-10pm.

La Tropical, C. Luna, 36 (tel. 36 05 56). *Tapas* bar, cafeteria, and an elegant dining room under one roof. Outdoor terrace open during the summer. *Menú* 800ptas. *Tapas* 225-600ptas. Credit cards accepted. Open daily 8am-midnight.

Mos i Glop, C. Alayor, 12 (tel. 36 64 57), off C. Hannover. Tucked away in a narrow alley, Glop is much more of a feast than its name might intimate. Sample a number of fresh Menorcan dishes (stuffed eggplant 775ptas, stuffed peppers 800ptas). Also serves the standard *bocadillos* (300ptas) and pizza (725-900ptas). Multi-optioned Menorcan *menú* 895ptas. Credit cards accepted. Open daily 8am-11:30pm.

SIGHTS AND ENTERTAINMENT

Església de Santa María la Major in Pl. Constitució, founded in 1287 and rebuilt in 1772, trembles to the 51 stops and 3006 pipes of its disproportionately large **organ,** built by Maese Juan Kilburz in 1810. A **festival de música** in July and August showcases this immense instrument. Festival concerts are given Mon.-Fri. at 11pm; seat prices are minimal, and the sound carries into the surrounding streets.

Up C. Sant Roc, **Arc de Sant Roc,** built to defend the city from marauding Catalan pirates, straddles the streets. A boat trip leaves from the harbor to the island beach **Illa d'en Colom,** stopping at secluded beached caves. Shipmates save *paella* and *sangría.* Ships leave at 10am and return by 5pm. Buy tickets at the **Bar Rosales,** Moll de Ponent, 73 (tel. 36 70 07; tickets 3500ptas, children under 12 2000ptas).

Free liquor samples (15 brews including *Schnapps de rosas* and herbal gin), are available at the **Xoriguer distillery.** Behind the store, visitors watch their drinks bubble and froth in large copper vats (open Mon.-Fri. 8am-7pm, Sat. 9am-1pm).

From May to September, artisans display their work alongside neon T-shirts in **mercadillos** held daily in at least one locale's main square. (Tues. and Sat. Mahón; Fri. and Sat. Ciudadela; Thurs. Alaior; Sun. Mercadal; Tues. and Fri. Ferrerias; Mon. and Wed. Es Castell; and Wed. Es Migjorn.)

Mahón is not famed for its nightlife, and curtain hour is sometimes an unseemly midnight. If you're still on Madrid time, a number of bars cluster along the port across

from the ferry. A string of *bares-musicales* is on the left coming down **Costa de ses Voltes,** the most popular of which is **Akelarre** (open daily 1pm-4am). Expect to be changing diapers if you arrive before 2am (dance floor open on weekends). **Icaro** offers neighborly competition. Away from the port, **Discoteca Sí,** 16 Virgen de Gracia, turns on the strobe only after midnight, while **Bar Nou,** C. Nou, 1, serves and swings until 3am.

Mahón's **Verge del Carme** celebration, July 16, floats a colorful trimmed armada into the harbor. The **Festa de Nostra Senyora de Gràcia,** the city's celebration of its patron saint, swings out September 7-9. For a list of **beaches,** see p.378.

■ Ciudadela (Ciutadella)

Ciudadela's blue and red townhouses sink into serpentine streets. Its colorful stucco architecture meshes brilliantly with dark, medieval cobblestone streets, a juxtaposition that to distant readers may seem odd. Ciudadela is out of reach for most budget travelers, but if you've reached Menorca, then a few extra bucks spent will be overlooked while effervescing in Ciutadella's uncrowded port. It lacks the glitz—but not the opulence—that has usurped most of Europe's Mediterranean coastline. Stay in a hostel, pack up at the grocery store, rent a scooter, and writhe at the beach for a few hours, and your budget will stay right on track.

ORIENTATION AND PRACTICAL INFORMATION

The bus from Mahón drops visitors off at **Plaça de s'Esplanada** (also called Pl. dels Pins). Walk across Pl. s'Esplanada to get to adjoining Plaça dés Born. Take C. Major des Borns to get to **Plaça de la Catedral** and the tourist office.

Tourist Office: The **main office,** Pl. Catedral (tel. 38 26 93), hands out maps, beach info, and a mega-guide to Menorca. Open Mon.-Fri. 9am-1:30pm and 5-7pm, Sat. 9am-1pm. The tourist **info van** parks in front of the Ayuntamiento in Pl. Born. Open Tues. 9:30am-1:30pm and 5-7pm.

Banks: La Caixa, C. dés Seminari 5, and **Central Hispano,** Negicle 7, offer the best exchange rates with no commission.

Telephones: Copiadores de Menorca, C. Nou de Juliol, 15 (tel. 38 23 03), directly off Pl. Born, sends **faxes.** Open Mon.-Fri. 9am-1:30pm and 4-8pm, Sat. 10am-1pm.

Buses: Transportes Menorca buses leave from C. Barcelona, 7 (tel. 38 03 93), goes to Mahón (6 per day, 450ptas). **Torres,** Poligona Industrial c/Sastres 3 (tel. 38 64 61), offers daily service to surrounding beaches. To: Cala Blanca (14 per day, Sun. 9 per day, 115ptas); Sa Caleta Santandria (14 per day, 115ptas); Cala Blanes (16 per day, Sun. 12 per day, 115ptas); Cala Bosch and Son Xoriguer (16 per day, Sun. 12 per day, 150ptas). Torres's ticket booth and bus departure point located at Pl. Pins.

Ferries: Flebasa (tel. 48 00 12) docks at Puerto Comercial and runs to Alcudia (2 per day Mon.-Fri., 1 per day Sat. and Sun., 3½hr., 3245ptas) and Vilanova i la Getrú (Barcelona) via Alcudia (1 per day, 6845ptas).

Taxis: tel. 38 28 96. Pl. s'Esplanada/Pins is a prime hailing spot.

Bike/Moped Rental: Bicicletas Tolo, C. Sant Isidor, 28, 32-34 (tel. 38 15 76). Across the street from Hostal Oasis (see below). Bike 500ptas per day, 2900ptas per week. Mountain bike 700ptas per day, 4200ptas per week. Scooter 3000ptas for 2 days, 9600ptas per week. Open Mon.-Fri. 8:30am-1:30pm and 3:30-8pm, Sat. 8:30am-1:30pm.

24-Hour Pharmacy: Farmàcia Martí, Pl. Pins, 20 (tel. 38 03 94), posts a list of night pharmacies in the window.

Medical Assistance: Emergencies (tel. 48 01 12). **Red Cross:** (tel. 38 19 93). **Ambulence:** tel. 061.

Police: Pl. des Born, in the Ajuntament (tel. 38 07 87). **Emergency:** tel. 091 or 092.

Post Office: Pl. des Born (tel. 38 00 81). Lista de Correos. Open Mon.-Fri. 8:30am-2:30pm, Sat. 9:30am-1pm. **Postal Code:** 07760.

Telephone Code: (9)71.

ACCOMMODATIONS AND FOOD

Pensiones are packed (and pricey) only during peak season (June-Sept.). Cruise pedestrian-packed C. Quadrado for more *platos combinados* and *tapas*. Sandwich bars have infiltrated **Pl. s'Esplanada** and **Pl. Pins.** Shop for staples at **Supermercado Diskont** (tel. 38 15 69), C. Purísima, 6 (open Mon.-Sat. 8am-1:30pm and 5-8pm). The prices below are for peak season only.

Hostal Residencia Oasis, C. Sant Isidre, 33 (tel. 38 21 97). From Pl. s'Esplanada, take Nerete to the 3rd left (C. Purissima). Isidre is first street on right. Trudge through the unforgiving desert (well, tunnel) to arrive at this floral paradise. Clean, breezy rooms have large wooden shutters. Breakfast is served in sunlit garden. Keys for 24hr. entry. Doubles with bath 5200ptas. Breakfast included.

Hotel Geminis, C. Josepa Rossinyol, 4 (tel. 38 58 96; fax 38 36 83). Take C. Sud off Av. Capital Negrete; turn left onto C. Rossinyol. Judge this book by its cover. All rooms with phones, shiny baths, and TVs. Winter heating. Plans to install a pool near the outdoor terrace. Singles 3700ptas. Doubles 7000ptas. Breakfast included.

Pensió Bar Ses Persianes, Pl. Artruitx, 2 (tel. 38 14 45), off Av. Jaume I El Conqueridor, close to the city center. Bright white walls enclose smallish rooms. Air-conditioned bar below serves breakfast (coffee and pastry 250ptas). Rooms are all doubles, 2000ptas per person. Only 8 rooms, so make reservations.

La Guitarra, C. Dolores, 1 (tel. 38 13 55), take St. Francesc off Born to Dolores. Golden oldies like rabbit in onion sauce and ox tongue with capers in a restaurant that challenges patrons to "try our meals the way *we* do them." Two-person *paella* 1400ptas per person. *Menú del día* 975ptas. Open in summer. Mon.-Sat. noon-3:30pm and 7-11:30pm. Credit cards accepted.

Cafe Balear, C. Marina (tel. 38 00 05). Near the end of the port. Watch the setting sun accentuate the city's pink and white facade from this waterfront restaurant. *Menú* 975ptas. Cheaper pastas and omlettes. Open noon-midnight.

SIGHTS AND ENTERTAINMENT

For beach options, see **Beaches,** p.378., and **Ciutadela: Orientation and Practical information: Buses,** p.376.

A mind-stretching alternative is to investigate the Bronze Age remnants at Menorca's archaeological sites. **Naveta dels Tudons,** one of the oldest buildings in Europe (despite some cosmetic restoration), sits 4km from the city. These community tomb ruins are the island's best preserved. **Torre Trencada** and **Torre Llafuda** were *talayot* settlements (rounded towers for overlooking the countryside). Both protect Stonehenge-esque **taulas,** formations that have stood for over 3000 years. Buses don't come near these sights, so consider hiking or hitching (about 5km) along C. Cami Vell de Maó.

Ciudadela's 16th-century law requiring all citizens shack up by midnight (still officially on the books, by the way) has generated a community of early-to-bedders. One spicy joint, however, is **Asere,** C. de Curinola 25, a Cuban salsa club (open Fri.-Sat. 8pm-midnight). From the first week in July to the first week in September, Ciudadela hosts the **Festival de Música d'Estiu** in the Claustre del Seminari, featuring some of the world's top classical musicians and ensembles. Tickets (1500-2000ptas) are sold at Foto Born, C. Bisbe Vila, 14 (tel. 38 17 54), and at the box office. In late June, locals burn gallons of midnight oil and down pints of *ginebra y limonada* during the **Festival de Sant Joan.** Even veteran partiers of Palma and Ibiza join in Menorca's biggest fiesta. A week before the festivities, a man clad in a sheepskin carries a decorated lamb on his shoulders through the city. The main events include jousting. The *mercadillo* of artisanry passes through the Pl. Born (Fri.-Sat. 9am-2pm).

ISLAS BALEARES

■ Northern Coast

FORNELLS

A small fishing village best known for its lobster farms, Fornells has just begun to attract tourists. Windsurfers busily zip around Fornells' long shallow port, but beach gurus have to make short excursions to **Cala Tirant** and **Binimella,** both a few kilometers west. Fornells is also a calm base from which to explore nearby coves and jagged cliffs by car or bike (buses run to Mahón only).Consider **renting a bike** for a full or half day (800ptas, 500ptas) from the multi-talented *hostal*-restaurant-bike rental establishment **S'Algaret,** Pl. S'Algaret, 7 (tel. 37 65 52).

Currency exchange is possible only at Sa Nostra, C. Gabriel Gelabert, 4, near the *plaça* (open June-Sept. Mon.-Fri. 8:15am-2:30pm). The **Red Cross** is at tel. 37 53 00, and the **police** answer at tel. 37 52 51. For other services, go to Mercadal, 8km away. Accommodations here are few and pricey, but **Casa de Céspedes La Palma,** Pl. S'Algaret (tel. 37 66 34), provides tidy rooms with terraces (singles 1200ptas, doubles with bath 6000ptas, triples with bath 6500ptas). Lobster restaurants in town are prohibitively expensive. *Bocadillos* are always an option at the numerous *bares* on **Pl. S'Algaret.** Or make a meal for yourself at **Supermercado Spar,** C. Major, 24 (open Mon.-Sat. 8am-1:30pm and 4-8pm, Sun. 8am-noon).

Autocares Fornells runs **buses** to Mahón (2 per day, 325ptas); Arenal d'en Castell (2 per day); and Son Parc (2 per day) from the port.

Every Day is Earthday in Menorca

Earth-lovers rejoiced on Oct. 7, 1993, when UNESCO declared Menorca's 701.84 sq. km a Biosphere Reserve. In light of relentless urbanization of Mallorca and Ibiza, where the only things sprouting are banks, airports, and beachside *bocadillo* stands, the new approach improves upon blindly conservationist quarantine measures by protecting the area's rich agricultural, archaeological, and cultural heritage in a way that capitalizes on the island's natural resources. The plan is complemented by designated zones where industrial exploitation is prohibited (Natural Areas of Special Interest, or ANEI).

So what does all this mean to the light-pocketed *Let's Go*er? For now, it means that Menorcan coves will remain uncontaminated by tourist colonies, but it may also mean ensure rising exclusivity—*hostales* will continue to either upgrade to hotels or fold. The budget traveler may be the newest endangered species on Menorca. For now, the island's sweetest pleasures remain unexploited and free of charge. For more info call CIME in Mahón (tel. 34 71 35).

■ Beaches

Some of the more popular (i.e. crowded) Menorcan beaches are accessible by bus from Mahón and Ciudadela. Many of the best, however, require a vehicle and sometimes legwork. They are worth the extra hassle. Northern beaches are rocky but less crowded. Finer sands are hidden under hundreds of tourists on the southern coast. The water, like the islanders, tends to take it easy, so rule out cutting the surf.

■ Near Mahón

Arenal d'en Castell, a sandy ring around calm water on Menorca's northern shore, behind a thin barrier of pine trees. Coastal ravines and cliffs are honeycombed with caves where prehistoric Menorcans lived. Camping is officially illegal (enforcement tightens in the summer). Autocares Fornells buses to Castell leave from C. Vasallo in Mahón (2 per day, 255ptas).

Es Grau is a small bay about 8km north of Mahón, popular with Menorcans. A 35-min. bike ride from Mahón takes you through part of Menorca's protected lands. Hike on the beach towards the small coves across the bay from the village. Auto-

cares Fornells buses leave from C. Vasallo (3 per day, 150ptas). Once at Es Grau, catch a boat out to the **Illa d'en Colom,** a tiny island with more beaches (tickets on sale at Bar C'an Bernat at the beach). Quiet until July.

Calascoves is a ½hr. walk to the east (left facing the sea) from Porter, with the best sand-to-tan ratio on the shore and a string of prehistoric caves where modern-day hippies keep the dream alive.

Cala en Porter's huge bluffs shelter curving beaches beneath. Here the **Covas d'en Xoroi,** a Swiss cheese of spooky prehistoric dwellings, gaze down on the sea. It is connected to Mahón by TMSA bus (7per day, 170ptas).

Platges de Son Bou is a gorgeous string of beaches with crystal waters on the southern shore. There is a 5th-century Christian **basílica** in the nearby settlement of Son Bou. Transportes Menorca buses leave from Mahón (5 per day, 215ptas).

Cap de Favàrtix. From Mahón take a moped or car in the direction of Es Gran/Fornells, turn off the highway at Favàrtix (9km), pass through farmlands, and break off from bushy edged roadway through an open gate to sink your toes in your very own black sand cove.

■ Near Ciudadela

Cala Bosch's jagged cliffs plummet into clear pale-blue water, a perfect backdrop for a refreshing dip in the Mediterranean. Accessible by Torres bus from Ciudadela (12-16 per day, 130ptas).

Son Xoriquer is small, overdeveloped, and crowded, but a mere 15min. from Ciudadela (use the same bus as Cala Bosch).

Cala Santa Galdana is a narrow beach 9km south of Ferrerias. Galdana is accessible by public transportation from Ferrerias (9 per day, 85ptas).

Cala Macarella: The 300ptas toll for private road to Macarella is well-spent. No tourist developments here, only crystal clear water in one of Menorca's least spoiled coves. *Naturistas* hang out on an even more secluded cove to the west (15min. walk). Access by bike, moped, or car off the country road to Sant Joan de Missa.

Cala en Turqueta is one of the tourist boat's favorite stops. Overcrowded but beautiful. Drive or ride here on road to Sant Joan de Missa.

Cala en Talaier is a tiny, unpopulated beach. The light blue bay is too shallow for boats to enter (access on wheels via road to Sant Joan de Missa). From here you can walk 15min. east to the long, white **Arenal de San Saura.**

IBIZA

"Dress the way you want to but with good taste," reads one tourist pamphlet. Most of Ibiza's summer residents want to dress in the trendiest styles, and many challenge the limits of good taste. They arrive in droves to showcase themselves in Ibiza's outrageous nightlife, and to debauch in a sex- and substance-driven summertime culture. Once a hippie enclave, Ibiza's summer camp for disco fiends and high fashion posers evokes a sense of new-age decadence. Although a thriving gay community lends credence to Ibiza's image as a center of tolerance, the island's high price tags preclude true diversity.

Since the Carthaginians retreated to Ibiza from the mainland in 656 BC, the island's list of conquerors reads like a "Who's Who of Ancient Western Civilization." The 1235 invasion by the Catalans, who instilled Christianity and constructed the massive Renaissance walls that still fortify Eivissa (Ibiza City), was the last incursion prior to the hippie influx of the 60s.

Beaches mitigate the summer heat with a warm blue surf, and can be reached in minutes by bus. Formentera, a tiny, sparsely populated island annex of Ibiza, is a convenient daytrip by ferry.

■ Eivissa (Ibiza)

When the sun rises, *dicotecarios* crawl into bed and *sol*-seekers scurry to Eivissa's nearby beaches. In the daytime, while the sun blazes, the city is ghostly; one couldn't imagine the fashion, techno-tracks, and drag queens that wait quietly behind fluttering shutters. At sunset the show begins. Grab a front row seat at one of the outdoor cafes to enjoy the action, as tourists and summertime residents parade the latest designs from Eivissa's swank boutiques.

ORIENTATION AND PRACTICAL INFORMATION

Three distinct sections comprise Eivissa. **Sa Penya,** the area in front of Estació Marítima, is mobbed with vendors, bars, and boutiques. Atop the hill behind Sa Penya, high stone walls bound **Dalt Vila,** the old city. **La Marina** and the commercial district occupy the gridded streets to the far right of the Estació (back to the water).

Buses to the **airport** (7km south of the city) run from Av. Isidor Macabich, 20 (every 40-60min., 7am-10pm) and return to town (every hr. on the ½hr., 7:30am-10:30pm, 30min., 115ptas). To get to the waterfront, walk down Av. Isidor Macabich, which becomes Av. Bartolomé Roselló, which runs straight down to the port.

The local paper *Diario de Ibiza* (125ptas) has an *Agenda* page that lists essential information: the bus schedule for the whole island; the ferry schedule; the schedule of all domestic flights to and from Ibiza for the day; water and weather forecasts; 24hr. pharmacies in the cities; 24hr. gas stations; and important phone numbers.

Tourist Office: Av. España, 49 (tel. 30 19 00), Po. Vara de Rey runs away from the port and into Av. España. Good maps, especially for hiking, and a complete bus schedule. Open Mon.-Fri. 9:30am-1:30pm and 5-7pm, Sat. 10:30am-1pm. Also a booth at the **airport** in the arrivals terminal (tel. 80 91 18; fax 80 91 32). Open May-Oct. Mon.-Fri. 9am-2pm and 3-8pm.

Flights: Airport tel. 80 90 00. **Iberia,** Po. Vara de Rey, 15 (tel. 30 25 80; 24hr. national and international reservations tel. (902) 400 500) has flights to: Palma (4 per day); Barcelona (5 per day); Valencia (2 per day); Madrid (3 per day); Alicante; Paris (3 per day); Rome (1 per day). Open for tickets and reservations Mon.-Fri. 9am-1:15pm and 4:30-7:45pm. Airport booth open 7am-11pm.

Buses: The 2 main bus stops are Av. Isidor Macabich, #42 and 20. For an exact schedule check the tourist office or *El Diario*. Intercity buses run from #42 (tel. 31 21 17) to: San Antonio (Mon.-Sat. every 15min., Sun. every 30min., 9pm-midnight, 180ptas); Santa Eulalia (Mon.-Fri. 7:30am-6:30am, every 30-60min., 165ptas). Buses to beaches (85-95ptas) leave from #20 (tel. 34 03 82) to: Salinas (every hr); Platja d'en Bossa (every 30min.); Cap Martinet (Mon.-Sat. 11 per day, Sun. 8 per day); Cala Tarida (5 per day).

Ferries: (also see **Islas Baleares: Getting There and Getting Around,** p.362) **Estació Marítima** (tel. 31 16 50), at the end of Av. Bartolomé Roselló. **Transmediterránea** sells tickets at Estació Maritima (tel. 31 50 50). In summer to: Barcelona (5 per week); Valencia (6 per week); Palma (1 per week). In the summer, *fast ferry* service to Valencia (3 per week, 3hr.) and Palma (3 per week, 2¼hr.). **Pitra,** Av. Sta. Eulalia, 17 (tel. 19 10 68), runs two routes: Denia-San Antonio and Denia-Formentera (both 3655ptas). **Flebasa** has stations in Eivissa (tel. 31 40 05) and San Antonio (tel. 34 28 71). The Eivissa office is located on the port. June-mid Sept. to Denia (2 per day from San Antonio, 1 per day from Eivissa, 5475ptas) with bus connections to Valencia (350ptas surcharge), Alicante (350ptas), and Benidorm (250ptas). April-Sept. from Ibiza City to Formentera (4 ferries, 12 *jets* per day, 25-60min., 2700-3600ptas round-trip).

Banks: La Caixa, Av. Isidor Macabich, offers the best exchange rates. **American Express** services available at Viajes Iberia, C. Vicente Cuervo (tel. 31 11 11). Open April-Oct. Mon.-Fri. 9am-1:30pm, Sat. 9am-1pm; Nov.-March Mon.-Fri. 9am-1pm and 4-7pm, Sat. 9am-1pm.

Taxis: (tel. 30 70 00 or 30 66 02).

Car and Motorbike Rental: Most places have similar prices. **Casa Valentín,** Av. B.V. Ramón (tel. 31 08 22), the street parallel to and one block off Pg. Vara de Rei rents mopeds (3000ptas per day, 2500ptas per day for more than 6 days). Panda and Marbella cars rent for 5000ptas per day. Open Mon.-Sat. 8am-1pm and 4-8pm, Sun. 8am-noon and 5-8pm. **Extra,** Av. Sta. Eulalia, 17, rents mopeds (3100ptas for 24hr. or 2600ptas for the day). Open Mon.-Sat. 8am-8pm, Sun. 8am-1:30pm and 5-8pm.

Luggage Storage: Extra, Av. Sta. Eulalia, 27 (tel. 19 17 17). 600ptas per 24hr. Open Mon.-Sat. 8am-8pm, Sun. 8am-1:30pm and 5-8pm.

Red Cross: (tel. 30 12 14.)

Hospital: Hospital Can Misses, Barrio Can Misses (tel. 39 70 00). Heading out of town on Av. Espanya, the hospital is on the left at the corner of C. Extremadura.

Police: C. Madrid (tel. 092), by the Post Office. **Emergency:** tel. 091, 092, or 112.

Post Office: C. Madrid, 23 (tel. 31 13 80), off Av. Isidor Macabich. Open for stamps and Lista de Correos Mon.-Fri. 8:30am-8:30pm, Sat. 9:30am-2pm. **Postal Code:** 07800.

Telephone Code: (9)71.

ACCOMMODATIONS

Decent, cheap accommodations in town are rare, especially in the summer. "CH" *(casa de huespedes),* marks many doorways, but often the owner can only be reached by the phone number on the door. Prices skyrocket in July and August, and you must make reservations two to three weeks in advance. Eivissa has a relatively safe and up-all-night life-style, so owners offer keys for 24hr. entry.

Hostal Residencia Sol y Brisa, Av. Bartomeu v. Ramón, 15 (tel. 31 08 18; fax 30 30 32), parallel to Pg. Vara de Rey. Upstairs from Pizzeria da Franco (signs point the way to the pizzeria). Two verdant terraces. Singles 2200ptas. Doubles 4000ptas. Off season: 1800ptas; 3000ptas.

Hostal Residencia Ripoll, C. Vicente Cuervo, 14 (tel. 31 42 75). Huge windows in doubles and triples, fans in singles—a breezy bargain. July-Sept. singles 3000ptas, doubles 5000ptas. April-June: 2000ptas; 3500ptas. Apartments with small kitchen, living room, and TV are an off-season bargain. Reservations accepted.

Hostal La Marina, C. Andenes del Puerto, 4 (tel. 31 01 72), conveniently across from Estació Marítima. Salty air floating through the window carries loud dance music from the bars next door. Dimly lit rooms keep the temperature down. Annexed housing near the bus stop is quieter but equally dim. Singles 1800ptas. Doubles 3300ptas, with bath 4800ptas.

Camping: Es Cana (tel. 33 21 17), 575ptas per person per day, site 600ptas per day. **Cala Nova** (tel. 33 17 74), 450ptas per person per day, site 425ptas per day. Both are close to Santa Eulalia. **Cala Bassa** (tel. 34 45 99), on the bay, 6km west of San Antonio (475ptas per person, 450ptas per tent).

FOOD

There is little supply of or demand for cheap eats. Full meals rarely cost less than 1200ptas in the port and downtown areas. **Sa Penya** and **Dalt Vila** proffer exquisite fare in elegant settings for no less than 1500ptas per person. Some Ibizan dishes worth hunting down are *sofrit pagès,* a deep-fried lamb and chicken dish; *flao,* a lush lemon- and mint-tinged cheesecake; and *graxonera,* cinnamon-dusted pudding made from eggs and bits of *ensaimada* (candied bread). Vegetarians soak up *sopas mallorquines,* a thick vegetable "soup" ladled over slices of brown bread.

A fruit and veggie **market** usurps Pl. Constitució in Sa Penya (open April-Sept. Mon.-Sat. 9am-2pm, some stands till 8pm). A **Supermercado Spar** is at the corner of C. Puig and C. Carlos V (open Mon.-Sat. 9am-2pm and 5-8:30pm).

Comida Bar San Juan, C. Montgrí, 8 (tel. 31 07 66), the 2nd right on the Puerto Moll walking from Pg. Vara de Rei. Tiny family-run restaurant with a surprisingly cheap selection. *Paella* 325ptas, *gambas a la plancha* 850ptas. Open Mon.-Sat. 1-3:15pm and 8-10:15pm.

ISLAS BALEARES

Pizzeria da Franco e Romano, Av. Bartomeu Vicente Ramon, 15 (tel. 31 32 53), below Hostal Sol y Brisa, signs point the way. Filling pasta and pizzas under 800ptas. Afternoon *menú* 925ptas. Owner promises "economy, happiness, and sympathy" at her popular pizzeria. Open Wed.-Mon. 12:30-4pm and 7:30pm-1am. Credit cards accepted.

Restaurante Victoria, C. Riambau, 1 (tel. 31 06 22), at the end of Pg. Vara de Rey. 50-year-old family eatery. *Sopa mallorquín* 375ptas. *Graxonera* 300ptas. *Platos* hover around 650ptas. Open Mon.-Sat. 1-4pm and 8:30pm-midnight.

Restaurante Ca'n Costa, C. Cruz, 19 (tel. 31 08 65), down the street from Victoria. Rows of tables tucked away in a basement eatery. Meats 550-1200ptas, fishies 600-1400ptas, lunchtime *paella* 500ptas—all cooked in a wood-burning stove. Afternoon *menú* 900ptas. Open Feb.-Dec. Mon.-Sat. noon-3pm and 8pm-midnight.

La Torre del Canónigo, C. Bisbe Torres, in Dalt Villa next to the cathedral. Fresh fruit concoctions and thirst-quenching drinks in a medieval tower. *Cava* (cheap champagne) breakfasts from 850ptas. Make your way toward the table on the mini-terrace. Open Mon.-Sat. 10am-8pm, Sun. 10am-2pm.

Restaurante Rocky's, C. Virgen, 6 (tel. 31 01 07), off the port in Sa Penya. Cozy, popular, and in the heart of Eivissa's nightlife, Rocky's specializes in *paella* (6 kinds, 1250-1500ptas). Friendly English-speaking owner spews info on area gay restaurants, bars, and discos. Outdoor terrace (arrive early). Open daily 7pm-1am.

SIGHTS

Wrapped in 16th-century walls, **Dalt Vila** (High Town) hosts 20th-century urban bustle in the city's oldest buildings. Its twisty, sloping streets lead up to the 14th-century **cathedral,** which offers super views of the city and beyond (open Mon.-Sat. 10am-1pm). Amid the antique action sits the **Museu D'Art Contemporani D'Eivissa,** C. Sa Carrosa, with a wide range of current art exhibitions. (Open Mon.-Fri. 10am-1:30pm and 5-8pm, Sat. 10am-1:30pm. 200ptas; students free.)

The archaeological museum, **Puig des Molins,** is on Via Romana, which runs off the Portal Nou at the foot of the Dalt Vila. The museum displays Punic, Roman, and Iberian art, pottery, and metals. Adjoined to Puig is the 4th-century BC Punic-Roman **necropolis** (both open Mon.-Sat. 10am-2pm and 5-8pm; 150ptas).

The power of the rising sun draws thousands of solar zombies to nearby tanning grounds. A 10-minute bike ride from the port reaches **Platja Figueredes,** a thin stretch of sand in the shadow of tourists and large hotels. Farther down, **Platja d'er Bossa** has one-foot waves which bring bottle caps and other plastic goods ashore. **Platja des Duros** is a small nook tucked in across the water from the cathedral, just before the lighthouse. **Platja de Talamanca** and **Platja de Ses Figures** have fine sand, plenty of snack-shops, and are 20 minutes away on bike. More private sands are in the northern part of the island, and are accessible by car or moped.

A Sign of the Times

Hippies who swarmed Ibiza during the 1960s and 70s knew it affectionately as "magic island." They organized communal societies in pre-historic lithic housing complexes, similar in design to adobe houses. Those two-fingered hippies have since morphed into the disco-raving, self-marginalized generation of the 90s, the newest counterculture to adopt Ibiza as its home. The epochal change from war politics surrounding Vietnam to the present-day peacetime atmosphere may account for the island's facelift. Today's Ibizans are full of pomp: men masquerade as women and vamps stalk the port-side walkways, vying for attention. From sundown to sun-up, spectators gawk from cafe patios at showboating passers-by, who promenade the sidewalks as if they were catwalks. The island's facelift is symbolized by a change in drugs of choice. Today's hardcore *disotecarios* savor synthetic treats like alcohol and Ecstasy, whereas hippies preferred herbal delights. Moreover, a quest for nirvana has superceded the anxiety over peace.

ENTERTAINMENT

The crowds return to Eivissa by nightfall, when even the clothing stores (open till 1am) dazzle with throbbing music and flashing lights. Live **jazz** wails through the smoky air of **Arteca** on C. Bisbe Azara. Gay nightlife hovers around **C. Virgen** and the part of Dalt Vila closest to the port; consult Restaurante Rocky's for other options (p. 382). **Capricios,** C. Virgen, has an outdoor terrace. **Bar Galerie,** C. Virgen, 64, and **Exis,** down the street, are a bit livelier. **Incognito** and **Angelo's,** Alfonso XII, break up the nightly exodus to **Discoteca Anfora** in Dalt Alta. The island's **disco** scene is world famous and ever changing. The best sources are regulars and the gazillion posters which plaster every store and restaurant. Generally, *discotecarios* pub-hop in Eivissa or San Antonio and jettison to clubs around 2am. PR reps sell discounted invitations to clubs outside the cafes by the seaport. The tourist office and hotels have the **Discobus** schedule—Bus D runs to and from all the major hotspots (midnight-6:30am, 225ptas). An attendant on the bus announces stops and nearby discos.

Privelege, Urbanización San Rafael (tel. 19 81 60), on the road to San Antonio (taxi 1500ptas). No purple rain, but this club—formerly known as **KU**—has everything else you can imagine. The mini village has double-digit bars, small garden terraces, and a stage set on a pool, where bizarre rock operas are performed during the night. Manumission parties draw a gay crowd, though the club is generally mixed. Cover 3500ptas (but can reach as high as 12,000ptas for parties), includes one drink. Open June-Sept. midnight-9am. Credit cards accepted.

Pachá, Pg. Perimetral (tel. 31 36 12), a 20min. walk from the port. A playful atmosphere with palm trees, terraces, and wax candle chandeliers. 3500-4000ptas cover includes one beverage. Open midnight-6:30am.

El Divino (tel. 19 01 76), Puerto Ibiza Nueva, has welcomed supermodels Linda Evangelista and Karie Miller. Extravagant parties affirm the club's reputation as "*un lugar de locuras.*" Have a drink at **El Divino's Bar** (on the port) and get a free pass to ride the disco shuttle. Cover 3000ptas. Open mid-June to mid-Sept. 1:30-6am.

Discoteca Anfora, C. San Carlos, 7 (tel 30 28 93), in Dalt Vila. Late-night partying for a gay crowd. The only discoteca inside the old city. Midnight-1am cover 500ptas, 1-6am 1000ptas.

Amnesia: On the road to Sant Antoni. Take the Discobus. Bring your raincoat for the foam parties two and three nights a week

■ Near Eivissa

FORMENTERA

Despite recent invasions by beach-hungry Germans and Italians, Formentera may be your last chance to set foot on a travel brochure's island paradise—the 11-mile moat separating Formentera from Ibiza City has sufficed to deter besiegement by Colonel Sanders and even General Gow. You may wish to join the "save our island" spirit by renting a bike or hiking, but the most efficient means of travel is by scooter. The tourist office provides a comprehensive list of "Green Tours" for cyclists and hikers.

Orientation and Practical Information The island's shape resembles the head and neck of a chicken facing west, pecking southward. Atop the head is the island's main port, **La Sevina.** The main artery runs from the port (km0) to the eastern tip, **Punta D'Esfar** (km21). The **tourist office,** Edificio Servicios La Savina (tel. 32 20 57; fax 32 28 25), is at the port (open Mon.-Fri. 10am-2pm and 5-7pm; Sun. 10am-2pm). Your arrival at La Savina is avalanched by car-scooter-bike rental booths that line the dock (car 5000ptas per day; scooter 2000ptas; bike 900ptas). Main roads have lanes where scooters can putter along freely with bicycles. The hubbub of basics and little else centers in the island's capital, **San Francisco,** which parts from the main artery at km3.1. In San Francisco, the **post office** (Mon.-Fri. 8:30am-2:30pm, Sat. 9:30am-1pm) and **bank (La Caixa)** are on Pl. Rey.

Two **ferry** lines at Est. Marítima provide the best alternative to swimming from Eivissa. **Umafisa** (Eivissa tel. 31 44 86; Formentera tel. 32 30 07) runs six ferries Mon.-Sat. and four on Sun. (1500ptas round-trip). **Flebasa** (Eivissa tel. 31 07 11; Formentera tel. 34 28 71) runs four 1hr. ferries (2200ptas one-way) and twelve 25min. jets daily (3600ptas). **Pitra** has service to and from Denia via San Antonio.

Food and Accommodations Pockets of cool air and the scent of pine trees mark the windy ascent through the mountainous regions of La Mola to Punta D'Esfar, which is marked by a lighthouse at the edge of a cliff. Bocadillo-eaters choose to enhance the moment with food from **Bar Es Puig.** Equally satiating is the *paella* (1300ptas) and vista from **El Mirador** (km14.3; tel. 32 70 37; open 12:30-4pm and 7-11pm). From here, the narrow strip of the Formentera Island looks like the stem of a champagne glass which widens out to the northern port, La Savina, and the southern tip, Cap de Barbaria. Others say it looks like a bull leering straight at the observer.

Hostal La Savina (tel. 32 22 79), near the port on Av. Mediterránea, offers ceiling fans, brown-tiled balconies, private access to a lake, and a breakfast buffet (3000ptas per person). Up the road and across the street is the **Supermarket La Savina** (tel. 32 21 91; open Mon.-Sat. 8am-2pm and 4:30-9:30pm; Sun 9:30am-1:30pm).

Risquée Beach Scene To bask on Formentera's best beaches, take Av. Mediterránea from the port, go left at the sign pointing toward Es Pujols, and hop onto the dirt road at the sign marking **Verede de Ses Salines.** Paths to the right lead to **Platja de Llevant,** a long strip of strippers on fine sand. Farther up the peninsula, roads to the left lead to **Platja de Ses Illetes,** more popular and rocky swimming holes. While the entire peninsula provides ample privacy, walking to the end (which requires wading through two shallow pools where sand level dips), will assure you of absolute solitude, although you'll have to nestle between rocks to catch some rays. To the south, **Platja de Migjorn** also has fine beaches but more surf. The bus runs to **Cala Saona,** a small cove on the west coast.

■ San Antonio de Portmany

British tourists storm San Antonio's huge crescent beach, busy harbor, and stirring night scene. During the day it's too hot to be anywhere but the beach. Sand space dwindles exponentially towards noon, so many people relocate to beaches farther out. **Boats** leave from Pg. Ses Fonts, before it becomes Pg. Mar, going to **Cala Bassa** (550ptas), a sandy beach on a thin strip; **Cala Conta** (500ptas), a slightly rocky beach; **Portinatx** (2700ptas); and the island of Formentera (2700ptas). **Buses** leave from Pg. Mar before it intersects with C. Madrid. They serve **Cala Tarida** (135ptas), a protected inlet, as well as Cala Gració, Port des Turrent, and Santa Eulalia.

Sa Cova de Santa Agnès, north of the waterfront, is a site of eerie devotion. The small underground cave has been a place of worship ever since a lucky sailor prayed to Santa Agnes in the midst of a tumultuous storm. Duly saved, the grateful lad paid homage by placing a figure of Agnes inside (open Mon. and Sat. 9am-noon). If you have wheels, explore **Cueva de Ses Fontanelles,** north of Platja Cala Salada, where faint prehistoric paintings cover the walls; or head north to **Cala Salada.** This tranquil cove (at the end of a windy road which wards off buses) offers an escape from San Antonio's crowded and over-populated beaches. It's also accessible on foot. Consult the tourist office for hiking excursions around San Antonio.

The **tourist booth** (tel. 34 33 63) at the beginning of Pg. Fonts can help with local transport. (Open Mon.-Fri. 9:30am-8:30pm, Sat. 9am-1pm, Sun. 9:30am-1pm; Nov.-April Mon.-Sat. 9:30am-1pm.) In **medical emergencies,** get help on C. Cervantes (tel. 34 51 21), or call 091 or 092. The **guardia civil** (tel. 34 05 02) is on Av. Portmany.

Rooms in San Antonio are good values but tough to come by—some may be booked years in advance. (Those Brits!) Ask the tourist office for a list. The San Antonio **Flebasa** (tel. 34 28 71), at the docks in Edificio Faro I, sends 2 per day to Denia for

5475ptas. Office open Mon.-Fri. 9am-1pm and 5-9:30pm; Sat. 9am-1pm and 7:30-9pm; Sun. 10:30am-noon and 7:30-9pm.

Hostal Marí (tel./fax 34 19 74), C. Progreso, 42, offers bright, renovated rooms with full bath. (2200ptas per person; July-Aug. 2750ptas per person. Breakfast 250ptas. Visa.) Or try **Hostal Nicolao,** C. Valencia, 9 (tel. 34 08 45), a few blocks inland, parallel to C. Progrés. Modern rooms have comfy beds, a terrace, and full bath (1500ptas per person, breakfast 250ptas). Closer to the water, simpler but cheaper rooms await at **Casa de Huespedes Serra,** C. Roselló, 13 (tel. 34 13 26), off C. Progrés (singles 1400ptas; doubles 2400ptas). The indoor **Mercat des Clot Mares** is located at the corner of C. Progrés and C. Santa Rosalía. (Open Mon.-Fri. 8am-2pm and 6-9pm, Sat. 8am-2pm; Sept.-May Mon.-Sat. 8am-2pm, Fri. also 6-8pm.)

Things get hot when the sun goes down. **Cafes** line C. Balanzat, one street in from the waterfront. The **bar** scene prevails on C. Vara de Rey and Pg. Mar. Those in the know head to **Es Paradis** (tel. 34 28 93), off Av. Dr. Fleming, a large garden of plants and white pillars where exhausted patrons crash on the pillows around the dance floor (open June-Sept. 11:30pm-6am; cover with drink 1500ptas, Aug. 2000ptas).

Valencia and Murcia

Valencia's *tierra de regadío* (rich soil) has earned the region its nickname: "Huerta de España" (Spain's Orchard). Spring and autumn river floods transport soil down the alluvial plain, nurturing Valencia's famous orange and vegetable groves, while pre-medieval irrigation networks designed by the Moors continue to nourish Valencia's farmlands. Dunes, sandbars, jagged promontories, and lagoons mark the coast's grand bay, and lovely fountains and pools grace the cities' carefully landscaped public gardens.

Valencia's past is a tangle of power struggles between the Phoenicians, Carthaginians, Romans, Moors, and Visigoths. El Cid conquered the Moors here in the 11th century and ruled for five years. The last region to be sacked by Franco in 1939, Valencia regained its autonomy with the Bourbon monarchy's reinstitution in 1977. *Valenciá*, the regional language spoken sparingly in the north and inland, differs from Catalan as American English differs from British. Although Valencia's regionalism is not as intense as Catalunya's, the Generalitat's recent mandate that all students enroll in one course of *valenciá* reflects the growing resurgence of regionalist sentiments.

Local *fiestas* amplify Valencia's enchantment with fire, water, and love to hyperbolic proportions. Whereas northern Spaniards are infatuated with the valorous bull and Andalucíans admire the intense look of *sevillana* dancers, it is a curious fascination with fire that characterizes the *valencianos*. All festivals promote *fuegos artificiales* (fireworks) and every little town along the coast has its own celebration. From the reactionary art and furor invested in the effigies at Valencia's *Las Fallas* (March), to the artful displays in Alicante during *San Juan* (June), and the recklessly adrenaline filled *Nit de l'Alba* (August) in Elche, two common threads unite the celebrations: fire as a purifier and as a destructive force.

With Valencia to the north, the Mediterranean to the east, and Andalucía to the west, the unique cultural mosaic that is Murcia today reflects an intricate past. The diverse physical appearance of *murcianos* dates to the intermarriages and inter-breeding of fair-haired Visigoths with the Alfonso X El Sabio's *moreno* (dark hair and olive-skinned) troops from Castilian. The Murcian accent hybrids the Castilian lisp with a light Andalucían tongue that is reluctant to pronounce suffixes. Inland townspeople speak with a sexy, throaty delivery.

Four centuries ago, a bizarre wave of plagues, floods, and earthquakes wreaked havoc throughout Murcia. Ironically, the earthquakes uncovered a rich supply of minerals and natural springs. Thermal spas, pottery factories, and paprika mills pepper the lively coastal towns, and its orange and apricot orchards bolster Murcia's reputation as the "Huerta de Europa" (Europe's Orchard). Overlooked by most vacationers, this unjaded region is Spain at its casual, everyday best.

Paella (saffron rice with meat or fish), the pride of Spaniards everywhere, is a *Levante* (east) coast matter-of-course. First concocted in a huge *paellera* (paella pot) somewhere in the rice fields around Valencia, it is available in varying degrees of glory from Peñiscola to Cartagena, though the best is found outside Valencia.

▓ Valencia (València)

Valencia is a stylish, cosmopolitan nerve center, a striking contrast to its surrounding orchards and brown speckled mountain ranges. Fountainous parks and gardens soothe the city's congested business environment, and soft-sanded beaches complement its kinetic nightlife. Unique architectural surprises hide behind the crowded city center, but the presence of neo-style buildings (e.g. the Ayuntamiento) discredits Valencia's bid for architectural fame.

Graffiti "correcting" Castilian road signs into *valenciá* reflects a recent surge in regionalism. However, regionalist sentiments are rarely seen or heard beyond a few

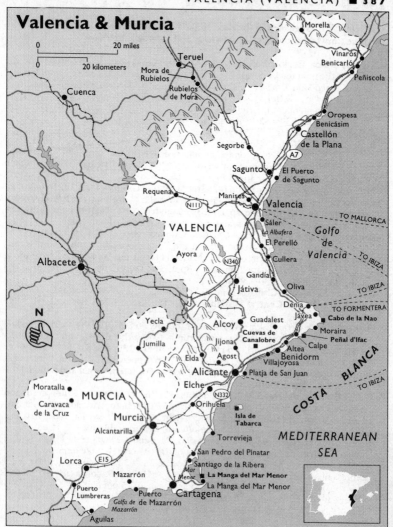

Valencia & Murcia

0 ——— 20 miles

0 ——— 20 kilometers

Morella, Vinarós, Benicarló, Peñiscola, Teruel, Mora de Rubielos, Rubielos de Mora, Cuenca, Oropesa, Benicásim, Castellón de la Plana, Segorbe, A7, Sagunto, El Puerto de Sagunto, Requena, NIII, Manises, Valencia, TO MALLORCA, Sáler, La Albufera, El Perelló, Golfo de Valencia, TO IBIZA, VALENCIA, Ayora, N340, Cullera, Albacete, Gandía, Oliva, TO IBIZA, Játiva, Denia, TO FORMENTERA, Yecla, Alcoy, Guadalest, Jávea, Cabo de la Nao, Cuevas de Canalobre, Moraira, Peñal d'Ifac, Jumilla, Jijona, Altea, Calpe, Elda, Agost, Villajoyosa, Benidorm, Alicante, Platja de San Juan, Moratalla, Elche, COSTA BLANCA, Caravaca de la Cruz, MURCIA, N332, Orihuela, TO IBIZA, Murcia, Isla de Tabarca, Alcantarilla, MEDITERRANEAN SEA, Torrevieja, Lorca, E15, San Pedro del Pinatar, Mazarrón, Santiago de la Ribera, Mar Menor, La Manga del Mar Menor, Puerto Lumbreras, Puerto de Mazarrón, Golfo de Mazarrón, Cartagena, La Manga del Mar Menor, Aguilas

N

spray-painted expressions, and the university students who invigorate Valencia during term-time still favor *castellano*.

ORIENTATION AND PRACTICAL INFORMATION

Those with foresight arrive in Valencia by train, since **Estación del Nord** is close to the city's center. **Avenida Marquéz de Sotelo** runs from the train station to **Plaza del Ayuntamiento,** where the city **tourist office** is located. The avenue then splits into **Avenida María Cristina,** which leads to the central market, and **Carrer de Sant Vicent,** which leads to **Plaza de la Reina** and the cathedral. The *casco antiguo* (ancient quarter) hosts almost everything of interest except for the bus station and beaches and is nestled into a bend of the Río Turia. Frequent city buses heading beachward leave from the Pl. Ayuntamiento. Valencia's geographical tangle and sprawl make unaided tours futile. El Corte Inglés's free **map** wins the annual *Let's Go*

Cartographical Excellence In the Face of Bitter Adversity Award. Maps from the tourist office (unwieldy) and Bayarri (unwieldy and 450ptas) lose out.

Tourist Office: Regional, Estación del Nord, C. Xàtiva, 24 (tel. 352 85 73), on the right of the train tracks (inside the station) as you disembark. Lots of pamphlets and maps. Open Mon.-Fri. 9am-6:30pm. Another regional **branch** with similar information on C. Paz, 48 (tel.352 40 00), is open Mon.-Fri. 10am-6pm, Sat. 10am-2pm. **City,** Pl. Ayuntamiento, 1 (tel. 351 04 17). Dedicated crew, useful lists of hostels. Open Mon.-Fri. 8:30am-2:15pm and 4:15-6pm, Sat. 9am-12:45pm.

American Consulate: (tel. 351 69 73).

Budget Travel: IVAJ, C. Hospital, 11 (tel. 386 97 00). From the train station, head left on C. Xàtiva, which becomes C. Guillem de Castro, and turn right on C. Hospital. Several travel handbooks in English. ISIC 700ptas. HI card 1800ptas. Open Mon.-Fri. 9am-2pm and 4:30-6:30pm.

El Corte Inglés: C. Pintor Sorolla, 26 (tel. 351 24 44). From Pl. Ayuntamiento, go down C. Barcas as it turns into a pedestrian walk; Corte's on the left. **Currency exchange,** award-winning **map,** novels and guidebooks in English, haircutting, cafeteria, restaurant, **telephones,** and **groceries.** Open daily 10am-9pm.

American Express: Duna Viajes, C. Cirilo Amorós, 88 (tel. 374 15 62; fax 334 57 00), next to Pl. América on the edge of Río Turia. No commission on AmEx traveler's checks. Accepts wired money. Mail held (1yr.) and **fax** service for cardholders. Open Mon.-Fri. 10am-2pm and 5-8pm, Sat. 10am-2pm; in winter Mon.-Fri 9:30am-1:30pm and 4:30-7:30pm.

Currency Exchange: Citibank is in Pl. Ayuntamiento on the corner of C. San Vicente Mártir. **Banco Central Hispano,** across the street, offers the best exchange rates.

Flights: The airport is 15km southwest of the city (tel. 370 95 00; Iberia schedule info tel. 152 00 65). *Cercanías* trains run between the airport and train station from 7am-10pm (Mon.-Fri. every 30min., 32min., 150ptas; Sat.-Sun. every hr., 170ptas). **Iberia** office, C. Paz, 14 (tel. 352 75 52; open Mon.-Fri. 9am-2pm and 4-7pm). To: Madrid, Palma, Paris, London, Rome. For international and national reservations call **Serui Iberia** (tel.902 400 500).

Trains: Estación del Nord, C. Xàtiva, 24 (tel. 351 36 12). Info open 8am-9pm. Ticket windows open 6:30am-10pm. **RENFE** (tel. 352 02 02), to: Barcelona (11 per day, 4-6hr., 3100ptas); Madrid (11 per day, 5-7½hr., 3800ptas); Sevilla (2 per day, 8½-9½hr., 5600ptas). *Cercanías* lines run often to Gandía and Játiva.

Buses: Estación Terminal d'Autobuses, Av. Menéndez Pidal, 13 (tel. 349 72 22), across the river, a 25min. walk northwest of the city center. Take municipal bus #8 (105ptas) from Pl. Ayuntamiento. **Auto Res** (tel. 349 22 30) sends 5 regular and 9 express buses per day to Madrid (4-5hr., 2845-3145ptas). **Bacoma** (tel. 347 96 08), runs to: Málaga (5 per day, 11hr., 5970ptas); Granada (5 per day, 4855ptas); Sevilla (3 per day, 12hr., 6800ptas). **Enatcar** (tel. 340 08 55), offers 10 trips daily to Barcelona (4½hr., 2650ptas). **Ubesa** (tel. 340 08 55), stops along the Costa Blanca on its way to Alicante (9 per day, 2¼-3hr., 1890ptas). **Eurolines** (tel. 349 68 55), has international service to: Paris (Mon.-Sat. 1 per day, 15,125ptas); Rome (5 per week, 18,050ptas); Geneva (3 per week, 11,450ptas); London (3 per week, 15,800ptas).

Ferries: Transmediterránea, Estació Maritima (tel. 367 65 12), to Palma (Mon.-Sat., 9hr., 6350ptas). Advance ticket sales open Mon.-Fri. 9:30am-2pm and 5-11pm, Sat. 9:30am-2pm; or buy tickets on day of departure at the port office. Take bus #4 from Pl. Ayuntamiento. Ask a travel agent for **Flebasa** (Denia office tel. 578 40 11), ferry schedule to Ibiza, leaving from Denia (5475ptas, does not include 800ptas bus ride from Valencia to Denia port).

Public Transportation: EMT Buses (tel. 352 83 99). Bus **map** available at EMT office, C. En Sanz, 4 (open Mon.-Fri. 8am-3:30pm) or at the tourist office in the train station. Half leave from Pl. Ayuntamiento. Bus #8 runs to the bus station at Av. Menéndez Pidal; bus #19 heads to Las Arenas and Malvarosa. Buy tickets aboard or at any newsstand (105ptas, 10-ride ticket 675ptas). Regular service stops around 10:30pm. Late-night buses run through Pl. Ayuntamiento (every 40min., 7 per night, 11pm-1:20am).

Taxis: (tel. 370 33 33, 357 13 13, or 374 02 02).

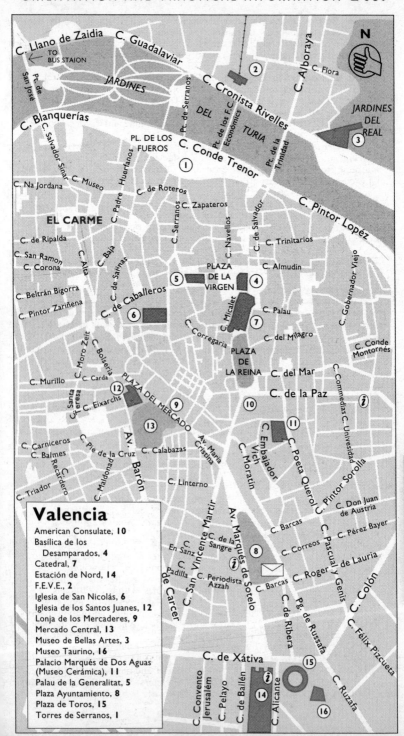

N

Valencia

American Consulate, 10
Basílica de los
  Desamparados, 4
Catedral, 7
Estación de Nord, 14
F.E.V.E., 2
Iglesia de San Nicolás, 6
Iglesia de los Santos Juanes, 12
Lonja de los Mercaderes, 9
Mercado Central, 13
Museo de Bellas Artes, 3
Museo Taurino, 16
Palacio Marqués de Dos Aguas
(Museo Cerámica), 11
Palau de la Generalitat, 5
Plaza Ayuntamiento, 8
Plaza de Toros, 15
Torres de Serranos, 1

VALENCIA AND MURCIA

Luggage Storage: At the bus station, lockers 200ptas and 400ptas. Or at the train station, lockers 300-600ptas. Open daily 7am-10pm.

Laundromat: Lavandería El Mercat, Pl. Mercado, 12 (tel. 391 20 10), on the left past the market. Self-service wash and dry 900ptas. Open Mon.-Fri. 10am-2pm and 4:30-8:30pm, Sat. 10am-2pm.

English Bookstore: The English Book Centre, C. Pascual y Genis, 16 (tel. 351 92 88), off C. Barcas. Open Mon.-Fri. 10am-1:30pm and 4:30-8pm, Sat. 10am-1:30pm.

Women's Center: Instituto València de la Dona, C. Naquera, 9 (tel. 391 48 87). Open Mon.-Fri. 8am-3pm; Sept.-June Mon.-Fri. 8am-8pm.

24Hr. Rape Crisis Hotline: tel. (900) 58 08 88 for hotline and free legal counsel.

Red Cross: tel. 380 22 44, or at the sea: tel. 323 16 16.

24Hr. Pharmacy: Check listing in the local paper *Levante* (135ptas) or check the *farmacias de guardia* schedule posted outside any pharmacy.

Hospital: Hospital Clínico Universitario, Av. Blasco Ibañez, 17 (tel. 386 26 00), at the corner of C. Dr. Ferrer. Take bus #70 or 81 from Pl. Ayuntamiento. An English-speaking doctor is often on duty.

Police: (tel. 362 10 12). **Guardia Civil:** (tel. 333 11 00 or 062).

Emergency: tel. 091 or 092, 085 for ambulance.

Internet Access: Pilgrim's Youth Hostel (see **Accommodations,** p. 390).

Post Office: Pl. Ajuntament, 24 (tel. 351 67 50). Open Mon.-Fri. 8:30am-8:30pm, Sat. 9:30am-2pm. **Postal Code:** 46080.

Telephones: Estación del Nord, C. Xàtiva, 24, near the RENFE info booth. Open daily 8am-10pm. **Faxes** (fax 394 27 44), sent and received. **Telephone Code:** (9)6.

ACCOMMODATIONS

The business of Valencia is business, not tourism—rooms are plentiful during the summer. During the papier-mâché orgy of Las Fallas, reserve well in advance. Avoid the areas by the *barrio chino* (Red Light district) around Pl. Pilar. The best options cluster around **Pl. Ayuntamiento** (plush), and **Pl. del Mercado** (a bit lower grade). From the train station, follow Av. Marquéz de Sotelo to Pl. Ayuntamiento. Last resort *hostales* cluster to the left of the train station off **C. Xàtvia.**

Alberg Colegio "La Paz" (HI), Av. Puerto, 69 (tel. 369 01 52), nearly halfway between the city and the port. Take bus #19 from Pl. Ayuntamiento (next to Citibank); it's the 3rd stop on Av. Puerto. Forbidding fortress safeguards a peaceful ambience. 2-4 people and a bathroom in every room. HI membership required. Curfew midnight. 1000ptas per person, *pensión completa* 1900ptas; over 26: 1500ptas; 2400ptas. Breakfast included. Sheets 400ptas. Lockout 10am-5pm; lock-in till 8am. Reception open daily 9am-1pm and 5pm-1am. Open July-Sept. 15.

Near Plaza del Ayuntamiento

Pensión Paris, C. Salvá, 12 (tel. 352 67 66). From Pl. Ayuntamiento turn right at C. Barcas, left at C. Poeta Querol, and right onto C. Salvá. 13 spotless rooms with angelic white curtains and balconies. A bargain. Singles 2000ptas. Doubles 3000ptas, with shower 3600ptas, with bath 4000ptas. Triples 4500ptas.

Hostal-Residencia El Cid, C. Cerrajeros, 13 (tel. 392 23 23). Coming from the train station take the 2nd left off C. Vicente Mártir after passing Pl. Ayuntamiento (and before Pl. Reina). Little dog Snoopy adds to its homey feel. Show your copy of *Let's Go* for a dog biscuit…we mean discount. Fans provided, heating in winter. Singles 1300ptas. Doubles 2600ptas, with shower 3000ptas, with bath 3700ptas.

Hostal Moratin, C. Moratin, 15 (tel. 352 12 20), 1st street on the left off C. Barcas from Pl. Ayuntamiento. Well-located with solid, clean rooms and a rooftop terrace. Owner serves a mean *paella.* Ask for a gate key before heading out late-night. Singles are limited, but don't pay more for a double bed. Singles 2000ptas. Doubles 3500ptas. Triples 5250ptas. Breakfast 250ptas. Dinner 950ptas.

Hostal-Residencia Universal, C. Barcas, 5 (tel. 351 53 84), off the plaza. Three floors of spacious rooms with balconies, ornate ceilings, and new sinks. Owner promises to try her hardest to find space for solo travelers. Singles 2000ptas. Doubles 3000ptas, with shower 3600ptas. Triples 4200ptas.

Near Plaza Mercat

Hostal del Rincón, C. Carda, 11 (tel. 391 60 83). From Pl. Ayuntamiento, Pl. Mercado extends past the market building; its continuation is C. Carda. The 54-room *hostal* was once a medieval lodging for wayfarers a la Don Quijote. The garage was once a stable to park coaches and their horsepower, but now hostelers can use it. First 2½ floors are newly renovated. Rooms cleaned daily. Singles 1500ptas, with bath 2000ptas. Doubles: 2800ptas; 3600ptas.

Hospedería del Pilar, Pl. Mercado, 19 (tel. 391 66 00). Past the market and Llonja, on the far, right-hand side. The sky may fall and room size may vary, but at least you can count on hot water and tiled bathrooms. Noisy and big. Singles 1500ptas. Doubles 2800ptas, with shower 3600ptas. Triples: 4000ptas; 4500.

Pilgrim's Youth Hostel, Pl. Hombres del Mar, 28 (tel. 356 42 88; email director@albergue.cybered.es). Take Bus #19 from Pl. Ayuntamiento (next to the Citibank) to the third stop on C. Doctor Lluch. (You will see a soccer field and tennis courts on your right.) Walk between the tennis courts and the soccer field on C. Pescadores, which leads to Pl. Hombres del Mar. Travelers should use caution when approaching the plaza at night. Two blocks from the beach, it offers modern comforts (A/C, email, coffee all day, TV, free laundry, kitchen) in a renovated building. 1000ptas per person. Over 26 1500ptas. Breakfast included. Call ahead.

FOOD

The taste (meat-shellfish-lemon-saffron-rice-chicken). The connotations (unadulterated Spain). The birthplace (Valencia). The word (*paella*). Unbeknownst to most tourists, *paella* is just one of 200 Valencian rice specialties. Other local specialties include *arroz a banda* (rice and fish with garlic, onion, tomatoes, and saffron), *all i pebre* (eels fried in oil, paprika, and garlic), and *sepia con salsa verde* (cuttlefish with garlic and parsley). Another favorite is *horchata,* a sweet, milky drink pressed from locally grown *chufas* (earth almonds). Buckets of fresh fish, meat, and fruit are sold at the **Mercado Central,** on Pl. Mercado (open Mon.-Thurs. 7am-2pm, Fri. 7am-2pm and 5-8:30pm, Sat. 7am-3pm). For **groceries,** huff and puff to the 5th floor of **El Corte Inglés,** C. Pintor Sorolla, 26 (tel. 351 24 44; open Mon.-Sat. 10am-9:30pm).

La Lluna, C. Sant Ramón (tel. 392 21 46), in El Carme district near IVAM. A veggie restaurant to moon over. Stuffed red peppers explode with ambrosial flavor. A 4-course *menú* and whole-grain bread served only weekday afternoons (850ptas). Natural juices 260ptas. Occasional evening guitar serenades. Open Mon.-Sat. 1:30-4:30pm and 8pm-midnight.

Restaurante La Utielana, Pl. Picadero Dos Aguas, 3 (tel. 352 94 14). Take C. Barcelonina off Pl. Ayuntamiento, turn left at its end, then make a sharp right onto C. Procida. Devilish to find, but worth it. Ideal service, and not a plate on the menu over 750ptas. Choose from a super scoop of scrumptious seafood *paella* (a shocking 325ptas) or *gambas a la plancha* (475ptas). Afternoon *menú* 800ptas. A/C. Open Sept.-July Mon.-Fri. 1:15-4pm and 9-11pm, Sat. 1:15-4pm.

La Pappardella, C. Bordadores, 5 (tel. 391 89 15). Stand in front of the doors to the Cathedral (Pl. Reina) and look left. Enjoy delicious pasta dishes such as *penne i gambi con vodka* (850ptas) on the outdoor terrace next to the Cathedral's Miguelete. Open Wed.-Mon. noon-4:30pm and 8pm-midnight.

Centro Aragonés, C. Don Joan d'Austria, 18 (tel. 351 35 50), off C. Barcas. A one-room clubhouse two floors up. Plain setting lets you focus on the appetizing food. High-quality, *paella*-filled *menú* 850ptas. Open daily 8am-9:30pm.

Comidas Esma, C. Zurradore, 5 (tel. 391 63 52), off C. Correjería. A local working-class diner. Full meal with hefty bowls of homemade soup and freshly grilled *merluza* (hake). A la carte dishes at rock-bottom prices. Afternoon *menú* 750ptas. Open mid-Sept. to mid-Aug. Mon.-Fri. 1-4pm and 8:30-11pm, Sat. 1-3pm.

SIGHTS

Touring Valencia on foot is complicated. Most of the sights line the Río Turia or cluster near Pl. Reina, which is linked to Pl. Ayuntamiento by C. San Vicente Mártir.

VALENCIA AND MURCIA

Valencia is on the cutting edge of contemporary art, and its galleries display Spain's freshest works. Contact the tourist office for exhibition schedules.

The Aragonese began work on the **cathedral** (Pl. Reina; tel. 391 81 27), shortly after the *Reconquista*. The three different entrances represent centuries of architectural styles, including Gothic, Baroque, and Romanesque. Inside, Californians can pay homage at the bust of San Luis Obispo, and all can admire the withered left arm of Valencia's patron saint San Vicente. Seized by a fit of Romantic hyperbole (or perhaps "new math"), French novelist Victor Hugo counted 300 bell towers in the city from atop the **Micalet** (the cathedral tower)—actually, there are only about a hundred. (Tower open Mon.-Sat. 10am-12:30pm and 4:30-7:30pm, Sat.-Sun. 10am-1pm and 5-7:30pm; in winter Mon.-Sat. 10am-2:30pm and 4:30-6:30pm, Sun. 10am-1:30pm and 5-6:30pm. 100ptas. Cathedral open daily 7:30am-1pm and 4:30-8:30pm. Free.) The **Museo de la Catedral** (tel. 391 81 27), squeezes a great many treasures into very little space. Check out the overwrought tabernacle made from 1200kg of gold, silver, platinum, emeralds, and sapphires; a Holy Grail; two Goyas; and the *Crucifijo de Marfil* statues depicting "man's passions" (open Mon.-Sat. 10am-1pm and 4:30-6pm; Dec.-Feb. 10am-1pm; 100ptas). Behind the cathedral on Pl. Virgen, elliptical **Basilica Nuestra Señora de los Desamparados** (Basilica of Our Lady of the Forsaken) houses a resplendent golden altar (open daily 7am-2pm and 4-9pm; free).

In Pl. Mercado, the old **Lonja de la Seda** (Silk Exchange; tel. 352 54 78), one of the foremost examples of Valencian Gothic architecture, testifies to Valencia's medieval prominence in the silk trade (open Tues.-Fri. 9am-2pm and 5-9pm, Sat.-Sun. 9am-1:30pm; free). The 15th-century **Torres de Serranos,** from which boiling oil was dumped on invaders, guards the edge of the historic district in Pl. Fueros. You can climb up and pretend to dump oil on annoying travel companions (open Tues.-Fri. 9am-1:30pm and 4-6pm, Sat. 9am-1:30pm).

For botanical diversion, the city maintains impressive **parks** on the outskirts of the historic district. Taxonomists marvel at the **Jardín Botànico,** C. Beato Gaspar Bono (tel. 391 16 57), on the western end of Río Turia. This university-maintained, open-air garden cultivates 43,000 plants of 300 precisely labeled species from around the world (open Tues.-Sun. 10am-9pm). One block farther, Valencia shows the world what should be done with dry riverbeds. A series of pillared public recreation areas mark the banks of the now diverted Río Turia, ending with hundreds of children climbing up a gigantic version of Jonathan Swift's "Gulliver" (tel. 337 02 04; open daily 10am-8pm; Sept.-June 10am-dusk). Moving past the Royal Gardens towards the sea, **Santiago Calatrava's** bridge, the black sheep of a series of stone bridges that cross the Turia, is nicknamed the *Peineta* because it resembles headdresses worn by *falleras,* young women in Las Fallas.

On C. Sant Pius V, next to the Jardines del Real, the compelling **Museu Provincial de Belles Artes** (tel. 360 57 93), displays superb 14th to 16th-century Valencian primitives and works by later Spanish and foreign masters: a Hieronymous Bosch triptych; El Greco's *San Juan Bautista,* Velázquez's self-portrait; Ribera's *Santa Teresa,* a couple colorful Sorollas; and a slew of Goyas. (Open Oct.-July Tues.-Sat. 10am-2pm and 4-6pm, Sun. 10am-2pm; Aug. Tues.-Sun. 10am-2pm. Free.)

West across the old river, the **Instituto València de Arte Moderno (IVAM),** C. Guillem de Castro, 118 (tel. 386 30 00), has a permanent collection of abstract works by 20th-century sculptor Julio González and temporary exhibits of cutting-edge art and photography (open Tues.-Sun. 11am-8pm; 350ptas, students 175ptas). The insti-

---

The Arm That Left

In 1104 AD, 800 years after San Vicente's martyrdom in Valencia, the Obispo de Valencia attempted to transport Valencia's patron saint's left arm to a holy resting spot in Vatican City. Despite the left arm's perseverance during the long journey, it never reached Rome because the Obispo died in Bari (Italy). Handily, San Vicente's forearm found a new right hand man in Don Pedro Zampieri de Venezia, who returned the reddened limb to Valencia 800 years later, in 1970.

tute also administers another small modern art museum in a rehabilitated convent, the **Centre del Carme,** C. Museo, 2, to the east off Pl. Carmen (open Tues.-Sun. noon-2:30pm and 4:30-8pm; free).

Sand-seekers will find the **beaches** close to Valencia along the Levante coastal strip overcrowded. Most popular are **Las Arenas** and **Malvarrosa,** both on the #19 bus route. Equally crowded but more attractive is **Salér,** a long, pine-bordered strand 14km from the city center. Cafeterias and snack bars line the shore, with shower and bathroom facilities nearby. Mediterráneo Urbano **buses** (tel. 349 72 22), make for Salér (on the way to El Perello) from the intersection of Gran Vía Germanias and C. Sueca, on the right side of the train station (every 30min., 25min., 175ptas).

ENTERTAINMENT

Rest up during *siesta,* because Valencia's nightlife will keep you drinking and dancing until sunrise. Bars and pubs around the **El Carme** district, just beyond the market, start rolling after dinner, around 11:30pm. Follow Pl. Mercado and C. Bolsería to Pl. Tossal, where outdoor terraces, upbeat music, and *agua de Valencia* (orange juice, champagne, and vodka) entertain the masses. **Plaza Cánovas del Castillo** and **Plaza de los Fueros** also buzz until the disco hour. The popular bus line **Calle Juan Llorens** is located West of Gran Vía Fernando El Católico, between San José la Montaña and Angel Guimera.

Discos dominate the university area, particularly on **Avenida Blasco Ibañez.** Young twenty-somethings begin dancing at the pubs off Av. Ibañez at **Plaza Xúquer.** Walk around the Pl. Xúquer pubs to pick up discounted passes to the discos. Discos don't draw a crowd until 3am, at the earliest. Be warned: hot spots flash in and out, so some of the places below (now totally cool, or why would we list them?) may have moved on to disco heaven. Local university students remain the best sources. Taxi drivers generally know *discotecas* by name. It's wise to tackle the labyrinth of the old city in groups; the dark areas in between the clusters can be dangerous. For info on activities in the city, consult the *Qué y Dónde* weekly magazine, available at newsstands (150ptas), or *La Cartelera,* a weekly entertainment supplement to the daily paper *Levante* (125ptas for both).

Caballito de Mar, C. Eugenia Viñes 22 (371 07 63), at Playa de Malvarrosa, remixes recent favorites and *bacalao* (Spanish techno). It mimics a cruise ship with outdoor tables and a decorative pool on deck. Rocking every day of the week after 2am. Open in summer.

Distrito 10, C. General Elío, 10. Another hot spot, with mirrors, 3 floors of balconies, and a gigantic video screen. Open Sept.-July Thurs.-Sat. 6-9:30pm and midnight-7am, Sun. 6-9:30pm. Early session 400ptas, late 1500ptas.

Club Perdido, C. Sueca, 17, past the train station, a bit out of the way. Plays jazz.

Carnaby Club, Poeta Liern, 17. A lesbian favorite.

Balkiss, C. Dr. Monserrat, 23 (tel. 391 70 80). Gay men congregate here.

Movie selections are bountiful and varied. Ask at the tourist office for info on the Mostra de València de Cine Mediterrani and the Independent Film Festival. Vintage and Foreign films, many in English, show at the **Filmoteca,** Pl. Ayuntamiento, 17 (tel. 352 23 30). Look in *Qué y Dónde* for *V.O. subtitulaela* films in their original languages.

During **Semana Santa,** the streets clog with lavishly attired monks riding platforms enacting Biblical scenes, and children performing the miracle plays of St. Vincent Ferrer. The festival of **Corpus Christi** features *rocas,* intricate coaches that double as stages for religious plays. The **Fira de Juliol** (July Fair) brings fireworks, cultural events, bullfights, and a **batalla de flors,** a violent skirmish in which girls on passing floats throw flowers at the crowd, which in turn flings them back.

Las Fallas

If you can choose any time of the year to come to Valencia, make it March 12-19, when Valencia's most illustrious event, **Las Fallas,** grips the city. Neighborhoods

compete to build the most elaborate and satirical papier-mâché effigy; over 300 such *ninots* spring up in the streets. Parades, bullfights, fireworks, and street dancing enliven the annual excess. On the final day—*la nit del foc* (fire night)—all the *ninots* simultaneously burn in one last, clamorous release. The inferno exorcises social ills and brings luck for the agricultural season. Tourists are not exempt from social ills, however, as accommodations are packed in March.

■ Near Valencia

SAGUNTO (SAGUNT)

Spaniards still puff with pride over the courage of this town's inhabitants. In the third century BC, residents of Phoenician-controlled Sagunto held out for 8 months against Hannibal's besieging Carthaginians. Some sources say that on the brink of annihilation, Sagunto's women, children, and elderly threw themselves into a burning furnace; others insist that the residents chose starvation over defeat. Monuments reflect the influence of a rambling list of conquerors (6 seizures, not including barbarian, Alan, Vandal, Visigoth, and Byzantine invasions during the 5th-7th centuries). By 1874, Sagunto had learned the hard way that if you can't beat 'em, join 'em, being the first town to recognize Alfonso XII's restoration of the Bourbon monarchy.

To get to the town center from the **train station,** turn right at the exit; then turn left at the traffic lights onto the diagonal street (C. Vicent Fontelles), heading the wrong way down a one-way street to a small plaza. Here, turn left onto Cami Real, which runs directly to the center of town and to the **Ayuntamiento,** where the old town peaks at the refurbished medieval **castle.** (Open Tues.-Sat. 10am-8pm, Sun. 10am-2pm; Oct.-May Tues.-Sat. 10am-2pm and 4-6pm, Sun. 10am-2pm.) Along the way, the once-crumbling **Teatre Roman** has survived a controversial restoration process to become an impressive modern performance stage, built entirely on the still-visible skeleton of the Roman structure.

Beaches, including the **Puerto de Sagunto,** which won an EU beach award, and **Almarda,** beckon by the port (4km away). Buses leave from Av. Santos Patronos next to the tourist office (every 20min., 90ptas). In summer, a number of nameless restaurants set up shop on the beach along Av. Mediterrani and Pg. Marítim.

The **tourist office** (tel. 266 22 13) is in Pl. Cronista Chabret; look for the orange facade at the end of the plaza, on the right as you arrive at the Ayuntamiento (open Mon.-Sat. 10am-2pm and 4-6pm, Sun. 10am-2pm). Frequent **RENFE trains** from Valencia (on the C-6 *Cercanías* line) stop in Sagunto (tel. 266 07 28; every 30min., 30min., 310ptas), as do **Vallduxense buses** (tel. 349 37 38; 30min., 250ptas).

MANISES

The small town of Manises has made the province of Valencia famous for its colorful, hand-decorated ceramics. Souvenir-o-phobes will cross neurons in the city's main square, where ceramics dealers push their wares. **CVT buses** (tel. 340 47 15) leave from Valencia's bus station (almost every hr., 30min., 100ptas), but *Cercanías* **trains** from Valencia along the line to Riba-Roja de Turia are more frequent and arrive at Manises's ceramic-lined station (20min., every ½hr., weekends every hr., 150ptas). Fine ceramics closer to Valencia are at the famous **Fábrica Lladró** workshop in Tavernes Blanques (take bus #16 from Pl. Ayuntamiento in Valencia; 105ptas).

L'ALBUFERA

The **Albufera,** Spain's largest lagoon, is 13km south of Valencia. Nature lovers flock to see fish and wild fowl frolicking in the water and rice fields lining the edges. Motorized gondola tours weave around reeds and through the marsh while flying fish serenade cruisers (45min., 1500ptas). **Buses** (tel. 349 14 25), from the corner of Gran Via de Germanía and C. Sueca, between the train station and Pl. Toros, stop here on the way from Valencia to El Perello (every 30min., 40min., 165ptas). To catch the return bus, cross the bridge on your right with your back to the lagoon.

CULLERA

The rapidly growing town of **Cullera,** south of Valencia, glories under the protective glare of its 13th-century **castell.** Those who complete the 15-minute zig-zag hike are rewarded with a 360-degree postcard view of the mountains, verdant rice paddies, a sea, a river, and a city. Attached to the castle, the 19th-century **Santuari de la Verge** displays sundry religious treasures "collected" by castle residents over the years (open daily 9am-9pm; off season 8am-6pm; free). Cullera lies on the *Cercanías* **train** line between Valencia and Gandía (every hr., weekends every ½hr., 35min., 310-355ptas). From the train station, take the bus into the city and ask the bus driver to let you off near Pl. Mercat (also Pl. de la Virgen). From the **plaza** go up the stairs in the back. Continue up C. Calvari at the top of the steps. This road narrows into a stone path that climbs to the *castell.* The bus also runs through town to the *faro* (lighthouse), and you can walk north to a seemingly endless strip of less populated beaches.

MORELLA

Morella is like a coveted cookie jar hidden above the kitchen cabinet—high up and hard to reach, but full of delights once within your grasp. Surrounded by a ring of thick walls and guarded by the stoic remains of a majestic castle, Morella still looks like an impenetrable fortress in an otherwise empty, rolling green countryside. The **Castell de Morella** (tel. 17 31 28), perched atop a massive rock, dazzles even the most jaded castlemasters. Celts, Romans, and Moors all chose Morella for its natural defenses. El Cid stormed the summit in 1084. Don Blasco de Aragón took the town in the name of Jaume I in 1232. Various civil wars in the 19th century damaged the castle, but the craters only add to the castle's allure. A serpentine path scales the castle past 14th- to 19th-century dungeons, slithering up to the **Plaça de Arms.** The view from there spans a fertile countryside and an ancient Roman aqueduct. (Entrance to the castle is on C. Hospital, uphill from the basilica with two Gothic portals. Open daily 10:30am-7:30pm; in winter 10:30am-6pm. 200ptas, students 100ptas.)

In the Pl. Arciprestal, the Gothic **Basílica Santa María la Mayor's** dual portals display amusingly dopey statues. Inside, a ghostly, fair-skinned statue of Nuestra Señora de la Asunción, windy stairwell, overgrown organ, and phasmatalogical gold altarpiece evoke images of Damien and *The Omen.* A five-minute walk from Puerta de San Miguel, remnants of the 13th-century Gothic **acueducto,** with 16 towers and six gates, arch above the road. Try visiting Morella during **Sexeni,** the town's most famous *fiesta,* celebrated every six years to honor the Virgen de Vallivana (not due to roll around again until August 2000).

Lost in the mountains of Valencia, Morella's charm is its unhurried daily life that continues uninterrupted by the sprinkling of tourists that shuffle in and out, but the downside is that the rest of Spain has been isolated from Morella's unique cuisine that features *rufas* (truffles), dug up from the local turf. Specialties include *croquetas morellanas, paté de trufas* (truffle paté), and *cordero relleno trufado* (lamb with truffled stuffing). Eat like El Cid at **Restaurante Casa Roque,** C. Segura Barreda, 8 (tel. 16 03 36), the best in town *(menú* 1500ptas; open Tues.-Sun.). If you're staying overnight, **Fonda Moreno,** C. San Nicolás, 12 (tel. 16 01 05), has ancient rooms and wood ceilings (singles 1000ptas, doubles 2000ptas). Also inexpensive is **Hostal El Cid,** Puerta San Mateo, 3 (tel. 16 00 08), down from the bus stop, with balconies with a view. (Singles 1300ptas. Doubles 2200ptas, with shower 3100ptas, with bath 3500ptas. Breakfast 300ptas.)

The **tourist office** (tel. 17 30 32) is at Pta. de San Miguel, uphill from the bus stop (open daily 10am-2pm and 4-7pm; in winter Tues.-Sat. 10am-2pm and 4-6pm, Sun. 10am-2pm). In **emergencies,** call the **Guardia Civil** (tel. 16 00 11) or the **Red Cross** (tel. 16 03 80). The **post office,** C. San Nicolás, 31 (tel. 16 03 13), off C. San Juan, offers basic services (open Mon.-Fri. 8:30am-2:30pm, Sat. 9:30am-1pm). The **postal code** is 12300. The **telephone code** is (9)64. **Autos Mediterraneo** (tel. 22 00 54) runs buses to Morella from Pl. Fadrell in **Castelló** (7:15am, 2, and 3pm, 2½hr., 1200-

1400ptas). From the train station, walk down the road to your right as you exit the station. Continue straight on this road (15min.), veering right where the road forks at Viajes Naraja, to get to Fadrell. In Castelló, **Pensión Martí,** C. Herrero, 19 (tel. (964) 22 45 66), is welcoming and clean (12:30am curfew). Castelló is on the **Cercanías Valencia** train line (every ½hr., 1hr., 470-535ptas).

■ Játiva (Xàtiva)

The last foreigner of note to come through Játiva was 18th-century fireball Felipe V, who burned it to the ground. With an imposing, mountainous backdrop and land that lends itself to *huertas* (orchards) and vineyards, it's no wonder that Felipe was just one in a long line of conquerors. Játiva's distinctions include being the birthplace of European paper production, Baroque painter José Ribera, and the Borja Popes Calixtus III and Alexander VI. Nonetheless, the city snares few tourists and doesn't even retain locals during the unbearably hot summer months.

Orientation and Practical Information 64km south of Valencia and 102km north of Alicante, inland Játiva is easily accessed by rail. **Alameda de Jaume I** divides the town into two: the old village, at the foot of the hill with the castles and ancient walls, and the modern village. To reach the old village and the tourist office from the train station in the modern village, go straight up **Baixada de L'Estació** (beginning at the Bar Bienvenidos) and turn left at its end.

The **tourist office,** Al. Jaume 1, 50 (tel. 227 33 46), across from the Ajuntament, shovels out pamphlets, a map, a restaurant guide, and speaks English. (Open Tues.-Sat. 10am-2pm and 4:30-6pm, Sun. 10am-2pm; Sept. 15-June 15 Tues.-Fri. 9am-2pm and 4-6pm, Sat.-Sun. 10am-2pm.) City **maps** are available any time of day at the **policía nacional.** Injured tourists should call the **Red Cross** (tel. 227 02 39 or 227 44 31), or head to **Hospital Lluis Alcanyis,** Ctra. Alzira (tel. 228 91 00; emergencies 228 91 21), 2km from the town center. The local **police** (tel. 228 01 32) hold fort on Baixada del Carme at Al. Jaume I, 33; **emergency** numbers are 091 and 092. The **post office,** at Av. Jaume I, 33 (tel. 227 51 68), is open for stamps and Lista de Correos Mon.-Fri. 8:30am-2:30pm, Sat. 9:30am-1pm. The **postal code** is 46800. The **telephone code** is (9)6. **RENFE trains** chug from Av. Cavaller Ximén de Tovia (tel. 227 33 33), to Valencia (35 per day, 1hr., 370-430ptas), Gandía (every 30min. with change in Silla; 305-370ptas), and Madrid. **Buses** stop at the corner of Av. Cavaller Ximén de Tovia and C. Don Carles Santhou, to the left and down from the train station. **Cambipos** (tel. 287 41 10), goes direct to Gandía (1 per day, 1¼hr., about 400ptas). Call the bus station in Valencia (tel. 349 72 22), for a schedule from there to Játiva.

Accommodations and Food Call before coming if you plan to stay the night. **Margallonero,** Pl. Mercat, 42 (tel. 227 66 77), looks out on the city's active market plaza and proffers large, utterly flowery rooms at reasonable prices (1400ptas per person). To get there, go left on Al. Jaume I coming from the train station (like going to the tourist office), take the first right onto C. St. Francese, go straight up the ramp onto C. Alos, and take the first left at C. Botigues, which runs into Pl. Mercat. Játiva's traditional desserts are unmistakably Arabic in origin. *Harnadi* is a pudding of squash, sweet potato, nuts, and raisins. *Al Monchamena* tastes like a sweetened omelette. The local version of *paella* is *arroz al horno,* which is baked, slightly drier, and loaded with chick peas. Blue- and white-tiled **Casa Floro,** Pl. Mercat, 46 (tel. 227 30 20), next door to the Margallonero, has A/C and a tasty 4-course *menú* for 1200ptas (open Mon.-Fri. 1:30-4pm, Sat. 1:30-4pm and 9-11pm). Tuesdays and Fridays are **market** days on Pl. Mercat (open 8am-1pm). The **Mercadona supermarket** is on Av. Abu Masaif, just off Baixada de L'Estació (open Mon.-Sat. 9am-8:30pm).

Sights and Entertainment The striking ramparts atop the hill in back of town lead to the awe-inspiring **castell,** a roughneck two-kilometer climb made either on the tedious, windy pavement or on the steep rock and roll dirt shortcut. The castle

has two sections: the **castell machor** (larger), on the right as you come in, and the pre-Roman **castell chicotet** (smaller). The former, used from the 13th through the 16th centuries, bears the scars of many a siege and earthquake. Its arched, stone **prison** has held some famous wrongdoers, including King Fernando el Católico and the Comte d'Urgell, would-be usurper of the Aragonese throne. Referred to in Verdi's *Il Trovatore,* the Comte spent his final years here and then was buried in the castle's chapel (open Tues.-Sun. 10:30am-7pm; 300ptas, Tues. free).

Leaving the tourist office to the right, take the first right and ascend Portal de Lleo and C. Peris Urios to find **Colegiata de Santa María,** a giant church known as **La Seu.** In front, the town's two popes scheme in bronze. Constructed from 1596 to 1920, the ornate *colegiata* is a religious museum—paintings and figurines lurk in nooks and crannies, and on the ceiling (open 9:30am-1:30pm; museum 100ptas).

The **Museu Municipal l'Almodí,** in a 16th-century palace on C. Corretgeria, 46 (tel. 227 65 97), off Pl. Calixto III, holds four floors of Spanish paintings, including three Riberas. Here the townspeople avenged Felipe V's 1707 destruction of the town by hanging his portrait upside down. Thus it remains. From La Seu, cross the plaza where C. Corretgeria runs to the right of the 15th-century hospital. (Open Tues.-Fri. 10am-3pm, Sat.-Sun. 10am-2pm; Oct.-May Tues.-Fri. 10am-2pm and 4-6pm, Sat.-Sun. 10am-2pm. 75ptas).

■ Gandía

Centuries before the EU began blue-flagging the Mediterranean's best beaches, Gandía (pop. 53,000) had already attracted the refined and powerful Borjas family. Five centuries later, as an agribusiness and mercantile exchange nexus, Gandía still cashes in on sugar cane, oranges, silk, daffodils, and mulberries—but mostly on beach, condos, and more beach. The youth hostel here offers the most privileged (and economical) access to the great Gandian *platja.*

ORIENTATION AND PRACTICAL INFORMATION

Everything you need is a stone's throw from the train station on **Marqués de Campo.** Everything you want is at the **beach,** 4km away.

Tourist Office: Marqués de Campo (tel. 287 77 88), across from the train station. Detailed map. Open Mon.-Fri. 10am-2pm and 4:30-7:30pm, Sat. 10am-1:30pm; in winter closed Sat. English spoken. A beach **branch** (tel. 284 24 07), at Pg. Marítim on the water. Open March 15-Oct. 15 Mon.-Sat. 10am-2pm and 5-8pm, Sun. 10am-1pm.

Trains: the **RENFE** variety (tel. 286 54 71) depart from Marqués de Campo to Valencia (31 per day, every 30min., 1hr., 480ptas) and Játiva (via Silla, 370ptas). Trains also run from Valencia to Platja i Grau de Gandia, Gandía's beach (3-4 per day, 480ptas in summer).

Buses: UBESA runs an extensive service between Alicante and Valencia via Gandía (tel. 287 16 54). Buses leave from C. Magistrado Catalan, 3. Go right as you leave the train station, take a left at the statue onto C. D'Alfaro, then take the 1st right (C. Magistrado Catalá). To: Valencia (9-12 per day, 1¼hr., 675ptas); Alicante (10-13 per day, 3hr., 1090ptas); Barcelona (1 per day, 7-8hr., 3575ptas); the Valencia-Denia-Alicante line makes several stops along the Costa Brava. **Auto Res,** Marqués de Campo, 12 (tel. 287 10 64). Buses stop at the beach at Pg. Marítim en route to Madrid (7 per day, 5½hr., 3295ptas).

Bike/Windsurfer Rental: At the HI hostel in Platja de Piles. Bikes 500ptas per day. Kayaks 700ptas per hr. Windsurfing lessons offered.

Luggage Storage: At the **train station,** with 300ptas token purchased at ticket windows. Lockers and ticket windows available 6am-10:30pm. An **UBESA** attendant may let you leave dead weight in the station's back room for the day.

Red Cross: (tel. 287 38 61; beach tel. 284 25 84).

Hospital: C. Sant Pere and Pg. Germanies (tel. 295 92 00).

Police: (tel. 287 88 00). **Emergency:** (tel. 091 or 092).

Post Office: Pl. Jaume I, 7 (tel. 287 10 91), a few blocks behind the Ajuntament. Open for stamps and Lista de Correos Mon.-Fri. 9am-2pm. **Postal Code:** 46700.

Telephones: Fax and **phones** at Parque de la Estación, 1, to the right as you leave the train station. Open Mon.-Fri. 9:30am-2pm and 4-8pm, Sat. 10am-1pm. **Telephone Code** (9)6.

ACCOMMODATIONS

HI cardholders rejoice at Gandía's hostel, especially given the number of expensive *hostales* about. Make reservations in the summer, especially in August and on weekends, or go bedless.

Alberg Mar i Vent (HI), C. Doctor Fleming (tel. 283 17 48), in Platja de Piles, a town 10km south of Gandía. Take **La Amistad** bus (tel. 287 44 10), which departs from the right of the train station (100ptas; check Bar La Amistad, across from the bus stop, for exact times). Flattery cannot do justice to this hostel/beachfront resort. There's a buff weight room, pool table, outdoor patio, and basketball/soccer court. They rent bikes and windsurfers, and water laps at the front door. Beach is relatively uncrowded. No alcohol, smoking outside. Dishware, microwave, and fridges available until late at night. Washing machine and library. 5-day max. stay. Curfew: in summer weeknights 2am, weekends 4am; in winter midnight. 800ptas per person, with breakfast 900ptas, with full *pensión* 1900ptas. Over 26: 1100ptas; 1400ptas; 2400ptas. Sheets 300ptas. Open Feb. 15-Dec. 15.

Hotel Europa, C. Levante, 12-14 (tel. 284 07 50). From the tourist office, hop on the **La Marina** bus and ask to be let off at the C. Levante stop (100ptas). A regal hotel with elevator, solarium, and many newly designed rooms. Singles with bath 3000ptas. Doubles with shower 4000ptas, with bath 5000ptas. Breakfast 300ptas.

Camping: The tourist office has directions to and details about the 3 campsites near the beach. The cheapest is **L'Alqueria** (tel. 284 04 70), on the La Marina bus route between Gandía and the beach (ask to be dropped off). 540ptas per person and 680ptas per tent. Open April-Sept.

FOOD

Gandía cooks up seafood specialities like *fidueà,* a shellfish and pasta dish covered with hot broth, and the invariably expensive but tempting *zarzuela,* a platter of assorted shellfish in broth. Before hopping on the bus, stock up at **Supermarket Macedona,** C. Perú, across from the La Amistad stop (open Mon.-Sat. 9am-9pm).

Spinach, Av. del Mar, 33 (tel. 283 15 86), around the corner from the Playa de Piles bus stop. Fresh fruit shakes and sinful desserts. Tasty crepes like asparagus and ham (550ptas) will make your forearms bulge and your pipe toot. Open Fri.-Sun. noon-midnight.

Asador Josman, C. Ermita, 16 (tel. 284 05 30), 100m down the street from Hotel Europa; Levante becomes C. Ermita as it nears the highway. On weekends this *pollería* (chicken store) is an unbelievable deal. Whole chickens 800ptas; whole chicken with french fries for 4 people 1050ptas. Open in summer Mon.-Sat. 9:30am-3pm and 7-10pm, Sun. 9:30am-3pm; in winter Sat.-Sun. only.

SIGHTS AND ENTERTAINMENT

There is not much here aside from the **beach** and a rare Keanu Reeves sighting, but who cares? Wedged between the blue sea and tiled Pg. Marítim, fine sands stretch for several km from the port to the condos. **La Marina buses,** Marqués de Campo, 14 (tel. 287 18 06), next to the tourist office, run along Pg. Marítim (every 30min. 6am-11pm, 120ptas; nocturnal service on weekends).

The pre-college crowd cashes in on the discos. The older duck into numerous **bars** lining C. Gutiérrez Más. Follow Marqués de Campo to the end, turn right on C. Magistrat Catala, and take the fifth right onto C. Gutiérrez Más. *Fiesta-*wise, Gandía has been honoring San Francisco, its patron saint, every September since 1310. The town also revs up for its version of **Las Fallas** between March 16-19.

■ Alicante (Alacant)

Lanky palm trees and shady cafes line Alicante's glossy avenues while white sand beaches ripple in the sea breezes. Energized by multifaceted night life and a bustling new port, Alicante (pop. 250,000) is the groovin' gateway to Costa Blanca's more serene beach towns. Increasingly confident in its urbanity, Alicante offers what its bigger sibling, Valencia, cannot: a beach at your front door. Above the frying flesh of roasting bodies, the *castillo*, spared by Franco when Alicante was the last Republican city to fall in the Civil War, guards the wicked tangle of streets in the *casco antiguo*.

ORIENTATION AND PRACTICAL INFORMATION

Avenida de la Estación runs straight out from the **train station** and becomes **Avenida Alfonso X el Sabio** after passing through **Plaza de los Luceros**. **Esplanada d'Espanya** stretches along the waterfront between **Rambla Méndez Núñez** and **Avenida Federico Soto,** which reach back up to Av. Alfonso X El Sabio. Together these form a box of streets around which nearly all services cluster.

Tourist Office: Regional, Esplanada d'Espanya, 2 (tel. 520 00 00; fax 520 02 43; email alicante.touristinfo@turisme.m400.gva.es). Info about the city and entire coast. Informative staff points backpackers to hostels, restaurants, beaches, and bars. A wealth of cultural info and guides to excursions. English spoken. Open Mon.-Fri. 10am-8pm, Sat. 10am-2pm and 3-8pm. **Airport branch** (tel. 691 93 67).

Budget Travel: TIVE, Av. Aguilera, 1 (tel. 590 07 70), near the train station off Av. Oscar Esplá. ISIC 700ptas. HI card 1800ptas. Open Mon.-Fri. 9am-1:30pm.

El Corte Inglés: Maisonnave, 53 (tel. 511 30 01). Wonderful **map. Currency exchange** with no commission, haircutting, cafeteria, restaurant, and **telephones.** Its annex down the street has novels and guidebooks *en inglés ¡qué guay!* Open Mon.-Sat. 10am-9:30pm.

Flights: Aeroport Internacional El Altet (tel. 691 90 00), 10km from town. **Alcoyana** (tel. 513 01 04) sends buses to airport every 40min. that pick up at the station and Pl. Luceros. Tourist office has a schedule (from town 6:30am-10:20pm, from airport 6:55am-11:10pm; 100ptas). **Iberia,** airport office (tel. 691 91 00). International and national reservations call **Servilberia** (tel. 902 400 500). To: Palma (3-4 per day); Barcelona (4 per day); Madrid (4-5 per day); Sevilla (3 per week).

Trains: RENFE, Estació Término, Av. Salamanca (tel. 592 02 02), west of the city center and not far from El Corte Inglés. Info open 7am-midnight. Most destinations require a transfer. Direct to: Murcia (1½hr., 525-560ptas); Valencia (2hr., 1325-2800ptas); Madrid (4hr., 3200-4700ptas); Barcelona (6hr., 3600-4200ptas). **Ferrocarriles de la Generalitat Valenciana,** Est. Marina, Av. Villajoyosa, 2 (tel. 526 27 31), a 15min. walk down Esplanada d'Espanya, away from Rambla Méndez Núñez; or bus G from the bus station and El Corte Inglés. Service along the Costa Blanca to: San Juan (100ptas); Villajoyosa (320ptas); Benidorm (415ptas); Calpe (635ptas); Denia (925ptas). Departures every hr., 6:15am-8:15pm; only 7 as far as Calpe and Denia. Round-trip tickets discounted 15%. Railpasses not accepted. In summer **El Trensnochedor** (night train) runs all night to discos *("¡viva españá!")* on the beaches near Alicante (150-700ptas round-trip, depending on destination).

Buses: C. Portugal, 17 (tel. 513 07 00). To reach Esplanada d'Espanya, turn left onto Carrer d'Italia and right on Av. Dr. Gadea; follow Dr. Gadea until the park, then left on the waterfront. City buses A and G reach the station (100ptas). Each company serves different destinations, including international ones. For the Costa Blanca, **UBESA** (tel. 513 01 43) sends 22 buses per day to Villajoyosa (330ptas) and Benidorm (430ptas). Also to: Calpe (620ptas); Jávea (875ptas); Altea (525ptas); Denia (1000ptas); Valencia (1875ptas). **Molla** (tel. 513 08 51), to Elche (every 30min., 205ptas). **Enatcar** (tel. 513 06 73), to: Madrid (8 per day, 5½hr., 2895ptas); Granada (6 per day, 6hr., 3325ptas); Málaga (6 per day, 8hr., 4435ptas); Sevilla (2 per day, 10hr., 5740ptas); Barcelona (8 per day, 8hr., 4590ptas). **Bilman Bus** (tel. 592 06 93) 2 per day to Pamplona and San Sebastián.

Ferries: Flebasa, Est. Marítima, Puerto de Denia (tel. 578 40 11). Service from Denia to Ibiza (3 per day, 3½hr., 5475ptas). Open Mon.-Fri. 9am-1pm and 4:30-8pm, Sat. 9am-noon. **Pitra** (tel. 642 31 20) offers the same price with 2 daily trips to Ibiza.

Taxis: (tel. 525 25 11or 510 16 11). Service to Platja Sant Joan (900-1000ptas).

Luggage Storage: At the bus station (200ptas per bag). Open daily 8am-8:30pm.

Red Cross: (tel. 525 25 25).

24Hr. Pharmacy: Check the *Agenda* section of the local newspaper, *Información* (125ptas) or call tel. 521 28 33 for info in Spanish.

Medical Services: Hospital General, Maestro Alonzo, 109 (tel. 590 83 00).

Police: Comisaría, C. Médico Pascual Pérez, 27 (tel. 514 22 22). **Emergency:** tel. 091 or 112.

Post Office: Pl. Gabriel Miró, 7 (tel. 521 99 84), off C. San Fernando. Open Mon.-Fri. 8:30am-8:30pm, Sat. 9am-2pm. **Lista de Correos** services available. A 2nd branch at Bono Guarner, 2 (tel. 522 78 71), next to the RENFE Station, is open Mon.-Fri. 8am-2:30pm, Sat. 9:30am-1pm; Oct.-June Mon.-Fri. 9am-2pm and 3-8pm, Sat. 9am-2pm. **Postal Code:** 03000.

Telephone Code: (9)6.

ACCOMMODATIONS AND CAMPING

Although there seem to be *pensiones* and *casas de huéspedes* on every corner, the number of clean rooms is considerably smaller. The tourist office keeps accommodations listings. Stay away from most places along C. San Fernando, where theft and prostitution are common, and around the Església de Santa María; opt instead for the newer section of town. Try to arrive early or call ahead for a good room.

Residencia Universitaria (HI), Av. Orihuela, 59 (tel. 511 30 44). Take bus G (100ptas, make sure you're going the right way) and get off at the last stop (the bus will stop for a while), directly behind the large *residencia*. Facilities are great, but the staff can be less than helpful. Hybrid college dormitory/one-star hotel—individual rooms, private bath, A/C. Pester them to keep the A/C running in your room. Cheap snack bar (wine 50ptas), big-screen TV, pool table, and foosball. HI members only. 3-day max. stay. Must arrive by 10pm to check in. 800ptas per person, with breakfast 900ptas, with three meals 1900ptas. Over 26: 1100ptas; 1400ptas; 2400ptas. Very few rooms available Sept.-June.

Pensión Les Monges, C. Monjas, 2 (tel. 521 50 46), behind the Ayuntamiento. In the center of the historic district a few blocks from the beach. Impeccable taste and charm have made this lovely *pensión* a budget traveler's dream. Immaculate and well-decorated rooms. A real Dalí hangs in the living room. The owner can direct you to the best restaurants (gourmets with the need to splurge head down the street to **Bar Luis**) and bars. A/C (600ptas per day), hair dryer, TV, and excellent mattress in each room. Laundry service. Singles 1700ptas, with sink 1900ptas, with shower 2200ptas, with bath 2800ptas. Doubles: 3000ptas; 3500ptas; 3800ptas; 4500ptas. Triples with shower 5000ptas, with bath 5500ptas. Parking 800ptas per day. Winter heating. Credit cards.

Habitaciones México, C. General Primo de Rivera, 10 (tel. 520 93 07; email mexrooms@lix.intercom.es), off the end of Av. Alfonso X El Sabio. Pristine rooms. Friendly owners organize a book swap and allow use of kitchen and email. Sleep (or stay up) to tunes from the *bar musical* down the street. Singles 1900ptas. Doubles 3200ptas, with bath 3800ptas. Triples 4500ptas. 15% cheaper in winter. Laundry service 800ptas per load.

Hostal-Residencia Portugal, C. Portugal, 26, (tel. 592 92 44), across from the bus station. Friendly atmosphere nurtured by Ramón and his staff. Angular rooms with cushy beds and cool sheets. The functional dining room/lounge has a color TV. Steamy interior rooms have fans. TV loan 400ptas. Singles 2200ptas, with bath 3300ptas. Doubles: 3600ptas; 4200ptas. Hearty breakfast 300ptas.

Camping: Playa Muchavista (tel. 565 45 26), 2nd class site near the beach. Take bus C-1. 520ptas per person and per tent. Open year-round.

FOOD

Most tourists refuel along the main pedestrian thoroughfare. Less traveled are the smaller, family-run, *bar-restaurantes* in the **old city** (between the cathedral and the castle steps). The most popular *terrazas* stuff **C. San Francisco** with cheap *menús* and *tapas*. Locals and tourists devour *tapas* on the **C. Mayor.** A number of pricier restaurants line the new **port.** The **market** near Av. Alfonso X El Sabio sells picnic materials (open Mon.-Sat. 8am-2pm). If you're otherwise uninspired, buy basics at **Supermarket Mercadona,** C. Alvarez Sereix, 5 (tel. 521 58 94), off Av. Federico Soto (open Mon.-Thurs. and Sat. 9am-8pm, Fri. 9am-8:30pm). Other supermarkets surround the bus station.

Capitol, C. Bazan, 45 (tel. 520 0592), between Alfonso El Sabio and the Esplanada. An appetizing 1150ptas *menú* (day and night) offers a number of Spanish dishes in four courses. Open Mon.-Fri. 1-4:30pm and 8-11pm, Sat. 1-4:30pm.

La Taberna del Gormet, C. San Fernando, 10 (tel. 520 42 33). Head to this restaurant for some of the best *tapas* in town. Restaurant courses are pricey, but *tapas*, like *montaditos* (panini-like sandwiches with pate, tuna, or salmon 150-200ptas) and *croquetas de bacalao* (cod fish *croquetas* 110ptas) are particularly delicious and reasonably priced at the lively bar. The *jamón* (*pata negra* 975ptas) is the most *riquísimo* in all of Spain. Open daily noon-midnight.

Restaurante Mixto Vegetariano, Pl. Santa María, 2. Iglesia Santa María towers over and Castillo looms above. Creative vegetarian fare; some meat dishes as well. Salad bar and the whole-wheat pizza crust. *Menú* 1100ptas. Trip to the salad bar 395ptas. Open Tues.-Sun. 1:30-4:30pm and 8pm-midnight; fewer hours in the off season.

La Venta del Lobo, C. San Fernando, 48 (tel. 514 09 85). A 2-room neighborhood grill ambitious enough to prepare specialties from all over Spain. Try *gazpacho andaluz* (370ptas) or Valencian *paella*. *Menú* 1075ptas. A menu of many tongues. Open Tues.-Sat. 1-5pm and 8:30pm-midnight, Sun. 1-5pm.

SIGHTS AND BEACHES

Complete with drawbridges, dark passageways, and hidden tunnels, **Castell de Santa Bárbara** keeps silent guard over Alicante's bustling beach. Built by the Carthaginians and recently reconstructed, the 200m-high fortress has a dry moat, dungeon, spooky ammunition storeroom, and an all-encompassing view of Alicante. A paved road from the old section of Alicante leads to the top; most people take the elevator (300ptas) from a hidden entrance on Av. Jovellanos, across the street from the beach and near the white crosswalk over the road (castle open daily 10am-7:30pm; Oct.-March daily 9am-6:30pm; free).

Bronze Age dowries and Roman statues from excavations throughout the province coexist inside the Neoclassical **Museu Arqueológic de la Diputación,** Av. Estación, 6 (tel. 512 13 00; open Mon.-Fri. 9am-6pm; free). Skipping ahead a few centuries, a crowd of Valencian modernist art pieces, along with a few Mirós, Picassos, Kandinskys, and Calders fraternize in the **Museu de Arte del Siglo XX La Asegurada** (tel. 521 45 78), at the east end of C. Mayor. The original collection was donated by Valencian artist Eusebio Sempre. (Open Oct.-April Tues.-Sat. 10am-1pm and 5-8pm; May.-Sept. Tues.-Sat. 10:30am-1pm and 6-9pm; closed Sun. afternoon. Free.)

Alicante's own **Playa de Postiquet** attracts a disturbing number of flesh-flashers. Six-kilometers-long **Playa de San Juan** and **Playa Muchavista** are popular options, accessed by bus C-1 from Pl. Espanya and bus S from either Pl. Espanya or Pl. Mar (both every 15min., 100ptas); or hop on the Alicante-Denia train (every hr., 20min., 100ptas). If crowds have soiled every inch, try the more public (and naked) **Platja de Saladar** in Urbanova. Buses from the Alicante station run to Urbanova (7 per day, 35min., 100ptas). The regional tourist office also has a complete listing of *bandera azul* (blue flag) beaches, accessed by the Alicante-Denia rail line.

ENTERTAINMENT

Warm-weather nightlife centers on the **Platja de Sant Joan.** In July and August, **Ferrocarriles de la Generalitat Valenciana** runs special **Trensnochedor** night trains from Est. de la Marina to several points along the beach. Pick up a schedule at the tourist office, which includes discounts on cover charges (trains every hr., 9pm-7am, 100-700ptas, depending on destination). A taxi from Alicante (900-1000ptas) to Platja de Sant Joan can be shared by up to four people. **Voy Voy** is on Av. Niza at the "Discotecas" night train stop. Go go inside and out (look for the fabulous **Katrina;** beer 350ptas; open until 6am). **Bares-musicales** line side streets off the beach to the right of the same train stop. The **Copity** disco is on Av. Condomina, a long walk or short taxi ride away from the "Condomina" night train stop. Sami says et off at the second **Benidorm** stop (650ptas round-trip) for hard-core *discotecas* like **Penélope, Pachá, KM,** and, for those who don't stop even when the sun rises, **Insomnia.** The party here goes on till at least 9am. PR people hand out discounts outside, but only members of the subculture and transvestites get in free (1500ptas and up).

For those in search of parties closer to home, Alicante itself offers a number of popular discotecas and bars. In the old section of town, **El Barne,** students hop from one bar-musical to the next. Particularly popular with both gay and straight dancers is **Celestial Copas** on C. San Pascual. **Rosé** on C. San. Juan Bosco also attracts a gay crowd, while **Desdén** on C. Santo Tomás attracts an astronomical number of Americans. Closer to the water, **Buggattl** (tel. 521 0646), C. San Fernando, floats candle-lit tables. (Cover and first drink 1500ptas. Open nightly until 5:30am. Women usually slip in without a cover.) **Paripe,** C. Baron de Finestront, attracts a lesbian crowd. On the Esplanada, at Pl. Canelejas, **Pachá** welcomes those who do not brave the bigger brother in Benidorm. After these clubs wind down around 4:30am, wild ones head out to the new port, lined with late-night bar-musicals.

From June 20-24, the city bursts with celebration for the **Festival de Sant Joan,** comprised of romping *fogueres* (symbolic or satiric effigies). The figures burn in a *cremá* on the 24th, but the charivari continues with breathtaking nightly fireworks as lights and decorations festoon the streets. On the last day, a marching band and parade of candy hurlers whet people's appetites for next year's festival. The **Verge del Remei** procession takes place on August 3; pilgrims trek to the monastery of Santa Faz the following Thursday. Alicante honors **La Virgen del Demedio** all summer long with concerts and theatrical performances, many of which are held in the new open-air theater on the port. Inquire at the tourist office for a schedule of events.

■ Near Alicante

Tabarca, an island 15km south that was once a prison, makes a fine, beachy daytrip. A natural reserve, the island is a great place for scuba diving. Crucero Kon-Tiki boats (tel. 521 63 96) leave from in front of the Esplanada d'Espanya (3 per day, winter 1 per day, round-trip 1700ptas).

Jijona, 37km north of Alicante, is home of the wondrous **Turrones El Lobo** (tel. 561 02 25), a nougat factory. Drool over free samples of the traditional honey and almond Spanish Christmas candy, *turrón,* that has made Jijona a household name. Guided tours every 30min. Open daily 9:30am-1pm and 4-8pm.

Covas de Canalobre (tel. 569 92 50) are spectacular, stalagmited caves 24km north of Alicante. The caves hang over the splendid coastline, 700m above the tiny village of **Busot.** Open daily 10:30am-9:10pm; Oct. 20-June daily 11am-6:30pm. 550ptas. Reached by Alcoyana buses, line C-14 (tel. 513 01 04; 3 per day, 280ptas).

COSTA BLANCA

The "white coast," which extends from Denia through Calpe, Alicante, and Elche down to Torrevieja, derives its name from the fine, clear sand of its shores. A varied terrain of hills blanketed with springtime cherry blossoms, craggy mountains, lush pine-layered hillsides, and natural lagoons surround a coastal burgh. Jávea, Altea, and Denia offer relief from the disco-droves and blinking strobes that energize Alicante and Benidorm. The extensive **rail** line out of Alicante (not RENFE) snakes through the mountains, hugging the picturesque coast and connecting most towns. **UBESA** buses start and stop in almost all of the coastal towns.

CALPE (CALP)

Stepping into Calpe is like stepping into a Dalí landscape. Sixty-two kilometers north-east of Alicante, the town cowers beneath the **Peñó d'Ifach** (327m), a gargantuan, flat-topped rock protrusion whose precipitous faces drop straight to the sea. Like Dalí, commercialized Calpe attracts hordes of *madrileños* and the northern European bourgeois. The main avenue, **Gabriel Miró,** descends to **Platja Arena-Bol,** which gets quickly as you move out (a plus), but has a rocky, floral bottom (a minus). **Platja Levante,** beyond the Peñó, is less crowded. The *bandera azul* (blue flag, the highest class of Spanish beaches) flaps high above both.

If you decide to climb the surreal rock (2hr.), wear sneakers, bring water, and scrap the excess baggage. Hike during the day, since ghosts in goats' clothing haunt the rock and butt unwary travelers over the cliff at full moon. Farther north hang the hard rock and caves of the easterly **Cabo de la Nao,** from which you can see Ibiza. Around the bend from the *cabo,* a castle and watchtower have protected the old fishing village of **Moraira** from freeloading pirates for centuries (buses from Calpe).

The **tourist office,** Av. Ejércitos Españoles, 62 (tel. 583 12 50), between the old town and the beach, has all the info you need on Costa Blanca beaches (open Mon.-Sat. 9am-9pm; off season hours vary). A dispassionate **branch** at C. José Antonio, 36 (tel. 583 85 32), offers a map (open Mon.-Sat. 10am-2pm and 6-9pm). The **American Express,** at Viajes Gandía, Av. Gabriel Miró, 25 (tel. 583 04 12; fax 583 51 51), holds mail for six months and cashes AmEx checks for no fee (open Mon.-Fri. 9:30am-1:30pm and 5-8:30pm, Sat. 9:30am-1:30pm). The **post office** (tel. 583 08 84) lies in the old town, on C. 18 de Julio (open Mon.-Sat. 8:30am-12:30pm). The most reasonable inns and restaurants line the steep incline toward the older *pueblo.* Beware of bland food and high prices by the seaside. Hang your hat at the bright and comfortable English-run **Pensión Céntrica,** Pl. Ifach (tel. 583 55 28). With your back to the water, take a right off Av. Gabriel Miró at the Banesto bank. TV lounge and carpeted floors are a refreshing welcome after a day in the sun (1500ptas per person). Deserving backpackers can try **Camping La Merced** (tel. 583 00 97), a 2nd-class site 400m from the beach (520ptas per person and per tent).

UBESA buses zip from Alicante (10-14 per day, 1½hr., 620ptas) and Gandía (9-12 per day, 1hr., 40min.) to Calpe, stopping 2km from the beach at C. Capitán Pérez Jorda. To get to town walk up the hill (not from whence you came) and curve to the left on Av. Masnou, following it until you see stores and people. **Trains** also connect the two cities (1¾hr., 635ptas). From the train station, take a municipal bus downhill past the bus station and to the beach (1 per hr., 90ptas)—it's an arduous walk.

DENIA

Halfway between Valencia and Alicante on the promontory that forms the Golfo de Valencia, Denia (named by the Greeks for Diana, goddess of the hunt, the moon, and purity), is an upscale family resort with a raging nightlife and important ferry connections to the Baleares, where only bright rowboats interrupt the smooth sweep of *platja.* Most services, including local buses, trains, ferries, the tourist office, and the post office, are clustered on C. Patricio Fernandez which runs straight to the port.

Take a left out of the Enactean/UBESA bus office, walk out of the plaza and turn left onto C. Patricio Fernandez to reach the center of town.

An 18th-century **castle** (tel. 642 06 56) sprawls across the hill overlooking the marina. (Castle open 10am-1:30pm and 5-8:30pm; Oct.-May 10am-1pm and 3-6pm. 300ptas.) A **tourist train** chugs to the castle from outside the tourist office (every ½hr. 10am-1pm and 5-8pm, 500ptas includes ride and entrance to castle). The **tourist office,** C. Glorieta Oculista Baigues, 9 (tel. 642 23 67), 30m inland from Estación Marítime, directs to beach and bed. (Open Mon.-Fri. 9am-8pm, Sat. 9am-2pm and 4-8pm, Sun. 10am-1pm and 4-8pm; Oct.-June Mon.-Fri. 9:30am-1:30pm and 4:30-7:30pm, Sat. 10am-1pm.) Contact the **Red Cross** at tel. 578 13 58. The **post office,** C. Patricio Ferrándiz, 38 (tel. 578 15 33), is west of the tourist office (open Mon.-Fri. 8:30am-2:30pm, Sat. 9:30am-1pm). The **telephone code** is (9)6.

Denia holds a mini **Fallas** festival March 16-19, burning effigies on the final midnight. During **Festa Major** (early July), locals prove they're just as ballsy as their fellow countrymen in Pamplona: bulls and fans dive simultaneously into a pool of water, a feat known as **Bous a la mar.** During the second week of July, the **Fiestas de la Santísima Sangre** (Holy Blood) feature street dances, concerts, mock battles, and wild fireworks over the harbor. The colorful parades and religious plays of the **Moros y Cristianos** celebration take place between August 14-16.

Denia is the place for padded wallets (bring your own). The tourist office has a list of (expensive) accommodations; otherwise try **Hostal el Comercio,** C. La Vía, 43 (tel. 578 00 71), about halfway between the tourist office and the bus station. Its roomy rooms have TVs, phones, and baths tiled in brilliant blue (singles 2850ptas, doubles 5100ptas). Among several campgrounds, **Camping Las Marinas** (tel. 578 14 46) is the closest to town, a 3km bus ride (100ptas) from Platja Jorge Joan (500ptas per person and per tent; Oct. closed). Say *bocadillo* and get used to it, because sandwiches are the only budget meal in town. Restaurants hover around **Calle Marqués de Campo.** One block north, on C. Magallanes, is the morning **market.** Or, shop for groceries at **Supermarket Consum** (tel. 900 50 01 26), C. Patricio Pernandez, near the post office (open Mon.-Sat. 9am-9pm).

The **train** station (tel. 578 04 45), C. Calderón, serves Alicante (7 per day, 925ptas). The **UBESA bus** station, Pl. Arxiduc Carles (tel. 578 05 64), serves Valencia (8-13 per day, 935ptas) and Alicante (6-12 per day, 1000ptas) via Calpe. Local buses leave from the tourist office to big sandy retreats (100ptas). Denia is the take-off point for **Flebasa ferries** (tel. 578 40 11) to Ibiza (3 per day, 3hr., 5475ptas). Office open 9am-1:30pm and 4:30-8pm. **Pitra** (tel. 642 31 20; fax 28 22), at Muelle Comercial, next to Flebasa, floats to Ibiza (San Antonio, 1-2 per day, 5475ptas) and Formentera (1 per week, 5475ptas). The office is open Mon.-Fri. 9:30am-1:30pm and 4:30-7:30pm, Sat.-Sun. 4:30-7:30pm.

ALTEA

A pristine, whitewashed town clustered on a small hill, Altea makes for a relaxing and pleasant daytrip from Alicante. Narrow, stone streets and steps wind up to **Plaza de la Iglesia.** Shaded by the cobalt dome of **Iglesia de la Virgen del Consuelo,** the square commands breathtaking views of the turquoise Mediterranean. A number of bars line the plaza, and an extended meal or drink here is reason enough to visit. Wandering through the crooked streets will lead to other squares which offer glimpses of the sea framed by Altea's bright white houses.

FGU runs **trains** to Altea every hour from Alicante (1¼hrs., 600ptas). **UBESA** (tel. (9)09 600 609) also runs **buses** from Alicante (14-15 per day, 1¼hrs., 525ptas). Both the trains and the buses stop at the foot of the hill and along the coast on C. La Mar. If arriving by bus from Alicante, get off at the 1st stop; if arriving from Valencia, get off at the 2nd stop. The **tourist office** is on C. Sant Pere, 9 (tel. 584 4114 or 584 4122; fax 584 4213), parallel to C. La Mar (open Mon.-Fri. 10am-2pm and 5-7pm, Sat. 10am-2pm). To get to the office from either the train station or the bus stop, walk 50m toward the sea to C. Sant Pere. The **Red Cross** answers at tel. 584 5511 or 584 0525. In **emergencies,** dial 091. The **Post Office** (tel. 584 0174) is on Av. Alt Rei en Jaume I

in the old town on the hill. The tourist office can direct to **lodgings** and **campsites** should you wish to spend the night.

A pebbled beach offers a cool reward for those who trek up and around the old city. Altea celebrates the factioned **Fiestas de Moros y Cristianos** during the last week of September, when the city erupts with music, gunpowder, and dance.

JÁVEA (XÀBIA)

The "Jewel of the Costa Blanca," Jávea's wide, sheltered position offers tranquil waters that have yet to be disturbed by kicking and screaming tourists. Although a municipal bus runs (2km inland) to the port and then on to a larger beach, Jávea's hidden beauties—it's coves, capes, and cliffs—are only accessible by bike, car, or foot. A number of secluded coves and beaches line the coast south of the **port** and **El Arenal,** the most populated beaches. **Playa La Granadella, Playa de Ambolo** (for nudies), and **Playa La Barraca** are serene and accessible.

Inconvenient public transportation to Jávea has spared the town from tourist havoc. **UBESA** (tel. 579 08 45) runs 4 **buses** daily to the town from Alicante (2½hrs., 875ptas) and Valencia (2½hrs.). The bus drops off in front of the UBESA office, C. Príncipe de Asturias. To get to the port, walk up C. Príncipe de Asturias, which (after a couple bends), becomes Av. Alicante. A municipal bus to the port passes here every 30 minutes to an hour (8am-2pm and 4-10pm). If you don't feel like waiting, continue walking down Av. Alicante, which runs directly to the port (20min.).

The regional **tourist office,** Pl. Almirante Bastarreche, 11 (tel. 579 07 36; fax 579 6057), is at the port. (Open Mon.-Fri. 9am-2pm and 5-9pm, Sat. 10am-2pm and 5-9pm, Sun. 10am-2pm.) The **Red Cross** answers at tel. 579 1961. **Municipal police** respond at tel. 579 00 81, the **Civil Guard** at tel. 579 10 85. For **medical emergencies,** call the Centro de Salud at tel. 579 25 00 or 579 25 40. To rent a **bike,** head to Jávea's Auda Marina Española, 13 (tel. 646 11 50), at the port.

A number of restaurants with reasonable *menús* line C. Andrés Lambert, which runs away from the port. Particularly appetizing is **La Yara,** C. Andrés Lambert, 8 (tel. 646 09 20), which offers a filling 1000ptas *menú* with delicious *mantequilla con ajo* (garlic butter) to spread all over your bread (open daily 11am-4pm and 6-11pm). Jávea's remote location may convince you to spend the night. If so, **Pensión La Favorita,** C. Magallanes, 4 (tel. 579 04 77), offers comfortable rooms near the port (singles 2700, doubles 4200-6200ptas; lower in off season). To get to the *pensión,* follow the signs near the tourist office. **Camping Jávea,** Partida Plá, 7 (tel. 579 10 70), is a 2nd-class site between the town and the port.

Jávea's **Moros y Cristianos** festival erupts the second fortnight of July; fireworks jolt wide-eyed tourists who roam among the costumed Moor and Christian factions.

ELCHE (ELX)

An oasis city surrounded by one of Europe's only palm forests, Elche is a tropical paradise. Locals, however, have no time to lounge—they're busy supplying Spain with its highly-regarded footwear. The *Dama de Elche,* the country's finest example of pre-Roman sculpture, hails from this town (23km from Alicante), although it rests at the Museo Arqueológico Nacional in Madrid (see **Madrid: Museums,** p. 99).

Both the **bus station** and **Estación Parque** (trains) are on Av. Ferrocarril Este. To get to the town center and the tourist office, go left leaving either station and left again on **Paseo de la Estación.** At the corner of Av. Ferrocarril and Po. Estación begins the **Parque Municipal,** where doves and palm trees glide and sway above subtropical flora and imitation arabic fountains. A mini-train tours the park and another baby palm forest across the street (trains every ½hr., 11am-10pm, 300ptas).

In the city center, the blue-domed **Basílica de Santa María** is flanked by a tall bell tower (open 7am-1:30pm and 5:30-9pm). A number of inexpensive *bares* line the tranquil plaza outside the basilica. Of the parks and public gardens that fill odd corners of the city, the most beautiful is the **Hort del Cura** (Orchard of the Priest), where magnificent trees shade colorful flower beds (open summer 9am-9pm; winter

9am-6pm; 300ptas.) If you have a car, leave via C. Fray Luis de Leon to reach L'Alcudia's **archaeological digs** and museum (open Tues.-Sat. 10am-2pm and 4-7pm, Sun. 10am-2pm; 400ptas).

Papal orders allowed Elche to host the **Misteri d'Elx**, a 14th-century religious musical that was once forbidden by the Council of Trent (held August 11-13; call the tourist office for ticket info). The work includes the only interpretation of Mary's ascent to heaven. On August 13, for **Nit de L'Alba** (Night of the Dawn), the city shuts off all its lights and sets the sky ablaze with 220-million-*pesetas* worth of Roman Candles. During even-numbered years, repeat performances occur Oct. 31 and Nov. 1.

The **tourist office** (tel. 545 27 47) sits at the end Pg. Estació, Parque Municipal. (Open Mon.-Fri. 9:30am-2:15pm and 4:15-7:45pm; Sat.-Sun. 10:15am-1:15pm; in winter Mon.-Sat. 9am-2:30pm.) Call tel. 542 77 77 for **taxis**. Contact the **Red Cross** at tel. 545 25 36. The **police station** (tel. 542 25 00) is also in Parque Project, near the Pont de Canalejas (tel. 545 13 53). The **post office** (tel. 544 69 11) is in Parque Project. The central **train** station, Estació Parque, is at Av. Ferrocarril Estació, but there's also the Estació Carrus (tel. 545 62 54), about 1km down the same road, on the other side of Po. Estació. It's better to get off at the Parque stop. Trains for Murcia pass through both stations (every hr., 1hr., 315ptas); to Alicante (every hr., 230ptas). The **bus** station (tel. 545 58 58), Av. Llibertat, serves Alicante (every hr., 205ptas) and the private, quietly rolling sand dunes of **La Marina d'Elx** (Mon.-Sat. 5 buses per day, 210ptas).

■ Murcia

Skirted by citrus orchards, quiet Murcia was unheeded until the 13th century when the Moors and then the Christians spontaneously declared it the region's capital. Today, Murcia thrives on university-infused energy when the temperatures are right (fall and spring are delectable), but dies in the roasting summer when everyone flees to the Mediterranean. The sight-seer must have a high tolerance for oceans of '60s-style apartment buildings to find Murcia's few islands of tranquility and architectural beauty. An abundance of beachward buses and frequent trains to quaint Lorca may be Murcia's most appealing feature.

ORIENTATION AND PRACTICAL INFORMATION

To lazy travelers' dismay, most places of interest scatter around the town's periphery. The Río Segura divides the city, with most sights and services in the north half and the **train station** in the southern half (bus #9 or 11). Most major avenues spray outwards from the **Plaza Circular. Gran Vía de Alfonso X El Sabio** runs toward the river and becomes C. Traperia. The cathedral is in **Plaza Cardenal Belluga**, at C. Traperia's end. The **bus station,** at the western edge, is 15 minutes from the center.

Tourist Office: Regional: C. San Cristobal, 6 (tel. 36 61 00; fax 36 61 10), behind the Casino. Enthusiastic staff is ready to unload truckloads of slick pamphlets on the city and province. Open summer: Mon.-Fri. 9:30am-2pm and 5-7:30pm, Sat. 11am-1:30pm; winter: Mon.-Fri. 9am-2pm and 5-7pm, Sat. 11am-1:30pm. **Municipal:** Palacio Almudí, C. Plano San Francisco s/n (tel. 21 98 01 ext. 23). From the train station take bus #9, from the bus station take bus #3 or 9. Smaller than the regional office, but friendly staff offers a map and sound advice. Open Mon.-Fri. 8:30am-3:30pm and 5-7:30pm.

El Corte Inglés: Av. Libertad (tel. 29 80 50). The old standby gives away **maps** and has **currency exchange** with commission rates similar to banks. Also offers novels and guidebooks in English, haircutting, cafeteria, restaurant, and **telephones.** Open Mon.-Sat. 10am-9:30pm.

Budget Travel: TIVE, Conde Roche s/n bajo (tel. 21 32 61) offers discounted airline tickets, ISIC (700ptas), HI cards (1000ptas). Open Mon.-Fri. 9am–2pm, Sat. 9am-noon.

Trains: Estació del Carmen, C. Industria (tel. 25 21 54). Ticket window open 6am-11pm. To: Lorca (1 per hr., 6:45am-9:45pm, 1hr., 515ptas); Alicante (9-17 per day,

1½hr., 515ptas); Valencia (3 per day, 3-4½hr., 1800-3000ptas); Barcelona (3 per day, 7-10hr., 4600-6000ptas); Madrid (3-4 per day, 4-5hr., 4900-5900ptas). **RENFE office,** C. Barrio Nuevo, 6 (tel. 21 28 42), by the cathedral. Open Mon.-Fri. 9am-1pm and 4:30-7:30pm.

Buses: C. San Andrés (tel. 29 22 11), behind the Museo Salzillo. Info window open daily 7am-10pm. To: Elche (50min.) and Lorca (1½hr.). **Alsina Graells** (tel. 29 16 12), info window open Mon.-Fri. 8am-4pm and 6-10pm, Sat.-Sun. 8-11:30am, 2-4pm and 8-10pm. To: Sevilla (3 per day, 7-9hr., 5115ptas); Granada (6 per day, 4-5hr., 2430ptas); Córdoba (1 per day, 9hr., 4135ptas). **La Albatarense/Alsa** (tel. 29 16 23), info window open Mon.-Fri. 7am-3pm and 4-9pm, Sat. 7am-3pm and 4-7pm, Sun. 8:30am-12:30pm and 2:30-9pm. To Valencia (3-7 per day, 3¾ hr., 1850ptas) and Alicante (9-17 per day, 600ptas). **Gimenez Garcia Hermanos** (tel. 29 19 11), services La Manga (6 per day, 655ptas). **Busmar** (tel. 25 00 88), runs to Lo Pagán and Santiago de La Ribera on the Mar Menor (every hr. 7am-9pm, 1hr., 375ptas). **Enactcar** (tel. 29 41 26) runs to Madrid (3090ptas).

Public Transportation: Municipal buses (tel. 25 00 88) covers the city and outskirts. Fare 100ptas. Route maps are available at municipal tourist office. Bus #9 runs a circular route, passing the train station; bus #3 passes near the bus station.

Taxis: tel. 29 77 00 or 24 88 00.

Luggage Storage: At the bus station (300ptas per bag). Open 24hr. At the train station (300-600ptas per day). Open 6am-11pm.

Late-Night Pharmacy: Check listings in *La Opinión de Murcia* (local paper, 125ptas) or postings outside any pharmacy.

Hospital: Hospital General Universitario, Av. Intendente, Jorge Palacios, 1 (tel. 25 69 00). **Red Cross:** tel. 22 22 22.

Police: C. Isaac Albéniz, 10 (tel. 26 66 00). **Emergency:** tel. 091 or 092.

Post Office: Pl. Circular, 8a (tel. 24 12 43), where Av. Primo de Ribera connects to the plaza, in a modern building. Open Mon.-Fri. 8:30am-8:30pm, Sat. 9:30am-2pm. **Postal Code:** 30001. **Telephone Code:** (9)68.

ACCOMMODATIONS AND FOOD

When Murcia steams up and empties out in summer, finding a room is a breeze, but winter competition is a bit stiffer. Prices are high year-round. **Pl. San Juan** is nothing but restaurants, while *mesones* fill **Pl. de Julián Romea.** Murcians end up with a vitamin surplus from veggies produced in the surrounding countryside. *Paella murciana* is vegetarian *paella.* Locals also nibble on *hueva de mujo* (millet roe). Sample the harvest at the **market** on C. Verónicas near the river (open Mon.-Sat. 9am-1pm). **Simago** on Av. de la Libertad (open 9am-9pm) challenges Corte Ingles' chi-chi grocery store across the street.

Hostal Legazpi, Av. Miguel de Cervantes, 8 (tel. 29 30 81; fax 29 91 27). Take bus #9 from the train or bus station to Ronda Norte, get off at the Renault dealership, and follow Ronda Norte around the center. Ample rooms with ceiling fans and TV. A bit outside of the center, but you'll lay prostrate under the ceiling fans on steamy summer nights. Single 1900ptas, with bath 2700ptas. Doubles 3800ptas, with bath 4200ptas. Triples with bath 6000ptas. Garage 500ptas per day.

Hostal-Residencia Murcia, C. Vinadel, 6 (tel. 21 99 63), off Pl. Santa Isabel. Take bus #11 from the train station. Rooms embellished with TVs, phones, and decorations from Sonny and Cher's heyday. Singles 2500ptas, with bath 3500ptas. Doubles 5000ptas, with bath 7000ptas.

El Tío Sentao, C. La Manga, 12 (tel. 29 10 13), near the bus station, hidden on a teensy street off Pl. San Agustín. Over 80 years and still cooking. A warm, family restaurant serving authentic Murcian fare in a colorful *comedor.* *Morcilla* (fried sausage with onions) 500ptas, *menú* 900ptas. Beware the powerful local *Vino de Jumilla.* Open daily 1-4pm and 7pm-11pm.

Mesón el Corral de José Luís, Pl. Santo Domingo, 23-24 (tel. 21 45 97). Chefs in the open kitchen toss together Murcian cuisine. Local handicrafts add some flavor. *Tapas* 150-450ptas. Daily *menú* 1150ptas at bar with drink, 1150ptas at table without drink. Open 11am-4pm and 8pm-midnight.

Casino de Murcia, C. Trapería, 22 (tel. 21 22 55). Dine in opulence and splendor, and feel like a member of an exclusive Victorian society. *Menú* for casino *socios* (members) 800ptas; non-members (that's you) 1100ptas. Open daily 1:30-4pm; July-Aug. closed Sat.

SIGHTS AND ENTERTAINMENT

The palatial **Casino de Murcia,** C. Trapería, 18 (tel. 21 22 55), began as a social club for the town's 19th- and 20th-century bourgeoisie. Rooms inside were each designed according to a particular theme. Mammoth, implausibly ornate chandeliers fill the Versailles ballroom. English billiard room offers a whiff of Pall Mall, while the Arabic patio and its multicolored, glass doors simulate the Alhambra. Look for the Oxfordian library with plush leather chairs and a gilt powder room (open 9:30am-pm; 100ptas).

Next door to the casino, 400 years of procrastination made Murcia's **cathedral** in Pl. Cruz, 2 (tel. 21 63 44; buses #2 or 3) an odd confusion of architectural styles: an oft-photographed Baroque facade, a Gothic entrance, and a Renaissance tower (cathedral open 10am-1pm and 5-7pm; tower open 10am-1pm).

The **Museo de Arqueología de Murcia** (tel. 23 46 02), Gran Vía Alfonso X El Sabio, 9, one of the finest in Spain, chronicles provincial history from prehistoric times (open Mon.-Fri. 9am-1:30pm; Sept.-June Mon.-Fri. 9am-2pm and 5-8pm on Tues., Thurs., and Fri., and Sat. 10am-2pm; 75ptas). The Museo de Bellas Artes on C. Obispo Frutos, 12, near the university (tel. 23 93 46), boasts a fine collection of Iberian painting and sculpture (open Mon.-Fri. 9am-1:30pm; Sept.-June Mon.-Fri. 9am-2pm and 4-8pm, Sat. 10am-2pm). The **Museo Taurino** (tel. 28 59 76), within the Jardín del Salitre (between Pl. Circular and the bus station), displays bullfighting memorabilia, elaborate early 20th-century posters, *matador* costumes, and mounted bulls' heads that pay homage to particularly valorous beasts. Of questionable taste is the enshrinement of José Manuel Calvo Benichon's shredded, bloody shirt worn the day he was gored to death in Sevilla by his 598kg opponent (open Mon.-Fri. 10am-2pm and 5-8pm; free).

On Wednesday and Saturday nights, local university students study the effects of alcohol at bars near **C. Saavedra Fajardo** (near the main campus). On the day before Easter the **Exaltación Huertana** starts a week-long harvest celebration bringing jazz and theater to the already crowded streets.

Just outside of Murcia, the Río España courses through rocky mountains dotted with the pines and sagebrush of the **Parque Natural Sierra España** (highest elevation 1585m). The flowers explode into dazzling color in springtime, the best season to visit the park. Accommodations range from a campsite and a hostel to mountainside refuges. Ask about **camping** at the tourist office.

■ Near Murcia

LORCA

Lorca's colorful, freshly painted train station and A stroll through Lorca, from its colorful, modern train station to its crumbling medieval castle, leads you through centuries of aesthetic and economic disparities. The march begins with contemporary elitism at the foot of the city by its transportation hubs Medieval ghettos, Renaissance artistry, Baroque vainglory, post-Franco urban expansion, and contemporary elitism demarcate Lorca's distinct neighborhoods.

Battles between Romans and Visigoths and between Christians and Muslims left Lorca without an orange grove, much less a full-fledged *huerta* (orchard). Yet each conquering force left its own peculiar imprint on the large, piecemeal **castillo** atop Lorca's central hill, a 15-20-minute walk from Pl. Espanya (open daily 9am-sunset; free). The Moors built the **Torre Espolón** shortly before the city fell to Alfonso el Sabio of Castilla, who in self-adulation ordered the construction of the **Torre Alfonsín.** The ruins of Lorca's first church, the **Ermita de San Clemente,** deteriorate at the castle's east edge. Once Granada fell in 1492, inhabitants left the fortresses and

moved to the bottom of the slope, leaving in their wake three idyllic churches—
Santa María, San Juan, and **San Pedro.** Starting anew, Lorcans erected six monasteries and the **Colegiata de San Patricio.** Of the many well-preserved private residences, **Casa de Guevarra's** wreathed columns and intricate carvings have a special
flair (open Mon.-Fri. 10am-2pm). Behind the train station, the opulent estates of **Las
Alamedas,** with aromatic gardens and red clay paths, are tucked away from the city
center around C. Lópes Gisbert.

The **tourist office** (tel. 46 61 57) in Casa de Guevarra on C. Lópes Gisbert, doles out
a detailed **map.** From the train station, take the pedestrian path, go right at C. Juan
Carlos I, left onto C. E. García Navarro, and right onto C. Lópes Gisbert (open Mon.-
Fri. 10am-1:30pm and 5-7pm). **Luggage storage** is available in the bus station (6am-
11pm, 400ptas). The **Red Cross** answer at tel. 46 70 85 or, for emergencies, 44 34 44.
The **police** come running from C. Villascusa (tel. 44 33 98). In an **emergency,** call 091
or 092. The **post office** (tel. 46 77 75) is on C. Musso Valiente (open Mon.-Sat. 9am-
2pm).

Accommodations are cheap in this arid area. Shining ceramic tiles and new wicker
furniture are the siren calls of **Hostal del Carmen,** C. Rincón de los Valientes, 3 (tel.
46 64 59), off C. Nogalte (singles with bath 2000ptas;. doubles with bath 4000ptas).
The pink-and-white, air-conditioned **Restaurante Rincón de los Valientes,** C. Rincón
de los Valientes, 13 (tel. 44 12 63), concocts a 900 or 1000pta homestyle *menú* (open
Tues.-Sun. 1:30-4pm and 8pm-midnight).

Trains toot by Av. Estació, parallel to C. Juan Carlos I (tel. 46 69 98; round-trip to
Murcia 730ptas). Next door, the **bus station** (tel. 46 92 70) runs buses to Murcia (7-16
per day, 600ptas), Barcelona, Alicante, Valencia, and points in Andalucía.

Valiant Visigoth Vixens

Lorca's proximity to Granada made the province an attractive stronghold during
the Muslim invasion in the 8th century. When almost the entire peninsula had
been conquered by the Moors, Lorca remained one of the few provinces under
Christian Visigoth rule. Eager to make complete his kingdom, Muslim leader Abd
al-Aziz attacked the dwindling Visigoth troops commanded by one Theodomir.
Suffering serious casualties, the Christian troops were forced to flee to Orihuela.
Supposing that his Christian nemesis' troops were near surrender, Abd launched
yet another attack. His machinations, however, were thwarted by a large line of
violent Visigoth warriors who bravely stood guard over Orihuela. Immediately
canceling the attack, Abd agreed to a pact with the Christians; and for many years
the province of Lorca survived as an important Christian nucleus in an otherwise
Muslim world. What the Moor leader never learned, however, was that the brave
Visigoth defenders were actually women disguised as warriors.

La Manga del Mar Menor

A geographic fluke created the popular vacation spot known as La Manga (sleeve) of
the Mar Menor. Centuries of marine deposits settled over a small sierra of volcanic origin then solidified into a 19km strip of land separating the calm, tepid Mar Menor
from the luxurious breaks of the Mediterranean. Windsurfers take advantage of the
waveless Mar Menor, while beachlovers kick it in the white sands and crystal waters
of the alternative. The two seas are only a somersault apart, and despite the 1963 Law
of Touristic Interest Centers that doomed La Manga to the architectural blasphemy
that plagues Spain's Mediterranean coastline, the strip's 40km of beach and conspicuous lack of industry are conducive to relaxing getaways.

La Manga has one main road (La Gran Vía) that runs its length. Addresses are indicated by km point (km0 is at the mainland pole), *plazas,* and *urbanizaciones* (tourist
complexes). The first 3¾km of La Manga belongs to the municipality of Cartagena,
and the rest to San Javier. The generous **tourist office,** at km0, Gran Vía, Salida 2 (tel.
56 33 55), has a detailed **map** and list of accommodations. A **pharmacy** at km1-2
posts a list of those on 24-hr. duty. **Red Cross** ambulances respond at 22 22 22. For
medical emergencies call 14 20 60. The police respond at 57 08 80 and the Civil

Guard at 56 31 14. For a **taxi,** dial 56 38 63. There's a **post office** hut in Pl. Bohemia (open Mon.-Fri. 8:30am-2:30pm).

Serma, C.B. (tel. 56 41 19) in Pl. Cavanna (Rm. 2-3) **rents bikes** (1400ptas per day) and **scooters** (3000ptas per day); open 10am-2pm and 5-9pm. The Escuela de Vela Pedruchillo (tel. 14 00 02) markets **water sports equipment** at km8-9 (open daily 10am-2pm and 4-8pm).

The closest thing to budget accommodations on La Manga is the **Albergue Juvenil Deportivo** in the Grimanga Club at Urbanización Hawaii V at km8-9 (tel. (968) 14 07 42). Bunk beds, locker room showers, and rambunctious summer campers are downers, but the front door opens on to one of the nicest beaches in Spain, **Playa de Pedrucho** (winter heating; room 1400ptas, *pensión completa* with 3 scrumptious meals 2600ptas). Also in Hawaii V, the **Restaurante Philadelphia** (tel. 14 37 15) wheels out mountainous platters of Murcian dishes (open 9am-midnight).

Nightlife on La Manga is straightforward and crowded. From 1-5am, thousands of Eurokids storm hundreds of *bares-musicales* in **Pl. Zoco Alcazaba** (km4), then hop onto nocturnal buses that run to **El Palmero,** a *discoteca* in an imitation castle just outside of La Manga. Keep an eye out for El Palmero invitations at Zoco.

Local **buses** zip back and forth along La Manga (every 20min. 7:30am-10pm, every hr. after 10pm; up to 120ptas, depending on destination). **Autobuses Gimenez Hermanos** (tel. 29 22 11) runs to and from Murcia (5-6 per day, 655ptas) and makes several stops along the strip. Longer distance voyages originate from a parking lot near Pl. Cavanna (km2-3). **Autobuses Egea** (tel. 10 33 00) runs to Cartagena (18 per day, 250-310ptas). **Autocares Costa Azúl** (tel. 50 15 43) goes to and from Alicante (1 per day, 2½-3½hr., 910ptas). **Autobuses Enatcar** (tel. 56 48 11) cruises to Madrid (3 per day), Bilbao (2 per day), and Pamplona/San Sebastián (2 per day). The Enatcar office is next to Bar La Parada, across from the bus stop (open Mon.-Sat. 9:30am-3:30pm and 5:30-11:15pm, Sun. noon-3:30pm and 8-11:15pm).

Andalucía

Andalucía derives its *duende* (spirit) from an intoxicating amalgam of cultures. The ancient kingdom of Tartessos grew wealthy off the Sierra Nevada's rich ore deposits, and the Greeks and Phoenicians later colonized and traded up and down the coast. The Río Guadalquivir (*Betis* to the Romans) nourished Roman vineyards and olive groves, and centuries later led Columbus through to Sevilla on his triumphant return from the Americas. Andalucía owes little more than its name to the Vandals, who flitted through on their way to North Africa, where they were promptly exterminated. The most enduring influences were left by the Arabs, who arrived in *al Andalus* in 711, stayed for almost eight centuries, and established a tangible link to Africa and the Muslim world. They prized Andalucía with *flamenco* and the gypsy ballads that are proverbially associated with the region. Under Moorish rule, which lasted until 1492, Sevilla and Granada reached the pinnacle of Islamic arts, and Córdoba matured into the most culturally influential Islamic city of the western Caliphet.

The Moors perfected Roman irrigation and architectural techniques, resulting in a mixture that was distinctly Andalucían. Cool patios, garden oases with fountains and fish ponds, and the alternation of red brick and white stone (as in Córdoba's Mezquita) were its hallmarks. Moreover, they sparked the European Renaissance by merging the wisdom and science of Classical Greece and the Near East. Two descendant peoples, the *Mozarabes*, or "Muslim-like" Christians, and later the *Mudéjares*, Moors conquered by Christians, made a lasting architectural impact, the former with horse-shoe arches and the latter with intricate wooden ceilings.

Spanish poets carried on the legacy of the arts after the Inquisition expelled the Arabs from Andalucía. The mystical verse of San Juan de la Cruz during the Renaissance, Luis de Góngora's elusive eroticism, and the caustic baroque sonnets of Francisco de Quevedo have influenced virtually every Spanish poet since. Federico García Lorca, the most popular literary figure in Andalucía's storied panorama, carried the tradition into the twentieth century by uttering three of the most famous verses in Spanish poetry: *"Verde que te quiero verde"* and *"Córdoba./Lejana y sola." Poesía andaluz* will always be a genre of its own, owing to the uniquely sentimental and transcendental *duende* of the Spanish south.

The dark legacy of Andalucía is its failure to progress economically. Stagnant industrialization and severe drought have mired the region in indefinite recession. Many have chosen to flee rather than face a future of indigence. In the 1960s, Andalucía lost 14% of its population to emigration; this was arguably the largest European peacetime migration in the 20th century. Residents complain that even with a university education, finding a high-class job is as probable as winning the ONCE national lottery. At the same time, they believe the good life is possible with good food, good drink, and spirited company. They are an open people, where even metropolitan *andaluces*, like the people of Sevilla, shun big-city snobbishness.

Owing to the long summers, regional cooking relies on light delicacies such as *pescaíto frito* (lightly fried fish) and cold soups such as *gazpacho*. Perhaps the most sublime of the many variations, attributed to Málaga, is *ajo blanco* (white garlic), a bread and garlic soup garnished with peeled grapes.

■ Sevilla

Springtime in Sevilla sweeps the light fragrance of orange blossoms through the streets. That mystical air has inspired a legacy of heroes of passion and sought after damsels. *Carmen, The Barber of Seville,* and *Don Juan* are only a few of Sevilla's great heroes and heroines. Never a champion of lust, Santa Teresa denounced Sevilla as the devil's work. The maxim *"Qui non ha visto Sevilla non ha visto maravilla"* ("he who has not seen Sevilla has not seen a marvel") remains true five centuries after its utterance.

During Semana Santa and the *Feria de Abril*, two of the most extravagant celebrations in Europe, Sevilla bewitches. Virgins, *matadores,* and *flamenco* dancers lead the town in endless revelry. Sevilla's reputation for gaiety is rivaled only by its notoriety as *la sartenilla de España* (the frying pan of Spain)—not even the mighty Guadalquivir River can quell the blistering summer heat.

ARRIVALS AND DEPARTURES

By Plane

All flights land at **Aeropuerto San Pablo** (tel. 467 29 81 or 467 52 10), 12km out of town on Ctra. Madrid. A taxi to the airport from the town center costs about 2000ptas. **Los Amarillos** runs a bus (750ptas) from outside the Hotel Alfonso XIII in the Puerta de Jerez about every hour from 6:15am-10:30pm. Call tel. 441 52 01 for departure times. **Iberia,** C. Almirante Lobo, 2 (tel. 422 89 01; international reservations tel. (901) 33 32 22; toll-free national tel. (901) 333 111), has an office in front of the Torre de Oro (open daily 9am-1:30pm and 4:30-7:30pm). They book flights to Madrid (3-4 per day, 45min.) and Barcelona (2-3per day, 55min.).

By Train

All train service is centralized in modern **Estación Santa Justa,** Av. Kansas City (reservations tel. 454 02 02, info tel. 454 03 03). Services include an info booth, **luggage storage, telephone office,** cafeteria, **ATM,** and a vending machine. Buses C1 and C2 link Santa Justa and the Prado de San Sebastián bus station. They stop on Av. Kansas City, to the left as you exit the train station.

In town, the **RENFE office,** C. Zaragoza, 29 (tel. 422 26 93), is near Pl. Nueva (open Mon.-Fri. 9am-1:15pm and 4-7pm). **AVE** to: Madrid (17 per day, 2½hr., 8000-9600ptas) and Córdoba (16 per day, 45min., 2100-2200ptas). **Talgo** to: Cádiz (13 per day, 2hr., 1195ptas); Málaga (3 per day, 3hr., 1850ptas); Granada (3 per day, 4hr., 2280ptas); Huelva (3 per day, 1½hr., 980ptas); Antequera (3 per day, 2hr., 1400ptas); Córdoba (6 per day, 1½hr., 980ptas); Jaén (1 per day, 3hr., 2125ptas); Almería (1 per day, 12hr., 3680ptas); Cáceres (1 per day, 5½hr., 2120ptas); Valencia (4 per day, 8½hr., 5200ptas); Barcelona (6 per day, 12½hr., 6400ptas).

By Bus

The older bus station at **Prado de San Sebastián,** C. José María Osborne, 11 (tel. 441 71 11), mainly serves Andalucía. Buses C1 and C2 link Estación Santa Justa and Prado de San Sebastián. **Luggage storage** *(consigna)* is open daily 6:30am-10pm (250ptas). As is usual throughout Spain, service decreases on Sundays.

Transportes Alsina Graells (tel. 441 88 11), to: Córdoba (11per day, 2hr., 1200ptas); Granada (9 per day, 3hr., 2700ptas); Málaga (10 per day, 2½hr., 2245ptas); Murcia (2 per day, 8hr., 4995ptas); Almería (1 per day, 7hr., 3995ptas); Jaén (4 per day, 4hr., 1995ptas); Nerja (1 per day, 4½hr., 2625ptas).

Transportes Comes (tel. 441 68 58). Open Mon.-Sat. 6:30am-9pm, Sun. 6:30am-10:45pm. To: Cádiz (7 per day, 1½hr., 1300ptas); Algeciras (4 per day, 3½hr., 2100ptas); Jerez de la Frontera (5 per day, Sat. and Sun. 2 per day, 2hr., 875ptas); El Puerto de Santa María (2 per day, 2hr., 1050ptas); La Línea (4 per day, 4hr., 2500ptas); Tarifa (4 per day, 3hr., 2020ptas).

Enatcar-Bacoma (tel. 441 46 60). Open daily 9:30am-9pm. To Valencia and Catalunya.

Los Amarillos (tel. 441 52 01). Open daily 6:30am-2pm and 2:30-8pm. To: Arcos de la Frontera (2 per day, 2hr., 905ptas); Ronda (6 per day, 2½hr., 1235ptas); Fuengirola (3 per day, Sat. and Sun. 3 per day, 3½hr., 2060ptas); Marbella (3 per day, Sat.-Sun. 2 per day, 3hrs., 1820ptas); Chipiona (8 per day, 2hr., 970ptas).

The newer bus station at **Plaza de Armas** (info tel. 490 80 40; open daily 8am-9:15pm), on the riverbank where Puente Cristo de la Expiración meets C. Arjona, serves destinations beyond Andalucía, including Portugal and other European coun-

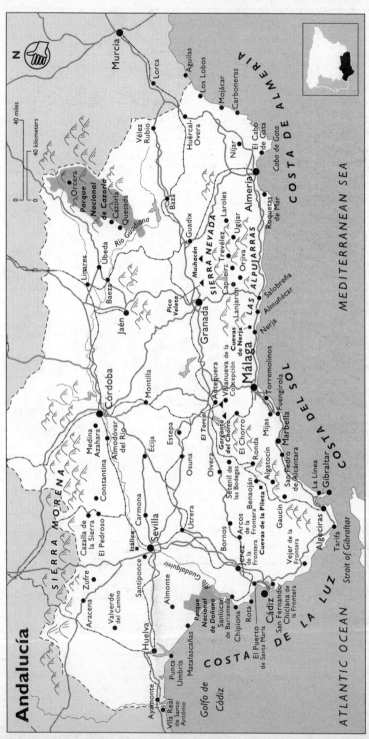

Andalucía

N

40 miles
40 kilometers

Murcia
Lorca
Aguilas
Los Lobos
Mojácar
Carboneras
El Cabo de Gata
Cabo de Almería
COSTA DE ALMERÍA
MEDITERRANEAN SEA

Vélez Rubio
Huércal-Overa
Níjar
Almería
Roquetas de Mar

Orcera
Parque Nacional de Cazorla
Cazorla
Quesada
Baza
Guadix
Laroles
Ugijar
LAS ALPUJARRAS
Salobreña
Almuñécar

Río Guadiana
Úbeda
Baeza
Linares
Mulhacén
SIERRA NEVADA
Trevélez
Capileira
Lanjarón
Orjiva
Nerja

Jaén
Pico Veleta
Granada
Cuevas de Nerja

Montilla
Villanueva de la Concepción
Torremolinos
COSTA DEL SOL

Córdoba
Antequera
El Torcal
Málaga
Fuengirola

Medina Azahara
Almodóvar del Río
Écija
Estepa
Garganta del Chorro
El Chorro
Mijas
Marbella

Constantina
El Pedroso
Osuna
Olvera
Ronda
Algatocín
San Pedro de Alcántara

SIERRA MORENA
Carmona
Utrera
Setenil de las Bodegas
Benaoján
La Línea
Gibraltar

Cazalla de la Sierra
Bornos
Arcos de la Frontera
Cuevas de la Pileta
Gaucín
Algeciras
Tarifa

Zufre
Itálica
Sevilla
Jerez de la Frontera
Vejer de la Frontera
Strait of Gibraltar

Aracena
Valverde del Camino
Santiponce
Río Guadalquivir
COSTA DE LA LUZ

Almonte
Parque Nacional de Doñana
Sanlúcar de Barrameda
San Fernando
Chiclana de la Frontera

Huelva
Matalascañas
Chipiona
Rota
El Puerto de Santa María
Cádiz

Punta Umbría
Golfo de Cádiz
ATLANTIC OCEAN

Vila Real de Santo António
Ayamonte

ANDALUCÍA

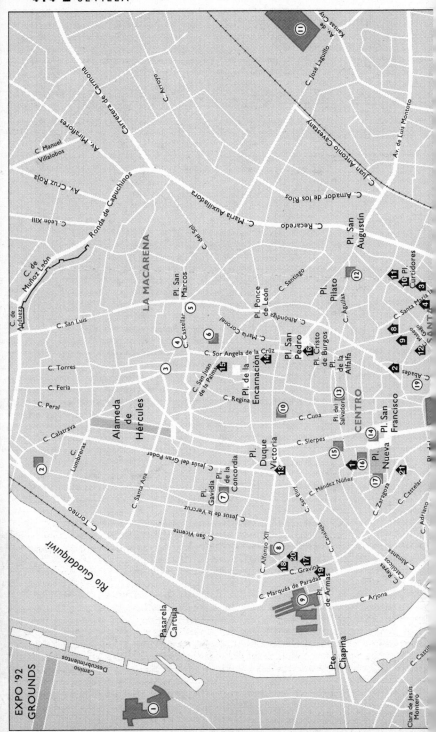

EXPO '92 GROUNDS

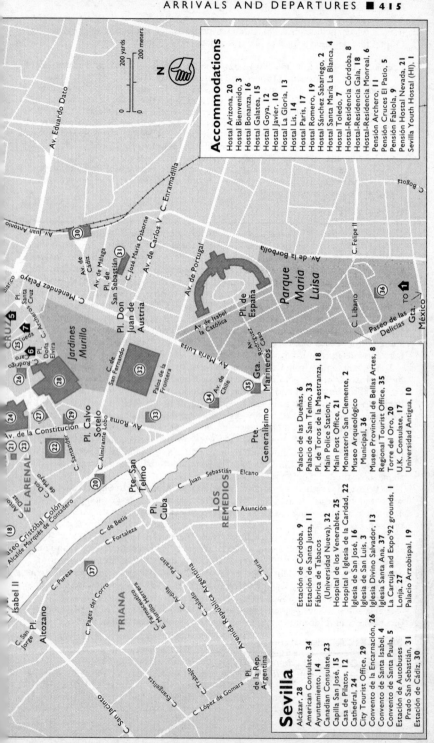

Accommodations

Hostal Arizona, 20
Hostal Bienvenido, 3
Hostal Bonanza, 16
Hostal Galatea, 15
Hostal Goya, 12
Hostal Javier, 10
Hostal La Gloria, 13
Hostal Lis, 14
Hostal Paris, 17
Hostal Romero, 19
Hostal Sánchez Sabariego, 2
Hostal Santa María La Blanca, 4
Hostal Toledo, 7
Hostal-Residencia Córdoba, 8
Hostal-Residencia Gala, 18
Hostal-Residencia Monreal, 6
Pensión Archero, 11
Pensión Cruces El Patio, 5
Pensión Fabiola, 9
Pensión Hostal Nevada, 21
Sevilla Youth Hostal (HI), 1

Sevilla

Alcázar, 28
American Consulate, 34
Ayuntamiento, 14
Canadian Consulate, 23
Capilla San José, 15
Casa de Pilatos, 12
Cathedral, 24
City Tourist Office, 29
Convento de la Encarnación, 26
Convento de Santa Isabel, 4
Convento de Santa Paula, 5
Estación de Autobuses
   Prado San Sebastián, 31
Estación de Cádiz, 30

Estación de Córdoba, 9
Estación de Santa Justa, 11
Fábrica de Tabacos
   (Universidad Nueva), 32
Hospital e Iglesia de la Caridad, 22
Iglesia de San José, 16
Iglesia de San Luis, 3
Iglesia Divino Salvador, 13
Iglesia Santa Ana, 37
La Cartuja and Expo'92 grounds, 1
Lonja, 27
Palacio Arzobispal, 19

Palacio de las Dueñas, 6
Palacio de San Telmo, 33
Pl. de Toros de la Maestranza, 18
Main Police Station, 7
Main Post Office, 21
Monasterio San Clemente, 2
Museo Arqueológico
   Municipal, 36
Museo Provincial de Bellas Artes, 8
Regional Tourist Office, 35
Torre del Oro, 20
U.K. Consulate, 17
Universidad Antigua, 10

tries. Services include an **ATM,** cafeteria, photocopies, drugstore, **luggage storage** (30ptas first day then 85ptas per day), and lockers (300ptas).

Socibus (tel. 490 11 60; fax 490 16 92). Open daily 8:30am-12:45am. To: Madrid (15 per day, 6hr. nonstop, 2715ptas) and Portugal (2 per day).

Damas (tel. 490 80 40). Open Mon.-Fri. 8am-1:30pm and 4:30-10:45pm; Sat.-Sun. 10:30am-1:30pm and 8-10:45pm. To: Huelva (26 per day, 1¼hr., 875ptas); Badajoz (6 per day, 3½hr, 1665ptas); Lisbon (2 per day, 9hr., 4350-4510ptas).

Alsa Internacional (tel. 490 78 00). Thurs. and Sat. year-round, 1 each per day to: Toulouse (21hr., 12,600ptas); Lyon (28hr., 18,800ptas); Geneva (30hr., 18,000ptas); Zurich (31hr., 20,500ptas). 1000ptas more July-Sept.

Cunisa (tel. 441 10 59 or 490 30 93). Open Mon.-Thurs. 6:30am-1pm, 2:30-5:15pm, and 9-10pm, Fri. 6:30am-10pm, Sat. 9am-3:45pm, Sun. 9am-1:15pm and 4-10pm. To: Cáceres (9 per day, 4hr., 2250ptas); Salamanca (6 per day, 8hr., 3940ptas); Valladolid (6 per day, 9hr., 4850ptas).

ORIENTATION

Over the centuries Sevilla has incorporated a number of neighboring villages, now colorful *barrios* in their own right. The **Río Guadalquivir** flows roughly north-south through the city. Most of the city, including the alleyways of the old **Barrio de Santa Cruz,** is on the east bank. The historic and proud **Barrio de Triana** and modern, middle-class **Barrio de los Remedios** occupy the west bank. The **cathedral,** next to Barrio de Santa Cruz, is Sevilla's centerpiece. If you're disoriented, look for its conspicuous *giralda* (the minaret turned bell tower). **Avenida de la Constitución,** home of the tourist office, runs alongside the cathedral. El Centro (downtown), a busy commercial pedestrian zone, lies north of the cathedral starting where Av. Constitución hits **Plaza Nueva,** site of the Ayuntamiento. **Calle Sierpes** takes off from here and cuts northward through El Centro.

To reach El Centro from **Estación Santa Justa,** catch bus #27 which heads to **Plaza de la Encarnación.** To get to Barrio Santa Cruz and the cathedral, first take bus C1, C2, or 70 to Santa Justa and the main bus station at Prado de San Sebastián. If you decide to sweat the walk from Santa Justa to the cathedral (40min.), exit through the parabolic front door and turn right on C. José Laguillo, which is past the apartment buildings. When this road ends, turn left on C. María Auxiliadora and continue 30 minutes as it turns into C. Recaredo and then C. Menéndez Pelayo along the Jardines de Murillo. At C. San Fernando, turn right. After this long block, take a soft right at the Puerta de Jerez onto Av. Constitución. The **Junta de Andalucía** tourist office is on the right; the cathedral looms a few blocks farther.

To walk to the cathedral from the bus station at **Prado de San Sebastián** (15min.), walk straight ahead towards the park (Jardines de Murillo) to C. Menéndez Pelayo. Take a left, an immediate right on C. San Fernando, then a right at the Puerta de Jerez onto Av. Constitución. Buses C1, C2, C3, and C4 connect the newer bus station **Plaza de Armas** to Prado de San Sebastián. To walk to El Centro from the **Plaza de Armas** bus station (10min.), walk upstream (right when facing river) three blocks and make a right onto C. Alfonso XII. To get to the cathedral (20min.), exit right onto C. Marques de Paradas, go right onto Po. Cristobal Colón along the river, and take your first left on to C. Adriano. This street leads to C. García Vinvesa, which then exits onto Av. Constitución at the cathedral.

Sevilla still has a well-earned reputation as the Spanish capital of purse-snatchers, pickpockets, and car thieves. Violent crime is extremely rare, but be cautious.

PRACTICAL INFORMATION

Tourist Offices: Junta de Andalucía, Av. Constitución, 21B (tel. 422 14 04; fax 422 97 53), 1 block south of the cathedral. Make this your first stop in Sevilla. Gushing staff with excellent regional and city info. Excellent city **map** (100ptas) with a detailed insert of the Barrio de Santa Cruz. English spoken. Perpetually swamped, but most crowded before and after *siesta.* Open Mon.-Sat. 9am-7pm, Sun. 10am-

2pm. **Municipal,** Po. Delicias, 9 (tel. 423 44 65), across from Parque de María Luisa by Puente del Generalísimo. Open Mon.-Fri. 9am-6:30pm. **Info booths** in Estación Santa Justa and Pl. Nueva stock city maps and bus guides.

Budget Travel: Viajes TIVE, C. Jesús de Veracruz, 27 (tel. 490 60 22), downtown near El Corte Inglés. Dispenses HI cards (1800ptas); ISIC (700ptas); BIJ tickets; Interrail train passes. Also offers language courses and excursions. Open Mon.-Fri. 9am-1pm. **Inturjoven,** Adriano, 23 (tel. 456 37 92), behind Pl. Maestranza, is good for HI cards and youth and student fares.

Currency Exchange: Banco Central Hispano, C. Sierpes, 55 (tel. 456 26 84), exchanges cash without commission and offers good rates. Open Mon.-Fri. 8:30am-2:30pm. **American Express,** Pl. Nueva 7 (tel. 421 16 17), changes cash and traveler's checks without commission, holds mail, and offers emergency services for cardmembers. Open Mon.-Fri. 9:30am-1:30pm and 4:30-7:30pm, Sat. 10am-1pm.

El Corte Inglés: Pl. Duque de la Victoria, 7 (tel. 422 09 31 or 458 17 00). 6 other locations in Sevilla. Offers **map, currency exchange** (see above), guidebooks in English, CDs, haircutting, cafeteria, restaurant, **supermarket** (basement), and **telephones.** Open Mon.-Sat. 10am-9:30pm. An excellent **map** of Sevilla, city and province, plus index (49ptas).

Public Transportation: The city bus network, like the city, is extensive but worth mastering. Most lines converge on Pl. Nueva, Pl. Encarnación, or in front of the cathedral on Av. Constitución. Most run every 10min , 6am-11.15pm. Limited **night service** departs from Pl Nueva (every hr., midnight-2am). City **bus guides** stocked at the regional tourist office, city tourist office, and at most tobacco shops *(estancos)* and kiosks. Fare 125ptas, 10-trip *bonobús* 550-600ptas. Particularly useful are C3 and C4 *(circulares interiores)*, which circle around the Centro, and #34, which hits the youth hostel, university, cathedral, and Pl. Nueva.

Taxis: Tele Taxi (tel. 462 22 22). **Radio Taxi** (tel. 458 00 00). Starting fare 350ptas, Sun. 25% surcharge.

Car Rental: Min. age of 23 and 1yr. of driving experience generally required. **Hertz,** Av. República Argentina, 3 (tel. 427 88 87), and at the airport (tel. 451 47 20). From 10,000ptas a day. Open Mon.-Fri. 9am-1:30pm and 4-7pm, Sat. 9am-1pm.

Moped Rental: You will never be as cool as the locals, but if you insist, **Alkimoto,** C. Fernando Tiraolo, 5 (tel. 458 49 27), near Est. Sta. Justa. 4700ptas per day.

Bike Rental: El Ciclismo, Paseo Catalina de Ribera, 2 (tel. 441 19 59), in Puerta del Carne, at the north end of Jardines de Murillo. 1500ptas per day (some mountain bikes available). Open Mon.-Fri. 10am-1:30pm and 6-8pm, Sat. 10am-1pm.

Hitchhiking: Not recommended. Those who hitch toward Madrid and Córdoba take bus #70 out on Av. Kansas City by the train station. This road becomes the highway. Those heading to Granada and Málaga take bus #23 to Parque Amate and walk away from the park to the highway (about 20min.); to Cádiz they take bus #34 to Heliopolis and walk west to the bridge; for Huelva bus C1 to Chapina, crossing the bridge and walking straight ahead until reaching the highway.

Luggage Storage: At Prado de San Sebastián bus station, Plaza de Armas bus station, and Santa Justa train station.

Lost Property: C. Almansa, 21 (tel. 421 50 64). Or contact the municipal police.

Laundromat: Lavandería Robledo, C. F. Sánchez Bedoya, 18 (tel. 421 81 32), a block west of the cathedral, across Av. Constitución. 5kg 950ptas. Open Mon.-Fri. 10am-2pm and 5-8pm.

Swimming Pool: Mar de Plata, C. Pablo I in Triana (tel. 445 40 85). Take Av. Republica Argentina from Pl. Cuba past Pl. Republica Dominicana and make the next right (or bus C1 or C2 to Pl. República and follow directions above). Open Tues.-Fri. 2:30-4:30pm, Sat.-Sun. 11am-8pm. 450ptas, under 12 200ptas.

English Bookstore: Virgin Superstore, C. Sierpes, 81 (tel. 421 21 11), is big. Downstairs, trendy teens shuffle among the CD racks. Virgin cola 100ptas. Open Mon.-Sat. 10am-2pm and 5-9pm. **Vertice,** C. San Fernando, 33 (tel. 421 16 54; fax 422 56 54), near Pta. Jerez. Large and diverse collection of fine English-language literature. Open Mon.-Fri. 9:30am-2pm and 5-8:30pm, Sat. 10am-1:30pm; in July, closed Sat.

VIPS: C. República Argentina, 25, (tel. 427 93 97), 3 blocks from Pl. Cuba. A modern convenience store. International newspapers and non-perishable groceries. Holds a restaurant as well. Open Sun.-Thurs. 8am-2am, Fri. 8am-3am, Sat. 9am-3am.

Women's Center: C. Alfonso XII, 52 (tel. 490 47 76 or 490 61 12; fax 490 83 93). Info on feminist, gay, and lesbian organizations, plus legal and psychological services for rape victims. Also employment listings for women. Open daily 9am-2pm.

Gay and Lesbian Services: COLEGA (Colectiva de Lesbianas y Gays de Andalucía), Cuesta del Rosario, 8 (tel. 456 33 66). Open Tues. and Thurs. 6-9pm.

Red Cross: (tel. 422 22 22), Av. Cruz Roja.

24Hr. Pharmacy: 5-6 pharmacies open each night, all night, on a rotating basis. Check list posted at any pharmacy in the city.

Medical Assistance: Ambulatorio Esperanza Macarena (tel. 442 01 05). **Hospital Universitario Virgen Macareno,** Av. Dr. Fedriani (tel. 424 81 81). English spoken.

Police: Av. Paseo de las Delicias (tel. 461 54 50). **Emergency:** tel. 091 or 092.

Post Office: Av. Constitución, 32 (tel. 421 95 85), across from the cathedral. Open for stamps, Lista de Correos, and **faxes.** Mon.-Fri. 8:30am-8:30pm, Sat. 9:30am-2pm. **Postal Code:** 41080.

Internet Access: Bar Metro Internet (tel. 434 14 01), C. Betis. Surf the net in the heart of Triana nightlife. Minimum 15min. (300ptas), 600ptas per hour. Open Mon.-Sat. 10pm-late, Sun. 6:30pm-late.

Telephones: C. Sierpes, 11, in a small alley. Open Mon.-Fri. 10am-2pm and 5:30-9:30pm, Sat. 10am-2:30pm. **Faxes** 100ptas plus phone call. **Telephone Code:** (9)5.

ACCOMMODATIONS AND CAMPING

During Semana Santa and the Feria de Abril, rooms vanish and prices soar. Make reservations months ahead if you value your footleather. At other times, call a day or two ahead. Tourist officials have lists of *casas particulares* that open on special occasions. Accommodations prices are often negotiable, so be sure to ask.

Sevilla Youth Hostel (HI), C. Isaac Peral, 2 (tel. 461 31 50). Take bus #34 from Prado de San Sebastián, C2 or #27 from Santa Justa, or C1, C2, C3, or C4 from Pl. Armas, and transfer to #34 at Prado S. Sebastián. #34 stops behind the hostel just after Po. Delicias. Newly renovated, bright, white, and disinfected. Up to 4 per room. Many private baths. Wheelchair accessible. 1300ptas per person. 1600ptas over age 28. Non-members pay 300ptas a night for six nights to become members.

Barrio de Santa Cruz

The narrow streets east of the cathedral around **C. Santa María la Blanca** are full of cheap *hostales.* **C. Archeros,** perpendicular to C. Santa María la Blanca, and **C. Fabiola** have a few options as well. Room quality varies little. The *barrio* is overwhelmingly touristed, but its narrow streets and fragrant, shady plazas are all within a few minutes' walk from the cathedral, river, *alcázar,* and El Centro.

Hostal Sánchez Sabariego, C. Corral del Rey, 23 (tel. 421 44 70), on the continuation of C. Argote de Molina, northeast of the cathedral. Follow signs to Hostel Sierpes. Friendly little hostel with antique furniture and spacious rooms. A/C upstairs. You get your own key. Singles 2000ptas. Doubles 4000-6000ptas.

Hostal Santa María La Blanca, C. Sta. María la Blanca, 28 (tel. 442 11 74). One of the few bargains in the Sta. Cruz district. Hallways decorated with cheap paintings of bullfights and provocative *gitanas.* Fan in each room. Singles 2000ptas. Doubles and triples 1500ptas per person, with bath 2000ptas.

Hostal Goya, C. Mateos Gago, 31 (tel. 421 11 70), off the cathedral. Lobby has brown leather furniture beneath a glass ceiling. Ample rooms cooled by fans. Doubles 5775ptas, with bath 6500ptas. Triples: 8090ptas; 9150ptas.

Pensión Archero, C. Archeros, 23 (tel. 441 84 65). Relaxed, friendly owner oversees pleasant rooms facing a wide-open fern-laden patio. Singles 1700ptas. Doubles 3200ptas, with shower 3700ptas.

Hostal-Residencia Córdoba, C. Farnesio, 12 (tel. 422 74 98), off C. Fabiola. Family-run. Spacious rooms and clean bathrooms. Renovations will soon give the *hostal* a two-star categorization; quality and prices will probably rise. Singles 2500-3500ptas. Doubles 4000-6000ptas, with bath 5000-7000ptas.

Hostal Bienvenido, C. Archeros, 14 (tel. 441 36 55), near Pl. Curtidores. English-speaking owner welcomes you to simple rooms; spacious doubles with balconies and small singles with big windows. 3rd fl. is oven-like July-Aug. Guests socialize on the terrace. Singles 1500-1700ptas. Doubles 3000-3500ptas. Triples 4500-5100.

Hostal Toledo, C. Santa Teresa, 15 (tel. 421 53 35), off C. Ximénez de Enciso, which is perpendicular to C. Sta. María la Blanca. Just west of Jardines de Murillo. Quiet, comfortable hostel houses researchers using the Archivo de Indios. Private baths. Curfew 1am. Singles 2675-3180ptas, depending on bath size. Doubles 5350ptas.

Pensión Fabiola, C. Fabiola, 16 (tel. 421 83 46). Basic rooms surround a plant-filled patio. Huge rooms on top floor can accommodate entire groups of backpackers. Beds are a bit floppy. Singles 2000ptas. Doubles 3000ptas. Triples 4500ptas. Owner allows 1 shower per day, included in room price.

Pensión Cruces El Patio, Pl. Cruces, 10 (tel. 422 96 33), on a street parallel to C. Sta. María la Blanca, 1 block towards the cathedral. Dim interior rooms, some with bunkbeds. As many as 4 to a room. Colorful patio is home to parakeets and two hairy dogs. Singles 1500ptas. Doubles 3500ptas, with bath 4000ptas.

Hostal Javier, C. Archeros, 16 (tel. 441 23 25). Decorated with oil paintings and prints. Rooms are well-furnished and comfortable, and fans spin smoothly. Singles 2000-3000ptas. Doubles 4500ptas. Triples 6000ptas. All with bath.

Hostal-Residencia Monreal, C. Rodrigo Caro, 8 (tel. 421 41 66). From the fountain in front of the cathedral, walk uphill on C. Mateos Gago to the 1st block on your right. A large, hotel-style place with unremarkable yet clean rooms with tiled floors, A/C, and little sinks. Restaurant downstairs with courtyard tables; the terrace has views of the *giralda*. Singles 2650ptas. Doubles 4028ptas, with shower 6360ptas. Triples: 5639ptas; 8900ptas. Visa, MC, AmEx.

El Centro

The *casco viejo* in El Centro, a mess of narrow, winding streets radiating from the Pl. de la Encarnación, is as charming as it is disorienting.

Hostal Lis, C. Escarpín, 10 (tel. 421 30 88), on an alley just east of Pl. Encarnación. Eye-bugging entry and patio with psychedelic Sevillian tiles. Large, decorative rooms, all with showers. Singles 2000ptas. Doubles 3500ptas. Triples 5000ptas.

Hostal La Gloria, C. San Eloy, 58 (tel. 422 26 73), on a lively pedestrian shopping street. Striking exterior with ornate wood trim. Flawlessly tiled floors. A/C upstairs where it's most needed. Beds a little floppy. Discounts for *Let's Go* readers. Singles 1500ptas, with bath 2000ptas. Doubles 3000ptas.

Hostal Bonanza, C. Sales y Ferre, 12 (tel. 422 86 14), in the depth of a maze—from Pl. Pilatos, head down C. Caballerizas and through Pl. San Ildefonso, where the street becomes C. Descalzos. From Pl. Cristo de Burgos, Sales y Ferre is on the left. In a dark apartment building, but all doubles have showers and A/C. Singles 1500ptas. Doubles 3000ptas. Triples 4000ptas. Quads 4500ptas.

Hostal Galatea, C. San Juan de la Palma, 4 (tel. 456 35 64; fax 456 35 17). From the west end of Pl. Encarnación, take C. Regina, then turn right. Renovated. Spic 'n' span rooms with fans could accommodate a posse. Colorful bar/patio and tiled roof terrace. Singles 3100ptas. Doubles with shower 5000ptas. Cheaper in winter.

Near Plaza de Armas

Most *hostales* on the quiet backstreets around the Pl. Armas bus station are on C. Gravina, parallel to C. Marqués de las Paradas, and two blocks inland from the station. Upstairs rooms feel like attics; downstairs rooms often have high, adorned ceilings.

Hostal Paris, C. San Pedro Mártir, 14 (tel. 422 98 61 or 421 96 45; fax 421 96 45), off C. Gravina. Brand new, clean, and classy. Bath, A/C, phone, TV. If you're looking for comforts, this place is one of the best values in town. Singles 3500ptas. Doubles 5000-6000ptas. Ask about student discounts. Visa, MC, AmEx.

Hostal Arizona, Pedro del Toro, 14 (tel. 421 60 42), off C. Gravina. Clean, attractive rooms, some with lounge chairs, balconies, and huge wardrobes. Singles 1500ptas. Doubles 3000ptas, with bath 3500ptas. Visa.

ANDALUCÍA

Hostal Romero, C. Gravina, 21 (tel. 421 13 53). Potted plants, antique furniture, and hanging brass pots embellish the inner courtyard. Mattresses are smooshy. Singles 1500ptas. Doubles 3000ptas. Triples 3200-3500ptas.

Hostal Residencia Gala, C. Gravina, 52 (tel. 421 45 03). Friendly owner. Clean bathrooms. Some rooms are windowless, but the A/C cranks. Singles 2000ptas, with bath 2500ptas. Doubles: 3000ptas; 3500ptas.

Elsewhere

Pensión Hostal Nevada, C. Gamazo, 28 (tel. 422 53 40), centrally located in El Arenal. From Pl. Nueva, take C. Barcelona and turn right on C. Gamazo, a street lined with pubs. Naturally cool courtyard. Sleek leather sofas and large collection of *abanicos* (fans). Dark, tapestry-laden rooms. Singles 2300-2500, with bath 3200ptas. Doubles: 5000ptas; 5000ptas.

Camping Sevilla, Ctra. Madrid-Cádiz, km 534 (tel. 451 43 79), 12km out of town near the airport. From Est. Prado de San Sebastián, take bus #70, which stops 800m away at Parque Alcosa. A happy medium between metropolis and outback. Grassy sites, hot showers, supermarket, and swimming pool. 460ptas per person, per car, and per tent. Children 375ptas.

Club de Campo, Av. Libertad, 13, Ctra. Sevilla-Dos Hermanas (tel. 472 02 50), 8km out of town. From C. Infante Carlos de Borbón, at the back of the Auditorium in the Prado de San Sebastián. Los Amarillos bus (the direct one) to Dos Hermanas (about every 45min., 6:30am-midnight, 140ptas). Grassy site, swimming pool. 485ptas per person and per car and 475ptas per tent. Children 395ptas.

FOOD

Sevillians offset the merciless midday sun by keeping their cuisine light. The town claims to be the birthplace of *tapas;* locals prepare and devour them with a vengeance. Favorites include *tortilla, caracoles* (quails), and *cocido andaluz,* a thick soup of garbanzo beans. Likewise, *sangría* relieves the lethargy of hot afternoons, as does *tinto de verano,* a cold blend of red wine and lemon soda. No beverage, however, rivals *la cerveza.* Defying the need for hydration and sobriety, locals imbibe Sevilla's own *Cruzcampo,* a light, smooth pilsner, whether in *tubos* (tube-like glasses) or *litrones* (liter bottles). The label's beer-bellied, feather-capped logo, *Gamrinus,* is a regional icon.

Popular venues for *el tapeo* (*tapas*-bar hopping) hide out in Triana, but avoid places on C. Betis that overlook the river—they are expensive. **Barrio Santa Cruza** and **El Arenal** around the bullring are also reliable feeding grounds. More casual still are Sevilla's bountiful markets. Buy renowned jams, pastries, and candies from convent kitchens or the stores in **Plaza Cabildo** off Av. Constitución. **Mercado del Arenal,** near the bullring on C. Pastor y Leandro, between C. Almansa and C. Arenal, has fresh produce, *toro de lidia* (fresh bull meat from next door), and screaming vendors. Merchants also hawk excellent fresh produce, fish, meat, and baked goods at **Mercadillo de la Encarnación** (both open Mon.-Sat. 9am-2pm). **El Corte Inglés** (see **Practical Information,** p. 417) has a huge basement supermarket (see above). For better prices, try **%Día,** C. San Juan de Ávila, on Pl. Gravídia, around the corner from El Corte Inglés (open Mon.-Fri. 9:30am-2pm and 6:30-9pm, Sat. 9am-1pm).

Near the Cathedral

Restaurants next to the cathedral cater exclusively to tourists. Beware of the unexceptional, omnipresent *menús* featuring *gazpacho* and *paella* for about 1000ptas. Food and prices improve in the back street establishments between the cathedral and the river in El Arenal and along side streets in the Barrio Santa Cruz.

Bodega Santa Cruz, C. Rodrigo Caro, 1 (tel. 421 32 46). Take C. Mateos Gago from the fountain in front of the cathedral; it's on the 1st corner on your right. Casual and crowded, with locals coming in at all hours to sample varied and tasty *tapas* (175-200ptas) and washing them down with *cañas de cerveza* (125ptas). Waiters

working at light speed write the tabs in chalk on the wooden bar. Mega-watt A/C. Particularly busy on weekend nights. Open daily 8am-midnight.

Restaurante-Bar El Baratillo/Casa Chari, C. Pavia, 12 (tel. 422 96 51), on a tiny street off C. Dos de Mayo. Friendly owner talks faster than the AVE while presenting tasty samples of her cooking in a room plastered with early 80s posters and images of Christ. Rock-bottom prices. *Menú* 500ptas. *Platos combinados* 450-750ptas. Call or ask in advance for the tour-de-force: homemade *paella* and drinks (2500ptas for two). Meals served Mon.-Fri. 8am-10pm, Sat. noon-5pm.

Casa Diego, Pl. Curtidores, 7 (tel. 441 58 83), a block up from C. Sta. María la Blanca along C. Cano y Cueto. Casa Diego's renowned *brochetas de pescado y carne* (fish and beef skewers 900ptas) have speared tourists and locals alike for the last 30yr. *Menú* 1000ptas. Open Mon.-Fri. 1-4pm and 8:30-11:30pm, Sat. 1-4pm.

San Marco Pizzería, C. Mesón de Moro, 4, (tel. 421 43 90 or 456 43 90), off C. Mateos Gago. Housed in a huge, atmospheric 12th-century Moorish bath house. Thin-crust pizzas drowned in chunky toppings (620-775ptas) are beautiful, but don't go if you're starving. Pastas around 795ptas. Always packed with tourists; try dining upstairs. Open Tues.-Sun. 1:15-4:30pm and 8:30pm-12:30am. Visa, MC.

Mesón Serranito, C. Antonia Díaz, 11 (tel. 421 12 43), beside the bullring. Take C. García Vinuesa across from the cathedral and continue along C. Antonia Díaz. Stuffed bulls' heads glare down on diners; behind the bar, Mary communes with hanging hams. If fresh fish guts your wallet, opt for the yummy *serranito,* a pork, prosciutto, and green pepper sub atop a mountain of french fries (400ptas). Open Mon.-Sat. noon-4:30pm and 9pm-midnight; in winter open Sun. Another locale at C. Alfonso XII, 7, near El Corte Inglés.

Texas Lone Star Saloon, C. Placentines, 25 (tel. 421 03 34). Could go so wrong but the Tex-Mex cuisine is actually delicious. Feast on the *chile relleno:* peppers stuffed with cheese, fried, and drenched in salsa, lettuce, and tomato (875ptas). A collection of American beers. Open daily 4pm-midnight, later on weekends.

Pizzería Renato, C. Pavia, 17 (tel. 421 00 77), on the corner of C. Dos de Mayo. Facing the post office, take the first right and continue through the golden archway onto C. Dos de Mayo. *Lasagna al horno* (750ptas) sizzles straight out of the oven. Several-topping pizzas will stuff you (480-750ptas). Pasta 450-750ptas. Open Sun.-Tues., and Thurs.-Fri. 1-4pm and 8-11:45pm, Sat. 8pm-midnight. Visa, MC, AmEx.

Modesto, C. Cano y Cueto, 5 (tel. 441 18 16), next to the Jardines Murillo. Come here if you don't mind spending the big bucks for the best seafood in Sevilla (1200-2000ptas). The oysters are succulent, the service impeccable. Open nightly 8pm-2am, always packed. Visa, MC, AmEx.

El Centro

Just beyond the usual tourist coops, this area belongs to businesspeople and shoppers by day and young people on their *paseo* by night.

Jalea Real, Sor Ángela de la Cruz, 37 (tel. 421 61 03). From Pl. Encarnación, head 150m east on C. Laraña, then left immediately before Iglesia de San Pedro. The Shangri-La of vegetarian restaurants. Young, hip management caters to same with lots of interesting salads and homemade desserts. Delectable spinach crepe 675ptas. Lunch *menú* 1200ptas. Open Mon.-Sat. 1:30-5pm and 8:30-11:30pm.

Bodega Sierpes, C. Azofaifo, 9 (tel. 421 30 44), off C. Sierpes in a quiet alley. Specializes in cheap, enormous portions of chicken eaten outside in a modest *terraza. Gazpacho* in a glass 150ptas. Half-chicken, bread, salad, and beverage 650ptas. Meals served daily 11am-midnight.

Bodegón Alfonso XII, C. Alfonso XII, 33 (tel. 421 12 51), near the Museo de Bellas Artes. Dark-stone walls with columns and arches. Fleet waiters sprint the dizzying circuit from kitchen to counter to you. Breakfast with non-green eggs and ham, coffee (or beer!) about 425ptas. *Menú del día* 800ptas. Open Mon.-Sat. 7am-10pm.

Rincón San Eloy, C. San Eloy, 24 (tel. 421 80 79). Waiters can barely be heard above the din of the crowd. Airy courtyard, old wine barrels, massive beer taps, and bullfight posters. *Tapas* 175ptas. *Raciones* 550-1000ptas. Spinach and garbanzo beans 530ptas. *Menú* with wine or beer 800ptas. *Sangría de la casa:* 1½L 900ptas, stein 200ptas. Open Mon.-Sat. noon-4:30pm and 7pm-midnight.

Bar El Camborio, C. Baños, 3 (tel. 421 75 34), directly off Pl. Gavidia. Standard Sevillian decorative triumvirate: the bullfighting wall, the *flamenco* wall, and the Semana Santa wall. A boisterous local crowd. *Menú del día* 800ptas. Whopping *platos combinados* from 500ptas. *Tinto de verano* 150ptas. A/C. Open Mon.-Sat. 8:15am-10:30pm, later in winter.

Barrio de Triana and Barrio de los Remedios

This old maritime *barrio*, on the far side of the Guadalquivir, was once a separate village. Avoid overpriced C. Betis and plunge instead down side streets to find *freidurías* (fish-fry vendors) and *bar-restaurantes* by day, *tapas* bars by night.

Casa Cuesta, C. Castilla, 3-5 (tel. 433 33 37), north of the Puerte Isabel II, 1 block inland. Locals speak highly of the beautiful dining room and exceptional food. A bit expensive, but worth it. *Pescado* 900-1700ptas. *Cola de toro* (bull's tail) 1700ptas. Open for lunch and dinner; especially popular on weekends.

Café-Bar Jerusalem, C. Salado, 6, at C. Virgen de las Huertas. Kick-back bar with an international crowd and inventive *tapas*. Meat and cheese *shoarma* called a *bocadillo hebreo* (bread, lettuce, roast pork, holland cheese, hebrew spices) ain't kosher but sure is tasty (500ptas). Open Wed.-Mon. 8pm-3am.

La Ortiga, C. Procurador, 19, off C. Castilla. An ecological organization operates this pleasant health food *tapas* bar/patio housed in a theater. *Tapas ecológicas* include pitas stuffed with cheese, lettuce, tomato, corn, and salsa (225ptas), all organically produced. Beer available. The group holds meetings and publishes info about Andalucían crop cycles. Open Mon.-Fri. from 7:30pm, 6pm in winter.

Freiduría Santana, C. Pureza, 61 (tel. 433 20 40), parallel to C. Betis, a block from the river. Fresh, greaseless fried fish. Free samples ease the wait. Eat *sevillano* style at a nearby bar serving icy *cerveza*. *Calamares* and *gambas* (shrimp) 1600ptas per kg. *Variado* (mix) 1200ptas per kg. Open Sept.-July Tues.-Sun. 7pm-midnight.

Casa Manolo, C. San Jorge, 16 (tel. 433 47 92), north of Puente Isabel II. Waiters in bolo ties serve all sorts of cheap seafood *tapas* (200ptas). *Pescado frito* (fried fish) 850ptas, *menú* 1600ptas. Meals served Tues.-Sun. 9am-midnight.

Café Nova Roma, C. Asunción, 58 (tel. 427 01 98), on a street leading downstairs from Pl. Cuba. Leather-backed chairs, antique furniture, and a grandfather clock in the back; up front, rows of syrupy pastries beckon from shiny glass counters. Coffee 115ptas. Open daily 9am-1am.

SIGHTS

The Cathedral, the Alcázar, and Surroundings

In 1401, Christians razed an Almohad mosque to clear space for a massive **cathedral** (tel. 421 49 71). All that remains of the former mosque is the famed minaret **La Giralda.** The tower and its twins in Marrakech and Rabat are the oldest and largest surviving Almohad minarets (its lower walls are 2.5m thick). In 1565, a Renaissance belfry and a bronze orchestra of 25 bells were added. A well-preserved stone ramp, built for horseback ascent, leads to the top.

In the middle of the **capilla mayor,** the main chapel stands face to face with a dark wooden choir made of hand-me-down mahogany from a 19th-century Austrian railway. The **retablo mayor** (altarpiece), one of the largest in the world, is the golden wall of intricately wrought figurines, depicting 36 biblical scenes. The floor mirror reflects a distorted version of yourself and the ornate dome above. By encircling the choir, you will approach the **Sepulcro de Cristóbol Colón** (Columbus' tomb). His black and gold coffin-bearers represent the eternally grateful kings of Castilla, León, Aragón, and Navarra.

Farther on and to the right stands the cathedral's most precious museum, the **Sacristía Mayor,** which holds Riberas, Murillos, and a glittering Corpus Christi icon, **la Custodia processional.** A small, disembodied head of John the Baptist eyes visitors who enter the giftshop and overlooks two keys presented to the city of Sevilla by Jewish leaders after King Fernando III ousted the Muslims in 1248. The neighboring **Sacristía de los Cálices** (or **de Los Pintores**) maintains a collection of minor canvasses

by masters Zurbarán and Goya. In the corner of the edifice are the impressive **Sala de Las Columnas** and the perfectly oval **cabildo,** or chapter house. Outside the cathedral proper, on the north end, the **Patio de Los Naranjos** (orange trees) evokes the bygone days of the Arab Caliphate. (Cathedral complex and Giralda open Mon.-Sat. 10:30am-5pm, Sun. 2-4pm; Giralda Sun. 10:30am-1:30pm. Tickets sold until 1hr. before closing. 600ptas, students and senior citizens 200ptas, under 12 free.)

The 9th-century walls of the **Alcázar** (tel. 422 71 63), the oldest palace still serving European royalty, face the cathedral's south side. The walls and several interior spaces, including the **Patio del Yeso** and the exquisitely carved **Patio de las Muñecas,** remain from the Moorish era. The latter patio displays handfans and a bed where Queen Isabel purportedly laid her Catholic head. One of the most exceptional Christian additions is the **Patio de las Doncellas** (Maids' Court). Court life in the Alcázar revolved around this colonnaded quadrangle, encircled by foliated archways adorned with glistening tilework and coffered ceilings and refreshed by a central fountain. Still more impressive is the golden-domed **Salón de los Embajadores,** where Fernando and Isabel welcomed Columbus back from America. (Open Tues.-Sat. 9:30am-4pm, Sun. 10am-1pm. 600ptas; students, senior citizens, and under 12 free.)

Between the cathedral and the Alcázar stands the 16th-century **Casa Lonja,** built by Felipe II as a *Casa de Contratación* (commercial exchange) for trade with the Americas. In 1785, Carlos III converted the building into the **Archivo General de las Indias** (Archive of the Indies), a collection of over 44,000 documents relating to the discovery and conquest of the New World. Offended by a number of unflattering interpretations of Spanish-American colonial history written by Englishmen, Carlos III commissioned philosopher Juan Bautista Muñoz to write the definitive, "official" version. Highlights include letters from Columbus to Fernando and Isabel, as well as a 1590 letter from Cervantes (pre-*Don Quijote*), asking for employment in America. (Access to documents is restricted to scholars. Exhibits open Mon.-Fri. 10am-2pm. Free.) Next door, the **Museo de Arte Contemporáneo,** C. Santo Tomaso, 5 (tel. 421 58 30), has some celebrated Mirós on the top floor (open Tues.-Sun. 10am-2pm; 250ptas, free for all EU citizens).

Barrio de Santa Cruz

The tourist office has a detailed inset map of the winding alleys, wrought-iron *cancelas* (gates), and courtyards of the Barrio de Santa Cruz. King Fernando III forced Jews in flight from Toledo to live in this former ghetto. Haloed with geraniums, jasmine, and ivy, every street corner in the *barrio* echoes with a legend. On **Calle Susona,** a glazed skull above a door recalls the beautiful Susona, a Jew who fell in love with a Christian knight. When Susona learned that her father and friends planned to kill several inquisitors, including her knight, she warned her lover. A bloody reprisal was unleashed on the Jewish ghetto, during which Susona's entire family was slaughtered. She requested that her skull be placed above her doorway in atonement for her betrayal, and the actual skull purportedly remained until the 18th century. C. Susona leads to **Plaza Doña Elvira,** where Sevillian Lope de Rueda's works, precursors of Spain's Golden Age of drama, were staged. A turn down C. Gloria leads to Pl. Venerables, site of the 17th-century **Hospital de los Venerables** (tel. 456 26 96), a hospital-church adorned with art from the Sevillian school, including Leal and Montañés (open daily 10am-2pm and 4-8pm; 600ptas, students 300ptas).

Lope de Rueda, off C. Ximénez de Enciso, is graced with two noble mansions, beyond which lies the charming and fragrant **Plaza de Santa Cruz.** Take a monumental break south of the plaza at the **Jardines de Murillo,** a shady expanse of shrubbery and benches. **Convento de San José,** C. Santa Teresa (off Pl. Santa Cruz), cherishes a cloak of Santa Teresa de Ávila and her portrait, by Father Miseria (open daily 9-11am). The church in Pl. Santa Cruz houses the grave of artist Murillo, who died in what is now known as the **Casa Murillo** (currently closed to visitors) after falling from a scaffold while painting ceiling frescoes in Cádiz's Iglesia de los Capuchinos. **Iglesia de Santa María la Blanca,** on the street of the same name, was built in 1391 on the foun-

dation of a synagogue. It features red marble columns, baroque plasterwork, and a *Last Supper* by Murillo (undergoing renovations; ask tourist office if it has opened).

The Barrio de Santa Cruz is also home to several excellent **art galleries.** Pl. Alianza, the small square at the end of C. Rodrigo Caro, houses the bullfighting-oriented **Estudio de John Fulton** (open irregularly 11am-2pm). Fulton is an accomplished expatriate artist and the first bullfighter from the U.S. ever to fight in Mexico City's ring. Some pieces are reputedly painted in bull's blood.

Sierpes and the Aristocratic Quarter

In Pl. San Francisco stands the **Ayuntamiento** (tel. 459 01 45 or 010), with 16th-century Gothic and Renaissance interior halls, a richly decorated domed ceiling, and a Plateresque facade. **Calle de Sierpes** stems from the plaza. Cutting through the Aristocratic Quarter, this pedestrian street is lined with shoe stores, fan shops, and chic boutiques. At the beginning of the street, a plaque marks the spot where the royal prison loomed; some scholars believe Cervantes began writing *Don Quijote* there.

Iglesia del Salvador, fronted by a Montañés sculpture, occupies the square of the same name, one block inland from Sierpes. The 17th-century church was built on the foundations of the city's main mosque, from which the courtyard and the belfry's base come. As grandiose as a cathedral, it is adorned with outstanding baroque *retablos,* sculptures, and paintings, including Montañés's *Jesús de la Pasión* (open daily 7:30-9pm). **Plaza del Salvador** fills up around noon with professionals, students, and stragglers taking their first well-earned *cerveza* break of the day.

A few blocks southeast of Pl. Salvador on C. Mármoles stand the excavated ruins of an old Roman temple. The remaining columns rise 15m from below street level and offer a glimpse of the literal depth of Sevilla's history. In the early 1600s, several of the massive columns were carried through the narrow streets across town to the Alameda de Hércules as part of an urbanization project that aimed at reclaiming an area that was once a lake. A few blocks east of Pl. Salvador, in Pl. Pilatos, the **Casa de Pilatos** (tel. 422 52 98) houses Roman antiquities, Renaissance and baroque paintings, several courtyards, and a pond (open daily 9am-7pm; 1000ptas). Use the bell pull if the gate is closed during visiting hours. Those interested in historical figures should visit the **Iglesia de la Anunciación** in Pl. Encarnación (open daily 9am-1pm). A pantheon honors illustrious *sevillanos,* including poet Gustavo Adolfo Bécquer.

La Macarena

Macarena is the name of both a Sevillian virgin and a popular rumba (not the one you're thinking of) which advises women to give their bodies *"alegría y cosas buenas"* (happiness and good things). C. María Coronel leads to **Convento de Santa Inés.** As legend has it, the founder was pursued so insistently by King Pedro el Cruel that she disfigured her face with boiling oil to get him to leave her alone. Cooking liquids are used more productively today—the cloistered nuns sell patented puff pastries and coffee cakes through the courtyard's revolving window.

The *ruta de los conventos* traverses this quarter. **Convento de Santa Paula** (tel. 442 13 07) includes a church with Gothic, Mudéjar, and Renaissance elements, a magnificent coffered ceiling, and sculptures by Montañés. The **museo** has a *St. Jerome* by Ribera. Nuns here peddle scrumptious homemade marmalades and angel-hair pastry (open Tues.-Sun. 10:30am-12:30pm and 4:30-6:30pm). Opposite the belfry of the Iglesia de San Marcos rises **Iglesia de Santa Isabel,** featuring an altarpiece by Montañés. Nearby on C. San Luís stands the exuberantly Baroque **Iglesia de San Luís,** crowned by octagonal glazed-tile domes. (Open Tues. and Thurs. 9am-3pm, Wed. 9am-3pm and 5-8pm, Sat. 10am-2pm and 5-9pm.) The site of the church was the endpoint of a 12-step prayer route based on the ascent to Golgotha; more recently it has been immortalized by the *Cruzcampo* beer logo. C. San Luis is also home to the **Centro Andaluz de Teatro** (tel. 490 14 93), an independent theater workshop that has produced some of Spain's best contemporary actors. C. Dueñas leads to another great mansion, **Palacio de las Dueñas,** birthplace of 20th-century poet Antonio Machado.

A stretch of **murallas,** restored since their 12th-century nativity, runs between the Pta. de Macarena and Córdoba on the Rda. de Capuchinos ring road. Flanking the west end of the walls, the **Basílica Macarena** (tel. 437 01 95) houses the venerated image of *La Virgen de la Macarena,* which is hauled around town during Semana Santa processions. A **treasury** glitters with the virgin's jewels and other finery. (Basilica open daily 9:30am-1pm and 5-9pm. Treasury open daily 9:30am-1pm and 5-8pm. 300ptas.) A large garden beyond the *murallas* leads to the **Hospital de las Cinco Llagas,** a spectacular Renaissance building recently primped to host the present-day Andalucían parliament. Toward the river is the **Alameda de Hércules,** a leafy promenade patrolled by prostitutes and other shady types at night, and the tremendous Sunday morning *mercadillo* (flea market). A few blocks west in Pl. San Lorenzo is **Iglesia de San Lorenzo y Jesús del Gran Poder** (tel. 438 54 54), with Montañés's remarkably lifelike sculpture *El Cristo del Gran Poder.* Worshipers kiss Jesus's ankle through an opening in the bulletproof glass. Semana Santa culminates in a procession honoring his statue (church open daily 8am-1:45pm and 6-9pm; free).

El Arenal and Triana

Immortalized by Siglo de Oro writers Lope de Vega, Quevedo, and Cervantes, **El Arenal** and **Triana** (across the river) were Sevilla's chaotic 16th- and 17th-century mariner's quarters. The 12-sided **Torre del Oro** (Gold Tower), built by the Almohads in 1200, overlooks the river from Po. Cristóbal Colón. A glaze of golden tile once sheathed its squat frame; today, a tiny yellow dome is the only reminder of its original splendor. Climb to the top to visit the **Museo Náutico** (tel. 422 24 19), with engravings and drawings of Sevilla's port in its heyday. (Open Tues.-Fri. 10am-2pm, Sat.-Sun. 11am-2pm. 100ptas, Tues. free, closed Aug.) On the far bank of the river, the Torre del Oro was connected to the **Torre de la Plata** (silver tower) by underwater chains meant to protect the city from river-borne trespassers. The river was later diverted to its present course (the Alameda de Hércules area was also drained), exposing El Arenal (the sandbank). The Torre de la Plata has been absorbed by a bank building, but one side lies in a cul-de-sac near the corner of C. Santander and C. Temprado.

Half a block away on C. Temprado is the **Hospital de la Caridad** (tel. 422 32 32), a 17th-century complex of arcaded courtyards. Its randy founder, Don Miguel de Marañe, is believed to be the model for legendary Sevillian Don Juan. He allegedly converted to a life of piety and charity after stumbling out of an orgy into a funeral cortège that he was told was his own. Inside, the **Iglesia de San Jorge's** walls display paintings and frescoes by Valdés Leal and Murillo. Murillo supposedly couldn't refrain from holding his nose when he saw Leal's morbid *Finis Gloria Mundi,* which depicts corpses of a peasant, a bishop, and a king, putrefying beneath a stylized depiction of Justice and the Seven Deadly Sins. Don Miguel is buried in the crypt (open Mon.-Sat. 9am-2pm; 200ptas).

The inviting riverside esplanade **Paseo de Marqués de Contadero** stretches along the banks of the Guadalquivir from the base of the Torre del Oro. Bridge-heavy boat tours of Sevilla leave from in front of the tower (1hr., 700ptas). The tiled boardwalk leads to **Plaza de Toros de la Real Maestranza** (tel. 422 45 77), a veritable temple of bullfighting. Home to one of the two great schools of *tauromaquia* (the other is in Ronda), the plaza fills to capacity for the 13 *corridas* of the Feria de Abril and for weekly fights. (Season runs March-Oct., fights Thurs. and Sun.; July-Aug. have few, if any, bullfights, usually on Thurs. Open to visitors on non-bullfight Mon.-Fri. days from 10am-1:30pm and 4-5:30pm, Sat.-Sun. 10am-1:30pm. Tours every 30min, 250ptas.)

The **Museo Provincial de Bellas Artes,** Pl. Museo, 9 (tel. 422 07 90), contains Spain's finest collection of works by Sevilla School painters, most notably Murillo, Leal, and Zurbarán, as well as aliens El Greco and Dutch master Jan Breughel. To reach the museum, walk toward the river along C. Alfonso XII, at the top of C. Sierpes (open Wed.-Sat. 9am-8pm, Tues. 3-8pm, Sun. 9am-3pm; 250ptas, EU citizens free).

On the riverbank just before the Puente de Isabel II is Eduardo Chillida's sculpture entitled **Monumento a la Tolerancia** (Monument to Tolerance). The abstract figure has its back turned to the ruins of the Castillo de la Inquisición (Castle of the Inquisi-

tion), and its arms are outstretched to embrace. Across the river is the former potters', tilemakers', and gypsies' quarter **Triana,** now gentrified, but still preserving a
cultural autonomy from Sevilla. **Pottery** studios and stores line both C. Alfarería
(ceramics street) and C. Antillano Campos; #6 on the latter street has Sevilla's oldest
kilns. Off C. Correa, two blocks inland from the river midway between Puente de Isabel II and Puente de San Telmo, stands the **Iglesia de Santa Ana** and its **Capilla de los
Marineros,** Sevilla's oldest church and the focal point of the exuberant fiestas that
take over the *barrio* in July. The terraced riverside promenade **Calle Betis** is an ideal
spot to view Sevilla's monumental profile.

Elsewhere

In 1929, Sevilla made elaborate plans for an Ibero-American world fair. When Wall
Street crashed, so did the fair, but the event bequeathed the lovely landscapes of the
Parque de María Luisa, framed by Av. Borbolla and the river. Innumerable courtyards, turquoise-tiled benches, and tailored tropical gardens send many visitors off to
siesta-land (open daily 8am-10pm). On the park's northeast edge, the twin spires of
Plaza de España poke above the city skyline. The plaza is the perfect setting for a
high bourgeois Sunday afternoon outing, evoking images of horse-drawn carriages,
top hats, puffy dresses, bottles of wine beside the fountain, and **boat rides** along the
narrow moat (300ptas per hr.). Mosaics depicting every provincial capital in Spain
line the decaying colonnade. Climb up to one of the balconies for a bird's-eye view.
Nearby, on C. San Fernando, stands the 18th-century **Antigua Fábrica de Tabacos**
(Old Tobacco Factory), setting of Bizet's *Carmen* and now part of the University.

Sevilla's **Museo Arqueológico** (tel. 423 24 01), inside the park at Pl. América,
shows off a small collection of pre-Roman and Roman artifacts excavated in the surrounding provinces (open Tues.-Sun. 9am-2:30pm; 250ptas, EU members free).
About a block toward the river down Palos de la Frontera is the 17th-century **Palacio
de San Telmo,** built as a sailor training school. Saint Telmo, patron saint of sailors,
hovers over the door amid a maelstrom of marine monsters. Across the river and
north of Triana, the **EXPO '92** nurses a prolonged hangover.

ENTERTAINMENT

The tourist office distributes *El Giraldillo,* a free monthly entertainment magazine
with complete listings on music, art exhibits, theater, dance, fairs, and film.

Movies, Theater, and Musical Performances

Cine Avenida, C. Marqués de las Paradas, 15 (tel. 422 15 48), and **Cine Cristina,**
Puerto de Jerez, 1 (tel. 422 66 80), both show predominantly foreign (i.e. American)
films dubbed in Spanish. **Corona Center,** Pagés del Corro, s/n (tel. 427 80 64) in the
mall between C. Salado and C. Paraiso in Barrio de Triana, screens subtitled films,
often in English. (Most theaters around 600-700ptas, Wed. half price, Thurs. two for
one.) For info on all three cinemas call or check under "Cinema" in *El Giraldillo.*

The venerable **Teatro Lope de Vega** (tel. 423 45 46), near Parque María Luisa, has
long been the city's leading stage. Ask about scheduled events at the tourist office, or
check the bulletin board in the university lobby on C. San Fernando. If you can't
make it to a show, at least stop by for a drink at **Casino,** the popular *terraza* outside.
In Pl. San Antonio de Padua, **Sala La Herrería** and **Sala La Imperdible** put on more
avant-garde productions (both can be reached at tel. 438 82 19).

The **Teatro de la Maestranza** (tel. 422 33 44), on the river next to the Plaza de
Toros, is a splendid concert hall accommodating both orchestral performances and
opera. (Purchase tickets at the box office in front of the theater daily 11am-2pm and
5-8pm.) The symphony was recently embroiled in controversy after three musicians
were laid off; the troupe decided to put on several free protest concerts. On spring
and summer evenings, neighborhood fairs are often accompanied by free **open-air
concerts** in Barrios de Santa Cruz and Triana.

Nightlife

Un vino risueño me dijo el camino.
Yo escucho los consejos áureos del vino,
que el vino es a veces escala de esueño.
Abril y la noche y el vino risueño
cantaron en coro su almo de amor.

[A gay wine showed me the way./I heed wine's golden advice, wine is
sometimes the stepladder to fantasy./April and the night and the gay wine
sang in chorus its love psalm.]
—Antonio Machado on springtime in Sevilla

Sevilla's reputation for gaiety is tried and true. A typical Sevillian sampling of *marcha* (revelry) begins with visits to several bars, followed by dancing at nightclubs, culminating in an early morning breakfast of *churros con chocolate*. Most clubs don't expect business until well after midnight; the real fun often starts after 3am. Women and foreigners, especially Americans, are sometimes admitted to discos free of charge. Ask bartenders or patrons at bars Capote, Alfonso, Líbano, or Chile (see below) to recommend hot spots.

Popular bars year-round cluster **Plaza Alfalfa** and **Plaza Salvador** in el Centro, **Calle Mateos Gago** near the cathedral, **Calle Adriano** by the bullring, and **Calle Betis** across the river in Triana. Summer crowds sweep towards the river in hopes of a pleasant breeze—even on "slow" nights, *terrazas* will stay open till 4am.

A trio of bars (popular with exchange students) line C. Betis: **Alambique, Múdáqui,** and **Big Ben.** On the other bank and downstream on Po. Dlicias, near Parque María Luisa, **Alfonso, Libano,** and **Chile** are popular *chiringuitos* (beach bars). Upstream, there's always a crowd at **Bar Capote,** Po. Cristóbal Colón, beside Puente Isabel II. (Open Mon.-Thurs. until 4:30am, later Fri.-Sat. Live music, DJs Wed.-Thurs. Beer 200ptas.) Farther up and across Puente Cristo de la Expiración, **Bar Latino** attracts a slightly older crowd relaxing with an evening's *copa*. **Dancing** during the summer also requires outdoor settings. A number of sandy dance floors open up in **Puerta Triana,** upstream from Triana on the old Expo '92 grounds. There is usually no cover (crowds build around 3am). **El Simpecao,** in the same area, devotes itself entirely to dancing *sevillanas*. A few kilometers out of town on Ctra. San Juan de Aznalfarache (the road towards Huelva), **La Recua** asks a hefty cover charge in return for an open-air dance floor crowded with *gente guapa* (beautiful people).

Sevilla's Cup of Tea

Got a few hours to kill before hitting Sevilla's thunderous nightlife? Bastions of Sevillian culture, the following local watering holes help ease the transition from daytime sight-seeing to nighttime swinging.

Two blocks inland from Pl. Encarnación, **El Rinconcillo,** C. Gerona, 40-42 (tel. 422 31 83), founded in 1670, is Sevilla's (if not Europe's) oldest tavern. Look behind the hanging hams for the plaque/anagram. Cheap *tapas* and *cervezas* enhance the timeless flavor. Around the corner on C. San Felipe, **Cervecería El Tremendo,** a popular lunchtime and after-work meeting place, claims to use a unique keg siphon treated with salt. It's the same beer as anywhere else, but regulars swear it's the best in Sevilla. Peruvian author Mario Vargas Llosa and Argentine president Carlos Menem hang at **Café Bar Las Teresas,** C. Santa Teresa, 2 (tel. 421 30 69), in the Barrio Sta. Cruz, down C. Méson del Moro from C. Mateos Gago, when they come to Sevilla. Ask the bartenders about Sevilla's two *fútbol* teams (Sevilla and Betis), and they'll fight all night. At **Casa Morales,** C. Garcia de Vinuesa, 11, one block from the Catedral, sit around a huge barrel and sample regional wines, *finos, manzanillos,* brandies, and other sherries (from 100ptas per glass). To be *muy sevillano,* buy fried fish across the street and eat it here.

In winter time, bar-hoppers stick to El Centro around Pl. Alfalfa and Pl. Salvador. The most popular disco is ultra-chic **Catedral,** Cuesta Rosario off of Pl. Salvador (expect a cover charge). Other popular spots congregate on **Avenida de la Raza,** parallel to the river off Puente de las Delicias. Two such clubs, **Hipódromo** and **Aduana,** admit ladies free; guys pay 1000ptas, one drink included.

Over the past several years, the **gay scene** in Sevilla has become more distinct from the general nightlife; places that used to host mixed gay and straight crowds now cater more exclusively to one group or the other. Nevertheless, the scene is thriving. Across the street from Puente Isabel II, near Bar Capote, **Isbiliyya,** Po. Colón, 2, and **To Ca Me,** C. Reyes Católicas, 25, host a mostly gay crowd until 4am. Both have outdoor tables; the latter has a video jukebox and blue neon lights. **Itaca,** on C. Amor de Dios, in El Centro, is the liveliest gay disco in town. (Shows Wed. at 1am; open until 5am weeknights, later on weekends. Knock on the door to be let in.) **Poseidon,** C. Marqués Paradas, is another option. Around 12:30am a number of hipper (and more expensive) joints start getting lively. The ambience at the bars listed here is nothing less than artistic:

Abades, C. Abades, 13 (tel. 422 56 22), off C. Mateos Gago. Notorious for its free-loving during Franco, this 18th-century mansion has hosted the likes of Plácido Domingo, princes, and *infantas.* Abades has since quieted down although the chic file in during winter and trickle in other times to sip divinely multi-liquored *agua de sevilla* (500ptas)—order first, ask ingredients later. Sit back in a plush wicker chair, listen to Mozart's Requiem, and forget you're slumming through Spain on the cheap. Summers open until 2am, until 4am in winter.

Garlochí, C. Boteros, 26, a few blocks inland (east) from Pl. Alfalfa and Pl. Salvador. A baroque den of cherubs, chandeliers, and brass-framed mirrors. House specialty is *Sangre de Cristo* (pomegranate liqueur, champagne, and whiskey served in a cut-glass goblet, 600ptas). Beer 300ptas. Closes around 3am, later on weekends.

Antigüedades, C. Argote de Molina, just north of the cathedral. A new decorative theme every few weeks (such as lifelike plastic insects, lizards, and frogs arranged on the wall by ecosystem). Outdoor tables host a mixed-age, international crowd, including a few expats. Beer 200ptas, mixed drinks 600ptas. Open weeknights until 3am, Fri.-Sat. until 4am.

Flamenco and Other Live Music

The lightning-quick stomping and footwork of Andalucía's flamenco dancers dazzle the eye and wailing *cantaores* overwhelm the ear. In Sevilla, the art has evolved into something distinct, *las sevillanas,* a dance of partners performing matador-like passes and turns, which locals have memorized as if it were law. Unfortunately, professional flamenco rarely comes cheap (unless you catch the Feria de Abril, when dancers take over the city). The flashiest show in town, catering exclusively to tourists, is on the west edge of Barrio Sta. Cruz, at **Los Gallos,** Pl. Sta. Cruz, 11 (tel. 421 69 81; fax 422 85 22). Cover starts at 3000ptas and includes one drink. Arrive early to get a good seat (and a ticket). Stores in Barrio Sta. Cruz sell advanced tickets. Half the passion of a *sevillana* comes from the rowdy, hand-clapping audience (an ambience that clueless foreigners cannot provide). High up in the Triana, **Casa Anselma,** C. Pagés del Corro, 49 (no sign), quakes with floor-stomping and guitar strumming nightly as patrons take turns dancing and singing. (No cover, *copas* 600ptas. Music between 12:30-3am. Follow C. San Jacinto from the bridge and take the 3rd right.) **El Tamboril,** Pl. Sta. Cruz, is slightly upscale with a pink interior and padded benches, but often hosts *sevillanas* and *rumbas* after midnight without a cover. **La Carbonería,** C. Levies, 18 (tel. 421 44 60), a few blocks up from C. Santa María la Blanca, was established 30 years ago to support artists and musicians who were censored during Franco's dictatorship, and has free live music on a nightly basis. Camarón de la Isla occasionally used to play here. Current acts may not be as prestigious but are at least inventive: usually flamenco, sometimes rock, jazz, or a combination of the above, performed next to cutting edge art exhibits.

El Fútbol

As if Sevillians weren't *loco loquísimo* enough over *fútbol,* the town has two first-division teams within its city limits. The pride of the Guadalquivir is **Betis,** which plays in Estadio Benito Villamarín (tel. 461 03 40), downstream on Av. Palmera. During the '96-'97 season, Andalucían hopes ran high as Betis reached the final round of the *Copa del Rey,* only to lose to Barcelona, 3-2. (The other major championship, the *Campeonato de la Liga,* is decided by final league standings and was snatched by *Real Madrid.*) Stars on Betis include the charismatic and gritty center forward, Alfonso Perez Muñoz. Team *Sevilla,* on the other hand, faced disruptive coaching changes and ultimately a humiliating demotion to second division. Followers will shift their gaze uncomfortably when they explain this. Sevilla's source of woes is the Estadio Sámche Pizjuán (tel. 453 53 53), east of Av. Menendez Pelayo on Av. Eduardo Dato. Soccer season runs from September-June. Tickets can be purchased at the stadium, but price and availability range wildly depending on the quality of the match-up. Fan(atic)s have been known to camp out at least a week ahead. Even if you can't make it to the stands, you'll likely know who's won judging by the colors worn by the sponges in the streets (Betis wears green and white, Sevilla white and red) or the waving banners and horn-blaring cars. Sevilla's fans are so wacky—even *madrileños* will readily laud the fans of *Ultra Sur*—that all international battles fought on Spanish turf are held in Sevilla.

La Corrida (The Bullfight)

To avoid the scalper's 20% markup, buy bullfight tickets at the ring. For a good *cartel* (line-up), however, one of the booths on C. Sierpes, C. Velázquez, or Pl. Toros might be the only source of advance seats. Ticket prices, depending on the coolness of both your seat and the *matador,* can run from 500ptas for a *grada de sol* (nosebleed seat in the sun) to 10,000ptas for a *barrera de sombra* (front-row seat in the shade). *Corridas de toros* (bullfights) or *novilladas* (cut-rate fights with young bulls and novice bullfighters) are held on the 13 days around the Feria de Abril and into May, often during Corpus Christi in June and early July, nearly every Sunday in June, and again during the Feria de San Miguel near the end of September. During the hottest summer months, they only occur on Thursdays. You'll know when a top-notch *matador* is scheduled to fight: hours before the big event, the ring is surrounded by throngs of female devotees who don their most seductive dresses and alluring lipstick in hopes of catching the eye of the stud. Some of the most popular Sevillian bullfighters include the aging Curro Romero and Emilio Muñoz, a.k.a. "El Espártaco" (Spartacus). For current info, call tel. 422 35 06.

Festivals

Sevilla swells with tourists during the *fiestas.* The world-famous **Semana Santa** lasts from Palm Sunday to Good Friday (March or April). Penitents in hooded cassocks guide bejeweled floats lit by hundreds of candles through the streets. Book your room well in advance, and expect to pay triple the ordinary price. Two or three weeks after Semana Santa, the city rewards itself for its Lenten piety with the six-day **Feria de Abril** (April Fair). Begun as part of a 19th-century popular revolt against foreign influence, circuses, bullfights, and *flamenco* shows roar into the night in a showcase of local customs. The fairgrounds are on the south end of Barrio Los Remedios. A spectacular array of flowers and lanterns festoon over 1000 kiosks, tents, and pavilions. Don't even dream of sleeping.

The **Romería del Rocío** (May 31) takes place 50 days after Easter on Pentecost and involves the veneration of the *Blanca Paloma* (white dove) by candle-light parades and traditional dance. The festival culminates with a pilgrimage from Sevilla to the nearby village of **Rocío,** 80km away. Hundreds of Sevillians participate in the two-day trek, accepting food from strangers and camping by the road at night. In the best Spanish fashion, the Romería is half religious penitence, half party. Singing and dancing break out around campfires, and *sevillanas* invigorate the streets till sunrise.

■ Near Sevilla

ITÁLICA

A mere 9km northwest of Sevilla, the village of **Santiponce** (pop. 6200) shelters the ruins of **Itálica,** the first important Roman settlement in Iberia. Itálica, itself born in 206BC, was the birthplace of emperors Trajan (98 BC) and Hadrian (117 BC). The Romans promptly became the town's aristocracy and the Iberians its underclass. The city walls and Nova Urbs were constructed between 300 and 400 AD, otherwise known as the *apogeo* (apogee). In the following centuries, Itálica's power declined, and by the 5th century Sevilla had usurped the region's seat of power. Archaeological excavations began in the 18th century and continue today. The **anfiteatro** (tel. 599 73 76), among Spain's largest, seats 25,000. It used to display fights between gladiators and lions and now hosts classical theater performances. Check Sevilla's *El Giraldillo* for schedules. Some buildings and streets have preserved **suelos de mosaicos** (mosaic floors). Take Empresa Casal's **bus** (tel. 441 06 58) toward Santiponce from C. Marqués de las Paradas, 33, across from the Pl. Armas bus station. Tell the driver you're going to Itálica (Mon.-Fri. 6:30am-midnight, every 30min., Sat.-Sun. 7:30am-midnight, every hr., 30min., 125ptas).

CARMONA

Thirty-three kilometers east of Sevilla, ancient Carmona (pop. 24,000) dominates a tall hill overlooking the gold and green countryside. Once a thriving Arab stronghold, it was later the favorite 14th-century retreat of Pedro el Cruel. Mudéjar palaces mingle with Christian Renaissance mansions in a network of streets partially enclosed by fortified walls. The **Puerta de Sevilla,** a horseshoe-shaped passageway with both Roman and Arab elements, and the Baroque **Puerta de Córdoba,** on the opposite end of town, once linked Carmona to both the east and west and still delineate the boundaries of the *barrio antiguo* (old town). The **Alcázar de la Puerta de Sevilla** (tel. 419 09 55), adjacent to the **Puerta,** originally served unsuccessfully as a Carthaginian fortification against Roman attack. During the reign of Augustus, the structure was expanded to nearly its current size. (Open Mon.-Sat. 10am-6pm, Sun. 10am-3pm. 200ptas, students 150ptas, under 12 and seniors 100ptas.) Opulent Baroque mansions dot the streets uphill past the Alcázar, while the **Alcázar del Rey Don Pedro,** an Almohad fortress, guards the east edge of town. In Pl. Marqués de las Torres looms the late Gothic **Iglesia de Santa María** (tel. 414 13 30), built over an old mosque. The splendid **Patio de los Naranjos** remains from Moorish days (open for mass 9am-noon and 6-9pm). Nearby, a number of convents sell their infamous *dulces.*

Just west of town lie the ruins of the **Necrópolis Romana.** Highlights include the **Tumba de Servilia** and **Tumba del Elefante,** where depictions of Mother Nature and Eastern divinities are trumped by the presence of a curious, pagan-looking stone elephant. Next door, the **Museo Arqueológico** (tel. 414 08 11) displays remains from over a thousand tombs that were unearthed at the necropolis. (Necropolis and museum open in winter only, Tues.-Sun. 10am-2pm. 250ptas, free for EU citizens.)

The **tourist office** (tel. 419 00 55; fax 419 00 80) will move to the Puerta de Sevilla/Alcázar entrance (open Mon.-Sat. 10am-6pm, Sun. 10am-3pm). For **medical assistance,** C. Paseo de La Feria, dial 414 09 97. The **police,** Pl. San Fernando, take calls at tel. 414 00 08. The **post office,** C. Prim, 29 (tel. 414 15 62), opens Mon.-Fri. 8:30am-2:30pm, Sat. 9:30am-1pm. The **postal code** is 41410. The **telephone code** is (9)5. Carmona's few accommodations are generally cheaper than Sevilla's. Take a gamble at **Casa Carmelo,** C. San Pedro, 15 (tel. 414 05 72), a vintage 19th-century casino turned *pensión,* to the right of the bus stop (singles 1750ptas, 2000ptas with bath; doubles 3000-3500ptas, with bath 4000ptas). **Restaurante San Fernando,** C. Sacremento, 3 (tel. 414 35 56), comes highly recommended (open Tues.-Sun. 1:30-4pm and 9pm-midnight; closed Sun. night). Carmona is a convenient, one-hour **bus** ride from Sevilla (Mon.-Fri. 20 per day, Sat. 10 per day, Sun. 7 per day, 295ptas). In Sevilla,

buses depart from Prado de San Sebastián. In Carmona, buses leave from in front of Bar La Parada at C. San Pedro, 31.

OSUNA

Julius Caesar founded Osuna (pop. 17,000), naming it after the *osos* (bears) that once lumbered about the land. Today there's no roar to the town. Rather, peaceful stone mansions attest to Osuna's days as a cushy ducal seat. The **Colegiata de Santa María de la Asunción** (tel. 481 04 44), the large church atop the hill, is one of many works of art commissioned by the Dukes of Osuna. Goya's portrait of the family—his most assiduous patrons—now hangs in the Museo del Prado in Madrid, but the Colegiata contains an impressive array of paintings (including five Riberas) and religious artifacts. (Open May-June and Sept.-Oct. Tues.-Sun. 10am-1:30pm and 4-7pm, Sun. 10am-1:30pm.; Nov.-April Tues.-Sat. 10am-1:30pm and 3:30-6:30pm, Sun. 10am-1:30pm. Colegiata 300ptas.) Facing the church's entrance is the **Monasterio de la Encarnación** (tel. 481 11 21). A resident nun will show you room upon room of polychromed wooden sculptures and silver crucifixes. Must-sees are the 18th-century statue of *Cristo de la Misericordia* in the adjoining Baroque church and the Sevillian *azulejos* in the sunny patio (same hours as the Colegiata; 250ptas). In the town proper, **Calle San Pedro** is decked out in palatial facades.

You can pick up a **map** at the **Casa de la Cultura,** C. Sevilla, 22 (tel. 481 16 17), a left off Pl. Mayor. From the bus station, walk downhill on C. Santa Ana past tiny Pl. Santa Rita, and continue along Av. Arjona, which leads into Pl. Mayor; C. Sevilla is to the left off the plaza. For **medical assistance,** call Hospital Nuestra Señora de la Merced (tel. 481 09 00). The **municipal police** on Pl. Mayor answer at tel. 481 00 50; in an **emergency,** dial 091 or 092. The **postal code** is 41640. The **telephone code** is (9)5. There are precious few hostel options, and they're across the street from each other. **Hostal Caballo Blanco,** C. Granada, 1 (tel. 481 01 84), furnishes comfy, cream-colored rooms with bath and A/C (singles 3000ptas; doubles 4900ptas). Osuna hides a number of old school *tapas* bars. **Casa Curro** in Pl. Salitre (take C. Sevilla from Pl. Mayor two blocks and turn left on C. Carmen), has a whopping *cerveza con tapa* deal (135ptas). Two of these will fill you up. The **Pardillo supermarket** is on C. Carrera (open Mon.-Sat. 9am-2pm and 5:30-9:20pm). Osuna is an easy daytrip from Sevilla or Antequera. **Trains** stop at the small, desolate station on Av. Estación (tel. 481 03 08), a 15-minute walk from the town center. To reach Pl. Mayor from the train station, walk up Av. Estación, which curves right onto C. Mancilla. At Pl. Salitre (Hostal Granadino marks the spot), turn left onto C. Carmen and then right onto C. Sevilla, which leads into the plaza. Trains run to Sevilla (4 per day, 1¼hr., 660ptas). Osuna is also only two stops (½hr.) from Bobadilla, RENFE's connecting point for other Andalucía destinations. The **bus** station (tel. 481 01 46), Av. Constitución, is a 10-minute walk from the center (see **Casa de Cultura,** above, for directions). **Empresa Dipasa/Linesur** (tel. 481 01 46) runs buses to Sevilla (6-12 per day, 1½hr., 815ptas). **Alsina Graells** (tel. 481 01 46) connects to: Málaga (2 per day, 2½hr., 1525ptas), Granada (3 per day, 3½hr., 1905ptas), and Antequera (5 per day, 1hr., 750ptas).

■ Córdoba

An observer sensitive of regional subtleties made the following distinction between Córdoba and her more flamboyant Andalucían sister to the west: "Sevilla is a young girl, gay, laughing, provoking—but Córdoba…Córdoba is a dear old lady." Córdoba (pop. 350,000) does indeed cloak itself in quiet refinement, a veneer befitting of the *cordobeses,* always known more for breadth of mind than festiveness. In Roman times, playwright and philosopher Seneca settled here, and under Islamic rule (711-1263) Córdoba reemerged as an intellectual and political center, producing Jewish philosopher Maimonides ("Astrology is a disease, not a science"). After Castile booted the western caliphate from Córdoba, the Siglo de Oro (Golden Age of Literature,

16th-17th century) saw poet Luís de Góngora manipulate Castilian Spanish as no one else had done before, or has since.

Córdoba's historical and cultural melange has left a unique architectural legacy. Remnants of ancient Islamic, Jewish, and Catholic civilizations are visibly intermixed. Springtime dresses its ancient facades in flowers, but, in the summertime, monuments and tourists bake.

ORIENTATION AND PRACTICAL INFORMATION

Córdoba is split in two: a modern, commercial north half extending from the train station on **Avenida de América** down to **Plaza de las Tendillas,** the center of the city; and a medieval maze, the **Judería** (old Jewish quarter), in the south. This tangle of beautiful and disorienting streets extends from Pl. Tendillas to the banks of the **Río Guadalquivir,** winding past the **Mezquita** and **Alcázar.**

Tourist Offices: Junta de Andalucía, C. Torrijos, 10 (tel. 47 12 35; fax 49 17 78), on the west side of the Mezquita. From the train station, take bus #3 (from Av. América, about 750m to the left of the station) along the river to Puerta del Puente, the large stone portal on the right. Office is 1 block up C. Torrijos. Abundant info on Córdoba and all of Andalucía. Bubbly English-speaking staff with good 100ptas **map** of monumental section. In summer open Mon.-Sat. 9:30am-8pm; in winter Mon.-Sat. 9:30am-6pm. Less crowded, but with stingy hours, the **Oficina Municipal de Turismo y Congresos,** Pl. Judá Leví (tel./fax 20 05 22), next to the youth hostel, is less useful, but gives out maps. Open Mon.-Sat. 8:30am-2:30pm, Sun. 9am-2pm; Oct.-May Mon.-Sat. 9am-2pm and 4:30-6:30pm.

Currency Exchange: Banco Central Hispano, Pl. Tendillas (tel. 47 42 67), charges no commission and gives good rates. Open Mon.-Fri. 8:30am-2:30pm; in winter also open Sat. 9am-1pm. Banks and **ATMs** dot Pl. Tendillas.

Trains: Av. América (tel. 49 02 02). To: Sevilla (15 AVE per day, 45min., 2200-2500ptas; 12 per day, 1¼hr., 890-2100ptas); Málaga (4 AVE per day, 2¼hr., 2200ptas; 11 per day, 3hr., 1535-2200ptas); Madrid (16 AVE per day, 2hr., 8000-9600ptas; 11 per day, 2-6hr., 3500-5800); Cádiz (2 AVE per day, 2½hr., 3600-3900; 4 per day, 3hr., 1960-4000ptas); Granada (8 per day, 3hr., 1765ptas); Algeciras (5 per day, 5hr., 2200-3270ptas); Antequera (4 per day, 1½hr., 1500ptas); Barcelona (6 per day, 11hr., 6800-11400ptas). For international tickets, contact **RENFE,** Ronda de los Tejares, 10 (tel. 47 58 84).

Buses: The main station, C. Diego Serrano, 14, is 1 block south of Av. Medina Azahara. To reach the town center, exit left, make an immediate left, then go right onto Av. Medina Azahara. When you reach the park, turn left, walking along Av. Republica Argentina, then go right at the gas station, cutting through the park to Av. Ronda de los Tejares. From there, follow our yellow brick Córdoba map. **Alsina Graells Sur** (tel. 23 64 74) covers most of Andalucía. To: Sevilla (11 per day, 2hr., 1200ptas); Málaga (6 per day, 3-3½hr., 1510ptas); Granada (8 per day, 3hr., 1765ptas); Jaén (6 per day, 2hr., 920ptas); Algeciras (3 per day, 5hr., 2805ptas); Marbella (2 per day, 4hr., 2085ptas); Antequera (3 per day, 2½hr., 1075ptas); Almería (1 per day, 5hr., 2995ptas); Cádiz via Los Amarillos or Comes Sur (5 per day, 4-5hr., 2120ptas). **Bacoma** (tel. 45 65 14) to: Valencia, Murcia, and Barcelona (1 per day). Intra-provincial buses depart from Av. República Argentina and Po. Victoria. **Socibus** (tel. (902) 22 92 92) provides exceptionally cheap service to Madrid (7 per day, 4½hr, 1540ptas), departing from Camino de los Sastres in front of Hotel Melia. **Autocares Priego** (tel. 29 01 58) runs anywhere on the Sierra Cordobesa. **Empresa Carrera** (tel. 23 14 01) functions in the Campiña Cordobesa. **Empresa Ramírez** (tel. 41 01 00) runs buses to nearby towns and camping sites.

El Corte Inglés: (tel. 47 02 67). Superstore on the corner of Av. Ronda de los Tejares and Av. Gran Capitán. **Supermarket** (5th fl.) and a thorough **map** with traffic directions (575 ptas). In summer open Mon.-Sat. 10am-10pm; in winter till 9:30pm.

Budget Travel: TIVE, Po. Victoria, 37 (tel. 20 43 41 or 20 43 73), books, and student discounts on train and airline tickets. ISIC 700ptas, HI card 1800ptas. Open in summer Mon.-Fri. 9am-1:30pm; in winter till 2pm.

Taxis: In Pl. Tendillas. **Radio Taxi** (tel. 47 02 91) 385ptas min.

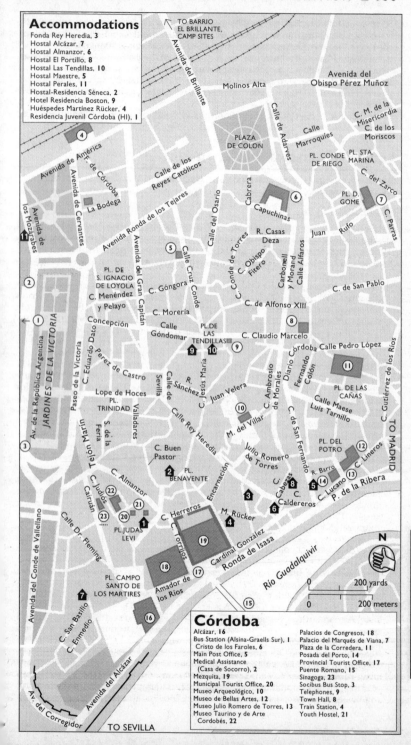

Accommodations

Fonda Rey Heredia, 3
Hostal Alcázar, 7
Hostal Almanzor, 6
Hostal El Portillo, 8
Hostal Las Tendillas, 10
Hostal Maestre, 5
Hostal Perales, 11
Hostal-Residencia Séneca, 2
Hotel Residencia Boston, 9
Huéspedes Martínez Rücker, 4
Residencia Juvenil Córdoba (HI), 1

ANDALUCÍA

Córdoba

Alcázar, 16
Bus Station (Alsina-Graells Sur), 1
Cristo de los Faroles, 6
Main Post Office, 5
Medical Assistance
  (Casa de Socorro), 2
Mezquita, 19
Municipal Tourist Office, 20
Museo Arqueológico, 10
Museo de Bellas Artes, 12
Museo Julio Romero de Torres, 13
Museo Taurino y de Arte
  Cordobés, 22

Palacios de Congresos, 18
Palacio del Marqués de Viana, 7
Plaza de la Corredera, 11
Posada del Porto, 14
Provincial Tourist Office, 17
Puente Romano, 15
Sinagoga, 23
Socibus Bus Stop, 3
Telephones, 9
Town Hall, 8
Train Station, 4
Youth Hostel, 21

Car Rental: Hertz (tel. 40 20 60), Av. América, by the train station. Must be 25. 10000ptas per day min. Open Mon.-Fri. 8:30am-1pm and 5-8pm, Sat. 9:30am-noon.
Luggage Storage: Lockers at the train and main bus stations (300ptas).
Late-Night Pharmacy: On a rotating basis. Refer to the list posted outside the pharmacy in Pl. Tendillas, or to the local newspaper.
Medical Assistance: Red Cross Hospital, Po. Victoria (tel. 29 34 11). English spoken. **Hospital de Reina Sofía** (tel. 21 70 21). English spoken. **Ambulance:** 061. **Emergency:** tel. 091 or 092.
Post Office: C. Cruz Conde, 15, just north of Pl. Tendillas. Open for stamps and Lista de Correos Mon.-Fri. 8:30am-8:30pm, Sat. 9:30am-2pm. **Postal Code:** 14070.
Telephone Code: (9) 57.

ACCOMMODATIONS AND CAMPING

Córdoba is especially crowded during Semana Santa and May through September, so call ahead to make reservations.

In and Around the Judería

The Judería's whitewashed walls, narrow, twisting streets, and proximity to major sights make it the most pleasing and convenient area in which to hunker down. Those without Ariadne's thread should procure a map. At night the area becomes desolate and a little spooky, so be cautious when walking alone.

Residencia Juvenil Córdoba (HI), Pl. Judá Lévi (tel. 29 01 66; fax 29 05 00), next to the municipal tourist office and a 2min. walk from the Mezquita. Huge, recently renovated, modern, and antiseptic. Rooms are doubles with private baths, or quads with shared bath. No curfew. 10am checkout, 1pm check-in. Call ahead to confirm reservations a day in advance. 1300ptas per person, over 26 1600ptas. Extra 300ptas per day for nonmembers for six nights to gain membership. As with all HI hostels, prices are expected to rise by summer 1998. Wheelchair accessible

Hostal-Residencia Séneca, C. Conde y Luque, 7 (tel./fax 47 32 34), 2 blocks north of the Mezquita; follow C. Céspedes. Impeccably maintained by a vivacious English- and French-speaking owner. All rooms have fans. 1000ptas for A/C. Singles 2400ptas. Doubles 4400ptas, with bath 5400ptas. Includes breakfast on the beautiful patio. Expect a 10% price rise in summer 1998.

Fonda Rey Heredia, C. Rey Heredia, 26 (tel. 47 41 82), on a long, narrow street parallel to the northeastern corner of the Mezquita. Tiled rooms with fans and high ceilings. Clean, modern common bathrooms. Singles 1500ptas. Doubles 3000ptas. Triples 4000ptas. Homers 5000ptas. All prices negotiable. Usually closed Nov.-*Semana Santa,* but call to check.

Huéspedes Martínez Rücker, Martínez Rücker, 14 (tel. 47 25 62), just east of the Mezquita. The gregarious young owner moonlights as an antique collector, and the comfortable patio and smallish rooms are his galleries. All rooms have quiet fans. Singles 1500ptas. Doubles 3000-3500ptas. Can accommodate as many as 5 to a room for 1500ptas per person.

Hostal Maestre, C. Romero Barros, 16 (reservations tel. 47 24 10; tel./fax 47 53 95). From the Mezquita, follow the river east to Pl. Potro, walk uphill and take a left (10 min.). Recently renovated. Intimate *hostal* feeling though the rooms belong in a hotel: new beds, full bathrooms, some rooms with A/C. Parking 850ptas. Singles 2000-2500ptas. Doubles 4000-4500ptas, with A/C 5000ptas. Owner also offers excellent apartments next door for 3-5 people, 7000-8000ptas. Choice of 10% discount or free parking for *Let's Go* readers.

Hostal Almanzor, C. Corregidor Luis de la Cerda, 10 (tel./fax 48 54 00), at the end of C. Rey Heredia close to the river, 3 blocks from the Mezquita. The new owner keeps spotless rooms with balconies and flowing white drapes. All singles have a king-sized bed. 24hr. reception. Free parking. Singles 1500-2500ptas, with bath 2000-3000ptas. Doubles with bath 3000-4000ptas.

Hostal Alcázar, C. San Basilio, 2 (tel. 20 25 61), on a tiny alley off the Jardines Santo Mártires, 2 blocks uphill from the Alcázar. The kind of place that makes you want to powder your nose: dainty furnishings and floral motif. Rooms with fans. Singles

2000ptas. Doubles 3000ptas, with bath 4300ptas. Generous 300ptas breakfast for *Let's Go* readers. Reservations would be wise. Visa, MC, AmEx.

Hostal El Portillo, C. Cabezas, 2 (tel. 47 20 91), off C. Caldereros, the continuation of C. Rey Heredía near the river. Another paradisal patio. Fans and winter heating. A few singles 1200ptas. Doubles 2500-3000ptas. Triples 3500-4000ptas.

Around Plaza de las Tendillas, the New City, and Camping

Just five minutes north of the Judería, rooms in this busy area offer a glimpse of bustling, modern Córdoba. In the afternoons, locals gather on its *terrazas* bordering the plaza for conversation and overpriced drinks. From RENFE, take bus #3; from the main bus station, #7. For a quick shack, try a hostel near RENFE or the bus station, on the west side of Av. República Argentina.

Hotel Residencia Boston, C. Málaga, 2 (tel. 47 41 76; fax 47 85 23), on Pl. Tendillas. Prices to please Boston bargain-hunters and amenities to please Boston Brahmins: A/C, winter heating, TV, phones, and baths. Full-time concierge. Singles with small bath 3600ptas. Doubles with bath 5500ptas. Triples 7000. Visa, MC, AmEx.

Hostal Las Tendillas, C. Jesús y María, 1 (tel. 47 30 29), on Pl. Tendillas. Respectable rooms and bathrooms. Deafening plaza revelry below. Refrigerator in the hall. Unusually enormous singles 1900ptas. Doubles 3300ptas. Triples 4000ptas.

Hostal Perales, Av. Mozárabes, 15 (tel. 23 03 25), ½block from the train station and around the corner form all bus stations. Look for the yellow sign. Old school tiles are institutionally clean. Singles 1500ptas. Doubles 3000ptas.

Pensión Medina Azahara, Av. Medina Azahara, 9 (tel. 23 34 78). Sign reads *camas.* Attractively convenient to the Alsina Graells bus station. *Let's Go* has received complaints about this hostel.

Camping Municipal, Av. Brillante (tel. 28 21 65). From the train station, turn left on Av. América, left at Av. Brillante, then walk about 2km uphill. Or take bus #10 or 11 from Av. Cervantes near the station and run to the campsite. Public pool. 550ptas per person, per tent, and per car; under age 10 425ptas.

Camping Los Villares, Carretera Vecinal Córdoba-Obejo (a.k.a. Carretera de Los Villares; tel. 33 01 45). Inaccessible by public transportation, but the best option if the Municipal is full. Drive past Camping Municipal and follow signs for 8km. 300ptas per car, 375ptas per tent and per person, children 275ptas.

FOOD

The famed Mezquita attracts nearly as many high-priced eateries as Muhammed does followers, but a five-minute walk in any direction except south yields local specialties at reasonable prices. **C. Doctor Fleming,** demarcating the west side of the Judería, is sprinkled with little *mesones* dispatching *platos combinados* for a moderate 600ptas. Students and student-priced eateries cluster farther west in **Barrio Cruz Conde,** around Av. Menéndez Pidal.

The roster of regional specialties includes gazpacho, *salmorejo* (a gazpacho-like cream topped with hard-boiled eggs and pieces of ham), and *rabo de toro* (bull's tail simmered in tomato sauce). Nearby towns of Montilla and Moriles produce superb sherries for about 150ptas per glass: a light, dry *fino;* a darker *amontillado;* a sweet *oloroso;* and a creamy *Pedro Ximénez.* Teetotalers favor the delicious and refreshing *horchata de almendra* (a bitter almond drink), and the similar *horchata de chufa,* as sweet as liquid *turrón.* Ice-cold *granizados* (slushies) work wonders on hot days. For staples, trot over to the supermercado **Simago,** C. Jesús María, half a block south of Pl. Tendillas (open Mon.-Sat. 9am-9pm). For mind-boggling selection but higher prices, try the fifth floor of **El Corte Inglés** (see **Practical Information,** p. 432).

Sociedad de Plateros, C. San Francisco, 6 (tel. 47 00 42), between C. San Fernando and the top end of Pl. Potro. Casual atmosphere and good food and drink have made this place popular since 1872. Wide selection of *tapas* 150-200ptas. *Raciones* and *media raciones* 300-400ptas. Fresh fish daily. Bar open Tues.-Sat. 8am-4pm and 7pm-2am; meals served 1-4pm and 8pm-midnight.

Taberna Salinas, C. Tundidores, 3 (tel. 48 01 35), down cobbled stairs from the Ayuntamiento. Waiters dash around the indoor fountain with traditional *cordobés* cooking. Superb *salmorejo* and eye-popping spinach-garbanzo mash. *Raciones* 600-700ptas. Beer 125ptas. Open Mon.-Sat. noon-4pm and 8pm-midnight.

Taberna San Miguel, Pl. San Miguel, 1 (tel. 47 83 28), 1 block north of Pl. Tendillas. Another classic *tapas* joint with bullfighting decor, always packed during lunchtime. Ask for their card, a name-tag which reads, "I am partying. If you find me somewhere, please return me to the following address...". *Tapas* 230-265ptas, *raciones* 750-1500ptas. Open Mon.-Sat. noon-4pm and 8pm-midnight. Closed Aug.

Mesón San Basilio, C. San Basilio, 19 (tel. 29 70 07), west of the Alcázar. The cool, breezy patio is so relaxing that the simulated bird chirping almost sounds authentic. Scrumptious *revuelta de ajetes, salmón, y gambas* (scrambled eggs with green beans, salmon, and shrimp; 800ptas). *Menú* (900ptas) served Mon.-Fri. Open 12:30-4pm and 8pm-midnight; in winter noon-4pm and 7-11:30pm.

El Pincantón, C. F. Ruano, 19, one block east of the top of C. Judíos. The selection in this little room includes nothing above 300ptas, making it a perennial favorite among young locals. Specializes in *salsas picantes* with names like *mala leche,* sour milk or sour person, depending on the context. Huge *bocadillos* 150-250ptas. Beer 100ptas. Open daily 10am-2pm and 8pm-midnight.

Halal, C. Rey Heredia, 28. With a working mosque upstairs, there's no alcohol allowed downstairs in the cushioned den or peaceful patio. Instead, the thirsty huddle around freshly-made *batidos* (shakes) of fruit or nuts (250-300ptas). *Té* and *infusiones* 150-300ptas. Open daily 4-11pm.

Oh Mamma Mia, C. Reyes Católicos, 5 (tel. 47 00 52), off Av. del Gran Capitán. Kids may overrun this popular chain restaurant, but it maintains high standards; every pizza is a work of art. Pictures of Leonardo da Vinci and other great Italians grace the walls. *Margarita* (plain pizza) 500ptas; delectable *aubergine* pizza 725ptas. Pastas 700ptas. Open daily 1-4pm and 8-11:30pm.

Bodega Guzmán, C. Judíos, 7 (tel. 29 60 09), half a block north of the synagogue. A wine cellar decorated with barrels, bullfight posters, and mosaics. Frequented by retired men who sit for hours, talking and drinking house wines. Hardcore *andaluz.* Beer 120ptas, half-glass of wine 80-120ptas. Reasonably priced *tapas* and *raciones.* Open Fri.-Wed. 11:15am-3:30pm and 8pm-midnight.

Mesón Paco, C. San Basilio, 25 (tel. 29 90 33). Look for the huge *cigüeña* (stork) nest atop the church. Outdoor dining in the quiet plaza. Gazpacho 150ptas. *Raciones* 600ptas. Open daily 9am-midnight.

SIGHTS

La Mezquita

Built in 784 AD on the site of a Visigoth basilica during Sultan Abderramán's reign, Córdoba's **Mezquita** (tel. 47 05 12) was intended to surpass all other mosques in grandeur. Over the next two centuries, the architectural masterpiece was enlarged to cover an area equivalent to several city blocks, making it the largest mosque in the Islamic world at the time. The 14th-century Mudéjar door, **La Puerta del Perdón,** opens to the northwest. Visitors enter through the **Patio de los Naranjos,** an arcaded courtyard featuring carefully spaced orange trees, palm trees, and fountains (open to the public all day). Inside, 850 pink and blue marble, alabaster, and stone columns— no two the same height—support hundreds of red and white striped two-tiered arches. At the far end of the Mezquita, in the extension made by Al-Hakam II, lies the **Capilla Villaviciosa,** where Caliphal vaulting, greatly influential in later Spanish architecture, appears for the first time. In the center, the **Mihrab** was the naturally lit central dome where the Muslims guarded the Koran. Its prayer arch faces Mecca. The intricate gold, pink, and blue marble Byzantine mosaics shimmering across its arches were given by the Emperor Constantine VII to the *cordobés* caliphs. His gift is estimated to weigh close to 35 tons.

The Christians converted the Mezquita into a church when they conquered Córdoba in 1236. The **Capilla Mayor** (High Chapel) was enlarged in 1384, but in 1523, Bishop Alonso Manrique, an ally of Carlos V, proposed plans for a full-blown Renais-

sance cathedral which would rise out of the center of the mosque. The town rallied violently against this decision, promising a swift and painful death for any worker who helped tear down the Mezquita. Nevertheless, within a century the Christians erected the towering **Crucero** and **Coro** (transept and choir dome), which combines all major Renaissance styles of the epoch. Even Carlos V lamented the befoulment of the Mezquita. He griped, "You have destroyed something unique to create something commonplace." (Open Mon.-Sat. 10am-7pm, Sun. 3:30-7pm; Oct.-March Mon.-Sat. 10am-6:30pm, Sun. 3:30-5:30pm. 750ptas, ages 8-11 350ptas; same ticket valid for Museo Diocesano de Bellas Artes. Free during mass, held weekdays 8:30-10am and Sun. 9:30am-1:30pm.)

In and around the Judería

Tucked away downhill from the Moorish arch, the **Sinagoga,** C. Judíos, 20 (tel. 20 29 28) is a solemn reminder of the 1492 expulsion of the Jews. It is one of Spain's few remaining Jewish temples, decorated with Mozarabic patterns and Hebrew inscriptions from the psalms. (Open Tues.-Sat. 10am-2pm and 3:30-5:30pm, Sun. 10am-1:30pm. 50ptas; free for EU.) The statue of **Maimonides** on C. Doctor Fleming was used as the model for the New Israeli Shekel. Half a block down C. Judíos to the left is **El Zoco,** a beautiful courtyard with leather, ceramics, and silversmithing workshops (open Mon.-Sat. 10am-2pm and 5-8pm, Sun. 10am-2pm).

Just west of the Mezquita along the river lies the **Alcázar** (tel. 42 01 51), constructed for the Catholic Monarchs in 1328 during the *Reconquista*. Between 1492 and 1821 it served as a headquarters for the Inquisition. Its walls enclose a manicured hedge garden with flower beds, terraced goldfish ponds, fountains, and palm trees. Inside, the **museum** displays 1st-century Roman mosaics and a 3rd-century Roman marble sarcophagus. (Open Tues.-Sat. 10am-2pm and 6-8pm, Sun. 9:30am-3pm; Oct.-April Tues.-Sat. 10am-2pm and 4:30-6:30pm, Sun. 9:30am-3pm. Illuminated gardens open 8pm-midnight. 425ptas, 1050ptas combined ticket to the Alcázar and the Museo Taurino. Fri. free.)

The **Museo Taurino y de Arte Cordobés** (tel. 20 10 56), Pl. Maimonides, recounts lore of *la lidia,* with galleries full of heads of bulls that killed matadors and other unfortunates and shrines to legendary Cordoban *toreros*. (Open Tues.-Sat. 10am-2pm and 6-8pm, Sun. 9:30am-3pm; Oct.-April Mon.-Sat. 10am-2pm and 5-7pm, Sun. 9:30am-3pm. 425ptas, joint admission with Alcázar and Museo Julio Romero 1050ptas. Fri. free). Across from the Mezquita, the **Museo Diocesano de Bellas Artes** (tel. 47 93 75), C. Torrijos, in a splendid 17th-century palace, displays the works of 13th-18th-century local artists. (Open Mon.-Fri. 10:30am-2pm and 4-6:30pm, Sat. 9:30am-1:30pm; Oct.-April Mon.-Fri. 9:30am-1:30pm and 3:30-5:30pm, Sat. 9:30am-1:30pm. 150ptas. Free with entrance to Mezquita.)

Townspeople take great pride in their traditional *patios,* many dating from Roman times. These open-air courtyards—tranquil pockets of orange and lemon trees, flowers, and fountains, flourish in the old quarter. Among the streets of exceptional beauty are **Calleja del Indiano,** off C. Fernández Ruano at Pl. Angel Torres, and the aptly named **Calleja de Flores,** off C. Blanco Belmonte.

Elsewhere

The **Museo de Bellas Artes** (tel. 47 33 45), Pl. Potro, 5-10 minutes east of the Mezquita, now occupies the building that was once King Fernando and Queen Isabel's Charity Hospital. Its small collection displays a couple of canvasses by Cordoban "primitives." (Open Tues.-Sat. 9am-2:30pm and 6-8pm, Sun. 10am-1:30pm; mid-Sept. to mid-June Tues.-Sat. 10am-2pm and 5-7pm, Sun. 10am-1:30pm. 250ptas, EU citizens free.) Housed in the same building, the **Museo Julio Romero de Torres** (tel. 49 19 09) exhibits the Romero's sensual portraits of Cordoban women. (Open Tues.-Sat. 10am-2pm and 6-8pm, Sun. 9:30am-3pm; Oct.-April Tues.-Sat. 10am-2pm and 5-7pm, Sun. 9:30am-3pm. 425ptas, free Tues. or Fri., check with tourist office. Admittance stops ½hr. before closing time.) Facing the museums is the **Posada del Potro,** a 14th-

century inn mentioned in *Don Quijote* that now contains the collection of *guadameciles* formerly held in the Museo Taurino.

The **Museo Arqueológico** (tel. 47 40 11), Pl. Paz, several blocks northeast of the Mezquita. Housed in a Renaissance mansion, the museum contains a chronological exhibit of tools, ceramics, statues, coins, jewelry, and sarcophagi. (Open Tues.-Sat. 10am-1:30pm and 6-8pm, Sun. 10am-1:30pm; mid-Sept. to mid-June Tues.-Sat. 10am-2pm and 5-7pm, Sun. 10am-1:30pm. 250ptas, EU citizens free.)

Those who share the city's passion for gardens can find bliss a 20-minute walk northeast of the Mezquita to the **Palacio del Marqués de Viana**, Pl. Don Gome, 2 (tel. 48 01 34). The elegant 14th-century mansion wins the grand patio award—fourteen stately specimens complete with sprawling gardens and fountains. (Open Mon.-Tues. and Thurs.-Sat. 9am-2pm, Sun. 10am-2pm; Oct.-May Mon.-Tues. and Thurs.-Sat. 10am-1pm and 4-6pm, Sun. 10am-2pm. 400ptas, children 200ptas. Patio only 200ptas. Free Thurs.) West of the Palacio del Marqués de Viana in Pl. Capuchinos (a.k.a. Pl. Dolores), is the **Cristo de los Faroles** (Christ of the Lanterns), one of the most famous religious shrines in Spain, and frequently the site of all-night vigils.

ENTERTAINMENT

Pick up a free copy of *La Guía de Ocio,* a monthly guide to cultural events, at the tourist office. Unfortunately, good (cheap) **flamenco** isn't easy to come by in Córdoba. Hordes of tourists flock to the **Tablao Cardenal,** C. Torrijos, 10 (tel. 48 33 20), facing the Mezquita, where big names flaunt their hips with intense proximity to the audience. (Reserve seats in the tourist office. Shows Tues.-Sat. 10:30pm. 2800ptas, includes 1 drink.) For classical or traditional music, the **Palacio de Viana** has free chamber music concerts on Fridays at 8:30pm during the summer. The city's open-air theater hosts concerts and festivals, including the irregularly scheduled **Festival Internacional de Guitarra** (tel. 48 02 37 or 48 06 44) in June or July. For **info** and tickets stop by the F.P.M. Gran Teatro, Av. Gran Capitán, 3 (tickets 400-1800ptas).

From the first weekend of June till the heat subsides, the **Brillante barrio** uphill from and north of Av. America is the place to be—the Sierra is cool, the beer is cold, and the prices fall to near zero. Bus #10 goes there from RENFE until about 11pm; a cab costs 500-900ptas. Around 4am, Cordoban youth climb even higher into the mountains to reach **Kachao,** a huge disco and *terraza* that hops past dawn. It is a few kilometers outside the city along Ctra. Santa María de Trassierra. The disco's name occasionally changes, so ask around (no cover and the snooty bouncers look kindly upon foreigners). The city has tried to divert revelers to the **Recinto Ferial** (a.k.a. **El Arenal**). The sandy fairground along the river is most efficiently accessible from the Mezquita by crossing the Puente Romano, cutting across the peninsula, and taking Puente del Arenal to the other bank. The *terraza* and discos here are sometimes lively, but usually flooded by *cordobeses* shouldering coolers and cook-out equipment. In the winter, pubs around **Plaza de las Tendillas** are a safe bet, but students also lounge around the bars and lawns of barrio **Ciudad Jardín,** the area south of RENFE between the Plaza de Toros and Po. Victoria.

Of Córdoba's festivals, floats and parades make **Semana Santa** the most extravagant. **May is a never-ending party.** During the **Festival de los Patios,** in the first two weeks of the month, the city erupts with classical music concerts, *flamenco* dances, and a city-wide decorated *patio* contest (don't forget to ask the owners of your hostel how theirs ranked). Late May brings the week-long **Feria de Nuestra Señora de la Salud** (commonly known as *La Feria*), for which thousands of Cordoban women don colorful, traditional apparel. A carnival, dozens of stands, lively dancing, and non-stop drinking keep spirits blithe for the entire week. In early September, Córdoba celebrates its patroness with the **Feria de Nuestra Señora de la Fuensanta.** The **Concurso Nacional de Arte Flamenco** (National Flamenco Contest) is held every third year during May. The next one will be in 1998.

■ Near Córdoba

MEDINA AZAHARA AND ALMODÓVAR DEL RÍO

Built in the **Sierra Morena** by Abderramán III for his favorite wife, Azahara, this 10th-century medina was considered one of the greatest palaces of its time. It was divided into three terraces: one for the palace, another for the servants' living quarters, and a third for a garden and almond grove. Displaced from Granada, Azahara missed the Sierra Nevada, so when springtime came she had blossoming almond groves to supplant her beloved snow. The site, long thought to be mythical, was discovered and excavated in 1944. Today it is one of Spain's most impressive archaeological finds. The **Salón de Abd al-Rahman III** (tel. 32 91 30), on the lower terraces, is being restored to its original intricate and geometrical beauty. (Open May-June 14 Tues.-Sat. 10am-2pm and 6-8:30pm, Sun. 10am-2pm; June 15-Sept. 15 Mon.-Sat. 10am-1:30pm and 6-8:30pm, Sun. 10am-1:30pm; Sept. 16-April Mon.-Sat. 10am-2pm and 4-6:30pm, Sun. 10am-2pm. 250ptas, EU citizens free.)

Reaching Medina Azahara takes some effort. Call ahead to make sure it's open. The **O-I bus** (info tel. 25 57 00, or see list in the tourist office) leaves from Av. República Argentina in Córdoba for Cruce Medina Azahara, stopping 3km from the site (about every hr. daily 6:30am-10:30pm, 100ptas). From the bus stop, it's about a 35-minute walk (mostly uphill), and the path ain't shady. A **taxi** costs about 800ptas one way.

Thirteen kilometers from Córdoba on the rail to Sevilla, the impenetrable **castillo** at **Almodóvar del Río** crowns a solitary, rocky mount commanding a tremendous view of the countryside and the village's downward spiral of whitewashed houses. On the second Sunday in May, the town celebrates the **Romería de la Virgen de Fátima** with a parade from Cuatro Caminos to Fuen Real Bajo roads. RENFE runs trains to Almodóvar del Río from Córdoba (5 per day, last train back at 4pm, 15-20min., 225ptas).

■ Jaén

The hills near Jaén are streaked with olive trees and wheat fields. Unfortunately, the bustling olive capital of Spain offers barely a glimpse of these amid its steep and narrow streets, crowded with shops, people, and cars. Jaén possesses little in the way of unique sights or tourist resources, but may be a necessary stopover for landlopers heading southbound.

Orientation and Practical Information Jaén lies 105km north of Granada and 57km southwest of Úbeda. The town centers around **Plaza de la Constitución,** roaring with autos and mopeds. **Calle Bernabé Soriano** leads uphill from the plaza to the cathedral and old section of town. **Calle Roldán y Marín** and **Calle Virgen** head downhill and become **Paseo de la Estacíon** and **Avenida de Madrid,** respectively. To reach the town center from the bus station, exit where the buses arrive and follow Av. Madrid uphill to Pl. Constitución (5min.). From the train station, follow Po. Estación, which turns into C. Roldán y Marín, into the main square. It's a 25-minute walk that can be cut short by the #1 bus along Po. Estación (85ptas).

The **tourist office,** C. Arquitecto Berges, 1 (tel./fax 22 27 37), is off C. Roldán y Marín, on the left when heading downhill. They offer information on sights and accommodations, and a **map** for 100ptas (open Mon.-Fri. 8:30am-2:30pm, Sat. 10:30am-1pm). **Taxis** gather outside the bus station (tel. 25 10 26) and Pl. Constitución (tel. 26 50 17). The **pharmacy** fills prescriptions half a block downhill from Pl. Constitución on Po. Estación (open Mon.-Fri. 9am-2pm and 5-8pm). **El Corte Inglés,** C. de Roldán y Marín, 2, stocks everything under the sun, and sells a good **map** for 475ptas (tel. 24 26 81; open 10am-9:30pm). The **Red Cross** answers (tel. 25 15 40). The **Police** answer (tel. 21 91 05). Call 091 or 092 in an **emergency.** The **post office,** Pl. Jardinillos, s/n (tel. 19 08 09), is down C. San Clemente (open Mon.-Sat. 8:30am-2:30pm). The **postal code** is 23001, the **telephone code** (9)53.

Trains (tel. 27 02 02) leave from Po. Estación at the bottom of the slope and connect with: Madrid (4 per day, 4-5hr., 2885ptas); Sevilla (1 per day, 3hr., 2125ptas); and Córdoba (1 per day, 1½hr., 1105ptas). **Buses,** Pl. Coca de la Piñera (tel. 25 50 14), are the most convenient transport to destinations within Andalucía. To get to the station from Pl. Constitución, walk three blocks downhill on C. Virgen/Av. Madrid. Buses go to: Úbeda (10 per day, 30min., 535ptas); Baeza (10 per day, 1hr., 445ptas); Cazorla (3 per day, 2hr., 930ptas); Granada (13 per day, 1½hr., 900ptas); Málaga (4 per day, 3hr., 2010ptas).

Accommodations and Food Quality budget beds are scarce in Jaén. The **Hostal La Española,** C. Bernardo López, 9 (tel. 23 02 54), is a treat for its quirky interior decorating. Vines canopy the dining room and a vertiginously slanting staircase spirals its way upwards. Everything exudes antiquity and, unfortunately, so do the saggy beds (singles 1600ptas; doubles 3500ptas, with bath 4000ptas). To get there, follow the street across from the cathedral's side entrance and take a left onto the alley Bernardo López. More mainstream is **Pensión Carlos V,** Av. Madrid, 4 (tel. 22 20 91), downhill from Pl. Constitución. (singles 2200ptas, doubles 3200ptas).

C. Nueva, a pedestrian street down C. Roldán y Marín to the right offers several palatable options. **Bar Pitufos** (Smurfs), C. Nueva, 2 (tel. 24 26 82), is a good place for a *caña* (smurf-sized beer 125ptas). The daytime *menú a la casera* (traditional) costs 1050ptas. **Yucatán,** Bernabé Soriano, 1 (tel. 24 17 28), has tasty hot and cold *bocadillos,* burgers (200-400ptas), and *platos combinados* (700ptas). Tables outside fill up after dark during prime people watching hours (open daily 8am-2am). Supermarket **Simago,** C. San Clement, 7-9 (tel. 24 31 02), off Pl. Constitución, is reliable.

Sights and Entertainment The **Catedral de Santa María,** uphill from Pl. Constitución on C. Bernabé Soriano, was built between 1492 and 1802. The lifelike *Imagen de Nuestro Padre Jesús,* behind the altar, reportedly saved the cathedral from destruction during the mass burning of churches in 1931 (open 8:30am-1pm and 4:30-7pm; free). The **Museo de la Catedral** displays sculptures by Martínez Montañés and canvases by Alonso Cano (open Sat.-Sun. 11am-1pm; free).

Jaén's most imposing and least accessible sight is the **Castillo de Santa Catalina** (tel. 21 91 16), a 3km climb from the center of town. From the cathedral, take C. Maestra, which leads to C. Madre de Dios which continues to C. San Lorenzo. Take a left when you reach the Carretera de Circumvalación, which becomes Carretera a Neveral and leads to the castle. This former Arab fortress now houses a four-star *parador.* If you don't feel like walking, a cab ride to the *castillo* from the bus station costs about 900ptas (open Mon.-Sun. 10am-2pm, closed Wed.; free).

The **Palacio de Villadompardo** (tel. 23 62 92), in Pl. Santa Luisa Marillac, is a Renaissance edifice containing Arab baths. The recently restored 11th-century *hamman* (baths), though not as elaborate as the baths of Granada, are Spain's largest. Follow C. Meastra from the cathedral to C. Martínez Molina. (Open Tues.-Fri. 10am-2pm and 5-8pm, Sat.-Sun. 10:30am-2pm. 100ptas. Free with passport number.)

Posters outside of **Palacio Municipal de Cultura,** C. Maestra, 18, uphill from the cathedral, advertise performances of Andalucían music groups. Across the street, the centuries-old **Peña Flamenca Jaén,** C. Maestra, 11 (tel. 23 17 10) serves up drinks and flamenco, indoors and out. **Del Posito,** a cafe bar tucked in a small plaza below Yucatán, has the hippest outdoor tables in town.

■ Near Jaén

The idyllic towns of northern Andalucía are beautiful and relatively tourist-free. Numerous whitewashed villages and ruins dot the mountainous countryside to the east and south. **Quesada,** 15km south of Cazorla, has Roman, Islamic, and Christian ruins. **Orcera,** less than 100km east of Úbeda, is a traditional highland village devoted to the wood trade. These towns are surrounded by the national parks of the Sierras de Cazorla y Segura. Alsina Graells has one **bus** per day to Orcena (3hr., 1395ptas) and

Muñez has four per day to Quesada (1½hr., 830ptas), making these spots reasonable day-trips from Jaén.

■ Baeza

Baeza merrily bathes under the Andalusian sun while overlooking the olive tree-covered valley of the Guadalquivir River. Once a capital of a *taifas* (Arabic kingdom) and later the first Andalucían town to fall during the Christian Reconquest, uncorrupted Baeza does not suffer from tourist infiltration, but has few lodging options for night-stays. Those virtuous few who spend the day here will satisfy their quest for quintessential Spain. Poet Antonio Machado found inspiration in the town's exceptionally well-preserved medieval streets and monuments, expecting to long for Baeza's charm even after his death: *"Campo de Baeza, soñaré contigo cuando no te vea…"* (Countryside of Baeza, I shall dream of you when I see you no more).

Orientation and Practical Information The center of town is the **Plaza de España,** which leads downhill to the long **Plaza de la Constitución.** When facing From the Pl. España facing Pl. Constitución, the **Barrio Monumental** is uphill to the left. To get to the center of town, follow C. Julio Burrel to C. San Pablo (on the right) which leads to Pl. España and Pl. Constitución below. The **tourist office,** Pl. Pópulo (a.k.a. Los Leones; tel. 74 04 44), vends maps (100ptas) translated into English, German, and French (open Mon.-Fri. 9am-2:30pm, Sat. 10am-12:30pm). The **pharmacy,** C. San Pablo, 19 (tel. 74 06 81), prescribes (open daily 9:30am-2pm and 6-9pm). Contact the **Red Cross** at tel. 74 05 74. The **hospital,** Centro de Salud Comarcal (tel. 74 09 17) is on Av. Alcalde Puche Pardo. The **police,** C. Cardenal Benavides, 5, (tel. 74 06 59), recommend cautious driving. The **post office,** C. Julio Burell, 19 (tel. 74 08 39; open Mon.-Fri. 8:30am-2:30pm), sorts it out. The **postal code** is 23440, the **telephone code** (9)53.**Trains** leave **Estación Linares-Baeza** (tel. 65 02 02), 15km from town on the road to Madrid. The **bus station** (tel. 74 04 68), at the top of C. Julio Burrel, offers service to: Úbeda (10 per day, 15min., 100ptas); Jaén (7 per day, 1 hr., 445ptas); Granada (7 per day, 2-3hr., 1320ptas); Malaga (1 per day, 4hr., 2425ptas); Cazorla (3 per day, 1½hr., 495ptas). Take the bus to Granada to transfer to Almería.

Accommodations and Food Budget accommodations are scarce in Baeza, considering its rising popularity with tourists. Call ahead to secure a room. **Hostal Residencia Comercio,** C. San Pablo, 21 (tel. 74 01 00), furnishes large, attractive rooms with baths, *fin-de-siècle* antiques, and has an "Antonio Machado lived here" sign over room 215—a common claim (singles 1700ptas, doubles 3500ptas.). **Hostal el Patio,** C. Romanones, 13 (tel. 74 02 00), has a lounge for guests with sofas and a TV. Conveniently located near the historic district, it's on the street up the stone steps next to the tourist office. (Singles 1500ptas, with shower 2000ptas. Doubles 2500ptas, with shower 3000ptas, with bath 3500ptas.)

A plethora of bars, *cafeterías,* and *pastelerías* line Pl. Constitución and neighboring streets. **Café Las Vegas,** on the plaza's southwest corner, has choice *bocadillos* (300ptas) and *platos combinados* (under 800ptas). **Helados los Valencianos,** C. Gaspar Becerra, 10 (tel. 74 15 05), might make the best ice cream in Spain. Their stand in the plaza sells cones (50-200ptas) and cool lemon and coffee *granizados* (300ptas).

Sights A stroll through the **Barrio Monumental** yields a sight on every corner. If you follow C. Romanones up the stairs next to the tourist office, before it opens on to the Pl. Santa Cruz, the **Antigua Universidad** (founded in 1595) stands on your left. Ask someone to let you into the courtyard where Antonio Machado had a day job teaching French (open 8:30am-2:30pm and 4-6pm). Across from it survives the **Palacio de Jabalquinto,** featuring a gracefully decaying courtyard punctuated with ancient stonework (open 11am-1pm and 4-6pm). Across the plaza looms the Romanesque **Iglesia de Santa Cruz,** Baeza's oldest church (13th century) with its frescoes of La Virgen, Santa Catalina, and the martyr San Sebastián, reverently discov-

ered in 1967 (open 11am-1pm). Adjacent to the *palacio*, the **seminario's** facade bears the names of some egotistical graduates and a caricature of an unpopular professor, rumored to be painted in bull's blood. The *seminario* now houses the **Universidad Internacional de Andalucía Sede Antonio Machado** (tel. 74 27 75; email machado@uniaam.uia.es), which teaches classes to students from Spain and beyond during the summer. Across the Pl. Santa María from the seminary looms the **Santa Iglesia Catedral.** It houses *La Custodia de Baeza,* Spain's second-most important (to Toledo's) Corpus Christi icon (open daily 10:30am-1pm and 4-7pm). farther uphill, the barrio fades into a modern residential neighborhood, at the edge of which one has a terrific viewpoint of the Guadalquivir valley where rows of olive trees converge in the distance. West of the plaza, on C. Cardenal de Benarides, the **Ayuntameiento** sports magnificent plateresque (see Spain: Literature, p. 60) windows. A block up to the northwest are the **Ruines de San Francisco,** an old church converted into an expensive restaurant and theater.

■ Úbeda

Fifteen minutes from Baeza and two hours from Granada and Córdoba, the cobbled streets of Úbeda's monumental district dip between ivied medieval walls and old churches and palaces. A stop on the crucial 16th-century trade route linking Castilla to Andalucía, the town fattened on American gold shipped up from Sevilla. The *barrio antiguo,* surrounded by friendly, newer neighborhoods, remains one of the best preserved gems of Spanish Renaissance architecture.

Orientation and Practical Information The town is centered around **Plaza de Andalucía.** The **barrio antiguo** (ancient quarter) stretches downhill from Pl. Andalucía along C. Doctor Quesada (which leads to **Calle Real**) and surrounding streets. To reach Pl. Andalucía from the **bus station,** go right exiting the front of the station, walk a block downhill, and take a left on **Avenida Cristo Rey,** which turns into **Calle Obispo Cobos** and then into **Calle Mesones,** which leads to Pl. Andalucía (5min.). **Calle Ramón y Cajal,** a major street in the newer section of town. To reach it from the bus station, walk one block left (uphill) and take a right at C. Huelva. This street leads into C. Ramón y Cajal after a six-way intersection.

The **tourist office** in the **Centro Cultural Hospital de Santiago,** Obispo Cobos, s/n (tel. 75 08 97), on the way from the bus station to Pl. Andalucía, offers books, brochures, and a map (100ptas) with translations in English (open Mon.-Sat. 8am-3pm). A **second office** across the street also provides information and a helpful free map, in Spanish only (open Mon.-Fri. 8am-9:30pm and sometimes on weekends). **Luggage storage** in bus station lockers costs 300ptas. Two **pharmacies** face each other in Pl. Andalucía, at Pl. Andalucía, 5 (tel. 75 00 57), and C. Rastro, 1 (tel. 75 01 51). Change money at **Banco Central Hispano,** C. San Fernando, 28, uphill from Pl. Andalucía, past the church. The **hospital,** Centro de Salud, is on C. Explanada, off Av. Ramón y Cajal (tel. 75 11 03). **Red Cross** answers at (tel. 75 56 40). Contact **police** at (tel. 75 00 23); for **emergencies** call 091 or 092. The **post office,** C. Trinidad, 4 (tel. 75 00 31), along the Hospital de Santiago, is being renovated but has a provisional branch on C. Obispo Cobos. The **postal code** is 23400, the **telephone code** (9)53.

There's **no train service** to Úbeda. The nearest station is **Estación Linares-Baeza** (tel. 65 02 02), 40 minutes northwest by bus. **Buses** leave from C. San José, 6 (tel. 75 21 57). Alsina Graells travels to: Baeza (14 per day, 15min., 100ptas); Estación Linares-Baeza (7 per day, 30min., 255ptas); Jaén (9 per day, 1hr., 535ptas); Cazorla (5 per day, 1hr., 425ptas); Granada (8 per day, 2-3hr., 1400ptas). Bacoma travels to Córdoba (3 per day, 2½hr., 1305ptas) and Sevilla (3 per day, 5hr., 2555ptas).

Accommodations and Food Úbeda's best bargain is the **Hostal Castillo,** Av. Ramón y Cajal, 20 (tel. 75 04 30 or 75 12 18), with comfy singles and fluffy bedspreads. (Singles 1800ptas, with bath and A/C 2200ptas. Doubles: 2800ptas; 3800ptas.) Some women travelers have complained about unwelcome advances by a

manager. The ritzier **Hostal Victoria,** C. Alaminos, 5, 2nd fl. (tel. 75 29 52), has the same owner but a different manager. They feature glistening private bathrooms, color TVs, and A/C. (Singles 2200ptas. Doubles 3800-420.0 Prices jump 300-400ptas during July and semana santa.) From Pl. Andalucía, walk two blocks on C. Mesones, and turn left onto Alaminos. Similarly, the **Hostal Sevilla,** Av. Ramón y Cajal, 7 (tel. 75 06 12), has private baths, A/C, and TVs for 200ptas extra (singles 2100ptas, doubles 4000ptas—but bargain for cheaper rooms). Úbeda's roster of regional cooking includes *andrajos* (soups with pasta, meat, and spices) and *pipirrana* (a hot or cold soup of tomato, green pepper, onion, egg, and tuna). C. Rastro leading from Pl. Andalucía has many *terrazas* with combination platters under 1000ptas and entrees for around 600ptas. **Pizzeria Restaurante Venecia,** C. Huelva, 2 (tel. 75 58 13, near the bus station, serves great homemade pasta (600-900ptas). The *ensalada mixta* (425ptas) is practically a meal in itself (open daily 1-4:30pm and 8pm-12:30am; Visa, MC.) **Helados los Valencianos,** C. Obispo, 1, and Av. Ramón y Cajal, 18 (next to Hostal Castillo), serves delicious *granizados* (slushies) for 200-300ptas and ice cream cones for 100-300ptas (open daily 9am-midnight). The **market** is down C. San Fernando from Pl. Andalucía (open Mon.-Sat. 7am-2:30pm).

Sights A walk through historic Úbeda should begin with the **Hospital de Santiago.** The building, a worthy sight in its own right, lists current cultural events, houses a modern art museum, and holds concerts. (Tel. 75 08 42. Museum open Mon.-Fri. 8am-3pm and 3:30-10pm, Sat. 8am-3pm. Admission 225ptas, children and seniors 75ptas.) From Pl. Andalucía, C. Real leads downhill to C. Juan Montilla which brings you to **Plaza de Vázquez de Molina,** the center of historic Úbeda. Two stone lions at the head of a garden-lined pathway guard the **Palacio de las Cadenas,** now the Ayuntamiento. Across the pathway is the Gothic **Colegiata de Santa María de los Reales Alcázares,** its side chapels embellished by wrought iron grilles. A Renaissance church, the **Sacra Capilla del Salvador,** originally designed as part of a palace commissioned by Carlos V, sits across the far end of the plaza. One can usually peek in during mass, but it is better to view during visitor hours (Mon.-Fri. 7:30-8:30pm). Uphill from the Pl. Vásquez de Molina along C. Juan Ruíz Gonzales is **Plaza 1 de Mayo,** in front of **Iglesia de San Pablo.** The **Museo Arqueológico,** uphill from the church on C. Cervantes, 6 (tel. 75 37 02), displays a physical narrative of Úbeda's history through prehistoric, Roman, Moorish, and Castillian times (open Tues.-Sun. 10am-2pm and 5-7pm; free.) A walk all the way downhill leads to a stunning view of the olive-laden **Guadalquivir valley** and the ruins of the **muralla,** a wall of God that the Moors built to enclose their city.

■ Cazorla

Nestled between foreboding cliffs and two ancient castles, Cazorla is one northern Andalucían *pueblecito blanco* (whitewashed village) that should not be missed. A hike through the mountainous town itself provides exceptional views of the Guadalquivir valley, but most tourists arrive to see the **Parque Natural de las Sierras de Cazorla, Segura, y las Villas** (1hr.). The national park's 210,000 hectares of protected mountains and waterways offer some of the choicest hiking, mountain biking, and horseback riding in Andalucía, inferior only to the Sierra Nevada and the Alpujarras.

A **bus** with stops in Granada, Jaén, and Úbeda arrives in the bare **Plaza de la Constitución** twice a day, and departs three times daily (tel. 75 21 57 for Allsina Graells in Úbeda; first departure 7am, last 8:15pm). Facing the peaks, walk down **Calle de Dr. Muñoz** (to the right) to reach **Plaza de Corredera.** farther downhill is **Plaza de Santa María** and the **old quarter.** The **tourist office,** C. Paseo del Santo Cristo, 17 (tel. 71 01 02; fax 72 00 60), up a garden-lined walkway from Pl. Constitución, in the opposite direction from Pl. Corredera, has a helpful staff as well as free maps and brochures (open Mon.-Fri. 10:30am-2:30pm, Sat. 10am-1pm). There's a **Banco Central Hispano,** C. Dr. Muñoz, 19 (open Mon.-Fri. 8:30-2:30pm). The nearest **hospital** is the Centro de Salud, Av. Ximenez de Rada, 1 (tel. 72 10 61 or 72 20 00), a few kilometers away. The

police are on Pl. Corredera (tel. 72 01 81). In an **emergency** call 091 or 092. The **post office,** C. Mariano Extremera, 2 (tel. 72 02 61), sits uphill on the left from Pl. Corredera. The **postal code** is 23470, the **telephone code** (9)53.

From the far end of Pl. Corredera, walk uphill on C. del Carmen to reach the **Albuerge Juvenil Cazorla (HI),** Pl. Mauricio Martinez, 6 (tel. 72 03 29; fax 72 02 03). The hostel has a TV lounge, outdoor patios, a heaven-sent pool (open July-Sept.), sparkling showers, and clean, spacious rooms that can accommodate 1-6 people. The English-speaking staff can help you plan excursions to the park. (HI members 1300ptas, over 26 1500ptas. Non-members pay 300ptas each night for six nights to become a member. Prices discounted 400ptas Sept. 15-June 15 and semana santa. Sheets provided. Towels rented for 175ptas). **Hostal Betis,** Pl. Corredera, 19 (tel. 72 05 40), has firm beds and rooms with valley-side views (singles with bath1300ptas; doubles 2500ptas, with bath 2700ptas). The friendly owner cooks up a fabulous *menú* (1000ptas) for guests only. **Terrazas** serving traditional platters such as *lomo de cerdo* (pork chops) and *rin-ran* (a cold soup of potatoes, red peppers, olives, and fish) ornament Pl. Corredora and Pl. Santa Iglesia. Making use of a 16th-century house, **La Cueva** (tel. 72 12 25), in Pl. Santa Iglesia cooks veggies in its ancient hearth as well as a crispy roast rabbit. The midday *menú* costs 1000ptas, entrees are around 800ptas each. For the sweet toothed, **Fran's Café Bar,** C. Muñoz, 28 (tel. 72 06 15), has scrumptious pastries (around 100ptas) and a jukebox whose Euro-pop roster also includes Roxette and Coolio featuring L.U. (open daily 9am-10pm). The **market** at Pl. Mercado (downstairs from C. Dr. Muñoz) has fresh produce (open Mon.-Fri. 9am-noon). Dry goods are available at the **supermarket** at the far end of Pl. Corredera (open Mon.-Fri. 9am-noon and 6-9pm, Sat. 9am-noon).

There are many opportunities for scenic strolls around town. The **Castillo de la Yedra,** started by the Romans, provides a pretty vista of Cazorla from its solitary peaks, and houses an art museum (open Tues.-Sat. 9am-3pm). A flood in 1694 and wartime fires left their mark on the unfortunate **Ruinas de la Iglesia de Santa María,** in the plaza of the same name. The offending river still trickles by. For longer excursions, stop by **Quercus,** C. Juan Domingo, 2 (tel. 72 01 15; fax 71 00 68), a private concessionary tour operator that can tell you all you need to know about the *parque natural.* They speak English and have good maps (375ptas; open daily 10am-2pm and 5-9pm, holidays 10am-2pm and 6-9pm). Inquire about **camping** options—alas, no free sites or back country. **Bus** service is subject to change (5:45am and 3pm, 1 hr., 400ptas). The Carecesa bus departs from Pl. Constitución and goes to the **Torre del Vinagre Visitor Center,** near the trailhead of the popular **Sendero Cerrada de Elias/Río Borosa,** a 4km or 12km walk, depending on direction, up a river canyon carved with natural pools. When you get off the bus, follow the sign to the kiosk. **Mountain bikes** will take you part way up the trail (1200ptas per ½day, 2000ptas per full-day). **Horses** are also available if you have a group of four or more (about 1300ptas per hour). Bring drinking water (you can get a *bocadillo* at the kiosk there). The last bus back to Cazorla leaves Torre del Vinagre at 4:30pm.

■ Granada

As Moorish ruler Boabdil fled Granada, the last Muslim stronghold in Spain his mother berated him for casting a longing look back at the Alhambra: "Weep like a woman for what you could not defend like a man."

Boabdil had relinquished the final Muslim fortress in Spain, and the last bit of empire remaining of a 700-year Moorish rule in the Iberian Peninsula. The kingdom had dwindled during the early 13th century, when, largely on the haunches of *reconquistador* Fernando El Santo, Castilian Reconquerers systematically booted Muslim fortresses from Úbeda, Baeza, and Jaén. From 1247-1492, the kingdom settled comfortably in Granada, and celebrated an era of peace and enlightenment. Washington Irving romanticized the epoch when he told us his *Tales of the Alhambra,* recounting the gallantry of an exotic people. More recently, García Lorca poetically glorified

the gypsy descendants as a mysterious, martyred people dislocated in the Spanish countryside.

The year 1492, when Spain reconquered Granada, could be considered the climax of Spanish history. It was the same year Fernando and Isabel launched the Inquisition and the same year Columbus returned from the Americas.

Fernando and Isabel's campaign to construct the greatest empire in the world met an enduring seven-month resistance in Muslim Granada. But in January the Castillians caught Sultan Moulay Abdul Hassan with his pants down—he was busy frolicking with his harem while his kingdom burned. His jealous wife Aïcha panicked, used popular support to have Hassan deposed, and appointed young Boabdil as her puppet on the throne. Fernando and Isabel capitalized on the disarray, capturing Boabdil and the Alhambra.

The saying holds "Si has muerto sin ver la Alhambra no has vivido" (if you have died without seeing the Alhambra, you have not lived). Between visits to the Alhambra, look for plenty of eating, drinking, and dancing—University of Granada students *hacen fiesta* (party) energetically.

Sing a Song of Conquest

¿Para qué nos llamas rey,/ a qué fue nuestra llamada? / —Para que sepáis, amigos, / la gran pérdida de Alhama. / ¡Ay de mi Alhama!

[What is it, our king? / Why have you called us here? / —So that you know, my friends / that they've taken Alhama. / Oh what of my Alhama!]

This verse is from a popular sixteenth century song, or *romance,* depicting the Moorish loss of the city of Alhama in 1482 which presaged the 1492 *Reconquista.* The lyrics of romance, written by Christians, were at times just plain fantasy, such as one about captive Christian girl, Moriana, playing backgammon with the Moorish Galván—when she won, he lost a city; when he won, Galván got to kiss her hand.

ORIENTATION AND PRACTICAL INFORMATION

The geographic center of Granada is the small **Plaza de Isabel la Católica,** the intersection of the city's two main arteries, **Calle de los Reyes Católicos** and **Gran Vía de Colón.** Two short blocks uphill on C. Reyes Católicos sits **Plaza Nueva,** framed by Renaissance buildings and a range of hotels and restaurants. Downhill, also along C. Reyes Católicos, lie **Plaza del Carmen,** site of the **Ayuntamiento,** and **Puerta Real,** the six-way intersection of C. Reyes Católicos, **Calle Recogidos, Calle Mesones, Calle Acera de Darro, Calle Angel Garivet,** and **Calle Acero del Casino.** The **Alhambra** commands the steep hill up from Pl. Nueva. To get there, take **Calle Cuesta de Gomérez** (no unauthorized cars from 9am-9pm) off Pl. Nueva and be prepared to pant. You an also take a cheap, quick **microbus** (every 20min., 115ptas) from Pl. Isabel la Católica or Pl. Neuva. Atop the hill across from the Alhambra sprawls the **Albaicín,** or Arab quarter.

To reach **Calle Gran Vía** from **RENFE,** walk 3 blocks up Av. Andaluces to Av. Constitución, and take bus #3, 4, 5, 6, 9, or 11. From the bus station, take bus #3 (60ptas). **Plaza de la Trinidad** sits at the end of C. Mesones from Pta. Real. On Gran Viá de Colón, you'll find the **catedral,** and next to it the old Arab silk market or **Alcaicería,** now specializing in souvenirs. Municipal **buses** (see Public Transportation, below) cover practically the entire city. Since the Alhambra and Albaicín are near both each other and the center, the best way to explore is on foot. If you are alone when night falls, stick to major streets in the Albaicín, and avoid paths higher up on the neighboring **Sacromonte.**

ANDALUCÍA

Tourist Office: Oficina Provincial, Pl. Mariana Pineda, 10 (tel. 22 66 88; fax 22 89 16). From Pta. Real turn right onto C. Angel Ganivet, then take a right 3 blocks later to reach the plaza. Possibly the most helpful tourist office in Andalucía. The multi-lingual staff gives out free maps, posters, and brochures. Open Mon.-Fri. 9:30am-7pm, Sat. 10-2pm. **Junta de Andalucía:** C. Mariana Pineda (tel. 22 10 22; fax 22 39 27). From Pta. Real, take C. Reyes Católicos to Pl. Carmen. C. Mariana Pineda is the first street on the left. More prominently signposted on C. Reyes Católicos, this office is also helpful but costlier. City maps (100ptas), Andalucían hotel guide (800ptas), brochures on hiking, hunting, and golf (400ptas). Open Mon.-Sat. 9am-7pm, Sun. 10am-2pm.

Budget Travel: Viajes TIVE, C. Martínez Campos, 21 (tel. 25 02 11), off C. Recogidos. BIJ train tickets (for those under 26) and interrail available. Open Mon.-Fri. 9am-1:30pm, but someone may be there in the afternoon to answer phone calls.

Currency Exchange: Banco Central Hispano, Gran Vía de Colón, 3 (tel. 22 54 25), off Pl. Isabel la Católica, exchanges money and AmEx traveler's checks without commission (open Mon.-Fri. 8am-3pm).

El Corte Inglés: (tel. 22 32 40), C. Geril, follow Acera del Casino from Pta. Real onto the tree-lined road. The Spanish superstore stocks everything including a thorough map (475ptas). Open Mon.-Sat. 10am-10pm.

American Express: C. Reyes Católicos, 31 (tel. 22 45 12), between Pl. Isabel la Católica and Pta. Real. Exchanges money, cashes personal checks for card holders, and holds mail (open Mon.-Fri. 9:30am-1:30pm and 4:30-7:30pm; Sat. 9am-2pm).

Internet Access: Email Net, C. Santa Ecolástica, 13 (tel. 22 69 19), up C. Pavaneras from Pl. Isabel la Católica, provides email, worldwide web, and drinks. (400ptas per hour, 15min. minimum, 150ptas. Open 9am-2:30pm, 4-11:30pm.)

Flights: Airport (tel. 24 52 00), 17km west of city. **Salidas** bus (tel. 13 13 09) shuttles from C. Gran Via, in front of the cathedral (7 per day, 3 on Sun., 425ptas). Taxi to the airport about 2000ptas. **Iberia** (tel. 22 75 92) to Madrid (2-3 per day, 45min.) and Barcelona (2-3 per day, 1¼hr.). Open Mon.-Fri. 9am-1:45pm and 4-7pm.

Trains: RENFE Station, Av. Andaluces (tel. 27 12 72). From Pl. Isabel la Católica, follow Gran Vía de Colón to the end, then bear left on Av. Constitución; or take bus #3, 4, 5, 6, 9, or 11 from Gran Vía to the stop marked Constitución 3 (ask the driver). Turn left on Av. Andaluces. RENFE is at the end of the street. To: Madrid (9 per day, 5hr., 1900ptas); Barcelona (2 per day, 12-13hr., 6200-6300ptas); Sevilla (3 per day, 4-5hr., 2280ptas); Antequera (3 per day, 2hr., 865ptas); Algeciras (3 per day, 5-7hr., 2280ptas); Almería (3 per day, 3hr., 1520ptas); Cádiz (3 per day, 7hr., 2885ptas); Ronda (3 per day, 3-4hr., 1520ptas).

Buses: All major bus routes originate from the new bus station on the outskirts of Granada on the Ctra. de Madrid.

Alsina Graells (tel. 18 50 10) to: Algeciras (2 per day, 5hr., 2500ptas); Almería (5 per day, 2¼hr., 1285ptas); Antequera (2 per day, 2hr., 900ptas); Cádiz (2 per day, 4hr., 4010ptas); Córdoba (6 per day, 3hr., 1765ptas); Jaén (12 per day, 1½hr., 900ptas); La Línea (2 per day, 4hr., 2390ptas); Madrid (9 per day, 5hr., 1900ptas); Málaga (15 per day, 2hr., 1165ptas); Sevilla (6 per day, 3hr., 2710ptas).

Bacoma (tel. 15 75 57) to: Alicante (5 per day, 6hr., 3335ptas); Barcelona (4 per day, 14hr., 7830ptas); Valencia (5 per day, 8hr., 4855ptas).

Antocares Bonal (tel. 27 31 00) sends one bus per day to Veleta from Palacio de Congresos. Follow Acera del Darro from Pta. Real across the river to Po. Violón, or take bus #1 on Gran Vía towards Pl. Isabel la Católica to the last stop. Tickets are sold only 8:30-9am at Ventorillo Bar across from the *palacio*. (Bus departs from Ventorillo bar 9am, returns from Veleta 6pm, 45min. each way, 675ptas round-trip.)

Public Transportation: Municipal buses (tel. 81 37 11). The buses you will grow to love are: "Bus Alhambra" from Pl. Isabel la Católica; #10 from the bus station to the youth hostel, Camino de Ronda, C. Recogidas, and Acera del Darro; and #3 from the bus station to Av. Constitución, Gran Vía, and Pl. Isabel la Católica (115ptas, *bonobus* book of 15 tickets 1000ptas). An indispensable free map is available from the tourist office.

Taxis: (tel. 28 06 54 or 15 14 61).

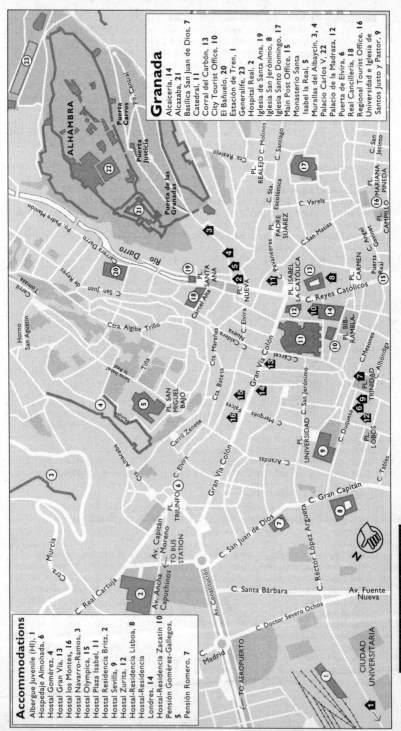

Granada

Alcaicería, 14
Alcazaba, 21
Basílica San Juan de Dios, 7
Catedral, 11
Corral del Carbón, 13
City Tourist Office, 10
El Bañuelo, 20
Estación de Tren, 1
Generalife, 23
Hospital Real, 2
Iglesia de Santa Ana, 19
Iglesia San Jerónimo, 8
Iglesia Santo Domingo, 17
Main Post Office, 15
Monasterio Santa Isabel la Real, 5
Murallas del Albaycín, 3, 4
Palacio Carlos V, 22
Palacio de la Madraza, 12
Puerta de Elvira, 6
Real Cancillería, 18
Regional Tourist Office, 16
Universidad e Iglesia de Santos Justo y Pastor, 9

Accommodations

Albergue Juvenile (HI), 1
Hospedaje Almohada, 6
Hostal Gomérez, 4
Hostal Gran Vía, 13
Hostal los Montes, 16
Hostal Navarro-Ramos, 3
Hostal Olympica, 15
Hostal Plaza Isabel, 11
Hostal Residencia Britz, 2
Hostal Sevilla, 9
Hostal Zurita, 12
Hostal-Residencia Lisboa, 8
Hostal-Residencia Londres, 14
Hostal-Residencia Zacatín, 10
Pensión Gomérez-Gallegos, 5
Pensión Romero, 7

ANDALUCÍA

Car Rental: Atasa, Pl. Cuchilleros, 1 (tel. 22 40 04 or 22 56 65; fax 22 77 95). Cheapest car 28,000ptas per week with unlimited mileage and insurance. Prices rise with shorter rentals. Must be at least 20 and have had a license for one year.

Luggage Storage: At the train station and bus station (400ptas; open daily 4-9pm).

Foreign Language Bookstore: Librería Flash, Pl. Trinidad (tel. 52 11 90), has a modest selection (including guidebooks) in several languages. Open Mon.-Fri. 10am-2pm and 5-9pm, Sat. 10am-2pm.

Lavandería: C. La Paz, 19, from Pl. Trinidad, take C. Alhóndiga, turn right on C. La Paz and walk two blocks. Wash 400ptas per load; dry 100ptas per 15min. Open Mon.-Fri. 9:30am-2pm and 4:30-8:30pm, Sat. 9am-2pm.

Swimming Pool: Piscina Neptuno (tel. 25 88 21), next to *flamenco* club Jardines Neptuno and near the intersection of C. Recogidas and Camino de Ronda. 600ptas, on Sun. 800ptas, children 400ptas. Open June-Sept. 11am-7:30pm.

Women's Services: Servicio Sociales, C. Lepanto (tel. 24 81 15), behind Ayuntamiento off Pl. Carmen up stairway D. No English. Open Mon.-Fri. 8am-2pm.

Red Cross: C. Escorianza, 8 (tel. 22 22 22, 22 20 24, or 22 21 66).

Pharmacy: Farmacia Gran Vía, Gran Vía de Colón, 6 (tel 22 29 90). Open Mon.-Fri. 9:30am-2pm and 5-8:30pm. For late-night pharmacies, check listings in any local paper or signs posted in pharmacies.

Medical Services: Clínica de San Cecilio, C. Doctor Oloriz, 16 (tel. 28 02 00 or 27 02 00), on the road to Jaén.

Police: C. Duquesa, 21 (tel. 24 81 00). English spoken. **Guardia Civil:** Av. Puliana Pol. Almanjayar (tel. 25 11 00). **Emergency:** tel. 091 or 092.

Post Office: Puerta Real (tel. 22 48 35; fax 22 36 41), on the corner between Acera de Darro and C. Angel Ganinet. Open for stamps and Lista de Correos Mon.-Fri. 8:30am-8:30pm, Sat. 9:30am-2pm. **Wires money** 8:30am-2:30pm. **Faxes** sent and received. **Postal Code:** 18009.

Telephone Code: (9)58.

ACCOMMODATIONS AND CAMPING

Granada has more cheap accommodations than shoe stores. Finding lodgings is a problem only during semana santa, when you must call ahead.

Albergue Juvenil Granada (HI), Ramón y Cajal, 2 (tel. 27 26 38 or 28 43 06; fax 28 52 85). From the bus station, take bus #10 (from Gran Vía or RENFE take #11) and ask the driver to stop at "El Estadio de la Juventud." It's the peach building across the field on the left. All rooms are doubles with baths or triples. Sheets provided, towels rented (175ptas). Rooms are spacious with comfortable beds. 24hr. reception. No curfew. Limited wheelchair access. (1300ptas per person, over 26 1600ptas, non-HI guests pay an extra 300ptas per night for six nights to join.)

Along Cuesta de Gomérez

Hostales line **Cuesta de Gomérez,** the street leading uphill to the Alhambra and to the right of Pl. Nueva. Crashing in this area is wise for those planning to spend serious time at the Alhambra complex.

Hostal Residencia Britz, Cuesta de Gomérez, 1 (tel. 22 36 52), on the corner of Pl. Nueva. Large rooms with luxurious beds and green-tiled bathrooms. Soda machine in the lobby says *"Gracias";* management is even friendlier. 24hr. reception. Singles with bath 2100ptas. Doubles 3300ptas, with bath 4700ptas. 6% discount for *Let's Go* readers if you pay in cash, are courteous, and show them the book. Washing machine available for 500ptas, no dryer. Visa, MC.

Hostal Navarro-Ramos, Cuesta de Gomérez, 21 (tel. 25 05 55). Quarters are comfortable and cool in the evening. Small balconies in some rooms are ideal for spying on the Alhambra-bound passers-by below. Singles 1375ptas. Doubles 2200ptas, with bath 3500ptas. Triples with bath 4700ptas. Shower 150ptas.

Hostal Gomérez, Cuesta de Gomérez, 10 (tel. 22 44 37). Clean rooms with firm beds. Amiable multilingual owner will wash and dry clothing for 800ptas per load.

Offers a 100-200ptas discount to *Let's Go*ers during the off season. Will assist guests planning longer stays. Singles 1400ptas. Doubles 2500ptas. Triple 3200ptas.

Pensión Gomérez-Gallegos, Cuesta de Gomérez, 2, 3rd fl. (tel. 22 63 98). Large rooms, some balconies, and numerous plants. Singles 1700ptas. Doubles 2900ptas. Triples 1400ptas per person. One clean and roomy shared bath. Ask about discounts on longer stays.

Near the Cathedral/University

The area alongside boutique-saturated C. Mesones and C. Alhónd'ga is nearest to the cathedral, the Alcaicería, Pta. Real, and Pl. Isabel la Católica. Hostels cluster around Pl. Trinidad, a cozy palm and orange-tree-laden square (at the end of C. Mesones from Pta. Real). Many *pensiones* around C. Mesones cater to students during the academic year but free up during the summer. The ones listed below are open year round.

Hospedaje Almohada, C. Postigo de Zarate, 4 (tel. 20 74 46). Walk 1 block from Pl. Trinidad along C. Duquesa; it's at the top of C. Málaga and has no sign. A successful experiment in communal living: guests enjoy socializing in the sky-lit courtyard, the living room, and the kitchen. Singles 1800ptas. Doubles 3500ptas, longer stays are common and encouraged (30,000-33,000ptas per month). Laundry 500ptas per load.

Pensión Romero, C. Sillería de Mesones, 1 (tel. 26 60 79), off of Pl. Trinidad with a big sign. Bright, cozy rooms, but not much peace from the plaza below. Singles 1500ptas. Doubles 2200ptas.

Hostal-Residencia Lisboa, Pl. Carmen, 29 (tel. 22 14 13 or 22 14 14; fax 22 14 87). Take C. Reyes Católicos from Pl. Isabel la Católica; Pl. Carmen is on the left. Sister *hostal* to Britz—you've seen one, you've seen them both (a good thing). Rooms are well furnished, with phones and fans. Singles 2500ptas, with bath 3800ptas. Doubles: 3700ptas; 5200ptas. Visa, MC.

Hostal Sevilla, C. Fábrica Vieja, 18 (tel. 27 85 13). From Pta. Real follow C. Alhóndiga into C. Fábrica Vieja, past Pl. Trinidad. Spotless and well-furnished with friendly staff. Singles 1800ptas, with bath 2500ptas. Doubles: 2800ptas; 4000ptas. Triples 4200ptas.

Hostal Residencia Zacatín, C. Ermita, 11 (tel. 22 11 55), enter through the Alcaicería from C. Reyes Católicos. Rooms are amply sized and baths are immense. Some rooms have balconies, interior rooms are more tranquil. Singles 1500ptas, with bath 2300ptas. Doubles 2700ptas, with shower 3200ptas, with bath 3800ptas.

Hostal Plaza Isabel, C. Colcha, 13 (tel. 22 30 22), above Bar La Viña, uphill to the right from Pl. Isabel la Católica. A statue of Ibn Tibon, 12th-century patriarch of translators, hails you to visit this convenient budget bargain. Mattresses decent but all rooms have balcony overlooking the street. Singles 1500ptas. Doubles 2400ptas.

Hostal Zurita, Pl. Trinidad, 7 (tel. 27 50 20). Beautiful rooms, high-quality beds, and 24hr. hot water. Double-paned balconies keep out plaza noise. Singles 1875ptas. Doubles 3750ptas, with bath 4500ptas. Triples: 5000ptas; 5500ptas.

Along Gran Vía de Colón

Hostels are sprinkled along Gran Vía de Colón, the main thoroughfare linking Pl. Isabel la Católica with Av. Constitución. In all cases, rooms with balconies over the street are much noisier than those that open onto an inner patio.

Hostal Gran Vía, Gran Vía de Colón, 17 (tel. 27 92 12), about 4 blocks from Pl. Isabel la Católica. Clean rooms. Singles with shower 2500ptas. Doubles 3000ptas, with bath 3500ptas. Triples with bath 4500ptas.

Hostal-Residencia Londres, Gran Vía de Colón, 29 (tel. 27 80 34), a bit farther down than Hostal Gran Vía. Pretty rooms and patios with views of the Alhambra, Albaicín, and hundreds of Granadan rooftops. Large shared bathrooms. Local students get first dibs from Oct.1 to June 30, so call ahead. Singles 1800ptas. Doubles 2800ptas. 1000ptas per additional person.

Pensión Olympia, Alvaro de Bazán, 6 (tel. 27 82 38). From Pl. Isabel, walk down Gran Vía 6 blocks and make a right. Same owner as Hostal Gran Vía, but this is a cheaper version. Communal bathrooms. Singles 2000ptas. Doubles 3000ptas.

Hostal los Montes, C. Arteaga, 3 (tel. 27 79 30). Going down Gran Vía de Colón from Pl. Isabel la Católica, it's the 8th street on your right. Very quiet, and a bit dark and secluded, with balconies and a patio. Singles 1600ptas. Doubles 2600ptas.

Camping

Buses serve five campgrounds within 5km of Granada. Check the departure schedules at the tourist office, and ask bus drivers to alert you to your stop.

Sierra Nevada, Av. Madrid, 107 (tel. 15 00 62), take bus #3 or 10. Lots of shady trees, modern facilities, and free hot showers. If the town fair is here, stay elsewhere or forget about REM sleep. 535ptas per person, per tent, and per vehicle. Children under 10 435ptas. There is also a hotel on the grounds. Open March-Oct.

María Eugenia, Ctra. Nacional, 342 (tel. 20 06 06), at km 436, on the road to Málaga. Take Santa Fé or Chauchina bus from the train station (every 30min.). 425ptas per person, per tent, and per car. Children 325ptas. Open March-Oct.

Los Alamos (tel. 20 84 79), next door to María Eugenia. Same buses. 350ptas per person, per tent, and per car. Children 300ptas. Showers 50ptas. Open April-Sept.

FOOD

Granada offers a welcome variety of ethnic restaurants to emancipate your tastebuds from the fried-fish-and-pig-products doldrums. Cheap, tasty, and healthy Middle Eastern cuisine can be found in and around the **Albaicín.** Near **Pl. Nueva,** the usual fare of *menús* awaits. Picnickers can gather fresh fruit and vegetables at the market on C. San Augustín. Get **groceries** at **Supermercado T. Mariscal,** C. de Genil, next to El Corte Inglés (open Mon.-Fri. 9:30am-2pm and 5-9pm; Sat. 9:30am-2pm).

Try one of Granada's holistic *platos típicos* (they eat the *whole* cow): *tortilla sacromonte* (an omelette with calf brains, ham, shrimp, and veggies), *sesos a la romana* (batter-fried calves' brains), and *rabo de toro* (bull's tail). Granada also hosts dozens of cafes, called *churrerias,* named for the classic *chocolate con churros,* a snack of thin, sugar-coated pastries with a cup of thick hot chocolate for dipping.

Near Plaza Nueva

Centrally located, but this area has nothing special in the full-fledged restaurant category. An endless array of establishments offer *menús* in the 850-1200ptas range.

La Nueva Bodega, C. Cetti-Meriem, 3 (tel. 22 59 34), on a small side street off C. Elvira out of Pl. Nueva. Sit-down area and bar separated by a wrought-iron partition. Winding staircase leads up to a fancier *comedor.* Popular with locals and tourists. *Menús* 825-1400ptas. *Bocadillos* around 300ptas. Open noon-midnight.

Bodega Mancha C. Elvira, 5, and **Bodega Castañeda,** C. Joaquin Costa, 8, both located in the alleyways around C. Elvira leading from Pl. Nueva. *Bocadillos* and *tapas* (under 300ptas) are the major fare preferred in these dens of Dionysus, the area's two *bodegas* (wine bars). The salty pork aroma might make you drowsier than the wine and sherry *de barril* (3 or 4 varieties of each, straight from the barrel, 125-200ptas). Ask for *un calicasa,* the house jungle juice mixture. Both open noon-4pm and 6pm-1am, weekends until 3am.

Restaurante Boabdil (tel. 22 81 36), serves lunch and dinner in a little outdoor nook on C. Elvira leading from Pl. Nueva. *Platos combinados* (725ptas) include such staples as *paella* and macaroni and cheese, as well as dessert. Open daily 1-5pm and 8pm-midnight, closed Thurs. afternoons. Visa, MC.

Restaurante Alcaicería, C. Oficios, 6 (tel. 22 43 41), in the Alcaicería, between the cathedral and C. Reyes Católicos. Eat outdoors in a corner of the souvenir market. Owner recommends the *rabo de toro,* and of course some *tinto. Menús* 1500ptas. Open daily noon-11:30pm. Visa, MC.

The Albaicín

Wander the narrow, winding streets of the Albaicín and you will discover a number of economical bars and restaurants on the slopes above Pl. Nueva. **C. Calderería Nueva,** off C. Elvira leading from the plaza, is crammed with teahouses and cafes.

El Ladrillo II, C. Panaderos (tel. 29 26 51), off Cuesta del Chapiz, near the Iglesia El Salvador, high on the Albaicín. Thunderous evening hangout. Consume whopping rations of delicious, fresh seafood to the sound of *sevillanas*. The restaurant's other location on Placeta de Fátima has a *terraza*. Open daily 2:30pm-1:30am.

Medina-Zahara, C. Calderería Nueva, 2 (tel. 22 15 41). This Mediterranean take-out joint slices lamb kebab before your very eyes and makes delicious samosas (275-325ptas) and falafel (325ptas).

Los Chirimías (tel. 22 68 82), on Po. Padre Manjón up C. del Darro from Pl. Nueva, has a breezy *terraza* along the Darro River, surveyed by the towering Alhambra. Pizzas range between 550-775ptas and the *plato del día* costs a mere 600ptas. Open daily 12:30pm-2am.

Naturi Albaicín, C. Calderería Nueva, 10 (tel. 22 06 27). Vegetarian cuisine, and we're not talking lettuce and carrot sticks. Tasty options include *berenjenas rellenas* (stuffed eggplant), quiche, and *kefir* (yogurt drink). *Menú* 850-1050ptas. Open daily 1-4pm and 7-11pm, closed Fri. afternoon.

Elsewhere

Restaurante Chino Estrella Oriental, C. Alvaro de Bazán, 9 (tel. 22 34 67), 5 blocks down Gran Vía Colon from Pl. Isabel la Católica. A bright red Pagoda facade hides cheap, tasty *menús* (695ptas). No fortune cookies and a curious amount of ham, but the meal does conclude with a refreshing Chinese liqueur. Delivery with order of 1500ptas or more. Open daily 12:30-4:30pm and 8pm-12:30am.

SIGHTS

Dale limosna mujer,
que no hay en la vida nada
como pena de ser ciego en Granada.

[Alms, lady, alms! For there
is nothing crueler in life
than to be blind in Granada.]

Francisco de Icaza,
inscribed in the Alhambra
(Torre de la Pólvora)

The Alhambra Complex

The **Alhambra** (tel. 22 09 12; fax 21 05 84) is both the name for the hill that dominates Granada and the sprawling palace-fortress atop it. The name, from the Arabic for "red," may refer more to the nickname of the founder of the dynasty, al Ahmar, then to the color of the walls, which originally gleamed white. Enter the Alhambra through Pta. de Granada, off Cuesta de Gomérez, and climb to the well-marked main entrance. (Alhambra open Mon.-Sat. 9am-8pm, Sun. 9am-6pm; Oct.-March 9am-5:45pm. 725ptas, Sun. free.) Nighttime admission to illuminated complex. (Open Tues., Thurs., and Sat. 10pm-midnight; winter Sat. 8-10pm. 725ptas. Entry limited to 8000 visitors daily, so get there early. Enter the Palace of the Nazarites (Alcázar) during the time specified on your ticket only.)

The Alcazaba

Against the silvery backdrop of the Sierra Nevada, the Christians drove the first Nazarite King Alhamar from the Albaicín to this more strategic hill. Here he built a fortress called the Alcazaba, the oldest section of today's Alhambra.

In the Alcazaba, the **Torre de la Vela** (watchtower) provides the finest view of Granada and the Sierra Nevada. The tower's bells were rung to warn of impending danger and to coordinate the Moorish irrigation system. Napoleon stationed his troops here, but before leaving he blew up enough of the place to ruin the citadel's utility as a military outpost. Exit through the **Puerta del Vino** (wine gate), where inhabitants of the Alhambra once bought tax-free wine (alas, no more...).

ANDALUCÍA

The Alcázar

Follow signs to the *Palacio Nazaries* to see the Alcázar (Royal Palace), which was built for the great Moorish rulers Yusuf I (1333-1354) and Mohammed V (1354-1391). An unexplained force allegedly murdered Yusuf I in an isolated basement chamber of the Alcázar, so his son Mohammed V was left to complete the palace.

The entrance leads into the **Mexuar,** a great pillared council chamber. The Mexuar opens onto the **Patio del Cuarto Dorado** (Patio of the Gilded Hall). Off the far side of the patio, foliated horseshoe archways of successively diminishing width open onto the **Cuarto Dorado** (Gilded Hall) itself, decorated by Carlos V. Its opulent wooden ceiling is inlaid with ivory and mother-of-pearl.

Next is the **Patio de los Arrayanes** (Courtyard of Myrtles), an expanse of emerald water filled with goldfish in the center and bubbling fountains at both ends. Stand at the top of the patio for a glimpse of the 14th-century **Fachada de Serallo,** the palace's elaborately carved facade. The long and slender **Sala de la Barca** (Boat Gallery), with a boat-hull ceiling, flanks the courtyard.

In the elaborate **Sala de los Embajadores** (Hall of Ambassadors), adjoining the Sala de la Barca to the north, King Fernando and Christopher Columbus discussed the (misguided) route to India. Every surface of this magnificent square hall is intricately wrought with inscriptions and ornamental patterns. The dome, carved with over 8000 pieces of wood and inlaid cedar, depicts the seven skies of paradise mentioned in the Koran (the ceiling style is called *mozárabe*). The enormous rounded windows once shone tinted light through stained glass until it was shattered by the explosion of a Darro Valley power factory in 1590.

From the Patio de los Arrayanes, once a harem and center of the Sultan's domestic life, the Sala de los Mocárabes leads to the **Patio de los Leones** (Courtyard of the Lions), the most photographed sanctum of the palace. The grandeur continues: a symmetrical arcade of horseshoe arches and white marble columns borders the courtyard, and a fountain supported by 12 marble lions tinkles in the middle.

At the far end of the courtyard, the **Sala de los Reyes** (Hall of the Kings) is covered by eroded but still spectacular wall paintings on leather surfaces, plus another amazing ceiling. Moving clockwise in the courtyard, one finds the **Sala de los Abencerrajes.** Sultan Abul Hassan piled the heads of the sons of his first wife here (16 of them) so that Boabdil, son of his second wife, could inherit the throne. The rust-colored stains in the basin are said to mark the indelible traces of the butchering. Untainted, the intricate ceiling, perhaps the most beautiful in the complex, dazzles irreverently. On the opposite side of the courtyard, the resplendent **Sala de las Dos Hermanas** (Chamber of the Two Sisters) was named for twin marble slabs embedded in its floor. Its staggering honeycomb dome (*mocárabe* style) is made of thousands of tiny cells. From here a secluded portico, **Mirador de Daraxa** (Eyes of the Sultana), overlooks the Jardines de Daraxa.

Passing the room where American author Washington Irving resided in 1829, a balustrated courtyard leads to the 14th-century **Baños Reales** (Royal Baths), the center of court social life. Light shining through star-shaped holes in the ceiling was once refracted through steam, creating indoor rainbows (currently closed during summer months for conservation studies).

Torres and Gardens

Just outside the east wall of the Alcázar, in the **Jardines del Partal,** lily-studded pools drip beside terraces of roses. The **Torre de las Damas** (Ladies' Tower) soars above it all, as one tower after another traverses the area between the Alcazaba and El Generalife, one for *cautivas* (captives), one for *infantas* (princesses), etc. The beautiful floral gardens also merit a visit.

El Generalife

Over a bridge, across the **Callejón de los Cipreses** and the shady **Callejón de las Adelfas** are the vibrant blossoms and towering cypresses of the *Generalife,* the sultan's vacation retreat. Arab engineers changed the Darro's flow by 18km and

employed dams and channels to prepare the soil for Aben Walid Ismail's design of El Generalife in 1318. Over the centuries, the estate passed through private hands until it was repatriated in 1931. The two buildings connect across the **Patio de la Acequia** (Courtyard of the Irrigation Channel), embellished with a narrow pool fed by fountains forming an aquatic archway. Honeysuckle vines scale the back wall, and shady benches invite long rests.

Palacio de Carlos V

After the *Reconquista* drove the Moors from Spain, Fernando and Isabel restored the Alcázar. Little did they know that two generations later omnipotent Emperor Carlos V would demolish part of it to make way for his **Palacio de Carlos V,** a Renaissance masterpiece by Pedro Machuca (disciple of Michelangelo).

Although glaringly incongruous amid all the Moorish splendor, experts have somehow agreed that the *palacio* is one of the most beautiful Renaissance buildings in Spain. Wrapped in two stories of Doric colonnades, it's Machuca's only surviving effort. Inside, a **museum** of Hispano-Arabic art contains the only original furnishings remaining from the Alhambra (tel. 22 62 79; open Tues.-Sat. 9am-2:30pm; ask about exhibits with extended hours; free for citizens of EU, otherwise 250ptas). Upstairs, the **Museo de Bellas Artes** (tel. 22 48 43) displays mostly religious sculpture and paintings of the *Escuela Granadina* (Granada School) from the 16th century to the present (open Tues.-Sat. 10am-2pm).

The Cathedral Quarter

Downhill from Arab splendor is splendor of the Christian kind—the **Capilla Real** (Royal Chapel), Fernando and Isabel's private chapel (tel. 22 92 39). During their prosperous reign, they funneled almost a quarter of the royal income into the chapel's construction (1504-1521) to produce their proper burial place: intricate Gothic carvings, meticulously rendered statues (St. Peter and St. Paul among them), as well as La Reja, the gilded iron grill of Master Bartolomé, which is considered one of the finest in Spain. Behind this grill rest the elaborate, almost lifelike marble figures of the royals themselves. Fernando and Isabel recline to the right; beside them sleeps their daughter Juana la Loca (the Mad) and her husband Felipe el Hermoso (the Fair). Their lead caskets lie in the crypt directly below, accessible by a small stairway on either side. The smaller fifth coffin belongs to the hastily-buried child-king of Portugal, Miguel, whose death allowed Carlos V to ascend the throne. To the horror of the rest of the royal family, Juana insisted on keeping the body of her husband with her for an unpleasantly long time after he died. Friends had a hard time convincing the insanely jealous wife that Felipe was actually dead. After they pried him from her arms, the remains of his body were laid to rest in the cathedral.

Next door in the sacristy, Isabel's private **colección de arte,** the highlight of the chapel, favors Flemish and German masterpieces of the 15th century including Memling, Bouts, and Roger van der Weyden. The glittering **alhajas reales** (royal jewels)—the queen's golden crown, scepter, and jewelry box, and the king's sword—shine in the middle of the sacristy. (Open April-Sept. Mon.-Sat. 10:30am-1pm and 4-7pm; Oct.-March Mon.-Sat. 10:30am-1pm and 3:30-6:30pm, Sun. 11am-1pm. 250ptas.)

The adjacent **cathedral** (tel. 22 29 59) was built by *los Reyes* upon the foundation of the major Arab mosque. The first purely Renaissance cathedral in Spain, its massive Corinthian pillars support an astonishingly high vaulted nave. Admission is also good for the cathedral's **tesoro** and **museo.** (Open April-Sept. daily 10am-1:30pm and 4-7pm; Oct.-March 10am-1:30pm and 3:30-6:30pm. Closed Sunday mornings. 250ptas.)

At the end of C. San Juan de Dios, the 16th-century **Hospital Real** is divided into four tiled courtyards. Above the landing of the main staircase, the Mudéjar-coffered ceiling echoes those of the Alhambra. Nearby rise the twin spires of **Basílica de San Juan de Dios,** a Baroque temple. The 14th-century **Monasterio de San Jerónimo** is around the corner; badly damaged by Napoleon's troops, it has been restored admirably. (Monastery open daily 10am-1:30pm and 4-7:30pm; Oct.-March 10am-1:30pm and 3:30-7pm. 250ptas. Basílica open for mass. Hospital open Mon.-Fri. 9am-2pm. Free.)

ANDALUCÍA

The Albaicín

Be cautious here at night, but don't miss the Albaicín, the old Arab quarter where the Moors built their first fortress. After the *Reconquista*, a small Moorish population clung to the neighborhood on this hill until their expulsion in the 17th century. The abundance of Middle Eastern cuisine and the recent construction of a mosque attest to a continued Arab influence in Granada.

The best way to explore this maze is to proceed along Carrera del Darro off Pl. Nueva, climb the Cuesta del Chapiz on the left, then wander aimlessly through Muslim ramparts, cisterns, and gates. On Pl. Nueva, the 16th-century **Real Cancillería** (or Audiencia), with the beautiful arcaded patio and stalactite ceiling, was the Christians' Ayuntamiento. farther north are the 11th-century **Arab baths**, C. Darro, 31 (tel. 22 23 39; open Tues.-Sat. 10am-2pm; free). Behind the Plateresque facade of Casa Castril, the **Museo Arqueológico**, C. Darro, 41, showcases funerary urns, coins, Classical sculpture, Carthaginian alabaster vases, Muslim lamps, and ceramics (tel. 22 56 40; open Tues.-Sun. 9:30am-2pm; 250ptas, free for EU members).

Cármenes—traditional whitewashed Arab villas with luxurious walled gardens—characterize the neighborhood. Bus #12 travels from beside the cathedral to C. Pagés at the top of the Albaicín. From here, walk down C. Agua through the **Puerta Arabe**, an old gate to the city at Pl. Larga. The terrace adjacent to **Iglesia de San Nicolás** affords the city's best view of the Alhambra, especially in winter when glistening snow adorns the Sierra Nevada behind it. To the west of San Nicolás, **Monasterio de Santa Isabel la Real,** founded by Queen Isabel in 1501, has exceptional coffered ceilings and Plateresque Gothic facade.

ENTERTAINMENT

Entertainment listings are near the back of the daily paper, the *Ideal* (120ptas), under *Cine y Espectáculos;* the Friday supplement lists even more bars, concerts, and special events. The *Guía del Ocio*, sold at newsstands (100ptas), lists the city's clubs, pubs, and cafes. The tourist office also distributes a monthly cultural guide.

For **flamenco,** tourists and locals alike flock to **Los Jardines Neptuno,** C. Arabial (tel. 52 25 33), near the Neptuno shopping center at the base of C. Recogidas. Rows and rows of plastic chairs sit under a huge tent (3500ptas cover includes one drink). A more smoky, intimate setting awaits at **Eshavira** (tel. 20 32 62), C. Postigo de la Cuna, in an alley off of C. Azacayes, between C. Elvira and the Gran Vía. This is *the* place to go for flamenco, jazz, or a fusion of the two. Photos of Nat King Cole and other jazz greats plaster the walls. One drink minimum. Call for music schedule.

Pubs and bars spread across several neighborhoods, genres, and energy levels. The most boisterous crowd belongs to **C. Pedro Antonio de Alarcón** running from Pl. Albert Einstein to C. Perogidas. Here, on Thursday, Friday, and Saturday nights, rowdy university students and high school groupies flood the many pubs, disco bars, and late-night pizza joints. **Iguazu** on C. Socrates off of C. Pedro Antonio de Alarcon offers a merengue or salsa beat, plus an occasional dance teacher. Also along Pedro Antonio de Alarcon, the daring cram into **Bar-Rama,** nicknamed **"Chupitos"** for the shot-sized concoctions they serve—some with such appetizing names as "Aborto de gallona" (chicken abortion) and "Vomito Lagarto" (lizard vomit). *Tapas* and *terrazas* attract friendly folks to **Campo del Principa,** up C. Pavaneras from Pl. Isabel la Católica, off Pl. del Realejo. Closer to Pl. Nueva, at the top of Calderería Nueva, a young throng of vacationers with beer bottles lounge on the steps of Placeta San Gregorio outside **El 22. Babylon,** Placeta Sillería, 5, off C. Reyes Católicos before Pl. Nueva, pumps Reggae, hip-hop, and funk, and moonlights as a speakeasy for study abroad students—thus its nickname, "Guirilandia." If you are looking for a bit more class and have a bit more cash, try **Hannigan and Sons** (tel. 22 48 26), C. Cetti Merien between C. Elvira and Gran Vía de Colon. The Irish bartender pours a succulent Guinness (500ptas) in a jolly atmosphere. Teatotalers can lounge the night away in the candle-lit pillowed dens of **Jardín de los Sueños,** on C. Calderería Nueva, while sipping exotic *infusions* for 250ptas. Higher up, in the Albacin, patrons of the refined

Casa de Yanguas casually sip beer (200ptas) to classical tunes amidst contemporary art in fountained Moorish patios. Follow Cuesta del Chapiz to its end near C. San Buenaventura (open daily 8pm-3am).

The **Aliatar,** C. Recogidas (tel. 26 19 84), near Pta. Real, is a conventional movie theater showing mostly American films (dubbed in Spanish), along with an occasional Spanish one (500ptas, 300ptas on Wed.). The twenty- to thirty-something crowd dresses elegantly for **Cine/Disco Granada 10,** C. Cárcel Baja, 14 (tel. 22 40 01), 3 blocks from Pl. Isabel la Católica along Gran Vía de Colon. They turn off the projector at midnight and bop to Euro-house through the wee hours (700-1000ptas cover includes one drink).

A number of festivals sweep the city during the summer. Granada's **Corpus Christi** celebrations, processions, and bullfights are well-known (they happen in May or June). **Espárrago Rock** now cultivates performances by contemporary Spanish musicians as well as foreign big-name bands, usually in March. Every May, avant-garde theater groups from around the world make a pilgrimage to Granada for the **International Theater Festival** (tel. 22 93 44 or 22 43 84). The **Festival Internacional de Música y Danza** (mid-June to early July) sponsors open-air performances of classical music and ballet in the Alhambra's Palacio de Carlos V. Seats run 1000-6000ptas. Granada also hosts the new **Auditorio Manuel de Falla** (tel. 22 21 88), one of Spain's premier concert halls. Performances at the **Cuevas Gitanas de Sacromonte** (Gypsy caves) are not as appealing as they may sound. Once home to a thriving Gypsy community, the hill is now essentially a snare for tourists.

■ Near Granada: La Cartuja and Fuentevaqueros

On the outskirts of Granada stands **La Cartuja** (tel. 16 19 32), a 16th-century Carthusian monastery and pinnacle of Baroque artistry in Granada. Marble with rich brown tones and swirling forms (a stone unique to nearby Lanjarón) marks the sacristy of Saint Bruno. To reach the monastery, take bus #8 from in front of the cathedral (open Mon.-Sat. 10am-1pm and 4-8pm; Oct.-March 10am-1pm and 3:30-6pm; free Sun. 10am-noon).

Author of *Bodas de sangre* (Blood Weddings) and *Romancero Gitano* (Gypsy Ballads), poet and playwright Federico García Lorca was born outside the tiny town of **Fuentevaqueros** and was shot by right-wing forces near Granada at the outbreak of the Civil War. The ancestral house-turned-**museo** (tel. 51 64 53) has photographs, manuscripts, and some personal sketches. The museum may be a psychoanalyst's dream, but few others get that excited. (Opens to 15 people every 30min. Tues.-Sun. 10am-1pm and 6-8pm; Oct.-March 10am-1pm and 4-6pm; April-June Tues.-Sat. 10am-1pm and 5-7pm. 200ptas.) Buses run from the train station hourly (150ptas).

■ Sierra Nevada

The peaks of Mulhacén (3481m) and Veleta (3470m), the highest in Spain, sparkle with snow and groan with tourists for most of the year. Ski season runs from December to April. During the summer, tourists hike, parasail, and take jeep tours.

Before you go, check road and snow conditions (tel. 24 91 19 English spoken) and hotel vacancies. Bring warm clothes. If you plan to hike extensively, head to **Librería Flash** in Granada, for their indispensible **map** of the Sierra for 800ptas (see **Granada: Practical Information: Foreign Language Bookstores,** p. 448).

VELETA AND PRADO LLANO

Near the foot of Granada's Alhambra, the highest road in Europe begins its ascent to one of its highest peaks. The road begins as a run-of-the-mill *camino* through the arid countryside, then scales the daunting face of the Sierra. Due to snow, cars can only cruise to the very top of Veleta in August and September.

The Autocares Bonal **bus** (tel. 27 31 00) from Granada to Veleta is a bargain (one per day, 9am, round-trip 640ptas). Buy tickets in the bar El Ventorrillo (see **Granada,**

p. 444). The bus runs to the resort community of **Prado Llano** (19km from the peak), stopping at a **cabina-restaurante,** but you may be able to coax the driver to go to the top (for 200ptas) if conditions allow it. The hike to the top is steep, treacherous, and takes about three hours—bring water and wear sunscreen. Call **Cetursa** (tel. 24 91 11) for info on other activities.

Veleta has 39 slopes and 61km of skiing area, with a vertical drop of 1300m. Lift tickets cost 2325ptas in *temporada alta* (winter), 2025ptas in *temporada baja* (off-peak season). **Rent skis** in the Gondola Building and in Pl. Prado Llano (full equipment, 2500ptas per day). This is the southernmost ski resort in Europe—wear sunscreen or suffer DNA mutations. The cheapest accommodation is the **Albergue Universitario** (tel. 48 03 05), Peñones de San Francisco (1300ptas per person, over 26 1600ptas; reserve early in winter; open year-round).

■ La Alpujarra

La Alpujarra's impoverished, secluded white villages huddle along the southern slopes of the Sierra Nevada. Although its roads are now paved and the towns well-traveled, a medieval Berber influence is still evident in the region's architecture. Low-slung houses rendered from earth and slate prevail only here and in Morocco's Atlas Mountains. After the fall of Granada, the Berbers were exiled to La Alpujarra, where Christian-Muslim conflicts resumed. In a gory battle at Bananco de la Sangre, Christian blood is said to have trickled uphill to avoid contamination with the plasma of the heathens below. Finally, in 1610, John of Austria ousted the Moors from La Alpujarra and ended their reign on the peninsula. On the heels of the Muslims, settlers from Galicia and Asturias brought Celtic and Visigothic traditions found nowhere else in Andalucía. The legacy of Moorish defiance lives on and peaks during the **Fiestas de Moros y Cristianos** in Trevélez, a dramatization of the Moorish-Christian conflict.

Although tourists have recently discovered the beauty of these settlements and the surrounding region, the Alpujarras remain among Spain's poorest areas. Until the 1950s, travel was possible only by foot or mule, and the area still suffers from severe drought, unemployment, and low literacy rates. Nevertheless, the region's slow-paced life-style and hospitality make for a refreshing visit.

Alsina Graells buses zoom from Granada (see p. 444) to Bérchules and stop in the most elevated towns: Órgiva, Pampaneira, Bubión, Portugos, and Trevélez. A different bus running to Almería serves Ugíjan and the eastern villages (each line has 2-3 departures daily). Plan for a night in the mountains since the single return buses to Granada and Almería leave early the next morning. Although these are the only forms of public transportation between the villages, travel **on foot** is a tradition of Alpujarras. The locals, aware of the transportation problem, often sympathize with **hitchers.**

LANJARÓN

Lanjarón (pop. 4300) is Spain's version of Evian, France. Famed throughout the country for mineral water that's sucked down by the gallon, Spaniards once came here in droves after mineral water was said to have medicinal value. Many said it cured kid-

---

Holy Water, Batman!

The water-endowed ecstasy in Lanjarón plunges to new levels the third week of June, during the **Fiestas del Agua y del Jamón** in honor of San Juan. While the rest of Spain celebrates with bonfires and fireworks, Lanjarón celebrates with water. From midnight to 1am water is dumped from balconies and spewed from squirt bottles, while throngs of soaked youngsters parade through town chanting *"mucha agua, mucha agua, eh, eh, olé!"* Fire hoses, plastic buckets, bedpans, and plastic cups are all acceptable instruments for aquatic assault, but the unwitting tenderfoot who dares splash murky puddles will be sternly scolded. Be prepared to be locked out of your *hostal* for the duration of the hour, and be sure to pack a change of clothes!

ney ailments and rheumatism. A mere 45km daytrip from Granada, Lanjarón abounds with accommodations. **Hostal Dólar,** Av. Andalucía, 5 (tel. 77 01 83), offers bright and clean rooms (singles 1200ptas, with bath 1500ptas; doubles: 2600ptas; 3000ptas). Drivers should turn left just before Órgiva. If taking the **bus** to Ugíjar via the main highway, disembark in Lanjarón to wander past flower-filled houses and drink from delicious public water fountains (marked *agua potable* only).

PAMPANEIRA

As the road winds in serpentine curves up to Pampaneira, the lowest of the high Alpujarran villages (1059m), the landscape quickly becomes harsh. This is the first in a trio of hamlets overlooking the **Poqueira Gorge,** a huge ravine cut by the Río Poqueira, which trickles down from Mulhacén. For more info on the region's natural wonders, visit **Nevadensis** (tel. 76 31 27; fax 76 33 01) in Pampaneira's main square. A local organization associated with the **Parque Natural de La Sierra Nevada,** they arrange for rural accommodations, horseback riding, and other services (open Sun.-Tues. 10am-3pm, Wed.-Sat. 10am-2pm and 4-6pm). **Hostal Pampaneira** (tel. 76 30 02), just off the highway in front of the bus stop, provides large rooms with polished chestnut furniture, all with bath (singles 1500-2300ptas, doubles 3000-3600ptas). Stock up at the **supermarket** three rows uphill (open daily 9am-2pm and 5-8pm).

Buddhism in Bubión

Bubión has a distinctly Buddhist slant. It was the birthplace of Osel, the Spanish reincarnation of the Tibetan lama Yeshe, one of the first lamas born in the West. Visitors from around the world (among them the Dalai Lama himself) come to meditate at the Buddhist retreat **Osel-Ling** (clear light), high in the mountains above Bubión. Osel is now in India, but his retreat is currently organizing courses in Buddhist studies and opens its *sala de meditación* to the public from 3-6pm (free). For more information, call Osel-Ling (tel. 34 31 34).

BUBIÓN

A steep 3km hike from Pampaneira separates the Berber architecture, village charm, and three contemporary art galleries of Bubión. For info, check out **Rustic Blue,** Barrio La Ermita, s/n (tel. 76 33 81; fax 76 31 34), the closest thing to a tourist office in the Alpujarras. The helpful staff organizes excursions, cooking lessons with Irish mountaineer/chef Conor Clifford, and lodging (open daily 10am-2pm and 5-8pm). **Las Terrazas,** Placeta del Sol (tel. 76 30 34), has spotless rooms with terra-cotta tiled floors, Alpujarran woven bedspreads, and baths (singles 2500ptas, doubles 3740ptas, breakfast included). Locals rave about the portions at **Restaurante La Artesa,** on the main road in front of the bus stop (*menú* 1100ptas, *menú alpujarreño* 1300ptas; open daily 1:30-4pm and 8-11pm). See **Buddhism in Bubión,** p. 457, for info on Bubión's spiritual heritage.

CAPILEIRA

Capileira (1436m) is perched atop the Poqueira Gorge and makes a good base for exploring the neighboring villages and the back side of the Sierra Nevada. Cobblestone alleys wind up the slope while peaks loom above and the valley plummets below. Enjoy the vista from your bedroom window at **Mesón-Hostal Poqueira,** C. Dr. Castillo, 6 (tel. 76 30 48). Rooms are pleasant and fresh, with baths and central heating. (Singles 1500ptas, with bath 2000ptas; doubles: 3000ptas; 4000ptas. Breakfast included.) While here, enjoy the scrumptious and filling 1200ptas *menú.* (The restaurant is closed Mondays.) **Supermercado Rubies,** downhill from the bus station, supplies provisions (open Mon.-Sat 9am-2pm and 5-9pm, Sun. 9am-2pm).

The road through Capileira continues up the mountainside and by June may be clear enough to make the two-hour climb to **Mulhacén,** Spain's highest peak. Proceed with extreme caution when approaching the summit—the wind is gusty, the snow is slippery, and the drop to the other side is unforgiving. The area above 2700m

may become a National Park with limited private access. To reach the trail, follow the Sierra Nevada signs. A fork appears after 20km. Go right to Mulhacén.

   Hiking around Capileira is pleasant if undramatic—*tómalo tranquilo* (take it easy) as the locals do, and saunter from the whitewashed village to the verdant gorge. Descend the stairs to the left of Fonda El Tilo and follow the dirt road to the bridge. Catch glimpses of traditional Alpujarran homes, built with flat grey stone and deep rounded windows to blend with the landscape. More ambitious hikers should consult Nevadensis or **Rustic Blue** (see **Pampaneira**, p. 457) for further suggestions.

TREVÉLEZ

Rural and temporal isolation escalates with the altitude in Trevélez (1476m), continental Spain's highest community. Aside from its Alpujarran charms the town is best-known for its cured ham, whose special qualities will probably elude all but the true *jamón* connoisseur. Steep roads weave in and out of three distinct *barrios* (upper, middle, lower) amidst the sounds of rushing water carefully channeled down thousand-year-old Moorish irrigation systems. In fact, some Moors were spared from the Inquisition because the Christians could not operate the channels without them.

   Trevélez is a logical base for the ascent to **Mulhacén.** Every August, throngs of locals climb to pay homage to the **Virgen de las Nieves** (Virgin of the Snow), whose shrine is at the peak. Those summit-bound should head north on the trail leaving the upper village; avoid the lower trail which follows the swampy Río Trevélez. You have three options: continue past the Cresta de los Postreros for a good 5½ hours and you will reach the Cañada de Siete Lagunas (the largest lake should be directly in front of you); go right to see a famous cave-refuge. To reach Mulhacén, go up the ridge south of the refuge. It is *not* advisable to hike Mulhacén the same day you visit the lake.

   Despite numerous signs near the bus stop advertising *camas* (beds), the steep walk to **Hostal Fernando** (tel. 85 85 65) is well worth it. The hostal is on C. Pista, almost one kilometer uphill on the left side of town from the bus stop. The friendly management keeps spacious, attractive rooms with an unbeatable view of the mountains from the terrace (singles 1800ptas; doubles 2500ptas). They also rent apartments by the day for two people (4000ptas) and for four people (7000ptas). A great restaurant is **La Fragua**, C. Carcel (tel. 85 85 73), which overlooks the town and valley from its second floor *comedor* (*plato alpujarreño*, 750ptas).

YEGEN AND UGÍJAR

In the villages of the Eastern Alpujarras, tourists are rare and donkeys are everywhere. On a mountaintop outside Berchules sits tiny **Yegen,** whose only monument is a plaque marking the house where British Hispanophile and Bloomsbury affiliate **Gerald Brenan** lived (and Virginia Woolf visited) in the 1920s and 30s. Brenan immortalized the name of Yegen and the customs and traditions of La Alpujarra in *South from Granada,* his autobiographical account of life in the region. Just around the corner, **Bar Nuevo La Fuente,** C. Real, 38 (tel. 85 10 67), offers inexpensive accommodations with private baths (1400ptas per person). Twelve kilometers southeast of Yegen is **Ugíjar,** a larger agricultural village where Odysseus stopped one day to patch up his ships. You can stop for more than one day at **Pensión Vidaña,** Ctra. Almería (tel. 76 70 10), which has bright rooms, some with enormous balconies, all with A/C and heat (singles 1700ptas; doubles 3200ptas; both with bath). The reasonably priced restaurant downstairs won the Washington, D.C. Golden Cock medal for best Alpujarran cuisine. Ugíjar is accessible by bus from Almería (2-3 departures daily).

COSTA DEL SOL

The coast has sold its soul to the Devil, and now he's starting to collect. Artifice covers its once-natural charms as chic promenades and hotels seal off small towns from the shoreline. The former Phoenician, Greek, Roman, and Arab ports cater to an

international clientele with wads of money and attitude. The Costa del Sol officially extends from Tarifa in the southwest to Cabo de Gata east of Almería. Post-industrial Málaga is in the middle. To the northeast, the hills dip straight into the ocean, where the scenery is less spoiled but beaches are usually rocky. To the southeast, the Costa is more built up and water washes almost entirely against concrete.

Nothing can take away the coast's major attraction, however: eight months of spring and four of summer per year. Sun-freaks swarm everywhere in July and August. Make reservations or be ready for a search. Prices double in high season. Some sleep on the beaches, but this is not a wise option for solo travelers and women. Alternatively, ask around for *casas particulares.* June is the best time to visit, when summer weather has come to town but most vacationers haven't. **Trains** go as far as Málaga and Fuengirola; private **bus lines** supply connections along the coast itself. Railpasses are not valid, but prices are reasonable.

■ Almería

Once one of the poorer cities in Andalucía, Almería is a seaside oasis undergoing a boom. It crept out of the Franco era slumping with the rest of Andalucía, but a population of migrant professionals has led a resurgence. The newest Almeríans swear by the city's year-round temperate climate and pristine beaches, and hope to promote Almería by hosting the eagerly awaited Mediterranean Games in 2005. A huge Moorish fortress still presides over the city, but travelers most appreciate Almería for the miles of soft sand stretching along the Mediterranean toward the Cabo de Gata, the eastern edge of the Costa del Sol.

Orientation and Practical Information The city revolves around **Puerta de Purchena,** a six-way intersection with a fountain, just down C. Tiendas from the old town. To reach the Puerta from the **bus station** (20min.), follow Av. Estación out of Pl. Barcelona, turn right onto Av. Federico García Lorca, then go left. **Rambla de Obispo Orbera** leads into Pta. Purchena. The **train station,** Pl. Barcelona, is across from the **bus station,** Pl. Estación; follow the above directions to get to Pta. Purchena.

The **tourist office,** Parque Nicolás Salmerón, s/n (tel. 27 43 55), distributes information on the city and province as well as a map (100ptas; open Mon.-Fri. 9am-7pm, Sat. 9am-1pm). Follow Po. de Almería out of Pta. Purchena toward the port, and turn right onto Parque de Salmerón. **Banco Central Hispano,** Po. Almería, 18 (tel. 23 43 43), offers currency exchange (open Mon.-Fri. 8:30am-2:30pm, Sat. 8:30am-1pm). **Luggage storage** is available at the train station for 400ptas. Call 22 61 61 or 25 11 11 for a **taxi.** For medication, go to the **pharmacy,** Po. Almería, 19 (open Mon.-Fri. 9:30am-1:30pm and 5-8:30pm, Sat. 10am-1pm). **Hospital Torre Cardenas** answers at tel. 21 21 19, and the **Red Cross** at tel. 22 22 22. The **police** can be reached at tel. 22 37 04. In an **emergency,** dial 061. The **postal code** is 14070. The **telephone code** is (9)50.

The **airport** (tel. 21 37 00 or 21 37 15), 9km out of town, has daily flights to Madrid and Barcelona. **Viajes Alysol,** Po. Almería, 32 (tel. 23 76 22), offers **AmEx** and **Iberia** services (open Mon.-Fri. 9:30am-1:30pm and 5-8:30pm, Sat. 9:30am-1:30pm). **Trains,** Pl. Estación, 6 (tel. 25 11 35), run to: Granada (3 per day, 3hr., 1520ptas); Málaga (2 per day, 7hr., 3000ptas); Sevilla (2 per day, 7-10hr., 3700ptas); Madrid (2 per day, 7hr., 3800ptas). Across the way, **buses** leave from Pl. Barcelona (tel. 21 00 29) to: Granada (5 per day, 2hr., 1285ptas); Málaga (8 per day, 3½hr., 1915ptas); Córdoba (1 per day, 6hr., 2995ptas); Sevilla (3 per day, 5½hr., 3995ptas); Madrid (3 per day, 8hr., 2980ptas); Mojácar (5 per day, 1½hr., 820ptas); Murcia (5 per day, 3hr., 2115ptas); Alicante (4 per day, 5hr., 2550ptas); Barcelona (2 per day, 14hr., 7045ptas). There's a **RENFE** office (tel. 23 18 22), C. Alcalde Muñoz, a block from Pta. Purchena

Accommodations and Food Well-located, bright, and attractive, **Hostal Bristol,** Pl. San Sebastián, 8 (tel./fax 23 15 95), beside the church in Pta. Purchena, provides A/C, a TV, and a full bath in every room (singles 2600ptas; doubles 4400ptas; call a week in advance July-Aug.; Visa, MC). **Hostal Andalucía,** C. Granada,

9 (tel. 23 77 33), has dimly lit rooms with antiques. (Singles 1500-1800ptas, with bath 2200-2700ptas. Doubles: 2700-3100ptas; 3400-4000ptas.) Numerous cafes line the Po. Almería. With ham chandeliers and over 70 types of *tapas*, **Casa Puga,** C. Jovellanos, 7 (tel. 23 15 30), in the old quarter, is always packed (open Mon.-Sat. 11am-4pm and 8pm-midnight). The classy **Augusto Cesare,** Parque Nicolás Salmerón, 17 (tel. 27 16 16), located along the water and down the street from the tourist office, has over 30 varieties of pizza (950-1200ptas; open daily 12:30-4pm and 8pm-1am). For groceries, browse the aisles of supermarket **Simago,** Po. de Almería (open Mon.-Sat. 9am-9pm).

Sights and Entertainment Built in 995 by order of Abderramán III of Córdoba, the **Alcazaba** (tel. 27 16 17), a magnificent 14-acre Moorish fortress, spans two ridges overlooking the city and the sea. From Pl. Carmen next to Pta. de Purchena, follow C. Antonio Vico (open daily 10am-2pm and 5-8:30pm; 250ptas, free with EC passport). The **cathedral** (tel. 23 48 48), in the old town, looks more like a fortress as a result of repeated raids by Berber pirates (open Mon.-Fri. 10am-5pm, Sat. 10am-1pm; 300ptas).

In general, **la marcha** (nightlife) congregates in the small streets behind the post office. An especially die-hard crowd gathers in pubs **Pisarela** and **Venue,** both on C. San Pedro off C. Padre Luque. **Georgia Jazz Club,** Padre Luque, 17 (tel. 25 76 84), is near the post office and Po. Almería. The club has live music most nights, beer (200ptas), whiskey (from 450ptas), and fruit and herbal teas (125ptas). At **Carpa,** a few miles east along the coastal road to Cabo de Gata, a half-dozen tented bars and competing bass lines rock the beach deep into the night. Buses stop running around 11pm, but a taxi will go there for about 700ptas.

Despite the miles of crystalline **beaches** stretching beneath the rugged **Sierra del Cabo de Gata,** a natural park only 30km east of town, locals crowd the pebbly **Playa Zapillo** in town. The town of **Cabo de Gata** is accessible by Bercerra bus (tel. 22 44 03 or 21 00 29; 6 per day, 1hr., 275ptas). From there, a string of beaches, including **Las Salines,** reaches several miles to *el faro* (lighthouse). A two-hour walk from there, **Caleta San José** just may be the nicest beach on the Spanish Mediterranean coast. The last bus returns from Cabo de Gata at 8pm (Sat. 5:30pm and Sun. 7pm). Hitching back to Almería is a risky alternative.

■ Mojácar

The houses of Mojácar rest on a hill, flanked on one side by mountains of scorched earth and an expanse of turquoise-blue Mediterranean on the other. This small resort community thrives in July and August, when hordes of international visitors join an already substantial contingent of expatriates who have wisely made Mojácar their home. Do not despair. The abundance of souvenir shops and non-*hispanoparlantes* (Spanish speakers) has not diluted Mojácar's dramatic landscape.

Practical Information The **tourist office** (tel./fax 47 51 62) is in Pl. Nueva. From the bus stop, follow the highway uphill for about 20 minutes; it eventually leads into Pl. Nueva, the town center (open Mon.-Fri. 10am-2pm and 5-7:30pm, Sat. 10am-1pm). The only reliable **ATM** in the pueblo can be found just below Pl. Nueva, at C. Glorieta, 3. **Buses** leave for Almería (4 per day, Sun. 3 per day, 2 hr., 820ptas) from the bus stop, located 20 minutes downhill from Bar Simón in the town center. For a **taxi** call 47 81 84. The **Red Cross** answers at tel. 47 89 52. Summon **police** by calling 47 51 29; in **emergencies,** dial 091 or 092. The **postal code** is 04638. The **telephone code** is (9)50.

Accommodations and Food Finding a bed in small but confusing Mojácar can be difficult. To reach the intimate **Hostal Luna,** C. Estación Nueva, 11 (tel. 47 80 32), walk up two flights of stairs from Pl. Nueva, turn right at the church wall, walk uphill to the top, and turn left. The hike leads to cheery Mediterranean decor, friendly

management, and spotless rooms (singles 2000-4000ptas; doubles 3500-5500ptas). The rooftop terrace serves meals and offers a priceless view. Walt Disney was born at **Pensión Torreón,** C. Jazmín, 4 (tel. 47 52 59), an appropriate cradle for the man who brought *Cinderella* to the big screen. Its five elegant bedrooms sit behind a seaview terrace. The owner can tell you all about the mystery surrounding Disney's birth over breakfast (500ptas; singles 3000-5000ptas; doubles 5000-6000ptas). To get there from Pl. Nueva, follow C. Indalo, take the second left (C. Eumedia), a right at the end onto C. Puntica, a right onto C. LaGuardia, and a left downhill along C. Jazmín.

Mojácar doesn't have a large selection of cheap eateries, but you'll find more variety and better value in the old or new town than at the *playa* or Pl. Nueva. **L'arlecchino** (tel. 47 80 37), in the aptly named Pl. Flores through the Moorish arch on C. Puntica, serves Italian and Spanish dishes on the *terraza* (*menú* 800ptas; open daily 11:30am-4pm and 7-11pm)..

Mickey Mouse Linked to Prehistoric Indalo Man

Late cartoonist Walt Disney was born in Mojácar, as was the figure called Indalo Man, first drawn on nearby cave walls around 2500 BC. Disney was born José Guirao around 1901, and after the death of his father, he and his mother emigrated to California. When she died, the farming Disney clan adopted teenage José, subsequently naming him "Walt." Back in the motherland, Mojácan villagers have always used the ancient Indalo Man, a crude figure holding a rainbow, to ward off bad luck and natural disaster. Archaeologists think the Indalo symbolizes a pact between God and humankind, and proud residents of Mojácar link Disney's success to his native town's animated history.

Hit the Beach Mojácar's vertiginous streets and breathtaking *miradores* (plazas with picture-perfect views) make it well-suited to romantic strolls and rosy daydreams. **Buses** run every hour between the *pueblo* and *playa* and along the shore (in summer 9:30am-1:30pm and 3:30-11pm; in winter 10am-1pm and 5-10pm; 100ptas). In the village, buses leave from the stop below Pl. Nueva. To reach the village from the beach, get on at one of the stops along Av. Mediterránea.

Entertainment Mojácar pulses with nightlife, and the *pueblo*'s streets brim with pubs. Visit **Lapu Lapu,** on C. Horno and **Sahara,** cafe/"disc...o...asis," under the Moorish Arch. **Budú Pub,** C. Eastación Nueva, has a soaring rooftop terrace that may be the most romantic spot in Mojácar. Along the shore, pubs turn into loud *chiringuitos* (beach bars) until 5 or 6am in the summer. Go by car if you can, because buses stop running at 11pm, taxis disappear at sundown, and walking the highway is a poorly-lit, dangerous alternative. Among the most popular is **Pachá,** on Po. Mediterráneo, where palm trees shade the bar. The infamous **Tuareg,** on the road to Carboneras, has the highest decibel levels in town. For a midnight dip, the pool at **Master Disco** (tel. 46 81 33), on the highway midway between the *playa* and *pueblo,* is open until 5am. A huge inflatable creature dressed in mauve greets revelers at the entrance. Expats run more laid-back watering holes—the **Time and Place,** in Pl. Flores, serves soothing cocktails, while Gordon pours Guiness and cultivates an intellectual atmosphere at **El Sartén** (familiarly known as Gordon's), C. Estación Nueva, behind the church. Keeping its promise as a *bar de copas* (night caps), **El Lord Azul,** C. Fronton, 1, plays blues and classic rock for an international crowd well into every night.

■ Almuñécar

In the 4th century BC, a booming fish-salting industry brought prosperity to this Phoenician port town. The Romans took over a hundred years later, constructing temples and an aqueduct, and calling it **Sexi.** You may, too. Seemingly endless boardwalks invite guests to gaze at silvery-gray sands, while exotic birds and mangos thrive in the sultry tropical environment.

Practical Information The **tourist office** (tel. 63 11 25) answers questions and provides a free map in a hideous mauve mansion on Av. Europa, off Av. Costa del Sol. From the bus station, exit right and follow Carrera de la Concepción through the rotary to Av. Costa del Sol; turn left onto Av. Europa and walk past the park (with its own mauve buildings); the office is on the right (open Mon.-Sat. 10am-2pm and 4-7pm). For medical assistance, rush to **Centro de Salud** (tel. 63 20 63), Ctra. Málaga. The **police** (tel. 83 86 00) are in Pl. Constitución at the Ayuntamiento, up C. Puerta de Velez from Av. Europa. In any **emergency,** dial 091 or 092. The **postal code** is 18690. The **telephone code** (9)58.

Buses run from the station (tel. 63 01 40) at the corner of Av. Fenicia and Av. Juan Carlos I to: Málaga (8 per day, 1½hr., 745ptas); Granada (7 per day, 1½hr., 830ptas); Madrid (1 per day, 7hr., 2300ptas); Nerja (8 per day, 30min., 295ptas). **Luggage storage** is available at the station (300ptas).

Accommodations and Food Three convenient and reasonably priced *hostales* are on **Av. Europa.** Walking toward the tourist office and the beach, the first to appear is **Hotel R. Carmen,** Av. Europa, 19 (tel. 63 14 13 or 63 25 11). All rooms have gigantic baths tiled in soothing blue floral prints. (Singles 2000-3500ptas; doubles 3500-5000ptas. Breakfast 300ptas. Visa, MC, AmEx.) **Residencia Tropical** (tel. 63 34 58), on Av. Europa a half-block from the beach, has a bar and spotless, well-furnished rooms with bathrooms (singles 2300-3200ptas; doubles 3300-5200ptas; Visa, MC).

Plenty of restaurants line **Po. Puerta del Mar** and **Po. San Cristóbal,** the place to savor the day's catch on a beach-front terrace. Locals frequent **Bar Avenida Lute y Jesús,** Av. Europa, 24 (tel. 63 42 76), across from Hotel R. Carmen. They specialize in *fritura de pescado* (fried fish 650-750ptas; *menú* 800ptas; open 8am-1:30am). Several heavenly **heladerías** (ice cream shops) dot the shore.

Sights and Entertainment Alumñécar's historical protagonists, the Phoenicians, Romans, and Moors, fought over this subtropical paradise, and each left a distinguishable mark. Built by the Moors, **Castillo de San Miguel** rests atop a massive hill at the front of Pl. Puerte del Mar. The interior is currently closed for the construction of a museum depicting the city's history. The 1900-year-old, 8km-long **acueducto,** 3km up the Río Seco from the tourist office, watered the ancient Roman town, and parts of it are still in use. Almuñécar is justly proud of its **Parque Ornitológico Loro Sexi,** beside El Castillo de San Miguel 100m from the beach, where nearly 100 species of birds nest (open June-Oct. daily 11am-2pm and 6-9pm; otherwise 10:30am-2pm and 4:30-7pm; 300ptas, children 150ptas). Nearby, uphill from the tourist office, **Parque El Majuelo's** 400 varieties of imported plants shade enticing benches.

Almuñécar's location on the **Costa Tropical** makes it beachgoers' turf. The two main beaches are separated by the jutting **Peñón del Santo. Puerta del Mar** is on the left when facing the water, **San Cristóbal** on the right. Most streets from the bus station terminate at the beach. The easiest way is via Av. Europa (signs point to Playa San Cristóbal). Walk beyond Po. Pta. del Mar to beautiful **Playa de Velilla.** Ten buses per day go through **La Herradura,** a suburb/beach on the way to Málaga frequented by windsurfers and scuba divers. The largest **nude beach** on the Costa Tropical is **Playa Cantarrijan.** If you get off at La Herradura, you will be 3-4km closer, but you will still need a car or a taxi. If you would like to join the fun, call the Asociación Naturista de Andalucía at (tel. (951) 25 40 44) or write Apdo. 301, Almería, 04070. In the evening, bar-hoppers and disco-boppers crowd the plazas and beaches behind the eastern end of C. Pta. del Mar at places like **New Fantasy.**

■ Nerja

Renowned for its pristine beaches and remarkable nearby caves, Nerja has become a playground for English-speaking visitors (during the summer, it might be hard to find someone who speaks Spanish). Visitors are seldom disappointed by the landscape.

Practical Information The multilingual **tourist office,** Pta. del Mar, 2 (tel. 252 15 31), beside the Balcón de Europa, sells a map (100ptas; open Mon.-Fri. 10am-2pm and 5:30-8pm., Sat. 10am-1pm). An **ATM** machine sits on C. Pintada on the way to the beach. For an **ambulance,** call 252 09 35. **Police** headquarters (tel. 252 15 45) are on C. Pescia; **emergency** numbers are tel. 091 and 092. The **post office,** C. Almirante Ferrándiz, 6 (tel. 252 17 49), sorts mail (open Mon.-Fri. 8:30am-2:30pm, Sat. 9:30am-1pm). The **postal code** is 29780. The **telephone code** is (9)5.

The **bus,** C. San Miguel, 3 (tel. 252 15 04), sends autocars to: Málaga (12 per day, 1½hr., 450ptas); Almuñécar (6 per day, 30min., 295ptas); Almería (5 per day, 4hr., 1455ptas); Granada (2 per day, 2¼hr., 1065ptas); Sevilla (3 per day, 4hr., 2320-2695ptas); Marbella (change in Málaga).

The Fifth Bomb

The area surrounding Mojácar has a sordid legacy. In the 1960s, as Spain was debating whether to join NATO, a USAF B-52 bomber carrying five hydrogen bombs blew up over the village of Palomares, 20km north of Mojácar, during an in-flight refueling mishap. Locals looked on as U.S. personnel in radiation suits combed the town in search of the bombs. Four were recovered and identified; the fifth emerged wrapped in a plastic tarp with no serial number evident. Spanish Greenpeace still doubts it was ever found. Much of Spain and Europe boycotted the area's produce (mostly tomatoes) as anti-NATO sentiment reached epic levels. To down-play the accident, the U.S. Ambassador and Franco's Minister of the Interior staged a seaside photo-op, swimming in the water before a dozen CIA agents. The U.S. then built a health clinic in the town. Palomares has since prospered with copious harvests of tomatoes, leeks, and melons, but some locals still blame defects and illnesses on the mysterious fifth bomb.

Accommodations and Food The cheapest place in town, **Hostal Residencia Mena,** C. El Barrio, 15 (tel. 252 05 41), is conveniently located off the Balcón de Europa (follow signs from the bus station to the Balcón), and has bare rooms and a shady garden (singles 1300-2000ptas; doubles 2000-3000ptas, with bath 2500-4000ptas). It's worth breaking a sweat for **Hostal Estrella del Mar,** C. Bellavista, 5 (tel. 52 04 61). From the bus station walk up the *carretera,* turn right toward "El Parador," and go left on C. General Asensio Cabanillas; C. Bella Vista is the third street on the right. Its spacious rooms have baths and terraces, most with ocean views (singles 2900-3700ptas; doubles 3700-4600ptas).

Overpriced restaurants near and along the Balcón de Europa tempt passers-by with views but offer stingy portions. For do-it-yourself cooking, the **market,** two blocks up C. San Miguel, is open daily 8am-2pm. On Playa de Burriana, **Merendero Montemar** briskly serves tourists fresh fish, *paella* (800ptas), *espeto de sardina* (600ptas), and an English breakfast (350ptas). In the heart of town, on C. Pintada, **Coconuts** has reasonably priced international dishes served on a tropical patio, as well as two-for-one happy hour drinks (8-10pm). For tea and crumpets, head to one of the many **coffeehouses** on C. Puerta del Mar or C. Almirante Ferrándiz (near the tourist office).

Sights The **Balcón de Europa,** a promenade that looks out over Playa de la Caletilla, earns its name as an internationally frequented vista. From the bus stop, follow the highway uphill to C. Pintada, which leads downhill to the *balcón.* Below the cliff are remarkable caves, best explored from the path **Paseo de los Carabineros** (off the stairs to the right of the tourist office). The walkway winds along the rocky shore to the east, past **Playa de Calahonda, Playa Carabeillo,** and **Playa Burriana.**

Nerja's long **beaches,** mostly gravel, coarse sand, and pebbles, sink into brilliant turquoise water. To reach the sprawling **Playa de la Torrecilla** from the Balcón, cut through town westward to the Playa de la Torrecilla apartments; from there follow the shoreline for 15 minutes. Much closer but more crowded is **Playa del Salón,** accessible through an alley off the *balcón,* to the right of Restaurante Marisal.

ANDALUCÍA

■ Near Nerja

The most impressive attractions near Nerja are the spectacular caves. **Cueva de Nerja,** just 5km east of Nerja, has piped-in music and photographers who try to sell you your own picture in a cave-shaped frame. The caverns consist of large chambers filled with rock formations formed over millions of years by calcium deposits and sea-borne erosion. (It's in the 1989 *Guinness Book!*) One cave is used as an amphitheater for music and ballet performances at the spectacular **Festival Cueva de Nerja,** held every July. Intrepid spelunkers have just discovered a new section of caves, report-edly four times as large as the ones already known. (Caves open July-Aug. 10am-2pm and 4-8pm. Sept.-June daily 10:30am-2pm and 3:30-6pm; 650ptas, ages 6-12 350ptas.) **Buses** run to and from Nerja (daily 8:15am-8:10pm, every hr., 95ptas). Call the tourist office for cave information (tel. 252 95 20). **Maro** is a speck of a village near the caves, with paths to nearly empty rocky beaches and coves. The Nerja tourist office has pamphlets suggesting local hikes.

■ Málaga

Birthplace of Picasso and once celebrated by Hans Christian Anderson, Rubén Darío, and native poet Vicente Alexandre, Málaga (pop. 531,140) has since lost some of its gleam. Dinginess and an infamy for petty thieves are especially hard to endure with the Costa del Sol's resort towns just down the road. Yet Málaga is a critical transporta-tion hub for all of Andalucía, and its residents are some of the liveliest, most genial people you are likely to meet in a city overrun by beach-bound tourists.

ORIENTATION AND PRACTICAL INFORMATION

To reach the town center from the **bus station** (25min.), exit right onto Callejones de Perchel, walk straight through the big intersection with Av. Aurora, take a right on Av. Andalucía, and cross the bridge, **Puente Tetuán.** From here, the palm tree and flower shop-lined **Alameda Principal** leads into **Plaza de la Marina.** For public trans-portation instead, walk one block on C. Roger de Flor to the train station.

From the **train station,** you can walk a block up **Explanada de la Estación,** turn left to the bus station and follow the directions above, or take the C-1 local train to Puente Tetuán (called **Centro-Almeda,** 135 ptas). Even better, bus #3 leads right into Pl. Marina (115 ptas). From Pl. Marina, **Calle de Molina Lario** leads to the cathedral and the old town. **Calle de Marques de Larios** connects Pl. Marina to **Plaza de la Consti-tución.** Also from Pl. Marina, **Paseo del Parque** leads past the Alcazaba. Farther on, the seaside promenade **Paseo Marítimo** stretches towards the lively beachfront dis-trict **El Pedregalejo** (accessible via bus #11 or a 30min. walk).

Tourist Offices: Municipal, Av. Cervantes, 1 (tel. 260 4410; fax. 221 4120), a little gray house along Po. Parque offering **free maps** and multilingual city info. (Open Mon.-Fri. 8:15am-2:45pm and 4:30-7pm; Sat 9:30am-1:30pm.) May also have a kiosk in front of the post office on Av. Andalucía. (Open Mon.-Fri. 9:30am-12:30pm and 4:30-7:30pm; in summer, also opens weekends 10am-2pm and 4-8pm.) **Junta de Andalucía,** Pasaje de Chinitas, 4 (tel. 221 34 45), off Pl. Constitución. Enter the alley through the arch and take the 1st right; at the corner with C. Nicasio. Bro-chures on the Costa del Sol and a map (100ptas). Open July-Sept. Mon.-Sat. 9am-7pm, Sun. 9am-1pm; in winter Mon.-Fri. 9am-2pm, Sat. 9am-1pm;

Budget Travel: TIVE, C. Huéscar, 2 (tel. 227 84 13), off C. Hilera which runs behind El Corte Inglés. Books international plane, train, and bus tickets. ISIC 700ptas. HI card 1800ptas. Open Mon.-Fri. 9am-2pm. Reservations till 1pm.

El Corte Inglés: Av. Andalucía, 4-6 (tel. 230 00 00), across from the post office. City map (495ptas). No charge for **currency exchange. Supermarket, telephones,** compact discs, health and beauty aids, a few English language books, clothes, etc. Open Mon.-Sat. 10am-9:30pm (till 10pm during the summer).

Airport: (tel. 213 61 28 or 213 61 66). From the airport, take **bus** #19 (at the City Bus sign). It leaves the airport every 30min. (6:20am-10:20pm, 200ptas) and stops at

the bus station and the corner of C. Molina Lario and Postigo de los Abades behind the cathedral. **RENFE's** train to the airport is cheaper (135ptas) and quicker (12min. to Málaga, 7:15am-11:45pm). In town, **Iberia** is at C. Molina Larios, 13 (tel. 213 61 47; national reservations tel. (901) 33 31 11; international tel. (901) 33 32 22). Open Mon.-Fri. 9am-1:30pm and 4:30-7:30pm.

Trains: Estación de Málaga, Explanada de la Estación, s/n (tel. 236 02 02). To get to the station, hop on bus #3 at Po. Parque or #4 at Pl. Marina. Tickets and reservations also at the less-crowded **RENFE,** C. Strachan, 4 off C. Molina Lario (tel. 221 31 22). Open Mon.-Fri. 9am-1:30pm and 4:30-7:30pm. To: Fuengirola (every 30min., 6am-10:30pm, 30min., 305ptas); Torremolinos (every 30min., 6am-10:30pm, 20min., 150ptas); Linares-Baeza (5 per day, 4hr., 2900ptas); Córdoba (12 per day, 2½hr., 2100ptas); Sevilla (3 per day, 3hr., 1800ptas); Barcelona (3 per day, 13hr., 6700ptas); Madrid (5 per day, 4hr., 8000ptas).

Buses: Po. Tilos, s/n (tel. 235 00 61), 1 block from RENFE station along C. Roger de Flor. To: Algeciras (6 per day, 3hr., 1300ptas); Fuengirola (every 30min., 30min., 290ptas); Marbella (every hr., 1½hr., 550ptas); Torremolinos (every 15min., 20min., 200ptas); Nerja (every hr., 1hr., 450ptas); Madrid (8 per day, 7hr., 2800ptas); Murcia (6 per day, 7hr., 3800ptas); Alicante (6 per day, 8hr., 4500ptas); Granada (every hour, 2hr., 1200ptas); Córdoba (5 per day, 3hr., 1500ptas); Sevilla (10 per day, 3hr., 2200ptas); Antequera (every 1½hr., 1hr., 525ptas); Ronda (12 per day, 3hr., 600ptas); La Línea (4 per day, 3hr., 1300ptas); Cádiz (3 per day, 5hr., 2500ptas); Gibraltar (1 per day, 3hr., 1200ptas).

Taxis: Radio-Taxi (tel. 232 79 50 or 232 80 62). From El Pedregalejo to town center, 750ptas. From town center to airport, 1300ptas.

Luggage Storage: Lockers at the train (open daily 7am-10:45pm) and bus stations (open daily 6:30am-11pm). Both 300ptas per day.

Red Cross: (tel. 221 76 32). **Women's Services: Ayuda a la Mujer** (tel. 230 40 00 or 261 42 07).

Pharmacy: Farmacia y Laboratorio Laza, C. Molina Lario, 2 (tel. 222 75 97). Open Mon.-Fri. 9:30am-1:30pm and 5-8:30pm, Sat. 10:30am-1:30pm.

Medical Assistance: (tel. 230 30 34).

Police: (tel. 231 71 00). **Emergency:** tel. 091 or 092.

Post Office: Av. Andalucía, 1 (tel. 235 90 08). A tall building just over the Puente Tetuán. Open for stamps and Lista de Correos Mon.-Fri. 8:30am-8:30pm, Sat. 9:30am-2pm. **Postal Code:** 29080.

Telephone Code: (9)5.

ACCOMMODATIONS

Most budget establishments are downtown, between Pl. Marina and Pl. Constitución. In general, rooms are somewhat run-down. Try bargaining if prices seem unreasonable (above 2000ptas for a single, 3700ptas for a double). Excluding Semana Santa, the market is usually slow. Be wary of the following neighborhoods after dark: **Alameda de Colón, El Perchel** (towards the river from the train and bus stations), **Cruz del Molinillo** (near the market), and **La Esperanza/Santo Domingo** (up the river from El Corte Inglés). Always watch out for lightning-quick **pickpockets** on the train and bus stations.

Hostal Residencia Chinitas, Pasaje Chinitas, 2, 2nd fl. (tel. 221 46 83), on an alley off Pl. Constitución. Centrally located. Owned by a big, warm family that deserves a medal. A little dark but clean. Singles 1800-2000ptas. Doubles 3400-4000ptas. Triples 4300-5000ptas.

Pensión Córdoba, C. Bolsa, 11 (tel. 221 44 69), off C. Molina Lario. Decently sized interior rooms with antique furniture. Spotless common bathrooms. Singles 1300ptas. Doubles 2500ptas. Triples 3900ptas.

Hostal La Palma, C. Martínez, 7 (tel. 222 67 72), off C. Marqués de Larios. Two brothers watch over clean, albeit noisy old rooms. Singles 1500-2000ptas. Doubles 2500-3000ptas. Triples and quads 1100ptas per person.

FOOD

Along the **Paseo Marítimo** in **El Pedro-galejo** beachfront restaurants specialize in fresh seafood (40min. walk, or bus #11 from Pl. La Marina, 115ptas). For land-bound creatures, try eateries around **C. Granada** leading out of **Pl. Constitución.** Pick up fresh produce at the **market** on C. Afaranzas (open daily 8am-2pm). There's also a supermarket in the basement of **El Corte Inglés** (see above). Watch *espetos de sardina* (sardines) roasted over an open flame (usually in old rowboats) on the beach. Wash your meal down with either *malagueño* or *moscatel*, Málaga's own sweet wines.

Restaurante La Paloma, Po. Marítimo, El Pedregalejo, 20, (tel. 229 79 94). Take bus #11. Indoor seating plus sea-breezy *terraza*. Their best dishes include *ensalada de atún* (400ptas) and *calamaritos a la plancha* (heaps of grilled baby squids in garlic sauce 675ptas). Open daily 11:30am-5pm and 8pm-1:30am. Closed Wed. mornings. Visa, MC.

La Cancela, C. Jose Denis Belgrano, 5 (tel. 222 31 25; fax. 222 31 50), off C. Granada. Their 4-page, single-spaced, 2-column menu accommodates vegetarians, finicky eaters, and just about everyone else. *Menú* 995ptas (on the *terraza* 1075ptas). Open daily 1-4:30pm and 8-11:30pm. Closed Wed. nights. Visa, MC, AmEx.

Restaurante El Tintero II, Po. Marítimo, El Pedregal, 99 (tel. 220 44 64). The farthest restaurant east on the waterfront. Waiters stroll by with pitchers of beer and seafood platters, while roving flamenco guitarists entertain diners. Loud, family style establishment. 600ptas per plate. Open daily 11am-5pm and 7:30pm-1am.

SIGHTS AND ENTERTAINMENT

With 10 major towers inside concentric walls, the **Alcazaba** is Málaga's most impressive sight. Guarding the east end of Po. Parque, this 11th-century structure was originally built as a fortified palace for Moorish kings. The attached **Museo Arqueológico** (tel. 221 60 05) has a good collection of neolithic pottery. (Open Tues.-Fri. 9:30am-1:30pm and 5-8pm, Sat. 10am-1pm, Sun. 10am-2pm. 30ptas.) Shifty types prowl around here at night, so think twice about evening strolls. Both the Alcazaba and Achaeological Museum are currently closed for renovations.

The **cathedral** on C. Molina Lario, s/n (tel. 221 59 17), is a pastiche of Gothic, Renaissance, and Baroque styles, and has organs dating from 1781. The cathedral's second tower, under construction between the 16th and 19th centuries, was never completed, hence its nickname La Manquita (One-Armed Lady; open Mon.-Sat. 10am-12:45pm and 4-6:30pm; 200ptas). **Castillo Gibralfaro,** built by the Phoenicians and the site of an Arab lighthouse, offers sweeping views of Málaga and the Mediterranean—although exploring the grounds alone may present a mugging danger. (Currently closed for renovations; check with the tourist office.)

The **Museo de Bellas Artes,** C. San Agustín, 8 (tel. 221 83 82), in the old palace of the Counts of Buenavista, displays late 19th-century works by Andalucían artists, including Picasso's teacher, Antonio Muñoz Degrain, and the student himself. Among Picasso's sketches is the affectionate portrait of his mentor, *El viejo de la manta,* (Old man in a blanket). (Open Tues.-Fri. 10am-1:30pm and 5-8pm, Sat.-Sun. 10am-1:30pm. 250ptas.) According to tourist officials, even though Picasso high-tailed it out of Málaga when he was quite young, he always "felt himself to be a true *malagueño.*" Diehards can visit **Picasso's birthplace** in Pl. Merced, (tel. 221 50 05; open Mon.-Fri. 11am-2pm and 5-8pm; free). It now houses the Picasso Foundation, which organizes a series of exhibitions, concerts, and lectures in his honor every October.

In summer, young *malagueños* crowd the boardwalk bars in **El Pedregalejo** (bus #11). A slightly older, more foreign crowd drinks *copas* on **Calle de Bolivia,** parallel to, and a few blocks up from, the beach. Check out bar **Donde. Bolivia 41,** C. Bolivia, 97 (not 41) mellows out among shrubbery, pillows, and a pool table. The **Nocturno I bus** takes over the Pedragalejo line between 12:45-5:45am, running once per hour. A cab back to Pl. Marina costs 750ptas.

All year long, on weekends, *la marcha* crowds the bars in the area between C. Comedias and C. Granada, which leads out of Pl. Constitución. **O'Neill's,** C. Luis de Velazquez, 3, has dark wooden decor, pints of Guinness (500ptas), Celtic music, and friendly bartenders imported from the Emerald Isle. With posters of characters from Quentin Tarantino flicks, **Casa Nostra,** C. Lazcano, 5, hosts live blues performances once a week. On the newsstands, the *Guía del Ocio* (200ptas), lists special events, although at least half of its pages are devoted to singles bars or **gay and lesbian entertainment.** As for festivals, Málaga's **Semana Santa** celebrations are (nearly) as grandiose as those in rival city Sevilla, and the **Feria de Agosto**—complete with bullfights, *flamenco,* concerts, and a *moraga* (sardine bake on the beach)—is among the most spectacular *fiestas* in all of Andalucía.

■ Near Málaga

GARGANTA DEL CHORRO

The **Garganta del Chorro** (a.k.a. El Chorro, 50km northwest of Málaga) is one of Spain's premier geological wonders. El Chorro's rocky terrain rises to 1190m, while below, the Río Guadalhorce splits the landscape in two. An exhilarating walk leads to the gorge, but the route is both difficult to find and dangerous. Those who generally avoid walking through functioning train tunnels will be scared stiff. If you're still game, talk to the bartender at El Chorro's train station for directions. While closer to Ronda and Antequera by car, the gorge is only accessible by public transportation via the Córdoba-Málaga rail line. **RENFE** runs trains to El Chorro from Málaga (1 per day, at 1:45pm, 1hr., 400ptas), but it's another few kilometers to the actual walkway.

TORREMOLINOS

On the coast a mere 20 minutes from Málaga by train, Torremolinos in the summer swells with tourists who are shamelessly, gluttonously, and almost embarrassingly on vacation. Bare-chested bathers mill in and out of McDonald's and KFC, while the slightly more attired drool in front of beckoning store windows. Even its ancient tower (the *torre* in Torremolinos) has an outcropping of souvenir shops.

Calle San Miguel, a bustling pedestrian street, is a shopper's heaven—if you're in the market for Lladró figurines, Mallorca pearls, or Louis Vuitton handbags. As it curves down to the beach, C. San Miguel becomes **Cuesta del Tajo,** laden with souvenir stands. When exiting the **train station,** walk through the alleyway on the right to reach the main thoroughfare, **Avenida Palma de Mallorca;** turn right and C. San Miguel will be on your right. From the **bus station,** exit to the right and follow C. Hoyo to **Plaza Costa del Sol** and Av. Palma de Mallorca; C. San Miguel is on your left. When following Cuesta del Tajo to the shore, **Playa Bajondillo** is to the left, and **Playa Carihuela,** loaded with bars and restaurants, is on **Paseo Marítimo,** to the right.

The **tourist office** (tel. 237 42 31; speaks English and French) is on Pl. Pablo Ruiz Picasso uphill from Av. Palma de Mallorca along Av. Isabel Manoja (open daily 9am-2pm). The **police** answer tel. 238 99 99 or 238 14 22. In an **emergency,** call tel. 091, 092, or 061. Stick tacky postcards into the lion heads at the **post office,** Pl. Palma de Mallorca (tel. 238 45 18; open Mon.-Fri. 8:30am-2:30pm and 9:30pm-1am). The **postal code** is 29620. **Portillo Buses** (tel. 238 24 19) and **C-1 local trains** (tel. 238 57 64) depart frequently to Málaga, Fuengirola, and other destinations. **Luggage storage** is available at the bus station between 7am and 9pm for 300ptas.

Hostels tend to get lost amid towering hotels and apartment complexes; some huddle on Cta. de Tajo and on streets off Pl. Costa del Sol. Visitors face evil price surges in August. **Hostal La Palmera,** Av. Palma de Mallorca, 37 (tel. 237 65 09), a few doors down from the post office (enter around the corner), has friendly owners who rent airy rooms with big closets. A TV and bar loiter in the reception room. (Singles 2500-3000ptas. Doubles 3500-4000ptas. Triples 4500-5000ptas. Breakfast 350ptas.) Reservations suggested. **Hostal Residencia Guillot,** C. Rio Mundo, 4 (tel. 238 01 44), offers cheap, quiet, dark rooms with shared baths (singles 2000-2800ptas, doubles 3000-

3500ptas). Follow C. Cruz from Pl. Costa del Sol, make a right onto Pasaje Pizarro, and a left onto tiny Rio Mundo.

At night, snoop along Av. Palma de Mallorca, or join the hordes farther west at **La Carihuela,** a sandy expanse dotted with *freidurías* and *heladerías,* whose see-and-be-seen attitude makes it *the* place to be when the sun goes down.

FUENGIROLA

At the end of RENFE's Málaga C-1 line, Guengirola's crowded beaches and chalk-hued villas are an extension of Torremolinos', but without the retail sector to exhaust the weary and *peseta*-less.

Since temperatures on the coast can be as much as 15°F cooler than they are a mere three blocks inland, visitors chill (relatively) in bars along **Pasea Marítimo** and on the beach in **Los Boliches,** a neighborhood several kilometers toward Málaga.

The **tourist office,** Av. Jesús Santo Reino, 6 (tel. 246 74 57), speaks English and provides a free map. (Open Mon.-Fri. 9:30am-2pm and 5-8pm, Sat. 10am-1pm; in the off season afternoon hrs. change to 4-7pm.) **ATMs** abound. **Medical assistance** answers at tel. 246 86 53 (24hr.). The **local police,** C. Alfonso XII, 1, respond to tel. 247 31 57. The **post office** is on Pl. Chinorros (tel. 247 43 84; open Mon.-Fri. 8am-3pm, Sat. 9am-1pm). The **postal code** is 29640. The **telephone code** is (9)5.

Fuengirola's reputation as a tourist trap for jet-setters is outdated—the British middle-class and the tattoo crew have taken over. Reasonable *pensiones* and *hostales* skulk between **Pl. Constitución** and the beach, and in **Los Boliches. Hostal Costabella,** Av. Boliches, 98 (tel. 247 46 31), is only one block up from the beach, and one block seaward from RENFE's Los Boliches stop. Some rooms have beach views, all have glistening private baths (singles 2000-3000ptas, doubles 3000-4200ptas). **Hostal Amigo,** Av. Los Boliches, 71 (tel. 247 03 33), has plain interior rooms (singles 1800-3700, doubles 2500-4500). There's no unrequited hunger on **Calles de Hambre,** south of Pl. Constitución. The local **market** is reportedly the greatest thing since *churros con chocolate* (across the street from Fuengirola RENFE, Tues. 9am-2pm). Supermarket **Cayetano** is on Av. Ramón y Cajal, 45 (open Mon.-Fri. 9am-2:30pm and 5-9:30pm, Sat. 9am-9:30pm; Visa, MC).

When the sun sinks, hit the bars on Po. Marítimo and the area around **C. Miguel de Cervantes** and **C. Oviedo.** The **Bowling Palmeras** (tel. 246 06 41) strikes on Av. Martínez Catena which leads up from the port (behind Hotel Las Palmeras), with a sauna, jacuzzi, gym, roller skating, bowling alley, and much more (open until 2am, 1am on Sun.).

The Málaga-Fuengirola route on **RENFE,** Av. Jesús Santos Reino (tel. 247 85 40), costs 305ptas and takes 40 minutes. Get off one stop early to get to **Los Boliches.** The **bus station** on C. Alfonso XIII off of Av. Jesus Santos Rein (tel. 247 50 66) runs buses to: Málaga (every ½hr., 45min., 290ptas, 7am-10:15pm); Marbella (every ½hr. 7am-11pm, 30min., 280ptas); Algeciras (11 per day, 2 hrs., 990ptas); and Ronda (5 per day, 2 hr., 815ptas).

■ Marbella

Glamorous Marbella, the jewel of the Costa del Sol, extorts *pesetas* quickly, efficiently, and in many different languages from hordes of the flashy and famous. Amazingly, though, it's also possible to steal away from the city with a budgeted good time. The city's controversial mayor has "cleaned up" the "marginal" elements (drug dealers, prostitutes, fellow politicians, etc.) and has been rewarded by voters with a second term. Now the greatest crime is skipping out on the raging nightlife.

ORIENTATION AND PRACTICAL INFORMATION

Marbella glitzes 56km south of Málaga. It can only be reached by bus. The brand new **bus station** surveys the sea from atop **Avenida Trapiche.** To reach the main strip, exit and walk left, make the first right onto Av. Trapiche, and follow any downhill

ANDALUCÍA

route to the perpendicular **Avenida Ramón y Cajal,** which becomes **Avenida Richard Soriano** on the way to **Puerto Bonús. Calle Peral** curves up from Av. Ramón y Cajal and around the **casco antiguo,** or old section.

Tourist Office: C. Glorieta de la Fontanilla (tel. 277 14 42), fronting the shore. They speak English and if you put together all of their little free maps you'll probably find your way around. Open Mon.-Fri. 9:30am-8pm, Sat. 9:30am-2pm. **Another office** doles out info in Pl. Naranjos (tel. 282 35 50; same hours but opens at 9am).

American Express: Av. Duque de Ahumada, s/n (tel. 282 14 94; fax 286 22 92), off Po. Marítimo. Mail received and checks cashed. Open Mon.-Fri. 9:30am-2pm and 4:30-8pm, Sat. 10am-1pm.

Luggage Storage: At the bus station (400ptas).

Currency Exchange: Banco Central Hispano, Av. Ramón y Cajal, 9 (tel. 277 08 92). Exchanges currency and AmEx traveler's checks without commission. Open Mon.-Fri. 8:30am-2:30pm; Oct.-May also open Sat. 8:30am-1pm.

Buses: Av. Trapiche, s/n (tel. 276 44 00). to: Málaga (every 30min. 7am-10:30pm, 1½hr., 570ptas); Fuengirola (every 35min., 30min., 280ptas); San Pedro de Alcántara (7 per day, 20min., 125ptas); Estepona (every 35min., 1hr., 255ptas); Granada (4 per day, 4½hr., 1735ptas); Ronda (4 per day, 1½hr., 585ptas); Sevilla (3 per day, 4hr., 1820ptas); Cádiz (4 per day, 4hr., 1985ptas); Madrid (10 per day, 7½hr., 3085ptas); Barcelona (4 per day, 16hr., 8325ptas); Algeciras (9 per day, 1½hr., 760ptas); La Línea (4 per day, 1½hr., 695ptas).

Taxis: Cánovas del Castillo (tel. 286 16 88).

Red Cross: (tel. 277 45 34). **Hospital: Comarcal,** CN-340, km187 (tel. 286 27 48).

Police: Pl. Los Naranjos, 1 (tel. 282 24 94). **Emergency:** tel. 091 or 092.

Post Office: C. Alonso de Bazán, 1 (tel. 277 28 98). Turn onto C. Finlandia from C. Ramón y Cajal, walk downhill and make the first right. Open Mon.-Fri. 8:30am-2:30pm, Sat. 9:30am-1pm. **Postal Code:** 29600.

Telephone Code: (9)5.

ACCOMMODATIONS AND CAMPING

If you are reservationless, especially from mid-July through August, arrive early and pray. The area in the *casco antiguo* around Pl. Naranjos (also known as Orange Square) is loaded with quick-filling little *hostales.* Several cheap guest houses line **Calles Ancha, San Francisco, Aduar,** and **de los Caballeros,** all of which are uphill off C. Peral and C. Huerta Chica and inland from C. Ramón y Cajal. Bartenders often know of *casas particulares*—the **English Pub** and **The Tavern,** face to face on C. Peral, can offer advice in English.

Albergue Juvenil (HI), C. Trapiche, 2 (tel. 277 14 91). Just downhill from the bus station and only slightly removed from the action. It has a sterile feel, but facilities include a TV room, basketball court, and pool. Orgasmic 900-1300ptas per person. Over 26 1200-1600ptas per person. Tents outside cost 500ptas per person. Nonmembers pay an extra 300ptas per night for six nights to become members. Full board available. Wheelchair accessible.

Hostal del Pilar, C. Mesoncillo, 4 (tel. 282 99 36), the 2nd left off C. Peral, an extension of C. Huerta Chica. In an alley behind the English Pub. Run by a Scottish woman and three multilingual countrymen who like to party with the young international clientele—not for the timid. Bar downstairs provides more social life than nourishment. Mattresses on the roof (if warm) from 1000ptas per person. Otherwise, 1500-2000ptas per person. Guests receive keys to the front door.

Pensión Aduar, C. Aduar, 7 (tel. 277 35 78). The beautiful courtyard, overflowing with flowers and songbirds, gives a sunny glow to well-kept rooms. Balconies upstairs. Singles 1700-2000ptas. Doubles 2700-3000ptas. No curfew.

El Castillo, Pl. San Bernabé, 2 (tel. 277 17 39), a few blocks uphill from Pl. Naranjos in the old town. Medieval decor and sunny, comfortable rooms. Stupendous private bathrooms, darling. Singles 1600-2600ptas. Doubles 3000-4500ptas.

ANDALUCÍA

Camping Marbella Playa (tel. 277 83 91), 2km east on N-340. Along the Marbella-Fuengirola bus line. Ask the bus driver to stop at the campground. A 2nd-class site. 520ptas per person, 860ptas per tent. Open year-round.

FOOD

The municipal **market** is on Av. Mercado, uphill from C. Peral (open Mon.-Sat. 8am-2pm). A **24-hour minimarket** beckons through the night on the corner of C. Pablo Casals and Av. Fontanilla, which intersects with Av. Richard Soriano. **Terrazas** fill Pl. Naranjos but offer little for the budget-conscious—some even charge for bread. Restaurants farther uphill may be less picturesque but more satisfying to stomach and wallet.

Bar El Gallo, C. Lobatas, 44 (tel. 282 79 98). Loud TV and louder locals won't distract you from cheap, delicious food. *Ensalada mixta* 325ptas. The most expensive dish is *San Jacobo* (pork stuffed with ham and swiss) and fries 475ptas. Open daily 9am-midnight.

La Famiglia, C. Cruz, 5, off Pl. Puente Ronda. A cozy setting with large portions. Pizzas from 750ptas. *Rigatoni alla siciliana* (with eggplant, garlic, and tomato) 950ptas. Open Mon.-Sat. 7:30-11:30pm.

Xin Xin, C. Ramiro Campos Turmo, 12 (tel. 282 93 50). Well sign-posted and downhill from Av. Richard Soriano. Lots of tasty Chinese food, but the budget bargain is definitely the (relatively) grease-free 3-course *menú* (595ptas). Open daily noon-4pm and 7pm-midnight.

Bar Bohemia, C. Peral, a few doors down from the English Pub. A starchy haven for wee-hour revelers. Cheeseburger and beer 525ptas. Open daily 9am-3 or 4am.

SIGHTS, BUT MOSTLY ENTERTAINMENT

Although no one comes to Marbella for its monuments, the **casco antiguo,** a maze of cobbled alleyways and ancient facades (and more than a few boutiques), merits a stroll. The thick walls of an Arab fortress seal off the neighborhoods, and houses with carefully tended to courtyards huddle against its crumbling remains. The **Museo del Grabacho Español Contemporáneo,** C. Hospital Bazán, will teach you anything you want to know about silk screens, lithographs, and woodcutting, and displays work by Miró and Picasso (open Mon.-Fri. 10:15am-2pm and 5:30-8:30pm; 300ptas). To the northeast is the small **Parque Arroyo de la Represa,** site of the **Museo de Bonsai** (tel. 286 29 26), the (self-proclaimed) "best in the world" collection of mini arboreal art (open daily 10am-1:30pm and 4-8pm. 400ptas, 200ptas for botanists under 12).

With 22km of beach, Marbella offers a variety of sizzling settings, from below the chic promenade to **Playa de las Chapas,** 10km east via the Fuengirola bus. The sand is generally gritty and scorching (wear sandals!), but the human landscape is scenic, to say the least. Because of the towering mountains nearby, Marbella's winter temperatures tend to be 5-8° warmer than Malaga's, and beach season goes on and on.

City buses along Av. Richard Soriano (destination San Pedro, 125ptas), or a 10-minute cab ride (1300ptas), bring you to chic and trendy **Puerto Banús.** Buffered by imposing white yachts and row upon row of boutiques and fancy restaurants, *this* is where the Beautiful People are. The port is frequented by the likes of Sean Connery, Richard Gere, Elton John, and King Fahd of Saudi Arabia (who built a huge palace modeled on the White House), and throngs of Euro-chicks roaming the marina in search of rich prospects. If you find star-gazing none too fruitful, gawk at the toys of the rich (Ferraris, Rolls Royces, motorcruisers), or kick back at **Sinatra Bar,** on the first row, and drink it all in. The Moroccan coast is visible on exceptionally clear days.

Back in town, Marbella's **nightlife** is unrivaled, swearing by the maxim, "All work and no play makes Juan a dull boy." Beaches don't fill up until three in the afternoon because people are just waking up—the night is still young at four in the morning, and that's not just on weekends. In the *casco antiguo,* action brews at the many bars as well as some English pubs along C. Peral. A mellower ambience suffuses the **Townhouse Bar,** C. Alano, on an alley off C. Nueva, which leads downhill from Pl.

Naranjos. Try a shot of apple pie, a secret recipe topped with cream and cinnamon (200ptas). A young international crowd socializes in bars **Planet,** C. Aduar, 22, and **Kashmir,** C. Rafina, 8, off of C. Aduar. Their smoky lounges upstairs might remind **Amsterdam** natives of home.

On the way to the beach, **Bar Incognito,** Av. Miguel Cano, 15, serves divine, fruit-garnished cocktails at half-price during Happy Hour (daily 9-11pm, regular price around 600ptas). Later in the evening (early in the morning), the city's entire young population swarms to the **Puerto Deportivo** ("The Port"), an amusement park of disco-bars and clubs. Wind your way around manic locals banging away on bongo drums to **Willie's Salsa** (tel. 282 73 63), a disco-bar which, belying its name, blares house music until 7 or 8am. Don't even think about breathing in here (no cover, expensive drinks). **Loco's** plays any kind of music as long as it's jarringly loud (beer 300ptas). Attracting a (barely) older crowd is **Arturo's Bar,** Local 42-43 (tel. 282 03 11), a rustic, backwoods American-style place, complete with bear-skin rugs and antlers on the walls. A British guitarist strums favorites, from dueling banjos to Queen.

The most sophisticated dance clubs cluster in **Puerto Banús.** Buses run there on the hour all night along Av. Richard Soriano (destination San Pedro, 125ptas). Be prepared to pay 2000ptas cover charges (women usually *gratis*), sometimes 1000ptas for water, and have your attire snootily scrutinized. **La Comedia,** Pl. Comedia in Banús, plays disco until dawn (1000ptas cover includes two drinks, women free).

As for festivals, the **Feria y Fiesta de San Bernabé** (mid-June) is the big event of the year, exploding with fireworks and concerts.

■ Antequera

Residents don't get too excited about Antequera, while visitors are stupefied by its nightly courting behavior—dozens of ornate, illuminated church spires stretch into the sky, wiggling ostentatiously for hard to get natives and easily aroused tourists. The Roman ruins are even more voluptuous—they include *los dólmenes*, funerary chambers built from rock slabs, the *oldest* of their kind in Europe. Few sunsets rival those from atop the old Moorish fortress on the hill, and several kilometers to the south, one can explore La Sierra del Torcal, a Mars-like wasteland of eroded rock (maybe there's life). But despite it all, townspeople still play hard to get, which may lend Antequera its charm as a place which, unlike Mars, has much to see without any real hurry to see it.

ORIENTATION AND PRACTICAL INFORMATION

It's a 10-minute hike up a shadeless hill (Av. Estación, which changes names twice) to the town center from the train station. From the top, continue straight past the market, turn right on **Calle Encarnaciá,** and go past the Museo Municipal to reach **Plaza San Sebastián.** The **bus station** perches atop a neighboring hill. To reach Pl. San Sebastián from the bus station, walk downhill (to the right as you exit) to the bullring, then turn left onto **Alameda de Andalucía.** At the fork, follow **Calle Infante Don Fernando** (the right branch) to the plaza. C. Encanción connects Pl. San Sebastián to **Calle Calzada.** C. Calzada leads uphill to **Plaza San Francisco** and the market. If your pack weighs a ton, arrive by bus and leave by train. Otherwise, a cab from the center to the train or bus station costs 550ptas.

Tourist Office: Pl. San Sebastián, 7 (tel. 270 25 05; fax 284 02 56). Helpful staff supplies free maps, transportation schedules, and free multilingual info on Antequera and nearby cities. Open Mon.-Sat. 10am-2pm and 5-8pm; in winter 9:30am-1:30pm and 4-7pm and Sun. morning. **Branch office** (tel. 270 40 51) is on Pl. Coso Viejo, inside the Museo Municipal, off C. Nájera near Pl. Descalzas. Open Tues.-Fri. 10am-1:30pm, Sat. 10am-1pm, Sun. 11am-1pm (same hours as museum).

Trains: Av. Estación (tel. 284 32 26). To: Granada (3 per day, 2hr., 750-865ptas); Málaga (3 per day, 1½hr., 615ptas); Sevilla (3 per day, 2½hr., 1100-1370ptas); Algeciras

(3 per day, 4hr., 1520ptas); Bobadilla (3 per day, 15min., 160-180ptas); Ronda (3 per day, 1½hr., 710ptas). Connections in Bobadilla (tel. 272 02 24).

Buses: Po. García del Olmo (tel. 270 35 73), near the Parador Nacional. To: Málaga (2 per day, 45min., 470ptas); Almería (2 per day, 5hr., 2385ptas); Córdoba (2 per day, 2¼hr., 1075ptas); Granada (3 per day, 1hr., 900ptas); Jaén (1 per day, 3hr., 1425ptas); Murcia (2 per day, 5½hr., 3275ptas); Sevilla (4 per day, 2¼hr., 1435ptas); Madrid (2 per day, 6hr., 2525ptas).

Banco Central Hispano: C. Infante Fernando, 51 (tel. 284 04 61), changes currency and AmEx traveler's checks without commission. Open Mon.-Fri. 8:30am-2:30pm.

Taxis: (tel. 284 10 76, 284 10 08, or 270 26 27).

Red Cross: (tel. 270 22 22).

Hospital: Hospital General Básico, C. Infante Don Fernando, 67 (tel. 284 44 11).

Police: Municipal, Av. Legión (tel. 270 81 04). **Emergency:** tel. 091 or 092.

Post Office: C. Nájera (tel. 284 20 83). Open for stamps and Lista de Correos Mon.-Fri. 8am-2pm, Sat. 9:30am-1pm. **Postal Code:** 29200.

Telephone Code: (9)5.

ACCOMMODATIONS AND FOOD

Food and lodging in Antequera are generally cheap and pretty awesome. Most establishments lie near **Calle Infante Don Fernando,** between the Museo Municipal and the **market,** Pl. San Francisco (open daily 8am-3pm). Try a nibble of *queso de cabra* (goat cheese). Ten-aisle **Supermercado Multimas** is on C. Calzado, 18 (open Mon.-Fri. 9:30am-1:45pm, and 5:30-9pm, Sat 9:30am-9pm).

Pensión Toril, C. Toril, 5 (tel./fax 284 31 84), off Pl. San Francisco. Two dear grand-fatherly types offer clean, bright rooms and free parking. Guests gather on patios to chat and play cards. Singles 1200ptas, with bath 2000ptas. Doubles: 2400ptas; 3000ptas. But before sleep, feast downstairs first—*menú* (800ptas), whopping *platos combinados* (500ptas), and generous drinks (100ptas). Meals served daily 1-4pm and 7:30-9:30pm.

Hotel Colón, C. Infante Don Fernando, 29 (tel. 284 00 10, fax. 284 11 64). Spotless, classy joint with wood floors and unupholstered furniture. Get psyched about the beer vending machine. Ritzy section has full baths, A/C, and TVs. Singles 2000-2500ptas. Doubles 3600-4800ptas. Older *pensión* wing has shared baths. 1000-2500ptas per person. Visa, MC, AmEX. Wheelchair accessible.

Pensión Madrona, C. Calzada, 25 (tel. 284 00 14). Walk through Bar Madrona to the *pensión.* Newly renovated with A/C and heating in every room. Cozy, family-run, dainty decor. Singles 1500ptas, with bath 2500ptas. Doubles with bath 3500ptas. Restaurant/bar downstairs offers a worth-it *menú* (800ptas). Visa, MC, Eurocard.

Mesón-Restaurante Amigos de Chaplín, C. San Agustín, 8 (tel. 270 39 59), on a narrow brick street off C. Infante Don Fernando. Bar downstairs, restaurant upstairs. Guess whose likeness adorns the entrance? *Menú* 800ptas. Bar open from 11am. Restaurant open daily 1-5pm and 7:30-11:30pm.

La Espuela (tel./fax 270 26 76), in Pl. Toros. The only restaurant in the world *inside* a bullring. Not surprisingly, prize-winning kitchen's specialty is *rabo de toro* (bull's tail). *Menú* 1700ptas, worth it if you have the dough, the cash, *lo que sea!* Open daily noon-5pm and 5:30-11:30pm. Visa, MC.

Manolo Bar, C. Calzada, 14 (tel. 284 10 15). Downhill from the market. Filled with wild west paraphernalia and good-humored patrons. Ultra-cheap *tapas* (100ptas) may cost more if they find you impolite *(bienvenidos, guiri)*. Open Tues.-Thurs. 4:30-11:30pm, until 3am on Fri.-Sat.

SIGHTS

Antequera's three ancient **Cuevas de Dólmenes** are the oldest in Europe. Giant rock slabs form both the antechamber (storeroom for the dead's possessions) and burial chamber. Hefty ancients lugged the mammoth 200-ton roof of the **Cueva de Menga** (2500 BC) over five miles to the burial site. The four figures engraved on the chamber walls typify Mediterranean Stone Age art. The elongated **Cueva de Viera,** discovered

in 1905, is equally oversized—and dark. Bring a flashlight. Small, flat stones cement the circular interior walls and domed ceiling of **Cueva de Romeral** (1800 BC).

To reach the **Cuevas de Menga** and **Viera,** follow the signs toward Granada from the town center (20min. walk), watch for a small sign on C. Granada just past the gas station. To reach Cueva de Romeral from the other *cuevas,* continue on the highway to Granada for another 3km. Just past Almacenes Gómez, one of the last warehouses after the flowered intersection, a gravel road cuts left and bumps into a narrow path bordered by tall fir trees. Take this path across the train tracks to reach the cave (open Tues.-Fri. 10am-2pm and 3-5:30pm, Sat.-Sun. 10am-2pm).

Back in town, all that remains of the **Alcazaba** are its two towers, the wall between them, and well-trimmed hedges. The view is tremendous. Next to it, the towering **Colegiate de Santa Mariá** is considered the first church in Andalucía to incorporate Renaissance style (open Tues.-Sun. 10am-2pm; free). From the plaza in front of the church, one can spot the massive **Roca de lo Enamorado** (Lovers' Rock), which looks exactly like the Sphinx lying down (tilt your head sideways). Legend has it that a Christian and his Moorish girlfriend leapt from the rock's face to their deaths rather than be separated by invading soldiers. Downhill, the **museo municipal** (tel. 270 40 21) manages to exhibit avant-guarde 1970s paintings by native son Cristobal Toral alongside dozens of Roman artifacts including the graceful **Efebo,** a rare bronze statue of a Roman pageboy. The postcards don't do him justice (open Tues.-Fri. 10am-1:30pm, Sat. 10am-1pm, Sun 11am-1pm; 200ptas).

■ Near Antequera: Sierra de Torcal

A garden of wind-sculpted boulders, the Sierra de Torcal glows like the surface of a barren and distant planet. The central peak of **El Torcal** (1369m) spans over most of the horizon, but the smaller clumps of eroded rocks are even more extraordinary.

Two trails circle the summit. The green arrow path takes about 45 minutes and is 1½km long; the red arrow path takes over two hours and is 4½km long. To prevent overcrowding, those on the *Ruta Roja* (red route) must call the Agencia del Medio Ambiente (tel. 222 58 00) prior to arrival. (In '97, the path was closed entirely. Inquire at the tourist office.) Both paths begin and end 13km from Antequera at the *refugio* at the mountain base. Two-thirds of the 13km can be covered by **bus;** ask the driver to let you off at the turnoff for El Torcal (repeat: "*¿Usted me puede dejar antés del éxito para El Torcal?*") Buses leave from Antequera (Mon.-Fri. at 1 and 7pm, 170ptas); the return bus leaves from the turnoff (Mon.-Fri. at 4:15pm). Call **Casado buses** (tel. 284 19 57) for details. A taxi to the *refugio* costs about 3600ptas round-trip. The driver will wait for an hour, giving you time to catch the sunset.

■ Ronda

Ronda's history runs even deeper than the spectacular 100m gorge dividing it. Called Arunda ("surrounded by mountains") by Pliny, Ptolemy, and pfriends, the town was a pivotal commercial center under the Romans. In Moorish times, the Machiavellian Al Mutadid ibn Abbad annexed the town for Sevilla by asphyxiating the ruling lord in his bath. This century, Ronda has attracted forlorn artistic types—German poet Rainer Maria Rilke wrote his *Spanish Elegies* here, and Orson Welles had his ashes buried on a bull farm outside of town.

Only an hour and a half from the resorts of the Costa del Sol, Ronda (pop. 45,000) has ample monuments, offers a welcome diversion from crowded beaches, and makes a good base for exploring the *pueblos blancos* to the south.

ORIENTATION AND PRACTICAL INFORMATION

Three bridges join the city's old and new parts: one Roman, one Moorish, and one modern. On the new side of the city, **Carrera Espinel** (the main east-west drag, known also as **Calle la Bola**) runs perpendicular to **Calle Virgen de la Paz.**

ANDALUCÍA

The **train** and **bus stations** rumble in the new city three blocks away from each other on **Avenida de Andalucía.** To reach the tourist office and the town center from the train station, turn right on Av. Andalucía and follow it through the **Plaza de Merced** past the bus station (it becomes C. San José) until it ends. Take a left on C. Jerez, and follow it past the lush **Alameda del Tajo** (city park) and **Plaza Toros** (C. Jerez turns into C. Virgen de la Paz at Pl. Merced), to **Plaza de España and the new bridge.** Cra. Espinel intersects C. Virgen de la Paz between the bull ring and Pl. España. From the bus station, turn right and follow the directions above.

Tourist Office: Pl. España, 1 (tel. 287 12 72). Staff has info on Ronda and is multilingual enough to say, "100 *pesetas* please," when they hand you a map. Open Mon.-Fri. 9am-2pm and 4-7pm, Sat.-Sun. 10am-3pm.

Trains: Station, Av. Andalucía (tel. 287 16 73). **Ticket office,** C. Infantes, 20 (tel. 287 16 62). Open Mon.-Fri. 10am-2pm and 6-8:30pm. To Algeciras (4 per day, 2hr., 845ptas). Change at Bobadilla for: Málaga (3 per day, 2hr., 1080ptas); Granada (3 per day, 3hr., 1495ptas); Sevilla (3 per day, 3hr., 1300-1700ptas).

Buses: Pl. Concepción García Redondo, 2 (tel. 287 26 57). To: Málaga (5 per day, 2½hr., 1110ptas); Cádiz (3 per day, 4hr., 1590ptas); Marbella (5 per day, 1½hr., 560ptas); Fuengirola (5 per day, 2hr., 895ptas); Torremolinos (5 per day, 1½hr., 965ptas); Sevilla (5 per day, 1235ptas).

Taxis: tel. 287 23 16. From the train station to the town center about 350ptas.

Luggage Storage: At the newsstand in the bus station for 200ptas per day (open daily 8am-10pm).

Car Rental: Velasco, C. Lorenzo Borrego, 11 (tel. 287 27 82). From 6000ptas per day, including mileage and insurance. Two years with license required

Hitchhiking: Those heading to Sevilla, Jerez, and Cádiz follow C. Sevilla out of the Mercadillo. Those aiming for Granada walk up Carrera Espinel and take the 3rd right after the tree-lined Av. Martínez Stein. Those destined for Málaga and the Costa del Sol zip across the highway leading downhill from Barrio de San Francisco. *Let's Go* does not recommend hitching.

Medical Services: Hospital General Básico de la Serranía, Ctra. de Burgos, km1 (tel. 287 15 40). **Emergency Clinic: Notfall,** C. Espinillo (tel. 287 58 52).

Police: Pl. Duquesa de Parcent (tel. 287 32 40). **Emergency:** tel. 091 or 092.

Post Office: C. Virgen de la Paz, 20 (tel. 287 25 57), across from Pl. Toros. Open for Lista de Correos Mon.-Fri. 8:30am-2:30pm, Sat. 9:30am-1pm. **Postal Code:** 29400.

Telephone Code: (9)5.

ACCOMMODATIONS AND FOOD

Most beds are bunched in the new city near the bus station, along the streets perpendicular to **Cra. Espinel**—try **C. Sevilla** and **C. Molino.** Expect room shortages during the Feria de Ronda in September. Restaurants and cafes line the streets around Pl. España and those heading towards Cra. Espinel.

Pensión Virgen del Rocio, C. Nueva, 18 (tel. 287 74 25), off Pl. España. Family-owned with spacious, attractive rooms. Singles 2000-3000ptas. Doubles 3500-4000ptas. Breakfast 300ptas.

Hostal Morales, C. Sevilla, 51 (tel. 287 15 38), near the corner with C. Lauria. Friendly management. Modern bathrooms with pre-modern cold showers (ask if the hot water's on before you jump in), a tiled courtyard, and spotless rooms. Singles 1500ptas. Doubles 3000ptas.

Pizzeria Pinocho, C. Dr. Fleming, 24 (tel. 287 91 45). Array of pizzas (475-675ptas) and delicious pastas (450-550ptas). Open daily 12:30-4:30pm and 8pm-1am.

Restaurante Flores, C. Virgen de la Paz, 9 (tel. 287 10 40), behind the tourist office. Tent-shaded outdoor tables afford a perfect view of tourists on their way to the Pl. Toros. *Menú* 975ptas. MC. Open daily 11am-4:30pm and 7:30-11pm.

Restaurante Peking, C. Los Remedios, 14 (tel. 87 65 37). Fu dogs, red tablecloths, hanging lanterns, and New Age music confused by a Spanish culinary slant. *Menú* 675ptas. *Tomate relleno con gambas* (shrimp-filled tomatoes 695ptas). Chinese fried bread 135ptas. Open daily noon-4:30pm and 7:30pm-midnight. Visa, MC.

A Lot of Bull

Bullfighting *aficionados* charge over to Ronda's **Plaza de Toros** (tel. 287 41 32), Spain's oldest bullring (est. 1785), and cradle of the modern *corrida*. The **Museo Taurino** inside tells the story of local hero Pedro Romero, the first matador to brave the beasts *a pie* (on foot), and to use the *muleta* (red cape). Romero killed his first bull in 1771, at age 17, the start of a glorious career: "From 1781-1799, it can be said that I killed in each year 200 bulls, whose sum totals 5600 bulls, yet I am persuaded that there may have been more." The museum exhibits costumes and capes, some large photos of giddy *aficionado* Orson Welles, and a display tracing the exploits of Cayetano Ordoñez, apotheosized by Hemingway's Romero in *The Sun Also Rises*. (Museum open 10am-8pm; Oct-May 10am-5pm. 275ptas.) In early September, the Plaza de Toros hosts *corridas goyescas* (bull-fights in traditional costumes) as part of the **Feria de Ronda** celebrations.

SIGHTS

Ronda's precipitous gorge, carved by the Río Guadalevín, dips 100m below the **Puente Nuevo,** across from Pl. España. During the Civil War, political prisoners were cast into the canyon's depths from the bridge's midpoint. Two other structures bridge the unsettling gap: the innovative **Puente Viejo** was rebuilt in 1616 over an earlier Arab bridge, and the **Puente San Miguel** (a.k.a. **Puente Árabe**) is a prime Andalucían hybrid with a Roman base and Arab arches.

In the old city (to the left across the Nuevo), a colonnaded walkway leads to the **Casa del Rey Moro** (House of the Moorish King), which, notwithstanding its name and Moorish facade, dates from the 18th century. From the gardens in back, 365 zig-zagging steps descend to *la mina* (the mine), a spring that once pumped in the town's water supply. Four hundred Christian prisoners were employed in the ardu-ous task of drawing water. Across the street, behind a forged iron balcony and a stone facade portraying four Peruvian Incas, stands the 18th-century **Palacio del Marqués de Salvatierra** (tel. 287 12 06). Its floors sparkle with ceramic tiles. (Open Mon.-Wed. and Fri.-Sat. 11am-2pm and 4-7pm, Thurs. and Sun. 11am-2pm. 300ptas.)

C. Marqués de Salvatierra leads to the **Iglesia de Santa María la Mayor** (tel. 287 22 46), a large 16th-century church hall crowned by a Renaissance belfry, in the heart of Ronda's old city. The small arch just inside the entrance and the Koranic verses behind the sacristy are the only vestiges of the mosque once on this site. An even fainter sign announces, *Julius Divo, Municipe,* revealing this site's original incarna-tion as a church consecrated for Caesar. (Open 10afm-6pm. Knock for the caretaker who'll extract 200ptas, 100ptas per person for groups.) To the east stands the **Giralda de San Sebastián,** part of a former mosque converted into a church after 1485, when Ronda was reconquered by the Christians. On the other side of the church lies the **Palacio de Mondragón** (tel. 287 84 50), once owned by Don Fernando Valenzuela (one of Carlos III's ministers). Its Baroque facade, bracketed by two Mudéjar towers, hides 15th-century Arab mosaics. (Open Mon.-Fri. 10am-7pm, Sat.-Sun. 10am-3pm. 200ptas, groups 100ptas per person, under 14 free.)

■ Near Ronda

CUEVAS DE LA PILETA

A subterranean museum of bones, stalactites, stalagmites, and paleolithic paintings, the **Cuevas de la Pileta** (tel. 216 72 02) burrow 22km west of Ronda along the road to Ubrique. Twenty-five thousand years ago, inhabitants colored the walls of the *Cámara del Pez* (Chamber of Fish) with an enormous prehistoric painting. Bring a flashlight or torch, bundle up, and don't wear sandals, high heels, or ill-fitting foot-wear. Upon arrival at the caves, climb to the mouth to see if the guide is inside. If no one is about, walk to the farm below and rouse the owner, who'll make appropriate arrangements. *¡Viva España!* (Open 10am-1pm and 4-5pm; in winter 10am-2pm and

4-6pm. Admission and 1hr. tour 800ptas, groups 600-700ptas per person; the larger the group, the cheaper the tour.)

By **car,** take highway C-339 north (Ctra. Sevilla heading out of the new city). The turnoff to **Benaoján** and the caves is about 13km out of town, in front of an abandoned restaurant. Don't leave valuables in your car during the tour. Or take the **Amarillo bus** to Benaoján (8:30am and 1pm, 22min., 195ptas). The approach through the Serranía de Ronda is stupendous as you wind through small Montajaque.

OLVERA

Olvera's wave of gleaming whitewashed houses rolls up a hill and breaks over the green and gold of surrounding farmlands, in bright contrast to the rows of orange houses lining the hillside. Procure the key to the **Castillo Árabe** from the town hall; the top of the castle has a fabulous view of the town set against acres of olive groves.

If you're stuck here, or seeking isolation, try **Pensión Maqueda,** on C. Calvario, 35 (tel. ((9)56) 13 07 33; 1300ptas per person). The town isn't loaded with wonderful bargain restaurants, but a few candidates await on **Av. Julian Besteiro.** Los Amarillos **buses** run to Olvera from Ronda (Mon.-Fri. at 5pm, 2hr., 550ptas).

SETENIL DE LAS BODEGAS

Nearby, the village of **Setenil de las Bodegas** perches on a mountain encrusted with caves that were first inhabited eons ago. Later residents built facades and then freestanding houses branching off the grottoes; long rows of chalk-white houses remain strategically built into the hillsides. The village stretches along a dramatic gorge cut by the Río Guadalporcún, and riverside streets or *cuevas* burrow under the gorge's cliff walls, creating long, covered passageways: **Cuevas Sombra, Cuevas del Sol,** and **Cuevas de Cabrerizos.** The 15th-century **Iglesia de la Encarnación,** atop the biggest rock, opens to views of the village below.

From Ronda, Setenil is accessible by Los Amarillos **bus** (Mon.-Fri. at 5pm, 410ptas) and **train** (1:30pm, 13min., 200ptas; one stop in the direction of Bobadilla). By **car,** take Ronda's Ctra. Sevilla to C-339 North. For Olvera and Setenil, take the turn for El Gastor or the longer route via the dramatic outcropping of the village of Zahara.

■ Gibraltar

Homesick Brits get jolly well excited over Gib's fish 'n' chips, while everybody else goes berserk over tax-free cigarettes (80 pence a pack). It's an ironic fate for grimey, tourist-trapping little Gibraltar (pop. 38,000), a British colony and once the world's most contested landmark. The ancients considered the Rock of Gibraltar one of the Pillars of Hercules, marking the end of the world. Its desirable position at the very mouth of the Mediterranean caused squabbles between the Moors and Spaniards, until English troops stormed Gibraltar's shores during the War of the Spanish Succession and the Treaty of Utrecht (1713) solidified Britain's hold on the enclave.

A 1967 vote showed that Gibraltar's populace overwhelmingly favored its British ties (12,138 to 44). In 1969, Franco sealed off the border and forbade any contact between Spain and Gibraltar, then, after a decade of negotiations and 16 years of isolation, the border re-opened at midnight, February 4, 1985. Tourists and residents now cross with ease, but Gibraltar remains culturally detached from Spain.

Despite the peninsula's history, Gibraltar pales in comparison with the picturesque Spanish coast. At best, Gibraltar is a daytrip—spend just enough time to stock up on Marlboros, stand on the Rock to say that you've done it, and practice your neglected English vocabulary.

ORIENTATION AND PRACTICAL INFORMATION

Gibraltar is regarded as a foreign destination from Spain; most buses terminate in bordering **La Línea.** From the bus station, walk directly towards the Rock; the border is five minutes away. After bypassing the line of sweating motorists, Spanish customs

and Gibraltar's passport control, catch bus #9 (40 pence or 100ptas), or walk across the airport tarmac and along the highway into town (20min.). Stay left on Av. Winston Churchill when the road forks with Corral Lane. Gibraltar's **Main Street,** a commercial strip lined with most services, begins at the far end of a square/parking lot past the Burger King on the left.

> Although **pesetas** are accepted everywhere (except in pay phones), the **pound sterling (£)** is clearly the preferred method of payment. Merchants sometimes charge a higher price in *pesetas* than is the pound's exchange equivalent. More often than not, change will be given in English currency rather than Spanish.
> 1£ = 246.95ptas

Tourist Office: 18-20 Bomb House Ln. (tel. 748 05), in the Gibraltar Museum, across the street from Marks and Spencer on Main Street. A bit better equipped than the info office, though it may be hard to hit a target using their maps (£1.50). Open Mon.-Fri. 10am-6pm, Sat. 10am-2pm. **Info Center,** Main St., The Piazza (tel. 749 82). Open Mon.-Fri. 9:30am-6pm, Sat. 10am-2pm.

Currency Exchange: (see box above). Most booths charge no commission and rates improve steadily as one proceeds along Main St. Banks close daily at 3:30pm, reopening Fri. only 4:30-6pm. **Gib Exchange Center, Ltd.,** John Mackintosh Sq., 6A (tel. 735 17). Open Mon.-Fri. 9am-1pm and 3-7pm, Sat. 10am-6pm.

American Express: Bland Travel, Irish Town (tel. 770 12). It holds mail and sells traveler's checks, but doesn't cash them. Open Mon.-Fri. 9am-6pm.

Buses: From La Línea, the closest Spanish town, to: Algeciras (every ½hr., 7am-10pm, 40min., 220ptas); Cádiz (4 per day, 3hr., 1440ptas); Sevilla (3 per day, 6hr., 2500ptas); Ronda (1 per day, 2½hr., 990ptas); Marbella (4 per day, 1¾hr., 670ptas); Málaga (4 per day, 3¼hr., 1225ptas); Granada (2 per day, 5-6hr., 2360ptas).

Luggage Storage: Lockers at the bus station (300ptas).

English-Language Bookstore: The Gibraltar Bookshop, 300 Main St. (tel. 718 94). Choice of superior classics. Open Mon.-Fri. 10am-6:30pm, Sat. 11:30am-2:30pm.

English-Language Periodicals: Sacarelo News Agency, 96 Main St. (tel. 787 23). The most globe-trotting selection of papers and magazines in town. Open Mon.-Fri. 9am-7pm, Sat. 9am-2:30pm, Sun. 1:30-5pm.

Hospital: St. Bernard's Hospital (tel. 797 00), on Hospital Hill.

Police: 120 Irish Town St. (tel. 725 00). **Emergency:** tel. 199.

Post Office: 104 Main St. (tel. 756 62). Sells Gibraltar stamps in sets for collectors. Possibly the world's easiest Poste Restante address (not one number unless your name is Two): Name, Poste Restante, Gibraltar (Main Post Office). Open Mon.-Fri. 8:45am-2:15pm, Sat. 10am-1pm; in winter Mon.-Fri. 9am-4:30pm, Sat. 10am-1pm.

Telephones: Red booths and pay phones don't accept *pesetas*. More expensive but without the hassle of coins is **Gibraltar Telecommunications International Ltd.,** 60 Main St. (tel. 756 87). **Faxes** also sent. Open Mon.-Fri. 9am-5pm. **Telephone Code:** From Britain (00) 350. From the U.S. (011) 350. From Spain 9567. From Cádiz province 7. The USA Direct code is 88 00.

ACCOMMODATIONS AND FOOD

Camping is illegal, and the two affordable places in the area are often full, especially from July-September. If worse comes to worst, crash in La Línea, a 20-minute trudge across the border. If the trudge back has made you hungry, you'll be happy to see restaurants serving Chinese, English, French, Indian, Spanish, and Italian cuisine, but you may choke on the price. There's always the **supermarket, Safeway** no less, in the Europort commercial complex (open Mon.-Sat. 8am-8pm).

Emile Youth Hostel Gibraltar, Line Wall Rd. (tel. 511 06), across from the square at the beginning of Main St. Cramped bunkbeds, but clean bathrooms. Lock-out 10:30am-4:30pm, and 11:30pm curfew, but the owner is friendly and flexible. £10 per person includes continental breakfast.

Queen's Hotel, 1 Boyd St. (tel. 740 00; fax 400 30). Through Southport Gate, bear right and enter around the back. Comfortable, well furnished rooms have phones;

ANDALUCÍA

some have TVs. Free parking and a huge bar/lounge downstairs. Laundry services. Special rates for *Let's Go* readers (ask for them). Twin bedded room £12 per person, with bath £18. Singles £16, with bath £20. Breakfast included.

Toc H Hostel, Line Wall Rd. (tel. 734 31). Same street, but nowhere near Emile Hostel. Walk toward the Rock on Main St., right just before the arch at Southport Gate, then left in front of the Hambros Bank. Rustic isn't the word. A maze of plants, cats, and itinerants. Solar-powered showers run warm only in the day time. £5 per person. £20 per week.

Cannon Hotel, 9 Cannon Ln. (tel. 517 11). Brand new with bright, airy rooms and floral decor. £20 per person. Doubles £30, with bath £35. Triple £35, with bath £40. Breakfast included. Visa, MC.

Smith's Fish and Chips, 295 Main St. (tel. 742 54). Run by a cheerful bloke who dishes out hardy servings of fish 'n' chips from £3, plus some vegetarian options. Open Mon.-Thurs. 11am-6pm, Fri until 9pm.; Sat. noon-3pm.

The Clipper, Irish Town (tel. 797 91). Maritime decor and whopping portions of roasts and pasta dishes in the £3.50-6 range.

Maharaja Indian Restaurant, Tuckey's Ln. (tel. 752 33), off Main St. Filling meat dishes starting at £4 and vegetarian entrees from £2. Open daily noon-3pm and 7-11:15pm. Visa.

SIGHTS

The northern tip of the massif known as **Top of the Rock** provides a truly remarkable view of Iberia and the Straits of Gibraltar. **Cable cars** carry visitors up from the south end of Main St., making a stop at Apes' Den. (Every 7min., Mon.-Sat. 9:30am-5:45pm; one way £3.65 per person, children £1.80. Round-trip £4.90 per person, children £2.45. If you are up for it, get a one-way ticket and walk down (1hr.). Tickets sold until 5:15pm.) The price of the cable car includes admission to St. Michael's Cave and Apes' Den. Tickets for the **Nature Reserve** on the Upper Rock are £5 for adults and £2.50 for children; £1.50 if you drive your own car. This ticket includes admission to St. Michael's Cave, the Apes' Den, the Great Siege Tunnels, the "Gibraltar: A City Under Siege" exhibit, and the Moorish Castle (open daily 9:30am-5:30pm).

The ruins of a Moorish wall descend along the road from the cable car station to the south, where the spooky chambers of **St. Michael's Cave** were cut into the rock. The deep grotto metamorphosed into a hospital during the 1942 bombardments. Now it's an auditorium with the requisite colored lights and corny music. If you're lucky, you'll hear a flute arrangement of the Hall and Oates classic, *Maneater*. The first Neanderthal skull ever found was excavated from St. Michael's. Take a U-turn down Queen's Rd. to **Apes' Den,** where a colony of monkeys cavort amusingly on the sides of rocks, the tops of taxis, and tourists' heads—the baby-talking, picture-snapping humans are more amusing still. These tailless Barbary apes have inhabited Gibraltar since before the Moorish invasion. The British believe they'll control the peninsula only as long as these animals survive. When the ape population nearly went extinct in 1944, Churchill put Yalta aside and ordered reinforcements from North Africa, so now the monkeys can be tormented by international visitors for years to come. At the northern tip of the Rock facing Spain are the **Great Siege Tunnels,** built into the cliffside in the 1770s to defend against a Spanish assault. The views from the turrets are spectacular, and a talking mannequin bellows, "Halt! Who goes there?" in a full-bodied British accent. Aren't you glad you came to Gibraltar?

At the southern tip of Gibraltar, **Europa Point** commands a seemingly endless view of the straits, guarded by three machine guns and a lighthouse. On a clear day you can see Morocco. Take bus #3 or 1B from Line Wall Rd., just off Main St., all the way to the end (every 15min., 45£).

ENTERTAINMENT

Main St. hosts throngs of lively **pubs.** Early evening busybodies people-watch from the **Angry Friar,** 287 Main St. (across from the Governor's Residence), also known as **The Convent** (tel. 715 70), and listen to occasional live music. Don't miss having

your photo taken with the fist-shaking monk. A pint of lager, ale, or bitter goes for £2 (open daily 10am-midnight, food served 10am-3pm). As evening wears into night, pub-hoppers slide down to the **Horseshoe Bar,** 193 Main St. (tel. 774 44; open Sun.-Thurs. 9:30am-midnight, Fri.-Sat. 9:30am-1am). **Bourbon Street,** 150 Main St. (tel. 437 63), has cajun cookin', a pool table, darts, and hosts live music nightly (karaoke Sun.; open Sun.-Fri. 8:30pm-1am, Sat. 3:30pm-1am).

■ Algeciras

Few visitors to Algeciras venture beyond the seedy, noisy port area. Moroccan migrant workers, young Spanish army recruits, and European and American tourists, all in transit between North Africa and Spain, traffic the area day and night. But hidden in the city proper is the city's calm, attractive older neighborhood, a pleasant refuge from the chaotic port. So while most visitors to Algeciras are in short transit between Morocco and Europe, less harried travelers can spend a pleasant first or last night in Spain by making a inland dash.

ORIENTATION AND PRACTICAL INFORMATION

Stretching along the coast, **Avenida de la Marina,** which turns into Av. Virgen del Carmen north of the port, is lined with travel agencies, banks, and hotels. **Calle Juan de la Cierva** runs perpendicular to the coast from the port, becoming **Calle San Bernardo** as it nears the **train** and **bus stations.** To reach the **tourist office** from either one, follow C. San Bernardo/C. Juan de la Cierva along the abandoned tracks toward the port, past a parking lot on your left. From the **port,** take a left onto Av. Virgen del Carmen, then a quick right onto C. Juan de la Cierva; the office is on the left. All services necessary for transit to Morocco cluster around the port, accessible by a single driveway. Be wary of imposters who peddle ferry tickets. Allow a half-hour to clear customs and board, an hour and a half if you have a car.

Tourist Office: C. Juan de la Cierva (tel. 57 26 36; fax 57 04 75), it's the tube-shaped, pink-and-red building. Sells map with all essentials clearly marked (100ptas), plus lots of Andalucía brochures. Also has a message board. Open Mon.-Fri. 9am-2pm.

Telephones: On C. Pescadería and Av. Virgen del Carmen. Open Mon.-Sat. 10am-2pm and 6-11pm, Sun. 11am-2pm and 7-10:30pm.

Currency Exchange: For exchange in *pesetas* or *dirhams,* there are plenty of banks along Av. Virgen del Carmen, directly in front of the port, many with **ATMs.** Banks open 8:30am-2pm, a few open Saturdays with shorter hours. Commissions range from 500-1500ptas. Travel agencies offer poor rates.

Trains: RENFE, Ctra. Cádiz (tel. 63 02 02 or 63 20 45), way down C. Juan de la Cierva and its connecting street. To: Granada (3 per day, 5½hr., 2300ptas). Connections in Bobadilla to: Málaga (3 per day, 5½hr., 2000ptas); Sevilla (3 per day, 6hr., 2580ptas); Madrid (3 per day, 6hr., 4500ptas; 1 additional overnight train, 12hr., 5000ptas).

Buses: Empresa Portillo, Av. Virgen del Carmen, 15 (tel. 65 10 55). To: Marbella (10 per day, Sun. 9 per day, 1½hr., 760ptas); Córdoba (2 per day, 6hr., 2805ptas); Granada (2 per day, 5hr., 2455ptas); Málaga (11 per day, 3hr., 1290ptas). **Linesur La Valenciana,** Viajes Koudubia, C. Juan de la Cierva, 5 (tel. 60 11 89). To: Jerez de la Frontera (6 per day, 5 per day Sun., 2hr., 1060ptas); Sevilla (11 per day, 3½hr., 1930ptas); **Transporres Generales Comes,** C. San Bernardo, 1, (tel. 65 34 56), under Hotel Octavio. To: Tarifa (10 per day, Sun. 4 per day, 30min., 215ptas); La Línea (every 30min., 7am-9:30pm, 45min., 220ptas); Cádiz (9 per day, Sun. 8 per day, 2½hr., 1225ptas); Sevilla (4 per day, 3½hr., 2100ptas). **Empresa Bacoma,** Av. Marina, 8 (tel. 65 22 00). To Barcelona (4 per day, 19½hr., 10,000ptas).

Ferries: Tickets, surprisingly, are the same price in any of the dozens of travel agencies in town or in the port terminal. It is recommended that you purchase tickets at the port, not the train station. Allow 30min. to clear customs and board, 90min. with a car. In summer to: Ceuta *(buque ferry:* 8 per day, with 4 additional during high demand, every 90min., 7am-8:30pm, 90min., 1884ptas per person, 4793ptas

per car, 1870-2810ptas per motorcycle; *embarcaciones rápidas:* 8 per day with 2 additional departures during high demand, 6am-11:30pm, 35min., 3002ptas per person, children 1505ptas); and Tangier: (10 per day, 7am-9pm, 2½hr.; 2690ptas per person, 1480ptas children under 12, 9300ptas per car, 2650ptas per motorcycle, 20% discount with Eurail pass. No cars on board in bad weather. Limited service in winter; hydrofoil: 1 per day, morning, 1hr., 2690ptas per person.

Taxis: tel. 65 55 12 or 65 55 51.

Luggage Storage: At Empresa Portillo bus terminal. Large lockers 300ptas per day. Open daily 7:30am-10pm. At RENFE 400ptas per day, 2 week limit.

Pharmacy: C. Cayetano del Toro at C. Tarifa (tel. 65 27 57). Open Mon.-Fri. 9am-1:30pm and 5-8:30pm. *Farmacias de guardia* listed on windowpane.

Hospital: Residencia Sanitaria (tel. 60 57 22).

Police: Municipal, C. Ruiz Zorilla (tel. 66 01 55). **Emergency:** tel. 091 or 092.

Post Office: C. Ruiz Zorilla (tel. 66 31 76). From the train station, turn left on the street to Málaga; it becomes C. Ruiz Zorilla. Open for Lista de Correos Mon.-Fri. 9am-8pm, Sat. 9am-1:30pm. **Postal Code:** 11080. **Telephone Code:** (9)56.

ACCOMMODATIONS AND FOOD

Lots of convenient *casas de huéspedes* and *hostales* bunch around **C. José Santacana,** parallel to Av. Marina and one block inland following the train tracks, and **C. Duque de Almodóvar,** two blocks farther from the water. Consider asking for a back room—wanna-be mods cruise the narrow streets on Vespas at ungodly hours. Furthermore, this neighborhood is notoriously squalid, and should only be considered as a last resort. The beach in Algeciras isn't the place to camp. Police patrol the waterfront, and when they don't, unsavories do. Walk a couple more blocks into town for a more pleasant area. Relish your final taste of *paella*, or welcome yourself back from Morocco with *pollo asado* (baked chicken) sold along Av. Virgen del Carmen, near the port, and on C. Juan de la Cierva. A **supermarket** sells food on the corner of C. Santacana and C. Maroto (open daily 9am-2pm and 5-8pm).

Hostal Rif, C. Rafael de Muro, 11 (tel. 65 49 53). In a restored 18th century building, Rif is quiet and cool run by helpful management. Follow C. Santacana into the small market square, bear left around the large kiosk and continue up C. Rafael del Muro for one block.Clean communal showers with hot water. Rooms are a bargain at 1200ptas per person.

Hostal Residencia González, C. José Santacana, 7 (tel. 65 28 43). A decent bargain close to the port. Roomy quarters with wood furnishings. Singles 1500ptas, with bath 1750ptas. Doubles: 3000ptas; 3500ptas.

Hostal Nuestra Señora del Carmen, C. Santacana, 14A (tel. 65 63 01). Comfy, decently sized rooms with showers. Singles 1600ptas, with bath 1900ptas. Doubles with bath 3000ptas.

La Alegría, C. José Santacana, 6 (tel. 66 65 09). Enthusiasts can indulge in whopping portions of homestyle, ham-free Moroccan cooking. Savory chicken *tahini* with bread and legumes 600ptas. Also *para llevar* (to go). Open daily 7am-11pm.

Casa Alfonso, C. Juan de la Cierva, 1 (tel. 60 31 21), the big green building near the tourist office. No-nonsense eatery frequented by port employees. *Tortillas* (400-500ptas) make a substantial meal. You can design your own *menú* for 900ptas. Open Sun.-Fri. noon-11pm.

Restaurante Casa Sanchez, Av. Segismundo Moret, 6 (tel. 65 69 57), on the corner of C. Río, one bl. inland from C. José Santacana. Lively local joint with low-key service. *Menú* 950ptas. *Platos Combinados* 775ptas. Open Mon.-Sat. noon-11:30pm.

SIGHTS

Debilitated by the War of Succession (1702-1714), Spain lost Gibraltar to the British in 1704. Exiled Spaniards fled to Algeciras, where they settled around beautiful **Plaza Alta.** Today the plaza is crowned by a handsome blue- and gold-tiled fountain. Many outdoor cafes and *heladerías* line nearby **Calle Regino Martinez,** the main *paseo*.

The nicest nearby beach borders **Getares,** a village 5km south of Algeciras, off the main road. The mile-long sand strip is relatively uncrowded. Three km from Algeciras in the opposite direction lies the fine sand of **Playa Rinconcillo**, extending to the Río Palmones. City buses (tel. 66 22 57), cruise from Av. Virgen del Carmen.

▨ Tarifa

When the wind picks up in Tarifa, the southernmost city in continental Europe and the western edge of the Costa del Sol, empty soda cans rattle through the streets with chaotic abandon. Shelter-seeking residents and tourists leave miles of white sandy beaches desolate but for the intrepid, gnarly few—the windsurfers. Rad vans with fresh window stickers replace SEAT Pandas and Quicksilver jams supplant Burberry's scarfs, but Ray Bans will always rock, brah. In Tarifa, even the Spaniards wear shorts and sandals.

Orientation and Practical Information The **tourist office,** Po. Alameda (tel. 68 09 93; fax 68 04 31), packs a basic plan of the city, a list of hostels, and bus schedules into one nifty brochure. From the bus station, exit to the east, follow C. Batalla del Salado for 2½ blocks, turn right on Av. Andalucía, and hang ten onto the tree-lined Alameda. The tourist office is the small glass building under the stairwell (open Mon.-Fri. 9am-2pm and 6-7pm; in winter Mon.-Fri. 8am-3pm). An **ATM** is at C. Batalla del Salado, 17, next to the bus stop. In a **medical emergency,** dial Centro de Salud at 68 15 15. The **police** (tel. 68 41 86) chill out in the Ayuntamiento. **Emergency** numbers are 091 or 092. The **post office,** C. Colonel Moscardó, 9 (tel. 68 42 37), is near Pl. San Maleo and the church, in the Moorish town through the arch (open Mon.-Fri. 8:30am-2:30pm, Sat. 9:30am-1pm). The **postal code** is 11380. The **telephone code** is (9)56. **Transportes Generales Comes buses** roll from in front of the office on Batalla del Salado, 19 (tel. 68 40 38; window open Mon.-Fri. 7:15-11:15am and 4-8pm, Sat.-Sun. 4-8pm), to: Algeciras (10 per day, Sat. 9 per day, Sun. 4 per day, 30min., 225ptas); Cádiz (8 per day, Sat. 5 per day, Sun. 4 per day, 2¼hr., 1055ptas) with a stop in Vejer (1hr., 500ptas); and Sevilla (3 per day, 4hr., 2020ptas). **Ferries** leave for Tangier from the port (Sat.-Thurs. at 10am, Fri. at 9am; returns at 6pm, Fri. at 5pm, 1hr., 3500ptas one way).

Accommodations and Food Affordable rooms line the main strip, **Batalla del Salado.** If you visit in August, call ahead or arrive early. **Hostal Villanueva,** Av. Andalucía, 11 (tel. 68 41 49), has all the comforts and brown-based decor of a Holiday Inn, plus a wind-blown rooftop terrace with an ocean view and friendly multilingual management (singles 1500-2000ptas; doubles 3000-5500ptas; Visa). The dining room downstairs serves specialty *paella* (open Tues.-Sun. 1-4pm and 8-11pm). Uphill, **Hostal El Asturians** (tel. 68 06 19), keeps brightly-tiled rooms, all with full bath (singles 1500-3000ptas, doubles 3500-6500ptas). Sample the Asturian *sidra* in the restaurant downstairs (open daily 1-4pm and 8pm-2am). A number of official **campgrounds** lurk a few kilometers to the west on the beach (400-500ptas per person). Unofficial camping occurs, but it's likely a windy experience. Eateries cluster in the streets through the arch and downhill in the old town. **Café-Bar Central,** C. Sancho IV El Bravo (tel. 68 05 60), has one of the few *terrazas* in town buffered by enough buildings so as not to blow away. Ham and cheese and vegetarian *bocadillos* range between 400-500ptas (open daily 8am-5:45pm). Up the street, **Ali-Baba,** C. Sancho, 8, serves falafel (350ptas) and kebab (375ptas) to go (open daily 2pm-2am).

Sights At the eastern end of town, next to the port, stand the ruins of the **Castillo de Guzmán el Bueno.** In the 13th century, the Moors kidnapped Guzmán's son and threatened to kill him if Guzmán didn't relinquish the castle. Guzmán, like Abraham, did not surrender. The castle is currently not open to visitors. Those with something more wet and wild in mind can head 200m south to **Playa Lances** and 5km of the finest white sand on the coast. Bathers should beware of high winds and a strong under-

tow. **Tarifa Spin Out Surfbase** (tel. 23 63 52), 9km up the road toward Cáohz, rents windsurfing boards and instructs all levels.

PROVINCE OF CÁDIZ

■ Cádiz

Located in the southwestern recesses of the Iberian Peninsula, today Cádiz is securely detached from the rest of Continental Europe. But from the 16th century until Spain lost Cuba in the Spanish-American War (1898), Cádiz filled its port with fabulous riches from the New World. It was also the capital of a new political discussion surrounding the exciting problem of how to manage an Empire—a world—that had extended to exotic lands.

Ever since the New World fervor, liberal politics has become a hallmark of Cadisian life. The city's decisive resistance to Napoleon in 1808 helped preserve the Spanish nation and awakened its disheveled political leaders to their political frailty. They subsequently designed the *Constitución de Cádiz* (1812), an assertion of democratic ideals that inspired a wave of Latin American nationalism, but sadly proved ineffectual in its own land. When Fernando VII restored the Monarchy in 1814, he ignored the constitution and submerged his country under 20 years of repression. Cadisian liberalism was thwarted again during the Civil War when it fell early and hard to Franco's Nationalist army. As fitting retaliation, Cádiz rekindled its immortal spirit once a year, celebrating their extravagant *Carnaval,* the only festival not suppressed by the Generalísimo. Perhaps Spain's most dazzling party, *Carnaval* makes Cádiz an imperative destination on February itineraries.

ORIENTATION AND PRACTICAL INFORMATION

To reach **Plaza de San Juan de Dios** (the town center) from the **Comes bus station,** walk along Av. Puerto for about five minutes, keeping the port to your left; the plaza lies to the right just after a park. From the **Los Amarillos bus stop,** walk inland about 100m. From the **train station,** walk past the fountain keeping the port to your right for about four blocks; Pl. San Juan de Dios is the first plaza on the left. The tangled *casco viejo* is altogether disorienting; a map is absolutely necessary.

Tourist Office: Municipal, Pl. San Juan de Dios, 11 (tel. 24 10 01), in the mauve Pozos de Miranda building at the end of the plaza. Bright yellow "i" marks the spot. Useful free **map.** English spoken. Open Mon.-Fri. 9am-2pm and 5-8pm, Sat. 10am-2pm. **Junta de Andalucía,** C. Calderón de la Barca, 1 (tel. 21 13 13). From the bus station, cross over to Pl. España and walk uphill on C. Ant. López. Office is across Pl. Mina, on the corner of C. Calderón de la Barca and C. Zorrilla. Good regional and transport info. 100ptas map. Open Mon.-Fri. 9am-7pm, Sat. 10am-1pm.

Currency Exchange: Banco Central Hispano, C. Ancha, 29 (tel. 22 66 22). No commission on cash exchanges or AmEx traveler's checks. Open Mon.-Fri. 8:30am-2pm.

Trains: RENFE (tel. 25 43 01), Pl. Sevilla, off Av. Puerto. To: Jerez (20 per day, 40min., 420ptas); Sevilla (13 per day, 2hr., 1215ptas); Granada (3 per day, 6hr., 2785ptas); Córdoba (5 per day, 5hr., 2601-3700ptas); Pto. de Sta. María (20 per day, 30min., 350ptas); Valencia (2 per day, 10-14hr., 6700ptas); Madrid (2 per day, via Sevilla, transfer to AVE, 5hr., 9200-9500ptas).

Buses: Transportes Generales Comes, Pl. Hispanidad, 1 (tel. 22 42 71). To: Pto. de Sta. María (every hr., 8:30am-8:30pm, 30min., 190 ptas); Rota (8 per day, 1¼hr., 450ptas); Arcos de la Frontera (3 per day, 1½hr., 670ptas); Jerez de la Frontera (16 per day, 1hr., 350ptas); Algeciras (8 per day, 3hr., 1225ptas); Vejer de la Frontera (9 per day, 1½hr., 550ptas); La Línea (4 per day, 3hr., 1440ptas); Málaga (3 per day, 4hr. 2515ptas); Sevilla (12 per day, 2hr., 1300ptas); Córdoba (1 per day, 5hr., 2185ptas); Granada (2 per day, 7hr., 4010ptas). **Transportes Los Amarillos** (tel.

28 58 52) leaves from beside the port, off Pl. San Juan de Dios, across from Po. Canalejas. Purchase tickets on the bus. To: Sanlúcar (9 per day, 1½hr., 375ptas); Chipiona (9 per day, 2hr., 460ptas); Pto. de Sta. María (9 per day, 30min., 175ptas); Arcos (3 per day, 2hr., 770ptas). Both companies have reduced service Sat.-Sun.

Ferry: El Vapor (tel. 87 02 70) leaves from the port next to the Comes station. To Pto. de Sta. María (5per day, 45min., 250ptas).

Municipal Buses (tel. 26 28 06). Pick up a map/schedule and *bonobus* (discount packets) at the kiosk across from the Comes bus station. Most lines run through Pl. España. Beach bum's favorite: #1 (Cortadura) runs along the shore.

Taxis: (tel. 22 10 06 or 28 69 69).

Luggage Storage: Lockers at train station (300ptas). Open daily 8am-10pm.

Red Cross: C. Sta. María Soledad, 10 (tel. 25 42 70 or 22 22 22).

Pharmacy: Farmacia S. Matute, Pl. San Juan de Dios, 2 (tel. 28 49 03). Open 9am-1:30pm and 5-8pm. **Medical Assistance: Ambulatorio Vargas Ponce,** Pl. Mendizábal, 2 (tel. 27 45 53).

Police: Municipal (tel. 22 81 06), Campo del Sur. In the new city.

Emergency: tel. 091 or 092.

Post Office: (tel. 21 39 45) Pl. Flores, next to the market. Open Mon.-Fri. 8:30am-2:30pm, Sat. 9:30am-2pm. **Postal Code:** 11080.

Telephone Code: (9)56.

ACCOMMODATIONS

Most *hostales* huddle around the harbor, in **Pl. San Juan de Dios,** and just behind it on **C. Marqués de Cádiz.** Others scatter throughout the old town. Singles and triples are scarce but sometimes negotiable in the off season. Call months in advance to find a room during February's *Carnaval.*

Hostal Colón, C. Marqués de Cádiz, 6 (tel. 28 53 51), off Pl. San Juan de Dios. Spotless rooms with sinks and colorful tiles. All rooms have balconies, but the best view is from the terrace: the cathedral amongst hundreds of TV antennas. Two windowless singles 2000ptas. Triples 1400-1600ptas per person.

Hostal Marqués, C. Marqués de Cádiz, 1 (tel. 28 58 54). Newly renovated 18th-century rooms with firm mattresses surround a resonant interior courtyard. Most have balconies except for one unloved single. Singles 1800ptas. Doubles 2800-3000ptas.

Hostal Cádiz, C. Feduchy, 20 (tel. 28 58 01), near Pl. Candelaria. Clean, comfy rooms—almost all triples. Some plastic furniture. Ask the amicable owner for tips on cheap eateries and hip nightlife. He may even help with laundry (500ptas). Key to the front door. 1500ptas per person, with shower 1700ptas.

La Isleña Casa de Huéspedes, Pl. San Juan de Dios, 12, 2nd fl. (tel. 28 70 64). Small and family run with simple, floral rooms, some with huge white balconies overlooking the main square. Singles 1300-1500ptas. Doubles 2400-3000ptas.

Camas Cuatro Naciones, C. Plocia, 3 (tel. 25 55 39), in a corner of Pl. San Juan de Dios. Funky decorating. Rooms facing the street get a lot of sunshine. Singles 1500ptas. Doubles 2500-3000 ptas. Triples 3500ptas.

FOOD

Once you leave Pl. San Juan de Dios, finding eateries can be a stomach-churning experience. But seek and you will be rewarded. Try the cafes and *heladerías* around **Pl. Flores** (also called Pl. Topete), near the post office and the municipal **market.** If you absolutely detest seafood, head to Supermarket **Simago,** next to the municipal market, off Pl. Flores (open Mon.-Sat. 9am-9pm.)

Bar Pajaro Pinto, Pl. Tío de la Tiza, 12, among similar **terrazas** hidden between C. Rosa and C. Cuba on the way down to Playa Caleta. Enormous *raciones* of the day's catch (700-1000ptas). Open June-Sept. daily 8:30pm-2am.

Freiduría Sopranis, C. Sopranis, 2 (tel. 25 64 31), off Pl. San Juan de Dios. Every imaginable type of seafood 1200-2200ptas per kg (feeds four). Try fresh *choco, acedías,* or *puntillitas.* Open daily 11am-4:30pm and 7pm-midnight.

ANDALUCÍA

Bar-Restaurante Pasaje Andaluz, Pl. San Juan de Dios, 9 (tel. 28 52 54). Outdoor metal tables with plastic covers hardly spell "Ritz," but this casual place knows the old standby *m-e-n-ú* (850-1000ptas). Open Sat.-Thurs. 1-4:30pm and 8-11:30pm.

SIGHTS AND ENTERTAINMENT

Most sights lie in the old town within walking distance of one another. Murillo, Rubens, and Zurbarán live in unholy union with some Phoenician sarcophagi at the **Museo de Bellas Artes y Arqueológico,** Pl. Mina (tel. 21 22 81), the result of a Fine Arts/Provincial Archaeological Museum fusion (open Tues.-Sun. 9am-2pm; 250ptas, EU citizens free). Follow C. Zorrilla inland five blocks to the **Museo Histórico Municipal,** C. Santa Inés, 9 (tel. 22 17 88), which flaunts an enormous, painstakingly wrought 18th-century ivory-and-mahogany model of the city. (Open Tues.-Fri. 9am-1pm and 5-7pm, Sat.-Sun. 9am-1pm; in winter Tues.-Fri. 9am-1pm and 4-6pm, Sat.-Sun. 9am-1pm. Free.) From Pl. Mona, C. Tinte leads downhill to C. Rosario, and the art of Goya, Cavallini, and Camarone at **El Oratorio de la Santa Cueva** (tel. 28 76 76; open Mon.-Fri. 10am-1pm; 100ptas).

Continue down C. Rosario and turn right onto C. Padre Elejarde to reach the gold-domed 18th-century **cathedral** (tel. 28 61 54), considered the last great one built by colonial riches. Its treasury bulges with crazy-opulent valuables—the *Custodia del Millón* is said to be set with a million precious stones. Composer Manuel de Falla is buried in the crypt. (Cathedral open Mon.-Sat. 10:30am-1:30pm, museum open Tues.-Sat. 10am-noon. Guided tours every 30min. 400ptas, children 200ptas. Cathedral mass Sun. noon. Free.)

Cádiz's **seaside paseo** runs along the Atlantic and the bay of Pto. de Santa María, and is accessible via the Muralla de San Carlos off Pl. España. Stupendous views of ships leaving the harbor recall the golden age of yore. Inland, infinite rows of antennae rising from the rooftops recall 1950. Exotic trees, fanciful hedges, and a few chattering monkeys enliven the adjacent **Parque Genovés.**

Since Cádiz was built on a long peninsula surrounded on three sides by the Atlantic, the exhaust-spewing ships on one coast don't profane the extensive line of pristine **beaches** on the other. **Playa de la Caleta,** the easiest one to reach, is picturesquely nestled between two castles in the *casco antiguo*. Other sands skirt the new part of town, serviced by bus #1 (towards Cortadura), which leaves from Pl. España (115ptas). The first beach beyond the rocks is the unremarkable 400m **Playa de Santa María del Mar.** Next to it, **Playa de la Victoria** stretches 2500m and has earned the EU's *bandera azul* (blue flag) of cleanliness, and by far the most visitors. A more natural landscape, with fewer hotels and straw mats, belongs to **Playa de Cortadura** (5000m), where the coveted *bandera azul* flaps proudly. Take bus #1 until it almost reaches the highway, when the bus will reverse its route. The boardwalk ends here and sunbather density falls steadily the farther one walks.

After midnight in summertime, anyone with a throat finds fresh air (and refreshments) by the beach. **Paseo Marítimo,** the main drag along Playa Victoria, has some of Cádiz's best bars, discos, cafes, and *terrazas.* **La Jarra,** on C. José G. Agullo, is one such hotspot. Another choice locale for bar-hoppers and disco-maniacs is **Punta de San Felipe,** reached by walking north along the sea from Pl. España, just beyond the Comes station; most of its real action kicks off at 4 or 5am. In **El Centro,** try the area around **Plaza Mina,** which is liveliest on weekends during the winter. **Calle de Manuel Rances,** nearby off C. Antonio López, freaks some of the hippest bars.

Carnaval (Feb. 6-16) insanity is legendary. The gray of winter gives way to dazzling color in February when the city hosts one of the most Rabelaisian *carnavales* in the world. Costumed dancers, street singers, ebullient residents, and folks from all over take to the streets in a week-long frenzy that makes New Orleans's Mardi Gras look like Thursday night bingo.

■ Near Cádiz

EL PUERTO DE SANTA MARÍA

Across the bay from Cádiz and a 12-minute train ride from Jerez, low-key El Puerto de Santa María is one of three cities (along with Jerez and Sanlúcar) that form the renowned "sherry triangle." Here, wine reigns next to God, and in a final concession to vice, El Puerto boasts the only functioning casino in western Andalucía.

Practical Information The **tourist office,** C. Guadalete, 1 (tel. 54 24 13 or 54 24 75; fax 54 22 46), is off Av. Bajamar near the port. From the train station, take a left on Ctra. Madrid, then a right onto C. Pozas Dulces. Follow it along the water; the tourist office is on the right. From the bus stop in front of Pl. Toros, follow C. Santa Lucía into Pl. España, turn right on C. Palacios, and continue to the end. Jog left and the tourist office is on the right (open daily 10am-2pm and 6-8pm; in winter 10am-2pm and 5:30-7:30pm). In a **medical emergency,** call tel. 54 33 02 or 87 11 11. The **municipal police** (tel. 54 18 63) can be alerted at Ronda de las Dunas, s/n. In **emergencies,** call tel. 091 or 092. The **post office,** Pl. Polvorista, 7 (tel. 85 53 22), does it all (open Mon.-Fri. 8:30am-8:30pm, Sat. 9am-2pm). The **telephone code** is (9)56.

El Puerto's bus stop is in front of Pl. Toros, but many buses passing through drop off and pick up passengers at the train station; ask at the tourist office for specific times and departure points. **Buses** connect El Puerto to: Cádiz (31 per day, 40min., 190ptas); Jerez (18 per day, 30min., 150ptas); Rota (8 per day, 30min., 325ptas); Sanlúcar and Chipiona (10 per day, Sat.-Sun. 5 per day, 215-275ptas). Reduced service on weekends. **Trains** (tel. 54 25 85) depart for: Jerez (20 per day, 6am-10:40pm, 12min., 150ptas); Cádiz (21 per day, 6:55am-11:32pm, 30min., 350ptas); and Sevilla (17 per day, 2hr., 1050ptas). An El Vapor **ferry** (tel. 87 02 70) links El Puerto with Cádiz, departing from the port near the tourist office (5 per day, Sun. 6 per day, off season 4 per day, 45min., 250ptas).

Accommodations and Food Unless you really feel like gambling, El Puerto de Santa María makes most sense as a daytrip. The family-run **Pensión Santamaría,** C. Nevería/C. Pedro Muñoz Seca (*not* C. Dr. Muñoz Seca), 38 (tel. 85 36 31), keeps clean rooms surrounding a relaxing patio. (Singles 1500-2000ptas. Doubles 3000ptas, with bath 3500ptas. Triples with bath 5000-6000ptas.) From the tourist office, head up C. Palacios toward Pl. España and take the fourth left. **Camping Playa Las Dunas,** Po. Marítimo La Puntilla (tel. 87 22 10), is a 20-minute walk along the shore from the tourist office or a painless local bus ride (#26). A *cafetería,* supermarket, and clean showers await (555ptas per adult and per tent, 455 ptas per child, 455ptas per car). The campground lounges in a pine forest across the street from **Playa de la Puntilla,** a blue-banner beach but with views of Cádiz's industrial harbor on the other side of the bay. Avoid the overpriced restaurants near the water. Instead, try **La Tortillería,** C. Palacios, 4, a bar famous for its inventive 200ptas omelette sandwiches (open Tues.-Thurs. and Sun. 8:30pm-1am, Fri.-Sat. 8:30pm-2am). For international food, Italian **Restaurante Pasta Gansa,** on C. Puerto Escondido, off C. Ribera del Río, has 700-900ptas pasta dishes, and Chinese **Restaurant Hong Kong,** across from the ferry dock, has a 4-course *menú* (525ptas).

Sights and Entertainment El Puerto's history as an embarking point for exploration and conquest has resulted in a few noteworthy monuments. Columbus's second voyage to the New World was launched here, and as business in the Americas developed, prominent families emptied their coffers to build structures that are now open to the public. Before the boom, Alfonso X El Sabio constructed the **Castillo de San Marcos** in the 13th century. Visitors can survey the city from the castle's tower. (Open Tues., Thurs., and Sat. 11am-1:30pm; Oct.-June Sat. 11am-1pm. Guided tours every 30min. Free.) **Iglesia Mayor Prioral** has a Baroque front topped with a one-armed nude and two sidekicks (open daily 10am-noon and 7:30-8:30pm; free). Two

of El Puerto's *bodegas* sponsor tours; make a reservation with **Bodega Terry** (tel. 48 30 00; tours Mon.-Fri. at 9:30, 11am and 12:30pm; in August, Mon.-Tues. and Thurs., 11am only; 300ptas) or **Bodega Osborne** (tel. 85 52 11; open Mon.-Fri. 10:30am-1pm; 300ptas), the sponsors of those *gigantesco* (or *grotesco*) black bull billboards that fill the countryside. Their promotional film is hysterical. The **Fundación de Rafael Alberti,** C. Santo Domingo, 25 (tel. 85 07 11), displays the poet's books, correspondence, and personal belongings (open Tues.-Sat. 10:30am-2pm; free).

■ Vejer de la Frontera

Before coming to Spain, you may have dreamt of a majestic white town crowning a massive hill, where friendly locals invite you into their ancient homes hemmed by narrow cobbled alleys. Vejer de la Frontera is as close as it gets. Although women no longer venture out cloaked in *cobijados* (long, black garb that obscures the face), the town hasn't lost its Arab mystique. Without the distraction of textbook monuments and must-see sights, beautiful Vejer welcomes you to sit back and soak it up.

Orientation and Practical Information Reaching the town center is no simple task. While some buses stop at the end of **Avenida de Los Remedios,** which leads uphill into La Plazuela (10min.), many just dump you out by the highway at **La Barca de Vejer.** Ask at the restaurant whether you can catch one of the infrequent buses to town, or use the buddy system for taxis (600ptas to take you up the hill). The alternative uphill walk can be arduous with a backpack. If you do make the 20-minute trek, climb the cobbled track to the left of the restaurant. When you reach the top, keep walking straight; all roads lead to quiet **Plaza de España,** not to be confused with **La Plazuela,** a tiny intersection across town inhabited by the **market,** the **tourist office,** and many **bars.** For the easiest route to the Plazuela from Pl. España, ascend the stairs to the right as you approach Pl. España, turn left on C. Corredera, and follow it for about five minutes. The first road to the left leads into the Plazuela.

Visit the **tourist office,** C. San Filmo, 6 (tel. 45 01 91), off the Plazuela, to receive maps, info, and occasional *tortas vejeriegas* (cookie samples; open Mon.-Fri. 10:30am-2pm and 6-9pm, Sat. 10:30am-2pm; in winter Mon.-Fri. 9am-2:30pm and 5-9:30pm). In a **medical emergency,** call the **Centro de Salud** (tel. 44 76 25) or visit them on Av. Andalucía. Reach the **police** at tel. 45 04 00. The **post office** (tel. 45 02 38) is on C. Juan Bueno, 22 (open Mon.-Fri. 8:30am-2:30pm, Sat. 9am-1pm). The **postal code** is 11150. The **telephone code** is (9)56. Leaving Vejer, some **buses** stop downhill from the Plazuela, just as Av. Los Remedios curves around the park and meets the highway. Bus info is in a tiny window with green ironwork on the Plazuela, at the **Comes** office (tel. 45 00 30), which never seems to open. Buses run to Cádiz (3 per day, 1½hr., 550ptas) and Sevilla via Jerez (2 per day, Sat.-Sun. 1 per day, 3½hr., 1640ptas). For other (mostly southeasterly) destinations, descend to **La Barca,** which heads to: Málaga (3 per day, 4hr., 2515ptas); La Línea (8 per day, 2¼hr, 1300 ptas); Algeciras (8 per day, 2hr., 1225ptas); Tarifa (3 per day, 1hr., 500ptas); Cádiz (7 per day, 1½hr., 550ptas); and Sevilla (3 per day, 3½hr., 1940ptas).

Accommodations and Food The best accommodations in Vejer are in its two **casas particulares** (private houses) on C. San Filmo, up the street from the tourist office. Next door, the friendly Sra. Rosa Romero owns **Casa Los Cántaros,** Galindo, C. San Filmo, 14 (tel. 44 75 92), a beautifully restored Andalucían home with a grape-vined patio. The spotless suites have sitting rooms, antique furniture, and private bathrooms, and you can use the kitchen (doubles 2500-3000ptas). Señora Luisa Doncel keeps tidy little apartments, often with TVs and kitchens, on **C. San Filmo, 12** (tel. 45 02 46). If Doña Luisa is not at #12, try #16 (singles 1300ptas, doubles 2600-3000ptas). Where you stay may depend on which woman you meet first.

The cheapest eats are *tapas* or *raciones* at the bars around the Plazuela. At **Bar El Cura,** Po. Cobijadas, 1, at the very bottom of C. Juan Bueno, locals place bets on who can make the solemn owner laugh (or at least crack a smile). A cup of *fino* (dry

sherry) costs a mere 50ptas. Open daily 6am-1am. If you're in the mood for a sit-down meal, try **La Posada,** Av. Los Remedios, 21 (tel. 45 01 11), a few buildings downhill from the bus stop. Inside is a bar and an ornate dining room with a 1200ptas *menú del día* (open daily 1:30-4pm and 8-midnight; Visa).

Sights and Entertainment To enjoy Vejer properly, simply wander along the labyrinthine streets and cliffside *paseos,* stopping frequently for drinks and *tapas.* As for monuments, the **Castillo Moro** offers the usual assortment of battlements and crenulated walls, plus a blinding view of the glowing white houses. (Open daily 11am-2pm and 5-9pm; Sept.-June 10am-2pm. Patio open at all hours. A boy scout troop leads the way around the ramparts.) The **Iglesia del Divino Salvador** is a choice blend of Romanesque, Mudéjar, and Gothic styles (open daily 9am-2pm and 5-9pm).

Ten kilometers from Vejer on the road to Los Caños lies **El Palmar,** 7km of fine white sand and clear waters easily accessible by car. Many beach-goers hitch rides at the bend of **Los Remedios** or catch the bus to **Conil de la Frontera** and walk southeast along the beach for three or four kilometers. For quasi tourist info and other outdoor activities, like **bike rentals,** consult **Magnum Bike and Surf Shop** (tel. 44 75 75), on Av. Los Remedios (bikes from 1000ptas a day, surf boards from 2000ptas a day).

The old quarter hops at night. Leave a piece of your heart at **Bar Janis Joplin** on C. Marqués de Tamarón, with plush wicker chairs, an amazing view, me, and Bobby McGee. Across the street, **La Bodeguita** is another favorite spot. Several other popular pubs lie downhill from the Plazuela on **C. Sagasta** and **C. Santisimo.** Students jam the underground **Pub Sótano,** on C. Altozano. From July-August, everyone dances among the thatched huts of **Carpa Bekkeh** in Prague de Los Remedios, behind the bus stop. Stupendous terrace views make **Café-Bar El Arriate,** C. Corredera, 5 (tel. 4471 70) is a good place for a *copa* and *tapas* anytime. You can also do some local wine sampling year-round at **Bodegas Gallardo** (tel. 45 10 80), down in La Barca.

The village throws brilliant *fiestas.* As soon as the **Corpus Christi** revelry ends in June, Vejer starts anew with the **Candelas de San Juan** (June 23), climaxed by the midnight release of the *toro de fuego* (bull of fire) at midnight. A local (obviously with a death wish) dressed in an iron bull costume charges the crowd as a bevy of attached firecrackers fly off his body in all directions. Audiences *love* it; nervous mothers flee indoors with the kids. The town demonstrates its taurine creativity again during the delirious **Semana Santa** celebrations (March 27-30). A *toro embolao* (sheathed bull), with wooden balls affixed to the tips of his horns, is set loose through the narrow streets of Vejer on the Sunday of the Resurrection. The goodnatured **Feria de Primavera** (April 10-13) is a bit tamer, with people dancing *sevillanas* and downing cupfuls of *fino* till sunrise.

■ Jerez de la Frontera

Though unremarkable in appearance, Jerez de la Frontera (pop. 200,000) is the cradle of three staples of Andalucían culture: *flamenco,* Carthusian horses, and above all, *vino de jerez,* also known as sherry. Visit *bodegas* (wine cellars) to sample grape-based liqueurs, then recover in time to hear live *flamenco* in the evening. Jerez also makes a good departure point for several popular tourist circuits: the *ruta de los pueblos blancos* (white villages), the *ruta del toro* (bulls), the *ruta de la costa* (coast), and, of course, the *ruta del vino* (wine).

ORIENTATION AND PRACTICAL INFORMATION

The labyrinthine, *bodega*-studded streets of Jerez are almost impossible to navigate without a highly detailed map. Get one from the tourist office or buy one from any bookstore or newsstand (around 500ptas). To reach the town center from the **bus station,** exit away from the restrooms and walk left. C. Cartuja becomes C. Medina, which beelines for **Plaza Romero Martínez** (the city's commercial center), and *Teatro Villanueva.* From here, walk left on C. Cerrón, which leads to C. Santa María

and C. Lencería, heading into **Plaza del Arenal.** From the **train station,** exit to the right and take C. Cartuja to the bus station; then follow the directions above.

Tourist Office: C. Larga, 39 (tel. 33 11 50; fax 33 17 31). From Pl. Arenal, take C. Lencería to C. Larga. Friendly, well-staffed, and English-speaking with highly technical info on brandy and sherry production, *bodegas* tours, and the royal equestrian school. Free maps. Open Mon.-Fri. 9am-2pm and 5-8pm, Sat. 9am-2pm and 5-7pm; in winter Mon.-Sat. 8am-3pm and 5-7pm.

Flights: Ctra. Jerez-Sevilla (tel. 15 00 00). Airport is 7km from town. **Iberia,** Av. Albaro Domecq (tel. 18 43 94). **Aviaco** (tel. 15 00 11) has flights to London (the "sherry express") every Mon., Wed., and Fri.

Trains: Pl. Estación (tel. 34 23 19), at the east end of C. Medina after it becomes C. Cartuja. **RENFE,** C. Larga, 34 (tel. 33 48 13). To: Cádiz (11 per day, 45min., 365ptas); Sevilla (11 per day, 1½hr., 735ptas); Madrid (4 per day, 4½hr., 7600-8800ptas); Barcelona (4 per day, 13½-14½hr., 9700ptas).

Buses: C. Cartuja (tel. 34 52 07), at the corner of Madre de Dios, 2 blocks from the train station at end of C. Medina. **T.G. Comes** (tel. 34 21 74) to: Cádiz (17 per day, Sat.-Sun. 9 per day, 1hr., 350ptas); Ronda (3 per day, 2¾hr., 1350ptas); Puerto de Sta. María (4-6 per day, 30min., 150ptas); Vejer (1 per day, 2hr., 790ptas). **Los Amarillos** (tel. 34 78 44) to Córdoba (1 per day, 4hr., 2005ptas) and Arcos (11-15 per day, 45min., 295ptas). **Linesur** (tel. 34 10 63) to: Sevilla (8 per day, 1½hr., 875ptas); Algeciras (8 per day, 2hr., 1425ptas); Sanlúcar de Barrameda (every hr., 7am-10pm, 30min., 215ptas); Chipiona (every hr., 7am-10pm, 1hr., 295ptas). **Sevibus** (tel. 30 50 05 or 25 74 15) to Madrid (5 per day, 5hr., 7775-9650ptas).

City buses: In a coquettish shade of mauve, the 12 lines run every 15min. most passing through Pl. Arenal and by the bus station (100ptas). Info office in Pl. Arenal.

Taxis: (tel. 34 48 60).

Car Rental: Hertz (tel. 15 00 38), at the airport. Starting price 9500ptas per day. Open Mon.-Fri. 7:30am-9pm, Sat. 7:30am-2:30pm and 3-7pm, Sun. 9:30-11:30am and 3:30-9pm. Must be 25.

Medical Assistance: Ambulatorio de la Seguridad Social (tel. 34 84 68), C. José Luis Díaz. **Red Cross:** C. Alcubillas, s/n (tel. 14 20 49).

Emergency: tel. 061, 091 or 092.

Police: (tel. 31 13 09).

Post Office: Main Office, C. Cerón, 2 (tel. 34 22 95; fax 32 14 10), off Pl. Romero Martínez. Open for stamps and Lista de Correos Mon.-Fri. 8:30am-8:30pm, Sat. 9:30am-1:30pm. **Postal Code:** 11480.

ACCOMMODATIONS AND FOOD

Finding a bed to crash in is as easy as finding a cork to sniff. Look along **C. Medina,** near the bus station, and **C. Arcos,** which intersects C. Medina at Pl. Romero Martínez. The area may not be interesting to look at, but remains a short walk from the fountains and *terrazas* of C. Larga. *Tapas*-hoppers bounce in, out, and all about **Pl. del Arenal** and northeast on Av. Alcalde Álvaro Domecq around **Pl. Caballo.** Supermarket **Cobreros** vends victuals on the second floor of the Centro Comercial on C. Larga next door to McDonald's (open daily 9am-2pm and 5:30-9:30pm).

Albergue Juvenil (HI), Av. Carrero Blanco, 30 (tel. 14 39 01), in an ugly suburb, a 25min. walk from downtown, or a 10min. bus ride (bus L-8 leaves near the bus station, every 15min., 125ptas; or bus L-1 from Pl. Arenal). Clean and modern, with spacious doubles, a pool, tennis and basketball courts, mini-soccer field, library, TV and video room, and a rooftop terrace. Doubles as a university dorm: call ahead to make sure there's room. 900-1300ptas per person; over 26 1300-11600ptas. Nonmembers pay an extra 300ptas per night for 6 nights to become members.

Hostal San Andrés, C. Morenos, 12 (tel. 34 09 83; fax 34 31 96). Take C. Fontana (off C. Medina) for 1 block, and turn left; C. Morenos is the first right. Two beautiful patios, one with stained glass, the other with hanging grapes. Singles 1200-1600ptas. Doubles 2200-2500ptas.

Hostal Sanvi, C. Morenos, 10 (tel. 34 56 24). Generic hotel rooms at hostel prices. Sparkling baths. Singles 1500-1800ptas. Doubles 3000ptas with bath. They "almost never" charge higher prices—just during festivals. Longer stays negotiable.

Casa Pepa, Pl. Madre de Dios, 14 (tel. 32 49 06), around the corner from the bus station. A meeting place and landmark. Locals keep coming back for scrumptious *menús* (750ptas), *platos combinados* (350-575ptas), and *tapas* (150-200ptas). Open daily 9:30am-5pm and 8pm-midnight.

Mesón Alcazaba, C. Medina, 19 (tel. 34 48 54). Posh, with an antique knights' armor, low leather and velvet couches, and avant-garde paintings, but it is affordable. *Menú* 800ptas, *platos combinados* 500ptas and up. Open daily noon-5pm and 8pm-midnight.

Dolce Vita (tel. 33 34 61), C. Divina Pastora, around the corner from the equestrian school. Not classy, but cheap and filling. Big pasta portions start at 620ptas, burgers at 250ptas. Pizza delivery. Visa, MC.

SIGHTS AND ENTERTAINMENT

Most people come to Jerez for the *jerez*. Multilingual tour guides distill the sherry-making process for you, then you can tipple for free. The best time to visit is early September during the harvest; avoid August when many *bodegas* close down for the annual hangover. *Bodegas* are plotted on any map and the tourist office can help find the right one for you. Group reservations for hour-long tours must be made at least one week in advance; reservations for individuals are often required. *Bodegas* open during specific hours, and most conduct tours in English. Call ahead for exact times.

Williams and Humbert, Ltd., Nuño de Cañas, 1 (tel. 34 65 39). Tours at 1:30pm Mon.-Fri. One of the prettiest, with gardens and a stable of prize-winning Carthusian horses. 300ptas. Reservations required.

Harveys of Bristol, C. Arcos, 53 (tel. 15 10 02). Tours at noon. Mon.-Fri. Live crocodiles. 300ptas.

B. Domecq, San Idelfonso, 3 (tel. 15 15 00). Tours Mon.-Fri. 10:30am and 12:30pm. The oldest in town. Overrun with house cats. 350ptas. Reservation required.

González Byass, Manuel María González, s/n (tel. 35 70 00). Tours Mon.-Fri. 11am, noon, 1, 5, and 6pm; Sat. 11am, noon, and 1pm. The largest with scenic gardens and trained mice that sometimes climb miniature ladders propped against wine glasses and sip the juice. Cheerful rodents. 375ptas. Sat. reservation required.

Wisdom and Warter, Ltd., C. Pizarro, 7 (tel. 37 50 90; fax 33 97 76). Mon.-Fri. at 1:15pm, except Thurs. at 11am and 2pm. No stupid pet tricks, but the smallest and coziest—a real family's *bodega*. 300ptas.

Jerez's love for wine is closely followed by its passion for horses. During the last week of April or the first week of May, the **Real Escuela Andaluza de Arte Equestre** (Royal Andalusian School of Equestrian Art), Av. Duque de Abrantes (tel. 31 11 11), sponsors a **Feria del Caballo** (Horse Fair) with shows, carriage competitions, and races of Jerez-bred Carthusian horses. Otherwise, shows held every Thursday in July and August at noon feature a troupe of horses dancing in choreographed sequences (1500-2400ptas, children 850ptas). Dress rehearsals are almost as impressive (Mon.-Wed. and Fri. 11am-1pm; 450ptas).

Just west of Pl. Arenal on the Alameda Vieja is the Moorish **Mezquita,** an 11th-century mosque. Almohad **baños árabes** (Arab baths) lie within, while the **Torre Octagonal** (Octagonal Tower) rises above (open in summer Mon.-Sat. 10am-2pm; in winter Mon.-Fri. 10am-2pm and 4-6pm; free). Near the Mezquita is the imposing Baroque **cathedral** (tel. 34 84 82 or 34 37 57), with a Mudéjar belfry, built on the site of an Arab mosque (open Mon.-Fri. 6-7pm, Sat.-Sun. 11am-2pm and 6:30-8:30pm; free).

Flamenco dancing and music reputedly originated in Jerez. If you're only a bit lucky, you'll catch a free, spontaneous show. Rare footage and concert appearances of Spain's most highly regarded *flamenco* singers, dancers, and guitarists, is available for viewing at the **Centro Andaluz de Flamenco,** Palacio Pemartín, in Pl. San Juan (tel. 34 92 65; open Mon.-Fri. 10am-2pm, also Tues. 5-7pm; audio-visuals on the hour;

Mother Nature and Family

Bust out your binoculars—the 60,000 acre **Parque Nacional Coto de Doñana** on the Río Guadalquivir delta is home to flamingos, vultures, and thousands more feathered favorites, along with geese (and mongeese), wild boars, and lynx. If ornithological delights such as the squacco heron don't entice you, the salt marshes, sand dunes, wooded areas, and relaxing beach might. Nature purists beware, lest you stumble upon the lair of the dreaded species *turgrupus touristicus*—the park neighbors Matalascañas (30km toward Huelva), a settlement with a concrete shopping center and hotel complex.

Access to most of the park is restricted—backcountry hiking and camping are prohibited. The western end of the park is accessible from Huelva and Matalascañas. Also, four-hour boat tours (no worries, Gilligan) on **S.S. Real Fernando** (tel. 36 38 13; fax 36 21 96), depart from Sanlúcar (May to mid-Sept. Tues.-Sun. 9am and 4pm; mid-Sept. to April 9am). Call to make reservations or visit the kiosk by the dock on Av. Bajo de Guía. Those more interested in sand than squacco can take the 400ptas round-trip launch across the bay (8am-8pm) to one of the few *chiringuito*-free beaches in Spain. To get a taste of Doñana without leaving Sanlúcar, check out the **Visitor Center** on Av. Bajo de Guía near the boat kiosk (tel. 36 07 15; open Mon.-Fri. 9am-3pm, Sat.-Sun. 9:30am-2:30pm).

300ptas). Most *peñas* and *tablaos* (clubs and bars that host *flamenco*) hide in the old town, a maze of narrow streets west of C. Larga and south of C. Porvera and C. Ancha. Most only perform for large groups, and require reservations in advance. Ask for details about big shows in the tourist office or at the Centro Andaluz de Flamenco. A bit secluded but worth the trek, **El Laga de Tío Parrilla**, Pl. Mercado, s/n (tel./fax 33 83 34), is the only *tablao* that hosts open shows nightly (10:30pm, includes 1 drink).

For more conventional **nightlife,** try the triangle formed by **Calle Santo Domingo, Calle Salvatierra,** and **Avenida Méjilo,** several blocks north of C. Larga. This area thunders on weekends, as does **Plaza de Canterbury,** a mini-mall of bars and *terrazas* located on C. Paul on the corner of C. Santo Domingo. **Porto Bello,** C. Parjarete, 18 (tel. 33 17 22), a huge, trendy *bar musical* off C. Zaragoza (a block from Pl. Canterbury) has a nautical theme. Alas, no whaling ditties—the usual techno-pop blasts from the speakers (couples, ladies and "members" only; free).

Autumn is festival season, when Jerez showcases its equine and *flamenco* traditions. The **Fiesta de la Bulería** in September celebrates the latter. During late September and early October, Jerez toasts the pagan roots of religious festivals with the **Fiestas de la Vendimia,** a celebration of the season's harvest. In September the **Festival de Teatro, Música, y Baile** celebrates *flamenco* dancing.

■ Near Jerez de la Frontera

SANLÚCAR DE BARRAMEDA

Sanlúcar de Barrameda sits at the mouth of the Río Guadalquivir, offering access to the **Parque Nacional Coto de Doñana** and some of Spain's most pristine beaches. For sailors and soldiers returning to Sevilla from years in the Americas, Sanlúcar must have been a sight for sore eyes. Its industrial outskirts are now more of an eyesore, but fret not—alongside superbly fine sand, small-town charm glitters under the sun.

Practical Information The **tourist office,** Calzada del Ejército (tel. 36 61 10; fax 36 61 32), which runs perpendicular to the beach, provides info on the city and the Parque Nacional de Doñana (open Mon.-Fri. 10am-2pm and 6-8pm, Sat. and Sun. 10am-1pm; closed Sat. in winter). For **taxis** call tel. 36 11 02 or 36 00 04. In a **medical emergency,** call tel. 36 71 65. **Police** stand guard at Av. Constitución, s/n (tel. 38 80 11). It's tel. 091, 092, or 061 for any **emergency.** The **post office,** Av. Cerro Falón, 6 (tel. 36 09 37), posts three blocks northeast of the tourist office (open Mon.-Fri. 8:30am-2:30pm, Sat. 9am-1pm). The **telephone code** is (9)56. The **postal code** is

11540. **Buses** leave from **Los Amarillos,** Pl. Salle (tel. 36 04 66), at the end of C. San Juan, and stop in front of Bar La Jaula. To: Chipiona (every hr. from 9am-10pm, Sat. 8-9 per day, 30min., 95ptas); Cádiz (8 per day, Sat.-Sun. 4-5 per day, 1hr., 375ptas); and Sevilla (8 per day, 2hr., 885ptas). **Linesur La Valenciana** (tel. 36 01 96) is two blocks towards the beach from Pl. Cabildo, by the tourist office. To Chipiona (every hr. from 8am-9pm, Sun. 10 per day, 30min., 95ptas) and Jerez de la Frontera (every hr. from 7:20am-10:20pm, Sun. 14 per day, 45min., 215ptas). Buy tickets on the bus.

Accommodations and Food Few true bargains exist; it may be worth inquiring at doorway signs reading *"se alquilan habitaciones"* (for rent). **Hostal La Blanca Paloma,** Pl. San Roque, 15 (tel. 36 36 44), keeps spacious, clean rooms, some with balconies (singles 2140-2500ptas, doubles 3000-4300ptas). Another option is **Pensión La Bohemia,** C. Don Claudia, 1 (tel. 36 95 99), just off C. Santo Domingo, offering beige bedspreads and cold showers to tame all bohemian urges. (Singles 2000ptas, with bath 2500ptas. Doubles: 4000ptas; 4500-5000ptas.) Sanlúcar is famous for its *langostinos* (king prawns). For a sit-down meal, head for the side streets off **C. San Juan.** *Terrazas* fill **Pl. San Roque** and **Pl. Cabildo,** its tree-lined neighbor. **Bar-Restaurante El Cura,** C. Amargura, 2 (tel. 36 29 94), between the two plazas, serves up divinely ordained *paella* (500ptas) in a family atmosphere (open daily 8am-midnight, supper from 8:30pm.).

Sights and Entertainment Two impressive palaces compete with the enormous 14th-century **Iglesia de Nuestra Señora de la O,** Pl. Paz (tel. 36 05 55), for the attention of sun-struck tourists (open 15min. before and after mass, daily 8pm, also Sun. noon; free). The **Palacio Medina Sidonia** (tel. 36 01 61) was inhabited until recently (open for visits Wed. 10am-1pm; free). The 19th-century **Palacio Infantes de Orleans** (tel. 38 80 00) now houses the Ayuntamiento (open for visits Mon.-Fri. 10am-2pm; free). Numerous **festivals** testify to Sanlúcar's fondness for merrymaking. The **Feria de la Manzanilla** (May 28-June 1) involves the most alcohol, but **Corpus Christi,** in June, explodes with the biggest fanfare. In August, **Carreras de Caballos** (horse racing) thunders along the beach, and the **Festival de la Exaltación del Río Guadalquivir** (Aug. 22-24) enlivens the streets with poetry readings, a *flamenco* competition, popular dances, and bullfights

CHIPIONA

A quiet seaside village for nine months of the year, Chipiona takes a summer somersault into domestic tourism. Spanish families turn Chipiona into one big cozy picnic, especially on weekends. The tradition that began in the 19th century, when Chipiona's extremely salty sea (the scent pervades the air) was reputed to have curative powers. **Iglesia de Nuestra Señora de la O,** constructed in 1640, stands in gorgeous Pl. Juan Carlos I, Chipiona's shadiest, most fragrant spot.

Chipiona's **Casa de Cultura** (tel. 37 08 80) houses the **tourist office,** in the municipal library at Pl. Pío XII, on pedestrian shopping street C. Isaac Peral (open Mon.-Fri. 8am-2pm), but a free map can be procured from any of the other offices there (Casa de Cultura open Mon.-Fri. 8am-2pm and 7-9pm). In a **medical emergency,** ring the **Red Cross** (tel. 37 42 22). For **local police** (tel. 37 10 88) go to C. Camacho Baños. **Emergency** telephone numbers are 091 and 092. The **post office,** C. Padre Lerchundi, 15 (tel. 37 14 19), is near Pl. Pío XII (open Mon.-Fri. 8:30am-2:30pm, Sat. 9:30am-1pm). The **postal code** is 11550.

The oligopoly of hostels in Chipiona have conspired against budget travelers. Consider sleeping in Jerez and commuting to the beach. One luxurious option is **Hostal Gran Capitán,** C. Fray Baldomero, 3 (tel. 37 09 29; fax 37 43 35), off C. Isaac Peral, sporting a charming patio and large rooms with baths (singles 2700-3200ptas, doubles 4500-5000ptas). The municipal **campground, El Pinar de Chipiona** (tel. 37 23 21), on Ctra. Rota at 3km, resides 800m from the beach, with a pool and supermarket. (550ptas per person or per tent, under 11 450ptas, 460ptas per car. Electricity 425ptas.) **Calle Isaac Peral** and the small streets stemming from it are dotted with bars, *heladerías,* and restaurants specializing in non-Spanish cuisine. Eateries also line

Po. Cruz del Mar (at the end of C. Isaac Peral) and the area around Pl. Palomas and Pl. Pío XII. In the latter, try the scrumptious *pan montadito* (mini sandwiches on hot bread) for 200ptas at **El Rincón de Jabugo.** The **mercado,** C. Victor Pradera, is to your left as you exit Los Amarillos bus station (open Mon.-Sat. 9am-2pm).

Los Amarillos buses (tel. 37 02 92), on Av. Regla at the top of C. Peral, run to: San-lúcar (14 per day, Sat.-Sun. 8 per day, 30min., 95ptas); Sevilla (9 per day, Sat. 5 per day, Sun. 6 per day, 2hr., 970ptas); Cádiz (8 per day, Sat.-Sun 4 per day, 1½hr., 460ptas). **Linesur La Valenciana** buses (tel. 37 12 83) roll to Jerez de la Frontera (every hr. 8am-8pm, Sat.-Sun. every 2hr., 1hr., 275ptas) from Pl. San Sebastián. Follow C. Larga to reach the perpendicular C. Isaac Peral.

▓ Arcos de la Frontera

The road to Arcos de la Frontera (pop. 27,300) snakes through sunflower fields and sherry vineyards on its way to the most attractive *pueblo blanco* on the circuit. Gen-eration of 1898 novelist Azorín described Arcos: "Imagine a long, narrow ridge, undu-lating; place on it little white houses, clustered among others more ancient; imagine that both sides of the mountain have been cut away, dropping downward sheer and straight; and at the foot of this wall a slow, silent river, its murky waters licking the yellowish stone then going on its destructive course through the fields…and when you have imagined all this, you will have but a pale image of Arcos."

ORIENTATION AND PRACTICAL INFORMATION

Arcos perches about 30km east of Jerez on the road towards Antequera. To reach the town center from the **bus station,** exit left, turn left, then continue uphill along C. Muñoz Vásquez. Walk for about 20 minutes; the street eventually turns into **Calle Debajo del Corral,** which becomes **Calle de Corredera,** which then turns into **Cuesta de Belén** and **Calle de Dean Espinoza** as it reaches the old quarter. The **tour-ist office** is one block to the right in the magnificent **Plaza de Cabildo.** Mini-buses run every half hour from the bus station to C. Corredera (100ptas). A taxi costs 500ptas.

Tourist Office: Pl. Cabildo (tel. 70 22 64; fax 70 09 00). Detailed free map of the old city and city info. Illegible 100ptas **map** of the whole town. Open Mon.-Sat. 10am-2pm and 5-8pm, Sun. 11am-2pm; in winter Mon.-Sat. 9am-2pm and 5-7pm.

Buses: C. Corregidores. **T.G. Comes** (tel. 70 20 15) to: Cádiz (6 per day, Sat.-Sun. 3 per day, 1½hr., 670ptas); Jerez (7 per day, Sat.-Sun. 4 per day, 280ptas); Ronda (4 per day, 1¾hr., 950ptas); Costa del Sol (1 per day, 3-4hrs., 1510-2060ptas, depend-ing on destination). **Los Amarillos** (tel. 70 02 57) to Sevilla (2 per day, Sat.-Sun. 1 per day, 2hr., 905ptas) and Jerez de la Frontera (every half hour, Sat. 9 per day, Sun. 6 per day, 15min., 295ptas).

Taxis: (tel. 70 13 55 or 70 00 66).

Medical Emergency: (tel. 70 04 98).

Police: (tel. 70 16 52), C. Nueva. **Guardia Civil:** (tel. 70 00 52).

Emergency: (tel. 091 or 092).

Post Office: P. Boliches (tel. 70 15 60), parallel to C. Corredera. Open Mon.-Fri. 8:30am-2:30pm, Sat. 9:30am-1pm. **Postal Code:** 11630.

Telephone Code: (9)56.

ACCOMMODATIONS AND FOOD

Arcos has only a few budget hostels; call ahead during Semana Santa and in the sum-mer to be safe. Restaurants huddle at the bottom end of C. Corredera, while *tapas* heaven is perched uphill in the old quarter.

Hostal Callejón de las Monjas, C. Dean Espinoza, 4 (a.k.a. Callejón de las Monjas; tel. 70 23 02), in the old quarter behind Iglesia de Santa María. Roomy, with fans or A/C. The upstairs has its own terrace and the loquacious owner has a barber shop downstairs. Singles 2500-3000ptas. Doubles 3500ptas, with bath 4500ptas.

Bar-Restaurant-Hostal San Marcos, C. Marqués de Torresoto, 6 (tel. 70 07 21), past C. Dean Espinoza and Pl. Cabildo. Friendly young owner and his family run this brand new establishment crowned with a scenic rooftop terrace. Clean rooms, private baths. Singles 3000ptas, doubles 4000ptas. Home-cooked *menú* 800ptas.

Los Faraones, C. Debajo del Corral, 8 (tel. 70 06 12). An Egyptian-Spanish couple serves Arab cuisine along with some Spanish staples. Extensive vegetarian menu includes couscous and the sweetest baklava this end of the Mediterranean (100ptas). *Menú del día* 800ptas. Huge *bocadillo de falafel* 400ptas (ask for it since it is not on the menu). Belly dancing Sat. nights. A/C. Open daily 11:30am-5pm and 8pm-12:30am. Closed Mon. evening.

Bar Típico Alcaraván, C. Nueva, 1 (tel. 70 33 97). Take C. Nueva down from Pl. Cabildo. In a beautiful cave carved into a mountain 900 years ago. Popular nighttime hangout. *Tapas* from 200ptas. Open Tues.-Sun. 11am-3pm and 8pm-1am.

SIGHTS

The most beautiful sights might just be the winding white alleys and hanging flowers of the old quarter, or the view from **Plaza Cabildo.** The plazas earned the nickname *Balcón de Coño* because the view's so startling that people exclaim, *"¡Coño!"* (damn). In this square stands the **Iglesia de Santa María,** built in 1553. Its most impressive attribute is the well preserved wall painting from the 14th century. Christians built the late Gothic **Iglesia de San Pedro** on the site of an old Arab fortress on the northern edge of the old quarter. Murillos, Zurbaráns, Riberas, and Pachecos decorate the interior. (Both churches open daily 10am-1pm and 3:30-6pm. 150ptas, groups 75ptas per person.) An artificial **lake** laps at Arcos's feet, its gentle waters beckoning over-heated travelers to take a dip. Urban buses descend to **Mesón de la Molinera** (the beach; 4 per day, first at 9:15am, last at 6:15pm, 100ptas). The incongruous **Mississippi Paddle Boat** (tel. 70 80 02) cruises around the lake on weekends at 5pm (250ptas)—not exactly *Showboat*, but they try.

Bornos, a hillside hamlet 11km to the northeast, is the next town along the *ruta de los pueblos blancos.* **Buses** for Bornos are run by both Comes and Los Amarillos from the bus station (12 per day, Sat. 11 per day, Sun. 7 per day, 20min., 145ptas). Buses coming from Arcos continue on to Sevilla (750ptas). To swim in its freshwater lake, walk across town (15min.) and climb down the hill.

Extremadura

Extremadura, aptly named, is a land of harsh beauty and cruel extremes. Arid plains bake under intense summer sun, while patches of sunflowers add color to the landscape. These lands hardened New World conquistadors Hernán Cortés and Francisco Pizarro. Cortés and Pizarro never returned home, but they patterned the cities they founded after Extremaduran plazas. The Roman ruins of Mérida attract most of the region's visitors.

Extremeños continue to struggle in one of the more economically depressed regions of Spain. Even the tourist industry is struggling, and although brochures and street maps are more readily available than they once were, offices are often under-staffed or unexpectedly closed. Tourists are a rare breed in the smaller towns of Extremadura.

Traditional Extremaduran cuisine comes from the wild. Tempting specialties include rabbit, partridge, lizard with green sauce, wild pigeon with herbs, and *faisán a la Alcántara* (pheasant with a truffle and port wine sauce). *Extremeño* soups are also scrumptious. *Cocido* (chick pea stew) warms in winter, while a variety of soups (including a white one) cool people down in the summer.

■ Cáceres

Founded by Romans in 34 BC, the thriving provincial capital and university town of Cáceres (pop. 80,000) is the closest thing Extremadura has to a big city. Between the 14th and 16th centuries, rival noble families vied for social and political status. Each family built a modest palace to glorify the family's image. The resulting old city is a wonderfully preserved jumble of palaces, museums, and churches. Cáceres's newer areas are less interesting, but their attractive parks and plazas, plus a healthy dose of nightlife, are redemptive. Cáceres makes a good base for exploring the rest of Extremadura. From here you can enter Portugal, by bus or train via Badajoz, or by train via Valença de Alcántara, due west.

ORIENTATION AND PRACTICAL INFORMATION

The **ciudad monumental** (old city) lies east of **Plaza Mayor** (a.k.a. Plaza General Mola). The plaza is 3km north of the **bus** and **train stations,** which face each other across the intersection of Av. Hispanidad and Av. Alemania, in the south end of the city. Catch bus #1 at the intersection and take it to the last stop, Pl. Obispo Galarza. From there, go right exiting the bus and take the first left, first right, and first left down the steps to Pl. Mayor. Bus #2, which stops on Av. Hispanidad, around the corner to the right as you emerge from the bus station, runs to **Plaza de América,** hub of the new downtown area (75ptas). From there, "Ciudad Monumental" signs point north up the tree-lined Av. España (a.k.a. Po. Canovas) toward Pl. Mayor. When the *avenida* ends, bear right on C. San Antón, then right on C. San Pedro.

Tourist Office: Pl. Mayor, 20 (tel. 24 63 47), on the east side of the plaza, right of the steps. No English spoken. Open Mon.-Fri. 9am-2pm and 5-7:15pm (4-6:15pm in winter), Sat.-Sun. 9:30am-2pm. The **Patronato de Turismo,** in Casa de Carva (tel. 25 55 97), within the old city, has good maps of the monuments (same hours).

Currency Exchange: Banks line Av. España and the streets leading to Pl. Mayor.

Trains: (tel. 23 37 61), Av. Alemania, 3km south of the old city, across the highway from the bus station. *Regionales* to: Mérida (4 per day, 1hr., 490ptas); Badajoz (3 per day, 2hr., 900-1500ptas); Madrid (5 per day, 4½hr., 2100-3400ptas); Lisbon (1 per day, 6hr., 5000ptas); Sevilla (1 per day, 4hr., 2200ptas).

Buses: Ctra. Sevilla (tel. 23 25 50), across the highway from the train station, 3km south of the old city. Info window open Mon.-Fri. 7:30am-11pm, Sat.-Sun. 8:30am-11pm. To: Madrid (7-8 per day, 4-5hr., 2395ptas); Sevilla (5-7 per day, 4hr.,

2250ptas); Salamanca (3-6 per day, 4hr., 1700ptas); Badajoz (3 per day, 2hr., 825ptas); Mérida (2-3 per day, 1hr., 675ptas); Trujillo (6-10 per day, 45min., 385ptas); Valencia de Alcántara (2 per day, 2½hr., 940ptas); Valladolid (3-4 per day, 5½hr., 2670ptas). Fewer on weekends.

Taxis: Taxi stands at Pl. Mayor and bus and train stations. **Radio Taxi** (tel. 23 23 23).

Car Rental: Hertz, Av. Virgen de Guadalupe, 3 (tel. 22 43 45).

Luggage Storage: At the train station (400ptas per day) and bus station (75ptas per item per day).

Late-Night Pharmacy: Four in Pl. Mayor, all with *farmacias de guardia* (late-night pharmacies) list posted in window.

Medical Services: Red Cross (tel. 24 78 58); **Residencia Sanitaria** (tel. 25 62 00); **Hospital Provincial** (tel. 25 68 00).

Police: Municipal (tel. 24 84 24), C. General Margallo. **Nacional,** Av. Virgen de la Montaña, 3 (tel. 21 72 00). **Emergency:** tel. 091 or 092.

Post Office: C. Miguel Primo de Rivera, 2 (tel. 22 50 71), off Av. España on the left from Pl. América (in building with the Caja Postal Argentaria sign). Open for stamps and Lista de Correos Mon.-Fri. 8:30am-8:30pm, Sat. 9:30am-2pm. **Postal Code:** 10071.

Telephone Code: (9)27.

ACCOMMODATIONS AND FOOD

Hostales and *pensiones* line Pl. Mayor and are scattered throughout the new city. Call ahead for stays on summer weekends, especially on the first weekend of each second month when soldiers on leave invade the town.

   Like any Pl. Mayor worthy of the name, the one in Cáceres is full of restaurants and cafes with *terrazas* ready to wine and dine the populace with cheap *bocadillos,*

raciones (300-600ptas), and *menús* (900-1200ptas). For **groceries,** there's always **Super Spar,** C. Parras, 4, at the junction of C. San Antón and C. San Pedro (open Mon.-Fri. 9:30am-2pm and 6-8:30pm, Sat. 9:30am-2pm).

Pensión Marquez, Gabriel y Galán, 2 (tel. 24 99 60), off Pl. Mayor, opposite the Ayuntamiento. Cheap and centrally located, Marquez has colorful bed spreads and slanted walls. Singles 1250ptas. Doubles 2500ptas.

Pensión Carretero, Pl. Mayor, 23 (tel. 24 74 82), opposite the tourist office. High ceilings, wacky tiles, and student-friendly. Lounge with TV. Singles 2000ptas. Doubles 3000ptas. Triples 4500ptas. Quads 6000ptas. No heating. Visa, MC.

Fonda La Salmantina, C. General Margallo, 36A (tel. 24 42 18). Sinkless rooms with large crucifixes and big windows. Singles 1600ptas. Doubles 3200ptas. Triples about 4000ptas. Portable heating units.

Hostal Residencia Almonte, C. Gil Cordero, 6 (tel. 24 09 25 or 24 09 26), 15min. south of Pl. Mayor, off Pl. América. 90-room monster with luxuries in every room: full bath or shower, phone, fluffy towel, and firm bed. The fan even oscillates! Parking garage. Singles 2700ptas. Doubles 4200ptas. Triples 5250ptas. Visa, MC.

Camping: Ciudad de Cáceres, Ctra. Nacional, 630, km549.6 (tel. 23 04 03 or 23 01 30). 1st-class site just outside of Cáceres. 450ptas per person, per tent, and per car. Children 425ptas.

El Toro, C. General Ezponda, (tel. 22 90 34), just off Pl. Mayor. Yuppified Spanish cuisine in an attractive pastel setting, complete with cow brands on the wall. Salads 350-500ptas. Entrees 500-2000ptas. *Menú* at 1200 or 1800ptas.

Paparazzi, Av. Virgen de la Montaña, 1 (tel. 24 02 63), in the new city, at the end of the arcade. Excellent fresh pasta (700ptas). Salads 550-900ptas. Visa, MC.

SIGHTS AND ENTERTAINMENT

The golden, stork-filled **barrio antiguo** (a.k.a. *ciudad monumental* or old city) is one of the most heterogeneous architectural ensembles in Europe. Roman, Arabic, Gothic, Renaissance, and even Native American influences (via *los conquistadores*) have left their mark. The main attraction is the *barrio* as a whole. Unfortunately, most edifices do not open their doors to tourists.

From Pl. Mayor, the Almohad western wall leads into the old city. A jumble of mansions crowds the inside of the walls, each emblazoned a different family crest. The most famous is the 16th-century **Casa del Sol,** the residence of the Solis family. It's on C. Monja next to the Iglesia de San Mateo, and has a mildly perturbed sun above the door. The easily-insulted aristocracy usually resolved their disputes through violence, prompting the monarchs to remove all battlements and spires from local lords' houses as punishment. Due to Don Golfín's loyalty to the ruling family, his **Casa y Torre de las Cigueñas** (the House and Tower of Storks) was the only one allowed to keep its battlements. Storks build impressive nests on its spires every spring. The **Palacio de los Golfines de Arriba** is a Golfín-owned palace near C. Olmos and C. Adarros de Santa Ana. Here, on October 26, 1936, Francisco Franco was proclaimed head of the Spanish state and Generalísimo of its armies. The **Casa de Toledo-Moctezuma,** built by the grandson of the Aztec princess Isabel Moctezuma (Tecuixpo Istlaxochitl), is down the street to your left, as you enter the Arco de Estrella.

In front of Arco de la Estrella, **Plaza de Santa María** lies between stone buildings. A statue of San Pedro de Alcántara, one of Extremadura's two patron saints, eyes the plaza from an outside corner pedestal of **Catedral de Santa María.** His big toes shine because locals have rubbed or kissed off all the dirt, bird turd, and oxidation, as touching them is said to bring good luck. The cathedral itself, built between 1229 and 1547, is Romanesque and Gothic, with a Renaissance ceiling. The *retablo mayor* (altarpiece) is in Plateresque style, constructed with pine and cedarwood. Cáceres's nobility is buried beneath the cathedral floor; you can see some of the same crests on the palaces nearby (open daily for mass; free).

Inside the **Casa de las Veletas** (House of Weathervanes), **Museo de Cáceres** (Museo Arqueológico Provincial; tel. 24 72 34) exhibits fascinating *estelas* (memorial stones), Celtiberian stone animals, Roman and Visigothic tombstones, an El Greco,

and some crafts. The museum's main attraction is the 11th-century Arab *aljibe* (cistern), which supplied Cáceres with water until 1935 (museum open Tues.-Sat. 9:30am-2:30pm, Sun. 10am-2pm. 200ptas. Students free).

On the Cuesta de Marqués is the soothing **Museo Arabe,** decorated with period pieces to look like an 11th-century Arab residence. You can read the miniature version of the Quran with a magnifying glass (and perhaps a dictionary). (Open Tues.-Sun. 10:30am-1:30pm and 4:30-7:30pm, but hours can be erratic; 200ptas.)

Earlier in the evening, revelers crowd the **Plaza Mayor** and its surrounding bars, or stroll along **Avenida de España.** C. Pizarro (down L. Sergio S. from Pl. de San Juan) is speckled with live-music bars. Later at night, party central moves to the area called **La Madrila** in the new city, near the Pl. Albatros.

■ Near Cáceres

TRUJILLO

Rising high on a granite hill, Trujillo (pop. 10,000) is known as the "Cradle of Conquistadors." Over 600 plunderers of the New World, including Francisco Pizarro, hailed from here. Romans, Arabs, Spaniards, and Jews bumbled and thundered through Trujillo in bygone centuries, but the most impressive buildings and monuments within the medieval walls date from the 15th and 16th centuries, when wealthy explorers and their descendants constructed sumptuous residences.

The town and its inhabitants still exude a warm energy, a continuation of its adventurous spirit. A resident acupuncturist has noted that the particularly parabolic structure of the Plaza Mayor focuses *energía cósmica* on the corner opposite the tourist office—perhaps this is what keeps Trujillo beaming.

Orientation and Practical Information Despite its small size, Trujillo offers access to many nearby cities and towns by bus, but there is no train station. The **bus station** (tel. 32 12 02) is on the road to Badajoz at the foot of the hill. To get to the **Plaza Mayor** (15min.), turn left as you exit the station (up C. Marqués de Albayda), then go up C. Pardos, past the Convento de la Encarnación and the small Pl. Aragón; continue onto C. Romanos, turn right at the end onto C. Parra, then left onto C. Carnicería. Across the plaza is the **tourist office** (tel. 32 26 77; open Mon.-Fri. 9am-2pm and 5-7pm, but plenty of info is posted in the windows when closed). The gift shop three doors down has free maps. **Currency exchange** can be done at Banco Central Hispano in the Pl. Mayor. The **Red Cross** is at tel. 32 11 77. For **emergencies** call 32 20 16. The municipal **police** (tel. 32 01 08) await the call of duty in Pl. Mayor. In an **emergency,** dial 091. The **post office** (tel. 32 05 33) shuffles papers on Po. Ruiz de Mendoza—you'll see it as you walk from the station to Pl. Mayor (open Mon.-Fri. 9am-2:30pm, Sat. 9:30am-1pm). The **postal code** is 10200. The **telephone code** is (9)27.

Accommodations and Food You'll find a maze of spacious rooms at the **Casa Roque,** C. Domingo de Ramos, 30 (tel 32 23 13), off the Plaza Mayor at the right of the church. Guests have access to a kitchen, TV lounge, and a pretty patio—just watch your head. If no one answers the door, ask at the gift shop three doors to the left of the tourist office (Singles 2000ptas. Doubles 3000ptas, with bath 3500ptas). Another comfortable place is **Pensión Boni,** C. Domingo de Ramos, 7 (tel. 32 16 04), up the street from the Casa Roque. (Singles 1500ptas. Doubles 3000ptas, with bath 3500-4000ptas. Luxury triple with full bath and A/C 5500ptas.) The Pl. Mayor boasts several restaurants and cafes. For a delicious repast, head to **Mesón-Restaurante La Troya,** Pl. Mayor, 8-12 (tel. 32 13 64), decorated like a typical Spanish house. Three-course *menú* 1800ptas, à la carte entrees 1500ptas (open daily 1-4:30pm and 9-11:30pm). **Nuria's,** Pl. Mayor, 27 (tel. 32 09 07), across the plaza, is less expensive, with *bocadillos* for 325-650ptas and *platos combiados* for 700-1100ptas.

EXTREMADURA

Need More Salt

Sedate Trujillo probably won't strike you as a town of overseas exploration. For starters, it's landlocked—not the best practice ground for budding seafarers. And when you consider its small size and self-sufficient character, you would think much more than water would need to be added for this place to breed skilled and adventurous sailors. Yet besides the daunting Pizarro, conqueror of the Incas in Peru, tiny Trujillo was the birthplace of a long list of monumental men. García de Paredes named Ciudad Trujillo in Venezuela in honor of his hometown; homeboy Orellana "discovered" the Amazon River; Nuflo de Chaves founded Santa Cruz in Bolivia; Francisco de Casas was among the first Spaniards to colonize modern Mexico...and the list goes on. These explorers' legacies, complemented by the town's intriguing architecture and layout, now attract the world to Trujillo—instead of the other way around.

Sights Unlike Cáceres, Trujillo offers plenty of elbow room. The **Plaza Mayor** inspired the one built in Cuzco, Perú, after Francisco Pizarro defeated the Incas. Palaces, arched passageways, and one wide flight of steps surround a stone-paved space and center fountain. The **Estatua de Pizarro,** the gift of an American admirer of Pizarro, was erected in 1927 to honor the town's most famous native son. At night the eerie blue checkered clock tower hovers over the fountain and statue.

Festooned with stork nests, **Iglesia de San Martín** dominates the northeastern corner of the plaza, while a baroque organ dominates the church's interior. The church contains several historic tombs. However, contrary to the dearly held Extremaduran belief, Francisco de Orellana, the first European to explore the Amazon, does not rest here. Conquistador graves in Spain are few; Orellana, like most Spanish explorers, died abroad (church open for evening and Sun. mass; 30ptas "donation" required). Across the street, the seven smokestacks of the **Palacio de los Duques de San Carlos** reputedly symbolize the religions conquered by Spaniards in the New World (open daily 10am-1pm and 4:30-7:30pm; 100ptas donation requested).

Uphill from the Iglesia de San Martín stands the **Casa-Museo de Pizarro.** The bottom floor is a reproduction of a 15th-century *hidalgo*'s (son of a nobleman) living quarters, and the top floor extensively displays the life and times of Francisco Pizarro. (Open Tues.-Sun. 11am-2pm and 4-8:30pm; 250ptas, students and seniors 150ptas.) On the summit of Trujillo's gentle 517m hill are the spectacular ruins of a 10th-century Arab **castillo** (open daily dawn to dusk; free). Battlements and ramparts offer a view of the unspoiled landscape—the air is thick with swallows, storks, and buzzards. You may encounter a passel of *burros*, lawnmowers in the flesh. Inside the walls lie remnants of the castle's *aljibe* (cistern) and the entrance to the lower-level dungeons. The fascinating and free **Museo de la Coria** (follow the wall down to the left of the *castillo*) explores the historical relationship between Extremadura and Latin America (open Sat.-Sun. 10am-2pm).

West on C. Ballesteros is the Gothic **Iglesia de Santa María.** Pizarro is said to have been christened at a stone font here. According to legend, the giant soldier Diego García de Paredes, known as the "Extremaduran Samson," picked up the fountain and carried it to his mother at age 11; the giant was buried here after he twisted his ankle and fell to his death. The church's 27-panel Gothic *retablo* at the high altar was painted by master Fernando Gallego. (Open Mon.-Sat. 10:30am-2pm and 5-8pm, Sun. for mass at 11am. 50ptas.) Downhill from Iglesia Santa María lies an *alberca* (cistern) used by the Romans and the Moors as a public bath, reservoir, and watering trough.s

GUADALUPE

Two hours east of Trujillo and a four-hour bus ride southwest of Madrid, Guadalupe rests on a mountainside in the Sierra de Guadalupe. Despite the inconvenient location, pilgrims have been coming to Guadalupe since the miracle of 1300, when the Virgin Mary appeared before a cowherd who was poised to kill and skin one of his cows. She sent him to fetch the local priests, explaining that an image of the holy

mother was buried in the ground under the cow's body. This icon had, according to the story, been a gift of Pope Gregory the Great to St. Isidore of Sevilla, and had been lost for centuries. In the end the cow was revived, the cowherd fled, the icon was found, and Guadalupe was on the map.

In 1340 at the Battle of Salado, Alfonso XI invoked the Virgin's aid and defeated a superior Muslim army. In gratitude to Mary he commissioned the sumptuous **Real Monasterio de Santa María de Guadalupe.** Later, it became customary to grant licenses for foreign expeditions on the premises. Columbus finalized his contract with Fernando and Isabel here. In the New World he named the present-day island of Turugueira Guadalupe. The Friars moved into the monastery early this century.

The monastery is home to an ornate Gothic and Mudéjar **cloister,** a **museum** of ecclesiastical finery, a **tesoro** (the monastery received so many donations of precious metals and jewelry that they had to melt them together to save space), and a unique series by the painter Zurbarán. The icon of the Virgin is the centerpiece. It's made of wood, blackened with age, and cloaked in gold and silver robes. The monastery's **basilica** hulks over Pl. Mayor. The *retablo* was designed by El Greco's son. (Monastery open daily 9:30am-1pm and 3:30-7pm. Winter 3:30-6:30pm. 300ptas.)

Plaza Mayor is the place to find a room; you'll have difficulty only during Semana Santa. **Mesón Típico Isabel,** Pl. Santa María Guadalupe, 13 (tel. 36 71 26), offers modern rooms with private baths (singles 3000ptas; doubles 5000ptas). The bar serves a toothsome *caldereta* (lamb stew 350ptas; open daily 8:30am-4pm and 11pm-1am). Dreamy **Hostal Cerezo,** Gregorio López, 20 (tel. 36 73 79), is between the Ayuntamiento and the plaza. All rooms have baths, many have nice views. Bare it all for the strong, hot showers. (Singles 2000ptas. Doubles 4000ptas. Triples 5400ptas. Prices do not include 7% IVA. Visa. Restaurant-bar *menú* 1100ptas.)

Buses run to and from Guadalupe from Cáceres (Empresa Mirat; tel. 23 25 50), and Madrid (Empresa La Sepulvedana; tel. (91) 530 48 00; Mon.-Fri. 1 per day). Buses run to and from Trujillo (Mon.-Fri. 1 per day), but schedules force an overnight stay.

■ Mérida

If you liked *Spartacus,* you'll love Mérida (pop. 25,000), the town with the most Roman ruins in all of Spain. As a reward for services rendered, Caesar Augustus rewarded a group of veteran legionnaires with a new city in Lusitania, a nation comprised of Portugal and part of Spain. They chose a lovely spot surrounded by several hills on the banks of the Río Guadiana and called their new home "Augusta Emerita." Not content to rest on their laurels and itching to gossip with fellow patricians in Sevilla and Salamanca, soldiers built the largest bridge in Lusitania. The nostalgic crew adorned their "little Rome" with baths, aqueducts, temples, a hippodrome, an arena, and a famous amphitheater.

Mérida's ruins and world-class Museo Romano merit at least a day's visit. In July and August, the spectacular *Festival de Teatro Clásico* presents some of Europe's finest classical and modern theater and dance, performed among the ruins.

ORIENTATION AND PRACTICAL INFORMATION

Deep in the heart of Extremadura, Mérida is 73km south of Cáceres and 59km east of Badajoz. **Plaza de España,** the town center, is two blocks up from the Puente Romano. From the **bus station,** cross the suspension bridge in front of the station (it's fun!) and turn right on Av. Guadiana. Walk along the river until you reach the Puente Romano, then turn left on C. Puente, which leads straight into Pl. España (20min.). From the **train station,** walk down C. Cardero, which curves left out of the station, and continue along C. Cordera it becomes C. Camilo José Cela. Bear right onto C. Felix Valverde Lillo, and follow it to Pl. España (5-10min.).

Tourist Office: (tel. 31 53 53), C. P.M. Plano, across the street from the Museo Romano. From Pl. España, the town center, head up C. Santa Eulalia, which becomes a pedestrian shopping street, then bear right at the little circle with the statue onto C.

J. Ramon Melida. The tourist office is at the end of the street, off to the right (10-15min.). Friendly, multilingual staff doles out small maps, theater schedules (but no tickets), and lists of accommodations. Open Mon.-Fri. 9am-1:45pm and 5-7pm (4-6pm in winter), Sat.-Sun. 9:15am-1:45pm. Get tickets at the **Casa Rural de Extremadura,** C. Felix Valerde Lillo, 17 (tel. 30 23 65) or at the theater.

Trains: (tel. 31 81 09), C. Cardero. Info booth open 7am-11pm. To: Madrid (5 per day, 4hr., 2700-3900ptas); Cáceres (4 per day, 1hr., 490-1200ptas); Badajoz (7 per day, 1hr., 380-1000ptas); Sevilla (1 per day, 4hr., 1570ptas); Zafra (2 per day, 1hr., 490ptas). For trains to Lisbon, transfer in Cáceres.

Buses: (tel. 37 14 04), Av. Libertad, in the so-called Polígono Nueva Ciudad. To: Cáceres (2 per day, 1hr., 675ptas); Badajoz (5-10 per day, 1½hr., 610ptas); Zafra (6-8 per day, 1hr., 675ptas); Sevilla (6-8 per day, 3hr., 1575ptas); Madrid (3 per day, 5½hr., 2720ptas); Salamanca (3 per day, 3hr., 2350ptas); Valladolid (8-10 per day, 7hr., 3220ptas), and Barcelona (1-2 per day, 12hr., 6420ptas).

Taxis: (24hr. tel. 31 57 56). **Teletaxi:** (tel. 31 33 09). **Radiotaxi:** (tel. 37 11 11).

Car Rental: Avis, (tel. 37 33 11), in the Hotel Trip Medea. Mid-sized car 9685ptas per day, 51,565ptas per week. IVA and insurance included.

Luggage Storage: In the bus station (100ptas per day) or the train station (400ptas per day).

Medical Services: Residencia Sanitaria de la Seguridad Social Centralita (tel. 38 10 00). **Emergency:** (tel. 38 10 18). **Red Cross:** (tel. 30 33 33).

Police: Ayuntamiento, Pl. España, 1 (tel. 38 01 00), or at the Comisaría, C. Almendialejo, 48. **Emergency:** (tel. 092 or 091).

Post Office: (tel. 31 24 58), Pl. Constitución. Follow signs to the *parador;* the office is directly opposite. Open for Lista de Correos Mon.-Fri. 8:30am-8:30pm, Sat. 9:30am-1pm. **Postal Code:** 06800.

Telephone Code: (9)24.

ACCOMMODATIONS AND FOOD

There are many options for budget accommodations, but few budget restaurants. Find meals and pop *tapas* around **Pl. de España** and **C. Juan Ramón Melida.** The **market** is on C. San Francisco, in between C. Lillo and Sta. Eucalia (open Mon.-Sat. 8am-2pm). The cheapest option is **groceries;** try **EuroSpar,** C. Felix Valverde Lillo, 8, off Pl. España (open Mon.-Fri. 9:30am-2pm and 6-8:30pm, Sat. 9am-2pm).

Pensión El Arco, C. Cervantes 16 (tel. 31 83 21 or 30 32 70), follow C. Santa Eulalia up from Pl. España; C. Cervantes is on the left. The gregarious owner of this spotless *pensión* collects things—postcards from guests, business cards, brochures—but best of all is the gallery of signed glossies from kings and queens. Spacious rooms and modern baths. Free city map. Singles 1600ptas. Doubles 3000ptas.

Hostal Nueva España, Av. Extremadura, 6 (tel. 31 33 56 or 31 32 11), a block from the train station, at the end of C. Cardero. A Roman legion could fit in the closets, but the phones might throw them off a little. All rooms with private baths. Singles 2500ptas. Doubles 4500ptas. Off season: 2300ptas; 3800ptas. For triples, negotiate the price of an extra bed—they're typically 6000ptas.

Hostal-Residencia Senero, C. Holguín, 12 (tel. 31 72 07), take the winding street to the left of Hotel Emperatriz (on Pl. España) to C. Holguín. Spanish tile interior. Clean and comfortable with space-saving baths and some balconies. Rooms overlooking the patio can get a bit hot and stuffy. Singles 2000ptas, with bath 2500ptas. Doubles 4500ptas. Triples 5100ptas. Cheaper in the off season.

Casa Benito, C. San Francisco, 3 (tel. 31 55 00), to the left of the market. Admire photos, prints, and posters of all things taurine while sipping a *caña* (beer, 100ptas) and munching a *menú* (1000ptas). Ivy-shaded terrace. Kitchen open daily 1-4pm and 9-11pm. Bar open all day and into the night.

Bar-Restaurante Briz, C. Félix Valverde Lillo, 5 (tel. 31 93 07). Typical Extremaduran fare. Hefty *menú* (1350ptas) specializing in *callos* (tripe). Frogs 1200ptas.

La Peña, coming up from Pl. Mayor it's the first left after Cafeteria Lusi. African theme-bar with jazz on the radio and beer for 100ptas.

Cafeteria Lusi (tel. 31 31 11), on a little plaza just behind Pl. España on the Hotel Emperatriz side. The *menú* (990ptas) is uninspired, but it's a popular spot in the evening for people watching and *tapas*-consuming (200-500ptas). Also does well in the breakfast department: *café con leche* or *churros con chocolate* (250ptas).

SIGHTS

Roman

Roman edifices fall apart beautifully. The road into Cáceres affords the best view of the **Acueducto de los Milagros.** Farther up the river are the **Acueducto de San Lázaro's** three remaining pillars. Over the wide, shallow Río Guadiana, the **Puente Romano,** one of the Romans' largest bridges, is still the main entrance into town.

Mérida's acclaimed **Museo Nacional de Arte Romano** (tel. 31 16 90), designed by Rafael Moneo, is an elegant museum with all the Romemorabilia you could ask for: statues, dioramas, coins, remains of wall paintings, little Roman whistles, disquisitions on the nature of the city-state, etc. (Open Tues.-Sat. 10am-2pm and 5-7pm, Sun. and holidays 10am-2pm; in Winter Tues.-Sat. 10am-2pm and 4-6pm, Sun. and holidays 10am-2pm. 400ptas, students 200ptas, free Sat. afternoon and Sun.) A Roman road passes under and through the museum, and a tour of the **cripta** offers a glimpse of the city that once was Augusta Emerita. To get to the *museo,* follow C. Santa Eulalia from Pl. España and bear right up C. Juan Ramón Melida.

You have to buy a **combined ticket** (600ptas; students 300ptas) to visit the following monuments. Most monuments are free on Saturday afternoons and Sunday mornings. The **Teatro Romano,** a gift from Agrippa to the city, lies in a park across the street from the museum and was used for political gatherings and theater. The audience (seating 6000) faces a *scaenaefrons,* an incredible marble colonnade built upstage. The notion that conquered Greece took captive her own fierce conqueror (Rome) is never more apparent than in theater; the building could easily be *griego.* **Teatro Clásico** performances take place here July-Aug. at 10:45pm (tel. 31 25 30; tickets 500-3300ptas; open 2-4pm and 5:30-11:30pm). Seats are divided into three sections, originally used to separate social classes, but they weren't in great demand. The citizens were far more interested in the blood-sport offered next door in the 14,000-seat **Anfiteatro Romano,** which is in worse shape. Inaugurated in 8 BC, the *anfiteatro* was used for man-to-man gladiator combat, combat between animals, and (everybody's favorite) contests between men and wild animals. Corridors at both ends of the ellipse have gloomy pre-combat waiting rooms. (Teatro and Anfiteatro open 9am-1:45pm and 5-7:15pm, 4-6:15pm in winter; included in combined ticket; separate admission 500 ptas.) Northeast of the theater complex is the **Circo Romano,** or hippodrome. Take Av. Extremadura through the underpass to the other side of the train tracks. Diocles, the all-time best Lusitanian racer, got his start here and finished in Rome with 1462 victories. Once filled with 30,000 crazed spectators cheering their favorite charioteers, the arena most resembles a quiet public park.

Casa del Mitreo (down Po. Alvarez with Teatro Romeno on left and right on via Ensarele) and **Casa del Anfiteatro** (to the left of the Anfiteatro) are ruins of Roman Residences. There, among the solitary columns, you can find some of the world's finest Roman Mosaics, including one with a jolly fish theme (in Casa del Anfiteatro) and, more importantly, the **Mosaico Cosmologico,** at Casa del Mitreo (both *casas* open same hours as *teatro* and *anfiteatro,* and are included in the combined ticket).

Other Ruins

Down the banks of the Guadiana and near the elegant *terrazas* of Pl. España is the **Alcazaba,** a Moorish fortress built to guard the Roman bridge. The always resourceful Moors built it utilizing materials discarded by the Romans and Visigoths. Some walls even contain Roman burial stones. The *aljibe* (cistern) is filled with river water (open same hours as *Teatro* and *Anfiteatro*; part of combined ticket). At the end of C. Rambla Mártir Santa Eulalia (from Pl. España, take C. Santa Eulalia and bear left onto the *rambla*), stand the **museo, basílica,** and the **iglesia,** all commemorating the martyr

EXTREMADURA

Santa Eulalia. During the course of repairs to the church in 1990 (which was originally constructed in the 6th century, turned over to the Arabs in 875 AD, and rebuilt in 1230 during the Reconquista), ruins and remains built willy-nilly atop one another were discovered: Roman houses dating from the 3rd to 1st centuries BC, a 4th-century necropolis, and a basilica dedicated to Santa Eulalia. You can visit this fascinating mix of left-overs from centuries past, plus a little museum that explains their provenance. (Open daily 10am-1:45pm and 5-6:45pm, in winter 4-5:45pm; part of combined ticket. Church open only during services, daily at 8:30am and 8pm. Free.)

■ Near Mérida

LOS PUEBLOS BLANCOS

Named for their glowing whitewashed walls, the *pueblos blancos* are a series of tranquil towns in southern Extremadura that warrant a visit from Mérida or Badajoz.

Known as "little Sevilla" for its gaiety and magical beauty, **Zafra** is full of lovely white buildings with iron balconies and delicate tilework. It is home to stunning 17th- and 18th-century mansions, such as the Casa de los Marqueses de Solanda, a Renaissance Alcázar (now a *parador de turismo*), and charming *plazas*. Buses from Mérida (5 per day, 1hr., 600ptas) and Badajoz (8 per day, 1hr., 745ptas) voyage here (fewer on weekends and erratic, so call to confirm at tel. 55 00 07). Buses also connect Zafra with Sevilla and Cáceres. Zafra has a **train station** (tel. 55 02 15), but it's a hike from town. Picturesque **Llerena** was an important seat of the Inquisition. It was also the center of the military Orden de Santiago, and was a 14th-century frontier town. Now home to a beautiful Pl. Mayor, Llerna is a textbook example of Mudéjar architecture. Buses run from Zafra (4 per day, 1¼hr., 510ptas) and Mérida during the week. The area around **Jerez de los Caballeros** is a mysterious prehistoric settlement. Numerous Roman inscriptions, funerary steles, and mosaics remain from later eras. Check out the decorated brick and painted stucco of the 13th-century Knights Templar Castillo Fortaleza. The knights were later put to death in the church towers (open daily 11am-8pm). Buses day go to and from Zafra (4 per day, 400ptas) and Mérida (1 per day, 950ptas). **Olivenza,** founded by the Portuguese Knights Templar, is still rich in the Portuguese Manueline style (buses from Badajoz 8 per day, 215ptas).

■ Badajoz

Reputedly very beautiful in the 11th century, Badajoz (pop. 120,000) has suffered from slow urbanization. The city bravely resisted Franco in one of the Civil War's bloodiest battles, but Badajoz is still recovering from neglect and industrial pollution. Efforts to beautify the city's plazas and gardens have been slow. For all it's worth, the nightlife is the region's best. Badajoz is often a necessary stopover en route to or from Portugal. The border is 6km to the west, and Elvas, Portugal, lies 11km beyond.

ORIENTATION AND PRACTICAL INFORMATION

Plaza España is the heart of the old town, across the unsightly Guadiana River from the train station. From Pl. España, C. Juan de Rivera leads to **Plaza Libertad** (5min.), home of the tourist office. Between Pl. España and Pl. Libertad lies **Plaza San Francisco,** with the post office, a big supermarket, restaurants, and *terrazas*. To get from the train station to the center of town, follow Av. Carolina Coronado straight to the Puente de Palmas, cross the bridge, go through (or around) **La Puerta de Palmas,** and straight along C. Prim and its continuation. Turn left on C. Juan de Rivera for Pl. España, right for Pl. Libertad (35min.). To Pl. España from the **bus station,** turn left out of the station, take a quick right, and then go left on C. Damión Tellez Lafuente. It becomes C. Fernando Cazadilla, passes through Pl. Constitución, becomes Av. Europa, and then C. Pedro de Valdivia, which runs uphill to the plaza (20min.).

Tourist Office: Pl. Libertad, 3 (tel. 22 27 63). City maps and glossy brochures. Staff helps with lodgings. Open Mon.-Fri. 9am-2pm and 5-7pm, Sat.-Sun. 9:15am-2pm.

Flights: Aeropuerto de Badajoz (tel. 21 04 00), Carretera Madrid-Lisboa, 10km outside the city. Small national airport services Madrid and Barcelona Mon.-Fri., and Palma de Mallorca in summer.

Trains: (tel. 27 11 70), Av. Carolina Coronado. Info open 6am-9pm. To: Madrid (2 per day, 5hr., 4300ptas); Barcelona (2 per day, 8000ptas); Mérida (5-7 per day, 1½hr., 385-1000ptas); Cáceres (3 per day, 2½hr., 820-1700ptas); Lisbon (2 per day, 5½hr., 2855ptas); Zafra (1-2 per day via Mérida, 820ptas).

Buses: (tel. 25 86 61), Ctra. Valverde. Info open 7:45am-9pm. To: Zafra (9 per day, 1hr., 700ptas); Mérida (8 per day, 1½hr., 610 ptas); Cáceres (4 per day, 1¾hr., 800-1250ptas); Madrid (10 per day, 4hr., 3190-3720ptas); Sevilla (5 per day, 4½hr., 1670ptas).

Public Transportation: Buses (70ptas). Bus #1 (every 30min.) runs from train station to Pl. Libertad; buses #4, 6a, and 6b run between bus station and Pl. Libertad.

Taxis: At the bus and train stations and Pl. España. **Radio-Taxi** (24hr. tel. 24 31 01).

Luggage Storage: In the bus station (50ptas per item) and train station (400ptas).

Red Cross: C. Museo, 3 (tel. 22 22 22).

Hospital: Hospital Provincial, Pl. Minayo, 2 (tel. 22 47 43), between Pl. Libertad and Pl. España.

Police: (tel. 23 02 53), Av. Ramón y Cajal, the street that runs in front of the tourist office. **Frontier Guards:** Caya (tel. 27 12 53). **Emergency:** (tel. 091 or 092).

Post Office: (tel. 22 02 04), Po. San Francisco. Main entrance on Pl. San Francisco. Open for stamps and Lista de Correos Mon.-Fri. 8:30am-8:30pm, Sat. 9am-2pm. **Postal Code:** 06001.

Telephone Code: (9)24.

ACCOMMODATIONS AND FOOD

Most *hostales* are near **Pl. España.** Acceptable *pensiones* huddle on **C. Arco-Agüero,** in the heart of the open-air party described below in **Sights and Entertainment.** You might not be able to sleep here until 5am unless you get an interior room and put your pillow over your head. For more upscale accommodations, check out **Pl. Cervantes.** Mediocre cafes and restaurants are scattered about. Check around **Plazas España, Libertad,** and especially **San Francisco. Simago,** next to the post office on Pl. San Francisco, is a grocery store (open Mon.-Sat. 9am-8:30pm; Visa).

Pensión San José, C. Arco-Agüero, 39, 1st fl. (tel. 22 05 68), off S. Blas to the right, coming from Pl. España. Sunlight gleans off golden wood. Big windows. Singles 1500ptas. Doubles 2500ptas. Triples 3750ptas.

Hostal Niza, C. Arco-Agüero, 34 (tel. 22 38 81). Big, solid beds, large rooms, and lofty ceilings. Keep ringing the doorbell when you arrive (persistence is key) or ask for help at Niza II across the street. Singles 1600ptas. Doubles 2945ptas. Triples 4125ptas. Visa, MC.

Hostal Victoria, C. Luís de Camoes, 3 (tel. 27 16 62), a 2min. walk from the train station just down the boulevard, on a quiet street to your left. Small, modern rooms with A/C (when the powers that be turn it on) and phones. Lounge and doubles have TV. Singles 1925ptas, with shower 2568ptas. Doubles with bath 4280ptas.

Cafetería San Juan, C. San Juan, 3 (tel. (9)08 70 31 13). Spanish cuisine in an airy room decorated with antique radios. *Raciones* 600-700ptas. *Tapas* 200-300ptas.

Café Bar La Ría, Pl. España, 7 (tel. 22 20 05). A popular hangout, central and cheap. Large entrees as good as their glossies (425-1600ptas). *Menú* 980ptas. Intimate *comedor* (dining room). A/C. Open daily 8am-1am.

El Tronco, C. Muñoz Torrero, 16 (tel. 22 20 76), off Pl. España. Yellow on the outside, white stucco on the inside (Bananarama?). Typical Extremaduran fare (tasty *menú* for 850ptas).

SIGHTS AND ENTERTAINMENT

Badajoz recently inaugurated its **Museo Extremeño e Iberoamericano de Arte Contemporáneo** (MEIAC; tel. 25 98 16), a cylindrical wonder. Its five floors exhibit

recent works from Spain, Portugal, and Latin America, including a few controversial creations, like Marta María Pérez Bravo's photograph of a woman's breasts as a communion offering. The fifth floor contains works by Badajoz-Born Juan Barjola, known best for his series on bullfights. The MEIAC sponsors free cultural events (open Tues.-Sun. 10:30am-1:30pm and 5-8pm; free).

While the newer parts of Badajoz tend to be loud and concrete, the old city is pleasant, especially in the older neighborhoods around **Plaza de España.** Visit the 13th-century **cathedral** in the Plaza, or stroll through nearby **Plaza de San Francisco**. The neighborhood gets progressively more run down as you walk farther uphill from the two plazas. The ruins of the **Alcazaba** are at the top. To get to the Alcazaba, follow the road leading uphill (parallel to the highway) from the Puerta de Palma. The road runs into C. San Antón, which leads to the right past the walls to the main entrance. (Open Tues.-Sun. 10am-3pm. 200ptas; EU citizens; students, and under 21 free.) Nearby is the **Torre del Apéndiz,** nicknamed **Torre de Espantaperros** ("to shoo away Christian dogs"), which served as the Alcazaba's watchtower. Its octagonal shape is similar to that of Sevilla's Torre de Oro. At the top sits the simple and informative **Museo Arqueológico Provincial** (tel. 22 23 14) which explains terms and eras (such as Mudéjar) that other museums assume you understand. The prehistoric collection is a marvel. Heading uphill from the center of town, the neighborhood becomes increasingly deserted. **Plazas Alta** and **San José,** just outside the castle walls, are particularly ruinous. Avoid the area after dark.

Nightlife spills out from the bars and fills several blocks of the *centro;* the fun-lovers come from kilometers around, even Portugal, to partake. The tourist office has a *"tapas* route" listed in its *Guía de Servicios.* **Calle de San Blas,** off Pl. Mayor, is wriggling with teens passing around *minis* of *cerveza* or *sidra* (325ptas). **Calle de Zurbarán,** off Pl. Mayor, is wall-to-wall with twentysomethings. Barhoppers clog the area between these two streets, especially along **Calle de Martín Cansado.**

Islas Canarias

The Canaries (1280km from mainland Spain and 112km from Morocco) have been pumping out myth and legend for millennia. When Spain stumbled upon the islands in the 15th century and figured they should be checked out, the natives (Guanche; see p. 512) were still busy living in the Stone Age (no wheel) and the islands were still busy being magical (no reality). Meanwhile, Europe put on its thinking (and swimming) caps and considered the existence of such a honey-sweet archipelago. Were they the last remnants of Atlantis? (No.) Homer's Elysian Fields? (Maybe.) Were their sands blown from the Sahara? (No.) Their Aborigines Cro-Magnon? (No.) Who knew about this paradise of beautiful year-round 76°F weather, and how did they hide it from the rest of the world for so long? Were all its previous visitors killed? (Maybe.) Since then, European tag-team tourism has pondered the isles more carefully, contributing 2,500,000 visitors to the city of Gran Canaria alone.

Tenerife is the largest island. It sports the best surf in the hemisphere and boasts the islands' highest mountain, the **Teide,** snow-covered, creepy, and 3718m tall. The island's amorphous black rocks (lava) and cold waters lured many to the notion that it was home to Hell, and today people still love to visit. **Lanzarote** and **Fuerteventura** battle it out to the east, offering completely contrasting vistas. The former is molten rock and dramatic colors, the latter is all blue skies and white sand. All the way to the west are snug **Gomera, La Palma,** and **El Hierro,** all of which have managed to preserve a bit more of themselves.

GRAN CANARIA

Formed by volcanic activity, Gran Canaria finds itself the center of much attention. Its capital, Las Palmas, finds itself in the center of the center; perhaps more importantly, its beaches are among the best in Europe. Often called the "miniature continent," Gran Canaria has a wide range of climates—from the lush green center and snow-covered Pico de las Nieves (6395 ft.) to the desert dunes of the south—all within a circular island with a maximum diameter of 33½ miles. Tourists (mostly German) flock to its eastern and southern beaches in order to lie down and roll over, while the island's northwestern and central zones are less trampled and perhaps more stunning.

■ Las Palmas

The capital of, and largest city in the islands (pop. 350,000), Las Palmas acts like it has very important business to take care of. Tourists are "clients" and it's the city's job to do something with all of them: send them to other islands, or sell them such staples as vodka, cocaine, and sex (sex shops make enough money to buy advertising space on telephone booths). Boats also have to be dealt with, as Puerto de la Luz was once Spain's most important port, uniting Europe, America, and Africa, and funneling an international population into the city. It all began 500 years ago, when the conquering Spanish flipped out over the city's beauty and location and built their dream houses here. They were tourists too. Add to this an old neighborhood with early Spanish dream houses, a beach, and an inappropriate number of palm trees, and you'll realize you're not in Kansas anymore. Take a deep breath and remember that the rest of the island is completely different.

ORIENTATION

Maybe it's because it's part of an island and all but Las Palmas is depicted every which way on maps. That is, there is no standard orientation (i.e. north at the *top* of the map), so some seem upside down. The city is divided into districts, with **Isleta,** the

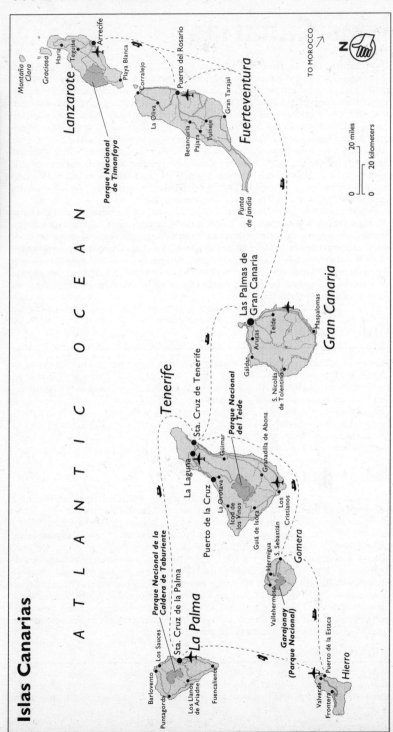

Islas Canarias

ATLANTIC OCEAN

Lanzarote

Montaña Clara
Graciosa
Haria
Teguise
Arrecife
Playa Blanca
Corralejo
Parque Nacional de Timanfaya

Fuerteventura

La Oliva
Puerto del Rosario
Betancuria
Pájara
Tuineje
Gran Tarajal
Punta de Jandía

TO MOROCCO

20 miles
20 kilometers

Gran Canaria

Las Palmas de Gran Canaria
Telde
Arucas
Maspalomas
Gáldar
S. Nicolás de Tolentino

Tenerife

Sta. Cruz de Tenerife
Parque Nacional del Teide
La Laguna
Güímar
Puerto de la Cruz
La Orotava
Icod de los Vinos
Guía de Isora
Granadilla de Abona
Los Cristianos

Gomera

Hermigua
S. Sebastián
Vallehermoso
Garajonay (Parque Nacional)

Parque Nacional de la Caldera de Taburiente

La Palma

Barlovento
Puntagorda
Los Sauces
Sta. Cruz de la Palma
Los Llanos de Ariadne
Fuencaliente

Hierro

Valverde
Frontera
Puerto de la Estaca

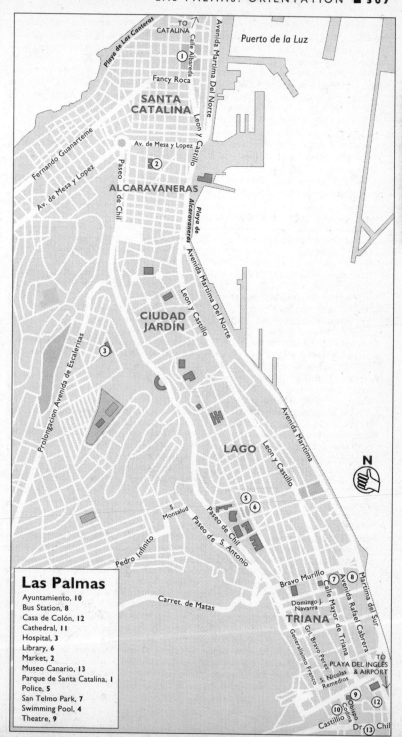

Puerto de la Luz

TO CATALINA

Playa de Las Canteras

Calle Albareda

Avenida Marítima Del Norte

Fancy Roca

SANTA CATALINA

Leon Y Castillo

Av. de Mesa y Lopez

Fernando Guanarteme

Paseo de Chil

ALCARAVANERAS

Av. de Mesa y Lopez

Playa de Alcaravaneras

Avenida de Alcaravaneras

Avenida Marítima Del Norte

CIUDAD JARDÍN

Leon Y Castillo

Prolongacion Avenida de Escaleritas

LAGO

Avenida Marítima

Leon Y Castillo

N

S Monsalud

Paseo de Chil

Paseo de S Antonio

Pedro Infinito

Carret. de Matas

Bravo Murillo

Domingo J. Navarra

TRIANA

Generalísimo Franco

Grl. Bravo Perez

Calle Mayor de Triana

Avenida Rafael Cabrera

Marítima del Sur

S. Nicolas Remedios

PLAYA DEL INGLÉS & AIRPORT

TO

Obispo Codina

Castillio

Dr Chil

Las Palmas

Ayuntamiento, 10
Bus Station, 8
Casa de Colón, 12
Cathedral, 11
Hospital, 3
Library, 6
Market, 2
Museo Canario, 13
Parque de Santa Catalina, 1
Police, 5
San Telmo Park, 7
Swimming Pool, 4
Theatre, 9

ISLAS CANARIAS

bulbous peninsula of fishermen, at the north end. The psychopathic multinational **New City** lies just south, in the **Catalina** district, across the itty bitty isthmus. On the west coast is **Playa de Las Canteras** and on the east is **Puerto de la Luz.** Practically all accommodations lie in between. Continuing south the city gets off its commercial high-horse and stays residential all the way down to **Triana,** where shops bust loose again, and **Vequeta,** where most of the historical sights gather. This means that the beach and museums are at polar opposites of the city. Bus #1 connects north to south. Up the hills to the west are houses. Two **bus** companies service the rest of the island. There are **no trains.**

> *Pleasant Weather Rankings* recently proclaimed that Las Palmas' climate is the best in the world. In fact, they said it's perfect—of the 600 cities surveyed, Las Palmas was the only one to receive a flawless score of 100. When planning a trip to Las Palmas, remember that high season runs from December to January, when temperatures hover around 20°C (July to November 23-24°C).

PRACTICAL INFORMATION

Tourist Offices: Main office (tel. 26 46 23) in front of Parque de Santa Catalina, in a beautiful colonial Canarian-style house meant to lure tourists. Consistently runs out of the information it publishes, which causes the tourist official to speak (in many languages) gravely of *"el gran problema."* Open Mon.-Fri. 9am-2pm. Less-frequented office with more straightforward answers (though slightly less knowledgeable staff) is in the **old Ayuntamiento,** across Pl. Santa Ana from the cathedral in the Vequeta district. Open Mon.-Fri. 10am-5:30pm. Or try the happy **Centro de Iniciaturas y Turismo** (tel. 24 35 93) in the Pueblo Canario. Open Mon.-Fri. 10am-1pm and 5-8pm.

Currency Exchange: Banks and **ATMs** hug Parque de Santa Catalina. **Banco Hispano Central,** C. Nicolás Estévalez, 5, is there, too. Another is in the Triana-Vequeta district, across Juan de Quesada from the market.

Airport: (24hr. tel. 57 90 00). Round-trip charter flights to Tenerife (11,600 ptas, 30 min.); Fuerteventura (14,5000 ptas, 35 min.); Lanzarote (16,500 ptas, 40 min.); La Palma (19,500 ptas, 45 min.); Hierro (20,800 ptas, 45 min.). They're working on an airport in Gomera. **Iberia:** tel. 57 95 38. Saccai **buses** run from Parque de San Telmo to the Airport (every 30min., 45min., 280ptas).

Buses: Estacion de Guaguas (tel. 36 83 35; info tel. 36 86 35) in front of Parque de San Telmo. Buses are called *guaguas* here (as in Central America). Office open Mon.-Fri. 6:30am-8:30pm. Buses leave station every 30min., 6am-10pm. Two *guagua* companies connect Las Palmas to the rest of the island. **Saccai** (tel. 37 36 25; green *guaguas*) travels south to Maspalomas (1½hr., 615ptas.) and Puerto Rico (1¾hr., 755 ptas). **Utinsa** (tel. 36 01 79; orange *guaguas*) travels north to Guia (45 min., 285ptas). Fares to popular destinations half price Sat.-Sun. and holidays. 10-ride *bonos* to a given destination 30-35% off regular price. There are no trains on any of the islands.

Ferry: Trasmediterránea, Muelle Ribera Oeste, s/n (tel. 27 88 12; fax 22 24 79). Tickets also sold at any travel agency, where ISIC cards confuse workers into offering a discount. Cheapest way to Santa Cruz de Tenerife is a 2hr. ferry from Aguete (4400 ptas); **buses** (included in price) leave from Las Palmas to Aguete 1½hr. before the ferry departs. Ferry from Las Palmas to Tenerife (3hr., 5400ptas). During *horas azules* (Mon.-Fri. except the first and last trip) **jet-foil** to Tenerife costs only 62000ptas. *Horas azules* do not apply to other destinations. 6200ptas round-trip to: Arrecife, Lanzarote; Santa Cruz, La Palma; San Sebastian, La Gomera; Puerto Del Rosario, Fuerteventura. Also to: Cádiz (2 days, 29,090ptas one way). **Jet-foil** takes half the time. To Santa Cruz de Tenerife (1½hr., 11,200ptas).

Public Transportation: Central office, C. León y Castillo, 330 (tel. 44 64 99), off Parque Santa Catalina. Open Mon.-Fri. 8am-2pm and 4-7:30pm. For lost items call tel. 44 65 01 or 44 65 25. **Guaguas Municipales** are yellow and travel within the city. Guagua #1 runs 24hr. from Puerto de la Luz-Teatro Perez Galdós, passing Parque de Santa Catalina and Parque St. Telmo. Complete **map** of routes available

Semester in Spain

A Program of Trinity Christian College

Spend a fall or spring semester, or a short-term program in Seville, Spain!

General Information

- Beginning, intermediate and advanced Spanish classes
- Home stay/small classes
- Experienced staff—native Spaniards
- Credit transfers by transcript
- Some financial aid available

Call: (800) 748-0087 or send in this card for more information or email us at: spain@trnty.edu *or find us on the web at:* www.trnty.edu/spain

Name _____

Street _____

City _____ *State* _____ *Zip* _____

School currently attending: _____ **LGO**

· **The Yellowjacket** is Let's Go's quarterly news-
· letter, jam-packed with articles, anecdotes, and
· all the top-quality Let's Go witty, informative
· prose you've come to expect. The newslet-
· ter is free, and can be delivered straight
· to your door at no additional cost! All
· you have to do is fill out and return
· this handy postcard, and the lat-
· est issue will be shipped to you
· post-haste. See what you're
· missing? Get to it, sister.

Let's Go

NAME . . . .

ADDRESS . . . .

CITY . . . . STATE . . . .

ZIP/POSTAL CODE . . . . COUNTRY . . . .

the yellowjacket

BUSINESS REPLY MAIL
FIRST CLASS MAIL   PERMIT NO. 7   WORTH, IL

POSTAGE WILL BE PAID BY ADDRESSEE

TRINITY CHRISTIAN COLLEGE
SEMESTER IN SPAIN
6601 W COLLEGE DR
PALOS HEIGHTS IL 60463-9908

the **yellowjacket**
LET'S GO PUBLICATIONS
67 Mount Auburn St.
Cambridge, MA 02138
USA

PLACE
POSTAGE
HERE

at *guagua* offices and tourist offices. Individual ride 125ptas. 10-ride *bono,* purchased at *estancos* (tobacco shops) 745ptas.

Taxi: Radio Taxi (tel. 46 22 12). **Taxi Radio** (tel. 46 56 66).

Libraries: Biblioteca Pública, Pl. Constitution, 3 (tel. 36 10 77 or 36 12 77). Open Mon.-Fri. 9am-9pm. **Biblioteca Insular,** Pl. Hurtado de Mendoza, 3 (tel. 38 26 72). Open Mon.-Fri. 9am-1pm and 4-8pm. Ground floor study room open 24hr.

Laundry: Lavesec, C. Joaquín Costa, 46 (tel. 27 46 17), off C. Nicolás Estévanez. Wash, dry, and iron up to 7kg for 1000ptas. Open Mon.-Fri. 9am-1pm and 4-8pm, Sat. 9am-3pm.

Weather Info: (tel. 35 40 00).

Car Rental: Hertz (tel. 57 95 77), at the Airport. Also in New City at C. Bernardo de la Torre, 94 (tel. 22 64 97). Opel Corsa 4650 ptas per day includes tax, insurance, and unlimited mileage. Can be taken to any other island.

Telephones: C. Riproche, 3 (tel. 27 50 66). Open daily 9:30am-midnight. C. Tomás Miller, 54. Open 24hr. **Telegrams** by phone (tel. 22 20 00).

Late Night Pharmacy: All pharmacies post the day's delegated all-night store. Pharmacies line Po. Santa Catalina.

Hospitals: Hospital Insular, Pl. Dr. Pasteur, s/n (tel. 44 40 00). **Nuestra Señora del Pino,** Angel Guinerá, 93 (tel. 44 10 00). **Ambulance:** (tel. 24 50 23).

Red Cross: (tel. 22 22 22).

Police: Policía Municipal (tel. 26 05 51), Parque Santa Catalina. **Policía Nacional:** C. Dr. Miguel Rosa, 25 (tel. 26 16 71 or 27 16 72).

Emergency: 091 or 092.

Post Office: Main Office, Avda. Primero de Mayo, 62 (tel. 36 13 20), 5min. from Parque San Telmo. Open Mon.-Fri. 8:30am-8:30pm, Sat. 9:30am-2:30pm. **Branch Office,** C. Nicolás Estevanez, by Parque Santa Catalina. Open Mon.-Fri. 8:30am-7:30pm, Sat. 9:30am-1pm. **Postal Code:** 35007.

Telephone Code: 9(28)

ACCOMMODATIONS

There are more beds for visitors to Gran Canaria than there are residents of Las Palmas, but apparently that's not enough. It is very difficult to find a place to stay without advance notice and nearly impossible during high season (Dec.-Feb., especially during *Carnaval*). It's the same with the other islands. Loyal Germans often book rooms in the south of the island a year in advance—but in the south there are no hotels below three stars. Unless you're traveling alone, renting an **apartment** is the most economical way to spend time on the island. Some require a minimum stay of five to seven days. Apartments are rated on "keys" (1-4). Most one- and two-key apartments in Las Palmas do not require reservations more than a week in advance. Two beds, a bathroom, a kitchen, and some furniture are standard in all apartments. Las Palmas' plentiful two-key apartments cost from 4000-7500ptas per night depending on length of stay and proximity to the beach. There's virtually always a complex somewhere with room available, but unlike hostels the owners don't necessarily wait around to see if a new client is going to pop in, so call ahead (*days* ahead). One-key apartments are harder to come by, and their owners are more elusive, but they're *cheap* (2500ptas per night). **Pensiones** can be found in Los Palmas because it's a city, but their owners make little effort to impress anybody—even these fill up quickly year-round. Calling a day or two in advance is a good idea.

Apartments

Apartamentos Teide (one key), C. Luis Morote, 42 (tel. 27 23 12 or 27 23 08; call Mon.-Sat.). White and simple rooms with pink and simpler beds. Clean. Two blocks from Las Canteras. 2500ptas per night for stays less than 15 days, 2000ptas per night for a month. Min. stay 1 week. Reserve at least 20 days ahead.

Apartamentos Bajamar, Venezuela, 34 (tel. 37 62 54). 4 blocks inland from the southern end of La Barra. Big, bright, comfortable rooms are well furnished. In less demand as it's a bit off the main beach activity. Doubles 3400ptas for stays up to a week, 2300ptas per month. For individual use, 2600ptas for stays up to a week, and 2000ptas for a month. Min. stay 5 days. Reserve one week ahead.

Hotel Madrid, Pl. Cairasco, 4 (tel. 36 06 64; fax 38 21 76), in the Triana-Vegueta district, inland from C. Triana. Entrance through the Café a Plaza. No sand, but beautiful location and scrumptious rooms verging on luxury. Large TV lounge downstairs and a twinkle in the owner's eye. Franco stayed in Room 3 the night before the Civil War began. All rooms are doubles for 4500ptas, with bath 5500ptas. For 1 person: 3500ptas; 4500ptas. Reserve one week ahead.

Hostels and Camping

Albergue Juvenil "San Fernando" (HI), Av. Juventud, s/n, Sta. María de Guía (tel. 55 06 85 or 55 08 27; fax 88 27 28). About 45min. outside Las Palmas by *guagua*. Take Utinsa #102 or 105 (285ptas) and ask the driver to let you know when you get to Guía (no sign). From the stop, walk back up the road towards Las Palmas and turn right at its end, uphill on C. Marques Del Muni. When the street forks left, go straight over the bridge with the green railing. Albergue complex is on the left. Across from a swimming pool (200ptas) with easy access to the Montaña de Guía if the hike to the beach isn't enough. Two foosball tables, a bar, and a cafeteria (breakfast 250ptas, lunch and dinner 800ptas each). Not too many rooms available for travelers (most taken by groups, for whom most of the amenities are reserved). Bright bunk beds 400ptas per night.

Pensión Plaza, Luis Morote, 16 (tel. 26 52 12). Red building facing Parque Santa Catalina. This place is m-e-l-l-o-w, but the Parque gets rambunctious at night. Run for cover in the simple, cool, and comfortable rooms. Singles 1700ptas, with bath 2200 ptas. Doubles: 2700 ptas; 3200ptas. Reserve one week ahead. 24hr. reception.

Pensión Viera, Pedro Castillo, 9 (tel. 26 96 01). Intersects the isthmus, connecting beach to port. *Pensión* is a block from Las Canteras. Nothing glorious, but rooms are ample and all have baths and a new paint job. If it seems deserted, go up a few flights and holler "Hola, eh?" Singles with bath 1800ptas. Doubles with bath 2500ptas. Reserve 2-3 days ahead.

Pensión Pacífico, Sargento Llagas, 10 (tel. 26 51 65). A block from beach, directly west of Parque Santa Catalina. Rooms are small, some don't have windows, the shower is a trickle, and the neighbors and neighborhood are noisy. But owners are friendly and funny and prices are low. Singles 1500ptas, with bath 1800ptas. Doubles: 2200ptas; 2500ptas. Call ahead, but keep your promise.

Camping: Camping Guantánamo (tel. 56 02 07), in Mogán (a port town in the south) on Playa Tauro. Third-class site near a eucalyptus forest and hunting zone. Over 750 campers. 350ptas per person, 400ptas per large tent, 345ptas per car.

FOOD

The range of food eaten in Las Palmas is matched only by the range of clothing (from topless to *saris*). You might end up downing Indian *tapas* in an Irish pub swinging to Moroccan pop music. Though they try hard to please visitors, inexpensive foreign-food restaurants tend to be less than great. Typical Canarian fare is itself a mixture of *Guanche,* Spanish, and Latin American tastes, and includes *papas arrugadas* ("wrinkled" potatoes encrusted with salt), *gofio* (a flour-like staple), and *potaje* (stew). The *plátanos* (bananas) of the Canaries are supposedly the best in the world. Many *terrazas* along the beach on Po. Canteras are cheap and serve up good *menús* for under 1000ptas. The fish here will, of course, make your head swivel, and is usually served with *mojo verde* (green sauce). The local wine, *Malvasia* (Malmsey), is hard to find but plenty of it used to intoxicate Shakespeare's **Falstaff. Cruz Mayor,** Nicolás Estévenez, 38, is a supermarket chain in the New City. There is a massive one at Pérez Galdós, 17, in the Triana district (both open Mon.-Sat. 8:30am-8:30pm). **Mercado de Vegueta,** C. Mendizábal, is the oldest city and sells a glorious assortment of fresh fruit, like *aguacates* (avocados), and *guayabas* (guavas).

El Herreño, C. Mendizábal, 5 (tel. 31 05 13), just beyond the market in Vegueta. Canarian cuisine in a Canarian structure. Very popular. Pork specialties (800ptas). Delicious maritime *menús* (575-1100 ptas). Meals served all day until 1am.

Dog eat dog

The earliest known mention of the Canary Islands was made by Pliny in the first century AD, in reference to an expedition sent out by the erudite and curious King Juba II of Mauritania. It is possible that the current name for the islands owes itself to that trip. It's a well-established fact that the "Canaries" do not refer to yellow birds but most likely to the wild dogs (canines) that Juba II's troop found roaming the islands. They brought some back, barking, and Pliny thought it fit to scribble "Canarii" in reference to the island dwellers. But when dog skulls were recently dug up in a prehistoric dining room, a new speculation was embraced—that Pliny wasn't referring to "people who live on an island with dogs" but "people who eat dogs," which is far more interesting and far more worthy of giving name to an archipelago.

Bar Amigo Camilo, El Confital. On the coast north of Las Canteras, at the end of C. Alonso Ojedo. Skip the beach and head straight for the ocean—this bar hides a hair's breadth away from the blue Atlantic. *Pescado fresco* (fresh fish) 2000-2800ptas per kg. *Papas arrugadas* 300ptas. *Menú* 1000ptas. Open Mon.-Sat. 1-5pm and 8-11pm, Sun. 1-5pm.

Hipócrates, C. Colón, 4 (tel. 22 64 15), across from Casa-Museo Colón in Vegueta. Middle-aged women huddle together for vegetarian dining by candlelight. Restaurant has temporary exhibitions (like colossal collages of scenes from *Dark Crystal*). The bathroom is a mystical experience.

La Strada, Tomás Miller, 58 (tel. 27 33 51). Aggressive self-service smorgasbord. Eat as much as you want (or can) of the average food on ugly green plastic tablecloths, then pay the overly enthusiastic cashier 1250ptas. No food fights. Open noon-4pm and 6-11pm daily. Grill opens after 7:30pm.

SIGHTS

Just don't forget to look at the people and the other tourists (un)like you. The historical neighborhood, where Juan Retón and the conquering Spanish set up camp in the 15th century, is **Vegueta,** overlooking the **Guiniguada Ravine.** Even after the infiltration of Spanish mainland mainstream culture, the islands retained a distinctive style, most visibly in typical colonial architecture which lines Vegueta. **Calle Mayor de Triana,** the shopping master, offers up a wild assortment of edifices, from the typical old to the modern interpretation of it.

Catedral de Santa Ana, C. Espíritu Santo, 20 (tel. 31 49 89), is a 16th-century Gothic house of worship with a touch of Renaissance, and a Neoclassical facade by the Canaries' favorite sculptor of Christ figures, José Luján Pérez (1765-1815). Three central naves are the same height, and the dome above the crypt is surpassed only by El Escorial. Massive restoration free-for-all should leave the Cathedral shiny by March 14th, 1998 at 11am and complete with an elevator. Part of the Cathedral is the **Museo Diocesano del Arte Sacro,** which blasts you with more Luján Peréz works and a view into the Cathedral's Capilla de Nuestra Señora de Los Dolores, where the "incorruptible" body of Bishop Buenaventura Codina does not rot. The Vatican is checking him out for potential sainthood. (Catedral and museum open Mon.-Fri. 9am-1:30pm and 4-6:30pm, Sat. 9am-2pm. 300ptas for both.)

Crazy for tourism, Las Palmas created a sight specifically for tourists. The **Pueblo Canario** (Canarian Village) is a whitewashed and wood-ridden wonder, in Doramoes Park, halfway between Parque de San Telmo and Parque de Santa Catalina. Designed by adored painter Néstor in 1937 and built by his brother, Miguel, it's practically a historical sight by now, and is most interesting as an example of tourist fanaticism. Outdoor performances of traditional Canarian music and traditional costumes take place on Thursdays at 5pm and Sundays at 11:45am. At one end is the **Museo Néstor** (tel. 24 51 25), a stunning museum that displays works by the first Canarian painter to receive international recognition, Néstor Martín-Fernández de la Torre, whose name conjures up mythical thoughts among those familiar with his beautifully pudgy figures. See here his vivacious *Poema del Atlántico* (1913-22), a series of 8 paintings

considered to be his most important work, and *Poema de la tierra,* whose intertwining bodies led to its censoring in the 1950s. Also, a Canary bird with a cigar and *Epitalamio* (Nuptial Song), 1910, was displayed in an international art exhibit in Brussels. (Open Mon.-Tues. and Thurs.-Fri. 10am-1pm and 4-7pm, Sat. 10am-noon, Sun. 10:30am-1:30pm. 150 ptas.)

Museums

Museo Canario, C. Dr. Chil, 33 (tel. 31 56 00). Past the cathedral, off C. Obispo Codina. Houses an important collection of artifacts from the early islanders (the *Guanches—guan* is man and *achinech* is white mountain, originally a reference to Tenerife) and does its best to give a sense of how these people lived. Upstairs things get macabre, with 4 mummies (one might be Prince Artemy, who died while defending Arguinequin in 1414) and shelves of aboriginal skulls that caused quite a stir in the 1800s as they looked somewhat Cro-Magnon (Dr. Chil was obsessed). The shapely *taras,* jugs used in ritual, are said to represent woman—the Guanche civilization was not patriarchal, and oft-times the head nobleman was a noblewoman. Open Mon.-Fri. 10am-5pm, Sat.-Sun. 10am-2pm. 400 ptas, students 100 ptas.

Casa de Colón, C. Colón, 2 (tel. 31 12 55). Everything you ever wanted to know about Columbus and then some. 15th-century governor's house where Columbus supposedly resided during a final pit stop to fix a broken rudder before setting out to sea in 1492. The tasty doorway and interior courtyard are original, while most everything else (balconies, ceilings, etc.) is a reconstruction, albeit a nice one. The building displays maps charting the voyage to America, replicas of the ships (including a life-size portion of the Niña), various documents, and loads of information. Downstairs is a great collection of pre-Columbian artifacts brought back from the trips. Open Mon.-Fri. 9am-5pm, Sat. 9am-1pm. Free. A plaque on the Ermita de San Antonio Abad, down the street towards the ocean, marks the sight of a no longer existent church where Columbus prayed.

Casa-Museo Pérez Galdós, C. Cano, 6 (tel. 36 6 9 75). The typically typical 19th-century Canary-style house with double patio and plain front (was white, now blue), where the "Spanish Balzac" grew up (author of *Nazarin,* which Luis Buñuel made into a film in the 60s). Furnished with astounding items from Galdós' Madrid residence, the house is evidence of a life well-lived. Galdós himself designed most of the exquisite wood furniture; one exception is the crib he slept in as a baby. The old wine cellar is now a library. Sorolla's famous 1894 portrait of the author hangs in the study. Open Mon.-Fri. 9am-1pm and 4-8pm, Sat. 9am-1pm. Guided tours offered in the morning. Free.

Centro Atlántico de Arte Moderno, C. Los Balones, 9 (tel. 31 18 24). Behind the Cathedral. Free museum with rotating exhibitions of all sorts of contemporary artists, though exhibitions in '98 will include works by two Canarians, Tony Gallardo and Juan Ismael. Open Tues.-Sat. 10am-9pm, Sun. 10am-2pm. Closed Aug.

BEACHES AND EXCURSIONS

Playa de Las Canteras, one of the most famous and popular beaches in Europe, is over 3km in length, most of which is wave-free, the waters calmed by *la barra,* a mammoth barrier reef 200m out from shore; this area is nicknamed "the world's largest swimming pool." For waves and black sand, head to the not-as-pleasant south end of the beach. Popular destinations throughout Gran Canaria include **Playa del Inglés** to the south and **Playa de Maspalomas** even more south. The latter is a favorite for naked people and the former for those who think about being naked. Connecting the two beaches is more sand—shapely sand dunes which have been officially declared a national park, and unofficially a nudist colony. Walk around Maspalomas' dunes, but Playa del Inglés, the European baby, is a better beach.

Gran Canaria, while famed for its beaches, also has plants. Hike through them throughout the central areas of the island. For help organizing a hike, contact **InfoJoven,** C. Pérez Galdós, 51 (tel. 38 29 79; open Mon.-Fri. 9am-1:30pm). They specialize in *Tourismo Rural.* Or take a **Utinsa** *guagua* (15min., 215ptas) to the Jardin Canario,

botanical gardens that present and preserve natural and endemic species of all the islands. Great cacti. (Open daily 9am-6pm.)

ENTERTAINMENT

Nightlife

Las Palmas has the difficult task of trying to please half the world, and has unfortunately been forced to resort to karaoke. Clubs are also used primarily by tourists, and thin out in the late spring and early summer months (low season)—most are located on and to the west of **Calle de Fernando Guanarteme** and **Calle de Secretario Artiles.** Packed by 2am, most are also empty by 5. The ones that stay open later are too cool to tell, and attract a younger (less married) crowd. Take advantage of year-round outdoor *terrazas* on **Plaza de España** and along **Paseo de Canteras.** The latter are most attractive and popular at twilight, when the beach winds are still blowing bodies about. Across from the Mercado de Vegueta on Pl. Stagno (the last stop on guagua #1) is the **Teatro de Pérez Galdós** (tel. 36 15 09), designed by Néstor. The interior can only be seen during performances.

Solo travelers should be careful late at night; you may be hassled for money and aggressively offered many drugs. Muggings are rare, but that's because everybody brings a buddy. Bring a friend or make one. Women should not go out alone.

Cuasquías, San Pedro, 2 (tel. 37 00 46 or 38 38 40), on a small street off C. Juan de Quesada, near Pl. Hurtado de Mendoza (in Vegueta-Triana). Soft yellow walls in the large performance space in the back room. Wide range of live music. (Tues.-Fri. at 12:30am, Sat. at 1:30am). Salsa, jazz, pop, or purely percussive, etc. Young crowd. No cover. Beer 350ptas.

La Cava, Av. Primero de Mayo, 57 (tel. 38 22 72). Take C. Bravo Murillo from Parque de San Telmo, turn left on Primero de Mayo. Less beer and more posters of Malcom X and Cree Indians. Politically active students perk up their ears to theatrical and musical performances and the occasional presentation by Amnesty International. Open Sun.-Thurs. 9:30pm-1am, Fri.-Sat. 9:30pm-3:30am. Live performances Fri.-Sat. Cover free-500ptas. Beer 125-200ptas.

Donosti, C. Nicolás Estévanez at Po.Canteras. Large student playground with beach-front *terraza.* Part of the "Bermuda Triangle" pedestrian-only nighttime hubub.

Tempus Fugit, C. Fernando Guanarteme, 12. The weary-eyed bouncer will let you in starting at 6am and shuffle you out at 11am—that's 5 hours of spinning spotlights and almost good techno, though it doesn't really start until 8 or so. There are race cars on the walls. Cover 600 ptas. Closed Sundays (technically, Mondays).

Festivals

Las Palmas has over 70 festivals each year. During **Carnaval** (January or February) the Canaries lose whatever small portion of sanity they might have had, freaking out with their new set of clothes and new set of faces (masks). Crazier is the amount of tourists who go to watch—this is the high season. Individual towns have their own idiosyncratic happy days, and during most you can catch a *lucha,* a traditional wrestling match. Most other Gran Canarian festivals fall in the fall, with October being particularly amenable to parades in traditional costumes. The *Fiestas del Carmen* in July celebrate the patron saint of sailors with a launching of little boats.

PORTUGAL

US $1 = 187.64 escudos ($)   100$ = US $0.53
CDN $1 = 134.63$ 100$ = CDN $0.74
UK £1 = 298.65$ 100$ = UK £0.33
IR £1 = 271.02$ 100$ = IR £0.37
AUS $1 = 140.05$ 100$ = AUS $0.71
NZ $1 = 120.11$ 100$ = NZ $0.83
SAR 1 = 50.03$ 100$ = SAR 1.99
SP 1pta = 1.20$ 100$ = SP 83.42pta
ECU $1 = 199.42$ 100$ = ECU $0.50

ESSENTIALS

■ Getting Around

MAIN TRAINS

Caminhos de Ferro Portugueses, EP, Estação do Rossio, 1000 Lisbon (tel. (351 1) 346 50 22 for rail service and timetable info) is Portugal's national railway, but aside from the Braga-Porto-Coimbra-Lisbon line, the bus is better. Local trains or commuter rails (e.g., in Lisbon) may be faster and cheaper than buses along the same route; in contrast, over long distances the opposite is frequently true. Most trains have first and second-class cabins, except for local and suburban routes. Special tickets may be available; look for bargains on trips over 100km on "blue days." When you arrive in town, go to the station ticket booth to check the departure schedule. Trains often run at irregular hours, and posted *horarios* (schedules) are not always accurate.

Unless you own a Eurailpass, the return on round-trip tickets must be used before 3am the following day. Anyone riding without a ticket is tagged over 3500$. Children under 4 travel free; ages 4-11 pay half-price. **Youth discounts** are only available to Portuguese citizens. A 1st-class **Portuguese Flexipass** can be bought outside Portugal. (4 days of any 15 US$99. 7 of 21 days US$155. Get one from Rail Europe—see p. 30.)

HOP ON THE BUS

Buses run frequently, are cheap, and link almost every town. **Rodoviária,** Av. Casal Ribeiro, 18-B, 1700 Lisbon (tel. (1) 54 57 75; fax 57 79 65), the national bus company, has recently been privatized. Each company name corresponds to a particular region of the country, such as Rodoviária Alentejo or Minho e Douro (the above address is for Rodoviária da Estremadura), with notable exceptions such as EVA in the Algarve. Generally Rodoviária is still known by its old name. Private regional companies— among them **Cabanelas, AVIC,** and **Mafrense**—cover the more obscure routes. Express coach service *(expressos)* between major cities is especially good, and the inexpensive city buses may run to nearby villages. Many cities offer several options.

Our pearls of wisdom for train travel apply to buses as well: upon arrival, ask the ticket vendor to write out the departure times. This saves time, money, and quite possibly your sanity if the posted *horarios* are wrong or outdated.

IN THE DRIVER'S SEAT

Portugal has traditionally had the highest accident rate per capita in Western Europe. Off the main arteries, the narrow, twisting roads prove difficult to negotiate. The locals' testy reputation is well-deserved. Speed limits are effectively ignored, reckless-

Portugal

N

ATLANTIC
OCEAN

Vila Nova
de Cerveira
Valença
do Minho
Rio Minho
Parque
Nacional
Peneda-
Gerês
Viana do
Castelo
MINHO
Serra do Gerês
COSTA VERDE
Rio Cávado
TRÁS-OS-MONTES
Bragança
Barcelos
Braga
Guimarães
Serra do Marão
Vila Real
DOURO LITORAL
DOURO ALTO
Porto
Rio Douro
BEIRA ALTA
Aveiro
Viseu
Rio Mondego
BEIRA LITORAL
Luso
Serra da Estrêla
Guarda
Buçaco
COSTA DA PRATA
Buarcos
Coimbra
Figueira
da Foz
Conimbriga
Serra da Gardunha
BEIRA BAIXA
Leiria
Castelo
Branco
Nazaré
Batalha
Fátima
São Martinho
do Porto
Alcobaça
Tomar
Ilhas
Berlengas
Caldas da
Rainha
Rio Tejo
Cabo
Carvoeiro
Óbidos
Castelo
de Vide
Peniche
Serra do Aire
RIBATEJO
Santarém
Marvão
ESTREMADURA
Crato
Portalegre
Serra de São Mamede
SPAIN
Vila
Franca
Mafra
Sintra
Évoramonte
Estremoz
Elvas
Cascais
Queluz
Lisbon
ALTO ALENTEJO
Estoril
Setúbal
Évora
Serra de Ossa
Cabo
Espichel
COSTA AZUL
TO AZORES
Beja
Sines
BAIXO ALENTEJO
Rio Guadiana
COSTA DOURADA
Rio Mira
Mértola
TO MADEIRA
Serra de Monchique
ALGARVE
Portimão
Silves
Tavira
Lagos
Albufeira
Vila Real de
Santo António
Cabo
São Vicente
Sagres
Faro
Olhão
Golfo de Cádiz

ness common, and lighting and road surfaces often inadequate. Buses and trucks are the safer option. Moreover, parking space in cities borders on nonexistent. **Gas** comes in super (97 octane), normal (92 octane), and unleaded. Prices may be high by North American standards, so factor this in prior to embarking roadward.

Portugal's national auto association (its own AAA or CAA) is the **Automóvel Clube de Portugal (ACP)**, R. Rosa Araújo, 49A (tel. 356 39 31). They provide **breakdown service** (Mon.-Fri. 8am-11pm, Sat.-Sun. 9am-10pm) and **first aid** (24 hr.; tel. near Lisbon (1) 942 50 95, in the north (2) 31 67 32). EU regulations give sanity to driving conditions; the new highway system (IP) is quite good. For **info** about driving regulations (someone should obey them) as well as tourist resources and helpful contacts and material, get in touch with the **Direção Geral de Viação,** Av. António Augusto de Aguiar, 86, 1000 Lisbon (tel. (1) 352 62 64; fax 315 03 08).

■ Accommodations

YOUTH HOSTELS

Movijovem, Av. Duque de Ávila, 137, 1050 Lisbon (tel. (1) 355 90 81 or 355 90 87; fax 352 14 66), the Portuguese Hostelling International affiliate, looks over the country's HI hostels. All bookings may be made through here. A cheap bed in a *pousada de juventude* (not to be confused with plush *pousadas*), costs 1100-2340$ per night, and slightly less in the off season (breakfast and sheets included). Lunch or dinner usually costs 900$, snacks around 250$. Rates may be higher for guests 26 or older. Though often the cheapest option, hostels may lie some distance from the town center. Check-in hours are 9am-noon and 6pm-midnight; some have lockouts 10:30am-6pm, and early curfews might cramp club-hoppers' style. The maximum stay at one hostel is eight nights unless you get special permission.

To stay in an HI hostel an **HI card** (3000$) is essentially mandatory. They're sold at Movijovem's Lisbon office; still, try to get one before leaving home for convenience. To reserve in high season, obtain an **International Booking Voucher** from Movijovem (or your country's HI affiliate) and send it from home to the desired hostel four to eight weeks in advance. In the off season (Oct. 1-April 30), double-check to see if the hostel is open. Large groups should reserve through Movijovem at least 30 days in advance. For more info, see **Hosteling Prep,** p. 10.

PENSÕES AND HOTELS

Pensões, also called **residencias,** will likely be your mainstay. They're far cheaper than hotels and only slightly more expensive (and much more common) than crowded youth hostels. All are rated on a five-star scale and are required to visibly post their category and legal price limits. (If you don't see it, ask!) During high season, try to book at least one month ahead, though travelers planning a week in advance will likely find a room. **Hotels** in Portugal tend to be pricey. A quality establishment typically includes showers and breakfast in the bill, and most rooms without bath or shower have a sink. Many will force you out by noon. When business is weak, try bargaining down in advance—the "official price" is merely the maximum allowed.

ALTERNATIVE ACCOMMODATIONS

Quartos are rooms in private residences, similar to *casas particulares* in Spain. These may be your only option in less touristed, smaller towns (particularly in the south), or the cheapest one in bigger locales. The tourist office can usually help you find a *quarto;* if not, ask at a local restaurant or bar for names and addresses.

Pousadas defy standard hotel rationale (and, unfortunately, rates) as castles, palaces, or monasteries converted into a luxurious, government-run hotels: *parador nacionales* are Spain's equivalent. "Historical" *pousadas* play up local craft, custom, and cuisine, and may cost as much as expensive hotels. Most require reservations. Priced less extravagantly are *regional pousadas,* situated in national parks and

reserves. For info, contact ENATUR, Av. Santa Joana Princesa, 10-A, 1749 Lisbon (tel. (1) 848 90 78, 848 12 21, or 848 46 02; fax 80 58 46 or 848 43 49). The **Turismo de Habitação Regional** helps tourists find rooms, apartments, or furnished houses. This service is best in the Algarve and provinces north of the Ribatejo.

▓ Camping

In **Portugal,** locals regard camping as a social activity more than anything else. Over 150 official campgrounds *(parques de campismo)* feature gobs of amenities and comforts. Most have a supermarket and cafe, and many are beach-accessible, or near rivers or pools. Given the facilities' quality and popularity, happy campers arrive early; urban and coastal parks may require reservations. Police have been cracking down on illegal camping, so don't try it—especially near official campgrounds. Big tourist offices stock the free *Portugal: Camping and Caravan Sites,* a handy guide to official campgrounds. Otherwise, write the **Federação Portuguesa de Campismo e Caravanismo,** Av. 5 de Outubro, 15-3, 950 Lisbon (tel. (1) 315 27 15; fax (1) 315 54 93 72; open 9:30am-12:30pm and 1:30-6:30pm).

LIFE AND TIMES

From the 14th century until 1750 Portugal was one of the wealthiest nations in the world, and just 30 years ago it still rivaled other nations in the reach of its colonies. Today, while much of the prosperity has perished, the pride has not. Its collective diligence, coupled with new-found political and economic stability, once again has Portugal on the road to progress. Portugal's cultural revival will be at the center of Expo 1998, an international cultural celebration which will be held in Lisbon.

▓ History and Politics

Early History

A variety of people inhabited the Iberian Peninsula around the first millennium BC. The first clearly identifiable immigrants were the **Celts,** who began to settle in northern Portugal and Galicia in the 9th and 8th centuries BC. The Celts established small agricultural and herding societies throughout the countryside. Around the same time, **Phoenicians** founded several fishing villages along the Algarve and ventured as far north as modern-day Lisbon, while **Greeks** from Asia Minor settled along the south and west coasts. The **Carthaginians** followed them, working chiefly on the west coast. Julius Caesar led a 15,000-man Roman force over the Sierras in the second century BC, paving the way for an Iberian *Pax Romana;* the "Latinization" of Portugal's language, law, roads, architecture, customs; and, most significantly, Christianity.

> **Julius Caesar led a 15,000-man Roman force over the Sierras, paving the way for an Iberian "Pax Romana."**

Swabians and Arabian Knights

As the Roman Empire declined in the 3rd and 4th centuries, the effects were felt on the peninsula. The Visigoths, a migrating Germanic people, slowly began to infiltrate and eventually take over the empire. The Church became the largest landholder in Europe, and monasteries and clerical schools became centers of learning and spiritual importance. The Visigoth monarchy collapsed in 712 AD, and the Muslims took over. Most of the peninsula became known as *Al-Andalus* (land of the Vandals). Many Christians willingly converted to Islam, and those who chose not to convert were treated relatively well. Muslim society reached its height during the 9th and 10th centuries AD. After nearly four centuries of rule, the Muslims had left their mark on Portugal. Along with agricultural advances and architectural landmarks, the religion of

Islam is a significant part of Portuguese culture, and Arab traditions, such as ceremonial dance, continue to characterize Portugal's broad cultural spectrum.

The Christian Reconquest

The reunification of Castile and León by Fernando I in 1037 provided a strong base for the Christian effort to reclaim territory. Groups like the Knights Templars travelled to the continent to battle Muslim forces. In 1135 Alfonso I refused to join other northern Spanish provinces and established the house of Burgundy in Portuguese territory. The papacy officially recognized the title of King of Portugal in 1179.

By 1249, the Christian Reconquest defeated the last remnants of Muslim power with a campaign in the Algarve. Along with the change in political rule came sweeping cultural reforms. The Christian kings, headlined by **Dom Dinis** (1279-1325), promoted use of the vernacular, established Portugal's first university in 1290, and solidified its current borders in 1297. By the middle of the 14th century Portugal could claim to be the first unified nation-state in Europe.

The Age of Discovery

The reign of **João I** (1384-1433) ushered in a time of unity and prosperity never before seen in Portugal. João increased the power of the crown, and in so doing established a strong base for future Portuguese expansion and economic success.

The 15th century was one of the greatest periods in the history of maritime travel and advances. Portugal established itself as a world leader in maritime science and exploration. Portuguese adventurers captured the Moroccan city of Ceuta in 1415, discovered the Madeiras Islands in 1419, happened upon the uninhabited Azores in 1427, and began to exploit the African coast for slaves and riches. **Henry the Navigator** organized seafaring adventures and those who followed.

Bartolomeu Dias changed the world forever when he rounded Africa's Cape of Good Hope in 1488. Dias opened the route to the East and paved the way for Portuguese entrance into the spice trade and empire in the east. In the meantime, **Christopher Columbus** begged the crown to patronize his trip east to the Indies, only to be turned down because Portuguese experts concluded his calculations were clearly wrong. Portugal's **Vasco da Gama** led the first European naval expedition to India in 1498, and thereafter Portugal added to its empire numerous colonies along the East African and Indian coasts. Two years later **Pedro Alvares Cabral** happened upon Brazil. Portuguese traders, colonists, and missionaries, often using oppressive tactics, boasted claims all around the globe. Portugal's explorers may not have been motivated by the most admirable of ambitions, but nostalgic relics of Portugal's global muscle endure to the present day: Portuguese surnames persevere in places where lonely sailors took lovers, and Catholic churches survive where missionaries passed.

> Bartolomeu Dias changed the world forever when he rounded Africa's Cape of Good Hope in 1488.

Portugal's monarchy reached its peak with **Manuel I The Fortunate** (1495-1521) on the throne. Known to foreigners as "the King of Gold," Manuel controlled a spectacular commercial empire. However, signs of future decline were already becoming evident, and it did not take long before competition from the other commercial powers began taking its toll.

The Houses of Habsburg and Bragança

In 1581 **Habsburg King of Spain Philip II** forcibly affirmed his quasi-legitimate claim to the Portuguese throne, and the Iberian peninsula was now ruled by one monarch. For 60 years the Habsburg family dragged Portugal into several ill-fated wars, including the Spanish-Portuguese Armada's crushing loss to England in 1588. Inattentive King Philip did not even visit Portugal until 1619—his priorities were elsewhere. By the end of Habsburg rule, Portugal had lost a substantial part of its once vast empire.

In 1640, while Phillip IV was forced to deal with rebels, the **House of Bragança** engineered a nationalist rebellion. After a brief struggle they assumed control. The Bragança dynasty went to great lengths to reestablish ties with England. **João V** (1706-

1750), often referred to as an "enlightened despot," used Brazilian gold to finance massive projects, such as the construction of fabulous buildings and palaces.

The Earthquake of 1755

One event in Portuguese history more than any other shook the annals of Western Civilization. The momentous **Earthquake of 1755** devastated Lisbon, killing 60,000 people. Such an impact, combined with the fact that it occurred on All Saint's Day (Nov. 1), shook Europeans' faith in God. The earthquake is said to have caused candles to flicker as far away as Ireland. Despite the massive amount of damage, dictatorial minister **Marquês de Pombal** was able to rebuild Lisbon, while instituting national economic reform.

Napoleon's Conquest and Its Aftermath

Napoleon took control of France in 1801, and had grand designs on much of Europe. Napoleon's army met little resistance when they invaded Portugal in 1807. Rather than risk death, the Portuguese royal family fled to **Brazil. Dom João VI** returned to Lisbon in 1821, only to face an extremely unstable political climate. Brazil declared its independence with a bloodless revolution only a year after João's return. While this meant a huge loss in revenue, the results were tempered by the fact that João's son **Pedro** became Brazil's first ruler. Today, Portugal and Brazil remain closely linked culturally, linguistically, and politically.

More problems developed with João's death in 1826. The **Constitution of 1822** had provided political guidance and improved the overall situation, but the constitution was handily suspended when chaos reverberated through Portugal following João's death. Absolutists halted the marriage of Pedro's seven-year-old daughter Maria da Glória and her uncle Miguel, adding fuel to the **War of the Brothers** (1823-1834). Eight gory years later, with Miguel in exile, **Maria II** (1834-1854) ascended to the throne at a mere 15-years-old. During the next 75 years, politics increasingly pitted liberals against conservatives and progressives against monarchists.

From the "First Republic" to Salazar

At the turn of the 20th century, Portugal was trying to recover from the political discord of the 19th century. On October 5, 1910, 20-year-old King **Manuel II** fled to England. The new government, known as the **"First Republic,"** granted universal male suffrage and diminished the influence of the Catholic Church. Workers were given the right to strike, and merit, rather than birth-right, became the primary qualification for civil service advancement. However, the expulsion of the Jesuits and other religious orders sparked world-wide disapproval; governmental conflicts with worker's movements heightened tensions at home. The weak republic wobbled along until it fell in a 1926 military coup. The military-backed rule of **Antonio Carmona** ended with his death in 1951. Antonio Salazar succeeded to the dictatorial throne. **António de Oliveira Salazar** was the son of a village bailiff. Unrest after the 1926 coup paved the way for this economist to become Prime Minister in 1932. Salazar's *Estado Novo* (New State) granted suffrage to women, but did little else to end the country's authoritarian tradition. While Portugal's international economic standing improved, the regime laid the cost of progress squarely on the shoulders of the working class and the peasantry, as well as on the colonized peoples of Africa. A terrifying secret police (PIDE) crushed all opposition to Salazar's rule, and African rebellions were quelled in bloody battles that crippled the nation's economy.

And furthermore...

A slightly more liberal **Marcelo Caetano** dragged on the increasingly unpopular African wars after Salazar's death in 1970. On April 25, 1974, a left-wing military coalition overthrew Caetano in a quick coup. The **Captain's Revolution** sent Portuguese dancing into the streets and splashing graffiti on government buildings; today every town in Portugal has its own Rua 25 de Abril. The Marxist-dominated armed forces established a variety of civil and political liberties and withdrew Portuguese claims on African colonies by 1975.

The socialist government nationalized several industries and expropriated large estates in the face of substantial opposition. The country's first elections in 1978 put the more conservative Social Democrats into power under the charismatic Prime Minister **Mario Soares.** A severe economic crisis exploded; foreign debt, inflation, and unemployment skyrocketed. Soares instituted "100 measures in 100 days" to shock Portugal into economic shape. Austerity measures to stimulate industrial growth cut back on worker protections. The landmark year 1986 brought Portugal into the European Economic Community, ending a traditional isolation from more affluent northern Europe. Soares won new elections to become the nation's first civilian president in 60 years. Forced to step down because of Constitutional limitations, Soares was replaced by the former Socialist mayor of Lisbon, **Jorge Sampaio,** who defeated former prime minister and PSD head Silva. Although the PSD's force as a party has diminished, the Socialists remain a minority government, holding 112 of 230 parliamentary seats.

▓ The Arts

PAINTING AND SCULPTURE

The Age of Discovery (15th-16th centuries) was an era of vast cultural exchange with Renaissance Europe and beyond. Flemish masters such as **Jan van Eyck** brought their talent to Portugal; likewise, many Portuguese artists polished their skills in Antwerp. King Manuel's favorite, High Renaissance artist **Jorge Afonso,** created realistic portrayals of human anatomy. Afonso's best works hang at the Conventos de Cristo in Tomar and da Madre de Deus in Lisbon. In the late 15th century, the talented **Nuno Gonçalves** led a revival of the primitivist school.

The Baroque Period boasted even more diverse artistic representation. Wood-carving became extremely popular in Portugal during the period. **Joachim Machado** carved elaborate crèches in the early 1700s. On canvas, portraiture was head and shoulders above other genres. The prolific19th-century artist **Domingos António de Sequeira** depicted historical, religious, and allegorical subjects using a technique that would later inspire French Impressionists. In another artistic tilt, Porto's **António Soares dos Reis** brought Romantic sensibility to sculpture in the 1800s.

Cubism, expressionism and futurism trickled into Portugal despite Salazar-inspired censorship. More recently, **Maria Helena Vieira da Silva** has won international recognition for her abstract works, and the master **Carlos Botelho** has become world-renowned for his wonderful vignettes of Lisbon life.

ARCHITECTURE

Few Moorish structures survived the Christian Reconquista, but Moorish influence persisted even in later examples. Colorful **azulejos** grace many walls, ceilings, and thresholds. Carved in fabulous relief by the pre-Reconquista Moors, these ornate tiles later took on flat, glazed Italian and Northern European designs. Ironically enough, this Arabic concept gained its greatest fame in Catholic churches, the palaces of Christian kings, and post-17th-century Portuguese urban architecture.

Portugal's signature **Manueline** style celebrates the exploration and imperial expansion which surfaced under King Manuel the Fortunate. This hybrid style boils down to late and extravagant Gothic, but also reflects aspects of Islamic heritage along with influences from Italy, Flanders, and the Spanish Plateresque. Manueline works routinely feature a sprinkle of marine motifs. The amalgam of styles found its most elaborate expression in the church and tower at **Belém,** built to honor Vasco da Gama. Close seconds are the **Mosteiro dos Jerónimos** in Lisbon and the **Abadia de Santa Maria de Vitória** in Batalha.

LITERATURE

For centuries, bards and balladeers entertained royalty with troubadour art. Returning the favor, poet-king **Dinis I** made Portuguese the region's official language (among

the first "official" non-Latin Romance vernaculars) in the 12th century. Portuguese poetry blossomed in the Age of Discovery, notably in the letters of **Francisco de Sá de Miranda** (1481-1558) and the musical lyrics of **Antonio Ferreira** (1528-1569). Renaissance-era writer **Luís de Camões** celebrated the Indian voyages of Vasco da Gama in the greatest epic poem of Portuguese literature, *Os Lusíadas* (The Lusiads, 1572), modeled on the *Aenid*.

Classics of Portuguese prose were often related to the sea. An explorer himself, **João de Barros** penned a history of Portuguese in Goa in *Décadas*. **Gil Vicente,** court poet to Manuel I and considered Portugal's equivalent to Shakespeare in style and importance, wrote simultaneously light and heavy dramas about peasants, nature, and religion. The witty realism of Vicente's *Barcas* trilogy (1617-1619) influenced contemporaries Shakespeare and Cervantes, and his works in Castilian duly earned him a distinguished place in Spanish literary ranks.

Spanish hegemony, intermittent warfare, and imperial decline conspired to make the literature of the 17th and 18th centuries somewhat less triumphant than that of past eras. Still, **João Baptista de Almeida Garrett** and historian **Alexandre Herculano,** leaders of the Romantic school, sought to culturally integrate Portuguese and European literature. A lyric poet, dramatist, politician, revolutionary, frequent exile, and legendary lover, Garrett is credited with reviving drama in Portugal. His most famous play is *Frei Luís de Sousa* (Brother Luís de Sousa, 1843).

Political thinkers dominated the rise of the literary **Generation of 1870.** Its most visible figure was novelist and life-long diplomat (residing almost always outside Iberia) **José Maria Eça de Queiroz.** He conceived a distinctly Portuguese social realism in works such as *O Primo Basilio* (Cousin Basilio), *O Crime do Padre Amaro* (The Sin of Father Amaro), and *A Cidade e as Serras* (The City and the Mountains).

Fernando Pessoa was Portugal's most famed and creative writer of the 20th century. Pessoa (literally, "person") wrote in English as well as Portuguese, developing four distinct styles under four pseudonyms: Pessoa, Alberto Caeiro, Ricardo Reis, and Alvaro de Campos. Ever the multiple personality, he introduced free verse to Portuguese poetry and his overall impact rivals T.S. Eliot's on English literature. Other contemporary writers, like **Miguel Torga,** have gained international fame for their wonderfully satirical novels, as well as **José Saramago,** who is probably Portugal's most important living writer of fiction.

The end of Salazar's reign brought literary liberation; repression, once the condition, is now the topic.

The end of Salazar's reign brought literary liberation; repression, once the condition, is now the topic.

Female writers, long discouraged or censored, have come out of the woodwork with a vengeance. In **Novas Cartas Portuguesas** (New Portuguese Letters), the "Three Marias" (the authors) expose the maltreatment of women in a male-dominated society. Although condemned as obscene in 1972, post-1974 Portugal opened its mind and pages to the cause of women's rights.

MUSIC

The **fado,** according to one brochure, "causes the chords of the Portuguese soul to vibrate melancholically or passionately." Portuguese romanticism makes these solo ballads accompanied by acoustic guitar soul-consuming and soul-enriching experiences. Named after fate, *fado* is identified with *saudade* (yearning or longing) and characterized by tragic, romantic lyrics and mournful melodies. *Fado* centers are in Lisbon and Coimbra and each area offers a slightly different approach. Today, Amália Rodrigues is the most famous *fadista* (fado singer).

Apart from its folk tradition, the music of Portugal has never been famous internationally. Opera peaked with **António José da Silva,** victim of the 1739 Inquisition. Italian **Domenico Scarlatti,** brought to Lisbon by João V, composed brilliant keyboard-geared pieces. His preeminent Portuguese contemporary, Coimbra's **Carlos Seixas,** thrilled 18th-century Lisbon with his genius and contributed to the development of the sonata form. **Domingos Bomtempo** (1775-1842) introduced symphonic innovations from abroad and helped establish the first Sociedade Filarmónica, modeled after the London Philharmonic, in Lisbon in 1822.

If Gilligan Were Ever So Lucky

Paradise on earth? Start with water, water, everywhere. Add some volcanic eruptions, for solidity's sake. Mix in hearty, friendly, and pleasingly relaxed inhabitants. Pepper it with astounding beauty, alluring beaches, and extract pollution, persecution, and stress. Voilá!—you have Portugal's Atlantic islands, the Azores and Madeiras, considered by many to be the world's most beautiful, serene locales. While beyond the *Let's Go* budget, these isles are integral to Portugal.

The **Madeiras,** consisting of three islands—Madeira, along with Porto Santo and Desertas—rise abruptly from the ocean off Africa's northwestern coast. Discovered uninhabited in 1419 by Portuguese seamen, the Madeiras became an essential stopover for budding explorers. Its climate, colorful fauna, tropical fruits, and luxurious hotels make it a strong contender as *the* ideal vacation spot.

Less commercial but no less awe-inspiring, the **Azores** lay alone in the Atlantic, thousands of miles from land. Immortalized in *Moby Dick* and all its visitors hearts, its nine islands boast rolling hills, lush fauna, cavernous lakes, glimmering seas, and friendly inhabitants. Tranquil and tempting, the Azores will leave 6- to 76-year-olds musing (as one brochure claims), "Is this God's home?"

Partly because the French invasion, Civil War, and decreased patronage stifled Portuguese music, activity has been limited to local and popular spheres. Visitors today may find more music from home than from Portugal itself.

PROSE TO PERUSE

Fiction: Portuguese and Foreign with Portuguese Flavoring

For the scoop on Portuguese classics in most every genre—short verse, epic poetry, short essays, novels, you name it—check out the **Literature** (p. 520). Most of the more famous works have been translated into English; for more options, consult your librarian. Moreover, English-speakers should feel fortunate (like Manuel), for Portugal has figured prominently in English literature. *Sonnets from the Portuguese* by Robert Browning features some of the world's most timeless, beautiful poetry. Also, Herman Melville's *Moby Dick* dives into whales, "Cap'ns," and the Azores.

History and Culture

Options here are many—hard-core students of Portugal will discover this for themselves. A good place to start may be *Roads to Today's Portugal: Essays on Contemporary Portuguese Literature, Art, and Culture* (1983) by Elanea Brown. Among the best history texts available is A. H. de Oliveira Marques' *History of Portugal* (1972).

■ Language

Thanks to the Romans who colonized Iberia in the late third century BC, practiced Latinites will find Portuguese an easy conquest. This softer sister of Spanish is among the purest Romance languages, although pronunciation is relatively complex. Portugal's diversity duly evidences itself in its language. A close listener will catch echoes of Italian, French, Spanish, Arabic, and even English and Slavic overtones. Portugal's global escapades also spurred its language's spread. Today, Portuguese (the world's fifth most spoken language) binds over 200 million people world-wide, most of them in Portugal, Brazil, Mozambique, and Angola. Prospective students of the language should note the handful of significant differences between Brazilian and continental Portuguese, mainly in pronunciation and usage.

Some may be heartened to know that English, Spanish, and French are widely spoken throughout Portugal, especially in tourist-oriented locales. In addition, look to the *Let's Go* glossary in the back of this book for terms (or their Castilian cousins) used recurrently in the text (see **Food Terms,** p. 688).

■ Food and Drink

TYPICAL FARE

Locals season their dishes with olive oil, garlic, herbs, and sea salt but relatively few spices. Seafood lovers will gleefully encounter a tantalizing selection of fish: *chocos grelhados* (grilled cuttlefish), *linguado grelhado* (grilled sole), and swordfish, to name a few. Probe the exotic *polvo* (boiled or grilled octopus), *mexilhões* (mussels), and *lulas grelhadas* (grilled squid). Pork, chicken, and beef appear on menus relentlessly, and often together. The comprehensive winter staple is *cozida à portuguesa* (boiled beef, pork, sausage, and vegetables). True connoisseurs add a drop of *piri-piri* (mega-hot) sauce on the side. An expensive delicacy is freshly roasted *cabrito* (baby goat). No matter what you order, leave room for *batatas* (potatoes), prepared countless ways—including *batatas fritas* (french fries)—which accompany each meal.

On the lighter side, **sopas** (soups) give cheap satisfaction to an empty stomach. Common soups are *caldo de ovos* (bean soup with hard-boiled eggs), *caldo de verdura* (vegetable soup), and the tasty *caldo verde* (a potato and kale mixture with a slice of sausage and olive oil). **Sandes** (sandwiches) such as the *bifana* or *prego no pão* (meat sandwich) may be no more than a hunk of beef or turkey on a roll. Cows, goats, and ewes please the palate by providing raw material for Portugal's renowned **queijos** (cheeses).

Portugal's favorite **dessert** is *pudim,* or *flan,* a rich, caramel custard similar to *crème bruleé.* Simple rice puddings are age-old staples. For the sweet tooth in all of us, the almond groves of the Algarve produce their own version of marzipan. For something different, try *pêras* (pears) drenched in sweet port wine and served with a sprinkling of raisins and filberts on top. Most common are countless varieties of inexpensive, high-quality **sorvete** (ice cream)—look for vendors posting the colorful, ubiquitous "Olá" sign. *Pastelarías* (bakeries) are a social center in most towns, and tasty **pastries** make for a cheap (80-180$) breakfast.

DINING HOURS AND RESTAURANTS

Portuguese eat their hearty midday dinner ("lunch" to Americans) between noon and 2pm, supper between 7:30 and 10pm. But, conversely, you're in the wrong country for a big, greasy lumberjack breakfast—eat a pastry and pig out later.

A full meal costs 1000-2000$, often depending on the restaurant's location. Yes, you pay for the view. Oddly, prices don't vary much between ritzy and economy restaurants, so don't strain yourself searching for something rock-bottom. **Meia dose** (half portions) cost more than half-price but are often more than adequate—a full serving may satisfy two. The omnipresent **prato do dia** (special of the day) and **menu** (*ementa* in Portuguese) of appetizer, bread, entree, and dessert stifle the loudest growls. The **ementa turística** (tourist menu) is usually a rip off to foreigners (and inevitably the most expensive option). Standard pre-meal bread, butter, cheese, and pâté may be dished without your asking, but it is not free (300-500$ per person).

Concocting a meal from outdoor food stalls stands is the cheapest option. Attention vegetarians: every town will likely have a **mercado municipal** (open-air market); get there before noon for the best produce. Groceries can be bought at the **supermercado** (supermarket) or **loja de conveniência** (convenience store).

DRINKS

The quality and low cost of Portuguese *vinho* (wine) is truly astounding. The pinnacle, **vinho do porto** (port), pressed (by feet) from the red grapes of the Douro Valley and fermented with a touch of brandy, is a dessert in itself. Chilled, white port makes a snappy aperitif, while the ruby or tawny port is a pleasing digestif. A cool heating process gives **Madeira** wines their unique "cooked" flavor. Try the dry Sercial and Verdelho before the main course, and the sweeter Bual and Malmsey after.

Sparkling *vinho verde* (green wine, referring to its youth, not its color) comes in red and white versions. The red may be a might strong for the faux connoisseur but the white is brash and delicious by most anybody's standards. The Adega Cooperatives of Ponte de Lima, Monção, and Amarante produce the best of this type. Excellent local table wines include Colares, Dão, Borba, Bairrada, Bucelas, and Periquita. If you can't decide, experiment with the **vinho de casa** (house wine); either the *tinto* (red) or the *branco* (white) is a reliable standby. Tangy **sangría** comes filled with fresh orange slices and makes even a budget meal festive at a minimal expense (usually around 500$ for a half-pitcher).

Bottled Sagres or Super Bock are excellent beers. If you do not ask for it *fresco* (cool) it may come *natural* (room temperature). A tall, slim glass of draft beer is a **fino** or an **imperial,** while a larger stein is a **caneca.** To sober and/or wake up, gulp a **bica** (cup of black espresso), a **galão** (coffee with milk, served in a glass), or a **café com leite** (coffee with milk, served in a cup).

TIPPING AND BARGAINING

As in Spain, a 5-10% tip is customary. Some restaurants add 10%. Otherwise, round up and leave the change. Don't worry, big tips aren't the norm: 150$ after a dinner for two is generally fine. Be mindful, others deserve your gratitude as well: tip porters 100-150$ and taxi drivers 15% the meter fare. Bargaining is not customary in commercial establishments or pensões, but hone your skills at the local *mercado* (market).

■ Today's Portugal: 1998 and Beyond

SPORTS

Futebol (soccer to Yanks) is the sport of choice for youngsters, professionals, and fans alike. The country has shown signs of making it big—at the 1996 European Championships, the national team ousted Denmark en route to the semifinals; at the Atlanta Olympics, they tied Argentina, beat France, and reached the semis. The quality matches the fervor: Lisbon's **Benfica** features some of the very finest players in the world. Native Portuguese have also made names for themselves off the pitch, specifically in long-distance running. Be it in a marathon (**Rosa Mota** was Queen of this race for some time) or less lengthy races (including the '96 women's 10,000m gold medalist), year in and out Portugal churns out a fleet of finely tuned legs.

For recreation diverging from jogging and pick-up soccer games, Portuguese often return to the sea. **Wind** and **body surfers** make waves along the wavy north coast, as **snorklers** and **scuba divers** set out on mini-explorations in the south and west.

BACK TO "O FUTURO"

Portugal is striving valiantly to catch up economically with the rest of western Europe. Its strong market should help Portugal enter the European monetary union in 1999. Currently, the EU is pumping funds into Portugal, fueling industry and infrastructure. This has resulted in new roads, railways, hospitals, schools, port and airport facilities, and sewage and waste disposal systems, among other things. Furthermore, Expo '98, to be held in Lisbon from May to September 1998, has inspired one of Europe's largest urban renewal projects, transforming a decaying industrial area into a thriving, beautified waterfront. Also, this past June Portugal kicked off its long-awaited derivatives exchange, centered in Porto, which pundits expect will boost international investment in the country. All told, prospects for the future are especially bright given the influx in industry and vastly improved educational system. At the same time, some things seem destined never to change—such as the pristine beaches along the Atlantic seaboard, the plush landscape in the north, the fine wines of Porto, and the hard-earned character and age-old traditions which evolved over the course of Portugal's rich history.

Prospects for the future are especially bright given the influx in industry and vastly improved educational system.

Lisbon (Lisboa)

Over 400 years ago, Lisbon was the center of the world's richest and farthest-reaching empire. Although the glorious Age of Discovery is part of the distant past, and modern problems such as traffic, smog, and urban decay assail Lisbon, the city retains a certain imperial grandeur. *Lisboetas* carefully preserve their traditions along with a relaxed urban atmosphere. The city continually renovates its historic monuments and meticulously maintains its black and white mosaic sidewalks, pastel facades, and cobbled medieval alleys. Streetcars weave between buses, motorcycles, cars, and pedestrians down broad avenues and narrow lanes.

Many nations claim to have settled Lisbon, with one legend crediting Odysseus as its founder. Lisbon became the Kingdom of Portugal's capital in 1255. City and empire reached their apex toward the end of the 15th century when Portuguese navigators pioneered explorations of Asia, Africa, and the New World. A huge earthquake on November 1, 1755 touched off the nation's fall from glory—close to one-fifth of the population died in the catastrophe, and two-thirds of Lisbon was reduced to a pile of smoldering rubble. Under the authoritarian leadership of the Prime Minister Marquês de Pombal, the city quickly recovered as magnificent new squares, palaces, and churches were speedily built. Another wave of construction in the late 19th century extended the city to the north and west.

During World War II, Lisbon's neutrality and Atlantic connections made the city a rendezvous for spies on both sides. When Mozambique and Angola won independence in 1974, hundreds of thousands of refugees converged upon the Portuguese capital. Immigration, combined with reactionary liberalism in response to the demise of Salazar's dictatorship, give Lisbon a cosmopolitan air. Today, Portuguese of African (Mozambican, Angolan, and Cape Verdean), Asian (Macaoan and Goan), and European origin mix freely on the streets.

■ Arrivals and Departures

BY PLANE

All flights land at **Aeroporto de Lisboa** (tel. 840 20 60 or 849 63 50) on the northern outskirts of the city. Walk out of the airport terminal and turn right, following the road around the curve to the bus stop, where you can take buses #44 or 45 (20min., 150$) to the **Praça dos Restauradores;** bus lets you off directly in front of the tourist office. Or, take the express bus (AeroBus or #91, every 20min., 15min., 430$) to the same location; it leaves directly from the airport exit. A taxi ride from the airport downtown will cost about 1300$, plus a 300$ luggage fee.

Major airlines have offices at Pr. Marquês de Pombal and along Av. Liberdade. Call for the current rates, as prices are almost always fluctuating.

> **TAP Air Portugal,** Pr. Marquês de Pombal, 3 (tel. 386 40 80; open Mon.-Fri. 9am-6pm). To Faro, Funchal (Madeira), Porto, Paris, London, New York, Madrid, and Barcelona.
> **Iberia,** R. Rosa Araújo, 2 (tel. 355 81 19).
> **Portugália Airlines,** Av. Almirante Gago Coutinho, 88 (tel. 848 6693), serves major domestic destinations.

BY TRAIN

Train service into and out of Lisbon is potentially confusing because there are four main stations, each serving different destinations. For info about Portugal's national railway system, **Caminhos de Ferro Portuguêses,** call 888 40 25. Beware that in Portuguese trains are called *comboios,* (by oxen).

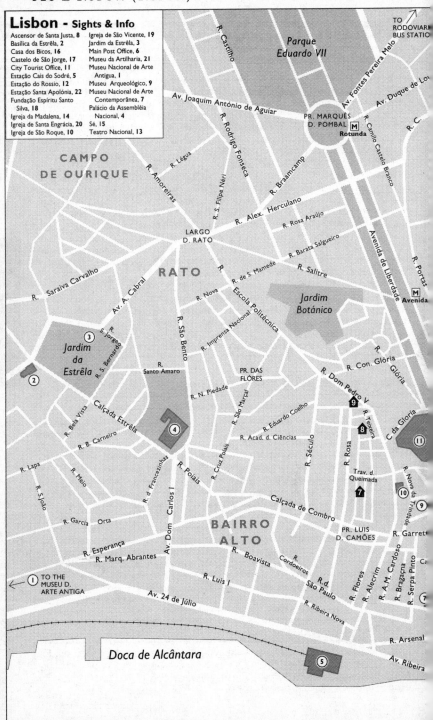

Lisbon - Sights & Info

Ascensor de Santa Justa, 8
Basílica da Estrêla, 2
Casa dos Bicos, 16
Castelo de São Jorge, 17
City Tourist Office, 11
Estação Cais do Sodré, 5
Estação do Rossio, 12
Estação Santa Apolónia, 22
Fundação Espíritu Santo
  Silva, 18
Igreja da Madalena, 14
Igreja de Santa Engrácia, 20
Igreja de São Roque, 10

Igreja de São Vicente, 19
Jardim da Estrêla, 3
Main Post Office, 6
Museu da Artilharia, 21
Museu Nacional de Arte
  Antigua, 1
Museu Arqueológico, 9
Museu Nacional de Arte
  Contemporânea, 7
Palácio da Assembléia
  Nacional, 4
Sé, 15
Teatro Nacional, 13

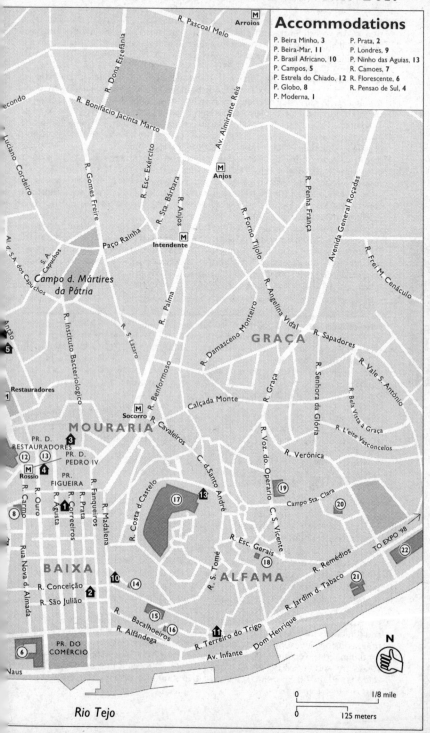

Accommodations

P. Beira Minho, 3
P. Beira-Mar, 11
P. Brasil Africano, 10
P. Campos, 5
P. Estrela do Chiado, 12
P. Globo, 8
P. Moderna, 1

P. Prata, 2
P. Londres, 9
P. Ninho das Aguias, 13
R. Camoes, 7
R. Florescente, 6
R. Pensao de Sul, 4

Estação Rossio, between Pr. Restauradores and Pr. Dom Pedro IV, the largest station, takes you to Sintra and points west (open 8am-11pm). Schedules and assistance available from an info office on the ground level (open daily 10am-1pm and 2-7pm). Luggage storage available (500$ for 48hr.). English spoken. To Sintra via Queluz (every 10min., 45min., 185$).

Estação Santa Apolónia, Av. Infante D. Henrique, east of the Alfama on the banks of the Rio Tejo, runs the international, northern, and eastern lines. The international terminal, with **currency exchange** and an info desk (English spoken), is located off the right side of the main platform. From the station, take buses #9, 39, or 46 to Pr. Restauradores and Estação Rossio. Luggage storage available (450-600$ for 48hr.). To: Aveiro (1680$); Braga (2500$); Bragança (2710$); Elvas (1600$); Coimbra (1300$); Mirandela (3000$); Madrid (8200$); Paris (24,000$).

Estação Cais do Sodré, just beyond the south end of R. Alecrim, east of Pr. Comércio, on the banks of the Tejo. Take buses #1, 44, or 45 to Pr. Restauradores or #28 to Estação Santa Apolónia. Luggage storage available (450$ for 48hr.). Trains leave approximately every 30min. to the monastery in Belém (110$), the youth hostel in Oeiras (150$), and Estoril and Cascais (180$). Smart travelers consult the video monitors above each platform.

Estação Barreiro, across the Rio Tejo from Lisbon proper, serves southern lines such as the Costa Azul and the Algarve. The station is accessible by ferries from the Terreiro do Paço dock off Pr. Comércio. Be sure to distinguish the Estasão from adjacent ferry docks. Ferries leave approximately every 30min. and take 30min. to reach the other side; the ferry ticket is included in the price of the connecting train ticket. To: Setúbal (every hr., 1½hr., 290$); Lagos (every 2 hr., 5½hr., 1700$).

BY BUS

Rodoviária da Estremadura, Av. Casal Ribeiro, 18 (info tel. 54 54 35; terminal tel. 55 77 15). M: Saldanha. From the metro, walk into the Pr. Duque de Saldanha. Av. Casal Ribeiro is the 2nd street on the left; the bus station is 2 blocks down on the left. English spoken. To: Évora (15 per day, 3½hr., 1350$); Coimbra (16 per day, 2½hr., 1350$); Peniche (11 per day, 2hr., 950$); Portalegre (4 per day, 4hr., 1500$); Lagos (10 per day, 5hr., 2200$); Porto (15 per day, 4hr., 1900$); Braga (6 per day, 5hr., 2100$); Tavira (5 per day, 5hr., 2200$); Jila Real St. Antonio (6 per day, 6hr., 2300$).

Caima, R. Bacalhoeiros, 16 off the Pr. Comércio (tel. 887 50 61 or 886 63 69), runs comfortable express buses to the Algarve and Porto (with movies and A/C!). Fastest way to the Algarve from Lisbon. To: Porto (6 per day, 2000$); Lagos (6 per day, 2400$).

▓ Getting Around

Lisbon has an efficient system of buses, subways, trams, funiculars and trains. Use them to full advantage—no suburb in or out of the city (even the beach) takes longer than 45 minutes to reach. If you don't speak Portuguese, however, taxi drivers and bus and train ticket booths may try to rip you off by charging an exorbitant fare or not returning your change. Make sure you know in advance what the fare should be, or else don't hand the ticket salesman more than 200$ for a local trip. If you are badly cheated and have a receipt or bill, write or call the **Departamento de Reclamações** (Department of Complaints), AMTRAL, R. Dr. António Cândido 8 R/C, 1097 Lisbon (tel. 356 38 31; fax 356 38 35), to see justice triumph (perhaps).

City Buses: CARRIS (tel. 363 93 43 or 363 20 44) runs the buses, subways, trains, and funiculars in Lisbon. 150$ within the city. If you plan to stay for any length of time, consider investing in a *bilhete de assinatura turístico* (tourist pass), good for unlimited travel on CARRIS transports (7-day 2265$; 4-day 1600$; 1-day 430$). Passes are sold in CARRIS booths (open 8am-8pm) located in most network train stations and the busier metro stations (e.g. Restauradores). You must show a passport to buy a tourist pass.

Lisbon Metro

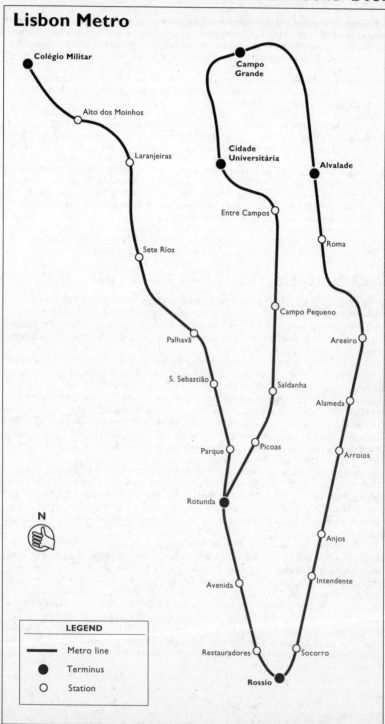

Colégio Militar

Alto dos Moinhos

Laranjeiras

Campo Grande

Cidade Universitária

Alvalade

Entre Campos

Roma

Sete Ríos

Campo Pequeno

Areeiro

Palhavã

S. Sebastião

Saldanha

Alameda

Parque

Picoas

Arroios

Rotunda

Anjos

Intendente

Avenida

Restauradores

Socorro

Rossio

N

LEGEND

— Metro line

● Terminus

○ Station

Subway: 70$ at window or from vending machines. Book of 10 tickets 550$. Tourist passes for 4, 7 or 30 days (1600$, 2265$ and 3600$). A red M marks Metro stops. The Metro (tel. 355 84 57) follows Av. Liberdade, then branches into lines covering the modern business district. Always keep your eyes peeled for pickpockets. Trains run 6am-1am.

Trams: Everywhere. These offer beautiful views of the harbor and older neighborhoods. Many are of pre-World War I vintage. Line #28 is great for sight-seeing in the Alfama and Mouraria (stops in Pr. Comércio, 150$).

Funiculars: These link the lower city with the hilly residential area (60-180$).

Taxis: Rádio Táxis de Lisboa (tel. 815 50 61), **Autocoope** (tel. 793 27 56), and **Teletáxi** (tel. 815 20 16). 24hr. service. Taxis swarm like pigeons along Av. Liberdade and throughout the Baixa, and cruise the streets elsewhere in the city. There is a flat rate of 300$ for luggage.

Car Rental: Cars can be picked up at the airport or in one of several locations downtown. Contact the central reservation numbers for all pickup locations. **Budget,** Av. Visconte Valmar, 36BIC (tel. 796 10 28; fax 797 13 77). **Hertz,** Qto. Francelha Baixio (tel. 941 55 41; fax 941 60 68). **Avis,** Av. Praia da Vitória, 12C (tel. 346 26 76). See **By Car,** p. 41, for toll-free numbers to get rates and other info from home. If you're confining your visit to Lisbon, a car is unneccessary. You won't want to be a part of the hair-raising traffic: it's dangerous enough being a pedestrian, but Portugal continually has the highest accident rate in Western Europe.

■ Orientation

According to legend, Lisbon, like Rome, was built on seven hills, though your calves might tell you there are many more. Navigating the maze of Lisbon's roller-coaster streets requires patience and stairmaster training. The three main *bairros* (neighborhoods) of the city center are the **Baixa** (low district, resting in the valley), the **Bairro Alto** (high district), and the **Alfama.**

The **Baixa,** Lisbon's old business center, sits in the center of town, sandwiched between the other two districts. Its grid of small, mostly pedestrian streets begins at the **Rossio** (also called the **Praça Dom Pedro IV**) and ends at the **Praça do Comércio,** on the **Rio Tejo,** otherwise known as the **Tagus River.** The **Praça dos Restauradores,** where buses from the airport stop, lies just above the Baixa. From Praça Restauradores, the tree-lined **Avenida da Liberdade,** which many have likened to the Champs-Elysées in Paris, runs uphill to the new business district centered around **Praça do Marquês de Pombal.** Boxy 60s-style art nouveau buildings add color to the broad avenues radiating from the *praça*.

From the west side of the Baixa, the **Ascensor de Santa Justa**—an elegant, historic outdoor elevator—lifts you up to the **Bairro Alto's** upscale shopping district, the **Chiado,** traversed by the fashionable **Rua do Carmo** and **Rua Garrett.** Most of the **Bairro Alto** is a populous, working-class area of narrow streets, tropical parks, and Baroque churches. Young Portuguese come here to party—there is scarcely a change in activity on the street between 2pm and 2am.

To the east of the Baixa, the **Alfama**—Lisbon's famous medieval *bairro,* comprising the Moorish quarter—is the oldest district of the city, stacking tiny whitewashed houses along a labyrinth of narrow alleys and stairways beneath the **Castelo de São Jorge.** Expect to get lost. Without a detailed map expect to get doubly lost. The twisting streets change names about every three steps, and streets that share a name may not actually be the same street: there are *travessas* (side streets), *ruas* (streets), *calçadinhas* (walkways), and *escadinhas* (stairways). The tourist office's map is free, but does not list all the tiny streets. A street-indexed **Falk city map** (sold in Estação Rossio and most magazine stands for 1000$) or the Poseidon **Planta de Lisboa** (with Sintra, Cascais and Estoril on the back) are worth the money.

■ Practical Information

Tourist Office: Palácio da Foz, Pr. Restauradores (tel. 346 63 07 or 346 33 14). M: Restauradores. English spoken. Bus schedules, *pensão* listings, and free map. Open daily 9am-8pm. **Aeroporto de Lisboa** (tel. 849 36 89), right as you exit the baggage claim area. English spoken. Open daily 6am-2am.

Budget Travel: Tagus (Youth Branch), Pr. Londres, 9B (tel. 849 15 31). M: Alameda. From the metro, walk up Av. Guerra Junqueiro. English spoken. **Tagus (Main Office),** R. Camilo Castelo Branco, 20 (tel. 352 59 86). M: Rotunda. Open Mon.-Fri. 9am-1pm and 2:30-5:30pm.

Embassies: see **Embassies and Consulates,** p. 36.

Currency Exchange: Banks are open Mon.-Fri. 8:30-11:45am and 1-2:45pm. For a relatively low commission and decent rates, try **Cota Câmbio,** R. Áurea, 283, 1 block off Pr. Dom Pedro IV in the Baixa. The **Banco Fonsecas and Burnay** branch in the international terminal at Estação Santa Apolónia charges high commission. Open 24hr. The main post office, most banks, and travel agencies also change money. Ask first—fees can be exorbitant (1000$ or more). **ATMs,** which offer the best exchange rates, line the streets of the Baixa and are sprinkled through the rest of the city. Nifty **automatic exchange machines** can be found throughout the Baixa, though their high fees more than negate the convenience.

American Express: Top Tours, Av. Duque de Loulé, 108 (tel. 315 58 85). M: Rotunda. Exit toward R. Rodrigo Sampaio and walk up Av. Liberdade toward the Marquês de Pombal statue, then hang a right. This sole (and often crowded) Top Tours office handles all AmEx functions. Traveler's checks sold and cashed. Mail held. English spoken. Open Mon.-Fri. 9:30am-1pm and 2:30-6:30pm.

Telephones: All over the city. The **Portugal Telecom** office, Pr. Dom Pedro IV, 68 (M: Rossio) has pay phones and a few booths for international calls. An impressive selection of phone books from around Portugal and throughout Europe. Pay the cashier after your call or use a phone card. Visa. **Phone cards** come in 50 units (875$) or 120 units (2100$) and can be purchased here or at neighborhood book stores and stationers. Local calls consume at least 1 unit. Office open daily 8am-11pm. **Telephone Code:** (0)1.

Luggage Storage: At **Estação Rossio** and **Estação Santa Apolónia.** Lockers 450-600$ (depending on size) for 48hr. access daily 6am-2am. At the **bus station,** 150$ per bag per day.

Laundromat: Lavatax, R. Francisco Sanches, 65A (tel. 812 33 92). M: Arroios. Self-serve or wash, dry, and fold 1100$ per 5kg load. Open 9am-1pm and 3-7pm, Sat. 9am-noon.

Public Toilets: In the Rossio, major squares, subway stations, and tourist offices.

Library: Biblioteca Municipal Central, Palácio Galveias (tel. 797 38 62). M: Campo Pequeno. Open Mon.-Fri. 9am-7pm, Sun. 11am-5pm. **English Bookstore: Livraria Británica,** R. Luis Fernandes, 14-16 (tel. 342 84 72), across from the British Institute in the Bairro Alto. Good collection of classics and popular novels. Open Mon.-Fri. 9:30am-7pm. Visa, MC, AmEx. **Livraria Bertrand,** R. Garrett, 73 (tel. 346 86 46). Good collection of best-sellers, some magazines. International maps, language books, travel guides—including *Let's Go.* Open Mon.-Fri. 9am-7pm, Sat. 9am-1pm.

Shopping Center: Amoreiras Shopping Center de Lisboa, Av. Duarte Pacheco (Bus #11 from Restauradores; tel. 69 25 58). 383 shops including a humongous **Pão de Açúcar** supermarket, English bookstores, and a 10-screen cinema.

Weather and Sea Conditions: tel. 150. Portuguese only.

Late-Night Pharmacy: tel. 118. Pharmacies throughout the city stay open all night on a rotating basis for emergencies only. The address of the next night service is posted on the door of every pharmacy.

Crisis Lines: Poison (tel. 795 01 43). **Drug Abuse: Linha Vida** (tel. 726 77 66) and **Centro das Taipas** (tel. 342 85 85). **Suicide Prevention:** (tel. 54 45 45). **Child Abuse Hotline: SOS-Criança** (tel. 793 16 17).

Medical Services: British Hospital, R. Saraiva de Carvalho, 49 (tel. 395 50 67; for appointments tel. 397 63 29). **Cruz Vermelha Portuguesa,** R. Duarte Galvão, 54 (emergency tel. 778 60 13; ambulance tel. 942 11 11). **AIDS Info: Linha SIDA** (tel. 759 99 43) and **Abraço** (tel. 342 59 29).

Police: R. Capelo, 3 (tel. 346 61 41 or 347 47 30). English spoken. **Fire:** tel. 342 22 22. **Emergency:** tel. 112 from anywhere in Portugal.

Post Office: Marked by red Correios signs. Lisbon's main post office is in the Pr. Comércio (tel. 346 32 31), and provides all services including **telephone, fax,** Posta Restante, and international express mail (EMS). Open Mon.-Fri. 8:30am-6:30pm. Another office in **Praça dos Restauradores** provides the same services with longer hours and a more central location. Open Mon.-Fri. 8am-10pm; Sat., Sun., and holidays 9am-6pm. **Postal Code:** 1100 for central Lisbon.

■ Accommodations and Camping

A price ceiling supposedly restricts how much *pensões* can charge for particular types of rooms, so if the fee seems padded, request the printed price list. During low- or mid-season prices generally drop, depending on room availability and the whim of the *pensão* owner—try bargaining the price down 500$ or so per night. Many establishments have rooms only with double beds and charge per person. Expect to pay about 3000$ for a single and 5000$ for a double, depending on amenities and location. If you're dissatisfied, ask the owner for a *livro de reclamações,* in which you can write your comments so the tourist bureau will see them.

Most hotels are in the center of town on **Av. da Liberdade,** while many convenient budget *pensões* are in the **Baixa** along the **Rossio** and on **R. da Prata, dos Correeiros,** and **do Ouro.** Lodgings near the Castelo de São Jorge or in the Bairro Alto are quieter and nearer to the sights, and hence more expensive. If central accommodations are full, head east to the *pensões* along **Av. Almirante Reis.** Be especially cautious after dark in the Bairro Alto, the Alfama, and the Baixa; many streets are isolated and most are poorly lit.

Pousada de Juventude de Lisboa (HI), R. Andrade Corvo, 46 (tel. 353 2696; fax 353 7541). M: Picoas. Exit the metro station facing south, turn right, and walk one block. This huge, ultra-clean youth haven has abandoned some of the typical HI restrictions—there is no curfew or lockout—but is typical in its inconvenient location. English spoken. Reception open 8am-midnight. Check out by 10:30am. Dorm bunks 2350$. Double with bath 5700$. In winter 1900$; 4800$. Breakfast included. Lockers 250$. Disabled access. HI card required.

Pousada de Juventude de Catalazete (HI), Estrada Marginal (tel. 443 06 38), in the nearby coastal town of **Oeiras.** Take a train from Estação Cais do Sodré to Oeiras (20min., 155$). Exit through the train station underpass from the side of the train coming *from* Lisbon. Cross the street and follow signs to Lisbon and Cascais. The street curves through a residential district. At the intersection across from a bus stop (no street signs), make a left and go downhill along R. Filipa de Lencastre. At the underpass, go straight and follow HI signs to the INATEL complex. The hike will reward you with beautiful ocean views from the patio and quiet rooms. Guard all belongings. Reception open 8am-midnight. Midnight curfew. June-Sept. dorm space 1700$. Doubles with bath 4100$. Cheaper in off-season. Breakfast included. Lunch and dinner each 750$. Reservations recommended.

BAIXA

Dozens of *pensões* surround the three connected *praças*—**Pr. dos Restauradoes, Pr. Dom Pedro IV,** and **Pr. da Figueira**—that form the heart of downtown Lisbon. Decrepit exteriors of pre-war buildings often conceal newly renovated interiors. Although most have fewer than 12 rooms, finding a vacancy shouldn't be a problem. For a good night's sleep, look for a *pensão* along the pedestrian-only streets of the Baixa. Some *casas de hóspedes* may be brothels; though occasionally located beneath hostels, they are not desirable lodgings.

Pensão Campos, R. Jardim do Regedor, 24, 3rd fl. (tel. 346 28 64), between Pr. Restauradores and R. Portas de Santo Antão. Comfortable rooms with phones and well-scoured baths. Overlooking a pedestrian street north of the Rossio. Cool multilin-

gual owner. An elevator whisks you up to the *pensão's* 12 rooms. Singles 2500$; doubles 4000$, with shower 5000$; triples 5300$.

Pensão Moderna, R. Correeiros, 205, 4th fl. (tel. 346 08 18), one block off of the south side of Pr. Figueira. A friendly local family tends comfortable if rather noisy apartment-style rooms. All 10 rooms are antique-filled and have large windows and balconies. Great location. Singles 3000$; doubles 3500-5000$.

Residêncial Florescente, R. Portas de Santo Antão, 99 (tel. 342 66 09; fax 342 77 33), one block from Pr. Restauradores. Basically, a hotel without room service. The 72 impeccable, spacious rooms with phone and TV are luxurious by budget standards. Windowed (and better furnished) rooms have an incredible view of Pr. Figueira. Singles and doubles 3500-5000$, with shower 6500$, with full bath, 7000-8000$; triples with bath 9000-10,000$. Large room with full bath and A/C 8500$. Visa, AmEx, MC.

Pensão Beira Minho, Pr. Figueira, 6, 2nd. fl. (tel. 346 18 46), beside the Rossio at the north end of the *praça*, through a flower shop. 28 plain, well-lit rooms with phones. Some have a veranda looking onto the square. Singles 2500$, with bath 4500$; doubles 4500-6000. Breakfast included.

Residência do Sul, Pr. Dom Pedro IV, 59, 2nd. fl. (tel. 342 25 11), through the souvenir shop. Somewhat dark but otherwise excellent rooms. Those opposite the square are quieter. English spoken. Singles with shower 4000$, with full bath 4500$; doubles 5500$; triples with shower 7000$. Prices drop in the off season.

Pensão Prata, R. Prata, 71, 3rd. fl. (tel. 346 89 08), 2 blocks from Pr. Comércio. The entrance to a busy cafe obscures the staircase. 12 clean, peaceful rooms with tiny baths. English-speaking owner very knowledgable of Lisbon hotspots. Singles 2800$, with bath 3500$; doubles 4000$, with shower 4500$, with bath 5500$. Prices drop 500-1000$ in the off season.

IN AND AROUND THE BAIRRO ALTO

The Bairro Alto is quieter than the Baixa and has a community feel which the town center lacks, but the uphill hike is inconvenient and daunting for luggage-bearers. Blessed (and financially prudent) are those who persevere; unto them shall be bestowed ample rooms of great value, enhanced by antiques and views of the castle. Most of Lisbon's nightlife is to be found here, but don't wander off alone at after dark—this area has a reputation for muggings.

Residencial Camões, Tr. Poço da Cidade, 38, 1st fl. (tel. 367 75 10; fax 346 40 48), off R. Misericórdia. A pristine set of rooms in the heart of the Bairro Alto party district. Singles 2500-3500$, with bath 6000$. Triples 6000$; 7000$. Prices drop Oct.-June 500-1000$. English spoken. Breakfast included. Reservations essential in the summer.

Pensão Estrêla do Chiado, R. Garrett, 29, 4th fl. (tel. 342 61 10). The 95-stair climb would tire Sisyphus, but the 12 spotless rooms, hot water, and large well-furnished singles entice. Three rooms with verandas have views of the castle. The common bathrooms have undergone recent renovations. Singles 2500$, with shower 3500$. Doubles 4500$; 5000$.

Casa de Hóspedes Globo, R. Teixeira, 37 (tel. 346 22 79), on a small street across from the Parque São Pedro de Alcântra at the top of the funicular. From the entrance to the park, cross the street to Tr. Cara and make a right onto R. Teixeira. Recent renovations have refurbished these spacious rooms with sturdy furniture, cheerful bedspreads, and nicely partitioned *lavabos* (bathrooms). English spoken. Singles 2000$, with bath 3000$. Doubles 4000$; 4500$. Prices drop 500$ during the off season. Reservations recommended.

Pensão Londres, R. Dom Pedro V, 53 2nd fl.(tel. 346 22 03; fax 346 56 82). Take the funicular next door to the tourist office in Pr. Restauradores and turn right. Walk 3 blocks up from R. Dom Pedro V. The *pensão* is on a hilltop street corner; take the elevator to the 39 spacious, well-lit rooms (all with phones) overlooking the old town. Singles 4500$, with shower 6000$. Doubles 5800-6200$; 7200-8000$. Triples 12,000$. Prices drop 1000-2000$ in winter. Breakfast included. Visa, MC, Eurocheques accepted.

ALFAMA

Staying in the Alfama grants flowering balconies and amazing views. It also means steep streets, a long walk to drop your pack in the *pensão,* and potential danger at night, when tourists no longer venture to the *castelo.* Yet behind the menacing, grimy facades hide cheap rooms with surprisingly comfy interiors.

Pensão Beira-Mar, Largo Terreiro do Trigo, 16, 4th fl. (tel. 886 99 33). Call the owner's cell phone (tel. 09 31 64 63 09). In a small square off Av. Infante Dom Henrique (the road that parallels the Tejo) between the Estação Santa Apolónia and the ferry station. One of the best values in Lisbon. Clean, spacious rooms, most with cheerfully mismatched bedclothes, some with water views. Hip English-speaking owner will pick you up from the train station (for free), tell you about Lisbon's hot spots, and might just give you a lift to the beach. Recently renovated rooms 2000$ per person (with bath 2500$); 500$ less per person in winter. Laundry 1000$ per load. Reservations recommended.

Pensão Brasil Africano, Tr. Pedras Negras, 8, 3rd fl. (tel. 886 92 66), off R. Madalena. A homey *pensão* with friendly management, at the foot of the Alfama hill. Spacious rooms with balconies. Singles 2000$. Doubles 3500$, with bath 4000$. Triples 5000$. Less in the off season. Discounts for longer stays.

Pensão Ninho das Águias, R. Costa do Castelo, 74 (tel. 886 70 08), down the street from the Teatro Taborda (behind the castle). This *pensão*'s spectacular views of Lisbon are worth the long hike and additional staircase. Cheerful rooms with phones are in high demand—make reservations in advance. Singles 4500-5500$. Doubles 6000-7000$. Triples 6500-7000$.

CAMPING

Although camping is popular in Portugal, campers are often prime targets for thieves. Info on all campgrounds in Portugal is available from the tourist office in the free booklet *Portugal: Camping and Caravan Sites.* There are 30 campgrounds within a 45-minute radius of the capital, although there is only one in Lisbon proper.

Parque de Campismo Municipal de Lisboa (tel. 760 20 61; fax 760 74 74), on the road to Benfica. Take bus #43 from the Rossio to the Parque Florestal Monsanto. Lisbon's municipal campground has a swimming pool and supermarket. 420$ per person, 355$ or more per tent (depending on size), 275$ per car. In winter: 135$; 110$; 110$. Reception open 9am-9pm; winter 8am-9pm.

▨ Food

Lisbon has some of the least expensive restaurants and best wine of any European capital. A full dinner costs about 1800$ per person, and the *prato do dia* (special of the day) is often a great deal, allowing you to finish it off with a sinfully cheap Portuguese pastry. Any good restaurant, regardless of location, will be feeding hordes of locals as well as tourists; the odd toddler running among tables is a good sign of authenticity. If you're searching for a bargain meal, avoid restaurants with menus translated into a Babel of different languages (tourist trap alert!). Lisbon reels with seafood specialties such as *amêjoas à bulhão pato* (steamed clams), *creme de mariscos* (seafood chowder with tomatoes), and a local classic, *bacalhau cozido com grão e batatas* (cod with chick-peas and boiled potatoes).

Supermercado Celeiro, R. 1 de Dezembro, 65, 2 blocks down the street from Estagão Rossio. Centrally located, this medium-sized market stocks a wide variety of fruit, meat, and processed foods, as well as fresh bread and pastries. Open Mon.-Fri. 8:30am-8pm, Sat. 8:30am-7pm.

Mercado Ribeira, a market complex inside a warehouse on Av. 24 de Julho outside the Estação Cais do Sodré (bus #40), is open Mon.-Sat. sunrise to 2pm. Go early for the freshest selection. The jumbo-sized **Supermercado Pão de Açucar** is in Amor-

eiras Shopping Center de Lisboa, Av. Duarte Pacheco (bus #11 from Restauradores or Pr. da Figueira).

BAIXA

In Lisbon, the closer you are to the industrial waterfront, the cheaper the restaurant. The south end near the port and the area bordering the Alfama are particularly inexpensive. Some bargain eateries line **R. Correeiros,** parallel to R. Prata, and neighboring streets. One block from Pr. Restauradores on **R. Portas de Santo Antão,** several superb seafood restaurants stack the day's catch in their windows. The small streets north of Pr. Figueira are all packed with eateries. Many of the Baixa's restaurants are not open on Sundays and close around 10pm on weekdays. Beware: the Baixa is home to some of Lisbon's most tourist-oriented restaurants.

Restaurante João do Grão, R. dos Correeiros, 222 (tel. 342 47 57), with a yellow sign out front, is one of Lisbon's most highly recommended eateries. Try the house special, *bacalhau com grão-de-bico* (cod with chick-peas, 1400$), while watching the soccer game on TV. House wine a winner at 295$. Entrees from 850$.

Restaurante Bonjardim, Tr. de Santo Antão, 11 (tel. 342 43 89), on a side street off Pr. Restauradores. The self-proclaimed *rei dos frangos* (king of chicken) rules the roost with delicious roast chicken (1100$). Entrees 1000-2500$. Open daily noon-11pm. V, MC.

Hua Ta Li, R. dos Bacalhoeiros, 109-115A (tel. 887 91 70), near the Pr. Comércio. Great vegetarian options. Try the noodles with vegetables (710$) and seafood salad (750$). *Menú* 1400$. Open daily noon-3:30pm and 6:30-11pm.

Churrascaria Gáucha, R. dos Bacalhoeiros, 26 C-D (tel. 887 06 09), one block north of the riverside near the Pr. Comércio. This large, popular grill serves South-American style *churrasco* dishes such as the bean-based *feijoada* (stewed with various meats 1200$). Open daily 10am-2am. V, MC, AmEx.

Celeiro, R. 1 de Dezembro, 65, take the first right off the Estação Rossio, go 2 blocks. Macrobiotic restaurant accompanied by a health food supermarket will sate the strictest herbivore. Cafeteria style salads, souffles, and sandwiches. Entrees 200-570$. Open Mon.-Fri. 8:30am-8pm, Sat. 8:30am-7pm.

Abracadabra, Pr. Dom Pedro IV, 64, next to Estação Rossio. Popular high school hangout featuring fab fast food and pastry counter. Pizza loaded with toppings (slice 400$), hot dogs, and burgers—Portuguese style. Open daily 7am-11pm.

Confeitaria Nacional, Praça Figueira 18-B. Succumb to the mirror-and-gold decor of this famous *pastelaría* (established 1820). Visit Nirvana nibbling on a sugar-coated almond-encrusted *austríaca* ($120). Open Mon.-Sat. 10am-5pm.

BAIRRO ALTO

Although the Bairro has its share of glamorous restaurants, it also has far more small and medium-sized eateries than the Baixa. Many inexpensive local haunts line **Calçada do Combro,** the neighborhood's main westward artery. Scour **R. Misericórdia's** side streets for cheaper restaurants and quieter, dimmer dinners. The area around **Praça Dom Pedro V** is also peppered with small culinary diamonds in the rough.

Cervejaria da Trindade, R. Nova Trindade, 20C (tel. 342 35 06), 2 blocks down a side street that begins in the square in front of the Igreja do São Roque and parallels R. Misericórdia. Regal imagery on shiny *azulejos* in an elegant, but noisy, atmosphere, which is part restaurant, part beer hall. Entrees range from 950-2500$, budget finds are the *sugestões do chefe* (chef's suggestions) such as *bacalhau com natas* (1250$). Open noon-2am. Visa, MC, AmEx.

Restaurante Tascardoso, R. Século, 244 (tel. 342 75 78), off R. Dom Pedro V. Small restaurant with hearty food. Walls inscribed with food-for-thought proverbs such as "He who talks much says little." So shut up and eat. Mouth-watering pastries 150-350$. Entrees such as *açorda de gambas* (prawn puff souffle) 900-1100$. *Vinho de casa* 650$ for a ½ bottle. Open daily 8am-midnight. Visa, MC, AmEx.

Café Brasil, R. São Pedro de Alcântara, 51 (tel. 342 52 49), across the street from the park of the same name. Hot, cheap food served in an airy local watering hole. Meat and fish dishes only 600-990$. The *prato do dia* is a real bargain at 650$. Open Mon.-Fri. 8am-midnight, Sat. 8am-8pm.

A Pérola do Bonjardim, R. Cruz dos Poiais, 95A (tel. 60 84 80), off R. Poiais, a continuation of Calçada do Combro. Stucco and tile family restaurant tucked away in a neighborhood of pastel colored buildings. Wonderful garlic aroma. *Pratos do dia* (830-1300$) and delectable entrees (500-1500$). Open Mon.-Sat. 7am-midnight.

Porto de Abrigo, R. Remolares, 16-18 (tel. 346 08 73), off Pr. Duque da Terceira, which is in front of the Estação. This lighthouse in a dingy semi-industrial neighborhood will lead you safely to *pato com arroz* (duck with rice and olives, 1200$). Entrees 950-1480$. Open Mon.-Sat. noon-3pm and 7-10pm.

ALFAMA

The winding streets of the Alfama conceal a number of tiny unpretentious restaurants often packed with neighbors and friends of the owner. Lively chatter echoes through the damp, narrow alleys. Watch the clock—the labyrinthine Alfama grows dangerously dark after nightfall.

Rio Coura, R. Augusto Rosa, 30 (tel. 886 98 67), uphill from the Igreja da Sé en route to the Castelo de São Jorge. Reward your aching ankles and growling stomach with the house's piping hot, generous portions of grilled seafood. Entrees only 800-1300$, house wines 300$. Open daily 1-4pm and 7-10:30pm.

Malmequer Bemmequer, R. de São Miguel, 23-25 (tel. 887 65 35), follow Av. Infante D. Henrique (the river road) east to Terreiro do Trigo. Take next left and climb the stairs to R. de São Miguel. The name means "He loves me not, he loves me well." The friendly cruise-ship-trained owner loves everyone; serves delicious seafood and meat dishes. Entrees from 850$. Open daily noon-3:30pm and 7-11pm.

Restaurante Arco do Castelo, R. Chão de Feira, 25 (tel. 887 65 95), across from the gate to the Castelo de São Jorge. For a hearty, spicy meal, try one of their specialties from Goa, Portugal's former colony in India. Curry in a hurry (from 1100$). Open daily 12:30-11pm.

Lisbon "Fiestas": http://www.festas_lisboa.pt
Lisbon "Agenda Cultura": http://portugal.hpv.pt//lisboa/agenda

---

■ Sights

EXPO '98

All eyes turn to the sea as Lisbon prepares the century's biggest World Expo fair. Making good use of its aquatic traditions, Portugal has worked with the theme of "The Oceans: A Heritage for the Future" to produce what promises to be history's biggest nautical extravaganza. Over 120 countries will show off their seafaring pasts at this ocean-front, ocean-minded four-month-long carnival. Make your reservations now—it is already late in the game—and plan carefully: the city and its environs will be inundated with visitors thirsty for the ultimate nautical experience. Your best bets probably lie outside Lisbon; check the youth hostels at Oeiras, Sintra, and Setúbal or scour nearby towns and villages for campgrounds and *quartos,* and take the train into Lisbon. Expect prices to rise accordingly.

The event kicks off 100 days before the official opening, with a festival of shows, including operas by Philip Glass and Portugal's António Pinto Vargas, commissioned specifically for Expo '98 at the Centro Cultural de Beléon and other Lisbon locations. The fair itself runs May 22 - Sept. 30, with cultural performances and sea-related exhibitions starting daily at 9am (when families of enigmatic Marine Monsters begin to circulate among visitors) and culminating in a nighttime multimedia show. Don't miss the nautical exhibition, featuring a slew of boats from around the world docked at the fair's Doca do Olivais, and the ambitious Oceans Pavilion, the largest oceanarium in

Europe. Stroll through half a millennium of history at the Portuguese Pavilion, witness the Big Bang, chill in the Garden of Eden, and hop onto Noah's Ark at the Utopia Pavilion (we don't get it either, but it sounds fun). Other pavilions will be dedicated to futuristic and international themes. Finally, ye soccer fans need not fret: giant screens will project ongoing matches at the World Cup in France.

The Expo grounds stretch along Av. Marechal Gomes da Costa on the industrial northern bank of the Tejo two kilometers east. To get there, take the buses departing from Terreiro do Io or Estaçao Santa Apolónia. You can purchase individual tickets for the Expo for 1 or 3 days, 1 night, or a 3-month pass. Children 5-14 years and seniors (over 65) pay half price. For more information, email info@expo98.pt, or check out their bubbly web page at http://www.expo98.pt.

BAIXA

The best place to embark upon your tour of Lisbon's Enlightenment-era center is from its heart—the **Rossio.** Let your eyes traverse the city's main square, also known as the **Praça Dom Pedro IV,** before your feet do. Once a cattle market with a public execution stage, bullfighting arena, and carnival ground, the *praça* is now the domain of drink-sipping tourists and heart-stopping traffic that whizzes around the statue of Dom Pedro IV in the center of the square. Another statue—of Gil Vicente, Portugal's first great dramatist—peers down from the top of the columnal **Teatro Nacional de Dona Maria II** at the north end of the Praça. Adjoining the Rossio is the elegant **Praça Figueira.**

The grid of mostly pedestrian streets south of the Rossio caters to ice cream eaters and window shoppers. After the calamitous earthquake of 1755, the Marquês de Pombal designed the streets to serve as a conduit for goods from the ports on the Rio Tejo to the city center. At the very height of Enlightenment urban planning each street was designated for a specific trade: shoemakers *(sapateiros),* couriers *(correeiros),* and cod merchants *(bacalhoeiros)* each had their own avenue. Two centuries later, the Baixa is one of the most crowded areas of town in the daytime. Pedestrians wander about on the wide mosaic sidewalks, cars drag race down the Marquês's stately avenues, and visitors swarm upscale shops along side streets. From the pedestrian streets of the Baixa, all roads lead to the **Praça do Comércio** on the banks of the Tejo. Also known as the **Terreiro do Paço,** Pr. Comércio lies supine before the towering statue of Dom João I, cast from 9400 pounds of bronze in 1755. The *praça* now serves as the headquarters of several Portuguese government ministries, while its center has been relegated to less dignified use as a fairgrounds.

Winding your way back up through the Rossio brings you to the **Praça dos Restauradores,** which commemorates the 1640 restoration of Portugal's independence from Spain with an obelisk and a bronze sculpture of the Spirit of Independence. Here begins **Avenida da Liberdade,** Lisbon's most imposing boulevard and one of the city's most elegant promenades, modeled after the wide boulevards of 19th-century Paris. This shady mile-long thoroughfare ends at **Praça do Marquês do Pombal,** from where the imposing 18th-century *Marguês* overlooks a bustling commercial district.

BAIRRO ALTO

Although it's just as easy to get from the Baixa to the Bairro Alto by walking, the classic way is to take the **Ascensor de Santa Justa,** a historic elevator built in 1902 inside a Gothic wrought-iron tower. Tourists ride to admire the view from the upper levels, while many locals use the elevator as transportation into the hilly Bairro Alto (runs Mon.-Fri. 7am-11pm, Sat.-Sun. 9am-11pm; 75$ each way). From the upper terrace, a narrow walkway leads under a huge flying buttress to the 14th-century **Igreja do Carmo.** The 1755 earthquake left the church roofless, but not without its dramatic Gothic arches. The ramshackle **Museu Arqueológico,** Largo do Carmo (tel. 346 04 73), includes Dom Fernando I's tomb (open Mon.-Sat. 10am-6pm; in winter Mon.-Sat. 10am-1pm and 2-5pm; 300$).

As you exit the elevator, turn left and walk one block to **R. Garrett,** the heart of the chic **Chiado** neighborhood. In the *Bairro,* (Chiado's hip name), Portuguese intellectuals mix with rebellious teens and idealistic university students—it's the only place in Lisbon that never sleeps. While waiting for the night life to begin, go left onto R. Serpa Pinto and walk two blocks to the **Museu do Chiado,** R. Serpa Pinto 4 (tel. 343 21 48). An educational (and aesthetic) experience awaits, courtesy of Portugal's most famous post-1850 painters and sculptors. (Open Tues. 2-6pm, Wed.-Sun. 10am-6pm. 400$; ages 14–25, seniors, and teachers 200$. Free Sun. and holidays 10am-2pm.) En route to the museum you'll pass Lisbon's opera center, the **Teatro Nacional de São Carlos,** R. Serpa Pinto, 9 (ticket office tel. 346 59 14), in a small square to the right.

Turning right just before the Pr. Camões will put you on **R. da Misericórdia,** where you'll find many of Lisbon's liveliest bars and *casas de fado.* Uphill on R. Misericórdia is **Igreja de São Roque,** Largo Trinidade Coelho (tel. 346 03 61), dedicated to the saint who is believed to have saved the Bairro Alto from the devastation of the great quake. Inside the church, the notorious **Capela de São João Baptista** (fourth from the left), ablaze with precious gems and metals, caused a stir upon its installation in 1747. It took three different ships to deliver the chapel to Lisbon after it was built in Rome from agate, lapis lazuli, alabaster, and mosaic tiles. Next door, the small but worthwhile **Museu de São Roque** (tel. 346 03 61), with its own share of gold and silver, features European religious art from the 16th to 18th centuries (open Tues.-Sun. 10am-5pm; 175$, students and seniors free, Sun. free).

If your calves aren't burning too badly, continue—you guessed it—up R. Misericórdia as it becomes R. São Pedro de Alcântara. The **Parque de São Pedro de Alcântara** will be on your right. Plop down under the mercifully shady trees, perfect for a picnic. The **Castelo de São Jorge** in the **Alfama** stares back from the cliff opposite the park, and the city of Lisbon twinkles at your toes. A mosaic points out the landmarks included in this vista. Continue uphill along R. Dom Pedro V and you'll hit the majestic **Parque Príncipe Real,** which connects to Lisbon's extensive **Jardim Botánico.**

A Camões Cameo

Turn left on R. Garrett and you'll face the **Praça de Camões,** marked by a monument to Luís de Camões, Portugal's famed 16th-century poet. Camões, whose *Lusíadas* chronicled his nation's discoveries in lyric verse, is considered the Portuguese Shakespeare. This stud had so many affairs with ladies of the court that he fled to North Africa to escape their vengeful husbands. He died a pauper somewhere in Asia, and to Portugal's chagrin his body was never recovered.

For more of a neighborhood flavor, walk through Pr. Camões and take R. Loreto, which turns into Calçada do Combro. At the base of the hill, the right fork becomes the Travessa do Convento de Jesus, where flowered balconies and hanging laundry frame the **Igreja das Mercês,** a handsome 18th-century travertine building. Its small *praça* overlooks the neoclassical **Palácio da Assembléia Nacional** (House of Parliament). Back down the hill towards the small square, the left fork leads to R. Poiais de São Bento, which turns into Calçada da Estrêla and leads to more churches, such as the ornate **Basílica da Estrêla** of 1796, Pr. da Estrela (tel. 346 04 73). The basilica's exquisitely shaped dome poised behind a pair of tall belfries steals the sky. Half-mad Maria I, desiring a male heir, made fervent religious vows promising God anything and everything if she were granted a son. When a baby boy was finally born, she built this church. Ask the sacristan to show you the gigantic 10th-century *presépio* (manger scene; open daily 9am-1pm and 3-8pm; free).

Across from the church, wide asphalt paths of the **Jardim da Estrêla** wind through flocks of pigeons and lush flora. Park walkways are popular for Sunday strolls, as the benches fill with smoochers. Behind the park tropical plants, cypress trees, and odd gravestones mark the **Cemitério dos Inglêses** (English Cemetery). Its musty Victorian chapel dates from 1885. A half-hour walk down Av. Infante Santo leads to Portugal's national museum, the **Museu Nacional de Arte Antiga,** on R. Janelas Verdes, Jardim 9 Abril (tel. 396 41 51). A representative survey of European painting ranges from

Gothic primitives to 18th-century French masterpieces (open Tues. 2-6pm, Wed.-Sun. 10am-6pm; 500$, students 250$). Buses #40 and 60 stop to the right of the museum exit and head back to the Baixa.

ALFAMA

The **Alfama**, Lisbon's medieval quarter, was the lone neighborhood to survive the famous 1755 earthquake intact. The *Bairro* slopes in tiers from the **Castelo de São Jorge**, facing the Rio Tejo. Between the Alfama and the Baixa is the quarter known as the **Mouraria** (Moorish quarter), established, ironically, after Dom Afonso Henriques and the Crusaders expelled the Moors in 1147. Watch out for Portuguese grandmothers gossiping, boys playing soccer on the hill, and—especially at night—muggers. It's best to visit by day and without handbags, cameras, or snatchables.

While the maze of streets in the Alfama can be entered by following any of the small uphill streets a few blocks east of the Baixa, the least confusing way to see the neighborhood is by climbing up R. Madalena, which begins two blocks away from the nearest corner of the Pr. Comércio. Hang a right when you see the **Igreja da Madalena** in the Largo da Madalena on your right. Take the R. Santo António da Sé and follow the tram tracks to the cleverly designed **Igreja de Santo António da Sé** (tel. 886 91 45), built in 1812 over the saint's alleged birthplace 800 years ago. The construction was funded with money collected by the city's children, who fashioned miniature altars bearing images of the saint to place on doorsteps—a custom re-enacted annually on June 13, the saint's feast day and Lisbon's largest holiday. The richly ornamented interior of the chapel is used for mass (open daily 7:30am-7:30pm; masses at 11am, 5, and 7pm). In the square beyond the church is the stolid 12th-century cathedral. Although the interior of the *sé* is unremarkable, its sheer antiquity and relic-filled treasury make it an intriguing visit. As a sign outside reads, "The *sé* is so old that no one really knows how old it is." (Open Mon.-Sat. 9am-5pm, treasury 10am-5pm.)

From the cathedral, follow the yellow signs for a winding uphill walk to the **Castelo de São Jorge**, which offers spectacular views of Lisbon and the ocean. Built in the 5th century by the Visigoths and enlarged by the 9th-century Moors, this castle was the primary lap of luxury for the royal family from the 14th to 16th centuries. The castle is a must-see; wander around the ruins and gawk at the cityscape below, or explore the ponds and gander at the exotic bird population of the castle gardens. Nooks for sitting, relaxing, and enjoying the view await after the long climb up the hill (open daily 9am-9pm; Oct.-March 9am-7pm; free).

On the way up to the castle, turn right onto Largo das Portas do Sol to reach the **Museu das Artes Decorativas**, Largo das Portas do Sol, 2 (tel. 346 04 73). Rooms filled with impressive furnishings and decorations convey a sense of 18th-century palatial luxury. The museum also features a tea room and bookstore with Portuguese art books in English. (Open Wed. and Fri.-Sun. 10am-5pm, Tues. and Thurs. 10am-8pm. 500$, under 12 or over 65 250$.)

On the far side of the castle, follow the main tram tracks along Tr. São Tomé (which changes names, winds uphill, and veers left as it goes along) to the **Igreja de São Vicente de Fora** built between 1582 and 1627, dedicated to Lisbon's patron saint. Ask to see the deathly still *sacristia*, with fabulous 18th-century walls inlaid with Sintra marble (open Tues.-Sun. 9am-noon and 3-5pm; free). The **Igreja de Santa Engrácia** is farther down toward the coast. Walk along R. São Vicente and keep right as the road branches. This church took almost 300 years to complete (1682-1966), giving rise to the famous expression, "endless like the building of Santa Engracia" (open Tues.-Sun. 10am-5pm). At the **Feira da Ladra** (flea market), which takes place in the church's backyard, the cries of merchants hawking used goods are drowned out by the din of a lively social scene. (Open Tues. and Sat. 6am-5pm. From the Baixa take bus #12 or tram #28 from the bottom of R. dos Correeiros, 150$.)

Continuing down the hill will put you on Av. Infanta Dom Henrique, which runs parallel to the Tejo. The avenue leads to the Estação Santa Apolónia. From outside the station, take the #13 bus for 10 minutes to **Convento da Madre de Deus**. The 16th-century convent complex houses the **Museu Nacional do Azulejo**, R. da Madre de

Deus, 4 (tel. 814 77 47), devoted to the classic Portuguese art of the *azulejo* tile, first introduced by the Moors. The Baroque interior of the church, reached through a fine Manueline doorway, is an explosion of oil paintings, *azulejos,* and gilded wood. The rapturous excess continues in the *coro alto* (chapter house) and the **Capela de Santo António,** where bright *azulejos* and paintings make the place eye-buggingly busy (complex open Wed.-Sun. 10am-6pm, Tues. 2-6pm; 350$, students 180$).

BELÉM

Belém is more of a suburb than a neighborhood of Lisbon, but its high concentration of monuments and museums makes it an important stop in any comprehensive tour of the capital. Belém is imperial glory at the service of culture; here, the opulence and extravagance of the Portuguese empire is showcased in a number of well-maintained museums and historical sites. To visit Belém is to understand *saudade,* the "nostalgic yearning" expressed musically in *fado.*

To get to Belém, take tram #15 from Pr. do Comércio (20min., 150$) or the train from Estação Cais do Sodré (every 15min., 10min., 110$). From the train station, cross over the tracks, cross the street, and go left. From the bus station, follow the avenue straight ahead. All museums are free before 2pm on Sunday.

Contemporary art buffs will bask in the glow of the gigantic, luminous **Centro Cultural de Belém** (tel. 361 24 00). With four pavilions regularly holding world-class exhibitions, several art galleries and a huge auditorium for concerts and performances, the *Centro* provides city-slick entertainment amid a slew of imperial landmarks (open daily 11am-8pm; check out their info-packed home page at http://www.fdesccccb.pt).

The **Mosteiro dos Jerónimos** (tel. 362 00 34), rises from the banks of the Tejo behind a lush garden. Established by King Dom Manuel I in 1502 to give thanks for the success of Vasco da Gama's voyage to India, the monastery stands as Portugal's most refined celebration of the Age of Discovery. The monastery showcases Portugal's native Manueline style, combining Gothic forms with early Renaissance details.

The main door of the church, to the right of the main monastery entrance, is a sculptured anachronism—Henry the Navigator mingles with the Twelve Apostles under carved canopies on both sides of the central column. The symbolic tombs of Luís de Camões and navigator Vasco da Gama lie in two opposing transepts. The octagonal cloisters drip with overdone stone carvings, a contrast to the simplicity of the rose gardens in the center. (Open Tues.-Sun. 10am-5pm. 400$, students 200$, Oct.-May 250$, free for students on holidays and Sun. 10am-2pm. Cloisters open Tues.-Sun. 10am-5pm. Free.)

Also in the monastery complex is the **Museu da Marinha** (tel. 362 00 10). This intriguing ship museum will bind you to its moorings; the Portuguese know ships. Globes from the mid-1600s show the boundaries of the continents with incredible accuracy (open Tues.-Sun. 10am-6pm; 400$, students 200$, free Sun. 10am-2pm). Next door, the cosmos whizzes before your eyes at the **Planetário Calouste Gulbenkian.** (Tel. 362 00 02. Shows in English and French Sat. and Sun at 5pm; in Portuguese Wed. and Thurs. at 11am, 3, and 4:15pm. 400$, ages 10-18 200$. Headphone rental for English and French shows 200$.)

Across from the monastery along the river is the **Padrão dos Descobrimentos** (tel. 301 62 28). Cross the street via the underground tunnel on the monastery side of the road. Built in 1960 to honor Prince Henry the Navigator, the monument's elevator transports visitors 70m up to a small terrace with great views. It hosts temporary exhibits and films (open Tues.-Sun. 9:30am-6:45pm; 320$, students 160$).

Back toward town is another nugget of the kings' former wealth, the **Museu Nacional dos Coches,** Pr. Afonso de Albuquerque (tel. 363 80 22), across from the train station, one block into town. The museum is the retirement home of 54 lavish carriages, ranging from the simpler ones of the late 18th century to the gilded Baroque coach that bore Queen Elizabeth II in this century (open Tues.-Sun. 10am-5:30pm; 450$, students 14-25, teachers, and seniors 300$). The **Palácio Nacional da Ajuda,** Largo da Ajuda (tel. 363 70 95), constructed in 1802, is a short bus ride away to the hills over-

looking Belém. The 54 chambers make a rather telling display of decadence (open Tues. and Thurs.-Sun. 10am-5pm, 250$; Sun. 10am-2pm free, students free). Take bus #14, 32, 42, or 60 from in front of the Museu Nacional dos Coches. Alternatively, tram #18 (Ajuda) stops behind the palace.

Last but by no means least is the **Torre de Belém** (tel. 362 00 34). Rising from the north bank of the Tejo and surrounded by the ocean on three sides, it's worth the 10-minute walk (heading away from Lisbon) along the coast from the monastery. Climb the narrow, winding steps to the top of the tower for a magnificent panoramic view (open Tues.-Sun. 10am-5pm; 400$, Oct.-May 250$, students 200$).

■ Entertainment

The *Agenda Cultural* and *Lisboa em,* free at kiosks in the Rossio and on R. Portas de Santo Antão (near Restauradores), as well as the tourist office, contain info on concerts, movies, plays, and bullfights, along with lists of museums, gardens, and libraries. The *Agenda Cultural* is also on the internet at http://www.consiste.pt/agenda.

BARS AND CLUBS

Tap into the Bairro Alto's **R. Norte, R. Diário Notícias,** and **R. da Atalaia**—but not before midnight—and choose your scene with care: smoking or non, punk or family style. With so many small clubs jammed into three or four short blocks, club-hopping means just crossing the street. Blaze your own trail. Most clubs don't charge a cover fee, but expect to pay about 350$ for a draft beer and at least 600$ for mixed drinks.

Termas D'Atalaia Bar, R. da Atalaia, 108 (tel. 342 47 74). One of the best, featuring drinks such as *orgasmo* and *sangue dos deuses* (blood of the gods, 600$). The quirky decor features a waterfall flowing down the front window and matchbox cars racing on the ceiling. Open Mon.-Sat. 10pm-3:30am.

Memorial, R. Gustavo de Matos Sequeira, 42A (tel. 396 88 91), one block south of R. Escola Politécnica in the Bairro Alto. This gay and lesbian disco-bar is far-out—in all senses. The lights and Europop blast from 10pm, but the fun starts after midnight. The 1000$ cover charge (except Mon. and Thurs.) includes two beers or one mixed drink. Live entertainment on Thurs. Open Tues.-Sun. 10pm-4am.

Frágil, R. da Atalaia, 126/8 (tel. 346 95 78), on the corner of R. da Atalaia and Tr. Queimada. Mostly dance music rocks a mixed gay and straight crowd of beautiful people. As the night goes on, they groove outside in the streets. Beer 600$, but hard liquor could empty your wallet. Open Mon.-Sat. 10:30pm-3:30am.

Os Três Pastorinhos, R. da Baroca, 111-113 (tel. 346 43 01). Pop, soul, and disco merge. Kaleidoscopic multimedia effects send the hard-partying (mostly student) crowd into a dancing frenzy. Open Tues.-Sun.11pm-4am.

Solar do Vinho do Porto, R. São Pedro de Alcântara, 45 (tel. 347 57 07). Not a club and not a bar, but something close enough—port-tasting in a sedate and mature setting. Glasses 130-2800$. Open Mon.-Fri. 10am-11:30pm, Sat. 11am-10:30pm.

Portas Largas, R. da Atalaia, 105 (tel. 346 63 79). A good ol' fashioned drinking establishment. Imbibe wisdom with your beer: signs say, "If you drink to forget, pay before you drink." Scrawl on the walls; hang with locals. Open daily 10am-2:30am.

Pé Sujo, Largo de St. Martinho, 6-7 (tel. 886 56 29), in the Alfama. Live Brazilian music nightly from 11:30pm-2am. Try the killer Brazilian drink *caipirinha* (made from sugarcane alcohol, 700$), or, if you're truly brave, down a *caipirosca* (with lime and vodka, 700$). Open Tues.-Sun. 10pm-2am.

Bar Artis, R. Diário Notícias, 95-97 (tel. 342 47 95). Sip beer with a cosmopolitan crowd under sultry red lights. Newspapers are on hand to peruse at this intimate but intense watering hole. Open Tues.-Sun. 10pm-2am.

CAFES

The **Pastelaria Suíça,** on the south corner of Pr. Dom Pedro IV in the Baixa (tel. 342 80 92), is a boisterous gathering place that stays mobbed until midnight. In the stylin'

PORTUGAL

Chiado neighborhood in the Bairro Alto, the 19th-century cafe **A Brasileira,** R. Garrett 120-122 (tel. 360 95 41; look for the bust of poet Fernando Pessoa outside), has the best after-dinner scene. Eça de Queiroz, another famous Portuguese literary figure who once patronized this coffeehouse, is long gone, but members of the new intelligentsia take his place nightly. Gold and green woodwork and silver sconces further color the scene (coffee 180-300$, alcoholic drinks about 600$; open daily 8am-2am).

FADO

Lisbon's trademark is the heart-wrenching *fado,* an expressive art which combines elements of singing and narrative poetry. *Fadistas* perform sensational tales of lost loves and faded glory. Their melancholy wailing is expressive of *saudade,* an emotion of nostalgia and yearning; indeed, listeners are supposed to feel the "knife turning in their hearts." On weekends, book in advance by calling the venues. The Bairro Alto, with many *fado* joints off **R. Misericordia** and on side streets radiating from the Museu de São Roque, is the best part of the city for top-quality *fado.*

Adega Machado, R. do Norte, 91 (tel. 346 00 95 or 342 87 13). Frequented by as many Portuguese as tourists. Dinner served (4600-6000$). Cover (with 2 drinks) 2500$. Open daily 8pm-3am. Nov.-May. closed Mon.

O Faia, R. Baroca, 54 (tel. 342 19 23). Typical Portuguese regional food combined with *fado* and folk dancing. Cover charge 2500$. Open Mon.-Sat. 8pm-2am.

Sr. Vinho, R. Meio à Lapa, 18 (tel. 397 26 81 or 397 74 56), in nearby Madregoa. Minimum food and drink charge 2500$, but with appetizers at 1200-2800$, it's not hard to reach. Open Mon.-Sat. 8:30pm-2:30am.

THEATER AND CONCERTS

The **Teatro Nacional de Dona Maria II,** (tel. 347 22 26) at Pr. Dom Pedro IV, stages performances of classical Portuguese and foreign plays (tickets 700-2000$, 50% student discount). Opera reigns at Lisbon's largest theater, the **Teatro Nacional de São Carlos,** R. Serpa Pinto, 9 (tel. 346 84 08; open 1-7pm), near the Museo do Chiado in the Bairro Alto, from late September through mid-June. The **Fundação Calouste Gulbenkian,** Av. Berna, 24 (tel. 793 51 31), also sponsors classical and jazz concerts year-round. When the pop heavies come to town (Sinéad, the Cranberries, Tina Turner),

---

The Many Lives of the Portuguese Feiras

While most nightlife in Lisbon revolves around the bars and *casas de fado,* those seeking more active revelry in June won't be disappointed. Open-air *feiras* (fairs)—smorgasbords of eating, drinking, live music, and dancing—abound. There's a lively one called *Oreal* at **Campo das Cebolas,** near the waterfront in the Alfama (open June Mon.-Fri. 10pm-1am, Sat.-Sun. 10pm-3am). Don't miss the *feira* in the **Praça Camões** in the Bairro Alto (take the Elevador da Glória, or walk up R. Garrett), which goes until 3am every night in June. After savoring *farturas* (Portuguese donuts; 190$) and Sagres beer (200$), pick up your feet and join in the traditional Portuguese dancing. On the night of June 12, the streets become a mega-dance floor for the huge **Festa de Santo António**—banners are strung between streetlights and confetti falls like snow.

More commercial *feiras* combine shopping and cultural involvement. The open-air markets come in many varieties, and bargaining is the name of the game. Bookworms burrow for three glorious weeks in the **Feira do Livro** (in the Baixa from late May to early June). In June, the Alcântara holds the **Feira Internacional de Lisboa,** while in July and August the **Feira de Mar de Cascais** and the **Feira de Artesania de Estoril** take place near the casino.

Year-round *feiras* include the **Feira de Oeiras** (Antiques) on the fourth Sunday of every month, and the **Feira de Carcanelos** for clothes (Thurs. 8am-2pm). Packrats should catch the **Feira da Ladra** (flea market), held at Campo de Santa Clara (Tues. and Sat. 7am-3pm; take bus #12 or tram #28).

they play at the **Coliseu dos Recreios,** R. Porta de Sto. Antâo, 92 (tel. 346 16 77), which is easily accessible by metro (M: Restauradores).

Outside of the city, the **Centro Cultural de Belém,** Pr. do Império (tel. 361 24 00), across from the Mosteiro dos Jerónimos, hosts a wide variety of performances ranging from classical music concerts to modern dance recitals to Tony Bennett extravaganzas. Take the train from Estação Cais do Sodré (every 20min., 15 min., 110$); bus #27, 28, 29, 43, 49, or 51 (150$); or tram #15, 16, or 17 (150$). **Tickets** for major events are available from box offices or the **Agência de Bilhetes dos Espectáculos Públicos (ABEP)** kiosk across from the Pr. Restauradores tourist office.

OTHER FUN THINGS TO DO

Portuguese **bullfights** (differing from the Spanish variety in that the bull is not killed) take place most Thursday nights from the end of June to the end of September at the **Praça de Touros de Lisboa** at Campo Pequeno (tel. 793 24 42) from 10am-2am (take buses #44, 45, 83, or 1; or M: Campo Grande).

To refresh your sea legs, try a two-hour **cruise** on the Tejo. The boat leaves from the Estação Fluvial Terreiro Paço, off the Pr. Comércio (tel. 887 50 58). The boats run from April-October and leave at 3pm.

If sports are your thing, catch a *futebol* (soccer) match. Lisbon has two professional teams featuring some of the world's finest players: **Benfica** at the Stadium of Light (tel. 726 03 21; M: Colégio Militar Luz), and **Sporting** at Alvalade Stadium (tel. 759 94 59; M: Campo Grande). Check the APEB kiosk in Pr. Restauradores or the sports newspaper *A Bola.*

If all else fails, try the **movie theater** (tel. 242 25 23), at the corner of Av. Liberdade and Av. dos Condes, directly across the square from the Pr. Restauradores tourist office. American movies are shown with Portuguese subtitles (4 movies per day, 550$, Mon. and matinees 400$).

PORTUGAL

Estremadura

Estremadura envelops Lisbon with sultry beaches and serene fields. The quintessence of provincial Portugal, its *vilas* are anything but extreme and make ideal, relaxing daytrips from Lisbon. Costa de Lisboa's shores tempt daytrippers and Wimbledon-types to suburban beach towns Estoril and Cascais, and to the patrician castles of Sintra, Queluz, and Mafra. Below the Rio Tejo, south of Lisbon, the Costa Azul (Blue Coast) is a surprisingly uncrowded stretch. Just to the north of the Costa Azul, Setúbal serves as a base for excursions to the fishing village of Sesimbra, the beaches of Tróia, and the sparkling sands of the Serra da Arrábida. Jagged cliffs and whitewashed fishing villages line the Costa de Prata (Silver Coast), north of Lisbon. Throngs of tourists and summer residents populate Nazaré and Peniche, while inland towns Óbidos and Alcobaça still embrace local traditions and coddle their monasteries and medieval remains. Although accommodations are expensive in these smaller towns, camping is available, and most towns are serviced by a reliable transportation network branching out from Lisbon.

■ Near Lisbon

Harbored on the Atlantic coast just west of Lisbon, the twin towns of Estoril and Cascais bask in their reputations as playgrounds for the rich and beautiful. Spending a night in the shadow of luxury resorts and swank country clubs might stun your wallet, but don't dream of passing up a day at the beach. Be warned, however, that everyone else in Lisbon has the same plan; you might try avoiding Estoril and Cascais on weekends, when the bronzed-flesh to bronzed-sand ratio skyrockets. Consider taking the Cascais-bound train from Lisbon's **Estação do Sodré** (about every 20min., 5:30am-2:30am, 30min., 180$) to Estoril, then treat yourself to a 20-minute walk along the elegant seaside promenade connecting the two towns.

ESTORIL

With a bustling casino, stately villas, and beautiful beaches, Estoril enjoys a reputation of luxury. Luckily, the greatest luxuries can be savored at little to no cost: Estoril's greatest assets are natural. The **Praia Estoril Tamariz** beach greets your arrival, while the palm-studded **Parque do Estoril** blooms behind you. At the recently renovated **tourist office,** Arcada do Parque (tel. 466 38 13; fax 467 22 80), on the park side opposite the tunnel from the train station, multi-lingual attendants offer detailed maps and schedules of events for the entire **Costa do Estoril,** including both Estoril and Cascais (open Mon.-Sat. 9am-7pm, Sun 10am-6pm). Bus #41B to Sintra departs from a stop next to the train station (every hr., 6am-11pm, 30min., 300$). **Police** are on Av. Biarritz (tel. 468 13 96). In an **emergency,** dial 115.

If you get bored of the beach scene, walk through the park to the **Casino Estoril** (tel. 468 45 21), if not to spend money, then to gawk at the gaming palace. Don't be fooled by the 70s exterior; it houses sparkling game rooms, a glitzy music hall and a well-stocked bar. (Foreigners must cough up a passport. Must be at least 18 years old for the slots and 21 for the game room. Open 3pm-3am. Free admission to bingo and slot machine rooms, game room 500$.)

If you get lucky at the casino (or are stranded with no way back to Lisbon), cash in some chips and head over to the recently renovated **Residencial São Cristóvão,** Av. Marginal, 7079 (tel./fax 468 09 13). Facing the park, turn right off the train platform; about one block on your right you'll find bright, airy rooms. (Continental breakfast and private parking included. Doubles 8000-10,000$, with shower 10,000-12,000$.) Farther from the beach is **Residencial Smart,** R. Maestro Lacerda, 6 (tel. 468 21 64). Follow Av. Marginal toward Lisbon past the Paris Hotel to the corner of Av. Bombeiros Voluntários and make a left. Walk three blocks uphill to R. Maestro Lacerda and follow the street three blocks until you see the *pensão* on the left. It has 13

rooms decorated in funky bright colors overlooking gorgeous grounds (all rooms are doubles: with shower 5000-7000$, with bathroom 6000-8000$, for 1 person 5000-7000$; breakfast and parking included). The best options for budget meals are the cafeteria-like stands along the beach. Several **bars** line the beaches. For a sit-down (read: pricey) meal, try the restaurants in the **Arcados do Parque** lining the park. Consider saving your appetite: more options await in Cascais.

CASCAIS

The favorite resort of celebrities, heads of state, and Third World dictators (the Pinochet family reputedly resides here), Cascais is euphemistically known as "a fishing village." If you reach Cascais by foot from Estoril, take a right at the fork in the promenade and follow the train tracks up to the station on the Largo do Estação. From the front of the train station, cross the square and take a right at the McDonald's onto Av. Valbom. The **tourist office,** Avenida dos Combatentes, 25 (tel. 486 82 04), on the site of an archeological dig, has a small sign across the street from where Av. Valbom ends. The English-speaking staff will make calls to find you a budget *quarto* (room prices start at 5000$; open June 1-Sept. 15 9am-8pm; Sept. 16-May 31 9am-7pm). **Police** are on R. Afonso Sanches (tel. 486 11 27). The **emergency** number is 112. **Buses** leave from outside the train station and #403 services Sintra (11 per day, 1 hr., 300$) and #415 runs to Praia do Guincho (every hr. beginning at 7:45am, 20 min., 180$). Tickets may be purchased in a booth outside the station. Complementing its four major beaches—all no more than a few steps from town—is a small pedestrian **shopping district** (left off Av. Combatentes heading from the tourist office to the beach).

Cascais has several historic sites and parks in addition to its renowned beaches. To reach the lush municipal garden, **Parque de Gandainha,** walk away from Estoril along the coast for 10 minutes on Av. Dom Carlos, which turns into Av. Rei Humberto de Itália (open Tues.-Sun. 9am-6pm). About 1km farther out of town (a 20min. walk along Av. Rei Humberto de Itália) lies the **Boca do Inferno** (Mouth of Hell), a huge cleft carved in the rock by the incessant Atlantic surf. This ominous sight is often swamped with tourists, but the surrounding rocky turf sprinkled with red sand makes a nice perch for sitting and marveling at the sea in peace. The **Praia do Guincho,** 8km farther west of Cascais, is considered to be one of the best surfing beaches in the world. Buses to Praia do Guincho leave from the train station in Cascais (see above). Two kilometers farther from Praia do Guincho, at a bend flanked by small restaurants, the road takes you to **Praia do Abano.**

Although it's cheaper to make Cascais a daytrip, if you get hooked or are too sunburned to move, bed down at **Residencial Parsi,** R. Afonso Sanches, 8 (tel. 484 57 44), off the beachfront Pr. 5 do Outubro. You'll pay the price for these slick rooms, all with TV and some with stunning views of the *praça* and the ocean (doubles with shower 5000-8000$; breakfast included; credit cards accepted). A cheaper option is camping in Orbitur's **Parque de Campismo do Guincho** (tel. 487 10 14), in the nearby town of Areia, near the Praia do Guincho.

Perhaps the least expensive (and most adventuresome) food option is to hike out to the Boca de Inferno, assemble a meal at one of the various food stands, and have a picnic (or a drink) on the rocks. The **Quiosque da Boca do Inferno** sells generous bags of pistachios and sunflower seeds (150$), as well as *caracois* (snails, 450$) and *sandes*. Indulge your hummus cravings at **Joshua's Shoarma Grill,** R. Visconde da Luz, 19 (tel. 484 30 64), left on R. Visconde da Luz, half a block uphill from the tourist office's back door. They have falafel (420$) and other delicacies in this upbeat Middle Eastern joint (open Mon.-Fri. noon-4pm and 6pm-2am, Sat.-Sun. 1pm-2am).

Cabo da Roca

A 3km hike (1hr.) or bus ride from Cascais, **Cabo da Roca** is the westernmost point on the European continent. The cape offers spectacular views of the ocean smashing against the cliffs. Certificates from the on-site tourist office will officially document

PORTUGAL

your achievement. It's often mobbed on Sundays. The cape is accessible by the bus from Cascais to Sintra (see Cascais, p. 545).

■ Sintra

British Romantic Lord Byron called Sintra a "glorious Eden" in the epic poem *Childe Harold*. His adulation made mountainous Sintra a chic destination for 19th century aristocrats and ladies. These days, proletarians and aristocrats alike admire Sintra's playground of castles. The colorfully amalgamated Palácolid Pena and the Castelo des Mouros, mossy and traditional, sit on the same hill, drawing wide eyes and appreciative silence. From either pinnacle, don't look down, but out, onto the breathtaking panorama of the valleys, the city of Lisbon, and the Atlantic.

ORIENTATION AND PRACTICAL INFORMATION

Sintra, 30km northwest of Lisbon and 15km north of Estoril, is connected by train to Lisbon's Estação Rossio (every 15min., 45min., 180$). Drivers should take the Estoril/ Cascais motorway out of Lisbon and pick up the IC19 road to Sintra. The town is split into two parts: a modern section around the train station, where most budget accommodations and banks are located, and **Sintra Vila,** where the historic sites perch on the mountainside. To get to the old town (15min.), take a left out of the train station and a right at the next intersection. At the bottom of the hill, take a left at the castle-like **Câmara Municipal** (tel. 923 40 21), and follow the road around the curve. Go up the small hill, and you will be staring at the **Praça da República,** with the **Palácio Nacional** on your right and a blue house directly in front of you. Be aware that theft is common in this heavily touristed area; consider stowing your gear in lockers at the Estação Rossio before you come (open daily 8:30am-11:30pm, 450$).

Tourist Office: Pr. República (tel. 923 11 57; fax 923 51 76). From the Pr. República with the palace on your right, walk straight ahead one block; the tourist office is beyond the palace in a columned marble building. English-speaking staff provides a map and list of accommodations. They can also help you find a *quarto* (3500-8000$). Upstairs is the **regional museum;** check out exhibits while waiting. The office also maintains a booth at the train station (tel. 924 16 23). Open daily 9am-8pm; Oct.-May 9am-7pm. Free.

Currency exchange: Banco Totta e Açores, R. Padarias, 4 (tel. 924 19 19), on a side street off the main *praça*. Has an **ATM.** Open Mon.-Fri. 8:30am-noon and 1-3pm. ATMs are also available to the right of the train station, at **Banco Nacional Ultra-marinho** (tel. 923 31 00).

Trains: Estação de Caminhos de Ferro, Av. Dr. Miguel Bombarda (tel. 923 26 05). To Lisbon's Estação Rossio (every 15min., 40min., 180$). There is no direct service to Estoril or Cascais and no locker service available.

Buses: Rodoviária, Av. Dr. Miguel Bombarda (tel. 921 03 81), across the street from the train station. Open 7am-8pm. To Cascais and Cabo da Roca (9 per day, 1 hr., 550$) and Estoril (13 per day, 40min., 320$). Green-and-white **Mafrense** buses depart from stops one block to the right as you exit the train station. To Mafra (11 per day, 45min., 350$), with connections to points north.

Hospital: Centro de Saúde de Sintra, Largo Dr. Gregório Almeida (tel. 923 34 00).

Police: R. João de Deus (tel. 923 07 61), behind the train station.

Emergency: tel. 112.

Post Office: Pr. República, 26 (tel. 924 15 90), on the right en route to the tourist office. Small, with local **telephones,** Posta Restante (indicate Sintra *Vila*). Open Mon.-Fri. 9am-noon and 2:30-6pm. **Postal Code:** 2710.

Telephone code: (0)1.

ACCOMMODATIONS AND CAMPING

Sintra is easily accessible as a day trip from Lisbon. If you choose to stay, the youth hostel has a beautiful location (albeit way, way uphill) and cheap rates; however, *pen-*

sões are pricier here than almost anywhere else in the country. The tourist office can provide a list of *quartos* (2500-8000$).

Pousada da Juventude de Sintra (HI), Sta. Eufémia (tel./fax 924 12 10), a hard-core uphill hike (2km) out of Sintra to the town of Sta. Eufémia, adjacent to the town of São Pedro. Shave the climb to 15min. by taking the bus from the train station (180$) or from the stop in the old town (exit the tourist office and take a left turn in the *praça;* the stop is on the left across from a fountain) to São Pedro, where you should get off across from the Banco Crédito Predial Português (look for the big blue neon letters). Take a right and walk 1km (15-20min.) to the hostel, or hail a taxi (1100$ weekdays, 1400$ weekends) in front of the Palácio Nacional. Seated amid flowering meadows, the hostel has a dining room, sitting room, TV with VCR and tapes, stereo, and winter heating. Fifty dorm beds (1200-1400$) and 3 family-sized rooms (2700$). Reception open 9am-noon and 6pm-midnight. Make the schlep worth your while: call before you come.

Pensão Nova Sintra, Largo Afonso de Albuquerque, 25 (tel. 923 02 20), take a right out of the train station; it's on your left after one block. A charming terrace and tidy rooms grace this recently renovated *pensão.* Singles 2500-3200$; doubles 4500-5500$. Breakfast included. Reservations necessary in summer. Visa.

Piela's, R. João de Deus, 70-72 (tel. 924 16 91), make a left out of the train station and another left around the bend onto the street heading uphill behind the station. Piela's 6 rooms are spacious, clean and well-furnished, though with unsightly views of the station. Friendly, English-speaking owner. Cafe with pool table and game room. Singles 4000-5000$; doubles 5000-6000$. Winter 3000-4000$; 4000-5000$.

Camping: Parque de Campismo da Praia Grande (tel. 929 05 81), on the Atlantic coast, about 12km from Sintra. 300$ per person. Reception open until 7pm.

FOOD

Cheap places crowd the street parallel to the train station on the other side of the tracks. In the old town, narrow side streets off the Praga sa República such as **R. das Padárias,** near the Palácio Nacional, host a wider range of eateries. Check out the daily **mercado municipal** (8am-1pm) in the small square behind the buildings facing the Palácio Nacional. On the second and fourth Sundays of every month, take the bus from the train station to the nearby town of São Pedro (15min., 180$) for a spectacular **regional market.**

Adega dos Caves, R. da Pendoa, 2-10, Largo da Vila Velha da Sintra (tel./fax 923 08 48), along an *escadinha* (stair alley) across the Palácio Nacional. Steer clear of the pricey "tourist menu," and savor house specialties like *bacalhav à caves* (cod, 1200$). Visit the snack bar next door for drinks and fast food. After 9pm on Thurs. and Sun., chill in the basement bar to the sound of live Portuguese folk music. Restaurant open daily 8am-10pm. Major credit cards accepted.

Casa da Piriquita, R. Padarias, 1 (tel. 923 06 26), up a small side street off the República. Inspiring bakery, snack bar, and candy counter flanked by a marble-floored coffee and tea room. Sintra's tiny traditional pastries with cheese and cinnamon or egg filling (120-200$ each) are available for take-out and are a welcome snack after an arduous climb up the mountain. Open Thurs.-Tues. 9am-10:30pm.

Casa da Avó, R. Visconde de Monserrate, 44 (tel. 923 12 80). Heading 1 block down the hill from Pr. República, turn right on R. Monserrate; the Casa with its adjacent *pastelaria* (bakery) is around the bend past the new toy museum on the right. Fewer tourists than most local restaurants, thus all the more *frango assado* (roast chicken 650$) for you. *Pratos do dia* up to 1400$, pitcher of *vinho da casa* 270$. Open Fri.-Wed. 8am-10pm.

SIGHTS

The road from the train station ambles and twists up the mountainside past the **Câmara Municipal** and its lush gardens and past the **Parque da Liberdade** on the left, then flattens out at the old city and the **Palácio Nacional de Sintra** (a.k.a. Paço Real

or Pálacio da Vila; tel. 923 0085) in the **Praça da República** (tel. 923 00 85). Once the summer residence of Moorish sultans and their harems, the *paço* and its complex gardens were torn down during the Reconquista and rebuilt in a unique mix of Moorish, Gothic, and Manueline styles. Its more than 20 rooms run the gamut from the *azulejo*-covered **Sala dos Árabes** (Hall of the Arabs) to the gilded **Capela** (Chapel). Two rooms not to miss are the **Sala dos Cisnes** (Hall of Swans) and the **Sala das Pêgas** (Hall of Magpies) which, according to legend, acquired its name when Dom João I's wife caught him kissing one of the ladies of the court. Although he claimed that it was merely a gesture of friendship, the court ladies ("magpies," according to the king) made it a subject of scandalous gossip. (Open Thurs.-Tues. 10am-1pm and 2-5pm. 400$, with student ID 200$.)

The **Sintra Museu de Arte Moderna** houses contemporary works by Andy Warhol, Morris Louis, and Gerhard Richters (among others) in a cheerful *belle-époque* building. (Open Wed.-Sun. 10am-6pm, Tues. 2-6pm. 600$, 300$ for students, free for children under 10.) The **Anjos Teixeira Museum-House** (tel. 923 61 23), nestled in the foothills below the Praga da República, displays sculptures by one of Portugal's most revered artists, Master Anjos Teixeira. His son, sculptor Pedro Anjos Teixeira, lives and works in the precinct and greets visitors in person (open Tues.-Fri. 9:30am-1pm and 2-6pm; weekends 2-6pm).

The 3km ascent to the **Palácio da Pena** and the **Castelo dos Mouros** (crowning one of the highest peaks in the Sintra range) begins at the Palácio Nacional. The hike uphill takes about 90min. If you do walk, be sure to leave Sintra Vila by about 1pm to have time to visit all the sites up top. Take the road that begins to the left of the tourist office and follow the blue signs up the mountain. Beware the *escadinha* (stairs alley) shortcut: you might get lost. The climb is steep and strenuous, so bring a full water bottle. Don't attempt the hike if you're tired, lazy, very pregnant, or in poor health. If pressed for time (or energy), you'll find taxis swarming outside the Palácio Nacional (one way; 1200$ weekdays, 1400$ weekends and holidays). A costlier shuttle runs from the tourist office to the Moorish Castle (every 45min., 10min., 500$ roundtrip). From the gate, walk 15min. uphill to see the Palácio. Although *Let's Go* does not recommend it, some travelers choose to hitch-hike up the road. Hit the Palácio first—it's mostly downhill from there.

The **Palácio da Pena** was built in the 1840s by Prince Ferdinand, the queen's German consort, on the site of a 17th-century convent. Nostalgic for his country, the prince commissioned an obscure German architect to combine the aesthetic heritages of both Germany and Portugal. The fantastic result is a Bavarian castle embellished with Arabic minarets, Russian onion domes, Gothic turrets, Manueline windows, and a Renaissance dome. Interior highlights—decked in *chinoiserie* and other regalia of Romantic Orientalism—include the chapel, the fully-furnished kitchen and Her Majesty's toilet, done entirely in *azulejo*. (Open Tues.-Sun. 10am-6pm; in winter Tues.-Sun. 2-4:30pm. 600$, students 400$, off season 200$.)

Signs point to the ruins of the **Castelo dos Mouros,** perched on the boulder-studded peaks towering over Sintra. Stroll along the walls of the 16th-century fortress and clamber up its turrets for the splendid view. On a clear day you can see the Atlantic and the neighboring Palácio da Pena (open daily 10am-7pm; free).

The winding *peões* (pedestrian paths) will bring you down to São Pedro, where you can take a bus back down or walk. Kilometers of well-kept paths run through a eucalyptus forest and the strollable **Parque da Pena.** Keep your eyes open for the **cruz alta** (stone cross) and the **Igreja de São Pedro.**

■ Near Sintra

QUELUZ

The reason to visit the residential suburb of Queluz, 14km west of Lisbon and about that far south of Sintra, is the amazing **Palácio Nacional de Queluz,** built by order of Dom Pedro III in the late 18th century. Portuguese architect Mateus Vicente de

Oliveira and French sculptor João Baptista Robillan collaborated to create this pink-and-white rococo wedding cake of a palace. The building and furnishings are clearly French-inspired; the well-ordered, albeit slightly overgrown garden is neoclassical. Highlights include the ornate **Sala dos Embaixadores,** with its gilded thrones and Chinese vases and the purely Portuguese *azulejo*-lined canal in the garden. Of historical interest is the **Quarto Don Quixote:** the room where Dom Pedro I, first emperor of Brazil, took his first and last breaths. (Open June-Sept. 10am-1pm and 2-5:30pm; Oct.-May 10am-1pm and 2-5pm. 400$, students, senior citizens, and children under 14 200$. Garden 50$.) To get here from Lisbon by **train,** take the Sintra line from Estação Rossio and get off at the Queluz-Belas (not the Queluz-Massomá!) stop (every 15min., 30 min., 110$). Turn left from the station and walk down Av. da República. Follow the signs to the palace; its a 10-minute walk downhill.

MAFRA

The sleepy, otherwise unremarkable town of Mafra (north of Sintra) is home to one of Portugal's most impressive sites and one of Europe's largest historical buildings, the **Palácio Nacional** complex. Like Spain's El Escorial, it incorporates a palace, royal library, marvelous cathedral-sized church, and hospital. The monstrous 2000-room building took 50,000 workers 13 years (1713-1726) to complete, under the whip of architect Johann Friedrich Ludwig. This Herculean task gave rise to a style of sculptur known as the Mafra School.

The exterior of the magnificent Baroque **igreja** (tel. 81 18 88) has fallen into grime-covered disrepair, but the belfries, two of the finest in Europe, still echo eloquence. Legend has it that Emperor Dom João V, upon hearing the astronomical price of one bell tower, replied, "I didn't expect it to be that cheap. I'll have two." Although he may have meant to be sarcastic, the literally minded architects actually cast 217 tons of bronze bells. The design for the church's ornate dome was lifted from Bernini's unexecuted plan for St. Peter's in Rome. The richly decorated interior—with bas-reliefs and statues of Carrara marble—is one of Portugal's gems.

To access the building's seemingly interminable corridors and extravagant living quarters, go through the door to the right of the church exit. The **Sala dos Troféus** (Trophy Room), furnished with stag antlers and skins from the chandeliers to the chairs, flaunts its purpose ably. The **biblioteca** (library) headlines with 38,000 volumes printed in the 16th, 17th, and 18th centuries, displayed on 290 feet of Rococo shelves. (Complex open Wed.-Mon. 10am-1pm and 2-5pm, closed on national holidays. 300$, students free. Tour in Portuguese.)

To reach the **tourist office** (tel. 81 20 23), in the Auditório Municipal Beatriz Costa building, Av. 25 de Abril, take a right off the main steps of the palace and bear left, then look for the blue turismo sign. The office is on your right in a beige stucco building with a fountain in front. The staff distributes brochures and info on accommodations in surrounding areas—Mafra has only one hotel—such as the popular coastal town of Ericeira. (Open Mon.-Fri. 9:30am-7:30pm, Sat.-Sun. 9:30am-1pm and 2:30-7:30pm.) For **police,** call 521 24. The **telephone code** is (0)61.

Green and white Mafrense **buses** stop in the square in front of the palace. They serve Lisbon's Largo Martim Moniz in the Mouraria off Pr. Figueira. The **train** goes to Sintra (1 per hr., 1 hr., 350$). If you plan on taking the train to Mafra from Lisbon's Estação Sta. Apolónia, be prepared for a 2hr. walk to Mafra; the station is way, way out in the countryside (1 per hr., 1½hr., 510$).

■ Setúbal

Granted, Setúbal's Ford and Renault factories have created a noisy commercial center surrounded by no-nonsense sugar cane and cork tree plantations, but wait—don't turn the page yet. Some of the brightest *azulejo*-covered alleys in Portugal are missed by tourists who head straight for the Algarve. Setúbal makes a perfect base for daytrips to the mountainous Serra da Arrábida, the beaches of Tróia and Figueirinha, and

PORTUGAL

the protected estuaries of the Rio Tejo. The lapping waters of the largely rural Costa Azul beckon. There are more than ten small, quirky cities within an hour's drive (or bus ride), each with its own combination of beaches, nature reserves, and medieval or ancient ruins.

Orientation and Practical Information Many shops and pensões are located along **Avenida Luisa Todi,** a loud boulevard with a strip of park and cafes down its middle, running through the city parallel to the **Rio Sado.** North of Av. Todi lies a dense pedestrian district of shops and restaurants centered around the pristine **Praça du Bocage,** named after one of Setúbal's finest 19th-century poets. Going north out of Pr. Bocage takes you to another main thoroughfare, **Avenida do 5 de Outubro.** Several blocks farther east is the bus station and a few blocks farther the **Praça do Quebedo,** where the **tourist office** sits. North of Pr. Quebedo along Av. da Portela is the **train station,** in Pr. Brasil.

The tourist office is the **Posto de Turismo Municipal** (tel. 53 42 22), off Pr. Quebedo. Out of the bus station, take two lefts onto Av. 5 de Outubro; take your first right and a quick left; the office is on your left. Out of the train station, take your first left onto Av. da Portela, which will lead into Pr. Quebedo. Open Mon.-Fri. 9am-12:30pm and 2-5:30pm. **Região de Turismo da Costa Azul office,** Tr. Frei Gaspar, 10 (tel. 52 42 84), off Av. Todi. Open Tues.-Fri. 9am-7pm Mon., Sat. 9am-12:30pm and 2-7pm, Sun. 9am-12:30pm. **Currency exchange** can be found at any of the numerous banks along Av. Todi. For after-hours banking, crowd in with the other tourists at Agência de Câmbios Central, Av. Todi, 226 (tel. 53 43 36). Open Mon.-Sat. 9am-7:30pm, Sun. 9am-1pm. For your transportation needs, **trains** are run by Estação de Setúbal, Pr. Brasil (tel. 52 68 45). To: Lisbon (31 per day, 1½hr., 300$); Faro (4 per day, 4hr., 1350$); Évora (13 per day, 2hr., 850$). You can find **buses** at Rodoviária do Alentejo, Av. 5 de Outubro, 44 (tel. 52 50 51). From the city tourist office, walk up the street facing traffic and turn left. To: Lisbon (every 30min., 1hr., 550$); Évora (5 per day, 2½hr., 820$); Faro (7 per day, 4hr., 1700$); Porto (6 per day, 6hr., 1910$), and Vila Nova de Milfontes (6 per day, 3hr., 1190$). **Luggage Storage** is also available here, 90$ per bag per day. For **ferries,** try Transado, Doca do Comércio (tel. 201 52), off Av. Todi at the east end of the waterfront. Trips run back and forth run Setúbal-Tróia (4am-2pm, 15min., 130$ per person, 80$ per child, 500$ per car, driver included). Call **taxis** at tel. 333 34, 314 13, 523 55, or 522 090. Medical attention is available at the **Hospital,** R. Camilo Castelo Branco (tel. 52 28 22). The **police** are located at Av. Todi (tel. 52 20 22), at the corner with Av. 22 de Dezembro, on the roundabout across the street from the Mercado Municipal. In an **emergency,** dial 112. The **post office** on Av. Mariano de Carvalho (tel. 52 27 78) is on the corner with Av. 22 de Dezembro. Open for Posta Restante and **telephones** Mon.-Fri. 8:30am-6pm. A branch office is in Pr. Bocage (tel. 52 55 55). No Posta Restante. Open Mon.-Fri. 9am-12:30pm and 2-6pm. **Postal code:** 2900. **Telephone code:** (0)65.

Accommodations and Food Summer prices are higher, but finding space for the night is no problem. Several *pensões* in town almost always have vacancies. **Centro de Juventude de Setúbal** (tel. 53 27 78, 53 28 35), is at Largo José Afonso. Heading left on the river side of Av. Tali, hang a right on Rodos Pescadores do Mar and make your first right; the hostel is on the corner. Spic 'n' span rooms in a new government-sponsored youth center. Dorm space in doubles 1200$ per person, doubles with bath 3200$. For reservations call 4pm-midnight. **Residencial Alentejana,** Av. Todi, 124, 2nd fl. (tel. 21 398), has an odd-smelling hallway but small and well-furnished rooms. Clean common bathrooms with plenty of hot water—no need to pay extra for a basic shower. Request a room off the street to avoid the noise from the racetrack that is Av. Todi (singles 1700$; doubles 2400$, with shower 3000$). Get-away-from-it-all types should escape to one of the many **campsites** in the Parque Natural da Arrábida or one of the smaller campsites near Setúbal in Azeitão or Sesimbra. Inquire at the tourist office for locations and rates. If you must stay in Setúbal, try **Toca do Pai Lopes,** R. Praia da Saúde (tel. 52 24 75), run by the Câmara Municipal de

Setúbal, at the west end of Av. Todi on the road to Outão. Right on the beach. Reception open June-Aug. daily 8am-10pm; Sept.-May 9am-9pm. June-Aug. 250$ per person and per car, 200$ per tent. Sept.-May: 180$; 130$. Free hot showers.

Hit the jackpot in the old town, especially off **R. A. Castelões** (turn off Pr. Bocage by the post office). Fresh grilled seafood costs more on Av. Todi. **Groceries** and fresh baked goods are at **Pingo Doce,** Av. Todi, 149 (tel. 52 61 05; open daily 8am-9pm). Next door, the **Mercado Municipal** vends at open stands on the corner of R. Ocidental do Mercado and Av. Todi. Setúbal's standard restaurants are located along Av. Todi across from the Doca do Comércio. One of these is **Jardim de Inverno,** R. Alvaro Luz, 48-50 (tel. 393 73), off R. A. Castelões. Green garden, walls, and lights—a go signal for this crazy cool, dirt-cheap *cafeteira-restaurante-bar. Menú* 900$. Ask about holiday festival specials—São João in late June brings a plate of fried pork, salad, fries, and a glass of *sangria* for 600$. Open Mon.-Fri. 8am-11:30pm, Sat.-Sun. 8am-3pm. **Casa de Santiago,** Av. Todi, 92 (tel. 216 88). What do all locals order when they dine at the self-proclaimed *rei do choco frito?* You guessed it. Devour their generous *meio dose* of the *choco frito* (fried cuttlefish) for 800$.

Sights and Entertainment Setúbal is known for fast cars, not the fast lane. The most impressive sight in town is the **Castelo de São Filipe,** a more than 30-minute uphill walk away. Take Av. Todi to its western end, turn right, continue to the crossroads, and then ascend R. Estrada do Castelo about 600m. If King Felipe II of Spain had known in 1590 that 400 years later it would be a luxury *pousada,* he certainly would have installed more bathrooms. To the west of town (follow R. Bocage west from the *praça*), crumbling old houses are tiled with over 100 different kinds of *azulejos,* some covered with melted glass, others protruding from the wall. Back in town, the **Igreja de Jesús,** begun in the 15th century as part of a larger monastic complex, resides at Pr. Miguel Bombarda at the western end of Av. 5 de Outubro. Maritime decorations and faux-rope pillars mark the beginnings of the Manueline style.

For city-slicker entertainment, check out the **Forum Municipal Luisa Todi,** Av. Todi, 61-61 (tel. 52 21 27), which shows both artsy and popular movies and community-produced plays. (Ticket office open daily 11am-10pm on show days, 11am-7pm on off days. 300$). The **Feira do Cinema** brings film screenings and other revelry during the first two weeks of June. In the last week of July and first week of August, **Feira de Santiago** is an industrial and agricultural extravaganza. More entertaining are the amusement park, bullfighting, and folk dancing that accompany it. The **Feira de Azeitão,** an artisan fair in neighboring Azeitão (accessible by local bus), takes place the first Sunday of each month.

The real sights around Setúbal are the natural ones. Get out of town to experience the **beaches** of peninsular **Tróia,** a 15-minute ferry ride away (140$, children 80$, 500$ per car, driver included). To the west of Setúbal is a large nature preserve, the **Parque Natural da Arrábida,** which includes a variety of nature trails (ask the tourist office for a copy of *A Walking Guide to Arrábida and Sado*) and the fabulously pristine **Praia da Figueirinha.**

Outdoor adventurers (hopefully on generous grants from *National Geographic*) can contact **Safari Azul,** R. Cidade de Leira, 3, 5th fl. (tel. 55 24 47), for somewhat pricey mountain biking, hiking, canoeing, and other **nature adventure trips.**

■ Near Setúbal

SESIMBRA

Nestled between mountains and the sea, Sesimbra retains a refreshingly traditional lifestyle, still anchored to its roots as a fishing village despite recent influxes of beach-flocking tourists. Sesimbra also pleases the less aquatically inclined—a steep half-hour hike above town to the **Moorish castle** rewards the hardy with a Kodachrome view of the ocean and surrounding mountains. To reach the castle from the town center, take R. Cándido dos Reis and follow the signs out of town.

PORTUGAL

Maps, regional info, and accommodations info are available at the **tourist office,** Largo da Morinha, 27 (tel. 223 57 43; open May-Aug. daily 9am-8pm; Oct.-April 9am-12:30pm and 2-5:30pm; English spoken). The **police** (tel. 223 02 69) are on Largo Gago Coutinino. Dial 112 in an **emergency. Postal code** is 2970. The **telephone code** is (0)1.

Inexpensive accommodations may be difficult to find, particularly in summer. The best option is to check for private rooms with the tourist office. Otherwise, **Residencial Chic,** Trav. Xavier da Silva, 2-6 (tel. 223 31 10), offers four breezy doubles with a common bath (singles 3500$; doubles 5000$; breakfast included). Across from Chic are the 12 rooms (all with shower) of the **Garcia family,** R. Cándido dos Reis, 2 (tel. 273 32 27), which are well-furnished, comfortable, and a bit dark. Ask to see the well-stocked wine cellar (singles 3000$; doubles 5000-7000$; triples 8000$). For excellent seafood, follow the local fishermen to **Restaurante A Sesimbrense,** R. Jorge Nunes, 19 (tel. 223 01 48). People drive from kilometers around for their exquisite *caldeira à pescador* (fisherman's stew, 1500$). Entrees go for around 1000-1500$ (open Wed.-Mon. 9am-3pm and 7-10pm).

Regular Rodoviária **buses** leave for Sesimbra from Lisbon's Praça de Espanha (1hr., 540$), but heavy traffic in the summer may lead you to take a **ferry** from Lisbon to Cacilhas (110$) from the Pr. Comércio station and catch a bus to Sesimbra (450$). Covos e Filhos (tel. 22 30 72) buses also leave from the corner of Av. 5 de Outubro and Av. Alexandro Mercularo, a block west of the main bus station in Setúbal.

■ Peniche

Many travelers overlook Peniche, a seaport town 24km west of Óbidos en route to the Ilhas Berlengas. What they miss is a lively port city that is close to good beaches and hiking trails. Harboring Portugal's second largest fishing fleet, this rugged peninsular city is so obsessed with seafood that they have dedicate a major festival to the sardine.

ORIENTATION AND PRACTICAL INFORMATION

Peniche's town center fits neatly into the square tip of its isthmus. The **fortaleza** (fortress) and **Campo da República** are on the coast side, **Avenida do Mar** is on the river, and **Largo Bispo Mariana** bounds the city proper.

Tourist Office: R. Alexandre Herculano (tel. 78 95 71). From the bus station, cross the river (on Ponte Velha). Turn left on R. Herculano and walk alongside the public garden, following signs to the office. English-speaking staff assists with accommodations. Open June-Sept. daily 9am-10pm; Oct.-May daily 9am-1pm and 2-5pm.

Currency Exchange: Try the main *praça.* **União de Bancos,** Av. Mar, 56 (tel. 78 10 75), on the way to the *fortaleza.* 1000$ commission. Open Mon.-Fri. 8:30am-3pm.

Bus station: R. Estado Português da India (tel. 78 21 33), on an isthmus outside the town walls. Express and regular service to: Lisbon (11 per day, 2½hr., 950$); Caldas (6 per day, 1hr., 405$); Nazaré (6 per day, 1½hr., 900$); Alcobaça (2 per day, 1¾hr., 950$); Leiria (6 per day, 2hr., 1200$); Santarém (3 per day, 1½hr., 780$).

Taxis: (tel. 78 26 87).

Luggage Storage: In the bus station (100$ per day).

Hospital: (tel. 78 17 00), R. Gen. Humberto Delgado.

Police: (tel. 78 95 55), R. Marquês de Pombal. **Emergency:** tel. 112.

Post Office: (tel. 78 70 11), R. Arquitecto Paulino Montez. From the tourist office, turn right on R. Herculano, left on Arquitecto Paulino Montez, and walk 3 blocks. Posta Restante, **fax,** and **telephones.** Open Mon.-Fri. 9am-6pm. **Postal Code:** 2520.

Telephone Code: (0)62.

ACCOMMODATIONS AND CAMPING

Pensões fill quickly in July and August; try to arrive early in the day. Look for signs on Av. Mar. Hostesses roam the streets promoting beds in their homes, but you should

insist on seeing the place and inquire about hot water and other amenities. The rooms may be good budget options. You should pay no more than 1500-2000$ for a single or 2500-3000$ for a double. Bargain—there are many of them and few of you.

Hospedaria Marítimo, R. José Estevão, 109 (tel. 78 28 50), off the square in front of the fortress. Newly decorated rooms with bright pine furnishings and new carpet. Some rooms have a TV, all have baths. Singles 2000$. Doubles 3000$.

Residência Mira Mar, Av. Mar, 40-44 (tel. 78 16 66), above a yummy seafood restaurant of the same name. Pink shag rug, oak furniture, great views. All rooms have TV and private bath. Plus, it's near the beach. Singles 3500$. Doubles with bath 4000-5000$. In winter: 1500$; 2000$.

Hospedaria Cristal, R. Marechal Gomes Freitas de Andrade, 14-16 (tel. 78 27 24), 3 blocks in from Pr. Jacob Pereira. Plain rooms do the job. Private baths more appealing than common ones. Singles 3000$. Doubles with bath 6000$. Triples 7000$.

Camping: Municipal Campground (tel. 78 95 29; fax 78 96 96), 1½km outside of town, along the bus route to Caldas da Rainha and Lourinhã. 10 buses per day speed to the campground (ask tourist office for times and/or check at the bus station). Otherwise, it's a 40min. walk out of town across the Ponte Velha; once across, turn right, then left at the T in the road. Go straight ahead a long, long time until the Mobil station, behind which you can collapse in *campismo* comfort. Fronts a beach. Small market. 520$ per person, per tent, per car. Open year-round.

FOOD

Eat some of the freshest seafood in Europe here, or don't eat at all. The real stuff sizzles in whale-sized portions on outdoor grills all along **Av. Mar.** Peniche's *sardinhas* (sardines) are said to be exceptional in a land of aficionados. Try the seafood *espetadas* (skewered aquatic treats served with a tub of melted butter). The outdoor cafes on **Pr. Jacob Rodrigues Pereira** are lively, particularly on Sundays, when the rest of town is virtually comatose. The **market,** R. António da Conceição Bento, has fresh produce (open Tues.-Sun. 6am-2pm).

Restaurante Beiramar, Av. Mar, 106-108 (tel. 78 24 79). Delectable grilled fare served on wood tables in a stone-walled room. The *cataplana de peixe* lands Nirvanic stewed fish right at your table (1200$). The 2nd floor boasts some cherry balcony tables. *Sardinhas grelhadas* (800$). Open daily 10am-11pm.

Restaurante Canhoto, Valadim, 23 (tel. 78 45 12), on the street connecting the tourist office to Av. Mar, is a local tavern-type joint with a tasty *sopa de peixe* (fish soup 200$). Entrees 800-1750$. Open daily noon-midnight.

Restaurante Mira Mar, Av. Mar, 40-44 (tel. 78 16 09). Though surrounded by similar seafood joints, Mira Mar has remarkable *lulas* (squid). Mouth-watering squid kebabs capped with pepper and lemon on a huge plate of fries for 1200$.

SIGHTS AND ENTERTAINMENT

Salazar, Portugal's longtime dictator, chose Peniche's formidable 16th-century **fortaleza** for one of his four high-security political prisons. Its high walls and bastions later became a camp for Angolan refugees. It now houses the **Museu de Peniche** (tel. 78 18 48), highlighted by a fascinating anti-Fascist Resistance exhibition. Photos, accompanied by text, trace the dictatorship and underground resistance from the seizure of power in 1926 to the coup that toppled the regime on April 25, 1974. The fortress is tough to miss; it's at the far end of R. José Estevão, near the dock where boats leave for the Berlengas. (Museum open in summer Tues.-Sun. 10am-12:30pm and 2-7pm; in winter Tues.-Sun. 10am-noon and 2-5pm. 100$, under 15 free.)

For sun and surf, head to any of the town's three beaches. The beautiful **Praia de Peniche de Cima,** along the north crescent, has the warmest water but gets windy. It merges with another beach at **Baleal,** a small fishing village popular with tourists. The southern **Praia do Molho Leste** is colder but safer and a good escape from the wind. Beyond it is the crowded **Praia da Consolação.** The strange humidity at this beach supposedly cures bone diseases. The only other beach with such recuperative prop-

erties is in Japan. Don't swallow the bones at the **Festa da Sardinha,** a massive sardine-devouring, wine-chugging party at the fishing port every Friday and Saturday night in July. Festivities acquire a less fishy (but no less sober) tint in the first Saturday of August, when boats—decked in wreaths of flags and flowers—file into the harbor in the procession that launches the two-day **Festa de Nossa Senhora da Boa Viagem,** celebrating the protector of sailors and fisherman.

The Peninsula

To truly savor the ocean air, hike around the peninsula (8km). Start at **Papôa,** just north of Peniche, and stroll out to the tip, where orange cliffs rise from a swirling blue sea. Nearby lie the ruins of an old fortress, **Forte da Luz. Cabo Carvoeiro,** the most popular and dramatic of Peniche's natural sights, and its **farol** (lighthouse) punctuate the extreme west end of the peninsula. Nearby is a convenient snack bar where you can watch the waves crashing below as you relish *ginja* (cherry liqueur of Óbidos). The **Nau dos Corvos** (Crow's Ship), an odd rock formation and a popular bird roost, promises a seagull's-eye perspective.

ILHAS BERLENGAS

The rugged, terrifyingly beautiful Ilhas Berlengas (Berlenga Islands) are in the Atlantic Ocean, 12km northwest of Peniche. One minuscule main island, numerous reefs, and isolated rocks form an archipelago that's home thousands of screeching seagulls, wild black rabbits, and a small fishing community. Deep gorges, natural tunnels, and rocky caves ravage the main island. Although the island is fringed with several protected beaches, the only one accessible by foot lies in a small cove by the landing dock. For beachgoers willing to brave the cold, dips in the calm water bring instant respite from the heat. For hikers, the tiring trek to the island's highest point yields a gorgeous view of the 17th-century **Forte de São João Batista,** now a hostel.

From Peniche's public dock, the Berlenga **ferry** zips to the island in (July-Aug. 9am, 11am, and 5pm; returning 10am, 4, and 6pm; June-July and Sept. 1-20 10am, returning 6pm). In late July and August the ferry gets so crowded that you may have to line up at 7am; at other times, one hour in advance will suffice. A same-day roundtrip ticket (2500$) for the 9am ferry means you'll return at 4pm; if you go at 11am, you return at 6pm unless there is space on the other boat. To stay overnight, buy a 1500$ one-way ticket for the 5pm boat and pay return fare on board a 10am return boat. Crossing can be rough—vomit bags given to all passengers are too frequently appreciated. Or, cruise in a **private motorboat. Turpesca,** docked at R. Marechal Gomes Freire de Andrade, 90 (tel. 78 99 60), in Peniche, tours underwater caves and other wonders in and around Peniche starting at 2500$ if at least 5 people sign up.

Pick one of three options for an overnight stay: the hostel, the campground, or the expensive *pensão.* While the community-run **hostel** (tel. 78 25 50), in the old fortress looks spectacular, it utterly lacks facilities. (Open Mon.-Fri. 12:30pm-1:30pm; or call tel. (0936) 87 66 05 Mon.-Fri. 10am-noon. Reservations required.) Bring a sleeping bag and flashlight: the half-hour walk from the boat landing to the hostel is lit only by periodic flashes from the lighthouse. The hostel has a kitchen, and the canteen and snack bar stock basic food (spartan doubles 1000$ per person; open June-Sept. 21). The island has a small, barren **campground** on a series of rocky terraces above the ferry landing. Be prepared to be shat upon by scores of seagulls. (Seven years' good luck may not be worth it miles away from your own tub.) Make the required reservations in person at the tourist office in Peniche. (2- or 3-person tent 1500$ per night, 4-person tent 2000$. 7-day max. stay. Open June-Sept. 20.) The **pensão** above **Pavilhão Mar e Sol** (tel. 75 03 31), the main restaurant on the island, will drain your *escudos* (doubles 10,000-12,000$; breakfast included).

ÓBIDOS

Walking through Óbidos's formidable stone gate is like stepping into the Middle Ages. The tiny village sits atop a hill dominated by a 12th-century fortress/castle (now

a luxury *pousada*). Tourism seems to have reinforced, not diminished, the town's commitment to historical authenticity. Narrow streets and stunning views have made Óbidos a romantic get-away destination since 1282, when Queen Isabel so admired Óbidos's beauty that King Dinis gave it to her. For centuries, in fact, Óbidos was considered the personal property of the Portuguese queen.

Practical Information The **tourist office** (tel. 95 92 31), not to be confused with the regional tourism bureau along the same street, is on R. Direita. Through the main gate to the town, take the high road to the left and follow it 200m. English-speaking staff has extensive bus info and will **store luggage** (open daily 9:30am-1pm and 2-6pm). The nearest **hospital** is in Caldas da Rainha (tel. 83 21 33), 6km away. For **police,** dial tel. 95 91 49, or in an **emergency,** 112. The **post office** (tel. 95 91 99), nearby in Pr. Santa Maria, has **telephones, fax** and Posta Restante (open Mon.-Fri. 9am-12:30pm and 2:30-6pm). The **postal code** is 2510. The **telephone code** is (0)62.

Frequent **buses** connect Óbidos to Peniche (8 per day, 5 on Sun., 40min., 375$). You can also travel via Caldas da Rainha (6 per day, 20min., 180$), to Lisbon, Santarém, and Nazaré. Buses stop down a few stairs from the main gate, under the shelter for Caldas de Rainha. No bus schedules are posted at the stop, so inquire at the tourist office. Óbidos is an easy **train** ride from Lisbon's Estação Rossio (2hr.). Take a commuter train to Cacém, then change trains for Óbidos (8 per day, 3hr., 600$). The train station is 10 minutes outside town to the north. To get there from the town center, walk out the gap in the walls at the far end of R. Direita from the Porta da Vila. Turn right, then left, then go down a steep flight of stairs on the hillside. Coming from the station, climb the stairs across from the station rather than walking along the length of the town wall. Buy tickets aboard the train.

Cherries on Top

Óbidos's castle has occupied a strategic position since the Moorish occupation in the Middle Ages. From the formidable walls you'll see why Portugal's first king, Don Afonso Henriques, was thwarted in several attempts to capture the town. But on January 11, 1148, forces at the main gate diverted the guards' attention, while men disguised as cherry trees tiptoed up to the castle. Noticing the advancing trees, an astute Moorish princess asked her father if trees walked. The distracted king paid her no heed, and by the time he realized what was happening, Afonso's men had broken through the castle door. To walk with the trees, follow R. Direita from the entrance at Porta da Vila to the back of the town, under the arch, and to the stairs. Arboreal attire is optional.

Accommodations and Food There's no real reason to stay overnight here; it's more a showpiece than a city. **Agostinho Pereira,** R. Direita, 40 (tel. 95 91 88), rents four homey rooms. Some of these have window seats, prime for enjoying the view of the nearby *igreja* (church). Winter heating cozies up the pleasant lounge with TV and small bar, washing machine, and kitchen (singles 3500$, doubles 4000-4500$, triples 5000$; try to reserve ahead). "Typical" restaurants (with tourist prices) and several reasonable mini-market **groceries** flesh out R. Direita. Eat light and save your *escudos* for Óbidos's signature *ginja* (wild cherry liqueur), even sweeter and more syrupy than the national norm. Stores along R. Direita sell gulp-sized bottles for 200$.

Sights The **castelo** on the coast, built as a fortress in the 12th century, gradually lost its strategic importance as the ocean receded 7km. Although the castle itself opens to *pousada* guests (28,000$ per night!), its walls are open to all. You can walk the circular route, or cozy up in a nook. The old castle's walls surround the entire city. The only *igreja* worth seeing is the 17th-century *azulejo* bonanza **Igreja de Santa Maria** (to the right of the post office in the central *praça*), built on the foundations of a Visigoth church and later used as a mosque. Nun Josefa de Óbidos's vivid

canvases mark the right of the main altar. The church was the site of the 1444 wedding of 10-year-old King Afonso V to his 8-year-old cousin, Isabel. (Open June-Sept. 9:30am-12:30pm and 2:30-7pm; Oct.-May 9:30am-12:30pm and 2:30-5:30pm. Free.)

CALDAS DA RAINHA

The town takes its name, "Baths of the Queen," from Queen Leonor, who soaked in its thermal springs. The first lady sold her jewels to finance the world's first thermal hospital, where victims of rheumatism, respiratory ailments, and skin afflictions still come to be cured. This may not be a desirable destination for healthy travelers, but Caldas's beautiful park, great pottery, and delicious pastries make it a short and sweet stopover between Lisbon and Óbidos.

Practical Information The **tourist office** (tel. 83 10 03; fax 84 23 20), is in Pr. 25 de Abril. Take a left out of the bus station; it's two blocks on the right (open Mon.-Fri. 9am-7pm, Sat.-Sun., and holidays 10am-1pm and 3-7pm). They kindly allow temporary **luggage storage**. Ask nicely. The **bus station** (tel. 83 10 67), R. Heróis da Grande Guerra, services: Óbidos (13 per day, 20min., 145$); Lisbon (8 per day, 1½hr., 900$); Porto (9 per day, 4hr., 1500$); Peniche (6 per day, 45 min., 600$). The **train station** (tel. 236 93) is on the northwest edge of town on Largo da Estação. From Av. 25 de Abril, take Av. 1 de Maio. Trains connect Caldas-Lisbon (12 per day, 2¼hr., 850$). **Taxis** (tel. 83 10 98 or 83 24 55) shuttle 24 hours. The **hospital** (tel. 83 03 01) is on the first street to the right after the **police station** (tel. 83 20 22), which is at Frei de São Paulo, just off Pr. República. In an **emergency**, call 112. The **post office**, R. Heróis da Grande Guerra, 149 (tel. 83 22 30), is across from the bus station. (Open Mon.-Fri. 8:30am-6:30pm, Sat. 9am-12:30pm for **fax, phone,** and Posta Restante.) The **postal code** is 2500. The **telephone code** is (0)62.

Accommodations and Food Pensão Irmãos Unidos, R. Nazaré, 8 (tel. 83 25 62), is three blocks from the bus station. Its large, mostly windowless rooms are simple and comfortable (singles 2500$, doubles 3500$; breakfast included). **Pensão Residencial Central,** Largo Dr. José Barbosa, 22 (tel. 83 19 14; fax 84 32 82), behind the Praga da República has more upscale rooms with TVs, bath, heat, and telephones. Try bargaining. (July-Aug. singles 3000$, with bath 4000$. Doubles: 6000$; 6500$. 500$ lower May-June and even lower in the off season. Breakfast included. Visa, MC, AmEx.) Orbitur (tel. 83 23 67) runs a **campground** just a 15-minute walk from the bus station in Parque Dom Carlos I. From the Thermal Hospital, continue on R. Camões, turn left on Av. Visconde de Sacavém, walk past the tennis courts, and *voilà!* (Reception open daily 8am-10pm. 450$ per person, 550-720$ per tent, and 420$ per car. Free hot showers. Open year-round.)

Caldas is the fruit capital of Portugal. Even if you don't want any produce, visit the large and colorful **Mercado da Fruta,** Pr. República, where frenzied local vendors and shoppers haggle each morning (open daily 6am-2pm). The town's sweets—including *cavacas* (frosted bowl-shaped pastries) and *trouxas de ovos* (sweetened egg yolks)—are famed throughout the country. **Pastelarias** sprinkle Av. Liberdade and Av. Duarte Pacheco; many also serve decent *pratos do dia* at reasonable prices (600-900$). **Pasteleria Machado,** R. de Camões, 47 (tel. 83 22 55), across from the park entrance, sells *cavacas* (80$) and doubles as a *salão de chá* (tea room) with a chrome-fitted 50s interior (open daily 9am-8:30pm). For more substantial fare, try local dishes such as *lombinhos de porco* (porkloin 1100$) at **Restaurante Portugal** on R. Alm. Cândido dos Reis (tel. 342 80).

Sights Although you can bathe at the historic **Hospital Rainha Dona Leonor** (tel. 83 03 00), it primarily serves as a hospital. To reach the complex, follow the signs from Pr. República. (Open Mon.-Fri. 8:15-11:45am and 3:15-4:30pm, Sat. 8:45-10:45am. June-Oct. 550$, Nov.-May 490$.) For serious relaxation, head to the immaculately landscaped **Parque Dom Carlos I** by following R. Camões on Largo Rainha Dona Leonor. The park has walking paths, a duck pond, and tennis courts. Caldas's

pottery prestige is unrivaled, and most art museums throughout Portugal shelve at least a few pieces from the town. The park's **Museu de Cerâmica** traces the history and manufacturing process of Caldas clay (open Tues.-Sun. 10am-noon and 2-5pm; free).

■ Nazaré

It's hard to tell where authenticity stops and tourism starts in Nazaré. Fishermen clad in traditional garb go barefoot and women typically don seven petticoats, thick shawls, and large gold earrings. The day's catch dries in the hot sun while locals string their nets along the shoreline esplanade. This "traditional" lifestyle, somehow thrives in the middle of one of the most touristed beach towns in Portugal. But if Nazaré is part theater, at least it puts on a good show—and everyone gets front row seats on the glorious beach. Drop your anchor elsewhere at the end of July and August, when prices double and bathers jostle with each other for tiny spots on the sand.

ORIENTATION AND PRACTICAL INFORMATION

Practically all the action in Nazaré, including the beach scene, nightlife, and most restaurants, is located in the so-called **new town** along the beach. Its two main squares, **Praça Sousa Oliveira** and **Praça Dr. Manuel de Arriaga,** are near the cliffside, away from the fishing port. Either the cliffside funicular or a winding road takes you up to the **Sítio,** the old town, which preserves a sense of calm and tradition less prevalent in the crowded resort farther south. To get to the tourist office from the bus station, go toward the beach and right onto **Avenida República.** The office is a 10-minute walk along the beach, between the two major *praças.*

Tourist Office: Beachside on Av. República (tel. 56 11 94). **Maps,** transportation schedules, and the scoop on entertainment. Open daily July-Aug. 10am-10pm; Oct.-June 15 9:30am-12:30pm and 2-6pm; June 16-June 10am-1pm and 3-8pm.

Currency Exchange: Banco Fonsecas & Burnay, Av. Vieira Guimarães (tel. 56 12 89), has an **ATM** (Visa, AmEx). Open Mon.-Fri. 8am-3pm.

Buses: Av. Vieira Guimarães (tel. 55 11 72), perpendicular to Av. República. More convenient than taking the train (12km away). To: Lisbon (8 per day, 2hr., 1050$); Coimbra (6 per day, 2hr., 1100$); Porto (9 per day, 3½hr., 1400$); Alcobaça (15 per day, 30min., 200$); Caldas da Rainha (20 per day, 1¼hr., 600$); Tomar (3 per day, 1½hr., 740$); Leiria (12 per day, 1¼hr., 750$); Peniche (6 per day, 1½hr., 850$); Fátima (6 per day, 1½hr., 900$).

Taxi: (tel. 55 31 25 or 55 13 63).

Car Rental: M&M Travel Agencies, Av. de República, 28 (tel. 56 18 88). Renting a car is the easiest way to visit Alcobaça, Fátima, and Batalha without camping out in the bus station. Open Mon.-Fri. 9am-12:30pm and 2-7pm.

Luggage Storage: In the bus station (100$ per bag per day).

Hospital: Hospital da Confraria da Nossa Senhora de Nazaré (tel. 56 11 16), in the Sítio district on the cliffs above the town center.

Police: (tel. 55 12 68), 1 block from the bus station at Av. Vieira Guimarães and R. Sub-Vila. **Emergency:** tel. 112.

Post Office: Av. Independência Nacional, 2 (tel. 56 16 04). From Pr. Souza Oliveira walk up R. Mouzinho de Albuquerque, which veers to the right. It's 1 block past Pensão Central. Open for Posta Restante and **telephones** Mon.-Fri. 9am-12:30pm and 2:30-6pm. **Postal Code:** 2450.

Telephone Code: (0)62.

ACCOMMODATIONS AND CAMPING

By stepping off the bus, you unwittingly signal a phalanx of room-renters into a stampede; once you've made it past them, you'll encounter insistent old ladies on most every street corner offering rooms. Bargain down to 1500$ for singles and 2500$ for doubles, but insist on seeing your quarters before settling the deal. For rooms in *pen-*

sões, look above the restaurants on **Pr. Dr. Manuel de Arriaga** and **Pr. Sousa Oliveira.** Fish is good. For fruit and veggies, check the **market** across from the bus station (open daily 8am-1pm; in winter Tues.-Sun. 8am-1pm). **Supermarkets** line R. Sub-Vila, parallel to Av. República, and Pr. Dr. Manuel de Arriaga.

Residencial Marina, R. Mouzinho de Albuquerque, 6A, 3rd fl. (tel. 55 15 41), on the beach side of Hotel Mare. Modern, carpeted rooms with tidy baths, and just a few steps from the beach. Doubles 3000$, with bath 4000$. July 15-Sept.: 6500$; 7000$. Reservations recommended in summer. Open May-Oct.

Pensão Leonardo, Pr. Dr. Manuel de Arriaga, 25-28 (tel. 55 12 59), above a restaurant of the same name, between Restaurant Mar Alto and Pensão Europa on a square parallel to the beach. Basic rooms, shared bathrooms. Singles 2500$. Doubles 3000$, with bath 4000$. Reservations recommended. Visa, MC, AmEx.

Camping: Vale Paraíso, Estrada Nacional, 242 (tel. 56 18 00; fax 56 19 00), has swimming pools, a restaurant-bar, and a supermarket. 345-575$, under 14 free. 360-600$ per tent, 290-470$ per car. Prices vary with season. Free showers. 20-40% off-season discount. Open year-round. Take the bus to Alcobaça or Leiria (8 per day, 7am-7pm, 15min.). Reception for both sites open daily 8am-10pm.

A Tasquinha, R. Adrião Batalha, 54 (tel. 55 19 45), several blocks off Av. República, 1 block left off Pr. Dr. Manuel Arriaga. Locals jostle for a seat at the family-style picnic tables. Perhaps the only restaurant in Nazaré with a Portuguese-only menu (a good sign). *Sardinhas* 600$. Open daily noon-midnight. Visa, MC, AmEx.

Charcutaria O Frango Assado, Pr. Dr. Manuel de Arriaga, 20 (tel. 55 18 42). Facing the beach, at the far end of the square. For under 450$ get a half-chicken with *piri-piri* (a tabasco-esque sauce). Take-out only. Open daily 9am-1pm and 3-8pm.

Restaurante Riba Mar, Av. República (tel. 55 11 58), at the south corner of Pr. Dr. Manuel Arriaga. Looks like the most expensive joint in Nazaré, and is...but attached to the absurd "international" menu (1500$ and up) is a reasonable "traditional" menu, with entrees from 800-1800$. Open daily noon-midnight. Visa, MC, AmEx.

Cliff Hangers

One-hundred twenty meters above the sea, the tiny, whitewashed **Ermida da Memória** (Memorial Chapel) stands in a corner of the square diagonally across from the church. The chapel was built in 1182 by the lucky nobleman Dom Fuas Roupinho. Out on a hunting expedition, Dom Fuas was chasing a deer that just kept runnin' until it fell off the cliff. Dom Fuas slammed on the brakes and his horse stopped with two legs on *terra firme* and two over the side. In a split second, Our Lady of Nazaré appeared and pulled the horse (and Dom Fuas) to safety. Out of this, the town of Nazaré was born—and so was the little chapel.

SIGHTS AND ENTERTAINMENT

Why are you staring at that church? Go to the beach! If you've been there and done that, take the funicular (every 15min. until 1am, 80$), which climbs from R. Elevador off Av. República to modest **Sítio.** Its uneven cobbled streets and weathered buildings were all there before tourism was invented. Around 7:30pm, fishing boats return to the **port** beyond the far left end (facing the ocean) of the beach; head over to watch fishermen at work and eavesdrop as local restaurateurs spiritedly bid for the most promising catches of the day.

Cafes in Pr. Souza Oliveira bustle till 1am. Bop through the early morn at **Discoteca Jeans Rouge** (Sat. only, opens at 11:30pm), up the street from the *praça*. For lively Brazilian and Portuguese tunes, imbibe with locals at **Bar A Ilha,** on R. Mouzinho Albuquerque (open 7pm-about 3am). Every Thursday and Friday at 10pm from July 15 -August, a local group performs **traditional dances** called *viras* at the Casino, a festival hall on R. Rui Rosa (500$). During the summer, look out for late-night gatherings of folk music and *fado* on the beach

The Three Beiras

Exquisite beaches and plush greenery make the three Beira regions perfect for acquainting yourself with traditional Portuguese life. From Porto south to Coimbra, this region endures the most extreme weather in Portugal. The Beira Litoral passes through the unspoiled Costa da Prata (Silver Coast) beginning at the resort town of Figueira da Foz north, through up-and-coming Aveiro, passing on the way to Porto. Coimbra, a bustling university city, overlooks the region from its perch above the celebrated Rio Mondego. Unlike the progressive towns of the Beira Litoral to the west, the mountainous Beira Alta (high edge) and Beira Baixa (low edge) have been slow to develop. These desolate, impoverished, and at times snow-covered (a true rarity in Portugal) provinces continue to cling tightly to tradition. Throughout the Beiras, farmers cultivate grapes along the mountainsides, while silvery almond trees cloud the horizon. As if this image is not ideal enough, rice fields spill down the valley and wildflowers scatter across the roads.

■ Coimbra

Camouflage in Coimbra is easy—twinkly eyed students and tourists shouldering backpacks blend harmoniously in and around town and at the renowned University of Coimbra. Established as the institution's permanent home in 1537, Coimbra remained the country's only university city until the beginning of the 20th century. Its infamous roles as center of the Inquisition and educator and employer of former economics professor Antònio Salazar, longtime dictator of Portugal, have long since been blotted out by time and charm. Crew races, rowdy cafeteria halls, and swinging bars make Coimbra appear noisy and chaotic, but its youthful energy, refreshing diversity, and smattering of medieval buildings welcome visitors who share the town's vigor.

ORIENTATION AND PRACTICAL INFORMATION

Coimbra's steep streets rise in tiers above Rio Mondego. There are three centers of activity in town, all on one side of the river. The **lower town,** site of the **tourist office** and **Coimbra-A** train station, lies within the triangle formed by the river, **Largo da Portagem,** and **Praça 8 de Maio.** Coimbra's ancient **university district** perches atop the steep hill overlooking the lower town. Downhill, on the other side of the university, the **Praça da República** plays host to cafes, a shopping district, and the youth hostel. Coimbra has two **train stations,** connected by bus #5: **Coimbra-A,** in the lower town center, and **Coimbra-B,** 3km northwest of town.

Tourist Office: Largo Portagem (tel. 286 86 or 330 19; fax 255 76), in a yellowish building 2 blocks east of Coimbra-A, off Largo Portagem (a square with a central statue across from the large Santa Clara bridge). From the bus station, turn right and follow the avenue to Coimbra-A and then to Largo Portagem (15min.). Travel pros will provide free **maps** and multilingual accommodation and daytrip info. Open July-Oct. Mon.-Fri. 9am-7pm, Sat.-Sun. 9am-1pm and 2:30-5:30pm. Oct.-April Mon.-Fri. 9am-6pm, Sat.-Sun. and holidays 10am-1pm. There's a **branch office at the university** (tel. 325 91), Pr. Dom Dinis, up the stairs connecting the university with Pr. República. Same hours as the central office. Pr. República's **branch office** (tel. 332 02) provides handy info. Open Mon.-Fri. 10am-1pm and 2:30-6pm.

Travel Agency: Tagus (tel. 349 99; fax 349 16), R. Padre António Vieira. Handles student/youth budget travel. Open Mon.-Fri. 9:30am-12:30pm and 2-6pm.

Currency Exchange: Montepio Geral, C. Estrela, behind the tourist office. 1000$ charge per transaction above 10,000$; otherwise no charge. Open Mon.-Fri. 8:30am-3pm. In a pinch, go to **Hotel Astória,** Av. Emídio Navarro, 21 (tel. 220 55), across the square and down the river from the tourist office. 1000$ charge per transaction. Open 24hr. Bank rates are better.

Trains: (tel. 246 32, 349 98, or 341 27). **Estação Coimbra-A** is near the town center. **Estação Coimbra-B** is 3km northwest of town. Trains from cities outside the region stop only in Coimbra-B, while regional trains stop at both stations. Trains arriving in Coimbra will stop in Coimbra-B 1st and Coimbra-A 2nd; for departures, the sequence is reversed. Bus #5 connects them (5min., 190$). To: Aveiro (15 per day, 45min., 470$); Figueira da Foz (1 per hr., 1hr., 280$); Viseu (4 per day, 2½hr., 720$); Porto (13 per day, 3hr., 900$); Lisbon (15 per day, 3hr., 1300$); Paris (1 per day, 22hr., 23,000$). Except for the Figueira da Foz-Coimbra route, buses are quicker and more reliable than trains, though more expensive.

Buses: (tel. 48 4o 45) Av. Fernão Magalhães, on the university side of the river about a 10min. walk out of town, past Coimbra-A. To: Lisbon (15 per day, 3hr., 1250$); Porto (5 per day, 6hr., 1200$); Évora (5 per day, 6hr., 1850$); Faro (4 per day, 12hr., 2800$); Condeixa (14 per day, 30min., 240$); Luso/Buçaco (on the Viseir-bound bus 5 per day, 45min., 450$). **AVIC,** R. João de Ruão, 18 (tel. 201 41 or 237 69), between R. Sofia and Av. Fernão Magalhães, next door to Viagem Mondego. Private buses with A/C and amenities to destinations across Europe.

Public Transportation: Buses and street cars. Fares: 190$; book of 10 600$; 3-day tourist pass 850$. Tickets sold in kiosks at Largo Portagem and Pr. República. Main lines are #1 (Portagem-Universidade-Estádio); #2 (Pr. República-Fornos); #3 (Porta-gem-Pr. República-Santo António dos Olivais); #5 (Coimbra A-Pr. República-São José); #7 (Portagem-Palácio da Justiça-Pr. República-Tovim); #29 (Portagem-near the youth hostel-Hospital); #46 (Cruz de Celas-Pr. República-Portagem-Santa Clara).

Taxis: Politaxis (tel. 48 40 45). Many wait outside Coimbra-A and the bus station.

Car Rental: Avis, Estação Nova, Largo das Ameias (tel. 347 86; fax (02) 28045 95). In Coimbra-A, outside platform door. Open Mon.-Fri. 8:30am-12:30pm and 2:30-7pm.

Luggage Storage: None in Coimbra-A or B. **Café Cristal,** Av. Fernão Magalhães, across the street and to the left of Coimbra-A. 250$ per bag. Mon.-Sat. 1-4pm.

Laundromat: Lavandaria Lucira, R. Sá da Bandeira, 86 (tel. 257 01). Wash and dry a full machine load (1000$) in a few hours, or drop it off (250$ per kg) and wait a few days for Lucira to collect enough clothes. Open for self-service wash, house wash, and dry cleaning Mon.-Fri. 8:30am-1pm and 3-7pm, Sat. 8:30am-1pm.

Swimming Pool: Piscina Municipal (tel. 70 16 05), on R. Dom Manuel I. Take bus #5 São José or #1 Estádio from Largo Portagem outside the tourist office. Trio of pools near the stadium are terrific but often packed. Open July-Aug. daily 10am-1pm and 2-7pm. 160$, under 6 and over 60 free.

Bookstores: Three good ones line the pedestrian-only R. Ferreira Borges. **Livraria Bertrand,** Largo da Portagem, 9 (tel. 230 14), a block from tourist office, offers a small selection of English classics. Open Mon.-Fri. 9am-7pm, Sat. 9am-1pm.

Hospital: Hospital da Universidade de Coimbra (tel. 400 400 or 400 500), Pr. Pro-fessor Mota Pinto. Near the Cruz de Celas stop on line #29.

Police: (tel. 220 22), R. Olímpio Nicolau Rui Fernandes, facing the market and post office. There is a special division for foreigners *(Serviço de Estrangeiros)*, R. Venâncio Rodrigues 25 (tel. 240 45). **Emergency:** tel. 112.

Post Office: Central office (tel. 281 81) is in the pink powder-puff structure on Av. Fernão Magalhães. Open Mon.-Fri. 8:30am-6:30pm. For Posta Restante, go to the **Mercado office** on R. Olímpio Nicolau Rui Fernandes (tel. 243 56), across from the police station. Open for Posta Restante, **telephones,** and **fax** Mon.-Fri. 8:30am-6:30pm, Sat. 9am-12:30pm. **Branch office** (tel. 272 64), at Pr. República, is open Mon.-Fri. 9am-12:30pm and 2:30-6pm. The **university post office** (tel. 343 05), downhill from the large stairs, has the same hr. as the Pr. República branch. **Postal Code:** 3000 for central Coimbra.

Telephones: In post offices and at Largo Portagem, 1. **Telephone Code:** (0)39.

ACCOMMODATIONS AND CAMPING

Undesirable *pensões* line the seedy neighborhood around **R. Sota** across from Coim-bra-A. Anything decent (try **Av. Fernão Magalhães**) starts at 3500$ for doubles; pay less and pay the consequences. Fortunately, an excellent youth hostel awaits those bearing the magic HI card and willing to walk about 20 minutes from the river.

Coimbra

Aqueducto de San Sebastián, 17
Arco de Almedina, 8
AVIC Bus Station, 1
Botanical Garden, 16
Capela San Miguel, 12
Central Bus Station, 2
Coimbra A Bus Station, 4
Coimbra B Train Station, 3
Igreja de Sta. Cruz, 6
King John V Library, 13
Market, 7
Municipal Tourist Office, 15
Municipal Tourist Office, 18
New Cathedral, 14
Old Cathedral, 10
Parque de Sta. Cruz, 19
Post Office, 5
Regional Tourist Office, 9
To Sta. Clara-a-Velha and Sta.
Clara-a-Nova Convents, 20
University of Coimbra, 11

PORTUGAL

R. D. Manuel Pina
R. D. Bastos Correia
R. Tenente Campos Rego
R. Eço de Queiróz
R. Antero de Quental
R. Tenente Valadim
Rua Antero de Quental
R. Dr. António de Vasconcelos
Rua Alexandre Herculano
Rua Venâncio Rodrigues
Rua Castro Matoso
Rua de Tomar
Rua Almeida Garret
Arcos do Jardin
Av. Júlio Henriques
Av. Sá da Bandeira
R. Manutenção Militar
Rua Padre António Vieira
Praça D. Diniz
Praça Marquês de Pombal
Rua dos Estudos
Rua de Saragoça
R. Inácio Duarte
LARGO DA SÉ NOVA
Rua de Montarroio
Rua Nicolau Rui Fernandes
Couraça dos Apóstolos
R. das Flores
R. da Matemática
LG. DE SAN SALVADOR
R. S. João
R. S. Pedro
Praça da Porta Férrea
R. José Falcão
Rua do Colégio Novo
Rua da Louveiro
B. da Anarda
R. de S. Jacinto
R. de S. Salvador
B. Borges Carneiro
R. Borges Carneiro
B. das Condeixinhas
Tv. Trinidade
Rua Martins de Carvalho
Rua do Corpo de Deus
Rua Dr. João
R. dos Coutinhos
R. do Norte
R. Dr. Guilherme Moreir
Couraça de Lisboa
Rua Sub Ripas
R. Bos Vista do Cabido
Rua dos Esteiros
Tv. Couraça de Lisboa
R. João António de Aguia
Rua Fernandes Tomáz
R. Fonte Nova
Rua da Alegria
Praça 8 de Maio
R. Visconde da Luz
Rua Ferreira Borges
Portagem
Rua da Sofia
R. Moreno
R. Arco de Ne
R. Nova
Rua Direita
Rua João Cabreira
Rua da Moeda
R. da Louça
R. do Corvo
R. E. Coelho
PRAÇA DO COMÉRCIO
LG. DA MARACHA
Tv. A. Veig
R. Almoçarife
Rua Adelino Veiga
Rua das Azeiteiras
LG. DO ROMAL
Rua Mor
Rua da Sota
Avenida Emído Navarro
Av. dos Oleiros
R. dos Oleiros
Rua João Cabreira
Largo das Olarias
Acshada do Pedro
Rua António Granjo
LG. das
Av. Fernão de Magalhães
Ponte de Sta. Clara
Rio Mondego

Pousada de Juventude de Coimbra (HI), R. Henrique Seco, 14 (tel./fax 229 55). The hostel was closed in early summer 1997 but was due to re-open in Aug. Expect prices to rise after renovation. From either Coimbra-A or Largo Portagem, walk 20min. uphill along R. Olímpio Nicolau Rui Fernandes to Pr. República, then walk up R. Lourenço Azevedo (to the left of the park). Take the 2nd right; the hostel is on the right. Alternatively, take bus #7, 8, 29, or 46 to Pr. República and walk the rest of the way. Consistently hot and high-pressure showers, TV room, kitchen, laundry room and/or service (1000$ per machine), and parrots make this hostel a cozy place. English-speaking manager. Reception open daily 9-10:30am and 6pm-midnight. Lockout all other times, but bag drop-off (a godsend in hilly Coimbra) all day. 1500$ per person. Doubles 3700$, with bath 4000$. Low season: 1300$; 3600$. Breakfast included.

Residencial Internacional de Coimbra, Av. Emídio Navarro, 4 (tel. 255 03), in front of Coimbra-A. Fluorescent lighting and lumpy pillows in rooms taller than they are wide. Still, conveniently located. All rooms equipped with phone, some with TV. River-front doubles with breathtaking views. Singles 2000$, with bath 2500$. Doubles: 3000$; 4000$. Winter discounts.

Pensão Avis, Av. Fernão Magalhães, 64 (tel. 237 18). Take a left exiting Coimbra-A. You get what you pay for: cheap rooms are squished, but more expensive rooms are bright, and have verandas. Tiny private baths are much more appealing than their common bath counterparts. Singles 2000$, with bath 2200$. Doubles: 3500$; 4000$. Triples: 4500$; 5000$. Breakfast 350$.

Residência Lusa Atenas, Av. Fernão Magalhães, 68 (tel. 264 12; fax 201 33), on the main Av. between Coimbra-A and the bus station, next to Pensão Avis (look for their neon sign). Phone, A/C, and cable TV in ritzy rooms. Singles 3000$, with bath 3500$. Doubles: 6000$; 6500$. Triples with bath 7000-7500$. Breakfast included.

Pensão Rivoli, Pr. Comércio, 27 (tel. 255 50), in a mercifully quiet pedestrian plaza a block downhill (and closer to the river) from busy R. Ferreira Borges, the pedestrian street of Largo Paragem. Well-furnished rooms are comfortably worn. Singles 2000$. Doubles 4500$, with shower 5000$. Triples with shower 6500$.

Camping: Municipal Campground (tel. 70 14 97), corralled in the recreation complex with the swimming pool and surrounded by noisy avenues. The entrance is at the arch off Pr. 25 de Abril; take the same buses as for the pool (see **Swimming Pool,** p. 560). Reception open daily 9am-10pm; Oct.-March daily 9am-6pm. 231$ per person, 163-174$ per tent, and 294$ per car. Showers free.

FOOD

Scout out **R. Direita,** running west off Pr. 8 de Maio, the side streets to the west of **Pr. Comércio** and **Largo da Portagem,** and the university district around **Pr. República.** Restaurants in these areas serve up steamy portions of *arroz de lampreia* (rice cooked with chunks of lamprey meat—it does not taste like chicken). Don't tell anyone, but you can probably get the best budget meal deal in the entire country at the **UC Cantina,** the university's student cafeteria, located on the right side of R. Oliveiro Matos, about half a block downhill from the base of the steps leading from the university to Pr. República. A mere 270$ buys an entire meal (soup, salad, dessert, and beverage). An international student ID is (theoretically) mandatory. The cantina has a small bakery (rolls 10$; opens daily at noon). Or grab a raw meal at the **mercado** in the huge green warehouse on the right just past the post office, uphill on R. Olímpico Nicolau Rui Fernandes (open daily 8am-1pm). **Supermercado Minipreço,** is in the lower town center on R. António Granjo, 6C. Go left leaving Coimbra-A, and take another left to land there (open Mon.-Sat. 9am-8pm).

Café Santa Cruz, (tel. 336 17). From the tourist office, walk down R. Ferreira Borges until you hit Pr. 8 de Maio. Formerly part of the cathedral (it still has a vaulted ceiling and stained-glass windows). It has probably seen better days, but it's still the most famous cafe in Coimbra and remains a popular place to tank up on coffee (90$ for a *bica*) or grab a sandwich (around 400$). Open daily 7am-2am.

Restaurante Esplendoroso, R. Sota, 29 (tel. 357 11), up a side-street across from Coimbra-A. Splendid Chinese food and prompt service in a relaxing atmosphere.

The real steals are the weekday-only lunch *combinados,* which include an egg roll, entree, and rice for around 710$. The flaming *gelado frita com rum* (fried ice cream in rum 390$) is quite a treat. Open daily noon-3pm and 7-11pm.Visa, MC.

Churrasqueria do Mondego, R. Sargento Mor, 25 (tel. 233 55), off R. Sota, 1 block west of Largo Portagem. Frequented by truck drivers and students. Unceremonious service at the counter. Their *frango no churrasco* (barbecued half-chicken, 350$) leaves Colonel Sanders on the wrong side of the road—watch them cook it over the huge flaming grill. The *ementa turística* translates to a full meal for 750$. Open daily noon-3pm and 6-10:30pm.

Restaurante Democrática, Trav. Rua Nova, 5-7 (tel. 237 84), on a tiny lane off R. Sofia (1st full left after city hall). Popular with the young, local crowd. For something different try *espetadas de porco à Africana* (pork kababs African-style, 880$). Entrees 850-1200$. Open Mon.-Sat. noon-3pm and 7pm-midnight. Visa.

Casino da Urca, R. Baixo (tel. 81 30 59), on the other side of the river behind the Santa Clara convent. Low-beamed ceiling and antique farm implements complement the rustic scenes painted on the walls. The *espetada da casa* (house kabab 950$) is mighty savory. Wide variety of entrees (750-1500$). Open daily noon-3pm and 7pm-midnight.

SIGHTS

Fortunate perhaps only for those with Olympic-sized quads, the best way to take in Coimbra's old town sights is to climb from the river up to the university—and what a climb it is. Begin the ascent at the decrepit **Arco de Almedina,** a remnant of the Moorish town wall, one block uphill from Largo Portagem next to the Banco Pinto e Sotto Mayor on R. Ferreira Borges. The gate leads to a stepped street aptly named R. Quebra-Costas (Back-Breaker Street). Up a narrow stone stairway looms the hulking 12th-century Romanesque **Sé Velha** (Old Cathedral). Take a breather in the cool, dark interior, or get there around noon to follow the guide around the principal tombs and friezes while Gregorian chants echo in the background (open 9:30am-12:30pm and 2-5:30pm; cloisters 100$). Jump ahead in time a few centuries and follow the signs to nearby **Sé Nova** (New Cathedral), built for the Jesuits in the late 16th century by a succession of builders. The architectural competition awarded the cathedral with an ever-more elaborate exterior. Unfortunately, similar attention was not lavished on the interior (open daily 9am-noon and 2-6:30pm; mass Tues.-Sat. 6pm, Sun. 11am and 7pm; free).

From the new cathedral, it is but a few glorious blocks uphill to the 16th-century **University of Coimbra** campus. Although many of the buildings were built in functional-yet-ugly 1950s concrete style, the venerable law school gets an A in architecture. Enter the center of the old university through the **Porta Férrea** (Iron Gate) off R. São Pedro. These buildings were Portugal's de facto royal palace when Coimbra was the capital of the kingdom. The staircase at the right leads up to the **Sala dos Capelos,** where portraits of Portugal's kings (six born in Coimbra) hang below a beautiful 17th-century ceiling (open daily 10am-noon and 2-5pm; free). The **university chapel** and 18th-century **university library** lie past the Baroque clock tower. Press the buzzer by the library door to enter three gilded halls with 300,000 works from the 12th-19th centuries (open daily 9:30am-noon and 2-5pm; 300$, students and teachers with ID free). For some green, walk downhill from the university alongside the **Aqueducto de São Sebastião** to admire the sculpture and fountains of the **Jardim Botânico.** Another option is to descend the large staircase and pass through Pr. República into the **Santa Cruz Park** and its beautiful moss covered fountain.

Back in the lower town, the **Igreja de Santa Cruz** (Church of the Holy Cross), on Pr. 8 de Maio at the far end of R. Ferreira Borges, is a 12th-century church with a splendid barrel-vaulted **sacristía** (sacristy) and ornate **túmulos reals** where the first two kings of Portugal rest. The exterior of the church is getting a serious face-lift, but the inside is open daily 9am-noon and 3-6pm. Crossing the bridge in front of Largo Portagem to the other side of the river, you will find the 14th-century **Convento de Santa Clara-a-Velha.** Since the convent was built on top of a swamp, it sinks a little deeper each year; today it is more than half underground. The convent was aban-

doned in 1687, and Coimbra just recently began renovating it. The building should re-open by 1998. As soon as Coimbra's citizenry realized what was going down, they rushed to build the replacement **Convento de Santa Clara-a-Nova** (1649-1677), in which the queen's 14th-century Gothic tomb and a new silver one can now rest in peace—contentedly above ground (open daily 8:30am-12:30pm and 2-6:30pm; free).

Finally, swallow your pride and mingle with the minors at **Portugal dos Pequeni-tos,** between the new convent and the river bridge. The park features scaled-down reproductions of famous castles and monuments (open Mon.-Sat. 10am-5pm; adults 500$, children 200$).

ENTERTAINMENT

Nightlife gets highest honors in Coimbra. After the beer with dinner in the **UC Can-tina,** upend a few bottles with the "in" crowd at outdoor cafes around **Praça República,** which buzzes from midnight to 4am. Around the corner and uphill is the hot (in all senses of the word) diso **Via Latina,** R. Almeida Garrett, 1 (tel. 330 34), near the Santa Cruz garden. Around the corner downhill from Via Latina is **Teatro Académico de Gil Vicente,** which hosts university plays and concerts (mainly rock bands) on most nights around 9 or 10pm. For jazz, try **Dixie Bar,** R. Joaquim António d'Aguiar, 6 (tel. 321 92), one block uphill from the main tourist office, to hear jam sessions until 3am. To absorb the most unrestrained **fado** singers, go from dinner to **Diligência Bar,** R. Nova, 30 (tel. 276 67), off R. Sofia (*fado* singing around 10pm-2am). You can find free-form *fado* in the wee hours at **Bar 1910,** above a gymnasium on R. Simões Castro (open until 4am; beer about 200$). Dance and house music shake the walls of **E.T.C.,** Av. Afonso Henrigues, 43 (tel. 40 40 47), until 2am. These listings do not even dent the club scene; blaze your own trail.

Students rampage day and night in Coimbra's famous and distinctive week-long festival, the **Queima das Fitas** (Burning of the Ribbons) in the first or second week of May. The festivities begin when graduating students burn the narrow ribbons they received as first-years and get wide, ornamental ones in return. The carousing continues with midnight *serenatas* (groups of black-clad, serenading youth), wandering musical ensembles, parades, concerts, and folk dancing. Live choral music echoes in festooned streets during the **Festas da Rainha Santa,** held the first week of July in even-numbered years. The firework-punctuated **Feira Popular** in the second week of July offers carnival-type rides and games across the river from the tourist office and traditional Portuguese dancing exhibitions in Pr. Comércio at the Camára Municipa.

■ Near Coimbra

CONÍMBRIGA

Ten kilometers south of Coimbra, Conímbriga boasts the largest Roman settlement in Portugal. Exciting ongoing excavations reveal more of the site each year. Outside the 4th-century town wall there's a luxurious villa, several small shops and houses, and baths complete with sauna and furnace room. Some of the mosaics are remarkably elaborate and well-preserved. (Ruins open daily 9am-1pm and 2-8pm; in winter daily 9am-1pm and 2-6pm. Admission Tues.-Sun. includes museum (below) 400$; students and seniors 200$; Sun. morning free until 1pm.) The nearby **Museu Monográfico de Conímbriga** (tel. 94 11 77) displays artifacts unearthed in the area (open March 15-Sept. Tues.-Sun. 10am-1pm and 2-6pm).

Buses departing from the stop in front of Coimbra-A will drop you off near the ruins; inquire at the Coimbra tourist office for schedules. The tourism bureau in the Condeixa Town Hall (tel. 94 11 14) carries information. Buses also run from Coimbra to Conímbriga and to sleepy **Condeixa,** 2km away from Conímbriga. Coimbra to Condeixa buses run surprisingly regularly (Mon.-Fri. every hr., Sat.-Sun. 3 per day, 30min., 320$; the last bus returns to Coimbra at 7:45pm). It is a 30-minute walk through Condeixa and the surrounding olive groves surrounding it up the road to Conímbriga.

BUÇACO FOREST AND LUSO

Buçaco (also spelled Bussaco), home to Portugal's most revered forest, has for centuries drawn wanderers in search of a pristine escape from the city. In the 6th century, Benedictine monks settled in the Buçaco Forest, established a monastery, and remained in control until the 1834 disestablishment of all religious orders. However, the forest owes its fame to the Carmelite monks who arrived here nearly 400 years ago. Selecting the forest for their *desertos* (isolated dwellings for penitence), Carmelites periodically planted trees and plants brought from around the world by missionaries. Today, the fruits of their labor are inspiring.

Dom Manuel II's exuberant **Palácio de Buçaco,** adjoining the old Carmelite **convent,** is a flamboyant display of neo-Manueline architecture. The *azulejos* adorning the outer walls depict scenes from *Os Lusíadas,* the great Portuguese epic about the Age of Discovery (see **Portuguese Literature,** p. 520). The palace is now a luxury hotel *(pousada)* with a doting staff that can provide maps of the forest.

In the forest itself, landmarks include the **Fonte Fria** (Cold Fountain) with waters that ripple down entrance steps, the **Vale dos Fetos** (Fern Valley) below, and the **Porta de Reina** (Queen's Gate). Robust walkers trek one hour along the Via Sacra to a sweeping panorama of the countryside from the **Cruz Alta** viewpoint. The little 17th-century **chapels** represent stations of the cross.

Bus service from Coimbra to Buçaco continues on to Viseu (first bus at 7:45am, Sat.-Sun. 9am, 5 per day, Sat.-Sun. 3 per day, 1hr., 440$). Buses leave from Buçaco's station on Av. Fernão de Magalhães, a 15-minute walk from downtown. (The last bus back to Coimbra leaves Buçaco at 6:15pm, Sat.-Sun. 4:20pm. Schedules change frequently, so confirm departing times at the tourist office.)

More buses make it to **Luso,** a 4km walk downhill from Buçaco and site of the **Fonte de São João,** the source of all that bottled water you have been gulping in Portugal. Be sure to get directions or a map from the hotel/palace in Buçaco before leaving. A crisp, cold **spring** spouts water for free public consumption. Bring some sort of vessel unless you want to be in the embarrassing position of having to suck straight from the spring. The staff at Luso's **tourist office** (tel. ((0)31) 93 91 33), on R. Emídio Navarro in the center of town, stacks lists of *pensões,* supplies a map, and is a *fonte* of knowledge about the area. (Open Mon.-Fri. 10am-8pm, Sat.-Sun. 10am-12:30pm and 2:30-8pm; Aug. 13-June Mon.-Fri. 9am-noon and 3-6pm, Sat.-Sun. 9am-12:30pm and 2:30-5pm.) **Buses** back to Coimbra stop on the same street, a couple blocks above the tourist office and across from the natural springs (Mon.-Fri. 5 per day, Sat.-Sun. 3 per day; last return at 6:55pm).

■ Between Coimbra and Porto

OVAR

Ovar, a sleepy, *azulejo*-fronted town hemmed in by two parts *pinheiro* (pine forest) and one part isolated beach, is a perfectly relaxing stopover. The town's new HI youth hostel is a veritable R-and-R nirvana, and the nearby **Praia do Furadouro** is clean and relatively untouristed. The town, itself rather uninteresting, lies along the railroad tracks about 4km from the coast.

Conveniently, **buses** to the beach and youth hostel stop right in front of the train station and just past the tourist office, to the right of the garden. (Buses every 15min., in winter every 30min.; last bus is around 7pm, 120$ to the beach and 90$ to the hostel.) The **tourist office** (tel. 57 22 15), on R. Elias Garcia, has maps and transportation information. Head straight ahead from the train station (take the right fork), through the traffic circle on Pr. São Cristóvão and follow Av. do Bom Reitor to Régua R. Dr. Manuel Avala, which turns into R. Elias Garcia. (Open daily 9:30am-12:30pm and 2-5:30pm; Nov.-April daily 10am-12:30pm and 2-5:30pm.) The **police** (tel. 57 29 99) are on R. José Estêvão. The **postal code** is 3880. The **telephone code** is (0)56.

If you are an HI member, put your feet up at the brand-new **Pousada de Juventude de Ovar (HI)**, Av. Dom Manuel I (Estrada Nacional 327; tel. 59 18 32). Take the bus to the beach (see above), get off at the stop right before the traffic circle 2km outside of town, turn right (follow the signs to Porto), and walk for about 10 minutes. You will see the sign for the hostel on the right. Pristine rooms, a relaxed bar with billiards and satellite TV, and home-cooked meals (lunch or dinner 900$) make this modern hostel a prime rest stop. Bike rental and horseback riding are also available. (Reception open 9am-midnight. Dorm beds 1700$. Doubles with bath 4200$. Off-season: 1400$; 3550$. Call ahead in high season.) There is **camping** on **Praia do Furadouro** (tel. 59 14 71), 4km from the city center, with amenities including a restaurant, minimart, sports fields, and hairdresser. (Reception open daily 8am-10pm. 470$ per person, 305$ per tent and per car. Open Feb.-Nov.) For food, buy out the **Mercado Municipal** (open Mon.-Sat. 9am-1pm). There are also a series of **food stalls** just off the Estrada nacional by the youth hostel.

The **train station** on Largo Serpa Pinto has service to: Aveiro (every hr., 30min., 250$); Porto (45min., 250$); Coimbra (1hr., 700$); and Lisbon (3½hr., 1750$).

■ Leiria

Capital of the surrounding district and an important transport hub, noisy Leiria (pop. 103,000) fans out from a fertile valley, 22km from the coast. An impressive ancient castle peers over this prosperous city, gazing upon countless shops and a beautiful park. While Leiria itself may not be the most exciting destination in Portugal, buses heading away from Leiria run frequently enough to satisfy both culture vultures (aching to get to the surrounding historic towns) and beach leeches (their minds and bodies firmly set on the gorgeous beaches of the Costa da Prata).

Practical Information Most commerce bustles about the sight-packed path from the tourist office to the castelo, so don't expect to wander far. **Buses** (tel. 81 15 07) leave from just off Pr. Paulo VI, next to the town garden. This is the easiest way to get to and from Leiria. Buses run to: Batalha (9 per day, 15min., 190$); Fátima (7 per day, 1hr., 600$; 6 expressos per day, 720$); Nazaré (8 per day, 14min., 750$); Coimbra (8 per day, 1hr., 800$); Lisbon (11 per day, 2hr., 1100$); Porto (8 per day, 3½hr., 1300$); Figueira da Foz (4 per day, 1½hr., 800$); Santarém (4 per day, 1hr., 105$); Tomar (2 per day, 1hr., 850$). **Trains** (tel. 88 20 27), run to Lisbon (12 per day, 3½hr., 1100$); and Figueira (7 per day, 1¼hr., 410$); to reach Coimbra you must change trains at Lares (hint: take a bus). The train station is 3km outside town. Buses for the station leave across the street from the tourist office (approximately every hr. 7:15am-11:45pm, every 20min. on summer weekdays, 10min., 100$). To reach the **tourist office** (tel. 81 47 48 or 82 37 73), cross the park facing the bus station. They have maps and schedules for beach-going buses. The English-speaking staff allows temporary luggage storage. Open Mon.-Fri. 9am-7pm, Sat.-Sun. 10am-1pm and 3-7pm; Oct.-April Mon.-Fri. 9am-6pm, Sat.-Sun. 10am-1pm and 3-6pm. A taxi (tel. 81 59 00 or 80 17 59) from the town center to the train station is 450$. For medical needs, the Hospital (tel. 812 215), Rua das Olhalvas, along road to Fátima, can help. The police can be found at at Largo Artilharia, 4 (tel. 81 37 99). In an emergency, call 112. The post office (tel. 81 28 09) is on Av. Combatentes da Grande Guerra three blocks from the youth hostel. Label Posta Restante mail "Estação Santana" (open Mon.-Fri. 8:30am-6:30pm, Sat. 9am-12:30pm). Another post office, Av. Heróis de Angola, 99 (tel. 82 41 68; Posta Restante: "Estação Angola"), down the street behind the bus station, has the same hours. The **postal code** is 2400. The **telephone code** is (0)44.

Accommodations and Food Bottom-barrel prices begin and end at the **Pousada de Juventude (HI)**, on Largo Cândido dos Reis, 7D (tel. 318 68). From the bus station walk to the cathedral, then exit Largo da Sé (next to Largo Cónego Maia) on R. Barão de Viamonte, a narrow street lined with shops. Largo Cândido dos Reis is about six blocks straight ahead. This recently renovated youth hostel is clean and *con-*

fortável. Kitchen and laundry facilities are available. Reception is open daily 9am-noon and 6pm-midnight. There is a flexible lockout noon-6pm (1300$ per person; off-season 1100$; breakfast included). **Residencial Dom Dinis,** Travessa de Tomar, 2 (tel. 81 53 42), has 18 cozy, modern rooms with baths, telephones, and satellite TV. Turn left after exiting the tourist office, cross the bridge over Rio Lis, walk two blocks, and turn left again (singles 3500$, doubles 5500$, triples 6500$; breakfast included; Visa, MC.) For **camping,** try **Praia do Pedrógão** (tel. 69 54 03), 10km from Leiria in nearby Monte Real. The park is nestled in the pines only 100m from the beach, and has a mini-mercado, restaurant, and snack bar. An international camping ID card is needed for entry. (210$ per person, per tent, and per car. Hot shower 120$. Open April 1-Oct. 31 9:30am-9pm.)

Shop for fruit and vegetables at the **market** (Tues. and Sat. 9am-1pm) in Largo da Feira, located on the far side of the castle from the bus station. **Supermercado Ulmar,** Av. Heróis de Angola, 56, has American (and Portuguese) foodstuffs (open Mon.-Sat. 8am-8pm, Sun. 10am-1pm and 3-6pm). **Restaurante Aquário,** R. Caitão. Mouzinho de Albuquerque, 17 (tel. 247 20), is on the main street into town, the 2nd right and 2 blocks from the bus station. Prices for superior regional specialties are quite reasonable. Try arroz á valenciana (rice with seafood and meat 1350$. Entrees 850-1450$. Open Fri.-Wed. noon-3pm and 7-10pm.)

Sights and Entertainment From the main square, follow the signs past the austere **sé** (cathedral) to the city's most magnificent monument, the **castelo.** This granite fort, built by the first king of Portugal, Dom Afonso Henriques, after he snatched the town from the Moors, dramatically presides atop the crest of a volcanic hill overlooking the north edge of town. Left to crumble for hundreds of years, only the **torre de menagem** (homage tower) and the **sala dos namorados** (lovers' hall) remain from the original. The main attractions are the terrace, which opens onto a panoramic view of town and the river, and the roofless shell of the 14th-century **Igreja da Nossa Senhora da Penha** (castle open daily 9am-6:30pm; 130$).

The **Santuário de Nossa Senhora de Encarnação** sits upon a wooded hill on the southern edge of town. Cross the river at the tourist office and take the fourth left. Inside, colorful murals painted above the choir illustrate three local miracles attributed to Mary. If the main doors are closed, try the unbolted door on the south wall. The church does not have any official hours. Trade the saints for the sun at nearby **beaches. Vieira, Pedrógã,** and **São Pedro de Moel** are all easily accessible via hourly buses departing from the tourist office.

Bars along Largo Cândido dos Reis near the youth hostel come alive after 10pm and have weekly drink specials. The **Teatro José Lúcio da Silva** (tel. 82 36 00), on the corner of Av. Heróis de Angola behind the bus station, features films and performances. The ticket office opens daily 7-10pm and the tourist office has a schedule.

▓ Fátima

Fátima used to be a sheep pasture; now it's a Roman Catholic religious center. Come if you're interested in pilgrimage, or don't come at all. Now that you've decided, prepare yourself for immersion in holy fervor. Only Lourdes rivals this site in popularity with Christian pilgrims. The miracles believed to have occurred here are modern-day phenomena, well-documented and witnessed by thousands. The asphalt-covered plaza in front of the church, larger than St. Peter's square in the Vatican, floods with pilgrims on the 12th and 13th of each month. The pious and hardy cross the 500m esplanade with dutiful piety and the curious consumerism that has bubbled since the advent of religious memorabilia (100ml bottle of holy water 150$).

ORIENTATION AND PRACTICAL INFORMATION

Activity in Fátima focuses in and around the basilica complex in the town center. **Avenida Dr. José Alves Correia da Silva,** running just south of the hubbub, contains

the bus station and tourist office. A right turn and 10-minute walk from the bus station leads to the tourist office at the plaza leading to the basilica.

Tourist Office: Av. Dr. José Alves Correia da Silva (tel. 53 11 39), same Av. as the bus station (go left as you exit), in a Hawaii Five-0 bungalow. Open Mon.-Fri. 9am-7pm, Sat.-Sun. 10am-1pm and 3-7pm; Oct.-April closes 1 hour earlier in the evening. Temporary **luggage storage.**

Currency Exchange: União de Bancos Portugueses, R. Francisco Marto, 139 (tel. 53 39 68). 1000$ commision for cash, 1000$ plus 1% for traveler's checks. Open 8:30am-3pm.

Trains: Station (tel. 461 22) is 20km out of town on Chão de Maças. To: Coimbra (3 per day, 1hr., 900$); Santarém (2 per day, via Entroncamento, 1½hr., 1100$); Lisbon (2 per day, via Entroncamento, 2hr., 1150$). Six buses per day run there from the bus station (45min., 340$).

Buses: Av. Dr. José Alves Correia da Silva (tel. 53 16 11). On bus schedules Fátima is often referred to as **Cova da Ivia**—forget and you'll risk confusion. Leiria (15 per day, 1hr., 600$); Batalha (3 per day, 45min., 240$); Tomar (2 per day, 1¼hr., 650$); Lisbon (8 per day, 2½hr., 1100$); Porto (7 per day, 3½hr., 1350$); Santarém (6 per day, 1hr., 850$); Nazaré (4 per day, 1½hr., 900$).

Taxis: (tel. 53 21 16 or 53 16 22).

Hospital: (tel. 53 18 36). A health center in Fátima is on R. Jacinta Marto.

Police: Av. Dr. José Alves Correia de Silva (tel. 53 11 05), near Rotunda de Sta. Teresa de Ourém. **Emergency:** tel. 115.

Post Office: R. Cónego Formagião (tel. 53 18 10), on the left before the tourist office. Has **telephones.** Open Mon.-Fri. 8:30am-6pm, Sat. 3-8pm, Sun. 9am-noon; Oct.-May Mon.-Fri. 8:30am-6pm. **Postal Code:** 2495.

Telephone Code: (0)49.

ACCOMMODATIONS AND FOOD

Scores of *pensões* and *hotéis* inundate both sides of the basilica complex. Credit cards are almost universally accepted, and lodging prices vary little. The town fills most during the grand pilgrimages on the 12th and 13th of each month and both *pensão* and hotel prices tend to increase 500-1500$ during these days. **Ruas Francisco Marto, Santa Isabela,** and **Jacinta Marto** have similar, touristy restaurants.

Pensão Dona Maria, R. Av. Dr. José Alves Coneia da Silva, 122 (tel. 53 12 12), between the bus station and tourist office—head left as you exit the station. *Simpática* owner dotes on cheery, Laura Ashley-type clients. Rooms 3500-5000$, all with bath and winter heat, some with balcony. Breakfast included.

Pensão A Paragem (tel. 53 15 58). The cheapest beds in town, upstairs in the bus station. Clean, pleasant, and ideal if you miss the last bus out of town. Try to get an early start in the morning—by 7:30am, diesel fumes begin to penetrate the room. All rooms with bath, doubles have TVs. Singles 2500$. Doubles 4500$. Triples 5000$. Breakfast included.

Mary and the Three Shepherds

On May 13, 1917, Mary appeared before three shepherd children—Lucía, Francisco, and Jacinta—to issue a call for peace in the middle of WWI. The children remained steadfast in their belief, despite the skepticism of clergy and attacks from the press, as word of the vision spread throughout Portugal. Bigger and bigger crowds flocked to the site as Our Lady of Fátima returned to speak to the children on the 13th of each month, promising a miracle for her final appearance in October. On that morning, 70,000 people gathered under a torrential rain storm. At noon, the sun reportedly spun around in a furious light spectacle and appeared to sink toward the earth. When the light returned to normal, no evidence remained of the morning's rain. Convinced by the "fiery signature of God," the townspeople built a chapel at the site to honor Mary.

Adega Funda, R. Francisco Marto, 103 (tel. 53 13 72). Take a break from prayer in this large wood dining room. Hefty traditional Portuguese dishes like *bacalhau à churrasco* (barbecued cod 1200$). Open daily 11am-3pm and 6-10pm.

Snack Bar A Lovca (tel. 53 16 21), R. Jacinta Marto in the Pope John Paul II building. Yep, it's one crazy snack bar. Lighter food, including omelettes (650-800$) and *pratos do dia* (750$). Open daily 11am-midnight.

SIGHTS AND ENTERTAINMENT

The sanctuary is set in parks shaded by tall leafy trees that block out the surrounding commercial area. At the end of the plaza rises the super-cool **Basílica do Rosário** (erected in 1928). A crystal cruciform beacon perches atop the tower's seven-ton bronze crown. Many of the devout approach the basilica on their knees across the length of the plaza. The centerpiece is a painting depicting Mary before the three shepherds. A dress code is enforced for both sexes—no shorts, bathing suits, tank tops, or other "inappropriate" clothing is allowed (open daily 7am-8pm). Sheltered beneath a metal and glass canopy, the 1919 **Capelinha das Aparições** (Little Chapel of the Apparitions) holds masses in six languages all morning and some evenings. To the right of the chapel is the very same **oak tree** under which the children prayed (though it's grown quite a bit since then). Museums commemorate the miracle. To the right facing the basilica (three blocks off, the **Museu de Arte Sacra e Etnologia,** R. Francisco Marto, 52 (tel. 53 29 15), exhibits Catholic icons from various centuries and boasts of missionaries' successes converting peoples in Africa, South America, and Asia. (Open April-Oct., Tues.-Sun. 10am-6pm; Nov.-March noon-5pm. 400$, students and seniors 200$). To the left of the basilica, through the park, and in the complex beneath the Hotel Fátima, the **Museu-Vivo Aparições,** R. Jacinta Marto (tel. 53 28 58), uses light, sound, and special effects to re-create the apparition (open 9am-8pm; Nov.-April 9am-6pm; multilingual soundtracks; 450$).

BATALHA

The *only* reason to visit Batalha (pop. 14,000) is the gigantic **Mosteiro de Santa Maria da Vitória,** which rivals Belém's Mosteiro dos Jerónimos in monastic splendor. Built by Dom João I in 1385 to commemorate his victory against the Spanish, the complex of cloisters and chapels remains one of Portugal's greatest monuments. To get to the *mosteiro,* enter through the church.

The **tourist office,** on Pr. Mouzinho de Albuquerque along R. Nossa Senhora do Caminho (tel. 961 80), across from the unfinished chapels of the *mosteiro,* has **maps** and bus info. (Open Mon.-Fri. 10am-1pm and 3-7pm, Sat.-Sun. 10am-1pm and 3-6pm; Oct.-April closes 1hr. earlier in the evening.) For **police,** call tel. 961 34. In an **emergency,** dial 112. The **post office** (tel. 961 11) is on Largo Papa Paulo VI, near the freeway entrance (open Mon.-Fri. 9am-12:30pm and 2:30-6pm). The **postal code** is 2440. The **telephone code** is (0)44. The **bus** stop is a concrete structure across from Pensão Vitória on Largo da Misericórdia. Inquire at the tourist office for info or call the bus station in Leiria (tel. 811 507). Buses run to: Leiria (7 per day, 20min., 180$); Fátima (3 per day, 40min., 250$); Alcobaça (12 per day, 45min., 350$); Nazaré, change at Alcobaça (5 per day, 1hr., 470$); Tomar (4 per day, 1½hr., 470$); and Lisbon (5 per day, 2hr., 2100$). Batalha is devoid of cheap beds or even a campground. If marooned here, sleep at **Pensão Vitória** (tel. 966 78), on Largo da Misericórdia in front of the bus stop. Its three simple, dark rooms are bare and monastic (3000$ per room). The **restaurant** below does wonders with *pudim* (pudding) and is a handy place to wait for the bus. Several inexpensive **churrosquarias** (barbecue houses) and **cafes** line the squares flanking the monastery.

The church **facade** soars upward in a heavy Gothic and Manueline style, opulently decorated and topped off by dozens of spires. Napoleon's troops turned the nave into a brothel, but none of that goes on today. The **Capela do Fundador,** immediately to the right of the church, shelters the elaborate sarcophagi of Dom João I, his English-born queen Philippa of Lancaster, and their son Henry the Navigator. The rest of the

PORTUGAL

monastery complex is accessible via a door in the north wall of the church, but you have to buy a ticket (400$, under 26 and senior citizens 200$; Sun 10am-2pm free). Enter through the broad Gothic arches of the **Claustro de Dom João I,** the delicate columns of which initiated the Manueline style. Don't mess with the stone-faced soldiers in the adjacent **Tomb of the Unknown Soldier**—they won't smile, and they've got machine guns. Through the **Claustro de Dom Afonso V,** out the door and to the right are the impressive **Capelas Imperfeitas** (Imperfect Chapels), with massive buttresses designed to support a large dome. The project was dropped when Manuel I ordered his workers to build a monastery in Belém instead (complex open daily 9am-5pm; 400$, under 25 200$). If you are visiting August 14-15 and are feeling festive, join the Our Lady of Victory celebration.

■ Near Batalha

Nature is at its most psychedelic in a spectacular series of underground *grutas* (caves) in Estremadura's natural park between Batalha and Fátima. The vast labyrinth of minuscule stalagmite and stalactite formations is accessible by bus; at **Mira de Aire,** 15km away, a tour guide accompanies you on the descent. About 15km farther, the **Grutas de Santo António** and **Alvados** are a bit more difficult to reach, but equally impressive. Take a **bus** to Alto de Alvados (from Leiria, 4 per day, 1hr., 400$). Most of the caves have been "enhanced" with background music and strategically placed colored spotlights. The tourist offices in both Batalha and Fátima have maps of the region and info on how to reach the caves.

■ Figueira da Foz

Figueira is one of the biggest (and seediest) party towns in Portugal, a place where pleasure-seekers celebrate the sun, the moon, and the neon sign. The constant sounds of arcade games and grunge rock seep down the dirty streets at all hours of the day, while at night tanned couples and some somewhat sketchy characters crowd the 12 bars, discos, outdoor cafes, and press their luck at the casino. Exhausted revelers collapse on Figueira's best feature—the beach—which, 3 sq. km, seems exposed even when packed. Just a short walk away, the little fishing town of Buarcos goes about its business, apparently oblivious to Figueira's steamy decadence.

ORIENTATION AND PRACTICAL INFORMATION

Packed with hotels, beachfront **Avenida 25 de Abril** is the busy lifeline that distinguishes town from beach; after the fortress, it turns into **Rua 5 de Outubro** leading to the train station. Four blocks inland and parallel to the avenue, **Rua Bernardo Lopes** harbors semi-affordable *pensões* and restaurants. Much of the action in Figueira centers in the casino-cinema-disco complex on this street.

Tourist Office: Av. 25 de Abril (tel. 226 10; fax 285 49), next to the Aparthotel Atlântico at the very end of the airport terminal complex. Useful map. English spoken. **Luggage storage** available. Open daily 9am-11pm; Oct.-May Mon.-Fri. 9am-12:30pm and 2-5:30pm.

Currency Exchange: Banco Crédito Predial Português (tel. 284 58), R. João de Lemos, on a small street between R. Dr. António Dinis and R. Cândido dos Reis. 750$ commission for cash exchange; no charge for traveler's checks. Open daily 8:30am-3pm. Major hotels near the tourist office exchange when banks are closed.

Trains: (tel. 283 16), Largo da Estação, near the bridge. Trains are the easiest way to reach Coimbra and Porto. Take an easy 25min. walk to the tourist office and the beach. Keeping the river to the left, Av. Saraiva de Carvalho becomes R. 5 de Outubro at the fountain, then curves into Av. 25 de Abril. To: Coimbra (13 per day, 1hr., 280$); Lisbon (7 per day, 3½hr., 1400$); and Porto (8 per day, 3hr., 1120$).

Buses: Terminal Rodoviário (tel. 230 95), 15min. from the tourist office. Facing the church, turn right onto R. Dr. Santos Rocha. Walk about 10min. toward the waterfront; turn right onto R. 5 de Outubro, which curves into Av. 25 de Abril. To: Leiria

(8 per day, 1½hr., 610$); Coimbra (6 per day, 2hr., 645$); Faro (1 per day, 12hr., 2700$); Lisbon (4 per day, 3½hr., 1350$); Aveiro (4 per day, 2hr., 950$); Alcobaça (3 per day, 1½hr., 900$); and Fátima (3 per day, 1½hr., 1000$).

Taxis: (tel. 235 00, 237 88, or 232 18), at the bus or train stations. 24hr. service.

Laundromat: Lavandaria Agueirense (tel. 223 82), R. Cândido dos Reis, near the municipal garden. 500$ per kg. Open Mon.-Fri. 9am-1pm and 3-7pm, Sat. 3-7pm.

English Bookstore: Three on 1 block of Cândido dos Reis. **Tabacaria Africana** (tel. 246 58). Small selection of romance and mystery novels. Open daily 9:30am-1am.

Hospital: Hospital Distrital (tel. 200 00), in Gala, across the river.

Police: (tel. 220 22), R. Joaquim Carvalho, near the bus station and the park. **Emergency:** tel. 112.

Post Office: Main office, Passeio Infante Dom Henrique, 41 (tel. 241 01), off R. 5 de Outubro. Open for Posta Restante and **telephones** Mon.-Fri. 8:30am-6:30pm, Sat. 9am-12:30pm. More convenient **branch office** at R. Miguel Bombarda, 76 (tel. 230 10). Open for stamps and **telephones** Mon.-Fri. 9am-12:30pm and 2:30-6pm. **Postal Code:** 3080.

Telephones: in post office and in Telecom trailer above the tourist office. Trailer open July-Aug. only, 10am-midnight. English spoken. **Telephone Code:** (0)33.

ACCOMMODATIONS AND CAMPING

Scour **Rua Bernardo Lopes** and neighboring streets for reasonable *pensões.* Proprietors may demand inordinate prices for rooms (especially in summer). Budget rooms are often questionable, and feature dirty carpeting. Arrive early to check vacancies; many managers will not reserve a room by phone in high season.

Pensão Central, R. Bernardo Lopes, 36 (tel. 223 08), next to Supermarket Ovo, down the street from the casino complex and all the action. High ceilings and huge rooms, comfortable and well-furnished. All 15 rooms have TV and bath, but no phone. Singles 4500$. Doubles 6000$. Triples 7000$. Winter discount. Breakfast included for singles. Credit cards accepted.

Pensão Residencial Rio Mar, R. Dr. António Dinis, 90 (tel. 230 53), perpendicular to R. Bernardo Lopes. Turn left at Benneton. 23 spacious and comfortable (albeit old and dark) rooms, of which half have their own bath. Singles 2500$. Doubles 4000$, with bath 6000$. Visa, MC, AmEx.

Pensão Residencial Bela Figueira, R. Miguel Bombarda, 13 (tel. 227 28; fax 299 60), 2 blocks from the tourist office and above an Indian restaurant. 12 simply-furnished rooms all with phones, some with TVs. Central heating. Singles 4500-6200$. Doubles 5000-6950$. Triples 5000-7500$. Prices drop 2000$ in the off season.

Pensão Restaurante Europa, R. Cândido dos Reis, 40 (tel. 222 65). A good deal for a typically dingy room with a big bed and huge window. The location (above a pool hall and busy restaurant) helps compensate. Closed Oct.-April. Singles 3500-4000$. Doubles $5500. Credit cards accepted.

Camping: Parque Municipal de Campismo da Figueira da Foz Municipal (tel. 327 42 or 330 33), on Estrada de Buarcos. With the beach on your left, walk up Av. 25 de Abril and turn right at the roundabout on R. Alexandre Herculano, then turn left at Parque Santa Catarina going up R. Joaquim Sotto-Mayor past Palácio Sotto-Mayor. Or take a taxi from bus or train station (500$). Excellent site complete with an Olympic-size pool, tennis courts, market, and **currency exchange.** Open year-round. Reception open daily 8am-8pm; Oct.-May 8am-7pm. Silence reigns midnight-7am. Showers 100$. June-Sept. each party must have a minimum of 2 people. 400$ per person, under 10 free. 300$ per tent and per car.

FOOD

Restaurants are more expensive than the Portuguese norm in Figueira, but hope (and good food) lies around **Rua Bernardo Lopes.** The truly lazy frequent sandy joints such as **O Bote,** between the sidewalk and the sea. A local **market** sets up beside the municipal garden on R. 5 de Outubro (open Mon.-Sat. 7am-7pm; in winter Sun.-Fri. 8am-5pm, Sat. 8am-1pm). For imported foods, check out **Supermercado Ovo,** on the corner of R. A. Dinis and R. B. Lopes (open Mon.-Fri. 9am-1pm and 3-7pm).

Restaurante Rancho, R. Miguel Bombarda, 40-44 (tel. 220 19), 2 blocks from the tourist office. Packed with locals at lunchtime. Hefty, delicious entrees (650-1100$) such as *chocos grelhados* (grilled cuttlefish, 650$). The *ementa turística* is a great deal (3 courses 1100$). Open Mon.-Sat. 11am-10pm.

Restaurante Bela Figueira, R. Miguel Bombardo, 13 (tel. 227 28), beneath the *pensão* of the same name. Tasty Indian food, including vegetable curry with roti (1000$) and chicken biryani (1200$). Several good vegetarian options are available, as is a less expensive menu with traditional Portuguese food. Entrees around 850$. Open daily noon-midnight. Credit cards accepted.

Café O Picadeiro, R. Acadêmico Zagalo, 20 (tel. 222 45), off R. Cândido dos Reis. This always-packed cafe/snack bar/restaurant serves snacks, drinks, and full meals (850-1300$). Sit under the white parasols, have a beer, and look blasé—you will fit right in. Open daily 10am-4am.

SIGHTS AND ENTERTAINMENT

In Figueira, the entertainment *is* the sight (and vice versa). Nightlife takes off between 10pm and 2am, depending on the disco or bar, and continues all night. Joints line **Avenida 25 de Abril,** next to and above the tourist office. A student crowd gathers at **Bergantim** (tel. 238 85), R. Dr. António Lopes Guimarães, inland from the train station. There are more lively places like **Buarcos,** a 30-minute walk along the waterfront to the other side of the cove. Do the disco thing at **CC Café** (tel. 34 18 88), just off the water at the end of the ramp. A happening crowd can be found at **Bar 31,** a block away from the beach on R. Cândido dos Reis. The **casino** complex on R. Bernardo Lopes (tel. 220 41) also has a **nightclub** (cover charge 1500$), **cinema** (500$), and **arcade.** Entry to the slot machines and bingo is free. You must be over 18 and show proper ID if you wish to gamble. There is also a show, usually a pseudo-Las Vegas revue, at night (casino open July-Aug. daily 4pm-4am, Sept.-June 3pm-3am).

Figueira's standard party mode shifts from high gear to warp speed during the **Festa de São João** (June 6 -July 9), featuring free public concerts every night. Around 5am, a huge rowdy procession heads for the beach at nearby Buarcos where all involved take a *banho santo* (holy bath). The **Festival de Cinema da Figueira da Foz** screens international flicks for 10 days in September.

If you feel naughty neglecting your vast intellect, the **Museu Municipal do Doutor Santos Rocha** (tel. 245 09) houses everything from ancient coins to the decadent fashions of Portuguese nobility. The building, in Parque Abadias, faces P. Calouste Gulbenkian (open Tues.-Sun. 9am-12:30pm and 2-5pm; free). **Casa do Paço,** Largo Prof. Vitar Guerra, 4 (tel. 221 59), is decorated with 6888 Delft tiles that fortuitously washed ashore after a shipwreck (open Mon.-Fri. 9:30am-12:30pm and 2-5pm; free). The modest exterior of the **Palácio Sotto Mayor** (tel. 221 21), R. Joaquim Sotto Mayor, belies the shameless extravagance inside. Lavish green marble columns line the main hallway, and gold leaf covers the ceiling (open Tues.-Sun. 2-6pm; 150$).

■ Aveiro

The old center of Aveiro is graced with several charming canals, along which traditional *gonalas*—like fishing boats laden with seaweed and sea salt—drift out to sea. The town boasts lovely sights. When you are through with these…well, unless you like gawking at seaweed, you'd best float out to sea as well; the region around Aveiro hosts some highly swimmable beaches. Prices may seem unjustifiably high in this tourist hole; rebel by camping at scenic **São Jacinto** on the outer banks.

ORIENTATION AND PRACTICAL INFORMATION

Two hundred kilometers north of Lisbon and sixty kilometers south of Porto, Aveiro is split by the *canal central* and a parallel street, **Avenida Dr. Lourenço Peixinho,** running from the train station to **Praça Humberto Delgado** (a *praça* that is really no more than a few bridges spanning the canals). The fishermen's quarter of **Beira Mar**

The Heart of the Matter

There's love, and there's *love*. Exhibit number one in the latter category is Dom Pedro I. While a prince, he fell head over heels for Inês de Castro, the daughter of a Spanish nobleman. Pedro's father, Afonso IV, objected to the romance, fearing such an alliance would open the Portuguese throne to Spanish domination. Pedro and Inês fled to Bragança where the couple was secretly wed, but soon thereafter the disgruntled Afonso had Inês killed. Upon rising to the throne, Pedro promptly—and personally—ripped out the hearts of the men who had slit his young wife's throat and proceeded to eat the broken *coracões*. Henceforth, the hardy king became known as Pedro the Cruel. In a disheartening ceremony, he had Inês's body exhumed, dressed her meticulously in royal robes, set her on the throne, and officially deemed her his queen. Eventually, she was reinterred in an exquisitely carved tomb in the king's favorite monastery. The king would later join her, both figuratively and literally, in a tomb directly opposite hers. The inscription on their tombs, *"Até ao fim do mundo"* (until the end of the world), attests to Pedro's intention that the couple finally reunite—face to face—at the moment of resurrection.

lies north of the *canal central*. The port to the south is the residential district and contains all of Aveiro's historical monuments.

To reach the **tourist office** from the **train station,** walk up Av. Dr. Lourenço Peixinho (the left-most street) until you reach the bridge; the office is an easy one-km walk on the righ-thand side in the next block. You can also hop on a bus (every 15min., 150$) from the station. Trains are the most convenient means of travel in and out of Aveiro and the Rota da Luz region.

Tourist Office: R. João Mendonça, 8 (tel. 236 80 or 207 60; fax 283 26), in an old-style building off the Pr. Humberto Delgado, on the street to the right of the canal as you are facing the ocean. Cheerful English-speaking staff doles out maps and lodging advice. If you have the time (or desire), watch a video about local fishermen. Free daytime **luggage storage.** Open Mon.-Fri. 9am-8pm, Sat. 9am-8pm, Sun. 9am-7pm; Sept. 15-June 15 Mon.-Fri. 9am-7pm, Sat. 9am-1pm and 2:30-5:30pm.

Currency Exchange: Hotel Pomba Branca, R. Luís Gomes de Carvalho, 23 (tel. 225 29), 1st right on Av. Dr. Lourenço Peixinho from train station. 24hr. service at bank rates. There is an **ATM** at Banco Fonsecas e Burnay across from the tourist office at R. Coimbra, 2 (tel. 231 31); more ATMs between the train station and tourist office.

Trains: Largo Estação (tel. 244 85), at the end of Av. Dr. Lourenço Peixinho. To: Coimbra (21 per day, 1hr., 460$); Porto (21 per day, 30min., 330$); Lisbon (21 per day, 5hr., 1600$); Braga (3 per day, 1½hr., 860$).

Buses: Since the nearest Rodoviária station is 19km away in Águeda, trains are more convenient for long-distance travel. Eight buses and 8 trains per day go from the train station to Águeda (230$). **AVIC-Mondego,** R. Comandante Rocha Cunha, 55 (tel. 237 47), runs from the train station to the Águeda station to Figueira da Foz (6 per day, 2½hr., 650$) and Praia da Mira (5 per day, 45min., 400$). For buses to Fortalezada Barra, see **Ferries** (below).

Ferries: Two direct boats per day from Aveiro to São Jacinto May 2-Sept. 20; reserve early via **Trans Ria** (tel. 33 10 95), on Av. Marginal in São Jacinto. Buses leave the railway station for Forte da Barra, where you can catch a ferry (12 per day, 7am-6pm, 30min., 220$). Also from Forte da Barra, you can get the bus coming from Gafanha de Nazaré to Barra, or a direct bus that runs July-Aug. 7:20am-8:40pm.

Taxis: (tel. 229 43 or 237 66). Taxis congregate around the train station and at the end of R. João Mendonça.

Bike Rental: (tel. 200 80), next to the tourist office on R. João Mendonça.

Laundromat: Lavandaria União, Av. Dr. Lourenço Peixinho, 292 (tel. 235 56), near the train station. 500$ per kg. Open Mon.-Fri. 9am-1pm and 1:30-7pm.

Hospital: Av. Dr. Artur Ravara (tel. 221 33), near the park across the canal.

Police: (tel. 220 22 or 211 37), Pr. Marquês de Pombal. **Emergency:** (tel. 112).

Post Office: Estação Vera Cruz: Pr. Marquês de Pombal (tel. 271 00). Cross the main bridge and walk up R. Coimbra past the town hall. Open for Posta Restante, **fax,** and **telephones** Mon.-Fri. 8:30am-6:30pm, Sat. 9am-12:30pm. A **branch office,** Av. Dr. Lourenço Peixinho, 169 (tel. 274 84), has the same services and is more centrally located (2 blocks away from the train station). Open Mon.-Fri. 8:30am-6:30pm. **Postal Code:** 3800.
Telephone Code: (0)34.

ACCOMMODATIONS AND CAMPING

The *pensões* lining Av. Dr. Lourenço Peixinho and the streets around Pr. Marquês de Pombal in the old city are more expensive than average but almost always have vacancies. The tourist office can assist in finding a place to stay.

Residencial Estrêla, R. José Estêvão, 4 (tel. 238 18), in an elegant building overlooking Pr. Humberto Delgado. Grand stairway illuminated by an oval skylight. Lordly rooms are on the 1st floor; servant-type quarters higher up. Friendly, English-speaking owner. Singles 4000$, with bath 4500$. Doubles: 5500$; 6000$. Triples 8000$. Winter: 2500$; 3000$; 4000$; 4500$; 5000$. Breakfast included.

Pensão Ferro, R. dos Marnotos, 30 (tel. 222 14). From the tourist office turn right, then take the 2nd street on the right. 35 rooms featuring high ceilings, windows (request them), and clean common baths make this airy, pastel-colored *pensão* a soothing place to stay. Singles 3000$. Doubles 3500$.

Residencial Santa Joana, Av. Dr. Lourenço Peixinho, 227 (tel. 286 04), a block from the train station on the left. Five floors stack spacious, no-frills, and reasonably priced rooms in a transport-friendly location. Naturally cool in summer. All rooms features phone, TV, and private bath. Singles 3500$. Doubles 5500$.

Camping: Orbitur São Jacinto (tel. 482 84; fax 481 22), on the beach northwest of Aveiro. Take the bus from the Canal Central stop to Forte da Barra (10min., 220$), then hop on the boat to São Jacinto (10min., 135$). Hike 5km or take a bus (150$) to the campsite. Sometimes crowded. Reception open Jan. 16-Nov. 15 8am-10pm. 570$ per person and per tent, 480$ per car. **Municipal Campground** (tel. 33 12 20; fax 33 10 78). Follow directions to Orbitur site until S. Jaunto; it is a 2km walk (20min.) down Estrada Nacional. Fewer facilities, lower prices. 300$ per person. 150$ per tent. 275$ per car. Reception open daily 8am-9pm; in winter 8am-7pm.

FOOD

Seafood restaurants are common, but prices will make you want to catch your own fish. Cast around for cheaper gruel off **Av. Dr. Lourenço Peixinho** and **R. José Estêvão.** Aveiro is known for its dessert pastries called *ovos moles* (sweetened egg yolks), available at most cafes in town. For normal egg yolks, patronize **Supermercado Mini Preço,** Av. Dr. Lourenço Peixinho, 132.

Restaurante Salimar, R. Combatentes da Grande Guerra, 6, 2nd fl. (tel. 251 08), across the river and a block uphill from the tourist office. Fragrant *bacalhau no churrasco* (barbecued cod 1200$) is served amid nautical decor. Their specialty is a bubbling, orange-red broth swimming with rice and seafood called *arroz de marisco* (1100$; 2 people 2000$). Open daily 8am-midnight.

Sonatura Restaurante Self-Service Naturista, R. Clube dos Galitos, 6 (tel. 244 74), directly across the canal from the tourist office. Vegetarian-macrobiotic-dieteticfood-store-restaurant serves up 2 daily menus (700$) which include soup, organic bread, and entree. Watch for their miso soup specials, made with delectable Aveiro seaweed. Open Mon.-Fri. 10am-10pm, Sat. 10am-3pm.

Restaurante Zico, R. José Estêvão, 52 (tel. 296 49), off Pr. Humberto Delgado . Very popular with the locals. If Mel's Diner opened a franchise in Aveiro, this is what it would look like—formica counters and all. Pork on *prego de porco* (pork steak with fries 650$) or try *omelete de camarão* (shrimp omelette 950$). Entrees 950-1500$. Save room for the calorie-ridden desserts. Open Mon.-Sat. 8am-2am.

SIGHTS AND ENTERTAINMENT

Aveiro is known for its beautiful *azulejo* facades and its great beaches. Don't miss the former because you are spending too much time on the latter. Simple but strikingly blue *azulejos* coolly make up the walls of the **Igreja da Misericórdia** in Praça da República, across the canal and a block uphill from the tourist office. In the same square, the regal **Paça do Concelho** (town hall) flaunts its French design, complete with bell tower. The real thriller of the compact old town is the **Museu de Aveiro,** R. Sta. Joana Princesa (tel. 232 97). The museum is housed in a c. 1458 convent where flamboyant gilded woodwork covers parts of the interior. In 1472, King Afonso and the Infanta Joana, who wished to become a nun despite her father's objections, had a royal battle here. She won. Beneath *azulejo* panels depicting the story of her life, Sta. Joana's Renaissance tomb, supported by the heads of four angels, is one of the most famous works of art in the country (open Tues.-Sun. 10am-12:30pm and 2-5pm; 250$, seniors and students 125$). The chapel beyond showcases the bewildering excesses similar to baroque woodcarving; its *coro alto* (high chorus) is lined with lacquered panels reminiscent of *chinoiserie*.

If *azulejo*-gawking loses its kick, head to the beach. Neighboring **beach** towns and the national park, **Dunas de São Jacinto** (sand dunes, approx. 10km away) merit daytrips. (To get to beach towns, see **Ferries,** p. 573.) At night, tap into the wateringholes lining **Rua Canal de São Rogue,** or strut your stuff with the beautiful people at neighboring **Salpoente, Estrondo Bar,** and **Urgência.** The bars around **Largo Praça de Peixe** in the old city in the **shopping center/entertainment complex,** Av. Dr. Lourenço Peixinho, 146 are also definite possibilities. For four weeks starting in mid-July, the city shakes for the **Festa da Ria.** As part of the festivities, dancers groove on a floating stage in the middle of the *canal central*.

Douro and Minho

Although their landscapes and shared Celtic past invite comparison with neighboring Galicia in Spain, the Douro and Minho regions of northern Portugal are more populated, wealthier, and far faster developing than much of Galicia. Spectacular greenery make them a haven for nature lovers. Hundreds of trellised vineyards in the fertile hills growing grapes for *porto* and *vinho verde* wines beckon connoisseurs. Additionally, houses tiled in brilliant *azulejos* draw visitors to charming, quiet streets. The traditional local female costume, which includes layer upon layer of gold necklaces encrusted with charms, attests to the area's mineral wealth. To add legacy to prosperity, the Kingdom of Portugal originated here in 1143 when Afonso Henriques defeated the Moors in Guimarães.

The mild climate is too cool to attract the beach crowd until July, and admittedly only a few ambitious travelers ever make it past Porto and the Douro Valley to the open greens and blues of the Alto Minho, which hugs the border with Spain. The cities of Vila Nova de Cerveira, Braga, Viana do Castelo, and Guimarães are all happily untouristed, but truly memorable for the few who do make it there.

▓ Porto (Oporto)

There's an old Portuguese proverb that says, "Coimbra sings, Braga prays, Lisbon sings, and Porto works." All that work has paid off: Porto is now one of Portugal's most sophisticated and modern cities. Although today it is a bustling center for all types of business, the source of its greatest fame can be sniffed in the bouquet of its *vinho do Porto*—port wine. Developed by English merchants in the early 18th century, the port wine industry drives the city's economy. Magnificently situated on a dramatic gorge cut by the Douro River, six kilometers from the sea, Portugal's second-largest city often seems more frenetic than Lisbon, even though its energy is framed within an elegance reminiscent of Paris or Prague. Granite church towers pierce the skyline, closely packed orange-tiled houses huddle along to the river, and three of Europe's most graceful bridges (one credited to Gustave Eiffel of Eiffel Tower fame) span the gorge above.

Porto's history is the stuff from which nationalism is made. When native son Henry the Navigator geared to conquer Ceuta (a soon-to-be Christian base in Africa), Porto residents slaughtered their cattle, gave all the meat to the Portuguese fleet, and kept only the entrails for themselves. The tasty dish *tripas à moda do Porto* commemorates this culinary self-sacrifice; to this day, the people of Porto are known as *tripeiros* (tripe-eaters), although the fetid bouquet of that particular delicacy belies the absolutely savory scent of their gloried wine. Whatever the smell, capture it and follow your nose to Porto, a graceful city well worth a visit.

ORIENTATION AND PRACTICAL INFORMATION

Get ready to...get lost. Constant traffic and a chaotic maze of one-way streets fluster even the most well-oriented of travelers; find your location on the map ASAP. At the very heart of the city is **Praça da Liberdade.** One of Porto's two train stations, **Estação São Bento,** lies right in the middle of town, just off the bottom of Pr. Liberdade. The other, **Estação de Campanhã,** is two kilometers east of the city. The **Ribeira** district is a few blocks to the south, directly across the bridge from **Vila Nova de Gaia,** where 80-odd port wine lodges ferment contentedly.

Tourist Office: R. Clube dos Fenianos, 25, just off the top of Pr. Liberdade. Robotically-efficient multilingual staff doles out maps and specialized brochures. Open Mon.-Fri. 9am-7pm, Sat. 9am-4pm, Sun. 10am-1pm; Oct.-June Mon.-Fri. 9:30am-5:30pm, Sat. 9am-4pm. **Branch office,** Pr. Dom João I, 25 (tel. 31 75 14), at R. Bonjardim. Open Mon.-Fri. 9am-7pm, Sat. 9am-2pm, Sun. 10am-2pm. There also are

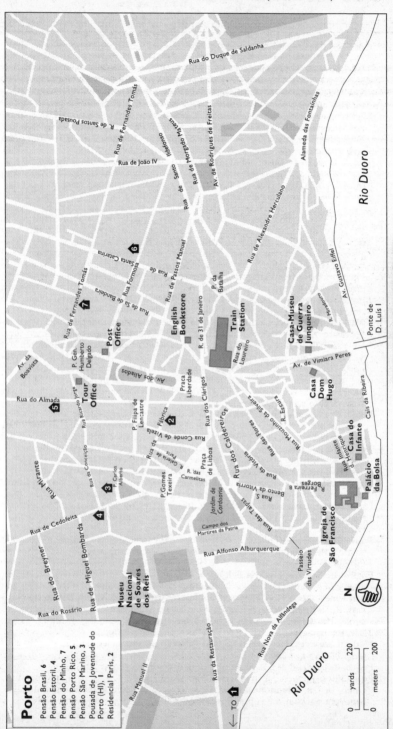

PORTUGAL

Rio Duoro

Rua do Duque de Saldanha

R. de Santos Pousada

Rua de João IV

Rua de Fernandes Tomás

Rua de Morgado Mateus

Rua de Rodrigues de Freitas

Av. de Rodrigues de Freitas

Alameda das Fontaínhas

Santo Ildefonso

Rua de Santo

Rua de Passos Manuel

Rua Formosa

Rua de Santa Catarina

Rua de Sá de Bandeira

Rua de Fernandes Tomás

Rua de Alexandre Herculano

Rua de Passos Manuel

Av. Gustavo Eiffel

R. Hintze Ribeiro

P. da Batalha

English Bookstore

R. de 31 de Janeiro

Train Station

Casa-Museu de Guerra Junqueiro

Ponte de D. Luís I

Post Office

P. Gen. Humberto Delgado

Av. da Boavista

Av. dos Aliados

Praça Liberdade

Rua do Loureiro

Av. de Vimiara Peres

Casa Dom Hugo

Cais da Ribeira

Rua do Almada

Tour Office

Rua Ricardo Jorge

P. Filipa de Lencastre

Fábrica

Rua dos Clérigos

Rua dos Caldereiros

Rua Mouzinho da Silveira

Rua do Infante D. Henrique

Casa do Infante

Rua da Conceição

Rua Carlos Alberto

Rua Conde de Vizela

Rua da Galeria de Paris

R. das Flores

Rua da Vitória

Rua das Flores

Palácio da Bolsa

Rua Mirante

P. Gomes Teixeira

Praça de Lisboa

R. das Carmelitas

Rua S. Bento da Vitória

R. Ferreira Borges

Igreja de São Francisco

Rua de Cedofeita

Jardim de Cordoaria

Rua das Taipas

Rua do Breyner

Campo dos Mártires da Pátria

Rua Alfonso Alburquerque

Passeio das Virtudes

Rua de Miguel Bombarda

Museu Nacional de Soares dos Reis

Rua do Rosário

Rua da Restauração

Rua Nova da Alfândega

N

Rio Duoro

Rua Manuel II

TO

0   220

yards

0   200

meters

Porto

Pensão Brasil, 6
Pensão Estoril, 4
Pensão do Minho, 7
Pensão Porto Rico, 5
Pensão São Marino, 3
Pousada de Joventude do Porto (HI), 1
Residencial Paris, 2

24hr. multilingual **computer info stands** in the main shopping centers and the larger squares; one sits in front of the McDonald's in Pr. Liberdade.

Currency Exchange: ATMs line Pr. Liberdade, and are omnipresent throughout the city. Most banks on **Pr. Liberdade** offer currency exchange (banks open Mon.-Fri. 8:30am-3pm), and some have automatic currency exchange machines outside.

American Express: Top Tours, R. Alferes Malheiro, 96 (tel. 208 27 85). Facing the town hall at the top of Pr. Liberdade, take the street to the left of the building and turn left after 2 blocks. Open Mon.-Fri. 9am-12:30pm and 2:30-6:30pm.

Flights: Aeroporto Francisco de Sá Carneiro (tel. 941 32 60 or 941 32 70 for arrival/departure info). Take bus #44 or 56 from Pr. Lisbon (about every 20min.). **TAP Air Portugal,** Pr. Mouzinho de Albuquerque, 105 (tel. 948 22 91). To Lisbon and Madrid.

Trains: Estação de Campanhã (tel. 57 41 61), Porto's main station east of the center, through which all trains pass. Frequent connections to Estação São Bento (5min., 120$). To: Aveiro (21 per day, 1½hr., 370$); Viana do Castelo (11 per day, 2hr., 650$); Braga, via Nine (11 per day, 2hr., 450$); Coimbra (12 per day, 2½hr., 910$); Lisbon (5 per day, 4½hr., 1950$); Madrid, via Entroncamento (2 per day, 12-13hr., 9100$); Paris (1 per day, 28hr., 24,000$). **Estação de São Bento** (tel. 200 10 54), centrally located a block off Pr. Liberdade, is the terminus for trains with mostly local and nearby regional routes. If your train stops at Campanhã, it is usually best to take a connection to São Bento. Buses also run to Pr. Liberdade and beyond (every 30min., 170$). There is a handy info office at Estação São Bento, open as long as trains are running. Minimal English, but fluent French.

Buses: There is no central bus station; over 20 different companies each has its own garage. Some of the largest are: **Garagem Atlântico,** R. Alexandre Herculano, 366 (tel. 200 69 54). To: Coimbra (10 per day, 1½hr., 1200$); Viseu (2 per day, 2hr., 950$); Lisbon (5 per day, 5½hr., 1900$). **Auto Viação do Minho,** Pr. D. Filipa de Lencastre (tel. 200 61 21), 1 block from Av. Aliados. To: Braga (every 30min., 2hr., 600$) and Viana do Castelo (12 per day, 2hr., 650$). **Rodoviária Nacional** (tel. 200 31 52), R. Alexandre Herculano, also runs to Braga and Viana do Castelo. **Rodonorte** (tel. 200 56 27), R. Atenou Comercial do Porto, a.k.a. Travessa Passos Manuel, a block from R. Sá da Bandeira. To Vila Real (6 per day, 4hr., 1100$). **Internorte,** Pr. Galiza, 96 (tel. 69 32 20 or 48 75). To: Spain; France; Belgium; Switzerland; Germany; and Luxembourg.

Public Transportation: A *Passe Turístico* discount pass is available for Porto's trolleys and buses. 4 days 1600$; 7 days 2150$. Single trip purchased on bus 160$, one-day unlimited ticket 350$. Tickets can be purchased at a small kiosk on the corner, half a block downhill and across the street from Estação de São Bento (discount single trip only 80$). You can pre-purchase tickets for half price.

Taxis: Raditáxis, R. Alegria, 1802 (tel. 52 80 61). 24hr. service.

Luggage Storage: Free in **tourist office** during the day, or at **Estação de São Bento** in lockers to the right as you enter the platform (400$ and 900$ per 48hr.).

Laundromat: Lavanderia Penguin, Av. Boavista (tel. 69 50 32), in shopping center Brasília. A block past the youth hostel. Self-service (a rarity). 1500$ per 5.5kg load. Open Mon.-Sat. 10am-11pm.

Public Showers and Toilets: Pr. Liberdade (in the middle of the garden in the traffic island), Pr. Batalha, and Largo do Viriato. Open 24hr. Coin-operated toilets throughout the city.

English Bookstore: Livraria Britânico, R. José Falcão, 184 (tel. 32 39 30). Decent choice of paperbacks: trendy, intellectual, classic, and trashy, plus hardcovers and magazines. Open Mon.-Fri. 9am-7pm, Sat. 9:30am-1pm. **Livraria Diário de Notícias,** R. Sá de Bandeira, 5, across from Estação São Bento. Smaller selection of books. **Maps.** Open Mon.-Fri. 9am-7pm, Sat. 9am-1pm.

24Hr. Pharmacy: tel. 118 for info on which pharmacy is open.

Medical Services: Hospital de Santo António, R. Prof. Vicente José de Carvalho (tel. 200 73 54 or 200 52 41).

Police: (tel. 200 68 21), R. Alexandre Herculano. **Emergency:** tel. 112.

Post Office: Pr. General Humberto Delgado (tel. 31 98 77), next to the town hall. Open for **fax, telephones,** Posta Restante (60$ per item), and stamps Mon.-Fri. 8am-9pm, Sat.-Sun. 9am-6pm. **Postal Code:** 4000.

Telephones: Telecom, Pr. Liberdade, 62. Open 8am-11:30pm. **Telephone Code:** (0)2.

ACCOMMODATIONS AND CAMPING

Rates for singles are higher than the norm, and the city's only youth hostel is somewhat small. However, you will never go without a room; there is an overpriced *pensão* for every light on the riverbank. Look west of **Av. Aliados,** or on **R. Fernandes Tomás** and **R. Formosa,** perpendicular to the Aliados Square.

Pousada de Juventude do Porto (HI), R. Paulo da Gama, 551 (tel. 617 72 47), 2km from town center. Take bus #3, 20, or 52 (10min., 160$) from the stop on the lower west end of Pr. Liberdade (make sure the bus is going toward the river and not into the square). From here it is a little tricky; you may want to ask the driver or sympathetic fellow passengers for help. After the bus makes a right onto R. Júlio Dinis (you will see a big park on the right and a green Tranquilidade sign in front), get off at the stop after the 2nd traffic light. Cross the street and walk 1 block uphill; turn left at the billboard on to a small side street. It is not the newest youth hostel, but the warden is cool and there's a lively social scene (lubricated by the Carlsberg vending machine). Reception open daily 9-11am and 6pm-midnight. No curfew. 1650$ per person. Doubles with bath 5000$. Off-season: 1750$; 4500$. Reservations highly recommended.

Residencial Paris, R. da Fábrica, 27-9 (tel. 32 14 21). Cross Pr. Liberdade from the train station and turn left onto R. Dr. Artur de Magalhães Basto, which quickly turns into R. Fábrica. Friendly English-speaking manager has maps and train schedules at hand. Large rooms and TV room and lush garden. Singles with bath 4000$. Doubles with bath 5500$. Reservations highly recommended.

Pensão São Marino, Pr. Carlos Alberto, 59 (tel. 32 54 99). Facing town hall, go up the street on the left and take 1st left onto R. Dr. Ricardo Jorge, which becomes R. Conceição; turn left onto R. Oliveiras, and make a quick right onto Pr. Carlos Alberto. Ask the efficient, English-speaking owner for one of the bright, carpeted rooms looking out onto the quiet *praça*. All 14 rooms have a bath or shower, phone, TV, and winter heating. Singles 3000-4000$. Doubles 4000-6500$. Triples 4500-7000$. Off-season discount 500$. Breakfast included.

Pensão Estoril, R. Cedofeita, 193 (tel. 200 51 52 or 200 27 51), above a cafe on a pedestrian street off Pr. Cados Alberto. Sail the sea-green carpeting into one of the *pensaã's* 17 colossal, bright rooms—all with TV, bath, and phone. Lounge and patio with satellite TV and pool table. Singles with shower 4000-4500$. Doubles with shower 4500-5500$. Triples 6000-7800$. Quads 8500$. Visa.

Pensão Porto Rico, R. Almada, 237, 2nd fl. (tel. 31 87 85). From Av. Aliados, go up R. Elísio de Melo; after 2 left-hand blocks turn right on R. Almada. Small but well-scrubbed rooms with wood furniture, phones, TV, and radio. Singles 2500$, with bath 3500$. Doubles: 3500$; 5000$. Triples: 4500$; 6000$. Off-season discount for multi-night stays. Reservations recommended. Visa, MC.

Pensão Brasil, R. Formosa, 178 (tel. 31 05 16). From Pr. Liberdade, cross Av. Aliados to R. Formosa; Brasil is about 3½ blocks up. Some of the cheapest rooms in Porto. Doubles are cleaner and brighter than singles. Winter heating. Singles 2000$. Doubles with bath 3500$. Triples 4500$. Call ahead. Prices vary seasonally.

Pensão do Minho, R. Fernandes Tomás, 926 (tel. 31 12 72). Facing the town hall, take the street to the right of the building and take your 1st right. Small, dingy, yet functional rooms on a loud street are cheap and exactly where you want them: near the train, tourist office, and city center. Singles 2500$. Doubles 3500$.

Camping: Prelada, R. Monte dos Burgos, Quinta da Prelada (tel. 81 26 16), 5km from the beach. Take bus #6 from Pr. Liberdade. 550$ per person, 475$ per tent, and 475$ per car. **Salgueiros** (tel. 781 05 00), near Praia de Salgueiros in Vila Nova de Gaia, is less accessible, less equipped, and less expensive, but closer to the surf. 200$ per person and per tent, 100$ per car. Open May-Sept.

PORTUGAL

Fine Wine, Port Gratis

Entertainment of an alcoholic nature might be one of the first things to go when money gets tight on the backpacker's trail. But in Porto, never fear—there is an abundant supply of fine port wines available for consumption at any one of 80-odd port wine lodges. And the best part is that it's all completely *gratuito* (free).

As you will learn while waiting impatiently for the tours to terminate and the toasting to begin, port was discovered when some enterprising English wine dealers added a strong brandy to cheap Portuguese wine to prevent it from souring en route to England. Nowadays, wine from grapes grown in the Douro Valley 100km west of Porto is mixed with 170 proof brandy (sorry, that stuff is *not* for sale) and aged in barrels to yield port, which takes different forms: vintage, white, ruby, and tawny. The lodges are all across the river in Vila Nova da Gaia—be sure to cross the lower level of the large bridge. A good starter is **Sandeman** (please, the "e" is silent) with costumed guides and high quality port. **Cálem,** next door, has a less stilted tour, and the port is almost as good. At **Ferreira,** down the road from Sandeman, you will learn about the illustrious *senhora* who built the Ferreira empire in the late 19th century—1996 was the *saudade*-filled 100th anniversary of her death. Last but certainly not least, **Taylor's** wins the highly unscientific *Let's Go* poll for best port in Porto. Ask for your wine on their terrace, which has a great view of Porto and the River Douro.

FOOD

Eating out costs more in Porto than in any other Portuguese city. Head for the *mercado* if you are on a tight budget. Pick up fresh olives and produce at one of the outdoor food and handicraft markets that line Cais de Ribeira daily (8am-8pm), or at the **Mercado de Bolhão,** on the corner of R. Formosa and R. Sá de Bandeira (open Mon.-Fri. 8am-6pm, Sat. 7am-1pm). Doling out a few hundred more *escudos,* however, will land some tasty dishes on your table—this is *the* place to feast on *bacalhau* (cod). Expensive restaurants border the river in the Ribeira district, particularly on **C. da Ribeira, R. Reboleira,** and **R. de Cima do Muro.** You will find budget fare in rowdier surroundings near **Pr. Batalha** on **R. Cimo de Vila** and **do Cativo.** Cheaper eateries lie around the **Hospital de Santo António** and **Pr. Gomes Teixeira,** a few blocks west of Pr. Liberdade. Adventurous gourmets savor the city's specialty, *tripas à moda do Porto* (tripe and beans).

Churrasqueira Moura, R. Almada, 219 (tel. 200 56 36), on a street parallel to Av. Aliados. Dirt-cheap meals of solid food to satisfy the grumpiest stomachs. Half-portions around 850$; full portions less than 1300$. Open Mon.-Sat. 9am-10pm.

Restaurante O Gancho, Largo do Terreiro 11-12 (tel. 31 49 19), across from Boa Nova. Typical Portuguese *comida* as well as lighter food such as omelettes served in a plain indoor bar/dining room over an outdoor esplanade. Entrees 850-1200$. Open daily noon-3pm and 7-11pm.

Restaurante Boa Nova, Muro dos Bacalhoeiros, 115 (tel. 200 60 86), in the row of houses overlooking riverside walk, next door to the house where the inventor/namesake of the cod dish *à Gomes de Sá* was born (read the plaque yourself). Wine served from huge, wooden barrels. Carapaus fritos (fried whitefish 850$). Open Mon.-Sat. noon-3pm and 7:30-10:30pm.

Restaurante China Pekim, R. Santo Ildefonso, 118 (tel. 200 16 80), on the corner with R. Sta. Catarina. Overdone "oriental" setting, with waterfall and all. Chicken entrees 650-750$. Vegetarian options. Open daily noon-3pm and 6-11pm.

Majestic cafe, R. Santa Catarina, 112 (tel. 200 38 87). Touts itself as "the joy of the city of Porto"—not far from the truth. A bit pricey, but why not treat yourself to the classy servers (clad in *Love Boat*-like stewards' uniforms) and mirrored walls with gaudy molded cupids? Tea sandwiches (600-900) and entrees, or *cafe* (200$). Some of the fanciest pastries in town (90-200$). Open daily 8am-midnight.

SIGHTS

Your very first brush with Porto's very rich stock of fine artwork may be in, of all places, the **Estação de São Bento** terminal which sports a celebrated collection of *azulejos.* Outside the station and at the top of adjacent **Praça da Liberdade,** the formidable *belle époque* **Prefeitura** (City Hall) is a monument to Porto's late 19th-century greatness. Fortified on the hilltop slightly south of the train station is Porto's pride and joy, the Romanesque **sé** (tel. 31 90 28), situated in one of the city's oldest residential districts. It was built in the 12th and 13th centuries, and the Gothic, *azulejo-*covered cloister was added in the 14th century. The **Capela do Santíssimo Sacramento** to the left of the high altar shines with solid silver and plated gold. During the Napoleonic invasion, crafty townspeople whitewashed the altar to protect it from vandalism. Climb the staircase to the **Renaissance chapter house** for a splendid view of the old quarter (open daily 9am-12:30pm and 2:30-6pm; cloister 200$).

Cash acquires cachet at the **Palácio da Bolsa** (Stock Exchange), R. Ferreira Borges (tel. 208 45 66), the epitome of 19th-century elegance. Although tours are pricey, get a feel for its opulence by popping in to peer at the ornate courtyard ceiling. It took a zealous artisan three years to carve the exquisite wood table in the portrait room with a pocket-knife. The ornate **Sala Árabe** (Arabic Room) took 18 years to decorate. Modeled after Granada's Alhambra, its gold and silver walls are covered with plaques bearing the oddly juxtaposed inscriptions "Glory to Allah" and "Glory to Queen Maria II." (Multilingual tours leave every 30min. Open April-Oct. Tues.-Sat. 2-8pm, Sat.-Sun. 10am-8pm; Nov.-March Tues.-Sun. 2-7pm. 700$, students 50$; main courtyard—thankfully—free.) To get to the Bolsa, turn left out of the *sé* and follow the winding streets straight ahead to Travessa da Banharia and Largo de Santo Domingos; the Bolsa is downhill on the right. From in front of the train station, follow R. Mouzinho da Silveira to the square. You'll see the signs along the way.

Next door to the Bolsa, the Gothic **Igreja de São Francisco** (tel. 200 84 41) glitters with one of the most elaborate gilded wood interiors in Portugal. Under the floor, thousands of human bones have been cleaned and stored in the *osseria* in preparation for Judgment Day. (Museum and church open April-Oct. Mon.-Fri. 9am-6pm, Sun. 9am-5pm; Nov.-March Mon.-Sat. 9am-5pm. 500$, students and seniors 250$.)

Porto's rocky **beach,** in the ritzy Foz district in the west end of the city, is a popular destination despite higher-than-normal levels of pollution. To get there, jump on bus #78 from Pr. Liberdade (160$ each way) and jump off wherever it suits you. At the bottom of the hill on R. Alfândega, past a marvelous quay filled with shops and restaurants, skirts the **Ribeira.** To see more of the riverside esplanade, take trolley #1 (160$) from the nearby Igreja de São Francisco. The cars run along the river to the Foz do Douro, Porto's beach community.

Back uphill rises the 82m **Torre dos Clérigos** (Tower of Clerics). Built in the mid-18th century, its granite bell tower (the city's most prominent landmark) glimmers like a grand processional candle. Mount the 200 steps to view Porto and the Rio Douro Valley (open daily 10:30am-noon and 2-5pm; tower 130$, church free).

A ten-minute walk west (away from the center) on R. D. Manuel II, past the churches and a forested park and en route to the youth hostel, stands the 18th-century **Museu Nacional de Soares dos Reis** (tel. 208 19 56), a former royal residence. It houses an exhaustive collection of 19th-century Portuguese paintings and sculptures, highlighting Soares dos Reis, sometimes called Portugal's Michelangelo (open Tues.-Sun. 10am-5pm; 230$, students and seniors 165$).

For modern art in a lovely setting, visit the **Fundação Casa de Serralves (Museu de Arte Moderna),** a recently opened contemporary museum west of the town center on the way to the beach. Its elegant marble walls contain artist-specific exhibitions. Ask to see an English video on the artists, as all descriptions in the museum are in Portuguese. The building crowns an impressive 44 acres of sculptured gardens, fountains, and even old farmland tumbling down toward the Douro River. (Museum open Tues.-Fri. 2-8pm, Sat.-Sun. 10am-8pm. Park closes at sundown. 300$, students and seniors 150$, Thursday free.) Bus #78 leaves for the museum from Pr. Dom João I—

PORTUGAL

ask the driver for the museum stop (about 30min. to R. Serralves; 160$ one way; buses return until midnight).

ENTERTAINMENT

Mellow **bars** keep the lights on until 2am on the waterfront in **Pr. da Ribeira, M. dos Bacalhoeiros,** and **R. Alfândega.** Try **Pub O Muro,** Muro dos Bacalhoeiros, 87-88 (tel. 38 34 26), right above the riverside near the bridge going to the port wine houses. **Discoteca Swing,** on R. Júlio Dinis near the youth hostel, is reputed to have swinging action for a mixed gay-straight crowd (cover about 1000$). The Beautiful People party in the Foz beach district. Try discos **Industria, Twins,** and **Dona Urraca.** The riverside **Nova Alfândega** (new customs house) plays host to gargantuan concerts, especially during the summer—Beck, Prodigy, and the Smashing Pumpkins have recently played here.

English-language **movies** are shown in at least three cinemas in the town center alone; try **Cinema Passos Manuel,** R. Passos Manuel, 141 (tel. 200 51 96; shows 2-9:30pm; tickets 600$, Mon. 400$), and **Cinema Praça da Batalha** (tel. 202 24 07). Live **concerts** and **theater** performances are held on many sultry summer nights at the Claustros do Mosteiro de São Bento da Vitória (tel. 31 21 32). The historic **Teatro Nacional São Joâo** (tel. 200 34 49), on Praga da Batalha, frequently hosts international drama troupes. Consult the bulletins at the tourist office for upcoming events.

But we digress. Back to your (probable) main focus of interest. You can enjoy the warm glow of Port wine and its Douro cousins by embarking on a "wine connoisseurship" **cruise** (a fancy booze-cruise) down the Douro River. Grab a few pamphlets at the tourist office, or head straight for the docks.

■ Near Porto

AMARANTE

Amarante is food for the soul. Mass tourism has yet to rear its head in this emerald green valley bedecked with whitewashed houses. Gracing the hillsides and greeting each other across the lazy Rio Tamega lie Amarante's two halves. The town's sites are interesting and mercifully few, but the town itself is well worth the trip.

Feeling historical? Cross the **Ponte de São Gonçalo,** once a Portuguese stronghold against Napoleonic troops, onto **Praya da Républica,** where you'll be dwarfed by the lacy facade of Amarante's *pièce de résistance,* the incorrigibly Romanesque **Igreja de São Gonçalo.** In the same complex are the **municipal library** and the well-curated **Museu Amadeo S. Cardoso** (open Tues.-Sun. 10am-12:30pm and 2-5:30pm; closed holidays; 200$). Finally, trek up and to R. S. de Outubro to the ghostly remains of the **Solar dos Magalhães,** a sordid but hauntingly beautiful reminder of Napoleon's pyromaniacal legacy. Once you've explored the main attractions, pick a riverside terrace, drink in the sun, and gorge on Amarante's culinary delights: sweets, sweets, and more sweets. Accommodations are still scarce and expensive; the town is best visited as a daytrip from Guimarães, Braga, or Porto. If you insist, try the three-star **Pensão Restaurante Sena** (tel. 49 17 25), on S. Gens. Rooms are tastefully decorated, spacious, and well-lit, but prices vary according to the season and demand is invariably high, so call ahead. Alternatively, pitch your tent at the new **campground** a few kilometers outside town on riverside R. Pedro Alvellos. Rodonorte **buses** (tel. 32 32 34) zip to: Porto (4 per day, 1½hr., 700$); Guimarães (3 per day, 1hr., 485$); Bragança (5 per day, 2½hr., 1400$); and Vila Real (10 per day, 45min., 700$). To get to the **tourist office** (tel. 43 23 59), follow Av. Alexandre Herculano toward the river, then hang a left on to R. 31 de Janeiro. Cross the bridge onto Pr. de República; the office is in the same building as (and just past) the museum entrance on Alameda Teixeira de Pascoaes. The staff hands out slick town maps and less-than-inspiring brochures. The post office is a short uphill hike along R. 5 de Outubro, which turns into R. Cândido dos Reis. The postal code is 4600. The **telephone code** is (59). For **currency exchange,** Banco Mello—past Igreja São Gonçalo on R. 5 de Outubro—has automatic

cash dispensers. The **hospital** (tel. 43 76 31) lies north of town on Av. General Vitorino Laranjeira

■ Braga

Well-heeled Braga—once the seat of the Archbishop of Spain—is considered by some the most pious, by others the most fanatic, and by all the most conservative city in Portugal. Not surprisingly, the 1926 coup that paved Salazar's path to power was launched from here. Yet in spite of Braga's austere reputation and large number of (primarily Gothic) churches, hedonism—manifested in bars and discos—marches cheerfully forward. During Holy Week, a procession crosses the flower-carpeted streets; at night, however, somber devotion caves into fireworks and dancing. Charming pedestrian thoroughfares and lively streets make Braga seem like a miniature Lisbon. It is also a sensible base for exploring the natural wonders of northern Portugal.

ORIENTATION AND PRACTICAL INFORMATION

Braga's focal point is the **Praça da República,** a spirited square filled with cafes, bordered by gardens, and crowned with a fountain. The **Avenida da Liberdade** emanates from the square. **Rua do Souto,** a pedestrian thoroughfare lined with deluxe stores, runs from the tourist office's corner at the *praça*. This becomes **Rua Dom Diogo de Sousa** and then **Rua Andrade de Corvo,** which leads straight to the **train station.** To reach the **bus station,** take R. Chãos from Pr. República up to tiny Pr. Alexandre Herculano and pick up Av. General Norton de Matos (to the left).

PORTUGAL

Tourist Office: Av. Central, 1 (tel. 26 25 50), on Pr. República. Maps and plenty of info on rustic excursions. Train schedules and bus info available. Temporary **luggage storage.** English spoken. Open Mon.-Fri. 9am-7pm, Sat.-Sun. 9am-12:30pm and 2-5pm; Oct.-June Mon.-Fri. 9am-7pm, Sat. 9am-12:30pm and 2-5pm.

Currency Exchange: Banco Borges e Irmão, on Pr. República, across from the tourist office. Open Mon.-Fri. 8:30am-3pm. **ATMs** are common.

Trains: (tel. 221 66), on Largo Estação. Go down the street to the right, cross the busy avenue, follow the curved road, R. Andrade Corvo, uphill to the right; the tourist office is 15min. straight ahead. Most trips require a change of train at Nine, 20min. to the west. To: Porto (14 per day, 1½hr., 520$); Viana do Castelo (10 per day, 2hr., 490$); Vila Nova de Cerveira (9 per day, 3hr., 710$); Valença (8 per day, 3hr., 820$, with 3 daily connections to Vigo, Spain); Coimbra (12 per day, 4hr., 1150$). Express **Inter-Cidades** runs to Porto and on to Lisbon (3 per day).

Buses: (tel. 783 54), Central de Camionagem, a few blocks north of city center. **Rodoviária** runs to: Porto (10 per day, 1½hr., 920$); Guimarães (6 per day, 1hr., 380$); Campo do Gerês, a.k.a. São João do Campo (5 per day, 1½hr., 520$); Coimbra (4 per day, 3hr., 1100$); Lisbon (7 per day, 8½hr., 2210$); Faro (2 per day, 12hr., 3200$). **Hoteleira do Gerês** buses zip to Gerês (9 per day, 1½hr., 550$).

Taxis: (tel. 61 40 28). To the youth hostel from the train station 650$.

Hospital: Hospital São Marcos, Largo Carlos Amarante (tel. 63 36 14 or 601 30 00).

Police: R. dos Falcões, 12 (tel. 61 32 50), on Largo de Santiago. **Emergency:** tel. 115.

Post Office: (tel. 61 77 20) Av. Liberdade, 2 blocks south of the tourist office. Open for **telephones, fax,** and other services. Mon.-Fri. 8:30am-6pm, Sat. 9am-12:30pm. For Posta Restante, indicate "Estação Avenida" in address. **Postal Code:** 4700.

Telephones: In the post office building and a kiosk in Pr. República. **Telephone Code:** (0)53.

ACCOMMODATIONS AND CAMPING

Braga resounds with *pensões*. The cheapest cluster around the **Hospital de São Marcos,** the more expensive center around **Av. Central.**

Pousada de Juventude de Braga (HI), R. Santa Margarida, 6 (tel./fax 61 61 63). From the tourist office, walk down Av. Central until the park ends, then turn left on Largo Senhora Branca. A 35min. walk from the train station (take a taxi), 15min.

walk from the bus station. Relaxing, though rooms are a bit cramped. Gargantuan windows open out onto a forested hill. Reception open daily 9am-1pm and 6pm-midnight. 1550$ per person. Doubles 3700$. Oct.-May: 1300$; 3200$. Breakfast included. Reservations recommended July-Aug.

Residência Grande Avenida, Av. Liberdade, 738, 3rd fl. (tel. 26 29 55), around the corner from the tourist office. Elevator whisks you up to 21 rooms with elegant mirrors and plush furniture. All equipped with TV, phone, and winter heating. Also boasts a Victorian sitting room. Singles 3500$, with bath 4500$. Doubles: 5000$; 5500$. 500$ less in winter. Breakfast included. Reserve ahead June-Aug.

Residencial Inácio Filho, R. Francisco Sanches, 42 (tel. 26 38 49). From the *praça,* walk down R. Souto 1 block; it's off the 1st perpendicular pedestrian street. Hallways cluttered with cool antiques connect 8 well-kept, prim rooms prime for relaxing. Doubles 4400$, with bath 5000$.

Camping: Parque da Ponte (tel. 733 55), 2km down Av. Liberdade from the center, next to the stadium and the municipal pool. Buses stop every 30min. Market and laundry facilities. 390$ per person. 250$ per tent. 250$ per car.

FOOD

Braga has many cafes and several superb restaurants, but little in between. A colorful **market** sets up in Pr. Comércio, two blocks from the bus station (open Mon.-Sat. 7am-3pm). Numerous restaurants in this *praça* serve the Minho's typically heavy dishes. For groceries, stop and shop at any of several mini-markets along the street between Pr. República and the youth hostel. **Supermercado Mini Preço** is on R. São Victor a block away from the youth hostel (open Mon.-Sat. 8am-10pm).

Cafe Vianna, Pr. República, behind the fountain. A snappy pink marble cafe, always lively. Full breakfasts (300-750$), light lunches, and dinner (sandwiches and *pratos combinados* 375-1050$). At night it turns into a popular hangout, sometimes with live music. Open Mon.-Sat. 8am-2am.

Churrasqueira da Sé, D. Paio Mendes, 25. This "cathedral barbecue" serves pork chops, veal, and omelettes fit for His Excellence and laymen alike. Half-portions (475-775$) easily fill up one person. Open Thurs.-Tues. 11am-11pm.

Grupo Jolima, Av. Liberdade 779, under the flamingo-pink archway a block from the tourist office. Food court pushes tasty pizza (150$ per slice), breads (35$ per roll), and traditional Portuguese barbecue (500-600$ per kg). Open daily 7am-2am.

SIGHTS

Braga's **sé,** Portugal's oldest cathedral, is a granite structure that has undergone a series of renovations since its inception in the 11th and 12th centuries. Guided tours in Portuguese to its treasury, choir, and chapels run most any time during opening hours (300$). The treasury showcases the archdiocese's most precious paintings and relics. On display is the *Cruzeiro do Brasil,* a plain iron cross from Pedro Álvares Cabral's ship when it ran into Brazil in 1500. The real treats are the *cofres cranianos* (brain boxes), one with the 6th-century cortex of São Martinho Dume, Braga's first bishop. The choir has an organ with 2424 fully functional pipes. Off a Renaissance cloister lie the cathedral's two historic chapels. The most notable, **Capela dos Reis** (Kings' Chapel), guards the 12th-century stone sarcophagi of Dom Afonso Henriques' parents. The mummified remains of a 14th-century archbishop have a more heart-stopping effect (cathedral open 8:30am-6:30pm; in winter 8:30am-5:30pm; free). The street behind the chapel leads to a square flanked by the 17th-century **Capela de Nossa Senhora da Conceição** and the picturesque **Casa dos Coimbras.** The chapel has an interior covered with *azulejos,* which tell the story of Adam and Eve (open Mon.-Fri. 10am-1pm and 3-7pm; free).

The Rococo facade of **Igreja de Santa Cruz** gleams from the monumental **Hospital de São Marcos** on Largo Carlos Amarante. In very different spirit sits the **Casa dos Crivos** (House of Screens) on R. São Marcos, with its Moorish latticed windows.

PORTUGAL

Braga

Câmara Municipal (Town Hall), 5
Casa Dos Crivos, 11
Casa Museu Nogueira Silva, 13
Escola de Música, 14
Estação Dos Caminhos
de Ferro (train station), 1
Estação Rodoviária (bus station), 9
Mercado Municipal, 8
Museu dos Biscainhos, 6
Museu Medina e Museu Pio XII, 3
Police, 2
Sé, 4
Sede do Parque Nacional Peneda-Gerês, 7
Tourism Office, 12
Torre de Menagem, 10

Accommodations

Residencia Grande Avenida, 2
Residencial Inácio Filho, 3
Youth Hostel, 1

Avenida Padre Júlio Fragata

Rua D. Pedro V

Avenida João Paulo II

Rua Bernardo Sequeira

Rua Ulisses Taxa

Rua de S. Domingos

Rua Dr. de Matos

Rua de S. Vítor

Rua de Miguel

Rua de Carvalho

Rua de Restauração

PRAÇA DA JUSTIÇA

Rua de Santa Margarida

Rua de Camões

Rua de Sardoal

LARGO DA SENHORA À BRANCA

Avenida 31 de Janeiro

Rua Dr. Constantino Ignácio Soares

Rua do Raio

Rua 25 de Abril

Avenida João XXI

Rua André

PRAÇA MOUSINHO DE ALBUQUERQUE

Rua de S. André

Rua S. Gonçalo

Avenida dos Combatentes

Avenida dos Combatentes

Avenida da Liberdade

Rua Sá de Miranda

TO CAMPING

Av. Artur

PRAÇA ALEXANDRE HERCULANO

Rua Gabriel Pereira de Castro

Rua S. Vicente

Rua do Carvalhal

Rua dos Chãos

Rua Dos Capelistas

PRAÇA DA REPÚBLICA

L. BARÃO DE S. MARTINHO

Rua do Souto

LARGO DE SANTA CRUZ

CARLOS AMARANTE

Avenida General Norton de Matos

PRAÇA DA GALIZA

Tr. do Carmo

Rua do Carmo

Rua San António

LARGO DE S. FRANCISCO

Rua do Castelo

Rua do Anjo

Rua Dos Falções

Rua Abade Loureira

PRAÇA DO COMÉRCIO

PRAÇA DO COMÉRCIO

PRAÇA CONDE DE AGROLONGO

Avenida V. Nespereira

Rua Alf Ferreira

Rua Era de Queirós

Rua Justino Cruz

Rua Franc Sanches

Rua de Misericórdia

LARGO DE S. DE SOUTO

Rua Afonso Henriques

Rua da S Santiago

LARGO S. PAULO

LARGO SANTIAGO

Rua de S. Geraldo

Avenida António Macedo

Torres E. Almeida

LARGO DO PAÇO

Rua de S. Diego de Sousa

LARGO MUNICIPAL

PRAÇA VELHA

Rua do Souto

Rua do Cabido

Rua do Leite

Rua do Forno

Rua de S. Miguel

Rua Dom Pereira

LARGO PAULO OROSIO

Rua de S. Sebastião

Rua da Boavista

Rua São Bartolomeu

Rua Dias Pereira

PORTA NOVA

LARGO DA PORTA NOVA

Avenida S. Miguel-o-Anjo

Rua D. Frei Caetano Brandão

CAMPO DAS CARVALHEIRAS

Rua da Cruz de Pedra

Rua Tenenta Coronel

Rua da Boavista

Praceta Padre Diamantino Martins

Rua Andrade

Corvo

Campo das Hortas

Largo Esteio

Rua do Caires

Nearby, the **Jardim de Santa Bárbara** sways under archaic, free-standing arches. Around the corner in the **Praça do Município, Câmara Municipal** (City Hall), and **Biblioteca Municipal** eye each other from opposite sides of a graceful fountain.

Braga's most famous landmark, **Igreja do Bom Jesús,** is actually 5km out of town on a hillside carpeted in greenery. The 18th-century *igreja*'s purpose was to re-create Jerusalem in Braga so that Christians unable to voyage to Palestine could make a pilgrimage here instead. Take the long, slow walk up the granite-paved pathway that forks into two zig-zagging stairways. Don't waste your money on the archaic, water-powered funicular (100$), or take it only on your way down—you'll miss the staircase depicting, among other things, the five senses (the "smell" fountain sprouts water through a boy's nose), major Biblical figures, and the saga of Christ's crucifixion (The Stations of the Cross). The church, along with some incredibly tacky cafes, is at the top. From Braga, buses labeled "#02 Bom Jesús" depart (at 10 and 40min. past the hr.; tickets 185$) from the stop in Largo Carlos Amarante, in front of Hospital de São Marcos, and stop at the bottom of the stairway and the funicular.

EXCURSIONS

Parque Nacional Penedo Gerês: Nature first! An unspoiled expanse of mountains, lakes, vegetation, and wildlife, Parque Nacional de Peneda Gerês lies in the Vale do Alto just south of the Spanish border at Portela do Homem, 43km north of Braga. Hiking routes between the main village of Gerês and the *miradouro* (lookout point) of Pedra Bela twist past glistening waterfalls and natural pools. On summer weekends, a bus connects several of the villages lying within the huge park. A new youth hostel, the **Pousada de Juventude de Vilardinho das Furnas (HI)** (tel./fax 353 39) camps out in the village of Campo do Gerês (a.k.a. São João do Campo) and borders the park. (1600$ per person. Doubles 3400$ per person, with bath 4200$. Off-season: 1300$; 2700$; 3500$. Doubles with bath 3500$. Breakfast included.) Rodoviária Nacional buses (5 per day, 1½hr., 490$) connect Campo do Gerês with Braga. Take a blue and white Braga-bound bus, get off at the Rio Caldo stop, and catch Rodoviária's bus coming from Braga to Campo do Gerês.

Citânia de Briteiros: Nine km from Bom Jesus, stone house foundations and huts speckle the hills in Portugal's best-preserved collection of Celtic ruins (open daily 9am-sundown, 200$). Bus #12 (to Pedraiva) leaves from in front of the Braga tourist office (4 per day, 1 hr., 370$). Get off at Lageosa and walk 2km up the road.

Mosteiro de Tibães: In an unspoiled forest, this beautiful and peaceful 11th-century Benedictine monastery has suffered from centuries of neglect. Stone tombs rattle eerily underfoot in the weathered cloister. Adjoining the cloister is a magnificently preserved church with a narrow, cylindrical ceiling and ornate high altar. Through the kitchen and the back woods is another chapel (open Tues.-Sun. 9am-noon and 2-7pm; tour free). A city bus heads 6km from Braga to the monastery. Buses labeled "Sarrido" leave from Pr. Conde de Agrolongo, one block west up R. Capelistas from Pr. República. The stop is in front of the "Arca-Lar" store, which posts a schedule (roughly every 2hr., 45min., 230$).

■ Near Braga: Guimarães

While some claim modernization and big-time shopping have dulled its luster, Guimarães' castle-dominated center still emanates a certain rustic *eu não se* which attracts an endless barrage of history buffs and atmosphere seekers. In 1143, Dom Afonso Henriques, the first King of Portugal, defeated the Moors here, thereafter making the town the golden nugget of his kingdom. Since then, Guimarães has been known as the "cradle of the nation."

Practical Information The **tourist office** (tel. 41 24 50), Alameda de São Dámaso, faces Pr. Toural. **Maps,** but not the regional guide, are free. There is also a **public bathroom** and free temporary **luggage storage** (open daily 9am-12:30pm and 2-5:30pm). A **branch office,** Pr. Santiago, 37 (tel. 51 51 23, ext. 184), conveniently located in the old city, has the same info (open daily 9am-6pm; in off-season daily

9am-12:30pm and 2-5:30pm). A **taxi** (tel. 52 25 22), from the town center up to the Penha Shrine, costs around 1200$. Contact the **hospital,** on R. dos Cutileiros, near Matadouros, at tel. 51 26 12. The **police station** (tel. 51 33 34) whistles at Alameda Alfredo Pimenta; in **emergencies,** dial 112 from anywhere in Portugal. The **post office** is at R. de Santo António, 89 (tel. 41 65 11; open Mon.-Fri. 8:30am-6pm, Sat. 9am-12:30pm). The **postal code** is 4800. The **telephone code** is (0)53.

The **bus station** (tel. 41 26 46) is located in the immense Guimarães shopping complex. To get there, follow Av. Londres (on the bank), then turn right at the intersection. Rodoviária dispatches buses for Braga (every ½hr., last one at 8pm, 45min., 370$) and Porto (2 per day, 1hr., 640$). Several private companies go elsewherc. **AMI** (tel. 41 26 46) travels locally to São Trocato and Madre de Deus (20 per day, 10-20min., 90$). **Rodonorte** runs to Vila Real via Amarante (5 per day, 1 hr., 380$). The **train station** (tel. 41 23 51), a 10-minute walk south of the tourist office down Av. Afonso Henriques, services Porto only (every hr., 15 per day, 2hr., 500$).

Accommodations and Food Guimarães offers few budget accommodations and restaurants. If you are looking for an angelic sleep, try the **Casa de Retiros,** R. Francisco Agra, 163 (tel. 51 15 15; fax 51 15 17), which is run by the Redentorista religious order. From the tourist office, head through Pr. Toural and straight up R. Santo Antônio; R. Francisco Agra curves left when you reach the traffic circle. The pristine bedrooms come with full bath, radio, phone, heating, and crucifix. The 11:30pm curfew is not negotiable, and unmarried couples are advised to introduce themselves as *Senhor* and *Senhora* (singles 3000$, doubles 5000$; breakfast included). **Camping** is 6km outside of town at **Parque de Campismo Municipal da Penha** (tel. 51 59 12). Take the road to Fafe, following signs to Penha, or hop on the bus to Penha (departing from the shopping complex, 15 min., 220$). The site is open year round with free showers, swimming pool, bar, and supermarket. (280$ per person, under 10 250$, 250$ per tent and per car. Reception May-Oct. 8am-7pm.)ʻ **Groceries** vegetate at **Hipermercado Guimarães** (tel. 421 22 00) in the huge shopping center (open daily 9am-9pm), deemed by Abdenurial Judges "Most Welcoming Site After Waiting in Communist Bread Lines."

Sights Guimarães predates Portugal itself by a few centuries. Galician countess Mumadona founded a Benedictine monastery here in the 10th century and supervised the construction of the **castelo.** This grand granite structure, perched on a rocky hill near the town center, is one of Portugal's foremost national symbols. Go slow on the ladder (open Tues.-Sun. 10am-12:30pm and 2-5:30pm; free) and save your energy for climbing the tower (100$).

The castle protected its inhabitants from the Normans and the Moors, but it was still a bit stuffy. To have a place to let loose or get recluse, the Dukes of Bragança built the versatile, palatial manor next door, the **Palácia dos Duques de Bragança.** After its construction, the elegant 15th-century palace, modeled after the manor houses of northern Europe, became the talk of European nobility. A **museum** inside includes furniture, silverware, crockery, tapestries, and weapons once used at the palace. In the banquet hall, tables that once seated 15th-century nobles now serve presidents of Portugal at their brouhahas. At dinnertime, at least a quarter of the 39 fireplaces burn in an attempt to heat the building. (Open daily 9am-7pm. 400$, students and seniors 200$, under 14 and Thurs. free. Mandatory tour is available in various languages.)

The **Museu de Alberto Sampaio,** in the Renaissance cloister of the **Igreja Colegiada de Nossa Senhora da Oliveira,** is in the center of town. The church entrance fronts an arched medieval square and outdoor temple. The museum, on Largo da Oliveira, houses late Gothic and Renaissance art. (Church open 9am-noon and 3-6pm. Museum open daily 10am-noon and 2-7pm; in off-season 10am-12:30pm and 2-5:30pm. Free.) The 15th-century Gothic **Capela de São Brax** holds the granite tomb of Dona Constança de Noronha, the first duchess of Bragrança. The courtyard *oliveira* (olive tree) symbolizes the patron saint of Guimarães. (Open Tues.-Sun. 10am-12:30pm and 2-5pm. 200$, students and seniors 100$, Sun. morning free.)

■ Viana do Castelo

Viana do Castelo is an elegant town built mercifully close to the beach, though it is not a seaside resort—rampant commercialism has yet to rear its ugly head in this beautiful stop-over between Porto and Galicia. Viana boasts some intriguing history and culture as well as a superb beach just a ferry ride away. Even though the small city beach fills in July and August, empty expanses of sand spread out north and south of town.

ORIENTATION AND PRACTICAL INFORMATION

Avenida dos Combatentes da Grande Guerra, the main drag along the Rio Lima, glitters from the train station south to the port. The old town stretches east of the avenue, while the fortress and sea lie to the west.

Tourist Office: Pr. Erva (tel. 82 26 20), one block east of Av. Combatentes. From the train station, take the fourth left at the sharp corner, then a quick right into the dead-end. Maps and lists of lodgings. Temporary **luggage storage** allowed. English spoken. Open Mon.-Fri. 9am-1pm and 2-7pm, Sat. 9am-12:30pm and 2:30-7pm. Sun. 9:30am-12:30pm. A handy **info desk** at the train station has similar info. Open Mon.-Sat. 9am-12:30pm and 2-5:30pm, Sun. 2-5:30pm.

Currency Exchange: Automatic exchange outside Caixa Geral de Depósitos on the main boulevard. **ATM** at **Montepio Geral,** Av. Combatentes da Grande Guerra, 332 (tel. 82 88 97), near the train station. Open Mon.-Fri. 8:30am-3pm.

Trains: (tel. 82 22 96), at the north end of Av. Combatentes, directly under Santa Luzia hill. From the bus station walk left passing through a pedestrian underpass, or take the bus (110$). To: Vila Nova de Cerveira (5 per day, 1hr., 330$); Barcelos (13 per day, 1hr., 300$); Caminha (7 per day, 30min., 210$); Porto (7 per day, 2½hr., 700$); and Vigo, Spain via Valença (3 per day, 2½hr., 1420$).

Buses: Rodoviária (tel. 250 47). Except for *expressos* (which leave from Av. Combatentes), buses depart from **Central de Camionagem,** on the east edge of town, a 15min. walk from train station. To Braga (8 per day, 1½hr., 630$). **AVIC** (tel. 82 97 05) and **Auto-Viação do Minho,** 181 (tel. 82 88 34), Av. Combatantes da Grande Guerra. To Lisbon (4 per day, 6hr., 2500$) and Porto (5 per day, 1½hr., 1000$).

Taxi: Táxis de Viana (tel. 82 23 22).

English Bookstore: Livraria Bertrand, R. Sacadura Cabral, 21 (tel. 82 28 38), off Pr. Erva. Best-sellers and maps. Open Mon.-Fri. 9am-7pm, Sat. 9am-1pm.

Hospital: Av. Abril, 25 (tel. 82 90 81).

Police: (tel. 82 20 22), R. Aveiro. **Emergency:** tel. 112.

Post Office: (tel. 82 27 11), Av. Combatentes, across from the train station. Open Mon.-Fri. 8:30am-6:30pm, Sat. 9am-12:30pm. **Postal Code:** 4900.

Telephones: In the post office, but the telephone office there closes 1-3pm. **Telephone Code:** (0)58.

ACCOMMODATIONS AND CAMPING

Except in mid-August, accommodations in Viana are easy to find, though not particularly cheap. *Quartos* are the best option. Small, informal *pensões* (usually above family restaurants) are slightly cheaper but far worse in quality. The tourist office lists accommodations. Otherwise, hunt on side streets off Av. Combatentes.

Residencial Magalhães, R. Manuel Espregueira, R. Manuel, 62 (tel. 82 32 93). From the tourist office, turn left onto Pr. República, then left again. Cross Av. Combatentes onto R. Manuel Espregueira. *Residencial* is on the left. Bed down at this homey, old-school establishment. English-speaking management. Doubles 4000$, with bath 5000$. Triples: 5000$; 7000$. Breakfast included.

Pensão Guerreiro, R. Grande, 14 (tel. 82 20 99), corner of Av. Combatentes. High ceilings, old-fashioned wallpaper, and big windows. Ask for a view of the port. Singles 2000$. Doubles 3000$. Triples 4000$. Homers 4500$.

Residencial Viana Mar, Av. Combatentes, 215 (tel. 82 97 70; fax 82 00 60), off Pr. República. Luxury, Thornton, luxury: large rooms furnished with phones and TV. Singles 5000$. Doubles 5500$, with bath 6000$. Triples with bath 8500$. Winter rates drop 1000-2000$. Breakfast included. Credit cards accepted.

Camping: Two campsites are found near the Praia do Cabedelo, Viana's (ocean) beach across the Rio Lima. Hop a "Cabedelo" bus (100$) from the bus station or behind the train station near the funicular stop. Or take the ferry (100$) and hike 1km from the 1st boat stop; signs point the way. **INATEL** (tel. 32 20 42), off Av. Trabalhadores. July-Aug. 300$ per tent, 400-470$ per trailer. June and Sept.: 250$; 400$. Oct.-May: 175$; 310$. Showers 100$. Tents for rent. Open Jan. 16-Dec. 15. **Orbitur** (tel. 32 21 67). Closer to beach, better equipped, more expensive. 550$ per person, 450$ per tent and per car. Free hot showers. Open Jan. 16-Nov. 15.

FOOD

Bloodthirsty diners drool over the local specialty *arroz de sarabulho,* rice cooked in blood (whose? who knows!) and served with sausages and potatoes. A less sanguine substitute is *arroz de marisco,* rice cooked with different kinds of shellfish. The large municipal **market** sets up in Pr. Dona Maria II, several blocks east of **Av. Combatentes** (open Mon.-Sat. 8am-3pm). Most budget restaurants lie on the small streets off Av. Combatentes. For **groceries,** hit **Brito's Auto Serviço,** R. Manjovos, 31 (tel. 231 51). From the train station walk down Av. Combatentes and take the fifth side street on the right (open daily 8:30am-12:30pm and 2:30-8pm).

Restaurante Arcada, R. Grande, 36 (tel. 82 36 43). Relatively untouristed and popular with local families. Entrees 800-1100$. Open daily noon-midnight.

Restaurante O Vasco, R. Grande, 21 (tel. 246 65), on the side street across from Pensão Guerreiro. A clinically white interior with cheap, tasty specialties such as *polvo cozido* (boiled octopus 720$) and *rojões à moda do Minho* (mixed roast meat 950$). Entrees 800-1150$. Open daily 11am-11pm.

Restaurante Dolce Vita, R. Poço, 44 (tel. 248 60), across the square from the tourist office. Wonderful Italian cuisine. Pizza and spaghetti 700-1100$. Portuguese dishes 1050$. Open daily noon-11pm; off-season noon-3pm and 8-11pm. Visa, MC.

SIGHTS

Even in a country famed for its charming squares, Viana's **Praça da República** is exceptional. Its centerpiece is a 16th-century fountain encrusted with sculpture and crowned with a sphere bearing a Cross of the Order of Christ. The small **Paço do Concelho** (1502), formerly the town hall, seals the square to the east. Diagonally across the plaza, granite caryatids support the playful and flowery facade of the **Igreja da Misericórdia** (1598, rebuilt in 1714). An intriguing *azulejo* interior lies within.

For great views of the harbor and ocean, visit **Castelo de São Tiago da Barra.** From the train station, take the second right off Av. Combatentes (R. Gen. Luis do Rego) and go five blocks. The walls of the *castelo,* built in 1589 by Spain's Felipe I, rise to the left. Inside, a regional **tourist office** (tel. 820 271) has basic info.

More views await at the cliff-like **Colina de Santa Luzia,** north of the city, crowned by an early 20th-century neo-Byzantine church and magnificent Celtic ruins. To reach the hilltop, take either the long stairway (drenched with blood, sweat, and tears) or the funicular (every hr. in the morning, every 30min. in the afternoon, daily 9am-7pm, 100$). Both start 200m behind the train station.

Beach connoisseurs will find plenty to be happy about in Viana. Avoid the beach on Rio Lima, prowling ground of some ferocious insects, and head directly for **Praia do Cabedelo.** Take the **ferry** behind the parking lot at the end of Av. Combatentes. (July-Sept. daily every 30min. 8:45am-midnight; May-June and Oct.-Dec. 8:45am-10pm; Jan.-April until 5pm. 100$ per ride.)

Those in search of a pristine beach experience abandon Viana altogether and head north to Vila Praia de Âncora, Moledo, and Caminha, some of the cleanest, least crowded, and overall best beaches in Portugal. The coastal rail line stops frequently

as far north as Vila Nova de Cerveira and Valença do Minho. **Vila Praia de Âncora,** 16km from Viana, is the largest and most popular. It has two rail stops, the main Âncora station and the Âncora-Praia just a few blocks from the beach. **Moledo** and **Caminha,** two and four local stops respectively north of Âncora, are equally gorgeous. Plus, the train lets you off 1-2km from the sand. Some trains do not stop at every station; check the schedule to make sure the train services your beach of choice (7 per day, 150$ to Âncora-Praia; 170$ to Moledo; 180$ to Caminha).

ALTO MINHO

The Alto Minho, set from Spain only by the crystal clear Rio Minho, could have inspired Thoreau to pen a second *Walden*. Wildflowers spring from the rivers' banks, broken only by cottage gardens of cabbage, corn, and grapes, with rocky mountains rising between unspoiled small towns. Intrepid travelers jump the train at stops between towns and get permission from farmers to camp in their fields.

CAMINHA

> One day Jesus and Peter were passing through these parts...
> St. Peter: My Lord, what should this place be called?
> Jesus: Caminha, Caminha (keep walking) we're in a hurry.

While everyone else keeps on walking, you can be the only tourist to slip off the train into Caminha and enjoy the hypnotically green hills, wide beaches, and peaceful medieval square. The village is slightly larger than its cousin five stops down the line, Vila Nova de Cerveira. The latter has a youth hostel, the former has a beach.

Put on your bathing suit, turn left on the riverside road, and keep going along the river about 1.5km to bask at the town **beach.** The zealous will hop on the bus (10min.) or skip 3km to the wide, pristine **Praia de Moledo,** where the Rio Minho rushes into the Atlantic.

The **tourist office** (tel. 92 19 52) is on R. Ricardo Joaquim Sousa. From the train station, walk straight ahead down Av. Manuel Xavier to the square/traffic circle, go down Tr. São João, take the second left, and it's a few steps away on the right (open Mon.-Sat. 9:30am-12:30pm and 2:30-5pm). The **Largo do Hospital** (tel. 72 13 06) is behind the town hall. The **police** (tel. 92 11 68) are on Av. Saraiva near the train station; in **emergencies,** dial 112. The **post office** is in Pr. Pontault-Combault (from the main square, take R. 6 de Setembro), open for stamps and **telephones** daily 9am-12:30pm and 2-5:30pm. The **postal code** is 4910. The **telephone code** is (0)58.

Caminha makes a good daytrip from Viana do Castelo or Vila Nova de Cerveira (don't sleep in Caminha). Those who do stay in town often settle in *quartos;* the tourist office can call around on your behalf. Otherwise look around **Largo Sidonio Pais,** where you will find **Pensão Rio Coura** (tel. 92 11 42), a block left of the train station. (Simple rooms above a popular restaurant/bar. Doubles with bath 5000$. In off-season 3000$.) Two campsites are nearby, but reaching them is challenging. **Orbitur's campsite** (tel. 92 12 95), on Mata do Camarido, is 1.5km south of Caminha on the river (reception open daily 8am-10pm; 525$ per person, 430$ per tent, 450$ per car). Grab the bus headed toward Viana do Castelo (13 per day, 285$). The **Vilar de Mouros** campsite (tel. 72 74 72) is between the Rio Minho and Rio Coura, 7km east of Caminha. It is accessible by one local morning bus, or by train to Lanhelas (5 per day), plus a 2km walk (500$ per person, 400-450$ per tent or per car). The only **restaurants,** all in the main square, dish out high-priced tourist fare. Pack a lunch.

The **train station** (tel. 92 29 25), on Av. Saraira de Carvalho, has trains rolling to: Vila Nova de Cerveira (6 per day, 10min., 120$); Lanhelas (6 per day, 10min., 130$); Porto (8 per day, 2-3hr., 750$). **AVIC buses** leave from near the main *praça* to Porto (2hr., 820$) and Lisbon (3 per day, 6hr., 2100$). **Taxis** answer at tel. 92 14 01.

VILA NOVA DE CERVEIRA

Linked by ferry to Spain, a scant 100m away (close enough to hear Galicians partying at night), Vila Nova de Cerveira is a sleepy town with lush mountain scenery, a historic town center, and—most importantly for backpackers—a great youth hostel. Practically the only thing to see in the town itself is the 14th-century **castle,** now the luxurious **Pousada Dom Dinis,** open for walks around, inside, and atop walls offering great views of the countryside. Crash here if you've got the *escudos* and, by day, jet to the handsome beaches of Âncora, Moledo, and Caminha, and to the even smaller towns of Valença do Minho and Ponte de Lima in the Alto Minho interior. The tourist office can help if you want to take a daytrip.

Hardy travelers hike up to the **Veado** (deer) statue. The 360° view at the top awaits those who travel along the winding road (4km, about 1½hr) through heath and rocky outcrops. From the main road just past town to the east, turn right and begin climbing at the sign reading Lovelhe (Igreja).

Vila Nova's **tourist office** (tel. 79 57 87) is on R. Antônio Douro, diagonally across from Igreja de São Roque. From the train station, turn left and then left again at the first (and only) major intersection. Maps are available for Vila Nova and most of north Portugal (open Mon.-Sat. 9:30am-12:30pm and 2-5:30pm). The **Police** (tel. 79 51 13) preside over Largo 16 de Fevreiro. The **post office** (tel. 79 51 11) is next door to the bank on Pr. Alto Minho (open Mon.-Fri. 9am-12:30pm and 2-5:30pm). The **postal code** is 4920. The **telephone code** is (0)51.

The nearest **campground** (tel. 72 74 72) digs in 4km southwest in **Vilar de Mouros,** an out-of-the-way village between Vila Nova and Caminha (500$ per person, 450$ per tent and per car). Eats are expensive—there is a five-restaurant monopoly, and it is not fair. Try **Cafe-Restaurante A Forja,** upstairs on R. 25 de Abril (entrees 800-1250$; open Tues.-Sun. 8am-11pm). Equally scrumptious is **Restaurante Abrigo das Andorinhas,** next door on R. Queiroz Ribeiro (tel. 79 53 35), with stone walls and an extensive wine list (half-portions 650-950$; open daily 8am-2am). To get to the town center (and the restaurant) go a block downhill from the youth hostel. The **Pousada de Juventude de Vila Nova (HI),** Largo 16 de Fevreiro, 21 (tel./fax 79 61 13) can be reached from the train station, by turning left, then left again at the Fonseca Porto mini-market (15min.). Guests enjoy large rooms, a grassy patio, TV with VCR, and a kitchen. Though this modern, well-kept hostel usually has plenty of space, it hosts a summer camp and fills to the brim with Portuguese tots. (Call ahead. Reception open daily 9am-noon and 6pm-midnight. 1500$ per person. Doubles with bath 3700$. Off-season: 1150$; 3200$. Breakfast included.)

The **train** station (tel. 79 62 65), off the highway ½km east of town, has service to: Valença do Minho (8 per day, 25min., 160$, with 3 daily connections to Vigo and Redondela, Spain, where you can catch another train to Santiago de Compostela); Vila Praia de Âncora (8 per day, 45min., 190$); Viana do Castelo (8 per day, 1hr., 300$); and Porto (8 per day, 2½hr., 730$). Three **bus** companies ride the same route as the train—upstream to Valença and down the coast to Porto. **Turilis** buses leave from the Turilis travel agency (tel. 79 58 50), across the road from the youth hostel. **AVIC** and **A.V. Minho** depart from Cafe A Forja, Av. 25 de Abril (tel. 79 53 11),

---

Bambi Thumps Spain

Vila Nova de Cerveira gets its name from the old Portuguese-Galician word for deer, an animal that turned out to be Cerveira's unlikely war hero. Back in the days before Spain and Portugal were EU buddies, the Rio Minho frontier hosted countless skirmishes. When the Spanish occupied the town, fleet-footed locals ran into the hills surrounding Vila Nova and tied torches to the horns of all the deer they could catch. When the Spaniards saw the hills filled with the torches of what they presumed to be a massive army, they gave up and fled. To this day, Vila de Cerveira tucks its tail quietly under the gaze of a huge metal deer sculpture, visible on the summit of the mountain behind town.

between the hostel and the town center. All go to: Valença do Minho (6 per day, 15min., 300$); Porto (4 per day, 2hr., 900$); and Lisbon (3 per day, 7½hr., 2250$). A **ferry** shuttles between Vila Nova and the Galician town of Goyan, with bus connections to Vigo and La Guardia in Spain (30min., 70$ per person, 300$ per car). Still, the train is the least painful way to get to Spain.

VALENÇA DO MINHO

Within easy reach of Vila Nova, **Valença do Minho** salutes Spanish **Túy** (Tui) from the entrance to northern Portugal. A 17th-century fortress protects the city's historic section. Its stone arches and cannon portal frame stunning views of rolling hills an the Rio Minho. Unfortunately, the historically rich center of Valença has fallen victim to unheard-of levels of commercial tackiness. Walk through town on the *pousada* side to avoid the nasty sight (unless you need a washcloth yourself). The *pousada*'s impressive stone walls yield spectacular views of both Spain and Portugal. A road winds 4km up to the breathtaking summit of **Monte do Faro,** overseeing the coastline, the Vale do Minho, and the Galician mountains.

The **tourist office** (tel. 233 74), Av. Espanha, in a log-cabin-like building, will zip out photocopied maps of the fort (open daily 9am-12:30pm and 2:30-6pm). **Pensão Rio Minho** (tel. 223 31) has spacious, tidy rooms next to the train station (singles 3500$, doubles 4500$; prices drop in off-season). Dine outside the fortress in the new town where prices are lower. **Restaurante Cristina,** in the *centro comercial* next to the Lara Hotel, serves a hearty *cabrito assado no forno* (oven-roasted kid—as in goat, 1100$) and a *prato do dia* for 750$ (open daily 8am-midnight).

Buses stop in front of the train station. Valença is a stop on the Porto-Vigo **train** line (7 trains per day from Viana to Valença, 2 of which continue to Vigo, 420$). From Redondela (1 stop before Vigo), you can connect to Spanish RENFE trains to Santiago de Compostela and points north.

Trás-Os-Montes

The country's roughest, rainiest, and most isolated region, Trás-Os-Montes (behind the mountains) is light years off the beaten path. Dom Sancho I practically begged people to settle here after he incorporated it into Portugal in the 11th century, and Jews chose this remote spot to hide during the Inquisition. Today, charm, beauty, and tranquility are the region's biggest draws.

Getting to Trás-Os-Montes is less than half the fun. Train service is slow and rickety (where it exists at all), and roads tend to be twisty and treacherous. Soaking up the beautiful landscape is more than the other half of the fun; hikers delight in the isolation of unspoiled natural reserves in the Parque Natural de Alvão (accessible from Vila Real) and the Serra de Montesinho (north of Bragança). Brimming with splendid mountain views, this region is one of the last outposts of the traditional Portuguese stone house, complete with hand-cut hay piled into two-story conical stacks. Even the gastronomic specialities devoured in these houses hint at the region's rusticity: *cozido à Portuguesa* is made from sausages, other pig parts, carrots, and turnips. Visitors might want to consume lots of bread and *feijoada à Transmontana* (bean stew) and then burn it off with some serious hikes.

◾ Bragança

Built on rough ground, Bragança, the capital of Trás-Os-Montes, is a proud and steadfast wilderness outpost. The days when Bragança was the key to the frontier, trademarked by the massive 13th-century castle, live on in the imaginations of visitors. While most simply come for the clean air and blue skies, Bragança's impeccably preserved medieval old town surrounding the *castelo* draws its share of gazers as well.

From its foothold on a hilltop terraced to grow hay and ubiquitous olives, Bragança is an excellent base for exploring the starkly beautiful terrain of the **Parque Natural de Montesinho,** which extends north and into Spain.

ORIENTATION AND PRACTICAL INFORMATION

Inter-city buses let you out on the modern square fronted by the cafe-lined **Avenida João da Cruz.** Down-sloping **Rua Almirante Reis** leads to budget *pensões* and the **Praça da Sé** at the heart of the old town. To reach the **fortress,** situated on a hill west of Pr. Sé, take **Rua Combatentes da Grande Guerra** from Praça da Sé, walk uphill, and enter through the opening in the stone walls.

Tourist Office: Largo do Principal (tel. 33 10 78; fax 33 19 13), northeast of the center. From Pr. Sé take R. Abílio Beça, and turn left on R. Marquês de Pombal which leads to Av. Cidade de Zamora; the office is 1 block down on the corner. **Maps,** free daytime **luggage storage,** and help finding accommodations. English spoken. Open Mon.-Fri. 9am-12:30pm and 2-8pm, Sat. 10am-12:30pm and 2-8pm, Sun. 2-7pm; Oct.-May Mon.-Fri. 9am-12:30pm and 2-5pm, Sat. 10am-12:30pm.

Currency Exchange: Banco Nacional Ultramarino, Av. João da Cruz, 2-6 (tel. 33 16 45), next to the post office has **ATMs.** Open Mon.-Fri. 8:30am-3pm.

Trains: No train service. The Portuguese rail system does, however, organize a somewhat awkward (4 connections required) combination bus-train route between Porto and Bragança. Eurail passes can be used to pay for this combo. You can pick up a train in **Mirandela,** the nearest station.

Buses: Three competing agencies offer similar express services to Porto and Lisbon. **Rodonorte** (tel. 33 18 70) leaves from Av. João da Cruz to Porto (5 per day, 5hr., 1400$), including stops at Mirandela, Vila Real, and also to Lisbon (3 per day, 8hr., 2600$). **San-Vitur Travel Agency** (tel. 33 18 26), Av. João da Cruz, sells tickets and has schedules. *Expressos* leave from the Rodonorte stop. To: Vila Real (3 per day, 2½hr., 1200$); Porto (3 per day, 5hr., 1450$); Coimbra (4 per day, 6hr., 1700$); Lisbon (4 per day, 8hr., 2300$); Amarante and Guimarães (13 per day,

2½hr., 2000$). **Internorte** runs to Zamora, Spain (1 per day, 2½hr., 2000$) and Braga (2 per day, 5hr., 1400$). Office open 9am-12:30pm and 2-6pm.

Public Transportation: Yellow and blue line #7 STUB buses forge 4km northward to the campground. They leave across from Banco de Fomento on the corner of Av. João da Cruz (Mon.-Fri., 3 per day, 10min., 120$).

Taxis: (tel. 221 62 or 31 23 53). Cabs congregate across from the post office and old train station. A ride to the campground costs about 700$.

Hospital: Hospital Distrital de Bragança (tel. 33 12 33), Av. Abade de Baçal, before the stadium on the road to Chaves.

Police: (tel. 33 12 67), R. José Beça. **Emergency:** tel. 112.

Post Office: (tel. 33 14 72), R. 5 de Outubro, in square where the bus stops. Open for Posta Restante, **fax,** and **telephones** Mon.-Fri. 9am-5pm. **Postal Code:** 5300.

Telephone Code: (0)73.

ACCOMMODATIONS, CAMPING, AND FOOD

Plenty of cheap *pensões* cluster about **Pr. Sé** and up **R. Almirante Reis.** The few restaurants are generally pricey and mediocre, but not always. Try hunting around Pr. Sé and **Av. João da Cruz.** Cafes in front of the bus stop all prepare inexpensive *pratos combinados.* The region is celebrated for *presunto* (cured ham) and *salsichão* (sausages), for sale at **Supermercado Bem Servir,** R. Abílio Beça, 120, below Pr. Sé (open Mon.-Sat. 9am-1pm and 2-7pm).

Pensão Poças, R. Combatentes da Grande Guerra, 206 (tel. 33 11 75). Large, airy, spartan rooms are kept spotless by the same family that monopolizes the block with Restaurant Poças next door and the Charcutaria Poças across the street. Singles 2000$. Doubles 3000$, with bath 3500$.

Pensão Rucha, R. Almirante Reis, 42 (tel. 33 16 72), on the street connecting Pr. Sé to Av. João da Cruz. The sign is *inside* the doors. Clean, old-school lodgings run by an old-school couple. Flexible curfew. Singles 2000$. Doubles 3500$.

Camping: Parque de Campismo Municipal do Sabor (tel. 268 20), 4km from town on the edge of the Montesinho park (see **Public Transportation,** above). 200$ per person and per car, 150$ per tent. Electricity 100$. Open May-Sept. **Parque de Campismo Cêpo Verde** (tel. 993 71), on the road to Vinhais, 8km from town. A private park. 750$ per person with swimming pool use, 500$ without. 350$ per tent and per car. Open year-round.

Restaurante Poças, R. Combatentes da Grande Guerra, 200 (tel. 33 14 28), off Pr. Sé to the east, across from the eponymous *pensão.* Classic grub in a no-frills setting crowded with locals and tourists alike. *Costeleta de vitela grelhada* (grilled steak 875$). Most entrees 800-1400$. Open daily noon-3pm and 7-10pm.

SIGHTS AND ENTERTAINMENT

High above Bragança sits the handsome old town with a brooding **castelo** as its centerpiece. The castle's **Museu Militar** (tel. 223 78), displays it all—from medieval swords to a World War I machine gun nest to African art collected by Portuguese soldiers (open Fri.-Wed. 9am-11:30am and 2-5pm; 100$, students 60$). The venerable **pelourinho** (pillory) in the square in front of the castle bears the coat of arms of the House of Bragança. At the base of the whipping post is a prehistoric granite pig—in the Iron Age people were bound to the pig as a punishment. The **Domus Municipalis,** behind the church on the other side of the square from the castle, had cisterns in the 13th century and later became the municipal meeting house. If closed, the *senhora* across the street at #40 has the key; be sure to tip her.

Feiras (fairs) rollick on the 3rd, 12th, and 21st of each month near the hospital, 2km out of town—the place for clothes, cheese, food, and a heckuva good time (take a taxi from the town center for about 400$).

▓ Vila Real

Vila Real teeters over the edge of the gorges of the Corgo and Cabril Rivers in the foot-hills of the Serra do Marão. The town has flourished as the principal commercial cen-ter for the southern farms and villages of Trás-Os-Montes. Its charming, untouristed old town center is surrounded by new boroughs reaching into the hills, a main street swooning with the heady scent of rosebuds, and a few hopping cafes. In the pedes-trian shopping district, keep an eye out for Vila Real's famed black pottery with a leaden sheen. The town makes a good point of departure for excursions into the fer-tile fields and rocky slopes of the **Serra do Alvão** and **Serra do Marão**.

ORIENTATION AND PRACTICAL INFORMATION

A hundred kilometers east of Porto, Vila Real's old town centers around **Avenida Carvalho Araújo,** a broad tree-lined avenue that streams downhill from the bus sta-tion to Câmara Municipal. All the action—cafes, shops, and *pensões*—is in this area.

Tourist Office: Av. Carvalho Araújo, 94 (tel. 32 28 19; fax 32 17 12), to the right and downhill from the bus stations. Info about Parque Natural do Alvão and other excursions. Some transportation schedules available. Temporary **luggage storage.** English spoken. Open April-May Mon.-Sat. 9:30am-12:30pm and 2-5pm; June-Sept. Mon.-Fri. 9:30am-7pm, Sat. 12:30-2pm. Sept.-March Mon.-Fri. 9:30am-12:30pm and 2-5pm, occasionally on Sat.

Currency Exchange: Realvitur, Largo do Pioledo, 2 (tel. 32 18 00), 4 blocks uphill from the tourist office and to the right. Same rates as the banks, most of which also exchange money. Open Mon.-Fri. 9am-7pm, Sat. 9am-1pm. **ATM** at Av. Carvalho Araújo, 84, at Banco Pinto and Sotto Mayor, next door to the tourist office.

Trains: Av. 5 de Outubro (tel. 32 21 93). To the town center, walk up Av. 5 de Out-ubro over the iron bridge onto R. Miguel Bombarda and turn left on R. Roque da Silveira. Continue to bear left until Av. Primeiro de Maio. Trains take longer than bus and require transfers at Régua. To Porto, via Régua (5 per day, 3½hr., 870$).

Buses: Rodonorte, R. D. Pedro de Castro (tel. 32 32 34), on the square directly uphill from the tourist office. To: Guimarães (3 per day via Amarante, 3hr., 840$); Bragança (4 per day, 4hr., 1250$); Porto (3 per day, 2hr., 850$); Lisbon (5 per day, 7½hr., 2150$). **Rodoviária do Norte,** out of Ruicar Travel Agency, R. Gonçalo Cris-tóvão, 16 (tel. 37 12 34), near Rodonorte uphill on the right. To: Viseu (2 per day, 2½hr., 1000$); Coimbra (2 per day, 4½hr., 1250$); Lisbon (2 per day, 7½hr., 2100$); Bragança (3 per day, 4hr., 1300$).

Taxis: (tel. 32 12 96). 24hr. They queue along R. Carvalho Araújo. To Mateus (600$).

Luggage Storage: Free at the tourist office and Rodonorte station, upon request.

Hospital: Hospital Distrital de Vila Real (tel. 34 10 41), in Lordelo, north of the town center.

Police: Largo Condes de Amarante (tel. 32 20 22). **Emergency:** tel. 112.

Post Office: Av. Carvalho Araújo (tel. 32 20 06), up the street from the tourist office. Open for Posta Restante, **telephones, fax,** and other services Mon.-Fri. 9am-6:30pm. **Postal Code:** 5000.

Telephone Code: (0)59.

ACCOMMODATIONS, CAMPING, AND FOOD

Accommodations cluster in the town center. Several cafes along **Av. Carvalho Araújo** advertise rooms upstairs, and three *pensões* line **Travessa São Domingos,** the side street next to the cathedral. Restaurants around **Av. António de Azevedo** and **Primeiro de Maio** cook up affordable meals, as do many cafes on the main drag. For groceries, hit **Mercado da Praça,** R. D. Maria das Chaves, 75 (open Mon.-Fri. 9am-1pm and 3-7pm, Sat. 9am-1pm).

Residencial da Sé, Trav. São Domingos, 19-23 (tel. 32 45 75). As you descend Av. Carvalho Araújo, it's down a sleepy side street to the right next to the cathedral.

Great, clean, bright rooms. Request one with windows. Singles 2500$, with bath and TV 4000$. Doubles: 4500$; 5500$. Breakfast included. Visa.

Pensão Mondego, Trav. São Domingos, 11 (tel./fax 32 30 97), next door to Residencial da Sé. Small, bright, carpeted rooms, all equipped with TV, phone, and bath. Singles 2000$. Doubles 4000$. Quads 7000$. Prices drop in the off season.

Camping: Parque de Campismo Municipal de Vila Real (tel. 32 47 24), on Av. Dr. Manuel Cardona, just northeast of town on a bluff above the Corgo River. Get on Av. Marginal and follow the signs. Free swims in the river or the pool complex. Free showers. Reception 8am-11pm; in off-season 8am-12:30pm and 2-6pm. 460$ per person, under 10 230$, 290$ per tent and per car.

Restaurante Nova Pompeia, R. Carvalho Araújo, 82 (tel. 728 76), next to the tourist office above a popular cafe of the same name. Low prices, middling environs, high A/C. *Prato do dia* around 750$. Excellent combination meals fill you up for 450-900$. Open Mon.-Sat. 8am-midnight. Major credit cards accepted.

Restaurante Museu dos Presuntos, Av. Cidade de Orense, 43 (tel. 32 60 17), at R. D. Afonso III and R. Morgado de Mateus. Savor one of the house's myriad *presunto* (ham) combinations and chase it down with the region's spunky wine. Entrees 950-1500$. Open Mon.-Sat. noon-3pm and 7-10pm.

SIGHTS AND ENTERTAINMENT

Most of Vila Real's sights lie outside of the city proper, but camera-toters still dote on three churches in town. The stodgy 15th-century **sé,** its simple interior divided by thick, arched columns, looms at the lower end of Av. Carvalho Araújo. Two blocks east of the cathedral, **Capela Nova** (New Chapel) blushes behind a floral facade. At the end of R. Combatentes da Grande Guerra, **Igreja de São Pedro** resounds with 17th-century *azulejos.* A superflux of cafes are the brunt of the town's main entertainment. Locals rendezvous at the ensemble of cafes on Largo do Proledo. **Copos e Rezas, Billiards Bar,** and **Ritmin** are lively draws within steps of each other.

■ Near Vila Real

While transportation for backpackers without wheels can be a pain, only a scarce few will regret a visit to the village of **Mateus,** 3km east of Vila Real, world-renowned for its rosé wine. The **Sogrape Winery,** on the main road from Vila Real, 200m from the turn-off for the Palácio Mateus, has a terrific free tour of the wine-processing center which includes complementary and unlimited tasting (open 9am-noon and 2-5pm daily; closes 1hr. early June-Sept.).

Up the road from the Sogrape Winery and surrounded by vineyards glitters the Baroque **Palácio de Mateus** (tel. 32 31 21), featured on the label of every bottle of Mateus rosé wine. The palace boasts a beautiful garden and features an original 1817 edition of Luís de Camões's *Os Lusíadas,* Portugal's famous literary epic. In the somewhat macabre 18th-century chapel, the 250-year-old remains of a Spanish soldier recline fully dressed in a glass case. (Open daily 9am-1pm and 2-7pm; in off-season 9am-12:30pm and 2-6pm. Last tour begins 1hr. before closing. Admission to mansion and gardens 900$, to gardens alone 700$.)

Rodonorte (see **Buses,** p. 595) runs seven inconveniently timed **buses** per day from Vila Real to the nearby town of Abambres (10min., 170$). These depart from the Câmara Municipal in Vila Real in the morning and from Cabanelas bus station in the afternoon. Ask the driver to let you off at Mateus and walk to Abambres to catch the return bus to Vila Real. Many people **walk** from Vila Real to Mateus; the road loops, so follow signs south from Vila Real's train station or north from the main highway out of town. A **taxi** costs around 850$.

Using Vila Real as a base, hardy souls explore the **Parque Natural do Alvão,** a protected area reaching to the heights of the mountainous Serra country north of Vila Real. The tourist office can provide maps and suggestions of places to visit. The outskirts of Lamas de Ôlo hosts mysterious granite dwellings and the spectacular **Rio Ôlo gorge.** The bus from Vila Real to Dornelas passes through the village.

Ribatejo and Alentejo

Fertile Ribatejo, named *riba do Tejo* (bank of the Tagus) by its imaginative first settlers, fills most of the basin of the Tejo and its main tributary, the Zêzere. Though farmed intensively, the area is best known in Portugal as pasture land and a breeding ground for Arabian horses and great black bulls.

Alentejo (*além do Tejo*, beyond the Tagus) covers almost one-third of Portugal, but with a population barely over half a million it remains the least populated and least touristed region. Townspeople are welcoming, and annual fairs are especially splashy. Aside from the mountainous west, the region is a vast granary, though severe droughts, resistance to contour farming, and overplanting of soil-drying eucalyptus trees have severely diminished its agricultural capacity. Locals complain of Lisbon's refusal to aid ambitious designs to divert water from the Taejo and Guadiana to irrigate their land. Évora, Elvas, and other medievalish towns grace the Alentejo Baixo, while Beja is the only major town on the seemingly endless Alentejo Alto plain.

■ Santarém

Santarém presides over Ribatejo and the Rio Tejo from atop a rocky mound. The town's name derives from Santa Iria, a nun who was accused of lapse of virtue and cast into the river. When she washed up in Santarém, an autopsy was done on her body and she was pronounced innocent. Santarém, Beja, and Braga were the three ruling cities of the ancient Roman province Lusitania. As a flourishing medieval center of 15 convents, it is the capital of Portuguese Gothic style.

ORIENTATION AND PRACTICAL INFORMATION

The core of Santarém is formed by the densely packed streets between **Praça Sá da Bandeira** and the park **Portas do Sol,** below which flows the Rio Tejo. **Rua Capelo Ivêns,** which begins at the *praça*, mothers the tourist office and many *pensões*.

Tourist Office: R. Capelo Ivêns, 6 (tel. 39 15 12), cross the park, walk past the church and go right onto R. Capelo Ivêns. **Maps** and info on festivals, accommodations, and transportation schedules. English spoken. Open Mon. 9am-12:30pm and 2-6pm, Tues.-Fri. 9am-7pm, Sat.-Sun. 10am-12:30pm and 2:30-5:30pm.

Currency Exchange: Banco Nacional Ultramarino (tel. 33 00 07), at Dr. Texeira Guedes and R. Capelo Ivêns. 1000$ commission. Open Mon.-Fri. 8:30am-3pm.

Train Station: (tel. 231 80 or 33 31 80), 2km outside town with bus service from the bus station (every 30min., 10min., 150$). Otherwise take a taxi (350-400$); it's a steep 20min. walk up dangerous roads. To: Lisbon (almost every hr., 1hr., 520$); Tomar (every 2hr., 1hr., 370$); Portalegre (via Entroncamento, 3 per day, 3hr., 920$); Faro (via Lisbon, 6 per day, 4hr., 1800$); Porto (6 per day, 4hr., 1300$).

Buses: Rodoviária Tejo, Av. Brasil (tel. 33 32 00; fax 33 30 54). To: Lisbon (5 *expressos* per day, 1hr., 1450$; others every hr., 1½hr., 1000$); Tomar (via Torres Novas, 2 per day, 1½hr., 750$); Caldas da Rainha (4 per day, 1½hr., 600$); Coimbra (4 per day, 2 hr., 1100$); Porto (4 per day, 3hr., 1000$); Faro (3 per day, 7hr., 2000$); Nazaré (1 per day, 1½hr., 720$).

Taxis: Scaltaxis (tel. 33 29 19). Stand is across from the bus station.

Luggage Storage: Bus station (100$ per day). Train station (250$ per day).

Hospital: Av. Bernardo Santareno (tel. 30 02 00; **emergency** tel. 30 02 60). From Pr. Sá da Bandeira, walk up R. Cidade da Covilhã, which becomes R. Alexandre Herculano. English spoken.

Police: (tel. 220 22). Follow the signs from the bus station onto pr. Sá da Bandeira. **Emergency:** tel. 112.

Post Office: (tel. 280 11 or 25 00 77). On the corner of Largo Cândido and R. Dr. Texeira Guedes. Turn right from the front door of the tourist office, take another

right at the next intersection and walk 2 blocks. Open Mon.-Fri. 8:30am-6:30pm, Sat. 9am-12:30pm. **Postal Code:** 2000.
Telephone Code: (0)43.

ACCOMMODATIONS, CAMPING AND FOOD

You stay, you pay. During the Ribatejo Fair (10 days starting the first Fri. in June), prices increase 10-40%. The tourist office can help find a room in a private house for about 3000-3500$ (2000$ during the rest of the year). Eateries cluster along and between the parallel **R. Capelo Ivêns** and **R. Serpa Pinto.** The **municipal market,** in the colorful pagoda-thing on Largo Infante Santo near the Jardim da República, supplies fresh produce and vegetables (open Mon.-Sat. 8am-2pm). Or pursue thrift at **Minipreço Supermarket,** R. Pedro Canavarro, 31, on the street leading from the bus station to R. Capelo Ivêns (open Mon.-Sat. 9am-8pm). Stop by **Pastelaria Venezia,** R. Capelo Ivêns, 99 (tel. 223 12), for delicious pastries and croissants.

> **Residencial Muralha,** R. Pedro Canavarro, 12 (tel. 223 99), next to the city's medieval wall. Winter heating and phones. Singles 2500$, with bath 3500$. Doubles 5000-8000$. Prices vary with the season. Breakfast 500$.
>
> **Residencial Abidis,** R. Guilherme de Azevedo, 4 (tel. 220 17 or 220 18), around the corner from the tourist office. Recently renovated rooms with high ceilings, large windows, and walnut furnishings. Singles 2500$, with bath 4500$. Doubles: 4500$; 6000-7000$. Breakfast included.
>
> **Pensão do José** (a.k.a. **Pensão da Dona Arminda**), Trav. Froes, 14 and 18 (tel. 230 88). Go left exiting Turismo and then take the first right. Small rooms, plastic flowers. Singles 2000$. Doubles 3000$, with shower 3500$.
>
> **Pastelaria Abdis,** R. Guilherme de Azevedo, 22 (tel. 222 50), next to the Residencial Abdis. Food is fast, fabulous, filling, and dirt cheap. *Febras de cebolada con congumelo* (meat in onion gravy, with rice and french fries 600$). Open daily 8-10am and noon-3pm.
>
> **Casa d'Avó,** R. Serpa Pinto, 62 (tel. 269 16). In "Grandma's house," food is home-cooked and served on petite tables surrounded by cast-iron garden chairs. Quiche, salad, daily fish and meat specials. Entrees 350-750$. Open Mon.-Sat. 9:30am-7pm.

SIGHTS

The austere facade of the **Igreja do Seminário dos Jesuítas** dominates Praça Sá da Bandeira, Santarém's main square. Stone friezes carved like ropes separate each of its three stories, and Latin mottos from the Bible embellish every lintel and doorway. To the left of the church, the former Colégio dos Jesuitas conceals two enormous, overgrown palm trees crammed into a tiny **cloister.** (Church under restoration. If closed, enter the door right of the main entrance and ask Sr. Domingos to unlock it.)

A statue of the Marquês da Bandeira embellishes the center of the *praça.* Stand back-to-back with him, and the street to the left, R. Serpa Pinto, leads to the wonderful **Praça Visconde de Serra Pilar,** formerly Pr. Velha. Centuries ago, Christians, Moors, and Jews gathered for social and business affairs here. The 12th-century **Igreja de Marvilha** has a 16th-century Manueline portal and a 17th-century *azulejo* interior (still closed for renovation). The early Gothic severity of nearby **Igreja da Graça** contrasts with Marvilha's exuberance. In the chapel is the tomb of Pedro Alvares Cabral, the explorer who discovered Brazil and one of the few *conquistadores* to stay alive long enough to be buried in his homeland.

Off R. São Martinho stands the medieval **Torre das Cabaças** (Tower of the Gourds), so-called because of the eight earthen bowls installed in the 16th century to amplify the bell's ring. Across the street, the **Museu Arqueológico de São João do Alporão,** in a former 13th-century church, exhibits the elaborate Gothic "tomb" of Dom Duarte de Meneses, who was hacked apart by Muslims. Entombed in a glass case is all that remains: a tooth. (Open June-Sept. Tues.-Sun. 10am-12:30pm and 2-6pm; Oct.-May Tues.-Sun. 9am-12:30pm and 2-5:30pm. Free.) It would be a shame to

quit before Av. 5 de Outubro ends at the **Portas Do Sol,** a paradise of flowers, gardens, and fountains surrounded by old Moorish walls.

Ready to imbibe? Join the throng at **Bar Boaviela,** Praça do Município (tel. 229 72), for food, drink, and live music on Fridays (open daily until 2am). **Município Cervejão,** Av. António Maria Baptista, 10 (tel. 264 33), stocked with beer and cocktails (open Mon.-Sat. till 2am). Santarém shimmies with festivals. Feed your sweet tooth at the **sweets fair** (the last Wed.-Sun. in April), featuring calories from all over Portugal. At the same time, **Lusoflora** displays flowers from all over the world. The largest festival is the **Feira Nacional de Agricultura** (a.k.a. **Feira do Ribatejo**), a national agricultural exhibition. People come for the 10-day bullfighting and horseracing **orgy** (starting the first Fri. in June). Smack your lips at the **Festival e Seminário Nacional de Gastronomia** (the last 10 days of October), when each region of Portugal has a day to prepare a typical feast and entertainment.

■ Tomar

For centuries the arcane Knights Templar—part monks, part warriors—plotted crusades from their lair in this small town straddling the Rio Nabão. Most of Tomar's monuments reflect the city's former status as the den of that secretive religious order. Their celebrated 12th-century convent-fortress, perched high above the old town, is exactly what you'd picture a medieval castle to be, right off the set of Monty Python and the Holy Grail. Nowadays, centuries of intrigue are trodden under foot: main streets are tiled with the Cross of Christ, the Knights' symbol.

ORIENTATION AND PRACTICAL INFORMATION

While the **Rio Nabão** divides Tomar, almost everything—the train, bus stations, accommodations, and sights—lie on the west bank. The lush **Parque Mouchão** straddles the two banks, while the antique (albeit fully functional) **Ponte Velha** connects the two. The bus and train stations border the **Várzea Grande,** a vast square/wasteland. Four blocks north, **Avenida Dr. Cândido Madureira** hems the south edge of the old city, with **Rua Everaro** and **Avenida Marquês de Tomar** on the river border, and **Rua Dr. Sousa** on the castle side. Rustic **Rua Serpa Pinto** cuts across town from river to castle and connects the Ponte Velha (old bridge) to the main square, **Praça da República.**

Tourist Office: Av. Dr. Cândido Madureira (tel. 32 24 27), facing Parque Mata Nacional. From the transportation stations, go through the small square onto Av. General Bernardo Raria. Continue 4 blocks and go left onto Av. Dr. Cândido Madureira; the office is at the end of the street. **Map,** accommodations list, and advice in an interesting mini-museum. Open Mon.-Fri. 9:30am-6pm, Sat.-Sun. 10am-1pm and 3-6pm.

Currency Exchange: União dos Bancos, R. Serpa Pinto, 20, has an **ATM.**

Trains: Av. Combatentes da Grande Guerra (tel. 31 28 15), at the southern edge of town. Tomar is the north terminus of a minor line, so most destinations require a transfer at Entroncamento; you can buy the transfer here. To: Lisbon (12 per day, 2hr., 870$); Coimbra (9 per day, 2½hr., 850$); Porto (5 per day, 4½hr., 1390$).

Buses: Rodoviaria Tejo, Av. Combatentes Grande Guerra (tel. 31 27 38), by the train station. To: Fátima (3 per day, 30min., 430$); Leiria (3 per day, 1hr., 580$); Lisbon (5 per day, 2hr., 1200$); Coimbra (2 per day, 2½hr., 1150$); Porto (1 per day, 4hr., 1400$); Lagos (1 per day, 11hr., 2300$); Santarém (2 per day, 1hr., 450$).

Taxis: (tel. 31 37 16 or 31 23 73). Taxis idle at R. Arcos.

Hospital: Av. Cândido Madureira (tel. 32 11 00). Same street as the tourist office.

Police: R. Dr. Sousa (tel. 31 34 44). **Emergency:** tel. 112.

Post Office: Av. Marquês de Tomar (tel. 32 23 54), across from Parque Mouchão. Open Mon.-Fri. 9am-noon and 2-5pm. **Postal Code:** 2300.

Telephone Code: (0)49.

PORTUGAL

ACCOMMODATIONS AND FOOD

Finding a place to stay is only a problem during the Festival dos Tabuleiros, which takes place every four years. Tomar is a buyer's market—practice bargaining.

Tomar is the picnic capital of Portugal. A section of the lush Parque Mouchão is set aside just for that. The **market,** on the corner of Av. Norton de Matos and R. Santa Iria across the river, provides all the fixings (Mon.-Thurs. and Sat. 8am-2pm). Friday is the big day, when the market gears up from 8am-5pm. Several inexpensive **mini-markets** line the side streets between the tourist office and Pr. República.

Residencial União, R. Serpa Pinto, 94 (tel. 32 31 61; fax 32 12 99), halfway between Pr. República and the bridge. Look for the oversized *azulejo* panels outside. Twenty-eight bright, plush rooms with wood furniture and white-tiled baths. Well-stocked bar, plus a spiffy shoe-shine machine on the ground floor. All rooms with shower or full bath, telephone, TV, and central heating. Singles 3500-4500. Doubles 6000-6500. Triples 7500$. Prices lower in winter. Breakfast included. Reserve several days ahead July-Aug.

Residencial Luz, R. Serpa Pinto, 144 (tel. 31 23 17), down the street from União. Cozy, clean rooms with phones. Swank TV rooms with leather couches. Singles with shower 3000$, with bath 3500$. Doubles: 4500$; 5400$. Gargantuan 4- and 6-person rooms with bath 2000$ per person. Oct.-May 20% off. Breakfast 300$.

Camping: Parque Municipal de Campismo (tel. 32 26 07; fax 32 10 26), conveniently across Ponte Velha near the stadium and swimming pool, on the river. Exit off E.N. 110 on the east end of the Nabão bridge. Thickly forested campground with a pool. Reception open in summer daily 8am-8pm; in winter 9am-5pm. 380$ per person, 200$ per tent, 280$ per car. Showers free.

Restaurante Estrêla do Céu, Pr. República, 21 (tel. 32 31 38). Ex-Sheraton chef serves up creative dishes in a relaxing rustic decor. *Lombinhos à corredoura* (veal with orange, red pepper, and carrots 1450$) is a specialty, but the daily lunch specials are the real bargain at 450$. Open Tues.-Sun. 11am-midnight.

Restaurante Bela Vista, R. Fonte do Choupo, 6 (tel. 31 28 70), across the Ponte Velha on your left. Dine on the riverside patio under a grape arbor with a handsome view of the park. Diverse meat and fish entrees, all with fries 700-1900$. Open Wed.-Sun. noon-3pm and 7-9:30pm, Mon. noon-3pm.

Restaurante Tabuleiro, R. Serpa Pinto, 140/148 (tel. 31 27 71), near Pr. República. Substance rules over style in this neighborhood joint. Mouth-watering *bitoque de porco* (675$) comes in an earthenware bowl topped with an egg and buried in a heap of fries. Other dishes 600-925$. Open Mon.-Sat. 11am-10pm.

SIGHTS AND ENTERTAINMENT

It's worth trekking in from the far corners of the earth to explore the mysterious **Convento de Cristo** grounds (tel. 31 34 81), established in 1320 as a refuge for the disbanded Knights Templar. Walk out of the tourist office door and take your second right; bear left at the fork. Pedestrians can take the steeper dirt path a bit after the fork on the left. Cars (and weary pedestrians) can enjoy the easy-grade paved road up the mountain. An ornate octagonal canopy protects the high altar of the **Templo dos Templares,** which is modeled after the Holy Sepulchre in Jerusalem. Just as Genghis Khan's soldiers slept on horseback, the Knights supposedly attended mass, each under one of the arches, in the saddle. A 16th-century courtyard is encrusted with the rich seafaring symbolism of Manueline style: seaweed, coral, anchors, rope, and even artichokes, which mariners ate to prevent scurvy. Below stands the **Janela do Capítulo** (chapter window), an exuberant tribute to the Golden Age of Discoveries.

One of Europe's masterpieces of Renaissance architecture, the **Claustro dos Felipes** honors King Felipe II of Castile, who was crowned here as Felipe I of Portugal during Iberia's unification (1580-1640). Tucked behind the Palladian main cloister and the nave is **Claustro Santa Bárbara,** where grotesque gargoyle rainspouts writhe in pain as they cough up a fountain. On the northeast side of the church is the Gothic **Claustro do Cemitério,** the only part of the complex dating back to the time of great

Prince Henry the Navigator. (Complex open daily 9:30am-12:30pm and 2-5:30pm. 400$, students and seniors 200$.)

Pyromaniacs light up over the **Museu dos Fósforos** (tel. 32 26 02), exhibiting the Europe's largest matchbox collection. It's in the Convento de São Francisco, just across from the train and bus stations (open Sun.-Fri. 2-5pm; free). Nature freaks can take a hike at one of the many trails leading away from the lush **Parque da Mata Nacional dos Sete Montes,** behind the gates across from the tourist office.

At night, Knights and laymen gather at **O Covil dos Templários II,** Av. Dr. Cândido Madureira, 94 (tel. 32 10 27), to bask in the glow of a giant video screen (open 8pm-2am). For a week in either June or July, handicrafts, folklore, *fado,* and theater storm the city during the **Feira Nacional de Artesanato,** but the big deal is really the **Festa dos Tabuleiros.** Unfortunately, this massive cultural celebration, involving the laborious construction of three-foot-tall decorative hats for women using cardboard, colored paper, and bread, takes place only once every four years (the next is 1999). Women and hats parade through town for days, as well as children, bulls, and horses in finery. If you miss the party, view some of the costumes donned by mannequins at the tourist office.

Judaism in Portugal

Tomar's **Museu Luso-Hebraico** (tel. 32 26 02 ext. 319, in the 15th-century Sinagoga do Arco at R. Dr. Joaquim Jaquinto, 73, is Portugal's most significant reminder of what was once a vibrant Portuguese Jewish community. Jews worshipped here for only a few decades before the convert-or-leave ultimatum of 1496. Since then the building has served as a prison, Christian chapel, hayloft, and grocery warehouse before a national monument. In 1923, Samuel Schwartz purchased the synagogue, devoted much of his life to its restoration, and in 1939 donated it to the state. The government awarded Schwartz and his wife Portuguese citizenship, assuring them sanctuary during World War II. The museum keeps a collection of old tombstones, inscriptions, and donated pieces from around the world. A recent excavation of the adjacent building unearthed a sacred purification bath *(mikvah)*, used by the Jews for ritual purposes only to be buried for centuries under sidewalks. Services are held at the site on selected Saturdays (open Thurs.-Tues. 9:30am-12:30pm and 2-6pm).

■ Évora

From a rolling plain of corktree groves and sunflower fields, Évora (pop. 45,000) rises like a megalith on a hill. Considered Portugal's foremost showpiece of medieval architecture, the picture-perfect town boasts the Roman Temple to Diana, twisting streets that wind past Moorish arches, and a 16th-century university, all things which prompted the UN to grant Évora World Heritage status. Elegant marble-floored shops flash their wares in the windows, students chat on the streets, and a steady but not overwhelming trickle of tourists flow from Lisbon and the Algarve.

ORIENTATION AND PRACTICAL INFORMATION

Évora is easily accessible from Lisbon, about 140km to the west. Several trains per day ply the Lisbon and Faro routes, also linking the town with Estremoz, Porto, Portalegre, and Elvas to the north, and Setúbal and Beja to the south. No direct bus connects the **train station** to the center of town. To avoid hiking 700m up R. Dr. Baronha, hail a taxi (400$), or flag down bus #6, which halts at the tracks two blocks over (100$). Near the edge of town, R. Dr. Baronha turns into **Rua República,** which leads to **Praça do Giraldo,** the main square, and home to most monuments and lodgings. From the **bus station,** simply proceed uphill to the *praça.*

Tourist Office: Pr. Giraldo, 73 (tel. 226 71), on the right as you face the *igreja*. Helpful, multilingual staff compensates for the illegible map by calling around until you

have a room. Open June-Sept. Mon.-Fri. 9am-7pm, Sat.-Sun. 9am-12:30pm and 2-5:30pm; Oct.-May Mon.-Fri. 9am-12:30pm and 2-6pm, Sat.-Sun. 9am-12:30pm and 2-5:30pm.

Currency Exchange: Automatic 24hr. exchange machine outside the tourist office.

Trains: (tel. 221 25). From the main *praça*, walk down R. República until it turns into R. Dr. Baronha; the station is at the end of the road, 1½km from town center. To: Lisbon (6 per day, 3hr., 810$); Faro (2 per day, 6hr., 1430$); Beja (4 per day, 2hr., 650$); Estremoz (3 per day, 1½hr., 420$).

Buses: R. República (tel. 221 21), downhill 5min. from Praça Giraldo, opposite Igreja de São Francisco. Much more convenient than trains. To: Lisbon (5 per day, 3hr., 1120$); Faro (3 per day, 5hr., 1470$); Vila Real de Santo António (2 per day, 6½hr., 1820$); Beja (6 per day, 1½hr., 940$); Elvas (1 per day, 1½hr., 900$); Porto (6 per day, 7hr., 2300$); Setúbal (6 per day, 2½hr., 900$).

Taxis: (tel. 232 65 or 291 38). Taxis hang out 24hr. in Pr.Giraldo

Luggage Storage: In the bus station basement (110$ per bag per day).

Laundromat: Lavandaria Lavévora, Largo D'Alvaro Velho, 6 (tel. 238 83), off R. Miguel Bombardo. 370$ per kg. Open Mon.-Fri. 9am-1pm and 3-7pm.

English Bookstore: Papeleria Nazareth, Pr. Giraldo, 46 (tel. 222 21). Small English and French sections upstairs. Has mysteries and inexpensive classics. Open Mon.-Fri. 9am-1pm and 3-5pm, Sat. 9am-1pm.

Hospital: (tel. 250 01), Largo Senhor da Pobreza, close to the city wall and the intersection with R. D. Augusto Eduardo Nunes.

Police: (tel. 220 22), R. Francisco Soares Lusitano, near the Temple of Diana. **Emergency:** tel. 112.

Post Office: R. Olivença (tel. 264 39), 2 blocks north of Pr. Giraldo. Exit the *praça* and walk up R. João de Deus, keeping right. Pass under the aqueduct and make an immediate right uphill. Open for mail, Posta Restante, **telephones,** and **fax** Mon.-Fri. 8:30am-6:30pm. **Postal Code:** 7000.

Telephone Code: (0)66.

ACCOMMODATIONS AND CAMPING

Most *pensões* cluster on side streets around **Praça do Giraldo.** They are crowded in summer, especially during the late June mega-fest *São João*—reserve ahead. Prices drop 500-1000$ in winter. The tourist office can help you find a room. *Quartos,* from 2000-4000$ per person, are pleasant alternatives to crowded *pensões* in the summer.

Pensão Os Manueis, R. Raimundo, 35 (tel. 228 61), left and around the corner from the tourist office. Trek up the marbled stairs to 27 homey rooms lining a noisy sun-roofed courtyard; more compact ones pack the annex across the street. Singles 3000$, with bath 5000$. Doubles: 4000$; 6000$.

Casa Palma, R. Bernando Mato, 29-A (tel. 235 60). From the tourist office, down the street and 3 blocks to the right. Pink bedspreads in bright doubles on the bottom floor; cheaper dim singles lie upstairs. Singles 3000$. Doubles 4000$. Prices drop in the off season.

Pensão Giraldo, R. Mercadores, 27 (tel. 258 33). From the tourist office, take a left and another left 2 blocks later. The *pensão*'s 24 rooms have TV, winter heat, windows, and either an in-room sink, shower, or full bath. Reserve in advance for the best-valued rooms in the recently renovated annex. Singles 3900-5500$. Doubles 4800-7800$. Visa, MC, Am Ex.

Orbitur's Parque de Campismo de Évora (tel. 251 90; fax 298 30), a 3-star park on Estrada das Alcáçovas which branches off the bottom of R. Raimundo. A 40min. walk to town; only 1 bus per day runs along this route. Washing machines and a small market. Reception open 8am-10pm. 500$ per person, 400$ per tent, 430$ per car. Shower 50$. Open year-round, with discounts Oct.-March.

FOOD

Many passable budget restaurants lie scattered about **Pr. do Giraldo,** particularly along R. Mercadores—in general, the farther you get from the square, the better (and cheaper) the meal, so think twice about dining with the doves. The **public market**

sets up in the square in front of Igreja de São Francisco and the public gardens, selling produce, flowers, and a wild assortment of cheese. For other feastables, try **Maxi-grula,** R. João de Deus, 130 (open Mon.-Sat. 9am-7pm).

Restaurante A Choupana, R. Mercadores, 16-20 (tel. 244 27), off Pr. Giraldo, across from Pensão Giraldo. Snack bar on the left for a budget lunch, and *restaurante* on the right for elegant Portuguese *nouvelle cuisine. Trutas do Minho* (trout with bacon 700$). Sundries on the table cost extra. Entrees 900-1300$. Half-portions 600$. Open daily 10am-2pm and 7-10pm. Visa, MC, AmEx.

Café-Restaurante A Gruta, Av. General Humberto Delgado, 2 (tel. 281 86). After exiting Pr. Giraldo, pass the bus station and follow R. República toward the train station, turn right at the end of the park. It's on your right. Inhale the aroma of roasting fowl. Lip-smacking *frango no churrasco* (barbecued chicken) buried under a heap of fries. Half-chicken 680$. Open Sun.-Fri. 11am-3pm and 5-10pm.

Restaurante O Garfo, R. Santa Catarina, 13-15 (tel. 292 56). From R. Serpa Pinto take the 1st right onto R. Caldeireiros, which turns into R. Santa Catarina. Yummy entrees (950-1400$). *Gaspacho à alentejana com peixe frito* (gazpacho with fried fish 1100$). Open daily 11am-midnight. Visa, MC, AmEx.

SIGHTS AND ENTERTAINMENT

Streets brimming with monuments and architectural riches earned Évora its UN status and nickname "museum city." Starting from the Praça Giraldo, the fortress-like 1553 Igreja Santo Antão conceals massive columns and no-frill vaults. Off to the east side of the *praça,* R. 5 de Outubro leads to the colossal 12th-century **cathedral.** The 12 Apostles adorning the doorway are masterpieces of medieval Portuguese sculpture, while the **cloister** is designed in ponderous 14th-century Romanesque style. Staircases spiral to its roof. The **Museu de Arte Sacra,** in a gallery above the nave, houses the cathedral's treasury and 13th-century ivory *Virgem do paraíso.* (Open Tues.-Sun. 9am-noon and 2-5pm. Cathedral free, cloister and museum 350$.)

Since the discovery of Roman, Visigoth and Moorish ruins under its floor, archaeologists replaced engineers out to expand the basement of the nearby **Museu de Évora.** The museum's collection (ranging from Roman tombs to 17th-century Virgin Mary) has vied for attention with the fascinating (and on-going) digging. (Open Tues.-Sun. 10am-noon and 2-5pm. Admission 250$, under 25 and seniors 125$, under 14 free.)

Évora's most famous monument, the 2nd-century **Templo de Diana,** is across from the museum. This temple honoring the Roman goddess of the moon, purity, and the hunt served as a slaughterhouse for centuries. A platform and 14 Corinthian columns are all that remains now. Warning: climbing up into the temple is a no-no.

The town's best-kept secret, the **Igreja de São João Evangelista** (1485), faces the temple. The church is owned by the Cadaval family, who reside in their ancestors' ducal palace next door (church open Tues.-Sun. 10am-noon and 2-5pm; 250$). The interior is covered with dazzling *azulejos,* but you must ask to see the church's hidden chambers. Downhill from the museum, two successive rights brings you to the villa-like **Palácio dos Condes de Bosto,** home of a Renaissance military order.

Another standby is the **Igreja Real de São Francisco,** in its own square downhill from Pr. Giraldo. Few dilly-dally admiring the art—the church encoffins the real show-stopper, the perverse **Capela de Ossos** (Chapel of Bones). Above the door an irreverent sign taunts visitors: *"Nós ossos que aqui estamos, pelos vossos esperamos"* ("We bones lie here awaiting yours"). Three Franciscan monks ransacked local cemeteries for the remains of 4000 people in order to construct it. Enormous femurs and baby tibias neatly panel every inch of wall, while rows of skulls and an occasional pelvis line the capitals and ceiling vaults. The three innovative founders grimace from stone sarcophagi to the right of the altar. (Church and chapel open Mon.-Sat. 8:30am-1pm and 2:30-6pm, Sun. 10-11:30am and 2:30-6pm. Chapel closed during mass. Admission 50$, photography permit 100$.) Just south of the church sprawls the **Jardim Público.** At the northeast end of the park, an exit leads to R. Raimundo past the 17th-century **Igreja Conventual de Nossa Senhora das Mercês.** Its multicolored

The Heart of Art in Portugal

A stroll around Évora reverses you to the time when the city was Portugal's cultural center. As early as the 13th century a renowned school of sculpture was born in the city. Around 1400, the monk and painter Brother Carlos, along with a number of Portuguese and Flemish artists, inaugurated a first-class art school in the city. The artistic euphoria peaked during the reign of Dom João III (ca. 1521-1557), when a corps of Portugal's finest writers—including Gil Vicente, Garcia and André Rezende, Jerónimo Osório, Aires Barbosa, Dom Francisco de Melo, Clenardo, Vaseu and Jean Petit, not to mention the king himself—flourished in Évora. Visitors can imagine the days before Évora was a museum city, and when it was *the* city in Portugal, in terms of urbanity and the arts.

tile interior is a museum of decorative arts (open Tues.-Sun. 10am-noon and 2-5pm; 150$). The **Jewish quarter** inhabited neighboring side streets, whose whitewashed houses and connecting arches have changed little since the 13th century.

Although most of Évora turns in with the sun, **Xeque-Mate,** R. Valdevinos, 21 (2nd right off R. 5 de Outubro from the *praça),* and **Discoteca Slide,** R. Serpa Pinto, 135, blare music until 2am. Only couples and single women need apply (1000$ covers at both include two beers). Évora's festival, the **Feira de São João,** starts the last Friday in June and goes for seven nights, all night. The entire town, including its toddlers, turns out for carnival rides, food, local dancing troupes, and a circus.

■ Near Évora: Elvas

Elvas is dead, you say? No, the town is just keeping a low-profile, perched on the crown of a steep hill rising out of arid fields 15km from the Spanish border. A perfect place for a taste of small-town Alentejo life, Elvas is also often a necessary stopover to or from nearby Badajoz, Spain. Quiet Elvas combines all things lovable in a Portuguese town: friendly people, good food, few tourists, ruins, and great views.

Elvas's main spectacle, the **Aqueduto da Amoreira,** emerges from a hill at the entrance to the city. Begun in 1529 and finished almost a century later, the colossal four-tiered structure, 8km by 31km, is Europe's largest aqueduct. You can soak in the view from the **castelo** above Pr. República—rows of olive trees stretch to the horizon in every direction. To the right of the entrance, a stairwell veiled by plants leads up to the castle walls. Upon request, an attendant will unlock the museum upstairs and show you around. (All churches open daily 10am-1pm and 3-7pm; Oct.-May daily 10am-1pm and 2:30-6pm.)

At Pr. República, **Igreja de Nossa Senhora da Assunção** dominates the mosaic-covered main square. Rebuilt in Manueline style, abstract *azulejos* and a beautifully ribbed ceiling give splendor to the church's interior. Behind the cathedral and uphill to the right is **Igreja de Nossa Senhora da Consolação,** also known as **Freiras.** Its octagonal interior has beautiful, multicolored geometric tiles. In the three-sided *praça* out front stands the 16th-century **pelourinho,** an octagonal pillory culminating in a pyramid. Just north of the city on the road to Portalegre is the impressive **Forte da Graça,** a stone fortress that peers at Elvas (the older one) from across the valley.

The **tourist office** (tel. 62 22 36), in Pr. Rebública, resides next to the bus station (open daily 9am-7pm; in off-season Mon.-Fri. 9am-6pm, Sat.-Sun. 9am-12:30pm and 2-5:30pm). The **bus station** (tel. 62 87 50) is on Pr. República. To: the Spanish border at Caia (2 per day, 20min., 220$); Évora (4 per day, 2hr., 820$); Lisbon (4 per day, 4hr., 1400$). *Espresso* to Faro (1 per day, 5½hr., 2100$) passing through Beja, Évora, and Albufeira. The **train station** (tel. 62 28 16) is in the town of Fontainhas, 3km north of the city and connects to Pr. República by bus (Mon.-Fri. 6 per day, Sat. 3 per day, Sun. 2 per day, 90$). Trains roll to Badajoz, Spain (3 per day, 15min., 450$) and Évora (1 per day, 3hr., 960$). **Taxis** answer at tel. 62 22 87. **Luggage storage** is available at the bus station (110$). Call the **hospital** at tel. 62 22 25; the **police** (tel. 62 26 13) are a block behind the tourist office. In an **emergency,** dial 112. The **post office**

When in 172-1011,
do as the 172-1011's do.

All you need for the
clearest connections home.

Every country has its own AT&T Access Number which makes calling from overseas really easy. Just dial the AT&T Access Number for the country you're calling from and we'll take it from there. And be sure to charge your calls on your AT&T Calling Card. It'll help you avoid outrageous phone charges on your hotel bill and save you up to 60%.* For a free wallet card listing AT&T Access Numbers, call 1 800 446-8399.

It's all within your reach.

Photo: R. Olken

Greetings from Let's Go Publications

The book in your hand is the work of hundreds of student researcher-writers, editors, cartographers, and designers. Each summer we brave monsoons, revolutions, and marriage proposals to bring you a fully updated, completely revised travel guide series, as we've done every year for the past 38 years.

This is a collection of our best finds, our cheapest deals, our most evocative description, and, as always, our wit, humor, and irreverence. Let's Go is filled with all the information on anything you could possibly need to know to have a successful trip, and we try to make it as much a companion as a guide.

We believe that budget travel is not the last recourse of the destitute, but rather the only way to travel; living simply and cheaply brings you closer to the people and places you've been saving up to visit. We also believe that the best adventures and discoveries are the ones you find yourself. So put us down every once in a while and head out on your own. And when you find something to share, drop us a line. We're **Let's Go Publications,** 67 Mount Auburn St., Cambridge, MA 02138, USA (email: fanmail@letsgo.com; http://www.letsgo.com). And let us know if you want a free subscription to **The Yellowjacket,** the new Let's Go Newsletter.

(tel. 62 26 96), on R. Calderia one block behind the tourist office, has **telephones** and Posta Restante (open Mon.-Fri. 8:30am-6:30pm, Sat. 9am-12:30pm).

The few *pensões* in Elvas are boarding houses for semi-permanent residents. Renting a room in a private home may be the only recourse. Bargain the price of a single down to 2500$ maximum, and pay no more than 4000$ for a double. Be very cautious when accepting a room from people who solicit at the bus station, and confirm the price and available amenities—especially hot water—in advance. **António Mocissoe Garcia Coelho,** R. Aires Varela, 5 (tel. 62 21 26), rents *quartos*. Take the first left below the bus station, and then the first right off R. João d'Olivença; it is across the street from Lucinda's (singles 2500$, doubles 4500$; Oct.-May: 1500$; 3500$). Campers may try **Campismo Varche** (tel. 62 54 02 or 62 47 77), a secluded orchard 4km from Elvas (420$ per person; hot showers 250$; electricity 300$; laundry 600$). Take buses to Évora, Lisbon, or Estremoz; they stop in Varche.

Every Monday fresh produce is sold at an outdoor **market** immediately outside town behind the aqueduct. Many stores and restaurants line **Rua da Cadeia** and the two streets perpendicular to it, **Rua da Carreira** and **do Alcamim,** just south of the *praça*. If all else fails, get **groceries** at the **Loja de Convêniencia,** R. Cadeia, 40, the first right going downhill on the street to the right of the tourist office (open daily 8am-11pm). For good food in a neighborhood joint, sidle over to **Canal 7,** R. Sapateiros, 16 (tel. 62 35 93), on the right side of Pr. República (half-chicken with fries 500$; open daily noon-3pm and 7-9:30pm).

■ Beja

Tucked amid the vast, monotonous wheat fields of the southern Alentejo, Beja ("kiss") is a town (founded by the Romans as pax Julia) of beautiful architecture and scorching temperatures. If you've always wondered what the Sahara is like but don't have the cash to get there, visit Beja in the summer. Steamy in more ways than one, the tale of a nun and her 17th century French Lieutenant boyfriend unveiled at the Museu Rainha Dona Leonor is just one entry in Beja's historic ledger of sex and intrigue. The nun's tell-all account, *Five Love Letters of a Portuguese Nun,* was published in Paris in 1669 and vaulted the town into the annals of sexual impropriety. A prime getaway destination for romantic exploits, Beja is also a haven of traditional food, music, and handicrafts.

The town's historical sites are scattered about, but the outstanding **Museu Rainha Dona Leonor** makes an excellent starting point. Walk past the tourist office and into the *praça*; the museum is on your right. Built on the site of Sister Mariana Alcoforado's famed indiscretion with a French officer, the museum features a replica of the cell window through which the lovers exchanged secret passionate vows. Inside, the gilded church's 18th-century *azulejo* panels depict the lives of Mary and St. John the Baptist. Nearby are fine intaglio marble altars and panels of *talha dourada* (gilded carvings). The *azulejos* and Persian-style ceiling make the chapter house look like a mini mosque. (Open Tues.-Sun. 9:45am-1pm and 2-5:15pm. 100$, Sun. free. Ticket also good for the **Museu Visigótico** behind the *castelo*.)

One block downhill from the convent is the adobe-like 13th-century **Igreja de Santa María,** transformed into a mosque during the Moorish invasion and back into a church when the city reverted to Portuguese control.

A miniature bull on its corner column symbolizes the city's spirit. From here, R. D. Aresta Branco leads past handsome old houses to the city's massive **castelo,** built around 1300 on the remnants of a Roman fortress. It still flaunts an enormous crenellated marble keep, vaulted chambers, stones covered with cryptic symbols, and walls covered with ivy. You can also climb the **Torre de Menagem** for 100$ (open Tues.-Sun. 10am-1pm and 2-6pm; Oct.-March 9am-noon and 1-4pm).

PORTUGAL

ORIENTATION AND PRACTICAL INFORMATION

Rua de Mértola and **Rua de Capitão João Francisco de Sousa** brand the center of town. The streets are unmarked and confusing, especially in the town center. The train station (tel. 32 5056) servicing Lisbon (3 per day, 3hr., 1200$); Evora (6per day, 1 hr., 690?); and Faro (2 per day, 5½ hr., 1100$), is about 1km outside of town; those with heavy bags might want to taxi (tel. 224 74) it to the town center (470$) rather than walk uphill for half an hour. The **bus station** (tel. 32 40 44) is on R. Cidade de São Paulo. at the roundabout on the corner of Avi Brasil. To: Lisbon (4 per day, 3hr., 1200$); Évora (4 per day, 2hr., 730$); Faro (4per day, 3½hr., 1300$); the rest of the Algarve; Real de la Frontera, Spain (1 per day, 1½hr., 1000$). Connections to Spain, France and beyond. **Luggage storage** is on the way out, at 160$ per day. From here to the center, walk straight out the terminal and through the traffic circle (past the statue). After one block, turn right, go past the post office on the left, and continue up the curving street. At the intersection, take a left on R. Capitão J. F. de Sousa (with a small pedestrian square). Keep to your right and watch for the **tourist office**, on R. Capitão J. F. de Sousa, 25 (tel. 236 93). The English-speaking staff hands out decent maps and helps find accommodations. (Mon.-Fri. 10am-8pm, Sat. 10am-6pm; in winter, Mon.-Sat. 10am-6pm). Take a refreshing dive into the town's excellent **swimming pool** (tel. 236 26) on Avi Brasil, near the bus station and camping ground. Admission to park and swimming pool 200$. Open Sat.-Thurs. 10am-9pm. To get to the hospital, on Dr. António F. C. Lima (tel. 32 02 00), follow the signs from the bus and train stations. The **police** is watching you on R. D. Nuno Álvares Pereira (tel. 32 20 22), one bl. downhill from the tourist office and a few meters to the left. **Emergency**: tel. 112. **Post Office:** Largo do Correio (tel. 238 50), down the street from the beginning of R. Capitão de Sousa. Open for Posta Restante and **telephones** Mon.-Fri. 8:30am-6:30pm. **Postal Code:** 7800. **Telephone Code:** (0)84.

ACCOMMODATIONS, CAMPING, AND FOOD

Most all rooms lie within a few blocks of the tourist office and the central pedestrian street. *Pensões* cluster around **Praça República. Residência Bejense,** R. Capitão J. F. de Sousa, 57 (tel. 32 50 01), down the street from the tourist office, features beautiful rooms with tile floors, ruffled bedspreads, TV, phone, and private bath. Winter heat and A/C. Singles 4500$. Doubles 6500$. Breakfast included. Visa, MC, AmEx. **Pensão Tomás,** R. Alexandre Herculano, 7 (tel. 32 46 13; fax 32 07 96). Walk uphill past the post office and take the 3rd right after Pousada São Francisco into a small square. Clean rooms with bath, phones, and fans. Singles 3500$. Doubles 4500$. Prices drop in winter. **Camping: Parque Municipal** (tel. 243 28) on the southwest side of town at the end of Av. Vasco da Gama, past the stadium. Out of the bus terminal, go straight one bl. and take a left. Small, shady, and clean. 320$ per person, 220$ per tent and per car. Free showers. Town swimming pool nearby. Beja is one of the best places to taste authentic (and affordable) Portuguese cuisine. Most restaurants keep limited hours (noon-2pm and 7-10pm). The local specialty is *migas de pão*, a sausage and bacon soup thickened with bread. The municipal **market** sets up in a building one block up and one black to the right from the bus station (open 6am-1:30pm). For **groceries**, go to **Urbeja, SA**, Largo de São João, 15 (tel. 243 41 or 286 30), a block uphill from the museum (open Mon.-Fri. 8am-8pm, Sat.8am-1pm; winter Mon.-Sat. 8am-8pm). **Restaurante Tomás**, R. Alexandre Herculano, 7 (tel. 32 46 13), beneath the *pensão.* This award-winning restaurant offers rich soup and regional fish and meat dishes (900-1100$). Open daily noon-4pm and 7-11pm. **Restaurante Alentejano,** Largo dos Duques de Beja (tel. 238 49), down the steps near the museum. Unpretentious regional restaurant with great meat options, reasonable prices (around 900$) and authentic fare. Generous portions of meat and pork. Open Sat.-Thurs. noon-3pm and 7-10pm.

Algarve

A freak of nature; a desert on the sea; an inexhaustible vacationland where happy campers from all over the world bask in the *sol*—behold the Algarve. Nearly 3000 hours of sunshine per year have transformed this one-time fishermen's backwater into a scene out of *Baywatch*. Tourist resorts are mobbed in July and August, packing the bars and discos from the 10pm sunset to the all-too-early sunrise.

That said, not all is excess in the Algarve. In the off-season, the resorts of the Algarve become pleasantly de-populated. The sun eases down a bit, presiding over tranquil grotto beaches lining the base of rugged cliffs and rocky islets. Salema, Burgau, and Sagres, to the west of Lagos, offer isolated beaches and steep cliffs, and the region between Olhão and the border remains understated. The west coast of the Algarve was recently declared a protected natural park, and flamingo wetlands float along Portugal's eastern border, near the town of Tavira.

Reaching more remote beaches is a snap. EVA has extensive bus services with convenient schedules and low fares. The train costs less than the bus but only connects major coastal cities, and in some towns the station is a hike from the center. Leave your car at home—the roads here are plagued by constant road work and legendary traffic jams—but rent a bike or moped at your hub town; there is no better way to explore nearby beaches. In this region, reasonably priced *quartos* are generally the best alternative to pricier or non-existent *pensões*. *The Algarve News* (125$) runs articles on trendy clubs, local festivals, and special events. Topless bathing is the fashion here, but bottomless is restricted to numerous nude beaches, sequestered in nooks between cliffs, but easy to find with a bit of effort.

The Algarve's sea-sonal cuisine includes *sardinhas assadas* (grilled sardines), often accompanied by *caldeirada,* a chowder of fish, shellfish, potatoes, and tomatoes perked up with onion and garlic. Native figs and almonds are combined in all manners to tempt those with a sweet tooth, so save space for a *sobremesa* (dessert). To wash it all down, try *amêndoa amarga* (almond liqueur) or *medronho* (firewater) made from the mini strawberries of arbutus trees. Wines such as the young *vinho verde* are inexpensive and make a wonderful complement to any meal.

Algarve Tourism: http://www.rtalgarve.pt

■ Lagos

For many, many moons, swarms of Europeans, Australians, and North Americans have sojourned here to worship the almighty Sun, god of Lagos. However, lately the *sol* is in danger of being dethroned by the porcelain god—to date, 20 bars and discos stay open until the wee hours. As the town's countless international expats will attest, Lagos (pop.15,000) is a black hole: come for two days and you'll stay a month. Although there isn't much more than beaches and bars, it is a very contented place. Whether you're soaking in the view from the cliffs, soaking in the sun on the beach, or soaking yourself in drinks at the bars, you'll be happy, too.

ORIENTATION AND PRACTICAL INFORMATION

Running the length of the river, **Avenida dos Descobrimentos** carries traffic in and out of Lagos. From the **train station,** go straight around the pink building, across the river, and hang a left. Out of the **bus station,** turn right. Follow it to **Rua das Portas de Portugal,** the gateway leading into **Praça Gil Eanes** and the town's glitzy tourist center. Most restaurants, accommodations, and services hover about the **Praça Gil Eanes** (also known as the "statue square") and the adjoining **Rua 25 de Abril** and the parallel **Rua Cándido dos Reis;** both are usually mobbed in the summer.

Tourist Office: Largo Marquês de Pombal (tel. 76 30 31). Take the side street R. Lina Leitão, which begins in the Pr. Gil Eanes. Take the 1st right—the door is on the side of the building. A 20min. walk from the train station, 15min. from the bus station. Brochures, maps, and transport info available, as well as a list of *quartos*. English spoken. Open daily 9:30am-12:30pm and 2-5:30pm.

Currency Exchange: Commission-free currency exchange is available at the youth hostel. **ATMs** and **automatic currency machines** can be found at the numerous banks on Pr. Gil Eanes and R. Portas de Portugal.

Trains: (tel. 76 29 87). On the east side across the river from the bus station. To: Lisbon (3 per day, 6½hr., 2000$); Vila Real de Santo António, via Faro (5 per day, 3hr., 1100$); Évora (2 per day, 6hr., 1740$); Beja (2 per day, 4hr., 1200$).

Buses: The **EVA** bus station (tel. 76 29 44), off Av. dos Descobrimentos, is on the east edge of town. To: Lisbon (8 per day, 5hr., 2000-2500$; also 4 express, 5hr., 2650$); Sagres (4 per day, 1hr., 445$); Faro (2 per day, 2½hr., 670$); Portimão (16 per day, 30min., 350$; 10 express 335-450$).

Taxis: tel. 76 24 69 or 76 30 48.

Car Rental: Hertz-Portuguesa, Rossio de S. João Ed. Panorama, 3 (tel. 76 00 08), behind the bus station. Must be 21 or over to rent. Cars start at 10,000$ (including tax and insurance) per day, less in winter. Cheaper though shadier deals can be found all over town.

Bike/Moped Rental: Motolagos, R. São José, 17 (tel. 76 03 65), on Pr. d'Armas, and a booth on R. 25 de Abril. Must be 16 or over to rent. Mountain bikes 500$ per hour, 1700$ per day. Motorbikes from 2000$ per day. Longer rentals for less. The youth hostel rents mountain bikes 1000$ per day.

Diving Lessons: Blue Ocean Diving Center, Quantro Estrados (tel. 78 27 18). Half day 5000$; full day 7000$

Laundromat: Lavandaria Miele, Av. dos Descobrimentos, 27 (tel. 63 969). 5kg wash and dry 1000$. Open Mon.-Fri. 9am-8pm, Sat. 9am-7:30pm.

English Bookstore: Loja do Livro, R. Dr. Joaquim Telo, 3 (tel. 76 73 47). Best-sellers, pulp romances, and travel guides. Open Mon.-Fri. 10am-1pm and 3-11pm.

Medical Services: Hospital, R. Castelo dos Governadores (tel. 76 30 34), next to Igreja Santa María. **Medilagos Ambulance:** Ameijeira de Cima, Bela Vista, Lote 2R/C (tel. 76 01 81 or 764 300). 24hr. service.

Police: General Alberto Silva (tel. 76 26 30). **Emergency:** tel. 115.

Fire Station: tel. 760 115 or 760 116.

Post Office: R. Portas de Portugal (tel. 76 30 67), between Pr. Gil Eanes and the river. Open Mon.-Fri. 9am-6pm. For Posta Restante, label all letters "Estação Portas de Portugal" or they may arrive at the **branch office. Postal Code:** 8600.

Telephone Code: (0)82.

ACCOMMODATIONS AND CAMPING

In the summertime, *pensões* (and the newly renovated youth hostel) fill up quickly and cost a bundle. Reserve rooms over a week in advance. Rooms in *casas particulares* sometimes include kitchen access and can be the greatest deals in town at around 1000$ per person from September through June and 2000$ in July and August. Try haggling with owners waiting at the train and bus stations and the tourist office, and (if possible) shop before you decide, because room quality varies greatly.

Pousada de Juventude de Lagos (HI), R. Lançarote de Freitas, 50 (tel./fax 76 19 70), from the train and bus stations, head into town on Av. República and turn right up R. Portos de Portugal. Head into Pr. Gil Eanes and turn right up R. Garrett into Pr. Luis de Camões, then take a left onto R. Cândido dos Reis. At the bottom of the hill, take a left onto R. Lançarote de Freitas; the hostel is on the right in front of the big green BP sign. Damn cool place with friendly staff and fun people who congregate in the central courtyard and TV room/bar. Fully equipped kitchen. Reception open 9am-2am; check out by noon; no curfew. Free storage of valuables; luggage storage 200$. Laundry 340$ per kg. Money exchange commission-free. Barracks-style rooms 1900$. Doubles with bath 4500$. Oct.-June 16: 1400$; 3550$. Breakfast included (take-out available). Summer reservations *strongly* recommended.

Residencial Rubi Mar, R. Barroca, 70 (tel. 76 31 65, ask for David; fax 76 77 49), down R. 25 de Abril, then left on Senhora da Graça. Run by 2 friendly expats from London. Centrally located, quiet and comfortable—a good deal if you can grab one of their 8 rooms. Breakfast included and served in the room. Doubles 5500$, with bath 6500$. Quads 7500-9000$. April-July 10 doubles 4500$, with bath 5500$; quads 6500-8500$. Oct.-March: 3500$; 4500$; 5500-7500$.

Residencial Caravela, R. 25 de Abril, 8 (tel. 76 33 61). Small but well-located rooms surrounding a courtyard. Singles 3500$. Doubles 5200$, with bath 5800$. Prices lower in winter. Breakfast included.

Residencial Gil Vicente, R. Gil Vicente, 26, 2nd fl. (tel. 76 29 82), on the block behind the youth hostel. Clean, very quiet location. Rooms somewhat stuffy but with beautiful high ceilings. Rarely full—knock on their door if the youth hostel rejects you. Singles 2500$. Doubles 3500$. Showers 80$.

Camping: Camping is *the* way most Europeans experience the Algarve; as a result, sites are crowded and expensive. Jam-packed **Parque de Campismo do Imulagos** (tel. 76 00 31) is frustratingly far away but linked to Lagos by a free shuttle bus serving the CEUTER and train and bus stations. Reception open 8am-10pm. 900$ per adult, under 10 230$, 400-640$ per tent, 370$ per car. On a beach 1.5km west of Praia da Luz and 6km outside Lagos, Orbitur's peaceful **Camping Valverde** (tel. 78 92 11) costs 700$ per person, 600-900$ per tent, 590$ per car. Free showers. **Camping Trindade,** just outside town (follow Av. dos Descobrimentos toward Sagres) charges 400$ per person with tent, 800$ without tent.

FOOD

Tourists are treated to multilingual menus in and around Praça Gil Eanes and R. 25 de Abril. Mexican, British, German, Chinese, and American food is everywhere, but a budget Portuguese meal is nearly impossible to find. Hit the **mercado,** Av. dos Descobrimentos, five minutes away from town center, or **Supermercado São Toque,** R. Portas de Portugal, across from the post office (open daily 9am-5pm; Oct.-June Mon.-Fri. 9am-8pm, Sat. 9am-2pm).

Casa Rosa, R. do Ferrador, 22. A Lagos standby, for better or for worse. Enjoy all-you-can-eat specials with backpacker hordes. Monday and Wednesday are spaghetti and garlic bread day (850$). Happy Hour 10-11pm. Famous 199 meal menu includes 52 vegetarian dishes. Open daily 9am-2pm and 7pm-3am.

Mullin's, R. Cândido dos Reis, 86 (tel. 76 12 81). A Lagos hot spot. Servers dance to the tables with huge portions of spicy food. The crowd quivers with a carnal pulse, or perhaps in reaction to burned mouths. Chicken *piri-piri* smothered in hot sauce 1200$. Entrees 1000-2200$. After dinner, the place transforms into a happening bar. Restaurant open noon-10pm; bar open until 2am.

Restaurante Escondidinho (tel. 76 03 86), hidden in a dead-end alley in front of the police station. From the *praça,* walk down Av. Descobrimentos to the bus station and turn left up R. Capelinha; it's on the left. An "authentic" Portuguese hangout, serving value-packed seafood specials such as all-you-can-eat sardines for lunch (600$). Fish entrees 850-1400$.

Hasan's Döner Kebab, R. Silva Lopes, 27 (tel. 76 46 82), a continuation of R. 25 de Abril. Perfect for that post-beach snack. Huge falafel sandwiches only 550$. Open daily noon-10pm.

SIGHTS AND ENTERTAINMENT

Although sunbathing and round-the-clock partying have long replaced naval warfare and fishing as the primary activities in this harbor, most of Lagos is still surrounded by a nearly-intact 16th-century city wall. Overlooking the marina is the **Fortaleza da Porta da Bandeira,** a 17th-century fortress holding maritime exhibitions (open Tues.-Sat. 10am-1pm and 2-6pm, Sun. 10am-1pm; free). Also on the waterfront is the old **Mercado de Escravos** (the slave market, on **Praça da República**)—legend has it that in 1441 the first sale of African slaves on Portuguese ground took place here.

PORTUGAL

Lagos's beaches are beautiful any way you look at them. Flat, smooth, sunbathing sands (crowded during the summer, pristine in the off season) can be found at the 4km-long **Meia Praia,** across the river from town. For beautiful cliffs that hide less-crowded beaches as well as caves (perfect to swim in and around), follow Av. Desco-brimentos west until you reach the sign for **Praia de Pinhão.** From the beach, con-tinue further on the paths and choose your own cove. The sculpted cliffs and grottoes of **Praia Dona Ana** appear on at least half of all Algarve postcards. For even more picturesque (and thinly populated) stretches, bike or hike your way west to **Praia do Camilo** and the grotto-speckled cliffs of **Ponta da Piedade.**

More good beaches soak up the sun at **Salema** and **Burgau,** small towns on the way to Sagres. Several convenient **buses** roll between Lagos and Sagres every day (1hr., 440$). There's no schedule at the bus stop in Sagres; go to the **Turinfo** office there to plan the return trip (the schedule is on the wall, and the bus stop is in front). In the opposite direction, **Portimão** makes a good hub for exploring the relatively uncrowded sands between Lagos and Albufeira. Take a bus from Lagos (30min., 350$). If you decide to stay overnight, check into the gigantic **Pousada de Juventude** (Lugar do Coca Maravilhas; tel./fax 49 18 04; 1800$ per person).

Now that you've tanned your hide, what are you waiting for? The streets of Lagos pick up as soon as the sun dips down, and by midnight the walls start to shake. The area between Pr. Gil Eanes and Pr. Luis de Camões bursts with cafes. The area around R. Marreiros Netto, north of Pr. Gil Eanes and the R. 25 de Abril, off the *praça,* form the center of nightlife—bars and clubs runneth over until well past 5am. Everyone has a personal favorite, and club-hopping is more a profession than a pastime. North of the *praça,* **Joe's Garage (Garagem de José),** opposite Mullin's restaurant at R. 1° de Maio, 78, will keep you on your toes from late-evening Happy Hour to early-morn-ing tabletop dancing. **Tribes and Vibes,** R. Marreiro Netto, 52, is a Tex-Mex theme bar, cafe, and dance club. A wooden Indian welcomes you into the 70s-chic dance floor (open nightly 4pm-4am). **Bad Moon Rising,** R. Marreiros Neto, 50, jams to grunge and indie rock from 8pm-4am, with a lively scam scene on the side. Stop by **Shots in the Dark,** R. 1° de Maio, 16, to hang out with a younger international back-packing crowd. Another hot watering hole is the **Calypso Bar,** R. 1° de Maio, 22. **Rosko's,** R. Candido dos Reis, 79, is a mellower Irish bar for all crowds.

Closer to the water, bars scatter along R. 25 de Abril and its extension, R. Silva Lopes. **Sins,** R. Silva Lopes, has a friendly frat party atmosphere, with beer funneling and the infamous nine deadly sins (nine shots, 4000$). Across the street, **Stones** plays Pearl Jam, U2, and Hendrix in a packed, two-story setting. Across the street, the crowd shuttles between **Eddie's** and **Bon Vivant.**

On the way up to the youth hostel along R. Lançarote de Freitas, the **Phoenix Club** (off a side street; look for the black sign on the left) plays house and dance music until 4am but occasionally charges a cover (1000$) for crowd-control. A hopping gay bar, **The Last Resort,** along R. Lançarote de Freitas, has live entertainment every Thurs-day night. Up the street half a block, the British pub **Taverna Velha (The Old Tav-ern)** hosts jolly happy hours (11pm-midnight) with televised soccer matches. When the game craving strikes, play the hustler at **Taco d'Ouro,** R. dos Ferreiros, 25; there are billiards, darts, pinball and a river of beer from 1pm-2am.

■ Near Lagos

SAGRES

Marooned atop a bleak, scrub-desert promontory on the barren southwest corner of Europe, Sagres's dramatic, desolate location discourages tour groups and upscale travelers—all the better for the town, which remains one of the most unspoiled des-tinations in the Algarve. The area caters mainly to young people who come to enjoy gorgeous beaches, rugged scenery, and an active social scene (except in January and February, when the town makes like a wallflower and wilts).

Empty beaches fringe the peninsula, several open for nude bathing. **Mareta** is at the bottom of the road from the center of town. Rock formations jut far out into the ocean on both sides of this sandy crescent. The less popular **Tonel** is along the road east of town. Turinfo (see below) arranges **jeep tours** to the tantalizing west coast, which has recently been declared "officially protected." West of town, **Praia de Martinhal** and **Praia de Baleeira** are good for wind surfing and standard tanning.

Prince Henry the Navigator's polygonal stone fortress dominates the town in regal fashion. From this cliff-top outpost, Prince Henry stroked his beard and formulated his plan to map the world. Vasco da Gama, Magellan, Columbus, Diaz, and Cabral apprenticed here in Henry's **school of navigation.** The 15th-century fortress and the surrounding area yield vertigo-inducing views of the cliffs and sea.

Six kilometers farther west, past the **Fortaleza do Beliche** (a fortress perched atop a cliff), lies the **Cabo de São Vicente,** once thought to be the end of the world. Overlooking the southwest tip of continental Europe, the second most powerful **lighthouse** in Europe beams 60 miles out to sea. (No fixed hours. Get permission to climb up from the gatekeeper, who disappears noon-2pm but is usually there 8am-9pm.) No buses connect the cape with Sagres—bike or take the hour-long cliffside walk.

Sagres is no Lagos, but it has its own brand of unsober nightlife. By day, the young set invades **Café Conchinha** (tel. 641 31), Pr. República (the main square), a restaurant with a cafe downstairs (entrees 800-1100$; open daily 8am-midnight, winter Tues.-Sun. 8am-10pm). At night the crowd moves across the street to the lively restaurant-bar **Rosa dos Ventos** (tel. 644 80; open daily 10am-2am). Get ready to draw at **The Last Chance Saloon,** which blasts English dance tunes and overlooks the beach. The small bar opens daily at 5pm, is hopping by 11pm, and closes at 4am.

Practical Information The privately run **Turinfo** (tel. 62 00 03; fax 62 00 04), on Pr. República in the main square is amazingly versatile—the energetic, English-speaking staff recommends accommodations and town events, **rents bikes** (2000$ per day, 1200$ per half-day), and hands out bus and train schedules. You can also take a **jeep tour** of the natural preserve (including lunch, 6500$), and soak up some **scuba** advice. They will even wash your clothes—seriously (open daily 10am-7pm). Down the street, the **Quiosque do Papa** kiosk station at the roundabout (tel. 647 57) **rents bikes** and **mopeds.** (Bicycles 1000$; mopeds 2500$ per day. Must be 16 to rent, with drivers' license and passport.) The kiosk also offers commission-free **currency exchange** daily 9am-10pm. **Banco Borges e Irmão,** R. Comandante Matoso (tel. 641 81), has an **ATM** and exchange, charging commission (open Mon.-Fri. 9:30am-4:30pm). Rodoviária **buses** (tel. 76 29 44) run from Lagos (4 per day, 1hr., 445$). For a **taxi** call tel. 645 01. **Police** answer at tel. 66 112; in an **emergency,** call 112. The **post office** is a left turn at R. Correio (open Mon.-Fri. 9am-12:30pm and 2:30-6pm). The **postal code** is 8650. The **telephone code** is (0)82.

Accommodations and Food Windows everywhere display multilingual signs for rooms, many in boarding houses with guest kitchens. Prices range from 2500-3500$ for singles and doubles to 3000-4000$ for triples. Experienced hagglers can wrestle them down to 2000$. If you aren't accosted at the bus stop, look for the signs or ask at the Turinfo. If you're looking for a private apartment, seek out **Atalaia Apartamentos,** Belceira (tel. 646 81). Follow the main road towards the traffic circle and take a left after the supermarket. These beautiful, fully furnished apartments and rooms above a grocery store are an exceptional value for those out for a little luxury (apartments for two 7500$; April-June: 6500$; Nov.-March: 5500$). Unofficial **camping** is tricky, as police hassle those who set up on the main beaches or in the fields. Sleep peacefully at the **guarded ground** (tel. 643 51; fax 644 45), near town, close to the beach, just off E.N. 268. (450$ per person, 625$ per tent, 350$ per car. June, Sept.-Oct.: 375$; 425$; 270$. Nov.-May: 250$; 300$; 200$. Showers $100.)

The **market** is off R. Comandante Matoso; turn left at R. do Correio off the main street (open Mon.-Sat. 10am-8pm). Several restaurants serve up tasty meals on Sagres's main drag. **Restaurante-Bar Atlántico** (tel. 76 42 36), serves heaping por-

tions of *amêijoas ao natural* (plain clams, 900$). **O Dromedário Bistro,** R. Comandante Matoso (tel. 642 19), whips up thick fruit shakes (280-500$), innovative pizzas (670-1140$), and crêpes (250-350$) in a fun bar atmosphere (open until 4am). The pizza proved such a hit that the English-speaking owner opened spiffy **Bossa Nova** (tel. 645 66) on the patio in back, with pizza, pasta, and more (800-1700; open daily noon-midnight; closed Thurs. in winter).

ALBUFEIRA

Those who come to Albufeira, the largest seaside resort in the Algarve, are hell-bent on relaxation. Sun, surf, and *cerveja* keep the English, German, and Scandinavian crowd satisfied; nary a Portuguese roams the cobblestone streets. English is the unofficial language, judging by the signs, menus, and the custom of breakfast. It may appear that there is little "authentic" Portuguese culture here, but you can stroll out of the center into the old town for a local immersion experience. For those too jaded to care, the nightlife is jumping and 12 beaches watch over glassy *azul* surf.

Practical Information The **tourist office,** R. 5 de Outubro, 8 (tel. 58 52 79), has maps, brochures, and a list of *quartos* (open Mon.-Fri. daily 9:30am-noon and 2-7pm, closes at 5:30pm on weekends). From the bus station, turn right and walk downhill into the main square, then to the street on the other side of the square to the right. Go straight one block and take a left. A booth run by **Portela** (tel. 57 11 55), hands out tourist info in front of the train station (open Mon.-Sat. 9am-7pm). Call a **taxi** (tel. 58 71 51) from the train station if you arrive at a late hour. The **Centro de Saúde** (tel. 58 75 50) is in the north end of town, and **police** (tel. 51 54 20) are in the *Caliços* zone, near the Mercado Municipal. In an **emergency,** dial 112. The **post office** (tel. 58 66 01) is next door to the tourist office at R. 5 de Outubro (open Mon.-Fri. 9am-6pm). The **postal code** is 8200. The **telephone code** is (0)89.

The **train station** (tel. 57 16 16), six kilometers inland, is accessible from town center by bus (every hr., 180$) from the EVA bus station. Albufeira is on the Lagos-Vila Real de Santo António line. Frequent departures to: Faro (45min., 300$); Lagos (1½hr., 480$); Olhão (360$); Tavira (550$); Vila Real de Santo António (690$); and Lisbon (3 per day, 3½hr., 1910$). The EVA **bus station** (tel. 58 97 55) is at the entrance to town, up Av. Liberdade; walk downhill to reach the center. Buses head to: Faro (every hr., 1hr., 570$); Portimão (7 per day, 1hr., 700$); Lagos (7 per day, 1½hr., 850$); Tavira (750$); and Vila Real de Santo António (750$).

Accommodations and Food Many places are booked solid from late June through mid-September, and truly cheap housing is scarce. Try looking far from the center or ask for *quartos* at the tourist office or any bar or restaurant, though chances are you will be accosted by room renters once you step off the train or bus. The modern **Pensão Albufeirense,** R. Liberdade, 18 (tel. 51 20 79), one block downhill from the bus station, has 24 comfortable rooms, a TV lounge, and a library of English books. (Singles 3500$. Doubles 5000$. Triples 6500$. Prices drop 500-1000$ in winter. Closed Oct.-April. Reservations with deposit.) **Pensão Silva,** R. 5 de Outubro (tel. 51 26 69), is a rather old building with wood floors, high ceilings, and chandeliers. Follow directions to the tourist office; once you exit the square you'll see the sign up a small side street. (June-Sept. Singles with shower 3000$. Doubles 5000$. Oct.-May: 2500$; 4000$.) Weary campers succumb to the ritz and glitz of the four-star rated **Parque de Campismo de Albufeira** (tel. 58 98 70; fax 58 76 33), a few km outside town on the road to Ferreiras. The *parque* is more like a shopping mall than a retreat, with four swimming pools, three restaurants, tennis courts, a supermarket, and a hefty price tag (850$ per person, per car, and per tent). Because of the new campground unofficial camping on nearby beaches is not tolerated.

Luckily there is no shortage of cheap and varied eats. Locals recommend **Tasca do Viegas,** R. Cais Herculano, 2 (tel. 51 40 87), near the fisherman's beach. Meat and fish dishes start at 750$ (open daily 11am-11pm). A few blocks uphill from the central square is **Restaurante Manjar,** R. do M.F.A., 17 (tel. 51 40 37). With an *ementa* at

1450$, you can *manjar* 'til your stomach's content (open daily noon-midnight). For something different, try a spicy Goan entry at **Minar Indian Tandoori Cuisine,** Trav. Cais Herculano (tel. 51 31 96), near the fisherman's beach (half a tandoori chicken 850$; most dishes 1100$-1500$; great veggie options).

Sights and Entertainment The last holdout of the Moors in southern Portugal, Albufeira preserves its graceful Moorish architectural heritage in the old quarters of town. Tiny minarets pierce the small Byzantine dome of **Santana,** an exquisite filigree doorway heralds the **São Sebastião,** an ancient Gothic portal fronts the **Misericórdia,** and a barrel-vaulted interior receives worshippers into the **Matiz.**

Albufeira's spectacular slate of beaches ranges from the popular **Galé** and **São Rafael** west of town, to the centrally located **Baleeira, Inatel,** and **Oura,** to the very chic **Falésia** 10km east of town. Many small and relatively uncrowded beaches lie scattered among the main *praias*—it pays to explore. In town, the fisherman's beach is lined with boats which venture out to sea every day.

After a day at the beach, you could…go to a bar. Bars and restaurants line all the streets, and clubs blast everything from salsa to techno to *fado* as soon as the sun sets, continuing until it rises. One prime spot is **Fastnet Bar,** R. Cândido dos Reis, 5 (tel. 58 91 16), packed with beer-gobbling Northern Europeans. Down the street is **Classic Bar,** R. Cândido dos Reis, 10 (tel. 51 20 73), which covers its floor with sand every night so the Grecian decor won't disorient you. The hottest clubs in town (jam-packed with a hot and sweaty student crowd), **Disco Silvia's** (tel. 58 85 74), and **Qué Pasa?** (tel. 51 33 06), face off on R. São Gonçalo de Lagos. For more **mellow nightlife,** head east along the coast into the old town. At **Café Latino,** on R. Latino Coelho, salsa tunes complement a stunning seaside view. There's nothing strange about nearby **Café Bizzaro,** R. Dr. Frutuoso Silva, 30, a cool, down-to-earth cafe-bar.

▌Faro

Although many northern Europeans begin their holidays in Faro, the Algarve's capital and largest city, few bother to stay long enough to fathom its charm and color. Faro is less packed than the rest of the Algarve. The city branches out from a slick marina fringed by lush gardens, and the adjacent **old town**—on the other side of the town wall—clusters around a quiet fisherman's harbor, which is in turn surrounded by a vast estuary melting into the sea.

ORIENTATION AND PRACTICAL INFORMATION

Faro's ritzy center hugs the **Doca de Recreio,** a marina lined with small vacation yachts and bordered by the **Jardim Manuel Bívar.** The main road into town, **Avenida da República,** runs past the train station and bus depot along the harbor, spilling into a delta of smaller streets at the **Praça Dr. Francisco Gomes,** which borders the dock and garden. **Rua Dr. Francisco Gomes** and **Rua de Santo António** are the major pedestrian thoroughfares off Pr. Gomes. The old town begins at the **Avio da Vila,** a stone arch on the far side of the garden, next door to the tourist office.

Tourist Office: R. Misericórdia, 8 (tel. 80 36 04), conveniently located at the entrance to the old town. From the bus or train station, turn right down Av. República along the harbor, and turn left past the garden. Helps find accommodations. English spoken. In summer open daily 9:30am-7pm; in winter Mon.-Fri. 9:30am-7pm and Sat.-Sun. 9:30am-5:30pm.

Currency Exchange: A small office, **Agência de Câmbios de Vilamoura-Faro,** is just off Pr. Gomes on Av. República. No commission. Open Mon.-Fri. 9am-6:30pm, Sat. 9am-2pm. **ATMs** are located all around the city.

American Express: There is no AmEx office in Faro. **Top Tours,** Infante de Sacres, 73 (tel. 30 27 26). The nearest is in the nearby village of Quarteira, accessible by EVA bus from the bus depot. Open Mon.-Fri. 9:30am-1pm and 2:30-6:30pm.

Flights: The international **airport,** 5km west of city, has a police post, bank, post office, car rental companies, and a tourism booth (tel. 81 85 82; open daily 10am-midnight). Buses #14 and 16 run from the street opposite the bus station to the airport (every 20min. 7:10am-7:56pm, 20min., 150$). From the airport to the bus station, there's a standard frequency and schedule. **TAP Air Portugal** (tel. 80 02 00), R. Dr. Francisco Gomes. Open Mon.-Fri. 9am-5:30pm.

Trains: Largo da Estação (tel. 80 17 26). To: Lisbon (6 per day, 5hr., 2060$); Albufeira (6 per day, 1hr., 300$); Vila Real de Santo António (13 per day, 1½hr., 460$); Lagos (8 per day, 2½hr., 680$); Beja (2 per day, 3hr., 1700$). Despite the frequency of trains, be sure to consult the schedule as departure times are often bunched together.

Buses: EVA, Av. República (tel. 89 97 00). To: Beja (2 per day, 3hr., 1300$); Albufeira (14 per day, 1hr., 530$); Olhão (15 per day, 20min., 175$); Vila Real de Santo António (9 per day, 1hr., 590$); Lagos (2 per day, 2½hr., 950$); Tavira (3 per day, 1hr., 300$); Vila Real S. Antonio (3 per day, 1hr., 600$); Albufeira (4 per day, 1hr., 570$). Express long-distance bus service is provided by **Caima** (tel. 81 29 80), across the street. To: Lisbon (every hr., 4½hr., 2300$); Porto (every hr., 8½hr., 3000$); Braga (every hr., 10hr., 3050$). International routes are run by **Intersul** (tel. 89 97 70), to Sevilla (2600$), with connecting buses to France and Germany.

Taxis: Rotaxi (tel. 82 22 89). From bus station to airport 1200$ weekdays, 1450$ nights and weekends. Taxis congregate near Jardim Manuel Bívar (by the tourist office) and at the bus and train stations.

Laundromat: Sólimpa, R. Batista Lopes, 30 (tel. 82 29 81), up R. Primeiro de Maio, to the *praça*. 350$ per kilo. Open Mon.-Fri. 9am-1pm and 3-7pm, Sat. 9am-1pm.

English Bookstore: Livraria Bertrand, R. Dr. Francisco Gomes, 27 (tel. 281 47), in the pedestrian area. Decent selection of pocket books, classics, and textbooks. Open in summer Mon.-Sat. 9am-10pm, Sun. 5-9pm.

Hospital: R. Leão Pinedo (tel. 80 34 11), north of town.

Police: R. Polícia da Segurança Pública (tel. 82 20 22). **Emergency:** tel. 115.

Post Office: Largo do Carmo (tel. 80 30 08), across from the Igreja de Nossa Senhora do Carmo. Open for Posta Restante and **telephones** Mon.-Fri. 9am-12:30pm and 2-6pm, Sat. 9am-12:30pm. **Postal Code:** 8000.

Telephone Code: (0)89.

ACCOMMODATIONS

Rooms vanish in high season—resort to the tourist office's top 20 list of *pensões.* Lodgings bite the heels of the bus and train stations. The low-end budget *pensões* are pretty sorry; for something cheap and cheerful, try to scrape up a *quarto.*

Pensão Residencial Oceano, R. Ivens, 21, 2nd fl. (tel. 82 33 49). From the marina-side Pr. Gomes, head up R. 1 de Maio and you'll see the sign up 1 block on the right. If you don't mind the funerary supply store next door, the doubles—somewhat austere, but tidy and comfortable—make a great bargain. Attractive *azulejos* in the halls and baths. All rooms have bath and telephone. Singles 5000$. Doubles 6000$. Triples 8500$. 500-1000$ discount in winter.

Residencial Madalena, R. Conselheiro Bívar, 109 (tel. 80 58 06; fax 80 58 07), just off Pr. Gomes. Centrally located with pleasant, neat rooms, all with full bath, telephone, fan, and heater. Friendly, English-speaking reception. TV room and small bar. Singles 5500$. Doubles 5000$, with bath 7000$. Winter: singles 3000$, doubles 4500$. Reservations and traveler's checks accepted.

Casa de Hóspedes Adelaide, R. Cruz das Mestras, 7-9 (tel. 80 23 83; fax 82 68 70). Ten rough but basically clean rooms, good for big groups. Singles 2500$. Doubles 3000$. Quads 4000$. Private bath 500$ more. 500$ discount in winter.

Residência Pinto, R. 1 de Maio, 27, 2nd fl. (tel. 82 28 20), off Pr. Gomes. Cramped rooms with cracking ceilings and old furniture. Some rooms are brightness-impaired. Singles 3000$. Doubles 4000$.

Pausada de Juventude, R. da Polícia de Seguranga Pública (tel. 80 19 70), is rather inconveniently located and lacks significant amenities, but at 1200$ per night is a decent budget option.

FOOD

Almonds and figs are native to the Algarve. Bakeries whip them up into delicious marzipan and fig desserts. Faro has some of the Algarve's chattiest cafes, many along **R. Conselheiro Bívar,** off Pr. Gomes. At the **market,** Pr. Dr. Francisco Sá Carneiro, locals barter fresh seafood (open Mon.-Fri. 9am-1pm). Live the high life on **R. Santo António,** a pedestrian district where costly *marisqueiras* (seafood restaurants) and credit cards reign, or live the budget life at **Supermercado Minipreço,** Largo Terreiro do Bispo, 8-10 (tel. 80 32 92; open Mon.-Sat. 9am-10pm, Sun. 9am-1pm).

Restaurante Dois Irmãos, Largo Terreiro do Bispo, 13 (tel. 80 39 12). Go up R. 1 de Maio into the small square (it's on your right). Half portions of *lombos de porco* (pork chops) and *arroz de lingueirão* (real sole-food with rice), around 700$ each. Groove to Portuguese hits. Open daily 11am-4pm and 6-11pm.

Restaurante Fim do Mundo, R. Vasco da Gama, 53 (tel. 262 99), down the street from Dois Irmãos. It's the end of the world, and you'll feel fine with chicken and fries (*meia dose* 650$) or a fish omelette (850$). Take-out, too. Open Mon. noon-3pm, Wed.-Sun. noon-3pm and 5-10pm.

Pastelaria Chantilly, R. Vasco da Gama, 63A (tel. 207 80), next to Fim do Mundo. You can indulge in delicious marzipan sweets (130$ each) and homemade pastries (such as the layered *gloría,* a puff pastry filled with egg cream 90$). Open Mon.-Sat. 8am-midnight.

SIGHTS AND ENTERTAINMENT

Faro's old city is a jewel—untouristed and deeply traditional, with superior churches and museums, as well as shops selling authentic handicrafts. Next to the tourist office, the 18th-century **Arco da Vila** pierces the old city wall. A narrow road leads through an Arab portico to the Renaissance **sé** (cathedral; open Mon.-Fri. 10am-noon), which sits forlornly in a deserted square. Its understated Renaissance interior is interrupted by the **Capela do Rosário,** decorated with 17th-century *azulejos,* a red Chinoiserie organ, and sculptures of two Nubians bearing lamps.

One day not long ago, archaeologists unearthed traces of Neolithic civilization under the cathedral, a site also sacred to Romans, Visigoths, and Moors. Behind the church, **Museu Arqueológico e Lapidar** (tel. 82 20 42) flashes assorted royal memorabilia, from diamond-studded hairpins to silver spurs and swords. The striking **cloister** is an ideal spot to relax with a book from the municipal library, housed in the same building (museum open Mon.-Fri. 9am-noon and 2-5pm; 110$). Across from the old city and facing the huge and dusty Largo de São Francisco (the town fairgrounds) stands the mighty **Igreja de São Francisco,** with its hulking facade and delicate interior (open Mon.-Fri. 10am-noon and 3-5pm). The city's **Museu de Etnografia Regional,** Pr. da Liberdade, 2 (tel. 80 60 02), introduces the folk life of the Algarve, with heartbreaking photos of the once tranquil, pristine fishing villages of Lagos, Albufeira, and Faro (open Mon.-Fri. 9:30am-6pm; 300$). Deep in the city center, step into **Igreja de Nossa Senhora do Carmo** to inspect the **Capela dos Ossos,** a wall-to-wall macabre bonanza of crusty bones and fleshless monk skulls borrowed from the adjacent cemetery (open daily 10am-1pm and 3-5pm; church free, chapel 120$).

Near the marina and next to the hulking Hotel Eva, the **Museu da Marinha** (tel. 80 36 01) flaunts three notable boat models: one bore Vasco da Gama to India in 1497; another took imperialists up the Congo River in 1492; and the vessel that outclassed the entire Turkish navy in 1717, highlighting a distant era when the Algarve was on the cutting edge of technology (open Mon.-Fri. 9am-noon and 2-5pm; 120$).

Sidewalk **cafes** crowd the pedestrian walkways off the garden in the center of town. Several **bars** populated by young crowds liven the R. Conselheiro Bívar and its side streets. Faro's rock-free **beach** hides on an islet off the coast. Take bus #16 from the stop in front of the tourist office (every hr., daily 8am-10pm, 150$).

PORTUGAL

■ Olhão and islands

Olhão, eight kilometers or two train stops east of Faro, prefers fish to tourists. Yet beyond this no-frills town, gorgeous beaches spread over the neighboring island, all easily accessible by ferry from Olhão's town dock. **Ilha da Armona,** the easternmost island, hosts a lively summer community that crowds around the ferry dock but leaves miles of oceanfront virtually deserted. Orbitur **bungalows** and rooms in private homes may be rented without hassle. Ferries run regularly year-round (10 per day in summer, 3 per day off season, 15min., 280$ round-trip). Another ferry heads to **Ilha da Culatra,** which boasts two beach communities accessible by the same ferry. **Culatra,** an island fishing community and the larger of the two, is known for its hospitality and fine bars. **Farol,** the second stop, has the most beautiful and least crowded beaches. Unfortunately, camping is discouraged on the islands. (Ferries every 2hr. in summer; 3 per day rest of the year, 30min. to Culatra, 45min. to Farol, 300$ round-trip. In summer, Farol can also be reached by ferry from Faro.)

Practical Information The **tourist office** (tel. 71 39 36) is on Largo Sebastião Martins Mestre, an offshoot of R. Comércio. From the train station, head straight down R. 1 de Maio and left on R. General Humberto Delgado (the bus station's street). Go right at the intersection with Av. da República, and straight into R. do Comércio. The office is around the bend on the left. Its English-speaking staff has maps, ferry schedules, and free **luggage storage** during the day (open Mon.-Fri. 9am-12:30pm and 2-5:30pm, Sat. 9:30am-noon). To get to the **port,** take any of the small side streets off R. do Comércio and weave your way to Av. 5 de Octubro, parallel to the shore. In an **emergency,** dial 112. The **post office,** Av. República, 17 (tel. 71 20 13), does not sell liquor (open daily Mon.-Fri. 8:30am-6pm). The **postal code** is 8700. The **telephone code** is (0)89.

The **bus station** is on R. General Humberto Delgado, one block west of Av. República. (Open Mon.-Fri. 7am-8pm, weekends 7am-7pm. To Faro every 30min., 20min., 175$ in advance, 240$ on bus; Tavira every hr., 1hr., 310$.) The **train station** is one block north of the bus station on Av. Combatentes da Grande Guerra. To Faro (5 per day, 30 min., 180$) and Tavira (4 per day, 1hr., 330$).

Accommodations and Food Cheerful tiled rooms with baths surrounding a plant-filled courtyard can be found off a dusty sidestreet at **Pensão Bela Vista,** R. Teófilo Braga, 65-67 (tel. 70 25 38). Exiting the tourist office, make a left, then the first left; R. Teófilo Braga is the first right. (Singles 2500$, with bath 3500$. Doubles: 3500$; 5000$. 500$ discount in winter.) Four blocks uphill from the tourist office, left on R. 18 de Junho and a left 4 blocks farther, **Residencial Boémia,** R. da Cerca, 20 (tel. 71 45 13), sits pretty with bright, clean rooms, all with bath and A/C. (Singles 4500$. Doubles 5500$. In winter: 3500$; 4500$. Visa, MC, AmEx.) Olhão's highly recommended year-round campground is the **Parque de Campismo dos Bancários do Sul e Ilhas** (tel. 70 54 02; fax 70 54 05). It's off the highway outside of town and can be accessed via nine buses per day (620$ per person, 50$ per tent and per car; showers included). **Supermercado São Nicolau,** R. General Humberto Delgado, 62,

---

A Slug in the Face

Escargot? Well, not exactly...One of Portugal's favorite snack foods is the lowly *caracol* (snail). Unlike their escargot counterparts, *caracóis* are eaten in massive portions, boiled in shells with just a bit of salt and perhaps a sprig of fresh oregano. No forks here—pile a heap of the little creepies on your plate and skewer them with a toothpick. True connoisseurs use a needle-like spine carved out of palm leaves. If the dainty method doesn't suit you, crack the shell between your teeth. If you see folks prodding along the roadside in search of a snack, why not join them? Or save your energy (the little fellas are surprisingly quick) and enjoy your *caracóis* at restaurants or cafes all over the country.

up the block from the bus station (open Mon.-Sat. 9am-9pm) will give you what you can't find at the fish and fruit filled **mercado,** adjacent to the city gardens along the river in two red brick buildings (open Mon.-Sat. 7am-2pm). Locals flock to the many eateries that line the port on Av. 5 de Octubro, which specialize, not surprisingly, in grilled fish. At **Casa de Pasto O Bote,** Av. 5 de Octubro, 122 (tel. 72 11 83), pick out your silvery meal from the trays of fresh fish, and watch it being charcoal-grilled right next to you. (Entrees from 750-1350$. Open Mon.-Sat. 10am-3pm and 7-11pm.)

■ Tavira

Farmers on motor scooters reputedly tease police by riding over the Roman pedestrian bridge: that's about as raucous as Tavira gets. And if you're looking to relax for a while in one of Algarve's loveliest communities, that's just fine. White houses and palm trees fringe the river banks, and festive Baroque churches bring glory to the hills above. The easy-going fishing port doesn't sweat it over the recent influx of backpackers. In mid-afternoon, fisherfolk sit in small riverfront warehouses repairing nets alongside their beached craft. Side streets trace the skeleton of the Moorish fortress from which the town arose. Most of Tavira's sights are planted along the side streets leading off of **Pr. República.** Steps off the *praça* lead past the tourist office to the **Igreja da Misericórdia,** whose superb Renaissance doorway glowers with heads sprouting from twisting vines and candelabra. Just beyond, the remains of the city's **Castelo Mouro** (Moorish Castle) enclose a handsome garden brimming with fuchsias, chrysanthemums, *bougainville,* and the church **Santa Maria do Castelo.** (Museum open Mon.-Fri. 8am-5:30pm, Sat.-Sun. 10am-7:30pm. Church open daily 9am-8pm.) The seven-arched pedestrian-only **Ponte Romana** footbridge leads to fragrant and floral **Praça 5 de Outubro.** Up the stairs at the opposite end of the square is the imposing **Igreja do Carmo.** Its elaborately decorated chancel resembles a 19th-century opera set, as false perspectives give the illusion of windows and niches supported by columns.

Local **beaches,** including **Pedras do Rei,** are accessible year-round. To reach Tavira's excellent beach on **Ilha da Tavira,** an island 2km away, take the Tavira-Quatro Águas bus from Pr. República to the ferry. (13 per day, 10min., round-trip 100$; keep ticket stub for the return.)

Practical Information The **tourist office,** R. Galeria, 9 (tel. 32 25 11), is off Pr. República, up the steps on the near left corner coming into town from the train station. It's on your right if you are coming into town from the bus station. The English-speaking staff doles out maps and recommends accommodations (open in summer daily 9:30am-7pm; in off season Mon.-Fri. 9:30am-7pm, Sat.-Sun. 9:30am-12:30pm and 2-5:30pm). **Bikes and scooters** can be rented from Loris Rent, R. Damião Augusto de Vasconcelos, 4 (tel. 32 52 03), across the way from the tourist office. For a **taxi,** call tel. 81 544. A **health center** answers at tel. 320 10 00. Contact the **police** at tel. 22 022. In an **emergency,** dial 112. The **post office,** R. da Liberdade, 64, one block uphill from Pr. República, has basic services and Posta Restante (open Mon.-Fri. 8:30am-6pm). The **postal code** is 8800. The **telephone code** is (0)81.

EVA **buses** (tel. 32 25 46) leave from the *praça* for Faro (10 per day, 1hr., 405$, express 500$) and Vila Real de Santo António (40min., 375$). It's one of the nicest, cleanest bus stations in Portugal (no English). **Intersul** runs twice weekly to Sevilla. **Trains** (tel. 32 23 54), leave every hour for Vila Real de Santo António (30min., 270$) and Faro (1hr., 300$).

Accommodations and Food No worries—there are *pensões* and *quartos* for all. To find the riverfront **Pensão Residencial Lagôas Bica,** R. Almirante Cândido dos Reis, 24 (tel. 222 52), from Pr. República, cross the pedestrian bridge and continue straight down R. A. Cabreira; turn right and go down one block. You'll find well-furnished rooms plus an outdoor patio and rooftop picnic area, a sitting room, washing facilities, and a fridge for guest use. The kind owner speaks English. (Singles in sum-

PORTUGAL

mer 2500$. Doubles 3500-4000$, with bath 5000$. 500$ cheaper in winter). Back on the other side of the river, expansionist **Pensão Residencial Castelo** is busy taking over the block and beyond with an ultra-modern, brand-new annex featuring bright, spacious rooms (singles 4000$; doubles 4500$, with bath 6000$) and savagely beautiful apartments (around 12,000$, max 6 people). **Ilha de Tavira campground** (tel. 323 505), with its entourage of snack bars and restaurants, sprawls on the beach of the island 2km from the *praça*. (340$ per person, 510$ per tent. Showers 100$. 24hr. reception. Open Feb.-Sept.)

Churrasqueira "O Manel," R. Almirante dos Reis, 6 (tel. 233 43), across the river from Pr. República, has a reasonably priced sit-down restaurant as well as a take-out counter, and serves up *febres na brasa* (pork chops) and *entrecostos* (baby back ribs 700$). Take your food to the park and chow down (open Wed.-Mon. 4pm-midnight). Seek and ye shall find other nice cafes and restaurants on Pr. República and opposite the garden on R. José Pires Padinha. Also facing the square across the river is **Restaurante Ponto de Encontro,** Pr. Dr. A. Padiuha, 39 (tel. 23 730), where you can binge outdoors on house specialties like *peixe con molho de amêndoa* (fish with almond sauce 1400$). For a more elegant night on the town, **Restaurante Pátio,** R. Antonio Cabreira, 30 (tel. 323 008), prepares pricey regional dishes like *cataplana* (seafood stewed in a pot) as well as fish and meat praised by diners the world over. Try *Caldeirada* (fisherman's stew) for 1000$. Credit cards and traveler's checks are accepted.

■ Vila Real de Santo António

Located at the east end of the Algarve and the mouth of the Rio Guadiana, the Vila Real is a transfer point. Before the construction of the highway bridge between Portugal and Spain in 1992, the town got a lot more tourist traffic, as marooned Spainbound travelers frequently spent the night. Most tourists now bypass the quiet city.

The **Pousada de Juventude (HI),** R. D. Sousa Martins, 40 (tel./fax 445 65), is a white building on the fifth street into the grid from the river (2 blocks to the left of R. Teófilo Braga, the main pedestrian street). Living room, bar, and washing facilities complement decent quarters. (Reception open daily 9:30am-midnight; lockout noon-6pm, but dropoff all day. 1450$ per person, low-season 1200$. Spartan doubles with bath 3200$, in winter 2700$. Breakfast included.) **Restaurante Snack-Bar El Conde** (tel. 419 70), in the main square on the corner of R. Teófilo Braga, cooks up excellent seafood in local combinations from 700$ (open daily noon-midnight).

Trains service Lagos (4 per day, 4½hr., 900$) and Faro (11 per day, 2½hr., 500$). For trains to Spain, cross the river by the cute **ferry** to Ayamonte (in summer, ferries run daily 8am-7pm; 150$ per person, 430$ per car). From Ayamonte, you can take a **bus** in the main square direct to Sevilla, or to Huelva (every hr., 540ptas) with connections to Sevilla (summer 8 per day, 1200ptas). *Pesetas* are changed in banks along the port in Ayamonte, and most establishments in Ayamonte accept *escudos* as well. Buses from Vila Real to the rest of the Algarve are more expensive, more reliable, and faster than trains. They zip to: Faro (5 per day, 1hr., 750$), via Tavira (2hr., 450$); Lagos (8 per day, 4hr., 1100$); and Lisbon (4 per day, 7½hr., 2200$). The last bus leaves at 6:30pm for Faro. Buses leave from the esplanade. Buses to Sevilla (1 per day, 3hr.) help you avoid the hassle of train-ferry-bus-train transfers.

MOROCCO (MAROC)

المغرب

US$1 = 9.97 dirhams (dh)	1dh = US $0.10
CDN$1 = 7.15dh	1dh = CDN $0.14
UK£1 = 15.87dh	1dh = UK £0.06
IR£1 = 14.40dh	1dh = IR£0.07
AUS$1 = 7.44dh	1dh = AUS $0.13
NZ$1 = 6.38dh	1dh = NZ $0.16
SAR1 = 2.66dh	1dh = SA R0.38
SP 1ptas = 0.06dh	1dh = SP 15.70ptas
POR 1$ = 0.05dh	1dh = POR 18.82$

ESSENTIALS

Just two hours from Spain across the Straits of Gibraltar, Morocco possesses an over-whelming geographical and cultural diversity in an extremely compact area. From the beaches and fortified towns of the Atlantic coast to the red mud of *kasbahs* of the Sahara, the depth and breadth of Morocco's beauty are unrivaled. A thorough net-work of inexpensive transportation, cheap, funky hotels, outgoing people, and plenty of opportunities for hiking, camping, and pack trips, makes it little surprise that Morocco has drawn visitors for centuries. Although popularity has had its by-products (mostly in the form of hustlers), problems are on the decline as Morocco increasingly tries to make its cultural riches more accessible to its visitors.

■ Getting Around

TRAINS

Trains are the swiftest and comfiest way to travel; service is fairly reliable and prompt. Second-class fares are a bit more expensive than corresponding CTM bus fares. Non-smoking compartments, couchettes (35dh), and (hopefully) air-conditioning are available. Tickets bought on board cost 10% more than at the ticket counter. The "Marrakech Express," one line of the national rail company, **Office National de Chemin de Fer (ONCF),** goes from Tangier to Rabat and on to Casablanca and Mar-rakech (the other goes between Rabat and Fès). No trains currently run to Algeria, although buses do. This may change. **InterRail** *is* valid in Morocco (p. 38), though the train fares are so low it's hardly worth it.

HOP ON THE BUS

In Morocco, wherever you want to go, whenever you want to go, there is a bus wait-ing to take you. They're not all that fast, they're not all that comfy, but they're extremely cheap and reach the most remote parts of the country. In the bus stations, each bus company has its own info window, as in Spain, so you must window-hop for destinations and schedules. **Compagnie de Transports du Maroc (CTM),** Morocco's national bus company, has the fastest, most luxurious, and generally most expensive buses. Usually, reservations are unnecessary, but always inquire ahead, especially on busy routes. The second largest company is **SATAS,** focused primarily in southwest Morocco. While equal to CTM in speed and reliability, the buses are slightly less comfortable. Countless other private companies, called **cars publiques,** have far more departures, are generally slower, less comfortable, and cheaper.

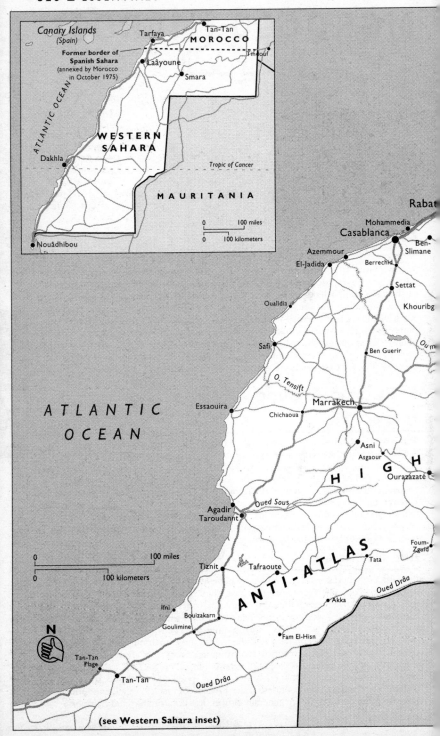

Canary Islands
(Spain)

Tarfaya
Tan-Tan
MOROCCO

**Former border of
Spanish Sahara**
(annexed by Morocco
in October 1975)

Laâyoune
Smara
Tindouf

ATLANTIC OCEAN

**WESTERN
SAHARA**

Dakhla

Tropic of Cancer

MAURITANIA

0   100 miles

0   100 kilometers

Nouâdhibou

Rabat

Mohammedia
Casablanca
Ben-
Slimane

Azemmour
Berrechid

El-Jadida
Settat

Khouribg

Oualidia

Ou

Safi
Ben Guerir

O. Tensift

Essaouira
Marrakech

ATLANTIC
OCEAN

Chichaoua

Asni

Asgaour
H

Ourazazate

I

G

Agadir
Oued Sous

Taroudannt

H

0   100 miles

Foum-
Zguid

0   100 kilometers

Tiznit
Tafraoute
Tata

Ifni
A N T I - A T L A S

Bouizakarn
Akka
Oued Drâa

N

Goulimine

Fam El-Hisn

Tan-Tan
Plage

Tan-Tan
Oued Drâa

(see Western Sahara inset)

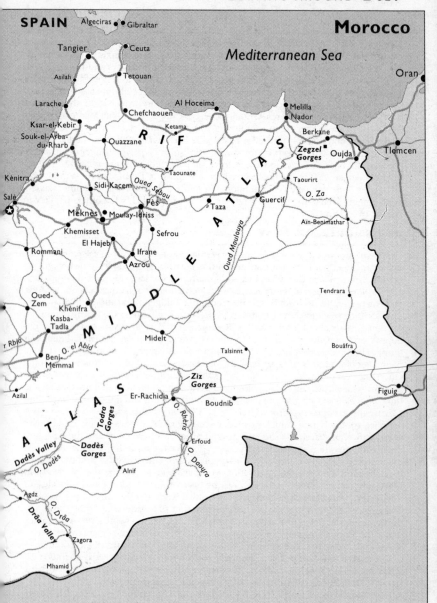

TAXIS

Morocco rushes travelers around cities in two kinds of cabs: *petit taxis* and *grand taxis*. Compared to Europe, both are very inexpensive. **Petits taxis** travel within cities. They are small, tan Renaults seating at most four passengers and posting "Petit Taxi" on their roof racks. Drivers must turn on the meter; if they try to fix a price instead, they may overcharge. Ask the hotel staff or police about standard fares to ensure you don't get cheated. Fares are usually 5-7dh, rarely over 10dh; there's often a 50% surcharge on night fares. **Grands taxis,** typically beige or blue Mercedes sedans holding five passengers comfortably, travel between cities for trips up to several hours. They don't usually cruise for passengers like *petits,* but rather congregate at a central area in town. Drivers charge by the trip, so price per passenger decreases as the seats fill up. Often you must wait for a full load (unless you're willing to pay for invisible passengers). A full taxi is usually as cheap as a CTM bus. In rural areas, market **trucks** *(camions)* are very common; just jump in the back with the other passengers bringing food to the market. They are very cheap. Watch what others pay so you are not overcharged.

IN THE DRIVER'S SEAT

Groups of four or more should consider **renting** a car, especially in the Sahara. Renting a car (most with manual transmission) is fairly easy, considering how hard the driving can be. **Afric Car, Moroloc,** and **Locoto** are the large Moroccan companies; also explore the cut-rate rental agencies or international companies. **Europcar, Avis,** and **Hertz** all rent a Renault IV, the most common budget car, at about 250dh per day plus 2.50dh per km. Local companies are much cheaper. Collision insurance (optional) costs about 78dh per day. Reserve a few days in advance, ask about discounts, and bargain. It's cheaper to reserve rental cars from the United States or Europe, but many companies are reluctant to insure driving in Morocco. Most companies require renters to be at least 21, but rental policies are seldom set in stone. Often one year of driving experience will suffice. North Americans should try **Europe By Car,** which sells cars for a prearranged period and then buys them back after the time expires. Rates are low and insurance terms good, but you must pay at home and pick up the car outside Morocco (tel. (2) 31 37 37 in Casablanca).

    Police routinely pull vehicles over for security checks, questioning about travel plans, and even searches, especially around major northern cities and the hash-producing Rif. All officers speak French. Try to dissolve the tension by asking directions immediately after you're stopped. *Always drive with your passport and car papers.* If you're stopped for a traffic violation, you may have to pay the fine on the spot; make sure you get a receipt. By law, **seatbelts** are required outside major locales. In the **desert**, bring along at least 10 liters of bottled water per person and per radiator, and a spare tire. Move rapidly over sand; if you start to bog down, put the car in low gear and put the pedal to the metal. If you come to a stop in soft sand, push rather than sink. Moroccan roads can be particularly dangerous; reckless maneuvers, excessive speed, bad road conditions, and poorly equipped vehicles are all too common.

    Gas costs about 8dh per liter. **Routes goudronées** (principal roads), marked "P," are paved and connect most cities. **Pistes** (secondary roads), designated "S," are less smooth. Flash floods and tortuous, risky mountain roads merit preparation.

    The **Michelin map,** widely available in Morocco, is by far the best. Also, ask if your intended routes are passable: roads on maps have a way of turning into riverbeds and mule tracks, while others marked impassable on old maps have been recently cleared and paved. The tiny Moroccan AAA clone, with touring info and assistance, is the **Touring Club du Moroc,** 3 Ave. de F.A.R., Casablanca (tel. (2) 20 30 64).

HUSTLERS AND GUIDES

Moroccans are generally extremely hospitable and friendly towards travelers; however, it is often hard to distinguish between this genuine hospitality and the invita-

Morocco
(by Rail)

ATLANTIC OCEAN

Cádiz
Algeciras
Tarifa
Tangier
Asilah
Larache
Kenitra
Rabat
Casablanca
Azemmour
El-Jadida
Safi
Essaouira
Cap Sim
Cap Rhir
Agadir
Tiznit
Tafroute
Goulimime
WESTERN SAHARA

SPAIN
Gibraltar
Ceuta
Mediterranean Sea
Tetuan
Al-Hoceima   Melilla
Chechaouen   Nador   Saïdia
Ouezzane   Oujda
Moulay
Idriss   Fes
          Sefrou   Taza
Meknès
      Ifrane
      Azrou
Khenifra
Kasba-Tadia
Beni-Mellal   Bouarfa
Marrakech   Er-Rachidia   Figuig
Asni   Dadès R.
          Tenirhir   Erfoud
Ouarzazate   Tafilat
Drâa R.
Zagora
Taroudannt
ANTI-ATLAS
ALGERIA

N

tions from hustlers. In some towns it can feel like there is someone lurking at every corner. *Faux guides* are illegal and should also be told *"Non, merci;"* they are usually ill-informed and will try to drag you to a carpet store anyway. If you want a guide, go to the tourist office and hire an official guide there for 120dh half day, 150dh full day. They generally know their stuff and will keep hustlers off you. Pests should be told no firmly; giving them money just encourages other hustlers. In any case, the key is keeping your cool and dealing with hustlers with a sense of humor. Although subtle threats are sometimes part of a hustler's rhetoric, there is really very little physical danger involved (although there have been muggings reported during drug deals in Tangier). In some cities police will help get hustlers off your back; often just walking towards one will chase them away.

■ Accommodations

Quality of accommodations in Morocco varies wildly both between and within hotels; always ask to see the room and if you don't like it, ask for another, or head to the next hotel (usually next door). Prices are uniformly cheap, incredibly so compared to Europe; expect to pay around 40-60dh per person. The listings are generally divided between the medina and the ville nouvelle. The medina hotels are generally cheaper and less pristine.

YOUTH HOSTELS

The **Fédération Royale Marocaine des Auberges de Jeunesse** (FRMAJ) is the Moroccan Hosteling International (HI) affiliate. Beds cost 20-40dh per night, a bit more for

nonmembers. Its 11 hostels vary widely in quality and are often far from the town center. While reception hours are limited (so call ahead), curfews and lockouts are rare. To reserve beds in high season, get an **International Booking Voucher** from FRMAJ (or your nearby HI affiliate) and send it to the hostel four to eight weeks in advance. Some hostels sell HI membership cards on the spot; otherwise, buy one at FRMAJ's main offices (or at home). A sleepsack is sometimes mandatory. For info such as hostel addresses, contact FRMAJ, Parc de la Ligue Arabe, BP No 15998, Casa-Principale, Casablanca 21000 (tel. (2) 47 09 52; fax 47 20 24; or at the Casablanca hostel, 6 pl. Amiral Philibert, Ville Ancienne (tel. (2) 22 05 51). For more advice, see **Essentials: Hostelling Prep,** p. 10.

HOTELS

Generally, the medina contains the cheapest hotels. Do some comparison shopping and bargain; hotels rarely fill to capacity. Some proprietors will let you sleep on the roof for a fraction of the room price (especially attractive when it's hot). Owners sometimes charge per room rather than per person, making it economical to find roommates. Acceptable rates for a budget room are 40dh for a single, 70dh for a double. Rooms may sometimes be rented by the week at 50% the per-night price. Hotels fall into two categories: *classé* and *non-classé*. Classé hotels are government-regulated, rated from one to five stars. Within each class there's an additional A-B rating. These are not necessarily better than *non-classé* pads; some of the worst hotels are decaying three- and four-star hotels with government-fixed prices too high to attract guests for it to afford upkeep. One- and two-star hotels can be prime budget bets. The price-listing of all *classé* hotels, *Royaume du Maroc: Guide des Hotels,* is free at tourist offices. Non-*classé* hotels are not regulated, rated, or price-fixed by the government, and thus have no uniform standards. They are much cheaper than *classé*. Showers, when available, may cost a few *dirhams* extra; in cheaper places hot water (if available at all) may be limited to certain hours.

CAMPING

Camping is popular and cheap (around 10dh per person) in Morocco; especially in the desert, mountains, and on the beach. Like hotels, campgrounds vary wildly, from little more than sunny dirt lots to plush budget resorts with swimming pools and discos. If you do camp "unofficially," use caution with your belongings, as theft can be a problem, especially along the beaches.

LIFE AND TIMES

Morocco has carved its identity out of a host of disparate influences. At the crossroads of Africa, Europe, and the Near East, Morocco is also the Far West of the Arab world. It is both an ancient civilization descended from nomadic tribes and a modern nation that has struggled against imperial powers for its sovereignty. The distinct richness of Moroccan culture, arts, and food testify to these influences.

■ History and Politics

Way Back

Morocco is a cultural as well as commercial crossroads. Berbers native to the mountains and plateaus met up with the Phoenician and Carthaginian colonists on the North African coast by 500 BC. The Romans who followed left behind economic prosperity and a few ruins. After Titus' destruction of the temple in Jerusalem in the third century BC, Jews trickled into the Moroccan cities. The Vandals established control over the area until AD 683, when the Islamic army of **Uqua Ibn Nabir** swept in to convert the pagans, found Qu'ranic schools, and make Arabic the dominant lan-

guage. The many southern Africans in the country share a common history; Arab slave traders kidnapped their ancestors from Mali, Guinea, the Sudan, and Senegal. Gold, spices, aphrodisiac rhinoceros-horn, salt, ebony, ivory and, of course, camels made Morocco a wealthy link in the commercial chain between Africa and Europe.

The Rise and Fall of Islam

Berber princess and prophetess **Kahina** killed herself at the news of the Arab conquest in 702, and by the end of the 8th century the Moors had converted most of the Berber rebels to Islam. **Idris (I) Ibn Abdallah,** a distant relation to **Muhammad the Prophet,** fled Baghdad in 789 to found the Kingdom of Fès near the old Roman settlement of Volubilis. Centered in Spain, the Moorish empire displaced the Idrisian dynasty, but by the 11th century **Almoravids** from the Western Sahara had quashed Spanish-Muslim control and established their own kingdom in Marrakech.

> **Berber princess and prophetess Kahina killed herself at the news of the Arab conquest in 702.**

A golden age of **Merinid** and **Wattasid** rule (1244-1554) promoted a cultural and intellectual boom and tied Morocco to Spain. As Muslim influence in Christian Iberia waned, however, the Spanish turned aggressive. A second wave of Jewish immigrants fled to Morocco during the Spanish Inquisition of 1492, during which Queen Isabel and King Fernando forced them to choose between conversion or death. The Wattasids formed an army of refugees and converted or mercenary Christians to battle the conquering Spanish and Portuguese, but by the early 1500s, the Iberians had established control over Moroccan ports and a number of inland territories.

The European Contenders

The **Saadis** drove out some foreign influence and reunited Morocco. Under **Ahmed el Mansour**—a.k.a. Ahmed the Gilded—Morocco expanded its trade in slaves and gold in Timbuctoo and parts of the Sudan. When the **Alawite dynasty** overthrew the Saadis in 1659, they took over Marrakech and the area around Fès, controlled by religious mystics known as **marrabouts.** The Alawite dynasty rules to this day. But battling European rulers conspired to disintegrate Moroccan unity. England copped Tangier in 1662 as part of a settlement with a war-weary Spain; France slowly invaded northern Africa, winning a major battle at Isly in 1844.

France's major stroke of luck came with the death of Sultan Hassan of Rabat in 1893. His 13-year-old son **Abdul Aziz,** an expert at bicycle polo and a famous playboy, ascended the throne. The French encroached massively upon Moroccan territories, eventually occupying Casablanca. By 1912, the French had exiled the ruling vizier, Abd el-Hafid, and secured an official protectorate in the **Treaty of Fès.** The equivalent **Treaty of Algericas** gave the Spanish the same rights.

Throwing off the Yolk

In 1921, **Abd el Krim,** now considered the founder of modern Morocco, began to organize a rebel army against the Spanish in the Rif Country. The troops of Major Francisco Franco (future General and Spanish dictator), with aid from Marshall Pétain's French army, forced the rebels to surrender by 1926.

Sultan Mohammed V ignited the nationalist movement with the founding of the Independence Party in 1944. The French deported nationalist leaders and exiled Mohammed without so much as a suitcase in 1952. The ensuing popular unrest combined with the revolt in Algeria forced the French to abandon their hard line. Mohammed returned to the throne on November 18, 1955, and signed a treaty of independence for French Morocco on March 2, 1956. The independence of most of Spanish Morocco followed one month later.

Muhammad V's successor, King Hassan II, came to the throne in 1961 and introduced a constitution favoring pro-monarchists, only to be vehemently protested by opposition party UNFP. In 1963, ten of UNFP's leaders, including **Ben Barka,** were implicated in a plot to overthrow the monarchy and sentenced to death. In 1965, King Hassan declared a national **state of emergency,** snagging direct control of exec-

utive *and* legislative powers. Hassan's 1970 constitution ended the emergency and restored limited parliamentary government, but two abortive military coups and governmental divisions delayed democratic parliamentary elections until 1977.

Modern Morocco

Today Morocco is nominally a **constitutional monarchy:** though assisted by a parliament and a Chamber of Representatives, the king can dissolve parliament and easily manipulate the country's political parties. Hassan has pledged to "improve the balance between legislative and executive powers," but Morocco's human rights abuses, alleviated only in part by a 1991 initiative, have failed to foster political freedom. Censorship meticulously stamps out opposition from such groups as trade union activists and university radicals. A drought further sapped monarchist support, but after sluggish industrial growth, riots, and the drain of civil war in Western Sahara on national resources, Morocco began recovery in the 90s. The North Africa-wide Islamist movement has kept Morocco on paranoid toes, though King Hassan's regime is stable in comparison to neighboring countries. Morocco's relations with neighbors are strained, particularly with Algeria, where illegal arms shuttling resulted in the closing of the Morocco-Algeria border in 1994. Southern Europe, also aligned against Islamist infiltration, has been taking a greater interest in Morocco, for one advocating tighter border controls

■ Language

Morocco is a paradise for polyglots. Arabic is the country's official language, but French is a close second. Almost all signs and documents are printed in French as well as Arabic; moreover, most government employees speak French as a second language. In certain northern towns, Spanish fills the linguistic role of French. Many Moroccans speak English and German, but don't count on it. In this book, city and country names appear first in English, then in Arabic. A massive shift from European street names is underway, so some of the streets mentioned in this book may go by a different title (listed in both French and Arabic when necessary and possible). *Rues* and *calles* may revolt and become *zankats, derbs,* or *sharias.*

■ Religion

There is much more uniformity of religion than language. **Islam** is the state religion (the king is also "commander of the faithful"), and less than 1% of the population is not Muslim. The Islamic calendar began in 622, the year Muhammad began ruling the Islamic polity. Muslims believe Muhammad was the last Prophet in a line including Noah, Abraham, Moses, and Jesus. He received God's (Allah's) words from the angel Gabriel; these words are recited to the people in the **The prophet's death provoked a "who rules?" crisis, spurring the Sunni and Shia division.** Qur'an, the holy scripture of Islam. There are five pillars of Islam: profession of monotheistic faith, prayer, almsgiving, pilgrimage to Mecca, and fasting during the Holy Month of Ramadan. Muhammad led the polity until his death in 632, during which time his words and deeds were recorded in *hadiths* (reports) which comprise the *Sunna,* or exemplary practice of Muhammad. Since the Prophet failed to plan ahead, his death provoked a "who rules?" crisis, spurring the Sunni and Shia division; the former believed his successor should be chosen among a community of men, the latter insisted pure spiritual leaders (Imams) should succeed. Most Moroccans are Sunni Muslims.

Local Islamic holidays akin to Catholic saint days are **moussems.** These last several days and feature group pilgrimages to local shrines, street bazaars, and agricultural fairs. Rowdier *moussems* treat observers to music-and-dance events that may include charging cavalcades of costumed, armed equestrians. Most fall in summer; exact dates vary with the Islamic calendar and the decisions of local governments.

All About Ramadan

During **Ramadan,** Islam's holy month, Muslims abstain from food, drink, cigarettes, and sex from sunup to sundown (around 4:30am to 8:30pm) to cultivate spiritual well-being, compassion, and charity. Ramadan after dark is another story: sirens prompt adherents to chug *harira,* streets burst with music, and the feasting and religious services begin. The **Night of Power,** on the 27th day, honors the passing of the Qur'an from God to Muhammad. When the moon comes out, the king officially ends Ramadan, and **Aid el-Saghir,** celebrated with enormous breakfasts and gifts to children, marks the end of the daylight fast.

City services operate through the holy month for the most part, but restaurants and cafes catering to locals close during the day. Ramadan is slightly earlier each year (calculated using the Islamic *(hijri)* lunar calendar), so over 30 years it makes a full cycle. Ramadan falls between Dec. 31, 1997 and Jan. 30, 1998.

Non-Muslims should be especially respectful during Ramadan; watch where and when you eat, drink, and smoke. In rural areas, where locals are not accustomed to tourists, a lack of sensitivity may draw outright hostility. All but the fancier tourist establishments close from dawn to dusk. But in large cities such as Tangier and Rabat, many restaurants stay open all day during Ramadan.

■ The Arts

ART AND ARCHITECTURE

Diverse architectural forms define Moroccan landscapes and cityscapes. Intense hot and cold combined with Berber austerity and Islamic privacy give **Berber architecture** an enclosed and stark nature. *Kasbah,* the monumental houses of Berber potentates, feature central courtyards, dark and narrow passageways, animal shelters, simple high slope-walled towers, thick walls, and plain façades. *Ksour* (plural of *ksar*), or fortified Berber villages densely pack "apartments." Both are made with *pisé* or packed earth—they are fast turning to ruins, unable to defy wind and sand storms

In the 10th century, Fès residents built the first Moroccan **mosques** (sometimes called *djemmas*), el-Andalus and the Kairaouine. Any place Muslims pray is a mosque, or *masjid* ("place of prostration"). The *qibla* wall contains the prayer niche *(mihrab)* and indicates the direction of Mecca. There are two basic designs for mosques: Arab style, based on Muhammad's house with a pillared cloister around a courtyard, and Persian style with a vaulted arch (an *iwan*) on each side. Non-Muslims may not enter Moroccan mosques. Tourists *can* gawk through doorways of famous ones. Out of respect, visitors should stay away during services. Attached to most mosques, Qu'ranic schools or **medersas** have classrooms, libraries, and a prayer hall around a central courtyard and fountain. Most Merinid and Saadien mosques display secular and/or devotional artistry.

Islam's opposition to idolatry spurred incredibly ingenious geometric and calligraphic decorations. Colorful patterns swirl across tiles, woodwork, stone, and ceramic. In less doctrinaire times, Almoravid artists slipped in designs that vaguely resemble leaves and flowers. **Calligraphy,** particularly elegant renderings and illuminations of the Qur'an, became another outlet for creativity as well as religious devotion. Merinids, following the strict Almohads, relaxed the formalism to include floral and geometric strains, manifest in curved and straight-edged *zallij* (mosaic tiles).

Sultans reserved their most dazzling designs for **imperial palaces,** with long, symmetrical series of reception and dwelling rooms studded with decorative gates, hidden gardens, and tiny pools and fountains. The diversity of styles is truly incredible.

CRAFTS

Of Moroccan handicrafts, **carpets** are the most popular with tourists. For centuries, Moroccan women have made rug-weaving their occupation. The central motif of

knotted Arabian-style rugs is a kaleidoscope of rich blues, reds, greens, and yellows, enclosed by an intricate border. Berber *kellim* carpets (often used as wall-hangings or bedspreads) are cheaper. Woven rather than knotted with wool, each is stunningly embroidered with "silk." Despite many mass-produced textiles, most Moroccans continue to dress in handmade clothing. Fès has been center of a renowned **leather** industry since the 15th century, when the Moors returned from Spain. High-quality Moroccan leather, a multimillion dollar export, can be inexpensive locally. Moroccan **pottery** dates back 1000 years, but, like leather work, the craft prospered in the 15th century. A medley of color splashes the white background of traditional Andalusian-inspired enameled pottery. Saharan and Berber **terra cotta** ware and roof tiles are also common. Especially in the South, distinctive and chunky **silver jewelry** often comes inlaid with colorful stones or plastic. Silver has long been valued by Berber women who couldn't afford gold. Craftsmen work wonders with **wood.** Boxes, chess sets, and desk paraphernalia—all splendidly inlaid—are available.

Souks (markets) display all of these handicrafts in abundance and widely varying quality. Souks target tourists for the sale of craftwork. **Bargaining** is big; the best policy is to gauge the personal worth of an item and stick to that price. It's unlikely you'll get a great deal by Moroccan standards, but the value ratio is still excellent in Western terms. Don't enter the store without an intent to buy. There's no obligation, but Moroccan merchants skillfully create needs previously nonexistent. When you walk in, act blasé. Declare that you've done your shopping already and/or claim student status. Walking out the door (with the faintest hint of reluctance) is very effective. Above all, never let a price escape your lips unless you intend to pay it.

PROSE TO PERUSE

Because our map of Morocco doesn't include the Western Sahara, *Let's Go* is banned from Moroccan bookstores. If worse comes to worst, you can check out some of the practical guidebooks of our competitors. Christopher Kininmonth's *Morocco: The Traveller's Guide* introduces Moroccan culture in laconic English. Fatima Mernissi's *Beyond the Veil* describes male-female dynamics in modern Morocco, and Gilles Perrault caused a stir with his tell-all *Our Friend, The King.*

Writing Moroccan guidebooks was popular among European and North American literati. Edith Wharton's *In Morocco* (1925) is a collection of episodic descriptions of Rabat, Salé, Fès, and Meknès. Walter Harris's *Morocco That Was,* a turn-of-the-century journalist's diary, features a wry account of a Brit's kidnapping by the international bandit Raissouli. *The Voices of Marrakech* by Bulgarian Nobel Prize recipient Elias Canetti eloquently records a European Jew's encounter with Moroccan Jews. *The House of Si Abd Allah,* edited by noted scholar Henry Munson, is an oral history of a Moroccan family which provides insight into the country's social history. Paul

> **Because our book doesn't include the Western Sahara, Let's Go is banned from Moroccan bookstores.**

Bowles, an American who settled in Tangier, sets much of his fiction in Morocco. *The Spider's House* is a numbingly gorgeous introduction to the country and to Bowles, a semi-cult figure and collector of Moroccan folklore and music. The movie *Sheltering Sky,* about Americans losing it in Morocco, is also from Bowles.

Albert Camus' classics *The Stranger* and *The Plague,* both set in neighboring Algeria, offer a vision of expatriate life under the Maghreb's sun. Another interesting Western observer of the Maghreb is Isabelle Eberhardt, an early 20th-century traveler drowned in a flood in the Algerian Sahara. Her diaries are collected as *Passionate Nomad.* The beat writers of the 1950s soaked up Moroccan culture (and sampled the Rif's famous crops); William S. Burroughs wrote *The Naked Lunch* in a Tangier hotel room.

Among the few Moroccan works available in English, *Love With a Few Hairs, M'hashish,* and *The Lemon* are Muhammad Mrabet's bits of contemporary Moroccan life. Historian Youssef Necrouf's *The Battle of Three Kings* is an entertaining account of medieval violence and intrigue under the Saadian dynasty.

■ Food and Drink

Moroccan chefs lavish aromatic and colorful spices on their dishes—pepper, ginger, cumin, saffron, honey, and sugar are culinary staples. The cuisine, climate, and unfamiliar microbes can combine to make gastrointestinal problems likely. Many travelers take every precaution and still end up running to the bathroom on an hourly basis. Tap water is fairly benign in the major northern cities, though bottled mineral water (Sidi Ali) is always recommended. Bottled mineral water is the safest option. A policy of peeling all fruit and cooking all vegetables can be helpful; the truly cautious avoid salads and raw vegetables on *kefta* sandwiches.

TYPICAL FARE

A dish of the North African staple, **couscous,** contains semolina grain, a cumin or saffron sauce, and whatever fish, meat, or vegetables the cook feels like throwing in. **Tajine,** the other common Moroccan main course (and the term for the ceramic bowl in which it's served), is the word used for a wide variety of stews with fish, chicken, or lamb mixed with potatoes, olives, prunes, nuts, and other vegetables. Brochettes, hamburger sandwiches, soups, and honey-soaked pastries are also on every street corner.

MEALS AND RESTAURANTS (PLUS TIPPING)

The restaurant scene in Morocco consists mainly of tourist-oriented restaurants replete with dancing and music and small locally patronized restaurants, generally in the medina. A complete meal includes a choice of entree (*tajine,* couscous, or perhaps a third option), salad or *harira,* a side of vegetables, and yogurt or an orange for dessert. Lunchtime spans from noon and 2pm, dinner between 7 and 9pm. Still, many restaurants serve at any time. If a service charge isn't automatically included, a 10% tip will suffice. Even more informal than the *brochetteries,* marketers hawk everything from *harira* to fresh potato chips to *brochettes* (roasted skewered beef, lamb, or brain). Almost every Moroccan main course includes meat; *couscous aux legumes* probably has the least meat. Your best bet is to cook with produce from the market. Less expensive *tajine* is made with *kefta* (delicately seasoned ground meatballs) often served on a baguette sub-style, as is *Merguez,* a spicy beef or lamb sausage. Gourmands and cheapskates alike swear by **harira,** a spicy chick-pea-based soup with or without meat stock. **Poulet** (chicken), whether *rôti* (roasted on a spit with olives) or *limon* (with lemon), rules the roost. Pricier and harder-to-find specialties include **mechoui,** whole lamb spitted over an open fire, or **pastilla,** a pastiche of squab, almonds, eggs, butter, cinnamon, and sugar under a pastry shell. For a lighter treat, slurp sweet natural yogurt with mounds of peaches, nectarines, or strawberries, or try an oily Moroccan salad with finely chopped tomatoes, cucumbers, and onions. Snackers munch briny olives (about 1dh per scoop), roasted almonds, and cactus buds (on the streets 1dh a bud). Oranges are the cheapest, sweetest, most eminently peelable fruit in the country.

DRINKS

Drink plenty of **purified water**—only purified water. If the bottle isn't completely sealed, it doesn't take James Bond to realize it's probably full of tap water. Water-sellers, with their red costumes and cymbals, earn more money posing for tourists' pictures than selling anything. Despite Islam's prohibition of alcohol, French, Spanish, and local **wines** can be bought in most supermarkets and some restaurants (but not in the medina). Moroccan wines tend to be heavy; go with the *gris* (try *Oustalet* or *Gris de Boulaouane*) rather than the *rouge.* Watery local **beer,** called Stork or Flag, goes for 12-15dh. Entirely male Moroccan **bars** major in heavy drinking, making them intimidating to most tourists. **Orange juice** (2-4dh) is always fresh and widely available. Other fruit juices blend whole fruit with milk. Make sure the juice is not diluted with tap water. **Tea,** the national drink, was introduced by the English in the 18th

century. The ritual of preparing it with fresh mint sprigs and loads of sugar penetrates most Moroccan daily routine (4-6dh per pot).

■ Sports

Pick-up soccer games are ubiquitous, as are karate and kick-boxing dojos. Moroccans have made a dent internationally, particularly in long distance running. Khalid Skah, for example, won a bronze medal in the mens' 10,000m in the 1996 Olympic Games in Atlanta. Women, long restricted by Moroccan society, are increasingly—if somewhat controversially—partaking in various sports, mainly low-contact endeavors.

■ This Just In...

A UN-sponsored referendum pertaining to the future of the Western Sahara, as to whether it should integrate with Morocco or become independent is facing problems. The voter identification process was ground to a halt in December 1995 due to serious differences over voter eligibility, and UN Secretary General Boutros Boutros-Ghali fatefully recommended the withdrawal of UN personnel in May 1996. The announcement of James Baker as the new UN special envoy to the Western Sahara signalled to many the UN's determination to come to resolution in the case. On June 23,1997, Baker mediated a meeting between the Polisario Front and the Moroccan government; this meeting was hailed as a breakthrough.

Morocco has made plans to start a limited interbank foreign exchange market, parts of its policy encouraging financial liberalization as the country struggles with its sizeable fiscal deficit, which in 1997 was 32% larger than the year before. However, the central bank is still very much in control.

Faced with an increasingly liberal world order, Morocco is feeling heat from more than the scorching sun. Still, its bustling cities attest to the nation's strong capitalistic tendencies, while sketchy guides exemplify its less progressive aspects..

Heat in the Western Sahara

Morocco has been embroiled in a conflict for years over its claims to territory in the sparsely settled, phosphate-rich Western Sahara. Morocco maintains that this area comprised part of the pre-Colonialist Alawite empire. The Polisario Front, championing the area's independence, disagrees, citing the area's history as the Spanish Sahara; it is backed by 71 countries which recognize it as the legitimate government. The Moroccan army built a 1500-mile concrete and barbed-wire wall to fence off the rebel army, and the "Green March" in 1975, led by Hassan II, staked Morocco's claim to the area. In the escalating conflict, Morocco broke diplomatic relations with Algeria, who supported the Polisario Front. A UN committee interceded on behalf of the rebels, and Algeria and Morocco reinstated uneasy relations in 1988. Western Sahara is now a de facto part of Morocco, though negotiations for a referendum continue, as do debates about whether voting should include the thousands who emigrated during the Green March.

The area continues to be a headache for the UN, and Morocco's relations with Algeria are off and on. Now, foreigners need an invitation from an Algerian in order to enter the country via Morocco. Buses, but not trains, cross the border.

THE NORTH AND THE MEDITERRANEAN COAST

The North comprises the ports and beaches of the Mediterranean Coast, the jagged Rif Mountains, and the agricultural inland, home to the grand imperial cities of Fès and Meknès. The region is the most easily accessible from Europe, and a likely destination for travelers to Morocco.

▨ Tangier (Tanger) طنجة

For travelers adventuring out of the European playground for the first time, disembarking in Tangier can be a distressing experience. Upon arrival at the port, any number of guides—do not trust any of them, they are hustlers—aggressively coax vacationers into following their misleading lead. Since the concentration of guides greatly diminishes as one moves away from the port, they become nothing more than a small nuisance if the visitor approaches this situation with the proper attitude and preparation (see **Hustlers and Guides** under **Morocco: Essentials,** p. 619, and **Tangier: Orientation and Practical Information**).

Once one has passed the hustlers, Tangier's fascinating character, imbued with a dramatic history, reveals itself. For centuries the region bounced from one imperial power to the next, culminating in 1923 with the declaration of Tangier as an "international zone." For 33 years a loose coalition comprised of the U.S. and eight European nations allowed Tangier political freedom, comparable to Hong Kong's pre-1997 situation. During the period Tangier attracted sultry heiresses, drug users, spies, pedophiles, currency traders, Beat Generation poets, and others. In 1960, four years after Morocco won its independence, Moulay Abdallah Ibrahim ended Tangier's status as a free port. The regime closed 100 brothels, and the city lost its international economy.

Despite these drastic changes, vestiges of a liberal era remain. The Anglican Church has Mass, the Café de Paris—*the* cafe of WWII secret agents—churns out lattes, hashish flows from the Rif, a gay community is visible, and hard currency circulates on the black market. The medina looms, overlooking the town, the Mediterranean, and the European continent beyond. Tangier is unlike anywhere else in Morocco, and its aura of contemporary romance amid urban squalor endures.

ORIENTATION AND PRACTICAL INFORMATION

Relative to other Moroccan cities, Tangier is navigable. Guides are entirely unneccessary, so know your initial destination before arriving and don't listen to badgering guides who insist that your hotel has gone out of business or that you *must* visit the medina and drink tea. From the ferry terminal, you can take a blue *petit taxi* or walk to the center of town. If you take a **taxi**—this is advisable—either agree on the fare in advance (about 5dh to the center of town) or make sure the driver uses the meter. If you **walk,** leave the ferry terminal along the main road running through the port compound; it will lead you through the large double arches onto the **avenue d'Espagne**. There is a **CTM bus station** on the right and a large white **train station** on the left.

The sprawling **ville nouvelle** ("new town") surrounds the port in all directions. The town's central road is the **boulevard Pasteur.** To find this road, follow av. Espagne running parallel to the beach and take a right on the narrow rue Ibn. Zohr. Turn left onto the paved street after the steps and then turn right after two short blocks. This brings you to the intersection of blvd. Pasteur and blvd. Mohammed V. Turn right onto blvd. Pasteur toward **place de France,** the heart of Tangier's ville nouvelle. A right turn at pl. France onto rue de la Liberté and a short walk down a winding hill leads to the **Grand Socco,** which is the largest square outside the west wall of the **medina**. The **Petit Socco** can be reached by crossing the Grand Socco and entering the medina on rue as-Siaghin, which runs through the medina.

For an alternate route to the medina and the Petit Socco from the port, take a sharp right and climb the steep road to the medina entrance. The Petit Socco is a short walk

up av. Mokhtar Ahardan. The main **bus station** lies about 2km from the port. Following rue d'Espagne, turn right onto av. Beethoven.

Tourist Office: 29 blvd. Pasteur (tel. 948 050). Friendly staff, English spoken. Free maps and tourist brochures, but little else. Open Mon.-Fri. 8:20am-noon, 2:30-6pm.

Currency Exchange: There is a branch of **BMCE** on most ferries. Its main office in Tangier is located at 21 blvd. Pastuer (tel 93 11 25). Exchange booth is open daily, with the commission of 4.60dh per check (open Mon.-Fri. 9am-12:45pm, Sat.-Sun. 3-6:45pm). There is an **ATM** on the street. Many hotels change money, some at a hefty commission. Travel agencies near the port must change money at official rates. Major banks line blvds. Pasteur and Mohammed V. Say *non* to hustlers offering exchange service.

American Express: Crédit du Maroc, 54 blvd. Pasteur (tel. 93 19 16). Open Mon.-Fri. 8am-2pm. Li'l window in a big bank sells traveler's checks (in *dirhams,* of course) but—like all AmEx offices in Morocco—it can't receive wired money.

Airport: A taxi to the airport, 16km from Tangier, costs 70dh for up to 6 people. **Royal Air Maroc,** pl. France (tel. 93 55 01). To Marrakech and Casablanca.

Trains: There is one station in the port compound. The main station is on av. d'Espagne (tel. 93 45 70), on the left after exiting the port compound through the large arches. **ONCF** 2nd-class to: Fès (3 per day, 5½hr., 93dh); Meknès (3 per day, 5hr., 77dh); Casablanca (3 per day, 6hr., 114dh); Rabat (3 per day, 5½hr., 87dh); Asilah (1 per day, 1hr., 13dh—it leaves you 2km from town, so the bus is a better option); Taza (4 per day, 7hr., 130dh); Onjda (4 per day, 10hr., 175dh).

Buses: CTM Station, av. d'Espagne (tel. 93 24 15 or 93 11 72), next to the port entrance. Buses to: Marrakech (1 per day, 10hr., 165dh); Casablanca (6 per day, 6hr., 110dh); Rabat (6 per day, 5hr., 80dh); Larache (3 per day, 2½hr., 29dh); Fès (4 per day, 6hr., 85dh); Meknès (4 per day, 5hr., 70dh); Oujda (1 per day, 12hr., 165dh); Asiliah (3 per day, 1½hr., 15dh). **Private buses:** rue Yacoub el-Mansor at pl. Ligue Arabe, 2km from the port entrance. These buses offer more departures at lower prices. A *petit taxi* to the terminal costs 12dh. Ask blue-coated personnel about ticket info. The standard price for luggage is 5dh—don't give more.

Ferries: Try **Voyages Hispamaroc** on blvd. Pasteur (tel. 93 31 13; fax 94 40 31), below Hôtel Rembrandt. English spoken. Open daily 8am-12:30pm and 3-7pm. Alternatively, buy a ticket at the port. You'll need a boarding pass (available at any ticket desk) and a customs form (ask uniformed agents). Near the terminal, pushy men with ID cards will try to arrange your ticket, obtain (and fill out) your customs card, and then demand 10dh. Don't bother. To: Algeciras (8 per day, 2½hr., Class B 2960ptas or 210dh); Tarifa (1 per day 3pm, except Fri. 7pm, 2hr., 210dh); Gibraltar (3 per week, Tues., Fri., Sun., 2½hr., 250dh). To reach the ferry companies directly, call **Transmediterránea,** 31 av. de la Résistance (tel. 93 48 83); **Limadet Ferry,** av. Prince Moulay Abdallah (tel. 93 39 14); **Comanau,** 43 rue Abou Ala El Maari (tel. 93 26 49); or **Transtour,** 4 rue El Jabha Ouatania (tel. 93 40 04).

Grands Taxis: Quick transport to nearby locations (Tetuan, Ceuta, Asilah). Prices subject to bargaining, but a fair price is 20dh when taxis are full (6 passengers).

Car Rental: Avis, 54 blvd. Pasteur (tel. 93 30 31). **Hertz,** 36 av. Mohammed V (tel. 93 33 22). Both charge 250dh per day plus 2.50dh per km and a 20% tax.

Luggage Storage: At the train station (5dh per bag). Open 24hr. Also at the bus station (5dh per bag). Open daily 4am-midnight.

English Bookstore: Librairie des Colonnes, 54 blvd. Pasteur (tel. 93 69 55), near pl. France. Novels and books on Moroccan culture, English classics, and popular fiction (from 50dh). Open Mon.-Fri. 9:30am-1pm and 4-7pm, Sat. 9:30am-1pm.

Late-Night Pharmacy: 22 rue de Fès (tel. 93 26 19), two blocks from blvd. Pasteur at the pl. France. They dispense through tiny windows in the green wall on the left side of the entrance. Open Mon.-Fri. 1-4pm and 8pm-9am, Sat.-Sun. 8pm-9am.

Medical Services: Croissant Rouge, 6 rue El Monoui Dahbi (tel. 93 11 99), runs a 24hr. English-speaking medical service. **Ambulance:** (tel. 33 33 00).

Police: (tel. 19), located at port and main train station.

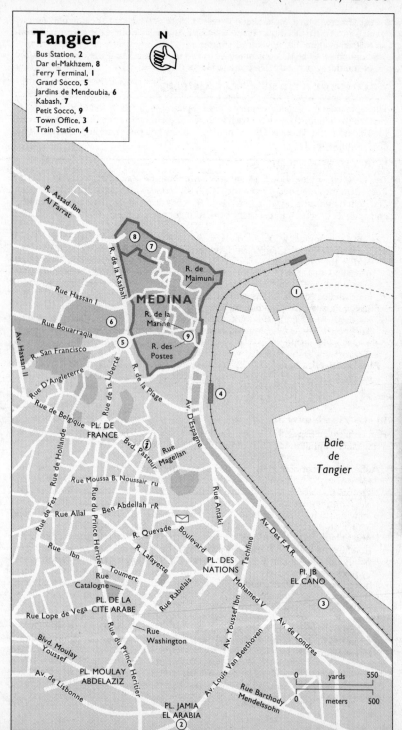

Tangier

Bus Station, **2**
Dar el-Makhzem, **8**
Ferry Terminal, **1**
Grand Socco, **5**
Jardins de Mendoubia, **6**
Kabash, **7**
Petit Socco, **9**
Town Office, **3**
Train Station, **4**

N

R. Assad Ibn Al Farrat

R. de la Kasbah

Rue Hassan I

Rue Bouarraqia

R. de Maimuni

MEDINA

R. de la Marine

R. des Postes

Av. Hassan II

R. San Francisco

Rue D'Angleterre

Rue de Belgique

Rue de la Liberté

R. de la Plage

Av. D'Espagne

PL. DE FRANCE

Bvd. Pasteur

Rue Magellan

Rue de Hollande

Rue Moussa B. Noussair   ru

Rue de Fes

Rue Allal

Ben Abdellah   rR

R. Quevade

Boulevard

Rue Antaki

Av. Des F.A.R.

Baie de Tangier

Rue Ibn

Rue du Prince Heritier

R. Lafayette

Toumert

Rue Catalogne

PL. DE LA CITE ARABE

Rue Rabelais

PL. DES NATIONS

Tachfine

Mohamed V

Pl. JB EL CANO

Rue Lope de Vega

Rue du Prince Heritier

Rue Washington

Blvd. Moulay Youssef

PL. MOULAY ABDELAZIZ

Av. de Lisbonne

Av. Youssef Ibn

Av. Louis Van Beethoven

Av. de Londres

Rue Barthody Mendelssohn

PL. JAMIA EL ARABIA

0   yards   550
0   meters   500

MOROCCO

Post Office: 33 blvd. Mohammed V (tel. 93 25 18 or 93 21 25), the downhill continuation of blvd. Pasteur. Poste Restante and telephones. Open Mon.-Thurs.
8:30am-6:30pm, Sat. 8:30am-12:15pm.

Telephones: 33 blvd. Mohammed V, to the right and around the corner from the
post office. Open 24hr. **Telephone Code:** (0)9.

ACCOMMODATIONS AND CAMPING

Those unfazed by Tangier's frenzy can find plenty of hotels in the medina and stay
close to the action. Those who wish to distance themselves from hustlers will prefer
the ville nouvelle. There is a broad range of quality and prices, though the two don't
always correspond.

In and Near the Medina

The most convenient hotels cluster near **rue Mokhtar Ahardan,** formerly **rue des
Postes,** off the Petit Socco. From the Grand Socco (see Orientation, p. 631), take the
first right down rue as-Siaghin to the Petit Socco. Rue Mokhtar Ahardan begins at the
end of the Petit Socco closest to the port. At night parts of the medina can be unsafe.

Hôtel Continental, 36 Dar Baroud (tel. 93 10 24 or 93 11 43; fax 93 11 43). From
the Petit Socco, take rue Jemaa el Kebir (ex-rue de la Marine) downhill toward the
port to the Continental's blue gate. Veer left at the raised overlook. The grand
piano and bird cage in the lobby have aged better than the mattresses, and showers are only hot in the morning, but the Art Deco rooms are unbeatable. Swarming with English chaps, this is a truly grand hotel. Singles 154dh. Doubles 179dh.

Pension Palace, 2 rue Mokhtar Ahardan (tel. 93 61 28). Downhill, on the alley exiting the Petit Socco to the right. Sanitary, if Lilliputian rooms. Clean communal
bathrooms. The establishment boasts an impressive courtyard featured in Ber-
tolucci's film adaptation of American novelist Paul Bowles's *The Sheltering Sky.*
Singles 50dh. Doubles 80dh, with bath120dh.

Pension Miami, 126 rue Salah Eddine el-Ayoubi (tel. 93 29 00), outside the medina,
off rue d'Espagne. Frayed turquoise and magenta rooms, handsomely carved ceilings, and a balconied cluster on each floor. Basic communal bathroom. Singles
50dh. Doubles 80dh. Hot showers 5dh.

In the Ville Nouvelle

Hotels line **av. d'Espagne** as it heads away from the port. The best values, though, lie
a few blocks uphill toward blvd. Pasteur and blvd. Mohammed V.

Auberge de Jeunesse (HI), 8 rue el-Antaki (tel. 94 61 27), down av. d'Espagne
away from the port, and ½block up the road to the right after Hôtel Marco Polo.
Visitors rave about Mohssine the warden, a friendly and reliable source of info.
New, firm dormitory beds, but no lockers. Office open Mon.-Sat. 8-10am, noon-
3pm, and 6-10:30pm, Sun. 8-10am and 6pm-midnight; closes at 10:30pm during
winter. HI members 31dh, non members 43.50dh. Hot showers 5dh.

Hôtel El Muniria (Tanger Inn), rue Magellan (tel. 93 53 37). Take the 1st right after
Hôtel Biarritz on av. d'Espagne, walking away from the medina, and follow it as it
winds uphill. William Burroughs wrote *Naked Lunch* in room #9 (now the
owner's room). Jack Kerouac and Allen Ginsberg stayed in room #4. Beat Generation aside, this establishment is a great deal for Tangier, with spacious rooms, hot
showers, towels, and the relaxed, ex-pat-frequented Tanger Inn bar next door.
Singles 100dh. Doubles 120dh.

Hôtel L'Marsa, 92 av. d'Espagne (tel. 93 23 39), away from the port, but right on
the main drag; you can't miss its restaurant which juts out onto the sidewalk. Very
clean rooms cost little considering their location. Singles 60dh. Doubles 80dh.
Hot showers 7dh.

FOOD

In and Near the Medina

For variety, low prices, and lots of haggling, stall-hop along the **Grand Socco.** Inexpensive Moroccan fare is also served in simple local eateries along **rue Mokhtar Ahardan** and outside the medina on **rue Salah Eddine el-Ayoubi,** which begins across from the train station and runs up to the Grand Socco. Those listed here are more established, more expensive, and less local.

Africa Restaurant, 83 rue Salah Eddine el-Ayoubi (tel. 93 54 36), just off rue d'Espagne, near Pension Miami. The name would indicate a sure-fire tourist trap, but the food and prices do not. Lip-smacking soup precedes delicious lamb couscous (30dh). Big 4-course *menu du jour* 45dh. Open daily 9am-12:30am.

Restaurant Andaluz, 7 rue du Commerce. Make a 90° left downhill at the end of Petit Socco and go through the yellow arch. This small dining grotto buzzes with activity. Hefty sizzling *brochettes* 24dh. Swordfish 40dh. Shrimp 35dh.

Restaurant Hammadi, 2 rue de la Kasbah (tel. 93 45 14), the continuation of rue d'Italie just past the medina walls. The only Moroccans here are waiters and serenading Andalusian musicians. Despite the touristy veneer, the food is excellent. Avoid lunch, when tour groups fill every seat. Specialties are *tajine* (40dh) and couscous (45dh). Beer and wine served. Service charge 20%. Open Mon.-Sat. (sometimes Sun.) noon-3pm and 8pm-1am.

In the Ville Nouvelle

International cuisine can be found throughout the ville nouvelle, more a product of enterprising Moroccans than a vestige of Tangier's international status. For hot sandwiches, try the storefronts off **blvd. Pasteur.** The restaurants along **av. d'Espagne** tout unspectacular *menus touristiques* for 50dh or more.

L'Marsa, 92 av. d'Espagne (tel. 93 19 28). Popular restaurant and cafe with outdoor dining, Italian menu, and *tajine* squeezed in. Praiseworthy pizzas (30-35dh) and 10 flavors of Italian ice cream (10-20dh). Open daily 6am-midnight.

Emma's BBC Bar, along the beach across from Hôtel Miramar. Beach club, catering to paunchy holidaying Brits, serves burgers and curry dishes. Has Morocco's only full English breakfast (45dh). 19% tax. Open daily 8am-2am.

SIGHTS

In the Nouvelle Ville

The **Galerie Delacroix,** run by the French Cultural Center, resides on rue de la Liberté heading toward the medina. The collection displays works by Moroccans as well as foreigners, whose depictions reflect their experience abroad (open Tues.-Sun. 11am-1pm and 4-8pm; free).

The tea-and-crumpet crowd should head down the rue Amerique du Sud, where aging British expatriates convene at **St. Andrew's Church,** designed by the British to look like a mosque (take a left as you enter the Grand Socco from rue de la Liberté, and then a quick left onto rue Amengnedu Sud). The Lord's Prayer is carved on the chancel arch in decorative Arabic. Surrounding gardens and benches offer respite from the medina. Caretaker of 32 years, Mustapha, leads tours from 9:30am-12:30pm and 2:30-6pm. A tip of a few *dirham* is appreciated. Sunday communion is held at 8:30am and morning service at 11am. The city's most recent monumental construction is the towering **New Mosque,** an ochre and white structure on **place el-Koweit,** southwest of the Grand Socco along rue Sidi Bouabib.

In and Near the Medina

While a guide is unnecessary, it is dangerous to wander off the medina's main streets or on the beaches at night. Try to restrict nighttime exploration to the ville nouvelle.

The medina's commercial center is the **Grand Socco.** This busy square and traffic circle is cluttered with fruit vendors, parsley stands, and kebab and fish stalls. In the colorful **Fès Market**—uphill on rue de la Liberté, across pl. de France, and two blocks down rue de Fès on the right—local merchants cater to Tangier's European community. Berbers from the Rif ride into the Dradeb district (west of the Grand Socco along rue Bou Arrakia and northwest on rue de la Montagne) on Thursdays and Sundays to vend pottery, parsley, olives, mountain mint, and fresh fruit. Opposite rue de la Liberté where rue Bou Arrakia joins the Grand Socco (through the door marked #50), a cache of 17th- and 18th-century bronze cannons hide in the **Jardins de la Mendoubia.**

To reach the **Kasbah,** enter the next large gate to the right of gate #50. Veer left, then follow rue d'Italie north from the Grand Socco through **Bab Fahs,** the Moorish gateway, and up steep rue de la Kasbah. This street ends at the horseshoe-shaped **porte de la Kasbah,** guarded by industrious hustlers. Rue Riad Sultan runs from the main portal alongside the **Jardins du Soltane,** where artisans weave carpets (open Mon.-Sat. 8am-2pm; off season Mon.-Sat. 8:30am-noon and 2:30-6pm; 5dh). Rue Riad Sultan continues to **place de la Kasbah,** a sunny courtyard and adjacent promontory offering a view of the Atlantic and Spain. With your back to the water, walk straight ahead toward the far right corner of the plaza, where just around the corner to the right, the sharp **Mosque de la Kasbah** rears its octagonal minaret.

Gold-trigger-finger

The **Forbes Museum of Military Miniatures,** set in the late tycoon's old Tangier pad, contains the world's largest collection of toy soldiers. Tiny figures endearingly disembowel each other in meticulous recreations of historic Moroccan jousts. Learning is half the battle—the other half is just plain cool. Gardens behind the museum, the setting of James Bond movie *Never Say Never Again,* offer a spectacular view of the ocean. To get here from the *Kasbah,* at the top of rue de la Kasbah turn left onto rue de la Corse. Bear right at the fork onto H. Assad Ibn Farrat and continue straight ahead past a hospital on the right until you reach the white mansion (open Fri.-Wed. 10am-5pm; free).

Near the mosque is the main entrance to the **Dar el-Makhzen** (tel. 93 20 97), an opulent palace with handwoven tapestries, inlaid ceilings, and foliated archways, once home to the ruling pasha of Tangier. The palace's **Museum of Moroccan Art** is not the country's best, but it does have some exhibits of ceramics, carpets, copper, silver jewelry, as well as Andalusian musical instruments (palace open Wed.-Mon. 9am-1pm and 3-6pm; free).

An interesting museum, especially but not exclusively for homesick Yanks, is the **Old American Legation,** 8 rue America (tel. 93 53 17), south of pl. de la Kasbah in the far corner of the medina—look for the yellow archway emblazoned with the U.S. seal. The first property acquired overseas by the U.S., it was the budding nation's ambassadorial residence. Among other documents relating to Tangier's international past, the museum displays correspondence between George Washington and his "great and magnanimous friend" Sultan Moulay ben Abdallah. An ever-changing selection of art ranges from strikingly inaccurate 16th-century maps to photographs of the 1943 Casablanca conference. The charming curators deliver excellent tours, even in the midst of their restoration efforts. (Open Mon. and Wed.-Thurs., 10am-1pm and 3-5pm. Free, but donations are appreciated and needed.)

Av. d'Espagne runs along Tangier's expansive **beach.** Stick to the main portions frequented by tourists—the deserted areas are prime locations for muggings.

ENTERTAINMENT

Place de France has hosted Tangier's social activity since the city's heyday. The most popular evening activity is to sip mint tea and people-watch from a **cafe** on **blvd. Pasteur.** The **Café de Paris** (on the left coming from the Grand Socco), slightly

more elegant than its neighbors, was *the* meeting place for secret agents during WWII. Also consider downing some tea at **Café Central,** off the Petit Socco, a favorite of William S. Burroughs. Mick Jagger's lips caressed cups from **Café Andaluz,** another famous establishment.

The best place for a quiet drink with little hassle is the **Tanger Inn,** similar to a pub, playing early 80s pop in the background. Those in search of alcohol or peace can try the relaxed **Negresco,** 20 rue Mexique (tel. 93 80 97), with free nuts and olives. Attached to the Hôtel Muniria (see **Accommodations and Camping,** p. 634), it's the city's longest-running bar and regularly attracts resident ex-pats and backpackers (beer 18dh; mixed drinks 30-35dh; open 10am-1am). Boisterous and seedy affairs run their shady course at the assortment of discos along **rue el-Moutanabi,** parallel to blvd. Pasteur, near pl. France. Bear in mind that Moroccan discos are not safe for solo travelers, but can be fun for groups.

■ Ceuta سبتة

Entering Morocco through Ceuta is a good option for those who want to avoid the stress of Tangier. Just a 90-minute ferry ride from Algeciras, this Spanish enclave on the Moroccan coast has a fascinating history, which is a bit hidden from the traveler by the huge military presence in town and by its role as a duty-free shopping haven.

Public **buses** and **taxis** ply the route between downtown Ceuta, a couple blocks from the port, and the border crossing into Morocco, 3km away. Bus #47 runs from Pl. Constitución and costs 100ptas. Taxis will run around 400ptas. Once at the Moroccan border, you can cross on foot and find a **grand taxi** to Tetouan for 15dh.

Heading to and from Spain, there are 8 **ferry** departures daily each way (90min., 1885 ptas), with more during periods of high demand. There are also 8 **fast-ferry** departures (35min., 3000ptas). It is always safer to buy your tickets in the port itself. There is a small **tourist office** on the way out of the port and a larger one in town that can help with places to stay or transportation details.

■ Near Ceuta: Tetouan تطوان

For those entering Morocco through Ceuta, Tetouan, the necessary first stop, can be very intimidating. Fortunately the town can be quickly escaped to the south. For those coming from deep in Morocco, Tetouan's hustlers and drug dealers will seem nothing new and can be brushed off in order to take a look around the large, whitewashed medina; exploration, however, should be limited to the day, as during nighttime the Tetouan medina can be a dangerous.

Practical Information The new town centers around **place Moulay el-Mehdi,** with the medina to the east (a few blocks down the pedestrian street) and the **bus station** a couple of blocks southeast along **rue Achra Mai.** The bus station is large and hectic, but with a little effort you can get out of Tetouan pretty quickly. **CTM** buses run to: Casablanca (3 per day, 100dh); Rabat (3 per day, 80dh); Chefchaouèn (4 per day, 1½hr., 16-18dh); Fès (2 per day, 5hr., 60dh); and Tangier (2 per day, 1½hr., 13dh). **Private companies** have more departures at lower prices. **Grand taxis** to Ceuta leave from in front of the bus station (15dh). Taxis to Chefchaouèn (25dh) run from a stand several blocks away; walk from pl. Moulay el-Mehdi away from the bus station along r. Achra Mai and bear left onto r. al-Jazeer; the stand is a few blocks away. Or take a **petit taxi** for about 4dh. The **tourist office** is a half block down C. Mohammed II toward the medina on the left. The friendly officials have a **map** to photocopy and **guides** for hire (open Mon.-Fri. 8:30am-noon and 2:30-6:30pm). The **post office** and the adjacent **telephone** office are on pl. Moulay el-Mehdi, as are banks with **ATMs** and **currency exchange.** As always, dial 19 for the **police.**

Accommodations and Food To get to **Hotel Trébol,** 3 blvd. Yacoub el-Mansour al Mouahidi, exit the bus station from the lower level and walk a few steps uphill to the right; it's the first left. The hotel is convenient and clean, with a definite Spanish feel to the balconied rooms (singles 41dh, doubles 62dh). **Pension Iberia,** pl. Moulay el-Mehdi, 3rd fl., has clean, breezy rooms and a good manager (singles 50dh, doubles 70dh). **Restaurants** are cheapest and more Moroccan in the medina, more spiffy and Spanish in the new town, clustered along blvd. Mohammed V.

THE MIDDLE ATLAS الاطلس الاوسط

■ Meknès مكناس

Meknès lies amid a gray-green agricultural checkerboard an hour west of Fès, three hours east of Rabat. Named for the Berber tribe Meknassa, the city has the largest Berber population in Morocco. Although less arresting than Morocco's other imperial cities, the people are friendlier, the atmosphere is less touristy, the *souks* are a bit tamer and offer better deals, and the monuments left by Moulay Ismail, the most ruthless and tyrannical sultan in Morocco's history, remain impressive. Ismail chose Meknès as his seat of power in 1672; then, using slave labor and notoriously brutal tactics, he attempted to turn this relative backwater into a capital that would rival Versailles. The city peaked during Ismail's reign, but a visit to Meknès still allows one to appreciate (or revile) one man's staggering ambition in what is now quite a peaceful setting.

ORIENTATION AND PRACTICAL INFORMATION

The old town and monuments of the **ville impériale** are separated from the modern **ville nouvelle** by the river **Oued Boufrekane. Avenue Hassan II,** the new city's main drag, turns into **avenue Moulay Ismail** as it approaches the medina. Local buses #5, 7, and 9 shuttle between the CTM bus station in the ville nouvelle and the colossal **Bab Mansour** (the entrance to the imperial complex). Major services in the ville nouvelle hover around **place Administrative** (a.k.a. place de la Grande Poste).

Tourist Office: 27 pl. Administrative (tel. 52 44 26). From the Abdelkader train station, go straight 2 blocks, turn left onto Mohammed V, and immediately right. Cross r. Allal-ben Abdallah and continue on to Hôtel de Ville. Veer right and it's on the right after the post office. Friendly staff, limited English. Unnecessary official local guides 120dh per ½day, 150dh for full day. Open Mon.-Fri. 8:30am-noon and 2:30-6:30pm. **Syndicat d'Initiative,** Esplanade de la Foire (tel. 52 01 91), off av. Moulay Ismail inside the yellow gate. Decent maps of most major Moroccan cities. Open Mon.-Fri. 8:30am-noon and 2:30-6:30pm.

Currency Exchange: It's easiest to change cash and traveler's checks in the ville nouvelle. Try the **BMCE,** 98 av. F.A.R. (tel. 52 03 52). Its **ATM** accepts Visa and MC. Exchange window open daily 10am-2pm and 4-8pm. **Hôtel Rif,** Zenkat Accra, around the corner from the tourist office, cashes traveler's checks, too.

Trains: Meknès has 2 stations, though only the **Meknès el-Amir Abdelhader Station,** rue d'Alger, 2 blocks from Av. Mohammed V, is of use to travelers; the misnamed **Meknès Main Station** is far from the center of town, and both stations have exactly the same connections. To: Fès (8 per day, 50min., 13dh); Tangier (4 per day, 59dh; 12:30pm train 45dh); Rabat (4 per day, 2½hr., 41dh); Casablanca (4 per day, 3¾hr., 61dh); Tetouan (7:55am, 82dh, includes bus connection).

Buses: CTM, 47 blvd. Mohammed V (tel. 52 25 85). Near av. Forces Armées Royales. To: Rabat (8 per day, 3hr.); Er-Rachidia (2 per day, 6hr.); Casablanca (8 per day, 4hr.); Tangier (3 per day, 5hr.); Fès (7 per day, 1½hr.). **Private companies** depart from a station just outside of Bab el-Khemis on av. Mellah outside the medina on the opposite side from the ville nouvelle. Prices and departures vary.

Taxis: Grand Taxis fester next to the private bus station and outside the Meknès el-Amir Abdelkader Station. To: Rabat (40dh); Moulay Idriss (10dh); Fès (15dh).

Swimming Pool: Municipal Pool, av. Moulay Ismail. Toward the medina, take a right after passing av. Forces Armées Royales, next to the river Oued Boufrekane. Open May-Sept. daily 10am-4pm. 5dh. Farther down is a cleaner, less crowded **private pool** with a lawn (15dh).

Late-Night Pharmacy: Red Cross Emergency Pharmacy, pl. Administrative (tel. 52 33 75). Side entrance to the Hôtel de Ville. Open 8:30am-8:30pm.

Hospital: Moulay Ismail, av. F.A.R. (tel. 52 28 05 or 52 28 06), near av. Moulay Youssef. **Mohammed V** (tel. 52 11 34).

Police: tel. 19.

Post Office: pl. Administrative. Open Mon.-Sat. 8:30am-12:15pm and 2:30-6:45pm. **Branch office** on rue Dar Smen, near the medina.

Telephones: Available at the post office daily 8:30am-9pm. Use the side entrance if the post office is closed. **Telephone Code:** (0)5.

ACCOMMODATIONS AND CAMPING

In the Medina

Budget hotels line **av. Roumazine** and **rue Dar Smen.** From the bus terminal below Bab Mansour, climb the hill to the pl. Bab el-Hedim which faces it. This road hooks left and becomes Dar Smen as it goes downhill. Turn right onto av. Roumazine when Dar Smen ends.

Maroc Hôtel, 7 av. Roumazine Derb Ben Brahim (tel. 53 07 05), near the merger of av. Moulay Ismail and av. Roumazine. Mellow owner presides over this collection of clean, small rooms around a leafy courtyard. Cold showers, Turkish toilets add to the atmosphere. Singles 40dh. Doubles 60dh.

Hôtel Nouveau, 65 rue Dar Smen (tel. 53 31 39). Its name belies its old rooms and beds. Still, it has sinks and hot showers (luxuries). Singles 30dh. Doubles 50dh.

Hôtel de Paris, 58 av. Roumazine. Basic, roomy, and pleasant. Public showers available next door (5dh). Singles 30dh. Doubles 50-60dh. Try haggling.

In the Ville Nouvelle

Staying in the ville nouvelle means greater comfort, higher prices, and easy access to banks, CTM buses, and trains. Most of the cheapest hotels lie around **av. Mohammed V** and **av. Allal ben Abdallah.**

Auberge de Jeunesse (HI), av. Okba Ben Nafii (tel. 52 46 98), near the stadium. Follow the arrows toward Hôtel Trans Atlantique off av. Hassam II going to the medina. A 20min. walk from Meknès Abdelkader Station (taxi 5dh), far from the city's hustle. Newly painted with clean mattresses. TV room around a pleasant courtyard. Members only. 25dh per person. Reception open 8-10am, noon-3pm, and 6-10pm; in summer 8-9am, noon-4pm, and 7pm-midnight. Tell the warden you're leaving before 10am or you'll be charged for an extra night. Cold showers free, hot showers 5dh (7-8pm only).

Hôtel Majestic, 19 av. Mohammed V (tel. 52 20 35). Wins the prize for most portraits of King Hassan II per square inch. Sizable rooms, modern, sanitary restrooms, and hot showers. All a stone's throw from the train station. Singles 83-172dh, depending on bathroom options. Doubles 137-205dh.

Hôtel Touring, 34 av. Allal Ben Abdallah (tel. 52 23 51). This hotel does admirably for its price, and the scarlet bedspreads and seedy furnishings lend some rooms the air of a bordello. Singles 68dh, with bath 100dh. Doubles: 94dh; 130dh.

Camping: Municipal Camping Agdal (tel. 53 89 14), on the ramparts of the medina. Outdoes any option in the hotel scene. Crowds gather in the beautiful, wooded park for the excellent amenities, including hot showers (5dh) and cooking facilities. The restaurant's 3-course *menu* goes for 45dh. Reception open 8am-1pm and 4-8pm. 17dh per adult, 12dh per child, 10dh per tent, and 17dh per car.

MOROCCO

FOOD

In the Medina

Vendors in the **pl. el-Hedim** hock *mergouz* sandwiches, freshly made potato chips, and corn on the cob roasted over open coals. Other inexpensive fare sizzles in the one-man *brochetteries* on **r. Dar Smen.** Few places have menus—dining is an adventure. The daily **vegetable market** sprouts beside Bab Mansour. The **Restaurant Economique,** 123 r. Dar Smen, serves Moroccan staples at perfectly adequate prices (couscous or *tajine* 30dh; open daily 7am-10pm).

In the Ville Nouvelle

Rotisserie Karam, 2 av. Channah (tel. 52 24 75), just off av. Hassan II. Higher standards than the norm. 20dh buys a decent *tajine.* Diversity has introduced the "sheese-burger *garni*" (24dh). Open daily 11am-11pm.

Pizzeria le Four, av. Zenkat Atlas (tel. 52 08 57), off av. Mohammed V, near the train station. Good pizza and other Italian dishes (50dh). Popular with tourists and locals. Wine and beer 35-45dh.

Restaurant Lorraine, 32 rue Moulay Abdelkader (tel. 52 17 10). From el-Amir Abdelkader Station, head left 2 blocks. Family-run restaurant serves simple, well-prepared dishes (*lapin garni, poulet* 25dh). Open daily 11am-4pm and 6-10pm.

Restaurant Marhaba, 23 av. Mohammed V (tel. 52 16 32). Just down the street from the Hôtel Majestic, towards the CTM station. Locals flock here for the spicy *harira* (3.6dh), while tourists are lured by a plaque outside proclaiming its blessing by a French budget traveler's guide. In any case, serious, cheap eating takes place here. *Brochettes* 18dh, *tajine* 30dh.

SIGHTS

The Imperial City

Attenuated by war, weather, the Great Earthquake of 1755, and looting by successors, the ramparts of the **Dar el-Kebira** (Imperial City) testify to Meknès's former pre-eminence as a capital city. Sultan Moulay Ismail used slaves to construct 25km of walls. Many died of exhaustion and were buried within the walls they were building. Strolling about the site with a pickax and whip in hand, the sultan supervised the city's construction, criticizing and decapitating at will. Plundering priceless materials from other parts of the kingdom (notably from Volubilis, which provided Roman marble, and from the Badi Palace in Marrakech), Moulay Ismail raised a radiant city for himself. Now only the walls, the prisons, and several large monuments remain. Ismail razed part of the *medina* to create the **place el-Hedim** (place of destruction) as a fitting approach to **Bab Mansour,** Morocco's greatest gateway.

Passing through the *bab,* shake off the guides and hug the wall to your right strolling through pl. Lalla Aonda. After the second gate, keep to the right and you'll see the emerald green roof of the **Salle des Ambassadeurs,** where Ismail conducted diplomatic meetings, at the far end of an empty lot. Ask the guard to unlock the door to the underground **Christian Dungeon,** a six square km behemoth which held 60,000 slaves, only a fraction of whom were Christian. If you think it looks bad now, bear in mind that the skylights were not there until the French came. (Open Sat.-Thurs. 8:30am-12:30pm and 2:30-6pm, Fri. 8:30-11:30am and 2:30-6pm. 10dh.)

As you leave the dungeon, walk through the two blue arches to the **mosque** and **tomb of Moulay Ismail** on the left, the only Moroccan shrine open to non-Muslims. Modest dress (i.e. clothes that cover your limbs) is appropriate. The rug-covered area around the tombs is off-limits, but you're welcome on the straw mats of the prayer area. Despite Ismail's bloody reputation, the tomb was carefully restored by Mohammed V, and pilgrims come here to venerate the sultan. Ismail didn't always get his way. When his marriage proposal to Louis XIV's daughter fell flat, the French king gave him the two grandfather clocks flanking the tomb as consolation (open Sat.-Thurs. 9am-noon and 3-6pm; free). The **Agdal Basin** was a private pool for Mou-

lay Ismail's wives (all 300) and a reservoir in case of siege. It now irrigates the city's gardens, and local kids swim in it. From Bab Mansour, follow the signs for the campground and continue down the road for another 100m past the campsite. **Café Agdal** serves cold drinks here (4dh).

The Medina

As you exit Bab Mansour, walk across busy pl. el-Hedime to the multi-colored mosaic on the outer wall of the 19th-century **Dar Jamai Palace,** the courtly mansion built by Moulay Hassan's powerful vizier. The palace houses the **Museum of Moroccan Art** (tel. 53 08 63), which flaunts one of the better collections in the country. Check out the carpet displays (especially if you're thinking of buying one) and the master bedroom, stuffed with embroidered divans and topped by a magnificent cupola (open Wed.-Mon. 9am-noon and 3-6pm; 10dh).

As you leave the palace, immediately turn left onto r. Sidi Amar to enter the *medina.* Follow the alley as it turns left, and then fork right to the green-glazed tile minaret of the **Mosquée Kebira** (Great Mosque). Directly across from the mosque is the breathtaking 14th-century **Madrasa Bou Inania,** an outstanding example of Merinid architecture from the Koranic school. Get a close-up view of the carved inscriptions surrounding the court from the top floor dormitories, and admire the mosque from the rooftop terrace. (Open Sat.-Thurs. 8:30am-12:30pm and 2:30-6pm, Fri. 8:30-11:30am and 2:30-6pm. 10dh.)

Meknès's **medina,** at the center of which is the mosque, is more pleasant, tranquil, and compact than those of other imperial cities. Start in front of the Dar Jamai. Facing the museum, take the alley to the left of the entrance. Push straight ahead to **Souk en Nejjarin,** a major east-west thoroughfare. Heading left here brings you to the **carpet market** (start low, bargain hard). Bear right on Souk en Nejjarin past the Medersa of Bou Inania, then right onto the alleyway hugging the eastern wall of the Great Mosque. Watch for a tiny opening on the left, marked by a set of crumbling, painted cedar doors. Here's the **Berber market.** Watch metalworkers hammer silver into tiny chests, cups, and plates. Beside the staircase, a doorway opens into the **Héri** (storehouse), a cool granary with enormous cisterns designed to withstand any siege (open daily 9am-noon and 3-6pm; 5dh). A long hike from northeast along the walls brings you to **Bab el-Khemis,** the west gateway to the city. Northeast of the Agdal reservoir, beside the campgrounds, are the **Agricultural Grounds,** perfect for a shady picnic.

■ Near Meknès

VOLUBILIS ويلبى

Thirty kilometers from Meknès lie the striking ruins of Volubilis, one of the most remote Roman outposts. The large complex is famed for magnificent 2nd- and 3rd-century **mosaics.** You may remember Volubilis if you made it through Martin Scorsese's *The Last Temptation of Christ.* A stroll around the ruins affirms the Roman Empire's astounding ability to export its culture. Look for the **Decaminus Maximus** road, lined by houses with the best mosaics. The **triumphal arch** on this road honors Emperor Caracalla (217AD), and the **capitol, basilica,** and **Roman baths** also have that Caesarean touch. The site closes at dusk (entrance fee 20dh). To get here, hire a **grand taxi** from their breeding grounds next to the private bus station (about 25dh per person).

MOULAY IDRISS مولاى ادريس

Five kilometers before Volubilis, the road from Meknès passes through Moulay Idriss, a pilgrimage site named after the man who installed Islam permanently into Moroccan religious life. Idriss was a third-generation descendant of Muhammad. Look for the only **cylindrical minaret** in Morocco, and try to find a spot with a good view of the **Mausoleum of Moulay Idriss.** Because the town is holy to Muslims,

dress very conservatively. Non-Muslims cannot visit the mosques or shrines or spend the night, but it's worth a look on the way to Volubilis.

■ Chefchaouèn (Chaouen) شفشاون

A whitewashed town on a hillside high in the Rif Mountains, Chaouen is no longer the hippie hangout or the escape from hustlers it once was, but it is as relaxed and as scenic as ever. It is a good place to spend your first couple days in Morocco coming from Ceuta or your last night before going to Spain.

ORIENTATION AND PRACTICAL INFORMATION

From the **bus station,** head up the steep hill, taking a right after several blocks onto the only big road you'll hit. Follow this to tree-filled, circular **place Mohammed V.** Cross the plaza and continue east on **Avenida Hassan II,** the ville nouvelle's main road. Hassan II terminates the small but busy Bab al-Ain, the main entrance into the medina. Passing through Bab al-Ain and following the main, twisting street will bring one to **place Uta el-Hammam,** the large plaza at the center of the medina.

Tourist Office: Both the ONMT and Syndicat d'Initiative seem to be non-existent here, but they are unnecessary anyway.

Currency Exchange: BMCE is on Hassan II. **Banque Populaire** is just outside Bab al-Ain. Both are open for change Mon.-Fri. 8:15am-2:15pm.

Buses: The bus station is downhill from town, but easy to find. Buses heading south fill up, so get tickets early. **CTM:** 7am bus to Casablanca (90dh) and on to Rabat (65dh); 1 and 3pm buses to Fès (46-52dh); 4 afternoon departures to Tetouan (16-18dh); and 1 bus to Tangier (3pm, 33dh). Private companies have buses to Tangier and Tetouan all day long, and about 5 buses to Fès every day.

Taxis: Gran Taxis are probably the easiest way to get to Tetouan (24dh). They leave a block downhill from pl. Mohammed V. Also to Ceuta 350dh.

Hospital: Hospital Mohammed V, a block west from pl. Mohammed V.

Police: Tel. 19.

Post Office: Av. Hassan II. Open Mon.-Fri. 8:30am-12:15pm and 2:30-6:30pm

Telephones: In and around the post office. Same hours as post office.

ACCOMMODATIONS AND FOOD

Chefchaouèn has a slew of colorful budget hotels, both in and out of the medina. In the medina, just head up from Bab el-Ain; hotels are clustered all along this street and around **pl. Uta el-Hammam.** Outside, just follow av. Hassan II towards Hotel Rif and beyond. Restaurants and cafes are ubiquitous, inescapable, and all-knowing. Find outdoor seating in **pl. Uta el-Hammam** and classier joints along **av. Hassan II.**

Hotel Abie Khanda (tel. 98 68 79), through Bab al-Ain on the right. Small bright pastel rooms, a nice terrace, and a pool table. 40dh per person.

Hotel Rif (tel. 98 69 82), just outside the medina walls. Follow av. Hassan II to the right around the medina; it's on your left after a few blocks. This classy hotel has clean comfy rooms, a large salon with satellite TV, and several terraces decorated in a style drawing from 16th-century Morocco and 70s America. Singles 50dh, with shower 70dh. Doubles: 80dh; 120dh.

Hotel Bab El-Ain (tel. 98 69 35), on the right just inside its namesake gate. Clean and bare. Good prices. Singles 26dh, with shower 51dh. Doubles: 62dh; 102dh.

Chez Aziz, just outside Bab el-Ain, serves tasty sandwiches at low prices. Shrimp 15dh, *vianda Hachee* 10dh.

Bar-Restaurant Om Rabih, on the right along av. Hassan II towards Hotel Rif (see above). Inexpensive Moroccan all-stars (*tajine* 25dh), seafood (shrimp 30dh), and wine and beer. Open Mon.-Sat. 11:30am-2:30pm and 6-10pm.

SIGHTS AND ENTERTAINMENT

Chefchaouèn's steep **medina** is one of Morocco's friendliest and brightest. Enter from av. Hassan II through the medieval **Bab el-Ain.** Narrow, cobbled passageways wind steeply up the mountain, converging on the hilltop at pl. Uta el-Hammam. The Kasbah across the square protects charming gardens and the remains of a palace built by Moulay Ismail. Also in the Kasbah, the **Musée de Chefchaouèn** has Rifian pottery and crafted knives. Don't miss the musical instruments, especially the mandolinesque *Aoud.* All labels are in Arabic (open Mon.-Sat. 9am-1pm and 3-6:30pm; 10dh). Chefchaouèn's **souk** operates Mondays and Thursdays in the square beside Hôtel Magou (down the stairs from av. Hassan II). Berbers descend from all parts of the Rif to trade with one another. Also in the new city, pl. Mohammed V sports a delightful garden with a fountain. The nameless **cafe** on the western side offers cold drinks, chess, and Parcheesi in the early evenings.

■ Fès فاس

The medina in Fès is one of the most overwhelming scenes in Morocco. Artisans bang out sheets of brass, donkeys strain under crates of Coca-Cola, *muezzins* wail, and children balance trays of dough on their heads. Your nose goes on sensory overload from the scent of brochettes on open grills combined with whiffs of hash, the sweet aroma of cedar shavings, and the stench of the open sewer (also known as the Oued Fès). Unlike the *medinas* of other Moroccan cities (most notably Tangier and Casablanca), tourists do not overwhelm Fès, although at times it can seem as if hustlers do. Since UNESCO designated Fès a World Heritage Site, the city's walls have been largely restored, and fresh plaster and cobblestones make the medina more fantastic. The banal ville nouvelle is nothing in comparison, but is a good refuge after a day's struggle in medina-land.

ORIENTATION AND PRACTICAL INFORMATION

Fès offers an extreme case of Morocco's cultural dichotomy: the French-constructed **ville nouvelle** is broad, orderly, and far from the huge, knotty **medina.** To compound confusion, the old city is divided into two walled-off sections: **Fès el-Bali** and **Fès el-Jdid** (old and new Fès). Two key landmarks are the **place des Alaouites** in el-Jdid (next to the Royal Palace) and **Bab Boujeloud,** the entrance to el-Bali and the private **bus station.** Inside **Fès el-Bali,** the main routes are **rue Talâa Kebira** and **rue Tâlaa Seghira.** To reach **Talâa Kebira,** turn left after passing under Bab Boujeloud into a small plaza, then turn right to reach the center of Fès el-Bali; the road is filled with butchers and grocers. It's a half-hour downhill walk to the **Kairaouine Mosque.** Use the Talâa Kebira to keep your bearings. Fès el-Bali is confusing, but you'll always find *some* way out if you keep walking uphill on steadily wider streets. **Avenue des Français,** just outside Bab Boujeloud, leads to Bab Dekkaken (one entrance to Fès el-Jdid). A stroll down the two main streets, **Grande rue de Fès Jdid** and **rue des Merínides,** leads to place des Alaouites, linked to the ville nouvelle by **avenue Moulay Youssef.** This avenue leads to **place de la Resistance;** a right on av. Sports leads to the **train station. Avenue Hassan II** is the main thoroughfare; a left on av. Mohammed V (by the PTT) leads to **place Mohammed V, Syndicat d'Initiative,** and the **CTM bus station.** Bus #3 at the train station and a different bus #3 at the Syndicat d'Initiative trek to the far end of el-Bali, **Bab Ftouh,** near the **Andalous Quarter.** Bus #2 roars to pl. Alouites. Reach Bab Boujeloud from the ville nouvelle by *petit taxi* (12dh) or bus #11 or 9 (1.90dh) from next to the Syndicat d'Initiative.

Tourist Office: ONMT, pl. Résistance (tel. 62 34 60), at av. Hassan II, in an office building across from the fountain. English-speaking staff provides poorly marked maps and decent brochures. Official guides 120dh per ½day, 150dh per day. Open Mon.-Fri. 8:30am-noon and 2:30-6:30pm; Ramadan Mon.-Fri. 9am-3pm. **Syndicat d'Initiative,** pl. Mohammed V (tel. 62 47 69), on the way to the CTM bus sta-

MOROCCO

tion from av. Hassan II, on av. Mohammed V. Helpful *Fassi* (citizens of Fès) answer almost any question. Same meager maps put out by the Moroccan National Tourism Office. Open Mon.-Fri. 8:30am-noon and 2:30-6:30pm, Sat. 8:30am-noon.

Currency Exchange: BMCE, pl. Mohammed V, across from the Syndicat d'Initiative, to the right of the main bank entrance. Handles Visa/MC transactions, traveler's checks, and ATMs. Open Mon.-Fri. 8:15-11:30am and 2:15-4pm. Several banks lurk just outside the Bab Boujeloud to exchange. Also try **Hôtel Les Marinides** (tel. 64 52 25) in the Borj Nord.

Flights: Aérodrome de Fès-Saïs (tel. 62 47 12 or 62 43 00), 12km out of town along the road to Immouzzèr. Bus #16 leaves from pl. Mohammed V (3dh). Taxis (7dh per person) also run there. **Royal Air Maroc** (tel. 62 04 56 or 62 04 57), av. Hassan II, flies daily to Casablanca.

Trains: av. Almohades (tel. 62 50 01), at r. Chenguit. Second-class trains are somewhat comfier than buses, but cost a few *dirhams* extra. To: Casablanca (8 per day, 5hr., 56dh); Rabat (8 per day, 3½hr., 42dh); Meknès (8 per day, 1hr., 13dh); Tangier (4 per day, 5½hr., 72dh); Marrakech (6 per day, 9hr., 130dh).

Buses: CTM (tel. 73 29 84). Stops on blvd. Mohammed V, away from the medina a few blocks past pl. Mohammed V. To: Rabat (8 per day, 3hr., 55dh); Casablanca (8 per day, 5hr., 80dh); Marrakech (2 per day, 8hr., 130dh); Meknès (10 per day, 1hr., 18dh); Tangier (2 per day, 6hr., 85dh); Chefchaouèn (2 per day, 4hr., 4dh). The **private station** (at which there is also a CTM window) is a 5min. walk from the Bab Boujeloud, on the rue Ceinture Nord past the cemetery.

Public Transportation: Numerous buses (1.90dh; fares increase 20% after 8:30pm, mid-Sept. to June after 8pm). Pl. Mohammed V and pl. Résistance are the major hubs. Major runs include: Bus #9 and 11 beside the Syndicat d'Initiative to Bab Boujeloud; #3 from the train station and pl. Mohammed V to Bab Ftouh; #4 from the pl. Résistance to Bab Smarine.

Taxis: Major stands at the post office, the Syndicat d'Initiative, Bab Boujeloud, and Bab Guissa. Fares increase 50% after 8:30pm, Sept. 16-June after 8pm. Staff at the Syndicat d'Initiative will get you on the correct **grand taxi** free of charge.

Car Rental: Avis, 50 blvd. Chefchaouni (tel. 62 67 46). **Hertz,** 1 Kissauiat de la Foire (tel. 62 28 12), blvd. Lalla Mergeme. Renault IV is 300dh per day.

Luggage Storage: At the train station, av. Almohades in the ville nouvelle. 2.50dh per bag per day. Open 24hr.

Swimming Pool: Municipal Pool, av. Sports, next to the stadium and near the train station in the ville nouvelle. Tends to be crowded. Open daily July-Sept. 15 8:30-11:30am and 2:30-5:30pm. 5dh.

English Bookstore: 68 av. Hassan II (tel. 62 08 42), near pl. Résistance. All genres: novels, poetry, plays, guidebooks, and phrase books. English-speaking staff. Open Mon.-Fri. 9am-12:30pm and 3-7pm. For newspapers and magazines in English, try the newsstand on rue Mohammed V closest to the post office, or the store 1 block away from rue Mohammed V, behind the central market.

Late-Night Pharmacy: Municipalité de Fès, blvd. Moulay Youssef (tel. 233 80), 5min. uphill from the royal palace, off pl. Résistance. Open daily 8pm-8am.

Police: tel. 19.

Post Office: At the corner of av. Hassan II and blvd. Mohammed V in the ville nouvelle. Open for stamps and Poste Restante Mon.-Fri. 8am-3pm; Sept. 16-June Mon.-Fri. 8:30am-6:45pm; for **telegrams** Mon.-Fri. 8:30am-9pm. **Branch offices** at pl. d'Atlas and in the medina at pl. Batha. Same hours.

Telephones: In the **main post office.** Enter from blvd. Mohammed V, to the right of the main entrance. Open 8:30am-9pm. The **branch office** in the medina also has international phones. Same hours. *Téléboutiques* cluster in the ville nouvelle. **Telephone Code:** (0)5.

ACCOMMODATIONS AND CAMPING

In the Ville Nouvelle

The new city is a long haul from the medina but provides relative respite from hustlers. Rooms here are more comfortable (and pricey) than those in the medina, and

Fès

Borj Nord, 8
Boujeloud Gardens, 6
CTM Bus Station, 1
Currency Exchange, 3
Dar Batha Museum, 7
Karaouyine Mosque, 9
Main Train Station, 4
Royal Palace, 5
Syndicat d'Initiative, 2

solid gray lines represent city walls

MOROCCO

Bab Ftouh

Bab Giussa

Route Ceinture Nord

Avenue des Merinides

Blvd Ahmed ben Mohammed el Alaoui

FES EL BALI

Rue Talaa Kebira

Rue Talaa Seghira

Bab Boujeloud

Liberté

Ave. de la

Route Principale No. 1

Bab Riafa

Grande Rue de Fes Jdid

Rue bou Ksissat

FES EL JDID

PLACE DES ALAOUITES

AGUEDAL

Blvd. Moulay Youssef

Boulevard des Saadiens

Avenue de l'Imarate Arabe

Avenue Youssef ben Tachfine

Boulevard

Avenue des Sports

Rue des Etats Unis

PLACE DE LA RÉSISTANCE

Rue Moussa Ibn Noussair

Ave. Mohammed el Korbi

Avenue Hassan II

Boul Abdallah Cinefria ouni

Ave. Mohammed es Slaoul

PLACE MOHAMMED V

Blvd. Mohammed V

Avenue Youssef ben Ghaupie

fill entirely in August. The cheapest ville nouvelle lodgings clump conveniently on or just off the west side of **blvd. Mohammed V,** between av. Mohammed es-Slaoui near the bus station and av. Hassan II near the post office.

Auberge de Jeunesse (HI), 18 rue Abdeslam Serghini (tel. 62 40 85). From pl. Résistance coming from the medina, bear left onto blvd. Abdallah Chefchaouni, walk 4 blocks, turn left, and look for the sign. Friendly English-speaking warden Abdul dispenses advice on dealing with *Fassi* guides. Don't step on Abdul's turtles. The dorms are outdoorsy—a sleep sack is essential. A good place to bond with fellow travelers. Cold showers. Reception open 8-10am, noon-3pm, and 6-10pm. Members only (wink wink, nudge nudge). 25dh per person.

Hôtel Central, 50 rue Brahim Roudant (tel. 62 23 33), on the way from the Syndicat d'Initiative (pl. Mohammed) to the CTM bus station on the right, just off blvd. Mohammed V. Springy beds and surplus chairs in unadorned rooms. Hot water in room sinks. Singles 59dh, with shower 87dh. Doubles: 83dh; 114dh.

Hôtel CTM, rue Ksarelkbir (tel. 62 28 11), next door to the CTM station. Get intimate with the buses' roar. Dark hallways belie wide-open rooms. Shabby Scandinavian-style furniture, but a decent deal. Singles 53dh, with shower 76dh. Doubles: 73dh; 96dh. Triples: 118dh; 141dh.

Hôtel Amor, 31 rue Arabie Saoudite (62 27 24). From PTT, head down av. Hassan II away from the medina and take a left onto rue Arabie Saoudite (sign for hotel is visible). The Howard Johnson's of Fès. Faux-Almorauid decor is a bit lurid, but comfortable. Wake-up calls. All rooms with bath. Singles 128dh. Doubles 160dh.

In the Medina

Step right up to **Bab Boujeloud** for budget rooms—they're noisier and dirtier than in the ville nouvelle, and hustlers may seem to track the scent of your luggage, but the hotels are economical and well located.

Hôtel Cascade, 26 Serrajine Boujloud (tel. 63 84 42), just inside Bab Boujeloud and to the right. Spartan, sanitary rooms are spacious for the medina. The terrace and some rooms have a bird's-eye view of the chaos below. Squat toilets. 35dh per person. Haggling acceptable.

Hôtel Lamrani, Talâa Seghira (tel. 36 44 11). Enter Bab Boujeloud; 1st right, then a left and through the arch. Unusually clean, with in-room sinks. Benevolent manager says warm showers will be added when there is enough money. A *hammam* next door is available for a few *dirhams*. 30dh per person.

Hôtel du Jardin Public, 153 Kasbah Boujeloud (tel. 63 30 86), a small alley across from the Bab Boujeloud bus station. Relatively clean rooms, some with views. Cold showers (a flight down from most rooms) and toilets. Singles 35dh. Doubles 55dh.

FOOD

Ville Nouvelle

Cheap food huts skulk on the little streets to either side of **blvd. Mohammed V.** Also try **rue Kaid Ahmed,** on the left a few blocks down blvd. Mohammed V from the main post office. **Boulangerie Pâtisserie Epi D'or,** 81 blvd. Mohammed V, serves a marvelous breakfast. The busy, aromatic **municipal market** is where city households stock up on fresh fruit, vegetables, fish, meat, and spices; it's just off blvd. Mohammed V, two blocks up from pl. Mohammed V.

Rotisserie La Rotonde, rue Nador (tel. 62 05 89). One block up from Hôtel Central (coming from av. Mohammed V). Chicken that puts Colonel Sanders to shame. Locals pounce on succulent ¼-pound fowls, sauce, bread, and rice (15dh). Order from and pay the white-coated workers only. Open daily 9am-9pm.

Café-Restaurant Mauritania, av. Hassan II, 1 block from pl. Resistance, away from the medina on the right. 4-course *menu* (39dh) and *tajine* (28dh). A good place to go with a large group. Open daily from 11am.

The Medina

Food stalls line **Talâa Kebira** and **Talâa Seghira,** near the Bab Boujeloud entrance to Fès el-Bali. A vegetarian feast of *harira*, roasted peppers and eggplant, potato fritters, and bread here will only set you back 10dh at the **stalls** inside. Deeper into the medina, go left from Talâa Kebira Medersa el-Attarin (see **Sights,** p. 647)) and head towards **pl. Achabine** for some of the cheapest eateries in Morocco.

Restaurant des Jeunes, 16 rue Serrajine (tel. 63 49 75), on the right as you enter the *bab. Tajine* 25dh. Other entrees 20-25dh. The *pastilla* isn't made with pigeon, but the chicken could fool most (30dh). Open daily 6am-midnight.

Restaurant Bouayad, 26 rue Serrajine (tel. 63 62 78), next door to Restaurant des Jeunes. Locals loiter around the clock watching satellite TV. Slightly pricey *menú* for 40dh; dive into the *tajine* with almonds. Open 24hr.

SIGHTS: FÈS EL-BALI

Well over 900 streets make Fès's medina the most difficult to navigate in Morocco. There are three ways to approach it. One is simple and expensive: hire a guide. **Official guides** are at the ONMT and Syndicat d'Initiative. (Ask for a local guide; they know Fès better and are cheaper. Prices for local guides are 120dh per half-day or 150dh for a full day and a meal.) **Unofficial guides** are not recommended; they're much cheaper, but may insist on taking you to shops and are not as well-informed. If you do hire one, nail down an itinerary beforehand and establish your aversion to shopping. The second option is to follow the route below, which hits the major "sights." The final option is simply to get lost in the magnificent atmosphere. When it's time to tear yourself away, ask merchants or women how to get to **Talâa Kebira** and follow it back uphill.

To see the medina at its liveliest, go in the morning or after 5pm. Don't acknowledge hustlers or the would-be guides and small children at the gates (see **Hustlers and Guides,** p. 622). To reach the medina from the ville nouvelle, take a *petit taxi* to Bab Boujeloud and work your way to the Kairaouine Mosque (see **Orientation,** above); or take bus #9 or 11 from the stop next to the **Syndicat d'Initiative** to Bab Boujeloud and begin your exploration.

The Dar Batha

To reach the Dar Batha, enter Bab Boujeloud and take the first right (past the Kissarine Serrajine) and bear right before the cinema. This should take you to **place de l'Istiqlal** and the museum. A 19th-century palace conceals a well-kept and beautiful museum, the **Dar Batha.** The spacious Moorish mansion headquartered Sultan Hassan I and his playboy son Moulay Abd el-Aziz during the final years of decadence before the French occupation. The museum, host to Moroccan music concerts in September, chronicles Fès's artistic and intellectual history. The keynote is the display of **ceramics** with the signature "Fès blue," derived from cobalt, standing out on a white enamel background (museum open Wed.-Mon. 9am-noon and 3-6pm; 10dh).

The Talâa Al Kebira

Fès el-Bali's main street and essential reference point, the Talâa Al Kebira (a.k.a. the Grand Talâa) heads downhill from Bab Boujeloud to the Kairaouine Mosque and into the medina's heart. Upon passing through Bab Boujeloud, make a quick left and a right to get onto the thoroughfare.

A short way down on the right reposes the old Qur'anic school **Medersa Bou Inania,** a masterpiece of carved cedar and stucco—not bad for a college dorm. The *medersa* was built in the 14th century by Merinid Sultan Abou Inan at a fantastic cost. The sultan simply threw all accounts into the river, claiming that one shouldn't put a price tag on beauty. A tiny canal separates the school from an adjoining mosque (open Sat.-Thurs. 9am-6pm, Fri. 8:30-10am and 1:30-6pm; 10dh). Plunging ahead, sniff the (almost) cured products from the **sheepskin fondouk,** hear the cries

of *"Batica!"* (watch out) from the drivers of heavily-laden donkeys, and ooh and aah at the ancient detail of the turquoise **Mosque Sidi Ahmed Tijani** minaret. From here, the Talâa Kebira bows slightly to the right and becomes **rue ech Cherabliyyan.** Up ahead, animal skins convalesce in the **leather souk.** From the *souk,* competent orienteers can take a right and then a left to the **place Nejarine,** a small triangular plaza headlined by its dazzling tiled fountain. Just below, an arched doorway leads into the **Nejarine Fondouk,** a fabulous 18th-century shopping area of delicate *mashrabiyya* and handsome balconies. Across the way, camera-shy woodsmiths chisel in the lively **carpenters' fondouk.**

Around the Kairaouine Mosque

Once back on rue ech Cherabliyyan, continue through the portal into the **Souk el-Attarin** (the spice souk). When spices were an expensive and prestigious commodity, its vendors got the privileged spot near the mosque. Be sure to visit the **Medersa el-Attarin,** another spectacular vestige of the Merinid dynasty. The arches and stucco give the structure a weightless feeling (open daily 9am-noon and 2-5:30pm; 10dh).

A corner of the enormous **Kairaouine Mosque** protrudes across from the *medersa.* Every Friday, 2000 people flock here to pray—though the mosque can hold up to 20,000 men and 2000 women (who worship behind the men). Founded in 859, the mosque is one of the oldest universities in the world. It trained students in logic, math, rhetoric, and the Qur'an while Europe stumbled through the Dark Ages. You can thank or curse the mosque for educating Pope Sylvester II, who later introduced algebra and the modern number system to Europe. Non-Muslims can gawk and take pictures through the portals but may not enter. Halfway around the mosque, the carpet shop/restaurant/tea salon **Palais de Fès** has a great view of the building from its terrace, almost (if not quite) worth the 10dh pot of tea sold there.

Keeping the mosque on your right (going south), you'll eventually come to the **place Seffarine,** famous for deafening travelers with vivid cauldron-pounding. Upon entering, several routes become apparent. To reach the **tanneries,** turn sharply left and continue to bear left (follow the worn, six-sided cobblestones). Once the smell becomes intense, head right down a microscopic alley (a tannery *"guardien"* has probably grabbed you by now; 10dh is the basic tour fee). Skins are soaked in green liquid, rinsed in a washing machine/cement mixer hybrid, dunked in diluted pigeon excrement or waterlogged wheat husks (for suppleness), and saturated in dye.

Andalous Quarter

The Andalous Quarter is across the Oued Fès (river) from the heart of Fès el-Bali. Many of the Moors who fled from Muslim Spain (Andalucía) to Morocco during the 15th-century Reconquista settled around the grand Almohad house of worship in Fès, the **Andalous Mosque.** Its main attraction is the grandiose 13th-century doorway. To find the mosque, head northwest from Bab Ftouh on the east end of the medina, and take the first major left. From Fès el-Bali, cross the river at Port Bein el-Moudoun near the tanneries and head straight down rue Seffrah. The portal on the left side of the mosque offers the best view of the interior.

Zaouia Moulay Idriss II and Environs

Back in pl. Seffarine, continue along the Kairaouine Mosque's walls, almost back to Souk el-Attarin. *Kissaria,* covered markets selling expensive cloths and *babouches* (slippers), lie to the left. Head straight in and you'll emerge on the other side by the **Zaouia of Moulay Idriss II.** A *zaouia* is a sanctum surrounding the tomb of a *marabout,* an Islamic saint. Pilgrims pray here, light candles, and touch the saint's tomb through a slot in a brass star. This place is so holy that, until recently, non-Muslims were not even allowed in the general vicinity. Wooden barriers on the streets leading to the *zaouia* were built to keep out donkeys delineate the sacred zone. For non-Muslims, sad rejection from the shrine is sweetened by the *nougat* sold around the building, a *Fassi* specialty (5dh will buy enough for a troop of Girl Scouts).

Up a steep side street from the women's entrance to the *zaouia,* a plaque commemorates the **Maristan Sidi Frej,** a teaching hospital and lunatic asylum between 1286 and 1944. Eccentrics of another sort fill the stalls here today, along with cheap pottery and cosmetics. The **henna souk** specializes in red dye, traditionally the only make-up permitted for unmarried Moroccan women.

SIGHTS: FÈS EL-JDID

Hit Fès el-Jdid after you've had enough of Fès el-Bali; the latter is more interesting. Christians, Jews, and Muslims once co-existed in Fès el-Jdid (New Fès), built by the Merinids in the 13th century. The ancient neighborhood still has narrow side streets, covered *souks,* and ornamental *mashrabiyya* balconies.

To the north, the arrow-straight **grande rue de Fès el-Jdid** traverses the area. To the south, the **grande rue des Merinides** cuts through the adjacent *mellah* (Jewish quarter). **Bab Semmarin** (often labeled **Bab Smarine** on maps), a chunky 20th-century gate, squats between the two areas. To reach this *bab,* take bus #4 from the pl. de la Resistance, or, better yet, walk to it from the ville nouvelle. To walk from the ville nouvelle to the *mellah* (15min.), take av. Hassan II north past the PTT, veer left at the fork two blocks later onto blvd. Moulay Hassan, and head straight for the grand pl. des Alaouites, where the *mellah* and grande rue des Merinides begin. To get here from Fès el-Bali, take bus #9, which returns by way of Bab Semmarin.

King Hassan II's sprawling modern palace, the **Dar el-Makhzen** (off limits to you, peasant!), borders the **place des Alaouites.** Diagonally off the *place,* **grande rue des Merinides** runs up to Bab Semmarin on the other end of the *mellah.* Off this boulevard, the meter-wide side streets open into miniature underground tailors' shops, half-timbered houses, and covert alleyways. The **jewelers' souk** glitters at the top of grande rue des Merinides. Cackling chickens, salty fish, dried okra, and shiny eggplants vie for attention in the animated covered **market,** inside Bab Semmarin at the entrance to Fès el-Jdid proper. Toward the top of the avenue, the *souks* are covered, shading rainbows of *kaftans* and gold-stitched *babouches.*

Bear left at the end of rue des Merinides into the **Petit Méchouar;** on the left is **Bab Dekaken,** the back entrance to the Dar el-Makhzen. Through **Bab es-Seba,** an imperial gate opens onto the **Grand Méchouar,** a roomy plaza lined with streetlamps. From here it's an easy walk to Bab Boujeloud—turn through the opening to the right of **Bab es-Seba,** continue straight for ¼km, veer to the right, and pass through a large arch at the end of road. The entrance to the refreshing **Boujeloud Gardens,** a fragrant refuge from the midday sun, is on the right (closed Mon.).

SIGHTS: OUTSIDE THE MEDINA WALLS

Borj Nord and Borj Sud, the hills surrounding the medina, are a simple bus or *petit taxi* drive away. If driving, bear east from blvd. Moulay Hassan in the ville nouvelle toward Taza and Oujda; the highway winds along the city fortifications. After 4km, turn right toward **Borj Sud,** a 16th-century hilltop fortress guarding the southern end of Fès el-Bali. The castle, built by Christian slaves, is largely in ruins but nevertheless commands an excellent view of the city.

The main highway continues east to **Bab Ftouh,** which arches in a **medieval cemetery.** Farther east, close to the ramparts, is **Bab Khoukha.** From here the walls curve wildly to **Bab Sidi Boujida.** A kink in the highway then leads to the **Jamai Palace,** an exquisite 19th-century dream house built by Sultan Moulay Hassan's powerful vizier. Now a luxury hotel, the palace tarries within **Bab Guissa,** where a **pigeon and parakeet market** squawks every Friday morning.

To continue the circuit, keep to the outer road and follow the signs for Hôtel des Merinides, which overlooks the ever-decaying ruins of the **Merinid Tombs.** Tourist climb the hillside (burrows at the base were **lepers' quarters** in medieval times) in droves and guides hover in similar numbers. The **spectacular view** of Fès el-Bali supposedly justifies its popularity. The panorama is most impressive in the half-light of dawn or dusk. During calls to prayer, when over a hundred *muezzin* simulta-

neously summon the faithful, the experience is mystical. **Borj Nord,** a short walk down from Hôtel des Merinides, is the crumbling fortress presiding over the north of the city. It houses the **Museum of Arms** and rifles galore. The tour lasts an hour (open Wed.-Mon. 9am-noon and 3-6pm; 10dh).

Ville Nouvelle

The chief attraction in the ville nouvelle is the superb **Ensemble Artisanal** on blvd. Allah ben Abdallah. Walk down av. Hassan II away from the medina; at the intersection with the Sheraton, it becomes blvd. Allah ben Abdallah. The Ensemble is only in Arabic, but is marked by its blue tiles and Moroccan flag. Sumptuous Arab carpets, Berber blankets, and other handicrafts fill the courtyard garden where you can watch the artisans at work. In the weaving rooms, scads of girls poke, thread, knot, snip, and pack spools of many-hued wool to create lavish (and expensive) works of art (open daily 8:30am-6:30pm). Or follow local crowds into the busy, aromatic **municipal market,** just off blvd. Mohammed V.

THE ATLANTIC COAST

In a matter of weeks, tourists transform the subdued coastal towns along Morocco's Atlantic coast into busy beach towns full of classy European tourists. Morocco's only extensive railway line connects these towns, whose old fortified medinas served as defensive ports in the 16th and 17th centuries. Rabat, Morocco's most westernized city, and Casablanca, its commercial center, preside over the Atlantic shoreline.+

■ Asilah أصيلا

Asilah's golden shores, quiet streets, and brilliant white medina offer respite from the tensions of Tangier. An overflow of tour guides follow the tour buses on the 46km ride from Tangier, but fortunately unofficial guides are easily dismissed. Eager merchants that peddle leather goods and carpets are neither persistent nor hostile. Although Asilah is not the unspoiled resort it once was—it now teems with tourists during July and August—it remains a relatively tranquil base for exploring the beaches and ruins along Morocco's Atlantic coast.

ORIENTATION AND PRACTICAL INFORMATION

The main street heading into town is **boulevard Mohammed V,** which ends at the town's center, **place Mohammed V,** a traffic circle. The road to the right leads to a fork in front of the medina. Bear right at the fork onto **rue Zallakah,** which leads to the port. To the left is **avenue Hassan II,** mirroring the walls of the medina.

Tourist Office: Nope. (That's okay, you won't need a map.)

Currency Exchange: Banks surround the pl. Mohammed V. Among them is **BMCE,** open Mon.-Thurs. 8:15-11:30am and 2:15-4:30pm; Fri. 8:15-11:15am and 2:45-4:45pm.

Trains: The station (tel. 41 73 27) is a 20min. walk from town on the Asilah-Tangier highway, near a strip of campgrounds. To get to town, follow the road by the beach, keeping the sea to your right. A taxi from town costs about 10dh. A minibus connects the station to town; it leaves from the front of the station just after the train arrives (10dh; you may have to bargain). To: Tangier (4 per day, 1hr., 2nd class 13dh), Casablanca, Rabat, and Marrakech (4 per day). Buses are more convenient.

Buses: CTM and **private companies** vend tickets together in the same stall off av. Prince Heritier Sidi Mohammed. Take the 1st right leaving pl. Mohammed V; station is in the lot on the left. To: Tangier (every 30min. starting at 12:30pm, 10dh); Casablanca (14 per day, 4½-5½hr., 60dh); Fès (4 per day, 3½hr., 52dh); Larache

(14 per day, 45min., 10dh); Rabat (14 per day, 4hr., 43dh). Many buses arrive fully occupied, so get to the station early during the summer when the lot is crowded.

Taxis: pl. Mohammed V, across from the bus station. *Grands taxis* only. To Tangier about 12dh. To train station 10dh.

Pharmacy: Pharmacie Loukili, av. Prince Heritier Sidi Mohammed (tel. 91 72 78), one block from pl. Mohammed V and across from the police. Open Mon.-Fri. 9am-1pm and 4-9pm.

Police: The police have temporarily moved to the medina. The office is difficult to locate, but police officers can almost always be found on the pl. Mohammed V or at the fork in front of the medina.

Post Office: (tel. 41 72 00). Walking on blvd. Mohammed V, turn right on the pl. Natzon Unis, keeping the park on your right. Post office is 20m up on the left. Open Mon.-Fri. 8am-noon and 2:30-6:30pm.

Telephone Code: (0)9.

ACCOMMODATIONS AND CAMPING

People may offer a room in a private home for 30dh, promising homemade meals for a little extra. Some of these offers may be legit, but the risk is considerable: you could end up in an uncomfortable or even dangerous situation. Besides, reasonably priced hotels (though not cheap by Moroccan standards) lie within walking distance of the beach and are clustered mostly around pl. Mohammed V and the east end of av. Hassan II. Asilah bursts with campgrounds, some of which rent small, inexpensive **bungalows.** Most are near or on the shore north of town, toward the train station.

Hôtel Marhaba, 9 rue Zallakah (tel. 91 71 44), on the right as you approach the medina from pl. Mohammed V. This popular *hôtel* may fill up during the summer. Prime location, low rates, adequate rooms, and free showers. Singles 60dh. Doubles 80dh.

Hôtel Belle Vue, rue Hassan Ben Tabit (tel. 91 77 47; fax 94 58 69). From the beginning of Hassan II, take a left on av. Imam Asili, then a right. Friendly, scholarly management and, indeed, there is a pretty view from the two-tiered terrace. Nice rooms with hot showers, although the prices are loftier than the panorama and there are no singles. Doubles 200dh; Sept.-June 130-150dh.

Hôtel Nazar, av. Mohammed V, 20m from the pl. Mohammed V, entering av. Mohammed V next to BCME. Small dark rooms surround a courtyard filled with grapevines. 30dh per person, though you may have to bargain.

Camping Echrigui (tel. 91 71 82), 700m from the train station toward town, where the new port finally ends, next to the similar **Camping es Sala**. Echrigui's office has a lounge with billiards, and a restaurant opens during the summer. Bring plenty of insect repellent. 10dh per person, 10dh per tent and per car. Bungalows with straw roof 90dh. Hot showers 5dh.

FOOD

Restaurants facing the ramparts along av. Hassan II dish out good meal meals for around 35dh. Down the street is the town **market,** good for produce. Seafood is the best choice at most restaurants.

Restaurant Marhaba, 33 av. Hassan II. Outdoor dining under towering ramparts. Multilingual menu. Try the swordfish or calamari (each 30dh).

La Al Kasabah, rue Zallakah (tel. 91 70 12), towards the ocean past Hôtel Marhaba. Reputedly the best restaurant in town, serving seafood and pasta. A terrace overlooks the street and port. The paella (40dh) is much touted but the grilled sardines are better and cheaper (22dh). Wine served. Service charge 10%. Open daily 8:30am-3:30pm and 6:30pm-2am.

Restaurant Najoum, rue Zallakah (tel. 91 74 59), below the Hôtel Marhaba. Grilled swordfish (40dh), plus *brochettes* (15dh) and *harira* (3dh). Open daily 7am-11pm.

MOROCCO

SIGHTS

Asilah has two attractions: its nearby **beaches** and a shining **medina**. Beaches north of town are smooth, sprawling delights, and the crowds are generally congenial. Still, don't bring a passport or valuables along—thefts occur. Lock your valuables in your hotel safe. Men tend to leer at and harass women who swim, but the scene mellows out northwards (at least a 15min.). The enclosed cove **Paradise Beach** is 5km away from town (1hr. walk). The medina, bounded by heavily fortified stone walls, is clean and perpetually smells of new paint (according to cynics, the Minister of Culture lives nearby and likes a tidy medina). On the coastal side across from **Bab Hamar** is the **Palais de Raissouli,** built by a bandit whose kidnapping of a Greek American prompted some big stick-waving by Teddy Roosevelt (to prevent conflict, the Sultan himself paid the enormous ransom). Bang on the door and ask the *guardien* for a peek, but be mindful that the story is more interesting than the structure. You can walk around the medina at the seafront, hopping along from rock to rock, and climb the steps to the **Krikia,** a Portuguese-built lookout with a majestic view. Children plunge the 40 feet from the Krikia into the ocean.

Apart from the regular town market, a Sunday morning Berber market at **souk el-Had el-Gharbia** opens 9km inland from Asilah. Berbers from as far away as the Rif Mountains converge on the tiny village to peddle their wares. Unfortunately, there's no public transportation to the market. In August, artists from all over the world flock to Asilah for the world-class **International Festival**. Scanty vestiges of the once-sizable Roman metropolis **Admercuri** lie 2km farther inland. Ask local children to point the way. Painters cover the white walls with murals, and jazz and folk musicians splash sound along the beach.

■ Larache

In the days of yore, peace-seekers fled bustling Tangier for Asilah, but faux guides eventually caught on and hustled down south. When Asilah is taken over by tourists during the summer, relief is spelled "Larache." This scruffy, relaxing nook on the Atlantic has no touristy veneer and is all the more rewarding for it. Spanish colonization has left Larache with an abundance of hotels and a taste for seafood. Furthermore, its whitewashed medina is manageable, a beach is nearby, and the Roman ruins of Lixus are worth a look.

Orientation and Practical Information Buses arrive eight blocks from **place de la Libération** (ex-Plaza de España), the center of activity. From the station, take the exit at the opposite end from the ticket windows, cross the traffic circle, and head straight down this road (8min.). Branching off pl. Libération is the main artery, **boulevard Mohammed V**. Also off pl. Libération, **Bab al-hemis** (also called Bab Medina) leads to the **medina** and the **Zoko de la Alcaiceria** (a.k.a. Zoko Chico), its source. Larache's **beach** is located to the north, across the Loukkos estuary, and is accessible by bus (2.50dh) or boat (2dh).

Larache has **no tourist office,** but the town is easily navigated. International **telephones** are located in and around the **post office,** on blvd. Mohammed V heading away from pl. Libértation. (Post office open Mon.-Fri. 8:30am-noon and 2:30-6:30pm; phones available for additional hours Sat. 8:30am-noon and 2:30-6:30pm.) **Banks** across the street from the post office exchange money, but there are **no ATMs** in town. To reach the **bus station,** leave pl. Libération going right onto av. Mohammed ben Abdallah; continue past Pension Salama, then take the first left. Go straight. **CTM** service to: Asilah (14 per day, 45min., 10dh); Casablanca (4 per day, 5hr., 74dh); Rabat (5 per day, 4hr., 50dh); Tangier (3 per day, 1½hr., 29dh). **Private buses** leave from the same station and send scads of often cramped buses to the same locations at cheaper prices. **Taxis** park outside the station. **Local buses** depart Casbah de la Cigone off av. Mohammed V, traveling to Lixus (buses #4 and 5) and the beaches (#4). The **police** answer at tel.19. Larache's **telephone code** is (0)9.

Accommodations and Food Basic hotels lurk in the medina, but a myriad of excellent budget options hover near **av. Mohammed ben Abdallah** and off **pl. Libération. Hotel Malaga** (tel. 91 18 68), is centrally located, off av. Hassan II. From pl. Libération, walk up the street to the right of the main thoroughfare blvd. Moham-med V. It's one block up on the left. Singles are small, doubles are comfy. (Singles 40dh. Doubles 90dh, with bath 120dh. Hot showers 5dh.) **Pension Amal** (tel. 91 27 88), off av. Mohammed ben Abdallah, is a bargain. It's 3 blocks up from pl. Libéra-tion, on the right. (Singles 40dh. Doubles 70dh. Hot showers 6dh. Cold showers 2dh.)

Budget eateries cook around the **Zoko Chico** and **pl. Libération.** Larache used to be a Spanish colony, so it's no surprise that Spanish seafood is the fare of choice. To reach **Restaurant Eskala,** Zoco Chico (tel. 91 40 80), enter through Bab Medina and take a quick left. This hole in the wall serves both seafood and more exotic fare like *trippe* (22dh). Try the yummy lamb *tajine* (30dh). **Sandwisch l'Ocean,** 5 rue Mou-lay Ismael (tel. 91 47 01), is a terrific sandwich shop that also serves *crevettes* (14dh) and various *tajines*. Follow the Credit Agricole sign from pl. Libération two blocks, hang a right, and—*voilà*—it's up ahead on the left.

Sights From pl. Libération head into the Moorish area (Bab al-Khemis) and take a right into **Zoco de la Alcaiceria,** a square built by Spaniards in the 17th century. Today it is the heart of the medina, a hassle-free affair that ripples with vendors. If you walk down the Zoco you will eventually come to another *bab*, outside of which lies the **Kasbah de la Cigogne,** built by Philip III in the 17th century. It's Larache's only intact fortification from that era, but it's closed to visitors.

The old city walls and ruined **kasbah** built by the Portuguese in the 16th century are visible from the boardwalk just off of pl. Libération. Continuing downhill on the boardwalk you will see the **beach** across the **Loukkos estuary.** Entrepreneurial boat-men transport passengers across for 2dh (be ready to pay 4dh to get back—they are adept hagglers). The otherwise pleasant beach crowds with locals. A smattering of cafes will quench that deep down body thirst sweltered by Maghreb sun.

Most tourists come to Larache to visit the Roman ruins of **Lixus,** 5km to the north on the highway to Tangier. Visiting the ruins can feel like discovering them anew, as they are unrestored, unguarded, and unmarked, and often they are entirely empty save a shepherd and his flock. Around 1000 BC, the Phoenicians set up camp here to trade gold, slaves, and ivory. Under Emperor Claudius, in 42 AD, Lixus became a Roman outpost that supplied the Empire with the condiment *garum,* a paste made of anchovies. The *garum* factories beside the highway are a good place to start your exploration. At the far end of the factory (away from Larache), a path leads up to the remains of the **amphitheater.** Beside it and towards the highway is the **Mosaic of the Sea God,** the only remaining mosaic at Lixus. Continuing up this path leads to the **acropolis,** where you might run into a goat or two foraging around the broken pillars. To get to Lixus, hop on bus #4 or 5 from the stop near Casbah de la Cigogne (2.50dh) in Larache and tell the ticket collector you want to go to Lixus. Unfortu-nately, it's a one-way street to Lixus. To get back, walk or flag down one of the rare taxis. Some folks choose to hitch a ride.

■ Rabat الرباط

Many of those 17th-century pirate expeditions you read about were a) true and b) based in Rabat. The Mediterranean Sea and Atlantic Ocean were the pirates' oysters until the Alaouites soundly disposed of them around 1700. Ironically, Rabat is exceptional in contemporary Morocco for its very absence of hustlers. King Hassan II resides here and his personal battalion chases hustlers, street peddlars, and beg-gars off of the main streets. The king, moreover, nurtures a healthy local economy. He co-opts rather than confronts political opposition by bolstering the bureaucracy, expanding the public sector by creating administrative positions. Rabat is also a

MOROCCO

business capital, with a swelling upper middle class and a flourishing Mercedes Benz trade. Admittedly, its restaurants are not as appetizing, beaches not as inviting, and *souks* not as exciting (or unnerving) as Morocco's other imperial cities, but Rabat is a modern city frequented for its facilities, not its charm. It's also the city where Western women tend to feel most comfortable. Rabat's historic venue pales in comparison to the imperial cities of Fès and Meknès, yet its order and Western facilities make Rabat a good transition into Moroccan life.

ORIENTATION AND PRACTICAL INFORMATION

The town is a navigational breeze. **Avenue Mohammed V** parades north-south from the Grand Essouna Mosque, past the train station and post office, and directly through the **medina.** Exiting the **train station,** turn left down Mohammed V to reach most budget hotels. **avenue Allal ben Abdallah** parallels av. Mohammed V, one block away (to your right walking toward the medina from the train station). Perpendicular to av. Mohammed V is **avenue Hassan II,** which runs east-west along the medina's south walls. To the east across the river is Rabat's sibling city **Salé**; to the west is the **route de Casablanca,** home of the inconvenient "central" **bus station.**

Tourist Office: Municipal, 22 rue al-Jazair (tel. 73 05 62). Distant but helpful. Turn right out of the train station, walk up av. Mohammed V to the Grand Essouna Mosque, turn left on av. Moulay Hassan, and bear right onto rue al-Jazair after 4 blocks. English-speaking staff. Sketchy maps of Rabat and other large cities. Open Mon.-Fri. 8am-2pm; mid-Sept.-June 15 Mon.-Fri. 8am-noon and 12:30-5:30pm; Ramadan Mon.-Fri. 9am-3pm.

Embassies and Consulates: U.S.: Marked by the flag waving over blvd. Tariq Ibn Ziyad, beside the fortifications on the southeast edge of town along the river. Will issue replacement passports within 3 days and can facilitate transfers of funds from sources in the U.S. **Canadian** (also serves **Australian** citizens); **U.K.** (also serves **New Zealand** citizens). For addresses, see **Embassies and Consulates: Morocco** (p. 36).

Currency Exchange: Banks and ATMs located on av. Mohammed V, and av. Allal ben Abdallah. A safe bet is the **BMCE,** at 260 av. Mohammed V and at the train station. Open Mon.-Fri. 8am-noon and 3-6pm, Sat.-Sun. 10am-2pm and 4-8pm.

Flights: International Airport Mohammed V (tel. (02) 33 90 40), in Casablanca. Slick trains run to the airport via Casablanca (6 per day, 1½hr., 50dh). **Royal Air Maroc,** av. Mohammed V (tel. 70 97 66), across from train station. Open Mon.-Fri. 8:30am-noon and 2:30-7pm, Sat. 8:30am-noon and 3-6pm. **Air France,** 281 av. Mohammed V (tel. 70 70 66). Open Mon.-Thurs. 8:30am-12:15pm and 2:30-6:30pm, Fri. 8:30am-12:15pm and 3:30-6:30pm, Sat. 9am-12:15pm.

Trains: Rabat Ville Station, av. Mohammed V (tel. 70 14 69), at av. Moulay Youssef. To: Casablanca (27 per day, 1hr., 27dh); Fès (8 per day, 4hr., 69dh); Marrakech (8 per day, 5hr., 99dh); Tangier (4 per day, 5½hr., 87dh); and Meknès (8 per day, 3hr., 53dh).

Buses: All companies operate from an enormous station on route de Casablanca at pl. Mohammed Zerktouni (tel. 77 51 24). It's several kilometers from the town center, so take a *petit taxi* (10dh) or bus #30 from av. Hassan near rue Mohammed V (2.50dh). CTM tickets at windows #14 and 15; other windows belong to private companies. **CTM** to: Casablanca (6 per day, 1hr., 27dh); Fès (8 per day, 3½hr., 57dh); Meknès (8 per day, 2½hr., 40dh); Tangier (5 per day, 5hr., 80dh); and Chefchaouen (2 per day, 6hr., 65dh).

Taxis: Stands at the train station, in front of the bus station along av. Hassan II across from Bab Oudaias, and at the entrance to the medina by the corner of av. Hassan II and av. Mohammed V.

Car Rental: Hertz, 467 av. Mohammed V (tel. 76 92 27). **Budget** is headquartered in train station. All 250dh per day plus mileage and 20% tax.

Luggage Storage: At the train station (2.50dh per bag, must be locked, locks for sale in station; could be a scam—you think?). At the bus station (3dh per day). Open daily 4am-midnight.

ATLANTIC OCEAN

Rabat

Chellah Burial Complex, 8
Currency Exchange, 5
Dar el-Makzhen, 2
Essouna Grand Mosque, 7
Hassan Tower, 1
Kasbah des Ousalas, 6
Museum of Moroccan Arts, 9
Post Office, 10
Train Stations, 3 and 4
U.S. Consulate, 11

Abou Yous El Marini

Bou Regreg

MEDINA

Boulevard Hassan II

Rue Mansour Ad-Dahbi

Boulevard Al-Rahba
Blvd Abi Regreg

Ave. Al Alaouiyyine a

Rue Al Jaza r

Ave. Al Jaza r

Ave. Marrakech

Ave. Moussa Ibn Noussair

Ave. Tariq Ibn Zaid

Ave. Ouarzazate

Ave. Mohammed V

Ave. Moulay Al Hassan

Ave. Yacoub al Mansour

Boulevard Ad-Doustour

Blvd. al-Alou

Boulevard Mest

Boulevard Mohammed V

Avenue Mohammed Ben Abdellah

Ave. Allal Ben Abdellah

Boulevard Mokhtar Gazoulet

Ave. Abdelkrim Al Khattabi

Avenue Al Mouqaouama

Avenue Hassan II Av

Ibn Toumert

Avenue Pasteur

Avenue Madgassez

Ave. Bin Al Widane

Rue Regragui

Rue Muhammed Tritki

Rue Opba

Ave. Ibn Khaldoune

Ave. Ibn Hazm

Ave. Ibn Batouta

Ave. Al Abial

Ave. Al Oumam Al Mouttahida

Ave. Al Amir Fal Ould Oumayr

Rue Oum Ar-Rabia

Ave. John Kennedy

Blvd. Mostafa As-Saih

Avenue Sidi Mohammed Ben Abdellah

Ave. Ar-Rahma

Ave. Ma Al Ainaine

Ave. Ibn Rochd

Ave. Ibn Sina

Rue Michlefen

Avenue Al Fahs

Boulevard Ad-Doustour

Avenue As Salam

Ave. an Nour

TO CASABLANCA

MOROCCO

N

Laundromat: Hotels are the best option—expect to pay 20-30dh.

English Bookstores: English Bookstore, 7 rue al-Yamama (tel. 70 65 93). Exiting the train station, take a hard right and cut diagonally through the parking lot to rue al-Yamama. Kerouac to Foucault to Dostoevsky. Open Mon.-Sat. 9am-12:30pm and 3-7pm. **American Bookstore,** 4 Zankat Tanja (tel. 76 87 17). Take av. Mohammed V past the Grand Mosque and turn left 3 blocks later. Great paperback selection. Open Mon.-Fri. 9:30am-12:30pm and 2:30-6:30pm, Sat. 10am-1pm.

Late-Night Pharmacy: Pharmacie de Préfecture, av. Moulay Slimane (tel. 70 70 72). From the post office, cross av. Mohammed V and veer to the right onto rue el-Qahira (as if going to the Syndicat d'Initiative). On your right a few blocks down. A sandy, pillared building across from Theatre Mohammed V. Open 8:30pm-8am.

Medical Services: Hôpital Avicenne, av. Ibn Sina (tel. 77 44 11), at the south end of blvd. d'Argonne. Free emergency medical care for all. U.S. citizens can also go to the U.S. Embassy p. 36) for medical care.

Police: Rue Soekarno (tel. 19), 2 bl. from the post office off av. Mohammed V.

Post Office: Av. Mohammed V (tel. 72 07 31) at rue Soekarno, left when leaving the train station. Open Mon.-Thurs. 8:30am-12:15pm and 2:30-6:45pm, Fri. 11:30am-3pm. Telephones and Poste Restante are next door.

Telephones: Rue Soekarno, facing the post office. International phones and collect calls (open 24hr.). **Poste Restante** is also located in this building (2dh per piece). **Telephone Code:** (0)7.

ACCOMMODATIONS AND CAMPING

Not surprisingly, inexpensive rooms are hard to find in prosperous Rabat. As usual, the medina is cheaper than the ville nouvelle, although less of a bargain than in other cities. Cushier hotels line **av. Mohammed V, av. Allal ben Abdallah,** and side streets. From the train station, turn left onto av. Mohammed V and walk toward the medina; av. Allal ben Abdallah runs parallel one block to the right.

In the Medina

Hôtel Maghrib El-Jadid, 2 rue Sebbahi (tel. 73 22 07), at av. Mohammed V, right past the entrance to the medina. Bright pink paint, spotless rooms, rather small beds. Rooftop terrace. The only thing fishy about this place is the aquarium at the entrance. English spoken. Singles 50dh. Doubles 80dh. Hot showers 5dh.

Hôtel Marrakech, 10 rue Sebbahi (tel. 72 77 03), past the Maghrib El-Jadid, off Mohammed V. Same owner as Maghrib El-Jadid, same decor (with a bit more hot pink) even cleaner. Rooms verge on miniature, but you get a fresh towel each day. Squat toilets. Singles 40dh. Doubles 70dh. Cold showers 2dh. Hot showers 5dh.

Ville Nouvelle

Auberge de Jeunesse (HI), 43 rue Marassa (tel. 72 57 69), on the road perpendicular to av. Hassan II in the ville nouvelle, just outside the medina. In an old mansion with a beautiful courtyard. Separate-sex dorm beds and cold showers. American/Australian spoken by the friendly manager. Reception open July-Aug. 7-9:30am, noon-3pm, 7pm-midnight; Sept.-June 8-10am, noon-3pm and 6-10pm. Members 26dh, nonmembers 31dh.

Hôtel Capitol, 34 av. Allal ben Abdallah (tel. 73 12 36). If you've got a few extra *dirhams,* stay here. Rooms are as bland as Keanu Reeves' acting, but they're cozy and spacious. Fresh towels daily, laundry service available. No shared showers available, so either take a room with one or use the spacious sinks. Singles 80dh, with shower 89dh. Doubles with shower 120dh.

Hôtel Central, 2 rue el-Basra (tel. 70 73 56). From the train station, cross av. Mohammed V and walk 2 blocks toward the medina; take the 2nd right immediately after Hôtel Balima. Gruff management and high prices are the obstacles on the way to these large, pleasant rooms. Singles 80dh, with shower 100dh. Doubles: 120dh; 147dh.

MOROCCO

Camping de la Plage (tel. 78 23 68), far away in sister city Salé, but at least on the beach. *Grand taxi* to the site 10dh. Running water, toilets, and a grocery store/restaurant. Facilities are primitive and a bit shabby, but their prices rule. 24hr. reception. 10.50dh per person, 5dh per tent and per car, slightly more for vans or larger vehicles. Cold showers and electricity included.

FOOD

Rabat has many mediocre food offerings from other countries, like Hong Kong, a restaurant with Chinese-style pigeon (60dh) on av. Mohammed V, and a brand new **McDonald's** across from the train station. In the **medina,** the continuation of **av. Mohammed V** is lined with virtually indistinguishable *brochetteries* and sandwich shops (many are unnamed). Beasts of budget forage in two areas of the new city: around av. Mohammed V and **av. Allal ben Abdallah,** a block or two from the medina, and around the train station, just off **av. Moulay Youssef.**

Restaurant el-Bahia, av. Hassan II (tel. 73 45 04), to the right, going toward the medina on av. Mohammed V. Built into the wall. Interior court and fountain with goldfish. *Salon marocain* upstairs. The lunch crowd devours appetizing dishes, sometimes leaving only monkey scraps for dinner. Try a *non kefta tajine* (30dh). Vegetarians savor the *couscous sept légumes* (32dh). Open daily 11am-11pm.

Café-Restaurant La Clef (tel. 70 19 72). Exiting the train station, make a hard right onto av. Moulay Youssef, then skip down the 1st alley on the left. The *salon marocain* has low-slung couches. Good, inexpensive *tajine pigeon* (minced pigeon stewed with prunes, almonds, and onions, 45dh). One of the few places to get a gin or whiskey shot (38dh). Open daily noon-4pm and 7-11pm.

Restaurant Ghazza, 3 rue Ghazza, just off av. Mohammed V, across from BMCE. Excellent omelettes (12dh) when all you can find elsewhere are pastries. Ask what the *tajine* (25dh) is for the day. The fish is great too. Open daily 8am-midnight.

SIGHTS

Rabat's principal place of worship, the **Essouna Grande Mosque,** towers at the end of av. Mohammed V away from the medina in the ville nouvelle. Sandy-hued arches and gold trim embellish its tall, tan-colored minaret. South of pl. Grande Mosque, the **archaeological museum** is recommended for its collection of Volubilis bronze works, all cast before 25 BC, its exhibit on the Roman necropolis of Salé, and its Phoenician and Carthaginian relics. To get here, walk down av. Mohammed V and turn left onto Abd Al Aziz at the Grande Mosque; the museum is on the next street off Abd Al Aziz to the right. (Open Wed.-Mon. 9-11:30am and 2:30-5:30pm. 10dh.) From the front of the Grand Mosque, av. Moulay Hassan proceeds to the salmon-pink **Bab el-Rouah** (Gate of the Winds) sporting Kufic (an Arabic script) inscriptions and arabesques on its arches (10-min. walk). Inside the gate to the right is a gallery of Moroccan impressionist painting. Exhibits change every few weeks, and you can periodically catch the artists in person (open daily 8:30am-noon and 2:30-8pm).

Back through Bab er-Rouah and through the wall to the right is the 1km avenue leading to the royal palace, **Dar el-Makhzen.** The palace was begun in the 18th century, but most construction was finished after French occupation. Foolish peons who get too close will be chased away by soldiers brandishing machine guns. Photography is permitted from afar; try not to ruffle the soldiers' feathers.

South of the palace grounds at the end of av. Yacoub el-Mansour loom the decrepit but impressive remains of the **Chellah burial complex,** a fortified royal necropolis revered since the Almohads' heyday. To get there from the palace, exit the gate adjacent to the palace (**Bab Zaers,** not the entrance gate) and turn left. The romantic, melancholy air that surrounds the ruins and the vista over the Oued Bou Regreg attracts visitors out for a stroll. Walk from the chellah gate through the overgrown gardens which cover what little remains of the Roman city **Sala Colonia.** At the bottom of the path is the ruined mosque. Step inside for a better view of the

MOROCCO

brightly tiled minaret and see Hassan's tomb, the white prism in the rear (open sunrise to sunset; 10dh).

Mohammed V Mausoleum and Hassan Tower

Across town along av. Abi Regreg (near the Moulay Hassan bridge to Salé) looms the **Mausoleum of Mohammed V,** a tribute to the sultan-king who led Morocco's independence movement and lent his name to seemingly every third street in the country. While facing the complex, the tomb is in the structure on the left. Non-Muslims can enter the lower room where hanging flags, an old man reading from the Qur'an, and sleepy guards give company to Mohammed V in his marble sarcophagus. The enormous courtyard outside was once the prayer hall of the enormous **Hassan Mosque,** begun in 1199 to commemorate a victory over Spain. An earthquake destroyed its roof, leaving only the stubby columns. The enormous, incomplete minaret (interior inaccessible) was to be El Mansour's greatest achievement, in the same style as the Giralda of Sevilla and the Koutoubia of Marrakech. El Mansour would surely roll over in his burial complex if he knew that construction had halted so soon after his death.

Medina and Kasbah

There is little of interest in the medina for the traveler who has visited Fès or Marrakech. The **Kasbah des Oudaias,** however, just northwest of the medina, is impressive. To get to it, walk through the medina on Av. Mohammed V and take a right on blvd. al-Alou; the *kasbah* is a few hundred meters away along the road to the left. It used to be a pirate stronghold until Moulay Idriss sent Saharan mercenaries to oversee the buccaneers' tributes of gold and slaves. **Bab Oudaia,** a succession of increasingly ornate Moorish arches at the top of the hill, is the best of the gates. Once inside, head straight on the main street, rue Jamaa. On the opposite side of the *kasbah* is a large esplanade overlooking the teeming beaches and the Rabat surf club, a hangout sponsored by King Hassan II's son. Exiting the *kasbah* through Bab Oudia and entering through the keyhole-shaped *bab* down the stairs leads to the sublime **Andalusian Gardens,** of medieval Islamic-Spanish design and French construction (on your right when you enter the *bab*). The **Museum of Moroccan Arts,** next to the gardens, was once the Rabat hideaway of the infamous Moulay Ismail in the 17th century. The excellent collection shows off the sultan's private apartment, signature Rabat-style carpets, and traditional costumes from the Middle Ages. Similar outfits can still be seen in Moroccan villages today. (Museum and garden open daily 10am-5pm; in winter Wed.-Mon. 8:30am-noon and 3-6:30pm. Admission to museum 10dh.) A charming cafe lies on the opposite side of the garden overlooking the estuary.

ENTERTAINMENT

The prosperous youth of Rabat scope each other out at cinemas and pricey, pseudo-Euro discos such as **Amnesia,** on rue Monastir near the Cinema Royale. Look for the New York checkered cab out front and airplane and school bus inside. For high culture, call the palatial **Tour Hassan Hôtel,** 22 av. Chellah (tel. 72 14 91), to sit in on a performance or concert. **Café Balima** (in front of Hôtel Balima on av. Mohammed V, near the train station), a relaxing spot to sip mint tea, is one of the best cafes in Rabat. **Cinema Renaissance** offers recycled pop culture.

■ Casablanca الدار البيضاء

As time goes by, Casablanca continues to bloat under the Maghreb sun. It is the largest city in Morocco with 3½ million inhabitants, where bright lights and a big medina attract rural Moroccans seeking urban prosperity. As the country's financial capital and Africa's largest port, "Casa" has developed into Morocco's only true cosmopolis during its 2000 years of communication with Europe. Western dress predominates, and women participate in city life. Indicatively, Casablanca has the

dubious distinction of having Morocco's first McDonald's and its only open prostitution.

A note of warning: many people are lured to Casablanca by visions of high-class international intrigue, inspired by a certain movie. The closest one can come to living like Rick and Ilsa, however, is to drink 10-dollar Martinis served by a trench-coated Moroccan at the local Hyatt. The movie was based more on Tangier anyway. With the construction of the gargantuan Grande Mosque Hassan II, Casablanca has tried to establish itself as a religious center. Nonetheless, non-believers and even the most die-hard Bogey fans concede that the city is little more than a transport hub.

ORIENTATION AND PRACTICAL INFORMATION

Almost 100km south of Rabat, Casa is accessible by plane, bus, and train. **Casa Port** is near the youth hostel and the city center. **Casa Voyageurs** is near nothing, a 50min. walk from Casa Port or 20dh *petit taxi* ride. To get from Casa Port to the **CTM bus station,** cross the street, follow blvd. Felix Houphëit-Boigny to pl. Nations Unies, turn left on av. Armée Royale, and watch for Hôtel Safir on the right; the station is behind it and to the right.

The city has two main squares, pl. Nations Unies and pl. Mohammed V. **place Nations Unies** spreads out in front of the Hyatt Regency at the intersection of blvd. Houphëit-Boigny, av. de l'Armée Royale, and, among other streets, av. Hassan II. Government buildings surround **place Mohammed V,** near the main post office (PTT) on av. Hassan II. Head to these squares for most of the action (and some mild hustling). If worse comes to worst, take a taxi—they're cheap.

Tourist Office: 55 rue Omar Slaoui (tel. 27 95 33 or 27 11 77). From pl. Mohammed V, walk south along av. Hassan II, left on rue Reitzer, then right on rue Omar Slaoui. Maps of the city and deserts. Open Mon.-Fri. 8am-noon and 4-7pm; Sept.-May Mon.-Fri. 8:30am-noon and 2:30-6:30pm; Ramadan Mon.-Fri. 9am-3pm. Much closer to pl. Nations Unies is the **Syndicat d'Initiative,** open on weekends. Some maps, brochures, and English. Mon.-Sat. 8:30am-noon and 3am-6:30pm, Sun. 9am-noon.

Currency Exchange: The airport and larger hotels change money at official rates when banks are closed. Try the Hyatt Regency, Hôtel Suisse, or Hôtel Safir near the bus station. Exchange rates throughout the city are fairly uniform.

American Express: Voyages Schwartz, 112 av. du Prince Moulay Abdallah (tel. 22 29 47 or 27 80 54; fax 27 31 33; telex 216 40). Standard services, except they won't receive wired money. French spoken. Open Mon.-Fri. 8:30am-noon and 2:30-6:30pm, Sat. 8:30am-noon. Cash transactions must be done before 4:30pm.

Flights: Aéroport Mohammed V (tel. 33 90 40) handles all international and most domestic flights. Pleasant trains (20dh) run frequently to the Casa Port train station and to Rabat. Some of the airport shuttle trains stop only at Casa Voyageurs. **Aéroport de Casablanca (ANFA;** tel. 91 20 00), accessible by taxi only (about 150dh), has other domestic flights. **Royal Air Maroc Ticket Office,** 44 av. des Forces Armées Royales (tel. 31 41 41), sells tickets for the national airline.

Trains: Casa Port, Port de Casablanca (tel. 22 30 11). Mainly northbound service. To: Rabat (17 per day, 1hr., 27dh); Fès (3 per day, 5hr., 96dh); Tangier (2 per day, 6hr., 114dh). **Casa Voyageurs,** blvd. Ba Hammed (tel. 24 58 01), away from the city center. Mainly southbound service. To Marrakech (4 per day, 5hr., 47dh).

Buses: CTM, 23 rue Léon L'Africain (tel. 44 81 27), off rue Chaouia. To: Rabat (18 per day, 1½hr., 30dh); Fès (8 per day, 6hr., 80dh); Tangier (2 per day, 6½hr., 100dh); Marrakech (6 per day, 4hr., 65dh); Meknès (9 per day, 5hr., 63dh); Essaouira (2 per day, 5½hr., 100dh); Agadir (6 per day, 10hr., 140dh); El-Jadida (2 per day, 1½hr., 25dh). Other companies leave from pl. Benjdia to Marrakech.

Car Rental: Casa has dozens of companies (for a list, ask for **Telecontact** at the tourist office or at the Syndicat). It's best to go through a well-known firm. **Europcar,** 44 av. des Force Armées Royales (tel. 31 37 37); **Hertz,** 25 rue de Aloraibi Jilali (tel. 31 22 23); and **Budget,** av. Forces Armées Royales (F.A.R.; tel. 30 14 80), have similar rates and rent to drivers with an international license.

MOROCCO

English Bookstore: American Language Center Bookstore, blvd. Moulay Youssef (tel. 27 95 59), under the American Language Center at pl. Unité Afric-aine. Vast array of novels and reference books. Open Mon.-Fri. 9:30am-12:30pm and 3:30-6:30pm, Sat. 9:30am-noon.

Late-Night Pharmacy: Pharmacie de Nuit, pl. Nations Unies (tel. 26 94 91). Open nightly 8pm-8am.

Medical Services: Croissant Rouge Marocain, 19 blvd. Al Massira Al Khadra (tel. 25 25 21). **S.O.S. Medicins,** 81 av. Armée Royale (tel. 44 44 44).

Police: Blvd. Brahim Roudani (tel. 19).

Post Office: blvd. de Paris, av. Hassan II. Poste Restante. Mon-Thurs. 8:30am-12:15pm, 2:30-6:30pm; Fri. 8:30-11:30am, 3-6:30pm.

Telephones: Make collect or international calls from phones in and around the post office. **Telephone Code:** (0)2.

ACCOMMODATIONS

Eschew the medina and look along **rue Chaouia** and **avenue des Forces Armées Royales (F.A.R.)** for the best deals.

Auberge de Jeunesse (HI), 6 pl. Amiral Philibert (tel. 22 05 51). From the port, head right (in the direction of the medina) along blvd. Almohades, walk along its walls, and go left up a small ramp-like street. Pleasant common area. Clean sheets and cold showers. Reception open 8-10am and noon-11pm. Members and non-members 40dh. Breakfast included.

Hôtel de Foucauld, 52 rue Araibi Jilali (tel. 22 26 66). Adjacent to Hôtel Perigord (below) and more comfortable. Singles 80dh. Doubles 120dh.

Hôtel Perigord, 56 rue Araïbi Jilali (tel. 22 10 85). From blvd. Felix Houphëit-Boi-gny, left on av. des F.A.R., then the 1st right. Bare-bones rooms with hard beds. Go to the 2nd floor for a flush toilet. Singles 63dh.

Hôtel Rialto, av. Mohammed El Qorri (tel. 27 51 22). From pl. Nations Unies, take blvd. Mohammed V and the 3rd right off it, then your first left. Hygenic, airy rooms are as quiet as they get in Casa. Singles 84dh. Doubles 112dh. Triples 150dh. All with bath.

Hôtel Terminus, 184 blvd. Ba H'mad (tel. 24 00 25), diagonally left across pl. Sem-pard from Gare des Voyageurs. Huge clean rooms at decent prices. Great for those planning early starts or late arrivals. Singles 62dh. Doubles 82dh. Showers 5dh.

FOOD

While it's true that cosmopolitan Casablanca boasts everything from French *haute cuisine* (reputedly the best French restaurant in Africa is here) to Korean food, most restaurants are geared to the city's wealthy business clientele. Kabab joints line **rue Chaouia** in the ville nouvelle, and good value meals can be found near pl. Nations Unies in the medina. Or try haggling Moroccan-style at the massive produce stands at the **central market,** 7 rue Chaouia.

Restaurant Widad, 9 rue de Fès. At the end of blvd. Houphëit-Boigny, take the 1st right into the medina. It's just after the 1st fork. With a whopping 10 tables, it's the biggest hole-in-the-wall in the medina. Attentive service, enormous portions, and delicious staples. 38dh for fruit, salad, couscous, vegetables, a quarter-chicken, and bottled water (ask for a sealed bottle). Open daily 11am-10pm.

Taverne au Dauphin, 75 blvd. Felix Houphëit-Boigny (22 12 00), up the road from the port. Tuxedoed waiters serve sizzling seafood to Casablancan professionals. *Crevettes grillées* (grilled shrimp, 55dh) and *filet de lotte* (filet o' fish, 70dh). Open Mon.-Sat. noon-4pm and 6-11pm.

SIGHTS

An industrial center and haven for financial moguls, Casablanca is too preoccupied with commerce to maintain a romantic veneer for tourists. A decaying **medina** dis-

appoints veterans of Fès and Marrakech. Public buildings around **place Mohammed V** are relics of French occupation. They exemplify the French neo-Mauresque style, an Art Deco "improvement" on ancient Moorish themes. By the port, vendors fervently try to rook crewmen disembarking merchant ships.

The biggest sight in Casa, literally, is the fabulous **Grande Mosquée Hassan II.** It's very easy to find: from anywhere in Casa, look toward the sea and spot the shiny new minaret. You will appreciate its immensity (200m high, the tallest minaret in the world) after walking towards it for a mile or two. Begun in 1980 and inaugurated in 1994, this mini Mecca carried a price tag of nearly a billion U.S. dollars (much of it collected by "universal voluntary conscription"). The prayer hall, much larger than St. Peter's in Rome, combines glass, marble, and precious wood in a space that holds over 25,000 worshippers. The courtyard accommodates another 80,000. Technology galvanizes religious devotion: the hall boasts a huge retractable sun roof, a **20-mile-long laser** shooting from the minaret toward Mecca, and a glass floor revealing the Atlantic Ocean crashing below heeds the Quranic saying that "Allah has his throne on the water." Morocco is so proud of this building that non-believers can go inside (tours Sat.-Thurs. 9, 10, 11am, and 2pm; 100dh, students 50dh, children 25dh). An elevator ascends the side of the minaret for 10dh. To get to the mosque, walk about 15 minutes past the medina along the coastal road, or take a *petit taxi* (5dh).

■ El-Jadida الجديدة

El-Jadida, a two-hour bus ride from Casablanca, is one of Morocco's largest Atlantic resorts. With a charming medina, crenellated Portuguese battlements, palmy boulevards, and a first-rate beach, it's a welcome overnight antidote to the bustle and hustling of Casa and Marrakech. The city's European air comes courtesy of the Portuguese, who made Jadida (née Mazagan) their first Moroccan foothold and their last Moroccan stronghold. The city was renamed El-Jadida ("The New One") and became a retreat for Marrakech's affluent families once Morocco won its independence. European interest, from merchants rather than invaders, resurged in the mid-19th century. Today El-Jadida is a prime destination for foreign and domestic tourists.

ORIENTATION AND PRACTICAL INFORMATION

The main centers are **place Mohammed V,** which adjoins blvd. Mohammed V at the post office (PTT); **place el-Hansali,** a pleasant pedestrian square; and **place Mohammed ben Abdallah,** which connects blvd. Suez to the old Portuguese **medina.**

Tourist Office: rue Ibn Khaldoun (tel. 34 47 88), down the street from Hôtel de Bruxelles and Hôtel de Provence. Follow signs from blvd. Mohammed V and the post office. Useful wall map. English spoken. Open Mon.-Fri. 8:30am-noon and 2:30-6:30pm; mid-Sept.-mid-June Mon.-Fri. 8:30am-noon.

Currency Exchange: Plenty of banks with **ATMs,** among them **BMCE,** located one block from pl. Mohammed V along av. Mohammed Errafil. Open Mon.-Thurs. 8:15-11:30am, 2:15-4:30pm; Fri. 8:15-11:15am, 2:45-4:45pm. Hôtel de Provence also changes money (see Accommodations and Camping).

Trains: Currently there is no passenger train service through El-Jadida.

Buses: blvd. Mohammed V. To reach the city center, exit left on blvd. Mohammed V and continue to pl. Mohammed V (10min.). To: Casablanca (private buses: 5am-7pm, every 20min., 2hr., 18dh; CTM: 11am, 3:30, 5pm, 2hr., 24dh); Essaouira (private buses: 6 per day, 45dh; CTM: 7:30am, 45dh). Buses to Essaouira begin in Casablanca and often have few seats left by the time they arrive in El-Jadida, so get a ticket well beforehand.

Late-Night Pharmacy: av. Ligue Arabe off pl. Mohammed V. Look for the plaque next door to the Croissant Rouge Marocain (Red Cross). Open nightly 9pm-8am.

Hospital: rue Sidi Bouzi (tel. 34 20 04 or 34 20 05), near rue Boucharette at the south edge of town. **Red Cross:** av. Ligne Arabe (24hr).

MOROCCO

Police: Located at the bus station and at the beach (tel. 19).

Post Office: pl. Mohammed V. Open for Poste Restante, **telephones,** and **telegrams** Mon.-Fri. 8:30am-noon and 2:30-6:30pm.

Telephone Code: (0)3

ACCOMMODATIONS AND CAMPING

For a fairly quiet coastal town, El-Jadida has a surprisingly large number of budget hotels. Most drift around **place Mohammed V,** a few blocks from the sea. Ask to see a room before you commit because there is a range of room quality among and within hotels. You will probably need reservations in July and August.

Hôtel Maghreb/Hôtel de France, 16 rue Lescould (tel. 34 21 81), just off pl. el-Hansali. Spacious rooms, most with sinks and *bidets,* and some with excellent views of the water. Singles 41dh. Doubles 57dh. Showers 5dh.

Hôtel Bourdeaux, 47 rue Moulay Ahmed Tahiri (tel. 35 41 17). About 50m from place el-Hansali through a couple narrow streets; follow signs at the north end of the place. Carpeted, bright modern rooms at low prices. Singles 41dh. Doubles 57dh. Triples 78dh. Shower 5dh.

Hôtel de Provence, 42 rue Fquih Mohammed Errafi (tel. 34 23 47 or 34 41 12; fax 35 21 15). From the bus station, head left on av. Mohammed V and turn left (away from the beach) at the post office. The "in" hotel for English speakers. Higher prices correspond with minor details (toilet paper, towels, nicer sheets). Excellent **currency exchange** rates. Singles 104dh, with shower 133dh. Doubles 131-164dh, with shower 159-186dh. Continental breakfast 22dh.

Camping: Camping Caravaning International, av. Al Oman al Mouttahida (tel. 34 27 55). From the post office, head toward the beach and take a right on av. El Jamia El Arabi. Take the 6th right (20min.). A large site with electricity, showers, and aging bungalows (160dh). 12dh per adult, 6.50dh per car, 10dh per tent. Add 4dh *emplacement* and 14% TVA.

FOOD

Many places serve the usual *brochettes* along **place Mohammed V,** but most restaurants cluster in and around **place el-Hansali.** Numerous cafes speckle the seafront. A weekly **souk** that sells everything from fruits and vegetables to cow lungs and bull genitalia is held by the lighthouse.

Restaurant la Broche, 46 pl. el-Hansali (tel. 34 22 99), next to the Paris Cinema. Intimate dining rooms complemented by a mile-long menu, fresh fruit decor, and speedy service. *Tajine* 25-30dh. Fish dishes 30-40dh. Fresh banana juice 7dh. Ostensibly open 7am-11pm, but the actual hours depend on the owner's whim.

Restaurant Chahrazad, 38 pl. el-Hansali. Don't expect all items to be available, but the procurable food is filling and appetizing. Couscous and *tajine,* 20-25dh.

Restaurant Tchikito, 7 rue Moulan Ahmed Tahiri, a few meters off pl. el-Hansali on street to Hôtel Bordeaux. Eat huge plates of fried fresh fish with locals without the help of a knife or fork (25dh per plate). Open noon-10pm.

SIGHTS

The signs that label El-Jadida's old town **Cité Portugaise** are correct; those around the **medina** are not. Completed in 1502, the retreating Portuguese blasted the old town in 1769. When Sultan Moulay Abderrahman renovated it in the 19th century, a *mellah* (Jewish quarter) unfolded. Iron balconies, garlanded cornices, and pillared doorways add splendor to its nooks and crannies. Enter through the fortified gate off pl. Sidi Mohammed bin Abdallah at the top of blvd. Suez. Immediately to the left off rue de Carreira kneels **l'Eglise Portuguese,** a 17th-century church with Spanish walls and a misfit French roof.

Up rue de Carreira on the left, a yellow plaque marks the entrance to the **Portuguese Cisterns,** one of the few buildings to survive the Portuguese bombardment. The water, illuminated by a shaft of light from the roof, reflects the cistern's col-

umns and arches. If it looks familiar, you are among the few who saw Orson Welles's *Othello*. A riot scene was shot here. (Cisterns open daily 8am-noon and 4-7pm; in winter Mon.-Fri. 8am-noon and 2:30-6pm. 10dh.) **Porta do Mar,** the grand archway at the end of rue de Carrcira, leads to the harbor. From here, walk up onto the ramparts and join the locals promenading above the city (the ramparts are permanently unlocked). Slightly north, the **Bastion de l'Ange** commands a view of the harbor from atop the incline. Walk along the walls to the **Bastion de St. Sébastien,** flanked by a Portuguese chapel, or along the jetty to see the entire town. Back below, in pl. Moussa, the Gothic **Church of the Assumption** has been converted to an assembly hall. Nearby, the abandoned Portuguese **Tribunal** has become a synagogue, built to accommodate Jewish resettlement in 1815.

The town **beach** gets cleaner progressing northward. **Sidi Bouzid,** a beach 5km south, is roomier and more chic. Take a *grand taxi* for 5dh per person, or the orange #2 bus from near the medina.

■ Essaouira الصو يرة

Visitors to Essaouira often stay for an extra day—or a lifetime. Freeloading has become the norm in this Atlantic jewel. Piracy boosted its port economy in the 18th century, when Sultan Muhammed bin Abdallah constructed the town fortifications (designed by a captured Frenchman) to protect his pirate proteges. More recently, appearances by Jimi Hendrix and Cat Stevens triggered mass hippie migrations.

Although most of the hash has slowly burned away, Essaouira remains one of the mellowest towns in Morocco. A population of independent backpackers and windsurfers have settled in, not only for the wind, but for the lifestyle. When the miles of beautiful beaches stretching south are too windy for sunbathing, the enchanting whitewashed medina and spectacular battlements await.

ORIENTATION AND PRACTICAL INFORMATION

Buses arrive at the main **bus station,** a 10-minute walk from the walls of the medina. To reach the medina entrance, exit the rear of the bus station (where the buses park) and walk to the right, past two *souks* (or deserted wasteland, depending on the time of day) to the medina gates, known as **Bab Doukkala.** These open onto **avenue Mohammed Zerktouni,** one of two main thoroughfares. The other is **rue Sidi Mohammed Ben Abdallah,** which runs parallel and to the right. To reach the city center from here, continue on Ave. Mohammed Zerktouni until just before the second-to-last tier of arches and make a right; if you pass the Hôtel Sahara, you've gone too far. Take the next left and walk until the street ends, then take a right. This will take you to **place Moulay Hassan,** the heart of Essaouira.

Tourist Office: Syndicat d'Initiative, rue de Cairo (tel. 47 36 30), head down av. Mohammed Zerktouni as if you were coming from the bus station. Take a left at the intersection beneath the clock tower. Old but decent maps available. Open Mon.-Fri. 8:30am-noon and 2:30-6pm.

Currency Exchange: Banks cluster around the pl. Moulay Hassan. The **Hôtel Beau Rivage** cashes travelers' checks (expensive rates, but 24hr. service), as does **Bank Credit du Maroc** (tel. 47 58 19), on pl. Monlay Hassan (open Mon.-Fri. 8:15-11:30am and 2:15-4:45pm, Sat. 9:30am-2pm and 3:30-7pm).

Buses: The fastest and most luxurious bus to Marrakech is run by the train company, **ONCF.** Buses leave across the square from Bab Marrakech, at Agence Supratours. Tickets sold here (departs 6:30am, 4dh). **CTM** (tel. 78 47 64) buses go to: Casablanca (10:30am, 75dh, via El Jadilla (54dh) and Safi (29dh); midnight express 100dh); Agadir (12:30pm, 37dh); **Satras** runs buses to Marrakech (7pm, 30dh), while other companies have almost a dozen departures daily.

Luggage Storage: 24hr. at the bus station (5dh per bag).

MOROCCO

English Language Periodicals: Jack's, pl. Moulay Hassan. Since Jack moved to Spain, this kiosk is no longer the English speaker's outpost it once was. Still, it carries a wide selection of periodicals and enough classics to supply a survey course.

Public Showers: Bain-Douche, about 100m down the beach from the harbor. Cold showers 1.50dh. A good steam in a *hammam* (traditional bath) is more in keeping with the lifestyle, though. Most hotel proprietors can recommend one.

Hospital: av. el-Moqaquamah (tel. 47 27 16), next to the post office.

Police: (tel. 19), next to Syndicat d'Initiative, on the left prong at the port.

Post Office: av. el-Moqaquamah at Lalla Aicha, the 1st left after Hôtel les Isles when walking away from the medina by the shore. Near the big red and white radio tower. Open for Poste Restante, **telegrams,** and **telephones** Mon.-Fri. 8am-3pm; Oct.-May 8:30am-noon and 2:30-6:30pm.

Telephone Code: (0)4.

ACCOMMODATIONS AND CAMPING

Hôtel Smara, 26 rue Skala (tel. 47 26 55), from pl. Moulay Hassan head from the port and left; make a left after Hôtel des Remparts and steer right along the ramparts. The beds are a bit worn, but rooms are clean and many have great views. Chill with other guests on the terrace. Arrive early—it is the most popular hotel in Essaouira among backpackers (no reservations). Staff will do laundry for a fair price. Singles 50dh. Doubles 70dh, with ocean view 85dh. Triples and quads 100dh. Hot shower 2dh. Breakfast 10dh.

Hôtel Beau Rivage, pl. Moulay Hassan (tel./fax 47 29 25). Large, old hotel located above the cafe society in the main square. Bright, clean rooms, many with balconies and a pleasant terrace. Singles 60dh. Doubles 80dh, with shower 120dh.

Hôtel Majestic, 40 rue Derb Laalouj (tel. 47 49 09), from pl. Moulay Hassan head away from the port down the street to the right; take a quick left, then another. Clean, newly renovated rooms overseen by a welcoming owner. Hot showers down the corridor. Singles 50dh. Doubles 90dh. Shower 55dh.

Camping: Municipal campground (tel. 47 21 00), off av. Mohammed V at the far end of the beach. Essentially a gravel parking lot near the shore with a wall to shelter campers from the wind. 8dh per person, 9dh per car, 10-20dh per tent.

FOOD

Informal dining, mostly geared toward tourists, is a tradition near the port and **pl. Moulay Hassan.** Fried sardines (with fish, bread, and tomatoes 20dh) and grilled shrimp (25dh) are sure bets. On the right-hand side coming from the port, the so-called **Berber cafes** near Porte Portugaise off av. de l'Istiqlal have low tables, straw mats, and fresh fish *tajine* or *couscous* (20dh). Establish prices before chewing.

Cafe Restaurant Essalem, pl. Moulay Hassan (tel. 47 25 48). Popular hangout for visitors since the 60s. The waiter will gladly point out the table where Cat Stevens sat studying Islam. Touristy clientele, but good and cheap. Standard range of *tajines* and couscous *menús,* 35-40dh. Breakfast for about 10dh. Open daily 8am-3:30pm and 5:30-11pm.

Chez Sam (tel. 47 35 13), at the end of the harbor. Shazam! Warped ceilings and walls plastered with Hollywood movie stars. Pricey and touristy, but it's got a nice ocean view and a liquor license. Steaming heap of mussels 25dh. *Menu* 65dh. Fish dishes 40-60dh. Open noon-2pm and 7pm-midnight. Visa, MC, AmEx.

SIGHTS

The medina provides the backdrop for one of the nicest walks in Morocco. Two *skalas* (forts) scowl atop the town fortifications. Dotted by formidable ramparts, dramatic, sea-sprayed **Skala de la Ville,** up the street from Hôtel Smara (see p. 664), lets visitors up to the large turret and artillery lined wall. Cannons, gifts from solicitous European merchants to the Sultan, perch peacefully facing the sea and the medina. La Ville is free and nicer than the **Skala de Port,** near the port.

Follow the sound of hammers pounding and the scent of *thuya* wood to land in the **carpenters' district,** comprised of cell-like niches set in the **Skala Stata de la Ville.** Working with both the trunk and root of the *thuya* tree, craftsmen inlay lemonwood and ebony (attention shoppers: watch out for painted fakes) with the indigenous wood to create the best marquetry in Morocco and some interesting masks and statuary. A good shopping plan is to go to **Afalkay Art** (pl. Moulay Hassan) for a quality overview of what's available and prices, then try the many shops lining **rue Abdul Aziz el-Fechtaly** (off rue Sidi ben Abdallah), or the carpenters' workshops themselves, where prices are the cheapest and the marketing the least aggressive. The local **museum,** near the Hôtel Majestic (see above), features antique marquetry as well as an eclectic collection of farm implements, and manuscripts, including a 13th-century Qur'an (open Fri.-Wed. 9am-noon and 3-6:30pm).

To get to the **beach,** go south past the port. High winds, though a boon to windsurfers, can be a bane for sunbathers, and swimmers should be careful of strong riptides. Nearby beaches fill with soccer matches in between high tides. Windsurfing clubs farther down rent by the hour (130-150dh), though true enthusiasts go to Sidi Kaoki (see **Near Essaouira,** below). While the Purpuraire Islands just off-shore may at first seem straight out of J.R.R. Tolkien, the Eleanora's falcons living here are only rare, not fictional. A Berber king from Mauritania, Juba II, set up dye factories on the islands around 100 BC, producing the purple dye used to color Julius Caesar's cape (among others). In 1506, the Portuguese, under King Manuel, contributed a fortress and Moulay Hassan added a prison. The islands, the Isle of Mogador being the biggest, have become a nature reserve and are generally off-limits.

■ Near Essaouira

Walking about two kilometers south along the beach from Essaouira brings the determined to the ruined fort **Bordj El Berod,** which supposedly inspired *"Castles Made of Sand,"* written by Jimi Hendrix, who tried to buy the nearby Berber village/hippie colony of **Diabat** from the Moroccan government. A 1970s police sweep closed down most accommodations, and the region is now fairly deserted.

Twenty-five kilometers south of Essaouira, many Europeans know **Sidi Kaouki** as the best **windsurfing** beach in the world. A blue sign points the way from the main road to the beach, where "Wind City" bumper stickers crowd the parking lot near the sand. A constant wind blows spurts of stinging sand down a shore filled only with windsurfers. Unfortunately, there are no lifeguards, and you must BYOB (bring your own board). Take bus #5 which departs outside the gates of the medina, down the street from the Syndicat (6dh), to test the waves yourself.

AGADIR اغادير

Backpackers who come to Agadir may feel betrayed. At the juncture of the routes to the western Sahara, Agadir stands in stark contrast to the great desert valleys around Ouarzazate, the breathtaking route through Tizi-n-Test to Marrakech, and the coastal road from the backpacker's haven of Essaouira. It is a town that has been entirely redesigned in the last decades as a European-style beach resort, and it fulfills this promise very nicely. Broad, clean beaches, a bevy of resort hotels, discos, and beachfront cafes are mostly filled with Northern European tourists. Agadir is also expensive, but for the budget traveler who wants a brief break from traditional Morocco or needs to spend a night in transit, it can be managed comfortably and affordably.

Orientation and Practical Information Buses arrive and depart along a two-block stretch of blvd. Mohammed Cheikh Saadi, around which most budget hotels and eateries cluster. Going downhill toward the beach you will cross av. Prince Moulay Abdallah, av. Hassan II, and blvd. Mohammed V, finally winding down to the esplanade. **Syndicat d'Initiative et Tourisme,** av. Mohammed V (tel. 84 06 95), has a good **tourist office.** To get there from the bus stations, turn right on

Mohammed V; the office is on the left after av. General Kettani. Pick up a free map, bus schedule, and a list of pharmacies. Some English is spoken (open Mon.-Sat. 9:30am-noon and 2:45-4:30pm, Sun. 9:30am-noon). Flights leave from **Airport El-Massira** (tel. 83 91 22), 25km out of town. The **Royal Air Force Morocco** office (tel. 84 07 93), av. du General Kettani, may also be able to help. **Bus stations** are scattered along blvd. Mohammed Cheikh Saadi. **CTM** (tel. 82 20 77) runs buses to: Taroudannt (1 per day, 2hr., 29dh); Marrakech (4 per day, 4hr., 70dh); Essaouira (8 and 11:30am, 3hr., 37dh); Laayoune (8:30pm, 180dh); Ouarzazate (9:30am, 5hr., 60dh); and Rabat (10:15pm). There are many options for **car rental,** including Hertz, Budget, and Eurocar. Many offer greatly reduced "low season" rates, but the "low season" changes from year to year. **Luggage storage** is available at many bus stations. If you need medical attention, head to **Hospital Hassan II** (tel. 84 14 77), on Route de Marrakech. The **police** can be found at Hôtel de Police, rue 18 Novembre (tel. 19). The **post office,** av. Sidi Mohammed, on the corner of av. Prince Moulay Abdallah and Poste Restante, will handle all of your mail needs. (Open Mon.-Thurs. 8:30am-12:15pm and 2:30-6:30pm, Fri. 8:30-11am and 3-6:30pm.) There are **telephones** next to the post office (open daily 8:30am-noon and 2-6pm), and the **telephone code** is (0)8.

Accommodations and Food Budget hotels that congregate around the bus stations are similar, so just walk next door if one doesn't strike your fancy. There is a campground on blvd. Mohammed V on the western edge of town. At **Hôtel Aït Laayoune** (tel. 82 43 75), next door to the CTM station, rooms range from dingy to large and bright. The communal showers are fine. (Singles 70dh. Doubles 90dh.) **Hôtel Paris** (tel. 82 26 94), av. du President Remedy, is nicer than the others and the price reflects it. This very Parisian establishment is arranged around a central courtyard. (Singles 74dh, with shower 137dh. Doubles: 110dh; 160dh. Breakfast 17dh.)

The budget eateries are clustered around the bus stations. Head down to one of the boardwalk cafes for more expensive non-Moroccan cuisine. **Restaurant Mille et une Nuits** (tel. 82 37 11), back from the CTM station, is one of four restaurants in a row, all with comparable menus and mostly outdoor tables. It is inexpensive (*menu* 30dh) and offers a pleasant environment (open daily 8am-11pm).

Sights For the budget traveler who cannot afford the excursions to harbor villages, kasbahs, and "natural spectacles" put on by large hotels, the beach is the main attraction in Agadir. Take the 15-minute walk down, lay out a towel, and enjoy one of the cleanest, most swimmable, and most surfable beaches in Morocco. Then compare sunburns with thousands of pink Northern Europeans.

■ Taroudannt تارودانت

The long, winding descent to the Tizi-n-Test Pass through the High Atlas ends at the ramparts of Taroudannt. The northern gateway to the Anti-Atlas, its bastions have controlled traffic through the mountain range for centuries. An enormous rectangle of fortifications encases the town, making Taroudannt one of Morocco's best-preserved walled cities. Taruoodannt has great *souks* and few tourists, and serves primarily as an amiable way-station for those waiting to cross into the mountains or pass down to the coast.

ORIENTATION AND PRACTICAL INFORMATION

Taroudannt is centered around **place al Alaouyine,** with a second square, **place an-Nasr,** nearby. CTM, SATAS, and other companies terminate in place al-Alaouyine, which is also where banks and several budget hostels are located; other companies are located in place an-Nasr. To get from Place al Alaouyine to place an-Nasr, take the right-hand street on the opposite side of the square from Hotel Taroudannt.

Currency Exchange: Banks, including **BMCE** and **Banque Populaire,** are in pl. al-Alouyine and change traveler's checks. **Hôtel Palais Salam,** set in the eastern wall of the Kasbah, changes small amounts of traveler's checks or cash (around $50).

Buses: Buses are infrequent, inconvenient, and confusing. It is best to ask around at different companies, as routes and locations change frequently. Fortunately, ticket sellers are helpful. **SATAS** buses go to: Marrakech via Agadir (5am, 6hr., 70dh); Agadir (6:30am, 2hr., 15dh); Ouarzazate (6:30pm, 5hr.). **CTM** to Marrakech via Agadir (9pm, 6hr., 91dh) and Ouarzazate (11:30am, 5hr.). One bus runs to Taroudannt-Marrkech via Tizi-n-Test from Pl. an-Nasr (5am, 55dh).

Swimming Pool: The **Hôtel Palais Salam** allows non-guests to use their pool (40dh per day).

Hospital: Hopital Mokhtar Soussi (tel. 85 30 80), inside the town walls through the Bab El Kasbah (Kasbah Gate).

Police: (tel. 19), in the basement of Public Works building, outside Bab El Kasbah, also a small office in pl. al-Alaouyine.

Post Office: Just beyond the police station out of the Bab El Kasbah, in front of the mosque. Poste Restante, no phones. Open Mon.-Fri. 8:30am-12:15pm and 2:30-6:30pm, Sat. 8-11am.

ACCOMMODATIONS AND FOOD

Hotel Taroudannt, pl. al-Alaouyine. A pleasant bar, courtyard jungle, clean rooms, and a roof-top terrace. Singles 55dh, with shower 70dh. Doubles 70dh, 85dh

Hôtel Roudani (tel. 85 22 19), slightly better than the other cheaper hotels. Free showers. Small rooms for one or two people 40dh. Larger rooms 70dh.

Hotel Taroudannt Restaurant, pl. al-Alaouyine. A left-over piece of France serving excellent French dishes and wine, complete with white table cloths and napkins (*menu* 60-75dh). Full bar with pleasant outdoor seating. Open daily noon-2:30pm and 7-9pm.

Restaurant Hotel Roudani, pl. al-Alaouyine. Moroccan specialties served at tables on the square. Open 24hr.

SIGHTS

The monumental **fortified walls** which enclose Taroudannt are more awesome than beautiful. Construction began in the16th century when Taroudannt thrived as a cultural and military center, but those that remain date from the 18th century. Walking around them is the best way to appreciate their immensity. Bicycles are a good way to circumnavigate the town and can be rented in several places, including Hotel Taroudannt (5dh per hr.; see **Accommodations and Food** above).

The **souks** around the two squares are also worth a look; although unimpressive in comparison to those in the imperial cities, Taroudannt is one of Morocco's silver-working centers. A good deal of high quality ornamental jewelry can be found.

There are also interesting fortified villages and kasbahs around Taroudannt, the closest of which is **Freija,** 11km away, an easy half-day bike ride. To get there, follow the Ourazazate-Marrakech road (Tizi-n-Test) 8km to the town of Aït Iazza. From there, turn right down the road to Igherm and Tata, cross the (usually) dry riverbed. The town is at the top of the hill.

HIGH ATLAS AND DESERTS الاطلس الاعلى

■ Marrakech مـراكش

For almost a thousand years Morocco's great imperial city has been the cultural capital of the Maghreb, drawing visitors from all over who have come to Marrakech to witness exotica. Tourists, still a minority at the Djemâa el-Fna, marginally observe the cacophonous crowd of snake charmers, musicians, boxers, acrobats, mystics,

MOROCCO

dentists (you'll just have to see it for yourself), scribes, and preachers in the medina's main square. The old city is huge, labyrinthine, and definitely worth a visit. Count the invasive hustlers and faux guides as part of the experience. In addition to its own fantastic merits, Marrakech also serves as a good base for expeditions into the Atlas Mountains or the Sahara.

ORIENTATION AND PRACTICAL INFORMATION

Most of the excitement, budget food, and cheap accommodations center on the **Djemâa el-Fna** and surround the **medina.** The **bus** and **train stations,** administrative buildings, and luxury hotels are in the **Guéliz** or **ville nouvelle** down **avenue Mohammed V;** from the Djemâa el-Fna, walk to the towering **Koutoubia Minaret** and turn right. Also in the ville nouvelle are most of the car rentals, newsstands, banks, and travel agencies. Bus #1 runs between the minaret and the heart of the ville nouvelle (1.50dh). Or, take one of the many *petits taxis* (despite the driver's demands, you shouldn't pay more than 10dh).

Tourist Office: Office National Marocain du Tourisme (ONMT), av. Mohammed V (tel. 43 62 39), at pl. Abdel Moumen ben Ali, about a 35min. walk from Djemâa el-Fna. Pl. Abdel Moumen is next to a bus stop and has **public toilets.** The office will get you a brochure with a mediocre map and access to **official guides,** (half-day 120dh, full day 150dh). ONMT open daily 8:30am-noon and 2:30-6:30pm; Ramadan daily 9am-3pm. **Syndicat d'Initiative,** 176 av. Mohammed V (tel. 43 30 97), on the right heading from the post office to the ONMT. Some mediocre maps, same dearth of info. Open daily 8:30am-12:30pm and 2:30-6pm.

Currency Exchange: Banks line av. Mohammed V and av. Hassan II in the Guéliz. Clustered in the medina around the post office on the Djemâa el-Fna. **BCME** is open Sat., and **Syndicat d'Initiative** on Sun. Most tourist-centered hotels change money at late hours—try Hôtel Ali or Hôtel Essaouira. Most banks also cash traveler's checks.

American Express: Voyages Schwartz, rue Mauritania, 2nd fl. (tel. 43 66 00), off av. Mohammed V, 2nd left after post office. Open daily 6am-11pm. Bank open Mon.-Fri. 8:30-11:30am and 2:30-4:30pm.

Flights: Aéroport de Marrakech Menara (tel. 44 78 65, 44 79 10, or 44 85 06), 5km south of town. Taxi service about 50dh. No bus. Domestic and international flights on Royal Air Maroc and Royal Air Inter. Like all other Moroccan airports, it's puny compared to Casablanca's Aéroport Mohammed V.

Trains: av. Hassan II (tel. 44 77 68 or 44 77 63), going away from the medina on Mohammed V, turn left on av. Hassan II and walk 5min. To: Casablanca (8 per day, 4hr., 73dh); Tangier (5 per day, 8hr., 140dh); Fès (2 per day, 8hr., 169dh); Melines (6 per day, 7hr., 150dh).

Buses: tel. 43 39 33, outside the medina walls by Bab Doukkala. Walk out of the medina on av. Mohammed V; pass through Bab Larissa, and turn right. Walk beside the walls until Bab Doukkala. The **gare routière** is to your left. **CTM** is next to window #8. To: Agadir (2 per day, 4hr., 61dh); Asni (8 per day, 1½hr., 15dh); Casablanca (3 per day, 4hr., 65dh); Fès (2 per day, 10hr., 130dh); Ouarzazate (4 per day, 4½hr., 65dh); Zagora (4 per day, 79dh); Essaouira (8 per day, 3hr., 36dh). Other windows are for different private companies which have lower prices, lower standards, more frequent service, or a combination of the three. Most private buses also stop outside the Bab er-Rob, just south of Djemâa el-Fna, but seats are often full. Go from here to Setti-Fatma in the High Atlas (every 30min., 13dh).

Grands Taxis: It's best to start from Bab er-Rob, where you can share a taxi to Asni or Setti-Fatma. 15dh if taxi has 6 passengers; slightly more for smaller groups.

Car Rental: Avis, 137 blvd. Mohammed V (tel. 43 99 84 or 43 13 94), and **Hertz,** 154 blvd. Mohammed V (tel. 43 46 80 or 43 13 94). Both also have airport offices. Both rent Renault IVs for 250dh per day plus 2.50dh per mile. Numerous other local agencies, including many hotels will arrange rentals and a discount.

Swimming Pool: Piscine Koutoubia, in the medina off av. Mohammed V, the next left heading toward the new city from the Koutoubia. Officially co-ed, but women

N

Marrakech

Bahia Palace, 10
Bus Station, 4
Dar el Makhken, 11
El Badi Palace, 12
Koutoubia Mosque, 5
Medrassa ben Youssef, 8
Mouassin Fountain, 6
Museum of Moroccan Art, 9
Post Office, 3
Saadien Tombs, 13
Souks, 7
Tourist Office, 2
Train Station, 1

MOROCCO

may be outnumbered by a thousand to one. Open late June to early Sept. Wed.-Mon. 9:30am-noon and 2:30-6pm. About 5dh. For a ritzier place with a poolside bar, try the **Grand Hôtel du Tazi,** near the Hôtel Foucauld (40dh).

Late-Night Pharmacy: Off the Djemâa el-Fna, on the way to av. Mohammed V, on the right. Open Tues.-Sun. 9pm-6am.

Medical Emergency: Doctor on call until 10pm at the above late-night pharmacy. It's best to avoid the government-run *polyclinique;* ask your consulate to recommend a private physician (see **Essentials: Embassies and Consulates,** p. 36).

Police: (tel. 19), to the south of the Djemâa el-Fna.

Post Office: pl. XVI Novembre, off av. Mohammed V. Unreliable Poste Restante, and it's a madhouse on Sat. Open Mon.-Fri. 8am-noon and 4-7pm, Sat. 8:30-11:30am. **Branch office** in the Djemâa. Open Mon.-Fri. 8:30am-noon and 2:30-6:45pm.

Telephone Code: (0)4.

ACCOMMODATIONS AND CAMPING

Apart from the youth hostel and campground, which are far from the medina but close to the train station, all cheap accommodations are within a stone's throw of the Djemâa el-Fna. Many places allow you to sleep on the roof for about 20dh. To find Hotels Essaouiria, Medina, and Afriquia, walk from Djemâa al-Fna down the street to the left of Banque al-Mayrib, take your first left, then turn right and follow the signs.

Auberge de Jeunesse (HI), rue el-Jahed (tel. 44 77 13). 5min. from the train station, in a dreamy part of the ville nouvelle, but 30min. walk from the interesting part of Marrakech. Exit the train station and turn left on Hassan II. Take the 1st right at the traffic circle onto av. France. Take the 2nd right, continue for 2 blocks, then take a left and the 1st right. The spartan hostel is at the end of the street. Cold showers. Stark rooms. BYOTP (Bring Your Own Toilet Paper). Reception open daily 8-9am, noon-2pm, and 6-10pm. Some rules—such as lock-out, 10pm curfew, and membership requirement—*may* be flexible. 20dh per person per night.

Hôtel Essaouira, 3 Derb Sidi Bouloukat (tel. 44 38 05), from pl. Djemâa el-Fna, face the post office (PTT) and Banque du Maroc. Head down the road in the left corner, through an archway. Take the first right after the Hôtel de France; there are some faded signs showing the way. The best terrace in town with a cafe and laundry basins. Manager stores luggage for excursions to the Atlas Mountains. 40dh per person. Hot showers 5dh.

Hôtel Medina, 1 Derb Sidi Bouloukat (tel. 44 30 67), on your way to the Hôtel Essaouira (and run by its manager's cousin). Great terrace and clean rooms. Singles 35-40dh. Doubles 60-80dh, depending on bed size.

Hotel Afriquia, 45 Sidi Boulouliate (tel. 44 24 03). Cool courtyard filled with slender orange trees differentiates Afriquia from the others. Clean rooms and bathrooms. Singles 40dh. Doubles 70dh. Hot showers 5dh.

Hôtel Ali, rue Moulay Ismael (tel. 44 49 79; fax 43 36 09), past the post office in the Djemâa el-Fna. Hôtel Ali draws tourists from around Morocco by milking its rep as *the* budget hotel. Good suites with soap, towels, usually A/C, and toilet paper (stock up!). Singles with shower 70dh. Doubles with shower 90dh. Say you don't want breakfast or they'll add 15dh to your bill. Hôtel Ali also has a complete restaurant (see **Food** below) and organizes expeditions. If it's full, don't agree to go to **Hôtel Farouk** (which is owned by the same family)—it is distant from the Djemâa el-Fna and is no better than the other budget hotels near Hôtel Ali.

Hôtel Gallia, 30 rue de la Recette (tel. 44 59 13; fax 44 48 53), from the Djemâa, take the street to the left of the Banque du Maroc, and the 1st left after the cinema. A cut above the other hotels in the area, and the price reflects it. Clean bedrooms (many with A/C) and sparkling bathrooms. Laundry service available. Singles 99dh, with shower 152dh. Doubles: 126dh; 182dh.

Camping: Camping-Caravaning Municipal (tel. 31 31 67), 13km out from Marrakech on rte. de Casablanca. Closed part of 1997; call ahead. Pool, warm showers, and supermarket. 10dh per person, 11dh per tent, 8dh per car.

FOOD

Two **markets** peddle fresh produce along the fortifications surrounding the city, far from pl. Djemâa el-Fna. A closer daily fruit and vegetable market lies just outside Bab Aghmat. Bab el-Kemis hosts a lively Thursday market. For delicious bargains, head for the **food stalls** in the Djemâa. Grub dealers contribute to the square's madness—dozens of stalls deal from late afternoon until after midnight. Follow the crowds to the best *harira* (2dh) and *kebab* (2dh). As always, settle the price first.

Chez Chegrouni, 4-6 pl. Djemâa el-Fna, just to the right of Café Montréal. Unassuming, but not unrewarding. Spot the brown and gold awning or follow your nose to 3dh *soupe marocaine,* a meal in itself. Excellent *couscous* (25dh).

Hôtel Ali (see **Accommodations** above). Popular with tourists for its (pricey) all-you-can-eat Moroccan buffet (75dh).

Café-Patisserie Toubkal, pl. Djemâa el-Fna, near the archway that leads to Hôtel Essaouira. Refresh your aching body on the shady outdoor patio. Scrumptious shish kebab with fried onions and peppers (18dh). Open daily 7am-11pm.

Restaurant Argana, pl. Djemaa el-Fna. Typical menu (75-90dh) and a pleasant terrace overlooking the square. Try the pigeon *pastilla,* avoid the spaghetti (open daily 6am-1am).

SIGHTS AND ENTERTAINMENT

Djemâa el-Fna

Welcome to the **Djemâa el-Fna** (Assembly of the Dead), one of the world's most frantically exotic squares, where sultans beheaded criminals and displayed the remains. Crowds of thousands participate in the bizarre bazaar that picks up in the afternoon and peters out after midnight. While snake-charmers and water-sellers pose to entice tourists' cameras (and wallets), the vast majority of the audience are townspeople and Berbers from outlying villages. Solitary figures consult with scribes, potion dealers, and fortune-tellers. Crowds congregate around the preachers, story-tellers, and musicians. Women have their children blessed by mystics, and touts encourage bets on boxing matches between 11-year-old boys (and an occasional American Champ). On a good night, it's an absolute sensory overload.

Almost every tour of Marrakech begins at the 12th-century **Koutoubia Mosque,** whose magnificent **minaret** presides over the Djemâa el-Fna. Crowned by a lantern of three golden spheres, the minaret is the oldest and best surviving example of the art of the Almohads, who made Marrakech their capital (1130-1213) and once ruled the region from Spain to present-day Tunisia. Unfortunately, as of June 1997, the minaret was still being restored. In 1157, Abd el-Mumin acquired one of four editions of the Qur'an authorized by the caliph Uthman, and used it as a talisman in battle and inspiration for the design of the second Koutoubia Mosque. Possession of this holy book turned Marrakech into a center of religious study. In fact, the name Koutoubia comes from the Arabic *kutubiyyin (*of the books). The minaret in particular is revered by art historians for its influence on eight centuries of Islamic architecture. As with most Moroccan mosques, entrance is forbidden to non-Muslims.

The imperial city also had considerable military importance (many sultans' campaigns to quell the tribes of the Atlas were launched from here), as evidenced by 2km of pink-tinged fortifications. The **walls** are punctuated by numerous **gates,** the most significant of which are:

Bab Agnaou, the most dazzling gate, 3 blocks south of the Koutoubia mosque. Formerly portal to the Kasbah of Yacoub el-Mansour. This 12th-century gate often displayed trophies of war—mutilated corpses and heads of slain enemies.

Bab er-Rob, next to Bab Agnaou, once the south doorway to the city. The Saadien tombs (see below) are just inside; *grands taxis* wait outside.

Bab el-Khemis, site of a lively Thurs. market, in the northeast corner of Marrakech, a long swing around town. The bastion was reputedly designed and built by

Andalusian architects and artisans. Best reached by heading around the corner of the Medrassa ben Youssef, and taking the first major left.

The Medina

A worthwhile survey of the medina (prime time 5-8pm) begins at the **souks.** Though dazzling and intimidating, the maze of streets doesn't necessitate a guide. If you get lost, stay cool until you want to leave, then ask a merchant for directions (or a child will lead you out for a few *dirhams*). From the Djemâa, enter the medina on the pathway directly across from the Café-Restaurant-Hôtel de France. This is the path running through the medina's main thoroughfare, and turning past the enormous **Souk Smarine,** which takes a turn at the **potters' souk.** Berber blankets, woven by families spinning wool in a tangle of dowels, string, and cards of yarn, pile the alleyways of the **fabric souk.** Follow your nose through the first major orange gateway and make a quick right to the Zahba Kedima, a small plaza containing the **spice souk,** with massive sacks of saffron, cumin, ginger, and orange flower, as well as the apothecaries' more unusual wares—goat hoof for hair treatment, ground-up ferrets for depression, and live chameleons for sexual frustration. Nearby is **La Criée Berbère** (the Berber Auction), a center for slave dealing prior to French occupation. Nowadays, it hosts less predatory carpet and rug merchants.

Farther on are the bubbling vats of color of the **dyers' souk.** Fragrant whiffs of cedar signal the nearby **carpenters' souk,** where workers carve chess pieces with astounding speed. Go left through these stalls to where the 16th-century **Mouassin Fountain** bathes its colorful carvings in an outer layer of grime.

On the road going right where **Souk Attarine** (perfume) forks, an endless selection of colorful leather footwear preens at the **babouche souk** (untinted yellow is traditional for men while women wear the fancier models). The right fork at the end of the street leads to the **cherratine souk,** which connects the *babouche souk* to the **Souk el-Kbir** (the right fork off Souk Smarine as you enter the medina), the **leather souk.** In 1565, Sultan Moulay Abdallah el-Ghalib raised the **Madrasa of ben Youssef** in the center of the medina (to get there, backtrack to Souk Smarine, bear right at the fork onto Souk el-Kbir, and follow this to its end). It reigned as the largest Quranic school in the Maghreb until closing in 1956. The Andalusian style includes the requisite calligraphy and intricate floral designs. Visitors can roam the students' cells, and feel lucky to be unaccompanied by 400 *madrasa*-mates. (*Madrasa* open Tues.-Sun. 8am-noon and 3-7pm; winter Tues.-Sun. 8am-noon and 2-6pm. 10dh.)

Around the corner, beside the Ben-Youssef mosque, juts the squat, unpainted cupola of 12th-century **Koubba el-Ba'adiyn,** the oldest monument in town and the only relic of the Almoravid dynasty. When you've had enough of keyhole arches, pinecone and palm motifs, and intricate dome carvings, ask the guard to open an ancient wooden door to the subterranean cisterns. (Open daily 8:30am-noon and 2:30-6pm. Bang on the door if it's closed. 10dh, plus tip for the custodian-guide.)

After the *madrasa,* those of strong nose and stomach can visit the **tanneries.** Head right around the corner and down toward Bab Debbarh. Each bubbling vat holds a different chemical for a stage of leather production.

The Great Glaoui

This place would have made Robin Leach drool. The Glaoui Kasbah, located just outside Marrakech, is one of the most extravagant sights in Morocco, even after its avaricious looting in 1956. By the turn of the century, the Glaouis had become the dominant political and financial force in the region. When France took over in 1912, they granted the Glaouis extensive power over the entire south. Yet all was not business. El Glaoui, Pasha of Marrakech during France's rule and buddy of Winston Churchill, relished a good party as much as anyone. He invested his fabulous wealth in extravagant parties at which El Glaoui purportedly doled out hashish, opium, gold, and even little boys and girls to his Western guests.

Palaces and Tombs

The **Saadien Tombs,** modeled after the interior of the Alhambra in Granada, constitute Morocco's most lavish mausoleum. The tombs served as the royal Saadien necropolis during the 16th and 17th centuries, until Moulay Ismail walled them off to efface the memory of his predecessors. In 1912 the burial complex was rediscovered during a French aerial survey. One **mausoleum,** the tomb of **El Mansour** (the Victorious), brims opulently with illuminated *zellij* (mosaic tilework). The second was built for his mother. Both date from the late 16th century. In the neighboring **Hall of the Twelve Columns,** trapezoidal tombs rise from a pool of polished marble. The sultan's four wives, 23 concubines, and the most favored of his hundreds of children are buried nearby. Unmarked tombs belong to the women. (Hall open 8:30am-noon and 2:30-6pm. Multilingual tours. 10dh.) To reach the Saadien Tombs, follow the signs from Bab el-Rob. The turquoise minaret of the **Mosque of the Kasbah,** Sultan Yacoub el-Mansour's own personal mosque, flags the way. Veer left into the adjoining alley.

The ruthless late 19th-century vizier Si Ahmed Ben Moussa, also known as Bou Ahmed, constructed **El Bahia** palace. Serving as the *de facto* seat of government for the man who ruled in the sultan's stead, El Bahia (The Brilliance) was built to stave off European domination by asserting Morocco's historical and cultural significance. Facing the Hôtel CTM in the Djemâa, head left through an archway onto rue Riad Zitouna el-Kedim on the right. Follow the main thoroughfare to the end, and bear left through pl. Ferblantiers, curving around 180 degrees. On the right, a reddish-brown archway opens into a long, tree-lined avenue which leads to the palace door. (Open 8:30-11:45am and 2:30-5:45pm.)

Dar Si Said, a 19th-century palace built by Si Said, brother of Grand Vizier Ba Ahmed and chamberlain of Sultan Moulay el-Hassan, houses a **Museum of Moroccan Art.** The collection features splendid Berber carpets, pottery, jewelry, Essaouiran ebony, and Saadien woodcarving (open Wed.-Mon. 8:30am-noon and 2:30-5:45pm; 10dh). The gleaming Dar Si Said is on a tiny alley off rue Riad Zitouna el-Jadid, the second right heading toward the Djemâa el-Fna from the Bahia Palace.

Gardens

The mid-day sun in Marrakech can be cruel, and for centuries residents have dealt with it by constructing massive irrigated gardens. The largest of these is the **Agdal,** a 3km enclosure accessible via a roofed portal overlooking the Grand Méchouar, once probably a royal date and olive plantation. It is closed to the public when the King is in residence. While olive trees predominate, the garden contains all manner of fruit-bearing trees that shade the avenues and large, still pools. To get to the Agdal from Bab er-Rob, walk left along the medina walls until you reach Bab Ahmar. Walk down rue Bab Ahmar for five minutes. If open, the garden is on your right.

The **Menara Gardens,** a vast enclave of olive groves around an enormous pond, are most beautiful at sunset, when the mauve and tangerine light reflects off the water. The cold green reservoir, 800m by 1200m, dates from the Almohad era. To reach the gardens, head west through Bab el-Jedid and straight down av. Menara, the wide boulevard that resembles an airport landing strip. To the left lies the expansive olive grove of Bab el-Jedid, a continuation of the gardens.

Menara and Agdal date back centuries, yet are overshadowed by the 1920s upstart **Majorelle Gardens.** Designed by French painter Jacques Majorelle, its exquisitely engineered explosions of colorful flowers contrast strongly with the stately greens of the Agdal and Menara. The garden is owned and maintained by Yves Saint Laurent (who occasionally zips around the Djemâa el-Fna on his moped), and its fanciful colors (pink concrete pathways?!) rival his wildest collections (open daily 8am-noon and 3-7pm; winter 8am-noon and 2-5pm; 15dh).

Entertainment

If you want to go where everybody knows your name ("Tourist!"), try the **hotel bars** at the **Tazi** and **Foucauld.** Here locals and tourists mix, lubricated by 15dh Flag *spé-*

MOROCCO

ciales. To hit the Tazi, head away from the Djemâa 200m down the street to the left of the Banque du Maroc. For the Foucauld, turn right by the Tazi onto the road that becomes av. Mohammed V and walk two blocks. Also, try the **Diamant Noir,** a nightclub on Mohammed V in Gueliz.

■ High Atlas الاطلس الاعلى

Trekking in the Atlas Mountains can be a wonderful addition to your tell-your-grand-children repertoire. Unlike their counterparts in Europe, the range's trails have yet to be fitted for tourists, and the valleys below remain green, unspoiled, and very accessible. Even travelers with limited funds, time, and skills can huff to the summit of **Djebal Toubkal,** North Africa's highest peak (4167m). Ascending Toubkal takes only two days; however, treks of up to a couple weeks are plausible. For Toubkal, little more than a sleeping bag, food, water, and sturdy shoes are necessary. For any-thing longer, though, unless one is skilled and equipped with a full outfit of back-packing equipment (i.e. a stove, tent, water purification system, compass, maps, etc.), the services of a guide and/or mule and muleteer can be very helpful, if not at times necessary, as the trails are many and universally unmarked. **Guides** and **mules** can be hired in **Imlil** for 160dh per day and 75dh per day respectively (not including tip). Alternatively, treks can be organized in Marrakech at **Hotel Ali** (see p. 667), where many experienced guides hang out. From Hotel Ali, prices are about 250dh per day per person, with everything from food-and-shelter deals to guide-and-mule setups. All this only applies during the summertime, since during the **winter** snow covers Toubkal and the upper valleys. In winter, full alpine gear and an experienced guide are a *must.* Also, no matter what time of year, **altitude sickness** must be taken into consideration, as the altitude change from Marrakech is drastic. Know the symptoms—headaches, nausea, dizziness, appetite loss—and if they become severe or last longer than a day *descend immediately.* If you have had problems with AMS before, spend a night or two in Imlil before ascending Toubkal.

The ascent of **Toubkal** is outlined here; for more ambitious treks, information can be garnered from books (*The Atlas Mountains, Morocco* by Robin G. Collomb is the acclaimed source), from guides (though remember they are guides and not information books), and from other trekkers.

A *grand taxi* to **Asni** kicks off the mountain adventure, heading off from Bab er-Rob when there are enough passengers (1hr., 15dh). Asni itself has little to offer besides mild hustling, *tajine,* and a Saturday *souk.* Those stranded overnight can stay at the primitive **youth hostel** at the end of the village's street (20dh; bring a sleeping bag). Most travelers climb onto the first **camionette** headed to Imlil, where the trail begins. The hair-raising pick-up truck journey is an experience in itself—all but the fainthearted should stand in back to enjoy the scenery (45 min., 15dh).

Imlil is a tiny village high in the Atlas. The air is cool (and damn cold at night), and the sound of running water is everywhere. Stay at the **CAF Refuge (HI),** which has bunks, a kitchen (5dh per hr. of cooking gas), and cold showers in a refurbished cot-tage in the center of town. (Members 44dh, nonmembers 52dh. Camping outside 10dh per tent, 5dh per person.) Unfortunately, the CAF Refuge will not allow you to store excess luggage while you explore. If this is a problem, consider getting a room at one of Imlil's two hotels. Both the **Hôtel Aksoual** and **Hôtel Soleil** have rooms for negotiable rates (about 40dh per person), and their cafes serve *tajine* for 30dh.

From Imlil, depart for Toubkal bright and early. Take the road up out of town, fol-lowing the river. Ask locals for the correct mule track. You will pass the hilltop vil-lage of **Aroumd** on the other side of the valley, then descend into a broad valley before zigzagging up the east side. After over an hour of spectacular scenery, hikers reach **Sidi Chamarouch,** home to a fiercely guarded *marabout* shrine. The trail turns right and upward upon entering the village. Past this point the area is snow-bound through late April. Next comes the **Toubkal** (or **Neltner**) **Refuge** (52dh, with HI card 44dh). Although often overcrowded, the refuge is a welcoming end to a day's hiking. Ask here for the best path up Toubkal (another 2½hr.). Most hikers

spend the night here and ascend Toubkal early the next morning, as it clouds over in the afternoon, and then descend back to Imlil that same day. A guide for the final ascent can also be arranged at the refuge.

THE SOUTHERN VALLEYS AND DESERT

Falling southeast from the Atlas ranges and stretching to the sand-dune seas of the Algerian Sahara is Morocco's desert: mountainous and desolate, its deep reds and oranges are contested only by the green veins of oases that creep through the valley floors. Set into this landscape are fantastic Berber towns and Kasbahs, where mud castles tower over the road and on hilltops. A rental car is useful for exploring this part of Morocco, but excursions can be made more easily using local transportation.

■ Ouarzazate ورزازات

The ride to Ouarzazate, on a cusp between the Atlas Mountains and the southern desert, reduces travelers to monosyllabic "oohs" and "wows," and perhaps—depending on the driver—a few "eeks" as well. The trip's finale is somewhat anticlimactic. Though envisioned by the Moroccan government as a tourist mecca (a four-lane highway was built, four- and five-star hotels were erected), Ouarzazate never became popular—the restaurants and enormous streets are often vacant. However, the town is an often necessary stop between Marrakech and the valleys and desert, and is a good place to stock up on supplies and even spend a relaxed, uninteresting day. The region has a strong crafts tradition, and because of the severe depression in tourism, bargains abound and hustlers are scarce. Ouarzazate is a great place to forget about trains and buses by exploring the *kasbahs* on a rented moped. It is also a good place to rent a car to explore farther south and east if the prospect of driving across the mountains from Marrakech seems a bit daunting.

PRACTICAL INFORMATION

One of the more helpful **tourist offices** (tel. 88 24 85) in Morocco is on av. Mohammed V, where the road forks to follow the Oued Drâa and the Oued Dadès. Get bus info and a directory of hotels in the Drâa and Dadès Valleys. Open Mon.-Fri. 8:30-noon and 2:30-6:30pm. **Currency exchange** is done at the banks lining av. Mohammed V. The four- and five-star hotels will only exchange cash.

CTM and **private buses** are located at the western edge of Ouarzazate. From Hôtel Royal, walk toward Marrakech on av. Mohammed V. Take a right after Hôtel La Gazelle, and go 1½ blocks. To: Marrakech (4 per day, 4½hr., 45dh); Rachidia, via Skoura, Boumalne du Dadés, and Tinehar (1 per day, 10:30am); M'Hamid, via Agdz and Zagora (1 per day, 12:30am, 6½hr., 55dh); Agadir (noon, 6hr. 60dh). Private buses travel more frequently. **Grands taxis** line up by the bus station and run fairly often to nearby destinations Skoura (45min., 10dh), Zagora (3hr., 45dh), and Marrakech (5hr., 70dh). If the taxis are not full (less than six people crammed in), be prepared to pay extra. Hôtel Royal rents **mopeds** (150dh per 12 hours, 250dh per 24hr.; haggling acceptable). Ask to speak with a "Star Skooter" representative. The are several **rental car** agencies in Ouarzazate, including Hertz, Avis, Eurocar, and Budget. The large companies charge about 500dh per day with unlimited mileage for a Fiat Uno. Local companies, while offering fewer services, charge half that. Check your car well before accepting it or making any payments—if it is not acceptable, ask for another one or go to another company. The **post office** sits on av. Mohammed V, next to the tourist office. **International telephones** are in the same building. (Open Mon.-Sat. 8am-noon and 2:30-6:45pm; Sept.-June Mon.-Sat. 8am-noon and 2:30-6pm.) The **telephone code** is (0)4.

ACCOMMODATIONS AND FOOD

Most administrative buildings, cafes, and restaurants are strung along **av. Moham-med V.** For inexpensive lodging, check either here or on streets parallel and to the north. **Hôtel Royal,** 24 av. Mohammed V (tel. 88 22 58), next to Chez Dimitri, is a safe bet. (Singles 36-51dh, with shower 80dh. Doubles: 72dh; 95dh. Warm shower 10dh.) The **Hôtel Bab Es Sahara,** pl. Mouhadine (tel. 88 47 22 or 88 49 65), has large cheap rooms. Head away from the bus station, and take a left after the Hôtel Royal. (Singles 50dh, with shower and toilet 70dh. Doubles 80dh; 105dh.) It has a restaurant and **currency exchange.**

The **supermarket,** on av. Mohammed V, across the street from Hôtel Royal, has an unrivaled selection of cured meats, canned goods, chocolate, wine, cold beer, and European goods. **Restaurante-Café Royal,** av. Mohammed V (tel. 88 24 75), is a great spot for neighborhood chess matches and chicken *tajine* (35dh)—the only dish they serve regularly, despite an extensive menu (open daily 7am-11pm). The tourists in Ouarzazate come to **Chez Dimitri,** the best (well, only) Italian restaurant in town. Built during the French occupation, and holder of the monopoly on alcohol. *Menu* (75dh); pasta (60dh).

SIGHTS

The nearest example of desert architecture is the **Kasbah of Taourirt,** once a stronghold of the Glaoui. The Kasbah, 1½km east of town near Club Med, was built in the mid 18th century and occupied until independence in 1956, when it was abandoned. It has been completely restored within the last year, and thus provides a unique opportunity to climb through the labyrinth of rooms, stairways, and balconies which chaotically fill the red kasbah's interior. To get there, walk down av. Mohammed V, away from Marrakech, and bear left at the tourist office. Step onto the bamboo floors through the doorway just to the left of the Kasbah as you face it from the street (open daily 8:30am-noon and 2:30-7:30pm; admission to palace 10dh). Across the highway, the tiny **Centre Artisanal/Carpet Cooperative** displays local crafts, including the region's woven and knotted carpets. Craft-seekers might take a look at one of Ouarzazate's four **souks** held on Tues. and Fri.-Sun. Ask at the tourist office for locations.

■ Near Ouarzazate

The area to the north of Ouarzazate is a hot and dusty palette of desert browns and greens. Small Berber **Kasbahs** (government citadels) pepper the descent. Perhaps the most spectacular of these is in the village **Aït Benhaddou,** 30km on the road towards Marrakech. Though seemingly abandoned, a handful of Berber families has not yet left the building. The forest of tapered turrets climbs to the ruined Kasbah at the crest of a hill. Look familiar? They're the region's film stars, featured in *Lawrence of Arabia* and *Jesus of Nazareth*. The village has since been designated by UNESCO as a world heritage site. Take a collective taxi from Ouarzazate (about 250-300dh round-trip; the driver waits) or get off at Oued El Malleh (10dh per person) and walk the 6km to Aït Benhaddou. It's a beautiful ride on a rented moped—but be sure the gas tank is filled.

■ The Drâa Valley وادى دراع

South of Ouarzazate, through Agdz, Zagora, and ending in M'Hamid, is the narrow Drâa Valley, at the bottom of which is a continuous grove of palm trees strewn with *kasbahs* and *ksours*. Stop and explore from a rented car; otherwise, hop from village to village using buses, taxis, or hitchhiking (very common in the south). Desert expeditions by camel or 4x4 can begin in Zagfora or, preferably, M'Hamid. Temperatures can reach 67°C here during July and August, but are tolerable the rest of the year, and it even gets cold during the night.

NORTHERN DRÂA TO ZAGORA

As you leave Ouarzazate southbound on P31, the scenery changes almost instantly. A lunar landscape strewn with volcanic rock stretches in all directions. Farther south, magnificent cusps of black cliff poke eerily through the horizon. Ancient lookout towers sprinkle the roadside terrain. The first *ksour* is **Aït Saoun.** From here the road passes a deep black gorge and winds over the Tizi-n-Tinifift pass to Ourika. Set below Jbel Kissane, 67km from Ouarzazate, **Agdz** stops buses for 30 minutes on their way to Zagora and M'Hamid. Agdz is a good place to get gas and a cold drink, but not much else. Immediately south of Agdz, the highway intersects the Drâa River and the long string of oases begins. The layout of the villages is remarkable: each community is divided into several clusters about an oasis, with smaller domiciles adjoining central fortified *kasbahs.* Oddly-shaped towers give **Tamnougalt** away, the first breathtaking *ksour* along the route. Next in line is **Timiderte,** then **Tansihkt** and its explosion of palm trees, **Ouaouzgar's** fine valley view, and **Tamezmoute**'s giant Kasbah. T^ezouline, a large central village with a pretty *kasbah,* is known for its lively Monday market. Just before Zagora, the **Azlag Pass** opens the valley to an ocean of palms. Note: Many hustlers pose as hitchhikers along the Ouarzazate to Zagora road, inviting the driver back to his place in "gratitude" for the ride, and once there trying to get the driver to take a camel trek, buy jewelry, etc. A good way to avoid this is to pile one's bags on the seats and say there is no space. Better yet, don't stop at all.

ZAGORA زاجورة

Stiflingly hot, tourist-trodden, and hustler-ridden, Zagora is the traditional place in which treks and expeditions into the valley and desert are organized. Built as a French administrative town, Zagora is not a very appealing place. Practically everyone you meet in Zagora seems to have camels to rent; it is better to go to an established hotel or campground. Even better, go to M'Hamid. *Everything* is lined along av. Mohammed V, the road that the highway turns into when it enters town. BMCE and **Banque Populaire** are both there for **currency exchange,** as is the **post office.** If you decide to stay in Zagora, the cheapest place is **Hôtel des Amis** (tel. 84 29 74). Slightly dingy, but passable rooms are 30dh. Doubles with shower are 50dh. Much nicer is the large, modern **Hôtel Palmeraie,** where singles start at 50dh and doubles 100dh. Rooms with a terrace cost 15dh extra. Many rooms have air-conditioning, and there is a nice pool and a bar. Both hotels are on av. Mohammed V. Signs indicate the way to **Camping Sindibad** (tel. 84 75 53), av. Hassan II., which charges 10dh per person, per tent and per car. Camping spots are shaded and covered with grass and there is also a pool. All three of these places arrange **camel treks** anywhere from a few hours to a few weeks long for around 300dh per day per person, with everything from food to bedding included. **Restaurants,** none particularly spectacular, line av. Mohammed V. Most hotels and campgrounds have restaurants as well. There is one morning **bus** and several evening buses to Marrakech through Ouarzazate, and several buses to Agadir, Rabat, and Casablanca. There is one CTM bus to M'Hamid at 4pm. Grand taxis are a much better way to travel to M'Hamid (25dh).

SOUTHERN DRÂA

To cross the Drâa at the southern edge of Zagora, travel out of town, away from Ouarzazate for 3km, and watch for a dirt road on the left (at the sign for Camping de la Montagne de Zagora). This rough track trundles its way to **Jbel Zagora,** a lone volcanic outcrop overlooking the fertile Drâa. The mountain is best visited at sunset, when the peaks shimmer in the dying light. At **Amazraou,** one-half kilometer south of the turn-off for Jbel Zagora along the main road, an ancient Jewish Kasbah contemplates the encroaching desert.

MOROCCO

Continue down the main highway to **Tamegroute,** an oasis of date palms and *ksours.* Here, in the middle of nowhere, is Morocco's best historical resource, Tamegroute's **library,** which contains 4000 Moroccan manuscripts dating from the 11th to the 18th centuries. There is a history of Fès, a copy of Bukhari's *Hadish,* poetry of al-Andalusi, and countless astronomical algebraic charts. The library's most treasured document is a history written on gazelle skin in 1063 by the great legal authority, Iman Malik. The caretaker speaks French and English. To get to the library, ignore the painted "biblioteque" signs (a scam) and turn left (coming from Zagora) down the one paved road in Tamegroute. Just after the paving ends, look for a large brown gate on the right; this leads to the courtyard in front of the library (open 9am-noon and 3-6pm; free, but tip the caretaker).

The **Saturday market** draws valley neighbors for its local pottery. Arrive early, because it's over by noon. You can eat in town at either **Restaurant L'Oasis** or **Restaurant du Drâa.** Taxi fare to Tamegroute via Zagora is 12dh per person.

Whisked into swollen shapes by fierce desert gusts, the **Dunes of Tinfou** rise from the valley floor in smooth golden mounds. These natural sculptures flow in gentle waves, buffeted into beautiful and delicate forms. To reach the dunes of Tinfou, follow the main highway south from Tamegroute and watch for the well-marked dirt turn-off on the left—the yellow humps are visible from the road.

M'HAMID

M'Hamid lies at the end of the road—and it feels like it. Forty-five kilometers from the Algerian border and 97km from Zagora at the edge of great sand deserts, its a lone outpost of dirt streets, no facilities, and recently-installed electricity. There is a Monday **market** here where nomads from the desert come to trade; other than that there is little besides organized expeditions into the desert. If you start here instead of Zagora, you can reach endless seas of sand dunes and isolated oases with a 4-5 day voyage, and very impressive landscapes on only a one- or two-day trip. There are no banks in the village and only a tiny **post office.**

In town, head for **Hôtel-Restaurant Sahara** (tel. 84 80 09). Singles cost 25dh, doubles 45dh. Cold showers are free. Food is a bit expensive, but this is to be expected in a remote location. Expeditions to the Sahara are organized here, and camel treks range from 250-350dh per person per day, with guide and food included. 4x4 trips, and even trips with your own car, are arranged as well. One bus leaves each day for Marrakech (5am, 18dh). Taxis (25dh) and trucks are, as always, more frequent.

■ The Dadés Valley وادى دادس

Broader, drier, and more scenic than the Drâa Valley, the Dadés Valley stretches eastward from Ouarzazate. Other than the *kasbahs* and palmeries along the way, the valley's main attractions are the **Dadés Gorge** and the **Todra Gorges,** which extend north into the dry escarpment of the High Atlas.

Forty-two kilometers east of Ouarzazate is the luxurious oasis of **Skoura,** surrounded by fields of grain and roses. Among the many magnificent kasbahs in town, **Amerhidil** (though inaccessible) and **Dar Aït Sidi el Mati** are the most impressive. Past Skoura, the first 40km east are a flat expanse of dust and rock, which are suddenly replaced by a burst of green plantations and palm groves, crowded on either side by *kasbahs* looming over the highway.

DADÉS GORGE

Boumalne Dadés, an uninteresting town which serves as a gateway into in the Dadés Gorge, is 116km east of Ouarzazate. If you get stuck in Boumalne, head for **Hôtel-Restaurant Adrar,** across from the bus station (singles 40dh; doubles 60dh). Gran taxis leave for the gorges in the same lot as the local buses, a couple blocks up the road from the CTM station. There is a bank across from the gran taxi stand.

There are several buses a day in both directions and a gran taxi from Ouarzazate costs 25dh.

The gorge stretches up along a road a few blocks west of the CTM station. The trip consists of wild stunning scenery where the earth seems to have been ripped away, leaving a massive gash through the mountainside. Towering kasbahs rise up on the slopes and dissolve into the surrounding earth. About 27km up the road, the gorge narrows and the road climbs above it. At this point there are several hotels, restaurants, and campsites. Try **Auberye Tissadrine** on the left. **Camping** by the river is 10dh person, and terrace sites are 15dh. Singles 40dh, doubles 80dh. Hot showers and breakfast are included. Trips up the gorge from here cost 150-200dh per day. A taxi to this point is 10dh.

TODRA GORGES

Another 53km along the road east from Boumalne is **Tinahir,** the gateway into the Todra Gorges. Like Boumalne, there is nothing of interest here, really only transportation into the gorge. As the Todra Gorge is much more accessible than the Dadés, there is even less chance of being stuck here, but if you are, try the cheap, basic **Résidence El Fath** (tel. 83 48 06), av. Hassan II (singles 35dh, doubles 60dh). One step up is **Hotel L'Avenir,** where techno blasts and singles 50dh and doubles 85dh. There is a Spanish restaurant downstairs that serves *paella,* among other dishes (45-60dh). Several **buses** leaving each day in both directions. Buses to Ouarzazate (37dh) and Marrakech (83dh), and a taxi from Boumalne (15dh).

The road out of Tinerhin snakes up the **Todra River** valley for 14km before reaching the mouth of the gorge itself. Along the way, a trio of beautiful campgrounds all charge about 9dh per person and 10dh per car. **Auberge de l'Atlas** (tel. 83 47 09) is the first of three with facilities slightly better than the others. There are several more hotels at the mouth of the gorge. **Cafe-Restaurant Auberge Etoile des Gorges** charges 25dh for singles, 50dh for doubles, and 5dh to sleep on the roof below the walls of the gorge.

From here, start hiking up between the towering walls. Almost a thousand feet high, the sienna walls frame a blue strip of sky above and fall to a rocky riverbed below. A half-day hike is enough to appreciate the magnificence of the gorge, but a few days, or even a week, will allow you to climb well into the High Atlas.

APPENDIX

HOLIDAYS AND FESTIVALS

Date	Festival	English
		Spain
1997		
Oct. 20-28:	*Valladolid.*	International Film Festival.
Oct. 27-29:	*Consuegra (near Toledo).*	The Saffron Rose Festival.
Nov. 1:	*National.*	All Saints' Day.
Dec. 6:	*National.*	Constitution Day.
Dec. 8:	*National.*	Feast of the Immaculate Conception.
1998		
Jan. 6:	*National.*	The Epiphany.
Feb. (week before Lent):	*Santa Cruz de Tenerife and Cadiz.*	Carnival.
Feb. 25-March 1:	*Villanueva de la Vera (near Cáceres).*	Pero Palo Festival.
March 12-20:	*Valencia.*	Fallas de San José (Las Fallas).
late March-- early April:	*National.*	Semana Santa (Holy Week).
April 11-16:	*Cuenca.*	Week of Religious Music.
April 23:	*Barcelona.*	St. George's Day and Cervantes Day.
end of April-beginning of May:	*Sevilla.*	Feria de Abril.
May 1:	*National.*	May Day.
first week in May:	*Jerez de la Frontera.*	Horse Fair.
May 5-18:	*Córdoba.*	Patio Festival.
May 15-22:	*Madrid.*	San Isidro Festival.
June 4-6:	*Almonte (near Huelva).*	Rocío Pilgrimage.

June 11:	*National, with special celebrations in Toledo, La Laguna (near Tenerife), and Granada.*	Corpus Christi.
June 15-July 15:	*Granada.*	International Music and Dance Festival.
June 20-29:	*Alicante.*	Festival de Sant Joan.
July 1-25:	*Almagro (near Ciudad Real).*	Festival of Classical Drama and Comedy.
July 6-14:	*Pamplona/Iruña.*	Fiestas de San Fermín (Running of the Bulls).
mid-late July:	*San Sebastián/Donostia.*	International Jazz Festival.
July 23-30:	*Villajoyosa (near Alicante).*	Festival of Christians and Moors in Honor of Santa María begins.
July 25:	*National.*	Feast of Santiago.
Aug. 15:	*National.*	Feast of the Assumption.
first week in Sept.:	*Jerez de la Frontera.*	Grape Harvest Festival.
Sept. 4-9:	*Villena (near Alicante).*	Festival of Christians and Moors in Honor of Our Lady of Virtue.
Sept. 21-30:	*San Sebastían/Donostia.*	International Film Festival.
early Oct.:	*Sitges (near Barcelona).*	Festival Internacional de Cine Fantástico.
Oct. 12:		Spain's National Day.

Portugal

1997

Oct.-Nov.:	*Santarém.*	National Festival of Gastronomy.
Nov. 1:	*National.*	All Saints' Day.
Dec. 1:	*National.*	Restorations of Independence.
Dec. 8:	*National.*	Feast of the Immaculate Conception.
Dec. 31:	*Funchal, Madeira.*	Festival of St. Sylvester.

1998

Feb. 21-24:	*Loulé, Nazaré, Funchal, Ovar, Graciosa.*	Carnival.
April 6-12:	*National, with special celebrations in Braga, Ovar, and Povoa de Varzim.*	Semana Santa (Holy Week).

April 10:		Good Friday.
April 25:		Liberty Day.
May 1-3:	*Barcelos.*	Festa das Cruzes (Festival of the Crosses).
May 1:	*National.*	Labor Day.
May 17:	*Ponta Delgada and Azores.*	Festival for Senhor Santo Cristo.
May 12-13:	*Fátima.*	Pilgrimage.
May-June (usually every weekend):	*Algarve.*	Music Festival.
June-Sept. 30:	*Lisbon*	EXPO '98 WORLD'S FAIR (http://www.expo98.pt)
June 10:	*National.*	Portugal's and Camões Day.
June 11:		Corpus Christi.
June 12-29:	*Lisbon, Porto, and other major cities.*	All Saints Festival.
June 23-24:	*Porto, Figueira da Foz, and Braga.*	Festa de São João.
June 27-29:	*Montijo, Ribeira Brava, and Sintra.*	Festa de São Pedro.
June:	*Évora.*	Feira de São João.
mid-June-mid-July:	*Sintra.*	Music Festival.
July:	*Vila Franca de Xira (near Ribatejo).*	Colete Encarnado (Red Waistcoast Festival).
July:	*Tomar.*	Festa dos Tabuleiros.
July:	*Lisbon.*	International Handicraft Fair.
July-Aug:	*Aveiro.*	Festa da Ria.
July-Aug:	*Estoril.*	Handicrafts Fair.
Aug. 14-15:	*Funchal, Madeira.*	Our Lady of the Monte.
Aug. 15:	*National.*	Feast of the Assumption.
Aug. 21-24:	*Viana do Castelo.*	Our Lady of Agony Festival.
Aug.-Sept.:	*Viseu.*	St. Matthew's Fair.
Sept. 4-8:	*Palmela.*	Wine Harvest Festival.
Sept.:	*Algarve.*	Folk Music Festival.
Oct. 5:	*National.*	Republic Day.
Oct.:	*Vila Franca de Xira.*	October Fair.
Oct. 12-13:	*Fátima.*	Pilgrimage.

CLIMATE

The following information is drawn from the International Association for Medical Assistance to Travelers *World Climate Charts*. In each monthly listing, the first two numbers represent the average daily maximum and minimum temperatures in degrees **Celsius**. The remaining number indicates the average number of days with a measurable amount of **precipitation**.

SPAIN

Temp in °C Rain in cm	January Temp	Rain	April Temp	Rain	July Temp	Rain	October Temp	Rain
Avila	07/-2	6.0	14/3	8.0	28/13	2.0	16/6	7.0
Barcelona	13/6	5.0	18/11	9.0	28/21	4.0	21/15	9.0
Burgos	6/-1	10	15/4	11	6/12	5.0	16/7	11.0
Cáceres	11/4	9.0	19/9	8.0	34/19	1.0	22/12	7.0
Cádiz	15/9	9.0	20/13	6.0	27/20	0.0	23/17	7.0
Granada	12/2	7.0	20/7	10	34/17	1.0	23/10	7.0
Madrid	9/2	8.0	18/7	9.0	31/17	2.0	19/10	8.0
Málaga	17/8	7.0	21/13	6.0	29/21	0.0	23/16	6.0
Palma	14/6	8.0	19/10	6.0	29/20	1.0	18/10	9.0
Santander	12/7	16	15/10	13	22/16	11	18/12	14.0
Santiago de C.	10/5	21	18/8	7.0	24/13	1.0	21/11	10.0
Sevilla	15/6	8.0	24/11	7.0	36/20	0.0	26/14	6.0
Valencia	15/6	5.0	20/10	7.0	29/20	2.0	23/13	7.0
Zaragoza	10/2	6.0	19/8	8.0	31/18	3.0	14/6	6.0

PORTUGAL

Temp in °C Rain in cm	Jan. Temp	Rain	April Temp	Rain	July Temp	Rain	Oct. Temp	Rain
Bragança	8/0	15	16/5	10	28/13	3.0	18/7	10
Coimbra	14/5	15	21/9	13	29/15	4.0	23/12	13
Evora	12/6	14	19/10	10	30/16	1.0	22/13	9
Faro	15/9	9	20/13	6	28/20	0.0	22/16	6
Lisbon	14/8	15	20/12	10	27/17	2.0	22/14	9
Porto	13/5	18	18/9	13	25/15	5.0	21/11	15

MOROCCO

Temp in °C Rain in cm	Jan. Temp	Rain	April Temp	Rain	July Temp	Rain	Oct. Temp	Rain
Essaouira	17/11	6.0	19/14	5.0	22/17	0.0	22/16	3.0
Fès	16/4	8.0	23/9	9.0	36/18	1.0	26/13	7.0
Marrakech	18/4	7.0	26/11	6.0	38/19	1.0	28/14	4.0
Rabat	17/8	9.0	22/11	7.0	28/17	0.0	25/14	6.0
Tangier	16/8	10	18/11	8.0	27/18	0.0	22/15	8.0

°C	35	30	25	20	15	10	5	0	-5	-10
°F	95	86	75	68	59	50	41	32	23	14

*°F=1.8°C+32; °C=5/9°F-32

TELEPHONE CODES

Barcelona	(9)3
Bilbao	(9)4
Lisbon	(0)1

Madrid	(9)1
Pamplona	(9)48
Porto	(0)2

Rabat	(0)7
Tangier	(0)9
Toledo	(9)25

Country Codes

Andorra	376
Australia	61
Canada	1

Ireland	353
Morocco	212
Portugal	351

Spain	34
UK	44
USA	1

TIME ZONES

Spain: 6 hours after EST; 1 hour after GMT.
Portugal: 5 hours after EST; same as GMT. Daylight savings is on last Sun. in March (clocks are set 1 hour faster) and the last Sun. in Sept. (clocks are set 1 hour slower); i.e., spring ahead/fall back.
Morocco: 4 hours after EST.

MEASUREMENTS

Although the metric system has made considerable inroads into American business and science, the British system of weights and measures continues to prevail in the U.S. The following is a list of U.S. units and their metric equivalents.

1 inch (in.) = 25 millimeter (mm)	1 millimeter (mm) = 0.04 inch (in.)
1 foot (ft.) = 0.30 meter (m)	1 meter (m) = 3.33 foot (ft.)
1 yard (yd.) = 0.91 meter (m)	1 meter (m) = 1.1 yard (yd.)
1 mile (mi.) = 1.61 kilometer (km)	1 kilometer (km) = 0.62 mile (mi.)
1 ounce (oz.) = 25 gram (g)	1 gram (g) = 0.04 ounce (oz.)
1 pound (lb.) = 0.45 kilogram (kg)	1 kilogram (kg) = 2.22 pound (lb.)
1 quart (qt.) = 0.94 liter (L)	1 liter (L) = 1.06 quart (qt.)

MISCELLANY

Addresses

Spain and Portugal: "Av.", "C.", "R.", and "Trav." are abbreviations for street. "Po." and "Pg." are abbreviations for a promenade, "Pl." is a square, and "Glorieta" is a rotary. "Ctra." is the abbreviation for highway. The number of a building follows the street name, unlike in English. The letters "s/n" means the building has no number. Note that the 4th floor to Europeans is the 5th floor to Americans, as Europeans don't count street level as the 1st floor. **Morocco:** Because things are named in French, "av.", "blvd.", "rue", and "calle" mean street; "pl." is a plaza. The number of a building comes before the street name, as in English. When hunting for an address, keep in mind that many streets are being renamed in Arabic; "rue" and "calle" may be replaced by "zankat", "derb", or "sharia."

Luggage Storage

Train and bus station lockers are usually operated by a token *(ficha* in Spanish) for which you pay. Less secure baggage checkrooms may also be found in stations.

Spain: *Consigna Automática* (lockers). *Consigna* (baggage check). The word for luggage is *equipaje,* for backpack *mochila.*
Portugal: *Depósito de Volumes* (baggage checkroom). Usually adjacent to the *chefe da estação* (station chief's office) on the platform. Pay when you reclaim your bag.
Morocco: The baggage check at CTM bus depots is usually safe. If you don't have padlocks on the zippers, however, your bags may not be accepted. Private bus companies also have baggage checkrooms. They're generally trustworthy and accept any kind of bag.

Nude Sunbathing

Most towns on the Spanish and Portuguese coast have at least a few nude beaches; some beaches have a separate section for nude sunbathers. Nude sunbathing is most common in resort areas. In **Spain** look for *playa natural* or *playa de nudistas* signs. In **Morocco,** nude sunbathing is never acceptable.

Pharmacies

Listings of late-night or 24-hour pharmacies are included for every town under the Orientation and Practical Information listings. In Spain, pharmacies are identified by their standard signs bearing a green cross. At least one pharmacy will be open all night in a Spanish town, on a rotating system. To find out which one will be open, look for a notice posted in the windows and doors of any pharmacy, or check the *Farmacia de Guardia* listing on the second or third page of the local paper.

Emergency Numbers

Spain: 091.
Portugal: 112.
Morocco: 19.

Clothing Size and Conversions

Men's Shirts (Collar Sizes)

U.S./U.K.:	14½	15	15½	16	16½
Continent:	37	38	39	40	41

Men's Suits and Coats

U.S./U.K.:	38	40	42	44	46
Continent:	48	50	52	54	56

Women's Blouses and Sweaters

U.S.:	6	8	10	12	14
U.K.:	28	30	32	34	36
Continent:	34	36	38	40	42

Women's Dresses, Coats, and Skirts

U.S.:	4	6	8	10	12	14
U.K.:	6	8	10	12	14	16
Continent:	34	36	38	40	42	44

Men's Shoes

U.S.:	8	9	10	11	12
U.K.	7	8	9	10	11
Continent:	41	42	43	44½	46

Women's Shoes

U.S.:	6	7	8	9	10
U.K.:	4½	5½	6½	7½	8½
Continent:	37	38	39	40	41

LANGUAGE

Terms that recur frequently throughout this book are listed below in alphabetical order. The parentheses after a word indicate its abbreviation (if any) and its language. We abbreviate *castellano* (Castilian) as Cast.; *català* (Catalan) as Cat.; *galego* (Galician) as G; *portugues* (Portuguese) as P., French as F.; and Arabic as A.

GLOSSARY

Term	English	Term	English
			General
abadía (Cast.)	abbey	Judería (Cast.)	Jewish Quarter
acueducto (Cast.)	aqueduct	kasbah (A.)	fort or citadel
ajuntament (Cat.)	city hall	kisosco (Cast.)	newsstand
albergue (Cast.)	youth hostel	lavandería (Cast.)	laundromat
alcazaba (Cast.)	Muslim citadel	llotja (Cat.)	stock exchange
alcázar (Cast.)	Muslim fortress-palace	lonja (Cast.)	stock exchange
anfiteatro (Cast.)	amphitheater	masjid (A.)	mosque
aqueduto (P.)	aqueduct	medina (A.)	Arab bit of modern city
arco (P.)	arch	mellah (A.)	Jewish quarter
avenida (Cast., P.)	avenue	mercado (Cast., P.)	market
avinguda (Cat.)	avenue	mercado municipal (Cast., P.)	local farmers' market
ayuntamiento (Cast.)	city hall	mercat (Cat.)	market
azulejo (P.)	glazed ceramic tile	mesquita (P.)	mosque
bab (A.)	gate	mezquita (Cast.)	mosque
bahía (Cast.)	bay	monestir (Cat.)	monastery
barrio viejo (Cast.)	old city	monte (Cast.)	mountain
baños (Cast.)	baths	mosteiro (G. and P.)	monastery
biblioteca municipal (P.)	public library	Mozárabe (Cast.)	Christian style of art
borj (A.)	fort or tower	Mudéjar (Cast.)	Muslim architectural style
cabo (P.)	cape (land)	museo (Cast.)	museum
calle (C.; Cast.)	street	museu (Cat. and P.)	museum
cámara municipal (P.)	town hall	muralla (Cast.)	wall
capela (P.)	chapel	oued (A.)	riverbed, often dry
capilla mayor (Cast.)	chapel with high altar	palacio (Cast.)	palace
carrer (Cat.)	street	palau (Cat.)	palace

carrera (Cast.)	road	parador nacional (Cast.)	state-run hotel in an old fortress or palace
carretera (Cast.)	highway	parc (Cat.)	park
casa do concello (G.)	city hall	parque (Cast. and P.)	park
casa particular (Cast. and P.)	lodging in private home	paseo (Po.; Cast.)	promenade
casco antiguo (Cast.)	old city	passeig (Pg.; Cat.)	promenade
castell (Cat.)	castle	patio (Cast.)	courtyard
castelo (P.)	castle	peregrino (Cast.)	pilgrim
castillo (Cast.)	castle	plaça (Pl.; Cat.)	square
catedral (Cast.)	cathedral	plage (F.)	beach
(el) centro (Cast.)	city center	plaia (G.)	beach
ciudad nueva (Cast.)	new city	platja (Cat.)	beach
ciudad vieja (Cast.)	old city	playa (Cast.)	beach
ciutat vella (Cat.)	old city	plaza (Pl.; Cast.)	square
claustre (Cat.)	cloister	polideportivo (Cast.)	sports center
claustro (Cast., P.)	cloister	ponta (P.)	bridge
colegiata (Cast.)	collegiate church	porta (P.)	gate
colegio (Cast.)	school	portal (Cast.)	entrance hall
colexiata (G.)	collegiate church	pousada (P.)	a state-run hotel
colexio (G.)	school	pousada juventude (P.)	youth hostel
convento (P.)	convent	praça (Pr.; P.)	square
coro (Cast, P.)	choir in a church	praia (P.)	beach
coro alto (P.)	upper choir	praza (Pr.; G.)	square
corrida (Cast.)	bullfight	puente (Cast.)	bridge
cripta (Cast.)	crypt	quarto (P.)	lodging in private house
cruz (Cast.)	cross	real (Cast.)	royal
cuevas (Cast.)	caves	red (Cast.)	company
duro (Cast.)	five pesetas	reina/rey (Cast.)	queen/king
encierro (Cast.)	running of the bulls	ría (G.)	mouth of river; estuary
ermida (Cat.)	hermitage	río (Cast.)	river
ermita (Cast.)	hermitage	rio (P.)	river
església (Cat.)	church	riu (Cat.)	river
estacão (P.)	station (train or bus)	retablo (Cast.)	altarpiece, retable
estación (Cast.)	station (train or bus)	ronda (Cast.)	rotary
estanco (Cast.)	tobacco shop	rossio (P.)	rotary
estanque (Cast.)	pond	rua (R.; P.)	street
estany (Cat.)	lake	rúa (R.; Cast., G.)	street
fachada (Cast.)	façade	rue (r.; F.)	street
feira (P.)	outdoor market or fair	sala (Cast.)	room or hall
feria (Cast.)	outdoor market or fair	sardanas (Cast.)	folk dance
ferrocarriles (Cast.)	trains	Semana Santa (Cast.)	week before Easter Sun.
floresta (P.)	forest	serra (Cat.)	mountain range
fonte (P.)	fountain	seu (Cat.)	cathedral
fortaleza (Cast., P.)	fortress	sevillanas (Cast.)	type of flamenco dance
fuente (Cast.)	fountain	sierra (Cast.)	mountain range

glorieta (Cast.)	rotary	**sillería (Cast.)**	choir stalls
grutas (P.)	caves	**s/n (sin número; Cast.)**	unnumbered address
habitaciones (Cast.)	rooms	**souk (A.)**	market
hammam (A.)	Turkish-style bathhouse	**tesoro (Cast.)**	treasury
iglesia (Cast.)	church	**tesouro (P.)**	treasury
igreja (P.)	church	**torre (Cast., P.)**	tower
igreja do seminário (P.)	seminary church	**torre de menagem (P.)**	castle keep
igrexa (G.)	church!	**universidad (Cast.)**	university
illes (Cat.)	islands	**universidade (P.)**	university
jardim botanico (P.)	botanical garden	**valle (Cast.)**	valley
jardim público (P.)	public garden	**zarzuela (Cast.)**	Spanish operetta
jardín público (Cast.)	public gardens	**zelij (A.)**	decorative ceramic tiles

Restaurant Terms

botella (Cast.)	bottle	**plato del día (Cast.)**	special of the day
comedor (Cast.)	dining room	**platos combinados (Cast.)**	entree and side order
cuenta (Cast.)	the bill	**prato do dia (P.)**	special of the day
meia dose (P.)	half portion	**pratos combinados (P.)**	entree and side order
menú (Cast., Cat.)	lunch with bread, drink, and side dish	**taberna (Cast.)**	tapas bar
mercado (Cast., P.)	market	**tasca (Cast.)**	*tapas* bar
mercat (Cat.)	market	**terraza (Cast.)**	patio seating
para llevar (Cast.)	to go (take-away)	**vaso (Cast.)**	glass

Food

aceitunas (Cast.)	olives	**lomo (Cast.)**	pork loin
albóndigas (Cast.)	meatballs	**lulas (G., P.)**	squid
anchoas (Cast.)	anchovies	**mantequilla (Cast.)**	butter
al ajillo (Cast.)	cooked in garlic	**manzana (Cast.)**	apple
a la parilla (P.)	roasted	**marisco (Cast.)**	shellfish
arroz (Cast.,P.)	rice	**mejillones (Cast.)**	mussels
asado/a (Cast.)	grilled	**melocotón (Cast.)**	peach
atún (Cast.)	tuna	**menestra de verduras (Cast.)**	mixed vegetables
bocadillo (Cast.)	tapa sandwiched between bread	**merluza (Cast.)**	hake (fresh white fish)
boquerones (Cast.)	smelts	**paella (Cast.)**	saffron rice with shellfish, meat, and vegetables
brochette (F.)	kebab	**pan (Cast.)**	bread
cabrito (P.)	kid goat	**pão (P.)**	bread
camaroes (P.)	shrimp	**patatas bravas (Cast.)**	spicy fried potatoes
caracois (P.)	snails	**peixe (P.)**	fish
caracoles (Cast.)	snails	**pescado (Cast.)**	fish
cebolla (Cast.)	onion	**pimientos (Cast.)**	peppers
champiñones (Cast.)	mushrooms	**pincho (Cast.)**	tapa on a toothpick

chocos (Cast.)	squid	pisto (Cast.)	vegetable stew
chorizo (Cast.)	yummy sausage	plancha (Cast.)	grilled
churrasco (Cast.)	barbecued meat	pollo (Cast.)	chicken
churros (Cast.)	lightly fried fritters	queso (Cast.)	cheese
cocido (Cast.)	stew with chickpeas	ración, pl. raciones (Cast.)	large size of tapa
comida (Cast.)	lunchtime meal; term for food	salsichas (P.)	sausages
empanada (Cast.)	meat or vegetable turn-over	sande (P.)	sandwich
ensalada (Cast.)	salad	sardinhas assadas (P.)	grilled sardines
fabada (Cast.)	bean stew	serrano (Cast.)	anything smoked or cured
feijoada (P.)	bean stew with meat	sopa (Cast., P.)	soup
frango no churrasco (P.)	barbecued chicken	tajine (A.)	stew, usually with meat
fresa (Cast.)	strawberry	tapa, pl. tapas (Cast.)	see Spain: Essentials
gambas (Cast.)	shrimp	tortilla española (Cast.)	potato omelette
gazpacho (Cast.)	cold tomato-based vegetable soup	tortilla francesa (Cast.)	plain omelette
habas (Cast.)	beans	verduras (Cast.)	vegetables
hígado (Cast.)	liver	ville nouvelle (F.)	new city
jamón (Cast.)	mountain-cured ham	zarzuela (Cat.)	seafood and tomato bouillabaisse
judías (Cast.)	beans		

Drinks and Drinking

agaurdiente (Cast.)	firewater	manzanilla (Cast.)	dry, sherry-like wine
bica (Cast.)	a mixed drink	medronho (P.)	firewater
bodega (Cast.)	winery	resolí (Cast.)	coffee, sugar, eau-de-vie
calimocho (Cast.)	red wine and coke	sidra (Cast.)	alcoholic cider
caña (Cast.)	normal-sized beer	suco (P.)	juice
cava (Cat.)	champagne variation	tubo (Cast.)	large-sized beer
cerveja (Port.)	beer	txacoli (Basque)	a type of Basque wine
cerveza (Cast.)	beer (general term)	vino blanco (Cast.)	white wine
chato (Cast.)	a little drink	vinho blanco (P.)	white wine
chupito (Cast.)	a shot	vino rosado (Cast.)	rosé wine
copa (Cast.)	a cocktail	vino tinto (Cast.)	red wine
horchata (Cast.)	a sweet almond drink	vinho verde (P.)	young wine
jarra (Cast.)	pitcher or mug	xampanyería (Cat.)	champagne factory
jerez (Cast.)	sherry	zumo (Cast.)	juice

Arabic Numerals

0	1	2	3	4	5	6	7	8	9	10
.	١	٢	٣	٤	٥	٦	٧	٨	٩	١٠
sifir	waahid	ithnayn	thalaatha	arba'a	khamsa	sitta	sab'a	thamaniya	tis'a	'ashara

Index

Numerics

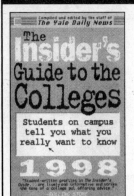

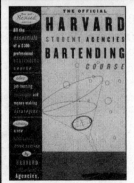

★Let's Go 1998 Reader Questionnaire★

Please fill this out and return it to **Let's Go, St. Martin's Press,** 175 Fifth Ave., New York, NY 10010-7848. All respondents will receive a free subscription to *The Yellowjacket,* **the Let's Go Newsletter.**

Name: _____

Address: _____

City: _____ State: _____ Zip/Postal Code: _____

Email: _____ Which book(s) did you use?_____

How old are you? under 19   19-24   25-34   35-44   45-54   55 or over

Are you (circle one)   in high school   in college   in graduate school   employed   retired   between jobs

Have you used Let's Go before? yes no **Would you use it again?** yes no

How did you first hear about Let's Go? friend   store clerk   television   bookstore display   advertisement/promotion   review   other

Why did you choose Let's Go (circle up to two)? reputation budget focus   price   writing style   annual updating   other: _____

Which other guides have you used, if any?   Frommer's $-a-day   Fodor's   Rough Guides   Lonely Planet   Berkeley   Rick Steves   other: _____

Is Let's Go the best guidebook?   yes no

If not, which do you prefer? _____

Please rank each of the following parts of Let's Go 1 to 5 (1=needs improvement, 5=perfect). packaging/cover   practical information   accommodations   food   cultural introduction   sights   practical introduction ("Essentials")   directions   entertainment   gay/lesbian information   maps   other: _____

How would you like to see the books improved? (continue on separate page, if necessary)_____

_____

How long was your trip?   one week   two weeks   three weeks   one month   two months or more

Which countries did you visit? _____

What was your average daily budget, not including flights? _____

Have you traveled extensively before?   yes   no

Do you buy a separate map when you visit a foreign city?   yes   no

Have you seen the Let's Go Map Guides?   yes   no

Have you used a Let's Go Map Guide?   yes   no

If you have, would you recommend them to others?   yes   no

Did you use the Internet to plan your trip?   yes   no

Would you use a Let's Go: recreational (e.g. skiing) guide   gay/lesbian guide   adventure/trekking guide   phrasebook   general travel information guide

Which of the following destinations do you hope to visit in the next three to five years (circle one)? South Africa   China   South America   Russia   Caribbean   Scandinavia   other: _____

Where did you buy your guidebook?   Internet   chain bookstore   independent bookstore   college bookstore   travel store   other: _____

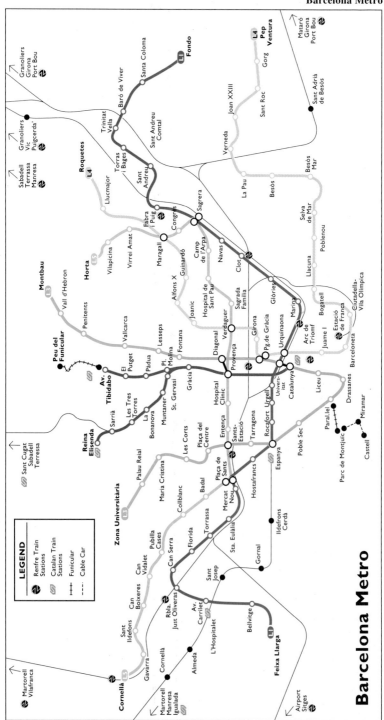

Barcelona Metro

Madrid Metro

LEGEND

🄿 Commuter Stations
🄼🄹 RENFE Train Stations
ℹ️ Information

Canillejas
Torre Arias
Suanzes
Ciudad Lineal
Las Musas

Esperanza
Arturo Soria
Avda. de la Paz
Alfonso XIII
Prosperidad

Barrio de la Concepción
Parque de las Avenidas
Quintana
Ventas

Cartagena

Duque de Pastrana
Pío XII
Colombia
Concha Espina
Cruz del Rayo

Avda. de América 8 7
Núñez de Balboa

Fuencarral
Begoña
Chamartín
Plaza de Castilla 1
Cuzco
Lima

República Argentina

Nuevos Ministerios
Ríos Rosas
Iglesia

Herrera Oría 9
Barrio del Pilar
Ventilla
Valdeacederas
Tetuán
Estrecho
Alvarado
Cuatro Caminos 2
Quevedo

Guzmán el Bueno

Metropolitano
Ciudad Universitaria 6
Moncloa 3

Barcelona

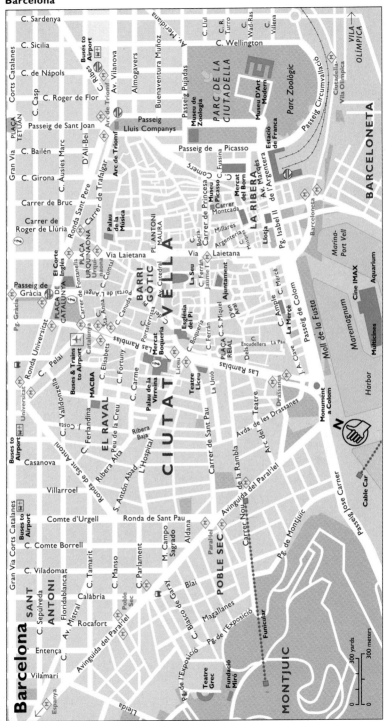

Barcelona

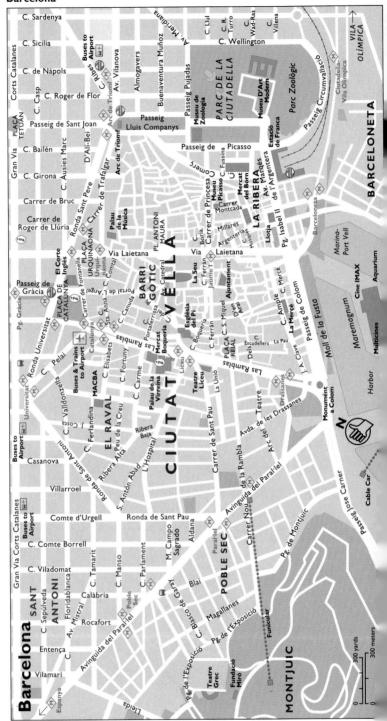

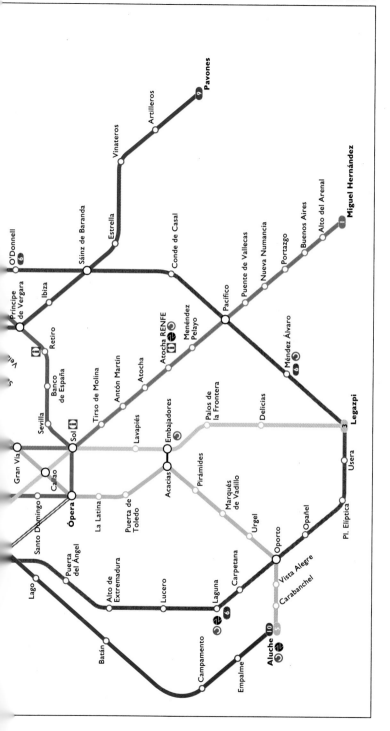

Madrid Metro

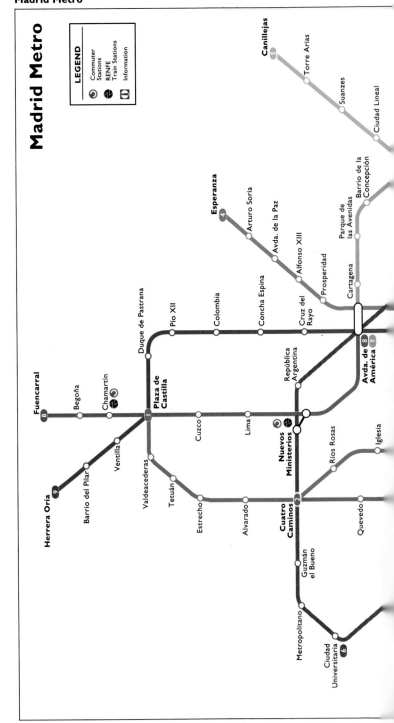

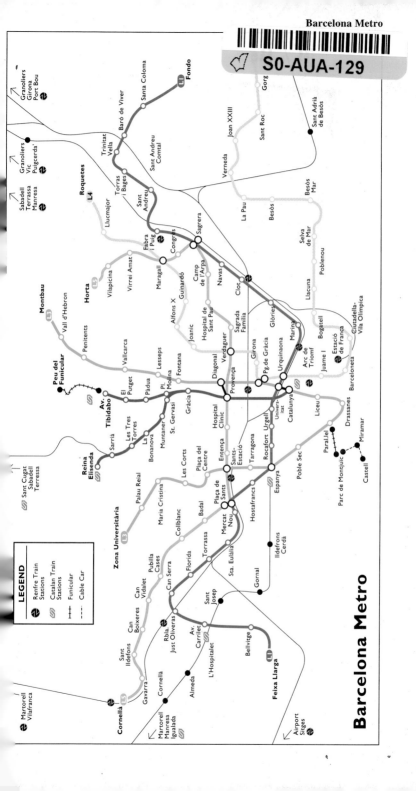

Barcelona Metro

S0-AUA-129

LEGEND
- Renfre Train Stations
- Catalan Train Stations
- Funicular
- Cable Car